WORD & WORSHIP WORKBOOK

FOR YEAR C

For Ministry in Initiation, Preaching,
Religious Education and Formation

Mary Birmingham

Paulist Press
New York, N.Y. • Mahwah, N.J.

Acknowledgments

Material from *Preaching the Epistles* by Raymond F. Collins, © 1996 by Raymond F. Collins, is reprinted by permission of Paulist Press. Excerpts from *New Jerome Biblical Commentary*, edited by Raymond E. Brown and Joseph A. Fitzmyer, copyright © 1989, are reprinted by permission of Prentice Hall Inc., Upper Saddle River, NJ. Lines from "Song of the Body of Christ" by David Haas, copyright © 1955 by G.I.A. Publications, Chicago, Ill., are reprinted by permission. The English translation of Eucharistic Prayer IV, opening prayers, antiphons, solemn blessings, prefaces and other texts from *The Roman Missal* © 1973, International Committee on English in the Liturgy, Inc. (ICEL); excerpts from the English translation of *Documents on the Liturgy, 1963–1979: Conciliar, Papal and Curial Texts* © 1982, ICEL; excerpts from the English translation of *Rite of Christian Initiation of Adults* © 1985, ICEL, are reprinted by permission. All rights reserved. Acknowledgment is made to The Liturgical Press of Collegeville, MN for permission to reprint material from *Preaching the New Lectionary* by Reginald H. Fuller, Copyright © 1971, 1972, 1973 and 1974 by the Order of St. Benedict, Inc., from *The Liturgical Year* by Adolf Adam, translated by Matthew J. O'Connell, ©1981 by Pueblo Publishing Company, Inc., © 1990 by The Order of St. Benedict, Inc., from *The Collegeville Pastoral Dictionary of Biblical Theology*, edited by Carroll Stuhlmueller, C.P., © 1966 by the Order of St. Benedict, Inc., and from *Days of the Lord*, volumes l–7, copyright ©1991 by the Order of St. Benedict, Inc. Excerpts from *Sharing the Light of Faith, National Catechetical Directory for Catholics of the United States*, and *Sharing the Light of Faith, An Official Commentary* are reprinted by permission of the United States Catholic Conference.

Book design by Céline Allen. Cover design by Tim McKeen. Cover illustration by Julie Lonneman.

Library of Congress Cataloging-in-Publication Data

Birmingham, Mary.
    Word and worship workbook for year C : for ministry in initiation,
preaching, religious education, and formation / by Mary Birmingham.
       p.   cm.
    Includes bibliographical references.
    ISBN 0-8091-3747–X (alk. paper)
    1. Catechetics—Catholic Church. 2. Church year—Study and
teaching. 3. Catholic Church. Liturgy and ritual. Lectionary for
Mass for Sundays of year C (U.S.) I. Title.
BX1968.B54 1997
268ʹ.82—dc21   9722382
                                         CIP

Published by Paulist Press
997 Macarthur Blvd.
Mahwah, N.J. 07430

Printed and bound in the United States of America

CONTENTS

PREFACE

Liturgical catechesis is one of the more significant topics to emerge in the wake of the liturgical, catechetical, and scriptural reforms inaugurated by the Second Vatican Council. Since the close of the Council the church has witnessed a genuine revival in each of these three areas. This should come as no surprise since liturgy, catechesis, and scripture are intimately related to one another. With a renewed and revitalized liturgy there comes a better understanding and love for the word of God. With an increased appreciation of the word of God celebrated and proclaimed in the liturgy there flows an enthusiastic response to proclaim the word in catechetics and to renew the place of liturgy in catechetical ministry.

Nowhere has this become more apparent than with the implementation of the *Rite of Christian Initiation of Adults* (RCIA). Since the rite was promulgated in 1972, those ministering on the pastoral level have become more deeply aware of the intimate unity of liturgy, catechesis, and scripture. In fact, the rite itself proclaims this basic unity as the foundation for formation for those embarking on the journey toward full sacramental initiation:

> A suitable catechesis is provided by priests or deacons, or by catechists and others of the faithful, planned to be gradual and complete in its coverage, accommodated to the liturgical year, and solidly supported by celebrations of the word. This catechesis leads the catechumens not only to an appropriate acquaintance with dogmas and precepts but also to a profound sense of the mystery of salvation in which they desire to participate. (RCIA, 75.1)

After more than twenty-five years of experience with the RCIA, those who have labored with the rite have become acutely aware of the importance of the unity of liturgy, catechesis, and scripture for all catechesis in the church. Even more, we have begun to see that this fundamental orientation for formation is applicable not just to the catechumenate, but to all sacramental and liturgical catechesis as well.

This awareness has led to a renewed enthusiasm and deeper appreciation for liturgical catechesis in many areas of our ministry. At the same time it has generated a host of practical questions. What does this catechesis look like on a concrete level? How do we "do" this type of catechesis in the parish? What form does catechesis accommodated to the liturgical year take? What does it mean to have catechesis "solidly supported by celebrations of the word"? How exactly do we lead people to an "appropriate acquaintance with dogmas and precepts" through celebrations of the word within the context of the liturgical year? How do we move beyond sharing our human experiences of the living word of God to an understanding of a "profound sense of the mystery of salvation"? How do we use the primary symbols of our faith to lead people to the heart of our beliefs? And the most common question of them all, "Is there a resource out there we can use in our parish?"

These questions, as well as many others, are addressed in the *Word & Worship Workbook* by Mary Birmingham. This is an exciting pastoral resource for liturgical catechesis that is suited to a variety of formational experiences: catechumenate, sacramental preparation, small Christian communities, ministerial formation, liturgical formation, and religious education. Through it all Mary Birmingham manages to wed the foundational principles integral to liturgy, catechesis, and scripture so that what is vital to each is fully incorporated into a practical program that may easily be implemented in many areas of parish life.

One of the main stumbling blocks for implementing any formational program for liturgical catechesis is a lack of basic understanding of what it is truly all about. Liturgical catechesis is not just a "new fad" or merely a "contemporary" way of doing something different. Rather, it is a result of the inspiring catechetical, scriptural, and liturgical advances that have been made in the church since the Second Vatican Council.

In spite of these advances we often hear of the "gap" that exists between catechesis and liturgy or between catechists and liturgists. This is not only unfortunate but also befuddling, since the primary catechetical and liturgical documents following the Council have emphasized the importance of the integral relationship between these two areas. The *National Catechetical Directory* proclaimed the importance of the four signs or sources of catechesis: biblical, ecclesial, natural, *and liturgical* (NCD, 43-48). The *Directory for Masses with Children* points out that "...liturgy itself always exerts its own power to instruct" (DMC, 12). The *Lectionary for Masses with Children* emphasizes that "The liturgy has the power to form children and all believers in the paschal mystery" (LMC, 21). And the *Catechism of the Catholic Church* states that the liturgy is the "privileged place for catechizing the People of God" (CCC, 1074) and that "liturgical catechesis aims to initiate people into the mystery of Christ (It is 'mystagogy.') by proceeding from the visible to the invisible, from the sign to the things signified, from the 'sacraments' to the 'mysteries'" (CCC, 1075).

The model that Mary Birmingham proposes builds on these teachings. The author devotes an entire chapter to helping the catechist understand how the four signs of God's saving activity in the world—natural, biblical, ecclesial, and liturgical—interact and play a vital role in our catechetical ministry. A special section is devoted to explaining how these signs are accommodated to the liturgical year and the scriptural readings found in the *Lectionary for Mass*. The author also provides a format for planning each session as well as practical information for preparing the catechetical session.

What catechists will find most helpful are the weekly catechetical sessions which are accommodated to the liturgical year and Lectionary readings. The sessions embody the wonderful unity of liturgy, catechesis, and scripture which is set forth in a detailed and practical manner. In each session the author leads the reader/catechist to an extraordinary awareness of why liturgical catechesis has become one of the more significant topics to emerge in the wake of the liturgical, catechetical, and scriptural reforms inaugurated by the Second Vatican Council.

Linda L. Gaupin, CDP, Ph.D.
Diocesan Director of Religious Education
Diocese of Orlando

1. INTRODUCTION

If you hope to become part of God's reign, you must let yourself be overtaken, knocked breathless, by a Presence, a Reality you can neither invent nor control. In a word, you have to open your life to the holy violence of conversion—a tumultuous experience that is liable to leave you feeling drenched and exhausted, as though the seas had seized, swallowed and spat you back alive on the shore. Newborn and salted, you sense that nothing looks the same, nothing can ever be the same.[1]

Nathan Mitchell's metaphor captures the heart of this book's purpose or, more humbly, its hope! While you may not find yourself spat back salted and drenched on the local beach, it is hoped that through the use of the methods and proposed sessions, you, as a catechist or small group facilitator, will share in the experience of empowering and being awed by the conversion of the adults and children with and to whom you minister and perhaps even by your own heightened faith life. Hope springs eternal in the human heart. One might therefore hope to light a spark, fan a flame, or at the very least prompt bold new questions to be raised regarding our Christian/Catholic story.

What was the experience and understanding of bread and gospel to the generations who went before us? Where work needs to begin and proceed is in helping people ask the right questions in finding meaning for their lives.

The genesis of this resource flows from the conviction that "...as many ministers of the divine word as possible will be able to effectively provide the nourishment of the Scriptures for the People of God, thereby enlightening their minds, strengthening their wills, and setting their hearts on fire with the love of God."[2] Catechists are ministers of that divine word. "The study of the sacred page is the soul of sacred theology. Sacred theology rests on the written word of God, together with sacred tradition, as its primary and perpetual foundation."[3] Catechesis that enlightens, strengthens, and inflames the love of God leads to deep conversion, which in turn leads to transformation of people's lives. This catechesis begins with the lived experience of people. It helps them celebrate and reflect on the presence of Christ in word and sacrament, in one another, and in the life and mission of the church. Hopefully this resource will assist in that noble endeavor.

This book is intended to help catechists plan engaging sessions for adults and children around the Sunday experience of word and worship. You, the catechist or group leader, may use this as a resource for planning your sessions or working with your specific group.

The structure of *Word & Worship Workbook* is based on the liturgical calendar. There are weekly planning sessions that include prayers and blessings from the liturgy, scholarly exegesis of the Lectionary scriptures, reflection questions, and suggestions for doctrinal themes. A doctrinal appendix is included for the catechist's reference.

One might ask, "How is this different from other resources that provide exegetical or catechetical material?" The answer is three-fold:

1. This book provides, under one jacket cover, condensed, scholarly exegetical material relating to both scripture and tradition and drawn from multiple and varied sources.
2. It includes ritual prayers and blessings, as well as questions, options, and possibilities for "unpacking" the experience of worship in the liturgical year.
3. It suggests themes from among the repertoire of hierarchical truths that naturally flow from interpreted texts of the Lectionary.

---

[1]Nathan Mitchell, "The Kingdom of Justice," *Modern Liturgy* 18 (October 1991): 8.

[2] *Dogmatic Constitution on Revelation (Dei Verbum)*, in *The Documents of Vatican II*, ed. Walter M. Abbot, S.J. (New York: Guild Press, America Press, Association Press, 1966), #23.

[3]Ibid., #24.

The impetus for this resource came from Jim Dunning who, in his book, *Echoing God's Word*, challenged us to view liturgical catechesis from a new perspective. Never was there an institute in which Jim was not heard saying, "Thou shalt not do to others what thou hast not done to thyself." Jim asserted that we as ministers must allow ourselves to be transformed by catechesis if we are to pass it on to others. For this reason, *Word & Worship Workbook* is not a book of lesson plans. It is a resource that committed Christians can use to prayerfully, ritually, and in an informed manner prepare for ministry in the church.

> We need formation and transformation, not just information. We need to take the journey ourselves. As ministers we need both the what (such as the vision of the church, faith, conversion, liturgical catechesis in these rites) and also some how's (some practical ways for pastoral ministers and catechumens to do that liturgical catechesis). We need methods, especially for catechists and homilists, that bring the word of God to echo in and through our lives in the community and that situate doctrine and law within the good news.[4]

This book is an attempt to tap into Jim's vision. It also seeks to tap into the current phenomenon of people's need for conversion and for renewed interest in scripture and in Jesus.

How might *Word & Worship Workbook* be used in a parish setting? The possibilities require only imagination. Obvious applications include:

1. Initiation Ministry
Catechists who work with catechumens and candidates could use this workbook to prepare sessions in which the central task is formation of the catechumen or candidate into the mystery of absorption in the paschal mystery of Christ as it unfolds in one liturgical cycle. "By means of the yearly cycle the Church celebrates the whole mystery of Christ, from his incarnation until the day of Pentecost and the expectation of his coming again."[5]

---

[4]Dunning, Jim, *Echoing God's Word* (Arlington: North American Forum on the Catechumenate, 1993), 20.

[5]"General Norms for the Liturgical Year and the Calendar" (GNLY), in *The Liturgy Documents* (Chicago: Liturgy Training Publications, 1991), #17.

2. Small Christian Communities
Facilitators could use this workbook to plan group sessions. Liturgy is about life. Reflection on the experience of liturgy is a wonderful way to share life in the context of our Catholic Christian experience. In order to be *community*, one must reflect on what it is the community celebrates as well as on what it believes, professes, and holds to be true.

3. Formation in Ministry
This workbook could be used by facilitators working with parish catechists who minister to adults and children through catechumenal ministry, scripture study, and adult enrichment.

4. Liturgy Teams
Liturgy teams could use *Word & Worship Workbook* as a source of reflection as they engage in planning liturgies, celebrations, and rituals for the parish.

5. Religious Education for Young People
There is much talk today regarding Lectionary-based catechesis in our schools and religious education programs. *Word & Worship Workbook* could assist religious educators in preparing Lectionary-based catechesis for their young people. At the very least it would help all who catechize be more informed about the "work" (read "liturgy") that we, as the people of God, do every Sunday throughout the liturgical cycle.

There are two final points. First, you will notice that there is an "agenda" in each of the weekly sessions. While attempting to avoid scriptural and doctrinal fundamentalism, there is nevertheless one constant lens through which the information contained in these pages has been redacted. This agenda is a radical option for the poor, the marginalized, and the less fortunate. In their document, *Communities of Salt and Light: Reflection on the Social Mission of the Parish,* the U.S. bishops state that

> The parish is where the church lives. Parishes are communities of faith, of action, and of hope. They are where the gospel is proclaimed and celebrated, where believers are formed and sent to renew the earth. Communities are measured by how they serve the "least of these" in our parish and beyond its boundaries—the hungry, the homeless, the sick, those in prison, the

stranger. The Church teaches that social justice is an integral part of evangelization, a constitutive dimension of preaching the gospel, and an essential part of the Church's mission.[6]

If this is true, it follows that justice is at the very heart of the gospel. The Hebrew understanding of justice (*hesed*) is right relationship. To be in right relationship with God means that one must show care and concern for God's *anawim*—the poor, the powerless, widows, orphans, and the marginalized. Thus, every weekly session is crafted in such a way as to raise questions of social responsibility. Justice is truly the agenda of the gospels. It is truly the agenda of this workbook.

Second, to be Catholic, says James Joyce, means, "Here comes everybody." We are diverse and we are to be inclusive. There is to be no "Jesus and me" mentality in the Catholic experience. Catholicism assumes community. We inherited the understanding that we are in relationship to God "as a people" from our Jewish ancestors. A personal relationship with God is essential. But we are corporate by nature and by intention. Thus, the first perspective in each session will be communal. The first question will always be, "What are the implications and challenges for our community, for the wider community?" Only after this question has been addressed is there movement toward the personal context, "What do the gospel and the liturgy call me to as a member of that corporate body?"

There is no doubt that Jesus maintained a radical stance toward the inclusion of all people. Language expresses our deepest held beliefs, convictions, and biases. To use exclusive language is against the spirit of the basic message of Jesus' gospel. Thus, I have tried to be as inclusive as possible throughout this text.

Since God is neither male nor female, our discriptive language is extremely limited. There are no adequate pronouns. The ancients struggled with naming God too, thus their designation, *YHWH*. However, I am a product of my own cultural and religious conditioning. While I desperately tried to avoid specific male pronouns in reference to the Transcendent Other, I found my efforts futile. Suf-

fice it to say that the use of "him" when it comes to God is solely a literary concession. There were no other choices that allowed the text to make sense and to flow smoothly. Also, quoted material was included as originally written; there were no changes made to texts from other sources.

Finally, the springboard for jumping into these often uncharted waters with both feet is to proceed with courage, emblazoned by the familiar communion refrain, "We come to share our story, we come to break the bread, we come to know our rising from the dead."[7] As we embark on this sometimes perilous voyage, may we be seized, salted, drenched, swallowed, and spat back alive on that not so distant shore we call "the Kingdom of God."

Mary Birmingham, 1996

---

[6]*Communities of Salt and Light: Reflection on the Social Mission of the Parish* (Washington: NCCB, 1993), 1-3.

[7]David Haas, "Song of the Body of Christ," GIA Pub. Inc., 7404 So. Mason, Chicago, Ill. 60638. All rights reserved.

2. THE SUBSTANCE OF CATECHESIS

Before proceeding further, it is important to understand *catechesis* as it is referred to in *Word & Worship Workbook*. The *catechesis* of subsequent pages embodies a broader interpretation than just the "Catholic stuff" that many have traditionally assumed is its definition. Catechesis refers to a radical relationship with Jesus Christ. Catechesis explores and recognizes God's action and presence in our natural lives, in scripture, and in the life, faith, and worship of the church. This chapter will dissect what that means in practical terms. Whether you are a small group facilitator with little or no formal catechetical training or a learned catechist, *Word & Worship Workbook* could be a useful tool as you "do" the work of catechesis.

CATECHESIS

Many people operate out of an erroneous assumption that catechesis refers to subject matter such as specific doctrines or theologies. In other words, catechesis implies content or head knowledge. However, catechesis supersedes that narrow interpretation. What, then, is it? One need look no further than church documents and the teaching authority of the church to gain insight.

The literal translation of the Greek word *catechesis* is "a sounding down, a resounding, and re-echoing." What and who is the object of this resounding? The "Who" is Jesus Christ. The "What" is the Good News of salvation offered by his life, death and resurrection. Pope John Paul II, in his apostolic exhortation, *Catechesi tradendae*, states that "the heart of catechesis is in essence a Person, the Person of Jesus of Nazareth, the only Son from the Father...who suffered and died for us, and who now, after rising, is living with us forever."[1] When people catechize, they reveal God's plan of salvation realized in the person of Jesus. Catechesis explores the meaning of Jesus' life, his words, and the marvelous works (signs) he accomplished. Catechesis is about relationship. It concerns a radical, personal, communal relationship with the living God encountered in Jesus Christ through the Holy Spirit. Catechesis helps us interpret the story of our lives in dialogue with the story of the scriptures and the story of the church throughout the ages.

The *National Catechetical Directory* (NCD) asserts that catechesis is God's word revealed through Jesus and operative in the lives of people exercising their faith. Catechesis supports the mission of the Church to proclaim and teach God's message, to celebrate the sacred mysteries and to serve God's people.[2] In this way the Church establishes the reign of God on earth. The aim of catechesis is to nurture a mature faith in adults, who will in turn help nurture a growing faith in children. "The content of catechesis is no more (but no less) than God's self revelation."[3]

THE FOUR SIGNS OF CATECHESIS

The catechesis referred to above is experienced through four signs of God's presence. God manifests the divine presence to humanity through signs. There are four signs of God's communication with humanity. God is present through natural, biblical, ecclesial, and liturgical signs.

I: Natural Signs

God, through Jesus Christ, is revealed in everyday life through natural signs. God resides and is revealed in the very substances of nature: creation, symbols, and our sensory world. God presides at the banquet of everyday life! God communicates to us through our own experience of life: through science, technology and the arts, through all that is human and all that supports or enhances human life. Our first awareness of God comes to us through *natural signs*.

---

[1] John Paul II, *Catechesi tradendae*, #43.

[2] *Sharing the Light of Faith, National Catechetical Directory for Catholics of the United States* (NCD), USCC, 1979, #30.

[3] *Sharing the Light of Faith, An Official Commentary* (Washington: USCC/NCCB, 1981), 19.

The elements of life such as water, light, fire, bread, and oil reveal and point to God. For example, we know that water is necessary for life. We cannot survive without it. God created this life-sustaining element. Through the natural properties of water we are reminded that God is necessary for life. Humanity depends on the benevolence of God.

God is revealed through the gift of science. God is encountered through the intervention of medical science and the healing arts. One cannot help but appreciate God's artistry through music, literature, and art. Believers recognize God's presence in the fields of science and technology. We are called to use the insights of secular sciences and appropriate them into catechetics. For example, catechetics is in great debt to the human secular sciences for a contemporary understanding of adult faith development, stages of faith, and childhood spirituality and faith development.[4]

This resource celebrates the God of everyday life. *Word & Worship Workbook* hopes to assist people to recognize God's presence in the natural order by providing questions that probe the awareness of God in the normal routine of life and its environment. At the heart of the natural sign is the realization that Christ is present in all things and throughout all creation. The task of catechesis is to help people become aware of his presence.

II: Biblical Signs

God, in Jesus Christ, through the Spirit, is revealed through *biblical signs*. Through the proclamation of God's word in worship and through the study of sacred scripture we are able to more fully live the Christian message. The gospel is the "principal witness of the life and teachings of Jesus."[5] Thus, in the course of one complete liturgical cycle, Christ of the gospels is encountered in the liturgical proclamation of the word. "By means of the yearly cycle the Church celebrates the whole mystery of Christ, from his incarnation until the day of Pentecost and the expectation of his com-

ing again."[6] Christ is present to us through *biblical signs* when we proclaim, listen, study, and live the sacred word.

First and foremost, scripture is experienced as the sacramental presence of God alive in the proclamation of the word. Every time the word is proclaimed in liturgy, Christ is truly present.[7] Scripture is the story of people in covenant relationship with their God. The task of Christians is to connect the story of their everyday lives with the story of Christ in the scriptures. There are a few basic, high priority themes that are woven through the Hebrew scriptures (Old Testament) and the New Testament. These biblical themes show us how God has been present and attentive to the work of salvation throughout all of human history. They give us a glimpse of how God views his relationship with us and how we, in turn, are to view our relationship with God. These basic themes are Creation, Covenant, Exodus, and People of God (community). These recurring themes emphasize the manner in which God has been present to us. They are standard themes that occur in both testaments.

Biblical Themes

a. Creation

God's power and divinity are witnessed through the things God has made, through *creation*. "Ever since the creation of the world, his invisible attributes of eternal power and divinity have been able to be understood and perceived in what he has made" (Rom 1:20). One need only gaze through the window of a 747 jetliner to be awesomely jolted by the explosive, generative, and creative power of the Almighty. Conversely, a quiet repose while watching bugs making trails on the shimmering waves of a gurgling brook serves as a peaceful reminder of God's order, symmetry, and artistry in the creation of nature's intricate designs.

During the Easter Vigil the story of creation is told to remind us that the Easter event, the paschal mystery, was part of God's plan from the

---

[4]Linda Gaupin, "Specialized Certification for Sacramental Catechesis," Class Session I, Diocese of Orlando, Florida, October 23, 1996.

[5]NCD, #60a; i.

[6]"General Norms for the Liturgical Year and the Calendar" (GNLY), in *The Liturgy Documents*, (Chicago: Liturgy Training Publications, 1991), #17.

[7]Gaupin, "Specialized Certification."

beginning. What God accomplished through Jesus began with the creation of the world. Creation was not a one-time event; it is not static, but exists on a continuum. It continues through history. God's creative power continues in the process of transformation. God's evolving work of creation continues in the presence of the risen Christ in the church today in the lives of men and women. All creation groans in grateful praise of the Creator.

b. Covenant

The theme of *covenant* began with the promise made to Abraham, continued on with Moses, and was fully revealed in the life and person of Jesus Christ. God is in covenant relationship with us today. It is the same covenant that began with Abraham, was fulfilled in Jesus, and continues to be lived by people of faith throughout the ages. *God promises to be with us.* That covenant relationship is experienced each day as people of faith live in the risen presence of Jesus. One need look no further than the sick bed of a dying child to find a mother sustained by the presence of her living God.

The covenant made with Abraham and Moses and fulfilled through Jesus continues today as people live in radical, reciprocal relationship with the living God. This relationship is ratified and renewed as people live in biblical justice. Biblical justice demands that one love the Lord God with one's whole heart, soul, and entire being and extend that same love to others and to self. Thus, people are to be treated as God would treat them: as children of God who deserve the highest dignity. To be in covenant with God means that the disciple has a duty to respect the dignity of all human persons. The poor, marginalized, oppressed, and powerless become the object of the disciple's care, concern, and love. Catechesis seeks to help people encounter the abiding presence of their covenant God and to instill in them zeal for a life of loving, apostolic service.

c. Exodus

The *exodus,* the premier symbol of God's saving love for the Hebrew people, ultimately reaches perfect fulfillment and profundity in the "passage from death to life accomplished by Christ's

paschal mystery."[8] This sign so clearly defines the Christian life that nearly every catechetical encounter addresses the mystery it contains. The ultimate goal of catechesis is transformation. Exodus asks the question, "How have I/you/we been transformed, changed, brought from death to life, in the story we just shared?" Every Christian has an exodus, a passover story; it is the heart of conversion. Each Christian's exodus story constitutes participation in the cherished life, death, and resurrection of Jesus Christ, the paschal mystery.

d. People of God

Another important sign throughout the scriptures is the image of God in relationship to a "people." In the Hebrew scriptures the community was a tangible sign of God's presence. In the New Testament that same sign was transferred to the church, the people of God. By remembering this sign we are better able to move beyond an individualistic "Jesus and me" mentality and embrace the God of Inclusion who is in relationship to us as a "people." The first perspective in scripture's challenge is communal: How does this word challenge "us" as a community? What are the implications of this word for our parish? What is the parish, diocesan, universal church's response in the civic, local, and national world? Are parishes responding to the culture as Christ would respond?

The people of God, the church, is in covenant relationship with God. The people of God, the church, is *one body* and is often called the sacrament of Christ. "As a divine reality inserted into human history, the Church is a kind of sacrament. Its unique relationship with Christ makes it both sign and instrument of God's unfathomable union with humanity and of the unity of human beings among themselves."[9] God is in intimate union with the church. Do our communities reveal the story of a people responding in faith to a God who is in relationship with and living within *them*? God's word is spoken first to a people. Every page of the Hebrew scriptures unveils God's self communication to *Israel.* Formation in the word of God as-

---

[8]NCD, #43.
[9]Ibid., #63.

sumes a communal relationship. The church is to respond to the world and the culture as a corporate body.

The biblical themes of creation, covenant, exodus, and community are like yeast is to bread. They are the leaven that allows the meaning of God's relationship with humanity to rise to fullness. Effective ministry of the word remembers and makes present the God of all creation and new life, the God of exodus who leads us out of slavery into that new life, and the God who invites the people of God into radical, reciprocal, covenant relationship.

III: Ecclesial Signs

Ecclesial signs usually are assumed to be the "content" of catechesis. Biblical signs help us encounter the presence of God in the proclamation of the word and remember and make present the saving works of God throughout salvation history. Ecclesial signs uncover the presence of God throughout the history of the church through its creed and through the way it lives its faith. Ecclesial signs get us in touch with the manner in which people lived the gospel message and celebrated their experience of God's revelation to the church. Over time, these people formulated their creed and the principles that would define behavior (tradition).

The Second Vatican Council's document on divine revelation, *Dei Verbum,* states:

> In His gracious goodness, God has seen to it that what He had revealed for the salvation of all nations would abide perpetually in its full integrity and be handed on to all generations.... This sacred tradition, therefore, and Sacred Scripture of both the Old and New Testament are like a mirror in which the pilgrim Church on earth looks at God, from whom she has received everything, until she is brought to see Him as He is, face to face (cf. 1 Jn. 3:2).... Now what was handed on by the apostles includes everything which contributes to the holiness of life, and the increase of faith of the People of God; and so the Church, in her teaching, life, and worship, perpetu-

ates and hands on to all generations all that she herself is, all that she believes.[10]

Catechesis continues what began with the apostles: handing down the tradition to present and future generations. That tradition encompasses the revelation of Jesus Christ as handed down through history, through faith, creed, worship, and way of life. Catechesis encompasses not only natural and biblical signs of God's presence, but also the witness of God in the life of the church in its creed, code and cult.[11]

Ecclesial signs (tradition) are but one of four ways God is revealed to us. There is often a tendency to believe that to be a good practicing Catholic is to know all the "Catholic stuff" from treatises on the Trinity to the historical development and understanding of indulgences. Many well-intentioned parish catechumenates, for example, are more concerned with the *information* about Catholic beliefs and practices (ecclesial signs) than they are with *formation* in the Christian/Catholic experience (all four signs). There is an assumption that *knowing* the Catholic information will automatically make good disciples. While not wishing to minimize the necessity of passing on Catholic teaching in its entirety, catechesis is the work of an entire lifetime. How many average Catholics know "all Catholic teaching in its entirety?"

The *Rite of Christian Initiation of Adults* states that there must be a "suitable catechesis, accommodated to the liturgical year...."[12] Too often that has been translated, "every jot and tittle of Catholicity." The question should not be, "Do they know everything?" Rather, the questions should be, "Have they encountered Christ in word, worship, and sacrament? Have they encountered Christ in the life and mission of the church? How does post-biblical teaching (doctrine) impact the Christian life? Where is the challenge for the community, the individual?"

Foundational issues deserve the highest priority as they help move adults toward a mature, faith-filled

---

[10] *Dogmatic Constitution on Revelation (Dei Verbum),* in *The Documents of Vatican II,* ed. Walter M. Abbot, S.J. (New York: Guild Press, America Press, Association Press, 1966), #7, #8.
[11] NCD, #45.
[12] *Rite of Christian Initiation of Adults,* #75.

Christian life. St. Augustine was once asked for a handbook of Christian doctrine. He complied by making his own handbook of basic beliefs. It includes an explanation of the creed, the Lord's Prayer, and the two great commandments—love of God and love of neighbor. Augustine asserted that "what we are to believe, what we are to hope for, and what we are to love, is the sum total of Christian doctrine."

The church recognizes that there is a hierarchy of truths around which other truths are rooted. There are many teachings that comprise the Catholic story. The focus of *Word & Worship Workbook* will be those foundational truths that form and flow from the core content of the Catholic/ Christian experience. Both the *General Catechetical Directory* and the *National Catechetical Directory* name four basic truths that hold priority of place within the tradition and are the norm for catechesis. They are: "[1] the mystery of the Father, the Son and the Holy Spirit, Creator of all things; [2] the mystery of Jesus Christ, the incarnate Word, who was born of the Virgin Mary, and who suffered, died, and rose for our salvation; [3] the mystery of the Holy Spirit, who is present in the Church, sanctifying it and guiding it until the glorious coming of Christ, our Savior and Judge; and [4] the mystery of the Church, which is Christ's Mystical Body, in which the Virgin Mary holds the preeminent place."[13]

However, lest I give the impression that mature Catholics need not grow in the fullness of Catholic faith and life, I would suggest that we allow Richard McBrien's distinction between catechesis and theology to give us serious food for thought as we approach our various ministries of the word.

A doctrine is an official teaching that derives from theology, not from direct inspiration of the Holy Spirit. Before the official Church can propose a statement of faith for the acceptance of its members, it must first think about and struggle with its possible meanings and with various possible expressions of meaning. That process of struggle to understand faith, leading to some official expression of faith, is called theology.... Theology, however, does not consist simply of a listing,

explanation, and defense of doctrines. The theologian's task is not only explicative, but critical—critical even of doctrines, or at least of a doctrine's language and conceptual framework so that the doctrine's truth can become accessible anew in a fresh formulation....

Theology is not catechesis. Catechesis is, literally, an "echoing" of the faith. Unlike theology, catechesis is for the potential member (known as the catechumen) or for a newly initiated member of the Church (whether a young child or an adult convert). Catechesis teaches the faith by highlighting and explaining the main elements of the faith-tradition and their relationships, as well as their personal and pastoral implications.

The catechist's task is not to invite potential or new members of the Church to think critically about their faith, but rather to understand and appropriate it in as clear and spiritually fruitful a way as possible. The theologian's task, by contrast, is critical. The mature member of the Church is invited to think critically, to question, even to challenge certain elements of the faith-tradition.[14]

Many good people in the church have not had the opportunities to know and grapple with the basic, core elements of our faith and the implication for living the Christian life. Catechesis must, then, be the starting point.

Located in the Doctrinal Appendix of this workbook is a list and a sampling of the main tenets of faith that *flow from* the hierarchy of truths and that are experienced in the liturgical cycle. Included with each post-biblical teaching are reflection questions that help connect ecclesial signs (tradition) and everyday life. Like biblical, natural, and liturgical signs, ecclesial signs intrinsically require a response. Such signs pave the way and point out the path toward bringing about God's reign on

---

[13] *General Catechetical Directory* (GCD), #43.

[14] Richard P. McBrien, "On What Theology Is and Is Not," excerpted in *America*, June 8, 1996, pp. 14-15. [Excerpts reprinted with permission from the *Tidings* (Southern California's Catholic weekly) of April 12 and 26, 1996.]

earth. This reign proclaims the Good News and demands liberty for those still held captive to oppression's grip.

IV: Liturgical Signs

God, through Jesus Christ, is revealed and encountered in the celebration of liturgy, the liturgical year, and the sacramental rites of the church. God, through Jesus Christ, is manifest through the church (ecclesial signs) by the way she appropriates her theology, formulates her creed, and lives her mission in the world.[15] Liturgical signs have their home in ecclesial signs, just as ecclesial signs reside within liturgical signs. All four signs are not independent of each other, though they are distinct. Liturgy, through ritual, symbols, and gestures, celebrates, remembers, and manifests God in the natural elements of life: fire, light, water, oil, bread, and wine. Liturgy celebrates, remembers, and makes present the signs of God in scripture. It is a living, ongoing testimony to the scriptural themes of creation, covenant, exodus, and community. Every time the church gathers for eucharist, those themes embody the language of God's continued relationship to the church. Liturgy proclaims the core creed of Christian faith. The church prays and from her prayer flows her belief: *lex orandi, lex credendi*. The creed is a living testimony to the faith and life of men and women of all generations, past, present, and future, the *communion of saints*. Liturgy, then, sends forth the church with a mission to live that faith, life, and creed for the transformation of the world.

One precious contribution of the Second Vatican Council was to describe liturgy as "the source and summit toward which the activity of the Church is directed and the font from which her power flows."[16] If the aim of catechesis is to reveal Jesus Christ, the gospel that is proclaimed in the liturgy is the "principal witness of the life and teachings of Jesus."[17] Jesus is truly present in proclamation of sacred scripture and in the eucharist, in the elements of bread and wine, transformed to body and blood, as well as in the celebrating assembly.

Catechesis prepares the community to celebrate and ritualize partnership with Jesus in the paschal mystery (his life, death, and resurrection) and to be sent as a sign into the world.

Catechesis is intrinsically connected to liturgical and sacramental activity. In the Apostolic Exhortation, *Catechesi tradendae* (#23), Pope John Paul II asserts that Christ works for the transformation of humanity in the sacraments, especially the eucharist. Catechesis has the power to change and originates in the liturgy. Liturgical catechesis has as its aim initiating people into the mystery of Christ. Catechesis helps the community reflect on the meaning and implication of the liturgy and sacraments. The purpose of catechesis is to assist believers so that their faith can "become living, conscious and active, through the light of instruction."[18]

God is present in the church as it gathers for prayer. The task of the church, then, is to reflect upon the deeper meaning of the experience of the risen Christ in the liturgy and the sacraments and to make appropriate life connections. Liturgy is the privileged environment for catechesis. It is where the people of God gather to encounter the biblical, ecclesial, and liturgical signs of God's presence during the liturgical year. From that encounter flows action and the mandate to go, do, and be what was just celebrated.

Liturgical Catechesis

The type of catechesis explored in this workbook is often referred to as liturgical catechesis. Liturgical catechesis uses as its source the liturgy, the sacramental rites of the church, and the church year.[19] Liturgical prayer is the church's official, public prayer celebrated in the midst of community. It is the way we are "church." The *Constitution on the Sacred Liturgy* states that "Liturgical services are not private functions, but are celebrations belonging to the Church" (#26). Through liturgy we celebrate the seasons of the church year and we ritualize the significant transition moments in the lives of individuals and the community (baptisms, funerals, weddings, etc.).

---

[15]NCD, #41-46.

[16]*Constitution on the Sacred Liturgy(Sacrosanctum Concilium)*, in *The Documents of Vatican II*, ed. Walter M. Abbot, S.J. (New York: Guild Press, America Press, Association Press, 1966), #10.

[17]NCD, #60a; i.

---

[18]*Christus Dominus:* The Decree on the Pastoral Office of Bishops in the Church (Vatican II, October 28, 1965), 14.

[19]NCD, #44.

While liturgical catechesis admittedly does not give a syllabus for doctrinal curriculum, it seeks to reveal and uncover the basic truths of our faith inherent in the celebration of the liturgy. "Although the liturgy is above all things the worship of divine majesty, it likewise contains rich instruction for the faithful."[20] As the church prays the scriptures and ritual prayers in the context of the liturgical year, as she shares eucharist and is sent forth, she internalizes, professes, and celebrates her creed about God, Jesus, and Spirit, the profound mystery of the church, and Mary's preeminent role.

The church at prayer ritualizes, lives, and celebrates the life and mission of Jesus. Liturgical prayer teaches us what it means to be Christian, Catholic, and disciples. Liturgical catechesis helps us articulate and enflesh it for our lives.

The Second Vatican Council's vision was for all people to be instructed and prepared for full participation in the church's liturgy. Since one of the principal signs of catechesis is liturgy, the church holds that catechesis begins with liturgical prayer and flows from it. "While every liturgical celebration has educative and formative value, liturgy should not be treated as subservient to catechesis."[21] There is a complementarity between liturgy and catechesis. Catechesis serves the liturgy and prepares people for full and engaging participation in it. Liturgy, on the other hand, provides rich food for the substance and basis of catechesis.

Every catechetical endeavor of the church must have liturgy as its anchor. The weekly sessions contained in this workbook are centered in liturgy. Catechist preparation sessions and the sample catechetical session take place within a liturgy of the word format. The ritual prayers of the church and the readings from the Sunday liturgy are formally and ritually proclaimed.

Many think of liturgy only in terms of the Sunday experience, but our church enjoys a vast repertoire of liturgical prayers and blessings: eucharistic celebrations, liturgies of the word, liturgy of the hours, blessings,[22] the Rite of Christian Initiation of Adults, the Rite of Baptism for Children, the Order of Christian Funerals, sacramental rites such as penance, marriage, ordination, confirmation, anointing of the sick and viaticum. In the midst of such liturgy, the living, dying, and rising Christ is encountered. Liturgical catechesis gives us a language with which to express the encounter.

Liturgical catechesis encourages people to name their experience of liturgy and ritual, articulate an understanding of the experience, and then make appropriate, informed decisions to live the message and become agents of change in the world. Thus, liturgical prayer is transformative. Like bread and wine, liturgy seeks to change us into a new reality: vibrant life-giving disciples.

Thus, the catechesis within the pages of *Word & Worship Workbook* is situated in the liturgical cycle: the Sundays, seasons, solemnities, and feasts of the year. As liturgy is the source and summit of all we do, and since catechesis prepares people for full and active participation in and reflection on the experience of liturgy, conversation in this workbook always begins with the presence of Christ encountered in people's experience of liturgical worship. This experience is on two levels: the liturgical worship of the catechetical gathering and reflection on and preparation for the Sunday experience of liturgy—the place from which the church's power flows.

In summary, then, catechesis echoes the four ways God makes his presence known to humanity— through natural, biblical, ecclesial, and liturgical signs. Catechesis is not solely a cognitive rendering of the articles of faith. Catechesis initiates an encounter with the risen Christ of biblical history and helps express an understanding of that encounter. Catechesis shows how the Christ encounter is celebrated in ritual and how the church remains a perpetual institution of living faith expressed in precept, dogma, life, and mission.

---

[20] *Constitution on the Sacred Liturgy*, #33.
[21] NCD, #36.

[22] Between *The Book of Blessings* and the *Catholic Household Blessings and Prayers*, there is a blessing for nearly every circumstance in life.

3. SCRIPTURE

PART ONE:
THE LECTIONARY

The Lectionary is the book that contains the chosen scriptural texts from the Old and New Testaments for proclamation in the liturgy throughout the liturgical cycle. The Lectionary begins with the readings from the three cycles of the First Sunday of Advent, continues through all the liturgical seasons, the Sundays of Ordinary Time, solemnities, weekdays, feasts, ritual and votive masses, and readings for masses for various needs and occasions. The Lectionary is the way Catholics encounter the bible, the living word of God, in their worship.

The liturgy by nature is biblical. The eucharistic liturgy is no exception. Most of the ritual prayers of the mass are inspired by biblical passages or images. "The Lord's Supper is an act of obedience to a biblical injunction (Lk 22:14c). From the opening sign of the cross (Mt 28:19) to the final dismissal (Ps 29:11b; Jdt 8:35), the participants are invited to live in the world of the Bible as one people with its people."[1]

The word of God is the heart of all liturgical gatherings. The mystery of Christ is unfolded during the liturgical year in the celebration of the church's sacraments and sacramentals. As each celebration is built upon the word of God "and sustained by it," every time the church gathers for liturgical prayer it "becomes a new event and enriches the word itself with new meaning and power."[2] In other words, Christ is sacramentally present to us in the proclamation of the biblical texts and continues to teach, form us, and provide new, life-changing insight into the living word of God.

The first and second (Old and New) Testaments are both proclaimed in order to demonstrate that there is continuity in God's plan of salvation begun with Israel and brought to completion through Jesus Christ.

We are to respond with assent and commit our lives to God's word in the person of Jesus experienced in the proclamation of the word and the celebration of the eucharist. The word brings us to the awareness of the paschal mystery of Christ we celebrate and make present in every celebration of the eucharist.

The Cycles

There are three liturgical cycles: A, B and C. Each new liturgical cycle begins on the first Sunday of Advent each year and lasts for one complete year. The three cycles make it possible for the fullness of the biblical texts to be proclaimed in the assembly over a three-year period. Each cycle's primary vehicle for encountering the mystery of Christ is one of the synoptic gospels: Matthew (A), Mark (B), Luke (C).[3] The gospel of John is interspersed in each cycle. At the beginning of the liturgical cycle the readings are concerned with the inauguration of Christ's manifestation and the beginning of his ministry. The end of the year focuses on chapters leading up to the passion.

How and Why the Readings Were Chosen

The biblical texts chosen for use at liturgy are intended to proclaim God's word so that the faithful may grow in the faith they profess. The history of salvation is broken open, especially during the seasons of Easter, Lent, and Advent, but also throughout the entire liturgical year. The readings correspond to the purpose and focus of the liturgical seasons and the principles of scriptural interpretation.

The Sundays and solemnities contain the most important biblical passages so that the faithful may

---

[1]Gerard S. Sloyan, "Overview of the Lectionary for Mass: Introduction," in *The Liturgy Documents,* (Chicago: Liturgy Training Publications, 1991), 118.

[2]"Lectionary for Mass: Introduction," Chapter 1 in *The Liturgy Documents* (Chicago: Liturgy Training Publications, 1991), #3, pp. 127-128.

---

[3]Refer to chapter 9 on this year's liturgical cycle.

experience God's revealed Word and plan of salvation over a reasonable period of time. The weekday readings contain a second series of readings that complement but are independent of the Sunday readings. "The Order of Readings for Sunday and the solemnities of the Lord extends over three years; for weekdays, over two. Thus, each runs its course independently."[4]

In addition, there are other sets of readings that follow their own set of rules depending upon their use, such as readings for celebrations of the saints, ritual masses, masses for various needs and occasions, votive masses, or masses for the dead.

Structure of Readings for Sundays, Seasons, and Solemnities

Each Sunday mass has three readings. The first reading is generally taken from the Hebrew scriptures (Old Testament). The second reading is from one of the apostles (either a letter or the book of Revelation, depending on the season), and the third reading is from the gospel. The responsorial psalm is a chant response following the first reading. It is from the psalter and usually is directly related to the first reading. However, there is allowance for the use of psalms common to a particular season, feast, or celebration. The psalm is generally sung, as the psalms were written as songs and best fit that mode of expression. The gospel acclamation (the Alleluia or the Lenten acclamation) is "a shout of joy which arises from the whole assembly as a forceful assent to God's Word and Action."[5] It is an acclamation of praise in preparation for the proclamation of the gospel.

There is a continuity between the Old and New Testaments that is best demonstrated when the first reading is directly related to the readings and the liturgy of the day, particularly the gospel. The Old Testament texts were chosen with that perspective in mind.

The order of proclamation is: first reading (Old Testament), responsorial psalm, second reading (from apostolic letters or Revelation), gospel acclamation, gospel.

---

[4]"Lectionary for Mass: Introduction," #65, p. 140.

[5]"Music in Catholic Worship," in *The Liturgy Documents* (Chicago: Liturgy Training Publications, 1991), #53, p. 286.

There is also a unity and harmony evident in the readings chosen for liturgical seasons. The seasonal readings reflect the meaning of the seasons of Advent, Christmas, Lent, and Easter, which have their own distinctive character.

The Readings for the Seasons of the Year

Advent Season

The gospels for the Sundays of Advent are concerned with the theme of Jesus' coming at the end of time and preparation for his birth at Christmas. The Old Testament readings are prophecies about the future messiah and messianic age. The apostolic letters are exhortations and proclamations that center around the themes of Advent. There are two series of readings for use during the weekdays of Advent. During the early weeks (first Sunday through Dec. 16) we hear from John the Baptist and extensively from the prophet Isaiah. The last weeks are concerned with events that immediately prepared for Jesus' birth (chapter 1 from Luke and Matthew).

Christmas Season

The readings of Christmas reflect important themes in the Christian tradition. On the feast of the Holy Family the readings are about the childhood of Jesus and the virtues of family life. The readings for the octave of Christmas, the solemnity of Mary, Mother of God, are about the Virgin Mother of God and the giving of the holy Name of Jesus. The readings for the Second Sunday after Christmas profess our belief in the Incarnation; the Epiphany readings are about the calling of all people to salvation. The texts for the feast of the Lord's baptism reflect the mystery of that event. The weekday readings center around themes of the Lord's manifestation.

Lenten Season

The first and second Sundays recount the Lord's temptation in the desert and the transfiguration. The third, fourth, and fifth weeks in Cycle A tell the story of the Samaritan woman, the man born blind, and the raising of Lazarus from the dead. These gospels may be used in place of the readings of Cycle B and C every year, as they are especially important to the Christian initiation process.

Passion (Palm) Sunday's gospel preceding the procession is a passage from the synoptic gospels that relates the story of Jesus' triumphant entry into Jerusalem. An account of the Lord's passion from one of the synoptics is read during the mass.

During Lent, the first readings are about the main aspects of our salvation history from the beginning up until the new covenant in Christ. The apostolic letters were chosen to reflect the first reading and the gospel.

The weekday readings from the Old Testament and gospel readings are related to each other. Readings that highlight proper Lenten spirituality and catechesis are used throughout the season during the week. The early days of Holy Week center around the mystery of the passion; the chrism mass celebrates Jesus' messianic mission and its continuation in the church by means of the sacraments.

Easter Triduum

Holy Thursday recounts the story of the last supper and its implication in the washing of the disciples' feet as well as Paul's telling of the institution of the eucharist, the new Passover in Christ. Good Friday always proclaims the passion event from John's perspective. Jesus as the prophesied suffering servant of Isaiah is the high priest who offered himself in sacrifice for all. The Easter Vigil's Old Testament readings (there are seven) tell the wondrous deeds of our salvation history beginning with the creation of the world. The resurrection story from one of the synoptic gospels and St. Paul's letter to the Romans about Christian baptism as the sacrament of Christ's resurrection are the two New Testament readings proclaimed at the Vigil.

Easter Sunday's gospel is from John and is about the finding of the empty tomb. However, we are allowed to use the gospel from one of the synoptics. If there is an Easter Sunday evening mass, the story of the disciples on the road to Emmaus may be used. The apostolic letter is from Paul and is concerned with living the paschal mystery.

Easter Season

The gospels for the first three Sundays of the season center around post-resurrection appearances of Jesus. The fourth Sunday is about Jesus, the Good Shepherd, and the fifth, sixth, and seventh Sunday gospels are taken from the teaching, conversation, and prayer of Jesus at the last supper. Throughout the Easter season the Old Testament reading is replaced by passages from the Acts of the Apostles in which the life, witness, and growth of the early church is unfolded. The apostolic readings that best reflect the spirit, faith, hope, and joy of the Easter season are taken from: year A–1 Peter; year B–1 John; year C–Revelation. During the first week (octave) of Easter, Acts is read semi-continuously at the weekday liturgies. The weekday gospel recounts the appearance of the risen Christ. The rest of the season proclaims John's gospel of the last supper discourse, especially themes that emphasize the paschal mystery.

Solemnity of Ascension

The first reading is a proclamation of the Ascension of Christ as described in the Acts of the Apostles. The apostolic letters are about Christ who sits at the Father's right hand in glory and the gospel proclaims the Ascension event from the view of a particular year's synoptic gospel.

Solemnity of Pentecost

The vigil readings for Pentecost give us the choice of four possible readings from the Old Testament that best reflect the many dimensions of the mystery of Pentecost. The apostolic readings depict the Holy Spirit alive and working in the church and the gospel remembers Christ's promise to send the Spirit. Pentecost day has us immersed in the account of Pentecost taken from the Acts of the Apostles (first reading). The apostolic letter from Paul highlights the workings of the Spirit in the church and the gospel remembers Jesus' gift of the Spirit to the disciples on Easter night.

Ordinary Time

Ordinary Time is not really a liturgical season, but it is the thirty-three to thirty-four Sundays of the year in which the fullness of the paschal mystery is unfolded through the life and mission of Jesus proclaimed in the Sunday gospel. Thus, even though Easter is the "mother of all feasts" and the pinnacle of the liturgical year (the very axis upon which it spins), each Sunday is a remembrance and celebration of Easter. Every liturgical celebration is an Easter, paschal event.

During Ordinary Time there is no distinctive character to the readings. The arrangement of the apostolic readings and the gospel is semi-continuous, and, as stated before, the first reading is chosen for its connection to the gospel.

The Second Sunday of Ordinary Time centers on the manifestation of the Lord (which Epiphany also celebrates) with the story of the wedding feast of Cana. The Third Sunday begins a semi-continuous reading of the synoptic gospels in which Jesus' life, mission, and work are unfolded in their fullness according to the perspective of each gospel. The readings form a continuity with the liturgical cycle. For example, the beginning of the year is concerned with the beginning of Jesus' life and work and develops from there accordingly as his story is proclaimed and celebrated throughout the year. The end of the year moves us toward endings and last things. It centers around the ending of Jesus' earthly life and work and eschatological considerations.

Solemnities of the Lord During Ordinary Time
The feasts of Holy Trinity, Corpus Christi, and the Sacred Heart (some call them idea feasts, as they do not celebrate an event in Jesus' life) all have biblical texts that express the meaning particular to each celebration.

Weekdays of Ordinary Time
During weeks one through nine, the gospel of Mark is proclaimed at the weekday masses. Matthew is read from the tenth to the twenty-first week; Luke is read from the twenty-second to the thirty-fourth week. Mark is read in its entirety with the exception of two passages that are read during a different season. Matthew and Luke contain all the passages not included in Mark. The first readings of the weekday masses are continuous readings that are taken first from the Old Testament books, then from the New Testament books. The number of weeks depends on how long it takes to get through a particular book.

The Old Testament passages were selected to recount the overall story of our salvation history and to reflect the general character of the individual books. The only Old Testament books that do not appear in some form in the Lectionary in the weekday cycle are two small prophetic books, Oba-

diah and Zephaniah, Esther, Judith, and the poetic Song of Solomon. Esther and Judith are read on Sundays and weekdays at other times of the year, however.

The readings from apostolic letters were chosen in order that the basic intent, message, and teaching of each letter be presented. Keeping in the spirit of beginning and last things, the end of the year weekday readings are from Daniel and Revelation and reflect the eschatological nature of the end of the liturgical cycle.

Lectionary-based Catechesis

This phrase is used to describe a method of catechesis based on the word of God proclaimed at the Sunday liturgy. In practice it is sometimes reduced to a simplistic approach that listens to the word of God, appropriates personal meaning from the word, and then chooses a doctrine that best complements our personal understanding. Often, however, the doctrine and teaching have very little to do with the inherent meaning expressed in the liturgy and the readings.

The church, however, has left us a marvelous tool for the ordering of catechesis: the Lectionary and the liturgical cycle. As one can see from the above descriptions of the readings chosen for use in liturgy through the seasons and Ordinary Time, the liturgy itself dictates what issues of doctrine emanate from our worship.

The church has systematically provided the ordering of our primary doctrine by the way and the reason it selected the biblical texts for a specific season, Sunday, solemnity, feast, sacrament, or celebration. The readings reveal the doctrine and meaning of that which is celebrated. For example, during the Christmas season, readings were chosen that best express our belief in the doctrine of the Incarnation, the manifestation of God, Mary as Mother of God, and the salvation offered to all people. The liturgy, then, dictates the content of our catechesis during the season of Christmas: Incarnation, soteriology (salvation), manifestation, Mary as Mother of God.

It is evident from the description, structure, and ordering of readings throughout the liturgical cycle that the major tenets of the Christian faith are unfolded in the readings and liturgies of the liturgical year. The liturgy provides us with the basis of catechesis. The implication, then, is that catechists must become very familiar with what the liturgy truly expresses, rather than with what they think it appears to be saying, or what seems to be compatible with our personal (often fundamentalist) interpretation of the readings of a particular Sunday.

Thus, catechists need to be familiar with documents such as the Introduction to the Lectionary, General Norms for the Liturgical Year, and all liturgical documents that define and express what it is we celebrate. This is one reason why a resource such as this is an important tool. While it does not answer all questions, it does provide interpretation of the biblical texts and it proposes inherent meaning in the liturgical celebration itself. It is in no way a substitute for the primary documents that truly inform and provide the praxis and rationale for the practice of our Catholic worship, faith, and life.

PART TWO:
THE INTERPRETATION OF SCRIPTURE

A word about the interpretation of scripture is in order at this juncture. *Word & Worship Workbook* is centered around the interpreted texts of the Lectionary scriptures. When I first entered the world of scriptural interpretation I had many questions. How can one scholar propose one interpretation, and another propose something altogether different? If these are respected scholars, who is right and who is wrong? Which interpretation is the most authentic? Do I really have the authority to present interpretations that are boldly new and unfamiliar to our common literal understanding of the texts?

Recently a man challenged me, "How is it possible that we could have heard a scripture in a certain way all our lives, and yet the discovery of the possible mistranslation of one word might change the entire meaning of a text? How can that be?" It is a valid question, one that I asked myself many times over in the early days. Hopefully, this chapter will answer some of those questions.

I make no claims to be a scripture scholar. In my role as catechist I have worked with scriptural exegesis in a parish setting for a long time and have used multiple resources and commentaries by various respected biblical scholars. As a compiler and redactor (editor), I have chosen exegeses according to a certain point of view. As a human person, I bring my own personality, beliefs, biases, and heart's desires to every reading of scripture. My first hearing of the scriptures is influenced by my limited perspective. Awareness of this limited perspective grew as the role of facilitating exegesis in our community was shared by members of a team. Each interpretation bore the personality traits of the facilitator who prepared it. The material might have been the same, but it was always nuanced from the perspective of the facilitator.

Bernard Lee maintains that we all enter every experience biased, "that is, with presuppositions, and rarely with much self consciousness about our ideological convictions. It is not wrong to have them. It is natural. It is disastrous not to know we have them."[6] Lee suggests that our safeguard is the Christian community as this is where discernment takes place. Thus, my effort to interpret the interpreters and to choose which interpretations to use comes with no official approbation. It is the result of one pastoral minister/liturgist's attempts to struggle with the insights of such interpretation in the midst of a faith-filled, life-giving Christian community. The efficacy of the redacted exegeses in this text will only be borne out (or not) in the midst of communities that seek to find God's compelling word in the midst of praying, studying, celebrating, and sharing the scriptures.

There is comfort in Jim Dunning's citation of Bernard Lee's[7] encouragement to ministers of the word:

> If we truly converse with scripture and
> allow the texts in their strangeness to interpret, change, challenge and call us to con-

---

[6]Bernard J. Lee, *The Future Church of 140 B.C.E.* (New York: Crossroad, 1995), 64-65.

[7]"Shared Homily: Conversation that Puts Communities at Risk," in *Alternative Futures for Worship, Volume 3: The Eucharist*, ed. Bernard J. Lee (Collegeville: The Liturgical Press, 1987), 157.

version, we need some guides to invite us into their world. Lee insists that the model for such guides is not the scholar who knows all the nuances of form criticism, redaction criticism, literary criticism and structural analysis but who cannot lead us toward any pastoral "so what's." We require, rather, a new kind of minister of the word and a new sense of community urgency to have someone prepared to help us converse with the word in our own world.[8]

This workbook's purpose is to assist people in the art of conversing with the word "in our own world." Such conversation leads to conversion that is at the heart of the liturgy and the scriptures.

Different models of biblical criticism (historical critical, literary, redaction, and others) are employed in some form or another throughout all the exegeses in this workbook. Different scholars employ different methods in their analyses. The vehicle used to travel the road of exegesis is far less important than the destination. What is important is the heart and soul of the text: "How have we/I been transformed as a result of our conversation with the scriptures?" To simply read the information within these pages without grappling with the interpretive questions in a communal setting of some sort is to miss the opportunity to allow the texts to overtake us. To reiterate this book's opening hope, "We miss the chance to be knocked breathless by the holy violence of conversion that will leave us drenched and exhausted as though swallowed by the sea and spat back newly salted upon the shore"[9] never to be the same again. Interpretation allows the texts to interpret us, to tell us who we are: God's beloved and chosen people.

The type of agenda, interpretation, and reflection process used in this workbook is pastoral and theological and employs historical and literary criticism. It is pastoral as it deals with real issues from real people's lives in the midst of their everyday existence. It is theological as it seeks to answer the question: "Who is the God of Jesus and what is the meaning of human life lived in the Spirit?" Historical criticism allows us to listen with the ears and cultural experience of a first-century Palestinian in order to better illuminate the meaning for listeners of the twenty-first century. The historical critical method allows us to move beyond a fundamental or purely historical meaning of the texts. The historical critical method studies scripture in the context of the history, culture, customs, religious beliefs, and economy of the original community for which the word was written. This methodology recovers and discovers the past of the text in order to bring it into today. "Since the Bible points to the mystery of God and of the divine-human relationship, it makes claims not simply on its original audience but on subsequent generations."[10] We not only strive to understand biblical interpretation historically, but we also engage in a hermeneutic to translate or explain it for today. Scripture is not approached as an historical, literally interpreted representation of the events that took place and the people who were involved. Rather, it uncovers the heart and soul of the message, the reason and meaning for the retold event.

Through literary criticism, the nuances and translations of language, cultural idioms, past and present meanings, and literary devices are explored. Literary criticism helps us get inside the story-world of the text to allow the drama to touch, impact, and transform us.[11]

Scriptural interpretation draws on the wisdom and lived experience of past Christian communities through the centuries of the church's existence. Such communities struggled to live the gospel as it was passed on to them. Because of the struggle, the church today is the beneficiary of a rich deposit of faith emanating from the scriptures. Biblical archaeology and study over the past forty years have contributed greatly to our understanding of the sacred text.

The doors to biblical scholarship were opened on September 30, 1943 by Pope Pius XII's encyclical, *Divino Afflante Spiritu* ("Inspired by the Holy

[8]Jim Dunning, *Echoing God's Word* (Arlington: The North American Forum on the Catechumenate, 1993), 180.

[9]Refer to opening sentence of chapter 1: quote by Nathan Mitchell.

[10]Dunning, *Echoing God's Word*, 166.

[11]Ibid., 177.

Spirit"). The encyclical exhorted the church and biblical scholars to use the modern methods of interpretation that Protestant churches had already been using. The intent was to "describe the literal sense of the scriptures, i.e. 'what the writer intended to express.'"[12] Prior to this time, much of our understanding of scripture had been figurative and allegorical. The encyclical moved us beyond allegory to the story-world of the text. *Divino Afflante Spiritu* challenged exegetes to uncover what the scriptures meant to the original authors and hearers of the texts.

Matthew, Mark, and Luke are called synoptic gospels. Their overall vision of Jesus is fairly similar. In the synoptic gospels Jesus is very busy establishing his reign and teaching his disciples what it means to live and work toward building that reign. Thus, there is little time or concern for proclaiming a theology about himself. John's Jesus, on the other hand, provides us with a refined christology. Each gospel was written from the vantage point of the community for which it was written. There was a significant difference in the way a story was told depending on the economic and class status of the listener. The stories were told with the community in mind, according to their needs and life situation. Since each evangelist was writing for his own community and from his own perspectives, each gospel is marked by the distinctive personality and specific agenda of its author.

It was once thought that Matthew was the earliest gospel. However, research has shown that Mark was the first evangelist, since his text appears in both Matthew and Luke. Matthew and Luke also share similar material that is not included in Mark. Thus, most scholars would agree that there must have been another source that was familiar to both Matthew and Luke. This lost reference is called *Quelle* (German for source) or "Q."

As the Hellenized, Greek speaking world became Christianized, the original biblical texts were translated into Greek. Translation from one language to another automatically involves interpretation. Jesus spoke Aramaic, not Greek. Every gospel was interpreted not only in a new language,

but in a different cultural system and world view as well. By the time the Greek texts were compiled, Christian culture had already embraced Greek philosophical thought that colored the translations according to Greek constructs.

Very often there are no words that capture the complexity of meaning in the original language, so the translator opts for an approximation. Language is limited. Scholarship, study, and archaeological efforts have advanced the quest to unearth authentic interpretation of the ancient texts. Exegesis is not an exact science. Yet that need not shake our faith too greatly, as the synoptic gospels are not always consonant with one another either. In many instances they contradict each other. For example, Luke's Jesus dies on the cross with a sense of peaceful confidence (23:46; cf. 23:34, 43) whereas Mark's Jesus cries out in desolation (15:34ff.).

Each evangelist has his own perspective and all draw upon the corporate memory of their different communities. New Testament scholarship recognizes that "the Gospels themselves are not histories of Jesus but the record of how communities remembered Jesus and taught new generations what and how they remembered."[13]

All scriptural interpretation is biased in one way or another. There is no such thing as an uninterpreted fact. History, for example, is shaded according to the bias of the historian. I was once struck by a comment made by a school principal who said that she would not use the Encyclopaedia Britannica in her school as it colored the events of the American Revolution according to a British bias. It was an eye-opening moment for me. Of course, it made perfect sense. Historians would naturally portray the "facts" of their history from a biased viewpoint. Facts, no matter how certain they are, are interpreted through the lens of the messenger, scribe, or historian.

Most scholars agree that none of the evangelists were eyewitnesses to Jesus' life and ministry. They had to rely on an oral account (a previous tradition) of his life. Raymond Brown asserts that the gospels developed over a long period of time and

---

[12]Richard P. McBrien, *The HarperCollins Encyclopedia of Catholicism* (San Francisco: HarperCollins, 1995), 423.

[13]Lee, *The Future Church*, 38.

were based on the memory and tradition of communities that lived and celebrated Jesus' words and deeds. "Apostolic faith and preaching has reshaped those memories, as has also the individual viewpoint of each evangelist who selected, synthesized and explicated the traditions that came down to him."[14] The implication for our understanding of the gospels is that each evangelist gives us a multi-faceted prism's view of the God/man called Jesus. Brown suggests that we should not be disconcerted when we read the contrasting views of Jesus in the gospels. Nor should we attempt to decide which view is the most correct. Each view is given to us "by the inspiring Spirit, and no one of them exhausts the meaning of Jesus. It is as if one walks around a large diamond to look at it from three different angles. A true picture of the whole emerges only because the viewpoints are different."[15]

What does all this mean for the average minister of the word in a parish? An effective minister of the word is armed not only with a personal understanding of scripture, but also with "the work of biblical scholars... [who] provide historical and literary insights which help uncover the meaning of the sacred texts."[16] When reflecting upon the scriptures people often focus on an affective, "warm fuzzy," personalist/literalist/fundamentalist hearing and understanding. "This is what it must mean because this is what it says," or "How did it make me *feel?*" There is nothing wrong with approaching the scriptures this way. It is the first way we are to approach the bible, as a hermeneutic of experience. It is beneficial insofar as it touches the person's lived experience (natural sign). However, sometimes this initial reaction becomes the final perspective and people unwittingly are left with a fundamentalist understanding of the text. "This is what it means because this is what it says and since it is in the bible it must be right." They are not challenged to move beyond their basic assumptions regarding the meanings of texts and the implications for Christian living. The opportunity to be challenged by the heart

and soul of the text is often missed. The role of the minister of the word is to move people beyond this initial literal understanding to one that provides the foundation for a renewed praxis of Christian living.

For example, on the sixth Sunday of Ordinary time, Cycle C, we hear Luke's version of the beatitudes. "Blest are you poor; the reign of God is yours" (6:20). An exclusively personal hearing of this scripture might prompt someone who is not literally poor to identify with the poor of Luke. They might think, "Surely, this means all who are poor in any way, such as the lonely, the stressed, those who are poor in spirit. I certainly am in that category." While Matthew's gospel does indeed make this extension, Luke's does not. The person's identification with the poor and assigning of personal meaning to the text perhaps is due to a life situation such as stress, sorrow, or grief, etc. This identification is not only logical, but desirable. It helps the person encounter God's love and compassion.

However, exegesis on the text presents a challenge. After conversing with the interpretation of the passage, that same person, given the opportunity, is invited to move beyond self, to a world view that embraces the heart of Luke's gospel: radical concern for the poor and the marginalized. Raymond Brown suggests:

> Luke's poor are the real "have-nots" of this world; his hungry know the misery of an empty stomach; his unfortunate are weeping. And just so that we do not miss the realism of the beatitudes, Luke narrates a series of corresponding "woes," stark anathemas hurled against the rich and the content who do not know the meaning of need.[17]

After such reflection on Luke's beatitudes, the person's original understanding is challenged. A decision is in order. He or she must make a decision: Am I willing to have my original assumption and understanding challenged? Is it in harmony

---

[14]Raymond E. Brown, *A Crucified Christ in Holy Week* (Collegeville: The Liturgical Press, 1986), 68.

[15]Ibid., 71.

[16]*Sharing the Light of Faith: An Official Commentary* (Washington: USCC/NCCB, 1981), 20.

---

[17]Raymond E. Brown, *The Beatitudes According to Luke: New Testament Essays* (Garden City: Doubleday Image Books, 1965), 336.

with the exegesis? If not, where is the difficulty? Transformation takes place through honest conversation with the interpretation. Concern for self moves to concern for others, in this case, the poor and marginalized. Conversion moves us beyond the personal (me only) to the corporate and/or the global (us together). Herein lies the impetus for Christian apostolic action. Catechesis of this sort always asks the communal question: How is the community and how am I challenged by such a word?

There is one powerful bias in the gospels: the thread that weaves their intricate design. Luke's beatitudes point to it. This bias, which permeates all of scripture, is a radical option for the oppressed, the poor, and those without power or use of the world's resources. One cannot ignore it or deny it. It is so blatant that one would have to fall over it, were it to be in one's path. A preferential option for the poor (in the words of the bishops) influences the way we are to hear the word of God. Love of God and love of neighbor demand that we be responsible for all members of the human family. For many, however, this bias is the biggest stumbling block in the scriptures. It is extremely counter-cultural and very politically incorrect. In an individualistic society such as ours, our creed often becomes, "Just pick yourself up by the bootstraps and take care of yourself." While such a platitude is grounded in the American work ethic, it ignores those factors that make it all but impossible for today's marginalized to even find their boots in the first place! To be Christian today means that we are to become bootmakers. Then and only then will the disenfranchised gain access to the world's possibilities. The decision ("so-what") questions, therefore, are critical to this process. When one is faced with having to commit to a transformed world view by the assent of one's actions, true metanoia is possible.

We are taught that the word of God proclaimed at liturgy is one of our primary symbols. What is the function of symbol? Symbols provide a language system between God and humanity. Symbols speak to us in ways that words cannot. Symbols convey many different layers of meaning. Water as symbol evokes images of life giving, thirst quenching, and death-dealing all at the same time. Some have

called the Vietnam wall a national symbol. Imagine a war protester and a U. S. Army officer standing before that symbol. The wall no doubt speaks two different things to both men. One can only imagine. But a loud word it speaks!

A comparison between sign and symbol helps us understand the complexities of the word of God as symbol. A sign is uni-dimensional. It points to one reality. A stop sign has one literal meaning: STOP. There is no other way to read STOP. One had better heed the sign. It means what it expresses. There are no ambiguities regarding the meaning of sign. A symbol, on the other hand, is complex, ambiguous, and powerfully enriches our lives. Symbols do not mean the same thing to every person who encounters them. Symbols touch the inner recesses of our being. They provide a vehicle for divine communication. A woman whose husband had just committed suicide was particularly moved by the symbol of breaking bread at her husband's funeral. She fully understood the meaning of one of the liturgy's primary symbols as if she had encountered it for the first time. The breaking bread recalled Christ's broken body. That day, the torn bread recalled her broken body as well. The symbol of breaking bread communicated a new truth to her. God spoke thunderous words through that symbol. Christ would have died on the cross even if she, in her unbearable grief, had been the only person in the world.

The linguistic symbol world of the gospel touches us on many different levels. How it touches us depends on the events of our lives. The story of Jesus healing the widow's son is going to speak something entirely different to a woman who has just lost her teenage son than it will to someone whose life experience is altogether different. Symbols never get exhausted of possible meanings.

The word *love* is a linguistic symbol. Its meaning will never be exhausted. We celebrate eucharist over and over because we have not experienced all there is to experience in the eucharist. What speaks to us today may not speak to us tomorrow. The word of God is living word. We are living people. Living things are fluid. Through the will of the Spirit, we move, change, and await new possibilities at the horizon of each new day. Symbols evolve. So do we. Consequently, we will never exhaust the symbol world of the scriptures. It is why we can return to Luke, three cycles later, and hear a word in a way that we never heard it before.

Sunday to Sunday and celebration to celebration, we encounter the sacramental, risen presence of Christ. How will we interpret the experience for our lives? Ancient wisdom assumed that Christians would engage in mystagogical reflection that would give meaning to their lives. Liturgy leads us to reflection. From the experience of Christ present in word and sacrament we order our Christian life. Mystagogical reflection as it is envisioned in this resource begins and begins again with the experience of Christ present in eucharistic liturgy; in the community of believers; in the church, *called and sent*; in the word, first experienced, then illuminated by informed scholarship and in the handed-down tradition of previous generations.

Catechists are charged with planting seeds. They are to plant the interpreted experience of liturgy, scripture, and tradition. God, the Creator/Harvester, then, will water, fertilize, and bring to fullness of life those who seek authentic worship and life in Spirit and in truth.

4. THE CATECHIST

Many unsuspecting persons find themselves in the role of catechist quite by accident. We have all heard the whimsical story of the person who comes to the church office to buy a mass card and is asked to be the Director of Religious Education. While this story is more myth and mirth than fact (we hope!), there are still many eager ministers who have not had the opportunity to pursue advanced instruction to prepare for catechetical ministry. In order to "re-echo" the person of Christ encountered in everyday life, in scripture, in the faith and belief of the church, and in liturgical celebrations, catechists need hearts that are on fire with the love of God and the desire to share that love with others.

However, more is needed. Catechists must be familiar with the authentic Christian/Catholic story: scripture and tradition. Formal instruction is important. Many, if not most diocesan offices provide good catechist training. Most people who will use this resource are probably familiar with the principles of catechesis articulated in previous chapters. However, review is often an enlightening and renewing endeavor.

Catechists should be confident that the heritage they are "handing down" is truly the official understanding of the church's tradition. Many folks make assumptions regarding church teaching, when in fact their assumptions are incorrect. For example, the church has no official position regarding recent Marian apparitions. While making no judgment one way or another regarding the authenticity of such apparitions, it is not necessary for a Catholic to consider them a part of the deposit of faith. To teach such apparitions as fact and precept would be grossly incorrect. It is one thing to share a personal and private experience of faith enrichment; it is quite another for a minister of the church to pass it on as divinely inspired revelation. Such apparitions come under the heading of private revelation and do not constitute "...all that the Catholic Church believes, teaches, and proclaims to be revealed by God."[1]

Also, while there is certainly disagreement and tension regarding the use of "male" centered God language, the church teaches that God transcends the human limitations of male and female. If one were to insist that the church teach that God is male, that person would be wrong.

Therefore, it is always wise to check with primary sources to either affirm or challenge one's understanding of church teaching. It is always good to seek out and refer to sources such as the Vatican II documents, the *General Catechetical Directory*, the *National Catechetical Directory*, *Sharing the Light of Faith*, and its companion, *Sharing the Light of Faith: An Official Commentary*,[2] the *Catechism of the Catholic Church*, and other catechetical documents, liturgical documents, encyclicals, apostolic exhortations, pastoral letters, canon law, etc. Secondary resources would include various works and commentaries of respected scholars and theologians.

Finally, catechists must be willing to enter into and immerse themselves in the conversion world of catechesis. It is a lifelong pursuit. The Christian life is not static. It is a life. To live is to grow. To grow means one has to learn. To learn means to live in a new way. "Catechesis is a lifelong process for the individual and a constant and concerted pastoral activity of the Christian community."[3]

Catechesis empowers men, women, and children and brings the light of faith to life. A noted atheist once mused that he might consider Christianity if

---

[1] *Rite of Christian Initiation of Adults*, #491, #585.

[2] The *National Catechetical Directory* (NCD), *Sharing the Light of Faith*, was formulated in response to the urging of the Sacred Congregation for the Clergy following formulation of the *General Catechetical Directory*. The GCD was prepared by that same Congregation after the Second Vatican Council called for a document that would provide the basic fundamentals of catechesis for the universal church. The intent of the Council was to assist Catholics in an informed and living faith. The bishop's conferences were urged to prepare national directories in order to apply the principles and guidelines of the *General Directory*.

[3] NCD, #32.

he were to observe disciples truly living the message they allege to proclaim. It is a sad critique that he has not encountered such disciples (if, indeed, his observation constitutes more than a tongue in cheek commentary!)

The church's vision of catechesis seeks to create living, conscious, and active followers of Christ evidenced by the way they live their lives. Enormous gratitude goes to all faithful servants who strive to bring that life to birth in the people they serve. May your lives be richly blessed as you encounter Christ in this catechesis of transformation.

5. A Story of Transformative Catechesis

Credos often have little life of their own. It takes the power of the human person to bring them to life. Stories put flesh and bones on the catechesis we profess. The following vignette is a real, though composite story that takes place in the context of Christian initiation. It is a story that is or should be repeated in the lives of all Catholics who walk the ongoing journey of faith.

Her name was Rita. She was preparing for the sacraments of initiation. Rita's preparation, her "suitable catechesis"[1] consisted in helping her strengthen the relationship she was developing with God by sharing common stories and experiences of Jesus' presence. She reflected upon the life of Jesus found in the Lectionary scriptures and the church's understanding of those scriptures. There were also stories of Christians and saints throughout the ages who tried to live the message of Jesus in their daily lives, some by offering their lives for others.

Folks shared with Rita how, in their struggle to live a gospel life, those earlier Christians wisely formulated and handed down the beliefs and practices that helped conform them to the life of Christ. Christians from the very beginning gathered to celebrate their common faith in Jesus and to be strengthened and nourished for mission in their world. Early Christians had inherited a tradition from their ancestors, the Hebrew people. To be in right relationship (*hesed*) with the God of Abraham and Moses assumed an action, a response. This response involved inclusive care and concern for the poor, widows and orphans, outcasts, and the marginalized.

Jesus lived *hesed* in word and practice. It was the hallmark of his ministry and was to be the hallmark of the Christian life. While often falling short of the mark, Christians relied on Jesus' two great commandments: love of God and love of neighbor. They gathered together to worship and be strengthened to go out and strengthen others. Rita was told how the same thing still happens today when the community gathers for liturgy. Rita understood what that meant. She, too, received similar strength in her encounter with Christ and his people in the celebration of the word each Sunday.

Over time Rita shared her experience of God. She had come to know that God was always a part of her life. She felt personally called into relationship with Jesus. This relationship brought her to the doors of the Catholic Church. Her faith was personal. The communal dimension frightened her, however, as it might ask more than she was willing to give.

Over time Rita's relationship with Jesus grew and her life began to change. Her angry, bitter edge began to melt away with the passing of each Sunday. The Christ of word and worship was impacting her life. She began to see areas and attitudes that were not in conformity with Jesus of the gospels. The Christ she encountered was reconciling and inclusive. The church she sought celebrated reconciliation and challenged one to conversion and transformation. The church was a vision and a source of biblical justice.

The social teaching of this church became Rita's proverbial thorn in the flesh, however. Jesus was far more inclusive of others than she was. Rita's new church insisted that *all* persons deserve to be treated with rightful, equal human dignity and respect. She wanted to change her inner disposition, but letting go was difficult. There was a cloud of darkness hanging over her. She tried to ignore it, but the gospel was persistent. Something was wrong. Denial is illusion's safety net. The "so-what" questions of each week began to haunt her. She responded to her new Christian life by working with needy mothers and their children. Yet, something was still wrong.

In the lenten season, those preparing for baptism—along with all the faithful—enter a period of purification and renewal. During the ritual celebration of scrutiny, Rita became conscious of the barrier that still existed in her life. In the procla-

---

[1] *Rite of Christian Initiation of Adults*, #75.

23

mation and preaching of the story about the man born blind, Rita became aware of her own "blindness from birth." It was a blindness that had its roots in her family system. Rita was raised in a climate of hate, prejudice, and racial bigotry. This hatred was normative behavior for her and her entire family. It was the "code and creed" she knew. The response of hate is to act hatefully, just as the response of love is to act lovingly. There had been responses of hate in her life. How could she reconcile such hatred? There was obviously no room for hatred in Jesus' reign. Jesus preached a gospel of reconciliation and inclusion.

Through catechesis that echoed Jesus' life to Rita, she was able to listen and respond to God's word. Scripture and tradition had been forming her. In spite of her environmentally conditioned hatred, Rita was captured by the inclusive God of scripture and a church struggling to live the gospel. She resolved to release the hatred.

After the Vigil's cleansing bath of baptism, the slathered, scented, and sealed anointing of the Spirit in confirmation, and the uniting, healing, and nourishing reception of Jesus in the eucharist, Rita was drained of emotion. She was well aware of her personal story of creation, covenant, exodus, and community experienced throughout her life's journey. Rita was not to remain in the safe haven of the Sunday table. She was sent forth to become the gift she had received.

The Vigil was not the end for Rita. Nor is any celebration of sacrament a port of arrival rather than departure. Rita realized a deeper reality. She was empowered for action in response to the Christ encountered in *word*, *eucharist*, and *community*. Her role was one of servanthood. Her mission was clear. She would do what she could to right the wrong that had been so much a part of the life she knew before. Christ had brought something to birth in her. Her exodus from death to life meant that she had to bury the seeds of hatred she had known. Rita's heart would permanently change through her decision to act. She resolved to become a voice for those she had once hated. Her most feared platform would be her family's own front porch. She was well aware of what it might cost. Yet she was willing. "Lord, help my unwillingness." A new joy crept into her life.

Rita's catechesis not only prepared her for full and vibrant celebration of the liturgy, but it also helped her realize that she was changed because of it. Rita could not wait to share her new life with the community that had nurtured her and assisted in God's creative work in her life. Rita unabashedly shared her passover story with the Sunday assembly during the Easter season. Rita had presided over the death of *hatred* at the Easter Vigil. In its place was resurrection of *love*: the new life of Christ's healing, sacramental joy. She thanked the community for nurturing her in her many months of formation. She credited God's word, the Catholic story, and her new family of friends for assisting in birthing her transformation.

The meaning Rita extracted from her experience was nothing less than a refined articulation of the church's foundational belief: the paschal mystery of Jesus Christ. Rita engaged in liturgical catechesis with the community. She recalled the threshold moments of the Easter Vigil. As she was immersed for the first time, gasping for air in the stirring waters, Rita experienced an interior cleansing. She waged her last battle with *hatred*. That old demon was being washed away while frantically holding on for one last breath of life. On the third plunge Rita thought of what it meant to die. "I came up the third time gasping for air." In those split seconds she sensed the fear of the Israelites sloshing through the watery wall toward an unknown land of promised freedom, leaving behind their despised, yet familiar life of bondage.

Water soaked and Spirit drenched, Rita exited the font aware that it was more than excess moisture dripping off her waterlogged robe. Her familiar, nasty companion was slithering back into the murky waters, never to surface again. She sensed new life. "If Jesus died for me and for everybody else, then I have to do the same. I have to let hatred die and I have to live for other people, just like Jesus did."

Rita's experience of baptism taught her more about the theology of baptism than any creedal statement could ever articulate. When the church teaches that baptism is the washing of sin, incorporation into the Body of Christ and the mission of discipleship, it is because generation after generation has experienced what Rita experienced.

Theology is not as lofty as it sometimes appears to be. It is simply a vehicle for the expression of faith.

Rita was catechized by the belief, story, and tradition of a people (both present and past) who share a common faith in Jesus Christ. She was further catechized by a rich, sensory ritual experience (liturgy) laden with meaning. With the entire church, Rita began the life-long process of experiencing celebration that leads to reflection that leads to meaning for life. The ancients called it mystagogical catechesis, uncovering the deep layers of mystery.

The *Rite of Christian Initiation of Adults* points out that catechesis for catechumens "enlightens faith, directs the heart toward God, fosters participation in the liturgy, inspires apostolic activity and nurtures a life completely in accord with the Spirit of God."[2] Rita experienced a suitable catechesis. Such catechesis should be the agenda of the entire Christian dispensation. It is not reserved only for those seeking entry into the church. Initiation is only the gateway, the beginning. Sacramental/liturgical/ritual catechesis is the conversion work of an entire lifetime.

---

[2] *Rite of Christian Initiation of Adults*, #78.

6. FORMAT FOR CATECHIST'S PLANNING SESSION

Catechists participate in a reflection session prior to the Sunday liturgy in order to prepare catechesis for their particular ministry group.

The weekly sessions in this book are intended to help prepare facilitators to lead a "Breaking open the Word" session that begins with a liturgy of the word and is followed by an adult learning session that explores the word just celebrated. Refer to chapter 7, "Preparing the Catechetical Session," for assistance in crafting catechetical sessions after participating in the weekly sessions provided in this workbook.

The prayers included in the weekly sessions are from the Sacramentary and serve to reveal the meaning inherent in the liturgy and the scriptures for each Sunday or feast. Thus, a closing prayer might be one of the opening prayers of the particular liturgy. Prayers are chosen to reflect the meaning of the Sunday or feast and are taken from the liturgy itself. The closing prayer, you will discover, is not necessarily the closing prayer of the liturgy.

PREPARATION

Liturgical Prayer

The entrance antiphon, the opening prayer, the final prayer, and assorted blessings are taken from the liturgy of the coming Sunday or feast. The ritual prayers are taken from the Roman Missal, the *Rite of Christian Initiation of Adults,* the Liturgy of the Hours, or approved books of blessing such as *Catholic Household Blessings and Prayers.*

Environment

As the preparation session occurs in the context of a liturgy of the word, it is worthy of a prayerful space decorated with the symbols of the liturgical season. Suggestions and available directives regarding the liturgical space are given at the start of each new liturgical season to assist you in creating a prayerful place for your gathering.

Music

While musical selections are not suggested in this workbook, it is nevertheless important to begin each gathering with music that is familiar to all gathered. If there are no courageous gifted voices among those present, there are tapes available at most Catholic bookstores that include most of today's church music repertoire. However, simple refrains are easily mastered by even the most challenged singer. Music is important to the catechetical gathering as it serves a critical function in the celebration of liturgy.[1] The psalm refrain could be chanted on one tone and ended on a lower note than the central tone, much like the chanting of the presider/celebrant when he chants, "The Lord be with you," and all respond, "And also with you." Or, the entrance antiphon could be sung.

LITURGY OF THE WORD

The readings are proclaimed in a brief liturgy of the word format with song, proclamation, and gesture (standing, sitting, sign of the cross, etc.)

Proclaim the Readings from the Lectionary

(Perhaps a copy of the text can be made available and given to each person *after* the proclamation. Some like to make notes on the text during the exegesis.

---

[1] "Among the many signs and symbols used by the Church to celebrate its faith, music is of preeminent importance. As sacred song unites to words it forms a necessary or integral part of the solemn liturgy" (*Constitution on the Sacred Liturgy,* in *The Liturgy Documents* [Chicago: Liturgy Training Publications, 1991], #112). "The quality of joy and enthusiasm which music adds to community worship cannot be gained in any other way. It imparts a sense of unity to the congregation and sets the appropriate tone for a particular celebration. In addition to expressing texts, music can also unveil a dimension of meaning and feeling, a communication of ideas and intuitions which words alone cannot yield. This dimension is integral to human personality and to growth in faith. It cannot be ignored if the signs of worship are to speak to the whole person" ("Music in Catholic Worship," in *The Liturgy Documents* [Chicago: Liturgy Training Publications, 1991], #23-24).

STEP 1
NAMING ONE'S EXPERIENCE

All share their initial impressions. All listen without agreeing or disagreeing. In this case, the hearing of scripture constitutes the experience. What are your initial impressions? What were the feelings, mood, words that captured your attention? How did the readings (particularly the gospel) affect you? Stay with your initial feelings. Do not try to explain or give a rationale at this point. This first exercise is an attempt to name your initial experience.

STEP 2
UNDERSTANDING THE EXPERIENCE

Why did the text touch you? Were there any experiences in your life that may have shaped the way you heard the story? What understanding of this gospel or readings do you already bring with you to this dialogue? What are your biases? What do you think the gospel readings are trying to convey? In your opinion, what does it mean?

STEP 3.
INPUT FROM VISION/STORY/TRADITION

The readings are interpreted in the context and from the vantage point of their original setting, culture, time, and hearers.

Liturgical Context

The facilitator gives *brief* input regarding the liturgical context of the readings. In a few sentences the facilitator explains why this reading occurs where it does in the liturgy in the present cycle. Most often the ritual prayers of the liturgy support the intent of the readings. Readings point to and focus the season, cycle, sacrament, feast, or theology.[2] The readings are interconnected with the liturgy and shed light on the celebration. Similarly, the liturgy being celebrated also helps focus

the readings. The liturgy is not only the liturgy of the word. It is much more. There are four equal signs of God's presence in the liturgy: God's presence in the assembly, the word, the eucharist and the presider/celebrant. The readings, therefore, and all the elements of liturgy are interdependent. To provide biblical interpretation without the liturgical context is to present a distorted view of the liturgy.

Gospel Exegesis

The facilitator provides input regarding critical biblical scholarship, using the insights of various biblical scholars. The world of the text is penetrated by looking at its structure, context, and literary devices, as well as by deepening our understanding of the author's intent or the church's reasons for using the text. What was the text saying to the early Palestinian community? Why was it said? Who was the audience and what was the background?

We ask: What does critical biblical scholarship have to say about this text? How would people have heard it in Jesus' time? Sometimes the meaning of the text is crystal clear and obvious. However, very often help is needed to appreciate the story-world, biases, and agenda of the original teller and listeners of the stories.

Proclaim the gospel again.

Listening to the gospel following the presentation of biblical interpretation often allows the text to be heard with new ears. The exegesis is brought to bear on this second reading of the gospel and helps implant (or perhaps cast doubt on) the insights that were shared.

STEP 4
TESTING ORIGINAL ASSUMPTIONS

This conversation gets the meaning out in front. Testing helps make the connection between the original story and the listener's initial assumptions and understanding. It either strengthens or chal-

---

[2]In the Rite of Confirmation there is a list of scripture citations for use in the ritual celebration. All of the citations, taken together, shed light on the meaning of the sacrament, making it beneficial to include and use all of the readings in preparation for Confirmation. The suggested readings are not simply for the purpose of choosing texts for the liturgical celebration. They help express the meaning as well.

lenges first impressions. Initial impressions are contrasted with or related to the exegesis. A person may experience excitement, challenge, discomfort, surprise, disagreement, vulnerability, or affirmation. It is at this point that we test our earliest assumptions and prior understandings in order to allow the text to transform us. Sometimes it is very difficult to let go of our previous biases, particularly when they have been informed by a prior fundamentalist hearing of the scriptures. It is at this juncture in the process that the adult is gently led toward a new outlook. As said earlier, the stories of scripture are like a prism; they can be viewed from various perspectives depending on how the light hits the prism at a given moment. People are asked: Now that you've heard the biblical scholarship concerning this text, how do you feel about it? How does your original interpretation fit with the opinions of scholars? What was the message to the community then and now? How would you articulate an understanding of the readings now?

STEP 5
DECISION

After an in-depth dialogue with the scriptural exegesis, a decision is in order. We decide if our original understanding is adequate or if it is in need of transformation. If the latter is true, opportunity is given to articulate a new or renewed course of action, practice, and/or attitude for the future. Scripture and tradition demand a response. Discipleship demands action. We are called to and empowered for service by the word of God and by the mission of the church. *This step is critical.* Transformation is observable in the life one lives, in the attitudes one professes, and in one's work of service in the world. "The proof is in the pudding."[3]

---

[3]While Christian life is not all action and no "being," one cannot ignore the gospel imperative to live the gospel we profess. As in all things there is to be balance, however. Action is balanced with prayer. Also, action may simply mean living a life of love in our home environments or changing an attitude or perspective and having the courage to speak up for what we believe. Some people are definitely called to public, active, pavement-pounding ministry. Others are called to ministry in the home and the marketplace. We are all invited to take the gospel with us to inform our posture, our actions, and our attitudes wherever we practice our ministry.

If people are not given the chance to move beyond steps one and two (naming their experience and articulating an understanding of the experience), there is a tendency to unwittingly engage in their own form of scriptural or doctrinal fundamentalism.

Reflection, study, and dialogue of this sort demand a decision, even if the decision is not to decide. If one has difficulty or disagrees with a particular interpretation, then the decision is to disagree. The decision then becomes a conscious resolution to ignore or be unaffected by what was shared. This is not a value judgment. Again, there is nothing that states that every biblical interpretation must be accepted as fact. That is one reason why it is wise to consult multiple commentators.[4] One scholar may shed light on one piece of the puzzle, while another sheds light on a different piece. Scripture scholarship is a growing, evolving discipline and unfolds as advances in biblical scholarship and biblical archaeology continue.

People are asked: How does this biblical scholarship challenge our community's (church's, parish's, neighborhood's, world's) attitudes and apostolic works? In what practical way can our parish respond to this biblical challenge? How has this biblical scholarship changed or challenged my attitudes and apostolic action? In what practical way can we/I respond to this biblical challenge?

DOCTRINAL ISSUES

Following the scriptural and liturgical segment of the preparation session, participants engage in dialogue and conversation with an issue from tradition, a doctrinal issue. Participants begin by suggesting possible doctrinal themes that flow from the readings. Whether or not this exercise results in choosing the actual topic for discussion, it is a worthwhile exercise. It helps people realize that there are connections to be made between the liturgy and the basic truths of our faith. Often multiple themes surface. Some are listed at the end of each week's session.

---

[4]Each week's exegesis in this workbook contains insights from a variety of respected biblical scholars.

There are two possible approaches to choosing a topic for discussion.

a) The facilitator invites participants to name and list possible doctrinal issues/themes. Participants take a few minutes to refer to the Doctrinal Appendix for a specific doctrinal issue. After reviewing those already listed, the group chooses an appropriate topic for its particular parish and ministry group. Once they have chosen a topic, group members read the doctrinal issue together from the Doctrinal Appendix and then respond to the corresponding questions. Or

b) A facilitator prepares and presents a specific doctrinal theme of his or her choosing.

Participants respond using the same five-step process described above.

The prepared doctrinal material should include the church's understanding of a particular doctrinal issue, including appropriate church documents, the perspective of the *Catechism of the Catholic Church*, expansion material by respected theologians, perhaps some background on historical context. The doctrinal segment is not "everything you ever wanted to know about a topic"; it is, rather, brief input on a particular post-biblical teaching, creed, or practice. Doctrine comes to us from the lived experience of past communities. Much of it comes to us from the scriptures; the rest comes to us from post-biblical generations[5] that

struggled to live the gospel in the presence of the risen Christ, and as a result formulated their creed out of their experience and understanding.

The hierarchy of truths is proclaimed at liturgy every time the church gathers. Either the liturgy itself or the readings from scripture address the principal tenets of our faith.[6] From the church's prayer comes her rule of faith (*lex orandi, lex credendi*). The Doctrinal Appendix provides *some* core doctrinal material. A resource of this size could not possibly address all doctrinal issues. *Word & Worship Workbook* is not intended to be a sole resource. However, by providing a sampling of core material, we hope that catechists will become familiar with the kinds of issues that need to be addressed, and that they will be able to use church documents in addressing any subjects not included in this workbook. The doctrinal material is presented in a reflection process format to facilitate dialogue with the material. The five-step reflection process (Naming, Understanding, Input, Testing, Decision) provides a framework for sharing. Following each doctrinal session there are instructions to return to the planning guide chapter that will assist you in preparing the catechetical session.

---

[5]Doctrine (tradition) is and has been formulated by the teaching authority of the church, the magisterium including the *sensus fidelium*, the sense of the faithful. The Second Vatican Council document, *Dogmatic Constitution on Divine Revelation (Dei Verbum)* asserts: "The tradition which comes from the apostles develops in the Church with the help of the Holy Spirit. For there is a growth in understanding of the realities and the words which have been handed down. This happens through the contemplation and the study made by believers, who treasure these things in their heart (cf. Lk 2:19, 51), through the intimate understanding of spiritual things they experience, and through the preaching of those who have received through episcopal succession the sure gift of truth." (*Dogmatic Constitution on Divine Revelation [Dei Verbum]*, in *The Documents of Vatican II*, ed. Walter M. Abbot, S.J. [New York: Guild Press, America Press, and Association Press, 1966], #8.)

[6]For further expansion on the topic of doctrine, refer to the Doctrinal Appendix. Also see the list of doctrinal issues that are encountered in the liturgical year.

7. PREPARING THE CATECHETICAL SESSION

At the end of each doctrinal teaching in the Doctrinal Appendix you will be instructed to refer to this chapter. This guide assists in planning an actual catechetical session. It provides general suggestions and ideas (painted with broad strokes) for crafting your session. It is in no way exhaustive. It is merely the impetus and launching pad for using your own gifts of creativity as you work with your particular ministry group. Few specifics are given, as your planning must consider the emotional, developmental, and age appropriate abilities of various groups within a ministerial setting.[1]

If your ministry is with adults, the same five-step reflection process is used: Naming, Understanding, Input, Testing, Decision.

THE LITURGY OF THE WORD

When a catechetical session for some reason does not follow directly upon the liturgy of the word at mass (if, for example, the catechumens are *not* dismissed following the liturgy of the word to break open the word), the session that meets during the following week should begin with a liturgy of the word as outlined below, followed by a "Breaking open the Word" segment. It is not necessary to do all three readings, however. Perhaps the Old Testament reading, a psalm, and the gospel are all you will need to proclaim for that session. Or perhaps only the gospel is necessary. Adapt the outline below to your particular needs for each specific session.

Please note that if the catechetical session follows directly upon the Sunday liturgy of the word, *there is no need to repeat a complete liturgy of the word.* A song, the sign of the cross, the opening prayer taken from the liturgy, and the proclamation of the gospel are all that is necessary.

---

[1]It would be beneficial for people in ministry to be familiar with the study of faith development in children and adults. Basic resources might be James Fowler's *Stages of Faith*, and *Becoming Adult, Becoming Christian* (Harper San Francisco).

A MODEL LITURGY OF THE WORD

When gathering for a liturgy of the word, the following format is used.

A liturgical environment is provided with appropriate symbols, music, and gestures.

Introductory Rites

Entrance Antiphon (sung) or

Psalm (sung) or

Appropriate Song

Entrance Procession
- Reader carries Lectionary or the Book of the Gospels.

Greeting
- Sign of the Cross

Opening Prayer
- The Opening Prayer from the Sunday or feast may be used.

Word of God

Reading (from Old Testament, Sunday or feast, or sacramental celebration)

Responsorial Psalm (always sung)

Reading (from apostolic letters of the Sunday, feast, or sacramental celebration)

Gospel Acclamation (always sung)

Gospel (from Sunday, feast, or sacramental celebration)

Homily

General Intercessions (adapted to occasion)

Lord's Prayer

Concluding Rites

Prayer/Blessing

Sign of Peace

Dismissal

FORMAT FOR CATECHETICAL SESSIONS WITH A MINISTRY GROUP

1. Life Check-in. Life is often shared in the midst of the session dialogue. Unresolved issues may surface and perhaps be dealt with in the coming session. Be careful with this piece. Good gate-keeping is essential. This is simply a check-in. Unless there is some major crisis in the group, this segment needs to be extremely brief. Life is shared throughout the reflection process.

2. "Are there any connections, themes or issues that need to be brought forward from last week into this week?" Too much time spent on #1 and #2 will prohibit the session from moving forward, so prudence is essential. However, crisis and major problems need to be resolved on the spot.

3. Celebrate the "Breaking open the Word" session: a) song, b) opening prayer, c) first reading, d) psalm, e) second reading, f) gospel,[2] g) naming the experience of the readings, h) articulating an understanding of the experience, i) giving input regarding the liturgical context and j) the exegesis, k) testing original assumptions and understanding in light of the exegesis.[3]

4. Sharing life experience. Help the group name any renewed insights or experiences of transformation that have resulted from their sharing of scripture and tradition.

5. Decision. Help group members articulate the implications of their sharing and what, if any, decisions for action or commitments they are considering.

6. Present doctrinal material. The facilitator names the doctrine and gives a one- or two-sentence definition. A question is asked to help place the issue in the context of the natural sign or personal experience. However, this is sometimes difficult, as some people have no experience of certain doctrines. For example, naming or understanding questions regarding the doctrine of eschatology might be: "Have you ever given any thought to your own death? What do you think happens after you die?" It would be most inappropriate to ask someone to name their experience of eschatology if they had never heard the word before that day. Common sense is certainly an asset in catechetical ministry.

7. Closing prayer or ritual.

CLARIFICATIONS

Scripture

Celebrate the liturgy of the word with your group as you did in your preparation session. Remember that it is a continuation of the liturgy from which they were just dismissed. Simplify the exe-

---

[2]If there is only time for reflection on the gospel, then you will need to decide whether you are going to proclaim all of the readings or just the gospel.

[3]Breaking open the Word in a Catechumenal Setting: In a catechumenal setting the catechumens are dismissed from the liturgy following the homily to further reflect on the word of God. At that point they go to another space to continue reflection on the liturgy of the word or, in places where there is no space available for further reflection, they simply go home to return at another time to continue the work begun at the liturgy. In the first scenario the catechumens and catechist are dismissed and gather in another place. They may begin with a song from the liturgy and an opening prayer. The readings or gospel (refer to footnote #2) are proclaimed again and reflection begins. Generally, there is time only for steps a–h before it is time to stop and gather with sponsors and the community for hospitality after the liturgy is over. The sponsors join the group and all return for a continuation of breaking open the word and the catechetical session. The second portion of the session begins with a proclamation of the gospel. The catechist presents the liturgical context and the exegesis and the conver-

sation with the liturgy and scripture resumes. The doctrinal issue is then explored using the reflection process and time is spent drawing conclusions, identifying implications, and coming to decisions based on the sharing, study, and reflection of the day.

In the second scenario, the catechumens are dismissed to do either steps a–h or they are dismissed to go home. When they return at a later time, they begin the session with the liturgy of the word from the Sunday liturgy. If they have already participated in the naming and understanding exercises on Sunday, they begin with the liturgy of the word and resume with the liturgical context, the biblical exegesis, and everything following.

gesis as much as possible. Be brief. The same reflection questions used in your preparation session may be used if they are appropriate for this group. Catechetical sessions take place *after* the experience of Sunday liturgy. Reflection takes place in light of the liturgical experience. Remember to include insights and memories gleaned from the ritual experience of the community's liturgy, including symbols, words, homily and music, etc. Consider the questions you will use in light of the composition of your group. For example, you might not use the same language or questions for people in the catechumenate as you would for people in a small Christian community.

Avoid "churchy" language. Make no assumptions that people know what you are talking about. Connect your questions to the material shared. For example, if the gospel is about the unjust steward, refer to the unjust steward in your questions.

Connect questions as much as possible to the experience of the liturgy. For example, *decision questions* might look something like this: "What might the story of the unjust steward have to say to our community about stewardship? How was this addressed to our community in today's liturgy? How would Jesus concretely address us today in light of what we learned from the parable about the unjust steward? What should we/I do about it?"

Tradition

Present the doctrinal material in the same fashion as scripture was presented. Give a one- or two-sentence overview of a particular precept or issue. Allow people the opportunity and time to reflect, observe, and react. Allow them the opportunity to articulate the meaning for themselves. Provide accurate, informed input regarding the issue (church documents, Doctrinal Appendix, etc.). Be careful to keep the input section brief, no more than ten minutes. It is not meant to be an exhaustive study of each topic. Rather, the intent is to help people live the life of faith encountered through God's presence in community, word, and eucharist and apply it to the Christian life. Doctrine often points the way.

Make sure that *transformation* rather than *information* is a primary focus.[4]

Allow testing and discussion with the doctrinal input piece in order to challenge original assumptions and understanding of the issue. Encourage people to grapple with the "decision for action" questions. There is a common tendency to reduce challenge questions to ethereal mind-sets rather than praxis (practice informed by theory/theology). "What difference does this issue make in my life?" "In what way am I/we called to change due to the scriptural and doctrinal material we have shared today?"

The Planning Session:
Things to remember as you plan your session.

1. Try to make connections with the previous week's session or sharing.

    Is there something that can be brought over into the sharing today? In a brief statement, how was your life different as a result of our sharing last week? Is there any unfinished business? Is there an overall thematic statement we can make as we move into this session?

2. Decide what direction to take in light of the sharing that took place in your preparation session.

    How does what we just shared [in our preparation session] specifically impact and affect the people in our ministry group? Is there a specific aspect of biblical scholarship that is more pertinent to their journey? Can all the material that we shared be covered? If so, how? If not, what are priority issues?

---

[4]Please make no mistake in regard to my bias concerning transformation vs. information. Information is not bad; it is desirable and laudable. Catholics should be doctrinally literate. I am not only in favor of passing on information, I love teaching Catholic doctrine. However, in the past, most of our efforts were centered around imparting information while assuming the information would provide the impetus for transformation. Experience has taught me that most people encounter the living God before doctrine impacts them on any meaningful level. Thus, balance is imperative: transformation and information.

3. Decide what areas might be problematic.

   Are there issues we have discussed that will cause unnecessary tension and difficulty for the group? If so, how do we deal with that?

4. Decide what questions need to be asked in order to effectively and concretely move group members through the reflection process.

   What questions should we ask to help them move, as we did, from naming their initial impressions and understanding to allowing the scholarship to test their assumptions and biases in order to appropriate renewed meaning and praxis (practice informed by theology) for action? What challenge questions need to be asked? What are the implications for the community and for the individual?

5. Decide on the practical format and techniques.

   How should the material be presented? What is the format for the questions: write in journal, one-to-one sharing, wider group, small group sharing, etc? What equipment (e.g., flip chart, paper, pencils, markers, overhead projector, journals, bibles, etc.) is needed?

6. Decide on supplementary materials.

   Are there any supplementary materials that we would like to use such as Catholic Updates, bulletin inserts, articles, books, etc.?

7. Discuss current issues and events that might impact the group's sharing.

   What are the current, pertinent issues in the church, neighborhood, civic community, and world that might enter the conversation? (Never ignore a local crisis issue that is weighing heavily on the community. It impacts people's lives and so should be included in their dialogue with the gospel.)

   For example, the major employer in my parish is the Kennedy Space Center. It would have been an affront not to spend considerable time lamenting the Challenger explosion so many years ago. There was not a person in the parish who was not impacted in some way either directly (having worked on the Challenger) or indirectly. Liturgy, the gospel, and worship are connected to our everyday lives. That event impacted our community in untold ways for years as we lamented, prayed, and celebrated the resumption of the suspended shuttle program in our Sunday gatherings. While that is a dramatic example, be sure to pay attention to what is happening in the local civic community that will impact those in your ministry groups.

8. Determine what doctrinal issues might surface from within the group other than the issue being prepared.

   What issues of post-biblical teaching might surface in addition to, or other than, what we have prepared? Would we be ready to address those issues?

9. Remember to connect the doctrinal material to everyday life.

   How do we connect the post-biblical teaching (doctrine) to the lived experience of those in our ministry group? What are the appropriate questions to help them see the relevance for their lives?

10. Determine what types of prayers and/or blessings will be used.

    What prayer experiences are we going to incorporate: rituals, prayers, spontaneous prayer, prayers from *Catholic Household Blessings and Prayers,* catechumenal minor rites such as blessings, exorcisms, and anointing? (The Minor Rites of the RCIA, #81-101 are normative closing and opening prayers for the catechumenate and should be used over and over as they, like liturgy, are formative.)

11. Invite (when appropriate and possible) other parishioners to share their stories and lives with the ministry group.

Should others from the community be invited to share their story or experience with the ministry group? Who are they and why should they be present?

12. Invite the people to serve in apostolic ministry.

   In what ways are we encouraging and challenging the mission activities in the lives of people in our group? When did we last address those questions? Are we asking concrete questions that require a practical response?

13. Determine the foundational issue.

   Did we ask the bottom-line question: What are the "so what's" of this session? In what way does this experience of liturgy, scripture, and tradition challenge the community and the individual? What action will be taken?

14. Remember the ongoing issues.

   Did we remember to: a) include questions that center on the four signs of catechesis: natural, biblical, liturgical, and ecclesial, and b) include questions that touch the basic themes of the scripture: covenant, creation, exodus, and community?

15. Determine necessary praxis for working with children.

   If our work is with children, have we chosen age and developmentally appropriate as well as sensory and concrete ways of passing on the message of what has just been shared?

16. Determine music and environment questions.

   What music will we use in our session? Where and when will we use it? Are books or song sheets to be used? How will we create a prayerful environment that will enhance and highlight the symbols of the season?

8. Time and the Liturgical Cycle

Sacred Time

God resides in the space of our temporal lives. Our daily lives are ordered by the sequence of time. It marks our coming and our going. Time determines when we will work, when we will play, and when we will pray. Time is sacred. Our lives as Catholic Christians are ordered by the sacred observance of time. Each day is holy. Each day, each hour, brings a renewed encounter with the Morning Star, the Dawn of Salvation, our Evening Light, the Prince of Peace. The hand of God at creation sanctified all created things, among them, the ordering of days and nights. God, the Master Artist, captured the fleeting moment and fixed it with other moments to form the hour. The hour was multiplied to fix the day, the day to form the week, the week to order the year. In order to understand the significance of our own liturgical calendar and what it expresses, it would be helpful to plumb the religious history of how our ancestors understood the division and ordering of time.

In the Hebrew scriptures time was regarded in a way that was far different from the way in which we regard it in modern times. There was no Hebrew word for *time* meaning duration. Time was seen as the "moment or period during which something happens."[1] Human life was a compilation of the events of time. "There is a time for everything under the sun; a time to be born and a time to die" (Eccl 3:13).

There were various perceptions of time: enduring time, appointed time, liturgical time, and measuring time. *Enduring time* was the measuring of time that formed a beginning and an ending, time that resembled eternity, an abstract sense of timelessness.[2] Current events were "perceived as stretch-

ing backward or forward or as continuing indefinitely, but this is not the same as eternity, as a life or event outside of time."[3] *Appointed time* was a reference term to identify a specific event, particularly the "prescribed feasts."[4] At the *appointed time* the assembly would gather for celebration of ritual feasts. *Measuring time* viewed the work of God at creation as that of ordering time into fixed hours, days, months, and years. God was the creator of time and sustained and ordained every facet of life. Time was the servant of God's purpose. Human beings were to use time for establishing God's shalom and justice as they ordered their lives and relationships in tune with God's will. The Israelites eventually moved toward an understanding of time as historical. Time was seen in relationship to the saving events of Yahweh.

The New Testament viewed time through the lens of Judaism. A day extended from sundown on one day to sundown the next. Thus, the Last Supper and the crucifixion took place on the same day. In first-century Palestine, time was measured in far less stressful terms than today. Time seemed to stand suspended in an extended *present*. There was no rush or anxiety about the future. The moment had its own concerns. Time in the New Testament was seen in terms of its eternal or everlasting quality (*aion*—the modern word "eon" comes from this Greek origin). Everlasting time had already begun for the Christian *in this life*. It began at the paschal event of Jesus. Even though the synoptic gospels looked at everlasting time as a future event, John referred to it as a present reality. For John, "eternal life begins now, as soon as one turns to Jesus in faith."[5]

---

[1] Kathleen O'Connor, "Time," in *The Collegeville Pastoral Dictionary of Biblical Theology*, ed. Carroll Stuhlmueller, C.P. (Collegeville: The Liturgical Press, 1996), 998.

[2] However, the concept of eternity as life after death, everlasting life, did not evolve until much later in Israel's history. The timelessness of enduring time was *not* an allusion to

life after death or eternity as we understand it. It had more to do with extended time; time that stood still, suspended in the timelessness of God.

[3] O'Connor, "Time," 999.

[4] Ibid., 1001.

[5] Sean P. Kealy, C.S.S.P. "Time," in *The Collegeville Pastoral Dictionary of Biblical Theology*, ed. Carroll Stuhlmueller, C.P. (Collegeville: The Liturgical Press, 1996), 1000-1002.

Another concept of time in the New Testament is that which refers to a determined, specific, set time, "ordinary calendar time as a quantity" (Greek—*chronos*). Chronos time ruled the ancients' daily lives and kept society functioning. A spiritual rendering of time in the New Testament is referred to as *kairos*. *Kairos* refers to those moments of spiritual significance, such as Jesus' coming and the moments and events of his life. It also refers to the circumstances in an individual's or community's life that are transitional, significant moments in the faith journey. All time was seen in relationship to Jesus Christ.

Historical time moved from the past to the present fulfillment in Jesus. Early Christians saw themselves as living in the last age; that is, they lived in the future. The future began with Christ's death and resurrection while they awaited the day of his second coming (as do we in this last age). The resurrection launched eternity. *Kairos* time envisions time and all the events of history in relationship to the Christ event.

Judaism understood time as cyclic. The events of God's intervention in human history were remembered and made present for each generation. They could not be repeated, but in the remembering, God's action was made effective for each succeeding age. Christians celebrate, recall, and make present the saving acts of Jesus every time they gather. The paschal mystery—Jesus' life, death, and resurrection—was considered the hallmark event of history. Through the paschal mystery humanity shares in Jesus' special relationship to the Father through the Holy Spirit as well as in his passion, death, and resurrection. We unite our lives to Christ's in order to share in the Father's community of love with the Son and the Holy Spirit. We seek to model our lives after Christ's and thus offer our lives as Christ offered his: then, today, and in the future. We do this when we remember (*anamnesis*) Jesus' saving events. Those same events are made present for each generation.

The early Christians ordered their entire lives around Jesus' *pasch*. The *pasch* identified who they were, how they were to live, how they were to wait for his return. Time was seen as a memorial to his passion, death, and resurrection. The morning and evening temple sacrifices were "reinterpreted as symbols of Jesus' own sacrifice."[6] The sun's slumber and awakening were seen in terms of Jesus' death and resurrection. Sundown symbolized Jesus' death and our hope for his return and for everlasting life. Sunup symbolized his resurrection. Israel's feasts were transposed into a Christian re-ordering. The yearly Passover became a metaphor for Jesus' passage from death to life.[7]

The early Christian community celebrated an annual *pasch* in which they remembered Jesus' passion, death, and resurrection. Otherwise, the only set time for prayer and worship in the first two centuries occurred on Sunday. A shift took place in the third century. As it became apparent that Jesus' return was not as immanent as once thought, there was a need to establish regulated practices of worship for the expanding church. A new ordering of time emerged.

As a response to scripture's exhortation to pray always, there emerged the practice of praying at various hours of the day. In the sixth century, monastic communities gathered for prayer at eight fixed times throughout a twenty-four hour period (the liturgy of the hours). The Middle Ages experienced a diminishment of natural symbols and metaphors. Symbols of sun and dawn in relationship to death and resurrection gave way to recitation of the Divine Office at no specific, fixed time during the day.

The liturgical year developed in similar manner. In the very early days of the church, Christians celebrated a yearly commemoration of the *pasch* and gathered only on Sunday. By the third century, Epiphany and commemorations of martyrs were added to the Christian observance. By the fourth century other remembrances of Christian events were added to the repertoire of observable feasts with the inclusion of the Nativity, the Ascension, Pentecost, and martyrs' feasts. Each of these feasts celebrated the entire mystery of Jesus' life,

---

[6]Edward Foley, O.F.M.Cap., "Time: Pastoral Liturgical Tradition," in *The Collegeville Pastoral Dictionary of Biblical Theology*, ed. Carroll Stuhlmueller, C.P. (Collegeville: The Liturgical Press, 1996), 1003.

[7]Ibid.

death, and resurrection. "At their inception these feasts were unitive feasts, each embracing the whole paschal mystery through the prism of a particular faith symbol or event. Thus, Augustine (d. 430) could call them sacraments."[8]

All ritual observances had been celebrated as remembrances and symbols of the paschal mystery. However, usage of symbols and metaphors waned during the Middle Ages. Efforts were made to determine literal historical times, dates, and places of the circumstances of Jesus' life. Time was marked by literal observances of events in his ministry, passion, death, and resurrection. (For example, the secular calendar proceeds from the date of Jesus' birth.)

Nature's rhythms (light and darkness) provide obvious metaphors for the paschal mystery. The light and darkness of day and night are cohesive with body rhythms of the human person. The slumber of night awakens in us the desire for the resurrection brightness of a new day. All parts of creation, its images and its life cycles, are metaphors of life and death. Recent reforms sought to restore the obvious, natural symbols that speak of Christ's paschal mystery: light, darkness, seasons, and feasts. In this way we immerse ourselves in the mystery of Christ's greatest act of redemption as we wait in hope for his return.

The Liturgical Calendar

Due to the reform of the liturgical calendar, Christian observances have been restored to their original context through the renewed, ritual ordering of time. All time is sanctified. The paschal mystery is the centerpiece of all liturgical celebration and ritual observances. "Christ's saving work is celebrated in sacred memory by the Church on fixed days throughout the year. Each week on the day called the Lord's Day, the Church commemorates the Lord's resurrection. Once a year at Easter the Church honors this resurrection and passion with utmost solemnity. Through the yearly cycle the Church unfolds the entire mystery of Christ and keeps the anniversaries of the saints."[9] Thus, the

paschal mystery is the root and the heart of the liturgical cycle. "By means of the liturgical cycle the Church celebrates the whole mystery of Christ, from his incarnation until the day of Pentecost and the expectation of his coming again."[10] The Lord's day, Sunday, commemorates this mystery each week even though the entire Easter season is devoted to its celebration and commemoration.

The church declares that each day is holy,[11] particularly as she gathers for daily worship. Our observance of Sunday is the earliest tradition of worship handed to us from the apostles. This day of the Lord is a weekly paschal event. "Thus Sunday must be ranked as the first holy day of all."[12] Since Sunday is held in such high esteem, nothing preempts it except solemnities and feasts of the Lord. "Only nine festivals can displace the celebration of the Sunday itself."[13] The Sundays of Advent, Lent and Easter, however, "take precedence over all solemnities and feasts of the Lord."[14] Easter is an extended meditation on the multifaceted dimensions of the paschal mystery and each Sunday is our ongoing remembrance and expression of devotion to it. We live our lives in the shadow of the cross and resurrection.

Thus, the "mother of all feasts" is Easter. Easter is to the liturgical year what Sunday is to the week. It is the premier ritual, whose life blood flows throughout the year to each and every ritual celebration. The Easter Triduum is the "culmination of the entire liturgical year."[15] The Triduum begins with the celebration of the Lord's Supper on Holy Thursday, continues with the celebration of the Lord's Passion on Good Friday, and culminates at the Easter Vigil in the darkness of night.

The Easter season continues for fifty days and culminates on the feast of Pentecost. Forty days after

---

[8]Ibid., 1005.

[9]"General Norms for the Liturgical Year and the Calendar" (GNLY), in *The Liturgy Documents* (Chicago: Liturgy Training Publications, 1991), #1.

[10]Ibid., #17

[11]Ibid., #3.

[12]*Constitution on the Sacred Liturgy (Sacrosanctum Concilium)*, in *The Liturgy Documents*, (Chicago: Liturgy Training Publications, 1991), #106.

[13]Laurence E. Mick, Timothy Fitzgerald DiCello, Kathleen Hughes, RSCJ, *Sourcebook for Sundays and Seasons* (Chicago: Liturgy Training Publications, 1995), 61.

[14]GNLY, #5.

[15]Ibid., #18.

Easter, the feast of the Ascension is celebrated. The days from Ascension until Pentecost anticipate the coming of the Holy Spirit.

Lent is a time of preparation for the celebration of Easter.[16] It is also a time of preparation for baptism. Catechumens prepare for celebration of the sacrament itself and the faithful prepare to renew their baptismal promises at Easter. It is also a time of renewal and penitence.

Christmas is second only to Easter and celebrates the Incarnation and manifestation of Christ/Spirit/God to the world. "Advent has a twofold character: as a season of preparation for Christmas when Christ's first coming to us is remembered, as a season when that remembrance directs the mind and heart to await Christ's second coming at the end of time. Advent is thus a period of devout and joyful expectation."[17]

Separate from the seasons that remember a particular aspect of Christ's salvific action, there are thirty-three or thirty-four weeks that are not devoted to any one facet of the Christian mystery. For those extended Sundays of the year, the church unfolds and observes all aspects of the mystery of Christ. Those Sundays are referred to as Ordinary Time.

Ordinary Time begins on the Monday after January 6 and continues until the Tuesday before Ash Wednesday. It resumes on the Monday after Pentecost and ends with the First Sunday of Advent.

Throughout the liturgical cycle, the church also remembers and venerates Mary, the mother of God, and commemorates the feasts of various saints and martyrs. The way the importance and significance of the celebration is determined is by its classification as a solemnity, feast, or memorial. Solemnities are principal celebrations of the church. Easter and Christmas are the most important solemnities and continue for eight days (octave).[18]

Feasts are next in importance and they generally fall on the natural days unless they fall on Sunday and commemorate the Lord during Ordinary Time and the Christmas season.[19] Memorials are observances that fall on weekdays. They are either obligatory or optional. Obligatory memorials must be celebrated on the designated day.

All ritual celebrations of the church cycle recall and make present the saving event of Jesus Christ through his life, death, and resurrection. "In the last analysis the paschal mystery is celebrated in every liturgical feast and in every feast the Lord who emptied himself, sacrificed himself in obedience unto death, and is now glorified, is present to his community and acts efficaciously in it."[20]

---

[16]Ibid., #27.

[17]Ibid., #39.

[18]Ibid., #11.

[19]Ibid., #13.

[20]Adolf Adam, *The Liturgical Year,* trans. Matthew J. O'Connell (Collegeville: The Liturgical Press, 1990), 31.

9. LITURGICAL CYCLE C: OVERVIEW OF LUKE'S GOSPEL

This liturgical cycle is year C, the year of Luke. We encounter Jesus through the eyes of Luke, the evangelist. (Mark is read during Cycle B and Matthew during Cycle A.) During this liturgical year, beginning on the First Sunday of Advent, most of Luke's gospel is proclaimed. The chapters dealing with the infancy narratives, Incarnation, and manifestation (1:5–3:22) are proclaimed during the Advent/Christmas season. Chapters concerning Christ's passion, death, and resurrection (22:1-24:33) are proclaimed during Passion Sunday and Easter time. More than sixty percent of Luke's gospel is encountered on the Sundays of Cycle C.

In addition to being the last of the synoptic gospels to have been written (Luke's gospel dates from approximately 85 C.E.,[1] Matthew's from 80 C.E., and Mark's from 70 C.E.), Luke's is the longest gospel. There are 1,149 verses in Luke's gospel as opposed to Mark (661 verses) and Matthew (1,068). Luke's is the only gospel with a preface that tells what the gospel is about. Even though the infancy narratives appear at the beginning of the gospel, they were not added until the very end. Luke was not as concerned with the history of the Christ event as he was with the meaning of it.

The gospels are documents that assume an existent faith in the people. They were not written in order to prove that Jesus was the Son of God. It was already assumed that the people knew, accepted, and believed that fact. There was no intention to provide an historical accounting of Jesus' life. However, there is factual, historical material within each gospel. The "Scriptures are documents of faith. The stories are true; some are not factual.

Faith does not require historical proof."[2] The miracle stories were told, for example, to prove that Jesus had access to the power of God and that we too have that same access through the Holy Spirit. "Miracles are faith stories that try to 'concretize God's power in the lives of all he touched.'"[3]

There are three major concerns of Luke, the evangelist: martyrdom, miracles, and fulfilled prophecy. "Luke's narrative would have given certainty to Christian and non-Christian alike because it appealed to the persuasiveness of selfless commitment (martyrdom), of power (miracle), and of being right and having roots (fulfilled prophecy). This narrative of Jesus is told with a persuasiveness intended to give certainty."[4]

The New Testament indicates that Luke was a physician, an associate of St. Paul's, and the author of the Acts of the Apostles. It is possible that Luke was not a Jew since there is little attention given to Jewish issues in his gospel. Luke's community is made up of Antiochan Jews and Gentiles. It is a mixed group. Some are wealthy; some are not. The wealthy Christians are afraid that they will lose everything if persecutions come upon their community. Luke tries to instill in them the conviction that one must be willing to lose all for the establishment of God's reign. He tries to tell the rich and the poor that there is much at stake.

Luke's begins his narration as an exhortation to the catechumen, Theophilus. Luke proclaims to Theophilus and the first-century world that Jesus was everything his followers believed him to be and more. Luke presents Jesus as a prophet who was misunderstood. He was not accepted as a prophet and was falsely accused of the charges against him.

---

[1] C.E. refers to the term *Common Era.* Contemporary biblical scholarship has adopted this ecumenically sensitive reference to historical and biblical time. Thus, there has been a "shift from the traditional calendar terminology, B.C. ("Before Christ") and A.D. ("In the Year of the Lord"), to the inclusive calendar terminology, B.C.E. ("Before the Common Era") and C.E. ("Common Era"). (Bernhard W. Anderson, *Understanding the Old Testament* [Englewood Cliffs: Prentice Hall, 1986], 6.)

---

[2] Eugene Hensler, "The Gospel of Luke," Workshop, Cocoa Beach, Fl., Oct. 1993.

[3] Ibid.

[4] Charles Talbert, *Reading Luke* (New York: Crossroad, 1992), 5.

Luke insists that behavior is a key element of the Christian life. To be a believer, one's action must reflect his or her belief. Christian discipline was an expectation. Every believer was to be engaged in the ongoing process of metanoia. "He [Luke] often stresses the importance of action, above all else in the social realm, and, in a word, effective charity. He does not give us a set of precepts or detailed rules, but he suggests concrete principles of action that each person must employ in his or her particular situation."[5] Luke insists that disciples must compassionately provide for the poor and needy. In Luke's gospel the "have-nots" will have access to the kingdom of God.[6] The "haves" will be left standing at the door. Luke's gospel has often been called the gospel of outcasts. God's revelation was announced to women and shepherds, society's lowest. Women appear in Luke more than any other gospel.

Luke's gospel is also known as the gospel of prayer. Jesus was repeatedly depicted praying. Luke's community was facing an identity crisis. There were persecutions taking place, from both within and without. Considerable time had distanced the community from the actual death/resurrection of Jesus. They were vacillating in their apostolic fervor. Questions abounded. Perhaps their prayers for the coming kingdom had been useless. Was the risen Christ still in their midst? Luke writes his gospel in order to deal with these serious faith questions. Perhaps a new understanding of the life and mission of Christ would "help them appreciate the value of their prayer, to recognize the risen Lord in the concrete situations of their communities, and to give fearless expression to their mission. So renewed, they would devote themselves to the apostles' teaching and fellowship, to the breaking of bread and the prayers" (Acts 2:42).[7]

Table fellowship is very important for Luke. Jesus is often portrayed as eating. "Meals are the privileged place for Jesus' teaching."[8] Luke's Jesus re-vealed a great deal about the counter-cultural reign he had come to establish through the meals he shared and through the often shady and questionable dinner companions he entertained. The God Jesus proclaimed was not going to be placed in the box of expected societal norms. God's grace was perfectly, freely given to all. All were to be included in the great banquet, both in this realm and in the eternal hereafter. No one was to be excluded except those who chose not to eat. Each of Jesus' meal episodes are laden with meaning. Luke sees eucharist as the common thread that weaves the parts of Jesus' ministry together. Jesus' every meal was a part of the "origins of the eucharist and revealed its implication for the life of the church."[9]

Luke's gospel is also known as the gospel of compassion, mercy and forgiveness. Jesus was compassionate and caring toward people. He freely offered salvation and forgiveness to those who turn away and break God's covenant, whether that be the righteous or the outcast.

The gospel's natural organization is according to the geographical sites and locations of Jesus' ministry. In *The New Jerome Biblical Commentary*, Robert Karris organizes Luke's gospel in the following manner:

Preface (1:1-4)

Dawn of Fulfillment of God's Promise (1:5–2:52)

Preparation for Jesus' Public Ministry (3:1–4:13)

Jesus' Galilean Ministry (4:14–9:50)

Jesus' Journey to Jerusalem (9:51–19:27)

Jerusalem Rejects God's Prophet (19:28–21:38)

Jesus' Last Meal and Association with Sinners (22:1–23:56)

Jesus' Vindication, Promise of the Spirit, and Ascension (23:56b–24:53)[10]

---

[5]*Days of the Lord*, Vol.1 (Collegeville: The Liturgical Press, 1991), 119.

[6]Hensler, "The Gospel of Luke."

[7]Eugene LaVerdiere, *Luke* (Wilmington: Michael Glazier, 1980), xii.

[8]Eugene LaVerdiere, *Dining in the Kingdom of God* (Chicago: Liturgy Training Publications, 1994), 14.

[9]Ibid., viii.

[10]Robert J. Karris, "The Gospel According to Luke," in *The New Jerome Biblical Commentary*, ed. Raymond E. Brown, S.S., Joseph A. Fitzmyer, S.J., Roland E. Murphy, O.Carm. (Englewood Cliffs: Prentice Hall, 1990), 677.

THE SEASON OF ADVENT

THE SEASON OF ADVENT: AN OVERVIEW

"Advent begins with the first evening prayer of the Sunday that falls closest to November 30 and ends before the first evening prayer of Christmas."[1] The document "General Norms for the Liturgical Year and the Calendar" states: "The season of Advent has a twofold character. It is a time of preparation for Christmas when the first coming of God's son to men is recalled. It is also a season when minds are directed by this memorial to Christ's second coming at the end of time. It is thus a time of joyful and spiritual expectation."[2]

The origin of Advent dates back to the fifth century and is influenced by the Eastern Church. The primary focus of this liturgy was expectation of the Lord's birth at Christmas. The first evidence of Roman observance of the season occurred around the sixth century. There was little emphasis placed on the parousia. The focus was on preparation for the celebration of Christ's birth.

At the same time, however, there were other shifts taking place that would eventually impact Advent's original focus. The Irish missionaries had descended upon Gaul with a compelling message concerning the final judgment of humanity. They exhorted people to repent in the face of eventual judgment. Thus, Advent became laden with penitential overtones. This influence reached the Roman church by the twelfth century as evidenced by the wearing of purple vestments and the exclusion of the Gloria during the liturgy. Yet, in spite of this, the penitential character of Advent was different in tone from that of Lent. There was an inherent joy to the penitential observance. There was clear intention that omission of the Gloria was an anticipatory gesture rather than a penitential gesture. "It is not omitted for the same reason as it is omitted in Lent, but in order that on the night of Christmas the angels' song may ring out again in all its newness."[3]

The first Sunday of Advent begins a new liturgical year and liturgical cycle: CYCLE C. During this year we encounter Jesus through the eyes of Luke, the evangelist. Luke has a different perspective than his predecessor Mark. Luke's community seeks to deal with the pastoral reality that Jesus' return is not as imminent as Mark's community believed. They were forced to appropriate a new understanding of Jesus' promise to return. Luke's Christians did not deny that Jesus would come again. It was a foundational truth. Luke, however, had an additional agenda. He was concerned with issues of relationship, relationship with God and with one another, while still focusing on and hoping for the parousia.

Luke's community had grown in Christian maturity. Mark's community was a community in its infancy whose principal concern was the immediate return of Jesus. Luke, on the other hand, aware that Jesus' return was not necessarily imminent, impressed upon his readers that growth in the Christian life and deep ongoing relationship (metanoia) with God and God's people is primary as they anticipate that great and terrible day. Luke called for diligence in living the kerygma. The end would come soon enough; disciples must keep a watchful, hopeful vigil, but they must also maintain an active prayer life if they are to withstand the temptations of their present reality. Only through constant prayer will the work of transformation and ongoing relationship with Christ grow. Only through expectant waiting and prayerful longing will their hope in the Risen One flourish.

---

[1] "General Norms for the Liturgical Year and the Calendar" (GNLY), in *The Liturgy Documents* (Chicago: Liturgy Training Publications, 1991), #40.

[2] Ibid., #39.

[3] *Commetarius In Annum Liturgicum Instauratum*, cap. I, sect. II, 2 (p. 61), published by the Consilium for the Implementation of the Constitution on the Sacred Liturgy.

Advent prepares us for the coming of the Savior. We must ask ourselves, "From what do we need saving?" The scriptures of Advent challenge us to wait for the day of the Lord, but they also demand that justice reign. In the biblical sense, justice (Hebrew: *hesed*) refers to right relationship with God as evidenced by one's behavior toward God and God's people. The demands of justice are not suggestions; they are commands. Advent asks the tough question: How are we living *hesed* relationship with our God? If we are God's people, if we are in covenant relationship with God, then we must be advocates of justice wherever injustice takes center stage.

Another theme that echoes through the season is penitential. God's people are to recognize, name, and lament over the evil that permeates the world and work to eradicate it. Throughout Advent we hear from the ancient prophets who cry, "Repent and change your lives!" The prophets' cry is as relevant today as it was then. They foretold the light that would shine in the midst of darkness. Christ is that light. We are to embrace the light and become the light of Christ in the world.

Advent explores two realities: the kingdom *here and now* and the kingdom *yet to come*. We live in the midst of that tension. We struggle just as Luke struggled to maintain the proper balance between passive waiting and proactive waiting. When we are proactive we cooperate in the work of *history making*. We enter salvation history with God and seek to alter injustice when we see it. We enter the struggle of the kingdom *here and now* with a vigilant eye and hopeful anticipation of the kingdom *yet to come*.

As consumerism seems to preoccupy the culture in the waning days of Advent, our liturgy seeks to bring us back to the "reason for the season." Advent is a wake-up call to the world. Advent's message is a counter-cultural plea to engage in the deeper meaning of the season. It is a mandate to reflect upon and prepare for the second coming of Christ, while looking forward to the celebration of the Incarnation, the ultimate gift of God's personhood to the world. We can do nothing less than ask ourselves the questions of human response and responsibility in the face of such a gratuitous gift.

St. Bernard (1090–1153) gave us a wonderful summation of the meaning of Advent when he wrote:

> We know that there are three comings of the Lord. The third lies between the other two. It is invisible, while the other two are visible. In the first coming he was seen on earth, dwelling among men; he himself testifies that they saw him and hated him. In the final coming "all flesh will see the salvation of our God," and "they will look on him whom they pierced." The intermediate coming is a hidden one; in it only the elect see the Lord within their own selves, and they are saved. In his first coming our Lord came in the flesh and in our weakness; in this middle coming he comes in spirit and in power; in the final coming he will be seen in glory and majesty. Because this coming lies between the other two, it is like a road on which we travel from the first coming to the last. In the first, Christ was our redemption; in the last, he will appear as our life; in this middle coming, he is our rest and consolation.[4]

The First and Second Sunday of Advent center around the future coming of Christ. The Third Sunday's focus is on the present coming and the Fourth Sunday is on the birth of Jesus, the past coming.

Advent and Christmas form a unity. We cannot engage in one season without reflection upon the other. Both seasons complement one another and do not stand alone. Yet Advent and Christmas are also viewed through the lens of Lent and Easter. Advent/Christmas looks toward the fulfillment of the Incarnation that is celebrated through the paschal mystery at Easter.

As in all good liturgy, we are to properly prepare ourselves for full and vibrant participation. Advent prepares the heart and the church for just such participation in the mystery of Christ's Incarnation.

---

[4] *Homelie pour l'Advent*, 5:1-3, *Edition cistercienne*, 4, 1966, pp. 188-190, in *Liturgy of the Hours* (New York: Catholic Book Publishing Co., 1975), p. 169.

FIRST SUNDAY OF ADVENT

INTRODUCTORY RITES

Opening Song (or Entrance Antiphon)

To you, my God, I lift my soul, I trust in you; let
me never come to shame. Do not let my enemies
laugh at me. No one who waits for you is ever put
to shame. (Ps 24:1-3)[1]

Environment

The liturgical color of Advent is a bluish shade of
purple (violet). Attention to the gathering space
will help create a sense of the season with no need
for elaborate explanation. The addition of an Advent wreath in the environment highlights the
new liturgical season. The wreath need not be the
traditional shape. Reminiscent of the "just shoot"
(Jesus was called the root of Jesse, from the shoot
of Jesse's lineage), perhaps just the right configuration of branches could be used to artistically cra-
dle the four candles of each week. Color, candles,
evergreen and/or the barrenness of wood can create a dramatic, yet simple Advent environment.
Four purple candles, or three purple candles and
one rose candle (for Gaudete Sunday, the Third
Sunday of Advent), or four white candles may be
used in the wreath.

Even though there is no prohibition against the
use of flowers during Advent as there is during
Lent, the *Ceremonial of Bishops* suggests that moder-
ation be used. While Advent does reflect a spirit of
joy, the joy is minimized in comparison to the exuberance of Christmas bliss. Thus, flowers should
be used sparingly, but when used, should manifest
simplicity. Less is more.

Prayer of Blessing
from "Blessing of the Advent Wreath"

Let us now pray for God's blessing upon this
    wreath.
Lord, our God,
we praise you for your Son, Jesus Christ: he is Em-
    manuel, the hope of the peoples,

he is the wisdom that teaches and guides us, he is
    the Savior of every nation.
Lord God, let your blessing come upon us as we
    light the candles of this wreath.
May the wreath and its light be a sign of Christ's
    promise to bring us salvation.
May Christ come quickly and not delay. We ask
    this through Christ, our Lord. Amen.[2]

Opening Prayer

*The facilitator of the session may lead the prayer. Others
in the group may be asked to proclaim the readings.*

Let us pray
[that we may take Christ's coming seriously]

    Pause for silent prayer.

All-powerful God,
increase our strength of will for
    doing good
that Christ may find an eager
    welcome at his coming
and call us to his side in the
    kingdom of heaven,
where he lives and reigns with you
    and the Holy Spirit,
one God, for ever and ever. Amen.

LITURGY OF THE WORD

*Members of the group proclaim the readings from the First
Sunday of Advent. All actively listen.*

Let us listen to God's word.

First Reading
Jeremiah 33:14-16

This pericope[3] might have been redacted (taken
from and interpreted) by a disciple of Jeremiah. It
is very similar to an oracle that Jeremiah uttered in

---

[1] First Sunday of Advent, "Entrance Antiphon," *The Sacramentary.*

[2] *Catholic Household Blessings and Prayers* (Washington:
NCCB, 1988), 110.

[3] *Pericope* is a term that refers to the section of a scriptural
passage that is chosen for a particular use. For example, the

earlier chapters. Jerusalem had been destroyed by Babylon and the people had been exiled. The author of Jeremiah seeks to strengthen hope in Yahweh, who will restore the rightful, righteous monarch. Nathan had promised David that his lineage and dynasty would last forever. The people were losing hope in the promise made to David. They were flirting with the gods of their conquerors and becoming lax in their observance of Jewish laws and customs. There was fear that the people would lose their identity as God's chosen. The book's author attempts to restore hope in the Davidic line and the promised messiah (anointed one). This messiah (the "just shoot") will restore justice and the righteousness to God's people. The coming of the messiah will signal a new age in which justice, mercy, and God's saving reign will flourish.

The metaphor of seeking light in the midst of darkness is an appropriate symbol for this first Sunday of Advent, when the church and the world exist in the dimly lit womb of darkness waiting to be born to the dawn of a new age (the renewed kingdom of God on earth).

Responsorial Psalm
Psalm 25:4-5, 8-9, 10, 14

"God is righteous," says the psalmist. This psalm proclaims the coming of Yahweh in truth. "The psalm should not be interpreted moralistically. It speaks of patient waiting for the advent of Yahweh's righteousness."[4]

Second Reading
Thessalonians 3:12–4:2

The Thessalonian letters are probably the beginning of Christian literature. Thessalonica was a city in northern Greece. Paul had attempted to evangelize the Jews of the city, but when his attempts failed he turned his efforts to the Greeks. This enraged the Jews and they expelled Paul and his disciples from the city. The Pauline letters are evidence of Paul's mission. Paul was concerned about the identity of the Christian community (not un-

like the author of Jeremiah who was concerned about the identity of the people of Israel in the face of oppression). Paul sent messengers to Thessalonica to relay his concern that the Thessalonian church might be tempted to turn away from God in the face of persecution. There was no immediate crisis; Paul simply wanted to affirm the work already accomplished by Timothy and challenge the community to continued diligence. His letter[5] is an admonition against future temptations while affirming community members in their present adherence to gospel living. Paul sought to offer strength and consolation to the communities as they awaited the fulfillment of Christ's promise to return. While encouraging them in their progress, Paul nevertheless exhorted them to an even greater commitment to the Christian life. This message echoes throughout the Advent season as we look in hope toward the second coming of Christ.[6]

Gospel
Luke 21:25-28, 34-36

Jesus tells his disciples that he will return a second time. He tells them that they will know it is time for his arrival by the signs that will accompany his return. His description of this cataclysmic event is enough to send terror through even the most stout-hearted. Thus, he accompanies his prediction regarding the end times with the consolation that disciples of Jesus have nothing to fear. Through vigilance and constant prayer they will be prepared to enter the gates of the new Jerusalem with bodies erect and heads held high.

Lectionary chooses specific verses from particular chapters in the bible. The selected text is called a pericope.

[4]Reginald H. Fuller, *Preaching the New Lectionary* (Collegeville: The Liturgical Press, 1974), 455.

---

[5]*Letter*: A letter was personal communication between two parties who were separated. The letter was usually occasioned by a particular situation. "According to Dreissman, only a few of Paul's works would be called epistles, while the rest were intended as letters" (Patricia Datchuck Sanchez, *The Word We Celebrate* [Kansas City: Sheed and Ward, 1989], 264.)

Epistle: An epistle was a form of literature that resembled a letter only in style and form. There was little else about it that resembled a letter. The epistle was a written essay for the purpose of public instruction or discussion of a disputed subject.

[6]See Sanchez, *The Word We Celebrate*, and Luke T. Johnson, *The Writings of the New Testament* (Minneapolis: Augsburg Fortress, 1986).

STEP 1
NAMING ONE'S EXPERIENCE

What were your first impressions? What was your first response? What caught your attention? How did you feel as Jesus taught his disciples in this gospel? How did the readings affect you?

Each person names his or her initial impression. Statement should be brief. No reasons should be given at this time. All simply listen without agreeing or disagreeing.

STEP 2
UNDERSTANDING

Were there any experiences in your life that may have shaped the way you heard the story? What understanding of this gospel do you already bring with you to this dialogue? What are your biases? In a brief statement, what do you think Jesus was trying to convey to his disciples? What is the intent of this gospel? In your opinion, what is it trying to convey?

All share their understanding of what the text is trying to convey.

STEP 3
INPUT FROM VISION/STORY/TRADITION

Liturgical Context

The facilitator discusses the liturgical context and the reason why these texts appear on this Sunday in this season.

Today begins the new liturgical cycle: Cycle C. Communities need to be reminded about the importance of the liturgical year, what it expresses and how important the seasons are to understanding the fullness of our Christian faith.[7] Catechetical groups should also reflect on the season of Advent, the church's celebration and understanding as well as communal and personal implications. How are we, the church, celebrating the season? How are we

---
[7]Refer to chapter 8, "Time and the Liturgical Cycle."

responding as a parish to the obvious issues of justice throughout the season? What are we doing in our families to observe the season in our homes?

The liturgy of Advent seeks to prepare us to enter fully into the mystery of Christ's coming. Jesus comes to us as we prepare to celebrate his Incarnation at Christmas and his coming again at the cataclysmic end of time. The liturgy engages in an *anamnesis* of God's role in salvation history. It also highlights the role of humanity in God's plan of salvation. Salvation is already ours. The prophets of old cry to us from their ancient graves with the same plea we hear from contemporary prophetic voices: "Reform your lives, the day of the Lord is near." Whether that final day comes in our lifetime or in the future makes no difference. Our lives are to reflect prayerful diligence and attentiveness to the task of waiting in joyful hope. The liturgies of Advent give us the opportunity to observe and reflect upon the future kingdom as we tell the stories of kingdoms past and live in the midst of the kingdom present.

Advent's liturgies remind us that we have an advocate amid the afflictions of this world. The Psalm and the Entrance Antiphon echo the depths of the human soul in its daring trust of God. "To you, my God, I lift my soul, I trust in you...for you are my Savior." During this season of *metanoia* we ask God to conform our will and our minds to the heart and mind of God. The liturgy resounds our fervent pleas. "Increase our will for doing good" (Opening Prayer). "Make your ways known to us" (Ps 25). Increase in us our capacity to love others (Second Reading). The eucharist strengthens us and forms us for the task of building God's kingdom. We ask the Lord to teach us to love heaven and guide our way on earth (Prayer after Communion). All this *metanoia*, submission to God's will, and interior and exterior preparation primes us for our great eschatological hope when the Lord will come "on a cloud with great power and glory" (Gospel).

Gospel Exegesis

The facilitator provides input from critical biblical scholarship. This input includes insights as to how people would have heard the gospel in Jesus' time.

Even though the gospel of Luke is read consecutively throughout most of the liturgical year during Ordinary Time, the Lectionary fast-forwards to the latter part of the gospel in order for us to reflect on "the future apocalyptic teaching on Advent where it is particularly seasonable."[8]

A discussion earlier in the chapter helps set the stage for how we are to understand this pericope. In verse 5 someone comments on how beautifully the temple is adorned. Jesus overhears and prophetically comments that one day not a temple stone will be left standing. Obviously, it was wondered when such a catastrophe would take place. This debate provides Jesus with the opportunity to place the discussion in a much larger setting with far greater implications: the cosmic disturbances that will occur just before the end [eschaton] approaches. Chapter 21 deals with two primary issues: the need to give witness to Christ in the face of impending religious persecution and the necessity of persevering while waiting for his return.

The way one withstands is through diligence and constant prayer. The church after Jesus' resurrection will be strengthened in the face of persecution. People need not fear. When they are dragged through the synagogue and civilian courts for their belief in Jesus, they are to give witness to him by the power of the Holy Spirit. They need not worry about their bodies. Yes, they can be destroyed in this life; however, everlasting life is the reward for such steadfast faithfulness. Another basic tenet of faith can be observed in this section: inherent belief in the resurrection of God's people.

The second concern of Luke in chapter 21 is perseverance. Earlier in Luke, disciples hear that they are to weigh their options before jumping with both feet into the rigors of discipleship. It is a challenging and strenuous undertaking and requires the greatest stamina and endurance. It requires giving one's self over completely to the will and the mission of Christ. This is no light matter. "Discipleship is not periodic volunteer work on one's own terms and at one's convenience."[9] The

gospel suggests that it would be better not to become a disciple than to acquiesce in the face of impending doom. Perseverance is required in the face of such rigors.

Disciples are to be prepared at all times. They will know the end is near when political uprisings occur and when there is great tumult in the universe. Those two signs will alert the readied disciples to the coming of their messiah on a cloud to take the faithful multitudes to their final resting place. Such readiness can take place only through vigilant prayer and conscientious living.[10]

In hearing Luke's exhortation to avoid carousing and drunkenness while awaiting Christ's coming, we might be tempted to identify too greatly with the intended ancient audience, thinking them no different from communities of today.[11] John Pilch warns us against such wrong assumptions. Pilch suggests that the majority of the people were poor peasants. They certainly did not live extravagant lives; their everyday concerns consumed all their time and energy. They were in a survival mode. Their only agenda was to secure the necessary provisions for each day's living. Pilch asserts that this text refers to the rich or the greedy. A primary issue in Luke's gospel is the refusal of the greedy to share with the poor. Pilch suggests that every time we see the word *rich* in Luke's gospel we should substitute the word *greedy*. According to Luke, such folks will be ill-prepared for the coming of the Son of Man. Disciples are to stay awake and pray. Prayer is the antidote to fear.

Proclaim the gospel again.

Sometimes we gain new insights when we hear the text after the interpretation has been given. Someone from the group proclaims the gospel a second time.

---

[8]Fuller, *Preaching the New Lectionary,* 455.

[9]Robert J. Karris, *Gospel of St. Luke* (Chicago: Franciscan Herald Press, 1974), 59.

[10]Charles H. Talbert, *Reading Luke* (New York: Crossroad, 1992), 199-205.

[11]John J. Pilch, "Cultural World of Jesus," *Sunday by Sunday,* Nov. 27, 1994 (Initiative Publications, PO Box 218332, Columbus, OH 43221-8332).

STEP 4
TESTING

Conversation with the Liturgy and Scriptures

Test your original understanding in dialogue with the interpretation.

(You might consider breaking into smaller groups.)

Now that you've heard what the scholars have to say about this passage, how do you feel about it? Was there anything that made you uneasy? How does your original understanding of this gospel fit with the exegesis (biblical interpretation)? Were there any new insights for you? How would you articulate an understanding of this gospel now?

Sharing Life Experience

Participants share experiences from their own lives that are reflective of the exegesis just given.

I am reminded of a time when someone accused me of "not being spiritual enough." This person felt that I should express my spirituality and my faith according to a particular style. Even though somewhat ruffled by the accusing voice, my discerning spirit affirmed my relationship with God. Light began to shine through the dimness of my interior reflection. I became aware of "moments." Every time I stopped to talk with a hurting stranger or to listen and respond to the homeless in our shelter; every time I shared my faith with someone and they in turn revealed to me a new insight into God's mysterious self, I was jolted with the hushed shout of my deafening inner voice. "This is how we love one another." God was showing me the mystery of radical, reciprocal covenant relationship. God's incredible advent came crashing through me like a lightning bolt through a towering pine. Every time I offered myself to others, and every time others offered themselves to me, God's covenant love was manifest. My inner life, my spirituality, was observable from the way I was attempting to live my life; through my relationships (family, parish, world). Through very imperfect attempts, I was trying to live the love I knew. God's love for me—though completely gratuitous and undeserved—prompted me to give it to

others. The woman's accusation of me became a moment of grace. It was the moment when Lady Wisdom gently showed me the face of God and her name was Stranger, Lonely, Cold, Weary, and Hungry. Will I be prepared to stand humbly and hopeful before God on my last day? On the last day? Only if I am faithful to the gift of love.

Is there any way you can connect this gospel to an experience in your own life?

All share at this time.

What was Jesus trying to say to the community of his time, to the community now, and to me personally? Is God's covenant with humanity expressed in this gospel? How? Are there images or evidence of the exodus theme? In what way does this gospel challenge us to leave something behind and look forward to freedom and liberation in Christ? In what way does Jesus speak to "a people" (community) like Yahweh spoke to Israel? Has our original understanding been stretched, challenged or affirmed?

STEP 5
DECISION

The gospel demands decision.

How does our sharing and this exegesis (biblical interpretation) challenge our community? How does this gospel specifically call our parish to action in the parish, church, or civic/global world? Has our sharing about (1) Jesus' second coming, (2) our suffering due to faith in Jesus, (3) our response to the poor and lowly personally stretched or changed me in any way? Does Jesus' exhortation to the greedy rich hit home in any way? How is this a word for twentieth-century America? What concrete thing could we/I do in response to what we have learned and shared today?

DOCTRINAL ISSUES

What church truth/teaching/doctrinal issue could be drawn from the gospel for the First Sunday of Advent?

Participants suggest possible doctrinal themes that flow from the readings.

Possible Doctrinal Themes

Advent; eschatology; kingdom of God; Christ's coming: future, present, past; Son of Man; parousia

Present the doctrinal material at this time.

1. The facilitator gives input on a particular doctrinal issue of his/her prior choosing. OR

2. Group members choose a doctrinal issue from the list they created. They read together from the Doctrinal Appendix.

(The doctrinal issues are found in the Doctrinal Appendix in the back of this workbook. If you are choosing an issue from this resource, please refer to it now.)

Reflection questions centered around the chosen doctrinal theme can be found in the Doctrinal Appendix. The questions are based on the five-step reflection process. If you choose a topic not included in the Doctrinal Appendix, you may craft your own questions according to the same five-step process.

Following the reflection questions you will be reminded to return to chapter 7, "Preparing the Catechetical Session," to assist you in crafting your own session.

Closing Prayer

Let us pray to the Lord who is a God of love to all peoples.

Pause for silent prayer.

Teach us, O God, to seek you,
and when we seek you, show yourself to us,
for we cannot seek you unless you teach us,
nor can we find you unless you show yourself to us.
Let us seek you in desiring you, and desire you in
    seeking you,
find you in loving you, and love you in finding
    you.

We ask this through Jesus Christ, your Son, our Lord, Jesus Christ. Amen.[12]

Selected Bibliography

St. Anselm of Canterbury, "Proslogion I," in *Opera omnia.* Edimbourg, t. I, 1946. *Liturgy of the Hours* (Wednesday).

Days of the Lord. Vol. I. Collegeville: The Liturgical Press, 1991.

Fuller, Reginald H. *Preaching the New Lectionary.* Collegeville: The Liturgical Press, 1974.

"General Norms for the Liturgical Year and the Calendar." In *The Liturgy Documents.* Chicago: Liturgy Training Publications, 1991.

Johnson, Luke T. *The Writings of the New Testament.* Minneapolis: Augsburg Fortress, 1986.

Karris, Robert J. *Gospel of St. Luke.* Chicago: Franciscan Herald Press, 1974.

Pilch, John J. "Cultural World of Jesus," *Sunday by Sunday,* Nov. 27, 1994 (Initiative Publications, PO Box 218332, Columbus, OH 43221-8332).

Sanchez, Patricia Datchuck. *The Word We Celebrate.* Kansas City: Sheed and Ward, 1989.

Stuhlmueller, Carroll, C.P. *Biblical Meditations for Advent and the Christmas Season.* New York: Paulist Press, 1980.

Talbert, Charles H. *Reading Luke.* New York: Crossroad, 1992.

---

[12]St. Anselm of Canterbury, "Proslogion I," in *Opera omnia* (Edimbourg: 1946), 97-100; in *Days of the Lord,* Vol. 1 (Collegeville: The Liturgical Press, 1991), #41, p. 321.

SECOND SUNDAY OF ADVENT

INTRODUCTORY RITES

Opening Song (or Entrance Antiphon)

People of Zion, the Lord will come to save all nations and your hearts will exult to hear his majestic voice (see Is 30:19, 30).[1]

Environment

John the Baptist is a prominent figure in today's gospel. Perhaps an icon of John the Baptist can be placed in the environment. Often inexpensive copies of icons can be purchased through religious goods stores. The traditional icon of John the Baptist pictures him with wings. God's messengers were considered angelic beings; as John was Jesus' messenger, early art depicted John in angelic form. John was considered the "messenger of the covenant" foretold by the prophet Malachi.

Opening Prayer

The facilitator of the session may lead the prayer. Others in the group may be asked to proclaim the readings.

Let us pray
[in Advent time
for the coming Savior to teach us wisdom]

Pause for silent prayer.

Father in heaven,
the day draws near when the glory of your Son
will make radiant the night of the waiting world.
May the lure of greed not impede us from the joy
which moves the hearts of those who seek him.
May the darkness not blind us
to the vision of wisdom
which fills the minds of those who find him.
We ask this in the name of Jesus, the Lord.[2]

---

[1] Second Sunday of Advent: "Entrance Antiphon," *The Sacramentary.*

[2] Second Sunday of Advent: "Opening Prayer," *The Sacramentary.*

LITURGY OF THE WORD

Members of the group proclaim the readings from the Second Sunday of Advent. All actively listen.

Let us listen to God's word.

First Reading
Baruch 5:1-9

At first glance it appears that the author of this pericope was writing on behalf of Israel who was waiting to return home from the Babylonian exile in 587 B.C.E. However, this book was penned at least four or five centuries later in the name of a folk hero who was believed to be Jeremiah's secretary. The actual Baruch obviously was not the author of the apocryphal books attributed to him. Some scholars suggest that Baruch was written for a situation similar to the exile (such as the diaspora) that took place following the destruction of the temple in 70 C.E.

There are three books that claim Baruch's authorship, but those books are not contained in the Hebrew or the Protestant Bible. The Council of Trent included Baruch in the official canon.

Baruch sounds Advent's clarion call: "Rejoice, for the day of the Lord is near, salvation comes to all of God's children." The author of Baruch wrote in the spirit of Deutero-Isaiah who professed the ultimate power of God to save in the face of human helplessness and adversity. Throughout the bible, whenever a transformation occurs in a person or in a given situation, a new name is given. In this passage, the new place of restoration is called "peace of justice, the glory of God's worship!" Instead of returning home dejected and defeated, the people return to their transformed new land in the midst of God's established reign. God restores exiled, hopeless people and offers them a new reality. That reality is salvation. It is a salvation that only Wonder Counselor, Prince of Peace, God-Hero can provide.

Responsorial Psalm
Psalm 126: 1-2, 2-3, 4-5, 6

The psalm is an appropriate response to the first reading. It, too, echoes Deutero-Isaiah's victory march from the captivity of Babylon and asserts the greatness of God for the wonders of salvation.

Second Reading
Philippians 1:4-6, 8-11

Philippi was Paul's first stop on his westward missionary trip. Paul believed the West was as anxious to accept the good news of Christ as was the East. He therefore set out to evangelize the western cities. There has been speculation that Paul treated the Philippian church with greater affection and deference than his other communities as the Philippians were his first converts.

Other communities had accused Paul of living off of the backs of the people, so he refused to accept stipends from those communities for his preaching. Instead, he insisted on paying his own way by working as he journeyed. However, he did accept subsistence from the Philippian church. They financed his southern missionary efforts. One particular benefactor, named Lydia, probably inspired the letter to the Philippians. Lydia is thought to be the one who set up the relief fund to help Paul when he was imprisoned. Paul's preaching created a ruckus while he was stationed in Ephesus on one of his missionary tours. The result is history. It was from his jail cell that Paul wrote his letter of gratitude to the Philippians. Paul's letter is filled with abundant joy and great rejoicing, which is noteworthy in light of his circumstances: an impending death sentence. His love of God and subsequent joy so completely consumed him that his death was inconsequential in light of his relationship to Christ.

This pericope contains the opening prayer of his letter. Using traditional Jewish prayer formulas, Paul assured the Philippians that God would complete the work that Paul had already begun in them "right up until the day of Christ." The "day of Christ" was a term used to depict Jesus' second coming. Paul exhorted his friends to be faithful to the law of love of God and to love one another.

Only through love would Christians be able to live a moral life while they awaited the parousia. No doubt Paul's precarious situation brought him face to face with reflections of his own death. Thoughts of the "day of Christ" must have longingly lingered in his imagination.

Gospel
Luke 3:1-3

Today's gospel has John the Baptist announcing the coming reign of God.

STEP 1
NAMING ONE'S EXPERIENCE

What were your first impressions? What was your first response? What grabbed your attention? How did you feel?

Each person names his or her initial impression. Statement should be brief. No reasons should be given at this time. All simply listen without agreeing or disagreeing.

STEP 2
UNDERSTANDING

In a brief statement, what do you think this gospel is trying to convey? In your opinion, what does it mean?

All share their understanding of what the text is trying to convey.

STEP 3
INPUT FROM VISION/STORY/TRADITION

Liturgical Context

The facilitator discusses the liturgical context and the reason why these texts appear on this Sunday in this season.

The gospel for the second Sunday sets the stage for the entire liturgical year and is the axis upon which it spins. The Baptist heralds for us what we ritually celebrate, remember, and make present throughout the entire liturgical year: the salvation offered by the paschal mystery of Christ.[3] Today's liturgy reminds us that we must prepare for Jesus' second coming just as the Baptist's disciples prepared for Jesus' first coming. We must be diligent and cooperate with the work that God has already begun in us, just as Paul exhorts, "up to the day of Christ Jesus" (Second Reading). Yet, we are still about the business of kingdom building and history making in this present sphere of existence. The liturgy reminds us that we are to work with God in the harvest of biblical justice (Second Reading). How else are we to make straight the path of the Lord if not by ensuring that all be given a just path in this life? (Gospel). We are not to lose hope; we are to remember that Advent is a time of joyful waiting, for "the day draws near when the glory of your Son will make radiant the night of the waiting world" (Alternative Opening Prayer).

Gospel Exegesis (critical interpretation of scripture

The facilitator gives input regarding what critical biblical scholarship has to say about this text. The input includes insights as to how people would have heard the gospel in Jesus' time.

Luke was an historian. He placed the events he was about to describe in the center of secular, political history. Luke named those in political power. However, there is more to this gesture than the desire to provide an accurate record of historical events. Luke wished to stress that what God was about to accomplish through Jesus, as announced by his herald John, was of critical importance to all of humanity. It was not intended to be only for a privileged, religious few. God's salvation was inclusive of all people: past, present, and future. Luke is so adamant about this that he uses the

words of Isaiah: "Then the glory of the Lord shall be revealed and all mankind shall see it together" (Is 40:5).

In mentioning the political ruler, Luke was also emphasizing who indeed was Savior and Lord. When emperors returned from victorious battle, their subjects shouted, "Lord, Savior!" Luke intended that all should know that only one person deserved that title, and his name was Jesus Christ. No earthly king warranted the title, "Lord, Savior!" Earthly rulers, people in the secular sphere, and pagans were invited to Christ's kingdom of salvation. However, it was clear that even emperors would be subservient to Jesus in his last reign.

Luke the evangelist depicted salvation history in three epochs. The period of Israel [the Hebrew Scriptures], the period of Jesus [the gospels], and the period of the church [Acts of the Apostles, also written by Luke]. John is the precursor of the events about to happen. John led his people by hand to *Christ, the One To Come* and said, "Behold, here stands the *Christ* who fulfills all we have been told by our prophets since the very first prophet. Listen and believe. The hour is upon us." He sounded the ram's horn and announced the beginning of a new epoch. The reign of God was established. John retreated in order to make room for the *Greater One* to follow. "The way Luke presents the mission of John the Baptist is oriented not to the immediate manifestation of Jesus after his baptism in the Jordan but to the foreshadowing of all his work of salvation, of which Easter is the summit of this world, and the moment of its full realization when 'all mankind shall see the salvation of God.'"[4]

John is the last of the prophets of the old law who announced the arrival of the new law in Christ. John has been identified with the prophet Jeremiah of whom we have glimpses in the first reading. Both were summoned by God from their mothers' wombs and both foretold God's final judgment of humanity. In line with all the prophets of old, both Jeremiah and John proclaimed a covenant, a reciprocal relationship with

---

[3]"Christ's saving work is celebrated in sacred memory by the Church on fixed days throughout the year. Each week on the day called the Lord's Day the Church commemorates the Lord's resurrection. Once a year at Easter the Church honors this resurrection and passion with the utmost solemnity. In fact, through the yearly cycle the Church unfolds the entire mystery of Christ." "General Norms for the Liturgical Year and the Calendar" (GNLY), in *The Liturgy Documents* (Chicago: Liturgy Training Publications, 1991), #1.

[4]*Days of the Lord*, Vol. 1 (Collegeville: The Liturgical Press, 1991), 83.

the God of Israel who lifts up the poor, cares for the downtrodden, and exalts the oppressed. Luke's moral exhortation demands that followers of Christ are to do no less in response.

What, therefore, is the heart of John's message of preparation? John had been baptizing people in the Jordan for the forgiveness of sins. His was a baptism of repentance. He called for nothing less than a complete *metanoia*, a turning away from sin and a turning toward the God who transforms and heals. The Jordan bath ritualized this turning away from sin. John demanded total conversion as evidenced by a change in behavior. John announced that the long awaited reign and final judgment was about to take place. It wasn't enough to be a good Jew to prepare for the coming reign. Kathleen Hughes states: "John required a baptism of initiation. This baptism was not a repeated purification but a decisive step like that of a proselyte seeking to become a Jew. Only such a change would make a person a member of the true Israel as a real son of Abraham. (Mt 3:9-11). Confession of sins preceded this baptism as a sign of sincere repentance (Mt 3:6; Mk 1:5) The result of such a baptism was forgiveness of sins in preparation for the new age (Mk 1:4; Lk 3:3)."[5]

Proclaim the gospel again.

Sometimes we gain new insights when we hear the text after the interpretation has been given. Someone from the group proclaims the gospel a second time.

STEP 4
TESTING

Conversation with the Liturgy and the Scriptures

Test your original understanding in dialogue with the text. (You might consider breaking into smaller groups.)

Now that you've heard what the scholars have to say about the role, mission and preaching of the

---

[5]Kathleen Hughes, "John the Baptist," in *The Collegeville Pastoral Dictionary of Biblical Theology*, ed. Carroll Stuhlmueller, C.P. (Collegeville: The Liturgical Press, 1996), 68.

Baptist, how do you feel about it? Do you agree or disagree? Is there anything in the ministry of John the Baptist that struck you in a new way?

Participants share experiences from their own lives that are reflective of the exegesis just given.

> *John reminds me that I cannot be lackadaisical about my relationship with God. My life as a wife, mother, liturgist, and catechist gets very frenzied and hectic. When one works for the church it is very easy to become complacent or adopt the attitude that "church" work in itself is the "relationship." The metanoia that John demands is nothing less than to live in a radical and new way, to wake from my conscious and unconscious attitudes and behaviors that do not conform to God's greatest commandment. If I am in covenant relationship with God, then my response to God will be prayer, praise, and thanks and the honest effort to live in right relationship. If we as a community are in covenant relationship with God, then our community will pray, offer thanks and praise, and become a living witness to the gospel. It is wonderful to be part of just such a community. We have our weaknesses and sins like every parish, but the Spirit is alive and well and ministry abounds.*

> *On a personal level, when I do not exercise the law of love with my family; when my own agenda is more important than the concerns of those around me; when I am too busy to take time to listen to the stories of lonely parishioners; or when I ignore the poor and marginalized who cross my path, then I may be busied about "church" work, but am I about God's work? John challenges me to wake from the slumber of complacency. Every minute of every day is to be spent in the work of conforming my life to Jesus. There will be evidence of that metanoia in the degree to which I am willing to lay down my life for others.*

Is there any way you can connect the gospel we just shared to an experience in your own life?

All may share at this time.

How does this gospel reflect the twofold character of Advent, preparation for celebration of Christ's birth and penitence? What was John trying to say to the community of his time, to the community now, and to you personally? How was God's covenant expressed in this scripture? How does this scripture reflect an exodus, a leaving behind of one thing in order to be liberated and find new life? How might the theme of creation be connected to this scripture? Do you still feel the same way about this text? Articulate an understanding now in light of your personal sharing and the scriptural interpretation. Has your original understanding been stretched, challenged, or affirmed?

STEP 5
DECISION

The gospel demands a response.

How are this gospel, our sharing, and this biblical interpretation relevant and challenging for our community today? In what concrete ways does this gospel call our parish to action? Has this conversation called us to change in any way? If so, how? How do we feel about the underlying message of both Jeremiah and John that repentance assumes care for the disadvantaged? What will we do about it? What is one concrete action we will take this week as a response to what we have learned and shared today?

DOCTRINAL ISSUES

What church truth/teaching/doctrinal issue could be drawn from the gospel for the Second Sunday of Advent?

Participants suggest possible doctrinal themes that flow from the readings.

Possible Doctrinal Themes:

Salvation/redemption (soteriology); conversion; parousia; eschatology

Present the doctrinal material at this time.

1. The facilitator gives input on a particular doctrinal issue of his/her prior choosing. OR
2. The group chooses a doctrinal issue from the list they created. They read together from the Doctrinal Appendix.

(The doctrinal issues are found in the Doctrinal Appendix in the back of this workbook. If you are choosing an issue from this resource, please refer to it now.)

Reflection questions centered around the chosen doctrinal theme can be found at the end of each topic in the Doctrinal Appendix. The questions are based on the five-step reflection process. If you choose a topic not included in the Doctrinal Appendix, craft your own questions according to the same five-step process.

Following the reflection questions you will be reminded to return to chapter 7, "Preparing the Catechetical Session," to assist you in crafting your own session.

Closing Prayer

Father,
you give us food from heaven.
By our sharing in this mystery,
teach us to judge wisely the things of earth
and to love the things of heaven.
Grant this through Christ our Lord. Amen.[6]

Selected Bibliography

Adam, Adolf. *The Liturgical Year.* Trans. Matthew J. O'Connell. Collegeville: The Liturgical Press, 1990.

Charlesworth, James H. *The Old Testament Pseudepigrapha.* Garden City, New York: Doubleday and Company, 1983.

Days of the Lord. Vol. 1. Collegeville: The Liturgical Press, 1991.

Fuller, Reginald H. *Preaching the New Lectionary.* Collegeville: The Liturgical Press, 1974.

"General Norms for the Liturgical Year and the Calendar." In *The Liturgy Documents.* Chicago: Liturgy Training Publications, 1991.

Hughes, Kathleen, "John the Baptist." In *The Collegeville Pastoral Dictionary of Biblical Theology.* Ed. Carroll Stuhlmueller, C.P. Collegeville: The Liturgical Press, 1996.

Sanchez, Patricia Datchuck. *The Word We Celebrate.* Kansas City: Sheed and Ward, 1989.

---

[6]Second Sunday of Advent: "Prayer after Communion," *The Sacramentary.*

THIRD SUNDAY OF ADVENT

INTRODUCTORY RITES

Opening Song (or Entrance Antiphon)

Rejoice in the Lord always; again I say, rejoice!
The Lord is near. (Phil 4:4, 5)[1]

Environment

John the Baptist still figures in today's gospel. An icon bearing his image would be appropriate (see Environment: Second Sunday of Advent). Today is Gaudete Sunday. As a sign of joyful anticipation, purple is replaced by rose colored vestments. Incorporation of rose colored material in the gathering space would be fitting on this joyful day.

Opening Prayer

The facilitator of the session may lead the prayer. Others in the group may be asked to proclaim the readings.

Let us pray
[that God will fill us with joy
at the coming of Christ]

    Pause for silent prayer.

Lord God, may we, your people,
who look forward to the birthday of Christ
experience the joy of salvation
and celebrate that feast with love and thanksgiving.
We ask this through our Lord Jesus Christ, your Son,
who lives and reigns with you and the Holy Spirit,
one God for ever and ever. Amen.[2]

LITURGY OF THE WORD

Members of the group proclaim the readings from the Third Sunday of Advent. All actively listen.

Let us proclaim God's word.

---

[1] Third Sunday of Advent: "Entrance Antiphon," *The Sacramentary.*

[2] Third Sunday of Advent: "Opening Prayer," *The Sacramentary.*

First Reading
Zephaniah 3:14-18

Many believe that this passage in Zephaniah is so unlike his usual forecast of gloom and doom that a later writer submitted this more optimistic section. We hear from Zephaniah only once in the three-year cycle. Zephaniah was a prophet in the sixth century B.C.E. His primary message is one of God's judgment. He sees pride, arrogance, rebellion, and lack of trust in God as the core cause of Israel's sin of idolatry. Earlier in the book Zephaniah warns that there will be swift retribution on the "day of the Lord." Yahweh will remove sinners from the midst of the people. One scholar suggests that the "day of the Lord" refers less to the destruction of people than it does to the forgiveness and removal of sin offered to the sinner. Zephaniah's eschatological concerns are centered upon the need for Israel to be prepared for the day of the Lord. There is a joyful, trusting anticipation of that day when sin will be exorcized and God's people will be thoroughly reconciled. Zephaniah's exhortation calls for nothing less than the total conversion of oneself to the Lord God. Both the first reading and the gospel exhort the reader to wait with joyful expectant anticipation.

Responsorial Psalm
Isaiah 12:2-3, 4bcde, 5-6

The responsorial psalm for this Sunday is not chosen from the customary psalter, but rather is taken from Isaiah. The setting is perhaps Israel's return from exile. The prayer gives thanks to the God of Israel for the soon-to-be fulfilled salvation promised in the scriptures. Special emphasis is placed upon the presence of Yahweh in Israel. This is a particularly fitting response for the Advent season as we await the fulfillment of that presence in the person of Jesus.

Second Reading
Philippians 4:4-7

This Sunday, traditionally known as "Gaudete Sunday," takes its name and theme from the first word of this reading—*gaudete* (rejoice). The reading proclaims the reality that the glorified Jesus is near. We are not to be somber, but are to cast off the veil of darkness.

Paul's letter is set against a situation in which two women in the community have been engaged in some unknown quarrel or dispute.[3] Paul intervenes, as their divisiveness threatens the unity of the community. Paul exhorts the women to see their dispute in light of what it ultimately means. How does their argument really matter in the grand scheme of this short life? It is inconsequential when one considers it in light of all eternity. Paul exhorts members of his church to be magnanimous toward one another, to stretch forbearance as far as it can be stretched for the sake of unity. He also points to another reason for quarrels and disputes to end: community members' lives are a reflection of Christ. People will be attracted to Christ (or not) by the way Christians act toward one another in love. If the task appears monumental, they are not to worry as Christ lives within the community and will give the necessary peace and strength to live his love and to be his peace.

Gospel
Luke 3:10-18

Today's gospel is divided into two parts: the Baptist's preaching to inclusive crowds, and his messianic preaching. John exhorts the crowds in the proper attitudes and behaviors they should display and he begins fading into the background so that Jesus may take center stage. Some believe the latter piece is a later addition by the evangelist in order to combat those who still insisted that John, not Jesus, was the messiah.

STEP 1
NAMING ONE'S EXPERIENCE

What were your first impressions? What was your first response? What grabbed your attention? How did you feel?

---

[3]Refer to "First Sunday of Advent: Second Reading" for background material regarding Paul's letter to the Philippians.

Each person names his or her initial impression. Statement should be brief. No reasons should be given at this time. All simply listen without agreeing or disagreeing.

STEP 2
UNDERSTANDING

In a brief statement, what do you think this gospel means? Were there any experiences in your life that may have shaped the way you heard the story? What understanding of this gospel do you already bring with you to this dialogue? In a brief statement, what do you think this gospel was trying to convey? What is the intent?

All share their understanding of what the text is trying to convey.

STEP 3
INPUT FROM VISION/STORY/TRADITION

The facilitator discusses the liturgical context and the reason why these texts appear on this Sunday in this season.

Liturgical Context

This Sunday is Gaudete Sunday. Gaudete means rejoice. The entrance antiphon for today's liturgy echoes the second reading from Philippians, "Rejoice in the Lord always, again I say rejoice." The second reading from today's liturgy has always been associated with Gaudete Sunday. The joyful nature of the season of Advent is especially evident in today's readings. Even though the liturgical purple color has lenten overtones and repentance is stressed, the season of Advent exudes an overall feeling of joyful expectation. The joy of this Sunday is not an exuberant exultation, but rather is "marked by serenity.... It is a joy that guards against anxiety.... Above all, it is an interior peace 'in the Lord,' a surrendering to his providence and love, which Jesus, in the Sermon on the Mount, makes a fundamental requirement for the kingdom (Mt 6:24-34)."[4] The reserved joy

---

[4]*Days of the Lord,* Vol. 1 (Collegeville, The Liturgical Press, 1991), 117.

of this transition point in Advent is evidenced by the plea that all be prepared and sadness removed, for sadness "hinders us from feeling the joy and hope which his presence will bestow."[5]

John is careful to remind us that his baptism with water is a baptism of repentance. The baptism of Jesus is a baptism in the Holy Spirit. John is the prophet who appears on the scene during Advent and Lent in the liturgical readings as the one who alerts us to the need for forgiveness and redemption. John is a symbol of the preaching ministry and reminds us that we are all called to preach the living word of God.

In addition to repentance we are reminded that through the eucharist we are given God's help and freedom from sin. The eucharist, too, prepares us for the Incarnation, the coming of Christ in our lives. "...may this Eucharist bring us your divine help, free us from our sins, and prepare us for the birthday of Our Savior...."[6] We must not forget that Advent celebrates the *kingdom here and now* and *the kingdom yet to come*. We look forward to the day when Jesus will return as we recall his first coming and prepare for his present coming that will explode anew at Christmas but is ongoing throughout our Christian lives.

Gospel Exegesis

The facilitator gives input regarding what critical biblical scholarship has to say about this text. The input includes insights as to how people would have heard the gospel in Jesus' time.

John the Baptist does the preparatory work for Christ who is to follow him. The portrait of the Baptist is given not so much to highlight his personality, but rather to stress the *word* that was spoken to him. It was a *word* that he enacted and proclaimed to his many and varied followers. Luke's concern was John the prophet, whose major themes were repentance, conversion, and preparation.

Throughout all biblical history God's dramatic mediation in human affairs is preceded by a messen-

ger who prepares the way. God in his graciousness was not accustomed to crashing in unannounced. Joseph Grassi tells us that the Markan community believed John to be the returned Elijah. "John first appeared in the Judean desert in the spirit and garb of the prophet Elijah" (Mk 1:6).[7]

The prophet's mission was to bring God's people to faith and in turn challenge them to repentance. How did John expect his mandate to be carried out? He addressed the various groups in the crowd directly. Tax collectors were to exact no more from the citizenry than what was fair and lawful. Tax collectors were Jews who bid for the right to collect the taxes. They were required to collect a fixed amount for the government. Anything above and beyond that amount was considered their commission and profit. Abuses abounded. Tax collectors usually gouged the poor people they served and were seen as ruthless, merciless, and abusive.

The soldiers in this text were part of a special task force appointed to protect the tax collectors. As the soldiers oversaw and guarded the greedy tax collectors, they used the opportunity to feather their own nests by exacting bribes from the citizenry through violence, deception, and force.

This scripture exhorted tax collectors to be fair and honest, to exact no more than was required by law, and to add only a fair and commensurate commission. Accordingly, the soldiers were asked to do their duty: guard the tax collector and exact no further bribes.

Luke insisted on practical commitments when it came to issues of conversion. Neither tax collector nor soldier was to exploit for purposes of self-gain. The citizens, on the other hand, were to act justly toward the needy. They were to share with God's *anawim*.[8]

Even though John's ministry was successful, there was evidence of lackadaisical behavior in his followers. His stern eschatological warning probably

---

[5]Third Sunday of Advent: "Alternative Opening Prayer," *The Sacramentary.*

[6]Third Sunday of Advent: "Prayer After Communion," *The Sacramentary.*

[7]Joseph A. Grassi, "John the Baptist," in *The Collegeville Pastoral Dictionary of Biblical Theology*, ed. Carroll Stuhlmueller, C.P. (Collegeville: The Liturgical Press, 1996), 494.

[8]Eugene LaVerdiere, *Luke* (Wilmington, Delaware: Michael Glazier, Inc., 1980), 43-49.

was prompted by complacent behavior inherent in his community. His baptism of repentance was in response to such complacency. John called for nothing less than a total turning of oneself to God as evidenced by keeping the law of love of God and of one's neighbor.

John was also responding to the people's anticipation for a political messiah who would restore Israel to her rightful place. People imagined John to be that long awaited messiah. John laid that notion definitively to rest. The Mighty One was to follow him. Hearing the word "mighty," the people realized that John was describing the messiah of Jewish folklore who would command the fight against the arch-villain Evil. John emphatically made it clear that he indeed was not the one. The true messiah would follow him. He, John, would retreat into insignificance in the face of the "Mighty One."

Proclaim the gospel again.

Sometimes we gain new insights when we hear the text after the interpretation has been given.

STEP 4
TESTING

Conversation with the Liturgy and the Scriptures

Test your original understanding in dialogue with the text.

(You might consider breaking into smaller groups).

Now that we've listened to the text on its own ground, in its own historical and interpretive setting, how do you feel about it? How did your original understanding about this scripture reading fit with the interpretation? Are there any new insights? How does this scripture reading speak to the season of Advent?

Sharing Life Experience

Participants share experiences from their own lives that are reflective of the exegesis just given.

This gospel reminds me that just because I am invited into the process of conversion does not mean that I am willing to do what is necessary. Conversion is an action word, not a pious ferverino or an abstract spiritual concept. I once was asked to reach out a hand in reconciliation to a person from whom I was estranged for ideological reasons. We each represented two different schools of belief. I was very smug in my own righteousness. I felt the blood rush to my face in embarrassing remembrance as I heard the tax collector ask, "What should I do?" Like the tax collector, I, too, asked that question. However, I did not like the answer I received. It was always a resounding demand, "Go, seek reconciliation!" "Anything but that, Lord," was my consistent reply. I waited for God to do it for me. I waited for the other person to make the initial gesture. The waiting made me realize that judgment was already "at hand." I was tried and found deficient in living the greatest commandment. How dare I bemoan the division in the church, the division in families, the division between enemies and nations and not be willing to transform a very divisive situation of my own making? There would be no peace until I complied. My pride and my need to be right were the gods that kept me from seeking reconciliation.

I swallowed the demon god of pride and today this person and I are very good friends who respect one another's differences and are gifted by the other's perspective. Interestingly, one very important belief we share and put into action is the belief in our responsibility to the poor and marginalized. Only God could have accomplished such metanoia.

Is there any way you can connect this gospel to an experience in your own life?

All share at this time.

What was the message for Luke's community? For our parish community? For me? How is God's covenant with humanity evident? Is there evidence of an exodus theme (turning away from one thing and movement toward another) apparent in this gospel? In what way is this gospel speaking to "a people"? Did you experience any new insights? Does this text still mean the same thing to you as when you began? Has your original understanding been stretched, challenged, or affirmed?

The gospel demands a response.

How do this scripture text and liturgy challenge your community? Has this conversation with the Baptist changed or stretched your perspective or outlook? How do you experience Advent joy in today's gospel? Can you relate to the tax collector, the soldiers, or the regular people in this story? Does the challenge that was offered to them in any way challenge you? In what way does this gospel call the community or you to action? Be specific.

DOCTRINAL ISSUES

What church truth/teaching/doctrinal issue could be drawn from the gospel for the Third Sunday of Advent?

Participants suggest possible doctrinal themes that flow from the readings.

Possible Doctrinal Themes:

Repentance, eschatology, parousia, soteriology (salvation), kingdom of God, justice, conversion

Present the doctrinal material at this time.

1. The facilitator gives input on a particular doctrinal issue of his/her prior choosing. OR
2. The group chooses a doctrinal issue from the list they created. They read together from the Doctrinal Appendix.

(The doctrinal issues are found in the Doctrinal Appendix in the back of this workbook. If you are choosing an issue from this resource, please refer to it now.)

Reflection questions centered around the chosen doctrinal theme can be found at the end of each topic in the Doctrinal Appendix. The questions are based on the five-step reflection process. If you choose a topic not included in the Doctrinal Appendix, craft your own questions according to the same five-step process.

Following the reflection questions you will be reminded to return to chapter 7, "Preparing the Catechetical Session," to assist you in crafting your own session.

Closing Prayer

Father of our Lord Jesus Christ,
ever faithful to your promises
and ever close to your Church:
the earth rejoices in hope of the Savior's coming
and looks forward with longing
to his return at the end of time.
Prepare our hearts and remove the sadness
that hinders us from feeling the joy which his presence will bestow,
for he is Lord for ever and ever.[9]

Selected Bibliography

Days of the Lord. Vol. 1. Collegeville: The Liturgical Press, 1991.

Fuller, Reginald H. *Preaching the New Lectionary.* Collegeville: The Liturgical Press, 1989.

Grassi, Joseph A. "John the Baptist." In *The Collegeville Pastoral Dictionary of Biblical Theology.* Ed. Carroll Stuhlmueller, C.P. Collegeville: The Liturgical Press, 1996.

LaVerdiere, Eugene, S.S.S. *Luke.* Wilmington, Delaware: Michael Glazier, Inc., 1980.

Richards, Hubert. *The Gospel According to St. Paul.* Collegeville: The Liturgical Press, 1990.

---

[9] Third Sunday of Advent: "Evening Prayer," *Christian Prayer: Liturgy of the Hours* (New York: Catholic Book Publishing Co., 1976).

FOURTH SUNDAY OF ADVENT

INTRODUCTORY RITES

Opening Song (or Entrance Antiphon)

Let the clouds rain down the Just One, and the earth bring forth a Savior (Is 45:8)[1]

Environment

All four candles are lit today as Advent reaches fulfillment in the Christ event. Perhaps an anticipatory manger of empty straw might be added as the final preparatory gesture. Our hope, longing, and conversion have created this straw berth for the Lord who comes continuously and who will come again on the last day.

Opening Prayer

The facilitator of the session may lead the prayer. Others in the group may be asked to proclaim the readings.

Let us pray
[as Advent draws to a close
for the faith that opens our lives
to the Spirit of God]

Pause for silent prayer.

Father, all-powerful God,
your eternal Word took flesh on our earth
when the Virgin Mary placed her life
at the service of your plan.
Lift our minds in watchful hope
to hear the voice which announces Christ's glory
and opens our minds to receive the Spirit
who prepares us for his coming.
We ask this through Christ our Lord.[2]

---

[1]Fourth Sunday of Advent: "Entrance Antiphon," *The Sacramentary.*

[2]Fourth Sunday of Advent: "Alternative Opening Prayer," *The Sacramentary.*

LITURGY OF THE WORD

Members of the group proclaim the readings from the Fourth Sunday of Advent. All actively listen.

Let us listen to God's word.

First Reading
Micah 5:1-4

Micah's message resonated with that of his popular and well known eighth-century B.C.E. contemporary, Isaiah. Micah was concerned about the insincerity of religious communities who did not exercise their piety according to the moral demands of justice. Micah witnessed great political upheavals such as the loss of the Northern Kingdom of Israel (he prophesied in the south, in Judah) and the Assyrian invasion of Judah. Yet these events captured little of his attention in comparison to Judah's lack of concentration on her relationship (*hesed)* with Yahweh God. Covenant love between God and God's people would be evidenced in behavior directed toward the needs of the poor, oppressed, and marginalized. Micah promised God's retribution for the sins of wealthy greed, an iniquitous legal system, an ineffective priestly and prophetic ministry, pride, arrogance, idolatry, and temple prostitution.

The passages of messianic longing resonate with literature that appeared following the exile. There was widespread hope for restoration of the Davidic succession. Bethlehem was the city of Jesse, David's father. From Bethlehem, the succession of the Davidic monarchy would be restored. Ephratha was the name of an insignificant clan from the tribe of Judah that settled in Bethlehem. From this "nothing" clan and this "nowhere" hamlet would come the future leader of Israel. Early Christian writers and believers used this text as the basis for claiming Jesus as messiah and Lord, sprouting from David's family tree.

Micah was influenced by Ezekiel's imagery. Thus, the "One to Come" would lead Yahweh's flock into eternity. Jesus attributed the metaphor to himself. "From its earliest days, Christian faith has recognized the birth of Jesus and his shepherding mission of peace (Mt 2:8) as the fulfillment of Micah's oracle of salvation."[3]

Responsorial Psalm
Psalm 80: 2-3, 14-15, 17-18

This appropriate advent psalm asks for blessings upon the Davidic king. In the Christian perspective, this and the first reading directly refer to Jesus Christ. Like ancient Israel we await the future coming with hope.

Second Reading
Hebrews 10:5-10

The letter to the Hebrews is primarily concerned with reflection upon the Jewish scriptures. The Lectionary omits a very important piece of the letter to the Hebrews in which the humanity of Jesus is addressed at great length. It is perhaps the "New Testament's most profound and systematic discussion of what it means for Jesus to have been human."[4] This reading is particularly appropriate on the fourth Sunday of Advent as it keeps us grounded in the Advent/Christmas focus rather than on the culture's over-sentimentalized preoccupation with the Christmas infant. The reason for the Incarnation is reparation for sin, the sin of the world. With the advent of Jesus, the sacrifices of old are rendered meaningless. Jesus replaces the burnt offerings and sacrifices of the old covenant. The Pauline community asserts that Jesus definitively assumed unto himself such oblations once and for all. One cannot meditate on the Incarnation celebrated at Christmas without reflection upon the reason for the event in the first place: the cross and resurrection.

Gospel
Luke 1:39-45

Luke tells of the meeting between the two soon-to-be mothers, Elizabeth and Mary. In so doing, Luke gives the church a refined understanding of the transition between the old covenant and the new covenant, the role of the Baptist and Christ in salvation history and of Mary, the church's model of zealous discipleship. This gospel points to the impending joy of "the birth that is the prelude to the final assembly" and is the basis for Mary's christocentric place within salvation's continuum.[5]

STEP 1
NAMING ONE'S EXPERIENCE

What were your first impressions? What was your first response? What captured your attention? How did you feel?

Each person names his or her initial impression. Statement should be brief. No reasons should be given at this time. All simply listen without agreeing or disagreeing.

STEP 2
UNDERSTANDING

In a brief statement, what do you think this gospel is trying to convey? In your opinion, what does it mean?

All share their understanding of what the text is trying to convey.

STEP 3
INPUT FROM VISION/STORY/TRADITION

Liturgical Context

On this the last Sunday in Advent, the liturgy is concerned with the business of final preparation. The prayers of the mass have something to do with the events that "immediately precede the Lord's birth or with texts that refer to these events."[6] The ritual prayers emphasize not only the Incarnation, but the fulfillment of salvation through the paschal mystery. "... fill our hearts

---

[3]Patricia Datchuck Sanchez, *The Word We Celebrate* (Kansas City: Sheed and Ward, 1989), 270.

[4]Raymond F. Collins, *Preaching the Epistles* (New York/Mahwah: Paulist Press, 1996), 120-121.

[5]*Days of the Lord*, Vol. 1 (Collegeville: The Liturgical Press, 1991), 157.

[6]Adolf Adam, *The Liturgical Year*, trans. Matthew J. O'Connell (Collegeville: The Liturgical Press, 1990), 132-138.

with your love, and as you revealed to us by an angel the coming of the Son as man, so lead us through his suffering and death to the glory of his resurrection" (Opening Prayer, Fourth Sunday of Advent). This is the only time we hear from Micah in the Sunday Lectionary. The reason for the prophet's appearance on this Sunday is due to his announcement of the advent of the messiah. It is not to be regarded simply as a proof text for the messianic fulfillment in Jesus. Rather, it is to be considered a present-day paradigm of hope, endurance, and vigilance as the second coming of Christ is awaited with conscious deliberation.

Gospel Exegesis

The facilitator provides input regarding what critical biblical scholarship has to say about this text. The input includes insights as to how people would have heard the gospel in Jesus' time.

Luke is not concerned with telling us a story about two pregnant relatives who meet one last time before their babies' birth. Nor is it a story that denotes Mary's concern and care for Elizabeth in her time of need. If that were the case, Luke would not have Mary departing when Elizabeth's need is obviously the greatest. Rather, through the literary devices inherent in storytelling, Luke provides a theology of God's plan of salvation through Jesus. The two mothers-to-be are gathered in praise of God for the work God is doing in and through them. In their gathering, they give witness to the theological reality: John is the precursor of Jesus, and Jesus is the Savior who is superior to John.

There are several literary devices commonly used in Luke/Acts to illustrate God's plan. These are: previews and reviews, repeated or highlighted scriptural references, commission statements, and interpretive statements by reliable characters. Robert Tannehill suggests that there may be details in the story that review what God has already done in the past and preview what God is about to do "in a way that interprets these events."[7]

Through the birth stories of both John and Jesus, Luke previews what God intends for humanity's redemption. Through various images and words, the reader knows that reference is being made to God's plan revealed in the scriptures.

Through allusions to scriptural passages and traditions, the reader is shown that "the law and the prophets are fulfilled in Jesus." These same passages also "express a particular understanding of God's purpose and are programs for action."[8] For example, when Elizabeth tells us that the baby leapt in her womb, the reader is reminded of the leaping of Rebekah's twin children, Jacob and Esau. According to biblical tradition, leaping in utero foreshadowed a future relationship and "symbolized destinies that would be lived out by the children."[9] John's leaping is a preview of the future relationship between Jesus and John.[10] Through the power of the Holy Spirit, Elizabeth is able to interpret John's leaping. John leapt in Elizabeth's womb because the destiny of the world was being fulfilled in the baby within Mary's womb.

Another literary device is the agent, the chosen instrument, "reliable persons commissioned by God to carry out God's purpose."[11] In this story both Elizabeth and Mary are those instruments. Both have been obedient to the will of God and, as a result, both bring God's intended plan of redemption to birth in the world. In biblical tradition, Mary leaving in haste refers to an "interior disposition that makes one act with fervor and zeal."[12] Mary is understood as being great because of the child she would bear. The blessings given her reflect a Semitic attitude of subservience. Mary is praised because of her relationship to Christ. Mary's role is christological. She has a role in God's liberating plan for the human race.

Finally, there is the commission, the call and mission of the individual in question. When Elizabeth

---

[7]Robert C. Tannehill, *The Narrative Unity of Luke-Acts: A Literary Interpretation* (Minneapolis: Augsburg Fortress, 1986), 20-38.

[8]Adam, *The Liturgical Year*, 21.

[9]Sanchez, *The Word We Celebrate*, 272.

[10]Robert J. Karris, O.F.M. "The Gospel According to Luke," in *The New Jerome Biblical Commentary*, ed. Raymond E. Brown, S.S., Joseph A. Fitzmyer, S.J., Roland E. Murphy, O.Carm. (Englewood Cliffs: Prentice Hall, 1990), 631.

[11]Tannehill, *The Narrative Unity of Luke-Acts*, 21.

[12]*Days of the Lord*, Vol. 1, 191.

said, "...blessed is the fruit of your womb. Who am I that the mother of my Lord should come to me?" she prophesied about the mission of the child in Mary's womb. This child will bring salvation. He will be the fulfillment of God's plan. Luke wants to make it clear that both John and Jesus have unique roles to play. John will prepare the way. John will be the bridge between the old covenant and the new covenant. John will help prepare hearts for giving birth to the advent of the messiah. Jesus, however, is that messiah. Jesus is the One who will fulfill Israel's hopes. Luke insists that his community have no illusions about "who's who" in the eschatological events about to take place.

Mary and Elizabeth, two great women of scripture, listen to God and become the ultimate paradigm of disciple. In this scripture text, Mary becomes the great gift and model for the church. She listens, she responds, she obeys with fervor and zeal the voice of God and she acts on that word. We, too, on this last Sunday of Advent are exhorted to "go in haste," to go with zeal and fervor to live the call of the gospel and to share the mighty news it contains. Mary models for us the perfect liturgy. She listens, she gives thanks and praise, she responds in faith to the Word of God and then she goes in haste. We must not forget Micah's exhortation to respond in faith according to our *hesed* relationship with God. Our response will be evidenced by how we live the law of love, how we respond to the needy in our world.

Proclaim the gospel again.

Sometimes we gain new insights when we hear the text after the interpretation has been given. Someone from the group proclaims the gospel a second time.

STEP 4
TESTING

Conversation with the Liturgy and the Scriptures

Test your original understanding in dialogue with the text.

(You might consider breaking into smaller groups).

Today's readings are theological and christological. What could they have to do with our lives? Were there any new or renewed insights? What would you say this text is about? How would you connect this gospel to an experience in your life?

Sharing Life Experience

Participants share experiences from their own lives that are reflective of the exegesis just given.

> *I am reminded of a time when my husband came home one day and announced that we would be moving to Florida. I was devastated and, in a word, refused the offer. I loved my job. It was November and most positions in liturgy and music would have already been filled. It would be next to impossible to find another job that year. I went home that evening and took my dilemma to prayer. I argued with God. "Surely, God, you don't intend that I give up this work?" All I heard was, "Go" and "Trust me." I made the decision that if it was God's will that I give up my work, stay home with my family, and concentrate on my role as wife and mother, then I would do it willingly. I felt sure that my decision would take me out of full-time ministry for quite some time. The next day I arrived at my office and found a national bulletin on my desk that contained a job offer in Florida. I called; the position was still open.*

> *Three weeks later, our house was sold. Four children, a dog, a cat, a husband and a wife were headed for Florida. Upon leaving the city I heard words spoken to another ancient woman of faith echo in my ears, "Go now, leave your homeland, and I will give you a home."*

> *I am going into my eleventh year at my parish. I am amazed as I look back at how God's plan for our life and for the direction of our ministries was fulfilled in and through our move to Florida. I cannot boast that I left in "haste" with fervor and zeal. But I will affirm my eventual submission to the will of God. It was quite a while before I could see what God had intended through the move, but somehow we knew that God was doing a mighty work. We needed only to wait. I am a different person, a better person today because of that experience. I had to wait to see the joyful fulfillment, but once I said yes, I could res-*

onate with the joy of Elizabeth's baby over the God who was about to reveal the plan for our lives. Jesus' mighty deeds were foretold in today's scriptures. John was being announced as the one who was to prepare the way. Both were brought to birth through the willing obedience of two women. Jesus did a mighty deed in our family through our exodus from Nebraska to Florida. Even though there was a period of anxious waiting to understand what that mighty deed was, we nevertheless were aware that we were in the midst of a great advent: God's new explosion into our lives.

How would you connect this gospel to an experience in your life?

All share an experience at this time.

How is the theme of God's role in creation experienced in the meeting of the two women of faith? What do today's readings tell us about God/Jesus? How is Mary's role in God's plan evidenced by today's reading?

STEP 5
DECISION

The gospel demands a response.

What does the meeting between Mary and Elizabeth have to teach our community today? How are we challenged by today's word? Has this conversation with the biblical interpretation regarding Mary and Elizabeth and the two babies in utero stretched me in any way? How is God calling us/me to the kind of discipleship experienced in the lives of Mary and Elizabeth? In what concrete way are we called to respond?

DOCTRINAL ISSUES

What church truth/teaching/doctrinal issue could be drawn from the gospel for the Fourth Sunday of Advent?

Participants suggest possible doctrinal themes that flow from the readings.

Possible Doctrinal Themes:

Salvation, discipleship, christology, soteriology, conversion, eschatology

Present the doctrinal material at this time.
1. The facilitator gives input on a particular doctrinal issue of his/her prior choosing. OR
2. The group chooses a doctrinal issue from the list they created. They read together from the Doctrinal Appendix.

(The doctrinal issues are found in the Doctrinal Appendix in the back of this workbook. If you are choosing an issue from this resource, please refer to it now.)

Reflection questions centered around the chosen doctrinal theme can be found at the end of each topic in the Doctrinal Appendix. The questions are based on the five-step reflection process. If you choose a topic not included in the Doctrinal Appendix, craft your own questions according to the same five-step process.

Following the reflection questions you will be reminded to return to chapter 7, "Preparing the Catechetical Session," to assist you in crafting your own session.

Closing Prayer

Father, all powerful God,
your eternal Word took flesh on our earth
when the Virgin Mary placed her life at the service of your plan.
Lift our minds in watchful hope
to hear the voice which announces his glory
and open our minds to receive the Spirit
who prepares us for his coming.
We ask this through Christ our Lord.[13]

---

[13]Fourth Sunday of Advent: "Evening Prayer," *Christian Prayer: Liturgy of the Hours* (New York: Catholic Book Publishing Co., 1976).

Selected Bibliography

Adam, Adolf. *The Liturgical Year.* Trans. Matthew J. O'Connell. Collegeville: The Liturgical Press, 1990.

Collins, Raymond F. *Preaching the Epistles.* New York/Mahwah: Paulist Press, 1996.

Days of the Lord. Vol. I. Collegeville: The Liturgical Press, 1991.

Fuller, Reginald H. *Preaching the New Lectionary.* Collegeville: The Liturgical Press, 1974.

Karris, Robert J., O.F.M. "The Gospel According to Luke." In *The New Jerome Biblical Commentary.* Ed. Raymond E. Brown, S.S., Joseph A. Fitzmyer, S.J., Roland E. Murphy, O.Carm. Englewood Cliffs: Prentice Hall, 1990.

Sanchez, Patricia Datchuck. *The Word We Celebrate.* Kansas City: Sheed and Ward, 1989.

Tannehill, Robert C. *The Narrative Unity of Luke-Acts: A Literary Interpretation.* Minneapolis: Augsburg Fortress, 1986.

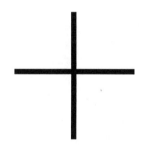

THE CHRISTMAS SEASON

THE CHRISTMAS SEASON:
AN OVERVIEW

There is no evidence of an official feast celebrating the nativity until the fourth century. There are two hypotheses regarding the origin of this feast. One school of thought suggests that it was adopted in response to a pagan feast inaugurated by the Roman emperor Aurelian in the hopes of strengthening and uniting his empire. The feast, *sol invictus,* was a celebration honoring the shortest day of the year when the sun reaches its lowest point. It reaches this point on December 25, the winter solstice. From that day forward the sun begins its victory over darkness by lengthening the time it will peer through the dimness of an unlit sky. Thus, the days begin to lengthen as the sun processes heavenward toward its ultimate destiny, full brightness and height during the summer solstice. Christians had no difficulty appropriating this feast to their understanding of Jesus who declared himself Light of the World. They could say very righteously to their pagan neighbors that they, in truth, were celebrating the "real" Sun of justice.

The second school of thought centers around the date of December 25 itself as the reason for establishment of the feast. Christians were very aware of the solstices and equinoxes because of the constant references to Christ as Light. Some hypothesized that John the Baptist was conceived during the autumn equinox and born during the summer solstice. As Jesus was to have been born six months later, that put his birth right at December 25th. It was once again evidence of God's incredible timing and wisdom. It seemed to be no accident that God's mighty work coincided with the temporal world's celebration of the symbols of light and darkness.

The feast spread rapidly due to the influence of the Arian heresy that "made the Son of God the highest of creatures, greater than we but less than God."[1] The Council of Nicea refuted the heresy

---

[1] Richard P. McBrien, *Catholicism* (San Francisco: Harper Collins, 1980), xxxiv.

and formulated the Nicene Creed. Through celebration of Jesus' birth, people would have an opportunity in their liturgy to proclaim what the council set out to accomplish.

There is an historical progression to the eventual celebration of the three masses of Christmas: night, dawn, and during the day. The first celebration of the feast of the nativity was a small papal mass. The prologue of John was proclaimed at this mass, the forerunner to our mass during the day. Jesus was honored as the Word of God made flesh. God revealed the Eternal Word to prophets throughout salvation history. The *Word* reached fulfillment in the Incarnation of the Son of God. The gospel and the celebration itself are highly christological.

Underneath the church of St. Mary Major in Rome is a small chapel designed as a replica of the cave at Bethlehem where Jesus was born. Wood was brought to the space, thus the name "mass near the creche." The story of Jesus' birth was read at this liturgy, the forerunner of the midnight mass. The symbol of the *Christ, our Light* is highlighted in the opening prayer. In the renewed liturgical calendar, the mass at night is patterned after this early St. Mary Major observance.

On December 25, the pope went in the early morning to St. Anastasia's Church in honor of the Greek feast day honoring the church's patroness, a martyr highly venerated in the East. The story of the shepherds who arrive at the creche seeking the heralded Child is proclaimed at this early morning liturgy, the mass at dawn. There is more reference to the "Light that will shine" in this liturgy than there is in the midnight liturgy.

In addition to the theme of Christ's manifestation to the world through the Incarnation, the liturgies of Christmas proclaim another truth that is evidenced in the opening prayer for the mass during the day and the third Christmas preface. A holy exchange takes place and humanity is elevated to the status of God's child. We share in Jesus' divine nature. "Your Son shared our weakness [literally: our humanity]: may we share his glory [literally: his divinity]." "Your eternal Word has taken upon himself our human weakness, giving our mortal nature immortal value."[2]

The texts of Christmas, while not directly referring to the paschal mystery, have strong underpinnings of Christ's act of redemption. It is through the life, death, and resurrection of Jesus that we are saved. We cannot look at Christmas without remembering Easter. The Christmas season celebrates the Incarnation of Christ that ushers in God's fulfillment of salvation history. It also honors Christ's manifestation to us in human form. These two realities define and give meaning and expression to the content of our Christian theology. One liturgy cannot possibly capture all the dimensions contained within the mystery of the Incarnation. The fact that so many texts are offered to us for celebration and reflection denotes the richness and complexity of the season. Like the view through a prism, all the readings together help reflect the many facets of the profound mystery of Christ's Incarnation.[3]

Holy Family

The feast of the Holy Family falls on the Sunday within the octave of Christmas. This relatively new feast originated in Canada. The feast of the Holy Family lifts up the family of Nazareth as a model for struggling Christian families. Pope Leo XIII promulgated this celebration of the family of Mary, Jesus, and Joseph.

Epiphany

Epiphany means "showing forth" or manifestation. It was considered a primary feast in the area of Gaul around the third and fourth century. Epiphany, from the "(Greek: *ephiphaneia*, or *theophoneia*, 'appearance or manifestation of God') is the original feast of Christ's birth."[4] In the ancient world an epiphany referred to a visit from a god or one who was revered as a god, such as a king.

In the East, Jesus' birth and his baptism were celebrated on this day. Thus, new members were baptized on this feast. The wedding feast at Cana, where Jesus manifested his power for the first time, was also commemorated on Epiphany.

By the end of the fourth century, the East celebrated the birth of Jesus and the coming of the magi on December 25. On January 6 they celebrated the baptism of the Lord and the wedding feast of Cana. The West celebrated the Epiphany in connection with the magi's appearance, the baptism of Jesus, and the Cana feast.

J. A. Jungman unites both feasts thematically when he states: "The mystery of the Incarnation is the proper subject of them both; but at Christmas we consider chiefly the coming down of the Son of God who became one of the poor children of men, while on the Epiphany we direct our attention to this Child's divine dignity which already is beginning to manifest itself in the world."[5]

Epiphany is also the day we remember the three magi. However, the focus is still on Christ and not the magi. In the gospel, wise men from the East come to exalt the newborn king of the Jews. The point of the story rests with Christ who comes to save the whole world, pagans and all.

Adolf Adam suggests that Epiphany is the premier celebration of Christ, the King. He proposes that the other feast designated by that title has more to do with reverence for the title, the theological concept, than it does with the inherent reality of Christ's kingship. "It is essential to the liturgical feast of Epiphany that it brings before us, in a concrete way, a royal action of Christ, an event that is an essential part of the process of salvation."[6]

Baptism of the Lord

The feast of the baptism of the Lord is celebrated on the Sunday following Epiphany. If the Sunday

---

[2]Adolf Adam, *The Liturgical Year,* trans. Matthew J. O'Connell (Collegeville: The Liturgical Press, 1990), 127.

[3]*Days of the Lord,* Vol. 1 (Collegeville: The Liturgical Press, 1991), 191-192.

[4]Adam, *The Liturgical Year,* 144.

[5]J. A. Jungman, *Public Worship: A Survey,* trans. C. Howell (Collegeville: The Liturgical Press, 1957), 208.

[6]Adam, *The Liturgical Year,* 147.

of Epiphany falls after January 6, then the feast of the Lord's baptism is celebrated on Monday that year. During Cycle C the gospel that is read is that of the wedding feast at Cana. During Cycle A the gospel is the account of Jesus' baptism.

This feast is important for three reasons. Jesus is named by the voice of God who calls him "Son." The Holy Spirit descends upon Jesus and thus anoints him for the destiny he is to fulfil. Since it is John who baptizes, Jesus shows his partnership with sinful humanity. This feast brings the Christmas season to an end.

Octave of Christmas

Following Christmas (and Easter) there is an entire week of liturgical feasts called an octave. The feast of St. Stephen, the first martyr (model of love for enemies and fearless witness to the faith), is on December 26. The feast of John the Apostle and Evangelist is celebrated on December 27. The feast of the Holy Innocents, the children killed by Herod, occurs on December 28. Other martyrs' feasts are celebrated on the remaining days of the week.

Christmas celebrates the manifestation of Christ, the Light of the world. The feasts of the octave lead us into the sobering reality of what happens when one becomes a child of the Light. For the Christian there can be no complacent lapses into nostalgic reminiscence of roasted chestnuts, pine scented rooms, or cozy hearths near an open fire. The Christmas octave feasts of St. Stephen, John the Apostle, and the Holy Innocents serve as a reminder that the only open fire a true disciple can expect is that of the martyr's stake. It has been said that the three feasts are examples of the three possible forms of martyrdom: voluntary and executed (St. Stephen), voluntary, but not executed (John the Apostle), and executed but not voluntary (the Innocents). However, regardless of how martyrs offer their lives, these feasts remind the believer that the cost of discipleship is very high. The Incarnation of Christ, the Light of the world, often requires nothing less than the complete self-offering of one's life.

The first reading of the feast of St. Stephen recounts the story of his ministry and his martyrdom. Christians are reminded of the persecutions they must endure for the sake of the gospel.[7] Stephen was chosen by the apostles to help them because "he was trusted by everyone."[8] Stephen distributed food to the poor and was the first deacon because of his great charism of service. St. Stephen's commemoration is one reason for the custom of giving gifts to the poor at Christmas.

The root meaning of the word *martyr* is "witness." Stephen gave witness to Christ by the gift of his life. The etymology of Stephen's name is "wreath." War heroes and famous athletes of his day were given wreaths in honor of their achievements. Art depicting martyrs often portrays them wearing wreaths around their heads. The Christmas wreath "announces the victory of Christ who brings justice, love and peace. We remember deacon Stephen, the first witness to lay down his life for Christ."[9]

The feast of John the Apostle, celebrated first in the East, dates to the fourth century. Tradition emanating from Iraenus holds that John ministered in Ephesus and was later banished to the island of Patmos where he wrote the book of Revelation. He subsequently returned to Ephesus where he composed the gospel of John and died at an old age.[10] The symbol of John's gospel is that of the eagle that flies to the heights.[11] The liturgy of this feast stresses that God was announced to humanity through the revelation given to John. John the Apostle, the Evangelist, manifested the Word of God, the Logos, to the world. The liturgy of this feast names him a credible eyewitness to the life of Jesus.

The origin of the feast of the Holy Innocents dates to the sixth century in North Africa. This date was chosen for the feast because of its connection to the Christmas story. The liturgy of the day tells the story of the flight into Egypt and the slaughtering of the innocent children by Herod who was in search of the prophesied Child. These children are remembered and praised for their innocent martyrdom.

---

[7]Ibid., 142.

[8]Mary Ellyn Hynes, *Companion to the Calendar* (Chicago: Liturgy Training Publications, 1993), 191.

[9]Ibid., 191.

[10]Adam, *The Liturgical Year*, 142.

[11]Hynes, *Companion to the Calendar*, 191.

Very often catechetical groups do not meet during the Christmas season. While this is understandable, it is somewhat regrettable. A great part of our Christian tradition is celebrated in the days and the feasts of the Christmas season. Every attempt should be made to break open the Christmas season liturgies with groups participating in liturgical catechesis. The liturgies and feasts of Christmas are integral to complete acquaintance with the entire rich deposit of faith. The liturgies of the Christmas season celebrate and emphasize each hierarchical truth of Catholic teaching. A great deal of flexibility and creativity is needed to ensure that adequate reflection is given to this great season.

There are four liturgies of Christmas: the Christmas vigil, the mass at midnight, the mass at dawn, and the mass during the day. As a result, people will be attending different masses and will not necessarily be experiencing the same readings. It will take a great deal of imagination to effectively incorporate all the readings into a catechetical session. Perhaps it will be next to impossible, considering people's busy lives and time constraints. If there is time for reflection on the readings from only one specific mass, it would be important that the other readings be made available to participants for their personal reflection. However, all the readings of the Christmas liturgies taken as a whole reflect the broader mystery of the Incarnation. A possible solution might be to provide a Christmas season retreat in which all the readings of Christmas would be reviewed and participants would be offered an opportunity to experience the entire rich fare in the treasury of our Christmas liturgical repertoire.

> ... Despite all the liturgical formularies, one thing remains: it is impossible to encompass and express in only one liturgy the richness and complexity of the mystery that it celebrates. The good liturgies are those that are not limited to one perspective. This accounts for the diversity of scriptural texts that are offered for reading and meditation. They are not as distracting as one might think: they open up, rather, a greater awareness of what is being celebrated.[12]

[12]*Days of the Lord*, Vol. 1, 193.

CHRISTMAS

VIGIL MASS, MASS AT MIDNIGHT, MASS AT DAWN, MASS DURING THE DAY

The liturgies of Christmas are presented here: the vigil mass, mass at midnight, mass at dawn, and mass during the day. Perhaps you will have time to reflect upon only one of the liturgies. However, all of the readings shed light on the fullness of Christmas and help to unfold the meaning of the Incarnation.

The Infancy Narratives of the New Testament

Matthew and Luke are the only evangelists who tell of Jesus' birth. Raymond Brown suggests that it was not for historical purposes, but for religious reasons that the infancy narratives are told in the first place. These religious reasons are: "first, the identity of Jesus, second, his role as dramatic embodiment of the whole of history."[1] Matthew and Luke use the birth stories as a bridge between the old law, the prophets, and other scriptural books. Matthew and Luke felt that an understanding of Jesus' life and mission could be grasped only in light of the major themes and stories of the Hebrew scriptures.

One cannot help but notice that the two accounts differ considerably. Today's Christmas creche is a combination of both stories put together. Brown warns against trying to make the stories mesh by explaining away the differences. "A greater fidelity to Scripture as we have received it would recognize that the Holy Spirit was content to give us two different accounts and that the way to interpret them faithfully is to treat them separately."[2] There is no accurate way to know where and how the two evangelists received their information. Brown suggests that when there is excessive concern for historical accuracy we are distracted from the inspired meaning of the biblical text: the identity of Jesus and his role in the fulfillment of salvation history.

Environment

While the seasonal color of Christmas is red and green in the culture, the liturgical color of Christmas is white. The traditional Christmas tree and creche are appropriate adornments for the catechetical environment. Holly, a plant associated with Christmas, not only adds to the environment but carries symbolic meaning as well; the berries are reminiscent of Christ shedding his blood and the prickly leaves are an allusion to the crown of thorns. The primary symbol of the Incarnation is light. Christ, the Light of the world, came to dispel the darkness. Every environment should include ample use of candles to reflect the light that always shines.

The following blessings may be used to bless the tree and the crib. They are adapted from *Catholic Household Blessings and Prayers*.

Christmas Tree Blessing

This tree is a blessing to our space.
It reminds us of all that is filled with the gentleness and the promise of God.
It stands in our midst as a tree of light
that we might promise such beauty to one another and to our world.
It stands like the tree of paradise that God made into the tree of life, the cross of Jesus.
Lord God, let your blessing come upon us as we illumine this tree.
May the light and cheer it gives be a sign of the joy that fills our hearts.
May all who delight in this tree come to the knowledge and joy of salvation.

Blessing of a Christmas Creche

We are at the beginning of the days of Christmas.
All through the season we will look upon these images of sheep and cattle,
of shepherds, of Mary and Joseph and of Jesus.
God of Mary and Joseph, of shepherds and animals,
bless us whenever we gaze on this manger scene.
Through all the days of Christmas
may these figures tell the story of how humans, angels, and animals
found Christ in this poor place.
Fill this place with hospitality, joy, gentleness and thanksgiving

---

[1]Raymond E. Brown, *A Coming Christ in Advent* (Collegeville: The Liturgical Press, 1988), 10-26.

[2]Ibid., 9.

and guide our steps in the way of peace.
We ask this through Jesus Christ the Lord.

VIGIL MASS

INTRODUCTORY RITES

Opening Song (or Entrance Antiphon)

Today you will know the glory that the Lord is coming to save us, and in the morning you will see his glory (see Ex 16:6-7).[3]

Opening Prayer

Let us pray
[that Christmas morning will find us at peace]

Pause for silent prayer

God our Father,
every year we rejoice
as we look forward to this feast of our salvation.
May we welcome Christ as our Redeemer,
and meet him with confidence when he comes to
    be our judge,
who lives and reigns with you and the Holy Spirit,
one God, for ever and ever.[4]

LITURGY OF THE WORD

First Reading
Isaiah 62:1-5

This was probably a song used to accompany a pilgrimage to Jerusalem. It is quite appropriate that this reading begins the Christmas celebration. It is a joyful exclamation that the day of salvation has arrived. Obviously, Christianity connected the object of Israel's joy to that which is celebrated today, the Incarnation of God's Son. The conferral of a new name designated God's almighty power over creation. When one was given a new name, that person was made a new creation. "To give a name is also to take possession."[5]

---

[3]Christmas Vigil Mass: "Entrance Antiphon," *The Sacramentary.*
[4]Christmas Vigil Mass: "Opening Prayer," *The Sacramentary.*
[5]*Days of the Lord*, Vol. 1 (Collegeville: The Liturgical Press, 1991), 196.

Responsorial Psalm
Psalm 89:4-5, 16-17, 27-29

In the first reading, Isaiah proclaims the covenant love between Yahweh and his people. The vigil of Christmas hearkens back to this covenant as it is fulfilled in the nativity of the messiah. The responsorial psalm sings of the covenant Yahweh made with Israel. This covenant is fulfilled in and through the Incarnation of Christ.

Second Reading
Acts 13:16-17, 22-25

"From the beginning, Christians have always proclaimed that Jesus was the Savior, born of the house of David according to God's promise, and the one to whom John the Baptist bore witness."[6] The Christmas vigil reading from the Acts of the Apostles professes that ultimate belief and reminds us of the reason we gather to celebrate the birth of Christ.

Gospel
Matthew 1:1-25

The genealogy of Jesus is proclaimed.

STEP 1
NAMING ONE'S EXPERIENCE

What were your first impressions? What was your first response? What captured your attention? How did the readings affect you?

Each person names his or her initial impression. Statement should be brief. No reasons should be given at this time. All simply listen without agreeing or disagreeing.

STEP 2
UNDERSTANDING

In a brief statement what do you think this gospel is trying to convey?

---

[6]Ibid.

Liturgical Context

The vigil mass is the least celebrated. It may be celebrated before or after the first vespers of Christmas. If this mass is not celebrated, the readings and prayers may be used for prayer and meditation in preparation for celebration of the feast.

A brief background will be given for the readings. Since the genealogy from Matthew's gospel is rarely heard by a gathered assembly, it is important to note that its message is worthy of serious consideration and contemplation.
In the first reading we hear that God espouses Israel. God weds humanity. One is reminded of a similar marriage metaphor sung at the Easter Vigil, the "mother of all feasts." God's betrothal to Israel culminates in the wedding event of salvation. God espouses his people. The song of the Easter Vigil is: "This is the night when heaven is wedded to earth and humanity is reconciled with God!" (Exsultet). The vigil announces the inauguration of that paschal event.

Gospel Exegesis

The facilitator gives input regarding what critical biblical scholarship has to say about this text. The input includes insights as to how people would have heard the gospel in Jesus' time.

Genealogies are rarely read at liturgies. According to Raymond Brown, we miss a very important piece of salvation history if we ignore the genealogy of Jesus. Matthew's intent is to trace Jesus' origins to the house of David through Joseph. Even though Joseph was not the biological father of Jesus (the Holy Spirit is the creative power behind the conception of Christ), he was the legal[7] father because of his betrothal to Mary. Jesus, then, is rightful heir to the house of David. He possesses the necessary pedigree to claim the messianic title.

Brown asserts that the genealogy is told in order to highlight the paradox of a God who writes the story of salvation with "crooked lines." "A God who did not hesitate to use the scheming as well as the noble, the impure as well as the pure, men to whom the world hearkened and women upon whom the world frowned—this God continues to work in the same melange."[8] The genealogy shows that God used ordinary, unknown men and women to be part of the greatest story ever told. "The message of the genealogy is an enabling invitation."[9]

God chose scoundrels and saints to be in this many-act play called salvation. There was one who pilfered his brother's birthright and one who sold his brother into slavery. God used people who would never stand up to human scrutiny. From the very beginning, God used questionable people to participate in the grand design, just like Jesus would do in his ministry to the prostitutes and tax collectors. The cast of characters in Matthew's genealogy includes scoundrel kings and the famous king David (who was not a paragon of virtue). Also included is a cast of extras, the long list of names we know nothing about. They remind us of our own minuscule place on the continuum of salvation history's time-line.

The genealogy names foreign prostitutes. It names women who give birth in questionable circumstances, and the last of these is Mary, pregnant and husband-less. God's design is certainly out of the imaginative world of human consciousness. Yet, it stands as a clarion call, an invitation of immense significance for our lives. This God who used fallible, crafty, wily, saintly, and not-so-saintly human beings to usher in his reign continues to work with our frailty and our shortcomings.

Jesus entered our world with the intention of getting his hands dirty. He is not the image portrayed in saccharine art that shows him as a sweet, otherworldly, haloed being who exists out of our grasp or realm of understanding. Rather, the Jesus of Matthew's genealogy has a sordid family tree. He understands the "drunk uncle" hidden in everyone's closet. He understands the inherited sins of

―――――――――
[7]Legal fatherhood was not a status that required physical fatherhood.

―――――――――
[8]Brown, *A Coming Christ in Advent*, 25.
[9]Ibid.

past generations. His ancestry includes the famed Davidic monarchy that, like the sinful church of any age, was used by God in spite of its corruption, sin, and vanity. Nevertheless, it was to be a vehicle for God's plan of redemption, just as the church has been and always will be. He stands as a beacon of light in the midst of relational darkness.

The genealogy portrays the unfathomable deeds of God and the gratuitous grace that has been poured out upon the world since the beginning time, in spite of us and in communion with us. Jesus is the ultimate expression of that grace. Through his life, death, and resurrection Christ pours out a newer and fuller portion to sustain the church until his promised return.

Proclaim the gospel again.

Sometimes we gain new insights when we hear the text after the interpretation has been given. Someone from the group proclaims the gospel a second time.

STEP 4
TESTING

Conversation with the Liturgy and Scriptures

Test your original understanding in dialogue with the text.

(You might consider breaking into smaller groups.)

How do you feel about Matthew's genealogy in light of the interpretation just given? Were there any new insights? How does your original understanding of this story compare with what was just shared? How does this story speak to your life?

Sharing Life Experience

Our parish provides a night's shelter for the homeless when the weather in Florida goes below forty degrees. My husband and our friend, Dan, provide dinner and breakfast and spend the night in the gym with the "guys." Most of the homeless who come to us are hard-core addicts and alcoholics. By the time they come to the shelter they are either stoned or massively drunk. Last year, Bob and Dan spent Christmas

eve, Christmas day, and the day after with the homeless in our gym. There were over thirty nights of cold last winter, so they had the opportunity to get to know these folks very well. The homeless know that Dan and Bob do not judge them or preach to them; they are the heroes of the beach. They talk to them, laugh with them, and accept them as human beings with dignity. They offer them the opportunity to get off of the street if they want the help. In three years, only two have accepted assistance.

The ministry cannot be evaluated in terms of success stories. However, it is not about success. It is about extending love to God's most judged, rejected people. Regardless of the reasons, the homeless in our shelter have given up on life. Like the sordid characters in the genealogy, the homeless of our cold night ministry are a part of God's world, just as we all are. Even in the midst of their addictions, they know that they are absolutely powerless. Denial is long gone. They have given up. They know with certainty that they are addicts. Their condition is almost systemic: it is so hopeless that only God could save them. They have lost all hope and unconsciously are trying to kill themselves. Who, more than they, are in need of a Savior? Somewhere there are mothers, fathers, sisters, and brothers who have given up on them too. The only one who will never give up on them is God. God's hand is always there offering them another chance at life.

I do not begin to know what part they play in God's plan, but no doubt people in biblical times would have been incredulous that God would use the characters that he did in his plan for the salvation of the world. The shepherds were unsavory characters, yet they were the first to hear the heralded message of the Incarnation. The scriptures show us that Jesus came for "just such as these." We need them. They show us how powerless we all really are and how much we need a Savior. "There but for the grace of God go I."

The homeless have taught me a great deal. God dwells with them. God is in the midst of their hopelessness. They possess an inherent goodness. They remind us of the reality of the Christmas message. Last year at the midnight mass we had to ask for blankets because we had run out. The presence of the homeless in the gym just a few yards away from our Christmas celebration was a sobering reminder that Christmas is far more than the remembering of a babe in a manger. It is the Incarnation of God in the midst of complete hopelessness and darkness. Perhaps God is speaking to us through the lives of all who have completely given up on life.

Participants share their life experience in relation to the exegesis at this time.

What was Matthew trying to tell his community? What does he have to say to our community and to me today? How is God's covenant expressed in these readings? How is the theme of liberation and deliverance (exodus) expressed in this gospel? If God is always in the process of creating things anew, how is that expressed in the readings from this liturgy? How is God speaking to a people (community)? Do you still feel the same way about this text as you did when you began? Describe your understanding of this story now. Has your original understanding been stretched, challenged, or affirmed?

STEP 5
DECISION

The gospel demands a response.

How can Matthew's rendering of the genealogy possibly speak to a contemporary church? In what concrete way are we called to respond? Have I been changed in any way as a result of this sharing? What are the implications for my life? What is one concrete action I can take this week as a response to what we have learned and shared?

MASS AT MIDNIGHT

INTRODUCTORY RITES

Opening Song (or Entrance Antiphon)

The Lord said to me: You are my Son; this day I have begotten you.[10]

---

[10]Christmas Mass at Midnight: "Entrance Antiphon," *The Sacramentary.*

Opening Prayer

The facilitator of the session may lead the prayer. Others in the group could be asked to proclaim the readings.

Let us pray
[with joy and hope
as we await the dawning of the Father's Word]

Pause for silent prayer.

Lord our God,
with the birth of your Son,
your glory breaks on the world.

Through the night hours of the darkened earth
we your people watch for the coming of your
    promised Son.
As we wait, give us a foretaste of the joy that you
    will grant us
when the fullness of his glory has filled the earth,
who lives and reigns with you for ever and ever.[11]

LITURGY OF THE WORD

The readings are proclaimed.

Let us listen to God's word.

First Reading
Isaiah 9:1-6

In order to appreciate this reading in light of the Christmas event, it is important to look at the situation and the story that defines it in the book of the prophet Isaiah. King Ahaz, the youthful king of Judah (Southern Kingdom), inherited a throne in which the political problems were no match for him. The king of the Northern Kingdom (Israel) had made an alliance with Assyria. This infuriated the people, as it drastically raised their taxes. A group from the western part of the country joined forces with Damascus to overthrow Assyria, which had joined forces with Israel in the north. Thus, the Southern Kingdom, Judah, was a prime target for overthrow. King Ahaz was panic stricken and felt drawn to join forces with the North, and thus with Assyria. Isaiah met Ahaz and told him to trust

---

[11]Christmas Mass at Dawn: "Opening Prayer," *The Sacramentary.*

Yahweh and be calm. He told Ahaz that the only way to deal with the crisis was to maintain a relaxed reliance on Yahweh who was far greater than any human power. God was in covenant relationship with Judah and therefore would not abandon them. Nor would God think of abandoning the promise made to David regarding David's everlasting dynasty. Isaiah assured Ahaz that he must have faith. If his faith was secure, his throne would also be secure.

Isaiah was telling Ahaz to be strong and to resist the temptation to unite with Syria and Israel in the north. Yahweh would protect them. Ahaz did not listen to Isaiah. Isaiah promised Ahaz a sign of assurance that Yahweh would do as promised. Ahaz told Isaiah that he was not interested in asking for a sign; he would not think of putting Yahweh to the test. Isaiah became angry and told Ahaz that Yahweh would offer a sign to the house of David—to David's dynasty, not to Ahaz. The sign would confirm that the northern alliance was doomed and that God would be faithful to the promise made to David. "The purpose of a sign [in biblical history] was to make visible and to confirm dramatically the truth and power of Yahweh's word spoken by the prophet. A sign does not necessarily have to be a miracle, in our sense of the word, for its significance is not so much in its unusual character as in its power to confirm a prophetic word spoken in threat or promise."[12] The ability to see signs was an important part of Israel's faith. It enabled them to perceive God acting in human history.

Isaiah's sign was the promised birth of a child whose name was Immanuel (God is with us). Isaiah prophesied that the birth was imminent. He believed the mother to be already pregnant. One might ask how the coming of a child could be a sign for Ahaz. Isaiah attested that, unlike Ahaz, the child would be a faithful, steadfast leader of the people. Isaiah prophesied in response to a current crisis in his time. He had no idea that this prophecy would become the basis for the Jewish hope in a future messiah. Isaiah's song in chapter 7 became a part of the prophetic messianic tradition. This "child to come" was to share the suffering of his

people. The child would usher in an age of judgment and an opportunity for new beginnings.

In Isaiah's prophecy the child was feasting on milk and honey, a reference to the milk and honey found in the promised land. Those listening to Isaiah realized from that reference that this child would be a sign of hope following a dismal time of misery and tribulation. "For Yahweh's purpose is not to destroy, but to refine and cleanse a remnant people. Once the Assyrian yoke is overturned the child will ascend the throne as the agent of God's rule over the people. Then the meaning of his name Immanuel will be clearly understood."[13] The early Christian community used this prophecy as the foundation for their belief in Jesus as messiah. This prophetic hymn of Isaiah sings of hope in the messiah, fulfilled in the person of Jesus Christ: Wonder Counselor, Mighty God, Everlasting Father, Prince of Peace!

Responsorial Psalm
Psalm 96:1-2a, 2b-3, 11-12, 13

The new song referred to in the psalm is the song to be sung when the messiah redeems the world. It will replace the old song sung when Moses delivered the people out of bondage.

Second Reading
Titus 2:11-14

The letter to Titus was written not to a community, but rather to an individual in regard to his pastoral duties. There are two other such letters, and they are referred to as the "pastoral epistles." There is some question as to whether Paul wrote these letters. Some believe that the letters might have been written by a disciple(s) who was trying to "publish the sort of letter he thought the master might have written had he still been alive."[14]

The reading of Titus reminds us that Advent prepared us for two comings. We do not forget the second coming of Christ even as we are steeped in celebration and remembrance of his first coming. Christ will come again; we are to live noble lives. Robert Karris asserts: "These verses are fitting for

---

[12]Bernhard W. Anderson, *Understanding the Old Testament,* 4th ed. (Englewood Cliffs: Prentice Hall, 1986), 331-334.

[13]Ibid.

[14]Hubert Richards, *The Gospel According to St. Paul* (Collegeville: The Liturgical Press, 1990), 128.

Christmas because they invite us to contemplate the new born babe as God's gracious appearance for our salvation."[15]

The overall theme of the letter to Titus is that we are not to retreat from the world. We are to be a sign in the world. We are to live upright lives as we go about the task of life, remembering as we go that our final fulfillment will take place when Christ comes again.

Gospel
Luke 2:1-14

The angels appear to the shepherds and the heavenly hosts sing God's praises and announce the arrival of the messiah.

STEP 1
NAMING ONE'S EXPERIENCE

What were your first impressions? What was your first response? What understanding of this story did you bring with you to this conversation? How did the readings affect you?

Each person names his or her initial impression. Statement should be brief. No reasons should be given at this time. All simply listen without agreeing or disagreeing.

STEP 2
UNDERSTANDING

In a brief statement, what do you think this gospel is trying to convey?

STEP 3
INPUT FROM VISION/STORY/TRADITION

Liturgical Context

Read the overview of Christmas. The Christmas readings proclaim for us the reason we gather to

remember the nativity event. They unfold for us a refined Christian understanding of the Incarnation. The opening prayer and the prefaces help us focus on the theological meaning of the celebration. God sent his Son as a human being to the world to redeem the world. Jesus is both fully human and fully divine. We became heirs to Christ's divinity through his Incarnation and subsequent life, death, and resurrection. We will share eternal life with him because of the nativity and the event for which he was born: his death and resurrection. We still wait in hope for his return.

Gospel Exegesis

The facilitator gives input regarding what critical biblical scholarship has to say about this text. The input includes insights as to how people would have heard the gospel in Jesus' time.

Our culture has so romanticized and consumerized Christmas that it is difficult to remember that the scriptures of the Christmas liturgies are not intended as detailed historical narratives (while they are nonetheless historical), but as a means of communicating the awesome reality of God's explosion into human history through the person of Jesus Christ.

The story of Jesus' birth is told as good news. Why good news? Charles Talbert tells us that in the Mediterranean world every time a great ruler was born, the benefits to the people were announced. The newborn ruler was often called a savior who would bring peace. Jesus, the new ruler, the one who came to fulfill the ancient prophecies, "who has on his birthday a proclamation of the benefits of his birth,"[16] is truly good news.

Shalom (peace), according to Hebrew understanding, meant wholeness, the right ordering of relationships with one another, with God, with the earth, and with oneself. "Peace became an eschatological hope."[17] To be at peace meant that one was in complete harmony with God, neighbor, creation, and self. Obviously, the only place where

---

[15]Robert J. Karris, O.F.M., *The Pastoral Epistles* (Wilmington: Michael Glazier, Inc., 1984), 112.

[16]Charles H. Talbert, *Reading Luke* (New York: Crossroad, 1992), 32.

[17]Ibid.

the perfection of such harmony is realized is in the eternal hereafter.

Luke situates his gospel in the context of the current political situation. Persecutions were taking place when Luke was writing his account. In Luke's gospel, the origin of the child Jesus is traced back to two small inconsequential towns, Nazareth and Bethlehem. Jesus was born to poor parents. He was not what one would consider "royal material" in the earthly sense of the word. Certainly, it would be difficult to imagine one so lowly laying claim to the political power of the reigning imperial authority. Luke made it clear that the kingship of Jesus has more to do with spiritual realities than with governmental overthrow. The logical extension to this carefully devised genesis is that Jesus' followers are part of his heritage and thus are not a threat to political authority. Read: there is no reason to persecute the church.

The image of shepherds has been over-sentimentalized throughout history. Shepherds were despised individuals and considered to be in the same category as tax collectors and prostitutes. "Their testimony was not considered valid because of their reputation for dishonesty."[18] The message cannot be missed. God comes for the outcast, for those everyone hates, disregards, and leaves behind as useless. God's salvation is for everybody. The shepherds are the first to whom the message is told. Perhaps they needed it the most. This is not the last time we will hear this message from Luke.

"Angels who bring messages to accompany events are the biblical way of expressing the meaning of salvation as an act of God."[19] There are two visitations from angels in Luke's story. The first announces the birth of the messiah. The second appearance comes in the form of the heavenly host. They announce that God's favor has come to people of good will. Reginald Fuller tells us that "people of good will" is not a term of exclusion. In Hebrew, "people of good will" referred to all people who, because of this event, were the object of di-

vine favor.[20] It also appears as if the angels came to proclaim Jesus' name and his identity. However, Eugene LaVerdiere tells us that "Luke's main point, which links God's glory in the highest with peace on earth for the humble, would have been lost had the passage merely raised the matter of Jesus' identity. The narrative called for a manifestation of Jesus' life and mission, a statement which would anticipate the actual unfolding of the implications of his name."[21] Luke's purpose is christological and ecclesial. Christ's mission is named and the church "is identified as the humble recipient and proclaimer of the gospel."[22]

Proclaim the gospel again.

Sometimes we gain new insights when we hear the text after the interpretation has been given. Someone from the group proclaims the gospel a second time.

STEP 4
TESTING

Conversation with the Liturgy and the Scriptures

Test your original understanding in dialogue with the text.

(You might consider breaking into smaller groups.)

Now that you've heard what the scholars have to say about Luke's version of the nativity narrative, how do you feel about it? Were there any new insights? Was there anything you had not considered before? How does your original understanding of this story compare with what was just shared? How does this story speak to your life?

Sharing Life Experience

Participants share something from their lives that connects with the exegesis just given.

> *I am reminded of the Christmas season a few years ago when, as part of an evening of music and poetry, a group of beautiful liturgical dancers artisti-*

---

[18]Ibid., 33.

[19]Reginald H. Fuller, *Preaching the New Lectionary* (Collegeville: The Liturgical Press, 1974), 467.

[20]Ibid.

[21]Eugene LaVerdiere, S.S.S., *Luke* (Wilmington: Michael Glazier Books, 1980), 33.

[22]Ibid.

cally pirouetted their way to the Christmas creche accompanied by angelic voices blended in harmonious exultation of the God who comes to us in the flesh. It all sounds very beautiful and holy, doesn't it? Well it was; that is, until we spotted something happening in the back of the dancers' line. Someone (who was certainly not wrapped in the swaddling garb of angelic chiffon) decided it was appropriate to join the dancers in their gestures of praise. Bringing up the rear behind six beautiful young women was one slovenly drunk who not-so-gracefully joined the parade—pirouettes, twists, turns, and all. I was horrified that such a beautifully choreographed work was being destroyed so haphazardly and with unconscious, alcoholic disdain. Later in the evening, there was a piece of poetry that echoed in wretched despair for those who, on Christmas night and every night, have no place to call home. Is there no place to be found where human choruses welcome the world's homeless into the sacred halls of their incense soaked cathedrals? Suddenly, there was something very paradoxical about the scene. Christ exploded into the world for this very outcast, society's lowest. If our drunken visitor had been the only one, Christ still would have come. We cannot imagine and feel we do not deserve love like that! Who would listen, if he, like the shepherds, were to be visited by heavenly hosts with tidings of great joy? Would anybody listen?

All share at this time.

What was Luke trying to tell his community? How does the image of the shepherds resonate with our experience of the Christmas story? How does it feel to have our sentimental understanding of the Christmas story challenged? If the shepherds were unsavory characters, yet the angels appeared first to them, what is the message for our community? How would it be received? Do we still feel the same way about this text as we did when we began? What is our understanding of this story now? Has our original understanding been stretched, challenged, or affirmed?

STEP 5
DECISION

The gospel demands a response.

What would be the contemporary implications of the angels' message to the shepherds? What would be the implication for our communities today? In what concrete ways should we respond? Has this conversation with the exegesis of this Christmas gospel changed or stretched my personal attitudes? What are the implications of Jesus' Incarnation for my own life? What should be my/our response?

MASS AT DAWN

Proclaim the readings from the mass at dawn. If time is limited, focus on the gospel.

First Reading
Isaiah 62:11-12

Trito-Isaiah, the third book of Isaiah, is concerned with the sin of the people. Their sin delays salvation. Nevertheless, they still believe that salvation is not far off. Trito-Isaiah sees salvation as a new creation very much like the creation of Genesis. Judgement is harsh. In this brief pericope for use at the mass at dawn we experience the joy of the new Israel at the arrival of "messianic salvation."[23]

Responsorial Psalm
Psalm 97:1, 6, 11-12

This is an enthronement psalm. One cannot miss the light imagery and its connection with the Christmas theme of the dawning of light.

Second Reading
Titus 3:4-7

Hubert Richards cites this passage from Titus as a "fine summary of the gospel Paul made his own; it is no wonder it has been chosen as one of the readings for the Christmas liturgy. It has a lyric quality...."[24] In this third chapter of Titus, Paul points out the wonders of God. He proclaims that God is all good and wishes nothing less than the very best for his children: wholeness and salvation. Paul insists that we are to imitate God's love for us

---

[23]Fuller, *Preaching the New Lectionary*, 467.
[24]Hubert Richards, *The Gospel According to St. Paul*, 133.

and treat others accordingly. Because we have been so gratuitously loved, we in turn must live in love and give in love. God would do no less for us. It is what God would want us to do. Paul echoes what appears to be a familiar understanding of Jewish spirituality. Covenant people are to work toward the ordering of right relationships (*hesed*). We are in *hesed* relationship when our relationships with God, one another, ourselves, and the earth are in right order. These relationships, of course, are informed by the great law of love, evidenced by our behavior to the least of God's people.

Paul provides us with a familiar schema. Robert Karris suggests that there is a movement of transformation in the *then/now* assumption apparent in this text. We were once this way, but now we are a different way. We have been made a new creation through our baptism in Jesus. We were once children in darkness, but not any more. Now we are children in the light. Citing its use of the pronouns *we/us* rather than *you*, Karris also suggests that this pericope was once a ritual prayer used in liturgy. Titus 3:4-7 is believed to be part of an ancient baptismal hymn of thanksgiving. We give thanks that we have been made new creations in Christ through the refreshing waters of baptism. At baptism we receive the Spirit and wait in hope for the life we will share in eternity. At our baptism we share in what God accomplished through Jesus' entrance into human history at his nativity and subsequent pasch: the salvation of the world. We are to go forth transformed and make a difference in our respective worlds. "Paul insists that liturgy begets daily Christian life."[25] Paul stated that we are justified by faith and are heirs of eternal life (Ti 3:7). Through the Incarnation, we share in Jesus' divinity.

Gospel
Luke 2:15-20

The shepherds speak among themselves of the wonderful good news and decide to go and see for themselves.

---

[25]Karris, *The Pastoral Epistles*, 124.

STEP 1
NAMING ONE'S EXPERIENCE

What were your first impressions? What was your first response? What grabbed your attention? How did you feel?

Each person names his or her initial impression. Statement should be brief. No reasons should be given at this time. All simply listen without agreeing or disagreeing.

STEP 2
UNDERSTANDING

In a brief statement, what do you think this gospel is trying to convey?

STEP 3
INPUT FROM VISION/TRADITION/STORY

Liturgical Context

The light motif is even more prominent in the liturgy for the mass at dawn than it is at the midnight mass. The responsorial psalm, the entrance antiphon, and the opening prayer speak of the light that will shine this day on us and on our actions.

Gospel Exegesis

The facilitator gives input regarding what critical biblical scholarship has to say about this text. The input includes insights as to how people would have heard the gospel in Jesus' time.

This gospel is an extension of the story begun at the midnight mass. Again, we know these culturally sentimentalized stories so well that it is often easy to be blinded by their significance. Jesus came for the outcast. Shepherds were outcasts, despised and considered dishonest. Yet they were the ones who saw the Christ child. They were the ones who heard the heavenly hosts singing the hymn of praise and announcing *shalom*/peace (wholeness, *hesed*). Perhaps we could call these outcasts the first evangelists. They were the first to spread and tell the good news. Would anybody believe their testimony?

Proclaim the gospel again.

Sometimes we gain new insights when we hear the text after the interpretation is given. Someone from the group proclaims the gospel a second time.

STEP 4
TESTING

Conversation with the Liturgy and the Scriptures

Test your original understanding in dialogue with the text.

(You might consider breaking into smaller groups.)

How does it feel that some of our traditional assumptions about the Christmas story are brought into question by contemporary scholarship? How do you feel about the image of the shepherds portrayed by the scholars? How does this story speak to your life? What was Luke trying to tell his community? What does he have to say to you and to your community today? What do the Christmas readings say about God/Jesus? Do you still feel the same way about this text as you did when you began? Describe your understanding of this story now. Has your original understanding been stretched, challenged, or affirmed?

STEP 5
DECISION

The gospel demands a response.

How do these readings for Christmas challenge me and the community to action? Where is growth needed in my community, in me? What am I going to do about it?

MASS DURING THE DAY

Proclaim the readings from the mass during the day. If time is limited, focus on the gospel.

First Reading
Isaiah 52:7-10

The people of Israel had the ability to view their lives in relationship to the mighty acts of God. They possessed a corporate conscience that allowed them to see the events of their lives in relationship to the Yahweh who saved, judged, forgave, punished, rewarded, and ordained their very life breath. Their optimism in the face of despair and oppression was of heroic proportions. Even though their exile was moving into a second generation, their hope for restoration was not to be squelched. The bondage that had ravaged their identity had the purging, yet freeing effect of giving definition to their lives.

Prophets such as Deutero-Isaiah helped them examine themselves and in the process they were formed in the heart and will of God. When it was time for their deliverance, joy overflowed and exultation filled the heart of a nation. It is this joyful song we hear from the prophet on Christmas morn. Their vindication had arrived. They were delivered from bondage. The dawn of God's saving might was upon the earth.

One need not wonder why Isaiah was chosen to sing this privileged song of joy in the liturgy of Christmas morning. It was this very event, the Christ event, that he foreshadowed in his eschatological hymn. During the time of Deutero-Isaiah, messianic prophecies began to include an eschatological element, a future hope of deliverance at the consummation of the world. Jesus ushers in the last days through his Incarnation. There was reason for joy.

Responsorial Psalm
Psalm 98:1, 2-3, 3-4, 5-6

All of the psalms of Christmas are enthronement psalms. They praise God for the acts of salvation and are most appropriate on this day of salvation.

Second Reading
Hebrews 1:1-6

St. Paul's letter to the Hebrews is not a letter at all, but rather, a *logos* of encouragement for the community. A logos was a public address, very much like a homily. This opening address is a christological hymn of praise with roots in Jewish praise of Lady Wisdom. Wisdom was personified and considered to be with God in the act of creation. Wisdom also was the agent of God's revelation of self to Israel. The early Christian community appropriated that understanding to Jesus. Jesus assumes the role of One who was with God from the beginning in the work of salvation.

Gospel
John 1:1-18 or 1:1-5, 9-14

STEP 1
NAMING ONE'S EXPERIENCE

What were your first impressions? What captured your attention?

Each person names his or her initial impression. Statement should be brief. No reasons should be given at this time. All simply listen without agreeing or disagreeing.

STEP 2
UNDERSTANDING

In a brief statement, what do you think this gospel is trying to convey?

STEP 3
INPUT FROM VISION/STORY/TRADITION

Liturgical Context

Prior to Vatican II, the prologue to John's gospel was read at the end of every mass, thus recalling for the faithful the salvation event of God through the Incarnation of the Son.

"Christmas is a feast that celebrates our redemption even though the focus of attention is on the Incarnation and the 'marvelous exchange' and not on the passion and resurrection."[26] This is clearly expressed in the second reading: "He cleansed us from our sins and took his seat at the right hand of the majesty in Heaven..."(Heb 1:3). The gospel for the mass during the day uses John's prologue to proclaim the mystery of the Incarnation. God speaks a definitive *Word* to the world and to Israel. Salvation was at hand. The *Word* had been spoken. John's prologue and the letter to the Hebrews emphasize that the Christmas liturgy is more than a mere celebration of a baby's birth. It is God's center-stage act of communication with the world. (On this day, one might consider using the shorter form of the reading, since the longer form, including reference to John the Baptist, contains what is believed to be a later addition to the original hymn.)

This liturgy celebrates the great expression of joy inherent in all of the Christmas readings. The mystery of Jesus' Incarnation is raised to a cosmic level. John reminds us in his prologue that we must return to the beginning and remember that God began the Christmas story at the creation of the world. God had always intended that humanity be heirs of eternal life with him. We must look at the nativity alongside the cross and resurrection. Christmas is viewed through the lens of Easter.

Gospel Exegesis

The facilitator gives input regarding what critical biblical scholarship has to say about this text. The input includes insights as to how people would have heard the gospel in Jesus' time.

The prologue serves as a preface to John's gospel. It is theological and its purpose is to establish the thesis for the entire book. John's gospel tells the stories of Christ from the perspective that God, even from the beginning, from before time, from the eternal past, had been in the process of communicating. To be God means to reveal God. Creation was an act of God's self-communication. God's revelation to Israel was a continuation of his continuous activity of self-revelation. Jesus, then, was the definitive, incarnate expression of God's self-communication to Israel.

---

[26]*Days of the Lord,* Vol. 1, 128.

Reginald Fuller suggests that the Word became flesh throughout Jesus' entire ministry. Through Jesus' life and miracles God continued the process of revealing self to the world. Jesus manifested God to humanity. In John's prologue, *flesh* refers to all human history since the very beginning, the creation of the world. All that God had done *for* and *with* Israel is brought to this moment, to this defining moment of salvation. All of God's deeds up to this point are understood in light of God's premier saving event: the spoken Word of God, in human form, given as ultimate gift of self, to suffer for the sins of the world.

John's gospel was written in response to the situation at the end of the century in which belief in Christ's divinity was questioned. John made his case by proclaiming that Christ was a part of God's action at creation. Jesus was present at God's first act of salvation (creation) and awaited his entrance into the world (Incarnation) to inaugurate God's last, conclusive act of salvation.

Patricia Datchuck Sanchez offers an interesting observation. The Semitic understanding of the word *logos* was "a challenge a believer can accept or reject."[27] A *logos* from God could be accepted or rejected. Thus the believer was faced with a decision and a response. The Greek understanding of *logos* was "an intermediary between God and the created universe."[28] The *logos* brought order to the universe. Therefore, according to Hellenistic thought, the one who embraced the *logos* would have access to the mysteries of the heavens. John is familiar with both constructs and cleverly uses both meanings in defining the ultimate mystery of Christ. Christ is the one who invites and calls people to faith, but he is also the one who reveals the face of God to the world.

Proclaim the gospel again.

Sometimes we gain new insights when we hear the text after the interpretation has been given. Someone from the group proclaims the gospel a second time.

---

[27] Patricia Datchuck Sanchez, *The Word We Celebrate* (Kansas City: Sheed and Ward, 1989), 274.

[28] Ibid.

STEP 4
TESTING

Conversation with the Liturgy and the Scriptures

Test your original understanding in dialogue with the text.

(You might consider breaking into smaller groups.)

How does John's prologue speak to you? Did the exegesis offer any new insights? How does your original understanding of this Christmas gospel compare with the interpretation? Does John's description of Christ as the eternal spoken Word of God have anything to do with your life? If so, how? What relevance does it have today? What was John trying to say to his community? What does he have to say to your community and to you today? Do you still feel the same way about this text as you did at the beginning? Describe your understanding of this story now.

STEP 5
DECISION

The gospel demands a response.

How should our community respond to this word from John? If we accept the Semitic understanding of *logos*, how might Christ be challenging us in this reading, or in all of the readings of Christmas? What one specific, concrete thing can I do during this season to respond to the word spoken today?

DOCTRINAL ISSUES

What church truth/teaching/doctrinal issue could be drawn from the readings for Christmas?

Participants suggest possible doctrinal themes that flow from the readings.

Possible Doctrinal Themes

Incarnation, christology, manifestation, salvation

Present the doctrinal material at this time.

1. The facilitator gives input on a particular doctrinal issue of his/her prior choosing. OR
2. The group chooses a doctrinal issue from the list they created. They read together from the Doctrinal Appendix.

(The doctrinal issues are found in the Doctrinal Appendix in the back of this workbook. If you are choosing an issue from this resource, please refer to it now.)

Reflection questions centered around the chosen doctrinal theme can be found at the end of each topic in the Doctrinal Appendix. The questions are based on the five-step reflection process. If you choose a topic not included in the Doctrinal Appendix, craft your own questions according to the same five-step process.

Following the reflection questions you will be reminded to return to chapter 7, "Preparing the Catechetical Session," to assist you in crafting your own session.

Closing Prayer

Father, all powerful and ever living God,
we do well always and everywhere to give you thanks
through Jesus Christ our Lord.
Today in him a new light has dawned upon the
    world:
God has become one with man,
and man has become one again with God.
Your eternal Word has taken upon himself our
    human weakness,
giving our mortal nature immortal value.
So marvelous is this oneness between God and
    man
that in Christ man restores to man the gift of
everlasting life.
In our joy we sing to your glory
with all the choirs of angels:
All sing or say: Holy, holy, holy, Lord, God of
    power and might,
heaven and earth are full of your glory.
Hosanna in the highest.
Blessed is he who comes in the name of the Lord.
Hosanna in the highest.[29]

---

[29]Christmas Preface III, *The Sacramentary.*

Selected Bibliography

Anderson, Bernhard W. *Understanding the Old Testament.* 4th ed. Englewood Cliffs: Prentice Hall, 1986.

Brown, Raymond E. *A Coming Christ in Advent.* Collegeville: The Liturgical Press, 1988.

Days of the Lord. Vol. 1. Collegeville: The Liturgical Press, 1991.

Fuller, Reginald, H. *Preaching the New Lectionary.* Collegeville: The Liturgical Press, 1974.

Karris, Robert J., O.F.M. *The Pastoral Epistles.* Wilmington: Michael Glazier, Inc., 1984.

LaVerdiere, Eugene. S.S.S. *Luke.* Wilmington: Michael Glazier Books, 1980.

Richards, Hubert. *The Gospel According to St. Paul*. Collegeville: The Liturgical Press, 1990.

Sanchez, Patricia Datchuck. *The Word We Celebrate.* Kansas City: Sheed and Ward, 1989.

Talbert, Charles H. *Reading Luke.* New York, Crossroad, 1992.

Feast of the Holy Family

INTRODUCTORY RITES

Opening Song (or Entrance Antiphon)

The shepherds hastened to Bethlehem, where they found Mary and Joseph, and the baby lying in a manger.[1]

Environment

Because it is still the Christmas season, the environment does not change.

Opening Prayer

The facilitator of the session may lead the prayer. Others in the group may be asked to proclaim the readings.

Let us pray
[for peace in our families]

> *Pause for silent prayer.*

Father in heaven, creator of all,
you ordered the earth to bring forth life
and crowned its goodness by creating the family of
  man.
In history's moment when all was ready,
you sent your Son to dwell in time,
obedient to the laws of life in our world.
Teach us the sanctity of human love,
show us the value of family life,
and help us to live in peace with all men
that we may share in your life for ever.
We ask this through Christ our Lord.[2]

LITURGY OF THE WORD

Today it would be important to pay attention to all of the readings. Taken together they better express the meaning of this feast. You might want to give particular attention to the second reading.

Let us listen to God's word.

---

[1]Feast of the Holy Family: "Entrance Antiphon," *The Sacramentary.*

[2]Feast of the Holy Family: "Alternative Opening Prayer," *The Sacramentary.*

First Reading
Sirach 3:2-6, 12-14

Ben Sira lived around 180 B.C.E. He was an educated man, and the main themes in his writing were reflection on the Torah and practical suggestions for upright living. The book of Sirach is not a part of the Hebrew and Protestant canons.

Sirach presents a commentary on the command to honor one's parents. He is so serious about the law's exhortation that he sees breaking the law as tantamount to breaking the covenant relationship with God.

As has been stated before, Israel was in covenant relationship with Yahweh. *Hesed,* or covenant loyalty, assumed a reciprocity and demanded that love of one another flow out of the love of God. The first person or group deserving of such *hesed* was one's parents. When one followed the law in such an upright manner one could expect mercy, blessings, and God's forgiveness. Children were to respect and care for their parents. Parents who raised their children in righteousness could expect their children to be firmly planted in the faith of Israel. Children who did not heed their parents would be uprooted from their firm foundation. The law even suggested that anyone who did not treat the aged with great care and concern was guilty of blasphemy. The challenge and the exhortation of this scriptural text is very clear. Dysfunctional family systems were not tolerated in ancient Israel. Every effort was to be made to live in the harmony expected by God.

Family was a very important reality for Israel. The clan, the tribe, the extended family, the people of God, all represented a form of family that was in covenant relationship with Yahweh. Covenant relationship requires great respect and care for one another. There is no life outside the community, the family of God's people.

Responsorial Psalm
Psalm 128:1-2, 3, 4-5

This wisdom psalm calls on God to bless human efforts. "Happy" refers to the blessing of many sons. The reference to "house" ("home" NAB) is a reflection on human effort. All who do what is upright in God's eyes will be blessed with many children.

Second Reading
Colossians 3:2-21

Colossae was a community in trouble. It was plagued by division and by religious problems caused by Jews who were angry over the inclusion of gentiles. Aberrant religious practices threatened the Colossian church. Epaphras called on Paul in prison to chastise and challenge his community to fidelity in Christ. Paul willingly wrote to his Colossian brothers and sisters and stressed that they must remain steadfast to the Christ who is above any pagan, philosophical, or religious practice that humans might construct. Jesus is the center of the universe. He is our primary reality. Any other spiritual quest is idolatry.

Some scholars believe this pericope is part of a baptismal teaching. When Paul exhorts the Colossians to "put on love" he references the baptismal liturgy in which the new garment is put on as a symbol of new life in Christ. The old self dies to sin and the white color of the garment represents triumphing over death and sin.

There is often great controversy over the latter verses of this pericope. Some people believe that the piece regarding the submission of wives should be left out of the text for the same reasons that the verses regarding the submission of slaves were deleted. The verses regarding slavery were deleted because of society's changed view of slavery. It is a thing of the past and is intrinsically evil. Some believe the verses about "submissive wives" should be deleted for the same reason. Proponents of deleting the text suggest that it was a reality of a former time and culture. Today Christian marriage is seen as a community of covenant love rooted in mutuality and reciprocity. Further, there is an even more more compelling argument against reading the verses. Many times they have been cited as an apologetic for dominance over wives by controlling, abusive husbands.

However, Raymond F. Collins suggests a different approach. He asserts that these and similar readings were part of early Christian *Haustafel* or household codes (compendiums of household duties).[3] There were political reasons for such codes. Christians were believed to be disruptive of the social order. They refused submission to the gods of the state. "On the domestic scene, various women, young people and slaves had become Christians. Such phenomena led to widespread suspicion of Christians and even to the persecution of Christians, considered people who disrupted social order and disturbed domestic harmony."[4] The household codes were a way for Christians to assert their compliance with the family values of the day. Collins suggests that there is merit in proclaiming these readings. We should read the "submissive wives" texts as presenting the world view of a former time, a former culture, and a former reality. Their value to us today is the deeper meaning they suggest. He submits that these readings affirm the concern that God has for the human family within the social culture in which it exists. "One cannot make of any given society's family structures the norm for all families of all times and places. We can, however, affirm that God is not indifferent to family life, as it is actually structured within any given society."[5] He suggests that the household codes point to God's care for the family as it is lived— not as it is idealized by some outside agency. Collins asserts that the basic message of the text should not be overlooked. The household codes affirm that there must be some order for a family to function well. He maintains that their use in the liturgy affirms that the Christian family has been and always will be a concern of the church. "The well-being of families who belong to the church is important for the well-being of the church itself."[6]

Although twentieth-century America has little resemblance to early Christian communities, there are corollaries to be drawn. Even the piece regarding slaves and masters has its present-day corollary. Both "submissive wives" and "obedient slaves" point to a reciprocity of relationships that is ex-

---

[3]Raymond F. Collins, *Preaching the Epistles* (New York/Mahwah: Paulist Press, 1996), 81-84.

[4]Ibid., 81.

[5]Ibid.

[6]Ibid., 83.

pected even today. When people work, they expect a fair wage for their labor and to be treated with respect and concern by their employers. Employers expect a fair day's work for a fair day's wage. It all boils down to the right ordering of relationships. We are all to "do right by one another."

Collins offers a caution. He says that there is a strength and a liability to the contemporary proclamation of the household codes of early Christian communities.

> It is a strength insofar as it recalls that one must live the Christian life within the context of a socially conditioned set of human relationships. It is a liability when one attempts to make the social relationships of yesteryear a norm for the social relationships of today. *When preaching household codes, the homilist should NOT proclaim that wives should be submissive to their husbands.* Such submission is no longer culturally acceptable; indeed, in our times, it may well be antithetical to the gospel itself. On the other hand, the liturgical reading of the household codes may provide a pastorally sensitive homilist with an opportune occasion for reflecting on the changing nature of the family structure.[7]

Collins suggests that there be serious reflection regarding our assumed norms for the human family. The nuclear family of the past is not the present norm. Nor was it a norm for all time. The extended family system was around long before the "Quaker, child centered family of the middle colonies." He also notes that in the seventeenth and eighteenth centuries the father was the primary care giver following the baby's nursing period. Before we canonize the "'typical' twentieth century white American family" we should rather reflect on God's presence in every family, no matter what social circumstances it finds itself in. Perhaps the atypical family is pure gift in our midst. It is a reminder of our responsibility to God's *anawim*, to one another, and to those who struggle just to keep themselves afloat in turbulent, often violent and dysfunctional family systems. It is the responsibility of the church, the people of God, to

_____
[7]Ibid., 84.

reflect God's care for all families, those considered typical and especially those considered atypical.

Gospel
Luke 2:41-52

Mary and Joseph lose their young adolescent son, Jesus. They frantically search for him and find him in the temple, preaching to the elders.

STEP 1
NAMING ONE'S EXPERIENCE

What were your first impressions? What was your first response? What captured your attention? How did you feel?

Each person names his or her initial impression. Statement should be brief. No reasons should be given at this time. All simply listen without agreeing or disagreeing.

STEP 2
UNDERSTANDING

In a brief statement, what do you think this gospel is trying to convey?

STEP 3
INPUT FROM VISION/STORY/TRADITION

Liturgical Context

Like other readings of the Christmas season, the gospel for this Sunday is another manifestation of Christ, the Son of God to the world. Today it is Jesus' wisdom that becomes manifest. The liturgy allows us to gaze upon this Christ who, though fully human, is the personification of divine wisdom.

The church has set aside this day to uplift and reflect upon the importance of the Christian family. The holy family is offered as a model. The first and second readings provide insights into familial relationships. Perhaps after reflecting upon what it means to love in the context of family, family systems, and societal structures, we then can turn to the gospel to remind us that we have one who is filled with wisdom, who lavishly showers us with love, who promises to be with us, even as we struggle to live in love in difficult situations. Perhaps the gospel reminds us that we must turn our children and their futures over to the providential care of God. Perhaps it tells us that we must be content to live in the mystery of God's revelation in our lives, even when we are faced with difficult family experiences. Perhaps we can view Mary and Joseph as willing to accept the ambiguity that life often presents. Perhaps they can serve as reminders to us that if we ponder the marvels of God in our heart and watch God's plan unfold in our lives, we will one day be able to look back and discern the mighty hand of God in the most trying situations.

The prayers of today's liturgy ask God for the intercession of Mary and Joseph for the peace and unification of families. The Prayer over the Gifts states: "Lord, accept this sacrifice and through the prayers of Mary, the virgin Mother of God, and of her husband, Joseph, unite our families in peace and love." The liturgy reflects great concern for the Christian family. On this day, this Christmas-season feast, we once again celebrate God's manifestation to the human race. Let us put it in the context of what can often be a most difficult place to experience such manifestation: the human family. We pray for and uplift families who struggle to submit their lives to the will of God. We thank God for the witness of their lives. We pray for those who suffer violence, hatred, and animosity within the walls of their own homes.

Gospel Exegesis

The facilitator gives input regarding what critical biblical scholarship has to say about this text. The input includes insights as to how people would have heard the gospel in Jesus' time.

Even though we are tempted to empathize with the frantic parents of the lost adolescent, we miss the point of the story if that becomes our central focus. Providing an historical account of an event in the early family life of Jesus is not the intent of this gospel. If it were, would not the child have responded to his parents' frantic fear with covenant love and respect? The first reading asserts that children must treat their parents with great admiration and deference. By normal standards, then and now, it would not be very respectful for a twelve-year-old to take off, without the permission of parents, to go to the temple and preach to the elders without so much as an "I'm sorry, Mom and Dad, for putting your through so much." That would have been as unthinkable in Jesus' time as it is now.

We are thus forced to look beyond the literal hearing of this story to the theological intent of the gospel. The purpose of Luke's story is christological; it attests that Jesus was the Son of God even as a boy. He worked similar signs and used theological language just as he would in his adult ministry. Robert Tannehill states: "The scene of the boy Jesus in the temple anticipates Jesus' ministry by presenting to the reader a twelve-year-old with precocious understanding of religious questions and with a developing sense of his own special destiny."[8] When Jesus' parents misunderstand the implication of the event, they foreshadow the disciples who will also one day misunderstand Jesus' mission. Luke begins to present preview glimpses of what it means to be Jesus, the Son of God.

We are also to become aware of Jesus' growing wisdom and of the "special favor of God which rests upon him."[9] Jesus affirms the urgency of his mission. *It has to be.* It is part of God's plan.

The fact that Mary pondered these things in her heart shows her openness to the will of God and her trust that all would be revealed in the fullness of time. All would make sense as Jesus' life unfolded, as his mission came to completion through his life, death, and resurrection.

Proclaim the gospel again.

Sometimes we gain new insights when we hear the text after the interpretation has been given. Someone from the group proclaims the gospel a second time.

---

[8]Robert C. Tannehill, *The Narrative Unity of Luke-Acts: A Literary Interpretation*, Vol. 1 (Minneapolis: Augsburg Fortress, 1986), 54.

[9]Ibid., 56.

Conversation with the Liturgy and the Scriptures

Test your original understanding in dialogue with the text.

(You might consider breaking into smaller groups.)

Was there anything you had not considered before? What are your feelings now? Was there anything that made you uncomfortable? How does the gospel relate to the feast of the Holy Family? How does your original assumption about the meaning of this gospel compare with the exegesis? How does this story speak to your life?

Sharing Life Experience

Participants share an experience from their lives that connects with the biblical interpretation just shared.

I am reminded of the years when our children were in their teens. They were particularly turbulent times. We often asked ourselves how all the "perfect" families managed to go through the teen years so peacefully. There were enormous societal pressures to "get tough," to allow our children to experience the radically serious consequences of their actions. There was the voice that said "If they don't obey the rules of the house, invite them to leave." There was another voice, a small, still, inner voice that gave an entirely different message. "Just love them, hang in there with them. I am leading them. Let me handle this one." That was the voice of peace. We recognized it as a manifestation of God. We hung in there. There was a home, a place of unconditional love (though extremely imperfect), in which our children could find refuge while working through their difficult teenage choices. Sometimes things worked out beautifully. Sometimes they did not. But God was present in the midst of the chaos. Again that "still, small voice" would tell us that perfect families do not exist, but loving families do. Whether we were correct or incorrect will become evident in time and through the witness of our children as they grow into adulthood. We did strive to be a holy family. Not a pietistic holy, but a holy in which we got our hands dirty in the day-to-day mess of real life. Our strength

was our faith community. The church does have a vested interest in families. My thoughts often turned to families of young individuals who make choices from which they will never recover, of families who want to be the "perfect" family but get embroiled in the devastating grip of society's anti-relationship pressures. We were fortunate. Our problems had to do with normal teenage growing pains and were minimal in comparison to the struggles facing many families today. Yet, we were blessed by the strong bonds of friends and community. What about those who have no one? Our job as church is to seek them out and show them that they are not alone. There is a church family that cares, and above all there is a Christ who not only cares, but who is there in the midst of the chaos.

All share their life experience.

What were Luke and Paul trying to say to their communities? What do they have to say to your community and to you today? How do you feel about Collins's interpretation of the "submissive wives" verses in the reading from Colossians? Is there evidence in the readings of the biblical themes of covenant, creation, community, and exodus? Do you still feel the same way about this gospel text as you did when we began?

The gospel demands a response.

How can our community grow through today's readings? What are the contemporary implications of the readings from Colossians and Luke's story about Jesus in the temple? In what concrete way am I/we called to respond to today's readings? Has this conversation with the exegesis of these readings caused any transformation in my thinking or assumptions? What are the implications for my life?

Closing Prayer

Eternal Father,
we want to live as Jesus, Mary and Joseph,

in peace with you and one another.
May this communion strengthen us to face the
troubles of life.
Grant this through Christ, our Lord.[10]

Selected Bibliography

Adam, Adolf. *The Liturgical Year.* Trans. Matthew J.
O'Connell. Collegeville: The Liturgical Press,
1990.
Collins, Raymond F. *Preaching the Epistles.* New
York/Mahwah: Paulist Press, 1996.
Days of the Lord. Vol. I. Collegeville: The Liturgical
Press, 1991.
Di Lella, Alexander A., O.F.M. "Sirach." In *The
New Jerome Biblical Commentary.* Ed. Raymond
E. Brown, S.S., Joseph A. Fitzmyer, S.J., Roland
E. Murphy, O.Carm. Englewood Cliffs: Pren-
tice Hall, 1990.
Sanchez, Patricia Datchuck. *The Word We Celebrate.*
Kansas City: Sheed and Ward, 1989.
Tannehill, Robert C. *The Narrative Unity of Luke-
Acts: A Literary Interpretation.* Vol. 1. Minneapo-
lis: Augsburg Fortress, 1986.

---

[10]Feast of the Holy Family: "Prayer After Communion,"
The Sacramentary.

MARY, MOTHER OF GOD

INTRODUCTORY RITES

Opening Song (or Entrance Antiphon)

A light will shine on us this day, the Lord is born for us: he shall be called Wonderful God, Prince of peace, Father of the world to come; and his kingship will never end (see Is 9:2, 6; Lk 1:33).[1]

Environment

The Christmas season environment continues.

Opening Prayer

The facilitator of the session may lead the prayer. Others in the group may be asked to proclaim the readings.

Let us pray...

Pause for silent prayer.

Father, source of light in every age,
the virgin conceived and bore your Son
who is called Wonderful God, Prince of Peace.
May her prayer, the gift of a mother's love,
be your people's joy through all ages.
May her response, born of a humble heart,
draw your Spirit to rest on your people.
Grant this through Christ, our Lord.[2]

LITURGY OF THE WORD

Let us listen to God's word.

The readings are proclaimed.

First Reading
Numbers 6:22-27

---

[1] Solemnity of Mary, Mother of God: "Entrance Antiphon," *The Sacramentary.*

[2] Solemnity of Mary, Mother of God: "Alternate Opening Prayer," *The Sacramentary.*

The last verse of this pericope is the key verse for our purposes in this liturgy. God's name is invoked. In biblical tradition the "name" implies the totality of the person. All God is and has done throughout salvation history is brought to bear in this blessing. Christians have extended their understanding of this to include all that has been accomplished through Jesus.

Responsorial Psalm
Psalm 67:2-3, 5, 6, 8

The theme of the first reading is resounded in the psalm. The psalmist asks for God's mercy. The Christian sees God's blessing fulfilled in the person of Jesus.

Second Reading
Galatians 4:4-7

The intent of this passage is to accentuate the fact that the Incarnate Word came to free us from strict adherence to the law. Through the Incarnation we become children of God. As children of Abraham we become heirs to God's promises. It is not through conformity to the law, but through our faith that we truly become God's children. The Spirit of the Risen One empowers us as God's adopted children and confirms us in our faith.

We begin this new year reminded that we are children of God, heirs to the promise of salvation, and that we live as children of the Spirit. We inaugurate the new year with the resolve to live each day in the fullness of Christ's light. Galatians reminds us that if we have been elevated to God's divine life through the coming of Jesus, then we must own who we are and live accordingly.

Gospel
Luke 2:16-21

The shepherds go to Bethlehem in haste to see the babe they have been told about. Mary treasures it all in her heart and on the eighth day they take Jesus to be circumcised and to be given his name.

What were your first impressions? What was your first response?

Each person names his or her initial impression. Statement should be brief. No reasons should be given at this time. All simply listen without agreeing or disagreeing.

In a brief statement, what do you think this gospel is trying to convey?

Liturgical Context

The Solemnity of Mary is the oldest of Marian feasts. This feast is christological and defines Mary's role in the church. It also defines Marian devotion. The Vatican II document *Lumen Gentium* states:

> Devotion to Mary as it has always existed in the Church, even though it is altogether special, is essentially distinct from the worship of adoration paid equally to the Word incarnate, the Father, and the Holy Spirit. For the various forms of Marian devotions sanctioned by the Church, within the limits of sound orthodoxy and suited circumstances of time and place as well as to the character and cultures of peoples, have the effect that as we honor the Mother we also truly know the Son and give love, glory and obedience through him, through whom all things have their being (see Col 1:15-16) and in whom it has pleased the eternal Father that all fullness should dwell.[3]

---

[3]*Dogmatic Constitution on the Church (Lumen Gentium)*, in *Documents of Vatican II*, ed. Walter M. Abbot (New York: Guild Press, America Press, Association Press, 1966), #31.

To reiterate: this feast is christological. It is primarily about the birth of Christ, the fulfillment of God's plan of salvation. However, it also points to Mary as an example of faith. She is a model for all believers and exemplifies the true Israel. Mary was a willing vessel, ready to receive God's grace. We too are to be such vessels.

The prayers of the liturgy today ask for her intercession. The liturgy itself shows us Mary's role in the church.

> God our Father,
> may we always profit by the prayers
> of the Virgin Mary,
> for you bring us life and salvation
> through Jesus Christ, her Son.
> (Opening Prayer)

> God our Father,
> we celebrate this season
> the beginning of our salvation.
> On this feast of Mary, the Mother of God,
> we ask that our salvation
> will be brought to its fulfillment.
> (Prayer over the Gifts)

> Father,
> as we proclaim the Virgin Mary
> to be the mother of Christ and the mother of
> the Church,
> may our communion with her Son
> bring us salvation.
> (Prayer after Communion)

Mary is our intercessor. She stands with the pilgrim church as we wait in hope for Jesus' return.

We cannot ignore the fact that this feast also initiates the new year. As each new year brings solemn promises of transformation, the feast of Mary, Mother of God, reminds us that Christian discipline involves striving to live in harmony with God's will. Mary opened herself to receive God's grace and blessing. In this new year, we too, ask for God's grace and blessing. Our prayer is for the openness to embrace salvation when it comes our way.

If catechetical groups are unable to center a session around this solemnity, it would be very important to address the themes and truths inherent in this celebration during another session.

Gospel Exegesis

The facilitator provides input regarding critical biblical scholarship on this text. The input includes insights as to how people would have heard the gospel in Jesus' time.

This gospel is almost identical to the gospel for the mass at dawn of Christmas day. It adds the event of Jesus' circumcision and the conferral of his name. Mary follows the prescriptions of the law by having Jesus baptized according to the law. In biblical tradition, the "name" often designated the person's mission. The name "Jesus" means "the one who saves." Thus, his very name identifies his role and his destiny. Throughout the Christian scriptures we are shown the power of Jesus' name to heal, expel demons, and liberate people. Jesus' name is to be used in faith.

However, in and of themselves, the events of today's gospel were not extraordinary. Many biblical figures were given a new name; Jesus' name was not exceedingly significant in biblical times, as there were others with the same name; presenting Jesus at the temple for the circumcision was prescribed by the law. Thus, the intent is to show that Mary did all that the angel told her to do. She was a willing, obedient servant.

Yet Christians know the story and they know well that the name indeed tells us who Jesus is: "the one who saves." We know from this story and beyond this story that Jesus' mission is extraordinary and is the fulfillment of all that was promised by the prophets of old. Jesus' name was power. His healing ministry was evidence of that power. When we call on Jesus in faith, we invoke the power of his name and place our lives under his care. It requires a great leap of faith. Mary did not ask how her son would become great as the angel had proclaimed. Hers was not to question or to know, but simply to accept in trust.

God's grace was shown to sinners in the revelation given to the shepherds. The peace offered is offered freely for all people, equally, not just for the pious righteous. We recall from a previous Sunday that peace implies wholeness, all things in right relationship, harmony. The peace brought by God's Son is a peace whereby people live in *hesed* love. Relationships are brought under the dominion of God. "The recovery of wholeness in human relationships, which is due to God's acts in Jesus, reflects honor to God."[4] This is understood in terms of our relationship to the human race, to one another, to the stranger, the lost, the alien, the misfit, and the outcast.

Mary accepted in faith what she had been told. She did not question. She allowed the events to unfold and was a willing, obedient servant in God's grand design. We are called to the same mission.

Proclaim the gospel again.

Sometimes we gain new insights when we hear the text after the interpretation has been given. Someone from the group proclaims the gospel a second time.

STEP 4
TESTING

Conversation with the Liturgy and the Scriptures

Test your original understanding in dialogue with the text.

(You might consider breaking into smaller groups.)

How does the feast of Mary the Mother of God touch your life? Does this feast have any relevance for the church today? Were there any new insights? How does your original understanding of this story compare with what we just shared?

How does this story speak to your life?

> *I am reminded that I cannot just practice my faith because the church demands that I must, or because it is what I should do. I am to enter into relationship with Christ because I can do no less. Jesus gives us peace that defies imagination. His peace is the*

---

[4]Charles Talbert, *Reading Luke* (New York: Crossroad, 1992), 34.

only hope for families today. It is very difficult to maintain the peace that God intends for our lives in the midst of twentieth-century family pressures. Faith allows families to persevere, to let go, and to allow God the space to work in our lives. Mary was a good mother; she followed all the rules. She presented her son to God, put him in God's care, and then pondered in her heart all that God was doing. Doesn't every mother do that? Or at least attempt to do that? Mary is every mother's model of patient waiting and pondering. She waited for God's plan to be fulfilled; she pondered the mysteries. Her life must have been a series of waitings and ponderings. She saw her son moving in a direction that would ultimately end in his death. Mary is a model for mothers who kiss their teenagers goodbye at the door and pray that they come home safely. Mary is the model for mothers who receive that late night call that their son was in an accident and someone died, only to find out it was their son's best friend. Mary is the model for the mother who lost her son. Mary is the model for the mothers who pondered the mystery of God as to why one child died and the other was spared. Mary is the disciple who shows all parents how to endure, how to let their children go and entrust them to God's care. Mary is the disciple who shows us how to rely on the God of mercy for sustenance through the good times and through times of horror. Mary shows us that our care and concern must extend to others, that we are all a part of God's family.

Think about it: how would you, or any other mother, feel on the night of her child's birth, in a damp, darkly lit cave, to be visited in this moment of intimacy by society's lowest scoundrels? I can only imagine how I would feel if our homeless friends were to stop by and enter my birthing space for a glimpse of my new child. How would I feel? I am sure I would not be as receptive as Mary. As disciple, Mary leads me to God. She shows me what radical trust is all about.

Participants share an experience from their lives that connects with the biblical interpretation just shared.

What was Luke trying to tell his community? What does he have to say to your community and to you today? The biblical themes of covenant, exodus, creation, and community are in full expression in the readings for today's liturgy. What difference does it make? Do you still feel the same way about this text as you did when you began? Has your original understanding been stretched, challenged, or affirmed?

STEP 5
DECISION

The gospel demands a response.

How does our understanding of these scriptures and today's liturgy call us to transformation? In what way are we, like Mary, to grow in faith? In what way does our community need to grow in the fullness of today's scriptures? In what concrete ways is our parish called to respond? Has this conversation with the exegesis changed or stretched my personal attitudes? What are the implications of this gospel in my life? What is one concrete action I will take this week as a response to the liturgy today?

DOCTRINAL ISSUES

What church truth/teaching/doctrinal issue could be drawn from the gospel for the Solemnity of Mary, Mother of God?

Participants suggest possible doctrinal themes that flow from the readings.

Possible Doctrinal Themes

Christology, salvation, Mary's role as disciple, Mary as model of church, Incarnation

Present the doctrinal material at this time.

1. The facilitator gives input on a particular doctrinal issue of his/her prior choosing. OR
2. The group chooses a doctrinal issue from the list they created. They read together from the Doctrinal Appendix.

(The doctrinal issues are found in the Doctrinal Appendix in the back of this workbook. If you are choosing an issue from this resource, please refer to it now.)

Reflection questions centered around the chosen doctrinal theme can be found at the end of each topic in the Doctrinal Appendix. The questions are based on the five-step reflection process. If you choose a topic not included in the Doctrinal Appendix, craft your own questions according to the same five-step process.

Following the reflection questions you will be reminded to return to chapter 7, "Preparing the Catechetical Session," to assist you in crafting your own session.

Closing Prayer

Father, as we proclaim the Virgin Mary
to be the mother of Christ and the mother of the
    Church,
may our communion with her Son bring us to
    salvation.
We ask this through Christ, our Lord.[5]

Selected Bibliography

Days of the Lord. Vol. I. Collegeville: The Liturgical Press, 1991.

Dogmatic Constitution on the Church (Lumen Gentium). In *Documents of Vatican II.* Ed. Walter M. Abbot. New York: Guild Press, America Press, Association Press, 1966.

Fuller, Reginald H. *Preaching the New Lectionary.* Collegeville: The Liturgical Press, 1974.

Talbert, Charles. *Reading Luke.* New York: Crossroad, 1992.

---

[5]Solemnity of Mary, Mother of God: "Prayer After Communion," *The Sacramentary.*

EPIPHANY

INTRODUCTORY RITES

Opening Song (or Entrance Antiphon)

The Lord and ruler is coming: kingship is his, and government and power (see Mal 3:1; 1 Chron 19:12).[1]

Environment

The liturgical color of the Christmas season is white. This celebration is centered around the manifestation of Christ, the Light. Epiphany is also the day on which we hear about the wise men from the East. Perhaps a Christ candle could be lit as you pray the opening prayer.

Opening Prayer

The facilitator of the session may lead the prayer. Others in the group may be asked to proclaim the readings.

Let us pray
[Grateful for the glory revealed today through God made man]

Pause for silent prayer.

Father of light, unchanging God,
today you reveal to men of faith
the resplendent fact of the Word made flesh.
Your light is strong,
your love is near;
draw us beyond the limits which this world imposes
to the life where your Spirit makes all life
        complete.
We ask this through Christ, our Lord.[2]

LITURGY OF THE WORD

The readings or the gospel are read out loud.

Let us listen to God's word.

First Reading
Isaiah 60:1-6

This reading is typological.[3] The return from exile in Trito-Isaiah foreshadows the liberation won by Christ through his manifestation to the world. The gentiles converging upon Jerusalem provide a glimpse of the manifestion of Christ—not just to the chosen people, but to the gentiles and to the entire world.

In the poems of Trito-Isaiah there is great excitement and expectancy regarding what is about to take place. "It is as if the hell and horror had been left behind, and one is moving up a high, sun drenched summit to the very doors of the Kingdom of God."[4]

Prophets were often gifted by the Spirit to utter oracles that transcended the immediate reality. They were able to understand the meaning of God's plan in the present as well as in the future. When we hear these prophetic utterances over and over in scripture, we begin to see God's plan for the human race. It all makes perfect sense in light of what has been proclaimed throughout the generations. The prophet saw the fulfillment of God's action. He saw the magnificent light that would illumine the darkness created by humanity's sin. He saw the future city in which God's power would be seen by all. The prophet of Isaiah's time knew well about God's manifestation. It was called *shekina* glory, the unveiled, glorious presence of Yahweh. The prophet saw a future where all would live in *shekina* glory. The new city would be illumined for all to see. St. John would also see this prototype city aglow with the magnificence of Yahweh's *shekina* in the prophecies of Revelation. Even though there is an eschatological promise inherent in such prophecies, we

---

[1]Epiphany: "Entrance Antiphon," *The Sacramentary.*
[2]Epiphany: "Alternative Opening Prayer," *The Sacramentary.*

---

[3]Typology is a way of interpreting the scriptures where old realities are seen as having foreshadowed, according to God's plan of salvation, future realities. The return from exile and the vision of gentiles converging upon Jerusalem was a foreshadowing of what would happen in the Christ event.

[4]John Bright, *The Kingdom of God* (New York: Abington, 1953), 137.

know that Christ is the manifestation of God's glory.

We are reminded of the typological aspects of this text when we read of gentiles riding on camels and bearing gifts of gold, frankincense and myrrh. When we read of them converging upon the city of Jerusalem singing praises, our attention is immediately drawn to the heart of the Christian story.

Responsorial Psalm
Psalm 72:1-2, 7-8, 10-11, 12-13

This psalm, originally a hymn composed for the Davidic monarchy, speaks of the future messiah and describes those bearing gifts and bowing in worship before the messiah who was to come. This psalm was appropriated by the Christian community as a foreshadowing of Jesus. The messiah/king would come to bring God's justice-liberation and help for the oppressed and the needy.

Second Reading
Ephesians 3:2-3, 5-6

Paul had left Corinth for Jerusalem. He was constantly in trouble with his pursuers, the Jewish authorities. They accused him of defacing the temple and he was thrown in prison. He spent three years in prison in Jerusalem and Caesarea. The letters to the Colossians and Ephesians are known as the "captivity epistles" as they were written from his jail cell. Paul had established missions in Ephesus and Colossae ten years earlier on his third missionary tour. Ephesus was his headquarters.

A great concern for Paul was dilution of the gospel in Ephesus and Colossae due to the influence of gnosticism.[5] He was concerned with promoting an authentic gospel, not one constructed from people's personal agendas and exclusive concerns.

Today's reading from Ephesians describes the prophets and the apostles as the mediators of God's revelation to the world. Jew and gentile alike share the covenant. Paul was probably not the author of Ephesians. Rather, it seems that a student of Paul was the author. The epistle is a reflection of Paul's attempts to unite the gentile and Jewish peoples into one faith. There are two themes represented in this pericope: Jesus, the revelation of God, and the universal message of salvation.[6]

Gospel
Matthew 2:1-12

Today's gospel tells the story of the magi who come bearing gifts to the messiah who was to be born. Herod tries to trick them into divulging the location of this great event.

STEP 1
NAMING ONE'S EXPERIENCE

What was your first impression? What captured your attention?

Each person names his or her initial impression. Statement should be brief. No reasons should be given at this time. All simply listen without agreeing or disagreeing.

STEP 2
UNDERSTANDING

What understanding did you bring with you to these readings? In a brief statement, what do you think this gospel is trying to convey?

STEP 3
INPUT FROM VISION/STORY/TRADITION

Liturgical Context

Please read the Christmas Overview for background on this feast. The Epiphany texts need to be understood in the context of the entire Christmas season. Epiphany is another celebration of Christ's manifestation to the world. Even though there is great emphasis placed on the story of the magi, the theme of this feast transcends the manifestation of God to the gentiles; it centers on

---

[5]For further expansion on Paul's preaching in regard to gnosticism and its impact on the church, refer to the Fifteenth Sunday in Ordinary Time, Second Reading.

[6]Reginald H. Fuller, *Preaching the New Lectionary* (Collegeville: The Liturgical Press, 1974), 478.

God's self-revelation to humanity in the person of Christ. This is another manifestation in a line of manifestations during the season: to the shepherds, to Mary, the Mother of God, through baptism and now to all the world.

In the overview of the Christmas season it was stated that the feast of the Epiphany has undergone a few shifts in the Eastern and Western Church. When East and West transposed their feasts, the West preserved Christmas overtones in its observance of Epiphany. "The connection is especially clear in the insertions in the first eucharistic prayer, since they speak of the celebration of this most holy day 'when your only Son, sharing your eternal glory, showed himself in a human body.'"[7] However, Epiphany was also the day to remember the magi. As the magi were considered gentiles, the feast proclaimed the manifestation of God's mission to the gentiles and to all nations.

Today's liturgy remembers and makes present the very mystery it celebrates—that is, the manifestation of God's power, God's salvation to the entire human race. The opening prayers of this liturgy exhort us to listen to the readings "as an announcement of a mystery, of the good news, of what is and will be."[8] The celebration calls us to live in the glory that is ours. In the Epiphany liturgy when we pray the "Prayer over the Gifts" we ask God to accept our offerings, not of gold, frankincense, and myrrh, but our very selves—our hearts and our humanity. The preface for Epiphany proclaims the feast's central theme, Christ, the Light of the Nations: "Today you revealed in Christ your eternal plan of salvation and showed him as the light of all peoples. Now that his glory has shown among us you have renewed humanity in his immortal image."

Gospel Exegesis

The facilitator provides input regarding critical biblical scholarship on this text. The input includes insights as to how people would have heard the gospel in Jesus' time.

---

[7]Adolf Adam, *The Liturgical Year*, trans. Matthew J. O'Connell (Collegeville: The Liturgical Press, 1990), 147.

[8]*Days of the Lord*, Vol. 1 (Collegeville: The Liturgical Press, 1991), 254.

Detailed historicity is not the object of this story. A far greater concern is the meaning of God's manifestation to the world expressed through the symbolic language of the story. That does not mean that the story is not based on a factual occurrence. Certainly, something happened to elicit such a narrative. However, the author cares little about the details. It is the point of the story that has captured his imagination, and in the process of telling that story he hopes to capture ours.

The way Matthew tells the story is "colored by the faith which enlightened the evangelist when he wrote his work; it expresses and clarifies the faith of the Church at the time; he intended it to be an aid to the faith of those Christians for whom he wrote. But faith is not simply a matter of acknowledging that Jesus is Messiah, Lord and Son of God. It involves obedience to him now. The Gospel is not only 'kerygma,' that is to say, proclamation of faith; it is also 'catechesis,' instruction on how to unify one's faith and life. This part of the message is especially stressed in Matthew."[9]

"After Jesus' birth..." begins the narrative regarding the approaching magi. Matthew puts this story in the context of the wider political arena. Herod was reputed to be compulsive and neurotic with regard to the possible political overthrow of his power. One cannot miss the subtlety of Herod's part in this drama. The scribes and Pharisees in Matthew's gospel quote Micah regarding the messiah's projected birthplace and are unaffected and unimpressed. Herod, on the other hand, takes the story of the "King of the Jews" quite literally and seriously. Those who knew better and *should have gotten it*, ignored it; and those who should have had no understanding or interest *did get it*, and as a result set out to do violence.

The mysterious magi enter the scene. The story tells us little of their origin. However, because of Psalm 72, where kings from Tarshish and the Isles come bearing gifts, it is assumed that the magi are those referred to in the psalm. This puts their place of origin in Persia. The only reason we have assumed there were three is due to the three gifts of frankincense, gold, and myrrh. In later Western

---

[9]J. Dupont, "L'evangile de saint Matthieu: quelques cles de lecture," in *Communautes et liturgies* 57 (1975): 21.

tradition they were given the names Balthasar, Melchior and Caspar. They became symbols of the diversity of the church, of God's manifestation to the gentile world, to all peoples.

Jesus is called the "King of the Jews" in order to name him the messiah. The *star* is a reference to a messianic prophecy in the Old Testament book of Numbers in which a star was identified with the messiah (Num 24:17). For Matthew, the magi signify that Christ has always manifested his glory to people from distant lands. There is noticeable irony in the fact that it is the very scribes and Pharisees who supply the magi with the scriptures that direct them to the place where their search will end.

In ancient times, people were often attracted to astral religions because of the cold predictability of the stars.[10] These religions were very burdensome as people believed themselves under submission to powers beyond their control. Some early Christians were offended by this story as it appeared to tolerate astrology. However, their problem was not Matthew's problem. The star merely served a purpose. The star was the instrument that would lead people to the One who would break the power of any force that would bind people to a predetermined fate. When people are in God's hands, their fate is secure in and through Jesus.

Later the gifts of gold, frankincense, and myrrh became symbols of Christ's kingship, his divinity, and his suffering. Like Christmas, Epiphany is a feast of redemption. Christ became incarnated in our world and manifested the presence of God in order to save the world from itself. Sin could be conquered only through the life, death, and resurrection of the One who was born and the One who revealed his glory to all the nations. The call of this gospel is to proclaim the *shekina* glory of God through Christ.

Proclaim the gospel again.

Sometimes we gain new insights when we hear the text after the interpretation has been given. Someone from the group proclaims the gospel a second time.

---

[10]Benedict T. Viviano, O.P., "The Gospel of Matthew," in *The New Jerome Biblical Commentary*, ed. Raymond E. Brown, S.S., Joseph A. Fitzmyer, S.J., Roland E. Murphy, O.Carm (Englewood Cliffs: Prentice Hall, 1990), 636.

Conversation with the Liturgy and Scriptures

Test your original understanding in dialogue with the text.

(You might consider breaking into smaller groups.)

Were there any new insights? Was there anything you had not considered before? There are many levels of meaning in this text, such as inclusivity, the manifestation of God's power, and the fact that the gentiles appropriated the faith while the chosen ones missed it. How are these themes relevant for our community today? Has your original understanding of these stories been transformed in any way? How? How does this story speak to your life?

Participants share an experience from their lives that connects with the biblical interpretation just shared.

> *I am reminded of a time when God was powerfully manifest in my life. My mother was dying of emphysema. She was on a respirator. We knew that if she did not get off the respirator she would live a miserable existence for an extended period of time. She wanted to get off the respirator, the doctors wanted her off, and so did we. It would be much better for her if she could live without it. Every breath was precious. We began to pray together. I held her hand as she took slow, laborious breaths. Inch by inch the doctors weaned her from the machine. In the midst of panic we prayed. We called on the light of Jesus and asked that the light lead my mother and strengthen her for the journey to freedom. The light of Christ was so present as we labored together in this holy birthing process that it seemed to illumine the intensive care unit.*

> *I use the word "birth" with firm intention. She was giving birth to a new trust; she who could no longer breathe was bringing to birth a new reliance on God's own life breath. I was bringing to birth the realization of what God's presence meant in the difficult moments of life. Here were mother and daughter. She who had given me life, and I who was praying earnestly with her for restoration of her life, sat as if alone in the room, in the brilliance of the*

soul's dark night. We sat in the presence of the Christ child. Fear left us. Shalom peace entered our space. My mother lived a few more days. Then, at the first sound of the bird's pre-dawn warning, at the advent of that Easter Monday morning's new dawn light, my fifty-six year old mother breathed her last labored breath. She was face to face with the shekina *glory of Jesus Christ. Epiphany reminds me that God's manifestation is not just an eschatological hope; it is a promised reality in this earthly sojourn.*

I am reminded that this feast of manifestation is also a feast of inclusion. Living in the light demands that I reach out to all who suffer, all who are lost, and all who do not know Jesus. My mother was the most tolerant, inclusive woman I have known. She instilled within us love for all people. Epiphany celebrates the light of love manifest to all people and challenges me to take the light out into the world.

How does this scripture touch an experience in your life?

All share their life experience.

What was Matthew's message to his community? Is it relevant today? How do these scriptures speak to you as church and to you personally? Are the biblical images of covenant, creation, exodus, and community in full view in today's liturgy? How? Do you still feel the same way about this text as you did when you began? How would you explain these readings to a stranger?

STEP 5
DECISION

The gospel demands a response.

In what way are we called to respond to this gospel? How are our attitudes challenged in this liturgy? Would there be any contemporary corollary for the issue of gentile inclusion today? Has this conversation with the exegesis of the Epiphany called for transformation of my actions or attitudes? Name one concrete action we/I will take this week as a response to today's liturgy.

DOCTRINAL ISSUES

What church truth/teaching/doctrinal issue could be drawn from the gospel for the feast of the Epiphany?

Participants suggest possible doctrinal themes that flow from the readings.

Possible Doctrinal Themes

Epiphany, manifestation, christology, missiology

Present the doctrinal material at this time.

1. The facilitator gives input on a particular doctrinal issue of his/her prior choosing. OR
2. The group chooses a doctrinal issue from the list they created. They read together from the Doctrinal Appendix.

(The doctrinal issues are found in the Doctrinal Appendix in the back of this workbook. If you are choosing an issue from this resource, please refer to it now.)

Reflection questions centered around the chosen doctrinal theme can be found at the end of each topic in the Doctrinal Appendix. The questions are based on the five-step reflection process. If you choose a topic not included in the Doctrinal Appendix, craft your own questions according to the same five-step process.

Following the reflection questions you will be reminded to return to chapter 7, "Preparing the Catechetical Session," to assist you in crafting your own session.

Closing Prayer

God has called you out of darkness
into his wonderful light.
May you experience his kindness and blessings,
and be strong in faith, in hope and in love. Amen.
Because you are followers of Christ,
who appeared in this day as a light shining in
    darkness,
may he make you a light to all your sisters and
    brothers.

Response: Amen.

The wise men followed the star,
and found Christ who is light from light.
May you find the Lord
when your pilgrimage is ended.

Response: Amen.[11]

Selected Bibliography

Adam, Adolf. *The Liturgical Year.* Trans. Matthew J. O'Connell. Collegeville: The Liturgical Press, 1990.

Bright, John. *The Kingdom of God.* New York: Abington, 1953.

Days of the Lord. Vol. 1. Collegeville: The Liturgical Press, 1991.

Fuller, Reginald H. *Preaching the New Lectionary.* Collegeville: The Liturgical Press, 1974.

Viviano, Benedict T., O.P. "The Gospel of Matthew." In *The New Jerome Biblical Commentary.* Ed. Raymond E. Brown, S.S., Joseph A. Fitzmyer, S.J., Roland E. Murphy, O.Carm. Englewood Cliffs: Prentice Hall, 1990.

BAPTISM OF THE LORD

INTRODUCTORY RITES

Opening Song (or Entrance Antiphon)

When the Lord had been baptized, the heavens opened, and the Spirit came down like a dove to rest on him. Then the voice of the Father thundered: This is my beloved Son, with him I am well pleased. (Mt 3:16-17)[1]

Environment

This feast brings the Christmas season to an end.

Opening Prayer

The facilitator of the session may lead the prayer. Others in the group may be asked to proclaim the readings.

Let us pray
[that we will be faithful to our baptism]

> *Pause for silent prayer.*

Almighty, eternal God,
when the Spirit descended upon Jesus
at his baptism in the Jordan,
you revealed him as your own beloved Son.
Keep us, your children, born of water and the Spirit,
faithful to our calling.
We ask this through our Lord Jesus Christ, your
    Son,
who lives and reigns with you and the Holy Spirit,
one God, for ever, and ever.[2]

LITURGY OF THE WORD

The readings are proclaimed.

Let us listen to God's word

First Reading
Isaiah 42:1-4, 6-7

Scholars believe that the suffering servant in Deutero-Isaiah represents Israel and her role as covenant people in relationship to Yahweh. There is strong evidence that the writer is referring specifically to Israel. Israel was servant from the very beginning, from her very origins in the womb of Sarah. Servant Israel is Yahweh's agent who quietly brings the idolatrous nations to justice. "Israel's election is for responsibility."[3] The image of suffering servant belongs to Israel who, through her exile, was tried by God for her transgressions and was recreated in order to participate in God's plan of salvation.

Bernhard Anderson suggests that there are flaws in this interpretation. The second poem clearly refers to an *individual* whose mission is *to* Israel. The "servant" of Deutero-Isaiah acclaims that Yahweh called him from the womb to be a light to the nations. Thus, the servant is an individual, not the collective Israel.

Some believe the servant was Moses; others believe the servant was Deutero-Isaiah himself. Some believe the suffering servant was a remnant few who would remain faithful to Yahweh. Others believe the servant was some future messianic person. (Jesus referred to himself as the suffering servant.) The early Christian community believed Deutero-Isaiah to be prophesying about their messiah and Lord, Jesus Christ.

In today's liturgy it makes no difference which hypothesis is correct. Deutero-Isaiah is chosen on this feast to shed light on the mission of Christ. Jesus is the fulfillment of Second Isaiah's word to Israel. It is Jesus who establishes God's justice. It is Jesus who reaches out to the poor and the powerless. It is Christ who, assuming the role of suffering servant, dies for the transgressions of many. Today this reading does not stand on its own. It prefigures Jesus' baptism in the River Jordan.

---

[1]Baptism of the Lord: "Entrance Antiphon," *The Sacramentary.*

[2]Baptism of the Lord: "Opening Prayer," *The Sacramentary.*

[3]Bernhard W. Anderson, *Understanding the Old Testament,* 4th ed. (Englewood Cliffs: Prentice Hall, 1986), 490.

Responsorial Psalm
Psalm 29:1-4, 9b-10

The "voice above the waters" in the psalm chosen for this liturgy is harmonious with the voice of God from heaven in today's gospel. The psalm proclaims the manifestation of God through Jesus' baptism in the River Jordan.[4]

Second Reading
Acts 10:34-38

This pericope from the Acts of the Apostles attests to the manifestation of God through Jesus Christ. Jesus' baptism is testimony to God's presence through Jesus' words and works. There are a few significant segments in this reading, obviously chosen for its connection to the gospel. First, the story of Cornelius was important for the early church. Cornelius was a gentile. His conversion opened the door to the gentile mission and to the inclusion, integration, and incorporation of gentile Christians with Jewish Christians. Peter proclaimed that God has no favorites, since all are called equally. "Therefore, the door is open to anyone who fears God and works righteousness as Cornelius does (cf. 10:33). Such a person is 'acceptable' to God."[5]

Second, verse 36 reflects evidence of a key theme of both Luke and Acts. Luke's primary message is the proclamation that Jesus is Lord and messiah. "He brings peace to the Jewish people in fulfillment of scriptural promises; it applies to all peoples, for they are invited to share with Israel in this messianic peace."[6] Verse 36 is an echoing of the birth narrative in which God proclaimed to the shepherds that peace had come to all the earth. Robert Tannehill suggests that verses 36-43 are a chronological summary of Luke's gospel from the birth stories through the sending of the apostles to the world. Empowered by the Holy Spirit, Jesus' ministry manifested God's healing and forgiveness and liberated those in bondage. He established a peace that only Yahweh could give. The response

to Jesus' life and work was and is apostolic witness to his life, work, and resurrection.

We encounter the story of Christ through events that reflect God's action and presence in and through Jesus' life, his work, and the ultimate fulfillment of God's plan of salvation for the human race. Jesus proclaims God's reign. God tells Mary of her role in salvation history; God tells the shepherds the good news of Jesus' birth; God manifests himself to the magi, to the gentile world, to all nations; and God manifests the fulfillment of his master plan through Jesus in the baptism at the River Jordan.[7] Reginald Fuller asserts that it is often said that a significant contrast exists between the message of Jesus and the message of the church. "Jesus preached the kingdom, but the church preached Jesus."[8] Fuller maintains that, in essence, there is really little difference. He maintains that Jesus was proclaiming God's action and presence in the lives of human beings through healings, exorcisms, and through his words and works. The church, on the other hand, proclaimed and proclaims that God was and is present through the signs, words, and deeds Jesus performed. God has, is, and will continue to be present in human history.

Gospel
Matthew 3:13-17

Jesus is baptized in the River Jordan and anointed through the power of the Spirit.

STEP 1
NAMING ONE'S EXPERIENCE

What captured your attention in these readings? How did you feel?

Each person names his or her initial impression. Statement should be brief. No reasons should be given at this time. All simply listen without agreeing or disagreeing.

---

[4]Reginald F. Fuller, *Preaching the New Lectionary* (Collegeville: The Liturgical Press, 1986), 132.

[5]Robert C. Tannehill, *The Narrative Unity of Luke-Acts: A Literary Interpretation*, Vol. 1. (Minneapolis: Augsburg Fortress, 1986), 137.

[6]Ibid., 140.

[7]Fuller, *Preaching the New Lectionary*, 132.
[8]Ibid.

STEP 2
UNDERSTANDING

In a brief statement, what do you think this gospel is trying to convey? What understanding did you bring with you to this discussion?

STEP 3
INPUT FROM VISION/TRADITION/STORY

Liturgical Context

The focus of the Christmas season is theological rather than historical. Throughout the season we experience the multi-faceted manifestations of God through Jesus Christ, his Son. Particularly in the East, the entire life of Christ is regarded as repeated manifestations of God, with the baptism of Jesus representing the most important of these manifestations. The East celebrates the Lord's baptism (and the manifestation at Cana) on the feast of the Epiphany. Prior to the renewal of the Roman calendar, this feast was not given the prominence it deserved in the Western church. Thus, without preempting Epiphany, the new calendar restored the feast of the Baptism of the Lord to a prominent place. It now follows Epiphany and closes the Christmas season.

God anointed Jesus for public ministry through the power of the Holy Spirit. The baptism at the River Jordan is Jesus' ritual celebration of empowerment. He is empowered through the authority of the voice of God, lord of the universe. Since John is intimately involved in this ritual event, the church avows that Jesus "shows his solidarity with the guilty human race and gives water the power to forgive sins."[9]

The preface of this liturgy expresses our theology succinctly and is very clear regarding God's role on the stage of salvation history. "You celebrated your new gift of baptism by signs and wonders at the Jordan. Your voice was heard from heaven to awaken faith in the presence among us of the

_____
[9]Adolf Adam, *The Liturgical Year,* trans. Matthew J. O'Connell (Collegeville: The Liturgical Press, 1990), 148.

Word made man. Your spirit was seen as a dove, revealing Jesus as your servant, and anointing him with joy as the Christ, sent to bring to the poor the good news of salvation."[10]

Gospel Exegesis

The facilitator gives input regarding what critical biblical scholarship has to say about this text. The input includes insights as to how people would have heard the gospel in Jesus' time.

In order to better understand Luke's account of Jesus' baptism, it would be beneficial to compare it to the account in the other gospels. Matthew's perspective is one of defense. Matthew is defending Jesus against the charge that if Jesus was sinless, he did not need a baptism of repentance for sins. There is no evidence of this problem in Luke. John, on the other hand, recounts the story as a revelation of Christ to the Baptist, so the Baptist may then proclaim him to the world. This is also not a concern of Luke's. Luke resembles Mark more than the others. Both Luke and Mark see this event in terms of empowerment. Luke, however, takes it a step further. The baptism is not the empowering agent; the descent of the Spirit *after* the baptism is. Luke "turns Jesus' baptism into an episode of prayer."[11]

The key thrust of this gospel is to proclaim Jesus as the prophetic messiah and Son of God. "Both in his personal identity and in his adult mission, Jesus is God's Son (1:35; 3:22) and his life must be seen as an expression of God's Spirit. Conceived by the power of the Holy Spirit (1:35) he exercises his mission by the power of that same Spirit (3:22) as he victoriously confronts the forces of evil."[12] The anointing of Jesus by John highlights John's prophetic role in the messianic plan. However, Luke makes sure that all recognize that John is merely a prophet. John's role diminishes in order to stress God's anointing of Jesus through the

_____
[10]Feast of the Baptism of the Lord: "Preface," *The Sacramentary.*

[11]Charles Talbert, *Reading Luke* (New York: Crossroad, 1992), 36-40.

[12]Eugene LaVerdiere, S.S.S., *Luke* (Wilmington: Michael Glazier Books, 1980), 44.

Holy Spirit. Jesus is the new prophet, the messianic prophet. "Jesus' mission was not merely a religious response to the reformer's baptism. Rather, it sprang from God's creative and empowering Spirit; it far surpasses the work of John the prophet and the many centuries of salvation history which led to it."[13] Luke insists that the premier event in this story is the descent of the Holy Spirit, not the baptism.

We see in this pericope a liturgical text of sorts. It is the ritual text of Jesus' baptism. John the Baptist, however, is not the presider. God, through the Spirit, is the presider at this liturgical event. As in all liturgy, the ritual words help explain and give clarity and meaning to the event. The ritual words used in verse 21 refer to verse 1 in the first reading from Isaiah and to a psalm citation. We are to draw from those words the meaning of the Spirit's descent. Jesus is God's beloved Son, "in whom I am well pleased," and his mission is from God. The baptism does not confer sonship on Jesus (that happened at his conception by the Spirit); rather, at the baptism the Spirit anoints and equips Jesus for his mission.

Another key theme in this gospel is Jesus at prayer. Luke's Jesus prays at every important juncture in his ministry. Luke Timothy Johnson asserts that Jesus' prayer is a "matter of faithful obedience" to his Father.[14] Prayer is integral to the life of the prophet, to the life of any minister. Jesus is empowered by the Spirit through his prayer. Luke's agenda is clearly to stress the importance of prayer in the life of the believer. Believers are empowered by the Spirit for God's work, just as Jesus was empowered. Prayer and discipleship go hand in hand. Prayer strengthens, empowers, and provides the stamina needed to endure the arduous responsibility of discipleship.

Throughout Luke's gospel, Jesus' moments of prayer are usually accompanied by some manifestation, visitation, or apparition. The audience of Jesus' day would have understood the import of such phenomena. In the Graeco-Roman story world, a flight of birds would be associated with

proclamations of someone's destiny. Omens from heaven would be expected to ratify a person's status. Luke's audience would have been aware of the ancient story of Numa, one chosen to be king. He turned to the heavens and expected a sign before his kingship could be ratified. He looked heavenward in prayer and as the appropriate bird omens appeared he was willing to assume his kingly robe and was received as "most beloved of gods." Thus, listeners would understand that the descent of the Spirit was heaven's ratification of Jesus as the Son of God.[15]

Proclaim the gospel again.

Sometimes we gain new insights when we hear the text after the interpretation has been given. Someone from the group proclaims the gospel a second time.

STEP 4
TESTING

Conversation with the Liturgy and the Scriptures

Test your original understanding in dialogue with the text.

(You might consider breaking into smaller groups.)

Was there anything in the exegesis that was new information or a new insight for you? How does your original understanding of this story compare with what we just shared? What are the main themes of this gospel?

How does this story speak to your life?

This gospel served as a reminder of my own reception of the Spirit at baptism. I can expect to share in Jesus' ministry because of the same Spirit given to me. I have always said that my ministry as disciple is as effective as my willingness to share in the passion of Jesus. Living the paschal mystery is prayer, the prayer of one's life. My life is incredibly hectic. I am always feeling guilty because I cannot seem to carve out an extended period of prayer each day. Between raising a family of young adults and my commitments to family and work, there is little time to

---

[13]Ibid., 46.

[14]Luke Timothy Johnson, *The Gospel of Luke*, Sacra Pagina Series, Vol. 3 (Collegeville: The Liturgical Press, 1991), 214.

---

[15]Talbert, *Reading Luke*, 40.

stop, take time out, and breathe in the generous wind of Spirit. However, God has been in relationship with me from very early in my life. This relationship has always consisted of ongoing, constant daily dialogue and awareness of one another's presence. I learn more about who God is in my life through my moment-to-moment conversations.

I pray that my day for contemplative prayer will come, and I continue to strive for that day, but in the meantime I am aware that God is with me in the moment-to-moment living of my life. Our relationship is important. My metaphor for daily prayer is best described by Paul who says "the Holy Spirit groans within me." I have become more and more aware of the Spirit's cry in my soul. Perhaps the Spirit is praying on my behalf for the things I cannot yet see.

I am very aware, however, that the passion I have for God's justice and for the powerless is placed there by the Spirit who strengthens me and shows me the heart of God. Today's gospel is not a singular event. It just places Jesus' life and work in the proper context. Jesus is empowered by the Spirit to go out and die for the world. The Spirit calls me and the church to the same mission.

Participants share an experience from their lives that connects with the biblical interpretation just shared.

What was Luke's main concern in this gospel? What was he trying to tell his community? Is there relevance for our community today? Do we still feel the same way about this text as we did at the beginning? How does this gospel call for transformation in our lives? What are the specific implications? How would we articulate a meaning of this gospel to someone who had never heard it before?

STEP 5
DECISION

The gospel demands a response.

Is there a call to action inherent for the community in this gospel or this feast? Be concrete. Has this conversation with the exegesis of this gospel changed your perspective in any way? What are

the implications for your life? Name one concrete action you will take this week as a response to what was learned and shared today.

DOCTRINAL ISSUES

What church truth/teaching/doctrinal issue could be drawn from the Baptism of the Lord gospel?

Participants suggest possible doctrinal themes that flow from the readings.

Possible Doctrinal Themes

Trinity, christology, baptism, Holy Spirit, Father, manifestation

Present the doctrinal material at this time.

1. The facilitator gives input on a particular doctrinal issue of his/her prior choosing. OR
2. The group chooses a doctrinal issue from the list they created. They read together from the Doctrinal Appendix.

(The doctrinal issues are found in the Doctrinal Appendix in the back of this workbook. If you are choosing an issue from this resource, please refer to it now.)

Reflection questions centered around the chosen doctrinal theme can be found at the end of each topic in the Doctrinal Appendix. The questions are based on the five-step reflection process. If you choose a topic not included in the Doctrinal Appendix, craft your own questions according to the same five-step process.

Following the reflection questions you will be reminded to return to chapter 7, "Preparing the Catechetical Session," to assist you in crafting your own session.

Closing Prayer

Almighty, eternal God,
when the Spirit descended upon Jesus
at his baptism in the Jordan,

you revealed him as your own beloved Son.
Keep us, your children born of water and the
    Spirit,
faithful to your calling.
We ask this through our Lord Jesus Christ, your
    Son,
who lives and reigns with you and the Holy Spirit,
    one God, for ever and ever.[16]

Selected Bibliography

Anderson, Bernhard W. *Understanding the Old Testament*. 4th ed. Englewood Cliffs: Prentice Hall, 1986.

Johnson, Luke Timothy. *The Gospel of Luke*. Sacra Pagina Series, Vol. 3. Collegeville: The Liturgical Press, 1991.

Talbert, Charles *Reading Luke*. New York: Crossroad, 1992.

Tannehill, Robert C. *The Narrative Unity of Luke-Acts: A Literary Interpretation*. Vol. 1. Minneapolis: Augsburg Fortress, 1986.

---

[16]Feast of the Baptism of the Lord: "Evening Prayer," *Christian Prayer: Liturgy of the Hours* (New York: Catholic Book Publishing Co., 1976).

THE SEASON OF LENT

THE SEASON OF LENT: AN OVERVIEW

The rich, liturgical color of royal purple cloaks the season in its penitential vesture. Simplicity and austerity quietly whisper images of the barren desert. Flowers are absent; music is sparse and the church quietly, but firmly, heralds its reflective "time out." Things have noticeably changed. As people and as church, we enter the poustinia of serious penitential and baptismal reflection. We take stock and assess our growth in the Christian life. We ask ourselves, "Where is there need for healing and reconciliation in our lives?"

> Lent is a preparation for the celebration of Easter. For the Lenten liturgy disposes both catechumens and the faithful to celebrate the paschal mystery: catechumens, through several stages of Christian initiation; the faithful, through reminders of their own baptism and through penitential practices.[1]

History of Lent

The history of Lent evolved over the centuries from varied and sometimes blended sources. Very early in the church's history, the Jewish Christians superimposed their worship of Jesus, the new Passover, on the annual celebration and understanding of Jewish Passover. Once this was established as an annual Christian feast, it was preceded by a day of fasting. At the same time, gentile Christians fasted on Wednesdays and Fridays, and celebrated the breaking of the bread after Sabbath, on the first day of the week. Eventually both traditions merged, and the annual Easter feast was celebrated on the Sunday closest to the Jewish Passover. The Saturday before Easter Sunday was designated a fast day and, since the Friday fast was already in observance, there emerged a two-day,

pre-Easter fast. Eventually the fasting period was extended to begin the Sunday before Easter (a week-long fast).

Early in the church's history, the Christian initiation of adults was a focus of the pre-Easter fast. By the third century, more was required for an adult to become a Christian than simply converting to belief in Jesus Christ. A process of initiation emerged that extended over a period of time and included several stages marked by ritual celebrations. There was no time limit imposed and eventually the process extended over a period of three years. Initially, baptisms were not specifically assigned to the Easter celebration, but rather, were most often celebrated during the fifty days between Passover and Pentecost.

Scrolling through time to the fifth century, we find the observance of a three-week preparatory fast for baptism. By the eighth century, three scrutinies were celebrated with those preparing for baptism. The scrutinies, which took place on three consecutive Sundays, are believed to have evolved from the three-week preparatory fast of previous centuries.

The history of a defined lenten season may be loosely divided into three periods: 1. the Council of Nicea (325) until the Middle Ages; 2. Middle Ages until the Second Vatican Council; 3. the promulgation of the Missal, Lectionary and Roman Calendar by Paul VI in 1969 until the present.[2] The Council of Nicea set forth a forty-day preparatory fast and determined a fixed date for the celebration of Easter.

At one time, the Alexandrian church (in the East) celebrated the Lord's birth and began its liturgical year on January 6. Alexandria's new year began with the proclamation of the Lord's baptism, the begin-

---

[1] "General Norms for the Liturgical Year and the Calendar" (GNLY), in *The Liturgy Documents* (Chicago: Liturgy Training Publications, 1991), #27.

[2] *Days of the Lord,* Vol. 2 (Collegeville: The Liturgical Press, 1993), 1.

ning passage from the gospel of Mark. St. Mark was considered the founding father of the Eastern church. Since the next passage in Mark's gospel was the story of Jesus' forty-day trial in the desert, the Alexandrian church established a similar forty-day fast (the "Fast of Jesus") beginning on January 7th. This fast had no connection to the week-long pre-Easter fast. Once the forty-day preparatory fast before Easter was established by the Council of Nicea, it collided with Alexandria's "Jesus fast" following the feast of the Lord's baptism. Adjustments, therefore, had to be made. Some monasteries observed a hundred-day fast in order to unify the two traditions of the East and the West.

Modern scholarship suggests that the penitential nature of the Lenten season emerged and grew stronger because of the influence of Alexandria's forty-day fast which was inspired by Jesus' temptations in the desert. The baptismal nature of Lent weakened with the decline of adult initiation in the fifth and sixth centuries. The heightened sense of penitence gave rise to the observance of three penitential Sundays prior to the first Sunday of Lent. These Sundays were called Septuagesima, Sexagesima, and Quinquagesima Sundays (seventy, sixty, and fifty days before Easter) and were observed until the Second Vatican Council.

Early in the fourth century, Lent lasted six weeks, beginning on the First Sunday of Lent. However, since Sundays were not fast days, the six weeks allowed for only thirty-six, rather than forty days of fasting. Thus, in the sixth century, Wednesday, Thursday, Friday, and Saturday before the First Sunday of Lent were added to the season in order to complete the forty days of fasting.

The Second Vatican Council restored a simpler, earlier version of Lenten observance. The Council halted the observance of three penitential Sundays prior to Lent. Lent begins on Ash Wednesday and continues until the Mass of Holy Thursday (which begins the Easter Triduum). Thus, there are five Sundays of Lent, followed by Palm Sunday (also called Passion Sunday). Lent begins on a day between February 10 and March 10, depending on the year and the occurrence of the spring equinox. It ends between March 19 and April 22. Lent is the only season that begins on a weekday (Ash Wednesday).

From the very earliest days, the season of Lent prepared the church for Easter. Lent fortifies God's people for immersion into the Lord's passion, death, and glorious resurrection. The ancient stories of God's salvation history with Israel were only a prelude to the ultimate event of all time—Jesus' paschal mystery. Each Sunday during Lent, the first reading takes us on a journey back to ancient Israel and brings forward the saving benefits of God's redemptive actions into our present day experience.

Themes of Lent

The season of Lent is highly charged with images of the exodus, Israel's premier, identifying moment. Passover is for Jews what the eucharist is for Catholics. Yahweh's action of delivering Israel out of Egyptian bondage was so essential to her consciousness and identity that she was instructed to commemorate it each year as a living memorial of God's great covenant with his people. The angel of death passed over the houses of the Israelites; they were delivered out of bondage and given possession of the promised land. The covenant was forged, and a *people,* a *holy nation* was brought to birth. Lent serves as the womb for the elect who await new birth into Christ's new covenant.

Lent is penitential, baptismal, and eucharistic by its very nature. The Second Vatican Council restored the early baptismal focus of Lent. The *Constitution on the Sacred Liturgy* restored the two-fold baptismal and penitential nature of Lent. "By recalling or preparing for baptism and by repentance, this season disposes the faithful, as they more diligently listen to the word of God and devote themselves to prayer, to celebrate the paschal mystery" (#109). Both baptism and repentance were to "be given greater prominence in both the liturgy and liturgical catechesis" (#109). This is to take place in the liturgy through homilies and catechesis that emphasize the two-fold nature of the season.

Penitential Nature of Lent

Lent is an extended time of self examination. "During Lent penance should be not only in-

ward and individual, but also outward and social."[3] In the Rite of Christian Initiation of
Adults, Lent coincides with the period of purification and enlightenment for catechumens. The
elect[4] enter a process of purification in which
they examine their heart, mind, and intentions.
They ask God to enlighten the areas of sin and
darkness with the light of Christ's healing presence. The elect preparing for baptism (along
with the rest of the faithful) scrutinize and uncover *(enlighten)* what is weak and sinful and ask
God to heal, strengthen, and liberate us from
the power of evil *(purify)*. The elect are a symbol
of the penitential posture we are all to assume
during the season. The elect stand before the
community in the celebration of the scrutinies
on the Third, Fourth and Fifth Sundays of Lent
as the premier sign of Christ's *deliverance from*
and *victory over* the power of evil.

During Lent's extended penitential period, the
church examines the dimension, power, and impact of personal, social, and systemic sin. She asks
to be delivered from sin's illusionary power and
control. Since the scrutinies are an important part
of the church's lenten observance, it is important
to explore the meaning of the ritual and our participation in it. The following is an extract from
my article in *Christian Initiation Magazine* regarding the scrutinies.

> In the scrutinies we name and uncover the
> sinister reality of sin; the personal sin that
> we commit when we reject God and fail to
> love; the social sin that we participate in
> when we do nothing to change the systems
> and structures that keep members of
> God's family oppressed, marginalized,
> hungry, and poor; and finally the systemic
> sin that encompasses total hopelessness
> and despair. Systemic sin is sin in which
> the only solution is God alone. Death al-
> ready reigns in the situation and nothing
> short of a miracle is required to heal it.
> "Sin and its effects are visible everywhere:
> in exploitive relationships, loveless fami-

lies, unjust social structures and policies,
crimes by and against individuals and
against creation, the oppression of the
weak and the manipulation of the vulnerable, explosive tensions among nations and
among ideological, racial and religious
groups and social classes, the scandalous
gulf between those who waste goods and
resources and those who live and die amid
deprivation and underdevelopment, wars
and preparation for war. Sin is a reality in
the world."[5]

Lest we be brought low by its devastating
effects we must not lose sight of the most
important element of the scrutinies: enlightenment or grace. Grace is union with
God and a share in his life. The *National
Catechetical Directory* reminds us that we are
unconditionally loved, adopted children
and that we live in the reality of being forgiven our sins.[6] Thus, the elect are filled
with the presence of Christ the Liberator,
who won the victory over evil and its consequences. In the Trinitarian prayer of exorcism, God the Father is invoked and asked
for strength and protection. Through the
power of the Holy Spirit (the epicletic action of laying on of hands), Jesus exercises
his healing and liberating power over the
effects of evil. Thus, the power and presence of Christ in Word and Exorcism are
the primary symbols of the scrutinies.[7]

Lent is a time of conversion, of metanoia, a compete turning away from sin into the loving arms of
our loving God. "What we are about when we observe this liturgical time is the correction of our
habits in order to relearn normative Christian behavior,"[8] first as a church, then as individuals.
While it is a somber time, it is nevertheless marked
by a spirit of joy. As Christians we know the rest of

---

[3] *Constitution on the Sacred Liturgy,* in *The Liturgy Documents*
(Chicago: Liturgy Training Publications, 1991), #110.

[4] Catechumens are called *the elect* after celebration of the
rite of election on the First Sunday of Lent.

[5] *National Catechetical Directory* (NCD), in *The Catechetical
Documents* (Chicago: Liturgy Training Publications, 1996),
#98.

[6] NCD, #98.

[7] Mary C. Birmingham, "Preparation for Celebration of
the Scrutinies," in *Christian Initiation Magazine,* February/
March 1997 (Kansas City: National Catholic Reporter): 1-3.

[8] *Days of the Lord,* Vol. 2, 6.

the story. Christ was victorious over the power of sin and death. While it is no doubt a time of serious reflection and interior conversion, we are joyful because we know that Easter joy awaits us. Christ the Liberator continues to heal, strengthen, and free us from the bondage imposed by ourselves and by the world.

Baptismal Nature of Lent

Lent is baptismal in nature. It is the time when the *elect* prepare to be fully initiated at the Easter Vigil through the sacraments of baptism, confirmation, and eucharist. During Lent, the faithful prepare to ritually remember their baptism and their baptismal commitment. Whether the newly baptized are present or not, the faithful will recall their baptism and renew their profession of faith at the Easter liturgies.

In the earliest days of the church, the Christian community walked hand in hand with the elect in their preparation for baptism—they were in it together. In his book, *The Liturgical Year,* Adolf Adam suggests that pre-Easter fasting was a way to prepare for the reception of the Spirit and the Easter sacraments of baptism and eucharist. It was a weapon against evil spirits, and a means to help the poor with money that would otherwise have been spent on food. What the church required of candidates for baptism by way of liturgical and spiritual effort was also done by the faithful in solidarity of spirit. "An atmosphere of cooperation and reciprocity was thus established that benefited the entire community."[9]

Eucharistic Nature of Lent

The season of Lent also prepares the elect and faithful for eucharist. While focusing on the baptismal nature of the season, we must not forget that baptism is the gateway, the door that leads to the table. The goal of initiation is not baptism; it is eucharist. The eucharist is the fullest sign of incorporation into the Body of Christ; it is the ultimate sacrament of unity. Through our participation in Christ's Body we become one people. The entire Christian life is somewhat catechumenal in nature. Christians are never finished; they never arrive; they are always on the journey. St. Augustine called the eucharist the repeatable sacrament of initiation. Eucharist is always a new encounter with the risen Christ. Jesus gave us his Body and Blood for the forgiveness of sins. Thus, whenever we eat Jesus' Body and drink his Blood at the communal feast we are made a new creation.

Each time we partake of Christ's Body and Blood, we recommit our lives to the ongoing incorporation into his life, death, and resurrection, the paschal mystery. We receive the necessary nourishment to take up our cross, to go out to the world, *to be fed off of,* and to become food for others. We come back to the table depleted; we are nourished again so that we can go out again.

The Disciplines of Lent: Prayer, Fasting, and Almsgiving

During the fifth century the church gathered for liturgical prayer on Mondays, Wednesdays, and Fridays. It was not until the sixth century that the other days of the week were added as eucharistic observances. Thus, from the earliest stages of the season, Lent was marked by prayer and communal worship. The people gathered to celebrate special "Liturgies of the Word, homilies and prayer.... Lent is a time characterized by more assiduous observance of prayer and liturgy."[10]

Fasting is regarded as the hallmark discipline of Lent. No doubt most Christians would immediately identify fasting with Lent. However, fasting is not just a lenten discipline. It should be a habit common to the Christian's entire life. Fasting does not have its origin in Christianity. The Jews fasted throughout their history. Fasting was a discipline of other pagan religions as well.

Fasting is *always* observed in tandem with prayer and almsgiving. The early Fathers of the Church considered fasting an exercise of compassion. It is expressed best in the following ancient sermon.

> There are three things, my brethren, by which faith stands firm, devotion remains constant, and virtue endures. They are

[9]Adolf Adam, *The Liturgical Year,* trans. Matthew J. O'Connell (Collegeville: The Liturgical Press, 1990), 91-113.

[10]*Days of the Lord,* Vol. 2, 4.

prayer, fasting and mercy (almsgiving). Prayer knocks at the door, fasting obtains, mercy receives. Prayer, mercy and fasting: these three are one, and they give life to each other.

Fasting is the soul of prayer, mercy is the lifeblood of fasting. Let no one try to separate them; they cannot be separated. If you have only one of them or not all together, you have nothing. So if you pray, fast; if you fast, show mercy; if you want your petition to be heard, hear the petition of others. If you do not close your ear to others, you open God's ear to yourself.

When you fast, see the fasting of others. If you want God to know that you are hungry, know that another is hungry. If you hope for mercy, show mercy. If you look for kindness, show kindness. If you want to receive, give. If you ask for yourself what you deny to others, your asking is a mockery...

...Fasting bears no fruit unless it is watered by mercy. Fasting dries up when mercy dries up. Mercy is to fasting as rain to the earth. However much you cultivate your heart, clear the soil of your nature, root out vices, show virtues, if you do not release the springs of mercy, your fasting will bear no fruit.

When you fast, if your mercy is thin your harvest will be thin; when you fast, what you pour out in mercy overflows into your barn. Therefore, do not lose by saving, but gather in by scattering. Give to the poor, and you give to yourself. You will not be allowed to keep what you have refused to give to others.[11]

Prayer, fasting and almsgiving are communal disciplines of Lent. The Lenten disciplines are not for private edification but are to build up the entire church. One fasts in order to share. In antiquity, those who did not have enough to share were instructed to fast and use the money they saved on food to give to the poor. Prayer, fasting, and sharing are the agenda of the entire community. Many parishes gather during Lent for light soup suppers in which the money normally spent on a hearty meal is given instead to the poor.[12]

Prayer, fasting, and sharing must include reflection on the social dimensions of sin in our world where many people do not have an adequate share of the world's resources. Our commitment to prayer and fasting must include a commitment to issues of justice and equality for all people. It is hypocrisy to pray and fast and then assert that the poor of the world are not our problem, but are, instead, the problem of politicians and other nations.

The only obligatory fast days are Ash Wednesday and Good Friday. Some dioceses have included the Fridays during Lent as days of fast and abstinence.

The Lenten Lectionary

The Old Testament readings of Lent proclaim the salvation events wrought by Yahweh, especially the exodus. Christianity understands the readings from the Hebrew scriptures to be the foreshadowing of the salvation accomplished through Jesus Christ. Reginald Fuller maintains that during Lent, the New Testament letters profess the Christian kerygma and participation in the passion, death, and resurrection of Christ through baptism. The lenten gospels are stories from Jesus' life that foreshadow his impending death and resurrection. The scriptures of Lent are intended to prepare us to celebrate our redemption in Christ. "The emphasis of the Lenten readings is the new life to which the baptized are called and its ethical demands."[13]

---

[11]St. Peter Chrysologus (ca. 380-450), "Sermon 43," Patrologia Latina 52, ed. J.P. Migne, in *The Liturgy of the Hours*, Vol. 2 (New York: Catholic Book Publishing Co., 1976) Office of Readings, Tuesday in the Third Week of Lent, 231-232.

[12]However, to reserve these activities only to the season of Lent diminishes Jesus' ongoing call to prayer, fasting, and sharing, the hallmarks of biblical justice. Lent serves as a reminder of what we should be doing as a matter of course throughout the entire Christian life.

[13]Reginald H. Fuller, *Preaching the New Lectionary* (Collegeville: The Liturgical Press, 1974), xxix.

Fuller also suggests that the lenten readings are penitential, but are placed in the context of the missionary implications of the gospel. On the First Sunday of Lent, the focus is the fasting of Jesus and his temptation in the desert. The Second Sunday of Lent takes us to the mountain of Jesus' transfiguration where we will hear the story from Matthew, Mark, or Luke's perspective. Thus, the First and Second Sundays of Lent in each cycle proclaim the same gospel event: temptation in the desert and the transfiguration. The gospels for the remaining Sundays of Lent are not the same for each cycle.

During Cycle A, we hear the powerful stories of the Samaritan woman at the well (Third Sunday of Lent, first scrutiny), the man born blind (Fourth Sunday of Lent, second scrutiny) and the raising of Lazarus (Fifth Sunday of Lent, third scrutiny). These Johannine gospels are catechumenal in nature as they best reflect the baptismal and penitential nature of the season. Through these stories we encounter sin (personal, social and systemic) head on and are filled with "Christ the Redeemer, who is living water, the light of the world, and the resurrection and the life."[14]

The Cycle A readings are known as "the Johannine signs" and were "long viewed as symbols of the Christian experience of baptism."[15] When baptismal preparation was only three weeks long, the three Johannine gospels were used as primary catechesis because of their strong baptismal images: "water and spirit, the light of faith, and death and life."[16] Whenever there are catechumens, the Cycle A readings are to be used, regardless of the liturgical cycle. Since they were for use in catechumenal ministry and were intended to "arouse the baptismal faith" of the faithful, there is an option to use the Cycle A readings each year.

During Cycle B, the Third Sunday's gospel is John's account of the destruction of the temple and its subsequent rebuilding in three days. The Fourth Sunday's gospel (also from John) professes the Son of Man who will be raised for the salvation of all. The Fifth Sunday is about the grain that dies and bears much fruit.

---

[14]*Rite of Christian Initiation of Adults*, #143.

[15]Fuller, *Preaching the New Lectionary*, xxix.

[16]*Days of the Lord*, Vol. 2, 35.

The Cycle C gospel for the Third Sunday of Lent is about the need for repentance and conversion. The Fourth Sunday is the story of the prodigal son and the Fifth Sunday is the story of the woman accused of adultery.

The second reading during Lent is chosen to support the gospel. The first reading, however, is concerned with recounting significant events in salvation history. On Palm Sunday, the first and second readings are the same every year. The gospel is the passion narrative from one of the synoptic gospels. (For more on the lenten lectionary, see chapter 3 on scripture.)

As a springboard for lenten reflection, the following poem captures the heart of Lent's purpose. The protagonist of the poem is a catechumen who has journeyed with a community of faith for over a year. The catechumen has just celebrated the rite of election and has moved into the final preparatory period of purification and enlightenment. The person in this poem has encountered Jesus through the prayer and worship of his or her celebrating community in one complete liturgical cycle. This person speaks for us all.

*so what **could** be left, sister lent?*

I thought I had uncovered it all . . . layer by layer I
shed it all away . . .
*so what **could** be left, sister lent?*
like a snake squirming from the casing of his
former self
and the butterfly wrestling from the safe bondage
of her quiet hibernation . . .
I stand empty . . .
a wonderful, curious, new creation,
chosen of god . . .
nakedly I gaze before discernment's interior
mirror . . .
*so what **could** be left, sister lent?*
Sunday after Sunday, story after story, decision
after decision,
gave way to an empty, vulnerable vessel, ready for
easter filling . . .
*so what **could** be left, sister lent?*
like an air-dried sponge I stand waiting . . .
for what do I wait?
for fire light's illumination . . .
for baptismal water's soaking immersion . . .
for confirmation oil's sealing configuration . . .

for eucharist bread and wine's sumptuous
celebration
for dying, rising, famine, for feasting,
for those who are *out* to be one with the *in*...
to eat, to be broken, to be poured, to be filled,
to live by example, to die, to be food...
for the hungry, the lost, the blind and the
obstinate...
I wait to give more of the gift already given,
the sacrament of life for the sake of the
kingdom...
so, forty more days of repentance and ashes
to renew, to strengthen and prepare for the
banquet...
is there more? could there be?
one forgotten remnant
of a life not yet surrendered, of blindness,
repression?
be it sojourn, or Passover or exodus event
I stand with eyes opened, my heart in my hand...
what could be left? only **YOU** know for sure...
so do what **YOU** will, root out from the core
all that might keep me from the life **YOU** intend
of thanksgiving, of service and praise till the
end...

Mary Birmingham[17]

[17]Mary C. Birmingham, "Preparation for Celebration of
the Scrutinies," *Christian Initiation* (February/March 1997),
Kansas City: National Catholic Reporter, 1.

ASH WEDNESDAY

INTRODUCTORY RITES

Opening Song (or Entrance Antiphon)

Lord, you are merciful to all, and hate nothing you have created. You overlook the sins of men to bring them to repentance. You are the Lord our God. (See Wisdom 11:24-25, 27.)[1]

Environment

The catechetical space may be adorned simply with a cross, the Lectionary, and a candle; you might want to use hints of the color purple. A clay pot filled with ashes may be included as a sign of our need for repentance. Barren branches simply arranged speak of that buried seed, hibernating in its preparatory earthen cocoon awaiting the new life of Easter. Since Lent is a time of preparation for baptism, holy water fonts should be emptied.

The names and pictures of catechumens who will be initiated at the Easter Vigil might be placed in a basket nearby so all can be united with them in prayer and solidarity throughout the season.

The cross might be surrounded by purple cloth and then in the later weeks shrouded with that same purple cloth. This ancient practice is reminiscent of Isaiah's prophecy concerning the future day of the Lord: the new heaven and new earth. The veil that covers our eyes will be torn down and all will see the glory of God. Sin shrouds us from the *shekina* glory of God. The custom of veiling statues was stopped after the Second Vatican Council. However, it was reinstated in 1985 for use in the last weeks of Lent.[2]

The following ritual prayer from *Catholic Household Blessings and Prayers* may be used to bless the lenten environment:

---

[1]Ash Wednesday: "Entrance Antiphon," *The Sacramentary.*
[2]Peter Mazur, *To Crown the Year* (Chicago: Liturgy Training Publications, 1994), 42-69.

Ash Wednesday Blessing of the Season and of a Place of Prayer

All make the sign of the cross as the leader begins:
The Lord calls us to days of penance and mercy. Blessed be the name of the Lord.

All respond:
Now and for ever.

Leader: Remember that we are but dust and ashes, yet by God's grace we have died in baptism and have put on the Lord Jesus Christ. Each year we keep these forty days with prayer and penance and the practice of charity so that we may come to the Easter festival ready to renew once more the life-giving commitment of our baptism. Throughout this Lent we shall gather here to read the Scriptures and ponder them and to intercede with God for the needs of the world.

Scripture
Isaiah 58:5-10

(Someone proclaims the reading from the prophet Isaiah.)

After a time of silence, members of the household offer prayers of intercession for the world, the church and its catechumens, and themselves. The leader then invites:

Let us kneel and ask for God's blessing on us and this holy season.
Merciful God,
you called us forth from the dust of the earth;
you claimed us for Christ in the waters of baptism.
Look upon us as we enter these Forty Days
bearing the mark of ashes,
and bless our journey through the desert of Lent
to the font of rebirth.
May our fasting be hunger for justice;
our alms, a making of peace;
our prayer, the chant of humble and grateful hearts.
All that we do and pray is in the name of Jesus.

Each person then kisses the cross.

All then stand, and the leader concludes.

All through these days let us be quiet and
  prayerful,
pondering the mysteries told in the Scriptures.
In the cross, we have been claimed for Christ.
In Christ, we make the prayer that fills these days
  of mercy:

Our Father...

The leader says:
Let us bless the Lord.

All respond, making the sign of the cross:
Thanks be to God.[3]

Opening Prayer

*The facilitator of the session may lead the prayer. Others
in the group may be asked to proclaim the readings.*

Let us pray
[in quiet remembrance of our need for redemption]

  Pause for silent prayer.

Father in heaven,
the light of your truth bestows sight
to the darkness of sinful eyes.
May this season of repentance bring us the blessing of your forgiveness
and the gift of your light.
Grant this through Christ our Lord.[4]

LITURGY OF THE WORD

Let us listen to God's word.

The readings are proclaimed.

First Reading
Joel 2:12-18

---

[3]"Ash Wednesday Blessing of the Season and of a Place
of Prayer," *Catholic Household Blessings and Prayers* (Washington: USCC, 1988), 132-135.
    [4]"Ash Wednesday: "Alternative Opening Prayer," *The
Sacramentary.*

Joel's book is heavily centered in the language of
temple worship. He speaks of vegetable offerings,
libations, the fast, and a solemn assembly—the
things of ritual worship. Temple priests, ministers
of Yahweh, and ministers of the altar were part of
Joel's cast of characters. Joel was one of the twelve
minor prophets. Most scholars believe that the
book of Joel was written after the exile and after
the temple had been rebuilt (ca. 515 B.C.E.).

In chapters 1 and 2, Joel tells of a devastating
drought and locust plague and thus sets the tone
for his manuscript. His primary agenda concerns
the reversal of fortunes. The first chapters depict
the effects of the drought and plague on the people and on their worship. First, those directly involved by the effects of the plague (such as farmers) were called to lament. The effects of the
invading army of locusts were so horrific, however,
that the entire community was summoned to publicly lament.

Scholars believe that the book's main theme flows
from verse 18. There was a corporate summons to
grieve and lament. Israel was in devastation; there
was pending doom. One can almost imagine the
scene in true epic style. The ground rumbled, the
earth shook, and the invading creatures blackened the sky. The people pleaded and Yahweh responded—a miracle happened! Yahweh intervened; the drought and plague were lifted. Their
fortunes were reversed; Yahweh saved the day.
This day was to be remembered.

Later in the book, Joel assigned this story to the
community's corporate memory so that when all
seemed lost, Israel would remember Yahweh's
mercy. They would count on Yahweh to usher Israel into that final victorious battle. Herein lies an
important lesson regarding the power of storytelling. Our stories of faith sustain us through the
difficult times. We remember God's action, and
are encouraged to be steadfast.

Yahweh does not act because of the ritual offerings. Yahweh acts because of his kindness and
mercy and because of "who God is." For God,
doing and being are the same thing. People repent because they are confident of his mercy.
Everyone is called to fast—no one is excluded!

Responsorial Psalm
Psalm 51

Psalm 51 is the psalm of repentance. Humans acknowledge their utter guilt before God. God not only forgives the sin and guilt, but he restores the relationship.

Second Reading
2 Corinthians 5:20–6:2

Paul expounds a beautiful theology regarding the effects of Christ's death and resurrection upon the sin of the world. When Christ died, the veil on the temple was ripped in two. Humanity was given access to the holy of holies; God was now approachable. Christ *became* the very sin he came to destroy. He lifted the weight of sin from humanity's shoulder. Jesus' act was the ultimate gift of grace. Now is the time to rejoice in the grace that was won for all the world! Like Joel, we must shout it from the rooftops—the day of salvation is upon us! It is Good News; we can do no less than share it.

Gospel
Matthew 6:1-6, 16-18

Jesus warns about ostentatious displays of prayer and fasting.

STEP 1
NAMING ONE'S EXPERIENCE

What were your first impressions? What was your first response? What grabbed your attention? How did you feel?

Each person names his or her initial impression. Statement should be brief. No reasons should be given at this time. All simply listen without agreeing or disagreeing.

STEP 2
UNDERSTANDING

In a brief statement, what do you think this gospel is trying to convey?

STEP 3
INPUT FROM VISION/STORY/TRADITION

Liturgical Context

On Ash Wednesday we receive ashes as a sign of our willingness to repent. We are sorry for our sins. At one time ashes were a public sign of repentance. They were not used in official liturgy until the thirteenth century. Until the reform of the liturgy, the ritual took place before mass. Since the reform, the blessing and distribution of ashes take place following the liturgy of the word. If mass is not celebrated, it takes place in the context of the liturgy of the word.

The ashes are given with the words, "Remember, man, that you are dust and to dust you shall return," or "Turn away from sin and be faithful to the gospel."[5] The ritual prayers that accompany the blessing of ashes place the season in its appropriate pre-Easter perspective:

> Lord,
> bless the sinner who asks for your
>   forgiveness
> and bless + all those who receive these
>   ashes.
> May they keep this Lenten season
> in preparation for the joy of Easter.
> We ask this through Christ, our Lord.
> Bless these ashes+
> by which we show we are dust.
> Pardon our sins
> and keep us faithful to the discipline of
>   Lent,
> for you do not want sinners to die
> but to live with the risen Christ,
> who reigns with you forever.[6]

On Ash Wednesday we humbly come before God seeking *metanoia*, conversion and complete repentance. Our repentance is an act of faith because we repent trusting in God's kindness and mercy. Today's liturgy is a call to repentance for the

---

[5]Ash Wednesday: "Blessing and Distribution of Ashes," *The Sacramentary.*
[6]Ibid.

whole church. Joel sets the stage. "Proclaim a fast, call an assembly!" This is not a "Jesus and me" event. The entire community is called. Together we recognize our need for God's mercy.

We engage in a process of reflection and renewal as a community. Joel summoned the nation, the church summons her people. Fasting increases our hunger. For whom do we hunger? The resurrected Christ. What is the living memorial of his resurrected presence? The eucharist.

Gospel Exegesis

The facilitator gives input regarding what critical biblical scholarship has to say about this text. The input includes insights as to how people would have heard the gospel in Jesus' time.

Jesus' words are part of the discourse on the Mount. They are part of the evangelical section of the sermon. We must read this gospel in its evangelical context, as well as in the obvious context of prayer, fasting, and almsgiving. To live as Jesus commanded is to live according to the demands of the law, according to God's justice. God's justice (*hesed*) embodies right relationship with God as evidenced by care and concern for the poor and oppressed. Our prayer, fasting, and almsgiving must be in the spirit of the gospel and its mission orientation. Our light must shine before all, but it must shine with integrity. There can be no false airs, no hypocrisy. We are not to perform the lenten disciplines to gain the admiration of others.

The good deeds of a righteous person will cause people to see the light of Christ. Jesus invites us to look within and judge our motives. As community and as individuals we are to examine our hearts and judge our motivation for worship, prayer, fasting, and devotional practices.

Christians are to be joyful in the midst of their trials. In spite of life's difficulties they know what awaits them. Believers are to act in love toward their neighbors and invite others to Christ by the way they live their lives.

Proclaim the gospel again.

Sometimes we gain new insights when we hear the text after the interpretation has been given. Someone from the group proclaims the gospel a second time.

STEP 4
TESTING

Conversation with the Liturgy and the Scriptures

Test your original understanding in dialogue with the text.

(You might consider breaking into smaller groups.)

Were there any new insights? Was there anything you had not considered before? How do the readings for Ash Wednesday speak to your life?

Sharing Life Experience

Participants share an experience from their lives that connects with the biblical interpretation just shared.

> *I see people in my parish who live their lives in the spirit of Jesus' gospel. They live it not only during Lent, but also throughout the year. They are the real saints. They live their lives in humble submission to the word of God. They pray, fast, and reach out to the sick, the sorrowing, the infirm, the lonely, and the aged. One woman exemplifies the life Jesus calls us to live in today's gospel. She ministers to the sick and the elderly. She ministers the word of God everywhere she goes. She seeks God with every breath she takes. She speaks for truth and will not listen to gossip or destructive conversation. She exudes joy and typifies the humility demanded in today's gospel. Few people know how much she does for the reign of God. I look to her this Lent to remind me of the spirit and challenge of the season. My lenten repentance and conversion must lead me to grow more like the woman I admire so.*

All share their life experience.

What was Matthew trying to tell his community? What does he have to say to our community and to me today? What might God be creating in us through this experience of Jesus in the gospel and the lenten liturgy? In what way does this gospel point to God's promise to be with us? In what way have I/we known death/resurrection in my/our experience and understanding of this gospel? How is God speaking to us as a community? Has our original understanding been stretched, challenged or affirmed?

STEP 5
DECISION

The gospel demands a response.

How does your sharing and this biblical interpretation challenge your community's attitudes? What will you/your community/your parish be called to do in response? Name one concrete action you will take this week as a response to what was learned and shared today.

DOCTRINAL ISSUES

What church truth/teaching/doctrinal issue could be drawn from the gospel for Ash Wednesday?

Participants suggest possible doctrinal themes that flow from the readings.

Possible Doctrinal Themes

Lent, conversion, repentance, fasting

Present the doctrinal material at this time.

1. The facilitator gives input on a particular doctrinal issue of his/her prior choosing. OR
2. The group chooses a doctrinal issue from the list they created. They read together from the Doctrinal Appendix.

(The doctrinal issues are found in the Doctrinal Appendix in the back of this workbook. If you are choosing an issue from this resource, please refer to it now.)

Reflection questions centered around the chosen doctrinal theme can be found at the end of each topic in the Doctrinal Appendix. The questions are based on the five-step reflection process. If you choose a topic not included in the Doctrinal Appendix, craft your own questions according to the same five-step process.

Following the reflection questions you will be reminded to return to chapter 7, "Preparing the Catechetical Session," to assist you in crafting your own session.

Closing Prayer

Come back to the Lord with all your heart;
leave the past in ashes,
and turn to God with tears and fasting,
for he is slow to anger and ready to forgive.
　　(Joel 2:13)

Let the priests and ministers of the Lord
lament before his altar, and say:
Spare us, Lord, spare your people!
Do not let us die for we are crying out to you.
　　(Joel 2:17; Est 13:17)[7]

Selected Bibliography

Days of the Lord. Vol. 2. Collegeville: The Liturgical Press, 1993.

Fuller, Reginald. *Preaching the New Lectionary.* Collegeville: The Liturgical Press, 1986.

Mallon, Elias D. "Joel." In *The New Jerome Biblical Commentary.* Ed. Raymond E. Brown, S.S., Joseph A. Fitzmyer, S.J., Roland E. Murphy, O.Carm. Englewood Cliffs: Prentice Hall, 1990.

Mazur, Peter. *To Crown the Year.* Chicago: Liturgy Training Publications, 1994.

---

[7]Ash Wednesday: "Antiphon 1 and 2," *The Sacramentary.*

FIRST SUNDAY OF LENT

INTRODUCTORY RITES

Opening Song (or Entrance Antiphon)

When he calls me, I will answer; I will rescue him and give him honor. Long life and contentment will be his. (Ps 90:15-16)[1]

Environment

Refer to Ash Wednesday

Opening Prayer

The facilitator of the session may lead the prayer. Others in the group may be asked to proclaim the readings.

Let us pray
[that this Lent will help us
reproduce in our lives
the self sacrificing love of Christ]

    Pause for silent prayer.

Father,
through the observances of Lent,
help us to understand the meaning
of your Son's death and resurrection,
and teach us to reflect it in our lives.
Grant this through our Lord
Jesus Christ, your Son,
who lives and reigns with you and the Holy Spirit,
one God, for ever and ever.[2]

LITURGY OF THE WORD

Let us listen to God's word.

The readings are proclaimed.

First Reading
Deuteronomy 26:4-10

---

[1]First Sunday of Lent: "Entrance Antiphon," *The Sacramentary.*

[2]First Sunday of Lent: "Opening Prayer," *The Sacramentary.*

As stated in the lenten overview, the exodus event was Israel's premier sign and symbol of God's covenant, liberation, and deliverance: a sign of God's sovereignty over their lives. Exodus is for the Jews what the death and resurrection of Jesus are for Christians. The reading from Romans highlights this understanding. All three readings today contain declarative professions of faith. These creedal formulas provide for us the impetus and motivation to embrace the faith and life embodied in all of today's scriptures.

Today's first reading was part of a liturgy of thanksgiving. The people offered their prayers and thanks for the first fruits of the harvest. This ritual had its origin in pagan rituals offered to the gods. Israelites adapted agricultural rites to conform to their worship of Yahweh, the One God, and to mirror their experience of the exodus. The exodus proved that God was in relationship with *a people.* Yahweh was the master of nature (master of the harvest) and the master of salvation history. The harvest ritual acknowledged this sovereignty. Today's reading from Deuteronomy confesses the Lord of the universe who is responsible for all the great deeds of power and might.

The primary focus of this reading for the First Sunday of Lent is the confession of faith. It is the oldest "credo" of ancient Israel. Yahweh, the Lord of history, formed an everlasting covenant with his people, Israel. It is a profession of faith rooted in the saving acts of Yahweh, their God. "...We cried to the Lord, the God of our fathers, and he heard our cry and saw our affliction, our toil and our oppression..." (Dt 26:7). We inherited this confession from our ancestors, and together with our profession of faith in the risen Christ, it is the creed we celebrate in the liturgy: "Father, we acknowledge your greatness: all your actions show your wisdom and love.... Father, you so loved the world that in the fullness of time you sent your only Son to be our Savior."[3]

---

[3]"Eucharistic Prayer IV," *The Sacramentary.*

Three acts of salvation history are professed in today's reading.
1. Yahweh established the southern kingdom of Judah.
2. The Lord God delivered Israel out of bondage, forming a people in the desert.
3. Yahweh gave them possession of the promised land.

This particular proclamation of God's saving deeds is one of the most important professions of faith in the Old Testament.

Responsorial Psalm
Psalm 91:1-2, 10-11, 14-15

This is one of the common psalms assigned to the lenten season. Satan quotes this psalm to Jesus in the third temptation.

Second Reading
Romans 10:8-13

Before Paul wrote his letter to the Romans, he had already struggled intensely with the subject matter. In his letter to the Galatians, Paul furiously defended his developing theology in regard to the Christian kerygma. One can almost hear the echoes of his interior debate regarding the meaning of Jesus' sacrifice as it relates to the law and the prophets. Paul was reformulating his theology in light of his experience of the risen Christ as experienced by the gentile community. The letter to the Galatians is a rather impulsive, defensive letter. It was written from a jail cell and reflects the frenzy of his predicament. The letter to the Romans is a more refined, less exaggerated articulation of the Galatian message: in order to become transformed, all one needed to do was embrace the message of Jesus Christ. The Holy Spirit, then, would slowly begin the process of transformation.

After no doubt alienating more than a few law-abiding Jewish Christians, Paul displayed more tact, finesse, and certainly more brilliance in expressing and defining his theology to the Roman community. He was careful not to minimize the importance of the Jewish roots of his readers. However, while the letter to the Romans is certainly more conciliatory toward Paul's Jewish audience, he is nevertheless determined to challenge

rigid legalism and the notion of merited salvation. The letter validated Yahweh's intervention in Israel's (Old Testament) history.[4] Paul asserted that the Christian kerygma is the fulfillment of what God already accomplished in the Old Testament. Thus, according to Hubert Richards, Paul did not repudiate Judaism and the gospel was stated as its fulfillment.[5]

Paul insisted that Jesus died once and for all people. It was a complete act of gratuitous, unmerited, unconditional love. The response to such love can be nothing less than the complete offering of one's entire life to the God who loves so greatly. Human beings are justified by faith, not by observance of the law or by their own merits. It was a difficult message to accept. Justification through the law was ingrained in the people's consciousness and history.

Paul was afraid that people would simply not believe they were forgiven. He felt compelled to proclaim the Good News to the entire world with determined urgency!

The letter to the Romans was written toward the end of Paul's third missionary journey. He was already planning his fourth trip and Rome was to be his home base. Paul's intention for writing to the Romans was to prepare them for his arrival. The letter to the Romans is a masterful articulation of the Christian belief in the paschal mystery. It is a brilliant, systematic expression of Christian theology.

This reading was chosen because of the confession of faith inherent within it: "For if you confess with your lips that Jesus is Lord, and believe in your heart that God raised him from the dead, you will be saved" (Rom 10:9). This was the basic Christian kerygma, the profession of faith that every neophyte would profess. From this statement of faith would flow the church's creed. This profession of faith is proclaimed in every liturgy. Jesus is Lord;

---

[4]Paul's letter to the Galatians seemed to repudiate the Old Testament. His tone in the letter to the Romans is far more conciliatory to the Jews.

[5]For more information refer to: Hubert Richards, *The Gospel According to St. Paul* (Collegeville: The Liturgical Press, 1990), 87.

he suffered, died, was buried, and rose again from the dead and sits at the right hand of the Father.[6]

Gospel
Luke 4:1-13

Jesus is tempted by the devil in the desert.

STEP 1
NAMING ONE'S EXPERIENCE

What were your first impressions? What was your first response? What grabbed your attention? How did you feel?

Each person names his or her initial impression. Statement should be brief. No reasons should be given at this time. All simply listen without agreeing or disagreeing.

STEP 2
UNDERSTANDING

In a brief statement, what do you think this gospel is trying to convey?

STEP 3
INPUT FROM VISION/STORY/TRADITION

Liturgical Context

Celebration of the first two Sundays of Lent (temptation and transfiguration) dates back to the fourth century. The First Sunday of Lent recalls Jesus in the desert, the place of his temptation and Israel's unfaithfulness (as well as her faithfulness). The symbol of the desert has ancient roots in the church. The desert was seen as a quiet, distraction-free place, where people commune with God. Monasticism emerged out of the desert.

The readings for the First Sunday of Lent are like a sacred liturgy replete with affirmations

---
[6]Reginald H. Fuller, *Preaching the New Lectionary* (Collegeville: The Liturgical Press, 1974), 2.

and confessions of faith. The inherent creedal statements (professions of faith) can be found in the basic canon of the liturgy. Whenever the Jews retold and remembered the salvation events of history (patriarchs, Jacob going into Egypt, slavery in Egypt and liberation through Moses, promised land, etc.—First Reading), it was considered a profession of faith. The saving actions were made present by recalling them (anamnesis). St. Paul's profession of faith (Second Reading) stressed the imperative to invoke (epiclesis) the name of the crucified and risen Christ. Through the invocation of the Lord's name, there is assurance of being saved—again a profession of faith.

Thus, the professions of faith woven through today's scriptures are foundational to our worship and our identity. We find them in our creed, the preface, and the eucharistic prayer; they are braided throughout all the ritual prayers of the liturgy. The proclamation of God's action throughout Israel's salvation history in the first reading and our assertion that "Jesus Christ is Lord" in the second reading are the heart and soul of worship. Every liturgy proclaims, remembers, and makes present the reality, effects, and implications of such professions.

The Memorial Acclamation of the liturgy echoes Jesus' lordship: "Christ has died, Christ is risen, Christ will come again." This powerful confession articulates the church's doctrine of the paschal mystery and her eschatology. The risen Christ is professed and experienced in word, sacrament, and celebrating assembly. Thus, as we tell our story and confess our faith, we enter the purifying season of Lent fully aware that it is Christ risen and crucified who enlightens and calls people to Easter birth.

Jesus' bout with the devil causes us to confess with our lips: "Truly, you are the Son of God." Luke tells his story of the temptation in the shadow of the cross. Jesus' ordeal on the temple parapet in Jerusalem was a foreshadowing of the cross he would endure. Jesus' temptation is an invitation and a challenge. The elect and the entire church are invited to the temple parapet as a prelude to the journey to Jerusalem and the challenge of the cross. Lent marks the way for us all.

Rite of Election and Rite of Sending

Today begins the period of purification and enlightenment for catechumens. This marks the beginning of the final, more intense preparation for the Easter sacraments of initiation. The celebration of the rite of election and the enrollment of names is the liturgical rite that signifies entry into this final period that coincides with the season of Lent. The principal celebrant for the rite of election is the bishop and the rite generally takes place at the diocesan cathedral. However, the great enthusiasm and ownership of the rite at the parish level has prompted an adaptation known as the rite of sending.

The rite of sending allows the parish to send its catechumens to the bishop for election and enrollment of names. The preliminary judgment of the catechumens' readiness takes place within the parish. The parish is the spiritual mother who now wishes to send her fledglings to election with assurances of love, support, and prayers. Baptized candidates are also sent to the bishop for recognition of their call to continuing conversion during this time of preparation for the completion of their initiation.

At the rite of election, the catechumens make a transition into their final preparation for initiation and are conferred with a new name: the *elect*. In scripture, the conferral of a new name signified a changed status or a new mission or vocation. The church accepts the catechumens as chosen of God; they are elected by God. On the basis of the testimony of the godparents and the catechists, as well as the catechumens' own reaffirmation, the church judges their state of readiness to go forward for initiation at the Easter Vigil. The church testifies to God's grace at work in the lives of the catechumens. The catechumens, then, hand their names over, and enroll for baptism.

Election is about being chosen. To be chosen assumes that one is in reciprocal covenant relationship with God. It is a relationship rooted in biblical justice. "Election as people of God requires a style of life that reflects this office. It is as much a responsibility as it is a privilege."[7] Election is a radical call to intimate relationship with God and unconditional love toward all of God's creation. In the Old Testament, election assumed that those chosen believed in their hearts and professed with their voices the ancient *Shema*: "The Lord God is One. We are to love the Lord God with all our heart, mind and soul, and love our neighbor as ourselves."

Election is God's free act of gratuitous, unmerited love. However, there is always an inherent obligation on the part of the person or group chosen. "To belong to God in the special relationship of election demands that one imitate the very character and qualities of God."[8] Election reminds us that God is in charge; we are not. Election is freely given, but it is also freely received. Barbara Bowe suggests that a person's membership among the elect depends on the extent to which a person is faithful to God throughout life, especially during times of distress and tribulation. Thus, there is an eschatological dimension inherent within election. Election is participation in the messianic reign in this world and anticipation of God's reign to come.

Election is understood as vocation and responsibility rather than privilege and superiority. Election assumes a special intimacy and full communion with God as well as the vocation to witness to the marvels of God in the world.[9]

Today's gospel is a wonderful testament to election. The first Christians compared Jesus to the suffering servant of Isaiah, the "chosen one of God" (Is 42-53). Jesus, as God's beloved, stands chosen above all others as God's elect. Prior to Jesus' temptation scene, he was baptized by the Holy Spirit in the Jordan River. The Spirit called and empowered Jesus for mission. The Spirit then led Jesus to the desert where he was tempted. The temptation was a prelude and preparation for

---

[7] Marilyn M. Schaub, "Election," in *The Collegeville Pastoral Dictionary of Biblical Theology*, ed. Carroll Stuhlmueller, C.P. (Collegeville: The Liturgical Press, 1996), 250.

[8] Barbara E. Bowe, R.S.C.J., "Election: New Testament," in *The Collegeville Pastoral Dictionary of Biblical Theology*, ed. Carroll Stuhlmueller, C.P. (Collegeville: The Liturgical Press, 1996), 251.

[9] Robert J. Schreiter, C.PP.S., "Election: Pastoral Liturgical Tradition," in *The Collegeville Pastoral Dictionary of Biblical Theology*, ed. Carroll Stuhlmueller, C.P. (Collegeville: The Liturgical Press, 1996), 254.

Jesus' ministry; it was intended to show Jesus the scope of his mission. His reign was to be a reign of service, not power. Jesus, "Beloved," "Elect of God," was shown what his ministry was to be, by being shown what it was not to be. Jesus' ministry was rooted in service, self-offering, and reliance on the word of God.

Jesus, as God's chosen and God's elect, was faithful to his call and mission. His call ultimately led him to the desert where his ancestors had failed miserably. They failed in their call to covenant relationship. Jesus not only succeeded, but he offered us a new covenant. Jesus invites us all into the desert of Lent. On this First Sunday of Lent, Jesus shows the elect what the call of discipleship means. It is fraught with dangers; it is the emptying of self; it is a mission of service; and it leads ultimately to the cross. Jesus does not leave us alone and abandoned in our testing, but rather gives us the sword of God's word as our saber of protection. He shows the elect and us the way through purification to enlightenment.

At the rite of election, the godparents testify to the catechumens' readiness to accept God's call and the subsequent challenge of election. The church, then, declares the catechumens chosen and ready to go forward for initiation.

Gospel Exegesis

The facilitator gives input regarding what critical biblical scholarship has to say about this text. The input includes insights as to how people would have heard the gospel in Jesus' time.

In the scriptures, the desert referred to a barren area with low rainfall. Sometimes it referred to wilderness. In the biblical perspective, barren places were places where humans encountered God. In the Christian perspective, the desert is a symbol of inner pilgrimage leading to the experience of God.

Many of the salvific acts of the Old Testament occurred in the desert. *It was a place of death.* If people lost their way in the desert, they would surely die. *It was a place of protection.* In the story of exodus, God led Israel through the desert for forty

years. He fed the Israelites, provided water for their thirst, and showed them the way through the desert. God entered into a covenant with Israel and she became a people. Many of God's dealings with Israel occurred in the desert. "Clearly the desert and God's plan for Israel were intimately bound together."[10]

All three synoptic gospels tell the story of Jesus in the desert. For Jesus, the desert was a place of contact with God. It was a place where demons and wild beasts lived. Prior to this passage, Jesus was baptized by John and was given his mission by the Holy Spirit. He was then led by the Spirit into the desert. The temptation scene helps Jesus discern his mission.

Luke portrayed a threefold temptation. When Satan tempted Jesus with bread, Jesus quoted scripture to the devil. He referred to the passage in Deuteronomy, "not on bread alone does a person live." Jesus alludes to the nourishment provided by God in the desert. Manna rained down from heaven upon the hungry Israelites.

When Satan tempted Jesus to throw himself down from the temple, in order to demonstrate his (Jesus') power, Jesus again sought the aid of God's word. Jesus once again quoted Deuteronomy: "It also says, 'You shall not put the Lord your God to the test.'" Jesus asserted his authority with the evil one: no one was to put the Lord God to the test.

Through his encounter in the desert, Jesus discovered what his mission was *not to be.* It would not be a showy demonstration of power. The point is not to be missed. Jesus succeeded in the desert where Israel failed.

In Luke's gospel, the temptation in the desert serves as a story of encouragement. Christians were to be heartened by Jesus' victory over Satan's temptation. They were to learn how to recognize temptation and how to overcome it. Jesus was empowered by the Spirit. He would be tempted, but the Spirit who empowered him gave

[10]John F. Craghan, "Desert," in *The Collegeville Pastoral Dictionary of Biblical Theology,* ed. Carroll Stuhlmueller, C.P. (Collegeville: The Liturgical Press, 1996), 216.

him the strength to overcome temptation. The Spirit would do the same for the church. Jesus was victorious over Satan's allure because of his understanding and use of the scriptures, and because he was led by the power of the Holy Spirit. The Spirit prompted Jesus and provided the scriptures that Jesus needed to combat his enemy. The *word* is the weapon but the Spirit engages in the battle.

Jesus was understood as the *New Adam*. At the creation of the world, God created Adam, his son. Adam was the one with whom God began his mission of salvation. Jesus, the *New Adam*, was understood as the Son of God and the One who would complete God's saving mission. We are to view this story in light of all of God's saving actions since the creation of the world.

Satan wished to throw Jesus' discernment about his mission off balance. He wanted to trick him and confuse him. He mistranslated scripture in the hopes of "instilling a false understanding of what it means to be the Son of God who is anointed with the Spirit."[11] The devil tempted Jesus to falsely use his power as well as to misunderstand his mission. The event asserts Jesus' growth in wisdom regarding the mission he was destined to fulfill.

The tempter hoped that Jesus' hunger would cause him to misconstrue and misuse his power for self-advantage. Satan offered the false security of freedom from harm's way and the lure of invincibility. The great aphrodisiac of power was dangled before Jesus if he would only acquiesce and worship the Evil One.

Ultimately the temptation tested Jesus' commitment to the will of God. Luke used the temptation narrative to correct people's misconceptions about who Jesus was and how he used his power and authority. Today's gospel is a carefully crafted and powerful confession of *who Jesus was,* by demonstrating assertively *who he was not.*

Proclaim the gospel again.

---

[11]Robert C. Tannehill, *The Narrative Unity of Luke-Acts: A Literary Interpretation,* Vol. 1 (Minneapolis: Augsburg Fortress, 1986), 59.

Sometimes we gain new insights when we hear the text after the interpretation has been given. Someone from the group proclaims the gospel a second time.

STEP 4
TESTING

Conversation with the Liturgy and the Scriptures

Test your original understanding in dialogue with the text.

(You might consider breaking into smaller groups.)

Sharing Life Experience

Was there anything about the temptation story that was new information for you? How do you feel about it now? How does this story speak to your life?

My husband and I went away for a brief respite with friends. Our discussion turned to our relationship with God and the fact that we are God's chosen. We referred to ourselves by using an image from one of the late Henri Nouen's books. We called ourselves, "Beloved and Chosen." We spent our time reflecting on the implications of that term. We are in God's hands; we are in a trusting relationship. God does not disappoint and promises to be with us through the trials of life. As God's beloved and chosen we are called to responsible living: we are to use the gifts God has given us to the fullest; we are to share our blessings with others, and we are to tell others that they, too, are "beloved and chosen."

As a result of our time of reflection in the quiet meanderings of a weekend river cruise, one of our friends made the decision not to "settle" for the minimal, but to trust God, go with the leanings of her heart and hold out for the decision that she knew God was asking her to make. Her decision not only resulted in a career that fed her soul, but also had long-range effects on many children waiting to be placed in adoptive homes.

Very often we are tempted to choose one good thing over another good thing. Discipleship insists that we carefully discern the voice of God and be willing to risk. Our friend was taking a big risk by choosing the path she chose. Two positive choices were placed before her—one was a certainty, the other a risk.

The discernment of our small group reflections allowed her to own her "beloved-ness and chosen-ness." Free from fear, and in complete confidence, she was able to choose the work and ministry she was destined and supremely gifted to do. She opted to trust her heart and refused to settle for the mediocrity called "certainty." As "beloved and chosen" my friend permitted the deep, interior purification that touched the core of her being. Her enlightenment came when she risked enough to abandon herself into the complete care and will of God.

Lent asks us to look within and discover areas of sin and weakness: personal, social, and systemic. Lent also asks us to empty ourselves so that the illumination of Christ can fill us. My friend emptied herself, and in the process discovered her authentic self through the eyes of God. Our reflection on sin must be rooted in the awareness of our privileged status as God's beloved, God's chosen, and God's elect. Only then will we be able to scrutinize the overpowering effects of sin in our lives.

Participants share an experience from their lives that connects with the biblical interpretation just shared.

What was Luke trying to tell his community? How does this word speak to our community today? There are many images of the biblical themes of creation, covenant, exodus, and community inherent in all three readings. How do those themes impact the life of our community? How are the three temptations of Jesus relevant to our contemporary experience? Are there any situations going on in our parish that need the light of today's word? In what way have I/we known death/resurrection in our understanding of this gospel? Do I still feel the same way about this text as I did when we began? Has my/our original understanding been stretched, challenged, or affirmed?

STEP 5
DECISION

The gospel demands a response.

How does sharing and dialogue with the biblical interpretation challenge your community? What are the implications of today's readings? In what way does this gospel call your parish to action in the church, parish, neighborhood, or world? Be concrete. Has this conversation with the exegesis changed or stretched your personal attitudes? What are you called to do in response? Name one specific action you will take this week as a response to what you have learned and shared today.

DOCTRINAL ISSUES

What church truth/teaching/doctrinal issue could be drawn from the gospel for the First Sunday of Lent?

Participants suggest possible doctrinal themes that flow from the readings.

Possible Doctrinal Themes

Conversion, sin, paschal mystery, reconciliation, salvation

Present the doctrinal material at this time.

1. The facilitator gives input on a particular doctrinal issue of his/her prior choosing. OR
2. The group chooses a doctrinal issue from the list they created. They read together from the Doctrinal Appendix.

(The doctrinal issues are found in the Doctrinal Appendix in the back of this workbook. If you are choosing an issue from this resource, please refer to it now.)

Reflection questions centered around the chosen doctrinal theme can be found at the end of each topic in the Doctrinal Appendix. The questions are based on the five-step reflection process. If you choose a topic not included in the Doctrinal Appendix, craft your own questions according to the same five-step process.

Following the reflection questions you will be reminded to return to chapter 7, "Preparing the Catechetical Session," to assist you in crafting your own session.

Closing Prayer

Let us pray
[at the beginning of Lent
for the spirit of repentance]

Pause for silent prayer.

Lord, our God,
you formed man from the clay of the earth
and breathed into him the spirit of life,
but he turned from your face and sinned.
In this time of repentance
we call out for your mercy.
Bring us back to you
and to the life your Son won for us
by his death on the cross,
for he lives and reigns for ever and ever.[12]

Selected Bibliography

Craghan, John F. "Desert." In *The Collegeville Pastoral Dictionary of Biblical Theology.* Ed. Carroll Stuhlmueller, C.P. Collegeville: The Liturgical Press, 1996.

Days of the Lord, Vol. 2. Collegeville: The Liturgical Press, 1993.

Fuller, Reginald. *Preaching the New Lectionary.* Collegeville: The Liturgical Press, 1974.

Richards, Hubert. *The Gospel According to Paul.* Collegeville: The Liturgical Press, 1990.

Tannehill, Robert C. *The Narrative Unity of Luke-Acts: A Literary Interpretation,* Vol. 1. Minneapolis: Augsburg Fortress, 1986.

---

[12]First Sunday of Lent: "Alternative Opening Prayer," *The Sacramentary.*

SECOND SUNDAY OF LENT

INTRODUCTORY RITES

Opening Song (or Entrance Antiphon)

My heart has prompted me to seek your face; I seek it, Lord; so do not hide from me. (Ps. 26:8-9)[1]

Environment

Refer to Ash Wednesday

Opening Prayer

The facilitator of the session may lead the prayer. Others in the group may be asked to proclaim the readings.

Let us pray
for the grace to respond to the Word of God

Pause for silent prayer.

God our Father,
help us to hear your Son.
Enlighten us with your word,
that we may find the way to your glory.
We ask this through our Lord
Jesus Christ, your Son,
who lives and reigns with you
and the Holy Spirit,
one God, for ever and ever.[2]

LITURGY OF THE WORD

Let us listen to God's word.

The readings are proclaimed.

First Reading
Genesis 15:5-12

Today's first reading gives us a bird's eye view of why Abraham was a character of supreme importance in the Old Testament and New Testament.

Reginald Fuller asserts that there are three major tenets of Israel's identity, consciousness, and history inaugurated in today's story:
1. Abraham was promised that his descendants would live on in future generations. What God was doing in and through Abraham would survive in history.
2. God promised Israel a place to call home; he promised them their own land.
3. God sealed his promise with a covenant liturgy.[3]

Today's reading celebrates *the making of a people in covenant relationship with Yahweh.* God gratuitously intervened in the history of a people. God provided the grace and Abraham supplied the faith. This story reveals a God in relationship with a people. Fuller suggests that we are not to view this story of Abraham from the perspective of individual salvation, but rather as salvation offered to the people of God. All scripture heralds God's relationship to the community.

According to Kenneth Kuntz, the Genesis stories provide believers with an understanding of how ancient Israel understood her calling and her destiny.[4] In earlier chapters of Genesis, we are introduced to an Abraham who is a paragon of faith, virtue, and conviction. Abraham has a star role in God's plan of salvation as highlighted in Chapter 15. Abraham laments the fact that he has no natural heir. In ancient civilization, a childless couple could adopt an heir in order to ensure they would be cared for in old age. Abraham was planning on Eleazar to fulfill this role. However, Yahweh asserted that he alone would provide the heir for Abraham: Abraham would have his own natural son. Abraham was incredulous, as Sarah was very old. Yet he believed. Abraham asked Yahweh for a guarantee or a sign that he would follow through with his promise. Yahweh proceeded to celebrate a covenant ritual with Abraham, to "seal the deal."

---

[1]Second Sunday of Lent: "Entrance Antiphon," *The Sacramentary.*

[2]Second Sunday of Lent: "Opening Prayer," *The Sacramentary.*

[3]Reginald H. Fuller, *Preaching the New Lectionary* (Collegeville: The Liturgical Press, 1974), 3.

[4]Kenneth J. Kuntz, *The People of Ancient Israel* (New York: Harper and Row, 1974), 66.

In antiquity, contracts were entered into by slaughtering an animal. Each of the contractual parties stood by one of the divided animal parts and the agreement was signed, sealed, and delivered. The ritual itself provided a grave warning: *notice the plight of the dead animal; the same awaits you if you break this agreement.* It was serious business.

Thus, the contractual, covenant liturgy Yahweh presided over was laden with symbolic meaning. Abraham did not pass through the animal parts; only Yahweh passed through the parts. This was a sign of God's unconditional agreement to do what was promised. Yahweh alone was responsible for the contract.

The animal used in this contractual ritual was a bird of prey. Birds of prey were considered omens. They were probably used in this ritual as a foreshadowing of future enemies who would try to break the bond God was making with Abraham on behalf of Israel. The bird used in this covenant ritual was a symbolic warning to anyone who would "thwart the covenant, and more precisely, all that would lead humans to doubt God's commitment."[5]

Responsorial Psalm
Psalm 27:1, 7-8, 8-9, 13-14

The connection of this psalm to the gospel lies most obscurely in connection to the verse: "I shall see the goodness of the Lord in the land of the living." The land Yahweh gave to Abraham is the same land extolled in this psalm.

Second Reading
Philippians 3:17–4:1

As stated in the overview of Lent, the second reading during Lent is chosen for its connection to the gospel. St. Paul, in his letter to the Philippians, reminds believers that their earthly bodies will become transformed at the final eschaton. In today's gospel, Jesus becomes transformed in his glorified state before the eyes of his disciples.

Philippi was Paul's first stop on his westward missionary trip. Paul believed that the West was as anxious to accept the Good News of Christ as was the East. He therefore set out to evangelize the western cities. Some maintain that since the Philippians were his first converts, Paul treated them with greater affection and deference than his other communities.

Some communities accused Paul of taking advantage of the people's generosity, so he refused to accept preaching stipends from those communities. Instead, he worked as he journeyed, thus paying his own way. However, he did accept subsistence from the Philippians' church; they financed his southern missionary efforts.

Paul's preaching created a stir while he was in Ephesus on one of his missionary tours. Paul wrote his letter of gratitude to the Philippians from his jail cell. Paul's letter was very joyful, which is noteworthy in light of his circumstances: imprisonment and an impending death sentence. His love of God and subsequent joy so completely consumed him that he considered his death to be inconsequential in light of his relationship to Christ.

Paul's letter to the Philippians gives us the best insight into his personality and inner feelings. He shared his heart with his beloved Philippian church. "It is only natural that I should feel this towards you all, since you have shared the privileges which have been mine...how much I miss you all" (Phil 1: 7-8).[6]

The church was threatened by all kinds of aberrant philosophies during Paul's missionary years. In today's pericope Paul offered himself as a model to follow: "Be imitators of me..." (Phil 1:17). Paul reminded them that even in the worldly plane of existence they were still citizens of heaven with all the rights and privileges of citizenship. Baptism was their powerful sign of citizenship and allegiance to Christ. Paul reminded believers that Christ was going to return and that his followers would experience transformation. This transformation included a complete and total metamorphosis: a glorified body, soul, nature, and spirit. Paul encouraged his favored com-

---

[5]*Days of the Lord,* Vol. 2 (Collegeville: The Liturgical Press, 1993), 89.

[6]Hubert Richards, *The Gospel According to St. Paul* (Collegeville: The Liturgical Press, 1990), 65-76.

munity to be strong in their commitment and to see the race through to the very end.

Gospel
Luke 9:28-36

Jesus is transfigured before the eyes of his disciples.

STEP 1
NAMING ONE'S EXPERIENCE

What were your first impressions? What was your first response? What grabbed your attention? How did you feel?

Each person names his or her initial impression. Statement should be brief. No reasons should be given at this time. All simply listen without agreeing or disagreeing.

STEP 2
UNDERSTANDING

In a brief statement, what do you think this gospel is trying to convey?

STEP 3
INPUT FROM VISION/STORY/TRADITION

Liturgical Context

Today's liturgy is resplendent with the biblical images of *covenant*. God entered into a covenant with a people, a covenant that began at the *creation* of the world. Because of Abraham's faith, a nation was born that would last forever. God would never forsake the community he formed. We are told to remember. Remembering for Israel and for us today is a special kind of remembering. It is a remembering that looks to the stories of the past and brings them into the present as a living reality. It is called anamnesis. The covenant made with Abraham is an ongoing, living covenant made with a nation—a people. Yahweh's covenant continued through the generations and was fulfilled in the exodus—the

Passover of Jesus Christ. Yahweh entered into a contractual agreement with Israel through a ritual of assurance. The new sign of Yahweh's covenant in Christ is his cross. We profess, remember, and make present its saving effects every time the church gathers for prayer. The eucharist is a living memorial, an anamnesis of the new covenant through the cross of Jesus Christ.

St. Paul attests that we are already citizens of the holy city because of Jesus' cross. Today's liturgy asks the ultimate question: To what place will we assign our citizenship? Will we choose heaven or the world, life or death?

Yahweh ratifies his promise with Abraham in a ritual ceremony. Yahweh continues to ratify his covenant with us through the celebration of the sacraments and primarily through the eucharist.

The transfiguration is a moment of decision to forge on to Jerusalem and ultimately the cross. Lent tests our willingness to die, to rise and ultimately to journey deeply into the heart of the paschal mystery. It is a time not only to prepare for the Easter sacraments, but also to renew and recommit to our belief in the resurrection.[7] Ritual prayers from today's liturgy express this well:

> Lord,
> make us holy.
> May this eucharist take away our sins
> that we may be prepared
> to celebrate the resurrection.
> We ask this in the name of Jesus the Lord.[8]

Lent places us at a crossroad and reminds us of the paradox of the Christian life. Jesus' Passover was humility, suffering, and death; but it was also light, glory, and life. Lent is a test. We must choose. The Christian journey always requires a choice. We must choose between the cross and the world. We assess past choices and discern future choices. We make adjustments where adjustments are needed and we do so with confidence and faith. Each liturgy is a transfiguration event in which we are brought to a moment of choice:

---

[7]*Days of the Lord,* Vol. 2, 92.

[8]Second Sunday of Lent: "Prayer over the Gifts," *The Sacramentary.*

Which way will we go? How will we live what we just celebrated? We are not to miss the point that Luke drives home throughout his entire gospel. Encounters with God occur when Jesus prays. Encounters with God occur when the church prays.

Gospel Exegesis

The facilitator gives input regarding what critical biblical scholarship has to say about this text. The input includes insights as to how people would have heard the gospel in Jesus' time.

Reginald Fuller maintains that there are three traditional ways to interpret the pericopes of the gospel: what actually happened, how the story was orally transmitted (understood) by the Christian community, and how the evangelist used the story. Fuller suggests a fourth way to understand the texts: *how they are interpreted and what they might mean to a gathered liturgical assembly.*

Fuller names the *givens* of this story: Jesus went up to the mountain after he broke off his ministry in Galilee. There was a change in plans. We are told of a trip to Jerusalem and the meaning of the trip. "The original meaning of the incident was that it inaugurated the final stage of the ministry."[9]

In light of Fuller's fourth level of understanding, one scholar suggests an interesting interpretation of the story. The following exegesis is based on Barbara Reid's proposed scenario and interpretation of the transfiguration.[10]

In Luke's version, Jesus went up the mountain *to pray.* Mark does not say why he went up the mountain. Jesus took Peter, James and John apart by themselves (just as he was to do on the day of his agony in the garden). Prior to this event, Jesus had been healing, teaching and experiencing success in his initial mission. Tension builds during the journey section of Luke's gospel known as "on the road to Jerusalem." Jesus' destination becomes more evident. He is apprehensive about having to go to Jerusalem, but he

faithfully forges onward. Jesus' instructions to the disciples intensify; his mission picks up in pace and urgency. Jesus passionately challenges his followers to understand the implications of his teaching.

Jerusalem was the headquarters of religious power and authority. If Jesus' mission was going to bring about the change that needed to happen, then he would have to go to the seat of religious power and authority. There was no other way; he had to go to Jerusalem. Yet, there was still so much to do in Galilee; there were still so many people searching for God and for meaning in their lives. "Should I go, should I stay?" Perhaps these concerns weighed heavily on Jesus' heart. Perhaps he was wrestling with God over the direction of his mission. Jesus knew where to find his answer and his strength: in intimate prayer with his Father. He gathered three of his disciples and together they went up the mountain to pray. Traditionally, mountains are places of profound theophanies.

Perhaps Jesus' discernment sounded something like this:

> *Jesus:* "My loving, compassionate Father, hear me. Help me discover your will. If I stay here, I can continue my ministry to your people: praying, healing, teaching, and exorcizing. Your people are broken. They are poor, hungry, and dejected. They are oppressed by systems that keep them on the bottom with no hope of rising to the top. Your precious, broken children, those most in need of your love and consolation, are even oppressed by the very religious structures that should offer them your love, hope, and consolation. I must do something. There is so much more to do; I must continue, I am not finished. Loving God, if I go to Jerusalem, it is over; they will kill me."

> *God:* "But, Son, you have done all you can do here. You must go to the seat of power. You must go to Jerusalem. You will understand soon enough."

Enter Moses and Elijah on the scene. Scholars have two opinions about the appearance of these

---

[9]Fuller, *Preaching the New Lectionary*, 4.

[10]Barbara Reid, "The Gospel of Mark in the Liturgical Year," Workshop: Church of Our Saviour, October, 1996.

two characters in the transfiguration scene. One opinion refers to the ancient tradition that believed that Moses and Elijah did not die in the natural sense, but were *taken up* into the next life, and would reappear before the inauguration of the messianic age. Thus, Moses and Elijah appeared on the mountain of transfiguration because they were the *heralds* of the messianic age that Jesus was about to initiate through his death and resurrection.

A second opinion regarding the appearance of Moses and Elijah centers around Israel's foundation: the law and the prophets. Jesus was the fulfillment of all the expectations of the law and the prophetic utterances of the prophets. Those who subscribe to this second theory suggest that the departure of Moses and Elijah from Mount Tabor signaled the arrival of the messianic age. Jesus would henceforth take up where the law and the prophets left off. Faith was now to be centered in Jesus Christ—not the law and not the prophets.[11]

Luke is the only evangelist who allows us to eavesdrop on the mountaintop conversation. Moses and Elijah speak of the *exodus* Jesus was about to experience in Jerusalem. "They appeared in glory and spoke of his *passage* which he was about to fulfill in Jerusalem." There were two different meanings to the word *passage* (Greek: *exodus).* One meaning was liberation and the other was death.

Luke does not use the word *transfiguration.* "His face *changed* in appearance." Jesus had an "A-ha" moment, the kind that knocks us off balance, makes us shake our head in incredulity and say, "Wow!" Jesus experienced an incredible insight, and it was *reflected on his face.* All of a sudden it all makes sense—Jesus understands the big picture. Now he knows what needs to happen and why. His death was not to be the end of his mission, but the fulfillment of it. His death meant liberation. He had to go to Jerusalem; it was the only way. His mission on earth was accomplished. There was nothing left for him to do. He left a living legacy, a living memorial. Jesus had to die. He had to "give

his life as a ransom for the many." Through his death, the gates of heaven would be opened and his ministry of healing and liberation would last forever. It made perfect sense.

Jesus' face had to change. The revelation was so profound, the *shekina* glory so great, that it was "written all over his face." Profound revelation is often accompanied by a change in facial expression, such as happened to Hanna when she learned she would have a child (Sam 1:1). Some of the stories of early martyrs reflect a changed expression on their faces. "The members of the Sanhedrin who sat there stared at him intently. Throughout, Stephen's face seemed like that of an angel" (Acts 6:15). In other instances we are told of martyrs who went to their day of victory cheerful and *bright of countenance.* Thus, from Luke's version of the transfiguration, it is possible to conclude that the theophany on Mount Tabor was for Jesus an encounter, a turning point, and the impetus to go forward to Jerusalem, to his ultimate death.

The secondary focus in the story of the transfiguration is the disciples. They are part of the story; it is told for their benefit. They are witnesses to this epiphany. They see it on Jesus' face. Peter wants to pitch a tent; to stay there; to bask in the glory (how human!). Peter wants to stay on the mountain of glory. *The whole point of the story, however, is that we need to proceed to Jerusalem; we may not stay in Galilee.* The transfiguration was for the benefit of the disciples! Some day, when they needed it most, they would reflect back on the experience and remember. In moments when the decision to stay or to go remained hanging in the balance, they would remember this night. When staying seemed more comfortable than going, they would remember this night. *This transition moment, this turning point in Jesus' life and mission, would be remembered and it would urge them onward.* Unfortunately, suggests Barbara Reid, the story was told, retold, and recast as a story of transfiguration rather than as a turning point.

The last scene in today's unfolding drama opens with the familiar voice from heaven telling the disciples: "This is my beloved Son, my Chosen One, listen to him." The last time we heard that Voice was at Jesus' baptism by John in the Jordan. It was

[11]Patricia Datchuck Sanchez, *The Word We Celebrate* (Kansas City: Sheed and Ward, 1989), 286.

the Spirit, not John, who baptized Jesus in the Jordan, thereby establishing and empowering his mission. Following Jesus' baptism, the Spirit led him into the desert to be tested by the devil. Jesus' desert scene, as we learned last week, was for the purpose of discerning the scope of his mission. He discovered what his mission was intended to be—a reign of service, love, and self-offering.

Today's gospel brings us full circle. We are brought back to memories of Jesus' baptism. With Moses, Elijah, and the disciples, we too encounter the Voice. We hear the same words that inaugurated Jesus' initial mission: "This is my beloved son, listen to him." The Voice first spoke to Jesus at his baptism. Now the Voice speaks to Jesus' companions, the disciples. This is what it means to be "beloved Son." It means head for Jerusalem.

Luke allowed us to be intimate viewers of Jesus' private moments of decision. We were present at Jesus' baptism when the Spirit inaugurated his mission and empowered his ministry. We were present in the desert as the Spirit led Jesus through the temptations that would help him discern his mission. We are present at Tabor as Jesus encounters yet another moment of decision and commitment. We are invited into the privileged intimacy as Jesus is helped to understand his final fulfillment and the ultimate consequences of his faithful mission.

Jesus went to the mountain to pray and, in the process, discovered who he was. As he tasted his future glorification, the heavens opened and the Father's Voice cried out: "This is my beloved Son." It was an awakening for Jesus. For the first time in salvation history, the law (Moses) and the prophets (Elijah) came together to testify to the day of fulfillment and to profess to the world, "Jesus Christ is Lord!"

Luke very artfully invites his readers into the intimacy. There are no detached bystanders. By being made privy to such profound intimacy, we are invited to embrace the journey. Every Lent is a renewed invitation to embrace the journey.

Jesus would experience one more turning point—Gethsemane. Today's gospel is cast in the light of Gethsemane. There is little question that Gethse-

mane is a moment of decision. Perhaps Gethsemane shows us how we should read the transfiguration event. Similarities between the two stories suggest that Luke considered them to be related. At Gethsemane and at the transfiguration, Peter, James and John go with Jesus to pray. At both events the apostles are overcome with sleep, while Jesus prays.

At Gethsemane the question of God's will erupts.

Jesus: "Father, let this pass. Surely there must be some other way! However, let your will be done, not mine."

God: "My Son, what I *will* is the liberation of all my people. I will life, not death. I do not *will* your murder, I do not *will* your death, but I *do will* the liberation of my people. Go, do what you must do, be faithful to my word as you have always been faithful. Your liberating death is necessary to the resurrection. The only way is through the cross."

One scholar suggests that God never willed Jesus' death. He could not will it. Jesus' death was an immoral, evil act. God would never will an evil act. Jesus was murdered; God does not will murder. However, God did will Jesus' faithfulness. His faithfulness ultimately led to the free offering of his life in death. Jesus' death is the result of the life and ministry that preceded it.

When we seek God, the joy of our encounter is reflected on our faces. What happened to Jesus also happens to us. What do our faces say to the world? Do our faces express the paradox? We, too, have those moments in which we have to face our decisions. They may not always be life-and-death situations; they may simply be a fork in the road. What road will we take, the road less traveled or the freeway at rush hour? Will our decisions be life-giving for those most in need of liberation, or will they be self-serving?

Proclaim the gospel again.

Sometimes we gain new insights when we hear the text after the interpretation has been given. Someone from the group proclaims the gospel a second time.

Conversation with the Liturgy and the Scriptures

Test your original understanding in dialogue with the text.

(You might consider breaking into smaller groups.)

Were there any "A-ha" moments for you? Any new insights? How is this a difficult word? How does your original understanding of this story compare with what you just shared? How does this story speak to your life?

Sharing Life Experience

Participants share an experience from their lives that connects with the biblical interpretation just shared.

Today's liturgy reminds me of the ultimate journey to Jerusalem and the price we all must pay. Parish life is the most wonderful sign of God's presence in our midst. We experience the joys of dying and rising each day. My parish is a wonderful place. It is home, it is a cocoon, and it is a testing ground for the exodus in today's readings. It is a tremendously graced place. Like all communities in scripture we have been on a journey. Sometimes we listen and other times we do not. Our story reads like a chapter out of any one of the bible's books. It is a story of joy, struggle, victory, defeat, grace, and sin. We would not be a community if that were not so.

I have been formed by the joys and struggles of living in community. For eleven years I have been part of a parish that attempts to live the gospel message. I am amazed at how God has fashioned and formed us as a people. People experience the sacrament of Christ alive in our church. We have grown over the years.

One area of growth is in our social response to the gospel. Over the years we have moved toward a corporate response to the social demands of the gospel, and not without controversy. We have had to endure some negativity because of a few of our gospel choices. There were times "our road to Jerusalem" was painful. There was controversy when we began our cold night ministry to the homeless. There was

strife when we made the decision to tithe ten percent of the parish income to the poor and disadvantaged of the world. There was discord when our pastor preached the seamless garment. There was conflict over preaching that professed our responsibility to third-world countries. There was dissension when we spoke in favor of saving the environment. There was discontent when we encouraged people to contact their politicians and encourage a fair, just, and loving response to welfare reform laws. We have been accused of being too political and not political enough. Every parish has the same tensions if it is consciously living the gospel of Jesus Christ.

Having expressed the discord, the cross, let me now celebrate the unity, the good news, the stories of resurrection. While I stated there was controversy, the percentage of complaining parishioners was minimal. In earlier days there was far more controversy over such issues than there is today. Today, service and justice form a part of who we are; they are the way we "do" church. We recently built an entire school in Haiti and are preparing to furnish it with books, desks, and teachers at this writing. We financially supported the introduction of a water filtering system in the Dominican Republic and Africa. Our parish supports a family and an outreach ministry in the Appalachian mountains. We tithe about $35,000 to the needs of the poor. We support our parish teens in their immersion experience in the Dominican Republic every year. We have built several homes for "Habitat for Humanity." There is an active St. Vincent de Paul ministry that accomplishes many wonderful things for the immediate needs of the city's poor. Our parish has assumed a leadership role in city decisions on issues concerning the homeless and restriction of immoral business establishments. Thirty percent of our parish schoolchildren attend our school on scholarship. All this is in addition to the normal Catholic charitable endeavors and collections.

Our parish supports and sustains ministry to the elderly in which the emotional, physical, and spiritual needs of our senior citizens are a high priority. Our old convent was transformed into an on-site home for mobile elderly women. I could go on and on. The list is endless. I have mentioned only the ways we corporately respond to the gospel. There would not be enough paper to address the response of individuals. While this seems like bragging (perhaps it is!), it is *offered for an entirely different reason. The activities mentioned here are not "above and beyond the call" of everyday parish life; they are expectations inherent in living the gospel. When we "do" what the gospel demands, we have "set our face toward Jerusalem" with all its consequences. We are called to respond to the needs of the world, whether our response is popular or not. The gospel does not say, "Feed the hungry, care for the oppressed, preach an uncomfortable gospel unless doing so would make people give less money to the parish coffers." Unfortunately, our poor pastors today are faced with the mounting costs of parish life. "Rocking the boat" has serious implications. I thank God I am in a community in which the gospel is professed and lived (albeit imperfectly at times). Praise God that we are still "in process"; that God is not finished with us yet; that we have only just begun and that we still have a long way to go. Jerusalem still lies before us.*

All share their life experience.

What was Luke trying to teach his community? What are the areas in your communal life that are in need of an "A-ha" moment of decision and transfiguration? The biblical themes of creation, covenant, exodus, and community are very prevalent in today's readings. How do they relate to your everyday life? How is your community:
a. being recreated,
b. living the covenant and promise with God in Christ,
c. experiencing death and resurrection and
d. understanding its role as a community?

What is your collective and personal response to all of the above questions? Do you still feel the same way about this text as you did when we began? Has your original understanding been stretched, challenged, or affirmed?

STEP 5
DECISION

The gospel demands a response.

In what way does this gospel call our parish to action in the church, parish, neighborhood, or world? Be concrete. Have I experienced *change* as

a result of this conversation with the scriptures? In what concrete way am I and are we challenged to respond?

DOCTRINAL ISSUES

What church truth/teaching/doctrinal issue could be drawn from the gospel for the Second Sunday of Lent?

Participants suggest possible doctrinal themes that flow from the readings.

Possible Doctrinal Themes

Paschal mystery, repentance, cross, conversion

Present the doctrinal material at this time.

1. The facilitator gives input on a particular doctrinal issue of his/her prior choosing. OR
2. The group chooses a doctrinal issue from the list they created. They read together from the Doctrinal Appendix.

(The doctrinal issues are found in the Doctrinal Appendix in the back of this workbook. If you are choosing an issue from this resource, please refer to it now.)

Reflection questions centered around the chosen doctrinal theme can be found at the end of each topic in the Doctrinal Appendix. The questions are based on the five-step reflection process. If you choose a topic not included in the Doctrinal Appendix, craft your own questions according to the same five-step process.

Following the reflection questions you will be reminded to return to chapter 7, "Preparing the Catechetical Session," to assist you in crafting your own session.

Closing Prayer

Father, all powerful and ever-living God,
we do well always and everywhere to give you
    thanks
through Jesus Christ our Lord.

On your holy mountain he revealed himself in
   glory
in the presence of his disciples.
He had already prepared them for his approaching death.
He wanted to teach them through the Law and
   the Prophets
that the promised Christ had first to suffer
and so come to the glory of his resurrection.
In our unending joy we echo on earth
the song of the angels in heaven
as they praise your glory for ever.[12]

Selected Bibliography

Days of the Lord. Vol. 2. Collegeville: The Liturgical
   Press, 1993.
Fuller, Reginald F. *Preaching the New Lectionary.* Col-
   legeville: The Liturgical Press, 1971.
Kuntz, Kenneth J. *The People of Ancient Israel.* New
   York: Harper and Row, 1974.
Richards, Hubert. *The Gospel According to St. Paul.*
   Collegeville: The Liturgical Press, 1990.
Sanchez, Patricia Datchuck. *The Word We Celebrate.*
   Kansas City: Sheed and Ward, 1989.

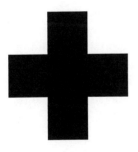

---

[12]Second Sunday of Lent : "Preface," *The Sacramentary.*

Third Sunday of Lent

INTRODUCTORY RITES

Opening Song (or Entrance Antiphon)

I will prove my holiness through you. I will gather you from the ends of the earth; I will pour clean water on you and wash away all your sins. I will give you a new spirit within you, says the Lord. (Ez 36:23-26)[1]

Opening Prayer

The facilitator of the session may lead the prayer. Others in the group may be asked to proclaim the readings.

Let us pray
[for confidence in the love of God
and the strength to overcome all our weakness]

Pause for silent prayer.

Father,
you have taught us to overcome our sins
by prayer, fasting and works of mercy.
When we are discouraged by our weakness,
give us confidence in your love.
We ask this through our Lord
Jesus Christ, your Son,
who lives and reigns with you and the Holy
    Spirit,
one God, for ever and ever.[2]

LITURGY OF THE WORD

Let us listen to God's word.

The readings are proclaimed.

First Reading
Exodus 3:1-8a, 13-15

All of today's readings can be viewed from the perspective of the first reading in which God is named: "I am who Am." Most scholars would translate that to mean: The One who causes to be what comes into existence. God is a God who is personally involved in the lives of people; God acts in human history.

Bernhard Anderson suggests that today's reading is a type of narrative biblical literature that represents the divine calling and commissioning of a prophetic figure.[3] The story resembles the call of Jeremiah. There is dialogue with God; God assures Jeremiah of his presence, and a sign is given.

Moses experiences a theophany. The wilderness place is transformed into sacred ground. Moses is both awed and frightened by the deity. However, this is not just any deity, but *Elohim,* the God of Abraham, Isaac and Jacob, the God who intervenes in human history, who cares about the suffering and oppression of his people. "God of pathos is sensitive to the human condition and participates in human history with saving power."[4] Today's reading depicts the basis for Israel's historical faith. Yahweh is a God who not only speaks and promises, but also acts and delivers.

In today's scene Moses was given a job to do. He was summoned to participate in the historical human drama God was unfolding. Moses exemplified the typical human response of fear and trepidation. He remained comfortable, preferring the role of passive spectator to that of a history-making change-agent.

If he were to go to Pharaoh, Moses would need to know Yahweh's name in order to identify God to Pharaoh. In antiquity, gods were named in relationship to their traits and personalities. There was strength and life in a name. A person's name revealed his or her personhood, each one's very soul. In antiquity a personal relationship with an individual required that the name be known. If one

---

[1]Third Sunday of Lent: "Entrance Antiphon," *The Sacramentary.*

[2]Third Sunday of Lent: "Opening Prayer," *The Sacramentary.*

[3]Bernhard W. Anderson, *Understanding the Old Testament,* 4th ed. (Englewood Cliffs: Prentice Hall, 1986), 59.

[4]Abraham J. Heschel, *The Prophets* (New York: Harper and Row, Pub., 1963), 315.

wanted a personal experience of God, the Name of God would have to be known (even though God was the Ineffable, Nameless Other).[5] According to one interpretation, God named himself in this pericope as the *One who promised to go with Moses, to be with him.* "Thus, the divine name signifies God, whose being is turned toward the people, who is present in their midst as deliverer and guide, and judge, and who is accessible in worship."[6]

Ultimately, for Israel, the name of Yahweh signified a relationship. Yahweh was the Remembered One who heard the cries of his suffering, oppressed people and subsequently delivered them from their oppression. The worship of Yahweh recognized God's action in history, extolled God's covenant, and lived by its demands.

Responsorial Psalm
Psalm 103: 1-4, 6-8, 11

This is Israel's song of the exodus. It praises the God of Moses who delivers, frees, and liberates: the God of mercy and love. This psalm became the hymn of the Christian community as it appropriated the liberating effects of the exodus to Jesus Christ.

Second Reading
1 Corinthians 10:1-6, 10-12

Corinth was a Greek city that was demolished in 146 B.C.E. and restored a century later. The diversity of Corinth was very apparent in the disparity between the very wealthy and the very poor. Most of those on the lower end of society's ladder were slaves. Corinth was an intellectual center that played host to many aberrant religious philosophies and doctrines. Paul preached and ministered in Corinth for about eighteen months and his community reflected the philosophical and religious diversity in the city. Paul's community was under a great deal of pressure because of the temptations and lures of the culture's religious and intellectual oddities. People were succumbing to pagan influences.

The Corinthians, like their ancient counterparts, were beginning to take God's gifts and promise of salvation for granted. Some believed that baptism and eucharist were all that was necessary for salvation. Paul referred to the Old Testament's identifying story of exodus to set the record and beliefs straight. Paul referred to the passing through the Red Sea as baptism into Moses. Similarly, Christians are baptized into Jesus through baptism, the new exodus. The exodus established Israel as God's people who were working out their salvation with him through their history. Baptism, on the other hand, establishes Christians in the same way.[7] Baptism ushers in Christ's redemptive action in the salvation history of the neophyte.

Paul referred to the manna and drink of the desert in the context of the Christian community's experience of eucharist. Manna and the drink of the desert were prefigured metaphors for the sacraments of baptism and eucharist. "Sacraments are quite literally a 'viaticum'—a nourishment of the pilgrim people of God on its way from Pentecost to the Second Coming."[8] The meaning of the exodus manna and drink was now to be appropriated to the Christian understanding of eucharist: nourishment, food for the journey, living sign of Jesus the Liberator, the Healer, the Provider, and the One who Sustains.

Paul does not hesitate to remind his readers that in spite of God's relationship to the wilderness people, they still failed. God was not pleased with them. They insisted on following their own way, rather than the way God had destined for them. Their food and drink did not "erase the wickedness of a people."[9] "Neither, therefore, could the gifts of the new covenant (baptism, eucharist, etc.) negate the sin of a stubborn and recalcitrant people. Sacramental grace cannot substitute for the believer's cooperative efforts at good living and loving service."[10]

---

[5]The personal name of God was pronounced Yahweh. The word, Halleluya, literally translated, means "Praise Yahweh," using the shortened form of Yahweh—Yah. Thus, Halleluya was an acclamation of praise for the personal God, Yahweh.

[6]Anderson, *Understanding the Old Testament*, 62.

[7]For further information refer to: Patricia Datchuck Sanchez, *The Word We Celebrate* (Kansas City: Sheed and Ward, 1986), 288.

[8]Reginald H. Fuller, *Preaching the New Lectionary* (Collegeville: The Liturgical Press, 1971), 6.

[9]Sanchez, *The Word We Celebrate*, 288.

[10]Ibid.

Gospel

Luke 13:1-9

Jesus tells the parable of the fig tree.

STEP 1
NAMING ONE'S EXPERIENCE

What were your first impressions? What was your first response? What grabbed your attention? How did you feel?

Each person names his or her initial impression. Statement should be brief. No reasons should be given at this time. All simply listen without agreeing or disagreeing.

STEP 2
UNDERSTANDING

In a brief statement, what do you think this gospel is trying to convey?

STEP 3
INPUT FROM VISION/STORY/TRADITION

Liturgical Context

There is a common theme that runs through all three readings today. God is a God who is personally involved in the lives of people; God acts in human history. God hears the cries of his people in bondage and sends Moses to deliver them (First Reading). God refreshes them with water from the Rock (Second Reading) and God sends his Son to "give people one last chance to repent and accept his salvation."[11]

Today's gospel leads us to ask, "Who, then, is God?" In light of the gospel we may profess with assurance: God is the One who has ultimate patience and mercy when dealing with human beings. God is the One who holds out the hand of mercy and offers another chance to the repentant sinner.

---

[11]Fuller, *Preaching the New Lectionary*, 5.

Both opening prayers for today's liturgy imply the demands of repentance as suggested in today's exegesis. "You have taught us to overcome our sins by prayer, fasting and works of mercy..." and "...to heal the wounds our sins and selfishness bring upon us you bid us turn to fasting, prayer and sharing...."[12]

We are reminded that through our sharing in the eucharist we are forgiven anew and peace is restored. We may not be complacent or think of the eucharist in a magical way. The eucharist is for the forgiveness of repentant sinners. It calls us to live the life we share in Christ. There is nothing magical. We choose to live it or we do not, but the choice is ours. Today's Communion Antiphon asks for the grace to make the right choice.

> Lord,
> in sharing this sacrament
> may we receive your forgiveness
> and be brought together in unity and peace.
> We ask this through Christ our Lord.[13]

Gospel Exegesis — *Critical interpretation*

The facilitator gives input regarding what critical biblical scholarship has to say about this text. The input includes insights as to how people would have heard the gospel in Jesus' time.

Today's pericope is cast in light of two disastrous situations: a tower that had fallen on unsuspecting victims (natural cause) and Pilate's assassination of Galileans (a human cause). Someone asked Jesus to comment about the judgment of those who had experienced the trouble. A commonly held belief during Jesus' time was that disaster was a sign of God's curse due to sin, and good fortune was a sign of God's blessings due to righteousness. Jews would have believed themselves righteous as evidenced by the tranquility of their lives. They might have thought: "Obviously the victims were sinners. Since I do not have such troubles, why should I repent?"

---

[12]Third Sunday of Lent: "Opening and Alternative Opening Prayer," *The Sacramentary*.

[13]Third Sunday of Lent: "Communion Antiphon," *The Sacramentary*.

144

fig tree parable

Jesus asserts emphatically that disaster is not the result of sin. *All* people must repent. It has nothing to do with whether a person is cursed or blessed. To drive home his point he tells them a parable about a fig tree.

The fig tree was a symbol of God's blessing of the land of Israel. In Deuteronomy it is named as characteristic of the promised land. The fig tree is the only tree mentioned in Adam and Eve's paradise (they covered their nakedness with its leaves). Destruction of the fig tree also represented a curse on the land (Am 4:9). Thus, the fig tree was used as a metaphor for blessings and curses. Good figs were allusions to the righteous, and bad figs to the unrighteous. Ultimately, the common biblical metaphor of the fig tree was associated with the blessings of God and the dawning of the messianic age.[14]

The tree in today's story is barren and fruitless (thus unrighteous). To illustrate how barren the tree is, we are told that it is beyond the third year of cultivation, which, under normal conditions, meant that the tree was beyond restoration and would have to be cut down. However, the tree was given a reprieve, one more chance, one more hope for growth. Talbert suggests that Jesus' point was clear: just because the tree was not cut down, did not experience God's judgment, and was given a reprieve, does not mean that it was not deserving of judgment or punishment.[15] By all normal standards, it should have been cut down. It was spared only because of the vine dresser's mercy. Regardless of righteousness or the lack of it, the tree (the unfruitful fig—the unrighteous) was allowed to remain *simply because of God's mercy*. The implication? All must repent, turn from no growth—death—to new growth—life. "The parable indicates that mercy is available for all who repent in time."[16]

Bernard Brandon Scott asserts a slightly different interpretation. This seemingly barren fig tree still has hope. The end of the story is not told in the parable. It is left to still be worked out. The parable is a metaphor about the present kingdom of God. The reign of God is still in process. We keep on fertilizing and tending because it is all there is to do; it is the way things are. We are left with the reality of the kingdom in the here and now.

Robert Tannehill links the parable of the fig tree with an overall theme of repentance that began with John the Baptist: a sign of repentance is the sharing of clothing and food with the needy.[17] Those who do not heed the commands of justice will be judged accordingly. True repentance will lead to biblical justice. This understanding is consonant with our present day understanding of the lenten disciplines of prayer, fasting, and almsgiving.

Proclaim the gospel again.

Sometimes we gain new insights when we hear the text after the interpretation has been given. Someone from the group proclaims the gospel a second time.

STEP 4
TESTING

Conversation with the Liturgy and the Scriptures

Test your original understanding in dialogue with the text.

(You might consider breaking into smaller groups.)

After hearing the exegesis, what are your impressions about the readings now? Were there any new insights? Was there anything you had not considered before? How does your original understanding of this story compare with what you just shared? How does this story speak to your life?

Sharing Life Experience

Participants share an experience from their lives that connects with the biblical interpretation just shared.

---

[14]For further information, consult Bernard Brandon Scott, *Hear Then the Parable* (Minneapolis: Augsburg Fortress, 1989), 331-342.

[15]Charles Talbert, *Reading Luke* (New York: Crossroad, 1992), 145.

[16]I. Howard Marshall, *The Gospel of Luke,* New International Greek Testament Commentary Series (Grand Rapids: Wm. B. Eerdmans, 1978), 552.

[17]Robert C. Tannehill, *The Narrative Unity of Luke-Acts: A Literary Interpretation,* Vol. 1 (Minneapolis: Augsburg Fortress, 1986), 50-51.

A hallmark of twelve-step groups is to acknowledge a person's powerlessness over the offending substance and to acknowledge the sovereignty of a "Power Greater than Themselves" as the only way to overcome the demon. We have much to learn from people in recovery. They live the image of repentance expressed in today's gospel. The Israelites learned how to name the "Ineffable One." Addicts name and describe their Power by the gratuitous act of mercy bestowed on them: "the One who liberated and set us free from the chains of death." In a sense, they know God by the great act of deliverance God accomplished for them. They realize their only road to continued recovery is diligence in sharing their "Power" with others caught in the same chain of death. A sign of their repentance is willingness to offer love, compassion, and mercy to other sick souls. God reached out and touched them with mercy.

I often ask myself why some make it into recovery and others never make it. Nearly every homeless person who enters our doors is addicted to some substance. Most are in the last stages of addiction. They know powerlessness like no one else. Despair has been such a common companion that it seems as if desire for change was long ago anesthetized. Yet, we must believe that the hope of today's gospel is a reality for them too. No one should ever give up on extending the offer of hope or the hand of mercy. We never know when their "day of the Lord" will arrive.

My tranquil, peaceful life (by comparison) is no assurance that I stand in better light before God than my homeless friends. No doubt my responsibility is greater: "to those who have been given much, much will be expected." My prayer and fasting must extend to sharing. It is the only way those disciplines do not become self-deceiving, self-serving exercises. Human beings are masters at self-deception. Without the continued, humble posture of repentance I become just like those who asked Jesus the question in the first place: people whose hearts are filled with self-righteous indignation, rather than the love of God. "Please, God, you heal the wounds of my sinfulness and selfishness by insisting that I pray, fast, and serve my brothers and sisters. I acknowledge my sinfulness and become discouraged over my repeated attempts to change. Compassionate God of Mercy, may your mercy fill me with hope and lead me

through this lenten time of repentance to the resurrected joy of Easter."[18]

All share their life experience.

What was Jesus telling his followers and what was Luke's message to his community? How is the parable of the fig tree a word for our community today? How are we called to change as a result of today's readings? How do the biblical images of creation, covenant, exodus, and community speak to us through these readings and what are the implications of those themes? Do I still feel the same way about these texts as I did when we began? Has our original understanding been stretched, challenged, or affirmed?

STEP 5
DECISION

The gospel demands a response.

How are our community's attitudes challenged by today's readings? In what concrete way does this gospel call our parish to responsible action? What are the implications of today's liturgy for my life? What is one concrete action I will take this week as a response to what we have learned and shared today?

DOCTRINAL ISSUES

What church truth/teaching/doctrinal issue could be drawn from the gospel for the Third Sunday of Lent?

Participants suggest possible doctrinal themes that flow from the readings.

Possible Doctrinal Themes

Repentance, conversion, kingdom, paschal mystery, image of God

Present the doctrinal material at this time.

---

[18]Third Sunday of Lent: An adaptation of "Alternative Opening Prayer," *The Sacramentary.*

1. The facilitator gives input on a particular doctrinal issue of his/her prior choosing. OR
2. The group chooses a doctrinal issue from the list they created. They read together from the Doctrinal Appendix.

(The doctrinal issues are found in the Doctrinal Appendix in the back of this workbook. If you are choosing an issue from this resource, please refer to it now.)

Reflection questions centered around the chosen doctrinal theme can be found at the end of each topic in the Doctrinal Appendix. The questions are based on the five-step reflection process. If you choose a topic not included in the Doctrinal Appendix, craft your own questions according to the same five-step process.

Following the reflection questions you will be reminded to return to chapter 7, "Preparing the Catechetical Session," to assist you in crafting your own session.

Closing Prayer

The Father of mercies has given us an example of
    unselfish love
in the sufferings of his only Son.
Through your service of God and neighbor
may you receive his countless blessings.
    All: Amen.

You believe that by his dying
Christ destroyed death for ever.
May he give you everlasting life.
    All: Amen.

He humbled himself for our sakes.
May you follow his example
and share in his resurrection.
    All: Amen.[19]

Selected Bibliography

Anderson, Bernhard W. *Understanding the Old Testament.* 4th ed. Englewood Cliffs: Prentice Hall, 1986.

Fuller, Reginald F. *Preaching the New Lectionary.* Collegeville: The Liturgical Press, 1971.

Heschel, Abraham J. *The Prophets.* New York: Harper and Row, Pub., 1963.

Marshall, I. Howard. *The Gospel of Luke.* New International Greek Testament Commentary Series. Grand Rapids: Wm. B. Eerdmans, 1978.

Sanchez, Patricia Datchuck. *The Word We Celebrate.* Kansas City: Sheed and Ward, 1986.

Scott, Bernard Brandon. *Hear Then the Parable.* Minneapolis: Augsburg Fortress, 1989.

Talbert, Charles. *Reading Luke.* New York: Crossroad, 1992.

Tannehill, Robert C. *The Narrative Unity of Luke-Acts: A Literary Interpretation.* Vol. 1. Minneapolis: Augsburg Fortress, 1986.

[19]Third Sunday of Lent: "Solemn Blessing or Prayer Over the People," *The Sacramentary.*

THIRD SUNDAY OF LENT (CYCLE A)

INTRODUCTORY RITES

Opening Song (or Entrance Antiphon)

I will prove my holiness through you. I will gather
you from the ends of the earth; I will pour clean
water on you and wash away all your sins. I will
give you a new spirit within you, says the Lord.
(Ez 36:23-26)[1]

Environment

Today's liturgy contains strong images of water:

The Entrance Antiphon: "I will pour clean water
    on you and wash away all your sins..."
The First Reading: "Yahweh instructed Moses to
    strike the rock and water flowed..."
The Gospel: "But whoever drinks the water I give
    will never be thirsty..."
The Communion Rite: "Whoever drinks the water
    I give...will have a spring inside..."

Imaginative display of this powerful symbol might
be appropriate for today's session.

Opening Prayer

*The facilitator of the session may lead the prayer. Others
in the group may be asked to proclaim the readings.*

Let us pray
[to the Father and ask him
to form a new heart within us]

    Pause for silent prayer.

God of all compassion, Father of all goodness,
to heal the wounds our sins and selfishness bring
    upon us
you bid us turn to fasting, prayer, and sharing with
    our brothers.
We acknowledge our sinfulness, our guilt is ever
    before us:
when our weakness causes discouragement,
let your compassion fill us with hope

and lead us through a Lent of repentance
to the beauty of Easter joy.
Grant this through Christ, our Lord.[2]

LITURGY OF THE WORD

Let us listen to God's word.

The readings are proclaimed

First Reading
Exodus 17:3-7

Today's reading refers to Israel's defining event:
the exodus and the wanderings in the desert.
Moses was instructed to strike the rock and water
sprang forth. Water was a powerful symbol of
God's activity. Water was a sign of life. At creation
God hovered over the waters and breathed life
into them. Water was a sign of destruction, purification, and God's awesome power. God sent
down the rain for forty days and forty nights and
submerged the earth because of the sin of
human beings. Water was a sign of salvation.
When the Israelites thirsted in the desert, water
flowed through the power of God. In an arid
land, water is an absolute need. Water is a symbol
of liberation and passage from death to life. God
held back the water for the Israelites to pass
through.

Through the water sign there is allusion to the
sacraments: water as salvation; water as sign of
baptism. Lent is both penitential and baptismal
in nature. The first reading touches on both
themes.

The psalm for this liturgy exhorts us "not to
harden our hearts." Meribah and Massah were the
places where the people had sinned. This first
reading reminds us of our total dependence on
the God who saves, Christ who liberates, and the
Spirit who leads us to the life-giving water.

---

[1]Third Sunday of Lent: "Entrance Antiphon," *The Sacramentary.*

[2]Third Sunday of Lent: "Alternative Opening Prayer,"
The Sacramentary.

Responsorial Psalm
Psalm 95

This psalm was chosen for its connection to the first reading. It especially helps focus the meaning for the first reading: "Harden not your hearts."

Second Reading
Romans 5:1-2, 5-8

Up to this point in his letter to the Romans, Paul has expressed his assurance that human beings were justified through the redeeming death of Christ. Today's pericope is concerned with the implications of our justification. Since we are justified, we share the peace of Christ. Our faith in the paschal mystery gives us free access to God's grace as we wait in hope for our future glory. Paul reminds us that the Spirit continues to shower us with the living, ever-present love of God. Reginald Fuller maintains that Paul related justification to the indwelling of the Spirit. The Spirit of God initiates and continues the work of healing transformation within those the Spirit justifies. Each person is thus raised to a state of created grace. God pours out gratuitous love through the gift of the Spirit and through the sacrifice on the cross by God's Son, Jesus Christ. The veil of the curtain was torn at the death of Jesus and sinners were given access to God. That access is the Spirit of God. The gift of the cross is God's Holy Spirit dwelling within human beings to transform them into the elevated state they were destined to attain. We also hear in Paul's letter the roots of our belief in the Holy Trinity.

Gospel
John 4:5-42

Jesus encounters the woman of Samaria.

STEP 1
NAMING ONE'S EXPERIENCE

What were your first impressions? What was your first response? What grabbed your attention? How did you feel?

Each person names his or her initial impression. Statement should be brief. No reasons should be given at this time. All simply listen without agreeing or disagreeing.

STEP 2
UNDERSTANDING

In a brief statement, what do you think this gospel is trying to convey?

STEP 3
INPUT FROM VISION/STORY/TRADITION

Liturgical Context

As stated in the lenten overview, the Johannine gospels for the three Sundays of Cycle A were used as immediate preparation for those preparing for baptism. Thematically they address the baptismal issues and symbols of water, light, and the passage from death into life. Today's readings are viewed through the lens of baptismal preparation.

The Communion Antiphon (from today's gospel) serves as a summary text for today's liturgy: "Whoever drinks the water that I shall give . . . will have a spring inside . . . welling up for eternal life" (Jn 4:13-14). Today's readings ask us where the areas of sin reside in our society, in the world, in the church, and in our personal lives. Where and how do we thirst? Where in our society, in the church, and in our personal lives, is there a need for Christ's healing liberation? When we scrutinize sin through the eyes of faith, Christ refreshes us and gives us the water of new life that springs up as a fountain within us.

Scrutinies

The Cycle A readings are designated for use when there are catechumens preparing for initiation at the Easter Vigil. In the Rite of Christian Initiation of Adults, Lent coincides with the period of *purification and enlightenment*. It is a period of final preparation for the elect. They (along with the entire church) are to seriously discern the areas of sin and weakness [purification] and allow those areas to be healed and illumined by Christ, the Liberator [enlightenment]. The church celebrates three scrutinies with the elect beginning on the Third Sunday of Lent. Scrutinies are intended to heal what is weak, defective, and sinful, to protect the elect from temptation, and to strengthen them in Christ (RCIA, #141-146). The magnitude of sin in all its forms—personal, social, and systemic—is laid bare. The elect are filled with the presence of Christ the Liberator who won the victory over evil and its consequences. God the Father is invoked and asked for strength and protection in the trinitarian prayer of exorcism. "Through the power of the Holy Spirit (the epicletic action of the laying on of hands), Jesus exercises his healing and liberating power over the effects of evil. Thus, the power and presence of Christ in word and exorcism are the primary symbols of the scrutinies."[3] Preparation for the elect's celebration of the scrutinies includes reflection upon the scriptures from today's readings. The elect seek to uncover the many layers of sin as well as to reflect upon the ultimate source of power and grace. They explore the question, "Where does sin exist and where is liberation needed in the world, in the community, and in my life?" They search the scrutiny gospel for ways that Christ, the great Liberator, is proclaimed and imaged. They come to the scrutiny as expectant, vulnerable, and willing vessels eager to approach the freedom that awaits them.

While scrutinies are celebrated with the elect, they are also for the entire church. We and the elect are on this journey toward liberation and wholeness together. The scrutinies prepare the elect for the sacraments of initiation and they serve as preparation for our own recommitment to the baptismal promises we will profess anew at Easter.

Presentation of the Creed

The presentation of the creed generally takes place during the week following the first scrutiny, "preferably in the presence of a community of the faithful, within Mass after the homily" (RCIA, #157). The elect are to commit the creed to memory and profess it publicly prior to their official profession of faith at their baptism (RCIA, #148). The creed and the Lord's Prayer have always been considered central to Christian faith and prayer. The creed is intended to enlighten the elect with

---

[3]Mary Birmingham, "Preparation for Celebration of the Scrutinies," *Christian Initiation Magazine* (January 1997).

the light of faith. God's wondrous salvation deeds (of which the human race is beneficiary) are professed. The RCIA does allow the presentations to take place during the catechumenate period as the season of Lent is rather brief and packed with multiple spiritual riches. Thus, some parishes celebrate and anticipate the presentations with their catechumens before Lent.

Gospel Exegesis

The facilitator gives input regarding what critical biblical scholarship has to say about this text. The input includes insights as to how people would have heard the gospel in Jesus' time.

The exegesis for the gospel of the Samaritan woman at the well will utilize the insights of Sandra Schneider, a biblical scholar. In my opinion, her interpretation most thoroughly uncovers the heart and soul, not only of the text, but of its place in baptismal and lenten catechesis. At a recent workshop, Donald Senior, one of this country's most respected biblical scholars, asserted that the scholarly work of Schneider in relation to this gospel is masterful and right on the mark. He was surprised that no one had stumbled across it before. He surmised that it was because most biblical scholars have been male. As male members of the community, they approach the texts primarily with a masculine hermeneutic. Biblical texts are to be interpreted not only through the science of biblical criticism, but also through the discerning wisdom of the community. For most of its history, the church has not had the privilege of the discernment of half of her members—the female half.[4] The scholar further noted that the

---

[4]Barbara Reid, in her book, *Choosing the Better Part* (Collegeville: The Liturgical Press, 1996), describes the vision that best informs the exegesis for this liturgy. "Patriarchy is 'any system, organization, or institution in which the men own, administer, shape, or control a major portion of all the facets of society.' [Joan Chittister, "Yesterday's Dangerous Vision: Christian Feminism in the Catholic Church," *Sojourners* (July 1987): 18.] The world of Jesus was a patriarchal world, as is our own, although that is beginning to change. Feminism, as a response to patriarchy, 'is a commitment to the humanity, dignity, and equality of all persons to such a degree that one is willing to work for changes in structures and in relationship patterns so that these occur to the

feminine consciousness has not had the opportunity to interpret the texts. That is presently changing with the emergence of many female biblical scholars.

Schneider approaches the text with a hermeneutic of suspicion.[5] She confronts the story, suspicious of its obvious moral dilemma: a woman chastised for her sexual indiscretions. It appears as though Schneider side-steps the patriarchal literal meaning, turning instead to the images, symbols, and typology common to the time and to the Johannine community, in order to appropriate a more inclusive interpretation.

Some scholars suggest that the story of the Samaritan woman probably was not an historical story. The story served as legitimization "of the Samaritan mission in John's community; to establish full equality between Samaritan and Jewish Christians, and to affirm Jewish legitimacy as bearer of covenant faith but with a surprising recognition of the essential validity of Samaritan faith and inclusion in the covenant."[6]

Samaria was a territory north of Jerusalem. It was part of the Assyrian and Persian empire in 721-612 B.C.E. The Assyrians imported foreign colonists and deported many of Samaria's native citizens; others sought refuge in Judea. A Yahwism influenced by other religions developed that led to animosity from traditional Jews. The bad feeling between the two groups was further exacerbated when the Samaritans offered to help re-

build the temple after the exile and were turned down by their Jewish brothers and sisters. This added fuel to the already smoldering fires of resentment. Another revolt forced the Samaritans to move to Shechem where they built a temple on Mount Gerizim.[7] Samaritans anticipated a prophet like Moses who would restore worship on Mount Gerizim in northern Israel. The Jews, on the other hand, believed the messiah would be a descendant of David who would restore worship in the Jerusalem temple. It is obvious that resentments ran deep and permeated the consciousness of the two peoples. They were bitter enemies.

In the story of the Samaritan woman, it is the unspoken text between the lines that captures our attention and imagination. The woman is nameless. Nameless people in scripture often represent more than the literal eye can see, especially in John's gospel (the beloved disciple, the royal official, the paralytic at the pool, and the man born blind). This woman is a symbolic figure who represents the Samaritan people and the New Israel (the new kingdom).

The woman was at a well—not just any well, but a famous well. Wells were important symbolic places in biblical literature. Important events in salvation history began with unions initiated at famous wells. Rebecca was found for Isaac at a well; Rachel met Jacob at the very well in this story. Before this scene in John's gospel, at the wedding in Cana, Jesus was called the new Bridegroom. Our attention in this reading, then, turns to Jesus, the new Bridegroom, present at the well of famous weddings to "claim Samaria as beloved in the New Israel."[8]

There is more to consider about the heroine of the story. She was a woman and a Samaritan, the lowest on society's totem pole. Even the pagans hated Samaritans. She was an outcast's outcast! Yet this outcast, woman and Samaritan, encountered Christ. Jesus, a Jew, not only spoke to her and noticed her, but he drank from her bucket (making him ritually unclean). The woman was trained by

equal good of all' (Chittister, 18). . . . Feminism advocates a community of equals that provides for all the members, women and men alike, to use their God-given gifts to the benefit of all. Christian feminists are women and men committed to eliminating sexism in their relations with one another, in the structures of their faith communities and in society. They see this as a work of justice that is truly faithful to the teaching and life of Jesus . . ." (Reid, 7).

[5] ". . . A hermeneutic of suspicion recognizes that the biblical texts have been written, for the most part, by men, for men, and about men, and that they serve the interests of patriarchy. One who reads with a hermeneutic of suspicion is wary that the text can be oppressive for women. This does not deny the inspiration of Scripture, but recognizes the limitations of the human authors that set forth God's word." (Reid, 9)

[6] James B. Dunning, *Echoing God's Word* (Arlington, VA: North American Forum on the Catechumenate, 1993), 306.

[7] For further information, refer to: Robert F. O'Toole, S.J. "Samaria/Samaritan," in *The Collegeville Pastoral Dictionary of Biblical Theology*, ed. Carroll Stuhlmueller, C.P. (Collegeville: The Liturgical Press, 1996), 872-873.

[8] Dunning, *Echoing God's Word*, 306.

her culture to believe she was worthless. Yet this Jew offered her acceptance, dignity, compassion, a way out, and a way in! Donald Senior suggests that this woman has much more to teach us than a lesson on morality. It is the story between the lines we dare to hear.

During the exile the Samaritans remained faithful to Yahweh, but became inculturated by their conquerors. While they still loved Yahweh, they nevertheless dabbled in the local worship of the Samaritan gods. The result was that Jews hated the Samaritans whom they judged unfaithful. Samaritans were outcasts and ritually unclean. No good Jew would drink from this woman's bucket. Yet Jesus drank from her bucket. In his encounter with her, Jesus welcomed the lost and included the sinner, the outsider.

She entered into a theological discussion with him. She interrogated him about his action toward her. He had broken Jewish tradition by speaking to her (a woman) and by using the same utensils she had used. She was dumbfounded. Samaritans would have been shocked to hear anyone claiming to be on the same plane as their patriarch Jacob who had given the well to Israel in the first place. Jesus acknowledged Samaria's rightful place in salvation history while still affirming Yahweh's covenant with the Jews. Yet he made it very clear that they had each missed the boat—both the Jews and the Samaritans. Neither had a monopoly on the truth. God was doing something new. While defending the Jewish claim to the covenant tradition, Jesus made no distinctions regarding the *territory* people worshiped in. What was important was the worship Jesus would inaugurate as messiah—worship in spirit and truth, authentic worship. The gospel would guide the worship. In the new kingdom people would live in biblical justice, in right relationship with God. They would live the law of love.

Centered in the middle of Jesus' theological discussion with the woman is his scrutiny of her adulterous liaisons—her five husbands. That she had had five husbands was unusual in the religious society of her day. "Either this is totally out of place, a trivial bit of moralism or even a shallow display of preternatural knowledge on the part of Jesus, or it is an integral part of this highly theological

exchange."[9] This story is about the *inclusion* of Samaria into the New Israel. Jesus scrutinized the woman's (Samaria's) adulterous (idolatrous) union with the gods of the five tribes. "Jesus' declaration that Samaria 'has no husband' is a classic prophetic denunciation of false worship, like Hosea's oracle in which the prophet expresses God's sentiment toward unfaithful Israel" (Hosea 2:2).[10] Thus, Jesus suggests that Samaria's relationship to Yahweh in the past was colored by her adulterous flirtations with other gods. Jesus scrutinized the false worship, named the sin, and invited repentance as he included Samaria in his New Israel.

At this wedding well, in broad daylight and at high noon so that all could see, Jesus, the new *Bridegroom*, wed Samaria and included her in the kingdom.[11] "Now the new Bridegroom who assumes the role of Yahweh, bridegroom of ancient Israel, comes to claim Samaria as an integral part of the New Israel, namely, the Christian community and specifically the Johannine community."[12]

What, then, was the woman's response? She recognized Jesus for who he was, messiah and lord. She could do no less than "go and tell everyone . . . and they all came to believe on her testimony." She was the first evangelist and the only person to bring an entire group of people to faith in Jesus. No wonder women had an important ministerial role in John's community.[13]

The implications? Jesus extended reconciliation, inclusion and healing to alienated Samaria; everyone is included in the reign of God. Jesus shared this revelation with a woman—society's outcast (then and in many places today).[14] He treated her

---

[9]Sandra Schneiders, *The Revelatory Text* (San Francisco: HarperCollins, 1991), 190.

[10]Ibid.

[11]Contrast the woman coming to the well at high noon, in the light of day for all to see, with Nicodemus, who came in the dead of night. John's gospel is filled with the metaphor of night and day, light and darkness.

[12]Schneiders, *The Revelatory Text*, 187.

[13]See Sixteenth Sunday in Ordinary Time: the story of Martha and Mary.

[14]At the time of Christ, in order for something to be attested and affirmed, it had to be verified in a court of law. I find it very interesting that first-hand testimony and events

as he would have treated any member of his society—with respect and dignity. We are, by extension, invited to cast aside any idols of our making that get in the way of our authentic worship of God, and we are to welcome all who are on the bottom rung of society.

This is a story about the kingdom in which there are no outcasts and no strangers, only repentant, welcomed sinners. "In summary, the entire dialogue between Jesus and the woman is the 'wooing' of Samaria to full covenant fidelity in the New Israel by Jesus, the New Bridegroom. It has nothing to do with the woman's private moral life, but with the covenant life of the community. Nowhere in the fourth gospel is there a dialogue of such theological depth and intensity."[15]

In light of the celebration of the scrutinies, this gospel helps us name the social and personal sin that keeps us from an intimate relationship with God. We are reminded that it is God who names our sin, who scrutinizes the evil in our lives, and who invites us to turn away from anything (our personal and corporate idols) that keeps us from a full liberated life in Christ. Today's liturgy highlights the evil of exclusion on any level: in our personal lives, in our society and in our religious structures. It demands that we ask the questions: *Who is out?* and *Who is in?* Like the woman, we are to go out and invite others in. Today's gospel invites *metanoia*—a complete turning away *from* sin *toward* the Healer, Liberator, Victor, and One who offers living water through the refreshing waters

---

often occurred to people who could not legally witness to them in the courts. Women could not serve as verifiable witnesses unless the issue pertained to a household matter. Shepherds were also not allowed to testify as valid witnesses, since they were considered too untrustworthy to give truthful testimony. Yet, is it not God's irony (or perhaps humor) that the two premier events of redemptive salvation were witnessed by people who, by human standards, were not able to verify or testify to what they had witnessed? Shepherds were the first to witness the Incarnation and a woman was first on the scene following the resurrection. Once again, God writes salvation history with crooked lines and refuses to be boxed in by humanity's standards of convention. In today's story, a woman experienced the messiah. Her experience and her story alone had the power to invite people to faith.

[15]Schneiders, *The Revelatory Text*, 191.

of baptism. This is the victory Christ holds out to us in today's liturgy.

Proclaim the gospel again.

Sometimes we gain new insights when we hear the text after the interpretation has been given. Someone from the group proclaims the gospel a second time.

STEP 4
TESTING

Conversation with the Liturgy and the Scriptures

Test your original understanding in dialogue with the text.

(You might consider breaking into smaller groups.)

Were there any new insights? How do you feel? Comfortable or uncomfortable? Why? How does your original understanding of this story compare with what was just shared? How does this story speak to your life?

Participants share an experience from their lives that connects with the biblical interpretation just shared.

> *A few years ago I had an encounter with this scripture. It caught my attention, challenged my attitudes, and invited me to change. This story summoned me to let go of the idol I had made of "being right." I had mentally and spiritually excluded some folks who held different points of view than I. They were my outcasts. They were wrong and I was right. Of this I was certain! I had been hurt by them and was not willing to consider how I had excluded them as a group. After wrestling with the angel of this text, I was forced to look at my idol and at the people that I had cut off and excluded. Through an interesting process of not-so-gentle persuasions, the Lord God insisted that I offer a hand in reconciliation to a person that best represented those I had discarded. Our reconciliation began a lasting bond of friendship.*

> *This word is a powerful word for communities today. Yet it is a word that often invites the greatest challenge. Try though we may, there are still many excluded people in our communities. Our hierarchical structure excludes, our parish structures exclude,*

and our personal relationships are often exclusive. The gospel continues to invite us to scrutinize the areas of elusion, sin, and idolatry and ask Christ, the liberator, to deliver us from evil.

All share their life experience.

What was John's message to his community? What are the implications for our communities today? Is there any situation in our community that needs to be enlightened by this gospel? In what way (if at all) did the experience of God's word:

1. affirm God's promise to be with us (*covenant*)
2. lead us through a death/resurrection experience in our attitudes (*exodus*)
3. speak to us as a community (*people of God*)
4. call us to new life (*creation*)?

Do we still feel the same way about this text as we did when we began? Has our original understanding been stretched, challenged, or affirmed?

STEP 5
DECISION

The gospel demands a response.

In what concrete way does this gospel call our parish to action in the church, parish, neighborhood, or world? Has this conversation with the exegesis changed or stretched my personal attitudes? What am I /we/community/parish called to do in response? What is one concrete action I will take this week as a response to what was learned and shared today?

DOCTRINAL ISSUES

What church truth/teaching/doctrinal issue could be drawn from the gospel for the Third Sunday in Lent, Cycle A?

Participants suggest possible doctrinal themes that flow from the readings.

Possible Doctrinal Themes

Grace and sin, baptism, social dimension of sin, Jesus the messiah

Present the doctrinal material at this time.

1. The facilitator gives input on a particular doctrinal issue of his/her prior choosing. OR
2. The group chooses a doctrinal issue from the list they created. They read together from the Doctrinal Appendix.

(The doctrinal issues are found in the Doctrinal Appendix in the back of this workbook. If you are choosing an issue from this resource, please refer to it now.)

Reflection questions centered around the chosen doctrinal theme can be found at the end of each topic in the Doctrinal Appendix. The questions are based on the five-step reflection process. If you choose a topic not included in the Doctrinal Appendix, craft your own questions according to the same five-step process.

Following the reflection questions you will be reminded to return to chapter 7, "Preparing the Catechetical Session," to assist you in crafting your own session.

Closing Prayer

First Scrutiny: Exorcism

All merciful Father,
through your Son you revealed your mercy
to the woman of Samaria;
and moved by that same care
you have offered salvation to all sinners.
Look favorably on these elect,
who desire to become your adopted children
through the power of your sacraments.
Free them from the slavery of sin,
and for Satan's crushing yoke
exchange the gentle yoke of Jesus.
Protect them in every danger,
That they may serve you faithfully in peace and joy
And render you thanks forever. Amen.

Laying on of hands

Hands outstretched over the elect:

Lord Jesus,
in your merciful wisdom
you touched the heart of the sinful woman

and taught her to worship the Father
in spirit and in truth.
Now, by your power,
free these elect from the cunning of Satan,
as they draw near to the fountain of living water.
Touch their hearts with the power of the Holy
    Spirit,
that they may come to know the Father
in true faith, which expresses itself in love,
for you live and reign for ever and ever.
Amen.[16]

Selected Bibliography

Birmingham, Mary C. "Preparation for Celebration of the Scrutinies." *Christian Initiation Magazine* (February/March 1997), Kansas City: National Catholic Reporter, 1997.

Dunning, James B. *Echoing God's Word.* Arlington: North American Forum on the Catechumenate, 1993.

Fuller, Reginald H. *Preaching the New Lectionary.* Collegeville: The Liturgical Press, 1971.

O'Toole, Robert F., S.J. "Samaria/Samaritan." In *The Collegeville Pastoral Dictionary of Biblical Theology.* Ed. Carroll Stuhlmueller, C.P. Collegeville: The Liturgical Press, 1996.

Reid, Barbara. *Choosing the Better Part.* Collegeville: The Liturgical Press, 1996.

Sanchez, Patricia Datchuck. *The Word We Celebrate.* Kansas City: Sheed and Ward, 1989.

Schneiders, Sandra. *The Revelatory Text.* San Francisco: HarperCollins, 1991.

---

[16]Prayer of Exorcism, "First Scrutiny," *Rite of Christian Initiation of Adults.*

FOURTH SUNDAY OF LENT

INTRODUCTORY RITES

Opening Song (or Entrance Antiphon)

Rejoice, Jerusalem! Be glad for her, you who love her; rejoice with her, you who mourned for her, and you will find contentment at her consoling breast. (See Is 66:10-11.)[1]

Opening Prayer

The facilitator of the session may lead the prayer. Others in the group may be asked to proclaim the readings.

Let us pray
[that by growing in love this Lenten season
we may bring the peace of Christ to our world]

Pause for silent prayer.

God our Father,
your Word, Jesus Christ, spoke peace to a sinful
   world
and brought mankind the gift of reconciliation
by the suffering and death he endured.
Teach us, the people who bear his name,
to follow the example he gave us:
may our faith, hope and charity
turn hatred to love, conflict to peace,
death to eternal life.
We ask this through Christ our Lord.[2]

LITURGY OF THE WORD

Let us listen to God's word.

The readings are proclaimed.

First Reading
Joshua 5:9, 10-12

The first nine chapters of the book of Joshua tell the epic of the Israelites as they conquered the land of Canaan. Joshua enjoyed his conquest after only three military victories. Today's pericope takes place at Gilgal. The old, faithless generation (those from the original desert journey) had died along the way only to be replaced by a new people. A new generation of Israelites was circumcised at Gilgal. Circumcision, an ancient rite of initiation that pledged the offering of self to the gods (symbolized in the presentation of a piece of foreskin), eventually became a sign of the covenant Israel shared with Yahweh.

Some believe Gilgal was named for the circle of twelve stones that symbolized Israel's success in crossing the Jordan River. Gilgal was perhaps where Joshua and his men pitched their base camp. The conquest of the land was considered the fulfillment of what had been promised to the Israelites' ancestor, Abraham.

Today's reading tells the story of the celebration of the first ritual memorial of the exodus. Last Sunday, the manna was rendered a type of eucharistic food, the bread of pilgrims.[3] Today's reading signals an end to the manna in the new, promised land. Instead, the Israelites eat a Passover ritual of unleavened cakes and parched bread: Passover food. The desert sojourn was over; they were ready to become a settled people in their new land. No longer would they wander; here their feet were planted firmly on the ground. The new settlers firmly relied on Yahweh to continue blessing them as they forged a new life in their new land.

Second Reading
2 Corinthians 5:17-21

In Paul's second letter to the Corinthians he describes the old Paul and the new, transformed Paul: the before Christ and the after Christ Paul. Paul sees himself as a new creation. Death and sin have passed away and a new reality has emerged: holiness. To become a new creation is

---

[1]Fourth Sunday of Lent: "Entrance Antiphon," *The Sacramentary.*

[2]Fourth Sunday of Lent: "Alternative Opening Prayer," *The Sacramentary.*

[3]Reginald H. Fuller, *Preaching the New Lectionary* (Collegeville: The Liturgical Press, 1971), 7.

not a once-and-for-all-time guaranteed event; it is to be constantly renewed. Through a process of ongoing reconciliation we become new creations in Christ.

Paul considered the ministry of reconciliation one of his most important endeavors. He felt honored to offer the reconciling presence of Christ to God's people. Paul asserted that all Christians are called to the same ministry of reconciliation. All believers are to be agents of Christ's reconciling peace and love.

Paul understood the incredible power of sin over our lives and our powerlessness over sin. Left to our own designs, we are powerless to change. Only God has the power to rescue us from the demoralizing effects of sin. God, through Jesus Christ, rescued us from the permanent hold of sin. Even though Jesus was sinless, *he became sin* in order to destroy it. That spine-shuddering phrase almost defies the imagination when one attempts an interpretation. When Jesus uttered his words of desolation on the cross, "My God, my God why have you forsaken me?" he experienced the effects of humanity's sin. As he hung there alone, abandoned and in humiliation, he experienced what sin ultimately causes. Sin causes complete alienation; the sinner is cut off from God. Jesus walked alone and unprotected into the dark fire of hell where he grasped humanity by the charred, choking collar, and carried it to the safety of eternal light.

Gospel
Luke 15:1-3, 11-32

Jesus tells the parable of the prodigal son.

STEP 1
NAMING ONE'S EXPERIENCE

What were your first impressions? What was your first response? What grabbed your attention? How did you feel?

Each person names his or her initial impression. Statement should be brief. No reasons should be given at this time. All simply listen without agreeing or disagreeing.

STEP 2
UNDERSTANDING

In a brief statement, what do you think this gospel is trying to convey?

STEP 3
INPUT FROM VISION/STORY/TRADITION

Liturgical Context

This Sunday used to be called Laetare Sunday. Vestiges of that mid-lenten joy can still be noticed in the readings today: the joy of arriving in the promised land (First Reading), the joy of being a new creation in Christ (Second Reading), and the joy over the return of the prodigal son.

The manna of the desert ends and is fulfilled in the living memorial of the exodus—the Passover ritual. The eucharist finds its fulfillment at the messianic banquet. The early church believed that Jesus would return at the celebration of the *pascha*, the ritual memorial of his death and resurrection. When it was apparent that Jesus' return was not as imminent as once believed, the Christian community celebrated the eucharist at this Passover ritual as a living memorial and an eschatological hope. The Easter eucharist has a closer connection to the heavenly banquet than any other eucharist of the year.

The prodigal son story richly addresses many primary expressions of faith we profess in the liturgy and life of the church. Love freely given, offered in humiliation (Christ on the cross) is redemptive. We are children of God, not slaves. Forgiveness is freely given, but we must acknowledge our need for it. We can either accept or reject it. Reconciliation is communal. We are all to rejoice over the reconciliation of sinners. Like St. Paul, we are to consider our ministry of reconciliation the highest priority.

Gospel Exegesis

The facilitator gives input regarding what critical biblical scholarship has to say about this text. The input in-

cludes insights as to how people would have heard the gospel in Jesus' time.

St. Paul's letter gives us the lens with which to approach the parable of the prodigal son: the redeeming grace of Jesus on the cross. The parable of the prodigal son at first glance could simply stand alone as a story about God's forgiveness. But Reginald Fuller maintains that the parable is far more than that. He states that it must be told in the context of the opening scene: the scribes and Pharisees were gathered around Jesus and were gossiping to each other about Jesus' questionable dinner companions. Jesus ate with sinners. This parable was not simply a teaching on forgiveness. Jesus told the parable as a commentary on the actions about which his detractors were gossiping. Jesus interpreted his parabolic action of eating with sinners and tax collectors as more than an extension of altruistic kindness or flagrant disregard for the religious laws. *Jesus' action of eating with sinners was a sign of God superseding his own laws in order to save the very people who break them.*

"Thus," says Fuller, "he who knew no sin, is made to be sin."[4] Jesus immersed himself in the lives of sinners. He walked into their lives and became one of them (one with the sinners), so he could pull them up to embrace the righteousness of God. Jesus' entire ministry was the ongoing offer of the cross.

Kenneth Bailey offers a marvelous interpretation of the events of the parable that help illustrate the point. Bailey uses the societal norms, legal customs, and religious traditions of the then-known-world as well as the mores of similar present-day Middle Eastern peasant communities to uncover the implications of the details in the parable. His conclusions prompt an insightful, challenging conversation with this brilliantly crafted parable.

"Thus," says Bailey, "the father in the parable is not God *incognito*, but an earthly father, as is conclusively demonstrated in verse 18."[5] However, the father often symbolizes and images God through

behaviors that resemble the characteristics of God. The prodigal son is not the tax collector or the sinner of the opening verses, nor is the Pharisee specifically the older son. But both resemble a "type" of individual that might prompt the listeners to conclude for themselves, "If the shoe fits, then I must wear it." "The parable about the prodigal son is not primarily about a spendthrift boy, but about the relationship between God and the sinner and the self-righteous."[6]

Early in the story the prodigal asked for his share of the father's inheritance. Unfathomable love was shown by the father when he granted the request. The older son not only failed to offer protest to the action, but he also did nothing to reconcile the younger son with the father (his duty by custom).

For one to pass on an inheritance while still alive was unthinkable in antiquity and in similar communities today. The younger son's request for an early inheritance was a serious affront to the father. The implication of his demand would be to say: "I want you to die." From this point on, the story line rapidly deteriorates. The son not only asks that the property be divided so he can have his share, but he also asks that he be given the rights to sell his share immediately. "Thus the prodigal's demand for the right of disposal was to treat his father as if he were already dead."[7] The boy's action was a complete break in his relationship with his father—he was truly lost!

When the father granted his son's request, he not only went against all conventions of the time (most fathers would have beaten a son for such presumption) but he put himself in jeopardy by not assuring his own future needs. The early Palestinian community listening to this parable had to be shocked by the inconceivable depth and breadth of the father's love. In order to legally give the son his inheritance, the father had to act as if the idea was his own; otherwise it would not be legally binding.

The fact that the son squandered his inheritance among gentiles was a serious breach with the com-

[4]Ibid.

[5]Kenneth E. Bailey, *Poet and Peasant and Through Peasant Eyes* (Grand Rapids: William B. Eerdmans Pub. Inc., 1980), 159.

[6]J. V. Jones, *The Art and Truth of the Parables* (London: SCM Press, 1963), 210.

[7]D. O. Via, *The Parables* (Minneapolis: Augsburg Fortress, 1967), 169.

munity as well. Thus, what the son did to the father was only compounded by the implications to the wider community.

The older son surprises the listener early on by his reaction (or non-reaction) to the situation. The older son should have protested the younger son's request or attempted to negotiate a reconciliation between the prodigal and his father; but again, there was silence. Even if he and his younger brother were not on good terms, the older son should have mediated the situation for the sake of the father. Allowing the prodigal to proceed with his plans ensured the older son that he would never have to share the estate with his brother in the future. The older son's silence and failure to intervene signaled an existing rift between the father and the older son as well as between the older son and the prodigal. The prodigal's action assured the older son that he would never have to reconcile with his brother again.

Thus, the prodigal asked for the immediate disposition of his inheritance (with all the inherent implications), received it, and left town quickly. This was not only unheard of, it was shocking! The father should have punished his son, but instead gave him what he wanted (to his own possible peril). The father's behavior demonstrated unparalleled love. The older son failed miserably in his response to the situation.

After a high-rolling spending spree, the next scene opens with a penniless and hungry prodigal. He was so hungry that pig fodder could not even fill him! He decided to repent and go home to his father. Bailey questions the sincerity of his repentance, however. When the prodigal acknowledged his "sin against heaven and in his father's sight," he was only acknowledging his failure to provide for his father's future. If he had not lost the money, there would have been no need to repent. True repentance was lacking, as his motivation was hunger.

The prodigal found a solution to his moral dilemma. He asked his father to employ him as a hired servant. Hired servants received a wage, and lived away from the estate. They were independent and socially were considered on a par with someone like the father and the brother. Bailey follows J. D. M. Derret's line of thinking: "Working as a hired servant (sleeping off the premises) he could see to it that eventually, with his wages, if not in other ways, he could give his father what, so long as the father lived, was only his due."[8] As a hired servant he would be able to repay the moral debt to his father, in his own way and on his own terms. His pride would remain intact. "Now he will make up for what he lost. In short, he will save himself. He wants no grace."[9] And, by negotiating this kind of reconciliation, he would not have to deal with his brother, either.

The prodigal's next problem was how to restore his relationship in the community. The community would have been exceedingly hostile. First, he had insulted his father; then he had sold the land and lost the money (squandered away on gentiles, no less). Shameful! They would have publicly castigated him.

Landowners lived in the village, not on an isolated estate. Thus, the son's arrival would have been known by all. The father was well aware of the treatment his wayward son would receive upon arrival. People would have taunted and abused him and created a mob scene. The father was probably prepared for the day his son might come home. "What the father did in this homecoming scene can best be understood as a series of dramatic actions calculated to protect the boy from the hostility of the village and to restore him to fellowship within the community."[10]

The father's next action was appalling. A dignified man would never think of running anywhere! But the father, dressed in his flowing robes, ran down the road to welcome his son. The father's "compassion" was no doubt influenced by the gauntlet his son was facing. "The father then runs the gauntlet for him, assuming a humiliating posture in the process!"[11]

The father's action would, of itself, draw a crowd, which is exactly what the father intended. *Reconcili-*

<hr>

[8]J. D. M. Derret, "The Prodigal Son," in *Law in the New Testament* (London: Darton, Longman and Todd, 1970), 65.
[9]Bailey, *Poet and Peasant*, 177.
[10]Ibid., 181.
[11]Ibid., 182.

ation with his son would be a public event. Rather than experience the ruthless hostility he deserved and anticipated, the son witnessed an unexpected, *visible demonstration of love in humiliation.*[12] Unabashed love expressed itself in self-effacing action.

A curve ball was thus thrown at the prodigal son. Earlier we were privy to the son's pre-rehearsed speech, yet when he faced his father, he left out a part of it. Why? Most commentators assume that the father simply interrupted him or that the son decided to keep his mouth shut. (After all, how could he ask for more? The father was offering him everything anyway). As noted earlier, he was not exactly looking for a return to the father-and-son relationship. He was simply seeking more independence and a way to take care of his moral responsibility in the least painful way possible. Bailey feels that he left out his pre-rehearsed speech because he simply changed his mind. The father's expression of humiliating love impacted him so intensely that his plan to fix things in his own cleverly devised way was no longer an option. The son had an "A-ha" moment, an awakening. This whole situation was not about money. It was about the broken relationship with his father. Nothing the son could do on his own could ever "fix" this one. It was up to the father. To suggest that he might pay off his misdeeds as a hired servant would have added insult to injury! There was nothing left for the son to say except, "I am not worthy." The prodigal's initial desire to redeem himself by becoming a hired servant was overshadowed (graced) by the father's over-abundant, unexpected act of love.

Next, in a series of symbolic gestures, the father made it crystal clear to every scrutinizing onlooker that he intended full reconciliation and restoration of the father-and-son relationship. He kissed his son—a sign of reconciliation and forgiveness. (The sign of peace at liturgy began as a kiss of peace.) The father, then, joyfully hosted a party and instructed the servants to clothe his son in the best robe (everyone knew that the best robe belonged to the father and was used for official events and parties). The father was making another statement to the servants and to the community. *The son was completely restored to his former status.*

The ring offered to the prodigal son was a sign of trust and the shoes were a sign of being a freed person—not a servant. Rather than succumbing to false humility, the son accepted the restored relationship. He accepted the grace that was offered. There was now reason to celebrate. The prodigal had returned, not as a servant, but as a son!

Because a calf was killed for the event, the entire village must have been invited to the party (otherwise, there would have been too much left over; it would have gone to waste, and that would have been shameful). The father's joy was so immense that nothing less than the grandest party would do. The banquet also served as a further means of reconciling the son to the entire community. (The eucharistic overtones jump off of the page!)

Repentance in the Jewish mind-set demanded a prior offer of atonement on the part of the offender. Jesus provided a new understanding of repentance: "as grace and the confession of unworthiness."[13] Without the humiliating display of love, the younger son might never have grasped the level of the father's love. This way there was a chance! Bailey suggests that the father already had one hired servant in the house (the older son); he did not want another. He wanted a restored relationship.

Let us turn now to the older son waiting in the wings. Obviously, the older son was not notified that the younger son had arrived. He entered the scene in the midst of the party. The father probably knew the older son would be offended and perhaps try to stop the banquet. The parable used the older son's not-so-grand entrance as a means to highlight the difference between the two sons.

The party was just beginning as the older son arrived. Instead of entering into the festivities, he was suspicious. Custom would have demanded that the eldest son stand at the door and greet the guests, see to their enjoyment, and be a gracious host. Even if it stuck in his throat, protocol would have demanded that he publicly welcome

---

[12]Ibid.

[13]Ibid., 187.

the younger brother and at least feign joy over his return. Any problems would have to wait until the party was over. However, the older son, unable to contain his rage, humiliated his father in front of the entire village. The older son's actions were shocking and abhorrent to the gathered guests.

The situation had come full circle. Now it was the older son who was breaking off relationship with his father—in front of the entire community. Another lost son! The guests would have expected the father either to ignore the boy until after the party and then seriously reprimand him or to publicly chastise him. The tension was building as all eyes were on the poor father. What would he do?

For the second time in one day the father humiliated himself. Undaunted, and without a moment's hesitation he went to his older son and offered him the same grace that was earlier extended to his younger son. Humiliated twice in one day! All eyes were then riveted on the older son. How would this son respond? Surely he would accept the same over-generous display of love.

He rejected the offer. The diatribe ensued: "I was the dutiful one who stayed at home to do all the work, and no one offered a party for me." "The difference between him [the older son] and his younger brother was that the younger brother was estranged and rebellious while absent from the house, but the older son was estranged and rebellious in his heart while he was in the house."[14] In a Middle Eastern context, the older son was worse than the younger son. At least the younger son was honest. He was up front. The father knew where the younger son stood. He wanted his money, he wanted it now, and he was willing to break a relationship to get it: the father was dead to him. The older son, on the other hand, kept his hatred and animosity to himself; he let it brew and lived in resentment and pretense. The older son's angry words revealed that, in essence, he was nothing more than a hired hand; *he had never been a son.* "After all, if I could have sold my share of the property like the younger one, I could have afforded to throw a party like this on my own. But

no, I couldn't sell my share, so I had to stay here and rot while this younger son of yours was out spending it on good times!" The story comes very cleverly back to the initial premise of the parable. He too had wanted the father dead. Both sons had broken their father's heart.

In spite of all this, the father does not rebuke him, but instead offers the same humiliating kind of reconciliation he had offered to the younger son. Perhaps this son would understand the depths of his love like his younger son had. The father extended the same humiliating love, but there was no confession of wrong-doing—thus no repentance. The listening Pharisees were invited to look at the older son and see themselves. The parable ends with an invitation to repent. Will they?

Bailey concludes his interpretation of the parable with five thematic points:

1. *Sin.* The parable shows two types of sinners and the nature and consequences of their sin.

2. *Repentance.* Jesus illustrates two types of repentance: one in which the sinner thinks he can save himself and another in which he knows he cannot.

3. *Grace.* The parable demonstrates the love of God that seeks out sinners and suffers for them in order to save them. ("The visible demonstration of love in humiliation is seen to have clear overtones of the atoning work of Christ."[15])

4. *Joy.* Joy is experienced when the sinner is found and saved and when the entire community rejoices over the one who was lost, but is now found and restored.

5. *Sonship.* One son is restored from death and from servanthood. The other son *chooses* to remain a servant. *We are all invited to repent and to embrace our status as fully redeemed, forgiven, graced, joyful children of God.*

Proclaim the gospel again.

Sometimes we gain new insights when we hear the text after the interpretation has been given. Someone from the group proclaims the gospel a second time.

---

[14]Derret, "The Prodigal Son," 65.

[15]Bailey, *Poet and Peasant,* 206.

STEP 4
TESTING

Conversation with the Liturgy and the Scriptures

Test your original understanding in dialogue with the text.

(You might consider breaking into smaller groups.)

Since this exegesis was very involved, what were the main themes and images? What did you hear? Were there any new insights? How does your original understanding of this story compare with what was just shared? How does this story speak to your life?

Participants share an experience from their lives that connects with the biblical interpretation just shared.

Anyone with children can relate to this parable. As the parents of four children, we have lived it many times over in small ways. Sadly, we did not always act like the father in the story. On the occasions when we did, family restoration was always healthier. But this parable is not only about the dysfunctional family home, but also about the dysfunctional community. It is easy to point fingers at those rebellious sons and daughters who are in a faraway country and not see the rebellion in our own house. We often look at the fringe people in our parishes and say, "If only they would get more involved." However, we overlook that we ourselves may be over-involved, in fact, self-involved, to the point of being dangerously close to the mind and heart of the older son.

Some who experienced the transition from the pre-Vatican II church to the post-Vatican II church often sound like the older son when they complain of how things used to be: they were always good, law-abiding Catholics; now, the church is soft on the law, the liturgies are not private anymore and if we had to learn all that Latin then, why doesn't everybody have to learn it now? It isn't fair! Contrast those folks with some post-Vatican II people who sometimes self-righteously and arrogantly insist on rigid adherence to Vatican II. They have replaced the old legalism with a more current, up-to-date, enlightened legalism. Repentance and humility are lacking in

both instances. The parable of the prodigal invites us to accept Christ's offer of love-in-humiliation and to examine our hearts. Do we, as community, stand humbly with the prodigal or arrogantly with the older son?

All share their life experience.

What was Jesus saying to his community? What does he have to say to your community and to you today? There are powerful biblical images of creation, exodus, covenant, and community in today's readings. How do you see these images as applicable to our lives? Do you still feel the same way about this text as you did at the beginning? Has your original understanding been stretched, challenged, or affirmed?

STEP 5
DECISION

The gospel demands a response.

What am I /we/community/parish called to do in response? What one concrete action will I/we take this week as a response to what we have learned and shared today?

DOCTRINAL ISSUES

What church truth/teaching/doctrinal issue could be drawn from the gospel for the Fourth Sunday of Lent?

Participants suggest possible doctrinal themes that flow from the readings.

Possible Doctrinal Themes

Repentance, grace, paschal mystery, sin, sacrament of penance

Present the doctrinal material at this time.

1. The facilitator gives input on a particular doctrinal issue of his/her prior choosing. OR
2. The group chooses a doctrinal issue from the list they created. They read together from the Doctrinal Appendix.

(The doctrinal issues are found in the Doctrinal Appendix in the back of this workbook. If you are choosing an issue from this resource, please refer to it now.)

Reflection questions centered around the chosen doctrinal theme can be found at the end of each topic in the Doctrinal Appendix. The questions are based on the five-step reflection process. If you choose a topic not included in the Doctrinal Appendix, craft your own questions according to the same five-step process.

Following the reflection questions you will be reminded to return to chapter 7, "Preparing the Catechetical Session," to assist you in crafting your own session.

Closing Prayer

Father, look with love upon your people,
The love which our Lord Jesus Christ showed us
when he delivered himself to evil men
and suffered the agony of the cross.
Grant this through Christ, our Lord.
All: Amen.[16]

Selected Bibliography

Bailey, Kenneth E. *Poet and Peasant and Through Peasant Eyes.* Grand Rapids: William B. Eerdmans Pub. Inc., 1980.

Days of the Lord. Vol. 2. Collegeville: The Liturgical Press, 1993.

Derret, J. D. M. "The Prodigal Son." In *Law in the New Testament.* London: Darton, Longman and Todd, 1970.

Fuller, Reginald H. *Preaching the New Lectionary.* Collegeville: The Liturgical Press, 1971.

Jones, G. V. *The Art and Truth of the Parables.* London: SCM Press, 1963.

Saìd, Ibrahim. *Sharh Bisharit Luqa* (Commentary on the Gospel of Luke). Cairo: The Middle East Council of Churches, 1970.

Sanchez, Patricia Datchuck. *The Word We Celebrate.* Kansas City: Sheed and Ward, 1989.

Via, D. O. *The Parables.* Minneapolis: Augsburg Fortress, 1967.

---

[16]Fourth Sunday of Lent: "Solemn Blessing or Prayer Over the People," *The Sacramentary.*

FOURTH SUNDAY OF LENT (CYCLE A)

INTRODUCTORY RITES

Opening Song (or Entrance Antiphon)

Rejoice, Jerusalem! Be glad for her, you who love her; rejoice with her, you who mourned for her, and you will find contentment at her consoling breast. (See Isaiah 66:10-11.)[1]

Environment

Today's gospel speaks of Christ, the Light of the World. If the environment is not normally adorned with a light symbol, today would certainly be a day to incorporate a Christ candle.

Opening Prayer

The facilitator of the session may lead the prayer. Others in the group may be asked to proclaim the readings.

Father, all powerful and ever-living God,
we do well always and everywhere to give you
    thanks
through Jesus Christ our Lord.

He came among us as a man,
to lead mankind from darkness
into the light of faith.

Through Adam's fall we were born slaves of sin,
but now through baptism in Christ
we are reborn as your adopted children.

Earth unites with heaven
to sing the new song of creation,
as we adore and praise you for ever:

Holy, holy, holy Lord, God of power and might,
heaven and earth are full of your glory.
Hosanna in the highest.
Blessed is he who comes in the name of the
    Lord.
Hosanna in the highest.
       (Preface, Fourth Sunday of Lent)

---

[1] Fourth Sunday of Lent: "Entrance Antiphon," *The Sacramentary.*

LITURGY OF THE WORD

Let us listen to God's word.

The readings are proclaimed.

First Reading
1 Samuel 16:6-7, 10-13

In today's reading David is chosen to be king by Yahweh from among Jesse's sons. Throughout all of scripture, it is very clear that God's election is God's own. Humans can do nothing on their own merit to achieve it. God often painted history with crooked lines by choosing people to fulfil his designs who would normally have difficulty passing human scrutiny. David was the least likely character from among Jesse's sons.

Saul anointed David king, thereby signifying the abiding, and guiding presence of God's Spirit. "Anointing means to touch some person or thing with a substance (oil, water, blood, fat, mud) to effect a change, either external or internal."[2] To be anointed by the Lord as king meant that the person was commissioned for a special mission. The new designation required protection and respect. David's anointing also signaled that he was divinely elected and was thus deserving of divine protection.

Today's reading was perhaps chosen for its baptismal images: David was elected by God and anointed for a new life in Yahweh's service.

Responsorial Psalm
Psalm 23:1-3, 3-4, 5, 6

The reasons for the choice of this psalm are ambiguous. One scholar has suggested that it could have been used because of its vague reference to the anointing of David.

Second Reading
Ephesians 5:8-14

---

[2] John C. Endres, S.J., "Anointing," in *The Collegeville Pastoral Dictionary of Biblical Theology*, ed. Carroll Stuhlmueller, C.P. (Collegeville: The Liturgical Press, 1996), 28.

Some question Pauline authorship of this letter. However, if Paul was the author, it was written around 60 C.E. This would correspond with Paul's stint in the Roman jail. The letter contains allusions to gnostic influences that were plaguing the first-century church. Chapters four through six describe the difference between the pagan and Christian way of life. It is the difference between life and death, light and darkness.

Today's subject is a primary theme of our Lenten reflection: conversion. The pericope suggests a complete metanoia—a turning away from all that is darkness into the marvelous light of Christ. Some suggest that today's letter was part of an ancient baptismal liturgy because of its use of the light and darkness baptismal metaphor.

Gospel
John 9:1-41

STEP 1
NAMING ONE'S EXPERIENCE

What were your first impressions? What was your first response? What grabbed your attention? How did you feel?

Each person names his or her initial impression. Statement should be brief. No reasons should be given at this time. All simply listen without agreeing or disagreeing.

STEP 2
UNDERSTANDING

In a brief statement, what do you think this gospel is trying to convey?

STEP 3
INPUT FROM VISION/STORY/TRADITION

Liturgical Context

The Fourth Sunday of Lent is highly charged with baptismal themes. Jesus healed the man born blind and then instructed him to wash in the pool of Siloam. The man came to believe in Jesus. On this Fourth Sunday, during the period of purification and enlightenment, the elect celebrate the second scrutiny. (Refer to the overview of Lent and Third Sunday of Lent, Cycle A for further explanation of the scrutinies.) We, along with the elect, seek enlightenment. "The early church referred to baptism as 'enlightenment' and spoke of the candidates as being enlightened."[3]

The three scrutiny gospels were used to prepare people for baptism when preparation lasted only three weeks. Today these readings are still used for penitential and baptismal preparation for the Easter sacraments. Jesus, Light of the World, is important catechesis for those preparing for enlightenment (baptism).

The first reading from Samuel, the anointing of David, may also be connected to baptism. The initiation corollaries are obvious. At baptism we are given (anointed with) the gift of the Holy Spirit. We are anointed priest, prophet, and king. "Baptism is a freely given call from God; it is a gift of the Spirit and brings participation in the royal priesthood of Christ."[4] In today's first reading, Saul anoints David king, symbolizing the presence of the Spirit in his life and mission. The anointing of David signals a changed reality for him. Baptism changes our reality—we change from children of the darkness to children of the light. (The second reading from Ephesians also points to today's baptismal focus when it speaks of those who had once lived in darkness but are now children of the light.) David was anointed for a special mission. Baptism anoints us for the reconciling, evangelizing mission of Jesus Christ. David's new identity entitled him to rights and privileges: he received divine protection and was respected. Through baptism we are protected from the snares of the devil and are entitled to rights and privileges as adopted daughters and sons of God. David's anointing was a sign of God's divine election. We, too, are baptized by God's divine election. We can do nothing on our own to merit salvation.

---

[3]Adolf Adam, *The Liturgical Year,* trans. Matthew J. O'Connell (Collegeville: The Liturgical Press, 1990), 102.
[4]Ibid., 103.

Today's liturgy is filled with anticipatory images of baptism as Easter fast approaches. The preface for this liturgy also speaks of being led out of darkness into the light. The prayer after communion seeks enlightenment from the light of the gospel.

Gospel Exegesis

The facilitator gives input regarding what critical biblical scholarship has to say about this text. The input includes insights as to how people would have heard the gospel in Jesus' time.

Today's gospel is a commentary on Jesus' earlier assertion that he is the Light of the World (Jn 8:12).[5] Jesus contrasts the growing vision of the blind man with the increasing blindness of the ones who claim they already see. This story is placed in the context of the controversies between Christians and the synagogue Jews in John's community. There are seven stories in John's gospel that serve to prove that Jesus was who he said he was—the messiah. They also attest to Jesus as the fulfillment of all prior Jewish worship (in this case, the water and light rituals of the Feast of Tabernacles), thus providing the rationale and the credence for the *new worship* of the Christian community. In other words, the stories gave permission to the Christian community to break away from the rituals of the past in order to embrace the new liturgy of Christ.

Jesus met the blind man after he left the temple area during the Feast of Tabernacles. It was a huge feast that attracted many pilgrims to Jerusalem. For a solid week there was great celebrating as all joyously waved their palm fronds.

The feast was at the end of the harvest. Booths had been erected and there was jubilant dancing, song, and festivity. The feast commemorated the entrance into the promised land and the future hope of the messiah at the end of the world. Priests would go to the pool of Siloam each day, draw a golden pitcher of water and recite their ritual prayers. "Rivers of living water will flow from

within him" (Jn 7:37-38). "I am the light of the world. Whoever follows me will not walk in darkness but will have the light of life" (8:12). They poured the water on the corner of the altar at night in the brilliantly illuminated courtyard of the women. The gospel of the man born blind is told in the contextual framework of this feast.

The collection of miracle stories in John is often referred to as the "Book of Signs." This is because, rather than referring to miracles, John speaks of signs. The stories describe the healing signs Jesus performed in his ministry and then discuss their significance (a forerunner of liturgical catechesis, to be sure!). The signs serve as windows to eternity for those who have faith: "...the man born blind truly sees the sign of Jesus as light of the world and the Pharisees remain in the darkness of their stubborn refusal of faith."[6]

The progression of the miracle begins with a theological discussion stating the nature of the problem. The man born blind from birth enters the scene. The disciples ask Jesus whose sin has caused the man's blindness. It was Jewish belief that sin—either of the individual or the parents—caused suffering. Jesus asserts that blindness is not due to human sin, but that God's glory will be seen through the man's blindness.

The next section of the story describes the miracle. Jesus spits into the dirt, makes a clay compress, and places it on the man's eyes, telling him to go and wash in the Siloam pool—the pool from which the water for the Feast of Tabernacles has just been drawn. The man does as he has been told and returns with his sight restored.

The story progresses to a description of reactions to the miracle. The man's neighbors are incredulous and can hardly believe this is the blind man they have always known. The blind man confesses Jesus' identity and answers their queries by reporting what Jesus instructed him to do. The Pharisees ask the man how his sight was restored. The man responds by relating the details again. Some Pharisees accuse Jesus of healing on the Sabbath. The Pharisees then approach the man's parents. Fear-

[5]For further elaboration, refer to: Charles Talbert, *Reading John* (New York: Crossroad, 1992), 158.

[6]Patricia Datchuck Sanchez, *The Word We Celebrate* (Kansas City: Sheed and Ward, 1989), 26.

ful of expulsion from the synagogue, they send the Pharisees back to the son. Finally, the Pharisees believe the man was healed.

The Pharisees challenge the man. They state that Jesus is a sinner. The man says that he does not know whether Jesus is a sinner or not, but perhaps they should go and ask Jesus themselves; *perhaps they, too, would like to be his disciples.* This lets the reader know that the newly sighted man is now a disciple. His healing has caused conversion.

Jesus is now elevated to the status of prophet. The man pleads Jesus' case. Never has there been a known case of someone healing a person blind from birth. The man reminds the Pharisees that everyone knows that God does not hear the prayers of sinners; yet this man's prayers were heard. He recalls and names a foundational scriptural truth that God hears the prayers of those who do the will of God and who are devout. The man confesses his christology (the main agenda of John's gospel) *as a result of his experience of Jesus:* Jesus is a prophet, the Master; he comes from God; he does God's will and God hears his prayers in ways that no one has ever before experienced.

The man is then thrown out of the synagogue. His expulsion is connected to his profession of faith in Jesus and his status as disciple. Jesus hears of the man's expulsion and looks for him. Some scholars believe that the next section of this gospel is an ancient liturgical text used at baptism. The man professes belief in Jesus and then worships him. "With this, the process of conversion is complete. For him, light means salvation/sight."[7]

Jesus then challenges the Pharisees. He asserts that his ministry is to bring light to those who cannot see. The Pharisees goad Jesus: "Do you presume to consider us among the sightless?" Jesus accepts their challenge and tells them that to be given sight means they must believe that they are blind in the first place. The Pharisees very self-righteously believe themselves among the fully sighted, thus not in need of Jesus' marvelous sign. "If people can feel the need for light, the help can be forthcoming. But if they absolu-

tize their blindness as sight, then help is impossible. For them, light means judgment/blindness."[8]

While there is progression in the story, there is also progression in the stages of awareness about Jesus's identity: first he was light, then the one sent, then prophet and Son of Man, and finally, Lord. In the first chapter of John, Jesus was named as the "Light that has come into the world." Today's story shows Jesus *in the process of doing* what God sent him to do: his mission as Light of the world. *The gospel asserts that we will know that Jesus is who he says he is by the signs he performs.*

Talbert maintains that the miracle functions as a sign—it is instruction. Miracles have three purposes. They serve as a way to legitimate and give authority to the person of Jesus. The miracle stories are also a means of evangelization—they bring people to faith. Third, they serve as a means of teaching. The story of Jesus' giving sight to the man born blind is a teaching on Jesus, the Light of the world.

Today's gospel prompts serious examination of our inner integrity and self deceptions. Where are we blind and yet think we see? Are any of our firmly held beliefs subject to the discerning challenge of Jesus' illumination?

It is no wonder this gospel was premier catechesis on baptism. The catechumen progresses, like the man born blind, from darkness to light, from unbelief to belief. This gospel reminds those preparing for baptism, as well as those preparing to renew their baptismal profession of faith at Easter, that "all will have to testify to their faith at the risk of being rejected by some or henceforth ignored by others."[9]

Proclaim the gospel again.

Sometimes we gain new insights when we hear the text after the interpretation has been given. Someone from the group proclaims the gospel a second time.

---

[7]Talbert, *Reading John*, 162.

[8]Ibid.

[9]*Days of the Lord*, Vol. 2 (Collegeville: The Liturgical Press, 1993), 126.

Conversation with the Liturgy and the Scriptures

Test your original understanding in dialogue with the text.

(You might consider breaking into smaller groups.)

Were there any new insights? Was there anything you had not considered before? How does your original understanding of this story compare with what we just shared? How does this story speak to your life?

Participants share an experience from their lives that connects with the biblical interpretation just shared.

> *The blindness of the Pharisees was a blindness rooted in certainty. The Pharisees were certain that they possessed the light and the only truth. It is a dangerous posture.*

> *Our society is steeped in blindness when we continue to perpetrate sins against the world's poor, oppressed, and marginalized. When we continue to foster policies that keep people under the thumb of oppression with the certainty that we are protecting the rights of our own citizenry (e.g., when we do not allow immigrant children access to medical care, etc.), we remain blind to the light of Christ.*

> *Our religious structures are steeped in blindness when we treat some of our members as marginalized people with no voice. We are blind when we dismiss members of our communities such as the uninvolved members of our parishes, the homeless, the poor, homosexuals, women, and all those who find themselves "outside the loop," whether that be at the hierarchical, diocesan, parish, or small-group level.*

> *I am blind when I hang on to personally held beliefs and positions as if they were written with hammer and chisel on the stone of my very own ego. At times I feel so strongly self-righteous about some issues that there is little room for the possibility of needed conversion, particularly if prayer and discernment helped formulate my position in the first place. Some-*

> *times I call that trust; at other times I call it arrogance. Discernment takes place within the Christian community. If and when I am unwilling to listen to all the voices within the community, my discernment is incomplete. I remain in blindness when I am unwilling to allow God to transform my belligerently held convictions.*

> *In my opinion, the primary sin of the Pharisees was idolatry. They presumed to know the mind, heart, and will of God better than God: all things are subject to God's interpretation and intervention. The message for me is: there is a God, and it is not me!*

All share their life experience.

What did I/we hear in this exegesis? What was John's concern for his community in today's gospel? Are there any connections that can be made to our community today? Do the baptismal implications of today's readings have anything to do with our community? What are our collective and personal responses to all of the above questions? Has our original understanding been stretched, challenged, or affirmed?

The gospel demands a response.

How might our community be challenged to change as a result of today's liturgy? In what contrete way does this gospel call our parish to action in the church, parish, neighborhood, or world? Has this conversation changed or stretched my personal attitudes? What is one concrete action I/we will take this week as a response to what we have learned and shared today?

DOCTRINAL ISSUES

What church truth/teaching/doctrinal issue could be drawn from the gospel for the Fourth Sunday in Lent Cycle A?

Participants suggest possible doctrinal themes that flow from the readings.

Possible Doctrinal Themes

Baptism, conversion, election, sin—personal and corporate

Present the doctrinal material at this time.

1. The facilitator gives input on a particular doctrinal issue of his/her prior choosing. OR
2. The group chooses a doctrinal issue from the list they created. They read together from the Doctrinal Appendix.

(The doctrinal issues are found in the Doctrinal Appendix in the back of this workbook. If you are choosing an issue from this resource, please refer to it now.)

Reflection questions centered around the chosen doctrinal theme can be found at the end of each topic in the Doctrinal Appendix. The questions are based on the five-step reflection process. If you choose a topic not included in the Doctrinal Appendix, craft your own questions according to the same five-step process.

Following the reflection questions you will be reminded to return to chapter 7, "Preparing the Catechetical Session," to assist you in crafting your own session.

Closing Prayer

Second Scrutiny: Exorcism

Father of mercy,
you led the man born blind
to the kingdom of light
through the gift of your Son.
Free these elect from the false values that surround and blind them.
Set them firmly in your truth,
children of the light for ever.
We ask this through Christ our Lord.
Amen.

Laying on of hands

Presider stretches hands over the elect:

Lord Jesus,
you are the true light that enlightens the world.
Through the Spirit of truth
free those who are enslaved by the father of lies.
Stir up the desire for good in these elect,
whom you have chosen for your sacraments.
Let them rejoice in your light, that they may see,
and, like the man born blind whose sight you restored,
let them prove to be staunch and fearless witnesses to the faith,
for you are Lord for ever and ever.
Amen.[10]

Selected Bibliography

Adam, Adolf. *The Liturgical Year.* Trans. Matthew J. O'Connell. Collegeville: The Liturgical Press, 1990.

Days of the Lord. Vol. 2. Collegeville: The Liturgical Press, 1993.

Endres, John C., S.J. "Anointing." In *The Collegeville Pastoral Dictionary of Biblical Theology.* Ed. Carroll Stuhlmueller, C.P. Collegeville: The Liturgical Press, 1996.

Fuller, Reginald. *Preaching the New Lectionary.* Collegeville: The Liturgical Press, 1974.

Sanchez, Patricia Datchuck. *The Word We Celebrate.* Kansas City: Sheed and Ward, 1989.

Talbert, Charles. *Reading John.* New York: Crossroad, 1992.

---

[10]Prayer of Exorcism, "Second Scrutiny," *Rite of Christian Initiation of Adults.*

INTRODUCTORY RITES

Opening Song (or Entrance Antiphon)

Give me justice, O God, and defend my cause against the wicked; rescue me from deceitful and unjust men. You, O God, are my refuge.
(Ps 42:1-2)[1]

Opening Prayer

The facilitator of the session may lead the prayer. Others in the group may be asked to proclaim the readings.

Let us pray
[for the courage to follow Christ]

    Pause for silent prayer.

Father,
help us to be like Christ your Son,
who loved the world and died for our salvation.
Inspire us by his love,
guide us by his example,
who lives and reigns with you and the Holy
    Spirit,
one God, for ever and ever. [2]

LITURGY OF THE WORD

Let us listen to God's word.

The readings are proclaimed.

First Reading
Isaiah 43:16-21

The author of Second Isaiah referred to the Babylonian captivity as similar to the exodus event. Thus, the language used to describe the Babylonian exile was couched in metaphors and remembrances of the exodus. Today's pericope is written from the perspective of the exiles who were awaiting release in an alien land. The exiles were encouraged to remember what God had done throughout salvation history. What God had done before, God would surely do again. Thus, through their remembering, God would continue to be present to them. They would continue to reap the benefits of all God had done in the past.

The author portrayed people in relationship with Yahweh. Through sin, the people had severed their covenant relationship with Yahweh. Their exile was understood as divine retribution. Israel was punished. However, there was cause to rejoice. Vindication was coming; soon they would be released from captivity.

Deutero-Isaiah recalled all the pivotal salvation moments. He saw them as hinge events that would serve as an anchor for people to cling to as they passed through their present ordeal.

The "old things" referred to in the text included God's saving acts of the past. The "new things" referred to the things God was presently doing and was going to do in the future. Christianity appropriated that terminology to reflect the new thing God was doing in Christ through his life, death, and resurrection.

Responsorial Psalm
Psalm 126

The psalm refers to the joy of restoration, specifically restoration after the Babylonian exile. Christians use this psalm to reflect the joy of deliverance from the power of sin and death through the saving acts of Jesus.

Second Reading
Philippians 3:8-14

Paul considered all of his advantages prior to his belief in Jesus as loss when he compared them to the advantage of his life in Christ. Paul was concerned over the philosophies that were threaten-

---

[1]Fifth Sunday of Lent: "Entrance Antiphon," *The Sacramentary.*

[2]Fifth Sunday of Lent: "Opening Prayer," *The Sacramentary.*

ing to undermine the gospel. Judaizers and gnostics (extremists) were coming at the gospel from two different threatening positions. Both groups believed they each had the only "way." Both believed themselves to be righteous and just.

Judaizers were trying to impose their old legalisms on the new gentiles. They insisted that the old way had to be embraced by the new converts to Christianity. All must be circumcised, all must adhere to the strict dietary regulations, etc. Justice demanded strict adherence to the law. The gnostics, on the other hand, believed that a person was perfectly "just" simply because of baptism—it began and ended there. There was no need for more. A person was made perfect at baptism.

Paul insisted that justice was realized only through Jesus and our faith in his saving power. Justice, like the unfinished race, was not yet perfected and was still in process. To be a Christian meant that the follower should conform his or her life to Jesus, his life, gospel, death, and resurrection. The Christian follows the example of Jesus' life. The Christian lives in the service of others, dies in the service of others and, through a gradual metanoia, grows in faith and conversion. The race is won when the transformed life reaches fulfillment with Christ in the new and eternal city. But, in this sojourn, we are to continue cooperating with God in the work the Spirit has done, is doing, and will continue to do in our lives.

Gospel
John 8:1-11

Jesus forgives the woman caught in adultery.

STEP 1
NAMING ONE'S EXPERIENCE

What were your first impressions? What was your first response? What grabbed your attention? How did you feel?

Each person names his or her initial impression. Statement should be brief. No reasons should be given at this time. All simply listen without agreeing or disagreeing.

STEP 2
UNDERSTANDING

In a brief statement, what do you think this gospel is trying to convey?

STEP 3
INPUT FROM VISION/STORY/TRADITION

Liturgical Context

The liturgy on the Fifth Sunday of Lent reminds us of the reason we gather for liturgy in the first place. We gather to offer praise and thanks to God; to become a new creation in Christ; to be transformed by the power of Christ in the word, in the eucharist, and in the community. Today's liturgy reminds us that conversion is an ongoing process, that God is not finished with us yet. When we gather at the eucharistic table we ask that we be changed, just as the bread and wine is changed into the Body and Blood of our Lord.

Today's liturgy reminds us that our behavior is the window of the heart. We can fool ourselves, but we cannot fool God. The woman was forgiven much. Yet the Pharisees could not see their own misery. Pride is a liar! When it speaks it sounds righteous and when it acts it appears divinely inspired. For the Pharisees, conversion was not possible, because it was cloaked in their own self-righteous judgment of the woman. Conversion meant that their judgment had to cease. Conversion meant that they had to own their own sin. We are all sinners, but we are forgiven much. Jesus does not condemn us, but he challenges us. Jesus did not have to condemn the Pharisees in their sin because they condemned themselves.

Lent is about purification and enlightenment. The woman today was purified; she expected judgment and received enlightenment: the mercy of Christ. Today's liturgy asks that we gaze around our assembly space. Who are the people in our parish family that we judge? In what way do we act like Pharisees to people in our world?

St. Paul tells us that we continue to be re-created as we run the race toward our goal. What trips us, makes us stumble and lose our way is a proud, stubborn, resistant, judgmental heart. In today's prayer over the gifts we ask Almighty God that the sacrifice we offer take away the sins of those God enlightens with the Christian faith.[3] We ask that the sacrifice of Christ's Body and Blood, offered together at the Sunday liturgy, rid us of the sins of false pride and judgment. The Solemn Blessing asks the Lord to protect us always from every evil that we may serve God with all our hearts. "With all our hearts" implies that we turn toward God and not toward our own self-righteous pride and judgmental attitudes.

Today's liturgy reminds us that conversion is at the heart of it all. We are converted to the God who saves and has always saved (First Reading). We are converted to God who is in relationship to us as people, who is working with us in the life-long process of transformation. We are converted to God who forgives, is infinitely merciful; who does not condemn and who demands that we, in turn, not condemn others. We are converted to a God who cares for the poor, the lost and the broken, the suffering, the poor and rejected, and all who are marginalized, despised, or forsaken. We are converted to a God who, in turn, demands that we do no less. This conversion is the very heart of justice.

> Let us pray
> [for the courage to embrace the world in the
>   name of Christ]
>
> Father in heaven,
> the love of your Son led him to accept
> the suffering of the cross
> that his brothers might glory in new life.
> Change our selfishness into self-giving.
> Help us to embrace the world you have given us,
> that we may transform the darkness of its pain
> into the life and joy of Easter.
> Grant this through Christ our Lord. [4]

Our time of purification and enlightenment is drawing closer to the great feast of Easter. By the time of its approach we will have been emptied, poured out, examined, scrutinized, purified, and enlightened. We will stand as empty vessels, ready to be filled, spilled, and running over with the new life of Easter joy.

Gospel Exegesis

The facilitator gives input regarding what critical biblical scholarship has to say about this text. The input includes insights as to how people would have heard the gospel in Jesus' time.

Most commentators believe that the story of the woman caught in adultery is not Johannine, either in style or theology. The story is a "biographical apophthegm" in which Jesus' enemies set a trap for him that he has to evade through the use of a wise saying or action.[5] The event takes place after one of Jesus' daily teachings in the temple in Jerusalem. It is believed that this story is part of the Lukan tradition.

The situation at hand concerned a married woman caught in adultery and the law's demand that she be stoned. Only an unfaithful wife was charged with adultery. A husband could be charged if found with another man's wife. Only the wronged or offended husband could bring the charge, however. In order for the charge to be made, there had to be two male witnesses to the event in addition to the woman's husband.

The Romans prohibited the Jews from exacting the death penalty when required for violations of Jewish religious law. The trap put Jesus in the position of having to reject either the law of Moses or the Roman authorities. If Jesus agreed that the woman should be stoned, then he could be accused of stoning a woman without hearing her case, which was against the law of Moses. If Jesus indiscriminately pardoned her then he would be accused of "casually absolving the woman," thus becoming her accomplice.[6] If he insisted that they stone her, he would have to contend with the Roman authorities. It was a brilliant trap. For Jesus

---

[3]Fifth Sunday of Lent: "Prayer Over the Gifts," *The Sacramentary.*

[4]Fifth Sunday of Lent: "Alternative Opening Prayer," *The Sacramentary.*

[5]Pheme Perkins, "The Gospel According to John," in *The New Jerome Biblical Commentary,* ed. Raymond E. Brown, S.S., Joseph A. Fitzmyer, S.J., Roland E. Murphy, O.Carm. (Englewood Cliffs: Prentice Hall, 1990), 965.

[6]*Days of the Lord,* Vol. 2 (Collegeville: The Liturgical Press, 1993), 183.

it was a no-win situation. No matter what he answered, he would be caught. However, Jesus turned the trap on the accusers and the woman was left alone with him.

A tradition dating back as far as St. Jerome hypothesized that the words Jesus was writing in the dirt were the sins of those present as they stood in accusation. Patristic commentators believed that Jesus' action of writing on the ground might have been in reference to a passage in Jeremiah in which the *names of those who turn away from Yahweh would have their names written on the earth* (17:13). Other exegetes have suggested that Jesus was writing the passage from Exodus 23:1, stating that no one was to offer malicious witness against another person. In both contexts, Jesus' calligraphy in the dirt was an indictment against the sinners who had brought the accusation and stood in judgment.

Jesus' exhortation that those without sin be the first to throw the stone was a reminder to the accusers of their own need for repentance. He was also subtly reminding them of Deuteronomy 17:7, in which those who stand in accusation as witnesses in a death penalty case carry a special responsibility for the person's death. Inherent in Jesus' statement is the implication: "If you are willing to assume responsibility for this case, then go ahead, throw the first stone. You, too, stand accused."

For a long time, this text was suppressed, as it seemed to be soft on the vows of marriage. However, this story is not a commentary on the state of marriage. Jesus simply recognized the woman's sin, told her to avoid it, and explained that he did not stand in condemnation. He offered forgiveness.

Jesus also challenged the accusers. There is an inherent warning against those who would judge another person: "Judge not, lest ye be judged." In this case, the accusers brought judgment upon themselves.

Reginald Fuller suggests that something is missing in the text. Jesus' lack of condemnation for the woman is not extended to the Pharisees.[7] The sin

of pride is far deadlier than sexual sins; thus, the Pharisees left accused by their own finger of judgment. By pointing one finger at the woman, they were pointing four at themselves.

Jesus was finally left alone with the woman. St. Augustine commented on the emotion the woman must have experienced as she waited for her one-to-one encounter. "*Relicti sunt duo, miseria et misericordia.*" "Only two were left, misery and mercy."[8] Misery met mercy and the woman left the encounter a new creation in Christ.

Jesus is the merciful judge who offers God's forgiveness and invites conversion instead of punishment, retribution, and death. This incredible story of mercy reminds us that we bring condemnation on ourselves when we judge others. We are also reminded of our utter need for God's mercy and forgiveness.

Proclaim the gospel again.

Sometimes we gain new insights when we hear the text after the interpretation has been given. Someone from the group proclaims the gospel a second time.

STEP 4
TESTING

Conversation with the Liturgy and the Scriptures

Test your original understanding in dialogue with the text.

(You might consider breaking into smaller groups.)

What did you hear in this story of the adulterous woman? Were there any new insights? Was there anything you had not considered before? How does your original understanding of this story compare with what was just shared? How does this story speak to your life?

---

[7]Reginald H. Fuller, *Preaching the New Lectionary* (Collegeville: The Liturgical Press, 1974), 10.

[8]St. Augustine, *Traités sur saint Jean*, 33, H. Tissot, edited and translated by *Les Pères vous parlent de l'Evangile*, Vol. 1. *Le Temporal* (Bruges: Apostolat liturgique, 1954), 329; in *Days of the Lord*, Vol. 2 (Collegeville: The Liturgical Press, 1991), 185.

Participants share an experience from their lives that connects with the biblical interpretation just shared.

> *There was a young man who died from AIDS. At his funeral vigil, the family did not hide the reality of the situation. Their son's friends were asked to come "as they were" to share their last remembrances. They were invited to speak. Some of what they shared perhaps was shocking to sensitive ears. Yet, I was so struck by the situation that I could not help but muse: if Jesus were walking on the earth today, this is exactly where he would be, at this gathering of grieving friends and loved ones, gathered around the table, sharing stories. Jesus challenged sinners, but he ate with them, "hung out with them," and called them his friends. To those of us with shocked sensibilities he would say, "Do not judge." Jesus would have shared their stories.*

> *Would he have openly challenged their lifestyle? I do not know for sure what Jesus would have done. The gospel perhaps sheds some light. Jesus waited until everyone left before he told the woman to "sin no more." He loved her unconditionally and he saved her life. This gave him the right and the authority to challenge, yet he never condemned.*

> *Some people left the church that night indignant beyond measure. How could anyone have allowed "those people" to speak? I witnessed the reconciling ministry of Christ in the family of the young man who reached out to their son's friends and thanked God for their giftedness. I saw the reconciling ministry of Christ in the presider who was willing to risk by allowing love the opportunity to speak. I experienced the reconciling presence of God in a loving community that reached out and embraced with God's unconditional acceptance.*

All share their life experience.

What was Jesus' message to the woman? To the Pharisees? What does he have to say to our community and to me today? How are the biblical themes of creation, covenant, exodus, and community evident in today's readings and what do they have to do with us/me? Do I still feel the same way about this text as I did when we began? Has my original understanding been stretched, challenged, or affirmed?

The gospel demands a response.

Has this conversation with the exegesis of the woman caught in adultery changed or stretched my personal attitudes? What are the implications for my life? What am I /we/community/parish called to do in response? What is one concrete action I will take this week as a response to what was learned and shared today?

DOCTRINAL ISSUES

What church truth/teaching/doctrinal issue could be drawn from the gospel for the Fifth Sunday of Lent?

Participants suggest possible doctrinal themes that flow from the readings.

Possible Doctrinal Themes

Forgiveness, redemption, reconciliation, sin, conversion, baptism, grace

Present the doctrinal material at this time.

1. The facilitator gives input on a particular doctrinal issue of his/her prior choosing. OR
2. The group chooses a doctrinal issue from the list they created. They read together from the Doctrinal Appendix.

(The doctrinal issues are found in the Doctrinal Appendix in the back of this workbook. If you are choosing an issue from this resource, please refer to it now.)

Reflection questions centered around the chosen doctrinal theme can be found at the end of each topic in the Doctrinal Appendix. The questions are based on the five-step reflection process. If you choose a topic not included in the Doctrinal Appendix, craft your own questions according to the same five-step process.

Following the reflection questions you will be reminded to return to chapter 7, "Preparing the Catechetical Session," to assist you in crafting your own session.

Closing Prayer

Father, all powerful and ever-living God,
we do well always and everywhere to give you
    thanks.
This season of grace is your gift to your family
to renew us in spirit.
You give us strength to purify our hearts,
to control our desires,
and so to serve you in freedom.
You teach us how to live in this passing world
with our heart set on the world that will never
    end.
Now, with all the saints and angels,
we praise you for ever. [9]

Selected Bibliography

Days of the Lord. Vol. 2. Collegeville: The Liturgical Press, 1993.

Fuller, Reginald H. *Preaching the New Lectionary.* Collegeville: The Liturgical Press, 1974.

Perkins, Pheme. "The Gospel According to John." In *The New Jerome Biblical Commentary.* Ed. Raymond E. Brown, S.S., Joseph A. Fitzmyer, S.J., Roland E. Murphy, O.Carm. Englewood Cliffs: Prentice Hall, 1990.

Sanchez, Patricia Datchuck. *The Word We Celebrate.* Kansas City: Sheed and Ward, 1989.

[9] Fifth Sunday of Lent: "Preface for Lent II (P9)," *The Sacramentary.*

FIFTH SUNDAY OF LENT (CYCLE A)

INTRODUCTORY RITES

Opening Song (or Entrance Antiphon)

Give me justice, O God, and defend my cause against the wicked; rescue me from deceitful and unjust men. You, O God, are my refuge.
(Ps 42: 1-2)[1]

Opening Prayer

The facilitator of the session may lead the prayer. Others in the group may be asked to proclaim the readings.

Let us pray
[for the courage to embrace the
world in the name of Christ]

Pause for silent prayer.

Father in heaven,
the love of your Son led him to accept
the suffering of the cross
that his brothers might glory in new life.
Change our selfishness into self-giving.
Help us to embrace the world you have given us,
that we may transform the darkness of its pain
into the life and joy of Easter.
Grant this through Christ our Lord.[2]

LITURGY OF THE WORD

Let us listen to God's word.

The readings are proclaimed.

First Reading
Ezekiel 37:12-14

The book of Ezekiel is a message of judgment and a message of hope. Ezekiel is considered third in a line of the great writing prophets: Isaiah, Jere-

miah, Ezekiel. Ezekiel was a priest and a prophet who was deported to Babylon along with the other inhabitants of Judah (ca. 597-538 B.C.E.). The prophetic ministry of Ezekiel was a testament to the awesome faithfulness and power of Yahweh. Only Yahweh possessed the power to bring life out of the ashes of despair and failure. Israel understood her tribulation and exile as punishment for her sinfulness. The people of Israel believed that God had punished their disobedience and unfaithfulness by inflicting political disaster. The exile was God's divine retribution and only God could breathe life into their hopeless situation. Ezekiel boldly asserted that even though the signs of God's covenant with Israel (promised land, temple, Davidic monarchy) appeared to be dead and gone, Yahweh was still sovereign and in control of their history.

The exile plays a great role in the corporate memory of this people; it is remembered as Israel's time of tribulation. Yahweh punished Israel for her sins. Yet, in spite of Israel's unfaithfulness, Yahweh was steadfast in his love for her. He never broke the covenant, but rather, in his power and love, stood with her to deliver her in her great time of distress.

Ezekiel vehemently professed God to be the sole agent in Israel's liberation. God spoke the word and caused it to be, so that all would know: "I am the Lord." Ezekiel puts these words in the mouth of the Great Author of Life at least eighty-six times throughout the book.

The great age of Israel had collapsed. The people were forced into an alien land (Babylon) without the support of their religious structures to sustain them in the midst of their ordeal. Ezekiel was a revolutionary. He demanded that Israel engage in reform that would see them through their faith-shattering trials.

Ezekiel forged a bold, new path in prophecy. His language and style were unlike those of any prophet before him. The literary text reads like an oratory which suggests that an oral tradition pre-

---

[1]Fifth Sunday of Lent: "Entrance Antiphon," *The Sacramentary.*

[2]Fifth Sunday of Lent: "Alternative Opening Prayer," *The Sacramentary.*

ceded its writing. Ezekiel's message was clear: trust Yahweh, return to the corporate memory and celebration of God's previous saving actions. Worship and observe the law, and faith will be strengthened. Since Ezekiel stressed the Torah as central to his message, he is often called the "father of modern Judaism."

Today's pericope is concerned with the restoration of Israel. Ezekiel assured his audience that the covenant with Israel was still operative (ch. 37). Ezekiel received two visions: one vision was Israel—dead, lifeless, dry bones. In Ezekiel's vision, Yahweh literally breathed life into the dead bones and they were restored to life (37:1-14). The hopeless Israel was given hope and promise for future restoration. Ezekiel's second vision was the convergence of the twelve tribes into one people.

Ezekiel's vision was a summary of his ministry to those in exile: the dead Israel would be restored by the divine breath, wind, spirit (*ruah*) of God. Ezekiel's vision in today's pericope was not intended as a commentary on the resurrection of individuals from the dead.

Ezekiel's vision left nothing to the imagination: death presided over the bone-littered plain. Yahweh and Yahweh alone must intervene if the tables were to turn and if life was to be restored into Israel's breathless corpse.

Responsorial Psalm
Psalm 130

Today's psalm, one of the seven penitential psalms, is an individual lament. The psalmist pleads for deliverance from distress.

Second Reading
Romans 8: 8-11

Paul's letter to the Romans typifies a refined, systematic articulation of Pauline theology. It is considered his greatest theological masterpiece.

Paul insists that God freely *forgives and forgets* people's sins; they are not held against them. Each sinner is welcomed into God's loving arms as a parent would forgive a precious, wayward child. The child is treated as if she or he had never strayed in the first place. The law can never re-

place the peace, freedom, and relief that only God can give. With the law, human beings work out their own salvation. With Christ, it is already won for those who accept it. Prior to Christ, the law had been a necessary guide. But now, the guide is Christ. We are set free from sin by Jesus' saving action. Jesus' death/resurrection opened the way for the Spirit to reign in the hearts of humankind.

Paul offers us the greatest gift: to see ourselves as God sees us—loved and forgiven. The law does not give us freedom; only Christ gives us freedom. This does not mean that we are no longer bound to an ethical code. Law will always serve as a reminder of our obligations and responsibilities to God, the world, other people, and ourselves. Paul insists that the law does not "capture the will of God."[3] Jesus did not come to create a new set of rigid codes that would replace the old set of rigid codes. Jesus did not denigrate the law; he simply wished to restore its heart.

Jesus came to *show us how to live*. Discipleship consists in living in the pattern of Christ—doing what he did. Thus, Christians are freed from rigid observance of the law. They are, instead, guided by a new motivator—the Spirit of God. When led by the Spirit, Christians participate in a mature, love-based faith. It is a faith based on biblical justice (*hesed*): a reciprocal, covenant relationship with God that is active, alive, and produces every good action because of the demands of love. Loving God with heart, mind, and soul is synonymous with extending that same love to all of God's creation. It is a higher law—one that is not self-determined, but rather Spirit-provoked.

Human nature is flawed because of the sinful, human condition—no one is exempt. However, we must never forget the power and affirmation of our Genesis origins: God created men and women in God's image and saw that "it was good." Thus, we have the ultimate disposition and created potential to be elevated to the divine status that has been our birthright since the beginning of the world. Yet we are nevertheless born into a sinful world and are thus subject to sin. It is simply (or

---

[3]Hubert Richards, *The Gospel According to St. Paul* (Collegeville: The Liturgical Press, 1990), 97.

not so simply) the way it is. We are human beings and so we are sinners. The indwelling of the Spirit prompts, nudges, and leads us, ever so gently—and sometimes not so gently—toward the created grace that is our destiny. The Spirit gives human beings the possibility of being free from sin. Humanity is to cooperate with the work of creation taking place within each of us. It is not automatic. The Spirit provides the yeast and, out of love, we become what the flour was destined to become: one complete loaf, ready to be broken and shared.

We are new creations in Christ to the extent that we cooperate with the generating work of the Spirit within us. When we live the cycle of death and resurrection and when we lay down our lives for others, we become that which we were created to be. "Paul shows how theology and morality are intimately connected. When we speak of 'Christian being,' we are led to discern what is 'Christian acting.'"[4]

Gospel
John 11:1-45

Jesus raises Lazarus from the dead.

STEP 1
NAMING ONE'S EXPERIENCE

What were your first impressions? What was your first response? What grabbed your attention? How did you feel?

Each person names his or her initial impression. Statement should be brief. No reasons should be given at this time. All simply listen without agreeing or disagreeing.

STEP 2
UNDERSTANDING

In a brief statement, what do you think this gospel is trying to convey?

STEP 3
INPUT FROM VISION/STORY/TRADITION

Liturgical Context

The raising of Lazarus is Jesus' last sign to the world before his impending passion. These are signs because they not only reveal Yahweh, the Almighty, Powerful Creator, but they point to the One who performed the sign, Jesus, the Christ. The signs of Jesus call people to radical faith.

This story is a prelude to the cross. It leads the way; it shows us the meaning of Jesus' coming passion. Lazarus was raised from the dead for a brief respite; Jesus was raised forever. Through Jesus' death and resurrection we all share in the Lazarus sign. The raising of Lazarus prompts every believer to answer the ultimate question: "Do you believe that I am the resurrection and the life?"

Most of John's signs are accompanied by an explanation of the event, except in this instance. This gospel reads more like an unfolding liturgy with a "certain number of declarations made as the action develops. . . . 'This illness does not end in death, but is for the glory of God, that the Son of Man might be glorified through it' . . . 'Lazarus has died. And I am glad for you that I was not there, that you may believe' . . . This sort of composition has been likened to the words of a commentator explaining the unfolding of a liturgy,[5] arousing the attention, spurring the curiosity, and provoking the reflection of the assembly."[6] The declarations made in today's unfolding liturgy prompt assemblies ancient and contemporary to answer the question: "Do you believe in Jesus, the Christ, the One who raised Lazarus from the dead, and the One who can and will raise us from the death of our sinful lives?"

In this liturgy, the elect who are preparing to plunge into the baptismal waters leading to new life stand in the face of impending death and with the entire assembly proclaim with Lazarus,

---

[4]*Days of the Lord,* Vol. 2 (Collegeville: The Liturgical Press, 1993), 129.

---

[5]This image is attributed to M. Moret, *Assemblées du Seigneur,* 2nd series, No 18 (Paris: Publications de Saint-Andrè—Cerf, 1971), 22. In *Days of the Lord,* Vol. 2, 131.

[6]*Days of the Lord,* Vol. 2, 131.

Martha, Mary, well wishers, and previous nay-sayers, "Yes, Lord, we do believe that you are the resurrection and the life."

Sin and death reigned in the world. Jesus shattered the choke-hold that death asserted over the neck of a powerless people. Lazarus is a sign and an explanation of the paschal event, of Jesus, the Resurrection and the Life.

The first and second readings attest to God's life-force in the world, the Holy Spirit. Through the power of the indwelling Spirit, we are left a living legacy that entails ongoing participation in the same resurrected life Lazarus was given. In the opening prayer of the Fifth Sunday of Lent, we ask to be inspired and guided by Christ's love and example. In the alternative opening prayer we are reminded of Christ's passion. We ask for the strength to embrace the cross, to work for the transformation of the world, and to be delivered from darkness that blinds us to sin and keeps us from the joy of Easter.

Today the elect celebrate the third and last scrutiny, one of the last steps before they enter into the Lord's ongoing *pasch*—the eucharistic banquet. The elect, with the entire church, celebrate Christ's victory over the systemic evil that keeps people lifeless, like dry, brittle, dead bones rotting in a worldly grave of death and despair. In the celebration of the third scrutiny we pray that the elect be "liberated from the shackles of sin that they may become like Christ by baptism, dead to sin and alive forever in God's sight" and "that they be filled with the hope of the life-giving Spirit and prepare themselves thoroughly for their birth to new life..." so the "eucharistic food, which they are soon to receive, may make them one with Christ, the source of life and of resurrection."[7] We thus pray to the Lord—for them and for ourselves.

The third scrutiny on this Fifth Sunday leads us to the premier moment in our liturgical life—the Triduum, the Easter pasch. We are poured out like a libation, ready for Easter filling.

Today brings us to the threshold of Holy Week. Stripped bare of our illusions, confronted with our blindness and insincere motives, the faithful and the elect prepare to enter the tomb of Christ's death and resurrection. We enter the darkened womb of this Holy Week enlightened by Christ who is the "water for which we thirst," the "light of our blindness" and our very "life's breath." We wait to be born anew in the dawn of Easter light. We will then go forth renewed, refreshed, and committed to live the *pasch* until, once again depleted, we will return next year to begin the paschal cycle once again.

Presentation of the Lord's Prayer

The presentation of the Lord's Prayer generally takes place during the week following the third scrutiny, "preferably in the presence of a community of the faithful, within Mass" (RCIA, #178). The Lord's Prayer has always been the prayer "proper to those who in baptism have received the spirit of adoption" (RCIA, #148). The Lord's Prayer gives the elect a better appreciation of God as their Father and thus prepares them to stand in the midst of the celebrating assembly and pray this prayer with confidence. At their baptism they will stand for the first time with the assembly and proclaim this foundational prayer. The creed and the Lord's Prayer have always been considered central to the Christian faith and prayer. The RCIA does allow the presentation of the Lord's Prayer to be deferred until the preparation rites for Holy Saturday.

Gospel Exegesis

The facilitator gives input regarding what critical biblical scholarship has to say about this text. The input includes insights as to how people would have heard the gospel in Jesus' time.

A few verses before this pericope begins, John tells us that "many came to believe in him." This is an excellent springboard for understanding the purpose of the Lazarus sign. Many came to believe in Jesus. Therefore, there was now urgency on the part of the chief priests to put Jesus to death. The stakes were higher. Jesus was having an influence on the people and they were becoming his disciples. Prior to this time, Jesus had had less impact on the Jewish community. People had been rejecting his message and fighting among themselves. Now things were changing, and many Jews were coming

---

[7] *Rite of Christian Initiation of Adults*, #174.

to believe in him. Peter Ellis suggests that John may have been mirroring what was taking place in the Johannine community "in the divisions among the people and in the animosity of the Jewish leaders toward those who wanted to accept Jesus and abandon the synagogue" (9:22 and 16:2).[8]

Jesus' greatest "sign," the raising of Lazarus from the dead, leads to the decisive act of unbelief, the formal decision that Jesus must "die for the people" (11:1-57).[9] Thus, the plot thickens and the collaboration of the religious leaders to have Jesus put to death begins. The Lazarus event is the catalyst for their decision to put the plans for his execution into motion.

The miracle stories in chapters 5 and 9 highlight the growing tension between Jesus and the religious authorities and set up this final event. Jesus healed the paralytic in a few short verses and then engaged in a debate with the Pharisees over curing on the Sabbath. Jesus healed the blind man in a brief narrative, and in the rest of the dialogue confronted the blindness of his interrogators. Thus, the miracle signs of chapters 5 and 9 were recounted not only to attest to Jesus' miraculous power to heal (while they indeed served that function), but also as a means of illustrating the judgment Jesus was hurling at the religious establishment.

The evangelist crafted his story around the premise that Jesus' *signs*, especially the gift of life, were gifts from the Father. Ellis believes that, in this instance, the miracle is the point of the story; it demonstrates Jesus' power to raise the dead and offer eternal life.[10] Jesus waited until the fourth day before he went to the side of his grieving friends. At first glance, Jesus' delay seems callous. Perhaps first-century listeners would have thought it more than callous; they may have thought it downright cruel. They would have known without question that by the fourth day Lazarus would have been as dead as those dry, rotted, brittle bones that were littered across Ezekiel's plain. Prior to the fourth day, there might have been

hope. "Rabbinical tradition taught that the life breath hovered around the body for three days. After that, all hopes for resuscitation were pointless."[11] Why would Jesus wait so long to go to his dying friend?

By making sure that the reader and the witnesses were fully aware that Lazarus was totally, irrevocably dead, John skillfully crafted the point of the miracle. All hope was lost. There was nothing anyone could do. Like the dead bones in the first reading, only God could breathe life into the situation. It was beyond human imagination and control. "...For the Johannine Jesus, the impossible is merely a matter of routine."[12] Jesus' miracle, by his own confession, was to bring people to faith and to reveal and glorify God.

John always refers to life in the eternal sense. Whether human beings are offered the gift of eternal life or not, everyone is subject to the body's mortality. Just as Lazarus was raised to life for a short while only to later die a natural death, so too, are people subject to the same mortality. "As mortal human beings they face the fact of death; but as believers in the Son who possesses the gift of eternal life, here and now, they can confidently look forward to their own resurrection from the dead. Of course, you have to die before you can rise from the dead never to die again; else, the resurrection would merely be a resuscitation."[13] Yet, amidst this mysterious, awe-inspiring gift, there is a lurking dark cloud: the gift of life is also cause for people to maliciously turn against Jesus.

Jesus went to Bethany because of the news of his friend Lazarus' death. Jesus confirmed that the illness would not result in death, but would be for the glory of God. Jesus stayed where he was for two more days in spite of the anxiety and grief of his friends. In typical Johannine style, Jesus' action was a sign that the miracle was going to be at God's initiative, not because of human pressures. "The illness and Jesus' behavior were under divine control."[14]

---

[8]Peter F. Ellis, *The Genius of John* (Collegeville: The Liturgical Press, 1984), 181.

[9]Pheme Perkins, "John," in *The New Jerome Biblical Commentary*, ed. Raymond E. Brown, S.S., Joseph A. Fitzmyer, S.J., Roland E. Murphy, O.Carm. (Englewood Cliffs: Prentice Hall, 1990), 969.

[10]Ellis, *The Genius of John*, 181.

[11]Patricia Datchuck Sanchez, *The Word We Celebrate* (Kansas City: Sheed and Ward, 1989), 29.

[12]Ibid.

[13]Stanley B. Marrow, *The Gospel of John* (New York: Paulist Press, 1995), 187.

[14]Charles Talbert, *Reading John* (New York: Crossroad, 1992), 172.

Pharisees believed in life after death and Martha professed that belief. Jesus asserted that he was the realization of that foundational belief—"I am the Resurrection and the Life." He was making eternal life possible through the gift of his life.

Jesus arrived at the tomb of Lazarus and wept. Charles Talbert suggests that John was portraying Jesus as a human figure who felt the deepest grief over the loss of a friend, the same grief he experienced over his own impending death and the same grief he experienced knowing that he would be betrayed by a disciple (12:27, 13:21). However, Jesus' weeping is contrasted to the weeping of Mary and the other mourners. Jesus wept sincere tears of sorrow, but did not wail like the other mourners. Wailing was an expression of despair. "Profound grief at such bereavement is natural enough; grief that degenerates into despair, that pours out its loss as if there were no resurrection, is an implicit denial of that resurrection."[15]

However, other scholars suggest a different interpretation of Jesus' emotion at the death of Lazarus. Jesus' weeping does not make much sense if he was aware that he was going to raise Lazarus from the dead. The Greek word *embrimasthai* suggests strong emotion. However, some scholars assert that Jesus' deep emotion is related to his justified anger "at the powers of darkness and evil with whom Jesus is about to do battle. In this emotion and the act which followed it, Jesus' victory over illness, darkness, sin, death and evil is complete and absolute."[16]

Jesus prayed a prayer of thanksgiving over the tomb of Lazarus. It was prayer rooted in ongoing intimacy with his Father. "It is not a prayer of petition, but rather for the purpose of indicating to those assembled his own close relationship with the Father."[17] Jesus' prayer demonstrated that the power he needed depended on God's gift. Jesus summoned Lazarus from the grave and gave the instruction to unbind him from his funeral wrappings. Thus, Jesus, who was called Lord throughout this gospel, completed the revival of the dead man, thereby asserting his sovereignty and authority.[18]

The reaction is two-fold: some believed through the sign he performed; others conspired to have him executed (see later verses). Jesus was a threat to the institutional and national Jewish identity. John the Baptist was killed because Herod feared a political uprising of John's followers. The Jewish leaders feared that the hard hand of government would come crashing down on their "holy place" and their "nation" as a result of Jesus' ministry. It would appear as if John was suggesting that the leaders were acting in order to protect the lives and worship of the Jewish community.

Richard Cassidy supports D. A. Carson's position that there were no such noble intentions. When Caiaphas stated that it would be better for one man to die for the many, he was in effect indicting himself and his co-conspirators. What Caiaphas really meant was that it would be better for the one man (Jesus) to die to protect Caiaphas and the Sanhedrin. They were the ones who stood to lose the most because of Jesus' alleged insurrection activities. The Romans might be angered enough to take away what little political, legal, and religious control the Sanhedrin enjoyed. Caiaphas uttered the prophetic oracle that Jesus would die for the whole nation so they would not perish. Indeed, Jesus did die to save all nations—past, present, and yet to come. There is a brilliant piece of irony in this segment. John has Caiaphas utter the prophetic meaning of Jesus' death and yet, from Caiaphas's point of view, he was merely positing the *party line* the Sanhedrin would assume when explaining their intentions to have Jesus killed. Caiaphas was rehearsing for the Sanhedrin what their response might be: "We were simply protecting the nation from Roman intervention and subsequent calamity. If we do not have him killed, the very fiber of our identity, our temple worship, may be threatened."[19]

Chapters 10 and 11 seek to show Jesus as the fulfillment of the Feast of Dedication because of the *signs* he performed. In this way, John's Jesus was authenticating the new worship emerging in the Christian community. This worship would supersede the traditional forms of Israel's worship, such

[15]D. A. Carson, *The Gospel According to John* (Grand Rapids: Eerdmans, 1991), 416.

[16]Sanchez, *The Word We Celebrate*, 29.

[17]Richard J. Cassidy, *John's Gospel in New Perspective* (Maryknoll, NY: Orbis Books, 1992), 37.

[18]Ibid.

[19]Ibid., 43, 107, #8.

as: temple sacrifices, purification rituals, temple worship on Gerazim or Jerusalem (see Samaritan woman), the water rituals that promise healing of the body, the feasts of Passover, Tabernacles, and Dedication. The new rituals were seen as the fulfillment of the old.

According to Charles Talbert, in John's gospel, the *disbelief of the people* motif served as a fulfillment of the biblical prophecies such as: "He has blinded their eyes and hardened their heart, lest they should see with their eyes and turn to me to heal them" (Is. 6:10). While human responsibility is not negated in John's gospel, divine sovereignty is a major theme. Thus, God is the architect (planner) of salvation history. Faith is a gift from God generated by divine initiative. Governments are also under the control of God. John maintains that even though God initiates and directs history, human beings are still responsible for their decisions. Those who did not believe in Jesus were responsible for their actions, but these actions were also part of God's plan.[20]

If we make wrong decisions, the implications for our lives are disastrous. We might find ourselves standing with the Sanhedrin in opposition to the saving love of God. Perhaps we will choose our own self interests of power and control while fooling ourselves and others into believing it is for the good of others. Or worse, we may try to stand in the way of God's gift of life by discouraging people in their quest for Jesus Christ, whether by our actions, attitudes or speech, conscious or unconscious. In other words, we have the freedom to choose death over life.

However, life is far more attractive. Jesus offers us life, fulfillment, and joy. We profess and celebrate the gift of life given to us through his paschal mystery. We accept Jesus as Lord of the hopeless, Lord of sinners, and Lord of history. We are heirs to eternal life because of Jesus' saving action and we accept his radical, unconditional love and truth with eyes of faith. Thus, fear loses its control over us. Nevertheless, the ball remains in our court; we are still left with a decision.

Jesus embraced hopelessness and became hope for the world. Jesus became sin and in the process delivered the world. Jesus delivered us from the snares of death and offered us resurrection and eternal life.

Proclaim the gospel again.

Sometimes we gain new insights when we hear the text after the interpretation has been given. Someone from the group proclaims the gospel a second time.

STEP 4:
TESTING

Conversation with the Liturgy and the Scriptures

Test your original understanding in dialogue with the text.

(You might consider breaking into smaller groups.)

Were there any new insights? Was there anything you had not considered before? How does your original understanding of this story compare with what we just shared? How does this story speak to your life?

Participants share an experience from their lives that connects with the biblical interpretation just shared.

> *One night, on the first Friday of Lent, we received the call every parent of teenagers dreads: "Come to the hospital, your son has been in an accident and someone is dead." We rushed to the hospital to discover that our son had been spared, but his best friend since fifth grade had died in his arms. Thus, Adam's family, our son, and the friends of the boys were forced to reflect on the precious gift of life. Some folks would innocently and lovingly say to us: "You are so blessed that God spared your son." I found myself cringing. If God spared my son, then it meant that he had snatched Adam. I had to wrestle with the mystery: "If you ordain all life and if you are the architect of our lives, [so went the argument], then you must have willed that Adam die and Joe live." For a time, I even bought into the concept. "God must really have wonderful plans for your life," I horrifically said to my son. He shuddered at the words: "Mom, don't say that. Don't you understand what a burden that puts on me?" I had to retract my untenable position. No, God is not, cannot be like that. God is the author of life; he is not a puppeteer who holds the strings and amuses himself by choosing this life over that life.*

---

[20]Talbert, *Reading John*, 173, 174.

This gospel gives great consolation and meaning to Adam's death. While we grieve over his death (it is now two years later and my son is still grieving), we are assured that Adam's death will not end in despair. Adam knows perfect happiness. We are the ones who are sorrowful. As Christians, we have the eyes of faith to see us through the tragic death of a loved one, particularly a young person. There is no rhyme or reason. Life happens; we are mortal human beings. God is with us in the living of life, but God does not pull all the strings. How it works is a mystery. Death is hideous. If we were not people of faith, despair would be an understandable reaction. It would be difficult to find meaning in a tragic death such as Adam's. We grieve for those who mourn the loss of loved ones, but faith gives us the assurance to know that Adam is far happier in his glorified state than he would have been in this world's sojourn. The Order of Christian Funerals asserts that the bonds of love forged in life do not end with death, but continue into eternity.

There are some who say that faith is this world's opiate for dealing with the tragedies of life. Jesus promised us that we would share eternal life; but he also showed us the price—the cross. So many issues emerged from the experience of Adam's death. The goodness and love of the local teens flowed in the midst of the tragedy. For days they held vigil, told stories, and reflected on the meaning of his death.

Many young people came to the funeral from homes where the word "Jesus" had never been spoken. Others were in their own personal deaths of despair, meaninglessness and disillusionment because of an adult world that had hurt them. Jesus is the life and the resurrection, but what does that mean to our young people who are hardened by cynicism? My son eulogized his friend, shared how much he cared for Adam and what Adam had meant to him. He offered a challenge. "We have to learn from Adam's death. We have to allow the experience to change us. If we do, his death will have meant something."

The liturgist in me could not help but apply symbolic meaning to the experience. It was a teachable moment for the kids and for us. The name "Adam" means red clay and the first man. Adam, the first young man among their friends to die and return to the red clay of the earth, was also the first to experience the life Jesus promised in today's gospel. He per-haps even paved the way for others. If his death prompted one young person to consider his or her life, then Adam, the first one to return to the red clay of the earth, was like a Christ figure. He paid the price with his life.

While there is no Sanhedrin to taunt us, we face similar enemies when we try to bring life to others. We often find ourselves headed straight for the cross. There is so much death around us. One need only encounter the hopelessness of many young people to observe it first hand. But today's gospel reminds us that we have the gift of life, not only for ourselves, but as a gift to offer all those who find life meaning-less and without hope. It is not only Good News, it is the best news.

All share their life experience.

What was John trying to tell his community? Are there any present-day similarities between the issues in John's community and the issues the contemporary church faces? How does this gospel call us (biblical theme of community) or me to be re-created (creation), to experience life, death, and resurrection (exodus) and commitment to my/our relationship with God (covenant)? Do I still feel the same way about this text as I did when we began? Has my original understanding been stretched, challenged, or affirmed?

STEP 5
DECISION

The gospel demands a response.

What specific thing am I /we/community/parish called to do in response to today's gospel? Has this conversation with the exegesis of the raising of Lazarus changed or stretched my personal attitudes? What are the implications for my life? What is one concrete action I will take this week as a response to what we have learned and shared today?

DOCTRINAL ISSUES

What church truth/teaching/doctrinal issue could be drawn from the gospel for the Fifth Sunday of Lent, Cycle A ?

Participants suggest possible doctrinal themes that flow from the readings.

Possible Doctrinal Themes

Eternal life, sin, cross, baptism, soteriology, Jesus the Christ, paschal mystery

Present the doctrinal material at this time.

1. The facilitator gives input on a particular doctrinal issue of his/her prior choosing. OR
2. The group chooses a doctrinal issue from the list they created. They read together from the Doctrinal Appendix.

(The doctrinal issues are found in the Doctrinal Appendix in the back of this workbook. If you are choosing an issue from this resource, please refer to it now.)

Reflection questions centered around the chosen doctrinal theme can be found at the end of each topic in the Doctrinal Appendix. The questions are based on the five-step reflection process. If you choose a topic not included in the Doctrinal Appendix, craft your own questions according to the same five-step process.

Following the reflection questions you will be reminded to return to chapter 7, "Preparing the Catechetical Session," to assist you in crafting your own session.

Closing Prayer

Father of life and God not of the dead but of the
    living,
you sent your Son to proclaim life,
to snatch us from the realm of death,
and to lead us to the resurrection.
Free these elect
from the death-dealing power of the spirit of evil,
so that they may bear witness
to their new life in the risen Christ,
for he lives and reigns for ever and ever.

Laying on of hands

Presider stretches hands over the elect.

Lord Jesus,
by raising Lazarus from the dead
you showed that you came that we might have life
and have it more abundantly.
Free from the grasp of death
those who await your life-giving sacraments
and deliver them from the spirit of corruption.
Through your Spirit, who gives life,
fill them with faith, hope, and charity,
that they may live with you always
in the glory of your resurrection,
for you are Lord for ever and ever.[21]

Selected Bibliography

Boadt, Lawrence, C.S.P. "Ezekiel." In *The New Jerome Biblical Commentary*. Ed. Raymond E. Brown, S.S., Joseph A. Fitzmyer, S.J., Roland E. Murphy, O.Carm. Englewood Cliffs: Prentice Hall, 1990.

Carson, D. A. *The Gospel According to John*. Grand Rapids: Eerdmans, 1991.

Cassidy, Richard J. *John's Gospel in New Perspective*. Maryknoll, NY: Orbis Books, 1992.

Days of the Lord. Vol. 2. Collegeville: The Liturgical Press, 1993.

Ellis, Peter F. *The Genius of John*. Collegeville: The Liturgical Press, 1984.

Fuller, Reginald H. *Interpreting the Miracles*. London: SCM, 1963.

Kselman, John S., S.J., Michael L. Barre, S.S. "Psalms." In *The New Jerome Biblical Commentary*. Ed. Raymond E. Brown, S.S., Joseph A. Fitzmyer, S.J., Roland E. Murphy, O.Carm. Englewood Cliffs: Prentice Hall, 1990.

Marrow, Stanley B. *The Gospel of John*. New York: Paulist Press, 1995.

Perkins, Pheme. "The Gospel According to John." In *The New Jerome Biblical Commentary*. Ed. Raymond E. Brown, S.S., Joseph A. Fitzmyer, S.J., Roland E. Murphy, O.Carm. Englewood Cliffs: Prentice Hall, 1990.

Richards, Hubert. *The Gospel According to St. Paul*. Collegeville: The Liturgical Press, 1990.

Talbert, Charles. *Reading John*. New York: Crossroad, 1992.

---

[21] *Rite of Christian Initiation of Adults*, #175.

PASSION SUNDAY (PALM SUNDAY)

On Passion Sunday [Palm Sunday] the Church enters into the mystery of its crucified, buried and risen Lord, who, by his entrance into Jerusalem, gave a glimpse of his own majesty. Christians carry branches as a sign of the royal triumph that Christ won by his acceptance on the cross. Since Saint Paul says: "Provided we suffer with him in order that we may also be glorified with him," the link between these two aspects of the paschal mystery should stand out clearly in the liturgical celebration and catechesis of Palm Sunday.[1]

INTRODUCTORY RITES

Opening Song (or Entrance Antiphon)

Hosanna to the Son of David,
the king of Israel.
Blessed is he who comes
in the name of the Lord.
Hosanna in the highest. (Mt 21:9)
Let us go forth in peace,
praising Jesus our Messiah,
as did the crowds who welcomed him to
    Jerusalem.[2]

Environment

The cross is the primary symbol of today's liturgy and should be prominently displayed in the catechetical environment.

Opening Prayer

The facilitator of the session may lead the prayer. Others in the group may be asked to proclaim the readings.

Let us pray
[for a closer union with Christ
during this holy season]

Pause for silent prayer.

---

[1] *Ceremonial of Bishops,* #263, in *The Liturgy Documents* (Chicago: Liturgy Training Publications, 1991), 213.

[2] Passion Sunday: "Commemoration of the Lord's Entrance into Jerusalem: The Procession," *The Sacramentary.*

Almighty, ever-living God
you have given the human race
Jesus Christ our Savior
as a model of humility.
He fulfilled your will
by becoming man and giving his life on the cross.
Help us to bear witness to you
by following his example of suffering
and make us worthy to share in his resurrection.
We ask this through our Lord
Jesus Christ, your Son,
who lives and reigns with you and the Holy Spirit,
one God, for ever and ever.[3]

LITURGY OF THE WORD

Let us listen to God's word.

The readings are proclaimed.

First Reading
Isaiah 50:4-7

Today's pericope is the second servant song in Deutero-Isaiah. In this song the prophet bemoans the rejection of his message. The people had grown weary of his optimism for the future while they were suffering amid the trials of the exile. However, their frustration would not stop him. He was given a word from the Lord and nothing would keep him from delivering the message. His suffering would result in vindication once Yahweh proved him right. He would not be deterred.

The Christian community thought of Jesus as the suffering servant of Isaiah. Jesus, too, would not be deterred from speaking and living the word he was given. The word he came to preach was one of love and faithfulness. His faithfulness ultimately led him to the cross. This is the fate of all prophets who faithfully proclaim and live their God-given message: a one way ticket to the cross, glory, and ultimate vindication.

---

[3] Passion Sunday: "Opening Prayer," *The Sacramentary.*

Responsorial Psalm

22:8-9, 17-18, 19-20, 23-24

This is the first Old Testament scriptural text to have been appropriated for Christian usage. To an innocent onlooker, it seems to have been specifically written with the passion events in mind. This psalm served as a proof text that Jesus indeed was the promised messiah. The psalm speaks of an innocent one's suffering. The details surrounding the suffering servant in the psalm bear an incredible resemblance to the passion and death of Jesus. It is no wonder that the early Christians related this text to the suffering of Christ.

Second Reading

Philippians 2:6-11

It is believed that Paul inserted this beautiful, previously crafted hymn into his letter to the Philippians. Some consider it a perfect expression of Pauline theology regarding the passion and death of Jesus. This hymn was probably used in ancient Christian liturgies and profoundly captures the essence and the paradox of Christian redemption. Jesus, through abject humiliation (see Fourth Sunday of Lent, Cycle C, parable of the prodigal son), offered the free gift of himself. Through such humiliation, salvation was won. Jesus left his rightful throne with Yahweh, descended into the midst of humanity, and took the form of a slave, subject to the suffering and limitations of the human person. He allowed himself to be rejected, misunderstood, and treated like a slave and a criminal. Because of this free gift of self, this abasement, Jesus ascended back to the throne victorious. Because of the resurrection, humanity was and is offered freedom from the ravages of sin and death, and the promise of eternal life. Jesus, the perfect servant, model of all perfect servants, earned the rightful title, Lord, *Kyrios* (Greek), *Adonai* (Hebrew).

Paul was addressing the factions in the Philippian community. He pleaded that all assume the posture of Jesus. If they would only assume the model of Christ's self-abasement, then harmony and peace would be restored to the community. Jesus could have claimed all the rights and privileges of royalty. But he did not. "He became sin." He entered the human condition with all its defects and in the process emptied himself. The Philippian community was exhorted to embrace *kenosis*, a voluntary emptying of self in the manner of Jesus. Paul challenged his community to turn away from the lure of power and control, to assume the humble stance of self-giver. Jesus, emptied and poured-out, went willingly to his passion and death. We are to follow in his footsteps.

Gospel

The Passion of our Lord Jesus Christ according to Luke.

STEP 1
NAMING ONE'S EXPERIENCE

What were your first impressions, your first response? What grabbed your attention? How did you feel?

Each person names his or her initial impression. Statement should be brief. No reasons should be given at this time. All simply listen without agreeing or disagreeing.

STEP 2
UNDERSTANDING

In a brief statement, what do you think were the primary concerns of Luke's version of the passion?

STEP 3
INPUT FROM VISION/STORY/TRADITION

Liturgical Context

The title of today's liturgy expresses its double emphasis: Passion Sunday/Palm Sunday. Today we remember Jesus' triumphant entry into Jerusalem and his passion and death on the cross. "Holy Week has as its purpose the remembrance of Christ's passion, beginning with his Messianic entrance into Jerusalem."[4] The origins of Holy Week

---

[4]"General Norms for the Liturgical Year and the Calendar" (GNLY), in *The Liturgy Documents* (Chicago: Liturgy Training Publications, 1991), #31.

began with a yearly celebration of the Lord's pasch in the spirit of the Jewish Passover. Jesus was celebrated as the new Passover, the one who passed from death into life. The purpose of the celebration was to remember and make present the eschatological implications of Jesus' passion, death, and resurrection. There was very little concern for recording the historical facts. "The redemptive event was a unitary feast, embracing the passion, death and resurrection and exaltation of the Messiah and the outpouring of the Spirit and the anticipation of his coming again."[5]

On the Sunday that began Holy Week, the Jerusalem Christians of the fourth century proceeded to the great church (Anastasis) called the *martyrium* (the place behind Golgotha where the Lord was crucified). Following their morning eucharist and right before the dismissal, the archdeacon announced the beginning of the "Great Week" and summoned Christians to meet each day, "beginning tomorrow" at the ninth hour in the *martyrium.* He instructed them to be ready at the seventh hour (early evening) and to meet at the church on the Mount of Olives. They met at the assigned place and together with the bishop they sang songs, antiphons, and hymns of praise and listened to lessons. At the ninth hour they moved to the place where Jesus ascended into heaven. At the eleventh hour they read the passage of the Lord's triumphant procession into Jerusalem; the bishop then led the procession from the Mount of Olives back to the *martyrium* in the city. Parents carried their small children and all waved their palm branches as they made their holy trek to the city gates. They processed through the city streets until they arrived at the Anastasis at a very late hour. They prayed the *lucernare* together, "with prayer at the cross; after which the people were sent home."[6]

From the earliest days, Passion Week began with the celebration of the eucharist, followed by a procession in honor of Christ the King to the Holy City. Antiphons and hymns were sung and the gospel of the Lord's entry into Jerusalem was pro-

claimed. With a few minor variations, the celebration of Palm Sunday still contains the same elements and meaning: "While the doors of his city are opened for the King, the Church already celebrates his triumph, being assured of the victory he will gain by his glorious cross."[7]

The church in the East adopted this liturgy with the exception of the procession with palms. Instead, they ritually anointed catechumens while reading John 12, the story of the anointing in Bethany. Following the anointing, they proclaimed the gospel of the entry into Jerusalem. Thus, the name Palm Sunday emerged, even though there was no procession with palm branches at the time.[8]

The *blessing of the palms* in the liturgy did not occur until around the eighth century. Ancient Latin and Greek texts referred to palms as the symbol of life, hope, and victory. However, popular devotion attached a certain magical power to the palms, in part because of the Greek and Roman secular belief that some species of trees carried magical powers. Christians carried over this secular belief by using palms in such practices as eating parts of the blessed palms to deter illness, planting or burning palms in fields to ward off storms, and placing palm branches on livestock to protect them from infestation. People took the blessed branches home in hopes they would ward off evil spirits.

The church responded to this common practice by formulating a blessing ritual for use with the palms. The blessing prayer asks that the branches be blessed and made holy. It is not an invocation of magic; rather—as with all blessings—it is a prayer that God will save us from all threat to our lives, our holiness, and our salvation. "Blessed or consecrated objects are symbols; they express and stimulate faith, hope and love, and do not possess magical power."[9]

The liturgy provides three forms for the entrance rite on Palm Sunday. The first form is reminiscent of the fourth-century liturgy. We are instructed to

[5]Reginald H. Fuller, *Preaching the New Lectionary* (Collegeville: The Liturgical Press, 1974), 11.

[6]*Days of the Lord*, Vol. 2 (Collegeville: The Liturgical Press, 1993), 210-211.

[7]Ibid., 211.

[8]For further elaboration, refer to: Adolf Adam, *The Liturgical Year,* trans. Matthew J. O'Connell (Collegeville: The Liturgical Press, 1990), 107.

[9]Ibid., 108.

meet at some other suitable place. All then process to the main church waving palms, not as an historical reenactment, but rather as a sign of loving discipleship. The branches are blessed with holy water, the entrance gospel is read, a brief homily is given, and—led by cross, incense, and candles—the solemn procession to the church begins.

The second form includes the solemn entrance inside the church before the principal mass of the day. The branches are blessed outside the sanctuary where the gospel is proclaimed. Then the presider and a representative group of the faithful process to the sanctuary.

In the third form, the simple entrance, the entry into Jerusalem is commemorated by singing the prescribed antiphon as the presider processes into the church. However, the Sacramentary suggests holding a bible service the night before to commemorate the triumphant entry into Jerusalem. The church obviously sees great value in not diminishing this important aspect of the Palm Sunday liturgy. However, it is not to overshadow the passion, which is of primary focus. The triumphant entry is significant insofar as it points to the cross.

The ritual prayers of the liturgy including the opening and concluding prayer and the prayer over the gifts reflect the central saving action of Jesus Christ: his victory over death for the reparation of sin. They exalt the death and resurrection of Christ and our ongoing participation in his paschal mystery.

Thus, Palm Sunday brings us to the culmination of Lent's arduous journey. The preparation and emptying of the lenten season have readied us to enter the holy city with Jesus, to die and rise to new life with our Lord and Savior. The triumphant procession has eschatological overtones; it hints of that final day when all will process with Christ into the holy city, the new Jerusalem.

Passion/Palm Sunday is celebrated with full acknowledgment of the ultimate reality: Jesus died and rose from the dead and is now seated at the right hand of God. We do not process as if we do not know the rest of the story. Jesus is addressed as "the Son of David . . . he who comes in the name of

the Lord." This antiphon from Psalm 118 is our joyful testament to the one who came, died, and rose for our sins, the one who is the fulfillment of the law and the prophets. Once again he comes to save in every celebration of the paschal mystery. We proclaim the Lord's passion and we acclaim what we already know to be true: Christ is Victor over sin and death.

In the blessing of the branches we acknowledge Christ's triumph and we ask that he lead us to embrace the cross and to share in the resurrection. The blessing and procession of branches is not an historical reenactment of that first procession. Rather, it is a living memorial to the saints of the past with whom we join in the ongoing dying and rising of people of faith through the centuries. The cross, the book of the gospels, and the presider are signs of the living presence of Christ in our midst as we process together to the Holy City. "It is a presence in absence."[10]

It is important to reiterate that the entrance into Jerusalem is a secondary theme and serves as a preparation for the prominent focus of this liturgy—the passion of our Lord. We are joyful, yet ever mindful of the price paid by our loving Lord to heal the wounded core of humanity. This week reminds us, ever more fully, that the path Jesus chose is also the path of discipleship. It is the path that leads to the light rather than the dark, to salvation rather than death.

The Proclamation of the Passion

Today we read the passion account through the eyes of Luke. Each year on Passion Sunday we hear from a different evangelist—Luke in Cycle C, Mark in Cycle B, and Matthew in Cycle A. John's account of the passion is read every Good Friday. It is apparent to the observant listener that the passion account read on Passion Sunday and on Good Friday vary considerably. "They do not offer the same outlook of Jesus either in content or outlook."[11]

Thus, contemporary disciples are faced with the awareness that God revealed himself in the words

---

[10]*Days of the Lord*, Vol. 2, 213.

[11]Raymond E. Brown, *A Crucified Christ in Holy Week* (Collegeville: The Liturgical Press, 1986), 9.

of human beings. Various factors colored their perspectives and the telling of their stories. What family does not have stories of family events, stories that are shaped and colored by the bias or perspective of the teller? "We recall the Catholic Church's official teaching that sayings uttered by Jesus have been expanded and interpreted by the apostolic preachers and the evangelists before they were put in the Gospels..."[12]

The fact that there are four different perspectives of the passion accounts serves an unconscious, blessed purpose in the lives of believers that is evident once each gospel is examined on its own ground.

> A true picture of the whole emerges only because the viewpoints are different. In presenting two diverse views of the crucified Jesus every Holy Week, one on Palm/Passion Sunday, one on Good Friday, the Church is bearing witness to that truth and making it possible for people with very different spiritual needs to find meaning in the cross.[13]

Thus, those whose lives cry out like the Jesus of Mark and Matthew, "My God, my God, why have you forsaken me?" find a Christ who resonates with their desperate, yet human pleas for deliverance. Those who need a savior who listens, is present, and can overturn hopelessness find consolation in the cross of those two evangelists. Those who find themselves in need of the tender embrace and loving forgiveness of God will find consolation in Luke's passion narrative. Others may need Christ, the reigning King of heaven and earth, who looks down from the throne of the cross to strengthen and uplift in life's burdensome travail. "To choose one portrayal of the crucified Jesus in a manner that would exclude the other portrayals or to harmonize all the Gospel portrayals into one would deprive the cross of much of its meaning."[14]

The passion narrative is the dramatic portrayal of the most significant event in human history. Its cast of characters reads like a Shakespearean tragedy complete with hero and antagonist. The church allows various readers to proclaim the text. While this serves to heighten the already powerful sense of drama, we are conscious that this is not "theater" provided for our passive enjoyment. We are all fully engaged participants in the proclamation. We are to put ourselves in the place of hero, protagonist, sympathizer, and accuser. In the process, we stand either accused or acquitted.

> The distribution of palm in church may too quickly assure me that I would have been among the crowd that hailed Jesus appreciatively. Is it not more likely that I might have been among the disciples who fled from danger, abandoning him? Or at moments in my life have I not played the role of Peter, denying Jesus, or even of Judas, betraying him? Have I not found myself like the Johannine Pilate, trying to avoid a decision between good and evil? Or, like the Matheean Pilate, have I made a bad decision and then washed my hands so that the record could show that I was blameless? Or, most likely of all, might I not have stood among the religious leaders who condemn Jesus?[15]

Brown insists that the last statement is very probable, since sincerely religious people often have binding, sometimes blinding affiliation with their tradition. However, Jesus challenged fundamentalist adherence to tradition. He always pointed out the human directives and elements that were not in keeping with the will of God. "If Jesus was treated harshly by the literal minded religious people of his time who were Jews, it is quite likely that he would be treated harshly by similar religious people of our time."[16]

Thus, our proclamation of today's passion requires that we become fully engaged, active participants. In so doing, we allow the story to impact our lives and become the leaven for transformation in the fullness of Jesus Christ's paschal mystery.

---

[12]Ibid., 16.
[13]Ibid., 71.
[14]Ibid.

[15]Ibid., 11.
[16]Ibid., 12.

Entrance Gospel Exegesis

The places and events of today's entrance gospel speak to us in far more symbolic ways than first meet the eye. Assemblies ancient and contemporary are first taken to the Mount of Olives, to the place where the Lord will come triumphantly to gather his people at the end of time (Zech 14:4). We are told that Jesus arrived in Jerusalem from Bethany and returned there. Bethany, "house of the poor," and Bethphage, "the house of figs," are reminders of the judgment against Jerusalem. Jesus, poor and humble, who walked among the poor will not stay in Jerusalem where they kill prophets. Bethphage, the fig tree that did not produce, was Jerusalem's final warning of her unfaithfulness. In this gospel passage, Jerusalem was referred to by her Greek secular name, *Hierosolyma*. She was not deserving of her sacred name, *Jerusalem*.[17] The seat of religious power, this place of holiness through the ages, did not produce the holiness expected of her; instead, she put the savior of the world to death. Judgment was upon her.

The events of the Jerusalem procession are significant for us as we reflect upon the entrance gospel. We enter the week with our eyes on Jesus Christ, *the King*. A cloak thrown on the ground before the king was a sign of royal enthronement. Successors to ancient thrones mounted a donkey to assume their newly ordained royal position. The eschatological messiah of the Old Testament was prophesied to usher in the last days on the back of a donkey (Gen 49:11; Zech 9:9). We are not to miss the symbolism: homage is paid to Christ, the King—to divine royalty.

Since the second century B.C.E. palms had been used in the Feast of Booths as a sign of victory and a symbol of power. The Maccabean revolt took place after the Greeks invaded and occupied Israel. Following the revolt, the temple was purified and the Feast of Booths reinforced the messianic hope for the end times. Today's entrance gospel, with the multitudes waving their palms, proclaims the fulfillment of that messianic hope in the per-

son of Jesus Christ, the one who came to save the world. Thus, "the entry was paradoxically the procession of a king to his coronation—the crown of thorns and the throne of the cross."[18]

Luke's entry narrative also recalls the first message of glad tidings given by the angels at Jesus' birth: "Peace in heaven and glory in the highest." Peace and glory were made possible only through the cross. Thus, we are reminded once again that Christmas can be celebrated only with eyes toward Jerusalem. The Incarnation finds fulfillment in the cross of Jesus Christ.

Gospel Exegesis

According to Reginald Fuller, the passion narratives possess a different form than the rest of the gospel. All gospel material, other than the passion narratives, was passed on as oral tradition in the short unit format. Those short pieces were preserved as individual units within the gospel. The passion narratives, on the other hand, were told in their complete form from the very beginning. The church continued its early tradition by preserving the pericopes in the Lectionary and keeping the passion narratives in their complete narrative form.[19]

Brown insists that our understanding of the passion narratives must begin with an understanding of the apologetic motives of the evangelists. One concern was to portray a balanced picture of Jesus for the Roman-controlled populace. Jesus was remembered by secular historians as a criminal who had been put to death. The evangelists sought to temper that portrayal, so they depicted Pilate as a fair judge who acknowledged Jesus' innocence. Pilate himself tells the Roman listeners that Jesus is not a criminal.[20]

The second bias of the evangelist centered around the controversy between the early Christians and the synagogue. Many of the gospel perspectives were shaped in relation and in response to that situation. However, Brown also points out that while there were scoundrel "ecclesiastical" politicians in-

[17]I. de La Potterie, "Des deux noms de Jerusalem dans l'évangile de Luc," *Parole de grace: Etudes lucaniennes à la mémoire d'Augustin George*, ed. J. Delorme and J. Duplacy (Paris: Recherches de science religieuse, 1981), 70; in *Days of the Lord*, Vol. 2 (Collegeville: The Liturgical Press, 1993), 218.

[18]Fuller, *Preaching the New Lectionary*, 12.
[19]Ibid., 15.
[20]Brown, *A Crucified Christ in Holy Week*, 12.

tent on getting rid of Jesus for their own selfish reasons, there were also no doubt some very religious men who thought they were honestly safeguarding the people from a liberal, false prophet who was leading the people astray and promoting a lackadaisical adherence to the law of God. Thus, we are prompted to remember that any one of us could stand quite unconsciously and maybe even innocently with the accusers of Jesus at any given time in the story. There were many factors involved in the portrayal handed down to us. Therefore, it behooves us to approach the text with an open mind and heart.

The intent of the evangelists was theological rather than biographical. They were primarily concerned with showing Jesus in relation to the messianic foreshadowing of the Old Testament. "The evangelists were emphasizing that through the Scriptures of Israel God had taught about his Son. Their emphasis also had an apologetic touch against Jews who rejected the crucified Jesus precisely because they did not think he fulfilled Scriptural expectations."[21]

Luke's passion narrative was written from the same perspective as that of his entire collection, comprising the gospel of Luke and the Acts of the Apostles. Jesus is the one who always, from his very birth, was faithful to the law of Moses. He was also the one who extended mercy, love, and forgiveness, who spent his earthly ministry in a forward movement to Jerusalem. Luke also portrayed the disciples in a very positive light. He made no mention of the fact that they fled the scene.

Throughout his gospel, Luke prepares the reader for the events that will continue in his second volume, the Acts of the Apostles. Jesus in judgment before the Roman court looks ahead to Paul who will stand before the same court. The forgiving Jesus who forgives his murderers looks ahead to Stephen, the first martyr who acts in like manner. Thus, Luke shows the progression of salvation through Jesus—from the Old Testament law and prophets, through his life, passion, death, and resurrection and then to the church.

Jesus goes with his disciples to the Mount of Olives to pray. Jesus, who has prayed throughout his en-

tire ministry, now prays in submission to God's will. The answer to Jesus' prayer is expressed in the form of the angel who comes to strengthen him. The word, *agony*, in the narrative, is a Greek word that translates: *the kind of tension that produces sweat in an athlete before a serious contest.* Jesus rose with resolve, ready to undertake his serious contest with the power of evil.

After acknowledging Judas by name, Jesus hints that he was previously aware of the arrest plan. Again, in typical Lukan style, Jesus continues his healing ministry by restoring the severed ear of the high priest's slave. Unlike the other synoptics who use temple couriers, Luke brings in the "big guns" of the Jewish leadership to arrest Jesus: high priests, temple officers and the elders.

There is no trial until the next day, but our attention is centered on the courtyard and on Peter who weeps, not only because Jesus predicted that Peter would deny him, but also because of the look on the face of his master during the ordeal. The fact that Jesus is mistreated and taunted for being a prophet gives ironic affirmation to his own prediction that he would die as a prophet in Jerusalem.

Jesus is then led before the Sanhedrin inquisitors. However, he does not foolishly give the accusers reason to put him to death. He does not openly refer to himself as the Son of God when asked directly by his accusers. Jesus is portrayed as the serene innocent man who is under the providential care of his Father.

Luke portrays Herod—the Herod of despicable memory and history—as judging Jesus innocent of the charges, just as Pilate had done. The animosity between the two rulers is healed, thus showing that Jesus has a "healing effect on those who maltreat him."[22]

Jesus' act of forgiveness of the Jewish leaders[23] implies that they were unaware of what they were really doing. It almost seems as if Jesus was implying that they should not be held accountable. Luke mentions the same type of ignorance in Acts (3:17).

---

[21]Ibid., 18.

[22]Ibid., 53.

[23]It is the Jewish leaders who seem to be the ones leading Jesus to the cross; this is reflected in Jesus' prayer: "Father forgive them for they know not what they do."

Brown suggests that this demonstrates Luke's awareness of the complexities surrounding the situation. Blame was not so clear cut. It also shows Jesus' willingness to do what he had done throughout his entire ministry, to offer forgiveness, healing and reconciliation, even to his enemies.

The religious and secular officials mock Jesus' offer of forgiveness, but the people do not. Luke is the only evangelist to record the eleventh-hour profession of faith of the thief on the cross and the subsequent promise of his eternal reward. Jesus' healing, saving ministry extended up to the very last moment of his death.

Jesus' last words demonstrate his unfailing trust in his Father's will. The consoling words of Christ in his last breath, "Into your hands I commend my spirit," have ushered many a soul peacefully into the loving arms of God at the moment of death.

In the end, the Roman centurion attests to Jesus' innocence, adding another Roman witness to Jesus' blamelessness: "so that time wise on either side of the cross a Roman governor and a Roman soldier have made the same declaration of not guilty."[24] Luke's ultimate purpose in the passion narrative was to portray Jesus in death as he was in life: the one who healed, the one who showed more concern for others than he did for himself; the one who offered divine love, reconciliation, and forgiveness even from the cross.

Proclaim the gospel again.

Sometimes we gain new insights when we hear the text after the interpretation has been given. Someone from the group proclaims the gospel a second time.

STEP 4
TESTING

Conversation with the Liturgy and the Scriptures

Test your original understanding in dialogue with the text.

---

[24]Brown, *A Crucified Christ in Holy Week*, 55.

(You might consider breaking into smaller groups.)

Was there anything in the passion narrative you had not considered before? Were there any new insights? How does Luke's passion speak to your life?

Sharing Life Experience

Participants share an experience from their lives that connects with the biblical interpretation just shared.

The passion of Christ as told by Luke evokes a very strong personal memory in me. Two years ago I participated in a retreat and study pilgrimage in Israel. One very defining moment for me occurred on the day we participated in the passion walk that closely resembled the steps of Jesus in his last days. Beginning at the place of the Last Supper, we walked down the hillside and across the Kidron Valley to the Mount of Olives. We mirrored the same walk of the fourth-century Christians described above. We stopped and prayed at the Mount of Olives, crossed the Kidron Valley, and processed up the mountainside once again to the holy city and to the Church of the Holy Sepulcher. It was about a four- to five-hour trek and I was not in the best physical shape.

As I labored up the mountainside and down into the valley, I entered the quiet space of sweat-filled, breathless interior reflection. My intention was to enter the heart of Christ as he walked those same steps for far different reasons than I. "Teach me what I need to know; show me your heart," was my earnest prayer. As each step became more strained, things began to change. Rather than centering on my inability to breathe in the hot August Jerusalem sun, I was moved to carry others with me on the burdensome trip. My attention started to shift. How must it have been for Christ as he carried the world on his shoulders that horrible, wonderful day!

"Who am I willing to carry?" Slowly, I became aware of those who suffer and those who cause the suffering. In that land of the Jews I became aware of the millions who had been oppressed, tortured, and murdered at the hands of an evil, distorted,

obsessed, and blind Nazi Germany. I was also aware of Arab families from that same ancient land who, after the war to gain Israel's independence, were taken from their homes and led on a death march across Israel. Mothers, fathers, children, grandmothers, and grandfathers had their homes and possessions ripped from them as they were marched to their new settlements. Many died on that horrendous march. How quickly the oppressed had forgotten their own tortuous past and put on the cloak of oppressor.

I invited them all to walk with me, oppressed and oppressor, and together we prayed, "Father, forgive them for they know not what they do. Father, forgive us." The day wore on and my back bent low. As we continued toward the place of freedom, a new group joined my imaginary motley entourage of the world's oppressed. It was this last group that brought me to my knees. They were the children, all the children in the world who were suffering, abused, neglected, and crying out for deliverance. "Climb on," I said, "we'll make it together." We climbed the last mount to Jerusalem huffing with each breath, singing all the way, "Father, forgive them, for they know not what they do."

As we approached the church's courtyard, the holy place where that Final Deliverance was realized, my imaginary companions and I stood still. All of us, the oppressed, the marginalized, the tortured, the poor, the children . . . all of us stood at the door, aware of who had gone before us. As if struck by lightning, I became aware of just one person—one small girl—who, as a very young child, had cried out to be saved from the horror that was happening to her. If her parents had only known, they would have saved her, but no one knew, no one saved her. She stood frozen at the doors.

It was as if the gentle hand of Jesus, from his nail-ridden wooden throne, reached out his hand to the small girl child and beckoned her into the holy place. Inside the holy of holies, the girl child and her friends stopped motionless at the rock, the earthen rock, split in two and opening into the earth's bowels, the rock that most believe is the very place where Jesus was crucified. On that hot August afternoon, energy-spent,

breathless and emptied, that small girl child and her companions gave it all up to the crucified Christ. They handed it over: the brokenness, the devastation. They left it all on the broken rock of Golgotha. "Father, forgive them, they did not, they do not know what they do."

This girl child was obviously my own wounded inner child. While details are unnecessary, that day, the Lukan Christ walked with me on the steps to Calvary and gave me freedom. He extends that same freedom to every broken person in the world. We are agents of his freedom. It is our job to bring the broken and the wounded to the wooden throne of Jesus.

I left the holy city that day with a new reality. Now whenever I hear the words, "Upon this rock I will build my church," I will think less of Peter and more of the broken, split, fissured rock of Golgotha. It is upon that rock that Jesus built his church—the broken rock of people's lost and forsaken lives. It is the Lukan Christ that reaches out and says, "I have prepared the way, I have gone before you. . . . Come, find healing and forgiveness in me . . . find your freedom."

While this was no doubt a powerful moment of liberation, it is not necessary to go to Israel to encounter the Jesus of Luke's passion. He is encountered in every life that struggles in the pain and sorrow of life and peacefully submits to the will of God. Luke's passion finds expression with every person who chooses love over hatred and forgiveness over resentment. As a wife and mother I am asked to live the cross of Christ in the difficult times as well as in the everyday circumstances of life. My family participates in Luke's passion every time we face a crisis in our lives with a willingness to love, to communicate, to listen, and to put aside our selfish interests and our selfish pride.

Every time we love one another in spite of our angers and our hurts, we live the passion of Christ. Every time we refuse to give in to despair and hopelessness in the difficult times, we live the passion of Christ. We live Luke's passion every time we refuse to submit to hatred, animosity, jealousy, and gossip and instead offer love and reconciliation to those who are differ-

ent from ourselves. Luke's passion is intimately connected to the living of our lives. As wife and mother I live Luke's passion every day. As a disciple and parishioner I am given opportunities to live it every day. Luke's passion helps me face each day with new resolve to extend the reconciling ministry of Jesus in my family, in my parish, and in the world.

All share their life experience.

What was Luke's primary agenda in his version of the passion narrative? What was he saying to his community, to our community, and to me today? How are we called to live Luke's account of Jesus' passion? What does the cross mean in our lives? In what way do we live the paschal mystery as a community? How do I personally live it? Do I still feel the same way about the passion of our Lord as I did when we began? Has my original understanding been stretched, challenged, or affirmed?

STEP 5
DECISION

The gospel demands a response.

In what concrete way does the passion of Christ call us (community, parish, me) to respond? Has this conversation with the exegesis of Luke's passion changed me in any way? What concrete action could I/we take this week as a response to what we have learned and shared today?

DOCTRINAL ISSUES

What church truth/teaching/doctrinal issue could be drawn from the gospel for Passion Sunday?

Participants suggest possible doctrinal themes that flow from the readings.

Possible Doctrinal Themes

Cross, paschal mystery, redemptive suffering

Present the doctrinal material at this time.

1. The facilitator gives input on a particular doctrinal issue of his/her prior choosing. OR

2. The group chooses a doctrinal issue from the list they created. They read together from the Doctrinal Appendix.

(The doctrinal issues are found in the Doctrinal Appendix in the back of this workbook. If you are choosing an issue from this resource, please refer to it now.)

Reflection questions centered around the chosen doctrinal theme can be found at the end of each topic in the Doctrinal Appendix. The questions are based on the five-step reflection process. If you choose a topic not included in the Doctrinal Appendix, craft your own questions according to the same five-step process.

Following the reflection questions you will be reminded to return to chapter 7, "Preparing the Catechetical Session," to assist you in crafting your own session.

Closing Prayer

Lord,
may the suffering and death of Jesus, your only Son,
make us pleasing to you.
Alone we can do nothing,
but may this perfect sacrifice
win us your mercy and love.
We ask this in the name of Jesus the Lord.[25]

Selected Bibliography

Adam, Adolf. *The Liturgical Year.* Trans. Matthew J. O'Connell. Collegeville: The Liturgical Press, 1990.

Brown, Raymond E. *A Crucified Christ in Holy Week.* Collegeville: The Liturgical Press, 1986.

Days of the Lord. Vol. 2. Collegeville: The Liturgical Press, 1993.

Fuller, Reginald H. *Preaching the New Lectionary.* Collegeville: The Liturgical Press, 1974.

Sanchez, Patricia Datchuck. *The Word We Celebrate.* Kansas City: Sheed and Ward, 1989.

---

[25]Passion Sunday: "Prayer Over the Gifts," *The Sacramentary.*

HOLY WEEK, EASTER TRIDUUM, THE EASTER SEASON

HOLY WEEK, EASTER TRIDUUM, THE EASTER SEASON:
AN OVERVIEW

HOLY WEEK

Palm Sunday, while still part of the Lenten season, inaugurates entrance into the liturgical year's holiest, most solemn week. "Holy Week has as its purpose the remembrance of Christ's passion, beginning with his Messianic entrance into Jerusalem. The Sixth Sunday of Lent, which marks the beginning of Holy Week, is called Passion Sunday [Palm Sunday]."[1] The first days of Holy Week, like all of Lent, serve as final preparation for the celebration of Easter. As the Triduum fast approaches, our focus turns toward the suffering of Christ. In the past, Mark's passion was read on Tuesday of Holy Week and Luke's was read on Wednesday. Now the passion narratives from the synoptic gospels are read on Palm Sunday in the three-year cycle.

During the weekdays of Holy Week the scriptures point us toward the Triduum. "In the first half of Holy Week the readings are about the mystery of Christ's passion."[2] We are immersed in the "Servant Songs" of the prophet Isaiah, whose image of the suffering servant finds fulfillment in the suffering of Jesus Christ. The gospel passages relate events from Jesus' last days before his pending passion and death.

Lent does not end with much fanfare. Like a graceful dancer, she makes one last pirouette, solemnly bows, and exits to make way for the grand finale, the showcase piece, the defining moment of the entire movement. Looking back in history, we observe two things that occurred before the Triduum began. The penitents, who on Ash Wednesday entered a period of preparation for reconciliation, were reconciled to the church on Holy Thursday. The oils were blessed on that same day. Thus, before the defining celebration of Christ's premier saving action could begin, the church became whole, complete, and restored again through the reconciliation of its penitents. The oils used in the sacramental, ongoing life of the church were blessed, sent, and received by individual parishes.

Chrism Mass

Lent ends on the evening of Holy Thursday with the celebration of the Lord's Supper. On the morning of Holy Thursday the Chrism Mass is celebrated by the bishop. For pastoral reasons it may be celebrated on a day prior to Holy Thursday. "At the Chrism Mass on Holy Thursday morning the bishop, concelebrating mass with his body of priests, blesses the oils and consecrates the chrism."[3] The blessing of the oils is a very ancient tradition dating back to Hippolytus and the *Apostolic Tradition* in the third century. Three oils are blessed: oil of chrism, oil of catechumens, and oil of the sick.

The chrism is blessed for the anointing of the newly baptized, for the chrismation of candidates for confirmation, and for the anointing of the hands of priests and the heads of bishops at ordination. Chrism is also used in the dedication of churches and altars.

The oil of catechumens is used to anoint catechumens in their preparation for baptism. "The anointing with oil symbolizes their need for God's help and strength so that, undeterred by the bonds of the past and overcoming the opposition of the devil, they will forthrightly take the step of professing their faith and will hold fast to it unfalteringly throughout their lives."[4]

---

[1] "General Norms for the Liturgical Year and the Calendar" (GNLY), in *The Liturgy Documents* (Chicago: Liturgy Training Publications, 1991), #30, 31.

[2] "Introduction to the Lectionary for Mass," *The Lectionary for Mass*, #98.

[3] GNLY, #31.

[4] *Rite of Christian Initiation of Adults*, #99.

"The oil of the sick is used to bring comfort and support to the sick in their infirmity."[5] The holy oils represent the ministry of the church. Each year we bless the new oils that are used in church life.

The premier focus of the Chrism Mass is the priesthood of Christ. The first reading and the gospel remind us that Jesus was empowered and anointed for this holy priesthood by the Holy Spirit. The second reading for the Chrism Mass from the book of Revelation reminds us that Jesus shares this priesthood with his disciples. "For the Chrism Mass the readings bring out both Christ's messianic mission and its continuation in the Church by means of the sacraments."[6] The Chrism Mass is also an expression of the unity of the priesthood and sacrifice of Jesus, which continues to be a present reality in the church today. All the priests of the diocese come together to concelebrate the Chrism Mass with their bishop and to consecrate the chrism, because they, like the bishop, share in the mission of Christ to sanctify, guide, and build up God's people.[7]

The preface of the Chrism Mass offers praise and thanks for Jesus' priesthood, for our share in it and for those who have been called "to share his sacred ministry by the laying on of hands."[8] The preface outlines the call of ministerial, ordained priesthood:

> He appoints them [presbyters] to renew in his
> name
> the sacrifice of our redemption
> as they set before your family his paschal meal.
> He calls them to lead your holy people in love,
> nourish them by your word,
> and strengthen them through the sacraments.
> Father, they are to give their lives in your service
> and for the salvation of your people as
> they strive to grow in the likeness of Christ
> and honor you by their courageous witness of
> faith and love.[9]

The oils are blessed and a renewal of commitment to priestly life may also take place during the liturgy.

While most of the faithful will not be participating in the Chrism Mass, it is an important part of our heritage and a vital piece of our tradition. The scriptures of the Chrism Mass speak to us of Christ's priesthood and our share in his priesthood by virtue of our baptism (according to the ritual text for baptism, we are anointed *priest, prophet* and *king*). The scriptures and the ritual texts of the Chrism Mass foreshadow and remember the rights, duties and responsibilities of ordained priesthood. The oils used in the sacramental function of the church are blessed and distributed for use in all diocesan churches throughout the liturgical year.

The Chrism Mass is a pivotal liturgy. Catechesis based on the liturgical year must address the Chrism Mass and what it means for the ongoing life of the church. This workbook does not provide a session for the Chrism liturgy. However, the scriptures and the issues just mentioned should be shared and addressed in catechetical reflections of Holy Week. To completely ignore the Chrism Mass would be tantamount to omitting an integral piece of the church's liturgical life.

THE EASTER TRIDUUM

The Easter Triduum is the "mother of all feasts." All other feasts of the year hinge on this great feast. While each Sunday stands on its own as an observance of the paschal mystery, the entire liturgical year is in forward motion toward the fundamental commemoration of our Christian faith: the redemptive action of Jesus Christ's passion, death, and resurrection. "Theologically and historically the entire liturgical year springs from the paschal redemptive action of Christ and the celebration of this action."[10] Any treatment of the liturgical year should begin and flow from the foundation and celebration of Easter. However, the liturgical year begins on the first Sunday of Advent and liturgical books are ordered according to chronological progression rather than the preeminence of the

---

[5]"Ceremonial of Bishops," in *The Liturgy Documents* (Chicago: Liturgy Training Publications, 1991), #274.
[6]"Lectionary for Mass: Introduction," in *The Liturgy Documents* (Chicago: Liturgy Training Publications, 1990), #91.
[7]"Ceremonial of Bishops," #274.
[8]Chrism Mass: "Preface for Priesthood" (P20), *The Sacramentary.*
[9]Ibid.

[10]Adolf Adam, *The Liturgical Year,* trans. Matthew J. O'Connell (Collegeville: The Liturgical Press, 1990), 57.

feast. Thus, in the interest of following the liturgical year and the Lectionary and Sacramentary's layout, *Word & Worship Workbook* begins with the First Sunday of Advent rather than with the logical, primary place—Easter.

It is understood that the early Christians remembered Jesus' saving event in a special way during the annual Jewish celebration of Passover. Jesus, the new paschal lamb, passed from death to life. While the early Christians continued to observe the Jewish Passover, it took on new significance in light of Jesus' saving action. There was probably a gradual break from the traditional Jewish Passover.

However, according to second-century literary evidence, there was debate over the date of the annual celebration, suggesting a probable first-century observance. The earliest recorded celebration consisted of a eucharistic meal, preceded by a period of fasting. According to Adolf Adam, the focus of the feast in Rome was primarily on Christ's resurrection and exaltation. The Council of Nicea (325) definitively set the date on the first Sunday after the first full moon in the spring. This way, Easter would not fall during the annual Jewish Passover feast.

The feast takes its name from the Aramaic and Greek word, *pascha,* which is a translation from the Hebrew, *pesach.* The Hebrew word is translated as a "passing by" or "passing through." The word refers to the primary saving event of Israel. The angel of death passed over the houses of the Israelites. Hebrew slaves were led safely out of bondage through the Red Sea and were given safe passage to the Promised Land. Christians appropriated the feast of Passover to their understanding of Jesus' *pasch:* "He passed through the sea of suffering and death and led the people of God to a communion of grace with the Father."[11]

The word *Easter* has various questionable origins. It was once thought to be a reference to the worship of the spring goddess, *Eostre.* However, modern scholarship refutes that connection. Though scholars are still uncertain, it is probably derived from some connection to or translation of the word *East,* where each day meets the rising sun (an obvious metaphor for "Christ, the sun of justice who will rise again in the East after his descent into death"[12]).

The Triduum:
A Celebration of the Paschal Mystery

Jesus' *pasch* includes his suffering, passion, death and—most of all—his passage from death to new life through the resurrection. Raniero Cantalamessa expresses it as follows: "The Passover was a pre-existing institution which the Christians inherited from the Old Testament. All its symbolism was directed to immolation, blood sacrifice. Because this was so, it was easy for Christians to make transfer to the passion of Christ."[13] Thus, the term "paschal mystery" was used to express the reality we know as Jesus' suffering, death, and resurrection. According to St. Augustine, "Passover is the day on which we at the same time celebrate the Lord's passion and resurrection."[14] Therefore, Easter is the prime, exalted celebration of the paschal mystery. However, every sacramental celebration is also the ritual remembrance of the same mystery. The Great Feast, however, summons our power of remembering with greater intensity, and rouses within us greater rejoicing, awareness, and corporate memory of the Easter event itself. It brings the paschal experience to full consciousness so that we may enter the mystery of Jesus' death and resurrection with active and vigilant participation. Thus, "Christ's Passover is prolonged in the Church with three rhythms of differing frequency; an annual rhythm which is the feast of Easter; a weekly rhythm which is Sunday; and a daily rhythm which consists in the daily celebration of the Eucharist."[15]

The feast of Easter is the ritual proclamation and embodiment of the saving act of Jesus' resurrection and glorification. This saving reality is remembered and brought into the present. Through this utterly gratuitous act of self-giving

---

[11]Ibid., 20.

[12]*Patrologia Latina*, ed. J.-P. Migne, Paris, 1878-90, 172:69, in Adolf Adam, *The Liturgical Year*, 63.

[13]Raniero Cantalamessa, *The Mystery of Easter* (Collegeville: The Liturgical Press, 1993), 37.

[14]St. Augustine, *Sermo Denis 7 (Miscellanea Agostiniana, 1,* p. 32).

[15]Cantalamessa, *The Mystery of Easter*, 58.

love, Jesus conquered sin and death and gave the human race the promise of eternal life and perfect union with Yahweh, the Lord of all creation. Through Jesus' saving act, the church was born. Through the Holy Spirit, the church was empowered to live in perfect union with Christ and to spread his Good News. The feast of Easter celebrates the passage from death to life. It inaugurates the church's participation in Christ's redeeming action. The church at Easter remembers past events and makes them present. Easter also prompts the church to look forward to the new and eternal city in the next life as she works for the salvation of the world in this one.

Historical Perspective

Prior to the fourth century all the different aspects of this powerful mystery were separated into specific units that centered on particular features of the mystery. Originally the Easter Vigil was spent in fasting and mourning over the death of Jesus until midnight.[16] The joy of the resurrection thus began at the end of the evening's vigil. At the end of the fourth century there was no Easter Sunday mass, as the Easter liturgy lasted all night long.

Over time, however, the vigil prior to the mass was shortened. In response to the vigil not lasting until the appointed midnight hour, the church of the sixth century initiated an Easter Sunday liturgy. By the eighth century, an early evening vigil emerged, and by the ninth century the rituals that preceded the mass were moved back to noon, thus pushing the mass back to three o'clock. From the Middle Ages on, three o'clock in the afternoon became the starting time for all masses that took place on fast days.

Fasting laws relaxed during the fourteenth century, so masses on fast days were moved to the morning hours. This posed a serious problem, however, for the Easter Vigil. The vigil rituals had to take place in the very early hours of the morning in order for the mass to be celebrated during regular morning hours. This was made obligatory by Pius V. The result: the Easter Candle was car-

ried into the church to the proclamation of *Lumen Christi* in the full light of day, with no one but a few clerics and a handful of the faithful gathered for participation.

Then, in 1951, Pius XII restored the early church's experience of the night vigil and moved it to the night before Easter. The rite was revised and finally made law in 1955. "The Roman Catholic liturgy had rediscovered a lost treasure."[17] Further steps were taken to restore this beautiful, awesome liturgy to its rightful place and status among the liturgies of the church. "During it [the Easter Vigil] the Church keeps watch, awaiting the resurrection of Christ and celebrating it in the sacraments. The entire celebration of this Vigil should take place at night, beginning after nightfall and ending with dawn."[18] "In accord with an ancient tradition, this night is a night of vigil for the Lord, and, as the memorial of the holy night of Christ's resurrection, the Vigil celebrated is the 'mother of all holy vigils.' The Church this night awaits the Lord's resurrection and celebrates the sacrament of initiation."[19]

By the fourth century, pieces of the Triduum gradually developed and merged into one distinct commemoration of the paschal mystery. The Triduum is the word designated for celebration of the Lord's paschal mystery that spans three days. The Triduum is one liturgy that lasts three days. There is no formal closing to the Holy Thursday or Good Friday liturgies. The liturgy continues for three days until its culmination at the Easter Vigil. For three days, the church enters and remains in the tomb with Christ. The Triduum begins with the Mass of the Lord's Supper, continues with the celebration of the Lord's passion on Good Friday, culminates with the Easter Vigil on Holy Saturday, and ends on Easter Sunday.

Holy Thursday

The Mass of the Lord's Supper begins the Triduum. It commemorates the Last Supper and is a living memorial of the institution of the eu-

---

[16]Adam, *The Liturgical Year*, 64.

[17]Ibid., 77.
[18]GNLY, #21.
[19]"Ceremonial of Bishops," #332.

charist and of the Lord's Passover in which Jesus left us sacramental signs of his new covenant. In this new covenant, Jesus promised to be with us through the signs he inaugurated (especially the eucharist). Through the *mandatum*, the washing of feet, Jesus reminds us of the self-sacrificing nature of his love. Jesus, servant of the human race, loves us to his death. Jesus, servant of all, washes the feet of those he serves and instructs his disciples to go and do the same. We share in the servanthood of Christ. In John's gospel there is no eucharist of bread and wine. John's eucharist *is* the washing of feet. The implication? Go, do this in memory of me! The "Ceremonial of Bishops" asserts that the liturgy of Holy Thursday recalls the unconditional love of God and the height and the depth of that love—even unto death.[20]

We slowly shift into part two of our three-day liturgy as part one quietly fades into the meditative silence of darkness. The liturgy of Holy Thursday draws to its temporary intermission, and the church enters into the silence of meditation as she sets her face toward Jerusalem and the ominous events that will forever change the world.

Good Friday

Celebration of the Lord's Passion on Good Friday commemorates the redemption Jesus won for us through the free gift of his life. Jesus was the messianic fulfillment prefigured by the law and the prophets in the Old Testament scriptures. The redemptive act of the cross was the fulfillment of all the saving acts of Yahweh prior to the Incarnation.

The liturgy of Good Friday begins in silent prayer. There are three parts: the liturgy of the word, with John's account of the passion and the general intercessions; the veneration of the cross; and communion using bread consecrated at the Holy Thursday liturgy. During the liturgy of the word we encounter John's Christ, the royal victor, who is fully aware of his divine preexistence.[21] Jesus' death will return him to his former state, to the state that was his before he was sent to this life's sojourn by his Father. He is not a victim; he is the

initiator of events. Jesus freely walks to his death. Jesus is aware of his victory over his enemy, Satan. The Good Friday liturgy is a cause for joyful celebration because of the infinite love of God demonstrated through his Son's passion.[22]

The intercessions of Good Friday are a sign of the priestly function of God's people. All are gathered together in the sacred assembly to offer prayers on behalf of the entire world. The veneration of the cross reminds us of the good news inherent in the cross: this instrument of torture became a sign of salvation and love for all humanity. Part two of this great three-day feast culminates with the reception of communion consecrated the night before at the Holy Thursday Mass of the Lord's Supper. The faithful then leave in silence. The church stands hopeful as she anticipates the night of the great Phoenix rising out of the ashes of sin and death. The church, then, awaits the Passover of the Lord.

The Easter Vigil

The Easter Vigil, in the words of St. Augustine, is the mother of all feasts. It takes center stage in relation to the other liturgies of the Triduum. "During it [the Easter Vigil] the Church keeps watch, awaiting the resurrection of Christ and *celebrating it in the sacraments* [italics mine]. The entire celebration of this Vigil should take place at night, beginning after nightfall and ending with the dawn."[23] There are four parts to the liturgy of this most holy night: the service of fire/light, the liturgy of the word, the service of baptism, and the liturgy of the eucharist.

The Service of Fire/Light

The service of fire/light catapults us back to the journey of the Israelites as they were led by the bright pillar of fire. The radiance of that fire, now dimmed, was replaced by the light of Christ shining in the lives of people. The primordial symbol of fire is blessed anew. The light of the Easter candle is triumphantly carried into the darkened space; the Easter proclamation of *Christ, the Light Who Dispels the Darkness* is shouted, resounded, pro-

---

[20]Ibid., #297.

[21]Raymond E. Brown, *A Crucified Christ in Holy Week* (Collegeville: The Liturgical Press, 1986), 57.

[22]*Days of the Lord,* Vol. 3 (Collegeville: The Liturgical Press, 1993), 23.

[23]GNLY, #21.

claimed, and heralded in the midst of the great assembly. The *Exultet's* euphoric proclamation elevates the gathering to a communion between the saints of heaven and earth who stand exultant in an assembly of triumphant victory over the crushed head of Satan, the evil arch-villain.

The Liturgy of the Word

The liturgy of the word carries us back to the roots of our Christian genesis: creation, passover, and paschal mystery. The believer is thrust into the drama of the first passover, Israel's liberation from bondage; the second passover, Jesus' passage from death to resurrection; and the third and ongoing passover, the church's passover from sin, darkness, and death to resurrected life both now and for eternity. The Vigil scriptures move us into a world of virtual reality. We are present at the threshold of dawn's first light, water's first flow, the star's first glimmer, the animal's first ravenous howl, the seed's first agonizing rupture from earth's womb and humanity's entrance on the world stage. We are hardly passive spectators as we intimately encounter man's and woman's first cognizance of their own goodness.

We are there and it is now as we stand with Abraham and Sarah in that first perpetual covenant of faith. *We are there and it is now* as we trudge through the parted waters of death, pursued and exhausted by Pharaoh's onslaught, only to be enfolded in the protective mantle of Yahweh's liberating providence. *We are there and it is now* as we call down that great and terrible day of the Lord's visitation, when sin comes to an end and we are gathered as *one people* to process majestically to the gates of the jeweled eternal city. (The first four Old Testament readings.)

The word reminds us that this is a night of genesis, of new life. Life is reborn as we witness the baptismal passage from death to life. Water flows abundantly as it promises to quench our thirst. The God who calls us to repentance pours down the waters of forgiveness on the church. The wisdom who blesses, invites, and leads to the light also delivers us from the stain of defilement. We are sprinkled with fresh water, given new hearts, taken by the hand, and led to the font. (The last three Old Testament readings).

We are then ready to stand in the Roman assembly as Paul definitively acclaims (then and now) that baptism is the "passage from death to sin, to life for God."[24] And finally, as fully engaged, sense-sharpened celebrants, we go with Luke to the empty tomb, where we, alongside the women witnesses,[25] are the first to hear the wondrous news: "Jesus Christ is not here, he is risen from the dead!"

The Service of Baptism

Thus, our senses sated and our emotions spent, we escort the elect to the font of life to *do* what we have heard, experienced, professed, and acclaimed. We bring new life to birth and in the process initiate our own rebirth.

As this is a night of new things and new beginnings, the new water is blessed. The water carries symbols and images both ancient and new. As the new water is blessed, the presider-celebrant once again touches our corporate memory. We are reminded of how God's hand once stirred the embryonic waters of creation and deluged the earth with flood, thereby hinting at the purgation of sin through water. Scripture's water images bring us face to face with the God who parted the Red Sea of deliverance. The symbol of water takes us to the shore of the Jordan River where Jesus, the "Beloved Son" whose lanced side would inaugurate the saving flow of his water and his blood, was baptized. Finally, the holy waters of creation, the Red Sea, and the Jordan still flow through the apostolic mission to baptize in the name of the Father, Son, and Holy Spirit.[26] The service of baptism lets us once again plunge into the ancient primordial symbol of water to remind us of who God is, what God did, and what God continues to do in and through the resurrection of Jesus Christ. God immerses us in the purging waters of baptism where death sinks to the bottom and resurrected life gushes

---

[24]*Days of the Lord,* Vol. 3, 43.

[25]In order for an event to be proclaimed as authentic, there needed to be two male witnesses. Thus, one can hardly miss the irony that the only witnesses to the empty tomb were not even officially allowed to testify to what they had seen and heard. God does not need a human court to authenticate the greatest act of redemption in salvation history.

[26]*Days of the Lord,* Vol. 3, 63.

to the top, dripping and spilling over at the font's edge. With all the saints—past, present, and future—the church, in her annual ritual, celebrates resurrected life and initiates new members into her hallowed communion.

Together with the elect, we commit and recommit ourselves through our baptismal promises. We pledge to enter and continue in the struggle between good and evil by renouncing evil's lure. We profess our faith in the Father, the resurrected Christ, and the Holy Spirit. Finally, the baptismal liturgy comes to a close as the newly baptized are anointed with confirmation's holy oil, permanently signed and sealed with the Spirit and delivered into God's service. Thus bathed and anointed, neophytes are ready for the joyful, exultant, and long awaited culmination of their journey: incorporation into the Body of Christ through the eucharist, the ongoing participation in Christ's paschal mystery. Purged, reconciled, and renewed through the waters of baptism, the faithful are ready for eucharist, that which St. Augustine called the repeatable sacrament of initiation.

Liturgy of the Eucharist

As the assembly breathes a sigh of intermission, the gifts of bread and wine are brought to the table and the paschal story continues in word and action. Calvary and Easter coexist boldly on our communal table. The *cross* stands triumphant in the brilliant light of the *resurrection* and we, God's people, consume both realities at the eucharistic banquet. Thus fed, we go forth, cross in hand, the resurrection in heart, and take what we have consumed to feed the starving soul of the world.

If this sounds like poetry, so it must. It is only through the language of poets that we dare come close to capturing the mystery of this sacred, awe-filled, holy night.

Symbols of the Vigil

The dominant liturgical symbols of the church—assembly, cross, fire/light, word, water, oil, white garment, laying on of hands, bread, wine—are all manifest at the Easter Vigil. The symbols speak to us of our identity as Catholic Christians. For example, the symbol of light has its genesis in Christ, the light of the world. Since we are to walk as children of the light, light identifies us and we become its reality—we become light, we become bread, etc.

Meaning is conveyed when people encounter symbols, which are repeatable and possess many layers of meaning. They are multi-faceted and have multiple forms and uses. At the Vigil alone, the symbol of light shines forth in the new fire, the Easter candle, the candles of the faithful, the incense, and the sanctuary lamp. Light's power is felt by its absence in the darkened church. The meaning of symbols is expressed in the way they are used and in the background and gestures that define them. Symbols are also understood through the words of the ritual text that are used in relation to them, and through the sacramental proclamation of God's word that accompanies their use.[27]

The Easter Vigil calls forth the symbols that illuminate our existence and that occur in all liturgies. We are people of the cross. We are chrismated into the ecclesial community. We are people of the light and the water of baptism incorporates us into the paschal mystery. We are people of the table: we are eucharistic people.

"Liturgical action depends on symbols because beings cannot be together and communicate without some kind of encounter in words (verbal symbols) and/or in gestures and actions (nonverbal symbols). All knowledge begins with our senses; this means that an encounter with God is only possible by means of sensible signs."[28] In antiquity, a symbol used to be understood as two halves, which when joined became one whole. The person who had one half would thus recognize the other half because the two put together formed the whole entity. By extension, then, a symbol can be regarded as two parts of a whole—the visible and the invisible. Just because the invisible half of the symbol is not readily observable, it is nevertheless

---

[27]Linda Gaupin, *Sacramental Catechesis,* course text for "Special Certification in Sacramental Catechesis," Diocese of Orlando, Florida, November 1996.

[28]Klemens Richter, *The Meaning of the Sacramental Symbols,* trans. by Linda Maloney (Collegeville: The Liturgical Press, 1990), 13.

half of the reality. When joined with the visible half of the symbol, it constitutes the whole reality. "In the language of religion and theology it is frequently the case that the concept of 'symbol' is reserved for the signs of faith, that is…in addition to their superficial, natural meaning, another and supernatural meaning that is only accessible to faith."[29] Through symbols we are able to touch the deep mysteries of our faith in ways that words can never express.

If symbols were to speak, they would say: "I am…" rather than "I am like…." Symbols in the sacramental sense *are* the reality they express. Eucharist in the form of bread and wine *is* the Body and Blood of Jesus. We can say with assurance that symbols express our identity. When we consume the precious elements, we become what we have consumed: the Mystical Body of Christ. The symbols of the Easter Vigil, highlighted and set forth, give us the means to communicate with God and for God to communicate with us through our senses. They express all of our sacramental realities. The symbols of the Vigil are food for mystagogical reflection throughout the Easter season and form the basis of our sacramental catechesis.

Easter Sunday

The Easter Sunday liturgy is a later development and thus did not originally have a liturgy of its own. The Easter Vigil is considered the principal mass of the Easter feast.[30] The Easter Sunday mass, however, is a cacophony of jubilation. From the opening prayers to the dismissal alleluia, praise and thanks are rendered for the resurrection of the Lord Jesus Christ. Many people who attend Easter Sunday mass do not attend the Vigil. It is important, therefore, that the homily reflect the unity of the passion and resurrection just as it is reflected in the Easter preface and the communion antiphon. The Vigil should be upheld "as the climax of the liturgical year and thus should be explained."[31] Very often the neophytes return on Easter Sunday and take their rightful place as fully initiated, candle carrying, garmented members of

the celebrating assembly. The neophytes themselves are an Easter symbol for the community: a symbol of new, resurrected life in our midst.

OCTAVE OF EASTER

The first eight days after Easter are called the octave. The liturgical calendar names each day a solemnity of the Lord ("General Instruction of the Roman Missal," #24). The observance of the octave dates back to the mid-third to fourth century. Some suggest that celebration of the octave has its roots in the Jewish Passover and the seven days of Unleavened Bread. Each day of the octave was, for the neophytes, a fuller introduction to the mysteries of faith and their initiation sacraments. Observance of the octave was a universal practice of the church (*ecclesiae consensus*) in which all the faithful attended daily liturgy and refrained from work. At one time the octave was referred to as "white week," since the neophytes wore their white baptismal garments to mass. The Eastern church called it a "week of renewal."

Due to the fast-paced life we lead, it is often difficult for the neophytes to attend daily liturgy during the octave. However, the practice should be strongly encouraged. The solemnities of the octave are an integral part of the Easter mystery. Most catechetical groups do not have the opportunity to come together to experience and reflect upon each day of the octave. This workbook will not provide sessions for the days of the octave. However, the octave should not be ignored. Those in catechetical groups—actually, all Catholics—should make every effort to attend daily mass and, when possible, reflect upon the scriptures, ritual prayers, and experience of the liturgies of the octave.

FIFTY DAYS OF EASTER

"The fifty days from Easter Sunday to Pentecost are sometimes called the great 'Sunday.'"[32] Each Sunday is considered a paschal Sunday; the Sundays are called the Second, Third, Fourth, etc. Sundays *of* Easter (not after Easter) until the eighth Sunday, called Pentecost. Forty days after

---

[29]Richter, *The Meaning of the Sacramental Symbols*, 13.
[30]Adam, *The Liturgical Year*, 83.
[31]Ibid., 84.

---

[32]GNLY, #22.

Easter, the Ascension of the Lord into heaven is celebrated except in places where it is not a holy day of obligation, in which case it is moved to the Seventh Sunday of Easter. Following the feast of the Ascension, the weekdays are intended as a preparation for Pentecost. Each Sunday of the Easter season is a solemnity, a Great Feast. Each Sunday exalts an aspect of the paschal mystery.

All three scripture readings of the Sundays are taken from the New Testament. The first reading is always from the Acts of the Apostles. The second reading for Cycle C is taken from the book of Revelation. The gospel readings for Cycle C are all taken from the gospel of John.

The celebration of the fifty days is the church's extended meditation on the paschal mystery as the source, summit, and driving power of the Christian life. The paschal mystery is the heart of all celebration, liturgical and sacramental. The resurrection of Jesus is the hinge on which the doors of faith swing. Without it, the church has no purpose for existence.

The Fifty Days of Easter and the Rite of Christian Initiation

The fifty days of Easter are also called the period of mystagogia (uncovering the mysteries). In the early centuries of the church, there existed an advanced type of religious instruction called mystagogical catechesis, or an introduction to the mysteries. This was usually directed by the bishop after baptism, not before. There was a belief that neophytes were unable to comprehend the church's teaching on eucharist until they had experienced it. Once they had taken part in the ritual celebration, then and only then would they be able to grasp what the awesome mystery was about. In his first address to the neophytes, St. Ambrose began: "I shall begin now to speak of the sacraments which you have received. It was not proper for me to do so before this, because, the Christian faith must come first."[33]

The reality of the risen and crucified Christ was conveyed through the initiation rites and their powerful symbols, thus sparking faith and enthusiasm.

---

[33]St. Ambrose, *Catechesis mystagogica* 1.1. (PG 33, 1066).

Mystagogical catechesis infuses the truths of the faith and the sacraments through the concrete, personal, and vivid memories of water-soaked skin, oil-slathered body, and flowing white robes. St. Cyril said it best to the neophytes: "It has long been my wish to discourse to you on these spiritual, heavenly mysteries. On the principle, however, that seeing is believing, I delayed until the present occasion, calculating that, after what you saw that night, I should find you a readier audience when I am to be your guide to the brighter and more fragrant meadows of this second Eden."[34]

Mystagogical catechesis seeks to make a connection between the events of salvation history (the prefiguring events of the Old Testament and their fulfillment through Christ) and the rites that make those saving events manifest and the benefits operative. Mystagogical catechesis explains the rite in dialogue with the experience of it. Mystagogical catechesis weds truth and experience. During their preparation for baptism, the catechumens immersed themselves in God's word and in the truths of our faith laid out in the celebration of the litugical year. As they unpacked the liturgy week after week, they discovered the truths of salvation history, and with baptism, confirmation, and eucharist they completed the rites of initiation. Now, for the first time, their prior knowledge and their experience come together.

The agenda of mystagogia is ongoing ritual catechesis. What happened? What did it mean? What are the implications and what am I going to do about them? Mystagogy is ongoing, repeated celebration leading to reflection that provides understanding which demands a response, a decision. Mystagogical catechesis is an activity of the entire church. It is what the Easter season is all about. We are *all* to spend the season asking, "What happened, what was my experience, and what does it mean?" The neophytes point to what we should all be doing.

During the season of Easter, the entire church enters a period of mystagogia in which we experience and reflect upon the meaning of the symbols

---

[34]St. Cyril of Jerusalem 14.10 (PG 33, 836 in Raniero Cantalamessa, *The Mystery of Easter* [Collegeville: The Liturgical Press, 1993], 65).

of initiation that express the dying and rising of Jesus for the fifty days between Easter and Pentecost Sunday. "Mystagogy is a time for the community and the neophytes together to grow in deepening their grasp of the paschal mystery and in making it part of their lives through meditation on the Gospel, sharing in the Eucharist and doing the works of charity."[35] It is a time for reflection on the way we are called to die and rise and thus fully embrace the paschal mystery in our daily lives. Reflection on the Easter gospels in light of their sacramental experience is the springboard for neophytes to unpack the meaning of the sacraments. This is post-baptismal, sacramental catechesis. Mystagogia is a time to gather with the community for eucharist and to be fed at the paschal table. It is a time to become more immersed in a life of service, outreach, evangelization and corporal and spiritual works of mercy.

The heart of mystagogy flows from ritual. We pray, we celebrate, we believe; then we seek to find meaning in our prayer, celebration, and belief. What does it mean for our lives? The ritual of mystagogia is eucharist, the "repeatable sacrament of initiation" (Augustine). The neophyte and the worshiping community become immersed in the Easter stories, symbols, and eucharists. Knowledge and understanding of the church's Easter tradition are thus based on experience. The risen Christ is experienced in word, in sacrament, and in symbol. To experience Christ is to "know" Christ.

The fifty days of Easter show us how to live the mystery of the Risen Lord as a result of plunging into the waters of rebirth, of being anointed with the Spirit, and of feasting at the Lord's table. Empty vessels become fully filled. The whole church is catechized, not just the neophytes.

Thus, while post-baptismal catechesis would appear to be only for neophytes, it is indeed the business of everyone; it is a life-long pursuit. The scriptures and liturgies of the season invite us to engage in this ancient form of catechesis in order to become fully absorbed in the paschal mystery of Jesus Christ. The historical perspective of the fifty days will be covered in the section that deals with Pentecost.

---

[35] *Rite of Christian Initiation of Adults*, #244.

ASCENSION

The feast of the Ascension is a solemnity that focuses on Jesus' second coming (entrance rite) and his continued risen presence in the community (communion antiphon). The liturgy's opening prayer expresses the effects of the resurrection: the elevation of human beings to the glory of Christ. The first two readings are the same every year but the gospel changes according to the cycle.

During the fourth century, the feast of the Ascension was celebrated on the fiftieth day along with the feast of Pentecost. However, there emerged a practice of celebrating the Ascension on the fortieth day after Easter. The reason for this was twofold. First, there was a strong connection to the sacred significance of the number forty. Second, there was reference in the Acts of the Apostles to "appearing during forty days . . ." and also the witness of the Ascension account in verses 9-11. The decision was made to place the celebration forty days after the resurrection.

The weekdays following Ascension serve as preparation for Pentecost, for the coming of the Holy Spirit. Thus, the old popular devotion, the Pentecost novena, was replaced by an official liturgy. During these pre-Pentecost days, the church enters the room of prayer with Mary, the women, and the disciples as they await the holy fire of the Spirit.

PENTECOST

Pentecost (*pentekoste,* the ordinal form of the number fifty) takes place fifty days after Easter and brings the Easter season to a close. It is the final, dramatic curtain call in which the church is brought on stage, commissioned, and sent out with the fire of the Holy Spirit. Pentecost inaugurates the full manifestation of the Spirit in the messianic age. Pentecost ushers us into the reality of all that was prophesied by the law and the prophets and then fulfilled through Jesus Christ. Pentecost, in its thunderous clamor from the womb of anticipation, brings the church to birth. Even though Pentecost commemorates the events that took place fifty days after Easter, it continues on through time through the liturgical celebration.[36]

Pentecost, the birthday of the church, is the day the church celebrates the conferral of the Holy Spirit. "It appears on the fiftieth day, when the Spirit was poured out on the first Christian community, giving it the strength and confidence to testify publicly to the resurrection."[37] The paschal celebration of redemption through Christ took place over the fifty days of Easter and was understood to include the "victorious passion and death, his resurrection and ascension, and the sending of the Spirit upon the Church."[38] Thus, Easter was not just a celebration of the resurrection of Christ, but also an extension of his ministry through the Spirit to the Church: ". . . Pascha was a total celebration of our redemption. . . ."[39]

The Christian feast of Pentecost has its roots and is to be understood in light of the Jewish celebration by that same name. The Jewish feast of Pentecost, or Weeks, also called *Shabuoth* ("Weeks") was the closing feast for the season of harvest that began with the feast of Unleavened Bread. Thomas Talley speaks of several hypotheses regarding the origin of Pentecost. He suggests that some scholars maintain that Pentecost represents a period of seven weeks measured from the day after Passover. The feast of Passover marked the first day. Thus, seven times a seven-day week equals forty-nine and the addition of one day for festival makes a *pentecontad*, or a period of fifty days.[40] There was dispute over how to count the days and there was an absence of dispute regarding a particular date for the feast of Weeks. Thus, it is suggested that "in the first century it was not simply the fiftieth day that was considered sacred, but the very period between that fiftieth day and the day from which it was counted, a day related in one way or another to Passover."[41] Since pilgrims from Judea and Galilee gathered in Jerusalem for the single-day feast of Pentecost, some scholars suggest that Pentecost was the cel-

ebration that brought the entire season, beginning with Passover, to a close. However, Talley maintains that there is also scriptural evidence that the feast stood on its own and was a feast celebrating the renewal of covenant and the giving of the law (Book of Jubilees, ca. 140-100 B.C.E.).[42] During the time of Christ it was probably being observed as a feast of renewal of the covenant.

There is no solid evidence to suggest that the period between Passover and Pentecost was appropriated as one feast of rejoicing by the first-century Christian church. However, by the second century there is evidence (fasting and kneeling in prayer were forbidden during the fifty days) that Christians observed an extended festival from Easter to Pentecost.

As the feast evolved and in places where it was celebrated on Sunday, the feast of Pentecost was counted from Easter-day itself, thus making Pentecost the eighth Sunday after Easter Sunday. Easter to Pentecost was celebrated as one continuous period of rejoicing. However, by the fourth century, the unitive dimension to the fifty days of Easter waned in the Roman church as Ascension and Pentecost were regarded as distinct festivals. Adolf Adam reminds us that the East always regarded Pentecost as the close of the Easter season. The Roman liturgy, on the other hand, "made this day an independent entity and thus a more or less isolated feast of the sending of the Holy Spirit."[43] Like the great feast of Easter, Pentecost was thus afforded an octave that caused liturgical confusion as it coincided with the ember days (days of penance), which had already been established on the liturgical calendar. Thus, this feast of rejoicing over the sending of the Spirit was clouded by days of penance.

In light of historical liturgical studies, the Congregation of Rites restored Pentecost to its unity with Easter and reaffirmed the close connection between the Resurrection, Ascension, and the sending of the Spirit. The "General Norms for the Liturgical Year and the Calendar" states: "The fifty days from Easter Sunday to Pentecost are cele-

---

[36]*Days of the Lord*, Vol. 3, 249.

[37]Ibid., 293-294.

[38]Thomas J. Talley, *Origins of the Liturgical Year* (Collegeville: The Liturgical Press, 1986), 57.

[39]Ibid.

[40]Ibid.

[41]Ibid., 59.

[42]Ibid., 61.

[43]Adam, *The Liturgical Year*, 89-90.

brated in joyful exultation as one feast day, or better as one 'great Sunday'" [#22].

There are two liturgies of Pentecost: the vigil mass and mass during the day. The vigil mass is not widely celebrated as the "mass during the day" is usually chosen for the Saturday evening liturgy prior to Pentecost Sunday. Even though we seldom participate in the vigil mass, the texts are nevertheless a wonderful preparatory meditation in anticipation of the Sunday celebration of Pentecost. The second reading and the gospel are always the same: Romans 8:22-27 and John 7:37-39. The first reading is chosen from among four possibilities: Genesis 11:1-9, Exodus 19:3-8, 16-20, Ezekiel 37:1-14, and Joel 3:1-5.

Pentecost's power is not simply in the recall of a monumental sacred event. While it is indeed just that, it is so much more. Pentecost is an ongoing event. It was inaugurated in the first Christian community, but it still continues to unfold in this messianic era. Pentecost is our eternal hope: it is the perpetual gift of the Spirit to build the Body of Christ. Pentecost celebrates within the community that which takes place in the individual through baptism and eucharist. The Spirit who breathes transforming life into the church is given at baptism and continues to be manifest through the ongoing celebration of eucharist. It is the same Spirit who challenges, teaches, seals us permanently to Christ and leads us forward in holiness to the new Jerusalem, the holy, eternal city. Pentecost celebrates the reign of God now and not yet; it is a present and future reality. The Spirit of Pentecost continues the work of Christ on earth as we are formed and prepared for the great day of his return. Pentecost is the ongoing renewal of our participation in Christ's new covenant. The liturgy of Pentecost calls us to worship in spirit and in truth. We are strengthened for mission to the world's poor, oppressed, and spiritually hungry.

In summary then, Easter is a living memorial of the primary Christian symbol of deliverance and liberation—Christ's passion, death and resurrection. Through his ultimate act of sacrifice, Jesus inaugurated the *new covenant*. Jesus, the New Passover, shed his blood, thereby ratifying the new covenant. Jesus' passage from death to life for the

forgiveness of sins fulfilled all the promises Yahweh had made with Israel since the creation of the world. Death ultimately lost its power. Christ's death and resurrection would guarantee human beings a place at the eternal banquet. The living memorial of Christ's Passover today is our sharing in the Body and Blood of Christ in the eucharist and our incorporation into and participation in the paschal mystery.

Each year, Easter renews our participation in the paschal mystery. We recall and renew our participation in the life, passion, death, and resurrection of Jesus and the sending of the Spirit to the church. Liturgically and sacramentally we celebrate and exalt the saving effects in our lives. We recommit our lives to cross and resurrection, to dying and rising, and in the process we are renewed in the mandate to go out, teach, and baptize all nations. Such is our faith; so shall it be.

HOLY THURSDAY

INTRODUCTORY RITES

Opening Song (or Entrance Antiphon)

We should glory in the cross of our Lord Jesus Christ, for he is our salvation, our life and our resurrection; through him we are saved and made free.[1]

Opening Prayer

Let us pray.

Pause for silent prayer.

God our Father,
we are gathered here to share in the supper
which your only Son left to his Church to reveal
    his love.
He gave it to us when he was about to die
and commanded us to celebrate it as the new and
    eternal sacrifice.
We pray that in this eucharist
we may find the fullness of love and life.
Grant this through our Lord Jesus Christ, your Son,
who lives and reigns with you and the Holy Spirit,
one God, for ever and ever.[2]

LITURGY OF THE WORD

Let us listen to God's word.

The readings are proclaimed.

First Reading
Exodus 12:1-8, 11-14

The synoptic gospels place the Last Supper in the context of a Passover meal. John's gospel places it a day before Passover. While the historical facts are not certain, one thing is: the meal was cloaked in the experience and language of Passover. It is very appropriate that the Triduum begin with this reading. The entire experience of Christ's passion, death, and resurrection was understood in light of the passover experience. Jesus naturally was seen as the fulfillment of all the promises inherent in the passover tradition.

As said multiple times throughout this workbook, the Passover was for Israel the hallmark event that celebrated Yahweh's redemptive act of salvation. Then and today every observant Jew remembers the exodus story as if he or she had actually been present for the original event.

The blood on the doorposts was considered a prefiguring of the blood that Christ would shed. This saving blood, shed for the sins of the world, is made real, active, and present at every celebration of eucharist.

This reading remembers the ritual of unleavened bread and passover lamb. Originally, the two rites were separate. Prior to the exodus, the ritual of the sacrificial lamb was used by herders to satisfy the gods as the herders moved their flocks from well-irrigated winter land to dry summer lands. The unleavened bread was used in a ritual for farmers. The rite functioned as a spring cleaning of the previous year's leaven. Tonight's text brings the sacrificial lamb ritual into the exodus story (vv. 11-13). The unleavened bread is established as a living memorial of the actual exodus narrative.[3] Thus, the ritual celebration of the passover lamb and the unleavened bread celebrated in the spring of each new year affords the descendants of the Israelites the opportunity to mark once again the liberation from the yoke of Egyptian bondage. The unleavened bread was a sign that those in bondage had to leave in haste. This urgency evolved through the generations to an expectation of the coming messiah who would return at night.

---

[1]Evening Mass of the Lord's Supper: "Entrance Antiphon," *The Sacramentary.*

[2]Evening Mass of the Lord's Supper: "Opening Prayer," *The Sacramentary.*

[3]Richard J. Clifford, S.J., "Exodus," in *The New Jerome Biblical Commentary*, ed. Raymond E. Brown, S.S., Joseph A. Fitzmyer, S.J., Roland E. Murphy, O.Carm. (Englewood Cliffs: Prentice Hall, 1990), 49.

Our eucharistic bread is unleavened, just as the bread of exodus was unleavened. The nomadic life was a hurried life; people had to be ready to pick up and leave at a moment's notice. There was no time to wait for the leaven to rise. The Israelites, fleeing from Pharaoh, had no time to wait for the unleavened bread to rise. Eucharistic people are on the move to the new and eternal city. They also have no time to wait around for the bread to rise, but rather, are in a hurry to work for the coming reign of God. For the nomads, for the fleeing Israelites, and for Christians, the unleavened bread was food for their respective journeys.

The shedding of Jesus' blood was easily connected with the Old Testament understanding of blood. Blood was a sign of life. "Blood took on special significance for the Israelites both in the popular imagination and in the official cult. . . . Blood, as the bearer of life, was offered to God as atonement for humanity's sins."[4] The blood poured out on the altar was a substitute for the human sinner. Thus, an animal that was sacrificed served as a symbol. The animal stood in the place of the sinner who was symbolically offering his own life in order to reestablish the lost covenant relationship with God. The blood of rams was placed on the horns of the altar and on the altar as a sign of the cleansing properties of blood. "The blood removed the impurities which would defile the Israelite community and its cult."[5]

In the ancient agricultural world, blood represented the sharing of all life. Both animals and humans were in relational community. Even though animals had to die for the people to survive, there was a special life relationship with the animals. To shed the blood of an animal was a sacred event. Also, those who shed their own blood to save others were considered sacred people.[6]

The ancient rituals of blood were fulfilled through the shedding of Jesus' blood on the cross. He of-

fered his blood for the sins of the world. In every eucharist we eat Jesus' Body and drink his Blood. Jesus is the new passover; he passed through death to life. Every time we celebrate eucharist we participate in that same passover. With Jesus, we pass from death to sin, to new life in Christ.

Responsorial Psalm
Psalm 116:12-13, 15-16, 17-18

This psalm celebrates the unity of the eucharist: a sacrifice of thanksgiving and a communion among believers.[7] This is a prayer of thanks after a difficult, terrifying ordeal.

Scholars are stumped when it comes to verse 15 in which the death of the faithful ones is precious in the eyes of the Lord. "Difficult. Just why their death should be 'precious' to Yahweh is not easy to see."[8]

Second Reading
1 Corinthians 11:23-26

This is the earliest fragment of Christian tradition preserved in the New Testament. Paul stated that he had received the tradition given in today's letter prior to his dealings with the Corinthians. He used language denoting the *passing on of tradition*, such as that which is passed on through the oral teaching of the rabbis. Paul received his revelation from the oral tradition in which human witnesses, under the inspiration of the risen Christ, shared and passed on their experience.

It is believed that today's pericope is an exegesis of a eucharistic liturgy already being celebrated. It does not completely describe the Last Supper, but rather seeks to define it in light of eucharistic theology. In the earliest celebration of the *breaking of bread*, there was a supper between the bread and the cup (as alluded to in this pericope), thus testifying to the primitive character of this text.[9]

---

[4]Dale Launderville, O.S.B. "Blood," in *The Collegeville Pastoral Dictionary of Biblical Theology*, ed. Carroll Stuhlmueller, C.P. (Collegeville: The Liturgical Press, 1996), 95.

[5]Ibid., 96.

[6]James A. Fischer, "Blood, New Testament," in *The Collegeville Pastoral Dictionary of Biblical Theology*, ed. Carroll Stuhlmueller, C.P. (Collegeville: The Liturgical Press, 1996), 97.

[7]Reginald H. Fuller, *Preaching the New Lectionary* (Collegeville: The Liturgical Press, 1974), 17.

[8]John S. Kselman and Michael Barré, S.S., "Psalms," in *The New Jerome Biblical Commentary*, ed. Raymond E. Brown, S.S., Joseph A. Fitzmyer, S.J., Roland E. Murphy, O.Carm. (Englewood Cliffs: Prentice Hall, 1990), 546.

[9]Fuller, *Preaching the New Lectionary*, 17.

Just as the unleavened bread was a living memorial of the events of Passover, so too is the unleavened bread of eucharist a living memorial of the events of Jesus' *passage through death to life.*

There are strong eschatological overtones in tonight's second reading. Paul reminds us of the Lord's second coming. Eucharist, for Paul and for us, was and is a ritual remembering of the cross with its effects made real and present. It is an anticipation of Jesus' second coming: "Christ has died, Christ is risen, Christ will come again."

Gospel
John 13:1-15

Jesus washes the feet of his disciples.

STEP 1
NAMING ONE'S EXPERIENCE

What were your first impressions? What was your first response? What grabbed your attention? How did you feel?

Each person names his or her initial impression. Statement should be brief. No reasons should be given at this time. All simply listen without agreeing or disagreeing.

STEP 2
UNDERSTANDING

In a brief statement, what do you think this gospel is trying to convey?

STEP 3
INPUT FROM VISION/STORY/TRADITION

Liturgical Context

Order of Service: Liturgy of the Word, Washing of Feet, Intercessions, Liturgy of Eucharist, Transfer of Eucharist

The observance of Holy Thursday began as a ritual celebration commemorating the Lord's Supper in Jerusalem. The story of the Christ's Last Supper is told and remembered as the event that instituted the eucharist. The Sacramentary defines the homiletic focus of tonight's liturgy: the institution of the eucharist; the institution of the priesthood; and the commandment of filial love. The first and second readings address the institution of the eucharist. The gospel hints at the institution of priesthood[10] and filial love is expressed in all three readings.

The liturgy for Holy Thursday is not unlike every liturgy of the year. However, it does have its own character and is set apart in one particular way. Holy Thursday is understood as the day Jesus was betrayed. This liturgy does *not* attempt to re-create the Last Supper. Jesus is referred to in the third person as if he were absent. "The night he *was* betrayed, he *took* bread," etc. However, the telling makes the actions and words present to us in a very concrete way. At every eucharist, the story we proclaim and the action we perform becomes a reality. The word is *anamnesis*, a remembering that brings the event forward and makes it present. This happens at every liturgy. The Holy Thursday liturgy is the same as every other liturgy in that regard. Where Holy Thursday is unique is that it highlights and exalts the connection between the free offering of Jesus' life through his passion and death and our own present celebration of eucharist.

"Eucharist is the sacrament of the Lord's presence during his absence."[11] We are not participating in an historical reenactment of an event that took place two thousand years ago. The events are

---

[10]Reginald Fuller cautions a careful handling of the issue of priesthood. He suggests that interpreting the command to "do this" as a command for priesthood oversimplifies the meaning for two reasons. First, the Vatican II document, *Decree on the Ministry and Life of Priests*, "set the eucharistic presidency in the wider context of a total pastoral ministry of word and sacrament." Also, there is no solid evidence as to who presided at the first liturgies. It is not until the second century that the bishop presides at liturgy and only later do the priests preside. "The command, 'Do this' (plural) is addressed to the Christian church as a whole. The eucharist is an action of the whole church and the preeminent expression of its priestly character" (1 Peter 2:1-10; Ap 1:6; and perhaps Hebrews 13:15). Fuller, *Preaching the New Lectionary*, 18.

[11]*Days of the Lord*, Vol. 3 (Collegeville: The Liturgical Press, 1993), 15.

historical and they do belong to the past. However, we remember them and they become presently effective. The events of Calvary build up the Body of Christ and are continued today through the sacraments, an ongoing living memorial of those events. We share in Jesus' passion, death, and resurrection and in his saving redemption every time we tell the story and share the meal in his memory.

> Lord, make us worthy to celebrate these mysteries.
> Each time we offer this memorial sacrifice, the work of our redemption is accomplished.
> We ask this in the name of Jesus the Lord.[12]

One can understand tonight's liturgy only through the eyes of the Passover. Ancient nomads participated in a ritual to mark the movement of their flocks to summer pastures after the first full spring moon. It was a dangerous journey and, to ward off evil, they marked their tents with the blood of lambs. "The death would propitiate the death-threatening deities."[13]

Later it was very easy to appropriate this rite into the Passover ritual: it gave new meaning to an old rite. Christianity had the same experience: new meaning was given to many of the Old Testament rituals.

The ancient ritual of Passover had two parts: unleavened bread and the sacrifice of the paschal lamb (First Reading). This passover ritual was celebrated by Jesus himself. He prayed the ritual prayers and enacted the ritual actions, perhaps many times over. Jesus was celebrating a passover supper on this night prior to his act of redemption. It was natural that the Christian psyche connect Jesus to the paschal lamb that shed its blood in order to save the Jews from the angel of death in the book of Exodus. The early Christians understood the paschal lamb of Exodus as a foreshadowing of Christ, the Paschal Lamb. John would later declare: "This is the Lamb of God who takes away the sins of the world." Christianity took an old rite and breathed new meaning into it.

So much of the Passover is integral to our understanding of eucharist. Passover was not celebrated alone; it was a family, communal event. Similarly, eucharist is a community event; it is celebrated in communion with other believers. Israel was in relationship to God as a people; so too, are Christians saved as a people. It is not a private affair.

We hear from Paul (tonight's second reading), who received the tradition of the supper from the Lord himself. Today we celebrate the same ritual of breaking bread that Paul's community celebrated. We celebrate eucharist as a living memorial of Jesus' presence in his absence as expressed in the preface for this liturgy:

> Father, all-powerful and ever-living God,
> we do well always and everywhere to give you thanks
> through Jesus Christ our Lord.
> He is the true and eternal priest
> who established this unending sacrifice.
> He offered himself as a victim for our deliverance
> and taught us to make this offering in his memory.
> As we eat his body which he gave for us,
> we grow in strength.
> As we drink his blood which he poured out for us,
> we are washed clean.
> Now, with angels and archangels,
> and the whole company of heaven,
> we sing the unending hymn of your praise.[14]

The gospel for Holy Thursday is John's account of eucharist: washing feet. Some scholars suggest that John's account of the foot-washing scene was a homily given at a eucharistic liturgy in his community. Holy Thursday is the place for us to best understand the meaning of the foot washing (*mandatum*). Holy Thursday used to be called Maundy Thursday, a derivative of the word *mandatum*. The *mandatum* makes sense only in light of Christ's approaching death and resurrection. The *mandatum* flows from Jesus' ultimate act of love: the gift of his life. We, too, are to wash feet by loving and dying for others.

---

[12]Evening Mass of the Lord's Supper: "Prayer Over the Gifts," *The Sacramentary*.

[13]Launderville, "Blood," 95.

[14]Evening Mass of the Lord's Supper: "Preface of Holy Eucharist," *The Sacramentary*.

During the Holy Thursday liturgy, twelve people come forward to have their feet washed. The ritual dates back to the fifth century in Jerusalem, the latter part of the seventh century in Gaul and Spain, and the twelfth century in Rome. The *mandatum,* at one time considered a sacrament, was commonly celebrated throughout the year by the early church as a sign of service and Christian charity.

The implication of eucharist is that we share in the paschal mystery. We are called to serve and to wash feet. We are called to love as Christ loved by offering the gift of ourselves for others. The sign of foot washing leads us into the mystery of these three days. Also, Holy Thursday used to be the day on which penitents were reconciled to the church so they could participate in the paschal celebration.

This is the only liturgy in which the church prescribes a hymn during the presentation of the gifts. Gifts for the poor are presented and the antiphon *Ubi Caritas* is sung: "Where charity and love prevail, there is God." The offering of food for the poor is the community's way of ratifying in action the directive of the *mandatum:* "This example I leave you (Antiphon 1) ... then surely you must wash one another's feet (Antiphon 3) ... If there is this love among you, all will know that you are my disciples (Antiphon 4) ... love one another as I have loved you ..."(Antiphon 5).

Sufficient bread is consecrated so that there is enough for both Holy Thursday and Good Friday. The liturgy ends with a transfer of the eucharist to a different place of reservation. We continue our vigil in prayerful meditation with solemn adoration ending at midnight. Anticipation of Christ's passion begins immediately. There is quiet solemnity as people spend a holy hour in adoration.

After the liturgy, the altar is stripped without any special notice by the assembly. In the past, special meaning was assigned to this action. It was intended to be symbolic of the stripping of Jesus. While this action no longer holds the same meaning, the practice itself was restored after the Second Vatican Council.

Gospel Exegesis

The facilitator gives input regarding what critical biblical scholarship has to say about this text. The input includes insights as to how people would have heard the gospel in Jesus' time.

One scholar calls this story "revelation in action" of the mystery of God, of Jesus and his Passover.[15] The meaning is not apparent at first glance. It unfolds as the story progresses. Jesus laid aside his garment, wrapped a towel around himself, and washed his disciples' feet. Jesus' laying aside his garment in this pericope alerts us to a prophetic symbolism. "Laying aside" is akin to "laying down" as in "laying down one's life." Jesus' action is symbolic of what will happen through his death.

The action of foot washing in Jesus' culture was a very menial task. It was considered too lowly even for Jewish male slaves; only gentile slaves, wives and children qualified. According to ancient Mediterranean custom, people bathed either at home or in the public baths before attending a dinner party. By the time they arrived at the party, the only washing ritual left was the washing of feet. Verses 6 and 8 refer to the washing of feet. Verses 9-10 refer to the washing of the entire body. Since the body had already been washed before the party, the only remaining washing was that of feet.

Charles Talbert suggests that "the bath of the whole person is linked with becoming a disciple."[16] The foot washing was a preparation for eating with Jesus. John's disciples *were already clean through a bath* (images of baptism). Jesus *made the disciples clean* by his word. Jesus was offering something beyond the cleanliness of the bath. He was offering ongoing, continued cleansing of the dust and dirt of life's everyday journey. This was to be preparation for the meal: disciples were to wash the feet of others. Talbert maintains that the point of the story is that through Jesus' death, the daily sins of disciples (who had already been washed clean earlier from the "principle of sin") were forgiven.[17] Thus, through Jesus' action of selfless love and service, post-baptismal sins are forgiven. After Jesus washed the feet of the disciples he took back his garments and resumed his place. The

---

[15]*Days of the Lord,* Vol. 3, 19.

[16]Charles Talbert, *Reading John* (New York: Crossroad, 1992), 193.

[17]Ibid., 194.

symbolic meaning in taking back his garments applies to Jesus' taking back his life.

The "do as I have done" command usually is understood to mean: to act as Jesus, the humble servant. One scholar suggests another meaning. If we are to wash one another's feet for the daily forgiveness of sin, an inherent piece of the preparation for eucharist must include forgiveness of our neighbor. There is a specific command to forgive one another's daily sins.

Images of baptism are obvious in tonight's gospel through the cleansing motif. Eucharistic overtones appear in the *mandatum* and preparation for eucharist through the daily forgiveness of sins. On this inaugural night of the Triduum, baptism, confirmation, and eucharist are foreshadowed as the elect wait on the threshold for their reception at the Easter Vigil.

We are reminded that Jesus performs the sign of foot washing right before his passion. As listeners, we expect the gospel to be an account of the institution of the eucharist. However, on this night that celebrates the institution of the eucharist, Jesus invites us into the challenge of living eucharist. John's *mandatum* provides the daily example of offering our lives for others (as Jesus would do the very next day) in service and in forgiveness, as we prepare to dine at his table.

Now we really know how much Jesus loved his disciples. Through the sign of foot washing Jesus took his place among the slaves of the world, humbled himself, and willingly gave up his life. The eucharist is an ongoing remembering of Jesus' passover from death to life. The liturgy jump-starts the Triduum with this solemn reminder: "We shall glory in the cross of our Lord Jesus Christ. Through him we are saved and made free."[18] Just as the Passover was a sign of liberation, so too is the eucharist the sign of liberation for Christians.

Proclaim the gospel again.

Sometimes we gain new insights when we hear the text after the interpretation has been given. Someone from the group proclaims the gospel a second time.

---

[18]Evening Mass of the Lord's Supper: "Introductory Rites," *The Sacramentary.*

Conversation with the Liturgy and the Scriptures

Test your original understanding in dialogue with the text.

(You might consider breaking into smaller groups.)

Were there any new insights in the readings that you had not considered before? How does your original understanding of this story compare with what was just shared? How does this story speak to your life?

Participants share an experience from their lives that connects with the biblical interpretation just shared.

Recently there was a very painful parish situation. It was difficult to let go of the anger and rage. One thing became very clear: it was impossible to pray or to share with the parties involved, due to the immense wall that had been erected. We eventually had to simply agree to disagree in the midst of efforts at reconciliation and forgiveness. Our mandatum *consisted in openly addressing the problem with listening ears and opened hearts in spite of our anger. We stayed in the struggle.*

Today's gospel and liturgy remind us that we are in a daily struggle of dying and rising, of forgiving as we have been forgiven, and of building up the reign of God through loving, humble service. The Triduum renews us and gives us the strength to remain in the struggle. Our communities are called to die and to rise. Eucharist nourishes and strengthens us for the daily struggle. Dying to self through parish life can be extremely painful. John's eucharist of foot washing reminds us that the struggle is worth the pain and that dying and rising are what it means to live a eucharistic life. Jesus took the form of a slave and washed feet. He performed an action not even worthy of Jewish slaves. We, too, are to humble ourselves and put ourselves in a similar position of humiliation in order to extend reconciliation and love to others. Sometimes pride gets in the way. The streets of Gehenna must be filled with pride-filled egos. The message of tonight's gospel is that love forgives a multitude of sins. When I reach out in charity to others, when I offer my life for others and extend a hand to the poor, I am offered forgiveness.

The offering of forgiveness can sometimes be the most difficult piece. It requires great humility to extend forgiveness to those who have hurt me, especially when my pride is at stake. All I need to do is turn to the liturgy for help. The psalmist sings it better than I: "How can I make a return to the Lord for all he has done for me?"

The living memorial of Jesus' death and resurrection is the eucharist we celebrate this night. Thank God for this night's sacred antidote to the poison of arrogant pride and self-righteousness. No one dare celebrate this Holy Thursday liturgy with the narrow view that it is simply a commemoration of Jesus' institution of the eucharist and priesthood. Our liturgy speaks powerfully about what our focus should be. Lest we get lost in pious thoughts about Christ present in the elements of bread and wine, we had better give serious attention to the Christ present in the feet of those who are sick, hungry, oppressed, poor, or alienated from our lives. This is the eucharist demanded by tonight's gospel. Who are those people in our lives? In my life? We had better seek them out. It is not a suggestion; it is a command.

All share their life experience.

What was John trying to tell his community? What does he have to say to our community and to me today? In what way is our community called to wash feet? Whose feet are we called to wash? How are images of creation, covenant, exodus/death/resurrection and community evident in tonight's readings? Has our original understanding of tonight's liturgy and scriptures been stretched, challenged, or affirmed?

STEP 5
DECISION

The gospel demands a response.

How does our sharing and this biblical interpretation challenge our community's attitudes? In what way does this gospel call our parish to action in the church, parish, neighborhood, or world? What is one concrete action we will take this week as a response to what we have learned and shared today?

DOCTRINAL ISSUES

What church truth/teaching/doctrinal issue could be drawn from the readings for Holy Thursday?

Participants suggest possible doctrinal themes that flow from the readings.

Possible Doctrinal Themes

Eucharist, bread, wine, washing feet, covenant, paschal mystery, charity, Triduum, service

Present the doctrinal material at this time.

1. The facilitator gives input on a particular doctrinal issue of his/her prior choosing. OR
2. The group chooses a doctrinal issue from the list they created. They read together from the Doctrinal Appendix.

(The doctrinal issues are found in the Doctrinal Appendix in the back of this workbook. If you are choosing an issue from this resource, please refer to it now.)

Reflection questions centered around the chosen doctrinal theme can be found at the end of each topic in the Doctrinal Appendix. The questions are based on the five-step reflection process. If you choose a topic not included in the Doctrinal Appendix, craft your own questions according to the same five-step process.

Following the reflection questions you will be reminded to return to chapter 7, "Preparing the Catechetical Session," to assist you in crafting your own session.

Closing Prayer

Almighty God,
we receive new life
from the supper your Son gave us in this world.

May we find full contentment
in the meal we hope to share
in your eternal kingdom.
We ask this through Christ our Lord.[19]

Selected Bibliography

Clifford, Richard J., S.J. "Exodus." In *The New Jerome Biblical Commentary.* Ed. Raymond E. Brown, S.S., Joseph A. Fitzmyer, S.J., Roland E. Murphy, O.Carm. Englewood Cliffs: Prentice Hall, 1990.

Days of the Lord, Vol. 3. Collegeville: The Liturgical Press, 1993.

Fischer, James A. "Blood, New Testament." In *The Collegeville Pastoral Dictionary of Biblical Theology.* Ed. Carroll Stuhlmueller, C.P. Collegeville: The Liturgical Press, 1996.

Fuller, Reginald H. *Preaching the New Lectionary.* Collegeville: The Liturgical Press, 1974.

Launderville, Dale, O.S.B. "Blood." In *The Collegeville Pastoral Dictionary of Biblical Theology.* Ed. Carroll Stuhlmueller, C.P. Collegeville: The Liturgical Press, 1996.

Talbert, Charles. *Reading John.* New York: Crossroad, 1992.

---

[19]Evening Mass of the Lord's Supper: "Prayer after Communion," *The Sacramentary.*

GOOD FRIDAY

Opening Prayer

Lord,
by shedding his blood for us,
your Son, Jesus Christ,
established the paschal mystery.
In your goodness, make us holy
and watch over us always.
We ask this through Christ our Lord.[1]

LITURGY OF THE WORD

Let us listen to God's word.

The readings are proclaimed.

First Reading
Isaiah 52:13–53:12

The Fourth Servant Song of Isaiah was written while Israel was still in captivity and awaiting deliverance in Babylon. Jerusalem had been destroyed and had not yet been reconstructed.[2] Deutero-Isaiah lamented the plight of the people and offered a message of consolation. Prior to the exile the people had been materialistic, greedy, and overly-prosperous. Once in captivity, that all changed. Deutero-Isaiah portrayed the people as depressed, "dazed, discouraged, and destitute, severely tempted to apostasy." [3] Deutero-Isaiah set out to console, not punish, to offer encouragement, not chastisement, and to strengthen the faith of the people as they awaited deliverance.

The early Christian community believed that Jesus Christ was the suffering servant of the first reading. They believed that Deutero-Isaiah was heralding and foretelling the passion and death of Christ and the inauguration of the messianic

age. Jewish scholars are not certain who the suffering servant of Isaiah was. Christians proclaim with faithful assurance: it was Christ, the one who suffered for the many, the one who bore our infirmities. Jewish scholars maintain that the "many" referred to gentiles. It is not certain whether Jesus saw himself as the servant of this Isaian passage. But there is evidence in the scriptures that he embraced Isaiah's servant image as a metaphor for his mission.

The first reading from Isaiah sets the stage for understanding the passion. Jesus, servant of God, who by all appearances was reduced to nothing, was exalted and raised up by the living God. Vindication was his. The passage ends on a note of peace and hope and helps form our understanding and theology of the cross: "Jesus' suffering was innocent, vicarious and redemptive; it is for all people inclusively; the righteous sufferer is finally vindicated."[4]

Responsorial Psalm
Psalm 31:2, 6, 12-13, 15-16, 25

The psalm highlights the suffering of the Just One. It includes the words of Jesus spoken from the cross in Luke's gospel.

Second Reading
Hebrews 4:14-16; 5:7-9

In the letter to the Hebrews, the theme of Jesus, the high priest, is very carefully set forth. "Jesus is the high priest of his own sacrifice, the perfect sacrifice that is ever before his Father, since he dwells eternally in his presence. He is, 'in the heavens,' the eternal and definitive Passover."[5]

This letter consoles us in our humanity. Jesus identifies with our suffering and weaknesses because he was a person, just like us. He was tempted just as we are tempted. "The only differ-

---

[1] Good Friday: "Opening Prayer," *The Sacramentary*.

[2] Carroll Stuhlmueller, C.P. "Deutero-Isaiah and Trito-Isaiah," in *The New Jerome Biblical Commentary*, ed. Raymond E. Brown, S.S., Joseph A. Fitzmyer, S.J., Roland E. Murphy, O.Carm. (Englewood Cliffs: Prentice Hall, 1990), 329.

[3] Ibid., 330.

[4] Reginald H. Fuller, *Preaching the New Lectionary* (Collegeville: The Liturgical Press, 1974), 19.

[5] *Days of the Lord*, Vol. 3 (Collegeville: The Liturgical Press, 1993), 3, 26.

ence that the author [of Hebrews] remarks between Jesus' temptations and those of his followers is that he never succumbed to them."[6] He prayed for deliverance *through* his hour to come. Jesus learned obedience through the struggle of his life.[7] Jesus lived his life in complete submission to the will of God. His faithfulness prompted decisions and choices that led him ultimately to the cross.

A major theme of the letter to the Hebrews is *Jesus Christ, the exalted High Priest and Lord, reigns from heaven's throne*. Verses 5-10 are believed to reflect a hymn to "Jesus the High Priest." The author of Hebrews often referred to Jesus as the High Priest in order to accentuate his superiority over the Jewish high priest. Later in the letter to the Hebrews Jesus was contrasted with the high priest in one very important aspect. The priesthood of the Jewish high priest ended upon his death. Jesus' priesthood, on the other hand, required his death in order to be officially inaugurated. Jesus, the resurrected High Priest, reigns from his exalted heavenly throne.

Jesus' throne is a throne of grace because Christ made it possible for the human race to have access to God and to God's grace. Unlike the Jewish high priest, Jesus did not sin, even though he was fully tempted to sin. Jesus offers loud cries, tears and prayers of supplication (v. 7) to God. In his glorified state, Jesus was no longer subject to the natural struggles of human nature, such as the fear of death.[8] The author of Hebrews maintains that God heard Jesus' cries and saved him from death. Jesus was not saved from death as we understand death. Jesus died a natural death. However, God did hear his cries and God did deliver him from death. Through the resurrection Jesus is no longer dead, but lives eternally. As reigning High Priest, Jesus empathizes with his people because he knows the trials, tribulations, and struggles of life's sojourn. Jesus cried out.

He knew pain, weakness, and suffering like any other human being. However, Jesus the High Priest sacrificed the gift of his own life and now sits on heaven's throne as an advocate on our behalf.

Jesus was God's Son (v. 8) in two very distinct ways. "He became Son when exalted; he always was Son because he existed with the Father even before he appeared on earth."[9] The Jesus of John's gospel is aware of his preexistence. Jesus learned obedience through his suffering and was consecrated to the priesthood because of his obedience (v. 8). Thus, he is qualified to "to save those who are obedient to him."[10] The author of Hebrews assures his reader that the follower of Christ will receive eternal salvation because that salvation is based on Jesus' eternal priesthood. In this sense, *eternal* refers to things that exist in the permanence of the heavenly realm rather than the impermanence of the earthly domain.

Gospel

The passion of our Lord Jesus Christ according to John.

STEP 1
NAMING ONE'S EXPERIENCE

What were your first impressions? What was your first response? What grabbed your attention? How did you feel?

Each person names his or her initial impression. Statement should be brief. No reasons should be given at this time. All simply listen without agreeing or disagreeing.

STEP 2
UNDERSTANDING

In a brief statement, what do you think this gospel is trying to convey?

---

[6]Myles M. Bourke, "The Epistle to the Hebrews," in *The New Jerome Biblical Commentary,* ed. Raymond E. Brown, S.S., Joseph A. Fitzmyer, S.J., Roland E. Murphy, O.Carm. (Englewood Cliffs: Prentice Hall, 1990), 928.

[7]Fuller, *Preaching the New Lectionary,* 19.

[8]This was probably a reference to Jesus' experience in Gethsemane in Mark 14: 35-36. (Bourke, "The Epistle to the Hebrews," 929.)

[9]Bourke, "The Epistle to the Hebrews," 929.
[10]Ibid.

Liturgical Context

"On this day, when 'Christ our passover was sacrificed' (1 Cor 5:7), the Church meditates on the passion of her Lord and Spouse, adores the cross, commemorates her origin from the side of Christ asleep on the cross, and intercedes for the salvation of the whole world."[11]

Scripture scholar Raymond Brown contends that John's Jesus is the all knowing, always in control Savior who conquered sin and death by carefully orchestrated design. Good Friday's message is Good News. St. John Chrysostom very eloquently summed up the reason we gather for this Good Friday feast.

> Today sees our Lord Jesus Christ on the cross; we celebrate, so that we may understand that the cross is a celebration, a solemn, spiritual feast. Before, the cross was synonymous with condemnation; now it is an object of honor. Before, a symbol of death; now, the means of salvation. It has been the source of countless blessings for us: it has delivered us from error, it has shone on us when we were in darkness. We were vanquished, yet it reconciles us with God. We were foes, yet it has regained God's friendship for us. We were estranged, yet it has brought us back to him.... We have discovered a wellspring.[12]

The liturgy is not a somber preoccupation with the wounds and suffering of Christ. It is surrounded by anticipatory joy. We do not feign ignorance of the resurrection. Liturgy is truth and authenticity, not historicization. In other words, we do not remember and make present Jesus' passion and death as if we didn't know about the resurrection. It is always a prominent piece of our consciousness, remembrance, and celebration.

There is no intention of minimizing Jesus' suffering. We grieve over his passion, so much so that we fast on this day as an expression of our grief. The Good Friday fast puts us in communion with our brothers and sisters who, from as early as the second century, observed a pre-Easter fast of no food or water. As the centuries wore on, and a definite celebration of Good Friday evolved, the fast was observed on Good Friday and Holy Saturday.

In the very early centuries, there was no official Good Friday liturgy. The observance of Good Friday developed according to the local custom of various places. The liturgy of Good Friday today is a blending of customs, observances, and liturgies that evolved over the centuries from varied sources.

The date of Jesus' death, the 14th of Nisan, which fell on a Friday, was observed as a day of mourning and fasting inspired by compassion (a "grieving fast").[13] By the turn of the fourth century there was a non-eucharistic liturgy that is recorded in the travels of the pilgrim, Egeria (ca. 400). She records multiple liturgies on Good Friday beginning before dawn and continuing through the night. The early dawn service took place at the site where Jesus was scourged. Later in the morning they gathered to venerate the cross. (In the fourth century Empress Helena gave the church in Rome a relic of the holy cross. Any church that possessed a relic of the cross venerated it at this liturgy. The present ritual of veneration developed from these early origins.)

The Christians of Egeria's day then gathered from about noon to three for a liturgy of the word. The celebration consisted of a series of scripture readings including psalms that alluded to Jesus' suffering, the passion of Jesus, and John's account of Jesus' death. Nearly spent from the day-long liturgies, the worshipers gathered again in the evening to listen to the proclamation

---

[11] *Circular Letter Concerning the Preparation and Celebration of Easter Feasts,* Congregation for Divine Worship (Rome, USCC, 1988), #58.

[12] John Chrysostom (ca. 350-407), "Homélie pour le Vendredi saint," in *Homiliaire patristique,* Lex Orandi 8 (Paris: Cerf, 1949), 65; in *Days of the Lord,* Vol. 3 (Collegeville: The Liturgical Press, 1993), 27-28.

[13] Adolf Adam, *The Liturgical Year,* trans. Matthew J. O'Connell (Collegeville: The Liturgical Press, 1990), 69.

of Jesus' burial. Following the evening service, there was an all-night vigil for those hearty enough to endure it.

By the seventh century there was a clearly defined Roman liturgy. The pope carried the relic of the cross barefoot from the Lateran Basilica to the Church of the Holy Cross in Jerusalem. The cross was venerated by clergy and laity alike as the scriptures were proclaimed. The intercessions of the faithful ended this liturgy until communion was added in the seventh century.

According to Adolf Adam, the liturgy became far more dramatic during the Middle Ages. The simple communion of the faithful became *missa praesanctificatorum* (mass with previously consecrated gifts). In other words, many parts of the mass, with the exception of the defining element, the eucharistic prayer, were added to this liturgy. The faithful were receiving communion rarely, if at all during those times; thus, only the clergy received the eucharist at the Good Friday liturgy. The Tridentine Mass of 1570 mandated this practice to last for the next four hundred years.

In 1955 the new Order reinstated the traditional three part liturgy: word, veneration of the cross, and communion. After a four-hundred year hiatus, the faithful were once again allowed to receive communion at the Good Friday liturgy. The liturgy was to begin at 3:00 P.M. unless, for pastoral reasons, it could not take place at that time. The liturgical color of the Good Friday liturgy was changed from black to red, the color of martyrs.

The liturgy of Good Friday begins with the very ancient and solemn gesture of prostration by the presiding celebrant and attending priests. The celebrant then moves to the chair and reads the opening prayer followed by the liturgy of the word. The first reading of Good Friday, the fourth Servant Song, was appropriated to the suffering of Christ very early in the Christian tradition. Psalm 31 is a lament and a prayer of trust to the faithful God. The second reading from Paul's letter to the Hebrews exalts Jesus, the great High Priest, the source of salvation. The gospel acclamation introduces the gospel with a proclamation of the exalted, obedient unto death, Jesus Christ crucified. The passion is proclaimed without candles or incense.

The intercessions of Good Friday have their roots in the early Good Friday liturgies. They are the inspiration behind the general intercessions prayed at every liturgy. The intercessions are prayers offered by God's people "for the holy Church, the pope, all states of life in the Church, catechumens, Christian unity, the Jews, all who do not believe in Christ, all who do not believe in God, rulers, those in every kind of need."[14] The intercessions allow the faithful to exercise their "priestly function and intercede for all humanity."[15] Liturgical prayer is universal and missionary. It is not self-centered; it is communal and other-centered. The first intercession is an example of this universal dimension.

Deacon: Let us pray, dear friends,
            for the holy Church of God
            throughout the world,
            that God the almighty Father
            guide it and gather it together
            so that we may worship him
            in peace and tranquility.

Priest: Almighty and eternal God,
            you have shown your glory to all nations
            in Christ, your Son.
            Guide the work of your Church.
            Help it to persevere in faith,
            proclaim your name,
            and bring your salvation to people
               everywhere.
            We ask this through Christ our Lord.[16]

The veneration of the cross is a high point of the Good Friday liturgy: "It expresses the Church's faith in and gratitude to Christ who turned the wood of an instrument of torture into the means of redemption and the sign of God's infinite love. The cross stands as an irresistible call to love God who has loved us so well."[17] The ritual text and antiphons for the veneration proclaim our faith in the cross:

Priest: This is the wood of the cross, on which
            hung the savior of the world.

---

[14]Ibid., 73.

[15]General Introduction to the Roman Missal, #45.

[16]Good Friday: "Intercessions for Good Friday," *The Sacramentary.*

[17]*Days of the Lord*, Vol. 3, 34.

All: Come, Let us worship.

Antiphon
> We worship you, Lord,
> We venerate your cross,
> We praise your resurrection.
> Through the cross you brought joy to the
> world.

Psalm 66:2
> May God be gracious and bless us;
> and let his face shed its light upon us.

Antiphon
> We worship you, Lord,
> We venerate your cross,
> We praise your resurrection.
> Through the cross you brought joy to the
> world.[18]

Communion ends the Good Friday liturgy. The Lord's Prayer is recited and communion bread, consecrated the day before, is distributed. The liturgy ends in silence. We keep vigil at the tomb as we await the Lord's resurrection.

The Office of Readings and Morning Prayer is to be celebrated with the faithful on both Good Friday and Holy Saturday morning.

Gospel Exegesis

The facilitator gives input regarding what critical biblical scholarship has to say about this text. The input includes insights as to how people would have heard the gospel in Jesus' time.

This exegesis of John's passion is based on Raymond E. Brown's *A Crucified Christ in Holy Week.* John's passion narrative is proclaimed every Good Friday. The context for this reading is given in the weeks preceding Holy Week in which other segments of John's gospel are proclaimed. Brown asserts that the Jesus of the Good Friday passion is a far different Jesus from the Jesus portrayed in the synoptic gospels. John's Jesus is aware of his pre-existence. Through Jesus' death he is simply re-turning to a state he temporarily left during his stay in this world (17:5).[19] The Jesus of Good Friday freely offers his life and freely takes it back again. Jesus is not a victim. There is no struggle. Jesus is confident of the outcome. Satan has no power over Jesus. He is a step ahead of all the characters. He knows what is going to happen. He is in complete control. Brown asserts that John's image and portrayal of Jesus is the one that was most frequently passed on to the faithful. The portrait of Jesus in the synoptic gospels is different: the Jesus of the synoptics was not aware of his pre-existence; he was not so all-knowing, either.

The light-darkness image in John's gospel is a strong sign that appears frequently. Jesus came as Light of the world. Judas arrived with a lantern to arrest Jesus. Judas resided in darkness and needed artificial light in order to see.

John's Jesus is the royal personage who grovels to no one. There are no blood and sweat stained moments in the garden. Jesus does not pray to be delivered from his ordeal (as he does in the reference to Mark's gospel in the second reading from Hebrews). He accepts his appointed task with awareness, purpose, and power. No worldly power has control over Jesus. Jesus Christ, Victor, is in complete control of his destiny.

Brown further points out that the Jewish trial of Jesus is different in John's gospel than it is in the other gospels. Rather than the formal court of the high priest, Caiaphas, Jesus is questioned by the police before Annas, Caiaphas's father-in-law. The interrogators try to determine if there is evidence against Jesus of insurrection, thereby prompting a Roman trial in a Roman court. Jesus is so clever with Annas that his captors abuse him.

Jesus' innocence is written all over his face while Peter's weakness stands out like a rooster's crow at first light. Peter cut off the servant's ear and denied Jesus in the garden. Contrasted with Peter is the beloved disciple of John's gospel. While no one knows for sure who this disciple is, he was nevertheless a hero in the Johannine community. It was the "Beloved Disciple" who was present at the

---

[18]Good Friday: "Veneration of the Cross—Antiphon," *The Sacramentary.*

[19]Raymond E. Brown, *A Crucified Christ in Holy Week* (Collegeville: The Liturgical Press, 1986), 57.

Last Supper, the trial, the foot of the cross, the empty tomb, and the post-resurrection appearances of Jesus. This disciple is *the enlightened one, the witness,* and *the lover* par excellence. It is believed that this disciple was upheld in the Johannine community as the perfect model of discipleship and apostolic witness. The Beloved Disciple, not Peter, is the perfect disciple.

The trial of Jesus reads like a Shakespearean play. Jesus was inside with Pilate; the Jewish community was outside. Pilate was moving back and forth between both and tension was mounting. Pilate was agitated and placating. Jesus was in control, engaged and hardly silent (as in Mark's passion). Jesus assumed his own advocacy. No, he was not a king in the earthly sense, but if Pilate wanted to call him a king, so be it; his kingdom was not of this world. He simply came to testify to the truth—not to preside from a royal throne. Jesus was in control. Pilate was on trial: would he succumb to the political pressure? Pilate was aware of who Jesus was, and he was afraid. He knew who Jesus was, yet he was too afraid to bear witness to the truth.

In Mark and Matthew, Jesus was scourged as a part of his sentence. His cloak was stripped from him and then he was marched off to Calvary. In John's gospel Jesus is scourged before he is brought out from the praetorium to the crowd.

All of the gospels highlight the guilt of the crowd by their own self-recriminating cries to crucify him. However, none of the cries are more intense than those in John's gospel. Jesus, wearing a kingly cloak and crown of thorns, was ultimately abandoned. The Jews favored Caesar over Jesus and in the process abandoned all their hopes for access to the messianic reign. Thus, in the final scene of this Roman court, Pilate extracted fidelity to Caesar from the Jewish crowd and in the process they abdicated their messianic hopes.[20] Pilate then handed Jesus over to the priests to be crucified.

The curtain was about to come down as Jesus, the one who willingly offered his life, carried the cross by himself. According to all four gospels, Pilate put a *titulus* (a charge) on the cross stating that Jesus was a would-be "King of the Jews." John's theology was not without a touch of irony. Jesus, who was rejected as king by his own people, was given the legal title of king by none other than Pilate himself.

John's Jesus is wearing a seamless garment. The synoptics only make allusions to the division of the garment. Some scholars believe that the seamless garment was the one worn by the high priest. Jesus hangs not simply as king, but as priest as well. Other scholars say the garment was a symbol of unity.

In Mark and Matthew there is no one with Jesus at the cross. John places Mary and the Beloved Disciple at the cross. John uses them in a symbolic way in his narrative. Jesus named Mary the mother of the Beloved Disciple and the disciple was named her son, thus becoming Jesus' brother. "Jesus has constituted a family of preeminent disciples and the Johannine community is already in existence at the cross (which becomes the birthplace of the church)."[21]

John loaded the final verses with further symbolism. Jesus was given wine-soaked hyssop. Hyssop was a type of leaf used to sprinkle the blood of the paschal lamb on the doorposts of Israelite homes in the exodus story. Jesus was sentenced to death at noon, the time when the priests would slaughter the paschal lambs at Passover. With his last breath Jesus fulfilled the Baptist's prophetic proclamation: "Behold the Lamb of God who takes away the sins of the world." Jesus' bones were not broken, again a symbolic connection to the paschal lamb.

Jesus, still in control of his destiny, proclaimed to the world that *"It is finished"* and handed over his spirit. His resurrected spirit, then, was present at his death and at his resurrection. The Spirit was not present until this defining, crowning moment.

---

[20]Brown alerts us to the anti-Jewish sentiment in John's gospel. He tells us that we are not to ignore it or sugarcoat it. It was real. There was tension between Christians and Jews. It was leveled not just at the leadership, but also at the synagogue. John's community suffered great persecution at the hands of their Jewish brothers and sisters. They were thrown out of the synagogue, which made them very vulnerable. The Romans allowed the Jews to coexist with them, but they were

suspicious of Christians. The hostility was deep and it was bitter. However, we are not to use it as a cause and source of anti-Jewish sentiment, but rather to understand it in light of the cultural and religious problems of the first century.

[21]Raymond E. Brown, *A Crucified Christ in Holy Week,* 64.

Jesus breathed the Holy Spirit on the disciples after his resurrection.

Upon Jesus' death he was quietly removed from the cross in a reverent fashion. Contrast this with the synoptics who record all kinds of cataclysmic events upon his death. Blood and water flowed from Jesus' side (the living water that we were told would flow from his side). It is believed that the water signifies the outpouring of the Holy Spirit upon Jesus' glorification. Some scholars suggest that the water and blood are signs of baptism and eucharist. The Spirit was given to the community through baptism (water) and the eucharist (blood). Thus, the church was born at the foot of the cross through his water of baptism and the blood of eucharist that flowed from his side.

John makes sure that Jesus' burial befits a king; there is plenty of myrrh and oil, and there are cloth wrappings. Nicodemus, a reluctant disciple earlier, now becomes a disciple in full view. At his death, Jesus continued to reconcile sinners to himself. Jesus died as he lived in John's gospel: as a conquering, royal king, in charge of his own destiny, who overcame the sins of the world. Jesus fought the great battle with Satan and was victorious.

The cross then is a sign of victory. Disciples do not stand at this Good Friday cross in sadness or in mourning, but rather in praise and thanksgiving for the incredible mercy of God who loved so greatly that he sent his Son to die for a sinful world.

Proclaim the gospel again.

Sometimes we gain new insights when we hear the text after the interpretation has been given. Someone from the group proclaims the gospel a second time.

STEP 4
TESTING

Conversation with the Liturgy and the Scriptures

Test your original understanding in dialogue with the text.

(You might consider breaking into smaller groups.)

Were there any new insights? Was there anything you had not considered before about this liturgy and/or scriptures? How does your original understanding of Good Friday compare with what we just shared? How does this story speak to your life? Have you ever known a time in your life when the Jesus portrayed in John's gospel was necessary to your situation?

Participants share an experience from their lives that connects with the biblical interpretation just shared.

> *There are times we need a Christ who stands strong, omniscient, all powerful, and ready to raise the arm of power and might over the strength and influence of evil. There was once a very destructive division taking place in a parish where I was working. The factions and divisions became more sinister each day. The situation brought the worst out in very good people. As the situation grew worse and the pain greater, we all became aware that the problem was so systemic that we alone could do nothing to change it. We found ourselves saying that we doubted that even the physical presence of Jesus could reconcile the animosity between people.*

> *John's portrait of Jesus and the celebration of this liturgy is the only thing that gives meaning and hope to such situations. All we could do was put the mess in God's hands, trusting that the One who was victorious over Satan's power could see us through the darkness. Our own efforts had failed miserably. I remember being strengthened by words of consolation in the scripture reminding us that God is the ultimate vindicator; if we would only put our trust in God, resurrection would prevail. Resurrection did prevail. There were no thunderbolts—God's action of deliverance brought with it no cataclysmic, dramatic signs: it was peaceful and it was slow but it was permanent. Reconciliation was possible. Thank God for the One who went before us to see us through life's despairs. God dealt with us as a community and as individuals. The innocent accused were vindicated and peace was restored. But, above all, we all marveled at the presence of John's Jesus— the One who was in control all the time.*

All share their life experience.

What was the message for the Johannine community in the passion narrative? What does he have to say to our community and to me today? How does today's liturgy call us to death and resurrection? What are the implications? What are our collective and personal responses to the Good Friday liturgy? Do I still feel the same way about this text as I did at the beginning? Has our original understanding been stretched, challenged, or affirmed?

STEP 5
DECISION

The gospel demands a response.

In what concrete way does this gospel call our parish to action in the church, parish, neighborhood, or world? Has this conversation with the exegesis of the scriptures and the liturgy for Good Friday called me to change in any way? What am I/we/community/parish called to do in response? What is the challenge of the Good Friday liturgy? What will I/we do about it?

DOCTRINAL ISSUES

What church truth/teaching/doctrinal issue could be drawn from the gospel for Good Friday?

Participants suggest possible doctrinal themes that flow from the readings.

Possible Doctrinal Themes

Cross, redemptive suffering, paschal mystery, christology

Present the doctrinal material at this time.

1. Facilitator gives input on a particular doctrinal issue of his/her prior choosing. OR
2. The group chooses a doctrinal issue from the list they created. They read together from the Doctrinal Appendix.

(The doctrinal issues are found in the Doctrinal Appendix in the back of this workbook. If you are choosing an issue from this resource, please refer to it now.)

Reflection questions centered around the chosen doctrinal theme can be found at the end of each topic in the Doctrinal Appendix. The questions are based on the five-step reflection process. If you choose a topic not included in the Doctrinal Appendix, craft your own questions according to the same five-step process.

Following the reflection questions you will be reminded to return to chapter 7, "Preparing the Catechetical Session," to assist you in crafting your own session.

Closing Prayer

Lord,
send down your abundant blessing
upon your people who have recalled the death of
    your Son
in the sure hope of the resurrection.
Grant them pardon; bring them comfort.
May their faith grow stronger
and their eternal salvation be assured.
We ask this through Christ our Lord.[22]

Selected Bibliography

Adam, Adolf. *The Liturgical Year.* Trans. Matthew J. O'Connell. Collegeville: The Liturgical Press, 1990.

Brown, Raymond E. *A Crucified Christ in Holy Week.* Collegeville: The Liturgical Press, 1986.

Circular Letter Concerning the Preparation and Celebration of Easter Feasts. Congregation for Divine Worship, Rome: USCC, 1988.

Days of the Lord, Vol. 3. Collegeville: The Liturgical Press, 1993.

Fuller, Reginald H. *Preaching the New Lectionary.* Collegeville: The Liturgical Press, 1974.

Stuhlmueller, Carroll, C.P. *"Deutero-Isaiah and Trito-Isaiah."* In *The New Jerome Biblical Commentary.* Ed. Raymond E. Brown, S.S., Joseph A. Fitzmyer, S.J., Roland E. Murphy, O.Carm. Englewood Cliffs: Prentice Hall, 1990.

---

[22]Good Friday: "Prayer Over the People," *The Sacramentary.*

EASTER VIGIL

The Easter Vigil sets out for the church in sign, symbol, word, and gesture the heart of our Catholic Christian faith and identity. The riches contained within the Vigil are nearly impossible to examine in one celebration or catechetical session. The Easter Vigil is the springboard not only for pre-sacramental preparation for the rites of initiation, but also for mystagogical reflection for neophytes and the entire church.[1] Rather than dealing with the segments as individual pearls scattered in other areas of this resource, this session will deal with the pearls as if on a finely crafted string. Therefore, the exegesis of the symbols, words, and ritual pieces in this liturgy will be treated as they occur in the liturgy. Obviously, the format for this session will be different from the formats for other sessions in the book. The gospel, the readings, and each ritual piece of the Vigil are vital to understanding who we are and why we gather on this night. There are enormous riches in this powerful celebration. It would be very difficult to absorb them all in one preparation session. Since the pieces of this liturgy are pivotal to understanding our Catholic heritage, it is essential that they become a benchmark for constant referral. All liturgy flows from this Mother of all Feasts.

This session is crafted in such a way that it can be used for ongoing reflection throughout the Easter season and liturgical year. The meaning, value, and function of symbols, as well as an exegesis of their bibical, ecclesial, and liturgical signs will be explained as they occur in the liturgy. Questions for mystagogical reflection are provided at the end of each section.

Each scriptural text and liturgical ritual will be examined as well. The historical development of the Easter Vigil will not be addressed in this session, as it was covered in the overview of the Easter season.

The symbols will not be repeated in the Doctrinal Appendix as they will be treated extensively in this session. However, symbols are critical to our Catholic tradition and therefore should form a major piece of our catechetical efforts. Thus, there will be questions provided for reflection on them, as well as on the scriptures and the liturgical segments.

This session is divided into seven Sections: A. Holy Saturday and Rites of Preparation, B. Symbols, C. Introduction to the Vigil, D. Service of Fire/Light, E. Liturgy of the Word, F. Service of Baptism, G. Liturgy of the Eucharist.

A. HOLY SATURDAY AND RITES OF PREPARATION

We are still in the midst of the Triduum; the liturgy is not over. The church gathers again for celebration of the liturgy of the hours on the morning of Holy Saturday.

Preparatory Rites

The elect are brought together for prayer and reflection in immediate preparation for the sacraments of initiation. If the presentation of the Lord's Prayer was deferred until this time [see #149, #178-180 in RCIA] it is celebrated on Holy Saturday. The "return" or recitation of the creed and the choosing of a baptismal name may also take place at this time (RCIA, #193-196, #200). Another preparatory rite is celebrated with the elect on Holy Saturday. "By the power of its symbolism, the *ephphetha rite*, or rite of opening the ears and mouth, impresses on the elect their need of grace in order that they may hear the word of God and profess it for their salvation" (RCIA, #197).

---

[1] The *National Catechetical Directory* asserts that "sacramental catechesis has traditionally been of two kinds: preparation for the initial celebration of the sacraments and continued enrichment following their first reception" (#36). The meaning of the sacraments is set forth in the scriptures assigned to the sacramental rites. Therefore, in order to prepare people for full, conscious, and active participation in the celebrations of the sacraments in the liturgy, the scriptures from those celebrations may be used for prior prayer and meditation. They may also be revisited following the celebration itself for mystagogical reflection and catechesis.

Blessing of Easter Foods

In some places there is a custom of blessing the foods that will break the lenten fast. Eggs, breads, meats, and produce are brought to the church for a special blessing. These foods used to be forbidden during Lent and blessing them is an indication that the lenten fast is over and Easter has arrived. This was easily understood when the Easter Vigil was celebrated early on Holy Saturday morning and the foods were brought to that celebration. Now, however, the blessing anticipates—rather than celebrates—the arrival of Easter. Gabe Huck suggests that rather than blessing with water (water blessing needs to wait for the Vigil) and incense, a simple extension of hands might be appropriate, if well explained. Another possibility might include inviting people to bring their foods on Easter day. "If such blessings are then given a prominent place in the liturgies of Easter day, with full use of water and incense, the blessings of food might slowly come to be seen—as they originally were—as part of the Easter liturgy."[2]

B. SYMBOLS

The symbols of the Easter Vigil are cross, fire/light, word, water, white garment, oil, laying on of hands, bread, wine, church. The nine dominant liturgical symbols of the church are all manifest at the Easter Vigil. The celebration of liturgy makes use of of symbols that speak most appropriately of creation (candle, water, fire), human existence (washing, anointing, breaking bread) and the history of God's saving action in the world (the rites of Passover). The stories and actions of remembrance, the human rituals, and the above mentioned cosmic elements are subsumed into a world of faith and, through the power of the Holy Spirit, they reveal the saving action of Jesus Christ.

Symbols are encountered through the four signs of God's presence (the four signs of catechesis referred to in chapter 2). We encounter symbols through the natural, biblical, ecclesial, and liturgical signs of God's presence. Symbols speak to us of our identity as Catholic Christians. For example, the symbol of light has its genesis in Christ, Light of the World. Since we are to walk as children of the Light, light identifies us and we become its reality—we become light, we become bread, etc.

Meaning is conveyed when people encounter symbols, which are repeatable and possess many layers of meaning. They are multi-faceted and have multiple forms and uses. At the Easter Vigil, the symbol of light looms in the new fire, the Easter candle, the candles of the faithful, the incense, and the sanctuary lamp. In the darkened church, light's presence is felt in absence. The meaning of symbols is expressed in the way they are used, in the scriptures and ritual prayers that accompany their use, and in the gestures that define them.[3]

The Easter Vigil accentuates the symbols that illumine our existence and that occur in all liturgies. We are people of the cross. We enter the waters and we are chrismated into the ecclesial community. We thus become people of the light and are thereby incorporated into the paschal mystery, which we experience as we gather around the eucharistic table.

"Liturgical action depends on symbols because beings cannot be together and communicate without some kind of encounter in words (verbal symbols) and/or in gestures and actions (nonverbal symbols). All knowledge begins with our senses; this means that an encounter with God is only possible by means of sensible signs."[4] In antiquity, a symbol used to be understood as two halves which, when joined, became one whole. The person who had one half would thus recognize the other half because the two put together equaled the whole. By extension, a symbol was regarded as two parts of a whole—the visible and the invisible. Just because the invisible half of the symbol was not readily observable, it was nevertheless half of the reality. When joined with the visible half of the

---

[2]Gabe Huck, *The Three Days: Parish Prayer in the Paschal Triduum* (Chicago: Liturgy Training Pub., 1981), 53.

[3]Linda Gaupin, *Sacramental Catechesis,* course text for "Specialized Certification in Sacramental Catechesis," Diocese of Orlando Florida, November 1996.

[4]Klemens Richter, *The Meaning of the Sacramental Symbols,* trans. Linda Maloney (Collegeville: The Liturgical Press, 1990), 13.

symbol, it constituted the whole reality. "In the language of religion and theology it is frequently the case that the concept of 'symbol' is reserved for the signs of faith, that is . . . in addition to their superficial, natural meaning, [they have] another and supernatural meaning that is only accessible to faith."[5] Through symbols we are able to touch the deep mysteries of our faith in ways that words can never express.

If symbols were to speak, they would say: "I am . . ." rather than, "I am like. . . ." Symbols in the sacramental sense *are* the reality they express. Eucharist in the form of bread and wine *is* the Body and Blood of Jesus. We can say with assurance that symbols express our identity. When we consume the precious elements, we become what we have consumed: the Mystical Body of Christ. The symbols of the Easter Vigil, highlighted and set forth, provide the means for us to communicate with God and for God to communicate with us through our senses. The symbols of the Vigil are food for mystagogical reflection throughout the Easter season and form the basis of our sacramental catechesis. Our symbol system connects us to the saints of the past with whom we share the same sacramental signs. When we experience the symbols of water, oil, and bread in their natural, biblical, ecclesial, and liturgical context, we discover new depths of meaning. God speaks to us as we crack open the meanings of the symbols and apply them to our lives. We encounter God in the natural elements of life. Those natural elements point to the hidden mystery of God in our lives. Sirach proclaimed: "Chief of all needs for human life are water and fire, iron and salt, the heart of the wheat, milk and honey, oil, the blood of the grape and cloth." If these are the chief of all human needs, no wonder they form the basis of our entire symbol system. Each one is essential for life just as God is essential for life.

The ecclesial signs provide us with the sources for understanding the nature and purpose of the symbols and rites. Ecclesial signs express what we believe about our symbols, how past communities understood them, and how we live what we believe. The first sources for understanding what the church believes about our signs and symbols are the ritual

texts themselves (The Sacramentary, RCIA, rite of baptism, rite of confirmation, rite of penance, etc.). Liturgical signs provide the vehicle for allowing our symbols to express what they were intended to convey. Liturgical signs occur in the worship of the community, in the liturgical celebration. In the liturgy, we pray the ritual prayers, perform the ritual action, and profess our ritual story. This is the night when new Christians are made in the waters of new birth; when the new oils anoint, seal, and brand the baptized to the image and likeness of Christ; and when the newly consecrated bread incorporates all the faithful in the life, death, and resurrection of Jesus Christ. The liturgy is the theater in which the symbols enact their intended roles and, in so doing, reveal the manifestation of God.

Before proceeding with the Vigil liturgy, let us explore the symbols of church and cross. The symbol of church/people of God is also addressed at this juncture because it is the context within which the Vigil is set. This is the night the church generates herself. We must approach the liturgy of this night from the perspective of church doing the work God has given her.

While the cross is a prominent symbol of this and every liturgy, it is underscored particularly in the liturgies of Good Friday, Palm Sunday, and the feast of the Triumph of the Cross. The cross is a primary symbol of the Easter Vigil as it relates to the resurrection of Christ. Without Christ's death on the cross, there could have been no resurrection. However, this liturgy does not meditate particularly on the cross, per se, but rather on its fulfillment in the resurrection.

Symbol of Church/People of God

One of the clearest symbols of God's presence in the world is the church. There are many interchangeable terms for church—community, church, people of God, assembly—but they are all the same reality. God is present to the world through the visible, tangible sign of God's love, the church. Human beings are, by nature, social beings. Belonging is a basic anthropomorphic need. From its earliest origins, Israel survived because it was *a people*. There was no life outside the

———
[5]Ibid., 13.

community. The ancient world was a treacherous place. Food and water were scarce, and the environment was dangerous. The community was needed for basic survival and protection. The community meant life. The community provided the basic needs of shelter, food, and human companionship. When someone was exiled from the community, it was a death sentence.

One common thread running through all religious symbols is that in some way they speak to something that is essential or meaningful for human life. A symbol mirrors, images, or reflects invisible realities. Symbols provide a way of touching the intangible. God is revealed through a visible, tangible sign, something people can experience, touch, taste, smell, or feel.[6] Since community was essential for life and since there was no life, food, shelter, or protection outside the community, perhaps the community was a sign of who God is, how God acts, and what it means to be God's people. God functions like the community. God is provider, protector, and the One who sustains life.

Our experience of human community colors how we experience and understand the spiritual, biblical sense of community. Community as a symbol of God is a lived reality for people whose primary experience of the family community is nurturing. However, when the contrary is true, community as a sign of God becomes a reality only as it is experienced in the ongoing life of a faith-filled community.

The Easter Vigil celebrates the symbol of church/people of God in the most visible way through the

presence of the elect. After months of loving guidance, care, and nurturing, tender Mother Church gently brings her children to the water's edge for full immersion in the life of the community, the life of God.

Natural Sign

We exist in community. We are part of the human family. We have friends and we are social beings. Groups can be exclusive or inclusive. They can pull together or be divisive. A unified community is capable of accomplishing many common goals. A divisive community is destructive. Community exists on many levels: family, friends, religious groups, ethnic groups, institutional groups, class groups, racial groups, civic groups, cities, states, country, world. Every family is a community. It can be nurturing and speak of the unconditional love of God, or the contrary can be true. Communities have power when they are united; they are powerless when they are not. Communities have the power to change laws and structures.

Questions: Have you ever had an experience of being part of a community other than your church community? What were the things that attracted you to this community? Did you ever have the sense that a community you were part of possessed corporate power?

Biblical Sign

The word *community* is not a term found in either the New Testament or the Old Testament. Israel was formed from tribal origins. Tribes were formed from unions between extended families, parents, brothers, sisters, cousins, in-laws, slaves, and servants. A person's identity was tied to the clan. Kinship was synonymous with tribal identity. Kinship prompted the celebration of rituals that supported the familial tribal bond, such as marriages, burials, and common festival meals. Passover was one such ritual.

In addition, there was a political understanding of community. Tribes were often forced to come together for military purposes or to support political leadership. "The basic Hebrew word for assembly, *qahal*, contains the notion of invited participation or summoning. This suggests that such large gatherings were irregular and exceptional;

---

[6]This is how sacraments nourish the ongoing life of the church. Sacraments get us in touch with the living God through visible, touchable human symbols. Jesus Christ is called the sacrament of God. The reason God sent the Son to the world is that humanity does not have the capacity to comprehend the mind, heart, and inestimable love of God on its own. Human suspicion and incredulity would have always been a barrier. Unconditional love makes no sense in light of the human condition. Human beings could always say to their maker, "Sure, you love us. Those are empty words. You do not know what it means to struggle, suffer, and live the human condition. Your love is empty until you walk in our shoes. It means nothing." So the Son was sent. His name was Jesus; he walked in our shoes. Made of human flesh, Jesus, the sacrament of God, expressed for us the unfathomable love of God through death on the cross.

Israelites gathered at someone's command or request for joint military purposes or raiding."[7] Only hierarchical males in the tribe gathered for such meetings. Such was the tribal, communal structure.

Israel was a unique people, a people set apart. Beginning with Abraham, they were elected by God to become a great nation. Biblical authors believed Israel was "chosen by God as the means by which a special people were brought into being."[8] Israel was called and elected by God for a special purpose in his plan for the salvation of the world.

The exodus solidified the understanding of Israel's election. God called Moses to deliver *God's people* from slavery in Egypt. He formed an everlasting covenant with them and made them his precious, chosen, endeared children (Ex 19:5-6). God formed a covenant with Israel that was tied to their understanding of the tribal, family system. God would provide, sustain, and protect them. They would enjoy God's blessing, sharing and peace, *shalom*. In return, they would live *hesed* (biblical justice) and would be obedient to God through adherence to the law and the prophets. Such obedience demanded that God's people extend the same covenant love to one another, especially the weakest members of the clan. Thus, in response to the covenant forged with Israel, they would live in obedience and biblical justice. Every time Israel sinned by going their own way, they understood their sin as disobedience to God's will. Calamity was understood as divine retribution for breaking the covenant.

The New Testament took the understanding of *people of God* one step further. The people of God were all those who were open to God's revelation in Christ, no matter what tribe or clan claimed their membership. "In referring to people of the second covenant, however, it also transcends having a common ancestry and history and is a reality of revelation, faith and historical awareness open to all human beings. This universality stems from the people's relationship to the person of Christ who died and rose in a great Passover event to be Lord of all, as well as from the creative Spirit of God manifested on Pentecost."[9] Thus, the invitation to become the people of God was open to all: Jew, Greek, gentile, who would accept the proclamation of God's reign (Acts 28).

When the Hebrew bible was translated into Greek, the term for *qahal*, an invited gathering, was *ekklesia* or *synagoge*. To the Greeks, the term meant a political gathering. There were many such gatherings that were not religious in orientation. The males would gather in a public square or gathering space for political or other reasons. They may have gathered for reading the Torah on the sabbath, but the *synagoge* was not necessarily religious in purpose.

According to Jerome Neyrey, when the Christian church adapted the term, it understood *ekklesia* (church) to mean the gathering of a new people as citizens of a new political reality—the reign of God. Christians were new citizens of the household of God (Eph 2:19).

People of Jesus' time did belong to groups outside the family structure. Neyrey calls these groups the *fictive* family. The disciples were a fictive family. When Jesus spoke of anyone who does the will of God as being his mother, brother, sister, etc., he was referring to the creation of a new fictive family, the household of God (Mk 3:34-35). Regardless of the social class structure in the tribal or political system, members of Jesus' new fictive family, or households, were to be treated with equal respect, honor, and protection, whether they were slave, servant, woman, or child. They were as deserving as blood relatives. There was no sense of individualism. "Family ideology indicates that individuals should always 'seek the good of the group' (1 Cor 10:24), and not pursue individualistic objectives."[10]

[7]Jerome H. Neyrey, S.J., "Community," in *The Collegeville Pastoral Dictionary of Biblical Theology*, ed. Carroll Stuhlmueller, C.P. (Collegeville: The Liturgical Press, 1996), 151.

[8]Joseph Jensen, O.S.B., "People of God," in *The Collegeville Pastoral Dictionary of Biblical Theology*, ed. Carroll Stuhlmueller, C.P. (Collegeville: The Liturgical Press, 1996), 720.

[9]Eugene LaVerdiere, S.S.S., "People of God: New Testament," in *The Collegeville Pastoral Dictionary of Biblical Theology*, ed. Carroll Stuhlmueller, C.P. (Collegeville: The Liturgical Press, 1996), 721.

[10]Neyrey, "Community," 152.

The Christian message of community centered around the eschatological hope of the new, eternal city, the new Jerusalem. It was a message of universality. God's new paradise would be open to all people inclusively without distinctions. "Later in the vision of the new creation (Rev 21:1–22:5), when salvation history is finally fulfilled, God's dwelling will be with the entire human race. 'He will dwell with them and they will be his people' (Rev 21:3)."[11]

Questions: What touched you in the biblical understanding of people of God? Was there any new insight? What does it teach you about God, Christ, Spirit, community or yourself?

Ecclesial Sign

The Second Vatican Council, in its document, *The Dogmatic Constitution on the Church*, recaptured the biblical symbol of the church as people of God. There is a direct bearing and relationship to the scriptural understanding of covenant between God and Israel.

Justin, one of the early church fathers, eventually understood the emergence of the Christian church as coming *from* Israel, but as now being the true Israel. The church continued the work and role of Israel. Augustine described the church as on its way, since the creation of the world, to her final destination in heaven. Since church and state were one during the Middle Ages, there was little need to refer to the church's identity—it was obvious. There was no one to dispute it. During the Reformation there was, however, discussion regarding the role of the church. Rather than using the symbol, *people of God*, the language chosen during the Reformation was *communion of saints*, "the invisible communion of believers who are the true Church."[12]

The symbol did not enjoy a renaissance until the nineteenth century. "The spirit of a people binding them together as a community, works to retrieve the symbol of body of Christ to describe the organic unity of the Church, through the enliven-

ing presence of the Holy Spirit"[13] (per the work of Johann Adam Mohler). This eventually led to the encyclical, *Mystici Corporis* in 1943. With the emergence of the field of biblical studies, the symbol *people of God* was retrieved from the church's earliest foundation, Israel and the Christian community. By 1960, the symbol was a consciously recognized aspect of ecclesiology. This led the way for reformulation of the church's theology.

The Second Vatican Council redefined our understanding of church. The following principles are a summary of our theology as articulated in *Sharing the Light of Faith: The National Catechetical Directory*. "The Church is a mystery. It is a reality imbued with the hidden presence of God" (from Pope Paul VI's opening allocution at the second session, September 19, 1963). "The Church is a gift coming from the love of God, Christ's redeeming action and the power of the Holy Spirit" (*National Catechetical Directory* [NCD], #63). "As a divine reality inserted into human history, the Church is a kind of sacrament. Its unique relationship with Christ makes it both a sign and instrument of God's unfathomable union with humanity and of the unity of human beings among themselves" (NCD, #63). "...As a mystery, the Church cannot be totally understood or fully defined. Its nature and mission are best captured in scriptural parables and images, taken from ordinary life, which not only express truth about its nature but challenge the Church: for example, to become more a People of God, a better servant, more faithful and holy, more united around the teaching authority of the hierarchy" (NCD, #63).

The church is a community of believers, the people of God. We are called to become a new people, a royal priesthood, a people claimed by God to proclaim the greatness of God (1 Pet 2:9). Jesus freed us from sin and because of the saving waters of baptism we are called to believe, worship, and witness to his saving works.

We are one body in Christ (Rom 12:5). Through Jesus' death, resurrection, and glorification, he remains a living presence and head of his church, of which we are all members. *We celebrate this identity most especially in the eucharist.* Through the eucharist, we become the Body and Blood of Christ.

---

[11]LaVerdiere, "People of God: New Testament," 723.

[12]Ann Graff, "People of God in the History of Theology," in *The Collegeville Pastoral Dictionary of Biblical Theology*, ed. Carroll Stuhlmueller, C.P. (Collegeville: The Liturgical Press, 1996) 724.

[13]Ibid.

The church is servant. The church has a mission to heal and reconcile as Jesus did. The church is to live the gospel through the works of mercy, assisting anyone who is in need of our help. The church as servant acts out of love and concern, not for personal glory. One way the church is servant is through its teaching ministry in which it witnesses to the gospel and the power of God in the world.

The church is a sign of the reign of God. The church is evidence that God is alive in our midst. In order to be that sign, the church "must be committed to justice, love and peace, to grace and holiness, truth and life, for these are the hallmarks of the kingdom of God" (NCD, #67).

The church is a pilgrim church. Aware of its sins, the church journeys to its final destination as it repents and overcomes patiently the trials and tribulations that come its way. In this way it demonstrates its steadfast faithfulness to the world.

"As mystery, people, one body in Christ, servant, sign of the kingdom, and pilgrim, the Church is conceived as God's family, whose members are united to Christ and led by the Spirit in their journey to the Father. The Church merits our prayerful reflection and wholehearted response" (NCD, #68).

Questions: Does the church's theology about church resonate with your experience of church in your own community? What are the areas of death/resurrection? What are some specific areas that are in need of growth? What does participation in your community teach you about God, Christ, Spirit, church, or yourself?

Liturgical Sign

The symbol of church as people of God is a primary symbol in the liturgy. The gathered community is a sign of God's presence in our midst. Before the book is opened or the bread shared, God is experienced in the community. "For these people are the people of God, purchased by Christ's blood, gathered together by the Lord, nourished by the word. They are a people called to offer the prayers of the entire human family, a people giving thanks in Christ, for the mystery of salvation by offering his sacrifice. Finally they are a people growing together into unity by sharing Christ's

Body and Blood. These people are holy by their origin, but becoming ever more holy by conscious, active and fruitful participation in the mystery of the Eucharist" (*Constitution on the Sacred Liturgy*, #59, "General Instruction of the Roman Missal," #5).

In every liturgical celebration the community is a primary experience of God's presence. We profess the mystery of the church in our ritual prayers and, through the eucharist, we live its reality. Through all the ministries of the church, Christ is present. Thus, when the people participate and celebrate, the lector proclaims, the priest presides, the eucharistic minister serves, the cantor sings, the hospitality people welcome, etc., Christ is made manifest in our midst.

Questions: Have you ever had an experience of the presence of God in the midst of your communal worship? What did your experience teach you about God, Christ, Spirit, community, yourself?

Symbol of the Cross

This object of torture and sign of disgrace and horror is a symbol of our salvation. It is the principal Christian symbol of hope. The cross is at the heart of our belief in the paschal mystery and our participation in it. Without the cross there is no resurrection. Tonight's liturgy leads us from the cross to the resurrection. We are transported through time as witnesses of God's great deeds of history and brought to this moment. God fulfilled in Christ what was begun at the creation of the world. We are called to take up our cross and follow Christ. "Apart from the cross there is no other ladder by which we may get to heaven."[14]

The cross was an absurdity to the people of Jesus' time. To imagine the cross as a symbol of salvation, victory, and honor, was as absurd to Jesus' contemporaries as imagining the electric chair as an object worthy of veneration would be in today's culture. The cross is a sign of our redemption. Christ was victorious over sin and death. St. Irenaeus reminds us of the implication of the cross:

---

[14]St. Rose of Lima, cf. P. Hansen, *Vita mirabilis* (Louvain, 1668).

"By the wood of the Cross the work of the Word of God was made manifest to all: his hands are stretched out to gather every one together."[15]

Natural Sign

Crucifixion is not a means of execution today. We have no natural concept of cross apart from what has come to us from religious sources. However, the cross is used in our culture as a sign of adornment with little or no meaning attached to it. Some in the counter-cultural strata of today's society have even made a mockery of it. The word *cross* has often been associated with a general understanding of suffering in our culture ("That poor woman has a cross to bear"). The term *cross* is somewhat universally understood to mean the trials in one's life.

Questions: How does "cross" have anything to do with your everyday life? What is your experience of the cross?

Biblical Sign

There was no mention of the cross in the Old Testament. Crucifixion was an oriental means of execution. The Greeks did not use it, but the Romans did. However, Roman citizens were never crucified. Crucifixion on the cross was reserved for slaves, insurrectionists, traitors, and anyone guilty of a grave crime. Jesus alluded to the cross in reference to his own death. The symbol of cross was fostered by Jesus who challenged his disciples to take up their cross and follow him. Cross was understood in that sense to mean the "denial of self." In order to gain one's life, one had to lose it. Disciples had to be willing to give up their personal welfare in response to the reign of God.

Paul gives us a refined theology of the cross as symbol. He preached that the cross was revolting to the Jews and folly to the Gentiles (1 Cor 1:23; 2:2). Through the power of the cross, all people who believe in it are saved. Circumcision is no longer needed; it is replaced by the cross as a sign of God's covenant with the human race (Gal 66:14). The cross is a symbol of unity; it unites Jews and gentiles. Jesus nailed the sins of the world to the cross. He became the victim of their sins (Col 2:14). Jesus freely gave up his life for all. He died once, and for the whole world. We cannot merit salvation. Jesus won it for us, once and for all.

Ecclesial Sign

The symbol of cross is understood to mean the unique sacrifice of Jesus' life for the salvation of the world. Only Christ was able to take unto himself the sins of the world by dying a horrid death on the cross. We are united to Jesus' cross and suffering through baptism. The cross is initiatory. We are incorporated into Christ's cross through baptism: we die to sin and are resurrected to new life in Christ. Through confirmation we are branded with the Holy Spirit. We are also sealed and joined to the cross of Christ. Through the eucharist, we share in Jesus' sacrifice of the cross. In the form of bread and wine we once again participate in the breaking, sharing, and pouring out of Jesus' life. We, too, are broken, shared, and poured out. The Christian community shares in the saving effects of Jesus' sacrifice: his paschal mystery, his death and resurrection. Like Jesus on Calvary, paschal Christians are to live, die and empty themselves for the sake of others, for the sins of the world. The sacrifice of the cross continues through the broken bread and the poured cup of the eucharist.

We cannot earn salvation. Jesus won salvation on the cross and through the grace offered by the selfless sacrifice of his life we are all beneficiaries. The cross is a supreme act of love. Jesus' death on the cross fulfilled all the expectations of the old Passover. Salvation history is fulfilled with Jesus' final act of love.

St. John Chrysostom professes it best:

> Today sees our Lord Jesus Christ on the cross; we celebrate, so that we may understand that the cross is a celebration, a solemn, spiritual feast. Before, the cross was synonymous with condemnation; now it is an object of honor. Before, a symbol of death; now, the means of salvation. It has been the source of countless blessings for us: it has delivered us from error, it has shone on us when we were in darkness.

---

[15]Quoted in Henri de Lubac, *Catholicism: A Study of Dogma in Relation to the Corporate Destiny of Mankind* (New York: New American Library, 1964), 210.

We were vanquished, yet it reconciles us with God. We were foes, yet it has regained God's friendship for us. We were estranged, yet it has brought us back to him.... We have discovered a wellspring.[16]

Question: In light of your personal experience of the cross, the suffering in your life, can you now perhaps assign a deeper meaning to that suffering in dialogue with our tradition's belief in its saving effects?

Liturgical Sign

The cross forms us as people. Every liturgy, every sacramental celebration has as its primary focus incorporation into the paschal mystery of Jesus Christ. That is, we participate in Jesus' death and resurrection through our participation in the liturgy. Eucharist is a living memorial of that death and resurrection.

Every liturgical gathering remembers the cross of Christ. We begin each liturgy with the sign of our identity, the sign of the cross. We are signed with the cross of Jesus as catechumens and at our baptism. The sign of the cross signifies the grace of salvation won for us through Jesus' passion, death on the cross, and resurrection. We make the sign of the cross before all prayer and as we enter the church.

We remember the cross of Christ especially on Good Friday, Palm Sunday, and the feast of the Triumph of the Cross. The Easter season is a meditation on its saving effects. The entire liturgical year invites us to live the cross each day. The cross is a primary symbol in every blessing, ritual, liturgy, sacrament, and sacramental of the church. (Refer to the Good Friday liturgy for the historical development of the ritual celebration of the cross.)

Questions: Do you remember a time when you were conscious of an experience of the cross in the liturgy? What did it teach you about God, Christ, the church, and yourself? What is the challenge of the cross we celebrate? How are we called to respond to the cross of Christ in our lives?

---

[16]John Chrysostom (ca. 350-407), "Homélie pour le Vendredi saint," in *Homiliaire patristique*, Lex Orandi 8 (Paris: Cerf, 1949), 65; in *Days of the Lord,* Vol. 3 (Collegeville: The Liturgical Press, 1993), 27-28.

C. INTRODUCTION TO THE EASTER VIGIL

Huddled around ancient fires, our ancestors told their stories and enacted the rituals that formed them into a holy nation, a consecrated assembly, a people set apart. We, too, gather this night around similar sacred flames to remember our origins, to tell our story, and to "do" the business of making church. The ancient phallic symbol of Easter candle is plunged into the embryonic waters of font. Tonight, the church gives birth. As she labors in love, Mother Church sings her pangs of joy as neophytes are born and hearts are reborn.

This is the night when heavenly hosts gather around their Master's jeweled banquet table in triumphant exultation, awaiting the final great communion. This is the night when Christians of earth look toward their participation in that banquet while rejoicing in the one at hand. It is sacred, earthy work. We dirty our hands in groves of olives, fields of wheat, and vineyards of grapes and we wash them again and again in the murky waters of life. And somehow the fruit of our labor is sanctified and transports us into the heart of Transcendent Mystery. This is the night when heaven is truly wedded to earth.

This night (the night early Christians believed would be the time and place of Jesus' return) is the high point and premier celebration of our liturgical year. All the liturgies of the year point to this one great feast; it is foundational to our Catholic experience and identity. The Easter Vigil is divided into four parts: 1. Service of Light, 2. Liturgy of the Word, 3. Liturgy of Baptism, 4. Liturgy of the Eucharist.

D. SERVICE OF LIGHT

Opening Prayer

Blessing of the Fire

Let us pray.
Father,
we share in the light of your glory
through your Son, the light of the world.
Make this new fire + holy, and inflame us with new
    hope.
Purify our minds by this Easter celebration

and bring us one day to the feast of eternal light. We ask this through Christ our Lord. Let us pray. . . .[17]

Liturgical Context

The liturgy begins with the service of light and the blessing of the new fire. Even though Christ was discovered missing from the tomb at dawn, this liturgy is celebrated in the dark of night, with the blessing of new fire and a procession. The baptized, passing from death to life, darkness to light, were once called the *illuminandi*. The church gathers to celebrate the risen Christ who, on this holy night, dispelled the darkness of death.

This is a night of new things and new beginnings. We bless the new fire that will be used to light all the lights that were extinguished on Holy Thursday. Lit by the flame of the newly blessed fire, the Easter candle is processed into the darkened space as the acclamation of praise resounds: "*Lumen Christi*, Light of Christ, *Deo Gratias,* thanks be to God."

Like our ancestors of old who followed the pillar of light to freedom, we, too, are led to our freedom, the font and table. The procession moves through the church, the light growing brighter with the multiplication of each person's individual candle light. We stand as God's triumphant, liberated people while we listen to our hymn of praise: the Christian story in its grandeur, the mother of all prayers, the Exultet. We boldly, almost shockingly, praise God for the "necessary sin of Adam that gained for us so great a Redeemer" who is Christ our Light, the One who dispelled the darkness. In the dimness of this darkened church we listen as our salvation is unfolded before our sense-sharpened eyes and ears.

There are three ritual moments of light in the service of light: the blessing of the new fire; the procession and passing of light through the congregation with the acclamation, *Lumen Christi, Deo gratias;* and the prayer of blessing in the Exultet. "The fundamental theme of the Exultet is thanksgiving and praise for the light and the event of Easter night: redemption through the paschal mystery."[18]

Questions: How do these introductory moments of the Easter Vigil speak to your community? What do they tell you about God, the church or you as an individual? What are the implications of blessing the new fire, processing by the light of the Easter candle, and singing our ancient hymn of praise? How does this experience call you to enter the death and resurrection of Christ?

Symbol of Light/Fire

The symbol of light in most religions is a sign of divinity. In the Christian tradition, the symbol of light is a sign of Christ's presence. Darkness symbolizes the converse: God's absence and/or the destructive force of evil. Fire is only used once in our tradition—at the Easter Vigil. However, the symbol of fire and light overlap in many ways, so they will be treated together.

Natural Sign

Fire and light order our life. We rise to the light and go to bed in the dark. Light and darkness are known to effect mood shifts. Studies have shown that sunny, bright days impact people in a positive way, whereas repeated dark and gloomy days can cause depression. We need the light to see; we are unable to see in the dark. Too much light can burn us or hurt our eyes. Too much darkness is known to have prompted some suicides. Without light, plants do not grow. If there is too much light they are burned. When the night is illumined with light, it protects us from the unknown shadows of the dark. The light of fire protected ancient communities from intruding marauders. Food is cooked and our homes are heated with the warmth of fire. Fire and hearth are images of cozy comfort. We have no control over the light of day or the darkness of night. We are subject to their benevolence or their tyranny.

Question: In what ways do we experience light and fire in our everyday lives? Describe your personal images and experiences of light and fire.

---

[17]Easter Vigil: "Blessing of the Fire," *The Sacramentary.*

[18]Richter, *The Meaning of Sacramental Symbols,* 112.

Biblical Sign

The bible uses fire first in very natural ways, then in symbolic ways. Fire is used in cooking, for heat and light, and as a weapon of war (2 Chr 35:13; Is 44:16, 19; Num 31:10). Fire, as light, is also a means of communication between cities. Fire can be a powerful sign of God's presence and protection: the burning bush (Ex 3:2) and the column of fire that escorted the Israelites (Ex 13:21-22). When fire and light appear in scripture, everyone is to take notice: it means God is present. Fire and light are signs of theophany. A fire was kept burning at the altar as a sign of God's abiding presence (Lev 6:2, 5-6). In addition to being a sign of God's presence, fire is also a sign of God's protection. God protected Elisha with fiery chariots; the three young men who were thrown into the fire by Nebuchadnezzar were not consumed by its flame. A very common Old Testament theme is that God will judge the world by fire (2 Sam 23:7) and test and purify his people by fire (Zech 13:9; Ex 32:20). Light is a reference to Torah or God's law—a lamp to light our feet (Ps 119).

The New Testament uses fire in the same way as the Hebrew scriptures used fire. God appeared to the twelve as tongues of fire. Jesus will test and purify when he baptizes with the Holy Spirit and fire (Mt 3:11). The last judgment is also seen in terms of fire. Jesus is understood as the Light, the new Word that lights our way.

Light is a prime symbol of Christ and his life. Christ is the Light; we are to walk as children of the Light (Mt 4:16; Lk 1:7-9; 2:32; Jn 12:36). For John, the evangelist, Jesus is the *Light* that dispels the darkness. Jesus, the *Light*, is the eternal Word of God. Faith calls people into the *Light*. The reign of God is characterized by light; there is no night in the heavenly sphere (Rev 21:22-27; 22:5).

Questions: What caught your attention in regard to the biblical understanding of fire and light? Why? What does it teach you about God, Christ, the church or yourself? How does it speak to the life of the community, your life?

Ecclesial Sign

The lighting of fire is not, in and of itself, characteristic of Easter. Every evening celebration in the ancient world began with a ritual of lighting. Whenever there is light, God is present: it is cause for our thanks. The blessing prayer over the fire is a prayer of longing for God, the Light that is never extinguished. The ritual of lighting probably has pagan roots. Large bonfires were lighted in the spring in hopes that pagan deities would bless the crops. Christians were forbidden to do this until the emergence of a ritual bonfire associated with Holy Saturday around the sixth century. This eventually became a part of the Easter Vigil liturgy. In the Middle Ages, people observed a custom of extinguishing all fires and lights in or around their homes. They would take a flame from the newly blessed Easter fire to light the extinguished fires in their homes as a sign of new life.

Fire and light are signs of the risen Christ. They are also signs of the Holy Spirit. Fire is a symbol of the transforming power and energy of the Holy Spirit. Everything that is touched by the fire of the Spirit is transformed. Tradition understands fire as a sign of hope, consummation, sacrifice, and purification. Fire and light are symbols of sanctification. Light is initiatory in character. It is a symbol of incorporation into Christ's Body: we are to walk as children of the Light. "The presentation of the lighted candle shows that they [neophytes] are called to walk as befits the children of the light" (RCIA, #214). Light is a symbol of Christianity. Jesus is the Light that illumines the world. Light is a sign of wisdom and understanding. Light reminds us of Christ's presence. It is a sign of discipleship and righteousness. Wherever a candle is left burning, Christ is present.

Questions: How would you articulate the church's understanding of light and fire? In what way does it have anything to do with living the Christian life, our life, your life? What does tradition's understanding of light and fire teach about God, Christ, the church or yourself?

Liturgical Sign

The church uses fire, particularly light, extensively in its liturgy. The only time fire is used as a single entity is at the Easter Vigil. Fire is blessed as a sign of the risen Christ. The Easter candle is lit from this new fire and all other candles are lit from the light of that candle. The assembly's individual candles are also signs of the resurrected Christ.

The Easter candle probably originates from the ancient ritual of the *Lucenare*, celebrated at the end of each day. Lamps were lit to ward off the darkness. Light has always been a symbol of the presence of God: Moses and the burning bush, the presence of smoke, the cloud and pillar of fire. Light is such an important symbol and sign of God's presence that it is used in every liturgical celebration. Wherever the Blessed Sacrament is reserved, a sanctuary lamp burns as a sign of Christ's presence. As the neophytes are baptized, they are given lighted candles as a sign of their new status: they now walk as children of the Light. Candles illumine the table of the word and the table of the eucharist as a sign of the living, sacramental presence of Christ. Candles are used for the blessing of throats, Candlemas, and with the sick. The Easter candle is used at baptisms and funerals. Candles are used in processions, in all liturgical celebrations, at evening prayer, weddings, religious professions, and in homes. The symbol of Christ, the *Light*, is present at every liturgy.

Questions: What is your experience of fire and light in liturgy? Has it ever touched you in a conscious way? What does it say to you about God, Christ, church or yourself?

E. THE LITURGY OF THE WORD

Liturgical Context

The biblical readings for the Easter Vigil are the same in the churches of the East and the West. The first four readings from the Old Testament (Hebrew scriptures) correspond to the Jewish tradition of the "Four Nights." The first night was when the Word of God created the world. The second night was when God appeared to Abraham and Sarah to fulfill the promise that Abraham would father Sarah's child in spite of their very old age. It was also the night when Abraham offered his son, Isaac, in sacrifice to God, thus demonstrating great faith. The third night was the night when the angel of death protected Israel's first-born from the death sentence reserved for Egypt's first-born. Pharaoh released Israel from

bondage and Yahweh led the fleeing band through the desert. The fourth night is yet to come and will take place at the end of the world.

Thus, the first four readings are essential to understanding our salvation history already set in motion at the beginning of the world, fulfilled through the Incarnation, and to be culminated through Jesus' second coming.

The next three Old Testament readings are laden with baptismal images. They prepare us for this night when the church opens its fonts to the flowing waters of new birth, death, and resurrection. Paul's letter to the Romans explicitly names baptism as death to sin as the beginning of new life in Christ. The liturgy of the word culminates with the exuberant proclamation of the resurrection. We are taken to the place where death was destroyed forever: we are brought to the empty tomb of Jesus Christ.

The Word as Symbol

The Word embodies the presence of Christ in our midst. We proclaim the word of God as the living, sacramental presence of God. "In the celebration of the liturgy, the word of God is not voiced in only one way nor does it always stir the hearts of the hearers with the same power. Always, however, Christ is present in his word; as he carries out the mystery of salvation, he sanctifies us and offers the Father perfect worship.... That word constantly proclaimed in the liturgy is always, then, a living, active word through the power of the Holy Spirit. It expresses the Father's love that never fails in its effectiveness toward us."[19] When the word is proclaimed, the church is built up and it grows. Through the symbols inherent in the liturgy, salvation events are brought into the present and we are their beneficiaries. Through the proclamation of God's word we are made a new people, heirs of God's covenant.

Natural Sign

Words can build up or tear down. They can affirm or destroy. Words have power. Words express mys-

---

[19] *Lectionary for Mass*: Introduction, #4, in *The Liturgy Documents* (Chicago: Liturgy Training Publications, 1991), 128.

tery and reality. Words can be spoken, written, sung, signed, or coded. Words can sell things, teach, regulate, and warn. Words can start wars. Words can create revolutions. Words can change consciousness and political perspectives. Words have power.

Questions: Can you a remember a time when words had a powerful impact on your life, positively or negatively? What did that experience teach you about the power of the word?

Biblical Sign

Word is understood as the self-revelation of God to human beings. The Hebrew word *dabar* means not only the spoken word, but also an event, a happening. The term assumes power, energy, and action. It is dynamic and alive. The word of God connotes God's acts of salvation. The power of God's word is evident in the first reading from tonight's liturgy. God's word created the heavens and the earth: "Let there be light, and there was light" (Gen 1:3). The covenant with Israel comes from the word of the Lord, "Everything the Lord has said, we will do" (Ex 19:8; 24:3, 7). The ten commandments were referred to as the spoken word of God. The word of God is synonymous with God's promises: Abraham and his descendants, the promised land, etc. God's word was spoken through the prophets. God spoke in person to Moses who, in turn, was to speak God's word to Pharaoh (Ex 33:11; Num 12:8; Deut 34:1). Samuel heard the voice of the Lord calling in the night (1 Sam 3: 7-14). Prophets spoke God's word to David. Nathan assured David that his monarchy would endure forever. Nathan also accused David of having an illicit affair with Bathsheba. Elijah and Elisha are always in dialogue with God's word. When the prophet speaks, Israel listens. What the prophet speaks is as good as accomplished.

In the Wisdom tradition, asserts Irene Nowell, the word is understood as the bearer of good things to God's people and calamity to God's enemies. *Word* is also another term for the law. The wisdom tradition begins to personify the word and give it a divine role. The word, for example, was present at creation and in salvation history (Wis 10-12).

In the New Testament, the term *logos* is used 331 times. It has many possible meanings: a statement, an assertion, a command, a report or story, a proverb, a saying, a prophecy, or a speech. It is used as a reference for the revelation of God, especially revelation as it occurred through Jesus Christ. "In many cases, the 'word of God' is simply the Christian message, the good news."[20] Apostles and preachers speak God's word. Hearers of the word are to listen and respond accordingly.

The evangelist John's use of *logos* is in direct relation to Jesus Christ. In the Jewish story of the Four Nights (the first four readings from the Vigil liturgy), God's word as a personified entity creates the world. Many believe that the identification of Jesus with *logos* comes from this concept. "The hymn in the Prologue is the clearest example in first century Christian literature of both an incarnation and a preexistence of Christology. It affirms both that the logos has become flesh in the person of Jesus of Nazareth and that Jesus of Nazareth existed before the incarnation, indeed before the creation of the world, as God's divine *logos*."[21]

Toward the end of the New Testament, the word was associated with the written word of God. "The 'good news' came to be seen in the written words of the four evangelists and in the Bible as a whole."[22]

Questions: Have you ever experienced God's living presence in the scriptures? What did it teach you about God, Christ, the church or yourself? Was there a call to respond, to action?

Ecclesial Sign

The Church Fathers sought to confirm the dynamic power of God's word through Christ in the

---

[20]William G. Thompson, S.J. and Gerard S. Sloyan, "Word: New Testament," in *The Collegeville Pastoral Dictionary of Biblical Theology*, ed. Carroll Stuhlmueller, C.P. (Collegeville: The Liturgical Press, 1996), 1097.

[21]Ibid., 1100.

[22]Anthony Tambasco, "Word of God," in *The New Dictionary of Theology*, ed. Joseph A. Komonchak, Mary Collins, Dermot A. Lane (Collegeville: The Liturgical Press, 1990), 1097.

church. "Where the Lordship (of God) is proclaimed, the Lord is present" (*Didache*, 4:1). St. Augustine linked the power of preaching to a person's absorption (or lack thereof) in the sacred scriptures. "Caesarius of Arles declared that 'the word of God is not to be treated as inferior to the body of Christ' (Sermon 78:2). For the Father, in fact, the liturgy becomes the fitting place where Jesus as the word of God is fully encountered, first in the scriptural flesh and blood of the *logos* and then in celebration of that word in the bread and wine of the eucharist."[23]

Because of the emergence of various heresies and the rise of the teaching ministry, the church of the Middle Ages was less concerned with the word as the living, dynamic, self-revelation of God and more concerned with the intellectual formulations of doctrines *about* God. Partly due to a concern over this, the Protestant reformers set forth *sola scriptura* (scripture alone) as the only source of God's word, thereby denying the teaching authority of the hierarchy. The Council of Trent insisted that the truth of God's word was in both the written sources and in the unwritten traditions. However, later developments elevated the unwritten source, tradition, to the status of a second, separate source of divine revelation.

Lines were drawn between Protestant and Catholic understandings of God's word. Protestants continued to preach God's word and to assert the importance of its power within each individual. Catholics relied on doctrinal formulations and theologies in relation to God's word. Tradition was placed in a higher position of authority than the biblical sources of God's word.

The Second Vatican Council retrieved the biblical source of God's self-revelation fulfilled through the person of Jesus Christ. The document *Dei Verbum* asserted the authenticity of scripture and tradition as one source. Thus, God is revealed through the scriptures *and* the tradition of the church. Tradition was redefined in terms of the "faith of the living church which surrounds, preserves and transmits the scriptures and makes them come alive."[24]

---

[23]Ibid.
[24]Ibid., 1098.

Questions: How does the church's experience of God's word throughout its history relate to the life of your community or yourself? What does it teach you about God, Christ, the church or yourself?

Liturgical Signs

Dei Verbum returned us to our earliest roots in which the living word of God was best experienced in the celebration of the liturgy. Therefore, the Council prompted a renaissance in the preaching ministry of the church. "The primary duty of priests is the proclamation of the Gospel of God to all" (*Decree on Ministry and Life of Priests*). Preaching is characterized by the "proclamation of God's wonderful works in the history of salvation, that is, the mystery of Christ, which is made present and active within us, especially in the eucharistic celebration of the liturgy"(*Constitution on the Sacred Liturgy*, [CSL], #35, 2).

The church teaches that Christ is present in the proclamation of God's word in the liturgy. "He is present in his word, since it is he himself who speaks when the holy Scriptures are read in the Church" (CSL, #7). The word of God proclaimed in the liturgy is efficacious: "and it is from the continued use of Scriptures that the people of God, docile to the Holy Spirit under the light of faith, receive the power to be Christ's living witnesses before the world" (*Lectionary for Mass*: Introduction, #12).

The word and the eucharist are in intimate relationship. "The Church is nourished spiritually at the table of God's word and at the table of the eucharist: from one it grows in wisdom and from the other in holiness. In the word of God the divine covenant is announced; in the eucharist the new and everlasting covenant is renewed. The spoken word of God brings to mind the history of salvation; the eucharist embodies it in the sacramental signs of the liturgy" (*Lectionary for Mass*: Introduction, #10).

Whenever the church gathers for prayer, God's word is primary. Whether the gathering is for sacraments, eucharist, rites, the liturgy of the hours, blessings, or sacramentals, it is the church's intention that the word be a pivotal part of all liturgical celebration.

Questions: Have you ever experienced the presence of Christ in the proclamation of God's word in the liturgy? What did it teach you about God, Christ, the church or yourself? In what way has the word of God called your community to respond in the past? How is God's word challenging your community now?

THE WORD OF GOD

Proclaim the word of God.

First Reading
Genesis 1:1–2:2

While meditating on the reason for God's incredible action in the lives of human beings, and drawing on Babylonian images of the creation of the world, the ancient author of Genesis (ca. 5th or 6th century B.C.E.) eloquently provided all future generations with refined insight into the creative, loving, and omniscient power of the Creator. The word was spoken and God's generative power created the universe. From creation onward, the generative word of God would have a leading role in human history and experience. (Remember the centurion who told Jesus to say but the word and his servant would be healed.)

"God creates the world for humans in six days and rests on the seventh, the first week of human history; the week of six work days ending in Sabbath observance is thereby hallowed.... In W. Semitic enumerations, the seventh place is often climactic; God's sabbath is therefore the climax of the story, which is primarily about God, not humans."[25] No matter how chaotic the pre-creation order was, God was in control.

Thanks be to God for this inspired author of Genesis. He gave us an anchor that would inspire all generations. Genesis is a constant reference. When we are tempted to accept the hopeless depravity of the human condition, we have something that shakes our sensibilities and reminds us: "Remember? God saw that it was *good.*"

"God pronounces the light good, beautiful; the phrase will be repeated six times of created elements, climaxing in the seventh climactic occurrence for the whole universe (v. 31). The declaration is not a deduction from human experience but a divine declaration that all of creation is good."[26] We are created in the image and likeness of God. "The human is a statue of the deity, not by static being, but by action, who will rule over all things previously created (v. 26). In the ancient Near East, the king was often called the image of the deity and was vested with God's authority; royal language is used here for the humans."[27] We are created to be fully alive human beings, imbued with transcendent dignity. "The human being is placed at the summit in the temple of creation: all humanity has value in God's eyes."[28] Men and women are created *equal* in the eyes of God. Men and women are given sacred rights and responsibilities.

In the creation account, men and women are to subdue the earth. They will control their harsh environment by force if necessary, but they are to treat God's creation with proper dignity. Human beings "are to respect the environment; they are not to kill for food but are to treat all life with respect...the world is made for man and woman. Plants will suffice for food for humans and animals; there will be no bloodshed. This prohibition is modified in the renewal of creation after the flood."[29] Thus, the whole created order is good. In Yahweh's world there is no evil; there is only beauty. In an effortless stroke of the Master's brush, God's word painted the heavens and the earth.

The creation story is eschatological as it defines what God intends. "This serene, beautiful world, in which all is ordered to humans, and humans are ordered to God, is how it will be at the end. God's world will triumph."[30] The sin that will follow in subsequent chapters will not reign forever. It will not stand in the way of God's original intent. God will be victorious.

---

[25]Richard J. Clifford, S.J. and Roland E. Murphy, O.Carm., "Genesis," in *The New Jerome Biblical Commentary,* ed. by Raymond E. Brown, S.S., Joseph A. Fitzmyer, S.J., and Roland E. Murphy, O.Carm. (Englewood Cliffs: Prentice Hall, 1990), 11.

[26]Clifford and Murphy, "Genesis," 11.

[27]Ibid.

[28]*Days of the Lord,* Vol. 3 (Collegeville: The Liturgical Press, 1993), 44.

[29]Clifford and Murphy, "Genesis," 11.

[30]Ibid.

The *word* of God created the world. Christian understanding gives Jesus Christ a star role in this first theater of God's creative drama. Jesus, the spoken *Word* of God (John's prologue), was present and active in this creative, generative moment. Jesus Christ was the *Light* that dispels the darkness and chaos. We share in that light and thus can marvel and proclaim with the psalmist, "Lord, continue to send out your Spirit and renew the face of the earth, continue to create it anew and make it good."

Questions: In what way does God continue the transforming work of creation in our community? Do we really believe in the goodness of creation? What are we going to do about it?

Responsorial Psalm
Psalm 104—Lord, send out your Spirit and renew the face of the earth.
or
Psalm 33—The earth is full of the goodness of the Lord.

Second Reading
Genesis 22:1-18

The Lord God promises Abraham many and great things in this reading. We, however, are shocked by the demand to murder his son. We have a difficult time getting past Abraham's willingness to perform such a heinous act. Someone once raised the question, "If that is an example of the kind of God you wish me to worship, thanks, but no thanks, I want no part of him. What God would ask a father to murder his own son?" It is an honest question. Yet this story is upheld throughout all of biblical literature as a premier story of faith. There has to be and there is more to the story.

In order to understand this story we must stretch ourselves and put our Western mind-sets on hold for a brief period. This story is not about killing one's son; it is about placing one's entire life in the hands of the all-knowing, omniscient God. "The father's life is bound up with that of his child and heir; Abraham entrusts his life and his future unconditionally to the God who calls him."[31]

This is the only time in scripture that God tests one individual rather than the entire nation. Abraham, as the future leader of Israel, must "entrust his entire life and future to God."[32] The reader of this story is aware from the beginning that God is testing Abraham, but Abraham is not aware. Isaac was not Abraham's only son as the text would intimate. Rather, a better translation is: *favored*. God makes sure that in this dialogue, the weight of Isaac's value to Abraham is emphasized.

Abraham and Isaac ascend Mount Moriah, the place believed to be the site of Solomon's first temple. Abraham, then, is the first worshiper on the temple site. Abraham obeys God in silence; Isaac follows and asks the whereabouts of the sacrificial animal. Abraham's reply that God would provide is another example of trusting God to supply all needs. Everything is completely in Yahweh's hands.

The angel arrives to save the day, Isaac is spared, and Abraham proves that his entire life is completely under God's providential care. "He has finally learned to give up control over his own life that he might receive it as grace."[33] God spoke the word to the angel and caused Isaac to be spared. God caused the first-born of Israel to be spared. In Israel it was understood that each new-born child belonged to God and was symbolically sacrificed to God. As a symbolic sign of this sacrifice, a ram (or other animal) was offered in order to redeem the first-born.

Abraham was always understood to prefigure what would be accomplished through Christ. Jesus, God's first-born, would be sacrificed, would stand in as the sacrificial lamb and redeem Israel. We can do no less than respond to such love with the unconditional trust of Abraham. Keep me safe, O God; you are my hope.

Questions: What is your first reaction to God's request to Abraham? How is Abraham a sign for your community? What difference do this reading and its implications make for the life of your community and for your own life? What is the challenge?

---

[31]Ibid., 25.

[32]Ibid.
[33]Ibid.

Responsorial Psalm
Psalm 16—Keep me safe, O God; you are my hope.

Third Reading
Exodus 14:15–15:1

The Passover is to Jews what the death and resurrection of Jesus is to Christians—the premier saving event of God. It is and has been remembered annually as a living memorial of God's saving, liberating power. It is actualized as it is remembered. Those who remember and celebrate the Passover are, in a manner of speaking, present at the first passover and are beneficiaries of its liberating action.

Thus, the exodus story is told on this night above all nights, when the passover of Jesus Christ was prefigured through the exodus event. This is why the reading from Exodus must be proclaimed at the Vigil.

Whether each detail of this epic event is based on historical fact or on the natural elaboration that goes with the telling of a great moment in the conscious collective memory of a people is not important. What is important is that the exodus event is remembered for generations as a defining moment for the people of God, the supreme initiative of God's loving and liberating action. It is a sign of God's covenant with Israel—a primary theme throughout biblical literature. (Refer to the exegesis on Holy Thursday for a more complete elaboration of the meaning and roots of Passover.)

Jesus is the new Passover, the new covenant. Jesus, the new paschal lamb, was sacrificed for the sins of all, and leads us out of bondage into the promised land of freedom and new life through baptism. The Red Sea was understood in Christian consciousness as an image of baptism. The neophyte passes through the sea of death to new life. It is no wonder that this story of Passover and passage is a baptismal scripture of great importance. We continue to live the benefits of the first Passover and Jesus' Passover from death to life. We must, then, sing triumphantly with Miriam: "Let us sing to the Lord; he has covered himself in glory."

Questions: In what way does your community resemble the Israelite community? How would you describe your communal covenant with God? What can be affirmed and where is growth needed? Are there any areas in your community life that are still in bondage and in need of liberation? How does your community live in covenant relationship with God? What is the evidence that you are in a covenant relationship with God as a community and as an individual? Where does death still reign? Where is there resurrection? What are you going to do about it?

Responsorial Psalm
Exodus 15—Let us sing to the Lord; he has covered himself in glory.

Fourth Reading
Isaiah 54:5-14

This reading is from Second Isaiah (Deutero-Isaiah) and it represents the fourth night—the fourth stage of salvation history. It is the night in which God's own people will be gathered to the heavenly city of eternal life. We are reminded on this Vigil night that lest we become mesmerized by the excitement of tonight and the joy of God's reign in the temporal sphere, there is an important reality always in our consciousness. We live in the reign of God on two planes—*the here and now* and *the not yet.*

This pericope is written from the tenuous situation of captivity. It is a word of consolation to a people in great distress. There is none of the overconfident self-assurance that was evident during the time of First Isaiah when Israel was in her shining glory. Such confidence faded into obscurity in light of domination by a foreign power in the alien land of Babylon.

Isaiah wants his people to know that, no matter what happens, God will not forsake them. No matter how difficult things become, God's covenant with Israel will stand. We are left with the hope and the imagery of that brilliant future city, laid out for us with streets and walls lined with "cornelians, rubies, sapphires and precious stones"—a city in which God's justice will reign eternal. "The word of God emanates from the splendor of the Lord's presence."[34] We pause, then, before our

---

[34]Carroll Stuhlmueller, "Deutero-Isaiah and Trito-Isaiah," in *The New Jerome Biblical Commentary,* ed. Raymond E. Brown, S.S., Joseph A. Fitzmyer, S.J., Roland E. Murphy, O.Carm. (Englewood Cliffs: Prentice Hall, 1990), 343.

great God and humbly acknowledge in heartfelt response: "I will praise you, Lord, for you have rescued me."

Questions: In what way has your community experienced the consoling love of God? Has there ever been a time in which great distress caused your complete reliance on God? What was the experience like? What does this reading teach you about God, Christ, the church and yourself? What are you called to do in response?

Responsorial Psalm
Psalm 30—I will praise you, Lord, for you have rescued me.

Fifth Reading
Isaiah 55:1-11

This reading turns our eyes from a backward glance at salvation history to a more present, sacramental stance. We are brought into the presence and action of Christ. Isaiah's conclusion to the "Book of Consolations" speaks of that day in which God's people will be lavished with rich fare and flowing water. "Deutero-Isaiah invites poor people to a joyful banquet."[35] Throughout the bible, the banquet image is used to demonstrate God's care for Israel. The messianic age and everlasting life in heaven are often described as a banquet.

Yahweh insists that the only requirement for this banquet is thirst for God. People are to seek God who is transcendent and elusive. God is near enough to be troubled by the sin of humanity, however. What Christian does not turn his or her eyes toward baptism and eucharist when hearing of quenched thirsts and rich food, spread for all, rich and poor alike? How could a Christian not think of the eucharistic banquet when hearing of Isaiah's admission-free banquet for the salvation of all people?

The word of God again plays a very important, sacramental role in this reading. "God's word is the initiator: from it comes salvation."[36] Stuhlmueller suggests that, in Isaiah, God's word is not

---

[35]Ibid.
[36]*Days of the Lord*, Vol. 3, 52.

so much a message as it is an event in the mystery of salvation history. God's word is not static, but living; it causes action. God's word will accomplish what God intends. God's word will restore Israel. The world rejoices as God brings Israel home. Sin will be no more in the new Jerusalem. Sin and death will not be invited guests at the eternal banquet; they will be gone forever. The *shalom* peace of God will reside eternally in God's restored Paradise.

Jesus, Word of God, on this night of nights, rises and returns to God. In so doing, Jesus, Word of God, brings salvation to the world. On this night, holier than all other nights, we listen to Isaiah and are invited to remember our baptismal and eucharistic life. We draw deeply and joyfully from the springs of our sacramental salvation.

Questions: Is your community—are you—inclusive? Where are there still areas of death? Where are the areas of resurrection? Do all of God's people have a place at your communal and individual banquet table? Who is not invited? In what way does your community need to grow? What does this reading say to you about God, Christ, the church, and yourself? What is the challenge? What are you going to do about it?

Responsorial Psalm
Isaiah 12—You will draw water joyfully from the springs of salvation.

Sixth Reading
Baruch 3:9-15, 32–4:4

This sixth reading extols the value of wisdom. When we stray (and we will) from God's path, wisdom leads us back. While on this earth, we can never completely know the extent of the mystery of God. What we do know is revealed through the power of wisdom. Wisdom reveals the mind and the heart of God through the Word of God.

Baruch upholds obedience to God's law as the highest value. Israel disobeyed the law and was punished. Prosperity and peace can occur only when the word of God is observed. Baruch understands the Mosaic law as wisdom. In later Judaism, wisdom is "personified and given divine attributes."[37] It is the greatest value, the most prized asset. Without wisdom, all is lost. Only God can offer wisdom; human beings can do nothing on their own to obtain it.

The word of God is the ongoing, sacramental presence of God's wisdom. Through the scriptures we come to know God. In our liturgy we believe that when scriptures are proclaimed we are in the living presence of Christ.

Through baptism, we live within the active, present word of God. We are strengthened and led by God's word in and through Jesus Christ and his Spirit. Thus, with assurance we together proclaim: "Lord, you have the words of everlasting life."

Questions: How is your community responding to God's wisdom? In what way, if any, do you forge ahead without seeking the will of God in your community life? How does your community listen to God? Where is there still death and where is there resurrection? What does this reading say to you about God, Christ, the church and yourself? What is the challenge?

Responsorial Psalm
Psalm 19—Lord, you have the words of everlasting life.

Seventh Reading
Ezekiel 36:16-28

In tonight's reading from Ezekiel, we are made privy to God's conversation with Ezekiel. God reminded Ezekiel that the people had turned away from Yahweh, thinking they had no need of his providential care. They found themselves in exile because they had sinned, blasphemed, and acted in depravity. Therefore, God punished them. Only God's power could gather the lost and scattered people.

However, the covenant continues with Israel. God blesses them. This reading is a summary of Ezekiel's theology. Paul resonates the same theology through-

out his ministry: salvation is freely offered grace. Salvation and justification are from God.

Ezekiel promises the bestowal of a new heart and a new spirit. "The heart is the seat of thinking and loving, so it will be a new way of looking at life from God's point of view."[38] The new spirit bestowed upon Israel empowers her to live *as a people.* God forms them as a community, not as individuals.

This reading also foreshadows the final eschatological gathering. Before the last gathering, people must be washed clean of their idolatry. Only God is capable of such cleansing. Only God has the power to remove stony hearts and replace them with hearts of love. God's Spirit will breathe new life into these newly gathered children.

On this night of baptisms and rebirth we ask for the new heart and new spirit promised to Ezekiel. Thus, the cries of our heart resound in song: "Create in me a clean heart, O God."

Questions: This reading reminds us why we must ask the communal questions first. God deals with us as a people, yet we often have only the sense that our relationship with God is a "Jesus and me" affair. What are the "stony heart" areas in your community, in your own life? Where is God's transformative healing needed? Where is the death and where is the resurrection? How are you called to change as a community?

Responsorial Psalm
Psalm 42—As the deer longs for running streams, so my soul longs for you, my God.
or
Psalm 51—Create a clean heart in me, O God.

Epistle
Romans 6:3-11

Paul's letter to the Romans is a transition point in the liturgy of the word. We now move from the Hebrew scriptures to the Christian scriptures;

---

[37]Aloysius Fitzgerald, F.S.C. "Baruch," in *The New Jerome Biblical Commentary,* ed. Raymond E. Brown, S.S., Joseph A. Fitzmyer, S.J., Roland E. Murphy, O.Carm. (Englewood Cliffs: Prentice Hall, 1990), 566.

[38]Lawrence Boadt, C.S.P. "Ezekiel," in *The New Jerome Biblical Commentary,* ed. Raymond E. Brown, S.S., Joseph A. Fitzmyer, S.J., Roland E. Murphy, O.Carm. (Englewood Cliffs: Prentice Hall, 1990), 325.

from the former age to the messianic age and thus to the present. The Sacramentary instructs us to turn on the lights at this point in the liturgy. This is the moment when we turn from darkness to light. We are led to the font, the place that initiates *bearers of the light*. Baptism assures us that we no longer live in the darkness, but are children of the light.

We are no longer dead. Paul reminds us that through baptism we die to sin and become a new creation in Christ. The neophyte plunges deeply into the waters of death, suffocated by the crushing weight of water and sin, only to come up, gasping for the air of invigorating new life and freedom. (A little sprinkle of water hardly speaks of the same reality.)

"The rite of Christian initiation introduces a human being into union with Christ's suffering and dying."[39] The newly baptized are initiated into Christ's resurrected life. Baptism gives the Christian the power to live the Christian life. Paul asserts that through baptism we are dead to sin; it no longer lives in us. "The destruction of the sinful 'self' through baptism and incorporation into Christ means liberation from enslavement to sin. Hence, one's outlook can no longer be focused on sin."[40]

Reginald Fuller reminds us that the verbs used in Paul's address remind us of the effects of baptism. When speaking of "dying to ourselves," Paul uses past tense verbs. He uses future tense verbs in relation to the resurrection. Through baptism we *died* (past tense) with Christ.[41] However, our resurrection is our future goal as we live out our baptismal commitment and moral response. We continue to renew our commitment to die to sin each day.

Paul's letter to the Romans prepares us for a key moment of the Easter Vigil liturgy: the renewal of our baptismal vows. And so, together with the psalmist, we can joyfully sing the triple alleluia as

---

[39]Joseph A. Fitzmyer, S.J., "The Letter to the Romans," in *The New Jerome Biblical Commentary*, ed. Raymond E. Brown, S.S., Joseph A. Fitzmyer, S.J., Roland E. Murphy, O.Carm. (Englewood Cliffs: Prentice Hall, 1990), 847, 848.

[40]Ibid., 848, 849.

[41]Reginald H. Fuller, *Preaching the New Lectionary* (Collegeville: The Liturgical Press, 1974), 21, 22.

well as our praise, awe, and trust in God's incredible, awesome mighty works!

Questions: How have you died to sin throughout this Lent as a community and as individuals? In what way have you grown? Where is growth still needed? Where is death? Resurrection? What difference has the baptism of neophytes made in your community this year? Is your community prepared to recommit to their baptismal promises? How is growth (resurrection) evident? Where is growth still needed? What is the challenge?

Responsorial Psalm
Psalm 118—Alleluia! Alleluia! Alleluia!

Gospel
Luke 24:1-12

Herein lies the ultimate reason we gather this night: to remember and bring forward the resurrection of Jesus Christ, the saving event that brings us to this place in time and history. We are a resurrection people. We live in the resurrected presence of the Spirit of Jesus Christ. It is the faith we profess and the power behind our profession. From the very beginning, the liturgy moves us to this moment. Excitement grows, as we are prepared in sense and spirit for the proclamation of the faith we confess with assurance: Christ has died; Christ is risen; Christ will come again. This is where it all began. Luke takes us back so we can bring it forward.

Luke's account of the resurrection does not tell the story of Jesus' resurrection, but rather tells the story of the witnesses of his resurrection. No one was present to witness the actual resurrection; they witnessed the empty tomb, but not the resurrection. The resurrection was not a resuscitation from the dead, but a transport into a new reality— a new realm of existence. Witnesses could only testify to what they knew to be true in this plane of existence: the body was gone, the wrappings were left. With the help of God they remembered what Jesus had said in relation to his death. Add to this the faith perspective, and the whole forms the reality of Jesus' resurrection.

The reality became more entrenched in the lives of Christians as they experienced the risen Christ in the life and work of their communities. Luke's version of the resurrection account is intended to serve as a transition between the story of Jesus and the subsequent story of his disciples in the Acts of the Apostles. Luke crafts this bridge by creatively reviewing events that had already taken place and previewing events to come. In the process, Luke gives us insight into the meaning of the events.

The meaning of Jesus' death and resurrection is extracted by reviewing things Jesus said throughout his ministry in regard to his death. Luke's technique to explain the resurrection is to refer to Jesus' own prophecies about himself. The disciples did not understand what Jesus meant while he was alive. Nor did they understand or "get it" when the women reported what they had seen. Luke seeks to "help them get it" throughout all of chapter 24.

The angel immediately alerts us to the human ignorance over Jesus' missing body: "Why do you seek the living among the dead?" (v. 5) The angel seems to be reiterating Jesus' constant frustration with his disciples: their lack of understanding. The angel reminds the women of how Jesus told them that the Son of Man would be delivered into the hands of evildoers. Jesus also told them that he would be crucified and raised on the third day. Even though the empty tomb and the appearance of the angel should bring instant awareness and faith, it does not. The women are not believed when they return to tell the other disciples. Peter runs to the tomb and is astonished. The word used for "astonished" is not that of a faithful believer, but perhaps that of "those who did not understand Jesus and opposed his mission."[42]

The official proclamation from heaven, "He is not here, he has risen!" once again resounds throughout heaven and earth. In each liturgy of the church, we remember the cross and resurrection; we bring it into the present and we live it. We continue to live it when we follow Christ's mandate to go out into the world and share the Good News.

The neophytes are escorted to the font as we bring Jesus' saving event to bear in the life of our communities. The newly baptized die and rise in the midst of a community committed to the same dying and rising. Thus, we stand before the exalted throne of the Lamb and profess our baptismal promises. We continue to participate in the ongoing paschal mystery of Christ as we break bread together in the eucharist.

Questions: What does Luke's story of the resurrection have to do with our life, your life? What does it mean to live in the resurrection of Christ? Do you think your community would have believed the testimony of the women? If so, explain. If not, why not? How has your community experienced death and resurrection throughout this liturgical year? Would you be willing to go and tell the good news if the angel had appeared to you, even if you knew you would be scoffed at? What is the challenge of this Easter gospel? What are you called to do in response?

F. SERVICE OF BAPTISM

Following the liturgy of the word is the liturgy of baptism. If there are candidates for baptism, they (the elect) process to the font, singing the Litany of the Saints. The elect and the faithful are in solidarity with the saints of old who went before us and the saints of today who walk with us.

The virgin water is blessed as the candle is plunged three times deeply into it. The intimate union is not to be missed. Water is blessed while remembering past images of God's action through the use of water. We remember the purifying floodwaters, the liberating Red Sea, and the salvation afforded by the water and blood from Jesus' side on the cross. We recall Jesus' mandate to the twelve to go out and baptize in the name of the Father, Son, and Holy Spirit. The blessing of water helps us remember (*anamnesis*) and bring into the present all that God has done throughout human history. We stand with God and the communion of saints as we participate in the ancient and always new and unfolding human and heavenly drama.

Blessing of the Water

Father, you give us grace through sacramental
    signs,
which tell us of the wonders of your unseen
    power.

---

[42]Robert C. Tannehill, *The Narrative Unity of Luke-Acts: A Literary Interpretation*, Vol. 1 (Minneapolis: Augsburg Fortress, 1986), 278-279.

In baptism we use your gift of water,
which you have made a rich symbol
of the grace you give us in this sacrament.
At the very dawn of creation
your Spirit breathed on the waters,
making them the wellspring of all holiness.
The waters of the great flood
you made a sign of the waters of baptism,
that make an end of sin and a new beginning of
    goodness.
Through the waters of the Red Sea
you led Israel out of slavery,
to be an image of God's holy people,
set free from sin by baptism.
In the waters of the Jordan
your Son was baptized by John
and anointed with the Spirit.
Your Son willed that water and blood
should flow from his side
as he hung upon the cross.
After his resurrection he told his disciples:
"Go out and teach all nations,
baptizing them in the name of the Father
and of the Son and of the Holy Spirit."
Father, look now with love upon your Church,
and unseal for her the fountain of baptism.
By the power of the Holy Spirit
give to the water of this font
the grace of your Son.
You created man in your own likeness:
cleanse him from sin in a new birth of innocence
by water and the Spirit.
We ask you, Father, with your Son,
to send the Holy Spirit upon the waters of this
    font.
May all who are buried with Christ
in the death of baptism
rise also with him to newness of life.
We ask this through Christ our Lord.[43]

Through our profession of the baptismal promises, we renew the promises made for us at baptism. We agree to continue the process of daily death and resurrection. The elect enter the font of death and resurrection and become the living witness of all that we have shared and heard up to this point. Water soaked and Spirit filled, they take their place in the assembly of believers and await the moment at which the trumpets of heaven announce the culmination of their baptismal journey. They are ushered along with the church triumphant to the banquet table of the Lord. Eucharist—not baptism—is the goal of initiation.

Water-soaked and oil slathered, the newly baptized are presented with the baptismal candle. Through baptism we are called out of darkness to live in the light; we become children of the Light. The Easter candle is a sign of the sacramental presence of Christ, the Light of the World. The fire is a symbol of the transforming energy of the Holy Spirit. Elijah prayed and the fire came down from heaven upon his sacrifice at Mount Carmel. This was a foreshadowing of the Spirit who causes transformation. St. John the Baptist said of Jesus that he would baptize with the Holy Spirit and fire. Jesus would cause great transformation and *metanoia* in his followers. Tongues of fire rested on the disciples at Pentecost. Thus, the symbol of fire has been retained as "one of the most expressive images of the Spirit's actions."[44]

As a sign of their new status, of the fact that they are made a new creation, neophytes put on the white garment. In scripture whenever a garment was placed on an individual it was a sign that a new status had been conferred upon that person. The new status for neophytes is that of newly baptized, confirmed children of the Light who await the culmination of their journey as fully initiated members of the community through participation in the eucharist.

Symbol of Water

"Water can cause destruction as well as life and cleansing, lending itself as a symbol of God's judgment as well as of life and forgiveness."[45] The symbol of water speaks to us of multifaceted realities.

---

[43]Easter Vigil: "Blessing of Water," *The Sacramentary.*

[44]Cf. St. John of the Cross, *The Living Flame of Love,* in *The Collected Works of St. John of the Cross,* trans. K. Kavanaugh, O.C.D., and O. Rodriguez, O.C.D. (Washington DC: Institute of Carmelite Studies, 1979), 577 ff.

[45]Joseph F. Grassi, "Water," in *The Collegeville Pastoral Dictionary of Biblical Theology,* ed. Carroll Stuhlmueller, C.P. (Collegeville: The Liturgical Press, 1996), 1060.

Natural Sign

In our natural lives, the experience of water is cleansing, soothing, and thirst quenching. It can be plentiful or in short supply. Water can be smooth and flowing as well as crushingly powerful. It is life-giving and death-dealing. We cannot live without it, and we cannot live in it. The properties of water speak to us of hidden realities. Water reminds us of how God acts and who God is. Like water, God is soothing and God's power is mighty. Immersion in water results in deep cleansing. Immersion in God's love causes deep, interior cleansing. Water is for the body what God is for the soul.

There is another facet to the many dimensions of water's inner realities. Water can be devastating. One can die in water. One is also born in water. No one can control the furious flow of water; no one can control the acts of God. When water is absent, there is thirst. When God is absent, there is parched thirst.

Biblical Sign

God is present in the biblical signs of water. Water is cited in scripture more than any other natural resource. The authors of biblical texts lived in a dry desert land. They were exposed to the continuous shortage of water. They were naturally preoccupied with finding it and the necessity for it. It is no wonder that our biblical texts use water as the revealer of the "God of Mystery who is its source and faithful dispenser."[46]

At creation, God hovered over the waters; the generative power of the Holy Spirit unleashed God's power and action into the lives of human beings. The great flood of Genesis purged the earth of sin. God's judgment came upon the earth and water purified the human race. "God overcame the primeval waters over the earth (Gen 1:1-10). He unleashed the deluge as a punishment for sin and then brought it to an end, saving Noah, the Hebrew ancestor."[47] God led the Israelites through the Red Sea, drowning Pharaoh in the process.

The Israelites were afforded safe passage through the sea to the promised land and, after crossing the hazardous Jordan, were made citizens of a new land.

In scripture, water is a sign of God's providential care. It can be abundantly showered down, or withheld because of sin (Deut 11:14-17). Water, then, is a source of death and of life. As a sign of life it is a sign of God's creative presence.

In scripture water is also a sign of purification. It was used for purification baths before celebrating community rituals. (However, repentance was still necessary for complete forgiveness.) Water is a symbol of the transforming action of the Holy Spirit. The Vigil reading from Ezekiel recalls the power of the Spirit to create transformed minds and hearts.

Water also has a role in the New Testament. Mark uses the image very little. Matthew exhorts everyone to go and baptize all nations. Matthew relates this baptism to the baptism of Jesus in the Jordan. Matthew sees water as a sign of incorporation into Jesus' own baptism. The Acts of the Apostles makes frequent reference to the waters of baptism. Water is a sign of the Holy Spirit. The gospel of John makes abundant use of the symbol of water. The water of Cana represented a repudiation of the old purification rites. The Samaritan woman was offered the new water of Jesus' Spirit. Water was curative in the story of the man born blind from birth who washed in the pool of Siloam. Jesus washed the feet of his disciples as a sign of love, service, and forgiveness. Water and blood came forth from Jesus' side on the cross. This sign was understood as the advent of the Holy Spirit upon the church. The water was a sign of baptism and the blood was the sign of eucharist.

Questions: Do the uses of water in scripture have anything to do with your life today? How might contemporary communities relate to the symbolism of water? What does it teach about God, Christ, Spirit, church, or yourself?

Ecclesial Signs

The church's theology of water is many-layered. Water is connected to the initiatory character of

---

[46]Kathleen Hughes, R.S.C.J., "Water: Pastoral Liturgical Tradition," in *The Collegeville Pastoral Dictionary of Biblical Theology,* ed. Carroll Stuhlmueller, C.P. (Collegeville: The Liturgical Press, 1996), 1062.

[47]Grassi, "Water," 1060.

baptism. Through water we are incorporated into the paschal mystery of Christ. As in the flood story, we enter the purifying waters of death to sin and rise again to the justice of new life in Christ. "Baptism, the cleansing with water by the power of the living word, washes away every stain of sin, original and personal, makes us sharers in God's own life and his adopted children."[48] Water is about death and resurrection and it is about passage. Water purifies, justifies, and sanctifies (makes us holy). "Sin is buried in the water."[49] Water purifies and cleanses us from sin. Through water we are enlightened. Our first natural birth took place in water. So too does our spiritual birth take place in the embryonic waters of the Holy Spirit. We are born again in the water of the Spirit. Water makes us adopted children of God, and members of the Body of Christ. Water gives us a share in the priestly, prophetic, and royal mission of Jesus.

Questions: Does the church's theology of water have anything to do with our lives today? What does it teach us about God, Christ, Spirit, ourselves? What is the challenge? What is the response?

Liturgical Sign

Liturgy expresses in ritual action the natural, biblical and ecclesial signs of God's presence through the symbol of water. The waters of baptism are blessed at the Easter Vigil. Through the ritual waters of baptism the neophyte is purified, justified, sanctified, and incorporated into the Body of Christ, the paschal mystery, the communion of saints. Water is used in the rite of sprinkling to remind us of our baptism and thereby recommit us to its call. The casket is blessed with holy water as a reminder that baptism is a share in the eternal life of Christ. People bless themselves with holy water as a sign of their incorporation into the Body of Christ. Water is used in the multiple blessings provided by the church for her ongoing life in Christ such as the dedications of churches, blessings of homes, seminaries, and religious houses, boats, fields, buildings, schools, animals, etc. (Please refer to the RCIA: General Introduction, # 1, 2, Introduction to the Rite of

Baptism, and the *Catechism of the Catholic Church*, #694 for further elaboration.)

Questions: Have you ever had a conscious experience of water in the liturgy? How were you impacted? How did it touch you? How does the experience of water call us to transformation as a community?

Symbol of Oil

Once baptized, the new Christian is permanently configured to Christ through the chrism oil of confirmation. Confirmation confers the gift of the Holy Spirit, not the gifts *of* the Spirit. The form of the ritual is "Be sealed with the Holy Spirit." The substance is oil. The baptized person is sealed with the Holy Spirit through the signing with oil.

In antiquity, the seal had the same function that a person's signature has today. A seal formed in wax identified the author of a document. Soldiers were tattooed with the seal of their division. The seal was a sign of ownership, much like a brand on cattle. Confirmation seals the Christian to Christ. The Christian is branded to Christ, marked permanently with the sign of salvation, the cross of Jesus Christ.

Natural Sign

How does oil express the inexpressible? Oil is difficult to rub off, stains clothing when spilled, and can only be rubbed in. Oil has healing, soothing, medicinal qualities. Oil is necessary for life. It is used in cooking, for energy, for lubrication, and for protection from the elements. Oil is a precious commodity; wars are fought over its control. Oil is the agent that holds things together, that unifies the ingredients in a recipe. All those aspects found in the natural world can be used to express the reality of the Spirit.

Our natural experience of oil reminds us of the Spirit. The Spirit stays with us. The Spirit heals and is a soothing, calming presence. The Spirit is balm for our wounded soul and strength in times of need. The Spirit is the unifier that holds God's people together. The Spirit is our life force. Oil expresses the ineffable reality of the Spirit. The

---

[48] *Rite of Christian Initiation of Adults*: Introduction, #5.

[49] St. Gregory of Nanzianzus, *Oratio* 40, 3–4 (Patrologia Latina Supplement, 36: 361C).

Spirit strengthens us when we must lay down our lives for the sake of this precious new commodity: life in Christ.

In the movie, *Lorenzo's Oil*, a young boy discovers that he has a horribly debilitating disease that, without a certain kind of oil in his system, will kill him. The movie begins with a scene from the mother's experience of the Easter Vigil. The Easter candle processes majestically through the church as the boy's mother is observed wrestling with the demon of anger and grief. She will not accept the prognosis that doctors have given her son. The Easter Vigil connection in the movie subliminally suggests that her quest for the holy oil of life is initiated by the Spirit of God, present in the pillar candle of fire leading her through the dangerous journey inaugurated that night. She leaves the Easter scene with firm resolve and burning determination. Nothing will deter her or her husband. The Spirit is in command and they forge onward. They will find the oil her son, Lorenzo, needs for life. They completely give up their lives for their son.

Through years of tortuous struggle, research, and rejection, they literally lose everything. When scientists rebuff them, they will not take *no* for an answer. Their arduous journey of the cross finally leads them to a cure. It is a simple derivative of the natural, everyday substance found in all kitchens: olive oil.

Lorenzo's family laid down their lives for their son. They loved him unconditionally and completely; they loved him against all odds. They saved their boy's life and the lives of many other children with the same disease. Their selfless act of love resulted in love for others. They "put on Christ" and became Christ for many other suffering children. The oil of chrism is the Spirit's necessary oil. We should be willing to lose all in our quest for it.

The oil of chrism is the necessary oil for the soul. It seals us to Christ. It makes us in his image. We are branded with the sign of his cross. The oil of the Spirit gives us the strength to carry the cross and to bear witness to Christ in our lives.

Questions: What is your experience of oil in everyday life? How might oil remind you of God, the Holy Spirit?

Biblical Signs

Throughout the Hebrew scriptures (Old Testament), oil was used for celebrating and greeting, as well as for preparing a body for burial. Sirach mentions that oil, water, fire, and bread are necessary for life. Oil was used for hygiene and cosmetic purposes and for the healing of wounds. Oil poured on the head of a person signified a changed reality. It meant the person was assigned to a new office. Kings were consecrated to office. Samuel anointed Saul and David for kingly service (1 Sam). It was assumed that God performed the anointing for a special purpose or mission. "So God had brought this person to a new state in life which demanded respect and protection."[50] Prophets were anointed into prophetic service. Elijah anointed Elisha (1 Kgs 19:16). Anointing with oil summons the prophet to hear God's word and sends the prophet to confess it. Priests were anointed or consecrated into God's service. Priestly anointing assumed that the anointed assume "a new role and the imposition of responsibility for effecting and preserving holiness for Israel."[51]

Sacred objects were anointed in scripture. Some oils were reserved for just such anointings (Ex 30:22-33). The tabernacle, the ark, the basin used in the purification rites, the table used for the bread of presence, the menorah, the incense altar, and the liturgical vestments were all anointed with oil.

In the New Testament, the anointings reserved for kings were now assigned to Christ. In the Mary Magdalene incident (Lk 7:50), Jesus connected the anointing of his feet with the forgiveness of sins. The anointing of Jesus by the woman was perceived as an act of anointing in preparation for Jesus' burial. Also, since Jesus was anointed by God, this anointing was similarly connected to his consecration as messiah by God. The word *messiah* means anointed of God.

Jesus was anointed prophet by the Holy Spirit. Jesus' ministry of the word and of healing was

---

[50]John C. Endres, S.J., "Anointing," in *The Collegeville Pastoral Dictionary of Biblical Theology*, ed. Carroll Stuhlmueller, C.P. (Collegeville: The Liturgical Press, 1996), 28.
[51]Ibid., 29.

anointed by God. The letter to the Hebrews asserts that Jesus was anointed high priest by God. Paul's second letter to the Corinthians refers to the Christian as anointed of God. Christ lives and works within the lives of Christians. John later takes up the clarion call and asserts that Christian anointing is realized as the guiding, teaching, and protecting Spirit of God (1 Jn 2:27).

Jesus and the apostles anointed and healed the sick. There are clear directions given in the letter of James for healing the sick; they are to be anointed with oil. As a result, they are healed, sanctified, and forgiven.

Questions: How does your natural experience of oil resonate with scripture's use of oil? Were there any new insights in examining the biblical uses of oil? What does oil teach you about God, Christ, Spirit, church, yourself? How do the biblical signs speak to your community?

Ecclesial Sign

The church teaches that oil signifies the conferral of the Holy Spirit. We are sealed with the Spirit at confirmation. Oil configures us to Christ. Oil literally bonds or adheres us to the person of Jesus Christ. Jesus is taken into ourselves. We "put on" Christ. We are branded with Christ himself. We bear the likeness of Christ. We take on Christ's image. We live as Christ would live in the world. The conferral of the Spirit in the oil of confirmation immerses us in the paschal mystery of Christ. We die and rise with Christ. Not only do we plunge into the waters of death and resurrection, but we literally take that death and resurrection into ourselves. We die and rise with the power and strength of the Holy Spirit. The oil of confirmation has an initiatory character; it completes baptism and leads to eucharist. The oil seals us to the mission of Christ and strengthens our priestly, prophetic, and royal role. "By signing us with the gift of the Spirit, confirmation makes us more completely the image of the Lord and fills us with the Holy Spirit, so that we may be witness to him before all the world and work to bring the Body of Christ to its fullness as soon as possible" (RCIA, #2).

(Please refer to "Apostolic Constitution of the Sacrament of Confirmation" and the "Introduc-

tion" of the Rite of Confirmation, and the *Catechism of the Catholic Church*, #695.)

Questions: What does the church's use of oil have to do with your community? How does it affect your life? What is the challenge?

Liturgical Signs

The church uses oil in various ways in her life and ministry. Oils are blessed at the Chrism Mass for use in ministry throughout the diocese. The catechumens are blessed with the oil of catechumens. Oil is used in the dedication of a church. Oil is also used in the sacramental life of the church. Infants are anointed at baptism with the oil of catechumens and chrism. The Spirit is given through the ritual anointing with oil at confirmation. Oil is used in the anointing of the sick and the dying. Priests are anointed for priestly service at their ordination.

Questions: Have you ever experienced the use of oil in liturgy? If so, what do you remember? What did it teach you about God, Spirit, Christ, church, community? What is the challenge for the community?

Symbol of Laying on of Hands

The power of the Holy Spirit is unleashed in the church today by the laying on of hands. The laying on of hands is a sign of the action of the Holy Spirit. It confers the gift of the Spirit in all sacraments.

Natural Sign

The hand can be an instrument of love or an instrument of hate. The touch of a hand can bring comfort and healing in a time of stress. The handshake can express friendship and the hand around another can impart guidance and care. Holding hands is a sign of love. For a child, the hand is a powerful instrument of protection or discipline. The hand used in massage is healing and curative. People clap their hands when happy or excited.

Questions: Do you remember a time when the sense of touch had a particular impact on you? How did it speak to you?

Biblical Sign

According to Dennis Sweetland, the hand has many uses throughout scripture.[52] The hand usually is a sign of God's power. "They assured Joshua, 'The Lord has delivered all this land into our power'" (Jos 2:24). Power is used as a metaphorical substitution for hand. The word *hand* is used over two hundred times in the Hebrew scriptures. When the right hand is mentioned, it usually refers to a place of honor. When the right hand of God is mentioned, it is usually intended to denote incredible, unusual power. "Your right hand, O Lord, magnificent in power... has shattered the enemy" (Ex 15:6).

The imposition of hands was used ritually in the Old Testament as well as in the New Testament. Hands were extended over offerings in response to the laws of sacrifice (Ex 29:10, Lev 1:4, 4:4, 24, 29, 33, 8:14). When hands were extended over a scapegoat, the guilt was transferred to the animal. The action usually had a direct relation to the acceptability of the sacrifice and the one offering the sacrifice. If the sacrifice was acceptable and pleasing, then the one offering was also acceptable. The sign of hands was intended to set things apart for a sacred purpose.

The laying on of hands is also used in scripture as a gesture of blessing. Hands outstretched over an assembly bless the entire group (Lev 9:22). The same gesture is also understood as a means of consigning power to another person, providing the one doing the consigning has the rightful authority to confer this power. Leaders conferred leadership to others through the action of laying on of hands (Num 27:23).

In the New Testament, the hand was understood in the same way as it was in the Hebrew scriptures. *Hand* was understood as power. The hand of God was not, however, a common New Testament image unless it was referring to an actual Old Testament use of the term (Lk 1:66). The hand was used to heal. Jesus was asked to heal Jairus's daughter by laying his hands on her. The Holy Spirit was conferred at baptism through the laying

on of hands (Acts 8:17-19; 19:6). The laying on of hands was also a sign of mission. The apostles laid hands on the seven and they were assigned a special service (Acts 6:6). The laying on of hands was also associated with installation in some office, either as presbyter or apostle (2 Tim 1:6).

Questions: Does the scriptural use of the sign of laying on of hands have anything to do with the life of your community? What does it teach you about God, Christ, the church or yourself? What are you called to do as a response?

Ecclesial Sign

Traditional theology regarding the laying on of hands is multi-layered. The gesture is believed to be the origin of the sacrament of confirmation. According to Paul VI *(Divinae consortium naturae)*, confirmation (imposition of hands) continues the grace of Pentecost. The action of laying on of hands is the conferral of the Spirit in each of the sacraments. The imposition of hands is used in all the sacraments: baptism, confirmation, eucharist (epiclesis in the eucharistic prayer), healing, penance, marriage, and ordination. The gesture has the same meaning and usage in the church today as it did in the Old and New Testament: it is a sign of power, installation of office, ministry, transfer of authority, healing, and blessing. The laying on of hands is a powerful symbol of the ongoing ministry of Jesus Christ through the power of the Holy Spirit in the church.

Questions: Does Catholic tradition's use of the gesture of laying on hands have anything to do with the life of your community? With your life? What does it say to you about God, God's Spirit, Christ, the church and yourself?

Liturgical Sign

Every sacrament exercises the epicletic action of calling down the Spirit of God to bless, sanctify, transform, and effect the desired grace. Hands are laid on the elect as they go down into the waters of baptism and are chrismated with the oil of the Holy Spirit, the chrism of salvation. Hands are extended over the gifts of bread and wine as a sign of the Spirit's role in transforming the elements into Christ's Body and Blood. The community is

---

[52]Dennis M. Sweetland, "Hand," in *The Collegeville Pastoral Dictionary of Biblical Theology*, ed. Carroll Stuhlmueller, C.P. (Collegeville: The Liturgical Press, 1996), 405-407.

blessed through the laying on of hands at the end of the liturgy. The presider/celebrant extends his hands over the assembly before sending them out to do the work of liturgy in the world. The sacred hand of the Spirit is imposed on the head of those seeking ordination, healing, and forgiveness in the sacraments of orders, anointing the sick, and sacrament of penance. The marriage couple join hands as they enter their solemn covenant and the community extends hands in a gesture of peace and unity at liturgical gatherings. Catechumens experience the hand's ministerial touch frequently throughout the catechumenate through the rituals of acceptance, blessings, anointing, exorcism, and various rites.

Questions: Have you ever experienced the sign of the Spirit at liturgy through the laying on of hands? Describe the experience. How did the experience speak to you? What did it teach you about God, Christ, the Spirit, the church or yourself? What are the implications? How is the community challenged? What are you and the community called to do in response?

Symbol of the Garment

The white garment is placed on the neophyte after baptism as a sign of his or her new status: a fully initiated member of the Body of Christ.

Natural Sign

The contemporary adage, "clothing makes the person," is usually a very consumer-oriented idea. When people have no clothes they find it difficult to compete in this consumer-oriented world. Clothes are a sign of status and wealth. In our everyday lives, new clothes have the effect of making us feel like new people. Persons in certain professions are identified by their clothing: judges, nurses, doctors, clergy, police, etc.

Biblical Sign

In scripture, clothing was a sign of office. Prophets such as Elijah and John the Baptist wore hair garments as a sign of their prophetic ministry (Zech 13:4). As Elijah passed on his prophetic ministry to Elisha, he gave him his cloak. "Clothes are an extension of the person; Elisha is thus assuming

Elijah's identity."[53] The ceremonial robe is placed on the prodigal son upon his return as a sign of his father's forgiveness. The garment in this case is a sign of God's mercy and forgiveness of sin.

Ecclesial Sign

The white garment is a sign of incorporation into the paschal mystery of Christ through baptism. The white garment is a sign that the newly baptized have put on Christ. They have risen with Christ through the waters of baptism. The clothing with the baptismal garment signifies the new dignity that is theirs.

Liturgical Sign

The neophyte puts on the white garment at baptism. Baptized infants also put on white baptismal garments. Many children who receive their first communion wear a white garment. Some people misunderstand the symbolism of the white communion dress, assuming that it signifies being a bride of Christ. However, since eucharist completes baptism, the white garment of eucharist is the baptismal garment, not a bridal dress. The pall placed on the coffin at funerals is a sign of the baptismal garment and the prescribed garment for liturgical functions is an alb ("General Instruction of the Roman Missal," #80, c), again reminiscent of the baptismal garment.

G. LITURGY OF THE EUCHARIST

There is not much that sets the Easter Vigil's liturgy of the eucharist apart from every other eucharist celebrated throughout the year. However, it is the night, different from all other nights, when new Christians are born and old Christians are renewed, new fire replaces the old light, new water is blessed, and the newly consecrated bread serves as the new leaven for the renewed missionary activity of the entire church. Our senses are attuned, as on no other night, to the words of the eucharistic prayer,

---

[53]Jerome T. Walsh and Christopher T. Begg, "1-2 Kings," in *The New Jerome Biblical Commentary*, ed. Raymond E. Brown, S.S., Joseph A. Fitzmyer, S.J., Roland E. Murphy, O.Carm. (Englewood Cliffs: Prentice Hall, 1990), 175.

Father, all powerful and ever-living God,
we do well always and everywhere to give you
    thanks
through Jesus Christ our Lord.
We praise you with greater joy than ever on
    this Easter night,
when Christ became our paschal sacrifice.[54]

On this Easter night, the trumpets should resound as neophytes triumphantly process to the table for the first time. It is the culmination of their journey. The ritual moment of baptism is not the crowning moment of their experience; it is the gateway. The crowning moment occurs at the table of unity and full participation in the paschal mystery. From the very beginning, the journey of the neophytes has been to the table. All believers come to the table to be nourished by Christ's Body and Blood in order to go out and live their lives in the world. We pour ourselves out for others; we become bread in the world so we can come back to the table again and again, depleted and in need of Easter filling. Every celebration of eucharist is an Easter filling.

Bread and Wine

Bread, food for our bodies, and wine, drink of refreshment, celebration, and merriment—are the stuff of life. These symbols assume a new reality in the paschal celebration of eucharist. They are not only reminders of physical nourishment, they become the very sustenance of the soul. We bring our gifts of bread and wine, made by human hands, and we ask God to bless them and make them holy. We ask that the Holy Spirit change these elements into the Body and Blood of Jesus Christ. We believe it happens every time the church gathers to tell the story and pray the blessing prayers of thanks and praise. Bread is and was a sign of God's providence and protection throughout scripture. It was a sign of nourishment, freedom from hunger, and satisfaction of the soul's longing for God. It is a sign of our very sustenance. Thus, bread broken and shared is a sign that we place our lives completely in God's care. The wine, as symbol of Jesus' blood, is a sign of his life force poured out for humanity in atonement for sin.

(Refer to the exegesis for Holy Thursday for further elaboration of the biblical symbol of blood.)

We become the bread we receive. We allow ourselves to be poured out as a libation. Christ's broken body was given up; his blood was poured out for the entire world. This happens every time we take the bread, bless it, break it, and share it. Thus, we too become broken, blessed, and shared.

Symbol of Bread

The sign of bread is at the heart of our identity. We are a eucharistic people. Baptism and confirmation lead us to the table and incorporation into Christ's Body and Blood. We consume the Body of Christ and, in so doing, we become the Body of Christ. Each time the Bread of Life is broken, and the Cup of Blood is shared, we become new creations. We take, bless, break, and share Christ's Body. In the taking, blessing, breaking, and sharing, we too are taken by God, blessed and made holy, broken for one another to share ourselves for others in the world. It is through the eucharist that we fully live the paschal mystery of Christ.

Natural Sign

Bread is the staff of life. Bread offers nourishment. Bread comes in many varieties: muffins, buns, pita, rolls, biscuits, leavened and unleavened loaves. With bread we are nourished; without bread we go hungry. Bread gives us strength for living. It is filled with the necessary nutrients for life. "Bread builds strong bodies twelve ways." Bread is a complement to every meal. Bread and water are all that is needed for life.

Questions: Have you ever had an experience of bread that spoke to you of something other than simply food? What did it mean to you?

Biblical Signs

Bread in the bible was considered a general term for food.[55] When God judged the people for their

---

[54]Eucharistic Prayer: "Preface for Easter I, P 21," *The Sacramentary.*

[55]John F. Craghan, "Bread," in *The Collegeville Pastoral Dictionary of Biblical Theology,* ed. Carroll Stuhlmueller, C.P. (Collegeville: The Liturgical Press, 1996), 109.

sins, it was understood that he withheld the "staff of life" (Lev 26:26). Bread is used to name certain human conditions: "bread of tears," "bread of wickedness," "daily bread," etc.

In the Hebrew scriptures, bread was a sign of hospitality. Melchizedek offered bread to Abraham and Abraham offered bread to strangers as a sign of hospitality. Shared bread suggested a relationship. The meal covenant bond was so strong that it was considered very serious to turn against someone with whom one had eaten. David tricked the enemies of his son, Absolom, into eating a meal with him so they would not carry out their plot to kill him. Contractual agreements between parties were ratified through the ritual of breaking bread. Israel commits herself to the Lord through the communal meal of Passover (Ex 24: 9-11).

The bread of exodus was unleavened bread (Ex 23:18, 34:25). Only unleavened bread was allowed in Israel's ritual worship. Anything but unleavened wheat bread was deemed impure. Bread was a sign of trust and a sign of God's providential care. God provided manna in the desert for the sojourners. Israel's part of the agreement with Yahweh was to trust him implicitly to care for them. Because God's part was to provide, God provided manna.

On every sabbath, twelve cakes of flour were placed on a table in the holy of holies as a sign of the covenant God had made with the twelve tribes of Israel (Lv 24: 5-9). The book of the prophet Isaiah used the image of banquet to refer to the eschatological day of the Lord, the end of the world. Jesus also referred to the banquet as a metaphor for the end of his earthly reign. Bread is an important symbol for Jesus, a sign of covenant and community (Lk 14:15).

Jesus multiplies the loaves and in doing so demonstrates, in action, the univerality of his messianic mission. Jesus came to save all people.

Paul details our Christian theology of eucharist in his letter to the Corinthians proclaimed at the Holy Thursday liturgy. Even though we are diverse, with many and varied gifts, eucharist unites us and makes us one body in Christ. Eucharist is a sign of unity. It is also a sign of sharing. Eucharist demands that we share with those who are in need.

The synoptic traditions equate the broken bread of eucharist with Jesus, the suffering messiah (Mt 26:28). Bread becomes a sign of Christ's paschal mystery. The covenant meal of eucharist replaces the old covenant meal of Passover. Jesus is the New Passover; his meal is the new covenant meal. Jesus is the Bread of Presence. No one who eats Jesus' bread will ever know hunger again.

Blood in the synoptics is interpreted as a sign that Christ shed his blood for the sins of the world. Blood is associated with the forgiveness of sins (Mt 24:27-28, Mk 14:24, Lk 22:20). The Old Testament concept of blood as expiation is carried over in the sacrifice of the cup. John equates blood with the giving of eternal life (6: 53-56).

Questions: What do the uses of bread and wine in scripture have to do with the life of your community? What do the biblical signs of bread and wine teach you about God, Christ, Spirit, church, or yourself?

Ecclesial Signs

The meal of the Last Supper was unleavened bread. However, Christians of the early centuries did not assign special significance to the unleavened nature of the bread. They no doubt used leavened bread brought from home and presented along with their offerings for the needy. The ritual action of breaking bread was the eucharistic worship of the early church. There is a detailed description of the ritual in a second-century document, the *Didache*. Early Christians understood eucharist to be a corporate sharing in the risen Christ as experienced in the breaking of the bread. This sharing unified them into one people.

Eucharist means *thanksgiving* in Greek. The early Christians gathered for thanks and praise and the breaking of bread. That early eucharistic liturgy evolved from Jewish table prayers of praise and thanks at festive meals. The early Christians gathered in their house churches for the breaking of the bread while still maintaining their ties to the synagogue. Around 100 C.E., there was a break from the synagogue and the ritual meal continued in the house churches. This meal was eschatological. The eucharist was believed to be the final means of bringing members to belief in Christ before his final coming. Thus, baptism was a requisite for eucharist.

The early liturgy consisted of two parts. The word of God was proclaimed: this consisted of the Hebrew scriptures and memoirs of the apostles. A homily was given based on the readings, and prayers of intercession were offered. The second part of the liturgy included the prayers of thanks and praise over the elements of bread and wine. The Body and Blood of Christ were then shared in communion. Very early (ca. 115), Ignatius of Antioch wrote of eucharist as recalling the passion and death of Jesus; it was offered as strength in times of persecution.

By the third century the liturgy had become more formalized with the established orders of bishop, priest, and deacon. The *Apostolic Tradition,* by Hippolytus of Rome, describes the liturgy in detail. The Tradition's prayer of thanks is the origin of the Second Eucharistic Prayer in today's Roman Missal. The *anaphora* (eucharistic prayer) remembers God's saving deeds since the creation of the world, culminating in the death and resurrection of Christ (*anamnesis*) and the calling down of the Holy Spirit to transform the gifts of bread and wine into the Body and Blood of Christ (*epiclesis*). This action is performed for the unity of the church because of its participation in sharing the Body and Blood of Jesus.

Later in the patristic period, there emerged a more sacrificial understanding of eucharistic bread and wine. The prayers over the elements were referred to as offerings rather than as thanksgiving prayers. The bread was still leavened, and beautifully adorned loaves (such as a braided loaf in the shape of a crown of thorns) were baked by skilled bakers. The Arian heresy was plaguing the church at the time and scholars believe that the special breads emerged at around the same time that theology was stressing the divinity of Christ.

During this same period (fourth to seventh centuries), beginning with Constantine's edict of Milan (315) legalizing Christianity, the liturgy changed to reflect the situation at hand. Christianity became the religion of the Empire. Worship moved from house churches to basilicas, the civic auditoriums large enough to hold the influx of people. It was now advantageous to become a Christian. The catechumenate declined and quality control for converts was minimal. Motivation was questionable. One had to be Christian in order to secure the best employment. The liturgy became more formalized. The hierarchy assumed religious and civic roles of leadership (stoles, miters and special vestments derived from these roles). The liturgy still maintained the two parts of word and sacrament, but embellishments were added for greater participation of the assembly: processions, litanies, chants, incense, etc.

The churches of the East and the West were established, each adopting its own style of worship. The metaphors of previous times became literalisms of this time. Eucharist was sacralized to such an extent that the meal aspect was difficult to detect. However, the eucharistic action of offering thanks and praise was understood as the "sacrifical action of the priestly community by virtue of their baptism."[56] Augustine asserted that eucharist was the offering of the church to the Father.

During the Middle Ages, the people received communion very infrequently. In order to further distinguish eucharistic bread from real bread, the church mandated that eucharistic bread be unleavened and then reduced it to a coin-shaped size, normally consumed by the priest (smaller varieties were used for the people). The Council of Florence in 1439 acknowledged the right of the Eastern church to use leavened bread while the Roman Church maintained its previous mandate.

In the next period (eighth to sixteenth century), the laity became less involved and were reduced to being spectators. Latin was established as the language of liturgy (only the clergy understood Latin). The Eastern church translated the prayers of the liturgy into the vernacular, but Rome maintained Latin as its official liturgical language. The mass was explained as an allegory on the life of Christ. The eucharist was defined as the real Body and Blood of Christ in which the priest broke the

---

[56]Mark R. Francis, C.S.V., "Eucharist," in *The Collegeville Pastoral Dictionary of Biblical Theology,* ed. Carroll Stuhlmueller, C.P. (Collegeville: The Liturgical Press, 1996), 277.

body and the people crushed it with their teeth. The Fourth Lateran Council (1215) and Thomas Aquinas refined that theology with terms such as "transubstantiation."

The sacrifical aspect of the mass increased and centered on the re-creation of the sacrifice of Christ on the cross. Because of the penitential overtones and the people's sense of unworthiness, the reception of communion severely declined. Receiving from the cup was reserved for the clergy only. Leaders of the Reformation spoke out against such abuses.

The Council of Trent sought to reestablish the teaching authority of the church and thus affirmed most practices while abolishing the more obvious abuses. The next four hundred years would see little change.

The Second Vatican Council retrieved the church's earlier biblical and patristic heritage. The meal aspect of eucharist was recovered and the role of the church was strengthened. The primary signs of God's presence in the liturgy were set forth in priest, sacrament, word, and church. "Christ is present in the sacrifice of the Mass, not only in the person of his minister...but especially in the eucharistic elements...in the sacraments....He is present in his word....He is present when the Church prays and sings" (CSL, 7).

For a further summary of eucharistic theology: the church teaches that eucharist completes initiation. The goal of initation is not baptism; it is eucharist. Augustine called eucharist the repeatable sacrament of initiation because it has the power to forgive sins, just as baptism forgives sins. Eucharist is our participation in the paschal mystery of Christ. We are incorporated into his death and resurrection. It is a sign of unity and of charity. We are to share what we have received. We are to become that which we have shared. Eucharist calls us to be bread for the world: the hungry, the suffering, the oppressed. Eucharist strengthens us to take up the cross and live the gospel. In the eucharist, we offer our praise and thanks to God for all his great saving acts since the creation of the world. Eucharist is the way we are church; it is our ongoing participation in Jesus' life. We come together as God's people to offer praise and thanks, to share the story of salvation and Christ's covenant meal. Eucharist commits us to the poor.

Questions: How does the church's teaching on the eucharist impact the life of your community? Does it have anything to do with your everyday life? What does it teach you about God, Christ, Holy Spirit, church, or yourself?

Liturgical Sign

The *Constitution on the Sacred Liturgy* (CSL) asserted that the eucharist is the action of the entire church and that "the liturgy is the summit toward which the activity of Church is directed; at the same time it is the fount from which all the Church's power flows..." (#10). "The Church earnestly desires that all the faithful be led to full, conscious, and active participation in liturgical celebrations called for by the very nature of the liturgy. Such participation by the Christian people as a 'chosen priesthood, a holy nation, God's own people' (1 Pet. 2:9; scc 2:4-5) is their right and duty by reason of their baptism" (#14). "Every liturgical celebration is a sacred action...surpassing all others; no action of the Church can equal its effectiveness by the same title and to the same degree" (CSL, #7).

From all this, it can be concluded that the celebration of the eucharist is the greatest endeavor of the church. Its celebration deserves our greatest attention. The symbols of the liturgy must be robust and reflect the reality they effect. Real bread, quality wine, full water immersion, abundantly slathered oil, a worthy book, a real garment, a large Easter candle, full participation in word, gesture, and song, qualified, trained cantors, lectors, and liturgical ministers: these are our primary symbols. We must give them the opportunity to speak to us. Most have heard the quip that it takes more faith to believe that the wafer-like hosts are bread than it does to believe in the real presence of Jesus Christ in the elements.

> The bread must be made from wheat and must have been baked recently, according to the long standing tradition of the Latin Church, it must be unleavened. The nature of the sign demands that the material for the eucharistic celebration truly have the appearance of food. Accordingly, even

though unleavened and baked in the traditional shape, the eucharistic bread should be made in such a way that in a Mass with a congregation the priest is able actually to break the host into parts and distribute them at least to some of the faithful.... The action of the breaking the bread, the simple term for the eucharist in apostolic times, will more clearly bring out the force and meaning of the sign of the unity of all in the one bread and of their charity, since the one bread is being distributed among the members of one family. ("General Instruction of the Roman Missal" [GIRM], 282, 283)

"Holy Communion has a more complete form as a sign when it is received under both kinds. For in this manner of reception a fuller light shines on the sign of the eucharistic banquet. Moreover, there is clearer expression of that will by which the new and everlasting covenant is ratified in the blood of the Lord and of the relationship of the eucharistic banquet to the eschatological banquet in the Father's kingdom" (GIRM, #240). "The act of drinking the consecrated wine, the Blood of Christ, strengthens the faith of communicants in the sacrificial nature of the Mass. Communion under both kinds can therefore manifest more fully the nature of the Mass both as a sacrifice and as a sacred banquet, ritually expressing that 'the sacrifice and the sacred Meal belong to the same mystery, to such an extent that they are linked to one another by a very close theological and sacramental bond'[57]" ("Directory for the Celebration of Communion under Both Kinds" #19).

On this night of new fire, water, oil and bread, we encounter the risen Christ anew. We are renewed as we go forth with Easter joy. The liturgy calls us to be world changers, to offer our lives for the sake of the world. There is an ancient symbol of eucharist that speaks of the mystery we just celebrated. A mother pelican is pictured with droplets of blood dripping from her breast. It was believed that in time of famine, the mother pelican would scratch her breast until droplets of blood dripped into her starving babies' anxiously waiting beaks.

---

[57]Congregation for Divine Worship, *Actio Pastoralis*, "Instruction on Masses for Special Gatherings" (May 15, 1969), 5.

Her babies fed off of her freely offered blood. We go forth this Easter night willing and strengthened to offer our droplets of love in the service of God's people.

Questions: Have you had a memorable experience of Christ in the eucharist? Describe your communal experience of eucharist. Does it reflect the theology just expressed? Where is there need for growth? What is the challenge of the church's teaching on the eucharist? How are you and your community called to respond?

Conversation with the Liturgy and the Scriptures

Test your original understanding in dialogue with the text.

Were there any new insights, anything you had not considered before in relation to the entire celebration of the Easter Vigil? How does your original understanding of this liturgy compare with what we just shared? How does this liturgy speak to your life?

Participants share an experience from their lives that connects with the biblical interpretation just shared.

Thank God for the Easter Vigil. It is a sign of hope. When parishes struggle in the process of dying and rising through the year, we are offered the opportunity to cast off the old and become a new community in Christ. One year, the pastor stood before us and asked us to stand during his homily and repeatedly sing the refrain: "And God saw that it was good!" He asked us if we really believed the power in those words. He repeatedly affirmed that if we truly believed in our own goodness we could transform the world. We know our sinful natures. It is very difficult to see our own goodness. But tonight's liturgy is a testament to the creative ongoing infusion of goodness in our lives.

It is the annual commitment to stay in the struggle to live the call of our baptism. It is a reminder that we are called to die and to rise. We are to eliminate injustice and become the eucharist. Our parish has had many opportunities over the years to die and rise. Sometimes we stay in death by our own choosing and other times we rise triumphant to new life. When we continue to reach out to the lonely, the sick, the sorrowing, and the poor, we die to our own selfish concerns and live in the resurrection of Jesus Christ. We should rejoice when people get angry that we feed the hungry, offer shelter to the homeless, give blankets to those on the streets, and preach the seamless garment of life. When Jesus made similar choices, he was sent straight to the cross. We are told that we should rejoice when we are persecuted for the sake of the gospel. That is what it means to live the paschal mystery, to be a resurrection people. We have a long way to go, but the Spirit of God continues to lead us in the struggle of death and resurrection. This is the night we take our annual pledge. We recommit ourselves to our covenant with God. The Easter Vigil brings us to our senses, shakes the dust off our feet and the sleep out of our eyes, and tells us to wake up and get on with the business of being God's people, created in the image and likeness of none other than God alone. Washed, anointed, and filled, we are fortified for another year of allowing the spiritually and physically hungry to feed from the satiated Body of Christ. Next year we will return, depleted, ready to be filled again.

All share their life experience.

In what way has this liturgy expressed creation, covenant, church, death and resurrection? How are those images relevant to our community's life today? In what way is our community challenged by this liturgy? What is our collective and personal response to all of the above questions? Do we still feel the same way about this liturgy and these scriptures as we did when we began?

STEP 5
DECISION

The gospel demands a response.

What am I /we/community/parish called to do in response to the Easter Vigil?

DOCTRINAL ISSUES

What church truth/teaching/doctrinal issue could be drawn from the gospel for the Easter Vigil?

Participants suggest possible doctrinal themes that flow from the readings.

Possible Doctrinal Themes

Resurrection, paschal mystery, baptism/confirmation, eucharist; symbols: community, fire/light, water, oil, garment, bread and wine, cross

Present the doctrinal material at this time.

1. The facilitator gives input on a particular doctrinal issue of his/her prior choosing. OR
2. The group chooses a doctrinal issue from the list they created. They read together from the Doctrinal Appendix.

(The doctrinal issues are found in the Doctrinal Appendix in the back of this workbook. If you are choosing an issue from this resource, please refer to it now.)

Reflection questions centered around the chosen doctrinal theme can be found at the end of each topic in the Doctrinal Appendix. The questions are based on the five-step reflection process. If you choose a topic not included in the Doctrinal Appendix, craft your own questions according to the same five-step process.

Following the reflection questions you will be reminded to return to chapter 7, "Preparing the Catechetical Session," to assist you in crafting your own session.

Closing Prayer

God, the all-powerful Father of our Lord Jesus
    Christ,
has given us a new birth by water and the Holy
    Spirit,
and forgiven all our sins.
May he also keep us faithful to our Lord Jesus
    Christ
for ever and ever.[58]

---

[58]Service of Baptism: "Concluding Prayer," *The Rite of Christian Initiation of Adults.*

Selected Bibliography

Boadt, Lawrence, C.S.P. "Ezekiel." In *The New Jerome Biblical Commentary.* Ed. Raymond E. Brown, S.S., Joseph A. Fitzmyer, S.J., Roland E. Murphy, O.Carm. Englewood Cliffs: Prentice Hall, 1990.

Clifford, Richard J., S.J. and Roland E. Murphy. "Genesis." In *The New Jerome Biblical Commentary.* Ed. Raymond E. Brown, S.S., Joseph A. Fitzmyer, S.J., Roland E. Murphy, O.Carm. Englewood Cliffs: Prentice Hall, 1990.

Craghan, John F. "Bread." In *The Collegeville Pastoral Dictionary of Biblical Theology.* Ed. Carroll Stuhlmueller, C.P. Collegeville: The Liturgical Press, 1996.

Days of the Lord, Vol. 3. Collegeville: The Liturgical Press, 1993.

de Lubac, Henri. *Catholicism: A Study of Dogma in Relation to the Corporate Destiny of Mankind.* New York: New American Library, 1964.

Endres, John C., S.J. "Anointing." In *The Collegeville Pastoral Dictionary of Biblical Theology.* Ed. Carroll Stuhlmueller, C.P. Collegeville: The Liturgical Press, 1996.

Fitzmyer, Joseph A., S.J. "The Letter to the Romans." In *The New Jerome Biblical Commentary.* Ed. Raymond E. Brown, S.S., Joseph A. Fitzmyer, S.J., Roland E. Murphy, O.Carm. Englewood Cliffs: Prentice Hall, 1990.

Francis, Mark, R.C.S.V. "Eucharist." In *The Collegeville Pastoral Dictionary of Biblical Theology.* Ed. Carroll Stuhlmueller, C.P. Collegeville: The Liturgical Press, 1996.

Fuller, Reginald H. *Preaching the New Lectionary.* Collegeville: The Liturgical Press, 1974.

Gaupin, Linda. *Sacramental Catechesis.* Course text for "Special Certification in Sacramental Catechesis," Diocese of Orlando Florida, November 1996.

Graff, Ann. "People of God in the History of Theology." In *The Collegeville Pastoral Dictionary of Biblical Theology.* Ed. Carroll Stuhlmueller, C.P. Collegeville: The Liturgical Press, 1996.

Grassi, Joseph F. "Water." In *The Collegeville Pastoral Dictionary of Biblical Theology.* Ed. Carroll Stuhlmueller, C.P. Collegeville: The Liturgical Press, 1996.

Huck, Gabe. *The Three Days: Parish Prayer in the Paschal Triduum.* Chicago: Liturgy Training Pub., 1981.

Hughes, Kathleen, R.S.C.J. "Water: Pastoral Liturgical Tradition." In *The Collegeville Pastoral Dictionary of Biblical Theology.* Ed. Carroll Stuhlmueller, C.P. Collegeville: The Liturgical Press, 1996.

Jensen, Joseph, O.S.B. "People of God." In *The Collegeville Pastoral Dictionary of Biblical Theology.* Ed. Carroll Stuhlmueller, C.P. Collegeville: The Liturgical Press, 1996.

LaVerdiere, Eugene, S.S.S. "People of God: New Testament." In *The Collegeville Pastoral Dictionary of Biblical Theology.* Ed. Carroll Stuhlmueller, C.P. Collegeville: The Liturgical Press, 1996.

Neyrey, Jerome H., S.J. "Community." In *The Collegeville Pastoral Dictionary of Biblical Theology.* Ed. Carroll Stuhlmueller, C.P. Collegeville: The Liturgical Press, 1996.

Richter, Klemens. *The Meaning of Sacramental Symbols.* Collegeville: The Liturgical Press, 1990.

Stuhlmueller, Carroll. "Deutero-Isaiah and Trito-Isaiah." In *The New Jerome Biblical Commentary.* Ed. Raymond E. Brown, S.S., Joseph A. Fitzmyer, S.J., Roland E. Murphy, O.Carm. Englewood Cliffs: Prentice Hall, 1990.

Sweetland, Dennis M. "Hand." In *The Collegeville Pastoral Dictionary of Biblical Theology.* Ed. Carroll Stuhlmueller, C.P. Collegeville: The Liturgical Press, 1996.

Tambasco, Anthony. "Word of God." In *The New Dictionary of Theology.* Ed. Joseph A. Komonchak, Mary Collins, Dermot A. Lane. Collegeville: The Liturgical Press, 1990.

Tannehill, Robert, C. *The Narrative Unity of Luke-Acts: A Literary Interpretation.* Vol. 1. Minneapolis: Augsburg Fortress, 1986.

Thompson, William, G.S.J. and Gerard S. Sloyan. "Word: New Testament." In *The Collegeville Pastoral Dictionary of Biblical Theology.* Ed. Carroll Stuhlmueller, C.P. Collegeville: The Liturgical Press, 1996.

Walsh, Jerome T. and Christopher T. Begg. "1-2 Kings." In *The New Jerome Biblical Commentary.* Ed. Raymond E. Brown, S.S., Joseph A. Fitzmyer, S.J., Roland E. Murphy, O.Carm. Englewood Cliffs: Prentice Hall, 1990.

EASTER SUNDAY

INTRODUCTORY RITES

Opening Song (or Entrance Antiphon)

Song: Jesus Christ Is Risen Today

The Lord has indeed risen, alleluia. Glory and kingship be his for ever and ever. (Lk 24:34; see Rev 1:6)[1]

Environment

The dark days of purple give way to festive joy as Easter days of white adorn our environments. Your catechetical space might include the draping of cross and book in an elegant, well-chosen, white material. As a reminder of the paschal candle, you might want to replenish your formerly consumed candle with a new (perhaps decorated) candle. An Easter lily or other spring flowers could adorn your space. The ancient icon of the resurrection called *Anastasis* would be a wonderful addition to your Easter environment.[2] The icon is a representation of Christ standing on top of the cross that crushes the evil of hell. Christ takes our first parents by the hand and escorts them out of their graves. "Amazing! Here the departure from the tomb is not that of Jesus but of all humanity."[3]

Opening Prayer

The facilitator of the session may lead the prayer. Others in the group may be asked to proclaim the readings.

Let us pray
[on this Easter morning for the life
that never again shall see darkness]

Pause for silent prayer.

God our Father, creator of all,
today is the day of Easter joy.
This is the morning on which the Lord appeared
    to men
who had begun to lose hope
and opened their eyes to what the scriptures
    foretold:
that first he must die, and then he would rise
and ascend into his Father's glorious presence.
May the risen Lord
breathe on our minds and open our eyes
that we may know him in the breaking of the
    bread,
and follow him in his risen life.
Grant this through Christ our Lord.[4]

LITURGY OF THE WORD

Let us listen to God's word.

The readings are proclaimed.

First Reading
Acts 10:34, 37-43

The Acts of the Apostles was the second volume written by Luke, the evangelist (the gospel of Luke was the first). The original Greek title was "Acts of Apostles, not Acts of the Apostles; the meaning is somewhat indefinite, but it is not limited to the Twelve."[5] The book is intended not as a history, but rather as a record of the church's growth through the power of the Holy Spirit. Luke wrote two gospels: the gospel of the Son and the gospel of the Spirit. The gospel of Luke was the former and the Acts of the Apostles the latter. Luke portrays the spread of the church to the gentile world and considers it complete once the mission extends to Rome. It is believed that Luke wrote his book from oral, rather than written, tradition.

---

[1]Easter Sunday: "Entrance Antiphon," *The Sacramentary.*

[2]Icons are symbols that draw us into the sacred presence. They help make present what they portray. There are companies that produce icons for purchase by catalogue. One such company is Monastery Icons, Rt. 1, Box 75, Geneva, NE 68361.

[3]Peter Mazur, *To Crown the Year* (Chicago: Liturgy Training Publications, 1995), 130.

[4]Easter Sunday: "Alternative Opening Prayer," *The Sacramentary.*

[5]John L. McKenzie, S.J. *Dictionary of the Bible* (New York: Macmillan, 1965), 9.

Irenaeus named Luke the author of Acts and further asserted that it was written in Rome sometime after the death of Paul. Eusebius claimed that it was written during Paul's Roman imprisonment. There is similarity in the structure of Luke and Acts. In Luke, there is movement from Galilee to Jerusalem. In Acts, there is movement from Jerusalem to Rome. The Acts of the Apostles places Rome at the center of the known world. It ends in Rome because the incredible has happened and the "gospel has become a world gospel."[6] It was believed to have been composed between 70-90 C.E.

Luke employed a common literary tool used by Greco-Roman historians in which the characters enacted and spoke the historical commentary and analysis they wished to convey. In the Acts of the Apostles, the speeches of the characters interpret and analyze the events of Luke's first volume, the gospel according to Luke. Peter's speech is a primary piece of the Christian kerygma (proclamation). The Acts of the Apostles was a catechetical tool for early believers. The characters in the text set forth the Christian creed.

Peter's speech today is considered the earliest formulation of that creed. Peter and his apostles were the first witnesses. They were the first to confess their faith and were charged with passing on the faith to the world. Every believer was and is to witness to that faith. Today's speech by Peter follows very early christological patterns. Reginald Fuller notes three: 1. Salvation was offered through the scandalous death and subsequent resurrection of Jesus and Israel rejected that salvation. 2. Jesus was vindicated through the resurrection while his religious peers rejected him. 3. The apostles are the first witnesses from his earthly ministry through the post-resurrection appearances.[7]

Peter's Credo is the living faith of the first Christian community passed on to succeeding generations of the church through its living tradition. The roots of Peter's confession can be found in the Apostles' Creed.[8]

[6]Ibid., 12.

[7]Reginald H. Fuller, *Preaching the New Lectionary* (Collegeville: The Liturgical Press, 1974), 23.

[8]*Days of the Lord*, Vol. 3 (Collegeville: The Liturgical Press, 1993), 68.

On this Easter Sunday, Peter's speech in the Acts of the Apostles contains within it not only the Christian kerygma, but a challenge to the Jewish Christian community. Peter's confession about Christ would have upset long-held religious views. God was demanding the unthinkable of good, law-abiding Jews. This whole section of chapter ten is about God removing obstacles to the gentile mission. Not only was Peter's confession for all people, including the gentiles, but it paved the way for Jewish Christians to consider their gentile counterparts worthy of association.

In order to understand this, it is important to consider the reading within the context of its setting. An angel appeared to Cornelius and told him that God favored him because he was an upright man. He was then instructed to go and seek out Peter in Joppa. Cornelius was a pagan, a God-fearing centurion. He was a holy man as is evidenced by his constant prayer and almsgiving. Meanwhile, Peter had a vision of his own. He was hungry. God dropped four-legged animals and reptiles from the sky and declared them no longer unclean. Cornelius's baptism by Peter and Peter's vision are the catalyst for a significant turning point in the early church.

Cornelius went to Peter's house and was invited to stay. Peter was still reeling from his vision and what it meant. Peter already knew of the universality of Jesus' mission. Jesus had commissioned the apostles to go and baptize *all nations*. However, prior to this time, the mission to the gentiles had not advanced much in the Jerusalem church. There were missionary successes, but not much was happening in Jerusalem.

Jesus' plan for the gentile mission had not taken root in Jerusalem. Why? The apostles did not have to go "to all nations" to find gentiles. They lived in their own backyards. Evangelization to the gentiles had not yet begun.

This reading is not about affirming the gentile mission. It is about clearing away the obstacles to it. Up to this point, the obstacle had been so great that it would have taken nothing less than a vision from God to overcome it. By law, gentiles were unclean pagans. A committed, communal relationship assumed reciprocal hospitality. If gentiles were converted, they would be initiated into the New Covenant. Thus, Jewish Christians and gentile Christians would have in common a covenantal relationship in which both parties shared reciprocal hospitality. In other words, there would necessarily be shared *agape,* communal meals. The obstacle for Jewish Christians was: How could they share meals with the unclean? It was forbidden by God. "Nevertheless he [Peter] is the one who takes the new step that requires the Jerusalem church to re-examine its relation to Gentiles. It is not enough that Peter takes the new step. The Jerusalem church must be convinced of its rightness."[9] God was lifting the status of *unclean* off of the backs of the gentiles, thus paving the way for a Jewish/gentile Christianity. Communal relationship between Jews and Christians was now possible.

In today's pericope, Peter confesses the Jesus story to Cornelius and friends to affirm that "God sent good news to the people of Israel about the peace now available through their Messiah, and this Messiah is Lord of all, offering peace to all. Peter reviews the Jesus story as told in Luke in order to say to Cornelius that this story is a word of salvation for him also."[10]

Peter's address to the new converts is indicative of the method used for evangelizing gentiles. Methods used for evangelizing Jews would include blaming the Jewish leaders for Jesus' death and using the Hebrew scriptures as a proof text for Jesus' life. Methods of evangelization for gentiles involved the proclamation of Jesus' life and work and the witness of the apostles to back up his claims.

In today's text, Peter confesses the Christians' story (the agenda of every Easter Christian) and asserts the universal message of God's salvation.[11] In other words, Peter demonstrates the inclusivity of God, and paves the way for disciples to move beyond religious fundamentalism and centuries-old prejudices. Only the Spirit could accomplish such a major shift.

Questions for mystagogical reflection: What does this reading have to do with Easter? How is this a word for our community? What are the implications for our community during this season that immerses us in the paschal mystery and Christian witness? What does this reading teach us about God, Christ, Spirit, church, ourselves? How might our community be called to respond? How does this reading challenge us to live the paschal mystery?

Responsorial Psalm
Psalm 118:1-2, 16-17, 22-23

Of all the psalms, Psalm 118 was one of the first that was used to refer to the death and resurrection of Christ. Psalm 118 is an individual song of thanks. "The stone which the builders rejected" (v. 22) was probably an ancient proverb. "A piece of stone judged unworthy of a position of prominence in the structure by the 'experts' has become the most prominent."[12] This line was a metaphor that the early church used to help explain Israel's rejection of its own people. "This is the day the Lord has made" (v. 24) referred to the day in which Yahweh acted to save his people. The resurrection was just such a day.

Second Reading
Alternative 1: Colossians 3:1-4

Paul's letter to the Colossians is written in the midst of turmoil. Gnosticism is threatening the church. According to gnosticism, spirit is good and matter is evil. Thus, the only way to attain God is through special knowledge (knowledge that only the elite can obtain); those without this knowledge are trapped in their human, evil bodies. There were two extreme responses to gnosticism: excessive spiritual exercises and extreme attempts to wear down the evil body. Both point to the denigration of Christian redemption through Christ. "If you have been raised in Christ" is a literary phrase. "It means if (and of course you are)."[13] The word, *raised,* is literally translated *co-raised.* We were raised with Christ and given a share in his

[9]Robert C. Tannehill, *The Narrative Unity of Luke-Acts: A Literary Interpretation,* Vol. 2 (Minneapolis: Augsburg Fortress, 1986), 143.
   [10]Ibid., 142.
   [11]Adolf Adam, *The Liturgical Year,* trans. Matthew J. O'Connell (Collegeville: The Liturgical Press, 1990), 83.

[12]Kselman, John S., S.S. and Michael L. Barre, S.S., "Psalms," in *The New Jerome Biblical Commentary,* ed. Raymond E. Brown, S.S., Joseph A. Fitzmyer, S.J., Roland E. Murphy, O.Carm. (Englewood Cliffs: Prentice Hall, 1990), 547.
   [13]Reginald H. Fuller, *Preaching the New Lectionary* (Collegeville: The Liturgical Press, 1974), 24

life. Because we have been given a share in Christ's divine life, we are called to live the redemption that was won for us. Thus, we are called to a higher moral standard.

Reginald Fuller suggests that the letter to the Colossians takes the Romans exhortation from last night's vigil one step further. Romans tells us "that we died with Christ." Colossians is more optimistic and is cause for Easter rejoicing. In this letter Paul maintains that we die *and rise* with Christ. However, this death and resurrection carries with it the responsibility to live the moral life and be aware of the "hidden reality which is not fully revealed until Christ's second coming."[14]

Questions for mystagogical reflection: How is our community dying and rising with Christ (living the paschal mystery)? Do we live the challenge of the gospel? Do we respond in love to our brothers and sisters around the world? Do we live the moral responsibility to care for one another, especially those who cannot care for themselves? Where is there death? Where is there resurrection? What are we called to do about it as a community? How are we called to respond?

Second Reading
Alternative 2: 1 Corinthians 5:6-8

Prior to Passover, Jewish women spent many hours removing every particle of leaven from their homes. Leaven was used in a figurative sense in the early church. Leaven was considered an impurity and was a metaphor for sin. A very little leaven impacted the entire batch of dough. Unleavened bread was a sign of purity.

"Do you not know that a little yeast has its effects all through the dough?" (v. 5). The opening line of today's pericope is actually a proverb. "Jesus used it to teach that if the kingdom had modest beginnings, it contains the seeds of great growth."[15] Leaven was also used to symbolize corruption. It is this last reference that Paul uses here. Paul exhorts the reader to get rid of all the old yeast so a new batch can grow. Last night at the Easter Vigil, the neophytes put on the new person of Christ. The old yeast was washed away in the waters of baptism, a new batch was begun, and new life began.

Paul speaks this word to the Corinthians in response to the case of a man who was guilty of incest. He had had relations with his father's wife, which was considered an abomination. Paul was more disconcerted over the community's lack of response than he was about the sin of the man. Paul exhorts the community to rid itself of the sinful leaven. He challenges the community to rid itself of such sin. Easter people are to cast off the darkness of sin and live in the light of the resurrection. Like the Jewish women of old, who swept their houses before Passover looking for the tiniest morsel of leaven, we too are to sweep the houses of our heart to rid them of the leaven of corruption. In so doing, we will then live as unleavened bread, in the resurrection of purity and holiness. Christians are to live and preach the truth and to call one another to holiness. This call to holiness has its basis in living the moral life. "These passages resound to the great Pauline intuition that we are not saved because of our works but neither are we saved without our works.... Moral and ascetic commitment is not the *cause* of salvation; it does, however, have to be the *effect* of it."[16] The Christian community and individual are to seek out the leaven of sin through purification from the old yeast in order to live in the resurrection of new, Easter life.

This is the first time that Christian Passover is mentioned and it refers to two different Passovers. One Passover is that already accomplished through Christ's sacrifice of his life on Calvary. The other is the Christian Passover: the passage of the person from death to life, sin to purity. The verb used in reference to Jesus' Passover is in the past tense. Jesus' Passover is already a reality. The Christian need only accept it, "believe it and celebrate it."[17] The verbs that refer to the Christian Passover, on the other hand, infer that the action is still in process. "The verbs in this case are in the imperative: 'purify yourselves, let us celebrate.'"[18]

---

[14]Ibid.

[15]*Days of the Lord,* Vol. 3, 71.

[16]Raniero Cantalamessa, *The Mystery of Easter* (Collegeville: The Liturgical Press, 1993), 85.

[17]Ibid., 92.

[18]Ibid.

Questions for mystagogical reflection: Christians are called to be a eucharistic people. In what way is your community like the leavened bread of the Pharisees? How have you grown in the image of unleavened bread—the eucharist? How has your community grown in holiness through the lenten season? What are you called to do in response to this reading?

Gospel
John 20:1-9

Mary Magdalene finds Jesus' tomb empty and runs to tell Peter and the others.

Sequence

> To the Paschal Victim let Christians offer a sacrifice of praise.
>
> The lamb redeemed the sheep. Christ, sinless, reconciled sinners to the Father.
>
> Death and life were locked together in a unique struggle. Life's captain died; now he reigns, never more to die.
>
> Tell us, Mary, What did you see on the way?
>
> "I saw the tomb of the now living Christ. I saw the glory of Christ, now risen.
>
> "I saw angels who gave witness; the cloths too which once had covered head and limbs.
>
> "Christ my hope has arisen. He will go before his own into Galilee."
>
> We know that Christ has indeed risen from the dead. Do you, conqueror and king, have mercy on us. Amen. Alleluia.

STEP 1
NAMING ONE'S EXPERIENCE

What were your first impressions? What was your first response? What grabbed your attention? How did you feel?

Each person names his or her initial impression. Statement should be brief. No reasons should be given at this time. All simply listen without agreeing or disagreeing.

STEP 2
UNDERSTANDING

In a brief statement, what do you think the readings are trying to convey?

STEP 3
INPUT FROM VISION/STORY/TRADITION

Liturgical Context

The Beginning of the Easter Season

The Easter Vigil is the primary ritual celebration of the Easter event. Easter Sunday is considered the first Sunday of Easter, and the next Sunday the Second Sunday of Easter. There are no special rituals for Easter Sunday other than to revisit the rituals initiated at the Easter Vigil the night before. On Easter Sunday we renew our baptismal promises, sprinkle the community with the newly blessed water of baptism, and continue the jubilant celebration in word, symbol, ritual, and song. Penitence is over and now begin the seven weeks of meditation on the awesome implications of the paschal mystery.

> He has made us pass:
> from slavery to freedom,
> from sadness to joy,
> from mourning to the feast,
> from darkness to the light,
> from slavery to redemption.
> Therefore we say before him: Alleluia![19]

The Easter season is not a time for giving an historical representation of the chronology of events in Jesus' post-resurrection life. It is, rather, intended to give sufficient time to uncover, unpack, and reflect on the paschal mystery in order to allow all of its dimensions to impact and affect the Christian life. It is a time for the entire church, neophyte and faithful, to reflect upon the Easter gospels, to live their paschal commitment with renewed vigor, and to process in joy to the Easter table. Eucharist,

---

[19]*Pesachim* 10.5; and Melito of Sardis, *On Pascha* 68 (Sources Chretiennes 123, p. 96, Paris: 1942), in Cantalamessa, *The Mystery of Easter*, 91, #2.

as the living presence of the risen Christ, is our prime focus. The eucharists of the Easter season help us remember and bring into the present the Christ who appeared on the road to Emmaus in the breaking of the bread, the Christ who appeared to believers to dispel the doubts of Thomas, and the Shepherd Christ who lays down his life for the church. Jesus appears to the apostles in the Easter season in the form of a meal. "The roots of the Christian Eucharist lie not only in the last supper, but in the meals which the Risen One celebrated with his disciples in the Easter season."[20]

Through the eucharist, we fully live the paschal mystery. St. Augustine asserted that we are to become that which we eat: the Body of Christ. During the Easter season we enter the mystery unfolding in our lives. (One meaning of the word mystery is "that which is unfolding in our midst.") We are challenged from the opening moments of the liturgy (Opening Prayer) to reflect on the mystery we celebrate with enthusiastic joy:

God our Father, creator of all,
today is the day of Easter joy.
This is the morning on which the Lord appeared to men
who had begun to lose hope
and opened their eyes to what the scriptures foretold:
that first he must die, and then he would rise and ascend into his Father's glorious presence.
May the risen Lord
breathe on our minds and open our eyes
that we may know him in the breaking of bread...[21]

The liturgies of Easter demand mystagogical reflection (*breathe on our minds and open our eyes*) not only for the neophytes, but for the faithful as well. They ask: What does it mean to live the *unfolding mysteries* of our sacramental life? What does it mean to be people of the water, light, word, cross, garment, oil, bread and wine? This is not just the task of the newly baptized Catholic Christian. It is the task of the entire church. Just as the lenten church entered the womb of penitence, so too the Easter church enters into the new birth of mystagogical reflection.

---

[20]Fuller, 23.

[21]Easter Sunday: "Opening Prayer," *The Sacramentary*.

The neophytes are a sign of the new life of Easter. As they begin the period of mystagogia, they are a symbol of Easter life. They sit in our midst, perhaps vested in their baptismal garments, and are a living sign of the unfolding mystery of Christ's death and resurrection. These new Christians, who died to the old leaven and rose again to the new leaven of Christ in the eucharist (alternative second reading), remind us that we are to continue in the struggle between life and death. Eucharist strengthens us for the struggle.

The neophytes spend the weeks of Easter growing in the paschal mystery through meditation on the gospel (RCIA, #244).

How do these Easter scriptures help me experience the risen Christ in my daily effort to die and rise with Christ?

Through sharing in the eucharist and doing works of charity, neophytes grow in the newness of the life they have just received.

How am I growing through my participation in the eucharist and the giving of myself in the spiritual and corporal works of mercy? How does the eucharist enlighten my understanding of the Scriptures? (RCIA, #246)

Are these not questions we should all be asking if we wish to grow in the Christian life? Is this not the agenda of the Easter Vigil and the entire Easter season?

For the neophyte, the period of mystagogia is a time for unpacking the sacramental mysteries experienced in baptism, confirmation, and eucharist at the Easter Vigil and eucharist during the masses of the Easter season. It is a time to delve deeply into the symbols of the Vigil, to name the experience and to discover the meaning and the challenge for the Christian life. Easter, then, is a time to lavishly feast and crack open the symbols of bread, wine, oil, water, garment, cross, and light.

The season is a single period of celebration, culminating with the feast of the Holy Spirit given to the church on Pentecost. The *Great Fifty Days of Easter* give ample time and expression to the mystery of

Christ's death, ascension and resurrection. We meditate on what it means to be Easter people. During these fifty days the church commemorates the fruits of Jesus' death and resurrection just as Israel celebrated the first fruit of the harvest during her fifty-day Pentecost feast. Today begins a fifty-day meditation on the wonders of Jesus' saving event and the life and witness of the early church.[22]

The Easter Sunday Liturgy

The readings today are the same for all three cycles. The mass is filled with the joy of the resurrection. It begins in exultation with the words: "The Lord has risen indeed, Alleluia!" Today's opening prayer is an adaptation from the old Gelasian Sacramentary. *"Deus, qui hodierna die,"* the original Latin beginning words, highlight the understanding of *day* in the liturgical sense. The concept of *this day* (also in the responsorial psalm) is important to all liturgical celebration, as it is truly on this Easter day that we especially remember the saving event of Jesus' *pasch.* After our forty days of prayer, fasting and almsgiving, we rise to new life with Christ. The prayers of the liturgy (Opening Prayer—"may we rise again"—and the second reading from Colossians 3: "You have been raised in company with Christ") remind us that through the liturgy we commemorate and share in Jesus' death and resurrection. The responsorial psalm, Psalm 118, is a fitting song of praise to ring in this feast of victory. The second song devoted to the joy of Easter faith is the Easter Sequence: *Victimae Paschali Laudes* ("Praises to the Paschal Victim").[23]

This is the only time of the year when the church experiences the life of the early church through the readings of the Acts of the Apostles. The Acts of the Apostles reads like an adventure-filled novel and is enacted in every community that strives to live the Easter kerygma. In the first reading from Acts, Peter confesses faith in the death and resurrection of Christ. Both choices for the second reading take us to the next step: our moral response. How will we behave, act, and live as people who are incorporated into Jesus' death and resurrection? The gospel from John is the story of the first Christian witness of the resurrection. The Beloved Disciple witnessed to the resurrection without seeing the event himself. Easter is a call for all people to believe without seeing and to go and witness it to the world.

The first Easter preface also refers to "this day" and stresses the victory of Jesus through the sacrifice of his death. The passover images from the Easter Vigil are strong in the preface and remind us that it is "the true Lamb who took away the sins of the world," who offered us redemption and forgiveness of sins.

The church is so insistent on the primacy of the Easter Vigil that it instructs its priests to preach on the unity of the redemptive paschal mystery and on the primacy of the Easter Vigil in the liturgical year on Easter Sunday.[24] Since many people do not attend the Easter Vigil, the church wishes that we be brought into the annual remembrance of Christ's saving event so explicitly encountered in the Vigil liturgy.

The Easter Vigil and Easter Sunday end with the solemn blessing. This solemn blessing asserts an important sacramental reality. The last part of the blessing reminds us of what it is we are to keep in mind at every liturgy. We feast at this banquet, while awaiting the final, glorious banquet with Christ in the hereafter.

The Triduum is brought to a close with the celebration of vespers on Easter Sunday night.

Gospel Exegesis

The facilitator gives input regarding what critical biblical scholarship has to say about this text. The input includes insights as to how people would have heard the gospel in Jesus' time.

---

[22]Please refer to the Easter season overview for a brief history of the Easter Sunday celebration. The gospel from the Easter Vigil is also an option for Easter Sunday morning. Afternoon masses on Easter Sunday may use Luke 13-35.

[23]On Easter Sunday the sequence is sung after the second reading and before the gospel. There are presently only four assigned sequences for the liturgy: Easter Sunday—*Victimae Paschali Laudes* ("Praises to the Paschal Victim"), Pentecost—*Veni Sancte Spiritus* ("Come, Holy Spirit"), Corpus Christi—*Lauda Sion* ("Praise Zion"), Feast of Our Lady of Sorrows—*Stabat Mater* ("The Mother Stood").

[24]Adam, 83-84.

Mary Magdalene enters the tomb, finds it empty, and runs to tell Peter that the Lord's body has been stolen. There is not a hint that she suspects Jesus was raised from the dead. Peter and the Beloved Disciple come to the tomb. The Beloved Disciple enters, sees the burial cloths, and believes. Peter does not believe, but his lack of faith is explained away as lack of understanding: he does not yet understand the scripture in relation to this event.

The two men are needed at the tomb because two witnesses are required to authenticate an event. Women were not acceptable witnesses. Thus, John "places the discovery of the empty tomb by men alongside its discovery by a woman or women. The one confirms the testimony of the other."[25] The cloths were perceived as proof of the resurrection. No one would steal a body by first unwrapping it. Even though grave robbing was a common problem, and even if the disciples had stolen the body (as they were accused of doing), no one would have unwrapped the body. The wrappings left on the floor seemed to suggest a new reality. The person inside those cloths had simply dematerialized, leaving the cloths in place as if his body had simply vanished. "His corpse has not been resuscitated; he has been transformed from mortal to immortal."[26]

This story does not set out to prove the resurrection. The New Testament had no need to prove it. This is more a story of faith. There was nothing that could be proved from the evidence of the empty tomb and the left-behind burial cloths. None of it made any sense until Jesus began to appear to the disciples after the resurrection.

The Beloved Disciple enters the tomb and believes without seeing. The Disciple is both an authentic witness of the resurrection event and a model believer for all those generations of people who will also believe without seeing Jesus.

The tomb is no proof of the resurrection. Mary Magdalene did not run off to tell Peter that Jesus was raised from the dead. She thought someone had stolen his body! The entire resurrection account is intended to prove that this man Jesus, whom they knew well, died on a cross and was raised from the dead. Without the cross there was no resurrection. Without the resurrection there was no gospel, no two-thousand year history. The resurrection was understood in the New Testament as the "climactic achievement in the saving deeds of God."[27] Yet John's gospel does not place the full meaning of Easter at the tomb. Jesus' mission is completed only when he returns to his Father in glory and the Spirit is sent upon the earth. Thus we must look at Easter Sunday with an eye toward Ascension and Pentecost.

Jesus' life and death were redemptive because they were a sign of victory over death. It takes great faith to believe in the resurrection. The disciples did not believe in the resurrection until the risen Lord himself appeared to them. They would not understand the scriptures in regard to his resurrection until Jesus' glorification. The resurrection had to be accepted on faith and on the word of Christian witnesses. The same is true today. During the Easter season the church enters into Jesus' dying and rising, the paschal mystery. We are to give Christian witness to the saving deeds of the Lord. Are we unbelieving, yet chosen for God's mission, like Peter? Or are we like the Beloved Disciple, who believes without seeing for himself and yet cannot contain the power of what he did not see?

Proclaim the gospel again.

Sometimes we gain new insights when we hear the text after the interpretation has been given. Someone from the group proclaims the gospel a second time.

STEP 4
TESTING

Conversation with the Liturgy and the Scriptures

Test your original understanding in dialogue with the text.

(You might consider breaking into smaller groups.)

---

[25]Charles H. Talbert, *Reading John* (New York: Crossroad, 1992), 249.

[26]Ibid., 250.

[27]McKenzie, *Dictionary of the Bible*, 733.

Are there any new or renewed insights in today's readings or liturgy? How does your original understanding of Easter, the gospel, readings and themes, compare with what was just shared? How does this story speak to your life?

Participants share an experience from their lives that connects with the biblical interpretation just shared.

> *It is very difficult in the midst of total loss, rejection, and failure to believe in God's intervention. Jesus' death and resurrection is a sign for us all. We all have had our Gethsemane. We have had those times when we cannot imagine that God will intercede for a positive outcome. The witness of our lives, however, should be enough to remind us that God does not forsake us, even when it appears that he has. There are times when we are called to stand for truth even if that leads to being rejected and misunderstood. Jesus is our model for such a posture and it took him to the cross.*

> *There was once a situation in which what appeared to be truth to a parish was not really the truth. Some people were sorely misunderstood for the positions they supposedly assumed. These people did not publicly defend themselves but chose, rather, to allow God to deal with the situation. They were sustained through the ordeal by the word of God. Like the Beloved Disciple, they had little more than an empty shroud lying on the floor to assure them of their resurrection and vindication, but they stood on what little they had.*

> *No one came down from the heavens to announce that they had been good and faithful servants, but over time the situation was healed by the reconciling presence of Christ. The resurrection did not happen overnight either. The Christian kerygma spread over time and through the Christian witness of faith-filled men and women. The men and women in the above situation simply stood on God's promise to be with them in the midst of their difficulty. That was their resurrection. The outcome of the situation was much better handled by the God whose wisdom is far greater than the limited perceptions of human beings.*

> *Jesus' death seemed to be a failure. He gave his life for what he believed and he was crucified for it. In today's resurrection gospel, he left us enough evidence for belief, but the door to unbelief was also left ajar.*

> *God will not coerce. He did not coerce the people in the above-mentioned parish situation to believe in his plan; but he gave them enough evidence throughout the ordeal to let them know who was in charge.*

> *Living the paschal mystery is not easy. It can mean that we will be misunderstood and persecuted, sometimes in grand ways and other times in ordinary ways. Yet Easter is a time for us to recommit to stay in the struggle and offer our joys and sorrows for the reign of Christ.*

All share their life experience.

What was Luke's message to the early Christian community in the first reading? What was John trying to tell his community? What does he have to say to our community and to me today? How are we challenged to be re-created (*biblical theme of creation*), to enter more fully into relationship with God (*covenant*), to live in Christian community (*community*) and to die and rise (*exodus*)? In what way have I/we known death/resurrection in my/our experience and understanding of this gospel? How is God speaking to us as a community and how are we challenged? What is our collective and personal response to all of the above questions?

STEP 5
DECISION

The gospel demands a response.

In what concrete way does this liturgy call our parish to action in the church, parish, neighborhood, or world? Has this conversation with the exegesis of this Easter liturgy changed or stretched my personal attitudes? What is one specific action I/we will take this week as a response to what was learned and shared today?

DOCTRINAL ISSUES

What church truth/teaching/doctrinal issue could be drawn from the gospel for Easter Sunday?

Participants suggest possible doctrinal themes that flow from the readings.

Possible Doctrinal Themes

Paschal mystery, resurrection, eucharist, baptism, confirmation, symbols: bread, water, oil, Christian witness

Present the doctrinal material at this time.

1. The facilitator gives input on a particular doctrinal issue of his/her prior choosing. OR
2. The group chooses a doctrinal issue from the list they created. They read together from the Doctrinal Appendix.

(The doctrinal issues are found in the Doctrinal Appendix in the back of this workbook. If you are choosing an issue from this resource, please refer to it now.)

Reflection questions centered around the chosen doctrinal theme can be found at the end of each topic in the Doctrinal Appendix. The questions are based on the five-step reflection process. If you choose a topic not included in the Doctrinal Appendix, craft your own questions according to the same five-step process.

Following the reflection questions you will be reminded to return to chapter 7, "Preparing the Catechetical Session," to assist you in crafting your own session.

Closing Prayer

May almighty God bless you on this solemn feast of Easter, and may he protect you against all sin.
   Response: Amen.

Through the resurrection of his Son,
God has granted us healing.
May he fulfill his promises,
and bless you with eternal life.
   Response: Amen.

You have mourned for Christ's sufferings;
now you celebrate the joy of his resurrection.
May you come with joy to the feast which
lasts forever.
   Response: Amen.[28]

---

[28]Easter Sunday, "Solemn Blessing," *The Sacramentary.*

Selected Bibliography

Adam, Adolf. *The Liturgical Year.* Trans. Matthew J. O'Connell. Collegeville: The Liturgical Press, 1990.

Cantalamessa, Raniero. *The Mystery of Easter.* Collegeville: The Liturgical Press, 1993.

Days of the Lord, Vol. 3. Collegeville: The Liturgical Press, 1993.

Dues, Greg. *Catholic Customs and Traditions.* Mystic: Crossroad, 1992.

Fuller, Reginald H. *Preaching the New Lectionary.* Collegeville: The Liturgical Press, 1974.

Kselman, John S., S.S. and Michael L. Barre, S.S. "Psalms." In *The New Jerome Biblical Commentary.* Ed. Raymond E. Brown, S.S., Joseph A. Fitzmyer, S.J., Roland E. Murphy, O.Carm. Englewood Cliffs: Prentice Hall, 1990.

Mazur, Peter. *To Crown the Year.* Chicago: Liturgy Training Publications, 1995.

McKenzie, John L. *Dictionary of the Bible.* New York: Macmillan, 1965.

Sanchez, Patricia Datchuck. *The Word We Celebrate.* Kansas City: Sheed and Ward. 1989.

Talbert, Charles H. *Reading John.* New York: Crossroad, 1992.

Tannehill, Robert C. *The Narrative Unity of Luke-Acts: A Literary Interpretation.* Vol. 2. Minneapolis: Augsburg Fortress, 1986.

SECOND SUNDAY OF EASTER

INTRODUCTORY RITES

Opening Song (or Entrance Antiphon)

Like newborn children you should thirst for milk,
on which your spirit can grow to strength, alleluia.
(1 Pet 2:2)[1]

Environment

Refer to Easter Sunday.

Opening Prayer

The facilitator of the session may lead the prayer. Others in the group may be asked to proclaim the readings.

Rite of Sprinkling

Dear friends,
this water will be used
to remind us of our baptism.
Let us ask God to bless it
and keep us faithful
to the Spirit he has given us.
Lord God almighty,
hear the prayers of your people:
we celebrate our creation and redemption.
Hear our prayers and bless + this water
which gives fruitfulness to the fields,
and refreshment and cleansing to man.
You chose water to show your goodness
when you led your people to freedom
through the Red Sea
and satisfied their thirst in the desert
with water from the rock.
Water was the symbol used by the prophets
to foretell your new covenant with man.
You made the water of baptism holy
by Christ's baptism in the Jordan:
by it you give us a new birth
and renew us in holiness.
May this water remind us of our baptism,
and let us share the joy
of all who have been baptized at Easter.
We ask this through Christ our Lord.

(When salt is mixed with the holy water:)

Almighty God,
we ask you to bless + this salt
as once you blessed the salt scattered over the
    water
by the prophet Elisha.
Wherever this salt and water are sprinkled,
drive away the power of evil,
and protect us always
by the presence of your Holy Spirit.
Grant this through Christ our Lord.

(After the sprinkling:)

May almighty God cleanse us of our sins,
and through the eucharist we celebrate
make us worthy to sit at his table
in his heavenly kingdom.[2]

LITURGY OF THE WORD

Let us listen to God's word.

The readings are proclaimed.

First Reading
Acts 5:12-16

Luke's main agenda in the Acts of the Apostles was to teach the early community how to live, grow and thrive as a church. In the Acts of the Apostles, Luke followed literary techniques commonly found in ancient literature. One such technique was to tell the stories of a group's founder so new followers would emulate his actions. These stories, called cultic biographies, also related the actions and movements of the founder's newly formed disciples. The greater purpose of cultic biography was to authenticate the mission of the leader and his followers.

---

[1]Second Sunday of Easter: "Entrance Antiphon," *The Sacramentary.*

[2]"Rite of Blessing and Sprinkling Holy Water," *The Sacramentary.*

One literary technique used by the author of Acts is the summary. Today's reading is a summary. There are three major summaries in Acts; this is the third. The summaries portrayed the developing life of the community as it lived in the resurrected presence of Christ. The community shared all things in common, and community members gathered for common worship and instruction. Signs and wonders not only prove the presence and power of the risen Christ, but they are also reminders of the messianic, eschatological age. The church furthers the reign of God in the here and now as she awaits God's reign in the age to come—the final age.

This pericope must also be set in the context of what went before it. Peter and John, under the power of the Holy Spirit, were boldly preaching about the healing power of Christ. After they had healed a lame man, the Sanhedrin forbade the apostles from further teaching or preaching. But they could not stop. They were compelled to obey God rather than human beings. Later verses show the church praying for the boldness to speak God's word in the face of hostility. The sign of the healed lame man impresses even outsiders and opponents. Signs, then, are also the means for uplifting and strengthening a persecuted church.[3]

This is what leads up to today's reading. Many people came from all over the region expecting to be healed, and many were healed. In spite of the Sanhedrin's prohibition, the apostles would do the work they were commissioned to do. God will accomplish what God intends. God's ministers are to persevere in the face of opposition and preach the gospel to all of God's people.

Today's reading also reminds us that one sign of the established reign of Christ is his healing ministry. When people are healed, it is a sign that Christ is alive through the power of his Holy Spirit in the ongoing work of the church. God's messengers, empowered by the Holy Spirit, continue Jesus' ministry of healing and reconciliation. God's people are thus uplifted as they await the triumphant return of their Master.

---

[3]Robert C. Tannehill, *The Narrative Unity of Luke-Acts: A Literary Interpretation,* Vol. 2 (Minneapolis: Augsburg Fortress, 1990), 63.

Questions for mystagogical reflection: Would your community be prepared to preach God's word in spite of harsh opposition? Would you be prepared to preach a bold word? What signs and wonders have you experienced (in your life or the community's) that you might witness to as you share the Good News? Where is there evidence of God's Spirit in your community? Living the paschal mystery requires that we be willing to lay down our lives for others and further the reign of God. In what way does the Easter season strengthen us for such a serious, yet difficult challenge?

Responsorial Psalm
Psalm 118:2-4, 13-15, 22-24

Psalm 118 is a song in praise of God's goodness. The salvation offered us by Jesus is celebrated in verses 13-15. When all seems lost ("I was hard pressed and was falling") is the moment when God comes crashing through with an eleventh-hour save. God's ways are not our own. When in terms of human appearances everything looks like failure, death, and rejection, God resurrects and brings life to the situation.

Second Reading
Revelation 1:9-11, 12-13, 17-19

The book of Revelation is different from any other type of literature in the New Testament. The gospels and the Acts of the Apostles attempt to relate a realistic narrative. The epistles serve as teachings, addresses, speeches, or preaching. The literary medium of the book of Revelation is laden with extraordinary images and visions not normally experienced by human beings.

The book of Revelation is an apocalypse with hints of prophecy, letter, and drama.[4] The book of Revelation understands itself as a prophecy. While not completely prophetic in form, the messages to the seven churches serve as prophetic oracles. The book also resembles an epistle, probably due to the fact that John had to communicate in letter form following his banishment to the island of Patmos. The epistle was also the approved means

---

[4]Adela Yarbro Collins, "The Apocalypse (Revelation)," in *The New Jerome Biblical Commentary,* ed. Raymond E. Brown, S.S., Joseph A. Fitzmyer, S.J., Roland E. Murphy, O.Carm. (Englewood Cliffs: Prentice Hall, 1990), 996.

of communication for religious leaders. There are hints of drama in the apocalypse. While it does not contain dialogue and narrative action, it does contain the emotive power of the Greek tragedy.

The word *revelation* in John's apocalypse alerts the reader to the fact that God, through Christ, is revealing "secrets about heaven, and earth, past, present and future."[5] In an apocalypse, the author is not given the vision from the deity, but from an intermediary, such as an angel or, in this case, the risen Christ. According to Adela Yarbro Collins, the revelation may take place in the form of manifestations, visions, otherworldly journeys. There are two themes in the revelation: the cosmos and secrets of the future. Inherent in the cosmos theme are the stars, moon, sun, calendar, causes of the weather, angelic beings, and places of reward and punishment. The secrets of the future theme involves the subject of heaven, earth, humanity and the future destination of God's people.

There is a common belief that the function of apocalyptic literature is to console people in times of crisis and distress. However, Collins suggests that this is too simplistic. Inherent in such literature is also an undercurrent of propaganda against current ideologies. The apocalypse is intended to present a particular interpretation in order to challenge people to live according to the position presented by the author of the work.

Theories regarding the authorship of Revelation abound and none are conclusive. Collins asserts: "It seems best to conclude that the author was an early Christian prophet by the name of John, otherwise unknown. The effectiveness of the book lies in the effectiveness of the text itself and in the fact that the church has included it in the canon."[6]

Another widely held assumption is that Revelation was written as response to the severe persecution of Christians by Domition. Collins suggests that Domition was blamed for persecution that took place under Nero. He was assumed guilty by association because he was Nero's successor. It would have been tempting and easy for Melito[7] to associate the two emperors and "to exaggerate the occasional local actions against Christians into systematic persecution."[8]

There is little evidence in Revelation of widespread persecution. There are only three situations named: John's banishment (1:9), Antipas's execution (2:13), and the anticipated arrest of some Christians in Smyrna (2:10). Those were local, current events, but do not necessarily reflect widespread persecution or the persecution in John's vision. Collins, therefore, maintains that the allusions to persecution in the book reflect past persecutions (such as under Nero) and the expectation of persecution in the immediate future.

The book of Revelation opens with the acknowledgment that the revealed word in the book comes from Jesus himself. The opening setting appears to be a liturgical gathering of Christians to hear the public proclamation of John's message. There is a sense of urgency as judgment is purported to be imminent. The revelation is not necessarily about Jesus, but rather reveals what is about to take place. John bore witness to Christ by writing the book. The reader is alerted that Christian witness has the potential to arouse hostility in those with power (v. 9).

Today's pericope begins with a word about tribulation, about the crisis and distress all will experience at the end of time. When the time comes, the church is to persevere and endure against those powers that will persecute Christians. Christians are to remain loyal to living the "Christian way of life" that will ensure their salvation. The author himself has experienced the consequences of living and preaching the Good News. John was banished to Patmos because of preaching the Christian kerygma. He paid a heavy price for his

---

[7]Melito of Sardis, a bishop ca. 160-170 B.C.E., wrote a Christian apology to the emperor, Marcus Aurelius, stating that only Roman emperors who had a bad reputation among the Romans themselves persecuted Christians. There was nothing wrong with Christianity; it was simply the ill will and bad judgment of those particular Roman emperors. Nero was unpopular with the Roman senate and Domition was often called a second Nero (Collins, 998).

[8]Collins, "The Apocalypse (Revelation)," 998.

---

[5]Ibid.

[6]Ibid., 998.

witness. The Romans often banished people whom they saw as a threat to the public welfare. John's eschatological message may have been viewed as subversive, thus he was banished.

"On the Lord's Day I was caught up in ecstasy." John's vision takes place on "the Lord's day," when Christians gather to celebrate the liturgy of Jesus' resurrection. Under the power of the Holy Spirit, the trumpet sounds and John is ordered to write the message in the book that will be sent to the seven major churches (seven lampstands) along the main road. One can almost picture the triumphant liturgy in which the seven churches gather to hear the message proclaimed.[9]

The "Son of Man" is a term that Jesus used in reference to himself. He also appropriated the suffering servant image from the prophet Isaiah. The "Son of Man" term has its roots in the book of Daniel. The Son of Man of Daniel's apocalypse was a divine-like human being who was given authority from God to have sovereign dominion. The early church appropriated the title to Jesus Christ.

In the remaining verses the reader is made aware that Jesus, the exalted and glorified Son of Man, is the One who conquered sin and death. He reigns in glory with his Father in heaven, and will sit in judgment of all humanity on the last day. The clothing of Christ described in today's reading takes us back to the transfiguration. Jesus, who holds the keys of life and death, will console all the persecuted in their hour of suffering. There is no need to fear. Those who believe and embrace the paschal mystery will share in the eternal life promised in today's reading.

Finally, John is instructed to write down what was revealed to him. It is written not as actual letters sent to the churches, but as an oracle probably proclaimed orally as was customary with prophecy.

Gospel
John 20:19-31

Jesus appears to the Twelve and eight days later, with Thomas present, he appears again.

---

[9]Trumpets were symbols of theophanies—manifestations of God. In the early church, the trumpet blast was often connected with the end of time.

STEP 1
NAMING ONE'S EXPERIENCE

What were your first impressions? What was your first response? What grabbed your attention? How did you feel?

Each person names his or her initial impression. Statement should be brief. No reasons should be given at this time. All simply listen without agreeing or disagreeing.

STEP 2
UNDERSTANDING

In a brief statement, what do you think these Easter readings are trying to convey?

STEP 3
INPUT FROM VISION/STORY/TRADITION

Liturgical Context

The liturgies of the Sundays of Easter are centered around the unity of the paschal mystery: the death, resurrection, and ascension of Jesus and sending of the Spirit. This four-fold reality is the focus of reflection during the Easter season.

The readings of the Easter liturgies are chosen to reflect the spirit and heart of the season.

> The first reading is from the Acts of the Apostles, arranged in a three-year cycle of parallel and progressive selections. Thus the life, growth, and witness of the early Church are presented every year.

> The selections from the writings of the apostles are year A, First Letter of Peter; year B, First Letter of John; year C, the Book of Revelation. These texts seem most appropriate to the spirit of the Easter season, a spirit of joyful faith and confident hope.[10]

---

[10]Lectionary: Introduction, Ch. 2, IV, 14, #1.

John's intention in the final chapters of his gospel is to define paschal faith. He wants his readers to understand that even if seeing is believing, not seeing and believing opens a person to a myriad of hidden truths. Those of us left to live the paschal faith in the messianic age are called to believe with new eyes. The early disciples had to move from their actual experience of the human Jesus to radical faith in the resurrected, glorified Jesus who now lives in the presence of the Spirit in the church.

During Easter we are reminded that we have died with Christ and rise again to new life with him through our baptism. We are sprinkled with the waters of baptism in order to remember and call forward our own baptism. We are reminded that through baptism we participate in Jesus' paschal mystery.

In the opening prayer of today's liturgy, we ask to share God's mercy and life. Christians wash away sins in the water of baptism, are given new birth in the Holy Spirit, and are redeemed by the blood of Christ. Our primary focus during the Easter season is to immerse ourselves in the paschal mystery. The opening prayer reflects this paschal faith and life.

> Let us pray
> [for a deeper awareness of our Christian
>   baptism].
> God of mercy,
> you wash away our sins in water,
> you give us new birth in the Spirit,
> and redeem us in the blood of Christ.
> As we celebrate Christ's resurrection
> increase our awareness of these blessings,
> and renew your gift of life within us.[11]

We are called to be Easter people. The "people of one heart and one mind" in the Acts of the Apostles are people who have become the new creation through faith and baptism (Prayer Over the Gifts). We are those people.

> Lord,
>   through faith and baptism
> we have become a new creation.

> Accept the offerings of your people
> (and of those born again in baptism)
> and bring us to eternal happiness.[12]

During Easter we meditate on what it means to be that new creation—to live paschal faith. Through baptism we died to sin and have been resurrected to new life. There are implications. Christian living brings hardships and trials. Acts alludes to this because of the prior context of the pericope and John prepares us for it in the book of Revelation. Paschal faith requires that we believe in Christ simply on his word and invitation. Paschal faith demands that we confess that faith, even if it leads to the cross—*especially* if it leads to the cross. Paschal faith also demands that we lay down our lives for one another. Neophytes are to be strengthened by the eucharist they celebrate and they, in turn, are to become the eucharist they receive.

Thus, the period of mystagogy necessarily includes meditation on the Easter gospels and living the charity demanded by the gospel. Easter is the time for the neophyte and the faithful to celebrate the saving deeds of God in the midst of the Christian community. How has God called our community to transformative faith and life? Easter is the time to witness to God's marvelous deeds. How are we telling our corporate and personal stories of death and resurrection?

The Easter sacraments, especially the eucharist, are the way in which we fully participate in Jesus' paschal mystery. Jesus appears to his disciples on the first day of the week. It is the day on which Christians gather to experience Jesus in the eucharist—both his real presence and his concealed presence. John's community was struggling with what it meant to live as Easter people in the reality of Christ's non-imminent return. They, too, celebrated the presence of Jesus in the eucharist: not only bread eucharist, but the eucharist of service (foot washing). Just as Christ beckoned Thomas to embrace a committed faith, eucharist is our similar invitation. "May the Easter sacraments we have received live forever in our minds and hearts" (Prayer After Communion). Jesus is both hidden

---

[11]Second Sunday of Easter: "Opening Prayer," *The Sacramentary.*

[12]Second Sunday of Easter: "Prayer Over the Gifts," *The Sacramentary.*

and present in the eucharist. Like Thomas, we are called to choose. When we fully commit, we are able to come before Christ in the eucharist and profess, "My Lord and My God!" Eucharist strengthens our doubting faith and helps us believe without seeing.

Gospel Exegesis

The facilitator gives input regarding what critical biblical scholarship has to say about this text. The input includes insights as to how people would have heard the gospel in Jesus' time.

Today's two post-resurrection appearances of Jesus are read every year throughout all three cycles. Jesus offers his peace, faith, the gift of the Holy Spirit, and a lasting legacy of his merciful forgiveness. He appears first on Easter night, and then a week later. Luke did not relate Jesus' resurrection, ascension, and Pentecost as a one-time event. He extended it over a period of time in order to lead and guide his community to a deeper faith. John's portrayal is probably more accurate: Jesus bestowed the Spirit and commissioned his disciples on the same day. According to Charles Talbert, one purpose of this resurrection account is to show that Jesus is alive and to offer further instructions to the disciples.[13]

A few verses before this pericope, Jesus encountered Mary Magdalene standing beside the tomb. She did not recognize him at first glance. We are led to understand that something has changed; Jesus is different. "In his new identity, Jesus is no longer subject to the constraints of space and time."[14] Today's gospel continues to portray Jesus in his new, altered state. He appears in the midst of the Twelve. There is no question that it is Jesus; he identifies himself by showing his hands and his side. His body is still real, though changed. Mary Magdalene in earlier verses was told not to touch him. Jesus passed through his shroud and through doors, but he could still be seen with the human eye. Talbert asserts that

Jesus continues in his incarnation even after the resurrection, albeit in a different corporeal form.[15] "The incarnation did not cease with the cross and the tomb; it continues even now in transcendental glory."[16]

Jesus first greets the disciples with peace (he offers it twice). He then offers them the gift of his Spirit; he commissions them and sends them out to forgive sins. The commission to forgive sins has its implications in the Christian community. Charles Talbert suggests that the forgiveness of sins implies that if disciples forgive the sins of other disciples against them, the community will remain intact. If those sins are not forgiven, then community peace and harmony will be disrupted.[17] The Holy Spirit is therefore given in order to help Christians live the peace Christ bestowed upon them and to empower them for their mission to the world. (Later theologians used the forgiveness text as the primary source for the church's understanding of the sacrament of penance or reconciliation.) The power to forgive one another will be given by the Holy Spirit.

In the same gospel, Jesus appears again, eight days later. This time Thomas is present. Jesus miraculously materializes through the doors. Thomas was given the opportunity to touch Jesus' wounds so he would believe. Thomas needed to be assured that the appearance was indeed the human Jesus he knew.

Thomas's scene is regarded by some scholars as the culminating scene of John's entire gospel. It brings closure and satisfaction. John began his gospel by stating the purpose for its writing: to proclaim Jesus, the incarnate Word of God. All the events of the gospel lead to this point. Thomas, upon seeing Jesus' wounds, acclaims him Lord and God. "Jesus is described as being of the essence of God at the outset of the Gospel, and then, fully twenty chapters later, one of his disciples comes to believe in him fully and affirms him loftily as 'my Lord and my God.'"[18] The last phrase

[13]Charles H. Talbert, *Reading John* (New York: Crossroad, 1992), 253.

[14]Richard J. Cassidy, *John's Gospel in New Perspective* (Maryknoll, NY: Orbis Books, 1992), 71.

[15]Talbert, *Reading John*, 253.

[16]Philip Edgcumbe Hughes, *The True Image* (Grand Rapids: Eerdmans, 1989), 382.

[17]Talbert, *Reading John*, 255.

[18]Cassidy, *John's Gospel in New Perspective*, 72.

of this gospel is the summary of the purpose of the work: 1. that people may believe in him, and 2. that they may have life.

John strongly connects belief with eternal life. "Yet the consequence of believing is itself of extreme importance for John; this consequence is that his readers have eternal life. The one purpose thus involves the other, for to have eternal life cannot be separated from believing."[19]

Jesus' greeting of peace is significant. Israel believed that the advent of the messianic era would be accompanied by the reign of peace, evidenced by people living in reciprocal covenant relationship with God and one another. Jesus manifested his messianic reign by offering the Holy Spirit to accomplish and realize harmony and peace among God's people. Thus, Jesus' salutation—"Peace!"—functioned as realized eschatology. That is, the promised, future reign of God was at hand in the presence of the Holy Spirit of God. The Spirit who was manifest, dynamic, and active in all of God's acts of salvation is the Spirit offered to the disciples on the day of this gospel event. The same Spirit who presided over the stirring waters at creation is the same Spirit who goes with the disciples in their work of healing the sick, forgiving sins, and announcing the messianic reign of God.

John's agenda was to connect the human Jesus with the divine Jesus. He wanted his readers to fully realize that the Jesus who walked the earth was the Jesus who reigned prior to his earthly life in union with his Father and the Spirit. Plagued by the influence of gnosticism, some in the Johannine church preferred to center on Jesus, the divine-man, wonder-worker, to the exclusion of Jesus, the crucified Lord who was raised and glorified. John's Jesus shows his wounds to Thomas in order to remind the community that Jesus' exalted status has its roots in his humiliating death.

The post-resurrection appearances also serve to strengthen the community in the Lord's absence until he returns in glory for a second time. Jesus' healing and forgiving mission will continue until he comes again.

_____
[19]Ibid.

Today's gospel also stresses the journey of faith. Thomas reminds us that doubt sometimes is a precursor of committed faith. Thomas struggled, and in his struggle he embraced a deeper, lasting faith. He did not come to belief because he touched the Lord's wounds. Faith was prompted by Jesus' invitation.

Easter reminds us to persevere in our faith in the Risen One, even though we have not put our hands into his wounds. Today's gospel is a challenge to live in the presence of the abiding Spirit, to forgive one another and to promote the reign of God.

Proclaim the gospel again.

Sometimes we gain new insights when we hear the text after the interpretation has been given. Someone from the group proclaims the gospel a second time.

STEP 4
TESTING

Conversation with the Liturgy and the Scriptures

Test your original understanding in dialogue with the text.

(You might consider breaking into smaller groups.)

Were there any new insights? Was there anything you had not considered before? How does your original understanding of this story compare with what was just shared? How does this story speak to your life?

Participants share an experience from their lives that connects with the biblical interpretation just shared.

> *I have never been put in a position of fearing banishment for my faith in Jesus Christ. I have never had to fear imprisonment for preaching the gospel. The only correlation I can make is the climate of fear that is prevalent today when it comes to expressing issues of inclusivity in the church. I know an elderly woman who suffers terribly for her belief in the equality of women. She believes that all people are anointed priest, prophet, and king at their baptism and deserve the highest dignity. Any time she per-*

ceives the rightful dignity of women being challenged in the church, whether by higher authorities or unwitting parishioners, she speaks out. She has put her credibility on the line, time and again. She is a prophet in our midst and very often is dismissed as inconsequential, yet she never gives up.

Wherever and whenever women are denigrated in even the smallest ways, she speaks up and addresses the injustice. She has suffered for her position. She is in her mid-seventies. She should be enjoying her last years, but she is on fire with her burden. She is a prophet of the Lord—a voice for women. I believe that God has emblazoned that word on her heart. She must be true to the word she has been given, just as John was true in writing down the revelation he was given. Prophets like this woman are placed in our midst to remind us that God's ways are not our own. This woman has suffered for taking the stands she has taken. She has been misunderstood by her peers and often dismissed by those she challenges. She has known little resurrection, but she stands on the hope that her efforts will someday pave the way for others. Her tenacity has been an inspiration to me and to others who have listened to her frustrations. Yet she perseveres. Thank God she does. Many a time I have heard the doubts of Thomas ring through her discouragements. But she forges on. She wrote the book on perseverance and endurance. She is an example of paschal, Easter faith.

All share their life experience.

What was John's message to his community? How does it relate to your community and to you today? How are the biblical themes of creation, community, covenant, and exodus (death/resurrection) evident in today's liturgy? What does John's message have to do with you and your community? What is your collective and personal response to all of the above questions? Has your original understanding of this liturgy been stretched, challenged, or affirmed?

STEP 5
DECISION

The gospel demands a response.

How does our sharing and this biblical interpretation challenge our community's attitudes? In what concrete way does this gospel call our parish to action in the church, parish, neighborhood, or world? What is one concrete action I/we will take this week as a response to what was learned and shared today?

DOCTRINAL ISSUES

What church truth/teaching/doctrinal issue could be drawn from the gospel for the Second Sunday of Easter?

Participants suggest possible doctrinal themes that flow from the readings.

Possible Doctrinal Themes

Death/resurrection/paschal mystery, sacraments, eucharist, confirmation, baptism, symbols: bread, water, oil, mystery of the church

Present the doctrinal material at this time.

1. The facilitator gives input on a particular doctrinal issue of his/her prior choosing. OR
2. The group chooses a doctrinal issue from the list they created. They read together from the Doctrinal Appendix.

(The doctrinal issues are found in the Doctrinal Appendix in the back of this workbook. If you are choosing an issue from this resource, please refer to it now.)

Reflection questions centered around the chosen doctrinal theme can be found at the end of each topic in the Doctrinal Appendix. The questions are based on the five-step reflection process. If you choose a topic not included in the Doctrinal Appendix, craft your own questions according to the same five-step process.

Following the reflection questions you will be reminded to return to chapter 7, "Preparing the Catechetical Session," to assist you in crafting your own session.

Closing Prayer

Let us pray
[as Christians thirsting for the risen life]
Heavenly Father and God of mercy,
we no longer look for Jesus among the dead,
for he is alive and has become the Lord of life.
From the waters of death you raise us with him
and renew your gift of life within us.
Increase in our minds and hearts
the risen life we share with Christ
and help us to grow as your people
toward the fullness of eternal life with you.
We ask this through Christ our Lord.[20]

Selected Bibliography

Cassidy, Richard J. *John's Gospel in New Perspective.* Maryknoll, NY: Orbis Books, 1992.

Collins, Adela Yarbro. "The Apocalypse (Revelation)." In *The New Jerome Biblical Commentary.* Ed. Raymond E. Brown, S.S., Joseph A. Fitzmyer, S.J., Roland E. Murphy, O.Carm. Englewood Cliffs: Prentice Hall, 1990.

Days of the Lord, Vol. 3. Collegeville: The Liturgical Press, 1993.

Hughes, Philip Edgcumbe. *The True Image.* Grand Rapids: Eerdmans, 1989.

Sanchez, Patricia Datchuck. *The Word We Celebrate.* Kansas City: Sheed and Ward, 1989.

Talbert, Charles H. *Reading John.* New York: Crossroad, 1992.

Tannehill, Robert C. *The Narrative Unity of Luke-Acts: A Literary Interpretation.* Vol. 2. Minneapolis: Augsburg Fortress, 1990.

---

[20]Second Sunday of Easter: "Alternate Opening Prayer," *The Sacramentary.*

THIRD SUNDAY OF EASTER

INTRODUCTORY RITES

Opening Song (or Entrance Antiphon)

Let all the earth cry out to God with joy; praise the glory of his name; proclaim his glorious praise, alleluia. (Ps 65:1-2)[1]

Opening Prayer

The facilitator of the session may lead the prayer. Others in the group may be asked to proclaim the readings.

Let us pray
[in confident peace and Easter hope]

Father in heaven, author of all truth,
a people once in darkness has listened to your
    Word
and followed your Son as he rose from the tomb.
Hear the prayer of this newborn people
and strengthen your church to answer your call.
May we rise and come forth into the light of day
to stand in your presence until eternity dawns.
We ask this through Christ our Lord.[2]

LITURGY OF THE WORD

Let us listen to God's word.

The readings are proclaimed.

First Reading
Acts 5:27-32, 40-41

The Sanhedrin was the Jewish high court. It was made up of the seventy-one members who were elders of the ruling families and clans, high priests, former high priests and leaders of priestly families, and the legal experts or the scribes. The Sanhedrin presided over Jewish religious, social, and legal life. Court was held in the temple complex and was in session from morning till evening. The Sanhedrin was able to pass legal judgment in most cases, except in capital cases (Romans reserved that right). It was a very powerful body.

Last week we saw the ministry of the apostles gaining momentum. Then persecution set in. The rising popular tide of support shifted and then wavered. Today's pericope shows the mounting tension between the Sanhedrin and the Christian community. The Sanhedrin refused responsibility for Jesus' death. They were furious over the apostles' rejection of their prohibition to preach. The apostles were denying temple sovereignty by teaching in the temple area. The apostles named Jesus as savior, the cause of Israel's repentance and the one who would bring forgiveness. The Sanhedrin considered the disciples renegades from Judaism. The apostles implied that there would be divine retribution for the actions of the Sanhedrin. "The teaching they [the Sanhedrin] are trying to suppress is not only a word about Jesus but also a stinging word about themselves."[3]

This brings the story to a crisis point. The leadership wanted to kill the apostles. The Sanhedrin was angry over the apostles' defiance and jealous over their success with the people. The courage of the apostles against such a formidable group is impressive. They were imprisoned and miraculously escaped as they awaited arraignment.

Today's pericope is a speech that "demonstrates persistent speaking in the face of opposition. It is dramatically important that the apostles repeat what they have said in spite of threats from the powerful."[4] Apostles are compelled to follow God's command rather than that of the Sanhedrin. There is an implied imperative to the characters within the story and to the readers of the text that human beings are to obey God rather

---

[1] Third Sunday of Easter: "Entrance Antiphon," *The Sacramentary.*

[2] Third Sunday of Easter: "Opening Prayer," *The Sacramentary.*

[3] Robert C. Tannehill, *The Narrative Unity of Luke-Acts: A Literary Interpretation*, Vol. 2 (Minneapolis: Fortress Augsburg, 1990), 64-65.

[4] Ibid., 62.

than any human institution. There is to be boldness modeled after the boldness of the apostles. "The apostles set forth the principle that the individual conscience is more binding that any authority, civil or religious."[5]

Questions for mystagogical reflection: How is the reading from Acts pertinent to church and political life today? What is the challenge of this reading in the United States today? Is your church community open to the challenge? In your opinion, how would your church community respond in the face of similar opposition?

Responsorial Psalm
Psalm 30:2, 4, 5-6, 11-12, 13

Today's psalm is not a reference to resurrection. Belief in future resurrection did not show up until later in the Old Testament. The image of deliverance in this psalm is a reference to deliverance from earthly tribulation (most likely illness in this case). This psalm was appropriated liturgically and christologically by the early Christian community.

Second Reading
Revelation 5:11-14

Written to provide strength for those who were about to endure suffering and persecution, Revelation was a word of encouragement and faith building. It looked to the future day of glory when all tears would be wiped away in the heavenly kingdom. Today's reading describes the rich and lavish eschatological banquet. God's people are feasting with the slain Lamb (a direct reference to the fourth Servant Song of Isaiah) at the heavenly banquet table. Jesus is referred to as a sacrificial lamb primarily in the book of Revelation. However, it was probably a popular subject of early catechesis. Images of the Jewish Passover resound in this reading.

Early apocalyptic literature envisions a triumphant lamb crushing the head of the evil beast of sin. The fourth Servant Song of Isaiah depicts a lamb led to the slaughter for the sins of many. The Passover lamb is reminiscent of Passover in which Israel remembers and actualizes the liberation from slavery to freedom through the exodus.

---

[5]Patricia Datchuck Sanchez, *The Word We Celebrate* (Kansas City: Sheed and Ward, 1989), 301.

John describes the heavenly liturgy. Our earthly liturgy is patterned after the liturgy of heaven. The four living creatures and the elders represent participants in the liturgy of John's own time. The vision of the heavenly liturgy was offered as hope to those who might have to offer their lives as sacrifice for others.

Some question whether today's reading is a fragment of an early paschal liturgy. No matter what the origin, the eschatological liturgy of Revelation brings us to the liturgies of today. We celebrate the risen presence of Christ and we participate in his life, death, resurrection, ascension, and life in the Spirit until he comes again. We do this in every eucharistic liturgy in which we break the bread of the Paschal Lamb.

Questions for mystagogical reflection: Have you ever experienced the paschal nature of the liturgy? Have you ever experienced strength in the midst of suffering, struggle, or persecution in the communal worship of the eucharistic liturgy? What is the challenge of this reading for your community, for yourself?

Gospel
John 21:1-19

Jesus appears at the edge of the Sea of Galilee and instructs the disciples to lower their nets. He celebrates a meal with them and appoints Peter shepherd.

STEP 1
NAMING ONE'S EXPERIENCE

What were your first impressions? What was your first response? What grabbed your attention? How did you feel?

Each person names his or her initial impression. Statement should be brief. No reasons should be given at this time. All simply listen without agreeing or disagreeing.

STEP 2
UNDERSTANDING

In a brief statement, what do you think the readings are trying to convey?

Liturgical Context

The eucharistic theme of today's liturgy filters throughout the readings and the liturgy. Acts exhorts us to live the martyr's life. Eucharist strengthens us for the challenge. Revelation reminds us of the future banquet as we celebrate eucharistic presence in the here and now: "by these Easter mysteries bring us to the glory of the resurrection" (Prayer After Communion) and "may we look forward with hope to our resurrection" (Opening Prayer).

The shared eucharistic liturgy is the place where the community principally encounters the presence of the risen Lord. We celebrate in hope as we await the future day of fulfillment: "May the great joy you give us come to perfection in heaven" (Prayer Over the Gifts).

Through baptism Jesus asks us the same challenging questions he asked Peter. "Hear the prayers of this newborn people and strengthen your Church to answer your call. May we rise and come forth into the light of day to stand in your presence until eternity dawns" (Alternative Opening Prayer). We, like Peter, are marked with the sign of the cross. It is not for decorative ornamentation. Through the cross we commit to die for the gospel we profess. Peter lived and preached under the sign of the cross; he was also martyred under it. Easter is a premier time of witness and preaching. It is a time to confess our Easter faith in the risen, glorified Christ.

In the liturgy we remember and make present the saving death of the Lord. We participate in his death and we rise again with him to new life. Our lives are broken along with Jesus' broken body on the altar of sacrifice. Like the torn bread, we too allow our lives to be torn and broken for the faith we profess.

Questions for mystagogical reflection: How is our community professing the risen Lord in our midst? How are we expressing our paschal faith? In what ways are we called to die for the gospel we profess? Does our Easter life include witness to the saving deeds of God?

Gospel Exegesis

The facilitator gives input regarding what critical biblical scholarship has to say about this text. The input includes insights as to how people would have heard the gospel in Jesus' time.

This portion of John's gospel was believed to have been a later addition—an appendix. It was perhaps written by a member of the Johannine school. Some believe that this post-resurrection appearance is intimately connected with the big catch of fish in the Lukan narrative (Lk 5). "Some think that the story is a retrojection of an appearance story into the earthly life, but the current trend is to regard John 21 as a projection of the earthly miracle in a resurrection context."[6] The Johannine authors choose to use the "fish story" in the context of the post-resurrection period. They choose to see their missionary effort as a result of the risen presence and power of Christ. Only with Jesus' authorization and power will they be successful missionaries. On their own power they can do nothing.

Like other post-resurrection appearances in John's gospel, this one functions as a means to give further instructions to the disciples and to show that Jesus is alive. This appearance takes place in Galilee after Jesus' resurrection. The setting of the story hints at specific Johannine agenda. The disciples are together. This is what Jesus prayed for in John's gospel: "to be" community. So far, the disciples are simply to be in community. They have not yet been sent. In today's gospel they will "learn of their task to be Jesus' fishermen."[7]

The disciples fished all night and caught nothing. At daybreak Jesus stood on the shore and urged them to try again and this time their nets were overflowing. Peter, on hearing it was the Lord, jumped into the water to swim to the Lord. The rest of the apostles remained at their assigned tasks.

---

[6]Reginald H. Fuller, *Preaching the New Lectionary* (Collegeville: The Liturgical Press, 1974), 27.

[7]John C. Talbert, *Reading John* (New York: Crossroad, 1992), 258-259.

On shore there was a charcoal fire. Jesus broke bread and ate a meal of fish with them. The fishermen's net was bulging with 153 huge fish, and yet the net did not tear. This was Jesus' third appearance. He was recognized before because of his wounds. This time he was recognized because of the role he always assumed in his earthly ministry: that of nourisher of his people.[8] The focus was now on Jesus the Nourisher and on the disciples who followed Jesus' instructions.

There is fairly universal agreement among scholars that the 153 fish represent the "universal outreach of the church's fishing expedition in obedience to Jesus' command."[9] There are varying opinions regarding the significance of the number. The un-torn net represents the unity of the church. Even though the church is comprised of many different types of people, it is nevertheless united. The church is diverse, yet one.

The disciples arc to fish for all kinds of people who are to be included in the community. Through the symbol of fish and fishing the disciples are to move out beyond themselves and the Christian community to do their fishing.

John's gospel is a gospel of signs that points to deeper mysteries. The focus of this gospel is fish as sign of church; Peter, the shepherd, as sign of love; and meal as the sign of eucharist (when Jesus had fed the multitudes with fish and bread on the same seashore it was a sign of eucharist).

The next dialogue with Peter centers on his responsibility to care for those who are brought into the Christian community. The first part of the dialogue is intended to heal Peter of his three-fold denial at Jesus' trial. The denial took place in three stages, asserts Charles Talbert, and so his rehabilitation (reconciliation) also occurs in three stages. Jesus has the ultimate power to rehabilitate sinners. Where does his rehabilitation lead? To ministry. Peter, the impulsive and impetuous sinner, was forgiven and empowered to serve.

Today's gospel assigns the disciples with the task of evangelization and Peter with the role of pas-

---

[8] Ibid., 260.
[9] Ibid.

toral leadership. Jesus rehabilitated Peter and assigned him his role as shepherd. He then described Peter's death. Every good shepherd is willing to lay down his life for his sheep. Jesus asks Peter if he is willing to assume this responsibility. Was he, Peter, willing to follow Jesus to the cross? Was he willing to die a martyr's death? He was. Are we?

Proclaim the gospel again.

Sometimes we gain new insights when we hear the text after the interpretation has been given. Someone from the group proclaims the gospel a second time.

STEP 4
TESTING

Conversation with the Liturgy and the Scriptures

Test your original understanding in dialogue with the text.

(You might consider breaking into smaller groups.)

Were there any new insights? Was there anything you had not considered before? How does your original understanding of this story compare with what was just shared? How does this story speak to your life?

Participants share an experience from their lives that connects with the biblical interpretation just shared.

> *A woman in our initiation process experienced a great transformation as she encountered the risen Lord in the midst of the celebrating community. She was forced to put aside attitudes and a way of living that were exclusive and contrary to the gospel. In doing so, she knew that she would risk the alienation of her family. She took the risk and in the process found herself. She experienced tremendous alienation from her friends and family. But she gained a new family and a new life. She witnessed to her miraculous transformation in one of our Easter season Sunday liturgies.*

> *This woman was on the brink of suicide. She cried out to God. She picked up the phone and called a*

random number by way of dare and challenge to a God she no longer trusted. Yet God acted. The heroine of this story told the person on the other end of the line that she was suicidal and that she had no idea what she hoped to accomplish by the phone call. The woman on the other end assured her that perhaps God had led her to call. She assured her of God's love and invited her to come to a place where she could experience the reconciling love of God in the midst of an incredibly loving community. She invited her to come to our parish and inquire. Our heroine accepted the invitation. To this day we do not know who the woman on the phone was, but the fruit of her evangelization can be found in the witness of the transformed, beautiful life of this new Catholic.

Our heroine journeyed with our community for an extended period and, through the celebration of Christ's presence in the liturgy and in the community, she was empowered to turn her life around. Her metanoia included a major turn from attitudes that were destructive and evil. Before her transformation, she could not envision a heaven in which she would be sitting at the banquet table with members of a different race. The inclusivity intended in John's gospel was abhorrent to her. When she openly discarded her old ways, she knew she would be castigated by her family. She made the sacrifice and the people of God have all benefited. Her family did abandon her, but she turned her pain into energy and started helping and working with poor families. She taught our community what paschal faith means and what it implies. It is not a flowery pious ideal, but is borne out in the daily crosses and struggles of life.

All share their life experience.

What was the message of the various biblical authors to their respective communities? What was the primary message of the gospel and what are the implications for your community and for you today? Where are the images of creation, covenant, community, and exodus (death/resurrection) in today's readings and how do they impact your community? In what way is your community challenged? In what way have your previous understandings about this liturgy been stretched, challenged, or affirmed?

The gospel demands a response.

How would the challenges in today's readings play in your parish community? In what concrete way does this liturgy call your parish to action in the church, parish, neighborhood, or world? What are you or your community called to do in response? Name one concrete action you will take this week as a response to what has been learned and shared today.

DOCTRINAL ISSUES

What church truth/teaching/doctrinal issue could be drawn from the gospel for the Third Sunday of Easter?

Participants suggest possible doctrinal themes that flow from the readings.

Possible Doctrinal Themes

Death/resurrection/paschal mystery, mystery of church, cross, eucharist (symbols of water, oil, bread, wine) baptism, confirmation, Christian witness

Present the doctrinal material at this time.

1. The facilitator gives input on a particular doctrinal issue of his/her prior choosing. OR
2. The group chooses a doctrinal issue from the list they created. They read together from the Doctrinal Appendix.

(The doctrinal issues are found in the Doctrinal Appendix in the back of this workbook. If you are choosing an issue from this resource, please refer to it now.)

Reflection questions centered around the chosen doctrinal theme can be found at the end of each topic in the Doctrinal Appendix. The questions are based on the five-step reflection process. If you choose a topic not included in the Doctrinal Appendix, craft your own questions according to the same five-step process.

Following the reflection questions you will be reminded to return to chapter 7, "Preparing the Catechetical Session," to assist you in crafting your own session.

Closing Prayer

Deacon: Bow your heads and pray for God's blessing.
Priest: Through the resurrection of his Son,
God has redeemed you and made you his
    children.
May he bless you with joy.
    Response: Amen.

The Redeemer has given you lasting freedom.
May you inherit his everlasting life.
    Response: Amen.

By faith you rose with him in baptism.
May your lives be holy,
so that you will be united with him for ever.
    Response: Amen.

May almighty God bless you,
the Father, and the Son, and the Holy Spirit.
    Response: Amen.[10]

Selected Bibliography

Days of the Lord. Vol. 3. Collegeville: The Liturgical Press, 1993.
Fuller, Reginald H. *Preaching the New Lectionary.* Collegeville: The Liturgical Press, 1974.
Sanchez, Patricia Datchuck. *The Word We Celebrate.* Kansas City: Sheed and Ward, 1989.
Talbert, Charles C. *Reading John.* New York: Crossroad, 1992.

---

[10]Third Sunday of Easter: "Solemn Blessing or Prayer Over the People," *The Sacramentary.*

FOURTH SUNDAY OF EASTER

INTRODUCTORY RITES

Opening Song (or Entrance Antiphon)

The earth is full of the goodness of the Lord; by the word of the Lord the heavens were made, alleluia. (Ps 32:5-6)[1]

Opening Prayer

The facilitator of the session may lead the prayer. Others in the group may be asked to proclaim the readings.

Let us pray
[to God our helper in time of distress]

God and Father of our Lord Jesus Christ,
though your people walk in the valley of darkness,
no evil should they fear;
for they follow in faith the call of the shepherd
whom you have sent for their hope and strength.
Attune our minds to the sound of his voice,
lead our steps in the path he has shown,
that we may know the strength of his outstretched
    arm
and enjoy the light of your presence for ever.
We ask this in the name of Jesus the Lord.[2]

LITURGY OF THE WORD

Let us listen to God's word.

The readings are proclaimed.

First Reading
Acts 13:14, 43-52

The Acts of the Apostles relate the life of the apostolic community in the first years after the resurrection. The chronicle shows how the first community was impacted by the resurrection experience.

Paul's first missionary trip probably lasted about thirteen years. Paul and Barnabas were commissioned by the Antioch church to go forth with the Christian kerygma. They sailed to Cyprus, disembarked, crossed the island, and went north to modern-day Turkey, then to Antioch in Pisidia. There was a large Jewish settlement in Pisidia and Paul was invited to preach in their synagogue. They were well received and the following week they were invited to return. In an exaggerated fashion we are told that the entire city also attended. The attitude of some of the people shifted and the leaders became jealous and resentful.

This scene sets the stage for what would be repeated over and over again in Paul's missionary travels. Paul would preach in the synagogue, his message would be rejected by the Jews, the gentiles would respond, a new community would form, the community would be persecuted by the Jewish leadership, and Paul would leave for other fertile missionary territory.

The Christian mission was universal. However, the mission to the gentiles was to follow a prescribed order. The Christian kerygma was first to be proclaimed to the Jews based on a two-fold principle: Israel's election and God's promise to send the messiah. In previous speeches Paul stated that Jesus' resurrection was the fulfillment of the promise made to David. Paul's speech at Solomon's portico reminded the Jews that God intended that Israel be heir to the messianic covenant. God sent Jesus to Israel first in fulfillment of the promises made to her ancestors, even though the intention was universal from the beginning. Paul, in like manner, was compelled to proclaim his message in similar order: the Jews would be the first to hear the kerygma proclaimed. Only then would he move to the gentiles. "Paul's preaching reflects a view that characterizes Luke-Acts from its beginning, the view that Jesus is the Davidic Messiah who fulfills specific promises of God to the Jewish people."[3]

There is no guarantee that people will accept God's word, but it must go forward. People will ei-

---

[1]Fourth Sunday of Easter: "Entrance Antiphon," *The Sacramentary.*

[2]Fourth Sunday of Easter: "Opening Prayer," *The Sacramentary.*

[3]Robert C. Tannehill, *The Narrative Unity of Luke-Acts: A Literary Interpretation*, Vol. 2 (Minneapolis: Fortress Augsburg, 1990), 174.

ther reject it or accept it. Ministers of God's word must be diligent in proclaiming the word; the rest is up to God.

The Jews had a custom of shaking the dust from their feet when returning from pagan lands. It was a sign that they were purified from the contamination of foreign people and lands. Paul's and Barnabas's similar action against the Jews was a major affront. In essence they were calling the Jews pagans! There was no greater insult to a Jew of Paul's time.

Questions for mystagogical reflection: How is today's reading a challenge to your community? Would your community be apt to embrace Paul and Barnabas or would there be resistance? Explain. What is the challenge of this reading for you and your community?

Responsorial Psalm
Psalm 100:1-2, 3, 5

This psalm is a hymn of praise. It is a psalm in which Israel is called to gather and praise God and God's dominion. The first part of the psalm praises God because of the covenant with humanity and the second part praises him for his kindness to the human race.

Second Reading
Revelation 7:9, 14-17

Christ, who is risen, has been exalted, and appears in glory, is the primary theme of Revelation. After giving a word of encouragement to the seven churches, Christ reveals the turmoil that will take place in the great battle between good and evil at the end of time.

Today's reading is usually associated with the Feast of All Saints. Easter is also an appropriate time to celebrate the joy of martyrs who share Christ's glorification. They shared in Christ's passion through their martyrdom. Last week's second reading referred to the Paschal Lamb whose blood was slain. Similarly, today's apocalyptic foreshadows the shepherd who leads the martyrs to the springs of living water.

This is John's second vision in which there is a large gathering of people. In this vision, the number of people is too great to count. The first vision was in reference to Israel. This vision refers to

everyone—all nations. The palm fronds that are held by the assembled are a sign of victory.

The great trial referred to in this pericope is the tribulation that will come at the end of the age. During these latter days of tribulation God's faithful will experience persecution. The robes represent the interior, spiritual disposition of the individual. The soiled robes represent sin and the clean robes exemplify holiness. This cleanliness is associated with the sacrificial death of Jesus. Through Jesus' death and resurrection, the robes (interior life) are washed clean.

Baptism is the means through which the person is transformed, washed clean by the blood of the Lamb, and made holy. "The fundamental allusion here seems to be repentance, conversion, and baptism taken together as a transformation of the person."[4]

The image of the last tribulation or the trial is an exhortation to persevere in conversion and *metanoia*. Perseverance will give people the necessary means to endure and share in the salvation offered through Jesus' paschal mystery. Some of those who persevere will be called to martyrdom.

Questions for mystagogical reflection: In what way can this reading be appropriated for a contemporary Christian community? What are the implications for living the Christian kerygma? How can we possibly relate to Christian martyrdom? In what way does this reading challenge you or your community?

Gospel
John 10:27-30

Jesus, the Good Shepherd knows and cares for his sheep.

STEP 1
NAMING ONE'S EXPERIENCE

What were your first impressions? What was your first response? What grabbed your attention? How did you feel?

---

[4]Adela Yarbro Collins, "The Apocalypse (Revelation)," in *The New Jerome Biblical Commentary,* ed. Raymond E. Brown, S.S., Joseph A. Fitzmyer, S.J., Roland E. Murphy, O.Carm. (Englewood Cliffs: Prentice Hall, 1990), 1006.

STEP 2
UNDERSTANDING

In a brief statement, what do you think this gospel is trying to convey?

STEP 3
INPUT FROM VISION/STORY/TRADITION

Liturgical Context

Good Shepherd Sunday helps us focus our attention on our Shepherd, Jesus, and his sheep, the church. We ask for the strength to follow the Shepherd to the end and our glorification in Christ: "give us new strength from the courage of Christ our shepherd, and lead us to join the saints in heaven" (Opening Prayer). The shepherd motif is carried throughout the liturgy. It appears again in an adapted form in the Prayer After Communion: "Father, eternal shepherd, watch over the flock redeemed by the blood of Christ. . . ." Note that, in this instance, the title of "shepherd" is used in reference to the Father. At the end of today's gospel, Jesus strongly asserts that he and his Father are one. When Christ protects, it is with the power and protection of the Father because they are one. John asserts that there is "one flock, one shepherd."

We, who gather for eucharist, are in communion with one another. We are all a part of the same flock. We, the church, a sacrament of Christ,[5] have been redeemed by his blood. Revelation reminds us that we are in the process of transformation. We are to persevere in our response to God's redeeming work within us: "may the continuing work of our redeemer bring us eternal joy" (Prayer Over the Gifts).

The lamb in Revelation and the shepherd in John's gospel meld into one image for our reflection. "The function of the shepherd and the lamb merge into one for the purpose of giving hope to suffering people. Because Jesus was victorious in his death, by the sacrifice of his own body and blood, so will his faithful followers share in that ultimate victory over evil and death."[6]

The custom of focusing on the Good Shepherd during the Easter season is a very ancient practice. During the seventh century, the passage, "I am the good shepherd . . ." (Jn 10:14-16) was read on the Second Sunday of Easter. There is evidence that proclamation of the Good Shepherd scriptures dates as far back as Pope Gregory (590-603 C.E.), and perhaps even as far back as the fifth century with Pope Leo the Great (440-461 C.E.). Pope Leo intimately connected the sheep to the Good Shepherd as he proclaimed the reading on the Wednesday before Easter. What happened to the sheep, happened to the shepherd, and vice versa. Christ and his people shared a mutual life. When people enter the waters of baptism, die to the old self, and are born again to the new, true conversion and transformation take place and they are incorporated into Jesus' paschal mystery. "For these newly baptized creatures are filled and fed by their Shepherd—since to participate in Christ's body and blood is to become, in fact, what we consume (St. Leo)."[7]

Later in the patristic period, the image of Christ as the Good Shepherd was appropriated as an image to describe leadership in the church. Christ who nourished and safeguarded his flock became a metaphor for those who would shepherd the people in his church. The word *pastor* was derived from this image. Gregory the Great formulated a working pastoral theology. Gregory, like those before him, connected the shepherd to Christ's passion and cross. Gregory insisted that pastors must not please people at the expense of the truth; they must bear the pain of those they serve in self-sacrificing love.

---

[5]"By her relationship with Christ, the Church is a kind of sacrament or sign of intimate union with God, and of the unity of all mankind." (*Dogmatic Constitution on the Church [Lumen Gentium]*, #1).

[6]Carol Osiek, R.S.C.J. and Ronald D. Witherup, S.S. "Shepherd," in *The Collegeville Pastoral Dictionary of Biblical Theology*, ed. Carroll Stuhlmueller, C.P. (Collegeville: The Liturgical Press, 1996), 907-909.

[7]Nathan D. Mitchell, "Shepherd," in *The Collegeville Pastoral Dictionary of Biblical Theology*, ed. Carroll Stuhlmueller, C.P. (Collegeville: The Liturgical Press, 1996), 909-911.

The Second Vatican Council drew on the patristic formulations as it developed a theology of pastoral ministry.

> In the Constitution on the Church, no. 6, the Johannine images of flock and Shepherd are invoked to support the view that the Church is a communion born of Christ's sacrifice on the cross, enlivened by the Spirit, and nourished by the paschal sacraments. Similarly, the council's documents on the Bishop's Pastoral Office in the Church, nos. 2, 16, and on the Life and Ministry of Priests, no. 3, interpret ordained ministry by reference to Christ the shepherd, who freely surrendered his own life that others might live.[8]

Gospel Exegesis

The facilitator gives input regarding what critical biblical scholarship has to say about this text. The input includes insights as to how people would have heard the gospel in Jesus' time.

There are two shepherd motifs in John's gospel. The shepherd motif in this pericope is secondary to the primary shepherd figure a few verses earlier. In this pericope, John employed a familiar technique and returned to an earlier (shepherd) theme. The interpretation of the parable of the Good Shepherd centers around the image of gate and shepherd. This section is more concerned with the sheep. The sheep belong to the shepherd. They will not be snatched away, but will enjoy the reward of eternal life. The sheep presently live the rewards of eternal life as they follow and are in relationship with the shepherd. This is an example of realized eschatology—the sheep presently live the reality of their eternal life.

Even though this pericope is told in typical Johannine style, it nevertheless promotes and reflects the message of Jesus in the synoptic gospels. Those who listen and respond to the word of God will be counted among those who will be accepted by God at the last judgment.

The Good Shepherd piece is directly associated with the Jewish Feast of Dedication. This feast celebrates the temple rededication after it had been desecrated by Antiochus Epiphanes IV. The high priests of that time had been false shepherds who, through their self-serving behavior, contributed to the desecration. Contrasted with the high priests were the Maccabean martyrs. They gave their lives for God's flock, believing that they would inherit resurrection and eternal life. The Feast of Dedication celebrates the gathering of God's people into one flock. Thus, according to Charles Talbert, the three themes of the Dedication are 1. desecration and subsequent purification of the temple, and the corruption of the high priests; 2. the Maccabean martyrs who offered their lives for the flock; and 3. the gathering of God's people into a people—one flock.

The tenth chapter of John is thus set in the context of that Jewish observance. Jesus is seen as the hope and fulfillment of the Feast of Dedication. Much of John's gospel is an apologetic for developing a new form of Christian worship that would replace traditional Jewish ritual. In this passage, John gives credence to his Johannine community's secession from the Jewish Feast of Dedication. It was henceforth to be interpreted in light of the mystery of Christ.

This pericope also serves as a commentary to explain the figure of the Good Shepherd in the parable. The sheep respond to the Shepherd at God's initiative. All who accept the invitation and align themselves with Jesus will be protected and preserved by God.[9] God and Jesus are one. Thus, all sheep who listen to the voice of the Shepherd also listen to the voice of God. The sheep will not be forsaken, but will be protected by the divine power of God. The Good Shepherd knows his sheep and is willing to lay down his life for them. The sheep will not be forsaken or left unattended. There will always be providential care.

This image is intimately connected to Jesus' sacrifice of the cross. Jesus, who was in intimate relationship with his Father, was willing to share that intimacy with his disciples. He willingly laid down his life for his disciples (like the shepherd). The early Christian image of shepherd developed

---

[8]Ibid., 911.

[9]Charles H. Talbert, *Reading John* (New York: Crossroad, 1992), 169.

to such a point that a specific interpretation of Christ's death emerged. Jesus was no common martyr. Somehow, over time, Christians came to understand Jesus' death as being more than the result of a faith-filled prophetic life. They came to understand Jesus' death in relation to salvation. "It was a death freely accepted 'for the many' (i.e., for all), a sacrificial death so complete in its power and efficacy that it brought the long history of alienation between God and humans to a close."[10] Thus, Jesus not only was the Shepherd who was willing to lay down his life for his sheep, but he was the Lamb of God who actually took away their very sins.

Proclaim the gospel again.

Sometimes we gain new insights when we hear the text after the interpretation has been given. Someone from the group proclaims the gospel a second time.

STEP 4
TESTING

Conversation with the Liturgy and the Scriptures

Test your original understanding in dialogue with the text.

(You might consider breaking into smaller groups.)

Were there any new insights in these readings? Was there anything you had not considered before? How does your original understanding of this gospel compare with what was just shared? How does this story speak to your life?

Participants share an experience from their lives that connects with the biblical interpretation just shared.

I am reminded of the self-sacrificial shepherding my husband and his best friend offered to the homeless of our city. Night after night, they slept with them, fed them, and offered anyone who wanted it a new chance at life. There were few accolades. Few people were aware that they provided dinner, an early breakfast, and slept next to their homeless friends on a hard floor. Bob

and Dan then had to go to work after a night of little sleep. Last year they opened the shelter thirty-one nights, including Christmas Eve, Christmas night, and News Year's Eve and New Year's night.

They were shepherds to their disheveled flock. They laid down their lives for their friends and were willing to do it as often as was needed. A ministry emerged in which the homeless fellows called on Bob and Dan throughout the week for help with their various skirmishes and difficulties. Both men have served as advocates in court, and advocates to change unfair civil laws that impact their homeless friends in unjust ways. They helped a few get off the streets and find employment. They challenged and encouraged, but, above all, they treated them with unconditional acceptance and dignity. Bob and Dan are exceptional examples of shepherds.

We all are given opportunities every day to be shepherds in our families and in all the encounters of our lives. When we give the gift of time and presence to those who need our help, we share Christ's shepherd role. When we take up our cross and lay down our lives for others, we share the paschal life of Jesus.

All share their life experience.

What was John's intention in this gospel? What was the word for his community? How could it apply to our community today? Is there any evidence of the biblical themes of covenant, creation, community, and death and resurrection? If so, what are they and how do they connect with our lives? Do we still feel the same way about this text as we did when we began? Has our original understanding been stretched, challenged, or affirmed?

STEP 5
DECISION

The gospel demands a response.

How does this liturgy, the biblical exegesis, and the sharing challenge your community's attitudes, your attitudes? In what way does this gospel call

---

[10]Mitchell, "Shepherd," 911.

your parish to action in the church, parish, neighborhood, or world? Be concrete. Have you changed in any way as a result of this sharing? What are you/your community/your parish called to do in response? Name one concrete action you will take this week as a response to what you have learned and shared today.

DOCTRINAL ISSUES

What church truth/teaching/doctrinal issue could be drawn from the gospel for the Fourth Sunday of Easter?

Participants suggest possible doctrinal themes that flow from the readings.

Possible Doctrinal Themes

Death/resurrection/paschal mystery, baptism, confirmation, eucharist, martyrs, redemptive suffering, symbols: cross, water, oil, bread, assembly, white garment, light

Present the doctrinal material at this time.

1. The facilitator gives input on a particular doctrinal issue of his/her prior choosing. OR
2. The group chooses a doctrinal issue from the list they created. They read together from the Doctrinal Appendix.

(The doctrinal issues are found in the Doctrinal Appendix in the back of this workbook. If you are choosing an issue from this resource, please refer to it now.)

Reflection questions centered around the chosen doctrinal theme can be found at the end of each topic in the Doctrinal Appendix. The questions are based on the five-step reflection process. If you choose a topic not included in the Doctrinal Appendix, craft your own questions according to the same five-step process.

Following the reflection questions you will be reminded to return to chapter 7, "Preparing the Catechetical Session," to assist you in crafting your own session.

Closing Prayer

Let us pray.
Father, eternal shepherd,
watch over the flock redeemed by the blood of
    Christ
and lead us to the promised land.
Grant this through Christ our Lord.[11]

Selected Bibliography

Cassidy, Richard J. *John's Gospel in New Perspective.* Maryknoll, NY: Orbis Books, 1992.

Collins, Adela Yarbro. "The Apocalypse (Revelation)." In *The New Jerome Biblical Commentary.* Ed. Raymond E. Brown, S.S., Joseph A. Fitzmyer, S.J., Roland E. Murphy, O.Carm. Englewood Cliffs: Prentice Hall, 1990.

Days of the Lord, Vol. 3. Collegeville: The Liturgical Press, 1993.

Fuller, Reginald H. *Preaching the New Lectionary.* Collegeville: The Liturgical Press, 1974.

Mitchell, Nathan D. "Shepherd." In *The Collegeville Pastoral Dictionary of Biblical Theology.* Ed. Carroll Stuhlmueller, C.P. Collegeville: The Liturgical Press, 1996.

Osiek, Carol, R.S.C.J. and Ronald D. Witherup, S.S. "Shepherd." In *The Collegeville Pastoral Dictionary of Biblical Theology.* Ed. Carroll Stuhlmueller, C.P. Collegeville: The Liturgical Press, 1996.

Sanchez, Patricia Datchuck, *The Word We Celebrate,* Kansas City: Sheed and Ward, 1989.

Talbert, Charles H. *Reading John.* New York: Crossroad, 1992.

Tannehill, Robert C. *The Narrative Unity of Luke-Acts: A Literary Interpretation.* Vol. 2. Minneapolis: Fortress Augsburg, 1990.

---

[11]"Fourth Sunday of Easter: "Prayer After Communion," *The Sacramentary.*

FIFTH SUNDAY OF EASTER

INTRODUCTORY RITES

Opening Song (or Entrance Antiphon)

Sing to the Lord a new song, for he has done marvelous deeds; he has revealed to the nations his saving power, alleluia. (Ps 97: 1-2)[1]

Opening Prayer

The facilitator of the session may lead the prayer. Others in the group may be asked to proclaim the readings.

Let us pray...
[in the freedom of the sons of God]

   Pause for silent prayer.

Father of our Lord Jesus Christ,
you have revealed to the nations your saving
      power
and filled all ages with the words of a new song.
Hear the echo of this hymn.
Give us voice to sing your praise
throughout this season of joy.
We ask this through Christ our Lord.

LITURGY OF THE WORD

Let us listen to God's word.

The readings are proclaimed.

First Reading
Acts 14:21-27

Chapters 13 and 14 of Acts chronicle Paul's missionary activities. There is a recurrent theme. First, he preaches in the synagogues until he is rejected and then he turns to the gentiles. Second, he witnesses to the gentiles about the one, true God. Third, he endures persecution throughout his missionary travels, but he does not let that get in the way of his divinely appointed purpose. Fourth, he strengthens, consoles, and uplifts the newly formed Christian churches.

In today's reading, Paul and Barnabas are homeward bound from their first missionary journey. They revisit churches they have established earlier. The ordination scene in verse 23 functions as a reminder that the church was built on the foundation laid by the original apostles.[2] Even though Paul and Barnabas seem like super-human travelers (Luke makes it sound as if all the missionary escapades take place in a day or two), the first missionary journey probably lasted about three years. There were great distances to travel and the terrain was rough. Luke's intention is to show that Paul is on a par with Peter and the other apostles. He is able to perform the same signs as other apostles; he endures myriad persecutions, including stoning, with great resolve and endurance. Paul is an example of the Christian principle of growth through suffering and persecution.

There are three things happening in today's reading. First, Paul and Barnabas show pastoral care for the Christian churches by returning to them for further strengthening. Second, their agenda is to encourage the disciples to persevere in the faith. Even though the churches themselves have not yet experienced much oppression, Paul and Barnabas remind them that persecution is the necessary path of salvation. Jesus was the prime example. Jesus taught his followers about the necessity of his own suffering. "Because the oppressions are the required way to 'enter into' the reign of God, the formulation is especially close to Luke 24:26, where the Messiah's suffering is the required way for him to 'enter into his glory'...Jesus suffered in accordance with a pattern of prophetic destiny that applied not only to him but to other prophets before him. The same destiny of suffering applies to Paul and Barnabas, and in 14:22 they warn that it will apply to other Christians, too."[3]

---

[1]Fifth Sunday of Easter: "Entrance Antiphon," *The Sacramentary.*

[2]Reginald H. Fuller, *Preaching the New Lectionary* (Collegeville, The Liturgical Press, 1974), 29.

[3]Robert C. Tannehill, *The Narrative Unity of Luke-Acts: A Literary Interpretation*, Vol. 2 (Minneapolis: Fortress Augsburg, 1990), 181.

The third point of this passage is to stress that God was the initiator of Paul's and Barnabas's missionary work. God was the one who had "opened the doors of faith to the Gentiles."[4]

Questions for mystagogical reflection: What are the main themes you can draw from this reading that pertain to the Christian life? What does it tell us about the challenge of Christianity? Is there any connection you can make to your present-day life? Have you ever suffered any type of persecution because of your faith or because of acting in accord with the gospel? How does this reading exhort us to live the paschal mystery?

Responsorial Psalm
Psalm 145:8-9, 10-11, 12-13

This is a psalm of joy in which the psalmist praises the God of creation and salvation. Fulfillment of God's acts of creation and salvation history is accomplished through the saving events of Jesus Christ.

Second Reading
Revelation 21:1-5

Today's reading, one of the most beautiful in all of scripture, captures the eschatological hope of every human person. The seer's seventh in the last series of visions is concerned with redemption. The new heaven and new earth emerge because the old heaven and earth and sea are no more. In Revelation, the sea has mythic symbolic connotations, harkening back to Old Testament themes similar to the "waters that were no more because of the flood" (sin) and the abyss (chaos). Thus, the sea that is no more is a reference to the destruction of sin and chaos that will take place at the end of the world when the new and eternal Jerusalem is established. It symbolizes "the complete victory of creation over chaos, of life over death."[5]

John was exiled to the island of Patmos. Jerusalem had recently been destroyed. The restoration he speaks of in this pericope is not an earthly expectation. He understands it as an after-life expectation.

Thus, the new Jerusalem coming down from heaven is a symbol of humanity's hope for union with God in eternity. A voice then speaks from heaven's throne to interpret the vision. The voice does so by renewing promises made in the past (Lev 26:11-12; Ez 37:27; cf. 2 Cor 6:16). The wiping of tears and giving of water to the thirsty serve as metaphors to express the meaning of salvation; "the satisfaction of physical and emotional needs symbolizes fulfillment of the whole person."[6]

Reginald Fuller asserts that the "new things" spoken of in this passage are already realized in principle through the resurrection of Christ, "anticipated in the life of the Church."[7] Thus, the passage is an expression of realized eschatology. We are living in the reality of the promise as we await its final consummation at the end of the world. The ongoing reality is present to us through the sacramental presence of God in the word and in the sacraments. The sacraments hint at future joy; they give us a sneak preview, an appetizer. But the full banquet will occur only when the end comes.

Some tears are wiped away through the ministry of Christ in the church, but suffering is a reality that will not end until Christ comes again in final glory. Then *all* tears will be wiped away, once and for all.

Gospel
John 13:31-33, 34-35

Jesus teaches his apostles the new commandment of love.

Step 1
Naming One's Experience

What were your first impressions, your first response? What grabbed your attention? How did you feel?

Each person names his or her initial impression. Statement should be brief. No reasons should be given at this time. All simply listen without agreeing or disagreeing.

---

[4]Fuller, *Preaching the New Lectionary*, 31.

[5]Adela Yarbro Collins, "The Apocalypse (Revelation)," in *The New Jerome Biblical Commentary*, ed. Raymond E. Brown, S.S., Joseph A. Fitzmyer, S.J., Roland E. Murphy, O.Carm. (Englewood Cliffs: Prentice Hall, 1990), 1015.

[6]Collins, "The Apocalypse (Revelation)," 1006.
[7]Fuller, *Preaching the New Lectionary*, 30.

STEP 2
UNDERSTANDING

In a brief statement, what do you think this gospel is trying to convey?

STEP 3
INPUT FROM VISION/STORY/TRADITION

Liturgical Context

Today's liturgy has far reaching implications for the life of ministry within any parish. The readings are rooted in self-sacrificing love. All of our work is to flow from the example of Christ. We are to lay down our lives for one another. We are to persevere in promoting the gospel of Christ and we are to be agents of Christ's love to all of God's people.

The alternative opening prayer calls for the joy necessary to sing praise to Christ, in other words, to proclaim his mighty deeds to all people.

> Father of our Lord Jesus Christ,
> you have revealed to the nations your saving power
> and filled all ages with the words of a new song.
> Hear the echo of this hymn.
> Give us voice to sing your praise throughout this season of joy.

The great commandment of love permeates all that we do and all that we are. Love is the hallmark and the witness of our Christian faith. We talk love, and we live love; or, at least, we should. Perhaps we need to be renewed and strengthened in our understanding of love. What does Jesus mean by love? Love is not a suggestion in the Christian life; it is a command. A noted atheist once said, "as soon as I see Christians live this law of love they profess, then and only then will I believe in their Christ." While there are many fine examples of Christian love in the true sense of the word, the atheist's accusation reminds us that we cannot be complacent. The following is a summary of a talk given by Walter Burghardt, S.J., in Orlando, Florida, that outlines the biblical dimensions of love.

The Biblical Vision of Justice

Love is rooted in biblical justice. Biblical justice is fidelity to relationships. Before Vatican II, scripture was not the foundation of how we should treat God's people, particularly the less advantaged. Philosophical tradition informed our practice. It could be summed up with the question and answer: "What does the Lord require of you? Give to each what rights they have coming to them" (philosophical tradition). The biblical focus of love/justice is faithfulness to the demands of relationships, to responsibilities that stem from our covenant with God.

In the Old Testament, Israelites were united by bonds of family or covenant. God's love/justice was rooted in the way God acted. God acted as God should; God was always faithful to God's promise, thus God provided, God punished violations, God was always faithful. We are just when we are in right relationship with our God, with our brothers and sisters, and with the earth.

In the Genesis creation story, everything was in right relationship with everything else. The covenant with God was based on love. God welcomed the stranger, fed the hungry, gave a home to the alien, not because they deserved it, but because this is how God acted toward Israel. Deuteronomy insisted that the stranger was to be loved because God loved him or her first. Thus, the justice of God, fidelity to relationships and the expression of love were synonymous. Not to execute justice/love was not to worship God.

American Catholic thought suggests that Christianity is concerned only with the relationship of the soul to eternity. That attitude does violence to scripture. A stance of individuality does not revere God's word. God was incredibly imaginative; God did not envision isolated independent groups. God had in mind a people—the human family. Israel, the people of God, was a symbol of the proper ordering of relationships: love of God and love of one another and reverential care for the earth. We were told to subdue the earth—not to exploit it—but to subdue it. In Greek, *subdue* means reverential care.

The Second Vatican Council asserted that all men and women are to work for social unity. Solidarity must increase. Israel was considered a single family when God brought them out of bondage. Why did God deliver them? God delivered them because of the promise made to their ancestors. Before, they had not been a people—God made them a people. God liberated them and offered them the freedom to live in intimate covenant with their God, with all its inherent responsibilities.

The prophets taught that the law was not to be obeyed for the law's sake. The promise of the covenant was behind the law. God's people were to respond to God's love for them by living according to the demands of the law. The rights of the oppressed, the marginalized, and the lowly were expressed in the law. This, in itself, was a sign of God's covenant. Through God's concern for such people, God proclaimed to Israel: I reject those things that you think I want from you, such as sacrifices and burnt offerings. The prophets Micah and Hosea were constantly reminding the people that God did not like their sacrifices. God wanted steadfast love and justice—not sacrifices.

The New Testament's perspective of justice/love/ *hesed* is based on the ministry of Jesus. "The Spirit is upon me to preach good news to the poor." The downtrodden go away relieved. Christians were not to give people what they deserved; rather, they were to give because of the command of love. Loving one another, one's neighbor, is synonymous with loving God. The Christian is to assume the mind-set that says: I am my neighbor; my neighbor is an extension of myself. Jesus said: "Love as I have loved you" [today's gospel]. In the New Testament perspective, to love as Jesus loved is over and above the demands of human ethics. It is the kind of love that compels God's Son to totally give of himself for the bedeviled and the beleaguered.

Love places demands on the community. "If anyone is hungry, " demands Jesus in Matthew 25, then *feed them!* You, go help! John's gospel insists that if anyone is rich in worldly goods, but has a closed heart toward others, how can God's love abide in him or her? We cannot say to anyone: "I have no need of you." We are to be one with others as Christ is one with the Father.

Ethical justice demands that we give people what is their right. A Catholic in good standing has a right to the eucharist. All races, creeds, and nationalities have a right to equal protection under the law. Charity is another matter. Charity has to do with what cannot be demanded. Charity is beyond obligation. Charity begins with and is rooted in biblical justice. God loves us, not because we can demand it, or have a right to it. God gives to us out of love; not because we deserve it. This is charity. God does not have to do anything.

God's justice is tempered by God's mercy. In the parable of the prodigal son, the father does not give to the son because the son deserves it; rather, he gives out of love. He freely offers his mercy.

Biblical justice, then, is not based on what we deserve. We exercise biblical justice because that is what God wants us to do! Biblical justice and charity merge and demand that we love everyone.

Biblical justice impacts our teaching ministry in the church: what we teach and how we love. Ethical justice is a value, but it is not enough. People come to hear God's word, echoed from the past, alive in the present. It is enshrined in God's book. There is ethical justice throughout all of scripture. However, over and above ethical justice is the *law of love.* The Lord gave it to Moses centuries before Christ proclaimed it: the two great commandments, love of God and love of neighbor as well as self.

Justice is not equal treatment, but appropriate treatment. It is an attempt to equalize relationships between the *haves* and the *have nots.* Scripture exhorts the farmer to leave the droppings of the harvest in the field by not sending workers back to pick up the missed harvest. This is so that the poor workers may gather them up to feed their own families. It is not a call for abundance; it is a call for enough.

We must stress biblical justice in our ministry of evangelization. If we do not, there is little that separates us from the secular humanist or the pagan who performs good actions for the sake of doing them. The Christian response of love insists that we take care of the poor because of our covenant relationship with God, because God wants it. We do not take care of them simply because they are deserving as children of God (which they are), but because taking care of everyone is part of God's promise. We, too, are in the covenant. Thus, we are to help God's people because God would, and God would want us to do the same.

Preaching a just word is not simply one more category in scripture. Rather, it is the lens through which we are to see all of life. All homilies should have a component of justice and emphasize the relationship between God, people, and the earth.

Our spirituality links what we are on the inside with what we do on the outside. Thus, biblical justice is an important element in our spirituality. We are gradually shaped to Christ for the sake of others. If we are just in the biblical sense, we will love God with all our heart, soul, and strength. We will see each person as the crucified image of Christ. We will touch everything with reverence. ("The earth is the Lord's." All creation bears the trace of the God who gives life—all things are traces of God's divinity.) There is presently a contemporary crisis of communication. How are we to be an effective medium to preach God's word? God's concern is that we do it face to face: person-to-person communication.

Finally, justice stemming from our covenant says that if we live it, if we teach it, we are shaped to Christ. Then the church will be transformed. Thus, in your most precious apostolate,

> May God lead you,
> may God feed you,
> and may God speed you!

Gospel Exegesis

The facilitator gives input regarding what critical biblical scholarship has to say about this text. The input includes insights as to how people would have heard the gospel in Jesus' time.

Love is taken to new heights in John's gospel. The synoptics assert that love of neighbor fulfills the law. However, John takes love another step. Throughout the gospel John identifies God as the personification of love. Love becomes human through the Incarnation of Christ, especially through the self-giving sacrifice of his life. This example of love is to be shown by all Christians toward one another. Love comes to the Son from the Father. The Son loves the Father and this mutuality of love is showered upon the human race. There is no greater love than the gift of one's life. This, of course, finds its greatest expression in Jesus' death on the cross for the sins of the world.

In today's gospel, Jesus exhorts his followers to love one another according to the pattern of Jesus' love for us. "This love of Christ even unto death becomes model and means of love for one another, so that Christ can offer a 'new' command to love one another."[8]

In today's gospel, Judas is on his way to betray Jesus and Jesus proclaims that now the Son of Man *is* glorified. The present-tense verb is used to demonstrate that John's Jesus is in control and very certain of the events and the outcome that are to follow.

Before he goes, he must leave a legacy of love to those he leaves behind. He leaves a "new commandment." According to Charles Talbert, the content of Jesus' new commandment is: "Love one another as I have loved you." The purpose of the new commandment is: "in order that you also love one another." The consequence of the new commandment is so "all will know that you are my disciples."[9]

The Hebrew tradition as well as other religions all had foundational laws of love. So why was this new? According to the law of love as established in Leviticus 19:18, the Jews were to love one another as they loved themselves. However, the term *one another* was exclusively understood to mean their own countrymen. Jesus' understanding of *one another* was meant to include all people. The commandment of love was *new* because it was a command of the new covenant in Christ, in the new messianic era. In the old covenant God gave the law as a response to covenant love. Christ gave the new law for the same reason. It was new because it

---

[8] Anthony J. Tambasco, "Love," in *The Collegeville Pastoral Dictionary of Biblical Theology*, ed. Carroll Stuhlmueller, C.P. (Collegeville: The Liturgical Press, 1996), 570-571.

[9] Charles H. Talbert, *Reading John* (New York: Crossroad, 1992), 198-199.

was grounded in the pattern of Jesus' life, death, and resurrection. It is a love rooted in the offering of one's life for others. This is the heart of the paschal mystery.

The synoptic gospels move into the institution of the eucharist narrative at this point in the Christian story. John does not. John takes love to a new dimension. Drawing on the work of T. Maertens, Patricia Sanchez asserts: "Where the synoptic accounts featured at this point in their narratives the *eucharist*, the Johannine author has featured the mission of love. 'It is as if for him love was just as real a memorial of Christ as the eucharist itself.'"[10]

It was always understood that the messianic reign would be evidenced by *shalom* peace, or by *hesed*, unconditional biblical love and justice. John definitively explains what *hesed* is to look like in this eschatological era. All people are to be loved with a self-sacrificial love.

How does this correspond with our contemporary issues of racial and ethnic bigotry, political and religious divisions, and the disparity between the rich and the poor? John's gospel is a strong commentary to the church of any age regarding her response to people of every race, creed, color, ethnicity or nationality.

Proclaim the gospel again.

Sometimes we gain new insights when we hear the text after the interpretation is given. Someone from the group proclaims the gospel a second time.

STEP 4
TESTING

Conversation with the Liturgy and the Scriptures

Test your original understanding in dialogue with the text.

(You might consider breaking into smaller groups.)

---

[10]Patricia Datchuck Sanchez, *The Word We Celebrate* (Kansas City: Sheed and Ward, 1989), 307.

Were there any new insights? Was there anything you had not considered before? How does your original understanding of these readings compare with what was just shared? How does this story speak to your life?

Participants share an experience from their lives that connects with the biblical interpretation just shared.

> *I know a single woman who is raising young children. She sacrifices to send them to Catholic school and gives them great love and attention. She works very hard during the week to support her family and on two Saturdays a month she takes her children with her to volunteer in an abuse center for women and children. She is of cheerful countenance and loves the Lord deeply. I cannot come close to finding an experience in my own life of such self-sacrificing love. All else pales in comparison.*

All share their life experience.

What were the authors of today's readings trying to teach their communities? Is there a relevant word for your community today? Where is there evidence of the biblical themes of creation, covenant, community and death/resurrection/ exodus? What do they have to do with the life of your community? In what way does this liturgy challenge you or your community? Do you still feel the same way about this text as you did at the beginning? Has your original understanding been stretched, challenged, or affirmed?

STEP 5
DECISION

The gospel demands a response.

How can this liturgy, the exegesis, and your sharing challenge your community's attitudes? What are the practical implications? In what way does this gospel call your parish to action in the church, parish, neighborhood, or world? Be concrete. Has this conversation changed or stretched your personal attitudes? What are you or your community called to do in response? Name one concrete action you will take this week as a response to what you have learned and shared today.

DOCTRINAL ISSUES

What church truth/teaching/doctrinal issue could be drawn from the gospel for the Fifth Sunday of Easter?

Participants suggest possible doctrinal themes that flow from the readings.

Possible Doctrinal Themes

The two great commandments/law of love, paschal mystery/death/resurrection, mystery of the church, Christian witness, sacraments, baptism, confirmation, eucharist, penance, symbols: water, light, oil, bread, wine, cross, white garment, laying on of hands

Present the doctrinal material at this time.

1. The facilitator gives input on a particular doctrinal issue of his/her prior choosing. OR
2. The group chooses a doctrinal issue from the list they created. They read together from the Doctrinal Appendix.

(The doctrinal issues are found in the Doctrinal Appendix in the back of this workbook. If you are choosing an issue from this resource, please refer to it now.)

Reflection questions centered around the chosen doctrinal theme can be found at the end of each topic in the Doctrinal Appendix. The questions are based on the five-step reflection process. If you choose a topic not included in the Doctrinal Appendix, craft your own questions according to the same five-step process.

Following the reflection questions you will be reminded to return to chapter 7, "Preparing the Catechetical Session," to assist you in crafting your own session.

Closing Prayer

God our Father,
look upon us with love.
You redeem us and make us your children in
    Christ.

Give us true freedom
and bring us to the inheritance you promised.
We ask this through our Lord Jesus Christ, your
    Son,
who lives and reigns with you and the Holy Spirit,
one God, for ever and ever.[11]

Selected Bibliography

Collins, Adela Yarbro. "The Apocalypse (Revelation)." In *The New Jerome Biblical Commentary*. Ed. Raymond E. Brown, S.S., Joseph A. Fitzmyer, S.J., Roland E. Murphy, O.Carm. Englewood Cliffs: Prentice Hall, 1990.

Fuller, Reginald H. *Preaching the New Lectionary*. Collegeville: The Liturgical Press, 1974.

Karris, Robert J. *Invitation to Acts*. New York: Image Books, 1978.

Sanchez, Patricia Datchuck. *The Word We Celebrate*. Kansas City: Sheed and Ward, 1989.

Talbert, Charles H. *Reading John*. New York: Crossroad, 1992.

Tannehill, Robert C. *The Narrative Unity of Luke-Acts: A Literary Interpretation*, Vol. 2. Minneapolis: Fortress Augsburg, 1990.

Tambasco, Anthony J. "Love." In *The Collegeville Pastoral Dictionary of Biblical Theology*. Ed. Carroll Stuhlmueller, C.P. Collegeville: The Liturgical Press, 1996.

---

[11]Fifth Sunday of Easter: "Closing Prayer," *The Sacramentary*.

Sixth Sunday of Easter

INTRODUCTORY RITES

Opening Song (or Entrance Antiphon)

Speak out with a voice of joy; let it be heard to the ends of the earth: The Lord has set his people free, alleluia. (See Is 48:20)[1]

Opening Prayer

The facilitator of the session may lead the prayer. Others in the group may be asked to proclaim the readings.

Let us pray
[that we may practice in our lives
the faith we profess]

Pause for silent prayer

Ever-living God,
help us to celebrate our joy
in the resurrection of the Lord
and to express in our lives
the love we celebrate.
Grant this through our Lord Jesus Christ, your
    Son,
who lives and reigns with you and the Holy
    Spirit,
one God, for ever and ever.[2]

LITURGY OF THE WORD

Let us listen to God's word.

The readings are proclaimed.

First Reading
Acts 15:1-2, 22-29

Today's reading is a witness to the power of the Spirit at work in the community to bring about resolution to its problems. This is the last time the apostles will gather as a body. Peter will no longer be a prime figure in Acts as Paul will take center stage.

Today's reading definitively establishes the Christian understanding of salvation. It is a free gift; it cannot be earned and it is not for a select, elite few. Salvation is universally bestowed. The chosen and the unclean stand side by side at the same banquet table, recipients of the same lavish feast. When one considers the forces at play that would work against the uniting of two such diverse groups, it is no small miracle. And no small miracle it was, as indicated by the group when they asserted: "It is the decision of the Holy Spirit, and ours too." The early community encountered the risen Lord in the midst of attempts to build and unify the church.

The situation that prompted the Jerusalem council was the overzealous preaching of some Judaizers (Jewish Christians) who believed the way of Moses and the way of Christ to be the only path of salvation. They preached that gentile Christians should follow the Mosaic law and submit to circumcision. The Judaizers went to Antioch and taught the gentiles that unless they were circumcised they would not be saved. Their religious zeal was based on their own love of God and the law that had originally formed them. They truly believed they were teaching the will of God. However, it caused quite an uproar. A crisis of major proportions was in the making.

The Antioch Church sent none other than Paul and Barnabas to Jerusalem to plead on their behalf. It became apparent that there was an underlying fear driving the Jews' concern. The gentile population was growing. Gentiles were converting to Christianity in large numbers. Soon they would outnumber the Jews. There was a concern that the Jewish Christians would be pressured into giving up their deeply held religious traditions. They might have to withdraw and isolate themselves—or worse—turn against the law of Moses.

A compromise was worked out at the Jerusalem conclave. In the verses not cited in today's pericope, Paul, Peter, and James supported the gentile

---

[1]Sixth Sunday of Easter: "Entrance Antiphon," *The Sacramentary.*

[2]Sixth Sunday of Easter: "Opening Prayer," *The Sacramentary.*

mission. They cited all of God's accomplishments in the gentile community. Peter recalled the Cornelius event and its impact on the church. Paul related how he himself remained true to the law of Moses and how he had witnessed the incredible conversion, healing, and signs of faith among the gentile people. Rather than compromise, all agreed to act in charity. True collaboration occurred in this ancient conclave.

Permission was granted for the gentiles to continue to forego circumcision. However, gentiles were asked to abstain from "certain things especially offensive to a Jewish sense of cultic purity so that Jewish Christians may remain in the fellowship of the church without being forced to give up their way of life."[3] For example, animals used for sacrifice in the temple were cut up and the pieces not used in the ritual were sold in the public market. By avoiding such food, gentiles would thereby respect the Jewish conscience that would equate eating such foods with idolatry. As an act of charity to their Jewish brothers and sisters, the gentiles would abstain from similar offensive practices. "Charity will sometimes demand not compromises but a willingness to restrict one's freedom when its use, even if legitimate, might scandalize the weak."[4]

The Jerusalem gathering was an example of the Spirit of God working within the community. The Spirit does not make the decisions, but guides the church as it honestly grapples with the issues in charity and a spirit of mutuality. There were intense disagreements, but the church was able to come together in love to support a common decision for the good of all. Unity was restored; disaster was averted. The contemporary church has much to learn from this early council, its inner workings, and the outcome.

Questions for mystagogical reflection: How is this reading relevant to the situation in the church today? What do our communities have to learn from the example of our founding ancestors? How does this reading challenge you? Is there anything in your life that relates to the situation in this reading?

---

[3]Robert C. Tannehill, *The Narrative Unity of Luke-Acts: A Literary Interpretation,* Vol. 2 (Minneapolis: Fortress Augsburg, 1990), 191.

[4]*Days of the Lord,* Vol. 3 (Collegeville: The Liturgical Press, 1993), 194.

Responsorial Psalm
Psalm 67:1-2, 4-5, 7

This psalm is a blessing and a prayer in thanksgiving for the harvest. The obvious harvest being celebrated is the collaboration and subsequent unity of God's people in working out their tensions and crises.

Second Reading
Revelation 21:10-14, 22-23

The seer in today's vision envisions the new city as a future transcendent reality. The mention of the twelve tribes suggests that the city represents the gathering of a people. This image is reminiscent of church. The church, as God's people, shares a history with the people of Israel. The temple (even though destroyed) was generally understood as a symbolic reference to the close relationship between God and humanity. The fact that there is no temple in this vision means that it is God and God alone who continues the relationship face to face.[5] Thus, this new, future city is the place where God will be in intimate, face-to-face union with God's people. The work Christ began in the church through the work of his apostles and his followers in this earthly realm will continue in glory in the heavenly reign.

Reginald Fuller suggests that this future city is already established in principle through the resurrection and in the ongoing life of the church. God dwells with us in word and sacraments. We taste the appetizer of heaven's bounty. But the full banquet will not be realized until every tear is wiped away at the final eschatological banquet.

Questions for mystagogical reflection: Have you ever experienced the type of intimacy with God described in this vision? How is this a relevant word for your community today? What are the implications for the Christian life? What is the challenge inherent in this reading?

Gospel
John 14:23-29

Jesus promises to send the Paraclete.

---

[5]Adela Yarbro Collins, "The Apocalypse (Revelation)," in *The New Jerome Biblical Commentary,* ed. Raymond E. Brown, S.S., Joseph A. Fitzmyer, S.J., Roland E. Murphy, O.Carm. (Englewood Cliffs: Prentice Hall, 1990), 1015.

What were your first impressions? What was your first response? What grabbed your attention? How did you feel?

Each person names his or her initial impression. Statement should be brief. No reasons should be given at this time. All simply listen without agreeing or disagreeing.

STEP 2
UNDERSTANDING

In a brief statement, what do you think this gospel is trying to convey?

STEP 3
INPUT FROM VISION/STORY/TRADITION

Liturgical Context

In today's reading Jesus tells the disciples that he will send his Holy Spirit. The liturgy is the ongoing reality of that first Pentecost. Without the Spirit, there is no liturgy. The Spirit forms the church and things change—realities change. The Spirit transforms bread and wine into Body and Blood. The Spirit hovers over water and it is blessed; the Spirit ignites the fire, consecrates the oil, ordains the ministers, sacramentalizes marriages, wipes out sin, obliterates illness, and presides over death. Without the Spirit there is no liturgy.

Just as the Spirit generated Christ through the body of Mary, so did the Spirit generate the church. The fullest expression of the Spirit in the church takes place in the liturgy. "For the liturgy, 'making the work of our redemption a present actuality,' most of all in the divine sacrifice of the Eucharist, is the outstanding means whereby the faithful may express in their lives and manifest to others the mystery of Christ and the real nature of the true Church. It is of the essence of the Church to be both human and divine..." (*Constitution on the Sacred Liturgy*, #2).

Dominic Serra asserts: "The Power of the Spirit in liturgical prayer makes *anamnesis* both possible and fruitful. The Spirit is the harbinger of the eschaton, making present for us a foretaste of the banquet of God's reign. It is the Holy Spirit who brings about in the present moment of celebration both past events of salvation and the glory they promise for the future. This is true not only of the Eucharist, but of all liturgical prayer."[6]

Gospel Exegesis

The facilitator gives input regarding what critical biblical scholarship has to say about this text. The input includes insights as to how people would have heard the gospel in Jesus' time.

The author of John's gospel seems to know more of the rest of the story than do the synoptics. Jesus knows of his pre-existence; he knows that he must die in order to be exalted; he goes to his passion and death in full charge and control of his destiny. Today's gospel is the farewell discourse read every Easter season. Jesus consoles his disciples regarding his upcoming death by telling them that he will be with them through the presence of his Holy Spirit. The Spirit is the gift and presence of Jesus in his absence. Jesus informs his disciples about the life they will encounter after his death. He speaks of the incredible intimacy he shares with his Father and promises that same intimacy through his risen presence, his Holy Spirit. The Spirit was to be the ongoing memory of Christ. The Spirit would be the means through which the church would remember and call the actions and the words of Jesus into the present. The Spirit is the church's corporate memory that reminds us to conform our lives to the heart of Jesus' teaching and his life. The Spirit nudges and prompts growth in the church. Wherever there is change, the Spirit is not far from the scene. The Spirit invites courageous and bold solutions to the problems facing Christians in the world today.

John was intent on having his disciples look past Jesus' suffering and death to his resurrection and

---

[6]Dominic Serra, "Holy Spirit," in *The Collegeville Pastoral Dictionary of Biblical Theology*, ed. Carroll Stuhlmueller, C.P. (Collegeville: The Liturgical Press, 1996), 955.

his heavenly reign. In so doing, they would be able to look beyond the suffering of the present to see their own future participation in Jesus' glorious exaltation. The Paraclete would see them through the travail of this world until entrance into the next.

Yahweh entered a covenant with the human race. Peace was the hallmark of this covenant. To those who do not have the vision of faith, sin seems to have destroyed creation's original plan of peace and harmony. Peace was also to be the hallmark of the messianic reign. The return of *paradise* would be characterized by *shalom* peace; all things would be in harmony. The greeting of peace was an expression that recognized another person to be in covenant relationship with God and others.

Jesus was preparing for and foreshadowing the peace his death and resurrection would inaugurate. In today's pericope Jesus prepared his disciples for the gift of his Spirit whom he would send after his death. He would send the Paraclete, a reference to his Holy Spirit. The term, "another paraclete" was used in the Johannine tradition as Jesus was generally understood as the first paraclete. There is no mistake that John identifies Jesus and the Spirit as one.

Throughout the gospel Jesus promised he would be with his disciples after his death. It was also said that the Spirit would be with them. Things said about Jesus throughout the gospel were also said about the Spirit. Jesus and the Spirit are one and the same. The Spirit would continue the work of Jesus and continue to reveal Christ to the nations long after his death and glorification.

There were two things happening in the Johannine church that contributed to the understanding of the Paraclete. Jesus' return was not as imminent as was once believed. This caused confusion. Eyewitnesses to the Jesus event were no longer alive, thus making human authentication next to impossible. The Paraclete answered both problems. The Paraclete was the real presence of the risen Christ in the midst of the community. The community was experiencing realized eschatology. They were living in the reign of God in this realm as they awaited the next. Through the Paraclete, God's people would continue to encounter the presence of Christ. Through the Paraclete, the messianic reign is not only a future expectation, but is also the living reality of Christ's glorified presence in the *here and now.*

Proclaim the gospel again.

Sometimes we gain new insights when we hear the text after the interpretation has been given. Someone from the group proclaims the gospel a second time.

STEP 4
TESTING

Conversation with the Liturgy and the Scriptures

Test your original understanding in dialogue with the text.

(You might consider breaking into smaller groups.)

Were there any new insights in today's scriptures? Is there anything you had not considered before? How does your original understanding of this gospel compare with what we just shared? How does this story speak to your life?

Participants share an experience from their lives that connects with the biblical interpretation just shared.

> Today's liturgy relates the power of the Spirit in the life of Christian communities. The Spirit is the life force that forms our communities. The Spirit is the agent that keeps our communities in constant touch with the risen Christ. I am particularly touched by the first reading and the way this early community handled its diversity and its crisis. The Spirit was with this early community as they forged their life in Christ as a people. They did not walk away from controversy; they walked through it. The presence of the Spirit does not mean that there will not be controversy. The Spirit helps communities grow through diversity and controversy.
>
> A few years ago our community was embroiled in controversy. People felt very passionately about their various positions regarding an issue in our parish experience. After a considerable time, there was finally an effort to come together to promote reconciliation and unity between the two groups. It was not easy and the unity was hard won. It took a couple of years before all vestiges of hurt were completely gone.

On the positive side, we did eventually openly address the problem and attempt to reconcile and resolve it, rather than sweep it under the rug. On the negative side, we should have begun our efforts sooner than we did. St. Paul's efforts on behalf of the gentiles in today's first reading reminds me of what is possible when good people come together to resolve issues of community diversity. People in Paul's Jewish and gentile communities were willing to offer themselves in charity. That same generosity is possible in our communities today. The Spirit will strengthen us in our efforts if we trust enough to face controversy and diversity head on. It takes great courage and willingness to abandon our self-right- eous need to be right. The risen Christ is with our communities and desires that we all be one, as Christ is one with God.

All share their life experience.

What was today's message to the Johannine community? What does it have to do with our community and with me today? How does God continue his promise to be in covenant relationship with us in today's gospel? What do today's readings wish to create or re-create in us? In what way does today's liturgy call us to become transformed, to move from death to life (death/resurrection/exodus)? How is God speaking to us as a community? In what way is our community challenged? What is our collective and personal response to all of these questions? Do I/we still feel the same way about these texts as when we began? Has our original understanding been stretched, challenged, or affirmed?

STEP 5
DECISION

The gospel demands a response.

How does our sharing and this biblical interpretation challenge our community's attitudes? In what concrete way does this liturgy call our parish to action in the church, parish, neighborhood, or world? Has this conversation with the exegesis of the Sixth Sunday of Easter changed or stretched my personal attitudes? What am I /we/community/parish called to do in response? What is one concrete action I/we will take this week as a response to what was learned and shared today?

DOCTRINAL ISSUES

What church truth/teaching/doctrinal issue could be drawn from the gospel for the Sixth Sunday of Easter?

Participants suggest possible doctrinal themes that flow from the readings.

Possible Doctrinal Themes

Passion/death/resurrection/sending of Spirit— paschal mystery, Holy Spirit, mystery of the church, Trinity, sacraments, baptism, confirmation, eucharist, penance, anointing of the sick, symbols: cross, light, white garment, oil, water, laying on of hands, bread, wine, assembly

Present the doctrinal material at this time.

1. The facilitator gives input on a particular doctrinal issue of his/her prior choosing. OR
2. The group chooses a doctrinal issue from the list they created. They read together from the Doctrinal Appendix.

(The doctrinal issues are found in the Doctrinal Appendix in the back of this workbook. If you are choosing an issue from this resource, please refer to it now.)

Reflection questions centered around the chosen doctrinal theme can be found at the end of each topic in the Doctrinal Appendix. The questions are based on the five-step reflection process. If you choose a topic not included in the Doctrinal Appendix, craft your own questions according to the same five-step process.

Following the reflection questions you will be reminded to return to chapter 7, "Preparing the Catechetical Session," to assist you in crafting your own session.

Closing Prayer

Through the resurrection of his Son,
God has redeemed you and made you his
    children.
May he bless you with joy.
    Response: Amen.

The Redeemer has given you lasting freedom.
May you inherit his everlasting life.
    Response: Amen.

By faith you rose with him in baptism.
May your lives be holy,
so that you will be united with him for ever.
    Response: Amen.[7]

Selected Bibliography

Collins, Adela Yarbro. "The Apocalypse (Revelation)." In *The New Jerome Biblical Commentary.* Ed. Raymond E. Brown, S.S., Joseph A. Fitzmyer, S.J., Roland E. Murphy, O.Carm. Englewood Cliffs: Prentice Hall, 1990.

Days of the Lord. Vol. 3. Collegeville: The Liturgical Press, 1993.

Fuller, Reginald H. *Preaching the New Lectionary.* Collegeville: The Liturgical Press, 1974.

Serra, Dominic. "Holy Spirit." In *The Collegeville Pastoral Dictionary of Biblical Theology.* Ed. Carroll Stuhlmueller, C.P. Collegeville: The Liturgical Press, 1996.

Tannehill, Robert C. *The Narrative Unity of Luke-Acts: A Literary Interpretation,* Vol. 2. Minneapolis: Fortress Augsburg, 1990.

---

[7]Sixth Sunday of Easter: "Solemn Blessing," *The Sacramentary.*

ASCENSION

INTRODUCTORY RITES

Opening Song (or Entrance Antiphon)

Men of Galilee, why do you stand looking in the sky? The Lord will return, just as you have seen him ascend, alleluia. (Acts 1:11)[1]

Environment

The Easter environment continues. Perhaps an icon of the ascension may be added.

Opening Prayer

The facilitator of the session may lead the prayer. Others in the group may be asked to proclaim the readings.

Let us pray
[that the risen Christ
will lead us to eternal life]

> *Pause for silent prayer.*

God our Father,
make us joyful in the ascension of your Son Jesus
    Christ.
May we follow him into the new creation,
for his ascension is our glory and hope.
We ask this through our Lord Jesus Christ, your
    Son,
who lives and reigns with you and the Holy Spirit,
one God, for ever and ever.[2]

LITURGY OF THE WORD

Let us listen to God's word.

The readings are proclaimed.

First Reading
Acts 1:1-11

The narrative of Christ's ascension in the Acts of the Apostles is concerned with the mission of the church and the future coming of Christ. Both the end of Luke's gospel and the beginning of the Acts of the Apostles deal with the commissioning of new members to promote the new reign of God. The commissioning of the chief characters highlights the central purpose of the entire narrative, which is concerned with rooting the events of the story in the divine purpose of God and Jesus' command.[3]

In this pericope Jesus reminds his hearers that not only did he promise the Spirit, but so did his Father. John the Baptist also prophesied regarding the sending of the Spirit. Jesus thus relates the prophetic utterances of two prophets: himself and the Baptist.

The Pentecost event is foreshadowed in verses 4 and 5. Even though the power of the Spirit is poured out at Pentecost, these early verses attest that the Spirit's role is more than just one of extending power. The Spirit has something to do with the essence of God. The connection of the Spirit with the essence of God as Father suggests that the Spirit's presence is a powerful experience of God's grace.[4] Even though Pentecost is anticipated, there is a sense throughout Acts that the conferral of the Spirit is not just a one-time event, but is the active movement of the Spirit in the ongoing life of the church.

The forty-day resurrection period is a time to teach the disciples about the reign of God (v. 3) that finds complete fulfillment in Jesus Christ. The number forty is symbolic and represents a sufficient period of time to prepare those who witnessed the Easter event for the mission of the church. This pericope sets the stage for the entire missionary thrust of the volume. God's reign is synonymous with the reign of Christ.

There is concern in verse 6 over God's intention for the salvation of Israel. Where was Israel's place

---

[1]Ascension: "Entrance Antiphon," *The Sacramentary.*
[2]Ascension: "Opening Prayer," *The Sacramentary.*

[3]Robert C. Tannehill, *The Narrative Unity of Luke-Acts: A Literary Interpretation,* Vol. 2 (Minneapolis: Fortress Augsburg, 1990), 12.
[4]Ibid., 13.

in what God was doing in Christ? There is hope that Christ will deliver Israel, but there is also concern and question. Hope is not dead in spite of Israel's rejection of Jesus. Acts highlights the drama of a people turning away from the messianic fulfillment that was theirs for the taking. However, this rejection is still fraught with the future hope of restoration. All is not lost for Israel.

The evangelists are commissioned to further the mission of Christ and to go out to the ends of the earth with the Good News, again proving that God's mission is to the whole world.

The scene ends with the Galileans being chided for looking upward, when their gaze should be toward the missionary activities they have been commissioned to pursue. The chastisement of the angels is a call to action. Servants of the master are called to go out and gather in new members. They will one day be held accountable for their successes and failures.

The reader is made aware that the action of God throughout Acts is prompted by God's direction, not by human desires. Jesus' exalted reign has a future dimension. He will one day return as divine judge. Thus, the church waits in hope for the future day when Christ will return in his exalted state to judge and to bring the faithful home to share his heavenly reality.

Responsorial Psalm
Psalm 47:1-2, 5-8

This psalm is an enthronement psalm. It celebrates the hypothetical annual feast that enthroned an earthly king as a sign of Yahweh's reign over his people. The church appropriated this psalm to its celebration of the ascension of Christ. Jesus is enthroned in heaven with Yahweh, the supreme ruler over all creation.

Second Reading
Ephesians 1:17-23

Most scholars believe that the letter to the Ephesians was written by a devotee of Paul's. It begins with a hymn that is reminiscent of an ancient liturgy's opening prayer of thanksgiving. The first section of this reading is a prayer for the church to grow in wisdom and knowledge through the power of the risen and ascended Christ. Knowledge of God fills us with God's illumination. We can scarcely take in the brilliance of God's light within us. The rest of the pericope highlights the exalted, glorified Christ. Christ is Lord over his own faithful as well as over the world, which does not yet recognize him. We, like the small child who recognizes the voice of his or her parents, recognize the voice and the light of our heavenly Father. The missionary thrust of the church is to bring the world to knowledge of Christ and his saving works. It is up to the church, the Body of Christ, to help others recognize the voice and the light of God.

Gospel
Luke 24:46-53

Jesus withdraws from his disciples and ascends to heaven.

STEP 1
NAMING ONE'S EXPERIENCE

What were your first impressions? What was your first response? What grabbed your attention? How did you feel?

Each person names his or her initial impression. Statement should be brief. No reasons should be given at this time. All simply listen without agreeing or disagreeing.

STEP 2
UNDERSTANDING

In a brief statement, what do you think this gospel is trying to convey?

STEP 3
INPUT FROM VISION/STORY/TRADITION

Liturgical Context

"Let us remind ourselves once more that if we are to be true to the perspective of the New Testament and the early liturgy we should not think of the Ascension Day as a historical commemoration."[5] The ascension of Jesus is an integral piece of the resurrection. The feast of the Ascension is not the commemoration of the historical ascending of Jesus into heaven, but rather it celebrates the glorification of Christ as a result of the resurrection. Jesus rose from the dead on the third day. He went immediately to the Father. His post-resurrection appearances flowed from his heavenly, glorious existence. Even though Luke and John seem to posit the ascension and resurrection separately, they are not regarded as two successive events. They are regarded separately in order to appropriately contemplate the dimension of each reality. Luke places the ascension on Easter Sunday night or the next day. John places the event after the appearance to Mary Magdalene. The Acts of the Apostles places the event forty days after the resurrection. (However, "forty" is "symbolic of the time of revelation, and there may be no intention to suggest the ascension actually 'occurred' on the fortieth day."[6]) It is obvious in the post-resurrection Emmaus account that Jesus was understood to have come from his realm of glory before the final ascension.

The New Testament gives us three different narratives of the ascension of Christ that describe Jesus' final withdrawal of his physical presence from his disciples. The ascension is an expression of Jesus' risen state that celebrates his victory and points toward Pentecost and the second coming.[7]

The passion, death, resurrection, and ascension were always considered a single entity. This reality is the fullness of the paschal mystery. In the first Christian centuries, ascension was not celebrated as a separate feast. By the end of the fourth century, there is evidence of a separate feast. The Apostolic Constitution (380 C.E.) describes a celebration that took place forty days after Easter. The pilgrim Egeria (384 C.E.) reported a celebration of the ascension and the sending of the Spirit on the fiftieth day after Easter. St. John Chrysostom asserted that even though there were two separate celebrations (Pentecost and Ascension), they nevertheless were "two facets of the same reality."[8]

By 388 C.E., St. Gregory Nyssa preached a sermon on the feast of the Ascension that did not look toward Pentecost. The fifth century entertained a celebration of ascension forty days after Easter, followed by a fast, thus the term, "the great forty day pascha." As a result of these shifts, the celebration of Easter as a fifty-day feast diminished and was replaced by historicization of the Easter event.

The "General Norms for the Liturgical Year and the Calendar" (#7) restored a non-literal understanding to the feast, stressing the connection between the passion, resurrection, ascension, and sending of the Spirit. The feast is a solemnity and in places where it is not designated as a holy day of obligation, it is to be moved to the next Sunday. The feast still is celebrated forty days after Easter in order to give it the proper focus for contemplation. There is no intention of making an historical connection.

The ascension was understood as symbolizing Christ's exaltation as well as the exaltation of those who believe in Christ. One scholar refers to the ascension as a metaphor that reflects an ancient belief in the divine destiny of Jesus. The theology of ascension includes Jesus' relationship to his church, his supremacy over the created universe, the sending of his Holy Spirit, his role as revealer, his heavenly priesthood, and the expectation of his return.[9]

No human being dares presume the right to live in heaven's exalted glory. Only unique chosen ones such as Enoch and Elijah were "taken up" to God. By affirming that Jesus is exalted and sits at his Father's right hand, the New Testament asserts that Jesus' death and resurrection transported him to an entirely new mode of existence with God. The resurrection symbolizes Jesus' victory over death. The ascension symbolizes Jesus' divinely controlled destiny.

[5]Reginald H. Fuller, *Preaching the New Lectionary* (Collegeville: The Liturgical Press, 1974), 33.

[6]Ibid., 34.

[7]M. Dennis Hamm, S.J., "Ascension," in *The Collegeville Pastoral Dictionary of Biblical Theology*, ed. Carroll Stuhlmueller, C.P. (Collegeville: The Liturgical Press, 1996), 52.

[8]Edward Foley, O.F.M.Cap., "Ascension," in *The Collegeville Pastoral Dictionary of Biblical Theology*, ed. Carroll Stuhlmueller, C.P. (Collegeville: The Liturgical Press, 1996), 52.

[9]Lionel Swain, "Ascension of Christ," in *The New Dictionary of Theology*, ed. Joseph A. Komonchak, Mary Collins, Dermot A. Lane (Collegeville: The Liturgical Press, 1990), 63.

The ascension narratives explain why the post-resurrection appearances of the risen Christ ended. Jesus entered into a new kind of existence in heaven. Scripture understood heaven as symbolic of God's mysterious inaccessibility as well as God's abiding presence. In his absence, Jesus is profoundly present. Jesus, now with God, is present to the world as God is present to the world.

Jesus is understood as the Lord of the universe. The ascension reveals Jesus' status as Lord and Christ. Since he ascended into heaven, he demonstrated control over the created order of the universe. Thus, Jesus is its master.

Jesus' ascension served as prelude to the sending of his Spirit. In the Acts of the Apostles, Jesus was reported to have ascended the mountain (symbol of heaven) where he "poured out his Spirit." The Spirit would be the *One* who would continue the work of Christ's new Covenant.

Jesus, now in heaven, is able to reveal the things of God as well as exercise his role as intercessor and high priest (letter to the Hebrews). The ascension of Jesus guarantees that Jesus will return again. It is because Jesus ascended to his Father that he became the Son of Man who will accomplish the completion of God's ultimate plan of salvation for the world. Jesus' ascension reminds us that we will one day share his heavenly home. We are on a journey to our ultimate destiny.

The entrance antiphon of this liturgy emphasizes Jesus' return. The communion antiphon highlights his presence within the community: "Father, in this eucharist we touch the divine life you give to the world. Help us to follow Christ with love to eternal life where he is Lord for ever and ever." The opening prayer reminds us that Christ is indeed exalted and, as his followers, we share in his exaltation.

Gospel Exegesis

The facilitator gives input regarding what critical biblical scholarship has to say about this text. The input includes insights as to how people would have heard the gospel in Jesus' time.

The ascension heralds a new age: the age of the church. Luke ends his gospel with the account of the ascension and he begins his second volume, the Acts of the Apostles, where he left off in the gospel: with the ascension of Christ. The ascension is the springboard that catapults the mission of the church into front and center. Jesus had to ascend before the mission could go forward.

Reference to Jesus' suffering and rising from the dead on the third day is the fulfillment of all God accomplished through Jesus Christ, the messiah. Henceforth, Jesus expects people to witness to his power and his works. The apostles are reminders for all generations that faith must be nurtured or succumb to doubt. It took a lot of prodding, teaching, repetition, and constant reminders for the truth of Jesus' message to sink in. Thus, scripture and the sharing of faith are essential to keeping the mystery of our faith alive.

Luke paints a grand picture of the final scene of Jesus' departure. "The Mass of the world is about to begin, with the proclamation of the gospel to all nations and the gathering of the faithful around the resurrected one who nourishes them with his Body and Blood, giving them a share in his paschal mystery while they wait for him to come again and take them with him."[10]

Luke's version looks forward to the mission of the church and the sending of the Spirit who will empower the church for mission.[11]

Proclaim the gospel again.

Sometimes we gain new insights when we hear the text after the interpretation is given. Someone from the group proclaims the gospel a second time.

STEP 4
TESTING

Conversation with the Liturgy and the Scriptures

Test your original understanding in dialogue with the text.

(You might consider breaking into smaller groups.)

---

[10]*Days of the Lord*, Vol. 3 (Collegeville: The Liturgical Press, 1993), 223.
[11]Fuller, *Preaching the New Lectionary*, 35.

307

Were there any new insights? Was there anything you had not considered before in regard to the feast of the Ascension? How does your original understanding of this feast compare with what we just shared? How does this story speak to your life?

Participants share an experience from their lives that connects with the biblical interpretation just shared.

> *Abraham Heschel once said, "There are no proofs for the existence of God, there are only witnesses." Today's liturgy reminds us that thanks to those first witnesses who walked with Jesus and were able to pass on what they witnessed, we too are able to witness to the marvels of God in our lives.*

> *At a recent retreat, the participants began to create the expectation of God's action in their lives. We told one another to expect miracles, to expect God to act powerfully. The greatest experience of God's presence during the week was in the shared stories of our lives. We were awed by the way God had been present to each of us throughout our life experiences. Whether our story was one of an estranged marriage, troubled family relationships, parenting problems and disappointments, or problems of health or doubting faith, our shared pain gave us a sense of solidarity with all who suffer. Once we gave each other permission to break open the stories of our lives with one another, God was with us in our vulnerability. The Spirit of God was with us, prompting us, teaching and challenging us to new growth. We were all witnesses to the incredible power of God's love and action.*

> *The first witnesses of Jesus life, death, resurrection, and ascension were together in their fear and their doubts. They needed the reminder of the scriptures and Jesus' words and actions to keep them grounded in what God was doing. They were able to go out and witness because of what he had done in their midst and because they were able to connect it to God's greater plan of salvation.*

> *We did not stand with Jesus on the mount of his ascension, but we knew we shared its promise. As we shared our stories and connected them to the larger story we share in the gospel, we became more certain of our common destiny and our common hope. As we shared our joys, our struggles, and the incredible pain of our lives, we were able to unite our dying*

and rising to Jesus' own paschal mystery. The power of the Spirit was unleashed in our midst through the witness of God's action in our lives. Jesus gave permission for the church to witness to that same power.

All share their life experience.

What was Luke's primary message to his community in both Luke and Acts? What does he have to say to our community and to me today? How might God be creating or re-creating new life within us through the sharing of these scriptures (creation)? In what way does the ascension point to God's promise to be with us (covenant)? In what way have I/we experienced death/resurrection (exodus) in my/our experience and understanding of this liturgy? Do I/we still feel the same way about this text as we did when we began? Has our original understanding been stretched, challenged, or affirmed?

STEP 5
DECISION

The gospel demands a response.

In what concrete way does this liturgy call our parish to action in the church, parish, neighborhood, or world? What am I/we/our community/ our parish called to do in response? What is one concrete action we will take this week as a response to what we have learned and shared today?

DOCTRINAL ISSUES

What church truth/teaching/doctrinal issue could be drawn from the liturgy for the feast of the Ascension?

Participants suggest possible doctrinal themes that flow from the readings.

Possible Doctrinal Themes

Ascension, paschal mystery, christology, Trinity, Holy Spirit, Christian witness, sacraments, baptism, confirmation, eucharist, penance, orders, marriage, symbols: light, water, cross, oil, bread, wine, laying on of hands, white garment, assembly

Present the doctrinal material at this time.

1. The facilitator gives input on a particular doctrinal issue of his/her prior choosing. OR
2. The group chooses a doctrinal issue from the list they created. They read together from the Doctrinal Appendix.

(The doctrinal issues are found in the Doctrinal Appendix in the back of this workbook. If you are choosing an issue from this resource, please refer to it now.)

Reflection questions centered around the chosen doctrinal theme can be found at the end of each topic in the Doctrinal Appendix. The questions are based on the five-step reflection process. If you choose a topic not included in the Doctrinal Appendix, craft your own questions according to the same five-step process.

Following the reflection questions you will be reminded to return to chapter 7, "Preparing the Catechetical Session," to assist you in crafting your own session.

Closing Prayer

May almighty God bless you on this day
when his only Son ascended into heaven
to prepare a place for you.
    Response: Amen.

After his resurrection,
Christ was seen by his disciples.
When he appears as judge
may you be pleasing forever in his sight.
    Response: Amen.

You believe that Jesus has taken his seat in majesty
at the right hand of the Father.
May you have the joy of experiencing
that he is also with you to the end of time,
according to his promise.
    Response: Amen.[12]

---

[12]Ascension: "Solemn Blessing," *The Sacramentary.*

Selected Bibliography

Days of the Lord. Vol. 3. Collegeville: The Liturgical Press, 1993.

Foley, Edward, O.F.M.Cap., "Ascension." In *The Collegeville Pastoral Dictionary of Biblical Theology.* Ed. Carroll Stuhlmueller, C.P. Collegeville: The Liturgical Press, 1996.

Fuller, Reginald H. *Preaching the New Lectionary.* Collegeville: The Liturgical Press, 1974.

Hamm, Dennis, S.J. "Ascension." In *The Collegeville Pastoral Dictionary of Biblical Theology.* Ed. Carroll Stuhlmueller, C.P. Collegeville: The Liturgical Press, 1996.

Swain, Lionel. "Ascension of Christ." In *The New Dictionary of Theology.* Ed. Joseph A. Komonchak, Mary Collins, Dermot A. Lane. Collegeville: The Liturgical Press, 1990.

Tannehill, Robert C. *The Narrative Unity of Luke-Acts: A Literary Interpretation,* Vol. 2. Minneapolis: Fortress Augsburg, 1990.

SEVENTH SUNDAY OF EASTER

INTRODUCTORY RITES

Opening Song (or Entrance Antiphon)

Lord, hear my voice when I call to you. My heart has prompted me to seek your face; I seek it, Lord; do not hide from me, alleluia. (Ps 26:7-9) [1]

Opening Prayer

The facilitator of the session may lead the prayer. Others in the group may be asked to proclaim the readings.

Let us pray
[to our Father who has raised us to life in Christ]

    Pause for silent prayer.

Eternal Father,
reaching from end to end of the universe,
and ordering all things with your mighty arm:
for you, time is the unfolding of truth that already
    is,
the unveiling of beauty that is yet to be.
Your Son has saved us in history
by rising from the dead,
so that transcending time he might free us from
    death.
May his presence among us
lead to the vision of unlimited truth
and unfold the beauty of your love.
We ask this in the name of Jesus the Lord. [2]

LITURGY OF THE WORD

Let us listen to God's word.

The readings are proclaimed.

First Reading
Acts 7:55-60

---

[1] Seventh Sunday of Easter: "Entrance Antiphon," *The Sacramentary.*

[2] Seventh Sunday of Easter: "Alternative Opening Prayer," *The Sacramentary.*

Stephen's job was to minister to the daily needs of the Hellenist widows and orphans. Stephen, as one of the seven Hellenists appointed by the apostles, provided great missionary service to the early church. The seven shared the good news, healed the sick, and spread the message of Jesus to those in Samaria and Gaza. This did not help them win friends in the Jewish Sanhedrin. For their actions, Stephen won the distinction as the first martyr. Prior to this pericope, Stephen had given a speech defending himself against the charge of blasphemy. He also retold Israel's salvation history, including the ways that Israel had not been faithful to Yahweh. Stephen pointed out how Israel had rejected Moses and the prophets, and finally rejected Christ.

Stephen's death strongly parallels the death of Christ. Both men were innocently accused by bribed witnesses. Both martyrs were brought before the Jewish court for trial and both for the same trumped up charges: both were accused of speaking against the law and the temple. The Sanhedrin was self-righteously indignant in both cases. Jesus and Stephen were both taken out of the city to be executed. Jesus and Stephen forgave their murderers. Both men handed over their spirits upon their deaths. The story of Stephen's death is not simply a wonderful retelling of a significant moment in the history of the early church. It is an example of what it means to live the gospel, the paschal mystery of Jesus Christ. Christian witness and discipleship demand such sacrifice.

There was a piece of realized eschatology with the death of Stephen. Prior to Stephen's martyrdom, the persecution of Christ and his disciples was seen as the result of what simply happens to all of God's messengers. However, Stephen's death moved the church into a new awareness. Stephen's martyrdom was seen as an action of the Son of Man who has come to judge the good and the evil in the eschatological age. The Stephen event was understood as the judgment already in progress. Stephen's experience also moved the church to a deep appreciation of our participation in the paschal mystery. Christian discipleship and witness lead to the cross.

Stephen was given a vision of Christ standing at the Father's right hand. Jesus, standing as advocate and as intercessor, vindicated Stephen and showed him the future promise of his heavenly reward.

Stephen was accused of "attacking the foundations of Jewish life: temple and Torah, God and Moses."[3] Stephen witnessed to the crucified and glorified Christ, thus "completing the basic elements of Christological witness."[4] Stephen did not call for repentance and forgiveness as happened in other similar New Testament speeches. The audience was closed off from hearing or responding to such a call. Their hearts were angry and made of stone. However, in a later verse Stephen prayed for their repentance and asked God to save them.

Questions for mystagogical reflection: How are we called to give similar life-offering Christian witness? How is Stephen a model for our lives as community? What are we able to reasonably do about it? Are we prepared to speak as boldly as Stephen when confronted?

Responsorial Psalm
Psalm 97:1-2, 6-7, 9

This is another enthronement psalm. The liturgy appropriates such psalms for the celebration of Christ's exaltation at the ascension and in the process sees Christ as the one who reigns triumphant over the forces of evil.

Second Reading
Revelation 22:12-14, 16-17, 20

This reading has overtones reminiscent of Advent. There is a sense of waiting for Christ's second coming during the fifty days of Easter. Jesus reigns triumphant, yet hidden. Jesus comes to us in this earthly realm in the liturgy as we await his final coming.

There is an urgency in the cry of the early church. Their desire for Christ to come soon was born out of suffering and persecution. Very quickly they dis-

covered that soon "was not soon enough." They had to make adjustments in light of the fact that Jesus' return was not as imminent as once believed. They became diligent in their sense of alert watchfulness. They were prayerfully prepared for their master's return. In the midst of this careful preparation we are reminded that Christ invites us to come to the waters of life offered by the Bridegroom who loves his spouse, the church.

Gospel
John 17:20-26

Uttering his last prayer of thanks and praise to his Father preceding his passion and death, Jesus intercedes for his disciples who will remain on the earth to carry on his mission.

STEP 1
NAMING ONE'S EXPERIENCE

What were your first impressions, your first response? What grabbed your attention? How did you feel?

Each person names his or her initial impression. Statement should be brief. No reasons should be given at this time. All simply listen without agreeing or disagreeing.

STEP 2
UNDERSTANDING

In a brief statement, what do you think this gospel is trying to convey?

STEP 3
INPUT FROM VISION/STORY/TRADITION

Liturgical Context

The Seventh Sunday continues the theme of Ascension: the glorification and enthronement of the risen Christ. Luke offers us a glimpse of the perfect disciple: the martyr, Stephen.

Today's liturgy reminds us that we are all called to self-sacrificing discipleship. We are given the bold

---

[3]Robert C. Tannehill, *The Narrative Unity of Luke-Acts: A Literary Interpretation,* Vol. 2 (Minneapolis: Fortress Augsburg, 1990), 85.
  [4]Ibid., 86.

reminder that to be a follower of Christ we must be willing to die. Incorporation into the Body of Christ is also incorporation into the paschal mystery.

We are also reminded that Jesus prayed for and longed for the unity of his church. His last prayer for his disciples was that they all be one. Through their unity the world would be evangelized. This unity is possible through the power of the Holy Spirit. The Spirit is the tangible presence of Christ in the church who strengthens the church to work for the unity that Christ envisioned.

Gospel Exegesis

The facilitator gives input regarding what critical biblical scholarship has to say about this text. The input includes insights as to how people would have heard the gospel in Jesus' time.

Today's gospel asks and answers the question: "For whom does Jesus pray, for what does Jesus pray, and why does Jesus pray for it?" Jesus prays for those who would believe in him on the word of the disciples. He is praying that they may all be united with the same intimacy that Jesus knows with his Father. The reason for the prayer is to bring people to faith, so people will believe that the Father sent Jesus to the world. This gospel has a strong missionary thrust.

The Johannine community would be an evangelical community as long as it lived in radical reciprocal love. People would be drawn because of the love they witnessed. "It [the Johannine community] sought to draw people out of the world and into the messianic community, and it did this not only by its words but by *being* that community."[5]

The unity that Jesus desired for his disciples would be a result of the living presence of Christ through the Holy Spirit. "The glory which you have given me I have given them." Charles Talbert asserts that glory does not mean *honor*, but rather presence. Jesus gave the Spirit as his living, ongoing presence. When Jesus said, "I have given

them," he was not referring to a past event. Rather, says Talbert, the "perfect tense functions here much as a prophetic perfect in Hebrew; a future event is spoken of as past because of the certainty of its fulfillment...."[6]

Unity is an important theme in today's pericope. It is two-fold. Unity is based on the love and intimate relationship shared between Jesus and his Father. This intimacy flows to the church and is evidenced in the Christian community that loves as Jesus and the Father love. "Jesus brings disciples into relationship with the Father."[7] Unless and until Christians come into intimate union with God, they will not fully understand the reality of Jesus' relationship with God.

The Johannine community experienced division and discord, and this gospel perhaps had this in mind when speaking of unity. Raymond Brown asserts, "When I was discussing the relationship between the Johannine Christians and the Apostolic Christians, I pointed out that the prayer of Jesus, 'That they may be one' (17:21), expressed the desire of Johannine Christians for unity with Apostolic Christians, if the latter would accept the high, pre-existence christology of the Fourth Gospel."[8]

Pheme Perkins insists that this gospel is not suggesting some call to communal reform. It is not intended as a handbook for how Christians should act toward one another (i.e., in love). "Its object is not to challenge the world with some program of communal reform but with the gospel message about the relationship between Jesus and the Father."[9]

There are two purposes for the prayer of unity for believers. The first is evangelical; the second is so that the world will know that Jesus' disciples are beloved of God as Jesus is beloved of God. There is a futuristic element, an eschatology, to Jesus'

---

[5]David Rensberger, *Johannine Faith and Liberating Community* (Philadelphia: Westminster, 1988), 147-150.

[6]Charles H. Talbert, *Reading John* (New York: Crossroad, 1992), 229.

[7]Pheme Perkins, "The Gospel According to John," in *The New Jerome Biblical Commentary,* ed. Raymond E. Brown, S.S., Joseph A. Fitzmyer, S.J., Roland E. Murphy, O.Carm. (Englewood Cliffs: Prentice Hall, 1990), 979.

[8]Raymond E. Brown, *Community of the Beloved Disciple* (New York: Paulist Press, 1979), 157.

[9]Perkins, "The Gospel According to John," 979.

prayer of intercession. Jesus prays that his disciples will one day join him in heaven.

The conclusion of today's pericope summarizes Jesus' ministry and has Jesus recommit to its goal. Jesus revealed God to the world. The disciples believed in Jesus who was the revealer of his Father. For the disciples, Jesus is the divine presence of God in the world. Jesus promises to continue his mission to reveal God, to make his name known to the whole world, and to be present to the world through the Holy Spirit.

For the Johannine community, the church is understood in terms of flock, not a Greek assembly. It is a community assigned to the Shepherd. The community is chosen by Christ and is preserved by Christ. The community is made up of all who believe in Jesus and know his roots. The mission of the Johannine church is to evangelize Christ to the world. The Johannine community regarded unity as a priority. It was inclusive by nature and intent. Their holiness was based on reciprocal love of one another.

Like the other readings today, there is an eschatological tone to this pericope. Those who are faithful until the end, despite life's struggles and trials, will experience everlasting life in heaven. Jesus' prayer in today's gospel is reminiscent of that of the high priest who offers prayers on the Day of Atonement. He prays first for himself, then for the priests and Levites. Jesus, in similar spirit, prays for himself, but then prays for his disciples. Jesus stands before God and offers prayers to God for us.

Today's gospel is almost like Jesus' last will and testament. He spoke of his hopes for those followers he would be leaving behind. Jesus' desire for unity was less a call to membership and more a call to intimate, loving union with the Father. This love would extend to others as an unconditional expression of the believers' love of God and one another.

Jesus brings the role of the Holy Spirit front and center in his farewell discourses. He uses the term Paraclete to describe the Spirit. It is a juridical term and affords the reader or audience a glimpse into the support and strength that will be provided to disciples both present and future as they seek to further the mission of Christ. "Subsequently, in a particularly rich passage in which Jesus consoles the disciples regarding his departure, he also alludes to the Paraclete's role in 'convincing' or 'convicting,' the world and the ruler of the world (16:8-10). . . . the juridical role of the Spirit here is more akin to that of a prosecuting attorney." The disciples will not fail because they have the Holy Spirit to guide and strengthen them and because Christ overcame the world.[10]

Proclaim the gospel again.

Sometimes we gain new insights when we hear the text after the interpretation has been given. Someone from the group proclaims the gospel a second time.

STEP 4
TESTING

Conversation with the Liturgy and the Scriptures

Test your original understanding in dialogue with the text.

(You might consider breaking into smaller groups.)

Were there any new insights, anything you had not considered before? How does your original understanding of this gospel compare with what was just shared? How does this story speak to your life?

Participants share an experience from their lives that connects with the biblical interpretation just shared.

> *John's community struggled as every community struggles to discover what it means to live the gospel within the context of community. How are we called to love one another? What does it mean that we are beloved and chosen of God, that God has called us into intimate relationship with God and with each other? My husband and I are blessed to be part of a small Christian community within the larger community. We have often discerned the meaning of God's love for us and God's will for our lives. We have often reflected that we are "beloved and chosen." In*

---

[10]Richard J. Cassidy, *John's Gospel in New Perspective* (Maryknoll: Orbis Books, 1992), 61.

many of our life's major decisions, we support one another by offering mutual care and support. We remind one another that God loves each of us and will lead us and be with us in our life's journey.

One family in our group was called by God to leave the security of family and friends and make a major move across country. They were leaving behind close, intimate, loving friends who revealed God's love in unimaginable ways. Yet, they were called to leave their roots behind and venture forth to a new place. We have discovered that the bonds forged in our relationships have been maintained and nurtured even from afar. We have shared so much of our beloved and chosen status that we are forged forever in unity. We will always be intimately involved in one another's lives even though the miles separate us. This family has been gone for nearly two years. However, the intimacy is maintained over long distance and over time.

The love we have known is very much like the love God has for each of us. It is a comfort to know that God resides in such unconditional love. Intimate relationships, rooted in unconditional love, reflect our status as beloved and chosen children of God. Such relationships are priceless pearls and are worth investing in.

Our small Christian community has experienced pain and persecution together. We have experienced God's presence and action in the midst of very difficult times. Together we weathered a time of division, distrust, and animosity within our community. We stood firm in our belief that God would see us and our community through the difficult experience. Our trust was not misplaced. We've had many opportunities to witness to the greatness of God with others. As a group we have ministered to the homeless, shared communal meals, prayed, and—above all—we have been the presence of Christ to one another. People who know us are well aware of what we have shared together. Our bond is forged not only in love and shared pain, but in persevering through the difficulties of the Christian life.

We have not been asked to lay down our lives like Stephen, but we do know what it means to love one another. Whenever one of us has a need, the others are there to uphold and support. When two of our group were at death's door; when one in our group

experienced a family tragedy due to suicide; when one in our group experienced the near death of a teen and the tragic loss of that teen's best friend in a car accident; when others in our group were forced to leave all behind and venture out alone to a new place—everyone in the group lived the trials together. Through such love and support, God the Father, Son, and Spirit was made manifest in our lives.

All share their life experience.

What was John saying to his community and what might he be saying to our community today? What might God be creating in us through this experience of Jesus in the gospel (creation)? In what way does this gospel point to God's promise to be with us (covenant)? In what way have I/we experienced death/resurrection (exodus) in my/our experience and understanding of this gospel? How is God speaking to us as a community? In what way is our community challenged? What is our collective and personal response to all of these above questions? Do we still feel the same way about this text as we did when we began? Has our original understanding been stretched, challenged, or affirmed?

STEP 5
DECISION

The gospel demands a response.

In what concrete way does this gospel call our parish to action in the church, parish, neighborhood, or world? What am I/we/our community/ our parish called to do in response? What is one concrete action we will take this week as a response to what we have learned and shared today?

DOCTRINAL ISSUES

What church truth/teaching/doctrinal issue could be drawn from the gospel for the Seventh Sunday of Easter?

Participants suggest possible doctrinal themes that flow from the readings.

Possible Doctrinal Themes

Passion/death/resurrection/sending of the Spirit—paschal mystery, Holy Spirit, Jesus Christ, Father, Trinity, mystery of the church, martyrdom, Christian witness, sacraments, symbols of the church

Present the doctrinal material at this time.

1. The facilitator gives input on a particular doctrinal issue of his/her prior choosing. OR
2. The group chooses a doctrinal issue from the list they created. They read together from the Doctrinal Appendix.

(The doctrinal issues are found in the Doctrinal Appendix in the back of this workbook. If you are choosing an issue from this resource, please refer to it now.)

Reflection questions centered around the chosen doctrinal theme can be found at the end of each topic in the Doctrinal Appendix. The questions are based on the five-step reflection process. If you choose a topic not included in the Doctrinal Appendix, craft your own questions according to the same five-step process.

Following the reflection questions you will be reminded to return to chapter 7, "Preparing the Catechetical Session," to assist you in crafting your own session.

Closing Prayer

Through the resurrection of his Son,
God has redeemed you and made you his children.
May he bless you with joy.
  Response: Amen.

The Redeemer has given you lasting freedom.
May you inherit his everlasting life.
  Response: Amen.

By faith you rose with him in baptism.
May your lives be holy,
so that you will be united with him for ever.
  Response: Amen.[11]

---

[11]Seventh Sunday of Easter: "Solemn Blessing," *The Sacramentary.*

Selected Bibliography

Brown, Raymond E. *Community of the Beloved Disciple.* New York: Paulist Press, 1979.

Cassidy, Richard J. *John's Gospel in New Perspective.* Maryknoll: Orbis Books, 1992.

Days of the Lord. Vol. 3. Collegeville: The Liturgical Press, 1993.

Fuller, Reginald H. *Preaching the New Lectionary.* Collegeville: The Liturgical Press, 1974.

Perkins, Pheme, "The Gospel According to John." In *The New Jerome Biblical Commentary.* Ed. Raymond E. Brown, S.S., Joseph A. Fitzmyer, S.J., Roland E. Murphy, O.Carm. Englewood Cliffs: Prentice Hall, 1990.

Rensberger, David. *Johannine Faith and Liberating Community.* Philadelphia: Westminster, 1988.

Sanchez, Patricia Datchuck. *The Word We Celebrate.* Kansas City: Sheed and Ward, 1986.

Talbert, Charles H. *Reading John.* New York: Crossroad, 1992.

Tannehill, Robert C. *The Narrative Unity of Luke-Acts: A Literary Interpretation,* Vol. 2. Minneapolis: Fortress Augsburg, 1990.

PENTECOST SUNDAY

INTRODUCTORY RITES

Opening Song (or Entrance Antiphon)

Song: Veni Creator Spiritus

The Spirit of the Lord fills the whole world. It holds all things together and knows every word spoken by man, alleluia. (Wis 1:7)[1]

Environment

The feast of Pentecost has always been associated with the first gathering of the harvest. The fifty days of spring were an anxious time of waiting for the fruits to ripen. The Jewish feast of Pentecost, "The Feast of Weeks—Shavuot," was a time of gathering the grain harvest.

Strawberries, cherries, and apricots are associated with the feast as these are usually the first ripened fruits of summer. Easter pastels should turn to vibrant shades of reds. Since the liturgical color of Pentecost is red, the catechetical environment should be draped in abundant shades of red. One is hampered only by a limited imagination. The image of the dove, while not directly associated with Pentecost, is associated with the coming of the Spirit upon Christ at his baptism. Icons have used the image of a firebird with vibrant feathers as a symbol of Pentecost. The symbol of the phoenix rising up out of the ashes has been a traditional symbol of the resurrection. Perhaps one of these images might be incorporated into a Pentecost environment.

Opening Prayer

The facilitator of the session may lead the prayer. Others in the group may be asked to proclaim the readings.

Let us pray
[in the Spirit who dwells within us]

> *Pause for silent prayer.*

Father of light, from whom every good gift comes,
send your Spirit into our lives
with the power of a mighty wind
and by the flame of your wisdom
open the horizons of our minds.
Loosen our tongues to sing your praise
in words beyond the power of speech,
for without your Spirit
man could never raise his voice in words of peace
or announce the truth that Jesus is Lord,
who lives and reigns with you and the Holy Spirit,
one God, for ever and ever.[2]

LITURGY OF THE WORD

There are two liturgies of Pentecost: the vigil mass and the mass during the day. The vigil mass is not widely celebrated since the mass during the day is usually chosen for the Saturday evening liturgy prior to Pentecost Sunday. However, exegesis is provided for both the vigil and the mass during the day. Readings from both liturgies together form the fullness of truth inherent in the feast of Pentecost.[3]

Let us listen to God's word.

The readings are proclaimed.

READINGS FROM THE VIGIL OF PENTECOST

Vigil First Readings
Genesis 11:1-9, Tower of Babel, or
Exodus 19:3-8, 16-20, Giving of the law and the manifestation at Mount Sinai, or

---

[1]Pentecost Sunday: "Entrance Antiphon," *The Sacramentary.*

[2]Pentecost, Mass During the Day: "Alternative Opening Prayer," *The Sacramentary.*

[3]The second reading and the gospel for the vigil mass are always the same: Romans 8:22-27 and John 7:37-39. The first reading is chosen from among four possibilities: Genesis 11:1-9; Exodus 19:3-8, 16-20; Ezekiel 37:1-14; Joel 3:1-5.

Ezekiel 37:1-14, Ezekiel and his vision of the dry bones, or

Joel 3:1-5, prophecy about the outpouring of the Holy Spirit

The Tower of Babel

The author of Luke-Acts no doubt made a connection between the sending of the Spirit and the story of the Tower of Babel. At Babel the people were following their own whimsical designs. They wanted to establish a permanent settlement, achieve their own prestige. Their human designs were thwarted and they were dispersed as a people. They were in disarray and they no longer understood one another's language. Pentecost answers the tragedy of Babel. Pentecost gathers and unites God's dispersed people. The preaching in tongues at the Pentecost event was understood as the restoration of the human race. People were able to understand one another in their own languages. Unity was again possible. People would be able to understand the gospel in their own language. The ravages of sin had been broken through the power of the Spirit.

Manifestation at Sinai

In the manifestation of God at Mount Sinai, God was present and spoke in majesty, in mystery, and in great Cecil B. DeMille fashion, midst thunder, lightning, and clouds. God is both accessible and inaccessible. Sinai was connected to Pentecost in the symbolism of the tongues of fire and the rushing wind. God is still both present and absent; we are still in relationship as Creator and creature. Yet, Christ is the ongoing presence of God in the community of his new covenant.

Ezekiel's Dry Bones

Israel had sinned. They were dispersed. They saw their captivity as a result of their sin. All was lost. There was no hope. They could do nothing on their own power. Ezekiel rose up as prophet in their midst and offered encouragement in their desperate situation.

God, through his prophet, sends down the Holy Spirit (an epiclesis) and breathes new life into the dry, dead bones. The Spirit breathes new life and gives new hope. The dry bones of Ezekiel summarize the entire drama of salvation history. When we lose our way (as we have and we will), God has been and will be there to breathe new life into what is dead, lost, and forgotten. Pentecost is the restoration and ongoing life of that same Spirit in the life of the community.

Prophecy of Joel

Peter quotes Joel in his speech at Pentecost. Joel was referring to the outpouring of the Spirit upon Israel. Usually it was understood that the Spirit was poured down upon a charismatic leader, a prophet, or particularly the messiah. However, Joel's vision extended beyond that narrow understanding. It was inclusive of the entire community. The community was to be empowered by the Spirit and would know the law in their hearts. Knowing the law would give them knowledge of God. In the community of the messianic age, the Spirit would come upon not just the leaders, but the entire community.

Responsorial Psalm
Psalm 104:1-2, 24, 27-28, 29, 30, 35

This is a psalm in praise of the God of creation. The understanding of Spirit throughout the Wisdom tradition is that the Spirit of God participated in the creation of the world. The New Testament tradition centers on the work of the Spirit in the messianic age. In the Hebrew Scriptures, says Reginald Fuller, "'renewal' by the Spirit probably refers to the renewal of nature at springtime."[4] However, Christianity expanded the notion of renewal to mean the renewal of creation in the messianic age, beginning first with the church, the people of God.

Vigil Second Reading
Romans 8:22-27

Paul's letter to the Romans picks up the theme of the Spirit at work in the universe. It is not just the Christian community that is renewed by the Spirit; the entire cosmos is renewed. Paul is concerned about the bondage of sin that traps people and keeps them enslaved to sin. On their own power, people can do nothing. Paul knows this principle from personal experience. He understands that we are still in the flesh and, as long as we are, the

---

[4]Reginald H. Fuller, *Preaching the New Lectionary* (Collegeville: The Liturgical Press, 1976), 38.

battle will continue and we will not achieve our destiny.

However, in spite of our innermost groaning, we do have the Spirit of God to renew and lead us to this ultimate destiny. The Spirit will help us withstand the suffering in our lives and persevere courageously. The Spirit uplifts all creation as we strive to live in accord with the will of God.

Vigil Gospel

The Jewish feast of Booths was a feast of great rejoicing over the end of the harvest. During the feast, the people erected and spent seven days living in tents (*sukkoth*). Later, this celebration was combined with a memorial of certain aspects of the Passover. The priests would go to the pool of Siloam ("the one who has been sent"); they would draw water in a golden pitcher, ceremoniously process into the temple, and then pour out the water at the corner of the altar. The water was reminiscent of the water that Moses caused to spring up from the desert and the water of Ezekiel's vision that flowed from under the temple. These were purifying waters that watered the whole country and purified the waters of the Dead Sea. "I will sprinkle clean water upon you to cleanse you from all your impurities, and from all your idols I will cleanse you. I will give you a new heart and place a new spirit within you, taking from your bodies your stony hearts and giving you natural hearts. I will put my spirit within you and make you live by my statutes, careful to observe my decrees. You shall live in the land I gave your fathers; you shall be my people and I will be your God" (Ez 36:25-28).

The feast of Booths was a celebration of all the mighty things God has accomplished, the new "Exodus of joy and glory, the definitive purification of the people, the coming of the Messiah, the effusion of God's Spirit and its manifestation on the last day."[5] This was a great feast of rejoicing that ended on the eighth day. It was on this eighth day that Jesus pronounced what was in this gospel.

"Let any one who thirsts come to me and drink." It is Jesus who now offers the life-giving waters of

refreshment. All the hopes and dreams embodied in the great feast are now to be found in Jesus. The life-giving water was a sign of the Spirit who came in the sign of water at the Red Sea, the water from the rock in the desert, Ezekiel's spring, the water promised to the Samaritan woman by Jesus, and water flowing from the side of Christ. The Spirit is given at baptism and confirmation and continues to be poured out on the church as she gathers to offer perfect worship in spirit and truth in the sacred liturgy.

A constant theme in the farewell discourses is that Jesus suffered, died, and rose again in order to send his Spirit to those who believe. In John's gospel, the water and blood that poured from Jesus' side at the crucifixion was a sign of the coming of the Holy Spirit upon the church. Blood and water, then, became the symbolic sign of Christ's fulfilled promise to those who believe. The coming of the Spirit to the gathered twelve at Pentecost was the actual event: the conferral of the Holy Spirit upon the church.

READINGS FROM THE MASS DURING THE DAY ON PENTECOST SUNDAY

First Reading
Acts 2:1-11

The actual historical event of the sending of the Spirit is not what is at issue in today's readings. In this reading, the Spirit comes at Pentecost; in the gospel it happens on Easter Sunday. The *when* is not important. This appearance denotes the establishment of the church as larger than just the twelve. It is also the beginning of the church's mission: the Christian kerygma.

The Pentecost account is told in a way that reminds the reader of the giving of the law on Mount Sinai. The new *Twelve*, like the twelve tribes of Israel, gather together for the event. There is a sound from heaven that fills the *whole* house, just as there was a thunderous noise from God on Mount Sinai that shook the *whole* mountain. The fire of Pentecost is reminiscent of the fire at Sinai—both evoking the manifestation or theophany of God. The tongues of fire are symbolic of the presence of God that will manifest itself in human language, the "prophetic ministry

---

[5] *Days of the Lord*, Vol. 3 (Collegeville: The Liturgical Press, 1993), 265.

of the disciples (tongues)."[6] Jesus mediates God's word to his people. The Holy Spirit will empower God's people with a new evangelical strength. The apostles will go out and spread the word among the nations.

By naming all the places of origin of those present, the Acts of the Apostles is positing a very powerful eschatology. Pentecost is the fulfillment of the promises made to Israel. All are now living in the eschatological age. This is the final gathering of Israel. The gift of Pentecost is first intended for the Jews and then for all the nations on earth. As said earlier, this pericope is understood as an answer to Babel. The people of Babel, filled with self-importance and sin, are scattered in confusion. They do not understand one another. In contrast, this reading highlights the gathering of a people, who now, under the power of the Spirit, are able to communicate. Formed as a repentant and reconciled new community, they now are able to understand one another, each in their own native language—under God's initiative, not their own.

Questions for mystagogical reflection: Has your community ever had an experience in which the Spirit of God brought understanding out of confusion? How are you personally challenged by the reading from Acts? Does your baptismal commitment have anything to do with today's liturgy? What might be going on in the world, in the church, or in your life that is in need of the Spirit today?

Responsorial Psalm
(same as vigil)

Second Reading
1 Corinthians 12:3-7, 12-13

One of the effects of gnosticism on Paul's community was that they treated those who did not have all the special gifts of the Spirit as somehow *less than*. Glossalalia (speaking in tongues) was just one such instance. Those who did not speak in tongues were considered inferior. This caused division within the community.

Paul puts priorities in the right place. He definitively asserts that to be in the Spirit means one confesses Jesus as Lord. He is referring here to the earthly, crucified Lord. The gnostic Corinthians regarded the death of Jesus as a past, forgotten reality and were more interested in an ethereal, intangible Jesus. Paul grounds them in the reality of the cross.

All the gifts of the spirit are for the uplifting of the Body. One gift is not to be stressed over another. All are to be used with prudence and balance for the good of the community, not for self-edification. Through baptism, the church is one Body. Through eucharist, all are "to drink of the one Spirit." There is to be no divisiveness. All gifts are to be used for the common good, to uplift and nourish the entire Body. Reginald Fuller notes that this letter was possibly written for the paschal feast.

Questions for mystagogical reflection: How does this reading challenge our community today? Is there any evidence of using gifts for personal gain rather than for the common good? How are we personally challenged by this reading? What does this reading have to say about our status as baptized, fully initiated people in the Body of Christ?

Sequence

Come, Holy Spirit, and from heaven direct on man the rays of your light. Come, Father of the poor; come, giver of God's gifts; come, light of men's hearts.

Kindly Paraclete, in your gracious visits to man's soul, you bring relief and consolation. If it is weary with toil, you bring it ease; in the heat of temptation, your grace cools it; if sorrowful, your words console it.

Light most blessed, shine on the hearts of your faithful—even into their darkest corners; for without your aid man can do nothing good, and everything is sinful.

Wash clean the sinful soul, rain down your grace on the parched soul and heal the injured soul. Soften the hard heart, cherish and warm the ice-cold heart, and give direction to the wayward.

Give your seven holy gifts to your faithful, for their trust is in you. Give them reward for

---

[6]M. Dennis Hamm, S.J., "Pentecost-New Testament," in *The Collegeville Pastoral Dictionary of Biblical Theology*, ed. Carroll Stuhlmueller, C.P. (Collegeville: The Liturgical Press, 1996), 715.

their virtuous acts; give them a death that ensures salvation; give them unending bliss. Amen. Alleluia.[7]

Today and on Easter Sunday the sequence is sung. The sequence is a hymn that is sung after the second reading and before the gospel. The Alleluia is prefaced by the sequence. The Veni Creator was written by Stephen Langton, the Archbishop of Canterbury (d. 1228), says Joseph A. Jungman, S.J. All of the attributes of the Spirit's presence, such as light, comfort, consolation, guidance, healing, refreshment, forgiveness, warmth, and joy are poetically set forth in the sequence assigned to Pentecost Sunday. There are presently only four assigned sequences for the liturgy: Easter Sunday– *Victimae Paschali Laudes* ("Praises to the Paschal Victim"), Pentecost–*Veni Sancte Spiritus* ("Come, Holy Spirit"), Corpus Christi–*Lauda Sion* ("Praise Zion"), Feast of Our Lady of Sorrows–*Stabat Mater* ("The Mother Stood").

Gospel
John 20:19-23

Jesus passed through the locked doors, stood in the presence of his disciples, and offered his peace and the Holy Spirit.

STEP 1
NAMING ONE'S EXPERIENCE

What were your first impressions? What was your first response? What grabbed your attention? How did you feel?

Each person names his or her initial impression. Statement should be brief. No reasons should be given at this time. All simply listen without agreeing or disagreeing.

STEP 2
UNDERSTANDING

In a brief statement, what do you think this gospel is trying to convey?

---

[7]Pentecost Sunday: "Sequence," *The Lectionary.*

STEP 3
INPUT FROM VISION/STORY/TRADITION

Liturgical Context

Pentecost is the grand finale to the extended celebration of the Lord's resurrection that takes place during the seven weeks of Easter. It is known as the birthday of the church and it is the day the church celebrates the gift of the Holy Spirit. By the first century, the feast also had "an historical association with the law given on Mount Sinai as well as the covenant with Noah and Abraham."[8] Pentecost ushers in the new covenant, the Good News that was foretold by the prophets. Pentecost is the final manifestation of God that gave birth to the church. "It appears on the fiftieth day, when the Spirit was poured out on the first Christian community, giving it the strength and confidence to testify publicly to the resurrection."[9] The paschal celebration of redemption through Christ took place over the fifty days of Easter and was understood to include the "victorious passion and death, his resurrection and ascension, and the sending of the Spirit upon the Church."[10] Thus, Easter was not just a celebration of the resurrection of Christ, but it was an extension of his ministry through the Spirit to the Church: "...Pascha was a total celebration of our redemption...."[11]

When the Easter Vigil became the prime locus for initiation, Pentecost also was used as an occasion for the celebration of baptism. This is the source of the term "Whit Sunday," which referred to the white garments worn by the newly baptized neophytes.

Refer to the overview of the Easter season for further historical background regarding the feast. Its origins, briefly, lie in the connection to the Jewish feast of gathering in the grain harvest that was inaugurated at Passover. In later Jewish history, the feast was associated with Israel's salva-

---

[8]John F. Baldovin, S.J. "Pentecost," in *The New Dictionary of Theology*, ed. Joseph A. Komonchak, Mary Collins, Dermot A. Lane (Collegeville: The Liturgical Press, 1990), 755.
[9]*Days of the Lord*, Vol. 3, 293-294.
[10]Thomas J. Talley, *Origins of the Liturgical Year* (Collegeville: The Liturgical Press, 1986), 57.
[11]Ibid.

tion history including the giving of the law at Sinai and the forming of Israel into a people. The Christian appropriation of the feast included the gift of the Spirit in place of the grain harvest and the law. The forming of Israel as a people was adapted in the Christian understanding to refer to the forming of a people in the new covenant.

In the early church there was no sense that the celebration of the Easter season included three separate feasts within the season. Resurrection, Ascension, and Pentecost were considered one great joyful feast that celebrated Christ's victory over death. "The early community did not share the tendency of later periods to divide this fifty-day feast into three feasts, each with its own season. Until the end of the second century, notices about Christians celebrating Pentecost refer to their keeping of the Jewish agricultural festival (e.g., *Epistula Apostolorum* 17)."[12]

Tertullian is the first to give evidence of a Christian rendering of the feast. It is noted as a fifty-day period of festival and as a "feast day appropriate to baptism."[13] As the feast evolved and in places where it was celebrated on Sunday, the feast of Pentecost was counted from Easter day itself, thus making Pentecost the eighth Sunday after Easter Sunday.

Edward Foley maintains that it was Origen (254) who asserted: "If a man is able to say truthfully 'we are risen with Christ,' and also that 'he raised us up and made us sit with him in the heavenly places of Christ,' he is always living in the days of Pentecost... [and] he becomes worthy also of some share in the fiery tongue given by God" (*Contra Celsum*).

The first four centuries understood Ascension and Pentecost to be intimately connected: "Ascension is the triumphant completion of Christ's earthly ministry, with the missionary outpouring of the Holy Spirit as the unavoidable result. Thus they were celebrated on the same day."[14] This tradition comes from John 20 where the resurrection, the sending of the Spirit, and the end of Jesus' earthly mission all took place on the same day.

By the fourth century, the unitive dimension to the fifty days of Easter waned in the Roman church as Ascension and Pentecost were regarded as distinct festivals. Adolf Adam reminds us that the East always regarded Pentecost as the close of the Easter season. The Roman liturgy, on the other hand, "made this day an independent entity and thus a more or less isolated feast of the sending of the Holy Spirit."[15] Foley suggests that the reason for this might be due to the Council of Constantinople that occurred around the same time. The Council definitively asserted the divinity of the Holy Spirit. This shift may have resulted in taking a primarily christological feast and turning it into a feast celebrating the Holy Spirit.

Liturgical renewal restored Pentecost to its unity with Easter and reaffirmed the close connection between the Resurrection, Ascension and the sending of the Spirit. The "General Norms for the Liturgical Year and the Calendar" states: "The fifty days from Easter Sunday to Pentecost are celebrated in joyful exultation as one feast day, or better as one 'great Sunday'" (#22). Even though the unity was restored, there is nevertheless still a tendency to focus primarily on the Holy Spirit rather than on the Easter mystery. However, today's preface strongly adheres to the proper connection between Resurrection, Ascension, and Pentecost.

> Today you sent the Holy Spirit
> on those marked out to be your children
> by sharing the life of your only Son,
> and so you brought the paschal mystery to
>   its completion.
> Today we celebrate the great beginning of
>   your church
> when the Holy Spirit made known to all
>   peoples the one true God,
> and created from the many languages of
>   man
> one voice to profess one faith.
> The joy of the resurrection renews the
>   whole world,

---

[12]Edward Foley, O.F.M.Cap. "Pentecost-Pastoral Liturgical Tradition," in *The Collegeville Pastoral Dictionary of Biblical Theology*, ed. Carroll Stuhlmueller, C.P. (Collegeville: The Liturgical Press, 1996), 717.

[13]Ibid.

[14]Ibid.

---

[15]Adolf Adam, *The Liturgical Year*, trans. Matthew J. O'Connell (Collegeville: The Liturgical Press, 1990), 89-90.

while the choirs of heaven sing for ever to your glory. . . .[16]

Pentecost brings the great Fifty Days of Easter to a close. The paschal candle is removed and placed by the font and there is great rejoicing and merriment. Perhaps parishes might consider gathering in a place where the entire parish could assemble for one large annual liturgy that celebrates their identity as church.

Christian Initiation

This is, perhaps, a day in which those who were not baptized at the Easter Vigil could be baptized.

During the seven weeks of Easter, the newly baptized gathered with the assembly for the masses of the Easter season. They entered into mystagogical reflection on the mysteries of the Easter season and the sacraments. They were fed at the table, they took their place with the people of God at the banquet table, and they continued to ask their questions. Their questions flowed from their experience as fully initiated members of the Roman Catholic Church.

The Rite of Christian Initiation calls the seven weeks of Easter the period of mystagogia or post-baptismal catechesis. During the seven weeks, the neophytes engage in an intense time of post-baptismal reflection. It culminates today on the feast of Pentecost. Paragraph #249 of the RCIA suggests that "some sort of celebration should be held at the end of the Easter season near Pentecost Sunday; festivities keeping with local custom may accompany the occasion." The formation of the neophyte continues to take place in the midst of the celebrating assembly with monthly gatherings for the first full year following baptism at the vigil. At the end of the year, on the anniversary of their baptism, "the neophytes should be brought together in order to give thanks to God, to share with one another their spiritual experiences, and to renew their commitment."

Pentecost was inaugurated in the first Christian community, but its power is ongoing for all generations. Pentecost celebrates the perpetual gift of the Spirit to build the Body of Christ. Pentecost celebrates within the community that which takes place in the individual through baptism and eucharist. The Spirit who breathes transforming life into the church is given at baptism and continues to be manifest through the ongoing celebration of eucharist. It is the same Spirit who challenges, teaches, seals us permanently to Christ, and leads us forward in holiness to the new Jerusalem, the holy, eternal city. Pentecost celebrates the reign of God *now and not yet;* it is a present and future reality. The Spirit of Pentecost continues the work of Christ on earth as we are formed and prepared for the great day of his return. Pentecost is the ongoing renewal of our participation in Christ's new covenant. The liturgy of Pentecost calls us to worship in spirit and in truth. We are strengthened for mission to the world's poor, oppressed, and spiritually hungry.

Perhaps Pentecost is a day on which all those who have celebrated an initiation sacrament during the year, such as infants, neophytes, first communicants, those who were confirmed or received into full communion could gather to be a visible sign in the assembly. Perhaps all those mentioned might don their baptismal garments and gather in the midst of the community as a visible sign of Christ's resurrection and the new life of the church as we bring this season to a close.

Gospel Exegesis

The facilitator gives input regarding what critical biblical scholarship has to say about this text. The input includes insights as to how people would have heard the gospel in Jesus' time.

John uses the event of Jesus' appearance to his disciples in Jerusalem to demonstrate that Jesus was fulfilling his promise to return in the hour of his exaltation/glorification. In John's gospel, Jesus gives the Holy Spirit on Easter Sunday. Reginald Fuller suggests that perhaps all of Jesus' post-resurrection appearances were associated with the gift of the Holy Spirit. Today is the day that the church is empowered for mission. She is given the Spirit to live out the Christian story.

---

[16]Pentecost Sunday: "Preface," *The Sacramentary.*

322

The mission in today's story, however, has more to do with the forgiveness of sins. Catholic and high Anglican tradition traditionally associated this with the conferral of the sacrament of penance. However, in the New Testament understanding, the forgiveness of sin is always associated with baptism. It is not surprising that the command to forgive sins is associated with a missionary emphasis. Baptism was withheld for those who did not believe after hearing the Good News. Pentecost was a day for baptisms in the early church. It is fitting that this gospel's baptismal mandate be given on a day that was often devoted to the celebration of baptism.

Pheme Perkins suggests that since John uses "only the general expression, 'disciples,' the commissioning in these verses may be intended to apply to the believing community as a whole, not to some specific group within that community such as the 'Twelve.' This 'power' of forgiveness is probably expressed in the bestowing of the Spirit on those who believe as a result of the disciples' 'mission' and who join the community, rather than in a process of dealing with Christians who have committed sins (as in Mt 18:19)."[17] Jesus insists that this is possible because of the gift of the Spirit. If people forgive each others' sins, then there will be no "obstacles to community oneness. If they continue to hold on to the sins against them . . . the sins remain as obstacles to community harmony."[18] The Holy Spirit, thus, is not only given to empower them for mission, but to enable them to live in harmony with one another. Jesus gives the Spirit to fulfill the promise that all would be one in him. This oneness is accomplished through the forgiving of one another. The sins that are to be forgiven are post-baptismal sins of Christians committed against one another. Many though we are, through the power of the Holy Spirit we are called to be one in Christ.

John posits this event on Easter Sunday as a foundational document. Through it he hopes to remind his progressive community that the Christian life is lived only through the cross and resurrection of Christ. John believes that it is essential to identify the Christ who appeared after Easter as the earthly one who suffered and who promised to return. Today's gospel is a reminder that Jesus' journey to Jerusalem took him eventually to Golgotha before the subsequent resurrection of Easter morn. We, too, are to walk the same journey to Jerusalem, strengthened and supported by the risen presence of Christ in the Holy Spirit.

Proclaim the gospel again.

Sometimes we gain new insights when we hear the text after the interpretation has been given. Someone from the group proclaims the gospel a second time.

STEP 4
TESTING

Conversation with the Liturgy and the Scriptures

Test your original understanding in dialogue with the text.

(You might consider breaking into smaller groups.)

Were there any new insights? Was there anything you had not considered before? How does your original understanding of this story compare with what was just shared? How does this story speak to your life?

Participants share an experience from their lives that connects with the biblical interpretation just shared.

> *There are so many things going on in today's liturgy. There is celebration of the many gifts, though one Body. There is celebration of being in community, of being church, the people of God. There is a call to mission and to forgiveness. There is a singleness of purpose in those who were empowered to understand the word of God though they each spoke a different language. There is the ultimate celebration of Christ's passion, death, resurrection, ascension, and the sending of the Spirit culminating in the Pentecost event. One experience does not quite express the many dimensions of this liturgy.*

---

[17]Pheme Perkins, "The Gospel According to John," in *The New Jerome Biblical Commentary,* ed. Raymond E. Brown, S.S., Joseph A. Fitzmyer, S.J., Roland E. Murphy, O.Carm. (Englewood Cliffs: Prentice Hall, 1990), 984.

[18]Charles H. Talbert, *Reading John* (New York: Crossroad, 1992), 255.

I am reminded of the power of the Spirit at work in a community that suffered terribly over the death and destruction caused by the explosion of the space shuttle Challenger so many years ago. The Space Center is the number-one employer in our area. Our schoolchildren watched as the shuttle their parents had worked on blew up before their eyes. In addition to the loss of lives of those on board, the event caused great suffering in the lives of many. Lots of folks lost their jobs. Our school lost a third of its population immediately due to transfers and loss of jobs. Our community strongly felt the impact. There was great depression and desolation over the tragedy. Those who remained working did so under very stressful circumstances.

This time of intense suffering in our community bound us together. It was several years before the shuttle would be allowed to fly again. Many jobs depended on its success. The day of the first launch was approaching. Finally it was time for the launch. We celebrated an outdoor liturgy in prayer for a safe launch. Parents who could join their children in the school parking lot to view the launch did so. Many people in our community gathered together to look to the skies for our long-awaited resurrection after so much devastation. Future hopes were riding on the shuttle. We gathered for this moment of reckoning as one community that had shared a common disaster and pain. Those of us who were not directly affected were touched by the tension and worries of those who were. As the shuttle lifted off successfully, cheers, loud prayers, and vocal sobs broke out on the playground. There were people huddled in embraces and people on their knees in prayers of thanks. We looked to the heavens for the mighty evidence of God's awesome power. That day was an Easter event for our community. We had been sustained through the difficult interim years by the power of the Spirit. The community was bound together in a common concern. Prayer and thanksgiving were the order of the day before and after the launch. Lives would be maintained, futures secured. Balloons lifted into the skies, celebration was everywhere. Joy echoed amidst the deafening explosion of the propellant that lifted the shuttle bird carrying its special cargo of the hopes of so many people. We were a community that shared a common joy. Our witness extended to the wider world as the TV crews were there to televise our prayers and experience our joy. Every interview expressed hope in our God who promised to sustain us through the power of the Spirit.

One other event that comes to mind on this day of church is that of a difficult time in our communal history. There was an event that caused serious division. Factions were formed and those involved on both sides stuck to their strongly held, self-righteous positions. After much pain, prayer, time, and eventual forgiveness, we experienced a paschal dying and rising. It was only through the power of the Holy Spirit that we are able to stand together so many years later and still call one another brother and sister. Forgiveness and healing took time, but they were accomplished. The experience was more than anything a growth experience. Rather than have the feelings go underground and end in despair and resentment, most folks were able to forgive and heal. We were thus able to stand united and corporately bonded at the eucharistic table.

Evidence of this strong Spirit-filled community can be found in the multitudes of ministries that are performed each day by the community and by individuals within the community. It would take volumes to include them all (from building a school in Haiti to ministry to the sick).

One of the strongest challenges for any community and for our community can be found in the second reading from the mass of the day. No one person's gift is valued over another's. There are to be no marginalized members of our communities. Each person is gifted by baptism and has something to contribute. If we could remember that one thing, our communal living would be so much easier and less fraught with the temptation of self-righteous self-importance.

All share their life experience.

What was John's intention in his telling of this event in the post-resurrection appearance of Jesus? What might the Spirit be creating or re-creating in us through this liturgy (creation)? In what way does this liturgy point to God's promise to be with us (covenant)? In what way does this gospel invite us to die and rise (exodus)? How does this liturgy speak to our community? In what way is our community challenged? Do we still feel the same way about these scriptures and this feast as we did when we began? Has our original understanding been stretched, challenged, or affirmed?

STEP 5
DECISION

The gospel demands a response.

What are the contemporary implications of the scriptures in today's liturgy? In what concrete way does this gospel call our parish to action in the church, parish, neighborhood, or world? Has our conversation with these scriptures and this liturgy changed or stretched my/our personal attitudes? What am I/we/our community/our parish called to do in response? What is one concrete action we will take this week as a response to what we have learned and shared today?

DOCTRINAL ISSUES

What church truth/teaching/doctrinal issue could be drawn from the gospel for the feast of Pentecost?

Participants suggest possible doctrinal themes that flow from the readings.

Possible Doctrinal Themes

Mystery of the church, resurrection/ascension/ Pentecost, paschal mystery, ministry in the church, sacraments, symbols of the church, evangelization

Present the doctrinal material at this time.

1. The facilitator gives input on a particular doctrinal issue of his/her prior choosing. OR
2. The group chooses a doctrinal issue from the list they created. They read together from the Doctrinal Appendix.

(The doctrinal issues are found in the Doctrinal Appendix in the back of this workbook. If you are choosing an issue from this resource, please refer to it now.)

Reflection questions centered around the chosen doctrinal theme can be found at the end of each topic in the Doctrinal Appendix. The questions are based on the five-step reflection process. If you choose a topic not included in the Doctrinal Appendix, craft your own questions according to the same five-step process.

Following the reflection questions you will be reminded to return to chapter 7, "Preparing the Catechetical Session," to assist you in crafting your own session.

Closing Prayer

This day the Father of light
has enlightened the minds of the disciples
by the outpouring of the Holy Spirit.
May he bless you
and give you the gifts of the Spirit for ever.
    Response: Amen.

May that fire which hovered over the disciples
as tongues of flame
burn out all evil from your hearts
and make them glow with pure light.
    Response: Amen.

God inspired speech in different tongues
to proclaim one faith.
May he strengthen your faith
and fulfill your hope of seeing him face to face.
    Response: Amen.[19]

Selected Bibliography

Adam, Adolf. *The Liturgical Year.* Trans. Matthew J. O'Connell. Collegeville: The Liturgical Press, 1990.

Baldovin, John F., S.J. "Pentecost." In *The New Dictionary of Theology.* Ed. Joseph A. Komonchak, Mary Collins, Dermot A. Lane. Collegeville: The Liturgical Press, 1990.

Days of the Lord. Vol. 3. Collegeville: The Liturgical Press, 1993.

Foley, Edward, O.F.M.Cap. "Pentecost-Pastoral Liturgical Tradition." In *The Collegeville Pastoral Dictionary of Biblical Theology.* Ed. Carroll Stuhlmueller, C.P. Collegeville: The Liturgical Press, 1996.

Fuller, Reginald H. *Preaching the New Lectionary.* Collegeville: The Liturgical Press, 1976.

---

[19]Pentecost: "Solemn Blessing," *The Sacramentary.*

Hamm, M. Dennis, S.J. "Pentecost-New Testament." In *The Collegeville Pastoral Dictionary of Biblical Theology*. Ed. Carroll Stuhlmueller, C.P. Collegeville: The Liturgical Press, 1996.

Perkins, Pheme. "The Gospel According to John." In *The New Jerome Biblical Commentary*. Ed. Raymond E. Brown, S.S., Joseph A. Fitzmyer, S.J., Roland E. Murphy, O.Carm. Englewood Cliffs: Prentice Hall, 1990.

Talbert, Charles H. *Reading John*. New York: Crossroad, 1992.

Talley, Thomas J. *Origins of the Liturgical Year*. Collegeville: The Liturgical Press, 1986.

ORDINARY TIME

ORDINARY TIME:
AN OVERVIEW

The word *ordinary* in Ordinary Time is not to be confused with *ordinary* as in lackluster, boring, or routine. *Ordinary* in this instance refers to ordinal (counted time). Each Sunday is designated a number that is counted from Sunday to Sunday. The liturgical color of Ordinary Time is green.

Ordinary Time's primary focus is the feast of Sunday.[1] Each Sunday is an Easter celebration of sorts. We remember and celebrate the life, death, and resurrection of Jesus. Each Sunday the paschal mystery is revealed in its fullness. During Ordinary Time there is no highlighted, singular aspect to the remembered story of Christ as in the other seasons. Rather, all the many facets of Christ's mystery are unfolded on these thirty-three to thirty-four Sundays of the year.[2]

> Ordinary Time begins on Monday after the Sunday following 6 January and continues until Tuesday before Ash Wednesday inclusive. It begins again on Monday after Pentecost and ends before evening prayer I of the First Sunday of Advent. (GNLY, #44).

The Ordinary Time cycle is often delineated in bite-sized chunks corresponding to the time of the year. Thus, winter Ordinary Time covers the block of time immediately following Christmas. The Second Sunday in Ordinary Time begins Ordinary Time and it falls after the feast of the Baptism of the Lord. Winter Ordinary Time extends to the lenten season. Summer Ordinary Time begins after the feast of Pentecost on the feast of the Trinity. Following Trinity and Corpus Christi, the counted Sundays begin again where they ended

before Lent began. Autumn Ordinary Time begins around the 23rd or 24th Sunday and continues until the season of Advent.

SUNDAYS OF CYCLE C

Much of Luke's gospel is proclaimed on the Sundays and weekdays of Ordinary Time. About thirty percent of Luke's gospel is read on the thirty-three to thirty-four Sundays. The *Introduction to the Lectionary* explains: "On the Second Sunday of Ordinary Time the gospel continues to center on the manifestation of the Lord.... Beginning with the Third Sunday, there is a semicontinuous reading of the Synoptic Gospels. This reading is arranged in such a way that as the Lord's life and preaching unfold the teaching proper to each of these gospels is presented."[3]

The meaning of each gospel for a given Sunday corresponds to the flow and the movement of the liturgical cycle. For example, after the feast of Epiphany, at the transition between the Christmas season and the beginnings of Ordinary Time, the church centers on the *beginnings* of Christ's preaching ministry. This connects well to the First Sunday of Ordinary time, the solemnity of the Baptism of the Lord, with its stories of "the first events in which he manifests himself."[4] By the same token, the theme of "last things, *eschatology*" naturally coincides with the readings and liturgies of the end of the liturgical cycle. The beginning of the year reflects beginnings and the end of the year reflects endings.

The first readings are chosen to bring unity to the Old and the New Testaments by their connection to the gospel. There is no logical order given for the readings from the Hebrew scriptures (Old Tes-

---

[1]See Chapter 8 regarding liturgical time and the liturgical calendar. The understanding and celebration of Sunday are covered extensively.

[2]"General Norms for the Liturgical Year and the Calendar" (GNLY), in *The Liturgy Documents* (Chicago: Liturgy Training Publications, 1991), #43.

---

[3]"Introduction to the Lectionary," in *The Liturgy Documents* (Chicago: Liturgy Training Publications, 1991), #105.

[4]Ibid.

tament) other than their connection with the gospel.

Paul's and James's letters are read semicontinuously. Peter and John are read during the Easter and Christmas season. The letters are distributed over the three-year cycle.

On the solemnities of the Lord during Ordinary Time (Holy Trinity, Corpus Christi, and Sacred Heart), the readings are chosen to highlight the central theme of the solemnity. Some call these feasts "idea feasts," as they do not celebrate an event of Jesus' life, but rather a creed in regard to the mystery of Christ.

All of the Sundays, feasts, and solemnities of the sacred liturgy celebrate the mystery of redemption through Jesus Christ. In his encyclical, *Mediator Dei*, Pius XII asserted:

> In the sacred Liturgy, the whole of Christ
> is proposed to us in all the circumstances
> of His life, as the Word of Eternal Father,
> as born of the Virgin Mother of God, as
> He Who teaches us truth, heals the sick,
> consoles the afflicted, Who endures suffer-
> ing and Who dies; finally, as He Who rose
> triumphantly from the dead and Who,
> reigning in the glory of heaven sends us
> the Holy Paraclete and Who abides in His
> Church forever: "Jesus Christ, yesterday
> and today; and the same forever." (#163)

WEEKDAYS OF CYCLE C

The first nine weeks of weekday readings in Cycle C proclaim the first twelve chapters of Mark's gospel.[5] The readings from Matthew and Luke consist of all material not contained in Mark. The first readings of the weekday masses rotate between sections from the Old and New Testament. During a period of weeks the first reading is taken from the Old Testament; another block of weeks will center on the New Testament. The number of weeks depends on the length of the specific book

---

[5]There is one exception. Two passages from the sixth chapter of Mark are read in other cycles and thus are not read in those first nine weeks.

being read. There are large sections of the New Testament readings proclaimed so that the fullness of the apostles' teaching may be provided. The Old Testament readings are limited and very select. The passage chosen reflects the character of the book from which it was taken.[6]

Just as Luke redacted the story of Jesus according to his community's needs, so too the church, through the chosen texts of the Lectionary, determines the scriptural texts that best reflect our Christian faith as celebrated in the context of the liturgical cycle. There is no attempt made to render an historical, chronological depiction of the life of Christ from his birth to his death and resurrection. Rather, the intent is to reveal the entire mystery of Christ. In the last analysis, every liturgical feast celebrates the paschal mystery of Christ, who empties himself, sacrifices himself in obedience, and is present and active in his community of believers. Herein lies the beauty, depth and intensity of this extended season we call Ordinary Time. Far from being *ordinary*, it is imbued with passion—the passion of a people in covenant, radical relationship with the Christ of the gospels, the Christ of the eternal universe! No Sunday is routine, humdrum, or subservient and antithetical to the major seasons of the year. Each Sunday, solemnity, and feast is *manifestation* in itself!

CHRISTIAN INITIATION

A thorough explanation of the ongoing process of Christian initiation is placed in the overview of Ordinary Time since initiation is the normative way a parish lives as *church*. It is part of the ongoing life of a parish. Since Ordinary Time is where the church spends thirty-four weeks of the year, this is an appropriate place to digress and include an examination of an initiation process that is fluid and continually celebrated in the midst of the Christian community throughout the weeks of the liturgical cycle. With the exception of the initiation rituals of Lent and Easter, most of the rites of initiation are celebrated on the Sundays of Ordinary Time. There is a comprehensive explanation of the rites of Lent and

---

[6]"Introduction to the Lectionary," #105-110.

Easter such as election, scrutinies, and Christian initiation in the chapters that deal with Lent and Easter.

ONGOING PROCESS OF CHRISTIAN INITIATION OF ADULTS: HOW IT WORKS

Operating Assumptions

The Spirit is not a respecter of time. The Spirit moves where the Spirit wills. How do we welcome people who inquire at inopportune times, times that do not fit our neatly packaged school calendar models? Each journey is unique.

Formation for the catechumen consists of living and experiencing the life, death, and resurrection of Jesus as it unfolds in one complete liturgical cycle. Thus, a candidate who enters the precatechumenate in September, celebrates the Rite of Acceptance in December, and is initiated at the Easter Vigil in April, is in the catechumenate stage for only four or five months. Such a person is formed by less than half of Christ's complete story of redemption!

In an ongoing model, the process is suited to the needs of each individual. The process takes into account the movement of God's grace and the circumstances of time and place of each person's faith journey (RCIA, #5). Realizing that God deals with us as individuals, an ongoing model is crafted in such a way that each person moves through the process when he or she is ready, not when it is convenient to the parish structure.

Thus, there is no official beginning or "start-up" time in an ongoing process. It is continuous. Once the four periods of the catechumenate are in progress, each period continues forever. There is no beginning or ending.

> The catechumenate is an extended period during which the candidates are given suitable pastoral formation and guidance, aimed at training them in the Christian life.... A suitable catechesis is provided, planned to be gradual and complete in its coverage, accommodated to the liturgical year.... (RCIA, #74)

The duration of the catechumenate will depend on the grace of God and on various circumstances.... The time spent in the catechumenate should be long enough, several years—if necessary—for the conversion and faith of the catechumens to become strong. By their formation in the entire Christian life and a sufficiently prolonged probation the catechumens are properly initiated into the mysteries of salvation and the practice of an evangelical way of life. (RCIA, #76)

The period of the catechumenate, beginning at acceptance into the order of catechumens and including both the catechumenate proper and the period of purification and enlightenment after election or the enrollment of names, should extend for at least one year of formation, instruction, and probation. Ordinarily this period should go from at least the Easter season of one year until the next; preferably it should begin before Lent in one year and extend until Easter of the following year. (National Statutes of the RCIA, #6)

...It [the catechumenate] should extend over a substantial and appropriate period of time. The rites prior to sacramental initiation should not be unduly compressed, much less celebrated on a single occasion. (National Statutes of the RCIA, #20)

It is clearly the vision of the Rite that the catechumenate proper extend for one full year in order for the catechumens to experience the paschal mystery as it unfolds in one complete liturgical cycle.

Having established the church's intention that the catechumenate be a fluid process, suited to the needs of individuals, how, you might ask, can this possibly work in a parish? Not only can it work, but experience dictates that it is less stressful and is the best possible stewardship of people's time and commitment.

Very often the biggest stumbling block for people are the mechanics and methodology of the process. For some these appear monumental.

However, when the liturgical year is laid out and all the "pieces" are juggled, one is amazed to discover how it all fits. The following is an imaginary scenario of how a few people in different circumstances might journey through the year in an ongoing process.

This imaginary calendar is based on the liturgical year. However, even though the First Sunday of Advent begins the liturgical year, this calendar will begin in January for a very practical reason. It will help to better illustrate the working principles of the ongoing process, and illustrate what happens when someone enters the process at a time other than September. It also forces our minds out of the nine-month school calendar model.

This scenario is solely for purpose of illustration. One is not to infer that the calendar's beginning date reflects a "start-up" time. The calendar merely had to begin somewhere. *The following situation in no way suggests "the way it should be done." Rather, it is merely an illustration of* one way *the ongoing process might work in a parish setting. Each parish must use its own creativity and resources to adapt an ongoing process for its particular circumstances.*

January

Tina comes inquiring. She begins sessions in the inquiry/precatechumenate that meets on Monday evenings (some places have moved inquiry sessions to Sunday mornings or afternoons, depending on what works best for their community). She joins Mark, Sally, Ralph, and Jim, already in process. After a couple of weeks, two other new inquirers, Bob and Jane, enter the inquiry/precatechumenate. The inquiry now includes Tina, Mark, Sally, Ralph, Jim, and Bob and Jane.

Second Sunday in Ordinary Time (or any other suitable Sunday in January)

Rite of Acceptance might be celebrated for the unbaptized who are ready to proceed to the catechumenate period. If there are any baptized folks ready to proceed to the catechumenate period, the optional Rite of Welcome might be celebrated at a different liturgy or on a different Sunday.

John, a catechized, baptized Christian from another ecclesial tradition, is to be in the catechumenal process for a very brief time. He is highly catechized in all areas except the communal dimension. He may only need a few brief weeks in order to experience church as community. In order to recognize his ecclesiology and to mark his intention to proceed to full communion, John chooses to celebrate at the optional Rite of Welcome. John celebrates the Rite of Welcome, chooses not to be dismissed after the liturgy of the word, and joins the catechumenate session with the sponsors after mass. A brief ritual catechesis takes place. Thus, in early January, John enters the catechumenate.

Ralph and Sally have been in the precatechumenate since October and are now ready to move to the catechumenate period as well. On Monday evening, or at another designated time prior to the celebration, Ralph and Sally and their sponsors meet for an evening of retreat in preparation for the celebration of the Rite of Acceptance on Sunday. A team member from the catechumenate group joins them in order to welcome them into the new period that will begin for them on Sunday.

Ralph and Sally celebrate the Rite of Acceptance and thus begin the catechumenate that already meets on Sunday mornings at a parish liturgy. Following the Rite of Acceptance and the liturgy of the word, they are "sent forth" [dismissed] with the other catechumens [already in process] to "crack" open the word they just celebrated. After the mass, sponsors and family join the catechumens and all reflect upon the experience of the rite just celebrated. This is called ritual/liturgical catechesis. The catechumens and all present reflect upon the experience of the rite, what it expressed, and the meaning and challenge for their lives. They discover new insights about God, the church, and themselves. The catechumens already in process recall, revisit, and remember their own celebration of the Rite of Acceptance and all present are "catechized" by the experience of liturgy. From that day forward, Ralph and Sally attend the Sunday morning liturgy and are "sent forth" each week with other catechumens for reflection on scripture and tradition.

Ritual Catechesis

Ritual catechesis is the reflection that takes place when people experience gradual initiation into the paschal mystery through the structures set up in the Order of Christian Initiation of Adults.

Ritual catechesis helps us name what happened in a particular ritual, the implications, how the community celebrated, how the scriptures set forth the meaning and what the ritual expressed. The rites celebrate the conversion and growth that have already happened and that continue to happen throughout the process. The rites celebrate the experience of God, Jesus, Trinity, and the church.

The candidates experience the rite first; then they meet to reflect on the experience and its meaning, both personal and communal. They enter into dialogue about the purpose of the rite, what it means, and how it challenges the community and individual to act and live a transformed Christian life in order to serve the mission of Christ.

The rites of each period of the catechumenate celebrate what was going on in the previous period and serve as a doorway to each succeeding period. The rites express our faith and help give new meaning to the way we live the Christian life. Each rite celebrates another dimension of God, church, and community. When time is spent reflecting upon the experience and the meaning derived from every liturgical celebration, liturgy becomes formative for the Christian life.

Possible Weekly Sunday Format for the Period of the Catechumenate

10:00 Liturgy begins.

10:30 Following the homily, catechumens are "sent forth" to break open the liturgy of the word.

11:00 Catechumens join their sponsors and the parish family for hospitality, coffee, etc.

11:15 Catechesis continues, drawing from the experience of scripture and the liturgy and leading into the issues of tradition (church teaching—those core truths that also form us in living the paschal mystery of Jesus in our lives).

12:15 Closing Ritual—The minor rites are celebrated.

Precatechumenate still meets on Monday evenings (or at another specified time) with Tina, Bob, Jane, Jim, and Mark.

Sunday Before Ash Wednesday

John is ready to be received into full communion in the Catholic Church by celebrating the sacraments of confirmation and eucharist. He is received into the Catholic Church at a Sunday liturgy after a brief four or five weeks in the catechumenate. John now joins the monthly mystagogia sessions if he wishes.

Eve of Ash Wednesday—"Fat Tuesday"

Neophytes from the previous year might host a Mardi Gras dinner for all folks in the initiation process in anticipation of Lent.

LENT:
PERIOD OF PURIFICATION AND ENLIGHTENMENT

Ash Wednesday

Lent begins.

First Sunday of Lent

The Rite of Sending for Election is celebrated at the parish.

The Rite of Election is celebrated at the cathedral.

(Ralph and Sally do not celebrate the Rite of Election. They will bypass Easter this year as will Tina, Bob, Jane, Jim, and Mark who are still in the precatechumenate.)

333

Four *catechumens*, George, Bonnie, Candy, and Dan, have been in the period of the catechumenate since last winter. They are ready to be initiated at this Easter Vigil. George, Bonnie, Candy, and Dan participate in a retreat in preparation for the Rite of Election. The purification and enlightenment team join them in order to welcome them into the period of purification and enlightenment that coincides with Lent.

> The elect are now in a period of intense prayer and preparation for baptism, confirmation, and eucharist that will take place at the Easter Vigil. They seriously look within themselves to see what is still in need of healing and reconciliation. They reflect on the effects of personal, social, and systemic sin and ask God for deliverance, freedom, and reconciliation. The entire church joins with the elect during this penitential time of preparation, renewal, and enlightenment.

Bonnie, George, Candy, and Dan are "sent forth" from the parish with a ritual celebration: the Rite of Sending for Election. With the blessing and prayers of the parish community, the catechumens are sent from the parish to the Rite of Election held at the cathedral. Their status henceforth changes. They will now be called the elect. The catechumenate is over for them. They continue to be "sent forth" for reflection on the Sunday scriptures, but they no longer stay for further catechesis. The elect move instead to Tuesday evenings (or some other time, designated by parish circumstances) in the church.

The change in environment helps convey the message that things are different. The tone and tenor of the gatherings change as the elect enter this time of purification and enlightenment.

The elect perhaps join the parish community for liturgy of the hours on Tuesday evenings (or another designated time) and from there begin their weekly retreat, renewal, and reflection. On the second, third, and fourth week of Lent they prepare for the penitential Rite of Scrutiny that is celebrated on the Third, Fourth, and Fifth Sundays of Lent.

Third Sunday of Lent: First Scrutiny

Bonnie, George, Dan, and Candy take part in the scrutiny and are "sent forth" with other catechumens (still in process who will not be initiated at Easter) to break open the scriptures. They engage in ritual catechesis with their sponsors and families who join them after liturgy or they wait for their next evening session and engage in ritual catechesis at that time. Catechumens who are not going to be initiated at this Easter Vigil continue their normal Sunday process.

Fourth Sunday of Lent: Second Scrutiny

Bonnie, George, Dan, and Candy take part in the second scrutiny and are then "sent forth" with the other catechumens to break open the scriptures. They engage in ritual catechesis with their sponsors and families in the same manner as last week.

Fifth Sunday of Lent: Third Scrutiny

Bonnie, George, Dan, and Candy take part in the third scrutiny and are then "sent forth" with the other catechumens to break open the scriptures. They engage in ritual catechesis with their sponsors and families in the same manner as last week.

– The *elect* continue to gather on the Tuesday evenings of Lent (or another designated time) for prayer, preparation, and reflection.

– *Catechumens* still in process continue to meet on Sunday mornings.

– *Inquirers* continue to attend the precatechumenate sessions that are held on Monday evenings. New people periodically join the group.

> In addition to the formation in *word, worship,* and *tradition* catechumens are to participate in the apostolic life—*mission*. During the catechumenate they are to engage in the works of justice, charity, and mercy. Such works are integral to the Christian life, and are the heart of apprenticeship in that life. Thus, formation in the apostolic mission of Christ needs to begin early in their formation, as early as the inquiry.

Holy Thursday, Good Friday

Catechumens and elect are "sent forth" to further reflect upon the scriptures and liturgies of Holy Thursday and Good Friday. One of the elect leads the "Breaking open the Word" session so catechists may participate in the liturgies with the community. By now the elect are experts at the process of liturgical/scriptural reflection and are very capable of leading the session.

Good Friday

9:00 A.M. Catechumens and elect attend Good Friday Morning Prayer with the community.

7:00 P.M. Catechumens and elect participate with the community in evening celebration of the Lord's Passion.

> *Note:* one possible liturgical adaptation (allowed in the Sacramentary) for Good Friday moves the individual veneration of the cross to after the communion service. The actual veneration occurs in the normal place, but the individual gesture of veneration such as kissing the cross, kneeling, etc. takes place after communion. If this is done, the elect and candidates can return from their "Breaking open the Word" session in time to participate in this communal gesture of veneration.

Ritual Catechesis: Following the evening service, catechumens, elect, sponsors, families, and team might gather for a brief ritual catechesis.

Holy Saturday

9:00 A.M. Catechumens and elect join the community for Holy Saturday Morning Prayer.

10:00 A.M. Retreat and preparation rites [community is invited to stay and participate]. Mystagogical team joins the elect to welcome them into the next period of mystagogia.

8:00 P.M.
Christian Initiation: Baptism, Confirmation, and Eucharist

The elect, Bonnie, George, Dan, and Candy, are initiated at the Easter Vigil.

Easter Sunday

Neophytes Bonnie, George, Dan, and Candy join the community as fully initiated members for Easter Sunday liturgy. They dress in their white baptismal robes and carry their baptismal candles. They are a focal point of the liturgy and participate in various ways such as leading the general intercessions, carrying up the gifts, etc. Catechumens who are still in process are "sent forth" as usual for reflection on the liturgy of the word.

PERIOD OF MYSTAGOGIA

Second Sunday of Easter

> Neophytes revisit, remember, and encounter once again the symbols of fire, light, water, oil, bread and wine. They appropriate new meaning for their lives in light of the experience of sacramental symbols from the Easter Vigil. The entire church enters this period of mystagogical reflection. "How have we experienced the paschal mystery in this Easter season and throughout our lives? How are we strengthened by the celebration of the Easter sacraments?"

Neophytes continue to be a visible presence in the assembly. Catechumens continue to be "sent forth" from parish liturgy for liturgical [Lectionary based] catechesis.

Mystagogia begins for the neophytes, who are still a visible presence throughout the Easter season. Homilies should focus on the paschal mystery (the life, death, and resurrection of Jesus) and emphasize that the neophytes are a living symbol of that reality in our midst. They are a sign of Easter life. They died to their old selves and were born again through water and the Holy Spirit at the Easter Vigil. They are gift to the church.

Following the liturgy, the neophytes meet for post-baptismal catechesis. They spend the Easter weeks immersed in uncovering the layers of meaning contained in the mysteries they have celebrated. This is called sacramental catechesis. Parishioners are invited to participate in these sessions.

A Sunday of the Easter Season

Rite of Acceptance is celebrated.

Tina, Bob, Jane, Jim, and Mark are ready to celebrate the Rite of Acceptance (remember that they began the inquiry in January and Lent is not the most appropriate time to celebrate a Rite of Acceptance). Ritual catechesis takes place after the celebration of the rite. Next Sunday Tina, Bob, Jane, Jim, and Mark join the other catechumens still in process.

> When the rites of initiation are celebrated at the same liturgy each time, then "all the faithful" (RCIA, #9) are not afforded the opportunity to experience them. Since initiation is the responsibility of all the baptized and since the rites are not only for the candidates but for the renewal of the entire church, it is desirable that they be celebrated with other Sunday parish assemblies as well.

Precatechumenate still meets on Monday evenings with all the inquirers who began inquiry since January and were not ready for the celebration of the Rite of Acceptance.

Sundays of Easter

Neophytes continue to be a visible presence. The rituals of mystagogia are the Sunday celebrations of eucharist. They share their stories of conversion and transformation, dying and rising. They continue to gather after liturgy for further reflection on the sacramental symbols of Easter. Parishioners also share stories of death and resurrection.

- Catechumens continue to be "sent forth" each week.
- Inquirers continue to meet on Monday evenings.

Pentecost

Neophyte witnessing continues. There is a big parish celebration and a party for the neophytes. All who celebrated a sacrament of initiation during the past year are invited to wear their initiation garment, such as baptismal gown or first communion dress, etc. They are recognized and given a blessing at every liturgy. This includes anyone who celebrated the sacraments of baptism (including infant baptism), confirmation (including the young people who experienced delayed confirmation), and/or eucharist (including those who celebrated their first communion and all baptized Christians who became Catholic during the year). All of the past year's initiates are recognized as a sign of the new life they represent to us in our community.

Mystagogia continues through monthly meetings throughout the year to break open scriptures and to share stories of witnessing and living the apostolic life.

- Catechumens continue to be "sent forth" on Sundays.
- Precatechumenate continues to meet on Monday evenings.

Summer Sunday in Ordinary Time

Rite of Acceptance is celebrated.

A new group of inquirers is ready to move to the catechumenate. They celebrate the rite, are sent forth with the other catechumens for further reflection on the word, and then, joined by sponsors and families after the liturgy, participate in ritual catechesis.

- Precatechumenate still meets on Monday evenings.

Another Sunday in Ordinary Time

Rite of Reception into Full Communion of the Catholic Church is celebrated.

Three baptized Christians are received into full communion with the Catholic Church. After liturgy, these new Catholics join the neophytes for their monthly session. All participate in ritual catechesis. New Catholics are invited to participate in the monthly mystagogia sessions.

Baptized candidates are received into full communion with the church at various Sunday liturgies throughout the year, whenever they are ready to be received.

The week prior to the celebration of reception, the baptized candidates participate in a communal ritual of reconciliation and renewal of baptism in preparation for the celebration of full communion that will take place the following Sunday.[7]

- Mystagogia meets for monthly sessions.
- Catechumens continue to be "sent forth" on Sundays.
- Precatechumenate continues to meet on Monday evenings.

Other Sundays of the Year

- Process continues as usual.
- Catechumens are "sent forth" each Sunday.
- Precatechumenate continues to meet on Mondays.
- Mystagogia meets monthly.
- Rite of Reception into Full Communion with the Catholic Church is celebrated when needed.

Fall Sundays in Ordinary Time

Rite of Acceptance is celebrated.

Inquirers celebrate the Rite of Acceptance, become catechumens, and join the catechumenate on Sunday mornings.

Perhaps a Rite of Reception into Full Communion with the Catholic Church will be celebrated on one of these Sundays if needed.

- Process continues as usual.
- Precatechumenate continues to meet on Monday evenings.
- Catechumens are "sent forth" each Sunday.
- Mystagogia meets monthly.

---

[7]See Mary Birmingham, "Baptized Candidates in the Catechumenate," *Catechumenate Magazine,* September 1996.

One of the Last Sundays of the Year

Rite of Acceptance or Rite of Welcome is celebrated if needed.

(This is the last celebration of the Rite of Acceptance until after Christmas.)

CHRISTMAS SEASON

The neophytes from the previous year host a potluck Christmas dinner for the entire initiation community of past years: inquirers, catechumens, sponsors, team, and all folks who went through the process in recent years.

Ralph, Sally, Tina, Bob, Jane, Jim, and Mark will be initiated at the Easter Vigil the coming spring. Ralph and Sally were in the catechumenate proper last January when they celebrated the Rite of Acceptance. Their catechumenate will have lasted one year and two months. Tina, Bob, Jane, Jim, and Mark celebrated the Rite of Acceptance in the Easter season last year. They will have been in the catechumenate proper for one full year before their initiation at the Easter Vigil.

And the process goes on and on.

Neophytes should be encouraged to participate in small Christian faith groups to help them continue the ongoing reflection, sharing, and story telling that helped form them and will continue to form them in the Christian life.

TEAM COMPOSITION

Precatechumenate: Two teams that alternate approximately every two months. Teams may consist of two or more people. If the inquiry group is small, each team can consist of one person as long as parishioners are invited to participate in many and various ways.

Catechumenate: Multiple catechists share this ministry. Some catechists participate only in "Breaking open the Word," while others may concentrate on the doctrinal piece. Some catechists do both. It is important that burnout be kept to a minimum. Trained catechists are a great gift to the community. When the burden is shared among many, it is very manageable. People can participate periodically or monthly where they are unable to do so weekly. We are not initiating folks into a "comfortable, small sharing group." Rather, we are initiating into a church. Therefore, various and abundant ministries and ministers help reflect this diverse, inclusive church they seek to join. (RCIA, #9)

In some parishes there are as many as eight "Breaking open the Word" catechists and four or five catechists who serve as catechists for the Catholic tradition piece. Some catechists serve once a month, others serve more frequently or less frequently. Adaptation and flexibility are essential.

Purification and Enlightenment: Two people may share responsibility for the six weeks of Lent.

Mystagogia: Team may consist of two people. Their commitment is the seven weeks of Easter and monthly thereafter for a year.

General Parishioners: As many people as possible are invited to share their gifts by being sponsors, hospitality ministers, and/or witnesses to their faith.

Ministries of the Parish: People involved in any and all parish ministries are invited to share their stories and their ministries throughout the catechumenate. We invite them into the precatechumenate that meets weekly in a comfortable, homey place that invites conversation and sharing.

FINAL REFLECTIONS

When do inquirers enter the precatechumenate?

Whenever they come seeking.

How long does the precatechumenate last?

As long as it needs to.

How do we know when people are ready to move to the catechumenate?

When they demonstrate initial stirring of faith, a spirit of repentance, the *beginnings* of the spiritual life, including calling on God in prayer, initial

conversion, the intention to change their lives and a sense of church. (RCIA, #42)

When is the Rite of Acceptance celebrated?

The Rite of Acceptance is celebrated whenever there are people ready to move to the catechumenate, the next stage. This works out to be approximately four times a year, but preferably not during Lent and Advent.

Entry into the catechumenate is marked by the Rite of Acceptance.

The Rite of Acceptance celebrates what people experienced in the inquiry and foreshadows what they will experience in the catechumenate.

When are baptized Christians received into full communion with the Catholic Church?

Whenever they are ready.

LITURGICAL PRAYER

Liturgical prayer is the official, communal, public prayer of the church. It is the primary way we should begin all our Catholic/Christian gatherings and mark all major life experiences and transitions. Liturgical prayer is different from other prayer forms such as private prayers, devotions, spontaneous prayer, or prayer services crafted in a catechetical resource. Our church enjoys a vast repertoire of liturgical prayer. As stated in the introductory section of this book, catechesis has the responsibility of forming children and adults in the liturgical life of the church. This does not simply mean the eucharistic liturgy of the church.

Since liturgy forms children and adults in their Catholic Christian faith, we must be attentive to all the church's liturgical prayer. This prayer constitutes the way we live our Catholic life on a routine, day-to-day, week-to-week basis. Thus, this section on liturgical prayer is placed in the overview of Ordinary Time as liturgical prayer is the normative way we are to pray as community throughout the year, not only seasonally, but throughout the days and weeks of the year. Suggestions for use of this vast repertoire will be included in the weekly sessions.

The treasury that comprises the church's liturgical prayer includes:

Eucharistic liturgy

Liturgy of the hours

Liturgy of the word

Rite of Penance:
Sacramental celebrations of the sacrament of reconciliation, including three revised liturgical celebrations:
a) Rite of Reconciliation of Individual Penitents
b) Rite of Reconciliation of Several Penitents with Individual Confession and Absolution
c) Rite of Reconciliation of Several Penitents with General Absolution

Non-sacramental Celebrations

Penitential celebrations are gatherings of the people of God to hear the proclamation of God's word. This invites them to conversion and renewal of life and announces our freedom from sin through the death and resurrection of Christ. (Rite of Penance, #36)

It is desirable to arrange such services especially for these purposes:
- to foster the spirit of penance within the community;
- to help the faithful to prepare for confession that can be made individually later at a convenient time;
- to help children gradually form their conscience about sin in human life and about freedom from sin through Christ;
- to help catechumens during their conversion. (Rite of Penance, #37)

Within the Rite of Penance there are various models for these non-sacramental liturgical celebrations that should be adapted to the specific conditions and needs of each community.
I   Penitential Celebrations during Lent
II.   Penitential Celebrations during Advent
III. Common Penitential Celebrations
IV. For Children
V.   For Youth

We are a people in need of continuous reconciliation and healing. The rite provides a fount of grace to heal and reconcile as we struggle with abuse, sin, pain, and broken relationships. We should celebrate reconciliation on a continuing basis in sacramental and non-sacramental celebrations. Non-sacramental celebrations do not require a priest and may be presided over by a lay minister.

Book of Blessings

The following is a sample list of blessings from the *Book of Blessings* that might be appropriately celebrated throughout the liturgical cycle.

Order for the Blessing of Children
Order of Blessing of the Sick
Order for the Blessing of a Person Suffering from Addiction
Order for Blessing of a Victim of Crime or Oppression
Orders for Blessings that Pertain to Catechesis and to Communal Prayer
Order for the Blessing of Animals
Order for the Blessing of Students and Teachers
Order for the Blessing of Seeds at Planting Time
Order for the Blessing on the Occasion of Thanksgiving for the Harvest
Order for the Blessing before or after Meals
Order for the Blessing of an Advent Wreath
Order for the Blessing of a Christmas Manger or Nativity Scene
Order for the Blessing of a Christmas Tree
Order for the Blessing of Throats on the Feast of Saint Blase
Order for the Blessing and Distribution of Ashes
Order for the Blessing of Food for Thanksgiving Day
Order for the Blessing of Readers
Order for the Blessing of Altar Servers, Sacristans, Musicians and Ushers
Order for a Blessing in Thanksgiving
Order for a Blessing to be Used in Various Circumstances

Other Liturgical Celebrations

Celebration of the Triduum

Holy Communion and Worship of the Eucharist outside Mass

339

- Rite of Eucharistic Exposition and Benediction
- Eucharistic Processions

Rite of Baptism for Children—celebrated in the parish

Rite of Confirmation—celebrated in the parish

Rite of Marriage—celebrated in the parish

Rite of Ordination

Pastoral Care of the Sick: Rites of Anointing and Viaticum
- Visits to a sick child
- Anointing of the Sick
- Celebration of Viaticum

Order of Christian Funerals

Catholic Household Blessings and Prayers—a vast repertoire of liturgical prayers for use in the home—for every occasion.[8]

Feasts and Events of Note Throughout the Year

The following is a compilation of some of the events and feasts of note that occur throughout the year. While they will not be addressed in full in this resource, they are nevertheless part of our Christian/Catholic/social life and are worthy of mention in our catechetical ministry.

January. January 1—New Year's Day. (Mary, Mother of God and Epiphany, Baptism of the Lord are covered during the Christmas season.) January 4—Memorial of St. Elizabeth Ann Seton (religious founder from the U.S.A., 1774–1821). January 5— Memorial of St. John Neuman (bishop, religious, missionary—U.S.A., 1811–1860). January 18-25 is the Christian Unity Octave in which eight days are set aside for special prayer for the unity of Christians. There are prayers in the *Book of Blessings* for use at ecumenical gatherings. The church prays for the unity of Christians throughout the year, but sets aside the octave for special remembrance and prayers. January 25— Conversion of Paul. Third Monday in January—Martin Luther King, Jr. Day. January 26—Sts. Timothy and Titus. January 28— Thomas Aquinas.

February. February 25—Feast of the Presentation of the Lord (Candlemas, the day on which

enough candles for the entire year are blessed). February 3—St. Blase (Order for Blessing Throats, *Book of Blessings*); February 12—birth of Abraham Lincoln. February 22—The Feast of the Chair of Peter, birth of George Washington. President's Day—third Monday in February.

March. First Friday in March—World Day of Prayer. March 8—International Women's Day. March 19—Solemnity of St. Joseph. March 24— Anniversary of the death of Oscar Arnulfo Romero. March 25—Solemnity of the Annunciation of the Lord.

April. April 1—April Fools' Day. April 22—Earth Day. April 25—Feast of St. Mark the evangelist.

May. Second Sunday in May—Mother's Day. Last Monday in May— Memorial Day (U.S.A.). Monday on or before May 24—Victoria Day (Canada). May 3—Feast of Sts. Philip and James, apostles. May 14—St. Matthias, apostle. May 15—St. Isidore the Farmer (a good day to bless gardens and fields— check Catholic Household Blessings and *Book of Blessings* for an appropriate blessing). May 31— Feast of the Visit of the Virgin Mary to Elizabeth.

June. Third Sunday in June—Father's Day. June 3—Anniversary of the death of Pope John XXIII. June 24—Solemnity of the Birth of John the Baptist. June 29—Solemnity of Sts. Peter and Paul.

July. July 1—Canada Day. July 3—St. Thomas, apostle. July 4—Independence Day (U.S.A.). July 16—Our Lady of Mount Carmel. July 22—St. Mary Magdalene. July 25— Feast of St. James, apostle.

August. August 6—Feast of the Transfiguration of the Lord. August 10—Feast of St. Lawrence, deacon, martyr. August 15—Solemnity of the Assumption of the Virgin Mary into Heaven. August 22— The Queenship of the Virgin Mary (octave[9] of Assumption).

---

[8]This section on liturgical prayer was taken from Sister Linda Gaupin's course, "Catechesis and Liturgy 106," Diocese of Orlando, Orlando, Florida, 1996.

[9]"In church tradition, an octave represents eternity.... Seven days make a normal, run of the mill week. But add an eighth day and you've got something special. You've got a week that ends and begins on the same day. In the early church, they thought that eight days was a symbol of perfection and of heaven." Mary Ellyn Hynes, *Companion to the Calendar* (Chicago: Liturgy Training Publications, 1993), 126.

September. First Monday in September—Labor Day. September 8—Feast of the Birth of the Virgin Mary. September 14—Feast of the Holy Cross. September 15—Our Lady of Sorrows. September 21—Feast of St. Matthew, apostle and evangelist. September 29—Sts. Michael, Gabriel and Raphael, archangels.

October. Second Monday in October—Thanksgiving Day (Canada). October 4—St. Francis of Assisi, patron saint of ecologists and all environmentalists. October 18—Feast of St. Luke the evangelist. October 28—Feast of Sts. Simon and Jude.

November. First Tuesday after the first Monday in November—Election Day (U.S.A.). Fourth Thursday in November—Thanksgiving Day (U.S.A.). November 1—All Saints, solemnity. November 2—All Souls. November 9—Feast of Dedication of the Lateran Basilica in Rome (reminds us of our history as a people; this church thinks of itself as the parish for the entire world as it is the cathedral of Rome, home to the bishop of Rome—the pope). November 11—Veterans Day (U.S.A.); Remembrance Day (Canada). November 21—Memorial of the Presentation of Mary. November 29—Anniversary of the death of Dorothy Day. November 30—Feast of St. Andrew the apostle.

December. December 1—Anniversary of the day Rosa Parks kept her bus seat. December 8—Solemnity of the Immaculate Conception of the Virgin Mary. December 10—International Human Rights Day. December 12—Feast of Our Lady of Guadalupe. December 25—Solemnity of the Birth of our Lord. Octave of Christmas begins. December 26—Feast of St. Stephen, first martyr. December 27—Feast of St. John the apostle, evangelist. December 28—Feast of the Holy Innocents.

SECOND SUNDAY IN ORDINARY TIME

INTRODUCTORY RITES

Opening Song (or Entrance Antiphon)

May all the earth give you worship and praise and break into song to your name, O God, Most high. (Ps 65:4)[1]

Environment

The season of Ordinary Time is thirty-three to thirty-four weeks long, interrupted by the Lent/Easter season. The liturgical color of the season is green. Simplicity is a great value; thus preparation of the catechetical environment may simply include a Christ candle, a green cloth, and perhaps a plant. As Ordinary Time spans many weeks, seasonal variation in the environment could be beneficial.

Opening Prayer

The facilitator of the session may lead the prayer. Others in the group may be asked to proclaim the readings.

Let us pray... to our Father for the gift of peace.

   Pause for silent prayer.

Father of heaven and earth,
hear our prayers,
and show us the way to peace in the world.
Grant this through our Lord Jesus Christ, your
   Son,
who lives and reigns with you and the Holy Spirit,
one God for ever and ever.[2]

LITURGY OF THE WORD

Let us listen to God's word.

The readings are proclaimed.

---

[1]Second Sunday in Ordinary Time: "Entrance Antiphon," *The Sacramentary.*

[2]Second Sunday in Ordinary Time: "Opening Prayer," *The Sacramentary.*

First Reading
Isaiah 62:1-5

This pericope from Isaiah is a song celebrating Israel's return from exile. God rejoices over the restoration of Jerusalem; thus, he rejoices over the restoration of his people. God rejoices as a lover would rejoice over his bride. Even though the city of Jerusalem has not been rebuilt following the return from exile, the prophet remains confident that Yahweh will completely restore the city.

In this reading God confers a new name. Throughout biblical history, when people were given a new name they were then to live in a new way. At the creation of the world, God *named* the light: day. Creating and naming are equal events for God. Naming is about creating something new. When a person was given a new name in scripture, it signified the beginning of a new direction or mission in that person's life. The conferral of the new name alerted Israel that she could no longer be the harlot she once was; she must instead turn from her sin and return to Yahweh. She who was called "Desolate" became a new creation and was restored by God to resplendent honor as evidenced by her new name, "Espoused." God's merciful covenant restored her to full relationship.

This reading from Isaiah portrays the primary motif of Israel's relationship with Yahweh. God loved Israel, and Israel responded in love. Then Israel sinned and turned away. Personal responsibility for sin demanded divine retribution. Israel was punished. God invited her to repent and to return to him in love. Israel repented and once again fell into the arms of the faithful, loving Yahweh. It was the pattern and hallmark of Israel's history with her God. The song of Isaiah praised the incomprehensible gift of God's mercy that extended out to the entire world.

Responsorial Psalm
Psalm 96:1-2, 2-3, 7-8, 9-10

This festival psalm (also used at the Christmas mass at midnight) proclaims that one can do no less than proclaim the wonders of God to the ends of the earth. God's mighty works call us to go out and tell the Good News!

Second Reading
1 Corinthians 12:4-11

We will be reading from Paul's first letter to the Corinthians (chapters 10–12) for the next six Sundays. Corinth was a Greek city that had been demolished in 146 B.C.E. and restored a century later. The diversity of Corinth was very apparent in the disparity between the very wealthy and the very poor. Most of those on the lower end of society's class ladder were slaves.

Corinth was an intellectual center that played host to many aberrant religious philosophies and doctrines. Paul preached and ministered in Corinth for about eighteen months and his community reflected the philosophical and religious diversity in the city. Paul's community was under a great deal of pressure because of the temptations and lures of the culture's religious and intellectual oddities. People were succumbing to pagan influences. Paul addressed these concerns in his letter to the Corinthians. He defined what constitutes proper behavior for a Christian gathering and named the gifts of the Spirit.

Paul's concern was leveled against the gnostics who were saying that only those with the gift of tongues possessed great spiritual prowess. He insisted that the gifts were not given in order to exalt the individual. The gifts were for the good of the community. The charisms mentioned by Paul in his letter were exercised by gnostics in their public assemblies. They obviously yelled out their utterances in ostentatious outcries. They self-righteously condemned others, including Paul, for not having similar gifts. There are many people today who have been victimized by similar self-righteous behavior.

Paul reminded his community that the source of such gifts is God, not the individual. No one can claim superiority. God's will directs and empowers the gifts within the community. Paul reminded his community that they were not to exhibit self-centered attitudes or engage in outward public displays.

The gifts of the Spirit, while given to individuals for the uplifting of the community, are not for personal edification. They are for the uplifting and the unification of the entire gathered community.

Gospel
John 2:1-12

Today begins the account of Jesus' public ministry. Mary insists that Jesus reveal the power he has been given by God and manifest it in the context of this festive community gathering.

STEP 1
NAMING ONE'S EXPERIENCE

What were your first impressions? What was your first response? What grabbed your attention? How did you feel?

Each person names his or her initial impression. Statement should be brief. No reasons should be given at this time. All simply listen without agreeing or disagreeing.

STEP 2
UNDERSTANDING

In a brief statement, what do you think this gospel is trying to convey?

STEP 3
INPUT FROM VISION/STORY/TRADITION

Liturgical Context

Today's story of the wedding feast at Cana serves as a bridge between the Advent/Christmas season and Ordinary Time. This feast illumines the reason for Christ's coming. Last week we celebrated Jesus' baptism. Empowered by the Spirit, Jesus' mission is inaugurated. The *One who was to come* had arrived and was ready to lead his people. Now we are to see first-hand the power of God available to all who follow Christ.

The marriage theme in scripture always replicates the covenant between Yahweh and Israel. One cannot miss the marital images in the first reading; these images are obviously the reason this reading was chosen. While marriages are sometimes difficult and filled with strain, they nevertheless represent an unbreakable bond. One can leave, one can turn away, but the bond remains.

Yahweh's steadfast love is always available for his people. Today's alternative opening prayer asserts that nothing will deter God from his loving plans for humanity as his "watchful care reaches from end to end and orders all things in such power that even the tension and the tragedies of sin cannot frustrate [God's] loving plans."[3]

Other Liturgical Rites

Perhaps a Rite of Acceptance or Welcome might be celebrated today, if needed.

Gospel Exegesis

The facilitator gives input regarding what critical biblical scholarship has to say about this text. The input includes insights as to how people would have heard the gospel in Jesus' time.

John did not write his gospel until the end of his life; thus he had an entire lifetime to reflect upon the mysteries he had witnessed. John provides us with a vision of the events he witnessed following years of discipleship and reflective wisdom. We are the recipients of his insight.

There was great tension between Jews and Christians. John's community had been expelled from the synagogues, making them an illegal religion with no right to exist under Roman law. Stakes were high and animosity ran higher.

According to Charles Talbert, John's entire gospel is concerned with the formation of disciples and the creation of a new community. In the early verses in which the Baptist reveals the messiah, John seeks to verify and clarify the life and mission of Jesus. Reginald Fuller tells us that the miracle stories of John are intended to convince potential converts that Jesus is the messiah, making it primarily a *missionary gospel.* John uses the language

of prophetic fulfillment to portray and validate the mission of Jesus.

Talbert suggests that the story is written from the perspective of common views of "Mediterranean worship" in the second century.[4] One group of worshipers honored deities by building temples (sacred space), offering sacrifice (sacred means) at sacred times (festivals) by a priest (sacred person). Jewish worship obviously exemplified this first group. There was another group that found flaws in this form of worship. There was a "denigration of sacred space" in the culture of the second century.[5] There were those who believed temple worship to be devoid of "morality and covenant faithfulness." "I hate, I despise your feasts, and I take no delight in your solemn assemblies. Even though you offer me your burnt offerings and cereal offerings, I will not accept them" (see Amos 5, Isaiah 1, Hosea 6). Such passages reflect disillusionment with empty, external temple worship.

For this group of people, there developed a different spirituality. The universe replaced the temple and the soul replaced the holy of holies. Thus, knowledge of God and ethical behavior exemplified authentic worship for those in the second group. A third form of worship in antiquity centered around the turning away from temple worship in favor of following a holy leader. "People, in their search for salvation, began to turn from temples and the cults of the temple and look to savior figures and communities, revolving around such figures as havens of salvation."[6] The holy person became the new path to the deity. In contrast with the old patterns of worship centered around the temple, new ritual forms emerged. The focus became "conversion, identification with the divine man, and initiation into the holy man's group."[7] Those in this third group reinterpreted their former experiences of worship. Temple worship and contemplation were replaced by total dedication to the holy man and his followers.

---

[3]Second Sunday in Ordinary Time: "Alternative Opening Prayer," *The Sacramentary.*

[4]Charles H. Talbert, *Reading John* (New York: Crossroad, 1992), 87.

[5]Jonathon Smith, *Map Is Not Territory* (Leiden: Brill, 1978), 186-189.

[6]Ibid., 91.

[7]Ibid., 186-189.

John's gospel is written from this third cultural understanding of worship. His entire gospel is written from the perspective that Jesus (holy man) replaced Jewish worship (temple worship). One's commitment to temple worship was now to be replaced by radical metanoia to the divine man, Jesus. Jesus participates in Jewish worship to show that he fulfills and supersedes it.[8]

The miracle at Cana typified three common themes in John's gospel. "Jesus' actions are not directed by human influence; that which Jesus fulfills preceded him; and the disciples are the ones who have beheld his glory."[9]

The miracle at Cana reflects John's agenda. First, Mary asks her son to help out in a potentially embarrassing situation. Jesus shifts the focus from the human level to the spiritual realm by making the earthly wine subservient to eternal wine. In other words, he answers Mary by reminding her that the wine he gives is the wine of eternal life, given for those in need. Thus, not even the intervention of Jesus' mother directs his action. It is directed by God alone. His first public action is to be at God's initiative.

Second, the miracle story forces a confrontation with Jewish purification rites. When Mary says, "They have no wine," it is a statement about the Jewish purification rites. Jesus directs that the stone jars be filled to the brim. Normally the jars were used for ritual washing before and after meals. Each jar held about one hundred and twenty gallons of water, an embarrassing extravagance if filled with wine. Thus, this new wine, the teaching of Jesus, fulfills the teaching (the covenant) that has gone before him.

Third, when the steward reacts to the miracle and admonishes the bridegroom for saving the "good stuff" until last, John cleverly uses an embarrassing situation to drive home his spiritual point. Even though the steward of the house could not see, the disciples came to believe. Through the deeper meaning of the sign of water turning to wine, the disciples were converted. They were willing to let go of former, entrenched rituals and enter into the new covenant with Christ.

This entire pericope is about the formation of a new community. Jesus performed signs at the behest of God. He demonstrated how his gift of new life fulfilled all they had once known and believed. Those who saw and believed with eyes of faith were called into community to share Jesus' new life.

By calling Mary *woman* (an unusual designation), John was connecting her to the woman of Genesis and the woman of Revelation. In both scriptural texts the woman engaged in cataclysmic battle with the demon evil. It is suggested that John established Mary as a permanent icon (symbol) of the church.

Mary represented the church militant who struggled with evil following Jesus' death until the time of his return. Mary received her commission, not here, at Cana, but at the cross upon the death of her Son. With Mary leading the charge, the church engages the theater of battle as she awaits the final glory.[10]

Proclaim the gospel again.

Sometimes we gain new insights when we hear the text after the interpretation has been given. Someone from the group proclaims the gospel a second time.

STEP 4
TESTING

Conversation with the Liturgy and the Scriptures

Test your original understanding in dialogue with the text.

(You might consider breaking into smaller groups.)

What understanding of this gospel did you bring with you to this discussion? How did it compare with the exegesis? Were there any new insights? What is John's primary purpose in writing this gospel? How is that relevant today?

---

[8]Talbert, *Reading John*, 93.
[9]Ibid., 85.

[10]Patricia Datchuck Sanchez, *The Word We Celebrate* (Kansas City: Sheed and Ward, 1989), 317.

How does this story speak to your life?

Participants share an experience from their lives that connects with the biblical interpretation just shared.

> *I am reminded that we do not have a monopoly on God. Very often I am very sure that I know everything there is to know about God. The miracle at Cana reminds me that I cannot put God in a box. God does not act because of our initiative, but because God chooses to act. I wonder if I would be the ignorant steward of the house or the receptive disciple. There was once a time when I was opposed to something that was being proposed in the community. I expressed my concerns and watched as it was implemented anyway. My delightful surprise came many years later as I reflected upon the incredible grace of God that occurred as a result of the implementation. God does not need my approval to act. I need, however, to be attentive to God's action, wherever I find it.*

> *I believe that as a community we are challenged to be open to the marvels of God, and to be prepared to see with eyes of faith. This openness sometimes forces us to let go of past preconceived ideas of who and what God is, and instead allow God to be God as God chooses to be.*

All share their life experience.

What was John trying to tell his community? What does the story of Cana have to say to our parish and to me? In what way are the biblical themes of covenant, community, exodus, and creation apparent in the gospel of today's liturgy? In what way, if any, have I been changed as a result of our sharing? How would I explain this gospel to a stranger?

STEP 5
DECISION

The gospel demands a response.

What would be the contemporary implications of this gospel? How would people today receive the message of this gospel? In what way is your community called to respond? Be concrete. What are the implications for your life? Name one specific action you will take this week as a response to what was learned and shared today.

DOCTRINAL ISSUES

What church truth/teaching/doctrinal issue could be drawn from the gospel for the Second Sunday in Ordinary Time?

Participants suggest possible doctrinal themes that flow from the readings.

Possible Doctrinal Themes

Christology, revelation, New Covenant/Old Covenant, church, Mary as icon of church

Present the doctrinal material at this time.

1. The facilitator gives input on a particular doctrinal issue of his/her prior choosing. OR
2. The group chooses a doctrinal issue from the list they created. They read together from the Doctrinal Appendix.

(The doctrinal issues are found in the Doctrinal Appendix in the back of this workbook. If you are choosing an issue from this resource, please refer to it now.)

Reflection questions centered around the chosen doctrinal theme can be found at the end of each topic in the Doctrinal Appendix. The questions are based on the five-step reflection process. If you choose a topic not included in the Doctrinal Appendix, craft your own questions according to the same five-step process.

Following the reflection questions you will be reminded to return to chapter 7, "Preparing the Catechetical Session," to assist you in crafting your own session.

Closing Prayer

The wine he offers, Christ makes excellent, to suggest the treasures hidden in his life-giving blood. The first sign he accomplishes is the wine that gladdens the celebrants; the significance is that his blood rejoices the nations. All earthly joys come together in wine; all of salvation is joined in the mystery of his blood. He offers the sweet wine that transforms hearts, as they believe in the inebriating doctrine that transforms them. (Ephraim, deacon of Edessa, Doctor of the Church, ca. 306-373)[11]

Selected Bibliography

Adam, Adolf. *The Liturgical Year.* Trans. Matthew J. O'Connell. Collegeville: The Liturgical Press, 1990.

Days of the Lord. Vol. 6. Collegeville: The Liturgical Press, 1991.

Fuller, Reginald H. *Preaching the New Lectionary.* Collegeville: The Liturgical Press, 1974.

Sanchez, Patricia Datchuck. *The Word We Celebrate.* Kansas City: Sheed and Ward, 1989.

Smith, Jonathon. *Map Is Not Territory.* Leiden: Brill, 1978.

Talbert, Charles H. *Reading John.* New York: Crossroad, 1992.

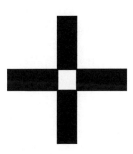

---

[11]Ephraim, *Commentaire sur l'Evangile concordant,* XII, 2, transl. L. Leloir, *Corpus christianorum orientalium,* Vol. 145, p. 115. Taken from *Days of the Lord,* Vol. 5 (Collegeville: The Liturgical Press, 1991), 17

THIRD SUNDAY IN ORDINARY TIME

INTRODUCTORY RITES

Opening Song (or Entrance Antiphon)

Sing a new song to the Lord! Sing to the Lord, all the earth. Truth and beauty surround him, he lives in holiness and glory. (Ps 95:1, 6)[1]

Opening Prayer

The facilitator of the session may lead the prayer. Others in the group may be asked to proclaim the readings.

Let us pray...

Pause for silent prayer.

All powerful and ever living God,
direct your love that is within us,
that our efforts in the name of your Son
may bring mankind to unity and peace.
We ask this through our Lord Jesus Christ, your
    Son,
who lives and reigns with you and the Holy
    Spirit,
one God, for ever and ever.[2]

LITURGY OF THE WORD

Let us listen to God's word.

The readings are proclaimed.

First Reading
Nehemiah 8:2-4, 5-6, 8-10

The authors of Nehemiah possessed the conviction that Israel was called to be a worshiping community, a church. The purpose for Israel's existence was to be a "liturgy," a divine service. In other words, their entire lives were to be devoted to the praise and thanks of Yahweh.

The book of Nehemiah was written after the Babylonian exile. Many Jews chose to remain in Babylon and tend to the lives they had carved out for themselves in the land of exile. Others opted to return to Israel, to Jerusalem. Their goal was to rebuild the sacral life of temple worship. However, work was cut out for the returning band of zealous religious refugees. During the exile some Jews had not been deported to Babylon but instead remained in Israel. They were not too thrilled at the prospect of returning religious zealots being in positions of power. Those who had remained in Israel during the exile had become comfortably inculturated. The tension between Samaritans and Jews began during this time of turmoil.

Samaritans were Jews from the north who had remained in Israel during the exile. They were apprehensive that their Jewish counterparts were returning with an exaggerated sense of nationalism and were intent on governing the land. However, they reluctantly volunteered to help the returning Jews rebuild the temple. Their offer was refused and hostility between the two groups became pronounced. Jews believed the Samaritans to have been corrupted by pagan influence during the exile. Samaritans believed the Jews to be driven by political rather than spiritual motives.

After some time, the Second Temple was built and life moved forward. "Israel's life and thought were nourished in the Temple until its final destruction in the Roman period (70 C.E.)."[3] Yet, a generation before Nehemiah, the people's worship had grown routine. They were offering sacrifices not worthy of the governor, let alone Yahweh. The prophets were crying for a return to sincerity. The prophetic books that preceded Nehemiah revealed a Jewish community torn by internal strife and division, poverty and religious apathy. Reform was critical.

Ezra was considered a noted scribe of the law. His first task was to restore the family institution, the

---

[1]Third Sunday in Ordinary Time: "Entrance Antiphon," *The Sacramentary.*

[2]Third Sunday in Ordinary Time: "Opening Prayer," *The Sacramentary.*

[3]Bernhard W. Anderson, *Understanding the Old Testament,* 4th ed. (Englewood Cliffs: Prentice Hall, 1986), 520.

mainstay of Jewish identity and traditions. He demanded strict adherence to the law of Moses and refused to allow intermarriage. At the Feast of Tabernacles, Ezra climbed the elevated platform at the Water Gate of Jerusalem and read the law to the people who were standing from morning until evening. The next day the people erected their booths for the seven-day vigil. During the week-long feast, the Torah continued to be proclaimed. The Levites (priests) interpreted the meaning of what was being proclaimed so the people could understand. At the end of the festival there was a ceremony of covenant renewal. The people confessed their sins and Ezra, "as covenant mediator," offered prayers to God on behalf of the people. All committed to the renewed covenant, and an oath was signed by representatives of the people. Today's reading reflects just such a liturgy.

Some scholars believe that Ezra's greatest contribution was to establish the Pentateuch as the authoritative canon[4] for Jewish faith and practice. Under Ezra, the life and religion of Jews were molded by the sacred Torah, the Mosaic tradition. The connection of this passage to the gospel is obscure. Some believe the only connection has to do with the reading of the Torah in both scriptural texts (Ezra in the first reading and Jesus in the gospel).

Responsorial Psalm
Psalm 19:7, 8, 9, 14

"This psalm praises God for the perfection, truth and purity of the Torah."[5] The word of God being praised in this psalm is not just a compilation of commandments. It includes God's complete self-revelation to humanity. The psalm is a response not only to the word spoken by Ezra, but to the Word revealed through the person of Jesus.

---

[4]"The word 'canon,' which is Sumerian in origin, refers in its primary sense to any measurement or yardstick. In a metaphorical sense, the Greeks referred to their classics as *kanones*— standards of excellence. However, when used in reference to Old Testament literature, it merely claims that this literature is *sacred scripture* and as such constitutes the community's rule of faith and conduct." (Anderson, *Understanding the Old Testament*, 530).

[5]Reginald Fuller, *Preaching the New Lectionary* (Collegeville: The Liturgical Press, 1974), 487.

Second Reading
1 Corinthians 12:12-30 (long form)
1 Corinthians 12:12-14, 27 (short form)

Reginald Fuller states that Paul's letter to the Corinthians answers a question: "Is the Body of Christ a simile or an ontological reality?"

It is both. Believers are "*like*" the body of Christ and they "*are*" the Body of Christ. Paul's message asserts that they are *like* Christ's Body because of the reality that Christ has already risen and believers have not. Salvation is not a sure thing; it still requires that one work for its completion. Paul insists that believers "*are*" the Body of Christ because they are completely dependent upon his sovereignty over their lives. Just as an arm cannot exist unto itself, so believers cannot exist without Christ. The implications are total dedication and obedience to the person of Jesus Christ.

In chapters 12 through 14, Paul "writes about the unity and diversity of the church, making use of the diversity of its members."[6] Some of the Corinthian members of the church, the gnostics, experienced ecstatic states that they believed set them apart from other believers. Paul insisted that the greatest gift of all was not the gift of such states, but rather the gift of love given by the Spirit. This gift of love drives all other gifts.

Gospel
Luke 1:1-4; 4:4-21

This gospel begins and sets the stage for the entire gospel of Luke (See Overview of the Gospel of Luke). Jesus enters the synagogue after a missionary tour throughout Galilee and proclaims the Torah.

STEP 1
NAMING ONE'S EXPERIENCE

What captured your attention? How did you feel?

Each person names his or her initial impression. Statement should be brief. No reasons should be given at this time. All simply listen without agreeing or disagreeing.

---

[6]Raymond F. Collins, *Preaching the Epistles* (New York/Mahwah: Paulist Press, 1996), 54.

In a brief statement, what do you think this gospel is trying to convey? What does it mean?

Liturgical Context

In the first words of his gospel, Luke proposed his clear intention for writing the account of Jesus' life and work. He wanted to make sure that everyone knew that Jesus' teachings were authoritative and that all prior events and prophecies had been fulfilled through Jesus' life and work.

For the next three weeks the chronological reading of Luke exhibits an internal unity. The Third Sunday establishes that Jesus is the revealed Word of God and as messiah his teaching is definitive and authoritative. The Fourth Sunday details the implications of accepting the revealed Word: one has to choose to believe or not believe. The Fifth Sunday demonstrates that believers are called to service in the ministry of the revealed Word.

Jesus' participation in the liturgy of the word in today's reading highlights for modern readers—for readers of all generations—that the word of God is timeless and contains permanent value and meaning. The liturgy in which Jesus was participating in today's gospel was the prescribed liturgy of the synagogue. Our own liturgy is rooted in this very same biblical, liturgical tradition. Jesus is as present today as he was in the synagogue at that morning liturgy and he "preaches the same present powers of the wonder of God."[7]

Luke's intention was not to create another liturgical, ritual text, but to provide instruction for catechumens.[8]

_____

[7] *Days of the Lord*, Vol. 6 (Collegeville: The Liturgical Press, 1991), 333.

[8] Fuller, *Preaching the New Lectionary*, 490.

Gospel Exegesis

The facilitator gives input regarding what critical biblical scholarship has to say about this text. The input includes insights as to how people would have heard the gospel in Jesus' time.

Before going any further it would be helpful to reread the overview of Luke's gospel. This Sunday we start with the beginning of Luke's gospel. Today's pericope sets the stage for the entire gospel. While the gospels are not actual biographies, Luke's intent was to write an "orderly account" of the events of Jesus' life and the subsequent life of the church that followed him (Acts of the Apostles).

Imagine for one moment. It is Sunday morning. Our best lector or preacher rises, goes to the ambo, opens the lectionary, reads a familiar passage (one that we have heard repeatedly); we are lulled in the trance of unconscious half listening; and then, POW! We are thunderously brought to full, active consciousness by the presumptuous upstart standing before us who dares to presume that the scripture just read refers directly to none other than himself! We would be calling in the liturgy police! It is no wonder that in just a few chapters the response of the religious elite is murder! They want to see him dead!

Jesus' proclamation in the synagogue must have embodied the sacramental presence of God to his listeners. Otherwise, in fairness, it would be hard to blame his detractors. The power of the Spirit must have given such authority to his words (the sacramental presence of God present in every Sunday proclamation of the word even today) that to *not hear* was worse than Israel's infidelity.

The second paragraph of this story lets us know that Jesus' ministry was driven by the power of the Holy Spirit. Luke authenticates the baptism of Jesus in which the Spirit anointed him for the work he was to do. It was the same Spirit that had led Jesus victoriously through the desert temptations and now gave him full legitimacy as evidenced by his presidency in the synagogue. All now were free to rejoice in his Spirit-anointed ministry. In Mark's gospel this scene occurs later in the text. Luke begins his gospel with Jesus in the synagogue. Jesus reveals his mission to the most difficult crowd of all—the hometown boys! He tells them that he is none other than the expected one from Isaiah's prophecy. It is Jesus—carpenter, son, brother—who is the suffering servant of Isaiah. Jesus jumps in with both feet, right from the beginning. There is nothing tentative about his mission. He describes the ministry he has come to establish: preaching, liberation, and healing. He asserts the eschatological implication: he is the fulfillment of all scripture. The last age is ushered in before their very eyes and ears!

Through the proclamation of Isaiah, Jesus emphatically tells his audience that the messianic era has arrived. The jubilee year of liberation from debt described in the passage from Isaiah was regarded as the messianic era. Luke establishes definitively that Jesus began his ministry with the full authority of the Spirit. His ministry embodied the restoration of justice that was to accompany the messianic age.

All who experience the messiah will know what it means to be released from the power of whatever oppresses and exercises control. Jesus' ministry of preaching, healing, and exorcism clearly demands a new way of living in the reign of God.

The mission of Jesus is the mission of the entire church. The church shares Jesus' mission. Just as Jesus was baptized in the Holy Spirit at the River Jordan, the church is also baptized, initiated, and empowered sacramentally by the presence of the risen Christ for the ministry of healing, preaching, and exorcism. The church is about the business of liberation and release.

Proclaim the gospel again.

Sometimes we gain new insights when we hear the text after the interpretation has been given. Someone from the group proclaims the gospel a second time.

STEP 4
TESTING

Conversation with the Liturgy and the Scriptures

Test your original understanding in dialogue with the text.

(You might consider breaking into smaller groups.)

Was there anything about Jesus' preaching in the synagogue or this gospel that was a new insight for you? What original understanding did you bring to this gospel? How does it differ from the exegesis?

How does this story speak to your life?

The story of Jesus in the synagogue reminds me that baptism, confirmation, and eucharist empower me for the same ministry as Jesus. Eucharist is an ongoing empowerment. We participate in Jesus' ministry of healing, preaching, and liberation. Every time I am willing to share a piece of my life, I share in Jesus' ministry. My husband and his friend Dan have a ministry to the homeless. They share the sacramental presence of Jesus with the homeless as they listen to their stories, feed their bodies, and try to offer the promise of a better way to live. This ministry involves the three dimensions of Jesus' ministry. They preach to those who have been cast off by society, the drug addicts, the hard-core alcoholics, and the mentally ill. They preach not with words, but with actions. Bob and Dan preach the love of God by treating the homeless with dignity.

They offer the homeless person specific assistance to get off the street. The homeless know that whenever any one of them is ready, Bob and Dan will help them get treatment, find a job, and secure a place to live. Out of eleven homeless people in two years, only two people have chosen to turn their lives around. But the ministry of healing, love, and liberation continues and the people keep coming back. Bob and Dan do not give up on them. They get frustrated, but they do not give up. Jesus invites each of us to participate in his preaching, healing, and liberating ministry. Our baptism challenges us to live in the power of the Spirit and to proclaim and work for the complete liberation of all the poor and oppressed of the world.

I wonder how I would respond if a familiar neighbor were to get up on a given Sunday morning and proclaim the same message Jesus proclaimed to his friends that day. I would hope that I would be attentive to the authentic voice of God in the midst of his proclamation. The ministry Jesus inaugurated that day lives on, however, and I can share it just as Bob and Dan share it in the way God has called them to share it.

Participants share an experience from their lives that connects with the biblical interpretation just shared.

What was Luke's message to his community? Is there any relevance today? There are strong elements of the biblical themes of covenant, exodus, creation, and community evident in these readings. How do they speak to you? Is there anything you would like to add to your original understanding of this gospel? Do you still feel the same way about this text as you did at the beginning?

STEP 5
DECISION

The gospel demands a response.

In what way is your community challenged by the interpretation of today's gospel? What would be the contemporary implications of Jesus' proclamation in the synagogue? In what way are you called to respond? Be concrete. Have you experienced any change or transformation as a result of this sharing? Name one specific action you will take this week as a response to what was learned and shared today.

DOCTRINAL ISSUES

What church truth/teaching/doctrinal issue could be drawn from the gospel for the Third Sunday in Ordinary Time?

Participants suggest possible doctrinal themes that flow from the readings.

Possible Doctrinal Themes

Christology, Spirit, sacramentality, discipleship, baptism, word of God

Present the doctrinal material at this time.

1. The facilitator gives input on a particular doctrinal issue of his/her prior choosing. OR
2. The group chooses a doctrinal issue from the list they created. They read together from the Doctrinal Appendix.

(The doctrinal issues are found in the Doctrinal Appendix in the back of this workbook. If you are choosing an issue from this resource, please refer to it now.)

Reflection questions centered around the chosen doctrinal theme can be found at the end of each topic in the Doctrinal Appendix. The questions are based on the five-step reflection process. If you choose a topic not included in the Doctrinal Appendix, craft your own questions according to the same five-step process.

Following the reflection questions you will be reminded to return to chapter 7, "Preparing the Catechetical Session," to assist you in crafting your own session.

Closing Prayer

Let us end with the words of Origen.

> Blessed assembly whom Scripture attests all had their eyes fixed on Jesus! How I wish this assembly might receive similar testimony that all catechumens and faithful, women, men, and children have their eyes, not of the body, but of the soul, filled with the sight of Jesus! When you look at him, his light and his contemplation will lighten your faces, and you will be able to say: "The light of your face has left its imprint on us, O Lord!"

> Therefore we humbly ask, imprint on us, O Lord, the Light of your Spirit that we may boldly proclaim your good news![9]

Selected Bibliography

Anderson, Bernhard W. *Understanding the Old Testament.* 4th ed. Englewood Cliffs: Prentice Hall, 1986.

---

[9]Origen (3rd c.), *Homelies sur saint Luc* XXXII, 6, in *Sources chretiennes* 87 (Paris: Cerf, 1962), 391-393. Taken from *Days of the Lord,* Vol. 6 (Collegeville: The Liturgical Press, 1991), 26.

Collins, Raymond F. *Preaching the Epistles.* New York/Mahwah: Paulist Press, 1996.

Days of the Lord. Vol. 6. Collegeville: The Liturgical Press, 1991.

Fuller, Reginald H. *Preaching the New Lectionary.* Collegeville: The Liturgical Press, 1974.

Sanchez, Patricia Datchuck. *The Word We Celebrate.* Kansas City: Sheed and Ward, 1989.

Tannehill, Robert C. *The Narrative Unity of Luke-Acts: A Literary Interpretation.* Minneapolis: Augsburg Fortress, 1986.

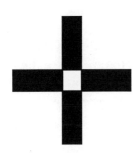

FOURTH SUNDAY IN ORDINARY TIME

INTRODUCTORY RITES

Opening Song (or Entrance Antiphon)

Save us, Lord our God, and gather us together from the nations, that we may proclaim your holy name and glory in your praise. (Ps 105:47)[1]

Opening Prayer

Let us pray...

Pause for silent prayer.

Father in heaven,
from the days of Abraham and Moses
until this gathering of your Church in prayer,
you have formed a people in the image of your
    Son.
Bless this people with the gift of your kingdom.
May we serve you with our every desire
and show love for one another
even as you have loved us.
Grant this through Christ, our Lord.[2]

LITURGY OF THE WORD

Let us listen to God's word.

The readings are proclaimed.

First Reading
Jeremiah 1:4-5, 17-19

Jeremiah was a prophet during very turbulent times. His ministry began at the end of King Josiah's reign and extended into the reign of the tyrant, Jehoiakim. Jeremiah was known as a somber prophet. People did not want to listen to his message. His prophetic career lasted over thirty-nine years (626–587 B.C.E.). Jeremiah threw himself into his prophetic work. He felt and experienced the passion of his oracles. He grieved vociferously over the plight of the nation. He was known as the "weeping prophet."

Under Josiah there had been a resurgence of nationalism. For a while it had appeared as if things would return to the splendor of the Davidic monarchy. The people were wooed by the prosperity prophets who promised that things would soon return to the "good old days of national glory."[3] However, Jeremiah's words of truth and reality remained in Israel's consciousness long after the prosperity prophets were gone. Jeremiah had not prophesied during the latter part of Josiah's reign. However, once the harsh reign of Jehoiakim began, Jeremiah could no longer keep silent and was compelled to step into the prophetic arena.

Today's pericope deals with the call of Jeremiah. Jeremiah outlines his credentials and his authority. It was Yahweh who knew him, formed him (literally fashioned him) and dedicated him, from the very womb of his mother. Yahweh knows the heart of every person from the instant of existence. Jeremiah had been set apart (consecrated) from the very beginning for his role in salvation history. This reading was chosen for its connection to the gospel in which Jesus, too, was called from the beginning of time to be messiah and the One who would restore God's people.

Jeremiah is not just a prophet to Israel; his ministry extends to the whole world. Jeremiah had a compelling sense of the God of history, of all peoples, past, present, and future. In this passage, Jeremiah is warned that his message will not be received. Some suggest that this reading prefigures the rejection Jesus would experience in his own ministry in his own home, by those who refused to listen.

Jeremiah's ministry and discipleship demanded a great price. Suffering was the hallmark of his min-

[1]Fourth Sunday in Ordinary Time: "Entrance Antiphon," *The Sacramentary.*

[2]Fourth Sunday in Ordinary Time: "Opening Prayer," *The Sacramentary.*

[3]Bernhard W. Anderson, *Understanding the Old Testament,* 4th ed. (Englewood Cliffs: Prentice Hall, 1986), 391.

istry. He was not ashamed to share his pain with his audience. He exhorted his community to ready themselves for the things to come. They had grown complacent in their commitment to the covenant.

Responsorial Psalm
Psalm 71:1-2, 3-4, 5-6, 15-17

The psalm is a psalm of lament. It was chosen to express Jeremiah's agonizing pain and the refuge he sought in God. Jeremiah frequently sought the refuge of Yahweh in the midst of his persecution.

Second Reading
1 Corinthians 12:31–13:13

Paul's community was experiencing internal strife and division. Some people (gnostics), glorying in their own manifestations of the gifts of the Spirit, had set themselves apart as the spiritual elite. Because of their self-righteous, emotional, and overt display of charisms, Paul wrote to them to remind them that God was the Giver of gifts and no one had reason to boast. Paul asserted that the gifts were for the uplifting of the community, not for personal edification. The gifts meant nothing if love was absent. The greatest charism for Paul as expressed in today's pericope is the response of love. Paul's perspective is ecclesial. He asserts that self-giving love toward one another should be the response of every member of the community. Paul reminds us of what church is called to be and to do. "This passage (about love) is often read and preached during nuptial celebrations, but it has an ecclesial importance. The church is a community of love; in all that it does, it is called to be the instrument of God, allowing his love to be active and present in the world. In this respect, Paul offers himself as an example of how God's love is at work in the Church."[4]

Gospel
Luke 4:21-30

Jesus reads from the scroll in the synagogue and finds resistance from his own neighbors.

---

[4]Raymond F. Collins, *Preaching the Epistles* (New York/Mahwah: Paulist Press, 1996), 55.

STEP 1
NAMING ONE'S EXPERIENCE

What were your first impressions? What was your first response? What grabbed your attention? How did you feel?

Each person names his or her initial impression. Statement should be brief. No reasons should be given at this time. All simply listen without agreeing or disagreeing.

STEP 2
UNDERSTANDING

In a brief statement, what do you think this gospel is trying to convey?

STEP 3
INPUT FROM VISION/STORY/TRADITION

Liturgical Context

Today's gospel takes up where last week's left off with Jesus preaching in the synagogue. He preached with authority and announced the messianic era. One would think that Jesus' message in his hometown would be reason for celebration in the streets of Nazareth. On the contrary, his own people rejected him. The scriptures today highlight discipleship that leads to the cross. Discipleship leads to and is often a path of rejection. Jeremiah prefigured Christ by the suffering he endured for the sake of God's word. Jesus, the true prophet, suffered and died for the *Word* he was and the *word* he preached. All of the readings today show us what it costs to be a disciple. They emphasize that it is God who validates our ministry and who upholds us in the midst of rejection and suffering. Paul's exhortation reminds us of our response: total commitment of self in love to God and to one another.

The alternative opening prayer for today's liturgy expresses the fact that we have been formed as a people and asks that the ministry and reign Jesus announced in the synagogue be made real in the lives of God's people. Loving discipleship is to be our response.

Gospel Exegesis

The facilitator gives input regarding what critical biblical scholarship has to say about this text. The input includes insights as to how people would have heard the gospel in Jesus' time.

Jesus, hometown boy, stands before the Nazareth crowd. With all eyes riveted on him, he announces that the passage he has just read from Isaiah is fulfilled in their hearing. Tension mounts in these first lines. Who is this Jesus? We have to choose. What appears to be enthusiastic response quickly moved to anger and antagonism. Obviously, the people of Nazareth had heard about his miracles. We know this from use of the imperfect verb form, "*was praised.*" This imperfect verb set up a "sense of repeated action; Jesus was making a circuit of local communities before he came to his own."[5] By acknowledging that everyone who heard him had praised him, a contrast was immediately set between *everyone* and his own people. At first there was enthusiasm for Jesus' proclamation. Things went downhill quickly, however. Luke's readers knew that the correct response in regard to Jesus was certainly not "son of Joseph," but rather, Son of God! However, Jesus' own townsfolk were taken in, not by his spiritual authority from God, but by the powerful deeds they had heard about. They wanted to be recipients of the deeds. They entertained great expectations that Jesus would set up his healing and exorcism ministry right there in Nazareth. When Jesus dashed their expectations, they were furious. The rage of the crowd is expressed by a word used in another scene in which a crowd reacts negatively against threats to its local prestige (Acts 19:28).[6]

Jesus entered into clarifying dialogue with them and in the process defined his ministry. In essence Jesus says, "You have expectations of me here in Nazareth. Let me set you straight. First, wisdom literature advises against me setting up headquarters here and so does Scripture. I will be taking God's anointed ministry with me *away* from Nazareth. Even the Gentiles will receive this message!"[7]

One scholar suggests that the people were trying to put him to the test. Jesus would not be put to the test and asserted that a prophet would never be accepted in his own place. He cited the examples of Elijah and Elisha. The people became infuriated by the comparison and wanted to do him in!

This scene is reminiscent of Jesus' diatribe (on the lake) against those who should have been the first to accept his message such as Chorazin and Bethsaida. Jesus said that if he had given the same message and worked the same signs in Tyre and Sidon they would have long ago repented. The point of his chiding is that it is sometimes those who *should* have access to the power and action of God who refuse to accept it or believe it when it is right under their nose. Perhaps the issue was one of loss of power and religious prestige. If everyone is invited, what does that do to the status of the religious elite?

Jesus laid out two important issues in this passage: liberation and inclusion. Jesus associated himself with the liberation ministry of Isaiah and he made it clear that the kingdom was to be inclusive; "Gentiles as well as Jews were to be included in Jesus' vision and concern."[8] This is evident in his referral to the prophet Elijah who "worked miracles for pagans while Jews were still in need of help."[9]

Luke's Jesus assumed a preferential option for the poor, the blind, and the oppressed. Luke Timothy Johnson contends that the *poor* are not only those who are economically oppressed but also those who are on the fringe, those who are out of the loop of human relationships such as the outcast.[10] Jesus assigned himself champion of all those outside the power structures and systems, all those who are controlled by forces outside themselves.

Some scholars suggest that this passage reflects the mission of Christ and the mission of the church. The message of salvation is revealed first to Israel. Yet they who should have been the first to believe instead reject Jesus and later the disci-

---

[5]Luke Timothy Johnson, *The Gospel of Luke,* Sacra Pagina Series, Vol. 3 (Collegeville: The Liturgical Press, 1991), 78.
[6]Ibid., 80.
[7]Charles H. Talbert, *Reading Luke* (New York: Crossroad, 1992), 56.

[8]Johnson, *The Gospel of Luke,* Vol. 3, 79.
[9]Ibid.
[10]Ibid., 79.

ples. Robert Tannehill suggests that Jesus was rejected for religious reasons. Jesus was anointed *by God* to take his mission out of Israel, to be inclusive of others, even gentiles! Jesus did not go out from Israel because he was rejected by Israel; he went because God had commissioned him to go! The contrast between the faith of those who should have rejoiced at the revelation and the gentiles is sharply drawn. Jesus' *word*, like the word of prophets before him such as Jeremiah, would ultimately be rejected. The irony cannot be missed. Here is a prophet who announces a year of favor, a "message acceptable to the Lord" and who himself is not acceptable.[11]

The bottom line of this pericope is that Jesus' mission, the mission of the entire church, is authorized by the Holy Spirit. It is a ministry of preaching, healing, exorcism, and evangelization that extends to the ends of the earth.[12] Luke longed for his disciples to know that no matter how much oppression or persecution there might be, the *word* goes forth according to the will of God.

Proclaim the gospel again.

Sometimes we gain new insights when we hear the text after the interpretation has been given.

STEP 4
TESTING

Conversation with the Liturgy and the Scriptures

Test your original understanding in dialogue with the text.

(You might consider breaking into smaller groups.)

What are your feelings about this gospel in light of the exegesis? How does it compare with your original understanding? What are the implications today of Jesus' preaching in his own synagogue? Who might be some prophets in our midst? Was there anything you had not considered before?

---

[11]Johnson, *The Gospel of Luke*, Vol. 3, 80.
[12]Talbert, *Reading Luke*, 57.

How does this story speak to your life?

I wonder how my parish (or any other parish) would react if one of our own were to say, "Folks, remember me? I am the fellow you have been reading about in the scriptures and the one you have been waiting for for years. All of your hopes and dreams will be fulfilled in me." I do not have to ponder long to assert with confidence that there would not be a listening ear in the house.

I am reminded of a time when we had a parish mission. The traveling preacher commanded an audience that had people sitting in the confessionals, jamming into the back sacristy and poking their heads through doors just to hear his message. His message was good news. It was proclamation of the gospel of Jesus Christ. Yet, aside from the delivery, it was the same message proclaimed week after week, Sunday after Sunday. Sometimes the showy medium attracts more attention than the plain truth of the message, especially when the message is proclaimed by people we have eaten with, played with, prayed with, and at times have been angry with. Somehow the message is de-sacralized because of the all-too familiar messenger. Jesus' message reminds me and our community that we should be attuned to the manifestation of God even when it appears in the everyday, mundane experiences of life.

Also, Jesus demands that we move beyond ourselves and to those we often find unsuitable or who do not meet our expectations of propriety or decency. The word of God is not for our personal enrichment alone. It demands action and response. Perhaps the Nazareth crowd was unimpressed by the company Jesus was keeping (prostitutes, homeless, outcasts, the unclean, tax collectors, gentiles, etc.). How would we/I respond?

All share their life experience.

What was Luke trying to tell his community? What are some relevant implications for our community today? Are the biblical themes of covenant, creation, exodus, and community evident in today's readings? How? Do I still feel the same way about this text as I did when we began? Has my original assumption about this gospel been expanded or challenged?

The gospel demands a response.

How does Jesus' message to his hometown call our community to respond? How would Jesus be received today in similar circumstances? How am I challenged by the scriptures today? What is one concrete action I will take this week as a response to what was learned and shared today?

DOCTRINAL ISSUES

What church truth/teaching/doctrinal issue could be drawn from the gospel for the Fourth Sunday of Ordinary Time?

Participants suggest possible doctrinal themes that flow from the readings.

Possible Doctrinal Themes

Christology, justice, conversion, mission, salvation, word of God

Present the doctrinal material at this time.

1. The facilitator gives input on a particular doctrinal issue of his/her prior choosing. OR
2. The group chooses a doctrinal issue from the list they created. They read together from the Doctrinal Appendix.

(The doctrinal issues are found in the Doctrinal Appendix in the back of this workbook. If you are choosing an issue from this resource, please refer to it now.)

Reflection questions centered around the chosen doctrinal theme can be found at the end of each topic in the Doctrinal Appendix. The questions are based on the five-step reflection process. If you choose a topic not included in the Doctrinal Appendix, craft your own questions according to the same five-step process.

Following the reflection questions you will be reminded to return to chapter 7, "Preparing the Catechetical Session," to assist you in crafting your own session.

Closing Prayer

Almighty and eternal God,
you gather the scattered sheep
and watch over those you have gathered.
Look kindly on all who follow Jesus, your Son.
You have marked them with the seal of one
    baptism,
now make them one in the fullness of faith
and unite them in the bond of love.
We ask this through Christ, our Lord.[13]

Selected Bibliography

Anderson, Bernhard W. *Understanding the Old Testament:* 4th ed. Englewood Cliffs: Prentice Hall, 1986.

Cassidy, Richard J. *Jesus, Politics, and Society.* Maryknoll: Orbis Books, 1978.

Collins, Raymond F. *Preaching the Epistles.* New York/Mahwah: Paulist Press, 1996.

Days of the Lord. Vol. 6. Collegeville: The Liturgical Press, 1991.

Fuller, Reginald H. *Preaching the New Lectionary.* Collegeville: The Liturgical Press, 1974.

Johnson, Luke Timothy. *The Gospel of Luke.* Sacra Pagina Series, Vol. 3. Collegeville: The Liturgical Press, 1991.

Kingsbury, Jack Dean. *Conflict in Luke.* Minneapolis: Augsburg Fortress, 1991.

Sanchez, Patricia Datchuck. *The Word We Celebrate.* Kansas City: Sheed and Ward, 1989.

Talbert, Charles H. *Reading Luke.* New York: Crossroad, 1992.

Tannehill, Robert C. *The Narrative Unity of Luke-Acts: A Literary Interpretation.* Vol. 1. Minneapolis: Augsburg Fortress, 1986.

---

[13]"Third Week in January: Week of Prayer for Christian Unity," *Catholic Household Blessings and Prayers* (Washington: USCC, NCCB, 1988), 160.

FIFTH SUNDAY IN ORDINARY TIME

INTRODUCTORY RITES

Opening Song (or Entrance Antiphon)

Come, let us worship the Lord. Let us bow down in the presence of our maker, for he is the Lord our God. (Ps 94:6-7)[1]

Opening Prayer

The facilitator of the session may lead the prayer. Others in the group may be asked to proclaim the readings.

Let us pray...

Pause for silent prayer.

God, our Father,
you give us a share in the one bread and the one
    cup
and make us one in Christ.
Help us to bring your salvation and joy
to all the world.
We ask this through Christ, our Lord.[2]

LITURGY OF THE WORD

Let us listen to God's word.

The readings are proclaimed.

First Reading
Isaiah 6:1-2, 3-8

Isaiah ("*Yahweh is salvation*") tells us today that he was called by God in the year King Uzziah died (ca. 742). Assyria was attempting to take over the then-known world. Isaiah's prophetic ministry occurred in the midst of this turmoil. He was an educated man from an upper class family who was married and had two sons. His ministry was centered near Jerusalem. Syria and Israel (Northern Kingdom) had invaded Judah (Southern King-dom) in order to force her into an alliance against Assyria. Isaiah was opposed to this alliance. Later Isaiah vociferously railed against Egypt's attempt to get Judah to join her against Assyria. Judah joined the revolt but was later crushed and experienced annihilation as a result.

Isaiah's primary message was to proclaim the immensity of God's power over all creation. He referred to Yahweh as "the Holy One of Israel." "Oppression of weaker members of society offended Yahweh's holiness, and so Isaiah spoke vehemently about social justice."[3] Yahweh was in control of all history. For Judah to design her own destiny was an affront to God.

Today's pericope is a call story. Traditionally, call stories served to validate the prophet's mission, even—and especially—when the message was unpopular. Isaiah saw God as Lord of all the earth, not a nationalistic icon god. Only Yahweh's transcendent power was an absolute.

In the scriptures wherever there is the presence of smoke, one knows immediately that there is an observable manifestation of God. Isaiah was aware of his unworthiness before the Transcendent Other. His "woe is me" reflected his fear and trembling at having seen the Lord. No one sees God and lives to tell about it. Yet, in this encounter there was a validation of sorts. Isaiah saw the Lord, repented, and was commissioned by the heavenly court to go and proclaim Yahweh's word. He went in peace and assurance. There was a three-fold component to the call. First, he repented; then, he was sent; and finally, he "responded by accepting the call."[4]

Responsorial Psalm
Psalm 138:1-2, 2-3, 4-5, 7-8

---

[1] Fifth Sunday in Ordinary Time: "Entrance Antiphon," *The Sacramentary.*

[2] Fifth Sunday in Ordinary Time: "Prayer after Communion," *The Sacramentary.*

[3] Joseph Jensen, O.S.B. and William Irwin, C.S.B., "Isaiah 1–39," in *The New Jerome Biblical Commentary,* ed. Raymond E. Brown, S.S., Joseph A. Fitzmyer, S.J., Roland E. Murphy, O.Carm. (Englewood Cliffs: Prentice Hall, 1990), 230.

[4] Reginald H. Fuller, *Preaching the New Lectionary* (Collegeville: The Liturgical Press, 1974), 496.

This psalm highlights Isaiah's revelation rather than his prophetic call. It is a psalm of thanks and praise before the omniscient Yahweh.

Second Reading
1 Corinthians 15:1-11

For Greek people schooled in the dualism of Greek thought (matter is evil, spirit is good), the resurrection of the body was a tremendous obstacle. Christians influenced by gnosticism suggested that they were already resurrected because of their participation in the sacraments. When Paul left Corinth, the people practiced selective Christianity. They discarded the theology they did not like and retained what suited them. Paul wrote his letter in order to remind them that the tradition they had been given was an authentic tradition. It was reliable, and verified by eyewitnesses. Verses 3 and 4 appear to be a creedal formula that had already been part of their tradition.

Paul's letter mentions verifiable witnesses. Two men were required to validate an eyewitness. Paul named more than two. Women could not witness to anything unless it pertained to issues that directly concerned them, such as household matters. Thus, if only women had witnessed to the Christ event, their witness would not have been valid. Therefore, the witness of women is starkly absent from this account. Their absence does not reflect a lack of presence; it simply reflects the cultural situation in which women were not deemed valid witnesses.

The reference to the Twelve has had multiple interpretations. One interpretation suggests that it was a designation for the twelve apostles. However, some scholars suggest that reference to the *twelve* refers to the twelve tribes of Israel, an implication of totality, of wholeness, of the entire nation, a whole people. The witnesses, then, are not reduced only to the *twelve*, but include all who saw and believed.

Paul, like Isaiah and Peter, was completely aware of his own unworthiness. He was abashed that he had persecuted the church and realized that his conversion was utter grace. He was sent by God, fully aware of his limitations and his humble stance before Isaiah's "Holy One of Israel."

Gospel
Luke 5:1-11

Jesus calls Peter to cast down his nets and gather in his catch. His new role is that of one who catches people.

STEP 1
NAMING ONE'S EXPERIENCE

What were your first impressions of the readings? What grabbed your attention?

Each person names his or her initial impression. Statement should be brief. No reasons should be given at this time. All simply listen without agreeing or disagreeing.

STEP 2
UNDERSTANDING

In a brief statement, what do you think this gospel is trying to convey? What was the understanding of this gospel that you brought with you to this sharing?

STEP 3
INPUT FROM VISION/STORY/TRADITION

Liturgical Context

Last week Jesus' mission was definitively proclaimed. His ministry of healing and exorcism was empowered by the Holy Spirit. It was to be inclusive and reach to the ends of the earth. As church, we share that same empowerment and participate in the ministry of healing, exorcism and inclusivity. In the First Testament God called the prophets to proclaim the *word*. In this Testament, Jesus calls those he designates *apostle*.[5] They are to be sent to proclaim the good news of salvation to all the world.

---

[5]Apostle in this instance is not to be considered as necessarily meaning the "twelve." The origin of the word *apostle* is from the Greek meaning *one sent*.... Thus, apostles are sent out to preach the good news.

In the first reading of this Sunday we are reminded of God's omnipresence. God's majesty fills the earth. Our imaginations are teased to glimpse at a mystery so powerful that words cannot adequately describe it. We can nearly hear the thunderous shouts and drink deeply of the smoke circling the sanctuary. Truly we shrink in light of such power. We recognize our frailty, yet in humility are called to respond like the prophet: "Here I am Lord, send me!" The primary reason for and response of our gathering in worship is reflected in today's first reading. With the angels we go out singing God's praises. Inadequate though it is, we offer our humble response of thanks and praise.

Why do we gather? To give thanks and praise to God and to be nourished and empowered to take what we receive with us into the world. The psalm itself is "a profession of faith, recall of the past (anamnesis), invocation (epiclesis); this psalm is a veritable cosmic liturgy!"[6]

Paul, too, was aware of his own unworthiness. He was very aware that he had persecuted the church in his pre-conversion days. Yet, he too had been called and he responded by the pure grace of God.

The movement from last week to this week's gospel is one in which the reader is asked to make a giant leap of faith. Last week we were asked to choose: Who is this person Jesus? For the last three weeks we have been absorbed in Luke's agenda. He is emphatic: Jesus is the *One Sent by God*. He is messiah and Lord. This narrative is an accurate account as handed down through oral and written tradition.

Once the parameters were clearly defined, Christ's mission could move forward as reflected in today's focus. *At God's initiative, disciples are called to service in God's realm.* The unity of the Third, Fourth and Fifth Sundays of Ordinary Time can be observed in the fact that "Luke, from the beginning, placed the Christian assembly in the presence of the person of Jesus and his mystery that is unfolded today in the Church and throughout the world."[7]

Perhaps a Rite of Acceptance or Welcome, or an anointing of catechumens with oil might be celebrated on this Sunday.

Gospel Exegesis

The facilitator gives input regarding what critical biblical scholarship has to say about this text. The input includes insights as to how people would have heard the gospel in Jesus' time.

Luke gave Peter's call special significance. Jesus not only called Peter but he foreshadowed his future mission at the moment of the call. Implications of the passion and the post-resurrection mission are boldly proclaimed.[8] Since this story takes place in the context of teaching the multitudes, Simon's call is intimately connected to Jesus' teaching mission. Simon knew Jesus and kept company with him before he was called by Jesus.

Luke's Jesus invited Peter to cast his nets. Peter thought it futile because of earlier unsuccessful attempts, but did what he was told. Prior to Jesus' invitation, there had been nothing but futility. Jesus initiated this next attempt and caused the nets to overflow.

After Peter had witnessed Jesus' manifestation of power, he was awestruck by the reality of who Christ was. Jesus' powerful deeds strengthened Peter's faith. Jesus' command to lower the nets not only had inconceivable results, but it validated Jesus' prophetic power. Jesus knew what would happen before he gave Peter the command. Jesus validated Peter's mission of evangelization. If Jesus knew that Peter's catch would be tremendous, he had to be confident that Peter's missionary efforts would be as tremendous.

Peter's call story underscores the fact that people followed Jesus in response to his miracles. "The story within which the call of the first disciples is

---

[6]*Days of the Lord*, Vol. 6 (Collegeville: The Liturgical Press, 1991), 36.

[7]Ibid., 39.

[8]Eugene LaVerdiere, S.S.S., *Luke* (Wilmington: Michael Glazier Books, 1980), 77.

placed leaves little room for doubt that they followed Jesus because of his wondrous power. Only after Peter, James and John see the miraculous catch of fish are they summoned to follow Jesus."[9] Peter had seen Jesus perform such miracles for other people. This time the powerful deed was done for him. Because of this gratuitous act performed on his behalf, Peter followed Jesus. Luke commonly depicted miracles as the impetus for conversion.

Jesus gave Peter a new name. The conferral of a new name in the scriptures signified transition to something new: a new direction or a new ministry. Simon, designated Peter, the rock, would lead the people. This was to be the new direction (new mission) for his life.

Like Isaiah and Paul, Peter attested to his own unworthiness and need for repentance. The presence of God, the *shekina* glory, can do nothing less than move a person to deep, interior repentance. The response to such glory is hearing and responding to the call. Peter's declaration of unworthiness foreshadowed his denial of Jesus after his arrest. In the midst of Jesus' inevitable suffering and passion, Peter would deny him. Peter's recognition of Jesus as Lord foreshadowed his first post-resurrection encounter with Jesus, when he said, "Lord, you know I love you."

Jesus initiated the call in the face of human limitations. An overabundance of fish was caught only in response to Jesus' initiative. The point? Success in ministry is rooted in Christ. We need only look ahead to the Acts of the Apostles to note the fruits of Peter's sending. Following his empowerment by the Spirit, Peter's first attempt netted three thousand converts.[10]

Proclaim the gospel again.

Sometimes we gain new insights when we hear the text after the interpretation has been given. Someone from the group proclaims the gospel a second time.

---

[9] P. J. Achtemeier, "The Lucan Perspective on the Miracles of Jesus: A Preliminary Sketch," in *Perspectives on Luke-Acts*, ed. C. H. Talbert (Danville: ABPR, 1978), 161.

[10] Charles H. Talbert, *Reading Luke* (New York: Crossroad, 1992), 60-61.

STEP 4
TESTING

Conversation with the Liturgy and the Scriptures

Test your original understanding in dialogue with the text.

(You might consider breaking into smaller groups.)

How does Peter's first fishing lesson, his call to discipleship, speak to your community? What is the relevance for your community? Were there any new insights? Was there anything you had not considered before? How do your original assumptions compare with the exegesis?

How does this story speak to your life?

> *Very often when people are invited to be eucharistic ministers they decline because of an overall sense of unworthiness. In today's gospel, Peter reminds us that those attitudes, while true in relationship to the transcendence of God, are not to keep us from ministry. Peter humbly acknowledged his unworthiness but accepted the call and forged ahead. All of us can relate with Peter on some level. I believe we have a pervasive lack of self esteem. Our sins are always before us. Many people say that we have lost a sense of sin in today's culture. While there is truth in that statement, I am painfully aware of the baggage that people carry around with them. Good, faith-filled people are very often burdened by an overwhelming sense of unworthiness. It is very hard for them to believe and live as though they are forgiven and redeemed. Vatican II gave us a new image of ourselves. We are children of God, elevated to God's divine nature because of grace and we share in Jesus' life as members of the Body of Christ. We can intellectually accept that. But, do we buy it? Do we believe it in our hearts? Many of us do not. If I truly believed it in the deepest recesses of my being, I would not be striving constantly for perfection. I would live my life more fully in the* shalom *presence of God. I must ask myself the question: What motivates me for ministry? Do I recognize my feeble efforts before God and allow God to use me in the way he chooses, or do I frantically bulldoze ahead out of a sense that I must be perfect in order to please God? When the*

latter is true, it is I—not God—who initiates my discipleship. Peter reminds me that I must check my reality meter daily. Do I reach out to others because that is what it means to a perfect disciple? Or do I act on God's initiative and reveal the compassion God has placed within me? It is very easy to fool myself. Christianity is an everyday, fully conscious participation in the life of Jesus. Peter shows us that we don't have to be perfect; we just need to know who starts our motor, drives our engine, and keeps the cylinders moving.

All share their life experience.

What was Luke trying to tell his community? What does he have to say to our community and to me today? What are some common biblical themes in the readings today? Do I still feel the same way about this text as I did at the beginning?

STEP 5
DECISION

The gospel demands a response.

What would be the contemporary implications of the call to discipleship themes of today's readings? In what concrete way is our community called to respond to this gospel? Have I been called to change my attitudes or behavior as a result of our sharing? What are the implications for my life? What is one specific action I will take this week as a response to what was learned and shared today?

Doctrinal Issues

What church truth/teaching/doctrinal issue could be drawn from the gospel for the Fifth Sunday in Ordinary Time?

Participants suggest possible doctrinal themes that flow from the readings.

Possible Doctrinal Themes

Discipleship, conversion, evangelization, baptism/confirmation/eucharist (the call), ministry

Present the doctrinal material at this time.

1. The facilitator gives input on a particular doctrinal issue of his/her prior choosing. OR
2. The group chooses a doctrinal issue from the list they created. They read together from the Doctrinal Appendix.

(The doctrinal issues are found in the Doctrinal Appendix in the back of this workbook. If you are choosing an issue from this resource, please refer to it now.)

Reflection questions centered around the chosen doctrinal theme can be found at the end of each topic in the Doctrinal Appendix. The questions are based on the five-step reflection process. If you choose a topic not included in the Doctrinal Appendix, craft your own questions according to the same five-step process.

Following the reflection questions you will be reminded to return to chapter 7, "Preparing the Catechetical Session," to assist you in crafting your own session.

Closing Prayer

Father, all powerful and ever-living God
we do well always and everywhere to give you thanks
through Jesus Christ our Lord.
Through his cross and resurrection
he freed us from sin and death
and called us to the glory that has made us
a chosen race, a royal priesthood,
a holy nation, a people set apart.
Everywhere we proclaim your mighty works
for you have called us out of darkness
into your own wonderful light.
And so with all the choirs of angels in heaven
we proclaim your glory and join in their unending
   hymn of praise:
Holy, holy, holy....[11]

Selected Bibliography

Achtemeier, P. J. "The Lucan Perspective on the Miracles of Jesus: A Preliminary Sketch." In

---

[11]Preface: Sundays In Ordinary Time I: "The Paschal Mystery and the People of God," *The Sacramentary.*

Perspectives on Luke-Acts. Ed. C. H. Talbert. Danville: ABPR, 1978.

Days of the Lord. Vol. 6. Collegeville: The Liturgical Press, 1991.

Fuller, Reginald H. *Preaching the New Lectionary.* Collegeville: The Liturgical Press, 1974.

Jensen, Joseph, O.S.B. and William Irwin, C.S.B. "Isaiah 1-39." In *The New Jerome Biblical Commentary.* Ed. Raymond E. Brown, S.S., Joseph A. Fitzmyer, S.J., Roland E. Murphy, O.Carm. Englewood Cliffs: Prentice Hall, 1990.

Johnson, Luke Timothy. *The Gospel of Luke.* Sacra Pagina Series. Vol. 3. Collegeville: The Liturgical Press, 1991.

LaVerdiere, Eugene, S.S.S. *Luke.* Wilmington: Michael Glazier Books, 1980.

Sanchez, Patricia Datchuck. *The Word We Celebrate.* Kansas City: Sheed and Ward, 1989.

Talbert, Charles H. *Reading Luke.* New York: Crossroad, 1992.

SIXTH SUNDAY IN ORDINARY TIME

INTRODUCTORY RITES

Opening Song (or Entrance Antiphon)

Lord, be my rock of safety, the stronghold that saves me. For the honor of your name, lead me and guide me. (Ps 30:34)[1]

Opening Prayer

The facilitator of the session may lead the prayer. Others in the group may be asked to proclaim the readings.

Let us pray...

   (Pause for silent prayer.)

God, our Father,
you have promised to remain for ever
with those who do what is just and right.
Help us to live in your presence.
We ask this through our Lord Jesus Christ, your Son,
who lives and reigns with you and the Holy Spirit,
one God, for ever and ever.[2]

LITURGY OF THE WORD

Let us listen to God's word.

The readings are proclaimed.

First Reading
Jeremiah 17:5-8

Some scholars believe that the verses of today's first reading were not written by Jeremiah. They do not seem to fit his normal writing style. These verses resonate more with traditional wisdom literature.

It is obvious that this pericope was chosen for its connection to the gospel. Jeremiah's naming of blessings and curses depicts a literary form used in

Luke that has its antecedents in First Testament literature as seen in today's readings.

One school of thought suggests that Jeremiah spent his entire lifetime witnessing the slow but sure destruction of Judah at the hands of enemies. Jeremiah emphatically stresses that trust in Yahweh is the only logical response for humanity in the face of trials and tribulation. Human beings cannot exist without the providential care of Yahweh. If they try to live by their own strength, they eventually wither and die like plants bereft of life-giving water.

Responsorial Psalm
Psalm 1:1-2, 3-4, 5-6

The psalm was written at a much later time than the first reading. It was written following the exile in which there was much stress placed on observance of the Torah (law). This psalm was chosen because of the similarity of images found in both pieces, such as the reference in line two regarding the tree planted near living water. However, the psalm is referring to the Torah as the source of life, not the Lord. The wisdom literature poem in Jeremiah places Yahweh at the center of trust.

Second Reading
1 Corinthians 15:12, 16-20

The Corinthian community began to question the fact of the resurrection. This was evidenced by their smorgasbord acceptance of Christian beliefs. Influenced by the dualism of Hellenistic philosophies (body is evil, spirit is good), the gnostics could not embrace the notion that the body could ever be thought of in terms of "glorification." Death was regarded as a release from "its confinement in mortal prison."[3] Some of the gnostic-influenced Christians believed that the sacraments already afforded them a share in the resurrection. Thus, there was no need for post-life resurrection of the body.

---

[1]Sixth Sunday in Ordinary Time: "Entrance Antiphon," *The Sacramentary.*

[2]Sixth Sunday in Ordinary Time: "Opening Prayer," *The Sacramentary.*

[3]Patricia Datchuck Sanchez, *The Word We Celebrate* (Kansas City: Sheed and Ward, 1989), 325.

Jesus promised that we would all share in the resurrection. His death and resurrection assured it for us. Through the living of the paschal mystery Christians already experience the forgiveness and liberation gained by the Christ event. Jesus' death and resurrection broke the bonds of sin and made eternal life possible. Thus, Paul reminds the Corinthians that we share Christ's victory. The salvation he won by his passion, death, and resurrection belongs to each and every one of us. We share in Jesus' mission of salvation when we take up our cross and offer our daily dyings and risings for the sins of the world.

Gospel
Luke 6:17, 20-26

Jesus teaches the disciples in the midst of the crowds.

STEP 1
NAMING ONE'S EXPERIENCE

What were your first impressions? What was your first response? How did you feel?

Each person names his or her initial impression. Statement should be brief. No reasons should be given at this time. All simply listen without agreeing or disagreeing.

STEP 2
UNDERSTANDING

In a brief statement, what do you think this gospel is trying to convey? What does it mean? What assumptions do you already bring with you to the hearing of this gospel?

STEP 3
INPUT FROM VISION/STORY/TRADITION

Liturgical Context

The Sixth, Seventh, and Eight Sundays in Ordinary Time form an interior unity. They cover twenty-seven out of forty-nine verses in chapter 6 of Luke's gospel. The scriptures for the three Sundays begin with the beatitudes proclaimed on the plain, continue the following week with further instruction regarding love of enemies, mercy, and kindness, and finally, on the last Sunday of the unit, they instruct people regarding the zeal they are to have in living the Christian life.[4]

The liturgy of the word on the Sixth Sunday in Ordinary Time places the contemporary community face-to-face with the implications of living the Catholic Christian life. As in all liturgy, we are reminded of what it means to live the paschal mystery of Christ, to enter into the dying and rising of daily Christian living. We are reminded that we are incorporated into the suffering Body of Christ and that we must act responsibly.

The beatitudes hold a primary place in the Christian dispensation. They are proclaimed, primarily from Matthew's perspective, on the Feast of All Saints, the Fourth Sunday in Ordinary Time, Cycle A, and are connected with the sacraments of marriage and confirmation as well as with funeral rites. Obviously Luke's perspective, not as prominent in the liturgy, is experienced on the Sixth Sunday in Ordinary Time, Cycle C, and on Wednesday of the Third Week of the Year. The beatitudes represent the program of Christian life, a list of particular Christian virtues (though of course with Old Testament roots).[5] They represent the way to holiness and sanctification (suffering for the sake of justice, etc).

Through the beatitudes, Christians enter the cycle of growing in the life of Christ just as we attempt to do in living and growing through the liturgical cycle.

Gospel Exegesis

The facilitator gives input regarding what critical biblical scholarship has to say about this text. The input in-

---

[4]*Days of the Lord*, Vol. 6 (Collegeville: The Liturgical Press, 1991), 40.

[5]Benedict T. Viviano, O.P., "Beatitudes," in *The Collegeville Pastoral Dictionary of Biblical Theology*, ed. Carroll Stuhlmueller, C.P. (Collegeville: The Liturgical Press, 1996), 80.

cludes insights as to how people would have heard the gospel in Jesus' time.

Luke places the sermon on the plain. Christ preaches to us in the everyday plane of our existence, our everyday life. The "Sermon on the Plain" comprises particular sayings of Jesus. It is possible that this sermon is a summary of other sermons. It presupposes the basic teaching of Jesus. In other words, it is assumed that Jesus' teaching is primarily directed to those who already believe in him. "The sermon is addressed not to the crowds, but to the disciples in the presence of the crowds."[6] The demands of the law are not for everyone, but those who call themselves disciples are expected to heed them.

The paschal mystery overshadows the sermon. The passion, death, and resurrection serve as a springboard for the beatitudes. In light of the paschal mystery, our response is to live as disciples. The beatitudes describe and define Christian moral behavior and discipleship.

Matthew's version of the sermon takes place on a mountain. High places are places of authority (the law was given to Moses on Mt. Sinai) and Matthew is concerned with putting the full weight of Jesus' teaching authority behind the beatitudes, especially because of his specifically Jewish audience. Matthew's people understood typology and placing Jesus on the mountain would have said to them that Jesus was certainly speaking with the voice of God.

Luke's audience is comprised of many gentiles. He assumes that they know nothing. He must, therefore, show them everything, especially how to pray. Luke's gospel is filled with images of Jesus praying. Both Luke and Matthew teach the basic kerygma (good news) of Jesus. The reign of God is changed because of the kerygma of Christ. It had always been understood that God's reign would be established when God came to rule as King. In the beatitudes the word for *reign* is a verb; it is not a place. The implication of the sermon is that God's rule has already occurred, it is already established in the here and now, and thus we

_____
[6]Reginald H. Fuller, *Preaching the New Lectionary* (Collegeville: The Liturgical Press, 1974), 498.

should live accordingly. Behavior is important. The sermon radically asks the question: Do you want to know how to make the reign of God visible? The answer is: By your behavior.

We might wonder how literally Jesus meant what he said. The bottom line for Luke's Jesus is that we preach by how we live. Evangelization takes place because of the example of our lives. Thus, Luke is very strict on discipleship. Behavior is critical!

There is an underlying agenda in Luke's description of the crowd in attendance and the geographical setting. Placing the sermon on the plain means it is for *all the people.* Jesus is eye-to-eye, brother-to-brother, brother-to-sister, sister-to-brother. By naming the places of origin of the guest list Luke establishes another favorite theme. Jesus' message is for all people—*it is a message of inclusivity!*

Luke reminds us that the outcasts, the outsiders, the oppressed will be the first to have access to the reign of God. The "haves" will be out, the "have-nots" will be in. The "woes" of verse 24 allude to Deuteronomy's exhortation that unfaithfulness will result in curses upon the people.

Luke's community was comprised of Jews and gentiles from Antioch. It was a mixed city, a city of great commerce, and people there were fairly well off. The Christian population was mixed; some were wealthy, others were not. There was tension in the ranks of wealthy Christians. What would happen to them if persecution came—would they lose all they had? Luke reminds them that they should muster the courage to stand with the community and be willing, if need be, to lose all. Luke tries to impress upon the poor and the rich that there is much at stake.

Luke's community lived in a world of limited goods. The concept of limited goods meant that whatever one possessed was all there was. There was no surplus to go around. This was the reality of the known world. All had to keep track of their own piece of the pie. In order to get more, one would simply have to steal. Personal wealth had a lot to do with one's good name, and respect was important. Luke was stressing that to live in the reign of God, there would not only be enough for everyone, but there would be an abundance of rich life.

The *blessed poor* of the beatitudes are not necessarily the spiritually poor. They include the economically poor and those who find themselves on the bottom levels of society in relationship to the world's goods and status: the outcast, the fringe folks (the marginalized), and the oppressed. Charles Talbert asserts that throughout Israel's history the term *poor* came to mean the spiritually poor—those who were aware of their poverty before God. In Israel's history, however, it was usually the economically poor who were best able to live and model such spiritual poverty.[7]

When Jesus tells the poor and marginalized that the reign of God is theirs, it does not mean that they will necessarily be given leadership authority, but it does mean that they will be accepted as equals within the realm of God's restored people.[8]

For those who hunger now, they will be filled (an allusion to the "all good things" promised by Mary's prayer in the Magnificat) when the restored order of creation pledged by Yahweh is established. This will happen in the realm of God, not a future time and place, but now, when two or more are gathered in Jesus' name. How could Jesus have expected such a radical counter-cultural reality? Even today the poor and the lowly are still the poor and the lowly. The mystery, the paradox, and the truth behind the expectation lie in the fact that when Christians are gathered in the name of Jesus and living according to the principles of the beatitudes, then Jesus' expectations will be an observable reality and an example for the world. Transformation of the world is possible only if and when Christians live exemplary Christ-centered lives in conformance to the Beatitudes. *In Christian communities there is to be no one on the bottom of the heap.*

For those who are weeping now will laugh: In biblical tradition, weeping often stood for a loud outcry of sorrow over sin or apostasy. Thus, those who have

such sorrow will be able to laugh over the forgiveness and healing that is theirs.

Jesus comforts those who are *blessed because they are hated, set aside and scorned.* To whom is this beatitude addressed? The word used for *hated* in this beatitude refers to the marginalized. The *hated marginalized* will be the beneficiaries of blessing. There are three prevalent realities in this exhortation: attitude, action, and speech. The marginalized are first oppressed by an attitude (hate). Second, they are oppressed by an action (they are set aside). Third, they are oppressed by speech (scorn). Christians are to treat the marginalized with proper dignity. There is to be a *metanoia* of attitudes, behaviors, and speech in the realm of God. People who live in just relationship (*hesed*) will be hated and persecuted for the sake of the God's reign.

Jesus takes the blessings conferred on those who suffer at the bottom, reverses the blessings, and turns them into *woes* or curses for those who enjoy favor on the top. "God is at work in this prophetic visitation, transforming values, challenging perceptions: the mighty are being cast down; the lowly are lifted up."[9]

Proclaim the gospel again.

Sometimes we gain new insights when we hear the text after the interpretation has been given. Someone from the group proclaims the gospel a second time.

STEP 4
TESTING

Conversation with the Liturgy and the Scriptures

Test your original understanding in dialogue with the text.

(You might consider breaking into smaller groups.)

Was there anything in the beatitudes that you had not considered before? How does your original

---

[7]Charles H. Talbert, *Reading Luke* (New York: Crossroad, 1992), 70-71.

[8]Luke Timothy Johnson, *The Gospel of Luke*, Sacra Pagina Series, Vol. 3 (Collegeville: The Liturgical Press, 1991), 106.

[9]Ibid., 111.

understanding of the beatitudes compare with what we just shared?

How does this story speak to your life?

I am reminded of a time many years ago when my husband and I tried to deliberately move in with the poor of our city. We had been active in ministry to the poor and were trying to discern whether we should more fully immerse ourselves in their lives. We looked for an apartment in the inner city of town. It was a very eye-opening experience. The rent we were asked to pay was higher than the rent we were paying for a suburban home. The only difference was that we could pay the rent weekly instead of monthly. The only local markets were convenience stores that would have increased our grocery bills by at least 20 percent. To add insult to injury, this apartment that was fifty dollars a month higher than the lovely home we were renting in suburbia was not fit for human habitation! We were scandalized! Blessed indeed are those who must endure such oppression! After much prayer and dialogue over a period of time, we discerned that it was not fair to ask our children to endure the life we were suggesting. However, the greatest irony was that we could not afford to do it! We did not make enough money a month to absorb the increase! No wonder the poor stay poor. I'm not sure if they are even aware of the extent to which they are exploited.

As a Christian I am required to stand with those on the bottom of the heap. Communities today must stand with those on the bottom of the heap. If we don't, the woes belong to us! Jesus was talking to his disciples. Those beatitudes were not suggestions; they were expectations. During these times of political action regarding welfare reform, where do we as Christians stand in relation to those on the bottom who are exploited and never given an opportunity or the means to move out of their wretched condition?

All share their life experience.

How were the beatitudes speaking to Luke's community? What was the common message? Is there relevance today? Are the biblical themes of exodus, covenant, community, and creation evident in the beatitudes? Do you still feel the same way about this text as you did at the beginning?

The gospel demands a response.

How does this sharing call for a response in your community? Be concrete. Where might contemporary communities have difficulties with this gospel's exegesis? Has this conversation in any way called your present attitudes or practices into question? What are the implications for your life? Name one specific action you will take this week as a response to what was learned and shared today.

DOCTRINAL ISSUES

What church truth/teaching/doctrinal issue could be drawn from the gospel for the Sixth Sunday in Ordinary Time?

Participants suggest possible doctrinal themes that flow from the readings.

Possible Doctrinal Themes

Morality, moral decision making, justice

Present the doctrinal material at this time.

1. The facilitator gives input on a particular doctrinal issue of his/her prior choosing. OR
2. The group chooses a doctrinal issue from the list they created. They read together from the Doctrinal Appendix.

(The doctrinal issues are found in the Doctrinal Appendix in the back of this workbook. If you are choosing an issue from this resource, please refer to it now.)

Reflection questions centered around the chosen doctrinal theme can be found at the end of each topic in the Doctrinal Appendix. The questions are based on the five-step reflection process. If you choose a topic not included in the Doctrinal Appendix, craft your own questions according to the same five-step process.

Following the reflection questions you will be reminded to return to chapter 7, "Preparing the

Catechetical Session," to assist you in crafting your own session.

Closing Prayer

Lord, we make this offering in obedience to your
    word.
May it cleanse and renew us,
and lead us to our eternal reward.
We ask this in the name of Jesus the Lord...[10]

Lord,
you give us food from heaven.
May we always hunger
for the bread of life.
Grant this through Christ, our Lord.[11]

Selected Bibliography

Days of the Lord. Vol. 6. Collegeville: The Liturgical
    Press, 1991.
Fuller, Reginald H. *Preaching the New Lectionary.*
    Collegeville: The Liturgical Press, 1974.
Johnson, Luke Timothy. *The Gospel of Luke.* Sacra
    Pagina Series. Vol. 3. Collegeville: The Liturgi-
    cal Press, 1991.
Sanchez, Patricia Datchuck. *The Word We Celebrate.*
    Kansas City: Sheed and Ward, 1989.
Talbert, Charles H. *Reading Luke.* New York: Cross-
    road, 1992.
Viviano, Benedict T., O.P. "Beatitudes." In *The Col-
legeville Pastoral Dictionary of Biblical Theology.*
    Ed. Carroll Stuhlmueller, C.P. Collegeville:
    The Liturgical Press, 1996.

---

[10]Sixth Sunday in Ordinary Time: "Prayer Over the
Gifts," *The Sacramentary.*

[11]Sixth Sunday in Ordinary Time: "Prayer After Communion," *The Sacramentary.*

SEVENTH SUNDAY IN ORDINARY TIME

INTRODUCTORY RITES

Opening Song (or Entrance Antiphon)

Lord, your mercy is my hope, my heart rejoices in your saving power. I will sing to the Lord for his goodness to me. (Ps 12:6)[1]

Opening Prayer

The facilitator of the session may lead the prayer. Others in the group may be asked to proclaim the readings.

Let us pray....

    Pause for silent prayer.

Almighty God,
Father of our Lord Jesus Christ,
faith in your word is the way to wisdom,
and to ponder your divine plan is to
    grow in the truth.
Open our eyes to your deeds,
our ears to the sound of your call,
so that every act may increase our sharing
in the life you have offered us.
Grant this through Christ, our Lord.[2]

LITURGY OF THE WORD

Let us listen to God's word.

The readings are proclaimed.

First Reading
1 Samuel 26:2, 7-9, 12-13, 22-23

In today's pericope David spares King Saul's life even though Saul had been on an obsessive mission to track David down and kill him. David fared much better in historical accounts than did his predecessor Saul. David was known for his charm,

good looks, courage, and magnanimity. David was very popular among the people. Saul was jealous and concerned about David's rapid rise to power. Fearing for his life, David fled into the desert with Saul in obsessive pursuit. David formed a guerrilla force and lived the life of a rebel.

In this story, David and his band of rebels enter Saul's camp to find them asleep. The reader is made aware that God intentionally placed "Saul at the mercy of David" by the word used for sleep (*tardemah*). *Tardemah* referred to a kind of sleep deliberately induced by God.[3]

David's mercy and respect for one of God's anointed (Saul) are highlighted in this reading. Since Saul was anointed by God for service as king, this conferred special status on him. David would not kill one of God's anointed. "Samuel anointed Saul and thereby conferred a special status on this inspired, courageous Benjaminite. A man of seemingly limitless valor, Saul had the honor of being Israel's first king."[4] People certainly would have understood if David had killed Saul, but David was not about to usurp Yahweh's right to vengeance.[5]

---

[1] Seventh Sunday in Ordinary Time: "Entrance Antiphon," *The Sacramentary.*

[2] Seventh Sunday in Ordinary Time: "Alternative Opening Prayer," *The Sacramentary.*

[3] Patricia Datchuck Sanchez, *The Word We Celebrate* (Kansas City: Sheed and Ward, 1989), 327.

[4] J. Kenneth Kuntz, *The People of Ancient Israel* (New York: Harper and Row, 1974), 179.

[5] Saul's reign was torn by problems from the beginning. In fairness, Saul was a victim and was slated to fail from the very start. The people disapproved of Saul, but his main concern was to defend (successfully) Israel from her enemies. He was a brilliant warrior. He was a religious man who desired to submit to the will and authority of Yahweh. He did not use his monarchy to acquire wealth like the later Israelite kings, but rather was more concerned "with honoring the requirements of holy war" (Kuntz, 181). However, Saul's downfall occurred when Samuel angrily turned against him. Saul chose to lead his soldiers in a ritual sacrifice before battle because Samuel was late and Saul could not wait any longer to advance with his soldiers. Samuel was furious. It was not Saul's role to perform the ritual sacrifice. That was the job of the priest/prophet. When David appeared on the scene it only made things worse for the wounded Saul. Biblical tradition depicted Saul as emotionally unstable. However, politics played

In today's reading David is an example of the type of discipleship Jesus expects. Disciples are to be like David, compassionate, forgiving, and humbly respectful of Yahweh's dominion, rather than like the pride-filled, murderous Saul.

Responsorial Psalm
Psalm 103:1-2, 3-4, 8, 10, 12-13

The psalm is a prayer of praise and thanks to Yahweh following some ordeal, trial, or crisis in the psalmist's life, perhaps illness. It speaks of reliance on God's mercy.

Second Reading
1 Corinthians 15:45-49

Paul's letters were written in response to specific problems in his community. Scholars believe that today's pericope has to do with a difficult issue that had surfaced in the Corinthian community. Paul was attesting to the Christian belief that Christ rose from the dead and that through his resurrection we are free from the bondage of sin and will share in his resurrection. Some people in the Corinthian community (under the Hellenistic influence that regarded the body as evil and the soul as good) had appropriated a skewed understanding of the resurrection and the afterlife.

Gnostic Corinthians regarded the body as a vessel in which the human soul was trapped. Death was seen as deliverance from the evil vessel. Paul was refuting the influence of Philo who had explained the two different accounts of creation in purely dualistic terms. Philo maintained that the creation stories in Genesis depicted two types of Adam. The first type revealed an ideal, spiritual human, the archetype of God. The second type depicted fallen humanity. Philo asserted that the first account upheld how we should *be* (spiritual), and the second account characterized how we actually *are* (corrupt). According to this view, "the soul of the gnostic elite consisted of divine sparks emanat-

ing from the heavenly man. These sparks had tragically become incarnated in the physical bodies of the earthly Adam."[6] All the elite few had to do was recover "their heavenly origin, thus their authentic self."[7] The Corinthians believed that some of them had already realized that divine spark through the sacraments and through the gift of knowledge.

Paul refuted this notion of two types of Adam. He asserted that both accounts in Genesis refer to the same Adam, a human person comprised of body and spirit. Paul asserted that human beings find their authentic self through sharing in the resurrection of Christ. The eschatological hope that Paul raises asserts that, yes, we participate in Jesus' life here on earth through the sacraments, but it is in eternity that we will fully share in the resurrection. Our bodies will be raised and we will then come to know our authentic self in union with God.

Gnostics believed that salvation was a matter of being delivered from the evil body so as to find one's spiritual reality. They further believed that it was possible for individuals to gain such salvation through their own merit. Those possessing the right charisms would be in; those who did not have them would be out. Paul reiterated the fact that salvation is nothing we can merit. It was freely given and it was given for all. He demanded that we be open to receive Christ, body and soul and spirit, and that we live upright lives as we wait in hope for the salvation that is ours.

Gospel
Luke 6:27-38

Jesus continues the "Sermon on the Plain" and teaches what it means to be a disciple.

STEP 1
NAMING ONE'S EXPERIENCE

What were your first impressions? What was your first response? What grabbed your attention?

---

a role in his eventual demise. Israel had established the monarchy as a way to replace the old tribal way of governance. However, those in tribal leadership were not willing to relinquish their power. Saul's lack of success was the result of the unwillingness to allow power to be taken from the purview of religious authority. In order for Saul to entertain any degree of success, he had to have Samuel's support, which he did not get.

[6]Reginald H. Fuller, *Preaching the New Lectionary* (Collegeville: The Liturgical Press, 1974), 502.
[7]Ibid.

Each person names his or her initial impression. Statement should be brief. No reasons should be given at this time. All simply listen without agreeing or disagreeing.

STEP 2
UNDERSTANDING

In a brief statement, what do you think this gospel is trying to convey?

STEP 3
INPUT FROM VISION/STORY/TRADITION

Liturgical Context

Refer to the Sixth Sunday in Ordinary Time regarding the internal unity of the three Sundays: Sixth, Seventh, and Eighth Sundays in Ordinary Time. Last week we learned that the happy ones in God's realm are the powerless and those who suffer for the sake of God. The unhappy ones are those who exercise unjust power over the powerless and who enjoy king-of-the-mountain status. God's realm reverses the order, turns the status quo upside down, and presents a new way to be children of God. This week we will explore what that new way entails. Behavior is the key and Jesus lays out his expectations. We see this theme echo throughout this Sunday's liturgy. Both opening prayers are pleas for God to teach us to be like Christ in word and deed. The prayer after communion asks God to help us live the example of love through our sharing in the eucharist. Our attention in the liturgy is focused on the need to embrace and live the message of Christ in today's gospel.

Last week Jesus taught the apostles in the midst of the crowds. The apostles were to pass on Jesus' authentic tradition to all people everywhere as evidenced by the crowds from diverse places who were in attendance at Jesus' great sermon. This week Jesus teaches the multitudes. The old law had permitted retribution and retaliation for iniquities committed against another person. Jesus turns this upside down and demands love, not retribution.

Perhaps this would be an appropriate time to celebrate a non-sacramental reconciliation service.

Gospel Exegesis

The facilitator gives input regarding what critical biblical scholarship has to say about this text. The input includes insights as to how people would have heard the gospel in Jesus' time.

Luke's intention is to give a synthesis of what life is to be like in the new Israel.[8] Luke seeks to provide a blueprint for living in the realm of God. He sets forth how one must live and behave as a Christian.

Today's pericope includes a series of sayings of Jesus that ultimately emphasize two points: Christians are to love their enemies and are to be generous in their response to others.[9] Jesus articulates a need to go beyond what is expected. Even sinners love those who love them in return. There is nothing heroic in that. However, it is truly heroic to love when love is not returned. Jesus promotes a gospel of going beyond the requirements of what is socially expected in order to offer the same gratuitous love that God offers to humanity. The love that Jesus proposes cannot remain an interior disposition. It must express itself through behavior. We must demonstrate love by our actions. The Ten Commandments were given so that those who had been delivered from slavery in Egypt would have a means of responding to the benevolent act of their Liberator. The freedom offered to humanity through the paschal mystery of Christ also calls for a response. Jesus provides the response in today's gospel.

Jesus exhorts the people "against the universal urge of retaliation. By doing so, he also turns the attitudes of those who are the outsiders toward the community around."[10] Rather than retaliate for wrongdoing, the marginalized, outcasts, and the oppressed are to respond in a non-violent way. They are to love their enemy. They are to pray for those who oppress and persecute them.

Christians are to love (attitude), to bless and pray (speech) and live according to the teaching of

---

[8] Eugene LaVerdiere, S.S.S., *Luke* (Wilmington: Michael Glazier Books, 1980), 95.

[9] Ibid., 97.

[10] Luke Timothy Johnson, *The Gospel of Luke,* Sacra Pagina Series, Vol. 3 (Collegeville: The Liturgical Press, 1991), 108.

Jesus (action). They are to go beyond the norm of what is expected. This principle of *going beyond* refers to the justice of God expected and initiated at the creation of the world (*hesed*). God established a realm of perfect order and harmony at the creation of the world (Genesis). God's free, completely undeserved, equally given, gratuitous love was offered to all people. The response to this love was to be expressed in people's attitudes, speech, and action. God's people were to love God completely, totally and without reservation. This love would be evidenced in the way people loved all of creation: men, women, children, resources, and environment. Reciprocity demanded a reverence for all people without exception. Thus, to be a child of God meant that the unconditional love of God was to be shown to *all people* inclusively.

Such love was to be demonstrated by *giving, doing good, and lending.* Who was to be the recipient of the giving, good works, and the lending? When Jesus referred to one's neighbor, the Jewish folks assumed it meant a fellow Israelite. "Behind the notion of 'neighbor' lies profound disagreement...the neighbor he is to love is the Israelite."[11] However, Jesus' intention was far more universal. It was directed toward the non-Israelite, the outcast, and the marginalized. When one's love for an enemy is demonstrated by *giving, lending, or doing good* for that enemy, then the lender, the recipient, and the observer pause to take notice. Truly it goes beyond what is a normal expectation.

God's love is offered to the just and the unjust. God's love for humanity is not dependent on humanity's love for God. We are to love similarly. In fact, the extent to which we love will be the measure by which we are judged. Thus, that which we do to others is to be either our indictment or our reward. The reward for going beyond and loving as God loves is to enjoy the "reality of being children of the Most High."[12]

Proclaim the gospel again.

---

[11]Jack Dean Kingsbury, *Conflict in Luke* (Minneapolis: Augsburg Fortress, 1991), 92.

[12] Johnson, *The Gospel of Luke*, 112.

Sometimes we gain new insights when we hear the text after the interpretation has been given. Someone from the group proclaims the gospel a second time.

STEP 4
TESTING

Conversation with the Liturgy and the Scriptures

Test your original understanding in dialogue with the text.

(You might consider breaking into smaller groups.)

This gospel suggested behavior and attitudes for Luke's community that were beyond normal expectations. How would those expectations be received today? Is this gospel relevant today? How does your original understanding of this story compare with what was just shared?

How does this story speak to your life?

This gospel causes me to ask the question: "Who are my enemies?" Most of us do not have enemies in the sense that we usually think of enemies. We do have people who we know dislike us. All leaders in public ministry experience at least a few folks who dislike their leadership. It would be a rare day if this were not the case. While 95 percent of the people are very loving, honest, and forthright in their suggestions, comments, and disagreements, there are some who are less than loving. I have found the latter to be a proverbial thorn in the flesh. There have been some wounds that have taken a great deal of work and repentance to heal. Yet, I am always hit in the face with this scripture when it comes to dealing with hateful animosity. I am always forced to ask myself: "How am I going beyond what is expected? Am I too proud to go the extra mile? Do I seek insidiously hidden or openly apparent revenge?" Sometimes I have been able to stand with the blessed; at other times I must admit I am in line with the cursed. When I am conscious of my animosity, I try to make an intentional effort to reach out. At other times I submit to my stubborn pride.

Not too long ago we were reflecting on how the media bend over backward to get interviewees to proclaim

*their hatred for the individual or individuals who
have hurt them. They usually do not have to exert
much effort. Revenge, hatred, and retribution seem
to be the norm. It is no wonder that stories such as
the reconciliation between George Wallace and one of
the victims of his racial prejudice meet with such
surprise. The only reason it makes the news is because it is so unexpected.*

*Obviously Jesus knows that what he suggests is ex-
tremely difficult. It must be possible or he would not
expect it. Thus, he must also provide the grace and
the strength.*

All share their life experience.

What was Luke trying to tell his community?
What does he have to say to our community and
to me today? What does this gospel teach us
about God, Jesus, the church? Do we still feel the
same way about this text as we did when we
began? How would we explain this gospel to a
stranger?

STEP 5
DECISION

The gospel demands a response.

How does this exegesis challenge your community's attitudes? What are the contemporary implications? What, if any, transformation has occurred
in you as a result of your sharing? What are the implications of the beatitudes in your life? What are
you/your community/your parish called to do in
response? Name one concrete action you will take
this week as a response to what was learned and
shared today.

DOCTRINAL ISSUES

What church truth/teaching/doctrinal issue
could be drawn from the gospel for the Seventh
Sunday in Ordinary Time?

*Participants suggest possible doctrinal themes that flow
from the readings.*

Possible Doctrinal Themes

Morality, justice, moral decision making, reconciliation, penance

Present the doctrinal material at this time.

1. The facilitator gives input on a particular doctrinal issue of his/her prior choosing. OR
2. The group chooses a doctrinal issue from the
   list they created. They read together from the
   Doctrinal Appendix.

(The doctrinal issues are found in the Doctrinal
Appendix in the back of this workbook. If you are
choosing an issue from this resource, please refer
to it now.)

Reflection questions centered around the chosen
doctrinal theme can be found at the end of each
topic in the Doctrinal Appendix. The questions
are based on the five-step reflection process. If you
choose a topic not included in the Doctrinal Appendix, craft your own questions according to the
same five-step process.

Following the reflection questions you will be reminded to return to chapter 7, "Preparing the
Catechetical Session," to assist you in crafting your
own session.

Closing Prayer

Let us pray
[that God will make us more like Christ, his Son]

Pause for silent prayer.

Father,
keep before us the wisdom and love
you have revealed in your Son.
Help us to be like him
in word and deed,
for he lives and reigns with you and the Holy
    Spirit,
one God for ever and ever.[13]

---

[13]Seventh Sunday in Ordinary Time: "Opening Prayer,"
The Sacramentary.

Selected Bibliography

Days of the Lord. Vol. 6. Collegeville: The Liturgical Press, 1991.

Fuller, Reginald H. *Preaching the New Lectionary.* Collegeville: The Liturgical Press, 1974.

Johnson, Luke Timothy. *The Gospel of Luke.* Sacra Pagina Series. Vol. 3. Collegeville: The Liturgical Press, 1991.

Kingsbury, Jack Dean. *Conflict in Luke.* Minneapolis: Augsburg Fortress, 1991.

Kuntz, J. Kenneth. *The People of Ancient Israel.* New York: Harper and Row, 1974.

LaVerdiere, Eugene. S.S.S. *Luke.* Wilmington: Michael Glazier Books, 1980.

Sanchez, Patricia Datchuck. *The Word We Celebrate.* Kansas City: Sheed and Ward, 1989.

EIGHTH SUNDAY IN ORDINARY TIME

INTRODUCTORY RITES

Opening Song (or Entrance Antiphon)

The Lord has been my strength; he has led me into freedom. He saved me because he loved me. (Ps 17:19-20)[1]

Opening Prayer

The facilitator of the session may lead the prayer. Others in the group may be asked to proclaim the readings.

Let us pray
[that the peace of Christ may find welcome in the world]

Pause for silent prayer.

Father in heaven,
form in us the likeness of your Son
and deepen his life within us.
Send us as witnesses of gospel joy
into a world of fragile peace and broken
   promises.
Touch the hearts of all men with your love
that they in turn may love one another.
We ask this through Christ, our Lord.[2]

LITURGY OF THE WORD

Let us listen to God's word.

The readings are proclaimed.

First Reading
Sirach 27:4-7

It is quite unusual for biblical works, but Sirach (Ben Sira) is actually the author of the book bearing his name. One of the books of wisdom literature, Sirach is among the longest books in the

bible. In some translations (NJB, NEB, RSV), it is referred to as Ecclesiasticus (the Book of the Church).

In 1947 at Qumran, in the heart of the desert, pieces of the book of Sirach were found. In 1964 an entire copy of the manuscript was found at an excavated site in Masada. Another copy was later found elsewhere. This text was obviously very popular among ancient peoples. It was written at a time when Hellenism was a threat to the stability and traditions of Judaism. Sirach addressed the threat and attested that wisdom could be attained only if one lived life according to the will of God.

Ben Sira lived during the third and second centuries B.C.E. He was an avid student of the law, the prophets, and writings and a respected scribe and teacher who "ran an academy for young Jewish men."[3] He traveled extensively, studied the wisdom literature of other cultures, and adapted what could be adapted to the Jewish tradition. Ben Sira wrote his book in response to the spread of Hellenism. He wished to emphasize that true wisdom was to be found in Jerusalem, not Athens. Thus, the good Jew should not be swayed by Greek thought. The book is a compilation of the teaching notes he acquired over the years.

Today's pericope is a piece of a larger section that addresses issues of integrity and friendship. One is to choose one's friends carefully. Speech indicates the disposition of the human heart. When one is silent it is difficult to discern what lies within. However, speech reveals the person immediately. This reading connects with today's gospel, as Sirach sets the stage for Jesus' reflection on the human heart.

Responsorial Psalm
Psalm 92:2-3, 13-14, 15-16

---

[1]Eighth Sunday in Ordinary Time: "Entrance Antiphon," *The Sacramentary.*

[2]Eighth Sunday in Ordinary Time: "Alternative Opening Prayer," *The Sacramentary.*

[3]Alexander A. Di Lella, O.F.M., "Sirach," in *The New Jerome Biblical Commentary,* ed. Raymond E. Brown, S.S., Joseph A. Fitzmyer, S.J., Roland E. Murphy, O.Carm. (Englewood Cliffs: Prentice Hall, 1990), 496.

Today's psalm is a psalm of thanksgiving. It praises Yahweh for the deeds of salvation and speaks of the rewards due to those who live righteously before God. No doubt this psalm was chosen as a response to Ben Sira's teaching regarding friendship and integrity and living an upright life.

Second Reading
1 Corinthians 15:54-58

The dialogue regarding Jesus' resurrection continues today in Paul's letter to the Corinthian community. In an earlier part of the chapter Paul referred to the living as "flesh and blood" and to the already dead as in "corruption." Paul believed that the *parousia* (second coming) would take place before the Corinthians died. He stressed that the living and the dead shared equal status, as both were headed for the same destiny. This destiny was assured by the passion, death, and resurrection of Jesus. The victory was won by Christ and human beings are the recipients of his victory. Through it we gain everlasting life.

Prior to this point, Paul had not stressed the law, sin, and death. However, in today's letter Paul reminds the Corinthians that not only were they saved through Jesus' resurrection, but they also enjoyed freedom from sin, death, and the law. The primary concern of Christians was to live in that freedom by working to bring about the reign of God as they awaited his return.

Paul reminded the Corinthians that salvation could not be gained through personal merit. Salvation comes only through the death and resurrection of Christ, who paid the price, once and for all.

Paul emphasized that the law was given to humanity in order to reveal God's plan of salvation. However, only God could empower people to keep the law. Of itself the law was empty. The law served only to intensify human sin.[4] Thus, the only freedom possible is the freedom offered by Christ's self-sacrifice and our participation in the paschal mystery.

---

[4]Patricia Datchuck Sanchez, *The Word We Celebrate* (Kansas City: Sheed and Ward, 1989), 329.

Gospel
Luke 6:39-45

Jesus looks into the human heart.

STEP 1
NAMING ONE'S EXPERIENCE

What captured your attention in today's gospel? What were your first impressions?

Each person names his or her initial impression. Statement should be brief. No reasons should be given at this time. All simply listen without agreeing or disagreeing.

STEP 2
UNDERSTANDING

In a brief statement, what do you think this gospel is trying to convey?

STEP 3
INPUT FROM VISION/STORY/TRADITION

Liturgical Context

Refer to the Sixth Sunday in Ordinary Time for an explanation of the interior unity of the Sixth through Eighth Sundays in Ordinary Time. The scriptures of the Eighth Sunday in Ordinary Time lay out a blueprint for the disciple. They warn against self-righteous adherence to the principles of Christ that often keeps us blind to the interior disposition of the soul. Sirach reminds us that our speech is a reflection of our heart. If we live uprightly our speech will reflect who and what we are to the world.

Paul reminds us that we are resurrection people. We are freed from the power of sin, death, and the law. We are to live in the freedom given to us by Christ's resurrection. Once again, behavior reflects an attitude of the heart. One cannot live a duplicitous life, since the deeds will eventually reflect the stance of the soul.

And finally, Luke once again reminds us that right behavior and the proper ordering of relationships are the keys to revealing the human heart. We will be known by our attitudes, our speech, and our actions. We can never fool God. We cannot fool a neighbor for very long, either. We will eventually give ourselves away. Today's liturgy reminds us that we are in constant need of conversion if we are to be effective disciples. The alternative opening prayer asks that we be sent as gospel witnesses into a broken, fragile world. We, too, are broken and fragile. It is only through serious inner reflection and submission of our wills to Christ that we are able to spread the good news with confidence. The opening prayer asks that the church be given the necessary peace and joy that come through serving God. Ongoing conversion demands that we acknowledge our need before God as expressed in the introductory rites. God strengthens us, leads us to freedom, and saves us because he loves us. Our inner work of conversion will be judged according to the way in which we love. It appears that *love* is the answer to the liturgy's challenge today. Disciples beget disciples and love begets love.

Gospel Exegesis

The facilitator gives input regarding what critical biblical scholarship has to say about this text. The input includes insights as to how people would have heard the gospel in Jesus' time.

In the final part of the "Sermon on the Plain," Jesus tells four related parables "concerned with the matter of Christian influence."[5] Jesus is concerned with forming disciples to assist others in the ongoing process of formation. Disciples learn discipleship from other disciples. Jesus instructs them in the Christian way of life. In order for disciples to lead and challenge others to live the *way*, they must themselves be models of the *way*. Thus, self-critical analysis must be a way of life for followers of Christ. How can one effectively lead others without engaging in his or her own ongoing process of renewal and conversion?

We are not to take this parable as an exhortation against fraternal correction. Just because the disciple is a sinner does not mean that he cannot engage in correction for the sake of the community. It is not expected of a disciple that "he should live and let live and be blind to moral imperfections about him. Such a stance would give the green light to evil and spell the end of mutual admonition in the community."[6] Rather, the point is: one must look at oneself before seeing the imperfections of others. Jesus brings the point home with a touch of ironic humor. Imagine a plank protruding from the eye of an unreflective disciple! Preposterous! It is just as preposterous to assume that disciples would correct one another without ever examining their own interior dispositions and behavior.

Jesus points the way for teachers through his use of metaphors. Blind people need the sighted to lead them. The ignorant need the knowledgeable to teach them. Teachers must have the sight and knowledge of God (gained only through relationship with Christ) in order to pass it on to those who seek it. Behavior again is the key word in this sixth chapter of Luke. *Attitudes*, *speech*, and *action* determine the heart of a disciple. If any one component is missing, the plank remains.

Proclaim the gospel again.

Sometimes we gain new insights when we hear the text after the interpretation has been given. Someone from the group proclaims the gospel a second time.

STEP 4:
TESTING

Conversation with the Liturgy and the Scriptures

Test your original understanding in dialogue with the text.

(You might consider breaking into smaller groups.)

---

[5]Charles H. Talbert, *Reading Luke* (New York: Crossroad, 1992), 75.

[6]Frederick W. Danker, *Jesus and the New Age According to St. Luke* (St. Louis: Clayton Publishing House, 1977), 89.

How does this exegesis compare with your previous understanding about this gospel? Were there any new insights? Was there anything you had not considered before? How does this story speak to your life?

Participants share an experience from their lives that connects with the biblical interpretation just shared.

> One of the strengths of living in a Christian community is that when some of us are blind, others are able to see and vice versa. The point is, we need one another in order to stay on track. When communities are torn by division, strife, gossip, factions, and internal disorder, the greatest sin is ignoring the problem, hoping that it will go away, instead of forging through the conflict. Healthy response to strife and honest admonition should be the hallmark of every Christian community. One of the ways that the Spirit guides and leads the church is through her loving, challenging voices.

> There was a time when we were experiencing division in the community. Parish unity was at stake. The Spirit provides the necessary gifts for a community's growth. One of our pastor's greatest gifts was his ability to objectively listen. All parties were offered a fair hearing and an opportunity to express their concerns. While many mistakes were made (every community is human and limited), the problem was not ignored in the hopes that it would go away. We were eventually able to gather as community, acknowledge our division and sinfulness, and prayerfully seek reconciliation between the groups involved.

> A big problem in dysfunctional family systems is unresolved anger. As the parish is a larger extension of family, there was risk of festering, unresolved animosity. We were at a crossroad. We could grow through the mess, or we could choose to remain hardhearted, cold, and indifferent to change. Efforts were made to reconcile the feelings that emerged out of the situation. Healing occurred over time and peace was eventually restored.

> There were many tensions, disagreements, and animosity in the early Christian communities. There were arguments as to who was in and who was out, who was right and who was wrong, who was first and who was last. The disagreements were healthy and moved the church to new growth. Today's gospel

> is a reminder for all to examine the stockpiled lumber lurking behind indignant, self-righteous eyelids. There are opportunities for growth at our parish doorstep.

> Disagreements are not bad; they are healthy opportunities for growth. For the most part, our community was able to rise to the challenge and in a small way learned what is possible when parties embroiled in controversy are willing to look within, and listen to, offer, and respond to prophetic voices in the midst of disruptive chaos.

All share their own experience.

What was Luke trying to tell his community? How does this gospel speak to our community and to me today? How do I feel about this gospel now? How would I articulate an understanding of this gospel to a stranger?

STEP 5
DECISION

The gospel demands a response.

How is our parish or community called to specific response to this gospel? Have my attitudes or outlook been changed as a result of our sharing? What is one concrete action we will take this week as a response to what we have learned and shared today?

DOCTRINAL ISSUES

What church truth/teaching/doctrinal issue could be drawn from the gospel for the Eighth Sunday in Ordinary Time?

Participants suggest possible doctrinal themes that flow from the readings.

Possible Doctrinal Themes

Reconciliation, conscience (moral decision making), morality, forgiveness

Present the doctrinal material at this time.

1. The facilitator gives input on a particular doctrinal issue of his/her prior choosing. OR

2. The group chooses a doctrinal issue from the list they created. They read together from the Doctrinal Appendix.

(The doctrinal issues are found in the Doctrinal Appendix in the back of this workbook. If you are choosing an issue from this resource, please refer to it now.)

Reflection questions centered around the chosen doctrinal theme can be found at the end of each topic in the Doctrinal Appendix. The questions are based on the five-step reflection process. If you choose a topic not included in the Doctrinal Appendix, craft your own questions according to the same five-step process.

Following the reflection questions you will be reminded to return to chapter 7, "Preparing the Catechetical Session," to assist you in crafting your own session.

Closing Prayer

Lord,
you care for your people even when they stray.
Grant us a complete change of heart,
so that we may follow you with greater fidelity.
Grant this through Christ, our Lord.[7]

Selected Bibliography

Days of the Lord. Vol 6. Collegeville: The Liturgical Press, 1991.

Di Lella, Alexander A., O.F.M. "Sirach." In *The New Jerome Biblical Commentary.* Ed. Raymond E. Brown, S.S., Joseph A. Fitzmyer, S.J., Roland E. Murphy, O.Carm. Englewood Cliffs: Prentice Hall, 1990.

Kselman, John S., S.S. and Michael L. Barre, S.S. "Psalms." In *The New Jerome Biblical Commentary.* Ed. Raymond E. Brown, S.S., Joseph A. Fitzmyer, S.J., Roland E. Murphy, O.Carm. Englewood Cliffs: Prentice Hall, 1990.

O'Connor, Jerome Murphy, O.P. "The First Letter to the Corinthians." In *The New Jerome Biblical Commentary.* Ed. Raymond E. Brown, S.S., Joseph A. Fitzmyer, S.J., Roland E. Murphy, O.Carm. Englewood Cliffs: Prentice Hall, 1990.

Sanchez, Patricia Datchuck. *The Word We Celebrate.* Kansas City: Sheed and Ward, 1989.

Talbert, Charles H. *Reading Luke.* New York: Crossroad, 1992.

---

[7]"Prayers Over the People, #6," *The Sacramentary.*

NINTH SUNDAY IN ORDINARY TIME

INTRODUCTORY RITES

Opening Song (or Entrance Antiphon)

O look at me and be merciful, for I am wretched and alone. See my hardship and my poverty, and pardon all my sins. (Ps 24:16, 18.)[1]

Opening Prayer

The facilitator of the session may lead the prayer. Others in the group may be asked to proclaim the readings.

Let us pray
[for God's care and protection]

> *Pause for silent prayer.*

Father,
your love never fails.
Hear our call.
Keep us from danger
and provide for all our needs.
Grant this through our Lord Jesus Christ, your
    Son,
who lives and reigns with you and the Holy
    Spirit,
one God for ever and ever.[2]

LITURGY OF THE WORD

Let us listen to God's word.

The readings are read proclaimed.

First Reading
1 Kings 8:41-43

The scene in today's pericope has Solomon praying in the temple that the prayers of foreigners who come to pay tribute to Yahweh be heard. This first reading was chosen for its obvious connection to the gospel, in which the foreigner (a gentile centurion) came to petition Jesus and pay him homage through his amazing faith.

Solomon, David's son, does not fare as well as David in the biblical historian's perspective. Solomon was seen as a king who flourished in riches and built the kingdom in splendor. "The name Solomon came to be the symbol of wealth and the glory of the empire."[3]

Solomon was not a military genius, but he did have enough diplomacy to carry on and build upon the efforts of his father, David. Unlike his father, Solomon's only claim to the throne was through heredity and the backing of his political supporters.

It is important to remember that Solomon's story is told from the perspective of the Deuteronomist's agenda to firmly establish the worship of Yahweh in the Jerusalem temple, not in outlying areas. Thus, the historians ignored Solomon's other political achievements and concentrated instead on the building of the temple. The authors were also writing the account of Solomon from an exilic perspective. The temple of Solomon had already been destroyed by the time of the final editing.

One reason Solomon was portrayed in a positive light was due to the fact that he was David's son. David's reign was destined by Yahweh to endure, so apologies and excuses were made for Solomon regarding his inability to live up to his father's reputation as a just and honorable king.

Also, since the account was written much later than the actual events described (following Israel's military and political troubles), there was a nostalgic remembrance for the "good old days" in which Israel was herself a force to be reckoned with, a great nation.

---

[1]Ninth Sunday in Ordinary Time: "Entrance Antiphon," *The Sacramentary.*

[2]Ninth Sunday in Ordinary Time: "Opening Prayer," *The Sacramentary.*

[3]Bernhard W. Anderson, *Understanding the Old Testament,* 4th ed. (Englewood Cliffs: Prentice Hall, 1986), 234

One of the differences between David and Solomon was the fact that David emerged as a leader from the midst of the people. He never forgot his tribal roots, or the nomadic life that had formed him. He came up through the ranks by paying his dues: he was a mighty warrior.

Solomon, on the other hand, was born in the royal splendor of palace living. He grew to adulthood in the palace. "From the first to the last he ruled with absolute power, caring little about the sanctities and special institutions of the former Confederacy."[4]

The setting for today's reading is the ritual of the dedication of the temple upon its completion. Solomon is presiding and this prayer is considered a liturgical prayer uttered at the dedication. Some scholars believe this prayer to be actually a set of teachings that promote the theology of the exilic authors. The primary motif is the endlessness of the temple compared to the perpetual dynasty promised to David.

Today's snippet reflects the transcontinental scope of Solomon's reign. The "foreigner" in Solomon's prayer referred to those who acknowledged Yahweh alone and upheld the moral demands of Jewish faith. People are drawn to Yahweh by the witness of faithful followers. Mortar and stone are not what attract believers. *It is the witness of faith-filled lives that manifests the unconditional providential love of God.*

Responsorial Psalm
Psalm 117:1, 2

The shortest psalm in the psalter, Psalm 117 extols the praise of nations [gentiles] when they witness Yahweh's faithful love and mighty deeds. They can do no less than acknowledge him as God.

Second Reading
Galatians 1:1-2, 6-10

The word *Galatian* is another word for Celtic or Gallic. Galatians were originally a Celtic tribe living in an area near France. The Greeks referred to it as Galatia. The Galatians eventually migrated east and settled near northern Turkey. The Ro-

mans combined this tribe with other tribes in Turkey and thus formed the province of Galatia.

Paul's letter to the Galatians is very similar in tone and content to the letter written to the Romans. However, the difference between Galatians and Romans is that one was written in the heat of the moment and the other was carefully planned and crafted with deliberate intention.

Paul's agenda was to answer the religious dilemmas facing the emerging Christian church. Were they to remain strictly Jewish and observe all the practices and rituals of Judaism, or "was their Christian experience so distinctive, and [were] their claims for Jesus so absolute, that they could no longer be contained within Judaism?"[5] Unlike the first believers who saw Christianity in strictly Jewish terms (as a sect within Judaism), the new pagan converts radically challenged the status quo. The implications were serious. How could they claim to be the heirs of the Old Testament covenant if they were no longer a part of Israel?

In the beginning Paul was sure that Jesus was doing something radically new and distinct. Thus, new converts were not to be saddled with formerly binding covenant rituals. However, this was scandalous to observant Jewish Christians. Their practice of the faith was rooted in their Jewish heritage. It was the foundation upon which Jesus himself had built his reign. Jesus asserted that he had not come to abolish the law but to fulfill it. Then why were converts excused from Jewish formation? It did not make sense. Corinth only proved their point. The heresies and godless practices would never have happened in the first place if converts had been well grounded in the ethics of Judaism.

Paul was furious, but it forced him into further discernment. The issue of circumcision further exacerbated the controversy. It was only through circumcision that people were in covenant relationship with Yahweh. It was a sign of membership in the people of God (one of Israel's primary motifs). Paul was hurt and angry over the attacks by other Christians. They said that he was not as informed as the "real" apostles. He had not known

---

[4]Ibid., 236.

[5]Hubert Richards, *The Gospel According to St. Paul* (Collegeville: The Liturgical Press, 1990), 81.

the historical Jesus. He was not privy to the actual life of Jesus. How could he be right and the others wrong? So the arguments went. Paul dug in his heels, typically overreacting, and boldly maintained that his position was the only correct one.

Paul's rhetoric was so divisive that he polarized the community. He cut to the heart of religious observance. He professed Christianity to be on one side of the religious pole and Judaism to be on the other. Only one was absolutely correct, the other absolutely incorrect. We need not guess where Judaism fell. (Finesse was certainly not one of Paul's strong suits!)

He wisely named the potential dispositions inherent in all religious traditions and in religious people. They will either be obedient or not; sincere or not (hypocrisy); aware or blind; mature or childish. So far so good. We can all agree. However, Paul's conclusion sent chills through even the most lackadaisical Jew. Paul asserted that Christianity completely adhered to the virtuous side of those determinants while Judaism was absolutely the opposite. (Not a way to win friends and influence people!)

Paul suggested that circumcision was no more than an act of savage brutality and almost implied that he was ashamed of his own permanent Jewish branding. While his methods left a lot to be desired, Paul's intentions were to hold fast to the central gospel message.

Salvation was freely won by Christ's death and resurrection and could not be earned by one's own merit. Paul maintained that the Jewish perspective of right relationship with God (during Paul's time) had evolved into total adherence to the law. This implied that salvation could be merited by one's own efforts. Paul vehemently protested. Salvation was a free, utterly gratuitous gift from God. "...People do not need to prove themselves. God accepts them as they are, with all their sins. When they acknowledge this is so, of course, they will make every effort to live a life of union with God. Still it is God's unearned love, not their own effort, that puts them right with God. They become good because God is good."[6]

The way of the law, on the other hand, stresses human responsibility. Serving God is synonymous with rule keeping. Such a perspective breeds the notion that if I am good enough, and follow the rules to the end, then God is obliged to save me.

Paul's way is not without its own set of dangers. Blindness, carelessness, and benign neglect can easily creep into the equation and prompt a person to sit on his or her laurels while passively responding to the demands of discipleship. However, Paul's vision puts God in charge and offers disciples the necessary freedom to respond to God, not to restrictive religious systems. Paul's letter to the Galatians reasserts belief in the paschal mystery. Jesus suffered, died, and rose again for the sins of the world. This reality has the power to change lives.

Paul so impulsively cranked out his letter that he did not even take the time to offer the customary introductory prayers of praise. The Galatians had questioned Paul's teaching. He had to set them straight. Paul's letter defended his ministry and his position. He had not been wrong. Faith was all that was required for salvation. Jesus had paid the price, and humanity had reaped the benefits. The law and all the ritual requirements of the law were no longer necessary. And, furthermore, his right to apostolic succession was given credence by Jesus' post-resurrection appearance to Paul.

This was a significant shift for the early church. One position embraced works as a means of salvation. The other position maintained that salvation through faith automatically leads to good works. Early Christians were put in a position of having to make a choice.

Paul's letter to the Romans took up the same impassioned conviction. However, it was more thoughtfully crafted and was not as influenced by his "knee jerk" reaction to the accusations leveled against him.[7]

---

[6]Ibid., 84.

[7]The primary source for the exegesis concerning Paul's letter is taken from *The Gospel According to St. Paul* by Hubert Richards.

Gospel

Luke 7:1-10

Jesus heals the gentile centurion's servant.

STEP 1
NAMING ONE'S EXPERIENCE

What captured your attention in the readings?

*Each person names his or her initial impression. State-
ment should be brief. No reasons should be given at this
time. All simply listen without agreeing or disagreeing.*

STEP 2
UNDERSTANDING

In a brief statement, what do you think this
gospel is trying to convey? What original understanding of this gospel did you bring with you to
this conversation?

STEP 3
INPUT FROM VISION/STORY/TRADITION

Liturgical Context

One cannot miss the centurion's contribution to
our liturgical tradition. We echo the centurion's
expression of humble, trusting faith at every
liturgy when we pray: "Lord, I am not worthy to receive you, only say the word and I shall be healed."

During the Sixth, Seventh and Eighth Sundays in
Ordinary Time we experienced a large portion of
the "Sermon on the Plain" and Jesus' teaching for
the first time in parabolic form. The next three
Sundays are similarly related. In the Ninth, Tenth,
and Eleventh Sundays in Ordinary Time we hear
the stories about the healing of the centurion's
servant, the son of the widow of Naim, and the
forgiveness and liberation of the sinful woman.
These three stories make up more than half of the
seventh chapter of Luke (31 of 50 verses). Following the three stories is a device used to link one
section of the gospel to the next. As a conclusion

to one section and an introduction to the next,
Luke summarizes the stories. He alludes to what
has just happened while at the same time pointing
us toward what is about to take place in the next
section. This interlude section serves as a breath
catcher. "Just what happened? What did we hear?
What did it all mean?"

So, what did happen? On the Third, Fourth, and
Fifth Sundays Jesus definitively identified himself
as the Awaited One when he preached the scriptures in the synagogue. Then from the lakeside he
called the first disciples who would assist in furthering his mission and in the "Sermon on the
Plain" Jesus laid out the reign of God. He came to
establish the law of radical love, *hesed* relationship,
and apostolic fervor. Thus, "When he had finished
all his words to the people . . . " Jesus healed the
centurion's servant in Capernaum, he raised the
widow's son in Naim, and he healed the sinful
woman, who in turn lavishly anointed his feet with
oil. These are the stories of the next three weeks.
We come front and center with the implication of
"who" Jesus was. His teaching was empowered by
the authority of the Holy Spirit and he had the
power to accomplish what he taught. Through his
words and actions Jesus was revealed to humanity.
The point in all of the stories is to answer the
question of "who" Jesus is and challenge readers
to answer "how" they will receive his revelation.
We are to know that God's gifts are unmerited and
freely given.

During weeks 9-14 in the C cycle, there is a semi-
continuous reading of Paul's letter to the Galatians. "Paul's letter to the Galatians is one of the
oldest Christian texts to deal with the issue of religious freedom and to explain the nature of religious liberty."[8] On this Ninth Sunday we shift our
attention away from Paul's letter to the Corinthians and begin our inquiry into the Galatian community. Paul's focus is to help the Galatians understand the universality and utter gratuity of
salvation. Over the next three weeks we will read
portions of two of the six chapters in Galatians.

We cannot miss the point of the Ninth Sunday
that God's salvation is open to all—even pagans!

---

[8]Raymond F. Collins, *Preaching the Epistles* (New
York/Mahwah: Paulist Press, 1996), 56.

The implication is crystal clear. Who are the "pagans" in our Sunday assemblies? Who are those we judge to be pagan while at the same time asserting our own righteousness as disciples of the one true faith? Such smugness has no place in our lives as we can observe in today's story of the centurion.

Today's prayer after communion asks that through the eucharist the Spirit guide us to live worthy lives of discipleship. Through the witness of our lives and our proclamation of God's great deeds we will enter the reign of God and seek to further that reign. We further the reign of God by living the gospel of Christ with all its implications.

Gospel Exegesis

The facilitator gives input regarding what critical biblical scholarship has to say about this text. The input includes insights as to how people would have heard the gospel in Jesus' time.

This story is one of two stories in Luke in which Jesus is named a prophet who manifests God to the people.[9] One of the major themes of Luke's gospel is Jesus' ministry to people who live on the edge, the fringe people, the excluded, the outcast, the outsider, and the marginalized. "Luke shows how Jesus effects a reversal of fortunes, or conditions, for a cross section of these persons."[10]

Most often the individuals show exemplary faith in the healing power of Christ. Today's story of the gentile centurion depicts just one example. The centurion was a benefactor of the Jewish people. He was known to love Israel by his kind acts toward her. The centurion, aware that contact with him would deem Jesus unclean,[11] approached other Jews to ask Jesus to heal his ailing servant. "The sending of emissaries . . . is not a sign of arrogance, but of humility; in effect, another compliment of an even greater benefactor."[12]

Jesus not only grants his request for healing, but he marvels at the centurion's faith. There are only two times in all of the gospels in which Jesus was amazed: once in Mark 6:6 where Jesus' amazement was directed at lack of faith, and in this gospel in which Jesus was amazed at the centurion's abundant faith.

The gentile centurion represents a type of gentile believer. He foreshadows the inclusion of gentiles into the mission of Christ that unfolds more deliberately and definitively in the Acts of the Apostles. The centurion defines the gentile believer in the midst of Jewish people. He also represents all believers *who have not seen Christ, but still believe.* This characteristic is common to the gentile convert.

The Jewish elders serve as intermediaries between Jesus and the centurion. They symbolically represent what had always been Israel's role in salvation history: to bring all nations to faith and trust in Yahweh.[13] The elders (local Galilean leaders, not the Sanhedrin) cite the credentials of the centurion official. This enables Luke to stress another favorite theme: Jesus' attitude toward other religious traditions. Charles Talbert lists three main points in relation to that attitude:

1. Luke maintained that Jesus came to fulfill Judaism.
2. Jesus challenged paganism on three levels. He disapproved of the use of spiritual power for personal gain (magic). Paganism was often greed-motivated and thus against the heart of Christianity. Jesus called for repentance for worship of the created thing, rather than the Creator.
3. By worshiping the Creator instead of the created, and through ethical behavior, Jesus completed paganism. Honest, virtuous pagans, who followed the light they knew in their quest for

---

[9]Luke Timothy Johnson, *The Gospel of Luke,"* Sacra Pagina Series, Vol. 3 (Collegeville: The Liturgical Press, 1991), 119.

[10]Jack Dean Kingsbury, *Conflict in Luke* (Minneapolis: Augsburg Fortress, 1991), 33.

[11]When Jews came in contact with gentiles they were deemed ritually unclean and were obliged to perform a ritual bath to become once again purified and cleansed.

---

[12]Johnson, *"The Gospel of Luke,"* 118.

[13]Patricia Datchuck Sanchez, *The Word We Celebrate* (Kansas City: Sheed and Ward, 1989), 332.

god [God], were in a sense prepared
for the light offered by Christ.[14]

The centurion is judged worthy by the elders, yet
the friends of Jesus report the centurion's own
sense of unworthiness. However, the centurion, familiar with the privilege of authority, is aware that
a simple command from a superior causes things
to happen. He trusts Jesus' authority. Luke stresses
Jesus' supreme authority over all creation. Jesus
parallels Yahweh who also had only to say the *word*
and the heavens and the earth were created. In
this gospel, Jesus' authority was firmly established
(by none other than a pagan) and in the process
his divinity further revealed.

Whereas the elders stressed the centurion's good
works as evidence of his worthiness, Jesus highlighted his faith. Thus, pious gentiles *complete
their relationship* to God by confession of their unworthiness and by "placing their faith in Jesus'
authority."[15]

Luke explicates a perfect example of Paul's' favorite theme: *faith is a higher value than the law.*

Proclaim the gospel again.

*Sometimes we gain new insights when we hear the text
after the interpretation has been given. Someone from the
group proclaims the gospel a second time.*

STEP 4
TESTING

Conversation with the Liturgy and the Scriptures

Test your original understanding in dialogue with
the text.

(You might consider breaking into smaller groups.)

Has this exegesis expanded your understanding of
this gospel? In what way? Were there any new or
significant insights?

---

[14]Charles H. Talbert, *Reading Luke* (New York: Crossroad,
1992), 81.
[15]Ibid.

How does this story speak to your life?

*I am struck by the irony of this gospel. In today's
gospel Jews are engaged in a dialogue about the gentile's worthiness, and thus his suitability for healing.
I am conscious of the reverse situation that has occurred throughout history ever since that time, often
in the name of Jesus. The worthiness and suitability
of Jews have often been questioned by sometimes well-
intentioned Christians. It is called anti-Semitism.*

*I have a Jewish friend. Her children attend a Christ-
ian school. On more than one occasion her daughter
has come home in tears because Christian children
have told her that she is not going to heaven, that
she is not saved. The children are reflecting the
rhetoric, prejudice, and belief of their parents. These
children are from very committed fundamental
Christian homes. They believe passionately that Jews
are unsaved, and thus are not going to heaven.*

*How triumphalistic and arrogant we are to assume
that God's covenant people, who were the first to
have God's plan of salvation revealed to them, have
been somehow cut off from God's mercy and love.
There were similar prejudices during Jesus' time.
There were prejudices of Jews toward gentiles; Romans toward the Jews; Jews toward Samaritans and
Samaritans toward Jews. Anti-Semitism is alive and
well today. So too, today, is Jewish prejudice toward
the Arabs. Conservatives are prejudiced against lib-
erals; progressive Catholics are prejudiced against
conservative Catholics. And the list goes on and on.
At some point in time, every group has the potential
to be an "outsider."*

*Today's gospel reminds me that Jesus offers a differ-
ent reality. It is what is in the heart that determines
salvation. None of us can read hearts. That job belongs to God. Perhaps the primary sin here is idolatry. Whenever I do not allow God to be God, I make
an idol out of my own self-righteous position. In my
righteousness I think I know the mind of God. I
somehow am able to perceive who is saved and who
is not. When I assume the role of judge I have taken
over God's role and in my utter arrogance think that
I know the mind and the will of God!*

*In today's scriptures God calls me to radical faith.
There is also a message of hope. God is not limited to
our narrowly confined constraints. One can be a good*

non-believer and that person's quest for good can serve as the good soil in which God plants the seed of grace. This is a consoling word for people who are concerned because of non-practicing family members.

All share their life experience.

What was Luke trying to tell his community? How is this relevant today for our community? According to this gospel, what is faith? How are the biblical themes of covenant, exodus, creation, and community observable in these readings? Do we still feel the same way about this text as we did when we began?

STEP 5
DECISION

The gospel demands a response.

How is your community challenged by this gospel? In what specific way might you be called to respond to its message? Is there any way that your community needs to change and grow in response to this gospel? Be concrete. Has this conversation with the exegesis of the story of the gentile centurion changed or stretched your personal beliefs or attitudes? What are the implications for your life? Name one concrete action you will take this week as a response to what you have learned and shared today.

DOCTRINAL ISSUES

What church truth/teaching/doctrinal issue could be drawn from the gospel for the Ninth Sunday in Ordinary Time?

Participants suggest possible doctrinal themes that flow from the readings.

Possible Doctrinal Themes

Ecumenism, faith, evangelization, image of God

Present the doctrinal material at this time.

1. The facilitator gives input on a particular doctrinal issue of his/her prior choosing. OR

2. The group chooses a doctrinal issue from the list they created. They read together from the Doctrinal Appendix.

(The doctrinal issues are found in the Doctrinal Appendix in the back of this workbook. If you are choosing an issue from this resource, please refer to it now.)

Reflection questions centered around the chosen doctrinal theme can be found at the end of each topic in the Doctrinal Appendix. The questions are based on the five-step reflection process. If you choose a topic not included in the Doctrinal Appendix, craft your own questions according to the same five-step process.

Following the reflection questions you will be reminded to return to chapter 7, "Preparing the Catechetical Session," to assist you in crafting your own session.

Closing Prayer

For the Church

Almighty and eternal God,
you have shown your glory to all nations
in Christ, your Son.
Guide the work of your Church.
Help it to persevere in faith,
proclaim your name,
and bring salvation to people everywhere.
We ask this through Christ, our Lord.

For those who do not believe in Christ

Almighty and eternal God,
enable those who do not acknowledge Christ
to find the truth
as they walk before you in sincerity of heart.
Help us to grow in love for one another,
to grasp more fully the mystery of your godhead,
and to become more perfect witnesses of your
    love
in the sight of men.
We ask this through Christ, our Lord.[16]

---

[16]Good Friday: General Intercessions from Celebration of the Lord's Passion, "For the Church" and "For Those Who Do Not Believe In Christ," *The Sacramentary.*

Selected Bibliography

Anderson, Bernhard W. *Understanding the Old Testament.* 4th ed. Englewood Cliffs: Prentice Hall, 1986.

Collins, Raymond F. *Preaching the Epistles.* New York/Mahwah: Paulist Press, 1996.

Days of the Lord. Vol. 6. Collegeville: The Liturgical Press, 1991.

Johnson, Luke Timothy. *The Gospel of Luke.* Sacra Pagina Series. Vol. 3. Collegeville: The Liturgical Press, 1991.

Kingsbury, Jack Dean. *Conflict in Luke.* Minneapolis: Augsburg Fortress, 1991.

Kselman, John S., S.S. and Michael L. Barre, S.S. "Psalms." In *The New Jerome Biblical Commentary.* Ed. Raymond E. Brown, S.S., Joseph A. Fitzmyer, S.J., Roland E. Murphy, O.Carm. Englewood Cliffs: Prentice Hall, 1990.

Richards, Hubert. *The Gospel According to St. Paul.* Collegeville: The Liturgical Press, 1990.

Sanchez, Patricia Datchuck. *The Word We Celebrate.* Kansas City: Sheed and Ward, 1989.

Talbert, Charles H. *Reading Luke.* New York: Crossroad, 1992.

Tenth Sunday in Ordinary Time

INTRODUCTORY RITES

Opening Song (or Entrance Antiphon)

The Lord is my light and my salvation. Who shall frighten me? The Lord is the defender of my life. Who shall make me tremble? (Ps 26:1-2)[1]

Opening Prayer

Let us pray
[to our Father who calls us to freedom in Jesus his Son]

Pause for silent prayer.

Father in heaven,
words cannot measure the boundaries of love
for those born to new life in Christ Jesus.
Raise us beyond the limits this world imposes,
so that we may be free to love as Christ teaches
and find joy in your glory.
We ask this through Christ our Lord.[2]

LITURGY OF THE WORD

Let us listen to God's word.

The readings are proclaimed.

First Reading
1 Kings 17:17-24

The stories about Elijah were less concerned with the factual recorded historical events than they were with the intent of the stories. The intent was to "mirror the experienced history of Israel in one of its great crises."[3] The stories also evoked Israel's fascination with Elijah.

Elijah (of Tishbeh in Gilead) appeared suddenly on the scene. He had lived an itinerant existence in the desert. He was an austere looking fellow with his hair garments, leather girdle, and great physical strength. He was a far cry from the cultured people of Israel. He certainly caught their attention! Elijah's first official action was to announce that Yahweh had called for a drought in the land in response to the actions of King Ahab and Queen Jezebel's promotion of pagan Baal (the god of storms and fertility) temples.

There are two key issues revolving around the Elijah narrative: the "opposition between Yahwism and Baalism" and a "portrait of prophetic life."[4] The first issue is named when Elijah claims Yahweh's power over rainfall. It is a direct challenge to the power of Baal. The second issue is addressed when "Elijah's claim to be Yahweh's servant is verified by his immediate and meticulous obedience to the divine word. Like Israel in the desert, Elijah is miraculously provisioned by Yahweh."[5] *Thus, the prophetic life is characterized by obedience to God's word.*

Much of chapter 17 takes place in the midst of the great famine. "The central concern of the stories is to portray Yahweh's authority over the fertility of the land, and to affirm that people's lives are wholly in Yahweh's hands."[6]

The backdrop for the story of Elijah is the arranged marriage of Ahab and Jezebel. Omri, Ahab's father, arranged for the marriage between Jezebel of Phoenicia and his son in order to strengthen the relationship between the two countries. In the view of the Yahwist writers, Ahab's sin was the worst of sins. He brought Jezebel to his home, the new capital, Samaria, and built a shrine

---

[1]Tenth Sunday in Ordinary Time: "Entrance Antiphon," *The Sacramentary.*

[2]Tenth Sunday in Ordinary Time: "Alternative Opening Prayer," *The Sacramentary.*

[3]Bernhard W. Anderson, *Understanding the Old Testament,* 4th ed. (Englewood Cliffs: Prentice Hall, 1986), 271.

[4]R. Cohn, *Journal of Biblical Literature* 101 (1982): 333-350.

[5]Jerome T. Walsh, "1-2 Kings," in *The New Jerome Biblical Commentary,* ed. Raymond E. Brown, S.S., Joseph A. Fitzmyer, S.J., Roland E. Murphy, O.Carm. (Englewood Cliffs: Prentice Hall, 1990), 171.

[6]Anderson, *Understanding the Old Testament,* 273.

to her Baal, Melqart, just as Solomon had built shrines in Jerusalem for his foreign wives.

Ahab never intended to turn away from Yahweh. He merely wished to offer his wife the freedom to worship as she chose. As a staunch defender of her god, she set out to evangelize the nation. This led to expected confrontation with Yahweh's prophets. As a response, she imported prophets from Phoenicia, paid them out of the public treasury, and attempted to liquidate every vestige of Israel's traditional faith. The altars were torn down, the prophets were killed, and faithful Israelites were driven underground.[7]

Elijah arrived on the scene bringing with him a word from God. He fearlessly challenged the king and the queen. He promised God's retribution in the form of a drought. The time was at hand. People had to choose. Either they were for Baal or they were for Yahweh. "Deity makes a total claim upon human allegiance: heart, soul and strength. Israel stood at the hour of decision. In the prophet Elijah the Mosaic tradition came alive with new power."[8]

For his courageous stand, Elijah was forced into the desert under the providential care of Yahweh. He was taken in by the widow of Zarephath. In return for her hospitality Elijah promised that her ration of food would remain until after the drought.[9] It is at this point in the story that today's pericope picks up.

During the Old Testament period, it was believed that God took vengeance upon people as a response to their sins and/or the sins of their parents. The widow was afraid that the death of her son had been brought upon her by Yahweh's judgment of her sinfulness. She also believed that Elijah's coming was a catalyst for Yahweh's judgment.

Elijah's restoration of the son's life *was intended as a refutation of the belief that God hurled death upon people as a punishment for sin.* Elijah's healing demonstrated God's incredible mercy and pardon of sins.

While the manner in which Elijah healed the boy seems a bit magical, the fact that a prayer was uttered with the ritual action indicates that the healing was an action of God.

Responsorial Psalm
Psalm 30:2, 4, 5-6, 11, 12, 13

Psalm 30 is an individual prayer of thanks for deliverance from mortal illness. Verse 5 depicts the "joyful reintegration into the community of one who had been at the point of death."[10] The psalm is chosen for its obvious connection to the first reading's raising of the widow's son.

Second Reading
Galatians 1:11-19

The early church struggled with its identity as it worked out its problems in regard to Jewish/gentile concerns. The challenge of celebrating the diversity as well as the unity in their new Christian faith at times seemed overwhelming to the post-resurrection church.

Controversies arose that threatened the church's growth. Paul's letter to the Galatians deals with such controversies.

The gentiles of Galatia possessed no Jewish heritage or understanding of Judaism. Paul's struggle with such communities centered around what needed to be passed on as authentic Christianity and what was deemed part of a former religious heritage that was not applicable to the new Christians: namely: circumcision and the Mosaic law. Paul preached faith as the necessary ingredient of salvation.

Those who were opposed to what they judged to be Paul's watered-down form of Christianity were dubbed "Judaizers" by Paul. He believed that their hostility was anti-Christian and against Jesus' central message. Paul insisted that freedom outweighed the law. Paul defended his authority by professing it to be of divine origin because of the way it had been revealed to him in the encounter

---

[7]Ibid., 272.
[8]Ibid., 274.
[9]Patricia Datchuck Sanchez, *The Word We Celebrate* (Kansas City: Sheed and Ward, 1989), 333.

---

[10]John S. Kselman, S.S. and Michael L. Barre, S.S., "Psalms," in *The New Jerome Biblical Commentary*, ed. Raymond E. Brown, S.S., Joseph A. Fitzmyer, S.J., Roland E. Murphy, O.Carm. (Englewood Cliffs: Prentice Hall, 1990), 531.

at Damascus. Paul maintained that as a law-abiding, observant Jew, he had been ill-prepared for the revelation of God in and through Jesus. The law had bound him. It was his duty, given to him directly by Christ, to teach freedom from the law and to reach out to gentiles with the good news of salvation.

Gospel
Luke 7:11-17

Jesus restores the dead son of the widow of Naim to life.

STEP 1
NAMING ONE'S EXPERIENCE

What immediately captured your attention in the gospel? Name your initial feelings.

Each person names his or her initial impression. Statement should be brief. No reasons should be given at this time. All simply listen without agreeing or disagreeing.

STEP 2
UNDERSTANDING

In a brief statement, what do you think this gospel is trying to convey? What assumptions did you bring with you to this conversation with the gospel?

STEP 3
INPUT FROM VISION/STORY TRADITION

Liturgical Context

The internal unity of the Ninth, Tenth, and Eleventh Sundays of Ordinary Time centers around the theme of Jesus' ability to effect what he teaches. In other words, through the power of the Spirit, Jesus reveals his identity by the acts he performs. Through the episode with the centurion, the healing of the widow's son, and forgiveness of the sinful woman, Luke shows that indeed the year of favor Jesus had announced in the synagogue had begun. Our liturgy professes that we live in the midst of God's continuing year of favor, the messianic age. We are living the promises. The year of favor was fully realized through the life, passion, death, and resurrection of Christ that we live and profess every time we gather as God's people.

Luke purposely connects the story of the widow with the previous story through the linking phrase, "and the next day." We are to assume a connection between the stories.

The signs that were to accompany the favored year included restored sight, healing for cripples and the deaf, and the raising of the dead. The greatest of these signs is the raising of the dead. It is a sign of God's promise of salvation's fullness: "victory over death, complete freedom from sin (1 Cor 15:54-58, 16:20—Eighth and Sixth Sundays)."[11]

In the words, "and she was a widow" Luke makes a direct reference to the widow of the first reading. Thus, the gospel reminds us of the first reading for today's liturgy.

Gospel Exegesis

The facilitator gives input regarding what critical biblical scholarship has to say about this text. The input includes insights as to how people would have heard the gospel in Jesus' time.

The story of the raising of the widow of Naim's son appears only in Luke. Thus, it must be viewed in accord with the overall agenda of Luke's gospel. There are two primary Lukan perspectives upon which this gospel hinges: Jesus' compassion for the helpless and the pronouncement of Jesus as the fulfillment of the messianic prophecy.

As said many times over, Luke shows radical concern for the disadvantaged. Who is more disadvantaged than a widow whose sustenance has been cut off by the death of her sole provider? Since the widow had no name, she was a representative figure. The nameless in scripture usually

---

[11]*Days of the Lord,* Vol. 6 (Collegeville: The Liturgical Press, 1991), 76.

represent a collectivity. She represented all the poor and the lowly. By saying "...and she was a widow," Luke echoed the biblical prototype of Elijah's raising of the widow of Zarephath's son. Although Luke does not say so directly, the widow's livelihood had been cut off by her son's death, as he was the sole support of his mother. Luke declared God's great compassion on those who are powerless and completely dependent on God for their care.

"These two stories (the widow and last week's centurion) serve to certify Jesus' status as a prophet through whom God is visiting the people."[12] Both stories show the fulfillment of Jesus' pronouncement in the synagogue. The good news was proclaimed to the poor. Thus, the messianic age had begun in and through Christ.

Jesus was compared to the prophets of old, such as Elijah who resuscitated another economically deprived widow's dead son. However, the comparison moves the reader beyond identification with Elijah who was understood as an eschatological character who would return to usher in the last days. Elijah had to perform a ritual action and pray that God would answer his prayer to raise the dead son to life. Jesus, on the other hand, had only to say the *word*. On his own power, Jesus caused the healing. Jesus transcended Elijah. Luke's intention was to identify Jesus as the prophetic *messiah*. There was to be no misunderstanding. Elijah was entitled to his just remembrance and honor. Elijah was the herald of God's reign. Jesus was not the reincarnation of Elijah. Jesus Christ embodied the reign Elijah was to herald. Thus, Jesus was accomplishing what prophecy had declared the messiah would accomplish and what would designate the messianic age. The poor would have the good news proclaimed to them and the lost and the dead would be found and restored to life. In the messianic age, the poor and suffering would be uplifted. This widowed woman, outcast, disadvantaged, and powerless, was recipient of the messianic reign of God through Jesus. This is Luke's first use of the term, "Lord." Jesus' deeds would now be seen in light of his divinity as "Lord" of all creation.

Unlike the story praising the faith of the centurion, this story does not demand faith for Christ to act. Christ acts because of his love, compassion, and mercy. "It is entirely consistent with the pattern Luke has already established that this visitation reaches those who are outcast because they are gentile or women."[13] Luke's gospel is known as the gospel of women. The healings involving women, "as well as the forgiveness extended toward a woman who was a public outcast (7:36-50, next week's gospel) establish Jesus' concern for women."[14] However, while women were an object of Jesus' concern, his message was universal and extended to all people. The invitation and the demands of the gospel were open to all people inclusively.

Luke 7:22 is a summary of Jesus' teaching and healing ministry from the beginning and the joyous fulfillment of Isaiah 61:1. However, Luke 7:23 shifts from joyous announcement to a stern warning to those who would oppose Jesus' ministry. Jesus offended the people of Nazareth. Luke reminds us that "he can only be accepted as the *Coming One* by those who can accept his offensiveness."[15]

The environment of this story is completely Jewish (unlike the centurion pericope). For gentiles to live in Jesus' reign, the new Israel, "required faith and radical healing. For Jews it implied resurrection."[16] It was believed that before the final age all the dead Israelites would be raised from the dead. For Luke, death was the same as being lost and life was tantamount to being found. Jesus welcomed the "lost, dead son" with great mercy and compassion. The lost, dead Israel would be elevated to resurrected new life in Jesus' new Israel. Jesus' compassion was translated into action through his simple command, *his word*. Because of Jesus' *word,* the old Israel would be invited to participate in Jesus' new Israel. Israel was to be heir to the promise of the resurrection.

---

[12]Luke Timothy Johnson, *The Gospel of Luke,* Sacra Pagina Series, Vol. 3 (Collegeville: The Liturgical Press, 1991), 119.

[13]Ibid., 120.

[14]Richard J. Cassidy, *Jesus, Politics, and Society* (Maryknoll: Orbis Books, 1978), 24.

[15]Tannehill, Robert C. *The Narrative Unity of Luke-Acts: A Literary Interpretation,* Vol. I (Minneapolis: Augsburg Fortress, 1986), 80.

[16]Eugene LaVerdiere, S.S.S., *Luke* (Wilmington: Michael Glazier Books, 1980), 101.

Proclaim the gospel again.

Sometimes we gain new insights when we hear the text after the interpretation has been given. Someone from the group proclaims the gospel a second time.

STEP 4
TESTING

Conversation with the Liturgy and the Scriptures

Test your original understanding in dialogue with the text.

(You might consider breaking into smaller groups.)

Have your original assumptions about this gospel been expanded or challenged? What does the story of the widow of Naim have to say to your community today? Were there any new insights? Was there anything you had not considered before?

How does this story speak to your life?

I am reminded of a funeral a few years ago in which a young man, recently estranged from his wife and two small children, committed suicide. The family of the man blamed the wife. The pain and tension in the church could be felt by all present. While the dead young man was not to be raised to earthly life, our ritual prayer professed Jesus' compassion for this lost, hopeless soul. Jesus was extending his compassionate mercy to one lost to despair. However, the hope and the promise rested with those who were left behind. Our pastor challenged the families to choose a different path, the path of life. Jesus was extending peace and reconciliation and the opportunity to turn this meaningless tragedy into good by forgiving the deeply felt resentments. Our pastor reminded the families that Jesus died for them and with them. Jesus was with them in their sorrow. His compassion and mercy were theirs. The only way to bring life into this death-dealing situation was to extend that same mercy and compassion to the guilt- and blame-ridden family members sitting in our communal, family gathering place. In this case, the broken and poor were the young wife and her children and the grief-stricken family of the dead young man. Jesus' promise of resurrection and new life was their only hope.

I do not know the rest of the story. I am not sure what happened to all the parties involved, but it is in circumstances such as these that Jesus' incredible love and mercy are made manifest through the support and concern of the Christian community. Jesus' resurrected life is made a sacramental reality through a community that is willing to embrace, uphold, and love people through the devastations of life.

All share their life experience.

What was the message for Luke's community? What is his message for your community and is it relevant today? Where would there be opposition? Are the biblical themes of covenant, exodus, creation, and community evident in today's readings? Do you still feel the same way about this text as you did at the beginning? How would you explain the meaning of this gospel to a stranger?

STEP 5
DECISION

The gospel demands a response.

In what ways are our community's attitudes challenged by today's readings? In what specific way might there be opposition to this word? What are we called to do in response? How would our response be received today? Have I personally experienced a change in attitudes or behavior as a result of this exegesis and sharing? What are the implications for my life? What is one concrete action I will take this week as a response to what we have learned and shared today?

DOCTRINAL ISSUES

What church truth/teaching/doctrinal issue could be drawn from the gospel for the Tenth Sunday in Ordinary Time?

Participants suggest possible doctrinal themes that flow from the readings.

Possible Doctrinal Themes

Justice, christology, God's mercy, forgiveness and compassion, grace

Present the doctrinal material at this time.

1. The facilitator gives input on a particular doctrinal issue of his/her prior choosing. OR
2. The group chooses a doctrinal issue from the list they created. They read together from the Doctrinal Appendix.

(The doctrinal issues are found in the Doctrinal Appendix in the back of this workbook. If you are choosing an issue from this resource, please refer to it now.)

Reflection questions centered around the chosen doctrinal theme can be found at the end of each topic in the Doctrinal Appendix. The questions are based on the five-step reflection process. If you choose a topic not included in the Doctrinal Appendix, craft your own questions according to the same five-step process.

Following the reflection questions you will be reminded to return to chapter 7, "Preparing the Catechetical Session," to assist you in crafting your own session.

Closing Prayer

Lord,
look with love on our service.
Accept the gifts we bring
and help us grow in Christian love.
Grant this through Christ, our Lord.[17]

Selected Bibliography

Anderson, Bernhard W. *Understanding the Old Testament.* 4th ed. Englewood Cliffs: Prentice Hall, 1986.

Cassidy, Richard J. *Jesus, Politics, and Society.* Maryknoll: Orbis Books, 1978.

Cohn, R. *Journal of Biblical Literature* 101 (1982): 333-350.

Days of the Lord. Vol. 6. Collegeville: The Liturgical Press, 1991.

Johnson, Luke Timothy. *The Gospel of Luke.* Sacra Pagina Series. Vol. 3. Collegeville: The Liturgical Press, 1991.

Kselman, John S., S.S. and Michael L. Barre, S.S. "Psalms." In *The New Jerome Biblical Commentary.* Ed. Raymond E. Brown, S.S., Joseph A. Fitzmyer, S.J., Roland E. Murphy, O.Carm. Englewood Cliffs: Prentice Hall, 1990.

LaVerdiere, Eugene. S.S.S. *Luke.* Wilmington: Michael Glazier Books, 1980.

Sanchez, Patricia Datchuck. *The Word We Celebrate.* Kansas City: Sheed and Ward, 1989.

Tannehill, Robert C. *The Narrative Unity of Luke-Acts: A Literary Interpretation.* Vol. I. Minneapolis: Augsburg Fortress, 1986.

Walsh, Jerome T. "1-2 Kings." In *The New Jerome Biblical Commentary.* Ed. Raymond E. Brown, S.S., Joseph A. Fitzmyer, S.J., Roland E. Murphy, O.Carm. Englewood Cliffs: Prentice Hall, 1990.

---

[17]Tenth Sunday in Ordinary Time: "Prayer Over the Gifts," *The Sacramentary.*

ELEVENTH SUNDAY IN ORDINARY TIME

INTRODUCTORY RITES

Opening Song (or Entrance Antiphon)

Lord, hear my voice when I call to you. You are my help; do not cast me off, do not desert me, my Savior God. (Ps 26:7, 9)[1]

Opening Prayer

The facilitator of the session may lead the prayer. Others in the group may be asked to proclaim the readings.

Let us pray
[to the Father
whose love gives us strength to follow his Son]

Pause for silent prayer.

God our Father,
we rejoice in the faith that draws us together,
aware that selfishness can drive us apart.
Let your encouragement be our constant strength.
Keep us one in the love that has sealed our lives,
help us to live as one family
the gospel we profess.
We ask this through Christ, our Lord.[2]

LITURGY OF THE WORD

Let us listen to God's word.

The readings are proclaimed.

First Reading
2 Samuel 12:7-10, 13

Around the tenth century B.C.E., leadership from the tribal federation gave way to the monarchy. This monarchy solidified Israel as a powerful nation. However, there were misgivings about moving to such leadership, as Yahweh was the only

king the people of Israel worshiped. They knew well the allurement of power and were afraid that it would be difficult to resist the temptation not to heed Yahweh's sovereignty over them. Reluctantly, Samuel and Yahweh concede and Israel is allowed a monarchy, but not without "unambiguous warnings."[3] Some refer to the time of the kings as "Israel's Golden Age." The monarchy lasted over four hundred years. However, the unified monarchy lasted only about a century. There was a schism in 922 B.C.E. that divided the north [Israel] and the south [Judah]. The northern monarchy lasted until 722 B.C.E. when it was defeated by the Assyrians. The southern kingdom lasted until the fall of Jerusalem in 587 B.C.E.[4]

In today's pericope we learn about the domestic problems of the Davidic court. David's armies were conquering Ammonite, Syrian, and Armenian armies. As monarch, David had inherited the palace harem. Yet he became hopelessly captivated by Bathsheba, the wife of Uriah, one of his military leaders. While his forces were engaged in battle, David took Bathsheba to his bed. She became pregnant. David was unable to convince anyone that Uriah was the father of the child, so he arranged for the death of Uriah.

The prophet Nathan was summoned by Yahweh to go to David. The shrewd Nathan told David a parable about a poor man who had one lamb and a rich man who had many lambs. The rich man took the poor man's only lamb and slaughtered it for his dinner guests, rather than take from his own flock. David was furious at such a cold and heartless deed; he insisted that the man should die. Nathan turned on David and pointed the accusing finger. "You are the man," said Nathan. David had taken the only wife of Uriah, while an entire harem was available for David's choosing.

David owned up to his sin. By Israel's law David could have been put to death for his actions. How-

---

[1]Eleventh Sunday in Ordinary Time: "Entrance Antiphon, " *The Sacramentary.*

[2]Eleventh Sunday in Ordinary Time: "Alternative Opening Prayer," *The Sacramentary.*

[3]J. Kenneth Kuntz, *The People of Ancient Israel* (New York: Harper and Row, 1974), 173.

[4]Ibid., 171.

ever, Yahweh, as master of the law, spared David. Justice would be realized through David's offspring (there was a Jewish understanding that offspring would bear the guilt of their parents). David would be judged and his act of violence would be reciprocated. David's child by Bathsheba would die. Other children of David would later die by the sword as well. Through Nathan's convicting word, David owned up to his sin and repented. "David would be led to recognize that moral sanctions apply as much to a monarch as they do to any other member of the Israelite community."[5]

Responsorial Psalm
Psalm 32:1-2, 5, 7, 11

Today's psalm was believed to be David's cry of repentance for the sin he had committed. He recognized his sin as an act against Yahweh and was overwhelmed by Yahweh's forgiveness and mercy.

Second Reading
Galatians 2:16, 19-21

Paul's letter to the Galatians is one of the oldest records we have regarding the early Christian understanding of religious freedom. The letter to the Galatians depicts Paul's intense passion. He is threatened, defensive, angry, aggressive, and challenging.[6] The letter to the Galatians gives us a glimpse of the real Paul.

Last week and this week Paul hammers home what he says is the heart of the gospel: we are justified by faith. Common interpretation of Galatians asserts that we are "justified as a result of our faith in Jesus Christ."[7] However, some have taken this text to mean that we are justified as a result of the faithfulness of Jesus Christ.

Paul knew well what it meant to follow the law. He was an observant Jew. He knew that even the most observant follower of the law could not begin to accomplish what Jesus accomplished through his life, passion, death, and resurrection. "The law

with its external observance is not capable of changing the heart or preventing death."[8]

Paul insists that we are made just by Jesus' actions. The rapist and the righteous stand before God saved because of Jesus' definitive action. Our only response to such a gratuitous gift is faith. Through faith we humbly accept the gift we have been given. In turn we offer it to others by spreading the gospel of Christ.

When Paul stated that it was because of the law that he had died to the law, he was referring to his own incorporation into the paschal mystery. Through Jesus' death and resurrection we are given a share in that same event. Thus, since Jesus died because of the law, so too, do we. Joseph Fitzmyer states: "The Mosaic law and the mentality that it produced among human beings were responsible for the refusal to put faith in Christ and for the crucifixion of him—and thus indirectly for the emancipation of Christians who believe in him."[9]

The Judaizers suggested that humans were still bound by legal observances and human accomplishment. Paul asserts that such a position simply negates what was accomplished through "Christ's surrender."[10]

Gospel
Luke 7:36–8:3 or 7:36-50

The woman anoints Jesus' feet with her hair.

STEP 1
NAMING ONE'S EXPERIENCE

What was your initial experience of this gospel? What grabbed your attention?

Each person names his or her initial impression. Statement should be brief. No reasons should be given at this time. All simply listen without agreeing or disagreeing.

---

[5]Ibid., 171, 194.
[6]Raymond F. Collins, *Preaching the Epistles* (New York/Mahwah: Paulist Press, 1996), 56.
[7]Ibid.

[8]Patricia Datchuck Sanchez, *The Word We Celebrate* (Kansas City: Sheed and Ward, 1989), 336.
[9]Joseph A. Fitzmyer, S.J., "The Letter to the Galatians," in *The New Jerome Biblical Commentary,* ed. Raymond E. Brown, S.S., Joseph A. Fitzmyer, S.J., Roland E. Murphy, O.Carm. (Englewood Cliffs: Prentice Hall, 1990), 785.
[10]Sanchez, *The Word We Celebrate,* 785.

In a brief statement, what do you think this gospel is trying to convey? What meaning of this gospel did you bring with you to this conversation?

STEP 3
INPUT FROM VISION/STORY/TRADITION

Liturgical Context

On the Ninth Sunday in Ordinary Time, Jesus healed a man who was near death. On the Tenth Sunday he revived a dead man. It is no wonder that the gospel of the Eleventh Sunday seeks to answer the question of "who" this person Jesus really is. Jesus is the "Promised One" who heals, saves, and resurrects. No one is excluded. Repentance is demanded. The prophets had always called for *metanoia*. Jesus, like the prophets of old, lays bare sin and shows the path to freedom from sin.

In his letter to the Galatians Paul defends his ministry and asserts the truth of the gospel and its implication: justification by faith. The Ninth, Tenth, and Eleventh Sundays in Ordinary Time give ample attention to this theme. During these Sundays the church deeply reflects on the mystery of salvation and its implications.

The alternative opening prayer and the prayer over the gifts stress the incredible love God has for us and God's expressed desire for the unity that the eucharist celebrates. The forgiveness and reconciliation celebrated in today's readings invite repentant sinners to approach the table as forgiven and equal in the eyes of God.

Perhaps this is an appropriate time to celebrate a rite of anointing the catechumens with oil. Are there any candidates ready for full communion?

Gospel Exegesis

The facilitator gives input regarding what critical biblical scholarship has to say about this text. The input includes insights as to how people would have heard the gospel in Jesus' time.

Eugene LaVerdiere asserts that today's gospel is a statement about eucharist. There are two related stories. In chapter five the Pharisees challenge Jesus about his questionable dinner companions (tax collectors and sinners). Jesus responds by affirming that his call is not to the righteous, but to the sinner. In this story, eucharist is connected to "evangelization and showed how the eucharist calls sinners to repentance [metanoia]."[11] Today's story demands reconciliation[12] and asks that those who come to the table repent and welcome others.

The meal in Simon's house takes place in Galilee, the place where Jesus appointed his apostles and where his ministry began. Chapters 6 through 8 are concerned with what it means to be a "community of the Twelve." Throughout Israel's history, "being the community of the Twelve meant transcending tribal distinctions and forming one people, distinct from all others surrounding it."[13] For the early Christian community the "meal" envisioned this same unity. Harmony and peace were expectations. There were to be no divisions or lack of hospitality.

The use of the woman in this story foreshadows verses 1-53 in chapter 8 in which Luke asserts the place and role of women in this community of the Twelve. The woman's alabaster flask represents the great respect she has for Jesus. By placing her at the feet of Jesus ("to be at someone's feet" meant to be someone's disciple), Luke makes the

---

[11]Eugene LaVerdiere, S.S.S., *Dining in the Kingdom of God* (Chicago: Liturgy Training Publications, 1994), 47.

[12]Eugene LaVerdiere details a very useful explanation and understanding of the usages of the terms repentance, forgiveness, and reconciliation in the New Testament. He asserts that the New Testament clearly distinguishes the terms "repentance" (*metanoia*), "forgiveness" (*aphesis*), "reconciliation" (*katallage*). *Metanoia*, or a complete turning from sin toward God, is a prerequisite of obtaining forgiveness and reconciliation. *Aphesis*, forgiveness from God, is God's response to metanoia. *Katallage*, reconciliation, is the goal of metanoia. In other words, one is transformed so that they in turn may be an agent of reconciliation with others [207, #10].

[13]LaVerdiere, *Dining in the Kingdom of God*, 48.

reader aware that she has assumed the spiritual posture of a devotee in relation to a great teacher. The fact that she anoints him and wipes his feet with her hair shows that she is an extraordinarily committed disciple.[14]

Jesus' eating at the house of a Pharisee indicates that Jesus is in solidarity with them. They, too, are heirs of his message. How will they respond? The Pharisee does not see the significance of the woman's gesture. He reacts with indignation. The reader sees an enormous difference in the "quality of disciple" between the woman and the Pharisee.[15] Jesus purposely does not respond to the woman. What elicits his response is the Pharisee's reaction to her.

Jesus then tells a parable based on the cultural reality of patron and client that was prevalent during his lifetime. In contrast with a contemporary employee/employer relationship, the patron/client model was "more familial than contractual."[16] The patron/client relationship was an unequal relationship. Someone had the power and was able to exercise it over the other. It was based on custom rather than law, so there was no higher court of appeal where an unjustly treated person could seek redress. "Since relations are unequal, a client accepts the patron's protection in exchange for submitting to control."[17] In his parables, Jesus reversed the expected order of things. He was the antithesis of the customary patron of his day. Jesus provided protection for his clients, but in loving solidarity with them. In the type of parable shown in this pericope, the kingdom is portrayed as an accounting with the purpose of setting things right.[18] In this parable the master places things in right order. As the hierarchical person in power, the master "establishes that order as one of grace and forgiveness."[19] This was obviously not the expected or experienced behavior in patron/client relationships.

---

[14]Ibid., 52.

[15]Ibid., 53.

[16]Bernard Brandon Scott, *Hear Then the Parable* (Minneapolis: Augsburg Fortress, 1989), 205.

[17]Ibid., 206.

[18]Ibid., 214.

[19]Ibid.

Debts incurred in first-century Palestine involved more than just paying off a loan. The person in debt owed not only the debt of money, but also that of gratitude for being lent the money in the first place. Thus, debts could never be fully repaid. According to LaVerdiere, debts could be forgiven, but would still entail a permanent debt of gratitude to the lender. In Jesus' parable, the gratitude was paid through love. The greater the debt forgiven, the greater the love.

Jesus contrasted the Pharisee's lack of love with the woman's lavish love. The bottom line for Simon was that, since he had repented little, he was forgiven little, and therefore he showed less love than the woman. She loved because she was forgiven so much.

Jesus addressed all listeners and invited them into the story. Anyone who possessed an attitude similar to that of Simon was to hear and repent. All who had been forgiven much were to be welcomed with open arms. The woman, like the tax collector (Lk 7:29), had acknowledged God's judgment on her and had received forgiveness from God. The Pharisee, on the other hand, had not accepted God's judgment on himself, and thus had not received forgiveness in any significant way.[20] Thus, those whose sins were external and obvious to all acknowledged their sin and the validity of God's judgment. Those whose sins involved hidden attitudes did not acknowledge their need for forgiveness and thus were not forgiven.

Luke often described the appropriate responses to Jesus' forgiveness and healing. The response could be horizontal, an ethical response directed to helping other people in need, or it could be vertical or spiritual, a response to God. In this parable, the vertical response was directed toward Jesus. In return for his incredible forgiving love, love was to be lavishly returned in the form of praise and thanksgiving. (One cannot miss eucharistic overtones, as the etymology of the word "eucharist" is praise and thanksgiving.)

There is an irony in today's story. Simon thinks to himself, "If Jesus really were a prophet, he

---

[20]Charles H. Talbert, *Reading Luke* (New York: Crossroad, 1992), 85.

would know who this sinful woman is who is making him ritually unclean by touching him." Jesus turns Simon's thoughts upside down; indeed, Jesus shows that he is a prophet, and reads the Pharisee's heart in judgment against him.[21]

Proclaim the gospel again.

Sometimes we gain new insights when we hear the text after the interpretation has been given. Someone from the group proclaims the gospel a second time.

STEP 4
TESTING

Conversation with the Liturgy and the Scriptures

Test your original understanding in dialogue with the text.

(You might consider breaking into smaller groups.)

Is there anything in this exegesis that was a new insight for you? What are the key issues in this text? How does your original understanding of this story compare with what we just shared?

How does this story speak to your life?

Participants share an experience from their lives that connects with the biblical interpretation just shared.

> *This is a much needed gospel for contemporary communities. How often we very righteously assume that we have the place of honor at the table, while others have no business there. Sometimes people complain about the way others dress for liturgy and their "seeming" lackadaisical attitude and approach to receiving communion. Not too long ago someone commented that these attributes are particularly true of young people. The speaker, someone of baby-boomer age, added that the young ones coming up aren't as committed as the older folks. How quick we are to judge an entire group by outer appearances.*

---

[21]Ibid., 84–89.

I wonder how it would be accepted if we were to tell our communities that the homeless we serve stand equally before the table of the Lord as the rest of us? With modern society's climate of rage and indignation toward the homeless and "those who refuse to work," we have a difficult time looking past their lives and their addictions to see broken, hopeless people in search of whatever it is they cannot find. It is no wonder that twelve-step groups are so powerfully touching people's lives. There is no judgment; there is only acknowledgment that all those present are powerless over their lives and need a power greater than themselves to restore them to sanity. I daresay addicts know what it means to have been forgiven much. I am certain that if Jesus were to walk our streets again, his first stop would be to break bread in the midst of smoke-filled AA meetings. Recovering alcoholics know what it means to seriously repent and to have been forgiven. They devote their lives to the service of reconciliation. They seek to bring others the good news. Our parishes have much to learn from these groups.

All share their life experience.

What was Luke trying to tell his community? What is the message for our community today? What might God be creating in us through the experience of Jesus and the woman in this gospel? In what way is our community challenged? What are our collective and personal responses to all of these questions? Do we still feel the same way about this text as we did when we began? Has our original understanding been stretched, challenged, or affirmed?

STEP 5
DECISION

The gospel demands a response.

In what way does this gospel call us to change our hearts, our attitudes, and our behavior? What would be the contemporary implications of today's readings? In what concrete way are we called to specifically respond to today's story? What is one action we will take this week as a response to what we have learned and shared today?

DOCTRINAL ISSUES

What church truth/teaching/doctrinal issue could be drawn from the gospel for the Eleventh Sunday in Ordinary Time?

Participants suggest possible doctrinal themes that flow from the readings.

Possible Doctrinal Themes

Eucharist, conversion, reconciliation, repentance, forgiveness, sin

Present the doctrinal material at this time.

1. The facilitator gives input on a particular doctrinal issue of his/her prior choosing. OR
2. The group chooses a doctrinal issue from the list they created. They read together from the Doctrinal Appendix.

(The doctrinal issues are found in the Doctrinal Appendix in the back of this workbook. If you are choosing an issue from this resource, please refer to it now.)

Reflection questions centered around the chosen doctrinal theme can be found at the end of each topic in the Doctrinal Appendix. The questions are based on the five-step reflection process. If you choose a topic not included in the Doctrinal Appendix, craft your own questions according to the same five-step process.

Following the reflection questions you will be reminded to return to chapter 7, "Preparing the Catechetical Session," to assist you in crafting your own session.

Closing Prayer

Lord God,
in this bread and wine
you give us food for body and spirit.
May the eucharist renew our strength
and bring us health of mind and body.[22]

---

[22]Eleventh Sunday in Ordinary Time: "Prayer Over the Gifts," *The Sacramentary.*

Selected Bibliography

Collins, Raymond F. *Preaching the Epistles.* New York/Mahwah: Paulist Press, 1996.

Fitzmyer, Joseph A., S.J. "The Letter to the Galatians." In *The New Jerome Biblical Commentary.* Ed. Raymond E. Brown, S.S., Joseph A. Fitzmyer, S.J., Roland E. Murphy, O.Carm. Englewood Cliffs: Prentice Hall, 1990.

Kuntz, J. Kenneth. *The People of Ancient Israel.* New York: Harper and Row, 1974.

LaVerdiere, Eugene, S.S.S. *Dining in the Kingdom of God.* Chicago: Liturgy Training Publications, 1994.

Sanchez, Patricia Datchuck. *The Word We Celebrate.* Kansas City: Sheed and Ward, 1989.

Scott, Bernard Brandon. *Hear Then the Parable.* Minneapolis: Augsburg Fortress, 1989.

Talbert, Charles H. *Reading Luke.* New York: Crossroad, 1992.

Twelfth Sunday in Ordinary Time

INTRODUCTORY RITES

Opening Song (or Entrance Antiphon)

God is the strength of his people. In him, we his chosen live in safety. Save us, Lord, who share in your life, and give us your blessing; be our shepherd for ever. (Ps 27:8-9)[1]

Opening Prayer

The facilitator of the session may lead the prayer. Others in the group may be asked to proclaim the readings.

Let us pray

   Pause for silent prayer.

Lord,
you give us the body and blood of your Son
to renew your life within us.
In your mercy, assure our redemption
and bring us to the eternal life
we celebrate in this Eucharist.
We ask this through Christ our Lord.[2]

LITURGY OF THE WORD

Let us listen to God's word.

The readings are proclaimed.

First Reading
Zechariah 12:10-11

The writing of the book of the prophet Zechariah is believed to have spanned a couple of centuries. There are at least two, possibly more, authors responsible for its writing. This portion of Zechariah was written soon after the return from the Babylonian exile. The primary concern of the day was reconstruction of a nation and a people. This piece is eschatological in its intention. Zechariah and Haggai were two late sixth century B.C.E. prophets who were the inspiration behind the reconstruction of the temple. It is believed that chapters 9–11 and 12–14 were written by disciples of Zechariah; thus the later portion of the book is often referred to as Deutero-Zechariah.

In today's pericope, Zechariah spoke of a battle between the forces of God and the forces of evil. Zechariah gave assurances that there would be victory, but it would first be preceded by a time of great trial and persecution. Through suffering, the people would come to know what it means to truly repent. Through repentance, the covenant with Yahweh would be restored. Yahweh promised to be with them in their suffering. Yahweh further promised that a new leader would emerge, a shepherd who would be "thrust through" (NAB) and who would be mourned as one would mourn an only son. Whereas Isaiah referred to the image of a suffering servant, Zechariah alluded to the shepherd who would guide his sheep through the purification of suffering. The shepherd's death in today's pericope would signal the beginning of the final age. The Spirit would be poured out in abundance, thus convincing the people of their need to repent.

The place of this mourning is very significant. Josiah died at Hadadrimmon in the plain of Megiddo and was mourned at that site because of his efforts to call his people to repentance. Two pagan gods of storm and of weather were also mourned in ritual every year at Megiddo. Thus, this place of remembered and ritualized grief served as a reminder of the kind of grief that Jerusalem was to experience in her time of trial.

The early Christians used Zechariah's image of slain shepherd and Isaiah's suffering servant as the primary motif for Jesus Christ. Jesus was the shepherd who was pierced and the suffering servant who atoned for the sins of many. Jesus was obviously seen as the fulfillment of Zechariah's prophecy.

---

[1]Twelfth Sunday in Ordinary Time: "Entrance Antiphon," *The Sacramentary.*

[2]Twelfth Sunday in Ordinary Time: "Prayer After Communion," *The Sacramentary.*

The central issue in today's reading from Zechariah is that people must undergo purification of sin that leads to repentance; but God in his incredible mercy is the one who instills such repentance in the human heart.

Responsorial Psalm
Psalm 63:2, 3-4, 5-6, 8-9

Our hope in the face of trials and purification exists through faith. The psalm today expresses this utter faith in Yahweh and is a good response to the impending forecast of difficult times. Only through faith and trust will humanity stand firm in the face of adversity.

Second Reading
Galatians 3:26-29

In his letter to the Galatians, Paul addressed serious issues of unity for the house churches. There was disagreement concerning the role of the law of Moses in relation to salvation: how it did or did not affect the gentile believers. Paul insisted that the law did not save; Jesus Christ alone saves through the paschal mystery. Human beings are reconciled to God through Jesus' passion, death, and resurrection. All are equal before God; there are no distinctions.

In today's pericope Paul was referring to a baptismal prayer which attested that all were one in Christ; there is neither male nor female. Paul purposely referred to the Genesis story in which men and women were created equal partners by God. The baptismal reference to the garment was a sign of belonging to a god of a particular religion. When initiated into any cult, the devotee put on a special robe, thereby attesting that he or she belonged to the god of that cult. The garment in Old Testament understanding referred to a change of behavior. The person donning the garment would begin a new way of living. Paul insisted that all are one in Christ. There are to be absolutely no distinctions in the church of Jesus Christ.

Paul was not concerned with hierarchical leadership as much as he was with the house churches acting "as a body." Leaders were to admonish, but so was everyone. Prophets were to build up, but so was everyone. There was no need for special human honors when it came to leadership in the community. Paul's notion of church leadership included the concepts of reciprocity, collegiality, and corroborative ministry. The members of the "body" would discern the direction of leadership. The one in charge would carry out the wishes as servant of the "body."[3]

Gospel
Luke 9:18-24

Jesus is alone praying; his disciples approach him and Jesus asks them who they think he is.

STEP 1
NAMING ONE'S EXPERIENCE

What captured your attention in today's gospel? What feelings did you experience?

Each person names his or her initial impression. Statement should be brief. No reasons should be given at this time. All simply listen without agreeing or disagreeing.

STEP 2
UNDERSTANDING

In a brief statement, what do you think this gospel is trying to convey? What pre-understanding did you bring to this session?

STEP 3
INPUT FROM VISION/STORY/TRADITION

Liturgical Context

Chapter 9 and part of chapter 10 are transition points in the gospel of Luke. The next three Sundays form an internal unity of their own. On the Twelfth Sunday, Jesus asks his disciples who they

---

[3]Vincent Branick, *The House Church in the Writings of Paul* (Wilmington: Michael Glazier Books, 1989), 95-96.

think he is. He tells of his impending passion and death and reminds them that all who want to follow him must do the same. In next week's gospel, Jesus begins the arduous journey to Jerusalem. We are told that we must keep our eyes focused forward, and that we must forge on with deliberation, unencumbered by possessions. The Fourteenth Sunday insists that neither complacency nor lack of success must get in the way of the journey. Jesus then sends seventy-two out ahead of him to prepare the way for his message. They will announce his coming, walk as he walks, live and die as he lived and died. They will proclaim the message of God's reign.

The cross is an important symbol in today's readings. We are told that we must take it up and carry it if we are to be disciples. The cross is a sign of our membership in Christ. It is a primary symbol in every sacramental celebration, from baptism through viaticum. The primary goal of every sacrament is incorporation into the paschal mystery of Christ. That is, we willingly take up our cross, deny ourselves, and die and rise daily with Christ. We profess, commit to, and celebrate this incorporation every time the church gathers for liturgy.

Raymond Collins suggests that this pericope is a good springboard for speaking about baptism. Paul's understanding of baptism forms an essential part of our baptismal theology: faith, becoming children of God, being united to Christ, and being one in Christ. Another less noticed theme of Paul's baptismal theology is that "the unity-in-diversity of the church is a sign of our unity-in-diversity in Christ, itself a sacramental sign of the kingdom of God."[4]

Since the cross is an important symbol in today's liturgy, it might be an appropriate Sunday to celebrate the Rite of Acceptance.

Gospel Exegesis

The facilitator gives input regarding what critical biblical scholarship has to say about this text. The input includes insights as to how people would have heard the gospel in Jesus' time.

The next ten chapters of Luke are about Jesus' journey to Jerusalem. They are particular to Luke. The other evangelists do not give such an exhaustive rendering of the journey. Luke intended to show that Jesus' journey mirrors the journey of every Christian. All are to follow Jesus to Jerusalem, to take up their cross, to die, to tell the good news, and to submit to the will of God with their very lives.

In today's scene Jesus has gone off to pray alone. Luke's Jesus prays throughout the gospel. Usually Jesus' praying signals a significant development. Luke wants his readers to know that "Jesus is a prophet who not only knows people's hearts, but can also foretell his own future death and resurrection."[5] Luke deliberately uses the term "all" to refer to those who are called to discipleship. Even though the story implies that the *Twelve* were his audience, by addressing all disciples, Luke's Jesus is telling all who will read this account that the rigors of discipleship are for all followers of Christ. Luke is emphatic: to daily take up one's cross is the source and summit of Christian spirituality. It is not just something one does occasionally, but is the hallmark of the Christian life.

It was through suffering that Jesus' obedience to the will of his Father was perfected. Through Jesus' prayer we are to understand that he was about to begin the fulfillment of God's plan for him. Something new was beginning for Jesus; he had to be receptive to it. Prior to this time, Jesus' ministry had met with success. In the next phase of his ministry Jesus was to encounter great suffering and rejection. Through these trials, this suffering and rejection, he learned obedience to God's will. "His obedience to God in the face of rejection, persecution, suffering, and finally death will signal his victory over death (1 Pet 4: 1-2)."[6] When confronted with such a reality, the human person comes face-to-face with loss. All is lost for the greater good: possessions, security, reputation, even life itself. This

---

[4]Raymond F. Collins, *Preaching the Epistles* (New York/Mahwah: Paulist Press, 1996), 86-88.

[5]Luke Timothy Johnson, *The Gospel of Luke,* Sacra Pagina Series, Vol. 3 (Collegeville: The Liturgical Press, 1991), 55.

[6]Charles H. Talbert, *Reading Luke* (New York, Crossroad, 1992), 106.

type of letting go allows a person to become detached and keeps him or her from attaching to the spurious security of false idols. Suffering of this sort purifies the soul. However, this type of purification is not possible without God's prior illuminating and empowering presence. The indwelling of God is necessary in order "for suffering to be experienced as purification. The way of Jesus, therefore was from empowering through suffering to glory."[7]

Jesus insists that the way of discipleship involves the same process for all disciples. Only when disciples detach from worldly attachments will they be able to willingly follow the master and his cross. Taking up the cross in this instance is not understood as taking up life's daily burdens. Rather, the self-denial expressed in this gospel resembles the posture of a condemned person awaiting a death sentence. There is nothing left in this world for the condemned person but the cross of Christ. There are no possible worldly attachments, as all are stripped away by the sentence of death.

We are to be free from false illusions of self. God is to become the motivating force of life. Self-sufficiency without God in the face of suffering and death is an absurdity. Jesus showed us by his death and resurrection that through a life of detachment we share in the reign of God, here, in this earthly sojourn. Disciples are to give themselves completely over to Christ. There is to be no holding back.

Jesus defended his disciples when they faced rejection. Jesus warned them that they were approaching a time when they would stand defenseless, just as Jesus would be defenseless. Jesus challenged his disciples to be steadfast and loyal to himself, to the gospel, and to gospel living.[8]

There is great mystery and consternation in today's story. Peter's confession that Jesus is the messiah is a pivotal point in the story. Because of Peter's insight, the disciples are ready to move to the next

stage of instruction on their way to Jerusalem. It is a coming of age, a moment of maturity.

However, the mystery remains. Why must Jesus suffer and die at the hands of the leaders of the Sanhedrin? A crisis is in the making. Jesus will suffer at the hands of Israel, the very people he came to save. What does it all mean? Robert Tannehill asserts that "a process of planning and preparation is taking place, a search for God's will disclosed in Scripture, and the process emerges out of prayer."[9] Jesus had his hands full in preparing mature disciples for the demands of discipleship as set forth in today's gospel. The disciples would falter and not fully understand the full extent of Jesus' words until after the resurrection. It was in retrospect that Jesus' words would be understood. Experience, as we know, is the best teacher. The experience of Jesus' passion, death, and resurrection allowed the disciples to look back at his words and understand their full implications for the Christian life of discipleship.

Proclaim the gospel again.

Sometimes we gain new insights when we hear the text after the interpretation has been given. Someone from the group proclaims the gospel a second time.

STEP 4

TESTING

Conversation with the Liturgy and the Scriptures

Test your original understanding in dialogue with the text.

(You might consider breaking into smaller groups.)

How do you feel about the exegetical understanding that taking up the cross is comparable to the posture of a condemned person awaiting a death sentence? What are the implications? What is the cost of discipleship now, after hearing the exege-

---

[7]Ibid., 107.

[8]Robert J. Karris, O.F.M. "The Gospel According to Luke," in *The New Jerome Biblical Commentary,* ed. Raymond A. Brown, S.S., Joseph A. Fitzmyer, S.J., Roland E. Murphy, O.Carm. (Englewood Cliffs: Prentice Hall, 1990), 700.

[9]Robert C. Tannehill, *The Narrative Unity of Luke-Acts: A Literary Interpretation,* Vol.1 (Minneapolis: Augsburg Fortress, 1986), 225.

sis? Was there anything you had not considered before hearing this exegesis? How does your original understanding of this story compare with what was just shared? How does this story speak to your life?

Participants share an experience from their lives that connects with the biblical interpretation just shared.

The demand made by today's gospel seems overwhelming. Yet it must be feasible or it would not be suggested as a possibility. In looking over my life, I find it difficult to find a time when I willingly lived like a condemned person. There have been experiences in which circumstances forced me into such a posture. But I certainly did not go willingly. There have been times when there were no other resources than the resources provided by God. Human strength failed; our own efforts failed and we were totally in the hands of God. I remember when we thought we were being moved out of town. We had a lovely home and enjoyed life where we were. But the opportunity presented itself and through careful discernment seemed to be a right decision for us. We put our house on the market and my husband began his job in a new city while my children and I stayed behind to tend to the selling of the house. At the last minute, everything fell through. We were left with no home and no move. I was very angry with God.

"You say you will follow me to the ends of the earth, but will you really? Will you follow me even when you have no idea of the outcome? Will you follow me if I demand that you give up the security of your home and your carefully laid plans?" These questions seemed to be the only answers to my furious questions. We were faced with decision: would we or wouldn't we trust? Detachment was essential. God was leading us. Only in looking back have we understood the extent to which that was true. We did not face rejection and persecution in that experience, but we were strengthened for that eventuality.

Experiences of suffering and purification are moments of learning on the journey toward Christian maturity. I have not always gone willingly. The type of suffering implied in today's gospel is a mystery and requires ongoing fidelity to the will of God, day after day. Most often I fall short, but sometimes I get it. I guess I am in good company. So was Peter.

Is there any way you can connect the gospel we just shared to an experience in your own life?

All share their experience.

What was Luke's message to his community? Where is the appropriate relevance today for our community? What might God be creating in us through reflection on the gospel? In what way does this gospel point to God's promise to be with us? How does this gospel call us to embrace our own exodus? What are our collective and personal responses to all of these questions? Do we still feel the same way about this text as we did when we began? Were there any new insights?

STEP 5
DECISION

The gospel demands a response.

How is your community challenged to respond to this gospel? Be concrete. What are the contemporary implications of this gospel? In what way are you called to conversion by this gospel? Name one concrete action you will take this week as a response to what was learned and shared today.

DOCTRINAL ISSUES

What church truth/teaching/doctrinal issue could be drawn from the gospel for the Twelfth Sunday in Ordinary Time?

Participants suggest possible doctrinal themes that flow from the readings.

Possible Doctrinal Themes

Cross, suffering, the cost of discipleship, paschal mystery, baptism

Present the doctrinal material at this time.

1. The facilitator gives input on a particular doctrinal issue of his/her prior choosing. OR
2. The group chooses a doctrinal issue from the list they created. They read together from the Doctrinal Appendix.

(The doctrinal issues are found in the Doctrinal Appendix in the back of this workbook. If you are choosing an issue from this resource, please refer to it now.)

Reflection questions centered around the chosen doctrinal theme can be found at the end of each topic in the Doctrinal Appendix. The questions are based on the five-step reflection process. If you choose a topic not included in the Doctrinal Appendix, craft your own questions according to the same five-step process.

Following the reflection questions you will be reminded to return to chapter 7, "Preparing the Catechetical Session," to assist you in crafting your own session.

Closing Prayer

The Father of mercies has given us an example of
    unselfish love
in the sufferings of his only Son.
Through your service of God and neighbor
may you receive his countless blessings. Amen.

You believe that by his dying
Christ destroyed death forever.
May he give you everlasting life. Amen.

He humbled himself for our sakes.
May you follow his example
and share in his resurrection. Amen.[10]

Selected Bibliography

Branick, Vincent. *The House Church in the Writings of Paul.* Wilmington: Michael Glazier Books, 1989.
Collins, Raymond F. *Preaching the Epistles.* New York/Mahwah: Paulist Press, 1996.
Days of the Lord. Vol. 6. Collegeville: The Liturgical Press, 1991.
Johnson, Luke Timothy. *The Gospel of Luke.* Sacra Pagina Series. Vol. 3. Collegeville: The Liturgical Press, 1991.

Karris, Robert J., O.F.M. "The Gospel According to Luke." In *The New Jerome Biblical Commentary.* Ed. Raymond E. Brown, S.S., Joseph A. Fitzmyer, S.J., Roland E. Murphy, O.Carm. Englewood Cliffs: Prentice Hall, 1990.
Kuntz, J. Kenneth. *The People of Ancient Israel.* New York: Harper and Row, 1974.
Sanchez, Patricia Datchuck. *The Word We Celebrate.* Kansas City: Sheed and Ward, 1989.
Talbert, Charles H. *Reading Luke.* New York: Crossroad, 1992.
Tannehill, Robert C. *The Narrative Unity of Luke-Acts: A Literary Interpretation.* Vol. 1. Minneapolis: Augsburg Fortress, 1986.

---

[10]The Passion of the Lord: "Solemn Blessing #5," *The Sacramentary.*

Thirteenth Sunday in Ordinary Time

INTRODUCTORY RITES

Opening Song (or Entrance Antiphon)

All nations, clap your hands. Shout with a voice of joy to God. (Ps 46:2)[1]

Opening Prayer

The facilitator of the session may lead the prayer. Others in the group may be asked to proclaim the readings.

Let us pray
[that Christ may be our light]

    Pause for silent prayer.

Father,
you call your children
to walk in the light of Christ.
Free us from darkness
and keep us from the radiance of your truth.
We ask this through our Lord Jesus Christ, your
    Son,
who lives and reigns with you and the Holy
    Spirit,
one God, for ever and ever.[2]

LITURGY OF THE WORD

Let us listen to God's word.

The readings are proclaimed.

First Reading
1 Kings 19:16, 19-21

Elisha was the prophet who succeeded Elijah. Today's reading is part of a longer sequence in which Elijah experiences a theophany on Mount Horeb following his harrowing escape from the royal authorities. It is after the phenomena usu-

ally associated with God's presence (fire, earthquakes, etc.) fade that "nearness is perceived in the lull of eerie silence."[3] Yahweh spoke to Elijah on Mount Horeb in the deafening silence, not in the thunderous ways of old (earthquakes, wind, etc.). Elijah hid his face in his mantle so that he could not see God. Elijah lodged a complaint with Yahweh.

The people of Israel had not been faithful; they worshiped Baal and cooperated in putting Israel's prophets in peril. Elijah felt alone, isolated, and in danger.[4] He even hinted that he was quitting, renouncing his prophetic ministry. Yahweh responded to Elijah's complaints by commissioning Elijah's successor. "To Israel's violence, Yahweh responds with the swords of Hazael and Jehu."[5] Yahweh sent Elijah back with work to do and tasks to fulfill. Elijah was not allowed to sit and brood over his misfortunes, but rather was to continue his prophetic mission. "Israel's faith finds expression in action rather than mystic contemplation."[6] He was to appoint Elisha prophet, anoint and commission king Hazael of Damascus, and join Jehu in his revolt against the Omri dynasty. Elijah was also to take part in the revolution against the existing governments of Syria and Israel. Interestingly, he did not accomplish the last two tasks, but his successor Elisha did.

Elisha would eventually carry out Yahweh's plan to return to Israel to "incite a revolution."[7] In this revolution many Israelites would perish. All who had worshiped Baal would fall, but a faithful remnant of Israel would be spared. When Elijah complained that he was alone in the midst of such de-

---

[1]Thirteenth Sunday in Ordinary Time: "Entrance Antiphon," *The Sacramentary.*

[2]Thirteenth Sunday in Ordinary Time: "Opening Prayer," *The Sacramentary.*

[3]J. Kenneth Kuntz, *The People of Israel* (New York: Harper and Row, 1974), 246.

[4]Jerome Walsh and Christopher T. Begg, "1-2 Kings," in *The New Jerome Biblical Commentary,* ed. Raymond E. Brown, S.S., Joseph A. Fitzmyer, S.J., Roland E. Murphy, O.Carm. (Englewood Cliffs: Prentice Hall, 1990), 172.

[5]Walsh and Begg, "1-2 Kings," 172.

[6]Bernhard W. Anderson, *Understanding the Old Testament,* 4th ed. (Englewood Cliffs: Prentice Hall, 1986), 276.

[7]Ibid., 277.

pravity, Yahweh reminded him of the seven thousand faithful remnant.

Elisha was to be part of the great prophetic movement that was intent on calling for reform, *metanoia,* and a return to Yahweh, the jealous God of Israel. The prophets demanded a return to the Mosaic covenant. Only a faithful return to the covenant would restore them after their idolatrous living. The prophets had no time for nostalgic reminiscence and longing for a return to the days of Moses. Instead, they remembered the covenant made with Moses and actuated its power and promise in the present. Elijah and Elisha, the great prophets, were revered as authentic prophets and all believed that God spoke through them.

In today's pericope, Elijah, in the name of Yahweh, called Elisha to prophetic service. Elijah offered Elisha his cloak. "The throwing of the cloak, the normal attire of a prophet, symbolized either ownership and responsibility or investiture and initiation of a successor."[8] There were many layers of meaning inherent in the gesture and those meanings can still be observed today in liturgical practice in the wearing of the stole by the deacon, the wearing of the chasuble by the priest, and the wearing of the habit by religious.

> The cloak symbolized the personality and rights of the owner, as well as the owner's protection. The gift of cloak was a sign of unity, communion, and friendship: Jonathan made a gift of his cloak and his weapons to David (1 Sam 18:4). Insofar as it was a sign of a function, it shared in the charism of the one who wore it. The imposition of this cloak was an investiture. When Elijah was lifted to heaven, Elisha picked it up and was thus able to perform the same miracle as Elijah (2 Kings 2:8, 13-14).[9]

Elisha was obviously a wealthy man as evidenced by his ownership of multiple oxen for plowing. Most people owned only one ox. The wealthy El-

isha asked if he could bid farewell to his parents before leaving. Elijah seemed to castigate him. Some scholars suggest that Elijah's terse remark might have just been his way of saying, "Go ahead, I won't stop you."

Elisha asserted his commitment to his new vocation by the grand gesture of slaughtering oxen on a grate made of his own plowing tools. He was ready, willing, and eager to go as Yahweh had commanded. It was definitely God's election, not Elisha's. Elijah summoned Elisha on behalf of Yahweh. Elisha went willingly and eagerly and let go of his former life. He gave up all to follow Yahweh.

Elijah returned from his mission to assume an ordinary life. Elisha continued where Elijah had left off. Elijah became the goal of pilgrimage, the locus of holy power to which Elisha was drawn and from which he would go forth, like Elijah from Horeb, a bearer of power and mission. Elijah drew his power from his theophany with God. Elisha, in turn, was empowered by Elijah.

Responsorial Psalm
Psalm 16:1-2, 5, 7-8, 9-10, 11

Psalm 16 is a psalm of faith and confidence in God. "You will show me the path of life" in Wisdom literature refers to the proper way of living. In this setting it probably refers to the fullness of life experienced in God's temple.[10]

Second Reading
Galatians 5:1, 13-18

The creedal intent of Paul's letter is that freedom from the law is not license, but freedom from material observance. People have a choice. They can choose either freedom and life in Christ or slavery and death in the law. Paul insists that if one chooses Christ, then the law of love must guide one's actions. Freedom is grounded in freedom *for others.*

The Spirit will lead and guide. People are to conduct themselves according to the Spirit's guid-

---

[8]Patricia Datchuck Sanchez, *The Word We Celebrate* (Kansas City: Sheed and Ward, 1989), 340.

[9]*Days of the Lord,* Vol. 6 (Collegeville: The Liturgical Press, 1991), 339.

---

[10]John S. Kselman, S.S. and Michael Barré, S.S., "Psalms," in *The New Jerome Biblical Commentary,* ed. Raymond E. Brown, S.S., Joseph A. Fitzmyer, S.J., Roland E. Murphy, O.Carm. (Englewood Cliffs: Prentice Hall, 1990), 529.

ance. Even though led by the Spirit, human beings still struggle with the "flesh," the symbol of all human resistance to God. Although the struggle with the flesh persists, the Spirit provides an indwelling strength that helps resist temptations of resistance and disobedience to God's will. The law does not have that kind of power.

Gospel
Luke 9:51-62

Jesus sets his eyes toward Jerusalem and teaches disciples and would-be disciples about discipleship.

STEP 1
NAMING ONE'S EXPERIENCE

What was your first impression? What captured your attention?

Each person names his or her initial impression. Statement should be brief. No reasons should be given at this time. All simply listen without agreeing or disagreeing.

STEP 2
UNDERSTANDING

In a brief statement, what do you think this gospel is trying to convey? What pre-understanding did you bring to this gospel?

STEP 3
INPUT FROM VISION/STORY/TRADITION

Liturgical Context

All three readings today are concerned with the call of discipleship. Elijah calls Elisha in the name of Yahweh; Paul invites all to embrace their freedom from the law and from sin, a freedom won by Christ's death and resurrection. Disciples are taught about the rigors of discipleship. The demand is for nothing less than the entire gift of self.

In today's opening prayer we acknowledge the call as God's children to live in the light of Christ. We

are reminded of Paul's warning that we are free from observance of the law, but we are to love. The responsibility requires our total commitment. We recognize that we cannot do it alone; we count on the Spirit to deliver us from the darkness that keeps us in the radiance of God's truth. The prayer after communion reminds us of the bottom line for Catholic Christians: Jesus offers us the gift of his life. We are to offer the gift of ourselves to others in love, no matter what the cost.

Today's scriptures are a sobering reminder of what "Ordinary Time" means. It is anything but ordinary. It is living the paschal mystery day in and day out in our everyday lives.

Gospel Exegesis

The facilitator gives input regarding what critical biblical scholarship has to say about this text. The input includes insights as to how people would have heard the gospel in Jesus' time.

Jesus journeyed to Jerusalem and, as he went, he taught would-be disciples the implications of discipleship. His journey shaped the role of the disciple. Disciples were to either prepare the way for Jesus or follow him. For Luke, journeying with Jesus was critically important. Disciples are given the power of Jesus' own ministry. They "not only receive his teaching but receive power to heal and share Jesus' rejection."[11] Jerusalem is the journey's goal. There is no mistaking where they are headed. In the midst of Jesus' teaching, there are mounting references to his eventual suffering and death.

There is also no mistaking of the path Jesus (and, subsequently, his followers) will follow: the path of rejection. Jesus clarifies the requirements of discipleship. He insists that the demands are rigorous, "beyond normal expectations."[12] The task of the missionary is critical. "The Son of Man has no place to lay his head" because, just as he was rejected in Samaria, he will be rejected again. Rejection is a hallmark of the Christian mission. It is

---

[11]Robert C. Tannehill, *The Narrative Unity of Luke-Acts: A Literary Interpretation,* Vol. 1 (Minneapolis: Augsburg Fortress, 1986), 229.

[12]Ibid., 231.

the plight of the disciple. Jesus insists that disciples are to be prepared and know full well what lies ahead.

James and John wanted to call down fire from heaven upon the Samaritan village that refused them hospitality, just as Elijah had done. *Jesus radically differs from Elijah.* He resists vengeance. On the way to Jerusalem, Jesus "not only taught forgiveness and love of one's enemies to the point of turning the other cheek, but he also rejected a proposal that would have resulted in physical violence to persons."[13] The message is clear: *judgment belongs to God.*

This section of Luke's gospel emphasizes that Jesus was indeed a Great Prophet. The "lifting up of Jesus" ("taken from this world") parallels the lifting up of Elijah in the book of Kings. Also, Jesus, like Moses[14] and Elijah, appointed Spirit-filled successors to his mission. Jesus gave an answer similar to Elijah's in regard to tending to family concerns before venturing off as an itinerant disciple. Thus, there is no room for doubt that Jesus is the great prophet who goes to Jerusalem to prophesy against Israel. "The narrative that results from this 'arrangement' is therefore filled with unexpected tension: the Prophet makes his way to Jerusalem, to his death and 'lifting up.' As he goes he speaks the word of God to those around him."[15] Some hear and become disciples. Others reject the *word*, and thus in turn, are themselves rejected by the disciples.[16]

Jesus set his face toward his final destination: Jerusalem. This was to be Jesus' ultimate journey. It is to be the ultimate journey of all Christians. Jesus' expectations are explicit and demanding. We may even be tempted to accuse Jesus of cruelty. It is a biblical virtue to bury the dead and to honor one's father and mother. How could Jesus possibly suggest that we go forward and not give so much as a glance back at dying parents or prior commitments? Jesus' response is not about a "conflict of duties"[17] or about which action is of higher value. Jesus is making a point and upholding a "principle that is to be applied always and everywhere."[18] *Nothing is more important than proclaiming the reign of God.* One cannot follow Christ without detachment from everything, "including one's past."[19] The moral choice posed in this gospel is not the point of the gospel. *The point is radical intimacy and union with the Risen One and living the life of committed discipleship with all its inherent paschal implications.* Jesus' journey was to "both a geographical point and a symbol of heavenly fulfillment beyond every earthly reality."[20] Jesus knew where he was going; can we follow?

Discipleship is about abandonment and risk. Nothing but radical trust will do. The road will not always be easy; there will not always be willing friends waiting for us at our journey's end; we may end up in our enemies' camp, but the challenge is: Are we, the people of God, willing to submit with our entire being to the will of God? Are we willing to fall into the arms of the Lord with nary a care or concern?

Proclaim the gospel again.

Sometimes we gain new insights when we hear the text after the interpretation has been given. Someone from the group proclaims the gospel a second time.

STEP 4
TESTING

Conversation with the Liturgy and Scriptures

Test your original understanding in dialogue with the text.

(You might consider breaking into smaller groups.)

How does your original understanding of this story compare with what was just shared? Has your

---

[13]Richard J. Cassidy, *Jesus, Politics, and Society* (Maryknoll: Orbis Books, 1978), 43.

[14]It was believed that Moses did not die but ascended straight to heaven.

[15]Luke Timothy Johnson, *The Gospel of Luke*, Sacra Pagina Series, Vol. 3 (Collegeville: The Liturgical Press, 1991), 161-164.

[16]Ibid.

[17]*Days of the Lord*, Vol. 6, 110.

[18]Ibid.

[19]Ibid.

[20]Eugene LaVerdiere, S.S.S., *Luke* (Wilmington: Michael Glazier Books, 1980), 142.

pre-understanding of this gospel been renewed with new insight? Was there anything you had not considered before?

How does this story speak to your life?

Participants share an experience from their lives that connects with the biblical interpretation just shared.

> *I am reminded of a young man who knows full well the implications of this gospel. He is like all other young men. He has struggled with the same issues that all young men encounter in their early adult lives. This young man knows what discipleship is about. I admire him immensely. In the midst of peer and societal pressure, he never gave up on his relationship with Christ. He was a voice for the poor and oppressed. He assumed political positions that upheld gospel values but were extremely unpopular. He challenged adults and young people alike and was not afraid to be rebuffed (as he was most of the time). He never hesitated to speak of his relationship with Christ, even when it meant that he was harassed or ridiculed. His friends eventually realized that he could not be worn down and grew to accept his faith as a piece of who he was. The harassment ended. He was eventually respected for his unwavering positions and actions. He was not a perfect young man. He was a limited, fallible human being like everyone else. He paid a heavy price to be a disciple.*

> *This young man has taught me a great deal about what it means to be a disciple. Living the paschal mystery goes beyond simply offering our everyday struggles to the cross of Christ. While not minimizing basic human suffering, Jesus gives us a glimpse today of the full impact of Christian, paschal suffering. Embracing the paschal mystery assumes a willingness to endure rejection, hardships, and ridicule* because of our love for Christ. *Thank God there are still such living witnesses in our midst. Thank God there is one very close to me. I am blessed.*

All share their life experience.

Have you ever experienced rejection for the sake of Christ? How do the implications of today's gospel make you feel? What was Luke's message to his own community? What is his message to yours? There are strong images of creation, exodus, covenant, and community in today's gospel. In what way do those images have anything to do with your life? Do you still feel the same way about this text as you did at the beginning? Has your original understanding been stretched, challenged, or affirmed?

STEP 5
DECISION

The gospel demands a response.

In what way is our community being called to respond specifically to Jesus' demands of radical discipleship described in today's gospel? How does this gospel call us to transformation? What is the challenge? What are the contemporary implications of the journey to Jerusalem? What am I/we/community/parish called to do in response? What is one concrete action we will take this week as a response to what was learned and shared today?

DOCTRINAL ISSUES

What church truth/teaching/doctrinal issue could be drawn from the gospel for the Thirteenth Sunday in Ordinary Time ?

Participants suggest possible doctrinal themes that flow from the readings.

Possible Doctrinal Themes

Paschal mystery, Christian witness, suffering, nonviolence, cross

Present the doctrinal material at this time.

1. The facilitator gives input on a particular doctrinal issue of his/her prior choosing. OR
2. The group chooses a doctrinal issue from the list they created. They read together from the Doctrinal Appendix.

(The doctrinal issues are found in the Doctrinal Appendix in the back of this workbook. If you are choosing an issue from this resource, please refer to it now.)

Reflection questions centered around the chosen doctrinal theme can be found at the end of each topic in the Doctrinal Appendix. The questions are based on the five-step reflection process. If you choose a topic not included in the Doctrinal Appendix, craft your own questions according to the same five-step process.

Following the reflection questions you will be reminded to return to chapter 7, "Preparing the Catechetical Session," to assist you in crafting your own session.

Closing Prayer

Lord,
may this sacrifice and communion
give us a share in your life
and help us bring your love to the world.
Grant this through Christ, our Lord.[21]

Selected Bibliography

Anderson, Bernhard W. *Understanding the Old Testament.* 4th ed. Englewood Cliffs: Prentice Hall, 1986.

Cassidy, Richard J. *Jesus, Politics, and Society.* Maryknoll: Orbis Books, 1978.

Days of the Lord. Vol. 6. Collegeville: The Liturgical Press, 1991.

Fitzmyer, Joseph A., S.J. "The Letter to the Galatians." In *The New Jerome Biblical Commentary.* Ed. Raymond E. Brown, S.S., Joseph A. Fitzmyer, S.J., Roland E. Murphy, O.Carm. Englewood Cliffs: Prentice Hall, 1990.

Johnson, Luke Timothy. *The Gospel of Luke.* Sacra Pagina Series. Vol. 3. Collegeville: The Liturgical Press, 1991.

Kselman, John S., S.S., and Michael Barré, S.S. "Psalms." In *The New Jerome Biblical Commentary.* Ed. Raymond E. Brown, S.S., Joseph A. Fitzmyer, S.J., Roland E. Murphy, O.Carm. Englewood Cliffs: Prentice Hall, 1990.

Kuntz, J. Kenneth. *The People of Ancient Israel.* New York: Harper and Row, 1974.

LaVerdiere, Eugene, S.S.S. *Luke.* Wilmington: Michael Glazier Books, 1980.

Sanchez, Patricia Datchuck. *The Word We Celebrate.* Kansas City: Sheed and Ward, 1989.

Tannehill, Robert C. *The Narrative Unity of Luke-Acts: A Literary Interpretation.* Vol. 1. Minneapolis: Augsburg Fortress, 1986.

Walsh, Jerome T. and Christopher T. Begg. "1-2 Kings." In *The New Jerome Biblical Commentary.* Ed. Raymond E. Brown, S.S., Joseph A. Fitzmyer, S.J., Roland E. Murphy, O.Carm. Englewood Cliffs: Prentice Hall, 1990.

---

[21]Thirteenth Sunday in Ordinary Time: "Prayer after Communion," *The Sacramentary.*

Fourteenth Sunday in Ordinary Time

INTRODUCTORY RITES

Opening Song (or Entrance Antiphon)

Within your temple, we ponder your loving kindness O God. As your name, so also your praise reaches to the ends of the earth; your right hand is filled with justice. (Ps 47:10-11)[1]

Opening Prayer

The facilitator of the session may lead the prayer. Others in the group may be asked to proclaim the readings.

Let us pray
[for greater willingness
to serve God and our fellow man]

Pause for silent prayer.

Father,
in the rising of your Son
death gives birth to new life.
The sufferings he endured restored hope
to a fallen world.
Let sin never ensnare us
with empty promises of passing joy.
Make us one with you always,
so that our joy may be holy,
and our love may give life.
We ask this through Christ, our Lord.[2]

LITURGY OF THE WORD

Let us listen to God's word.

The readings are proclaimed.

First Reading
Isaiah 66:10-14

The connection of this reading to the gospel is ob-
scure. Reginald Fuller suggests that the inaccurate translation of "prosperity like a river" in the first reading is the reason it was chosen for its connection to the gospel. "Prosperity like a river" is connected to the peace offered in the gospel and is the only link between the two readings.[3] Fuller suggests that linking them requires a stretch of the imagination.

Today's pericope from Trito-Isaiah is believed to have been written by disciples of Second Isaiah just after their return from exile in Babylonia. Chapters 40–55 are considered the work of Second Isaiah, and were primarily addressed to people in captivity in Babylonia. Chapters 56–66 are the work of Trito-Isaiah and were written for the people as they were facing the difficulties of the restoration.[4]

There is a mood of disillusionment in the Trito-Isaiah chapters. Second Isaiah brimmed with hopeful expectation of the imminent return. Trito-Isaiah lived with the reality of *what is.* Things were not as the people had hoped. There was controversy in the Palestinian community. Those who had returned from exile were eager to get back to their orthodox way of life. Those who had remained in Israel during the exile (the laborers and lower class folks) had become enculturated with the conquering peoples and were not so eager to return to Jewish orthodoxy. Trito-Isaiah speaks of the faithful remnant as "servants who are oppressed within the Jewish community."[5]

Second Isaiah lifts up the suffering servant who suffers for the people and thus is a blessing for them. Trito-Isaiah connected the faithful remnant with the suffering servant. Yahweh comforts the remnant "servants" with the tender love of a nursing mother.

---

[1]Fourteenth Sunday in Ordinary Time: "Entrance Antiphon," *The Sacramentary.*

[2]Fourteenth Sunday in Ordinary Time: "Alternative Opening Prayer," *The Sacramentary.*

[3]Reginald F. Fuller, *Preaching the New Lectionary* (Collegeville: The Liturgical Press, 1974), 48.

[4]Bernhard, W. Anderson, *Understanding the Old Testament,* 4th ed. (Englewood Cliffs: Prentice Hall, 1986), 476.

[5]Ibid., 503.

Second Isaiah was concerned with current political circumstances. Chapter 65 begins a world view that goes beyond the historical plane. We see an eschatological hope emerge. Belief in a future life, a new age, and a new creation sprouts forth and ushers Israel into a new apocalyptic era. Belief in an afterlife and a messianic age emerge.

Responsorial Psalm
Psalm 66:1-3, 4-5, 6-7, 16, 20

This psalm is a prayer of praise and thanks for national deliverance. It directly refers to the original exodus event. Yahweh is thanked for his saving deeds and for sending the Spirit. Verses 19-20 abruptly shift from the communal to the individual. The gift of the Spirit is both corporate and individual. "Both must be held in balance."[6]

Second Reading
Galatians 6:14-18

We remember from the Ninth Sunday that the letter to the Galatians was written to a community that was on the verge of ignoring the gospel in favor of adherence to the law. Paul cut to the heart of the Christian life: the cross of Christ. Paul wrote to gentile converts and warned them about getting caught up in the trappings of Judaism. He told them that adherence to the law through circumcision demanded that they embrace the whole law. They could not simply pick and choose. But now they were freed from the law. They did not have to succumb to the rigors of observance. The cross of Christ, not the law, was their hope. Paul himself cared little for his own mark of circumcision. It was the mark of Christ's suffering that caused him to boast.

Freedom does not mean that disciples have a license to act any way they choose. Because of Christ, because of the presence of the Risen Savior, disciples are free to *love*. The demands of love are engaging and require the total gift of self. We are to adhere only to the cross of Christ.

Gospel
Luke 10:1-12, 17-20

The seventy-two are sent out to evangelize and witness to the good news.

---

[6]Fuller, *Preaching the New Lectionary*, 49.

STEP 1
NAMING ONE'S EXPERIENCE

What were your first impressions? What was your first response?

Each person names his or her initial impression. Statement should be brief. No reasons should be given at this time. All simply listen without agreeing or disagreeing.

STEP 2
UNDERSTANDING

In a brief statement, what do you think this gospel is trying to convey? What does it mean? What pre-understanding did you bring to this conversation?

STEP 3
INPUT FROM VISION/STORY/TRADITION

Liturgical Context

Last week Jesus explained the rigors and demands of discipleship. Today he gives instructions to those who willingly agree to take up the cross and follow in his steps. Today's readings proclaim a true missionary effort to the ends of the earth. Reginald Fuller reminds us that the mission is not initiated by the disciples (therefore the church), but that rather it is commissioned by God in response to the prayer of the church. Liturgy continues that prayer. We are sent forth to love and serve the world. We are offered the same *shalom* peace every time we gather. It is offered to us by Christ himself and we in turn offer it to one another and, by extension, to all the world. The *Constitution on the Sacred Liturgy* (CSL) tells us that liturgy is the source and summit of all we do and that from which our power flows (CSL, #9). Jesus continues to send us out with his power, his authority, and most especially with the peace we are offered every time we gather for worship. The alternative opening prayer reminds us of who it is we bring to the world: Christ crucified. When we share his suffering we witness to his love. We pray that sin will not overtake us, but that our joy will give birth to life-giving love.

415

Are there any candidates ready to celebrate the Rite of Full Communion, Acceptance, or Welcome?

Gospel Exegesis

The facilitator gives input regarding what critical biblical scholarship has to say about this text. The input includes insights as to how people would have heard the gospel in Jesus' time.

In chapter 9 of Luke's gospel, Jesus sent the apostles out on a mission. In today's pericope he extends that ministry as he sends the seventy-two out to prepare for his coming (in this case, it is a future oriented, eschatological coming). This text is part of a section referred to as the "travel section." This missionary effort foreshadows the mission to the gentiles in the Acts of the Apostles.[7] The number of the disciples sent is significant. It represents all the nations of the world, and thus represents the universal mission of Jesus to the entire world. In the Greek version of the book of Genesis, seventy was the number of people in all the world. Some suggest that the number seventy also refers to the seventy elders sent out by Moses, thereby connecting Christ to the great prophet. Whatever the intent, there will never be enough missionaries to reach out to the entire world. Disciples are to pray that God will supply the necessary workers to fulfill the demands of the waiting fields.

Luke was concerned with establishing missionary guidelines needed for the fledgling church. Thus, as the seventy-two were sent out, they were given instructions for their missionary activities. They were to pray that God would provide other missionaries like themselves to spread the news of the reign of God. They were to rely completely on God for strength, sustenance, and protection. Procrastination was to be avoided, as their mission was urgent. Disciples were to willingly accept the generosity and hospitality of others. They were to eat whatever was provided, thereby ignoring Jewish food laws. They were to witness by their lives and by the proclamation of God's word. Since Christ was to go with them, to reject the disciples was to reject both Jesus and God. Judgment would come upon those who rejected the disciples. Disciples were to enact a parable against those who rejected Christ's mission by shaking the dust from their feet.

Satan loses his power every time Jesus' power is demonstrated. Thus all were to rejoice in the power Jesus gave to his disciples to heal, cast out demons, and bring the good news. However, miracles could be a distraction. Therefore, disciples were not to make them a major priority or concern.[8]

The only possession the missionary was to take with him or her was *shalom* peace. *Shalom* is evidence of God's reign. It is the same peace offered to humanity at the creation of the world. It is a sign of perfect union and harmony with God. Peace is the sign that Jesus' reign is at hand; the messianic age has arrived. Jesus came to fulfill and restore the lost *shalom* of Eden. Peace was the first post-resurrection gift Jesus offered to the world. "Whether one accepts it or rejects it—it does not depend on the messenger—it is a sign of the proximity of the kingdom, like the healing of the sick."[9]

Proclaim the gospel again.

Sometimes we gain new insights when we hear the text after the interpretation has been given. Someone from the group proclaims the gospel a second time.

STEP 4
TESTING

Conversation with the Liturgy and the Scriptures

Test your original understanding in dialogue with the text.

(You might consider breaking into smaller groups.)

How does your original assumption about the sending of the seventy-two compare with the exegesis? Were there any new insights? Was there anything you had not considered before?

---

[7]Charles, H. Talbert, *Reading Luke* (New York: Crossroad, 1992), 114-115.

[8]Ibid., 114-119.

[9]*Days of the Lord*, Vol. 6 (Collegeville: The Liturgical Press, 1991), 117.

How does this story speak to your life?

Participants share an experience from their lives that connects with the biblical interpretation just shared.

A few years ago our parish participated in a huge evangelical effort. As a response to our own baptismal calling, each parishioner was invited to go to every home in our city and invite people to join our church family. Even if no one had responded, the experience was well worth the effort. It gave us an opportunity to go out in the spirit of today's gospel. One couple was particularly thrilled that someone visited their house. They had been thinking about calling us anyway. They knew a lady in our parish who was a perfect example of Jesus' shalom peace. They believed her to be the most loving person they had ever known. This couple observed her taking care of her sick mother, co-workers, and neighbors with enthusiastic energy. She was the most giving person they had ever seen. The couple already felt invited to our parish through Grace's gifts of love and hospitality. (Grace's name was so apt; she personified it.) Sometimes it seems as if efforts must be grandiose in order to make a dent in the world's spiritual hungers. However, such efforts fade in comparison to the quiet witness of a well-lived Christian life. We all would do well to watch the Graces in our midst to remind us how to "do" today's gospel.

All share their life experience.

What was Luke's primary agenda in today's gospel? What was the message to his community? What is the relevance for your community today? How are the biblical themes of creation, exodus, covenant, and community evident in today's liturgy? Do you still feel the same way about this text as you did at the beginning? How would you explain it to a stranger?

STEP 5
DECISION

The gospel demands a response.

Have you experienced any change in outlook, attitudes, or proposed behavior as a result of this conversation? In what concrete way might your community be called to respond in practice to today's

gospel? In what way are you personally called to respond? Name one specific action you will take this week as a response to what was learned and shared today.

DOCTRINAL ISSUES

What church truth/teaching/doctrinal issue could be drawn from the gospel for the Fourteenth Sunday in Ordinary Time?

Participants suggest possible doctrinal themes that flow from the readings.

Possible Doctrinal Themes

Evangelization, Christian witness, faith and trust , service, Kingdom of God, community/assembly/ church

Present the doctrinal material at this time.

1. The facilitator gives input on a particular doctrinal issue of his/her prior choosing. OR
2. The group chooses a doctrinal issue from the list they created. They read together from the Doctrinal Appendix.

(The doctrinal issues are found in the Doctrinal Appendix in the back of this workbook. If you are choosing an issue from this resource, please refer to it now.)

Reflection questions centered around the chosen doctrinal theme can be found at the end of each topic in the Doctrinal Appendix. The questions are based on the five-step reflection process. If you choose a topic not included in the Doctrinal Appendix, craft your own questions according to the same five-step process.

Following the reflection questions you will be reminded to return to chapter 7, "Preparing the Catechetical Session," to assist you in crafting your own session.

Closing Prayer

May the Lord bless and keep you. Amen.
May his face shine upon you,

and be gracious to you. Amen.
May he look upon you with kindness,
and give you peace. Amen.[10]

Selected Bibliography

Anderson, Bernhard W. *Understanding the Old Testament.* 4th ed. Englewood Cliffs: Prentice Hall, 1986.

Days of the Lord. Vol. 6. Collegeville: The Liturgical Press, 1991.

Fuller, Reginald H. *Preaching the New Lectionary.* Collegeville: The Liturgical Press, 1974.

Johnson, Luke Timothy. *The Gospel of Luke.* Sacra Pagina Series. Vol. 3. Collegeville: The Liturgical Press, 1991.

Kuntz, J. Kenneth. *The People of Ancient Israel.* New York: Harper and Row, 1974.

LaVerdiere, Eugene, S.S.S. *Luke.* Wilmington: Michael Glazier Books, 1980.

Talbert, Charles H. *Reading Luke.* New York: Crossroad, 1992.

---

[10]Ordinary Time I, Solemn Blessing: Blessing of Aaron (Num 6:24-26), *The Sacramentary.*

FIFTEENTH SUNDAY IN ORDINARY TIME

INTRODUCTORY RITES

Opening Song (or Entrance Antiphon)

In my justice I shall see your face, O Lord; when your glory appears, my joy will be full. (Ps 16:15)[1]

Opening Prayer

The facilitator of the session may lead the prayer. Others in the group may be asked to proclaim the readings.

Let us pray
[to be faithful to the light we have received,
to the name we bear]

Pause for silent prayer.

Father,
let the light of your truth
guide us to your kingdom
through a world filled with lights contrary to your
    own.
Christian is the name and the gospel we glory in.
May your love make us what you have called us to
    be.
We ask this through Christ, our Lord.[2]

LITURGY OF THE WORD

Let us listen to God's word.

The readings are proclaimed.

First Reading
Deuteronomy 30:10-14

Today's pericope is part of Moses' farewell address. It is a liturgical homily that urges a return to radical and reciprocal covenant relationship with Yahweh. It is believed to have been written during the exile. The Deuteronomist's perspective is that biblical justice (righteousness) is based on love, love of God evidenced by love of others, especially widows, orphans, the marginalized, and the oppressed.

The law was the heart of ancient Israel. The law was not merely a code of conduct. One could follow the rigid observance and miss the intent of the law altogether. The law assumed an interior posture. The law was a sign of an inner reality. It was a sign that believers loved the Lord, their God with all of their being and, as a response to the love God had showered upon them, they would lovingly and willingly observe the law. Obviously, scrupulous ritual observance was not what God had in mind when the law was given to Moses. The *Shema,* even today, forms the heart of Jewish prayer.

> Hear, O Israel! The Lord is our God, the Lord alone! Therefore, you shall love the Lord, your God with all your heart, all your soul and all your strength. Take to heart these words I enjoin on you today. (Deut 6:4-6)

There is nothing in those words that even remotely suggests a legalistic observance of a legal code. What matters is a person's heart and love response to God.

God alone interpreted the law. Moses asserted that it was "not the book of the Law, but the *word* that Moses declared to *'be very near to you.'"*[3] Israel's understanding of the heart of the law could be summed up as the living, sacramental *Word (presence)* of God that consumes the depths of the human heart. Yahweh called for responsible observance of the law. One could do no less in the face of such gratuitous gift.

Responsorial Psalm
Psalm 69: 14, 17, 30-31, 33-34, 36, 37

---

[1]Fifteenth Sunday in Ordinary Time: "Entrance Antiphon," *The Sacramentary.*

[2]Fifteenth Sunday in Ordinary Time: "Alternative Opening Prayer," *The Sacramentary.*

[3]*Days of the Lord,* Vol. 6 (Collegeville: The Liturgical Press, 1991), 121-122.

This psalm is a cry out of suffering to God. Like many such psalms it begins in sorrow and ends in trust. It follows the pattern of exodus/liberation and death/resurrection and points to Christian joy over being delivered from sin through justification.

Second Reading
Colossians 1:15-20

The letter to the Colossians is known as a "Captivity Epistle" as it was written from Paul's Roman jail cell. Paul had journeyed to Jerusalem from Corinth. The Jewish authorities were in hot pursuit and were intent on stopping this rabble-rouser. They did all in their power to have him arrested on charges that he had desecrated the temple. This bogus charge did not stick. However, he was charged with disturbing the peace and was thrown in prison for three years in Jerusalem and Caesarea. He finally appealed to the emperor and demanded the trial to which he was entitled as a Roman citizen. He reached Rome in chains for his trial. This letter was written from his Roman jail around 62 C.E.

Paul's greatest anguish was to see the gospel he so cherished be distorted. Many of his travels and letters were efforts to grapple with the gospel and refashion his message in a way that would halt the destructive distortions that were cropping up.

The great evil, as Paul saw it, was gnosticism. Gnosticism asserted that access to God was possible only through knowledge. People's sinfulness was due simply to ignorance. Thus, if people only held the secret knowledge of God, they would be released from this false world in which they were imprisoned. The body was considered evil, so union with God was impossible without some kind of intermediary: angels. As belief in the unworthiness of the body grew, so did the college of angels: dominions, principalities, etc. Angels existed at varying levels on the hierarchical chain. To the gnostic, angels were intermediaries, beings through whose aid "the godless world could slowly emerge from its earthbound state and by degrees ascend to God."[4]

Many saw Jesus to be just such an intermediary, making him neither of this world nor of heaven. Paul had already addressed this false philosophy in Corinth and Galatia. It was within this context that he addressed Colossae. He was appalled that people were worshiping angels and strictly adhering to the law as their path to God, *when Jesus and the cross was the only path.*

Today's pericope is a christological hymn. Christ is identified with God, the Creator of all things. Christ is imaged to have been present from the beginning at creation. Before there was wisdom, *Christ was.* Christ possessed creative power over the cosmos. "As the agent of creation he created the cosmic powers."[5] As the Risen Savior, he was the firstborn of all who had previously died and were still asleep. Jesus opened the gates of heaven and the dead of all previous generations rose with him.

The wisdom of God is alive and incarnate in the person of Jesus. Christ, *Wisdom of God,* reached perfect fulfillment in the cross. Through the cross, peace is possible. The peace imaged at creation, *shalom* peace, is realized only in Jesus. *Shalom* peace is the ordering of relationships in perfect harmony. Humanity was to flourish in Yahweh's charitable righteousness/justice (*hesed*).

Righteousness, biblical justice (*hesed*), assumed a reciprocal, loving intimacy with the Creator. Love was to flow from the love the Creator bestowed on the created. People were expected to love as God would love. God's love is a jealous, inclusive love that is extended equally to all people. *Righteous men and women must extend the same love to all human beings without exception.* This was the world envisioned at the creation of the world. This was the world destroyed by sin. One cannot understand today's first reading or the gospel without taking into account this very basic Hebrew understanding. It is foundational!

Ancient Hebrew literature had attested to the creative power of God known as Wisdom. Jesus became the personification of that Wisdom to the Christians. The creative Wisdom of God was to come and restore the perfect order intended at

---

[4]Hubert Richards, *The Gospel According to St. Paul* (Collegeville: The Liturgical Press, 1990), 108-109.

[5]Reginald H. Fuller, *Preaching the New Lectionary* (Collegeville: The Liturgical Press, 1974), 51.

creation. Jesus, in an act of creative submission to Yahweh's will, gave humanity the most precious gift of all: redemption from the sin and chaos that had demolished God's perfectly ordered world. Through the cross Jesus reinstated the intimacy and union established at the creation of the world. He was the *Restorer* of Paradise. Today's hymn from Colossians sets the stage for us to go deeply into the parable in today's gospel. Paul's letter is definitive. Jesus is no mere angelic intermediary. *He is the Wisdom of Yahweh.*

Gospel
Luke10:25-37

A man is robbed, stripped, and beaten by robbers. A priest and a Levite pass by and ignore him. A Samaritan happens on the scene and offers unimaginable mercy and compassion.

STEP 1
NAMING ONE'S EXPERIENCE

What captured your attention? What was your initial experience of this gospel?

Each person names his or her initial impression. Statement should be brief. No reasons should be given at this time. All simply listen without agreeing or disagreeing.

STEP 2
UNDERSTANDING

In a brief statement, what do you think this gospel is trying to convey? What understanding of this parable did you bring with you to this conversation?

STEP 3
INPUT FROM VISION/STORY/TRADITION

Liturgical Context

The next three Sundays form an inner unity. We read the remaining verses of Luke's chapter 10 and part of chapter 11 in which Jesus teaches the disciples. There is no particular chronological order to the stories. They are set within the context of the "journey to Jerusalem" that began a few Sundays ago. The unity of these three weeks can be summed up in "to do" teachings. Jesus asserts what one must "do" in the realm of God.

This week begins an encounter with Paul's letter to the Colossians. We begin our own liturgical odyssey into the mindset of the Colossian community and Paul's response to them (and vicariously to us) as one-third of Paul's letter is proclaimed in the next three weeks.

Today's first reading gives us a glimpse into the biblical understanding of the law and God's word. It is a wonderful opportunity to make the appropriate connection between the biblical understanding and the understanding we bring to the liturgy of the word every time we gather for worship. The *word* that Moses proclaims "to be near" is none other than God alone! This is what the liturgy heralds with the *"Word of the Lord"* after every ritual proclamation. The scriptures are not pious history lessons or codes for upright living. The scriptures proclaimed at Sunday Mass are the living, sacramental presence of Christ in our midst. They are the *word of God* alive; the *word of God* that burns in our hearts and demands the total gift of self-effacing love. We no longer use the narrow formula, "This is the Word of the Lord," as it confines God solely to the pages just read. God, instead, is far greater, and speaks God's *Logos/Word* to us through the sacramental proclamation, through the gathered community, through the presiding minister, and through the sacramental elements of bread and wine become Body and Blood of Christ.

The alternative opening prayer asks that we be led to Christ's authentic light and teaching. The world offers "lights that are contrary" to the message Jesus proclaimed. We are to glory in the fact that we are called Christians. More than just a title, the name assumes a radical turning toward God and a life lived according to the rigorous demands of the gospel.

Perhaps it would be an appropriate time to celebrate a non-sacramental communal reconciliation service.

Gospel Exegesis

The facilitator gives input regarding what critical biblical scholarship has to say about this text. The input includes insights as to how people would have heard the gospel in Jesus' time.

Jesus applies the principles just articulated in regard to the first and second reading and demonstrates their implications through the medium of story or parable. He is asked, "What must one do to inherit everlasting life?" Jesus responds by telling a story. In the telling he asserts that discipleship is an action word. To be a disciple does not mean that one embraces empty platitudes and pious thoughts. Disciples must "put their money where their mouth is" and live what they profess. It is often easier to accept a cultural group's norms of behavior and ways of thinking than it is to accept God's counter-cultural expectations.

Every culture establishes boundaries and decides who is "in" and who is "out." That same culture asserts that not only are the "in" in, but they are *righteously and defensively* "in." The "outsider," on the other hand, deserves to be on the outside, giving the insiders moral certitude regarding their privileged status. During Jesus' time the Greeks believed outsiders were barbarians. Jews believed outsiders were unclean. Things are no different today. The same boundaries exist in political, cultural, and religious communities. People have always held attitudes and participated in actions that divide the human community. In today's gospel Jesus upsets the status quo (the function of a parable) and asserts that "to do" means that one must be prepared to examine accepted patterns of social behavior and judge them in light of the law of love.

On the Thirteenth Sunday of Ordinary Time, at the start of Jesus' journey to Jerusalem, the disciples went first to a Samaritan village and were rejected there. *We are not to assume that the Samaritans were among the righteous as we listen to this parable.*

Earlier, Luke had told another "to do" story after a rich man had asked what he must do to gain eternal life. A rich man and a lawyer asked the same question and were given the same answer. What Jesus asked was impossible. He asked the rich to become poor and Jews to consort with Samaritans.[6] Unthinkable! Without God, it was impossible!

We know from the rejection of the Samaritans at the beginning of the journey to Jerusalem that Jesus' response to them was other than the expected response. The disciples wanted Jesus to rain down fire upon them. Jesus, however, suggested a new attitude and behavior toward Samaritans through his own stance of restraint. With this understanding as background we are now prepared to enter the story world of the parable.

It is believed by some scholars that today's pericope was a construction of Luke, the evangelist. It is believed that Luke used the parable to define what a good neighbor is. All ancient peoples had clear distinctions regarding outsiders and insiders. The early Christian communities tore down those distinctions. Ancient Judaism defined neighbor as one who is a "cobrother of the covenant."[7]

A major agenda item for Luke is the inclusion of gentiles into the Jewish/Christian experience. We note that in this parable the questioner is a Jewish lawyer and the audience is probably mostly Jewish. The Jewish world view was very different from that of gentiles. For the Jew, a Samaritan was not a neighbor. For the gentile, the Samaritan was indeed a neighbor. *A main point of this parable is to break down divisions.* The intended hearer of the story determines the point of the parable. The meaning is completely different depending on whether one is a Jew or a gentile.

The story itself gives us clues. First, the unfortunate victim in the story was probably Jewish, as he would have been identified if he had been anything other than Jewish. The fact that he was stripped of clothes meant that there was nothing to indicate where he came from, no indication of class or status. Luke's audience was Jewish and yet did not identify with the Jewish victim.

---

[6]Bernard Brandon Scott, *Hear Then the Parable* (Minneapolis: Augsburg Fortress, 1989), 190.

[7]T. W. Manson, *The Sayings of Jesus* (Grand Rapids: Wm. B. Eerdmans, 1979; London: SCM Press, 1957), in Scott, *Hear Then the Parable*, 192, #16.

A priest and a Levite both pass by. The hearers do not know the reason why these people ignored the victim, but they can guess. They can assume that it was out of fear of being robbed themselves or perhaps out of fear of becoming ritually unclean. One way or another, they both had the responsibility to act, even according to law.[8] If the audience was poor Jewish peasants, this story would feed their negative attitudes about upper class clerics. If the audience was upper class, priestly or Sadducee (rigid observers) they would approve and deem the behavior of the priest and Levite acceptable. Lay folks and Pharisees would have disapproved of the behavior. At any rate, lines were drawn; one had to step into one camp or another and the outcome was tenuous. "Where will I stand?" is asked simply by the clever construction of the story.

Immediately the hearer of the parable was trapped by the story when the Samaritan entered the picture. Usually, the expected order in any story about Jewish people would be priest, Levite, and Israelite. There could be no priest and Levite without an Israelite to complete the picture. This was how the Jewish hierarchical social structure was ordered.[9] Jews would have expected an Israelite, not a Samaritan, to be the logical third person on the scene. Their interest and dis-ease were piqued. The hearers' expectations were dashed and incredulity ensued with the grand entrance of the Samaritan hero. Herein lay the crisis. With whom would they now identify? There would have been no question had the hero been the expected Israelite.

For a Jew to identify with a Samaritan was unthinkable. It would require sidestepping generations of righteous hatred between their peoples. Not only was the hearer's frustration tapped, but he was forced to endure every minute, agonizing detail regarding the Samaritan's outrageous level of

compassion. The Samaritan's actions were to invade and permeate the consciousness of the unsuspecting audience.

Most commentators assert that Luke used the parable as an example story. Jesus' followers are to behave like the Samaritan. Bernard Brandon Scott offers a different possibility. From the story one is tempted to embrace the perspective: Jews are bad, Samaritans are good. However, let us not forget the Samaritan story that started the disciples' journey in the first place. The Samaritans were hardly paragons of virtue. Since Samaritan hatred was as strong as Jewish hatred, there can be little credence for such a posture.

Scott suggests a different view. The behavior of the Levite and the priest was certainly not exemplary, so no one would want to identify with them. A Jew would find it unconscionable to identify with a Samaritan. Since the Israelite was excluded from the parable, the only one left in the story was the victim. A choice had to be made. The Jewish audience must put themselves in the place of the half-dead victim. Either the Jew identified with the half dead man and was "saved by a mortal enemy"[10] or the story was dismissed as not true to life.

Does it make sense that it is better to die than to be helped by a mortal enemy? The audience was forced to ask, "If I were the half-dead person, would I refuse the only help available, even if from an enemy?" The next conclusion to draw is that perhaps such enmities are ludicrous.

The parable placed the expected hierarchical structure of priest, Levite, and Israelite under suspicion and suggested a new world order. Insiders and outsiders were not to be determined by previously accepted religious lines of demarcation. The new reign of Christ defies the conventional religious ordering of groups. There was definitely something novel and explosive taking place here. Structures were being challenged. The Samaritan was the hero and the Israelite was the victim. There was no attempt or need to convert the Samaritan. In this parable the Samaritan was righteous by his actions. He was living biblical justice.

---

[8]According to Leviticus, a priest becomes unclean if he touches the dead body of a friend or relative. However, the Mishnah and the Talmud (the interpretations of the law) asserted that if the same priest were to pass a dead corpse that obviously had no one to attend to it, then the priest had the obligation to attend to it.

[9]The only corollary in today's world would be priest, deacon, layperson.

[10]Scott, *Hear Then the Parable*, 201.

Jesus gave no opportunity for triumphalism, no victory over the enemy. Rather, he asked the question, "Who really is the enemy?"

Israel had been anticipating a messiah. In fact, fervor and expectation were at a fever pitch around the time of Christ. Due to the political and economic difficulties of the times, the messiah became an expectation of their own fashioning. The awaited messiah had been reduced to hopes for a victorious warrior who would crush their enemies. Luke's Jesus shattered this illusion. Jesus was not that kind of messiah. Destruction of Israel's enemies was not part of Jesus' plan.

A strong statement was being made in this parable. It is no wonder that the religious authorities eventually sought Jesus' life. Their power was at stake and being called into question. According to the parable, religious proscriptions did not determine righteousness: actions did. The bottom line: "The temple no longer divides the world into religious and nonreligious."[11] The hearer was forced to ask: If the old structures are no longer adequate, then, who is in and who is out? Who is first in God's reign? Who is my neighbor?

All are equal before the eyes of God. All are deserving of the same love that God gives to all people. To be a disciple means we are to love as Jesus loves. There are no deserving or undeserving recipients of our love. The principle refers back to the perfect order of creation. If Jesus, the new messiah, came to restore creation to its harmonious intention, then the equal, inclusive, jealous love of God is to be extended to all people. We are not to decide according to preconceived human, cultural, and religious structures. There are no deserving and undeserving recipients. All are deserving in the eyes of God.

Proclaim the gospel again.

Sometimes we gain new insights when we hear the text after the interpretation has been given. Someone from the group proclaims the gospel a second time.

---

[11]Ibid., 202.

Conversation with the Liturgy and the Scriptures

Test your original understanding in dialogue with the text.

(You might consider breaking into smaller groups.)

How did the interpretation regarding the priest, Levite, and Samaritan compare with your pre-understanding of this parable? Were there any new insights? Was there anything you had not considered before?

How does this parable speak to your life?

Participants share an experience from their lives that connects with the biblical interpretation just shared.

> *This parable brings me immediately to the state of the church today. As a person who works in full-time church ministry I am incredibly saddened by the divisions within parish communities and within the wider church community. Often the thinking goes: some are too holy, some are not holy enough, some are too conservative, others are too liberal. Some are good Catholics and others are not. (Some are Democrats and others are Republican— believe that one, if you will, in church communities!) The divisions, hatred, and enmity are scandalous. I am as guilty of classifications as the next person. Try as I may, I always fall back into the pit. I am put back to where the lawyer stands today. "Just what do I need to do?" I sometimes believe that it is easier to reach out and offer unconditional love to those the world considers totally undeserving such as drug addicted homeless than it is to offer the hand of reconciliation to those in our midst who stand on differing ideological platforms. If I were half dead, I would not only welcome the assistance of such folks, I would shout for it from the core of my being. Thus, are not our divisions a waste of time? Are there not greater purposes that can be served than wasting our time forming and fueling camps and defending positions? Like the hearer of today's parable I have to ask, "With whom will I identify?" The hearers of the parable were stretched beyond all the assumptions they brought with them*

to the story. *No matter who they were, every posture and position was stretched. The peasant Jew, the Pharisee, the Sadducee, the priest, the Levite—all were shaken up by the parable and its unexpected outcome. All were stretched.*

My prayer is that we all allow ourselves to be stretched beyond the expected. Perhaps our challenge is to take up the late Cardinal Bernardin's plea to work for a common ground and celebrate our unity in the midst of diversity. Something as simple as loving dialogue and a posture of mutual respect and dignity would be in the spirit of Jesus' word for us today. I can only do my part where I live, work, pray, and play. I am challenged every day. Sometimes I am up for the challenge and other times I am like the priest and the Levite. I ignore what obviously screams at me from the side of the road.

All share their life experience.

What was Luke trying to tell his community? What does he have to say to our community and to me today? What does this gospel teach us about God? Christ? The church? How are the themes of covenant, creation, exodus/liberation, and community evident in today's readings? In what way does this gospel challenge our community? Are there any glaring examples of the attitudes prevalent in today's parable in our community? How would we explain this parable to a stranger and how do we feel about it now?

STEP 5
DECISION

The gospel demands a response.

What can you do to respond to the challenge of today's gospel both within your community and within yourself? In what way does this gospel call your parish to action in the church, your parish, your neighborhood, or your world? Be concrete. In what way, if any, have your attitudes and/or behavior changed as a result of this sharing? Name one specific action you will take this week as a response to what was learned and shared today.

DOCTRINAL ISSUES

What church truth/teaching/doctrinal issue could be drawn from the gospel for the Fifteenth Sunday in Ordinary Time?

Participants suggest possible doctrinal themes that flow from the readings.

Possible Doctrinal Themes

Ecumenism, justice, christology, Trinity,

Present the doctrinal material at this time.

1. The facilitator gives input on a particular doctrinal issue of his/her prior choosing. OR
2. The group chooses a doctrinal issue from the list they created. They read together from the Doctrinal Appendix.

(The doctrinal issues are found in the Doctrinal Appendix in the back of this workbook. If you are choosing an issue from this resource, please refer to it now.)

Reflection questions centered around the chosen doctrinal theme can be found at the end of each topic in the Doctrinal Appendix. The questions are based on the five-step reflection process. If you choose a topic not included in the Doctrinal Appendix, craft your own questions according to the same five-step process.

Following the reflection questions you will be reminded to return to chapter 7, "Preparing the Catechetical Session," to assist you in crafting your own session.

Closing Prayer

Lord,
by our sharing in the mystery of this eucharist,
let your saving love grow within us.
Grant this through Christ, our Lord.[12]

---

[12]Fifteenth Sunday in Ordinary Time: "Prayer After Communion," *The Sacramentary.*

Selected Bibliography

Days of the Lord. Vol. 6. Collegeville: The Liturgical Press, 1991.

Fuller, Reginald H. *Preaching the New Lectionary.* Collegeville: The Liturgical Press, 1974.

Richards, Hubert. *The Gospel According to St. Paul.* Collegeville: The Liturgical Press, 1990.

Scott, Bernard Brandon. *Hear Then the Parable.* Minneapolis: Augsburg Fortress, 1989.

SIXTEENTH SUNDAY IN ORDINARY TIME

INTRODUCTORY RITES

Opening Song (or Entrance Antiphon)

God himself is my help. The Lord upholds my life.
I will offer you a willing sacrifice; I will praise your
name, O Lord, for its goodness. (Ps 53:6, 8)[1]

Opening Prayer

*The facilitator of the session may lead the prayer. Others in
the group may be asked to proclaim the readings.*

Let us pray
[to be kept faithful in the service of God]

Pause for silent prayer.

Lord,
be merciful to your people.
Fill us with your gifts
and make us always eager to serve you
in faith, hope, and love.
Grant this through our Lord, Jesus Christ, your
    Son,
who lives and reigns with you and the Holy
    Spirit,
one God, for ever and ever.[2]

LITURGY OF THE WORD

Let us listen to God's word.

The readings are proclaimed.

First Reading
Genesis 18:1-10

The link between the gospel and the first reading
is hospitality. Through an act of hospitality God's
revelation was made manifest. Genesis 18, written
by the Yahwist, portrays Abraham in his humanity.

"Abraham's hospitality, boldness and ethical sensitivity are captured by the Yahwist...."[3]

The bond of Oriental hospitality is very hard to
describe, as there is very little one can use by way
of comparison in today's culture. The rules of hospitality were governed by laws and to break such
laws was unthinkable. Table fellowship was so
strong that to eat with another assumed an unbreakable covenant.

Abraham was visited by God. In his best posture of
hospitality Abraham offered his visitor the finest
gifts of food and hospitality. Sarah busied herself
baking bread and Abraham was the gracious host.
By virtue of the amounts of bread and beef that
were offered, it was understood that Abraham's
gifts of hospitality were lavish, far more than was
needed.

Usually in typical ancient myths, when the hero
was visited by the gods, he was rewarded in relation to the lavishness of the gifts of hospitality he
offered. The Yahwist obviously drew on the secular
stories and used them for his own purposes. God
rewarded Abraham with the gift of a birth announcement. He announced that the very aged
Sarah would conceive and have a son.[4] Such theophanies in the form of birth announcements usually had deeper implications. Reginald Fuller
states that "Annunciation scenes are a device to
disclose the meaning of God's acts in salvation history."[5] The announcement of this supernatural
birth (Abraham and Sarah were too old to be parents) prefigured the supernatural birth of Jesus to
Mary.

This is a God who was actively engaged in the lives
of his people. In his visitation, God ate with and

---

[1]Sixteenth Sunday in Ordinary Time: "Entrance Antiphon," *The Sacramentary.*

[2]Sixteenth Sunday in Ordinary Time: "Opening Prayer," *The Sacramentary.*

[3]J. Kenneth Kuntz, *The People of Ancient Israel* (New York: Harper and Row, 1974), 70.

[4]Patricia Datchuck Sanchez, *The Word We Celebrate* (Kansas City: Sheed and Ward, 1989), 348.

[5]Reginald Fuller, *Preaching the New Lectionary* (Collegeville: The Liturgical Press, 1974), 52.

enjoyed Abraham's companionship and hospitality. This was a God who cared. This story foreshadowed the time when God would send his Son through the Incarnation to share, live and die with and for his friends. Abraham's God was involved. As amazing as the theophany was, equally amazing was Abraham's unwavering faith. Sarah laughed (in v. 12) and Abraham believed. Both reactions reflect the Christian dispensation: joy and trust. Abraham and Sarah exemplify lives fully lived with exuberance and in complete abandonment to the will of God.

Three people came calling upon Abraham but he spoke to only one. One scholar suggests that the Christian imagination would have no difficulty in associating this theophany by the trio with the Trinity. While this reading indeed extols the virtue of hospitality, that is not the primary focus of the text. It is about a God who acts in salvation history.

Responsorial Psalm
Psalm 15:2-3, 3-4, 5

This psalm was an entry psalm used upon entry into the temple. The pilgrim is described as sincere, honest, and just—qualities demonstrated by Abraham.

Second Reading
Colossians 1:24-28

Some believe that this pericope was not written by Paul while others are equally convinced that it was. Regardless, it does reflect Pauline thought found in other letters.

The letter to the Colossians is an interesting study in communication. We are brought into a one-sided conversation. We do not know the problem posed; we only know the answer given. Paul addressed the elite philosophies that threatened the gospel and he defended his ministry throughout the letter. He asserted that the salvation won by the cross of Christ was awarded to all equally. It was not for just an elite few.

The letter was written from a prison cell and reflects how the author's own suffering was part of God's divine plan for the reconciliation of the world. The author demonstrates joy in the face of his trials and hardships. This letter reflects what should be the posture of all disciples. Because of their baptism, Christians are called into relationship with Christ and are invited to embrace the paschal mystery. Discipleship is the way of the cross. The letter challenges us in the same way the liturgy challenges us: to become transformed, to live the cross of Christ and spread his gospel.

Gospel
Luke 10:38-42

Jesus is a guest in Mary and Martha's house. Martha is busy about the tasks of hospitality and Mary is attentive to the person of Christ.

STEP 1
NAMING ONE'S EXPERIENCE

What were your first impressions? What was your first response? What grabbed your attention? How did you feel?

Each person names his or her initial impression. Statement should be brief. No reasons should be given at this time. All simply listen without agreeing or disagreeing.

STEP 2
UNDERSTANDING

In a brief statement, what do you think this gospel is trying to convey?

STEP 3
INPUT FROM VISION/STORY/TRADITION

Liturgical Context

The opening prayer elevates the virtue of service but recognizes that only by grace and through the gift of God will we have the faith, hope, and love necessary for such service. Martha and Mary remind us that service and committed attention to the presence of Christ are the path to follow. Jesus does not admonish Martha because of her hospitality. Some say that he admonished her because of her loss of balance and perspective. The cares and concerns involved with the actions of service overshadowed the more important aspect: intimacy with Christ.

With issues of hospitality so much in the forefront of today's readings, we cannot miss the opportunity to acknowledge the liturgy's challenge to be hospitable people. Today prompts us to ask how we are a welcoming community. What are our strengths? Where do we need to grow? We may not exclude anyone; we will be judged according to how we welcome the least of Christ's family, whether they be the poor, the oppressed, children, or women.

Today's story of Mary receiving the word of God reminds us that we are to listen and respond to the proclamation of God's word in our assembly every time we gather. Such listening calls us, like Martha, into the world of authentic action for the sake of the kingdom where the words of the communion antiphon will be a reality for us. "I stand at the door and knock, says the Lord. If anyone hears my voice and opens the door, I will come in and sit down to supper with him and he with me" (Rev 3:20).[6]

Gospel Exegesis

There are interesting contrasted opinions regarding the story of Martha and Mary. Traditionally the story was seen as a commentary on the balance between contemplation and action. One scholar, however, posits an interesting commentary on Luke's treatment of Martha. It makes a big difference whether the story of Martha and Mary is more a story written for the benefit of the community, or whether it was written as an actual episode in Jesus' life. First, Luke is the only one who tells this story. Second, the gospel of John seems to suggest that perhaps it was written from the perspective of the community rather than from an event in Jesus' life. John's treatment of Martha was so different that it is hard to imagine they are the same person.

In John's gospel Martha was seen as a leader of the community. She was engaged in service to the community and was regarded as a household/community leader. Like the beloved disciple, she was introduced as "beloved" (11:15) in the story of the raising of Lazarus. Martha went to meet Jesus after her brother had been dead for days, but Mary stayed home. Martha expressed her faith in Jesus and together they had a theological discussion in which Jesus professed to be the Resurrection and the Life. Martha attested to the real identity of Jesus, the messiah. The synoptics gave that role to Peter. John had Martha making the profession of faith that mirrored the faith ("so that all may believe") John gave as the reason for writing the gospel in the introduction to the gospel. Thus, Martha was elevated as a model disciple. "She becomes one who believes on the basis of Jesus' word, without seeing signs (Jn 20:29). The next chapter illustrates how Martha's belief in Jesus' words leads to the ministry of service."[7] The entire gospel of John shows strong women in positions of authority and leadership whereas Luke typifies the tensions revolving around women in ministry in the Lukan community.

Many people assert that Luke's is the gospel of women since it contains more stories about women than any other gospel. It is said that Luke upholds women and regards them as equals to men. Because of that perspective, many have tried to rescue this story, not dealing with it in the way it was told, but rather making apologies and explanations for what was "really" meant by Jesus' castigation of Martha. The two values of *hearing the word of God* (Mary) and *doing it—serving* (Martha) are almost held up as opposites. We have been teased with the possibility that what Jesus *really* meant was that Martha was overly attached to her worldly cares and not concerned with spiritual realities. However, there is no strong support for that position in the story itself. Throughout the scripture, Jesus exhorts disciples into service of the kingdom, so issues of hospitality and service are strong biblical values. Barbara Reid suggests that there is something else going on here and that if we read the text the way it was written we have to let it stand as is. Many translate

[6]Sixteenth Sunday in Ordinary Time: "Communion Antiphon," *The Sacramentary*.

[7]Barbara Reid, *Women in the Gospel of Luke* (Collegeville: The Liturgical Press, 1996), 160.

diakoinia in verse 40 to refer to "details of hospitality." However, the term was also used to designate a variety of ministries. Reid suggests that Luke was reflecting the tension going on in the church over women involved in ministry. While there were many women involved in extensive ministries of proclamation, apostolic work, and leadership, some scriptural texts hint of dis-ease with the situation.

A later "copyist" of the Pauline letters shows disapproval of women in leadership even to the point of stating that they are to be subordinate to men, and thus, in effect, silencing them. One stark conclusion is that, perhaps, in the same spirit of the ongoing community struggle, Luke "placed on the lips of Jesus a resounding approval of the silent woman in Luke 10:42."[8] In essence, he was telling Martha that Mary had chosen the better part— prayer and contemplation—and that, like Mary, she should not busy herself about the details of official ministry. She should leave that to others. In other words, ministerial roles were not something that she should busy herself about, but rather, she should be content with the quiet role of prayer and contemplation. (That is not to negate the need for and the calling to such contemplation, but if contemplation were the only value, then *all people* would be advised to choose only that rather than public ministry.) In light of the tension in Luke's church, the issue regarding Martha is "not about having too much work to do, but rather that she is being denied her role in ministerial service."[9]

Barbara Reid asserts that "women are beneficiaries of Jesus' ministry and engage in charitable works, but are seen to have 'chosen the better part' when they remain silent and receptive."[10] While women do participate in the ministry in Luke, they "do not participate in the mission of Jesus the same way that the men disciples do. If we are looking to Luke's narrative to show that women and men shared equally in Jesus' mission in the first century, we will be disappointed."[11] Reid cautions that we are not to view the scriptures from a position of female dominance, but rather as women and men committed to furthering the dignity of men and women equally. She suggests that a primary theme throughout scripture is the radical option for the poor, oppressed, and powerless. Thus, she cautions us to read the scripture from a "hermeneutic of suspicion." That is, we are to read the stories aware of the cultural biases of a patriarchal society and patriarchal authors. While not ignoring the fact that the bible is the inspired word of God, the authors were nevertheless limited human beings who set forth the word of God.[12]

Thus, one way to approach Luke's interpretation of the story is to remember how John portrayed Martha (with strength and authority) and how subsequent generations portrayed her. The artist, Fra Angelico (1387-1455) pictured Martha and Mary at Gethsemane. The disciples are asleep, Mary is reading a book and Martha is imitating the posture of Jesus whose hands are uplifted in prayer. Another picture has Martha at the foot of the cross with Veronica. Master Eckhart (ca. 1260-1327), a Dominican monk and mystic, preached that Martha had already attained the balance between action and contemplation. He further suggested that Mary was a novice in the contemplative life and that Martha's complaint had more to do with a warning to Mary that she not "get stuck in the tranquil resting, indifferent to the needs around her."[13]

From a traditional, theological point of view, the text upholds the value that the greatest action one can engage in is to love the Lord with one's mind, heart, soul, body, and spirit. All else is rubbish in comparison to that goal. "In Jesus' presence, the 'one thing required' was to listen and hear the word."[14] Service that is not rooted in the word of God will not last.

Proclaim the gospel again.

Sometimes we gain new insights when we hear the text after the interpretation has been given. Someone from the group proclaims the gospel a second time.

[8]Ibid., 155.
[9]Ibid., 157.
[10]Ibid., 3.
[11]Ibid.

[12]Ibid.
[13]Ibid., 161.
[14]Sanchez, *The Word We Celebrate,* 349.

Conversation with the Liturgy and the Scriptures

Test your original understanding in dialogue with the text.

(You might consider breaking into smaller groups.)

Now that you've heard the interpretation, how do you feel? Comfortable? Uncomfortable? Were there any new insights? Was there anything you had not considered before? How does your original understanding of this story compare with what was just shared? How does this story speak to your life?

Participants share an experience from their lives that connects with the biblical interpretation just shared.

> *It is very "politically incorrect" today to speak of women's issues in the church. While I do not intend to discuss the hot issue of women's ordination, I will share my own struggle with women's issues in general. I was once accused of being a radical feminist. I found it rather amusing because, at the time, I did not have strong feminist leanings. However, I have experienced a metamorphosis. It goes something like this. I had a problem making a major issue of women's role in the church because in many ways it seemed quite picayune. The issues seem to fade when one considers the real issues of women around the world. I felt I had no right to complain about such inconsequential matters when there were women in some parts of the world so denigrated and abused that they were completely stripped of all dignity. Some women are burned for not having the appropriate dowry to pass on to their fiancés. Some women and girls are surgically kept from experiencing any female sexual pleasure. Some are treated like beasts of burden while others are prohibited from obtaining an education. Many are constantly reminded of their secondary role in society. I was embarrassed that we, in this country, should make such a noise over issues that pale in comparison. That is, until I experienced metanoia.*

> *After one celebration of eucharist, I returned from communion and noticed a fresco on the wall that pictured men and women standing around the pil-*

> *lar to be scourged along with Christ. A realization came crashing down upon me. The eucharist I had received put me in solidarity with all the suffering people in the world. When, in our own everyday life, we stand for the rights and dignity of all, we are standing for the rights and dignity of all people everywhere. If we, in this country, were to never address the issues of women's rights, then we would not stand a chance of convicting other countries of their horrific human rights violations. When I stand with my sisters in my own realm of experience, I stand with my suffering sisters around the world. Mary, in today's gospel, reminds me that through prayer and listening to God's word I am strengthened to stand with the oppressed and accept the cross for the sake of the kingdom. Martha reminds me that I had better put my money where my mouth is and back up my prayer with action. Now I speak out for women's rights where I am able. I am not personally oppressed, but I stand with my sisters who are.*

All share their life experience.

What was Luke trying to tell his community? How do the issues in Luke's community relate to the issues our communities face today? How are the themes of exodus (death/resurrection/liberation), creation, covenant, and community evident in today's readings? How is God speaking to us as a community in these readings? In what way is our community challenged? What are our collective and personal responses to all of these questions? Do we still feel the same way about this text as we did when we began? Has our original understanding been stretched, challenged, or affirmed?

The gospel demands a response.

How does our sharing and this biblical interpretation challenge our community's attitudes? How would this interpretation be received today? What are the contemporary implications? In what concrete way does this gospel call our parish to change or to respond? Has this conversation with the exegesis of the Martha and Mary story changed or stretched my personal attitudes? What are the implications for my life? What is one concrete action I will take this week as a response to what was learned and shared today?

DOCTRINAL ISSUES

What church truth/teaching/doctrinal issue could be drawn from the gospel for the Sixteenth Sunday in Ordinary Time?

Participants suggest possible doctrinal themes that flow from the readings.

Possible Doctrinal Themes

Service, prayer, word of God, hospitality, suffering, justice

Present the doctrinal material at this time.

1. The facilitator gives input on a particular doctrinal issue of his/her prior choosing. OR
2. The group chooses a doctrinal issue from the list they created. They read together from the Doctrinal Appendix.

(The doctrinal issues are found in the Doctrinal Appendix in the back of this workbook. If you are choosing an issue from this resource, please refer to it now.)

Reflection questions centered around the chosen doctrinal theme can be found at the end of each topic in the Doctrinal Appendix. The questions are based on the five-step reflection process. If you choose a topic not included in the Doctrinal Appendix, craft your own questions according to the same five-step process.

Following the reflection questions you will be reminded to return to chapter 7, "Preparing the Catechetical Session," to assist you in crafting your own session.

Closing Prayer

Lord,
by the power of this sacrament
make your people strong in the truth.

Help your faithful people who suffer persecution
to carry their cross in the footsteps of Christ your
   Son
and in the midst of their sufferings
rejoice to be called Christians.
We ask this through Christ, our Lord.[15]

Selected Bibliography

Fuller, Reginald. *Preaching the New Lectionary.* Collegeville: The Liturgical Press, 1974.

Kuntz, J. Kenneth. *The People of Ancient Israel.* New York: Harper and Row, 1974.

Reid, Barbara. *Women in the Gospel of Luke.* Collegeville: The Liturgical Press, 1996.

Sanchez, Patricia Datchuck. *The Word We Celebrate.* Kansas City: Sheed and Ward, 1989.

---

[15]Mass for Persecuted Christians: "Prayer After Communion," *The Sacramentary.*

SEVENTEENTH SUNDAY IN ORDINARY TIME

INTRODUCTORY RITES

Opening Song (or Entrance Antiphon)

God is in his holy dwelling; he will give a home to the lonely, he gives power and strength to his people. (Ps 67: 6-7, 36)[1]

Opening Prayer

The facilitator of the session may lead the prayer. Others in the group may be asked to proclaim the readings.

Let us pray
[that we will make good use of the gifts
that God has given us]

Pause for silent prayer.

God our Father and protector,
without you nothing is holy,
nothing has value.
Guide us to everlasting life
by helping us to use wisely
the blessings you have given to the world.
We ask this through our Lord Jesus Christ, your
    Son,
who lives and reigns with you and the Holy Spirit,
one God for ever and ever.[2]

LITURGY OF THE WORD

Let us listen to God's word.

The readings are proclaimed.

First Reading
Genesis 18:20-32

Sodom and Gomorrah have gone down in history as symbols of the worst depravity. The two cities were known for myriad transgressions, from sex-

---

[1]Seventeenth Sunday in Ordinary Time: "Entrance Antiphon," *The Sacramentary.*

[2]Seventeenth Sunday in Ordinary Time: "Opening Prayer," *The Sacramentary.*

---

ual aberrations to inhospitable acts. While not certain, it is believed that the two cities were located near the desolate Dead Sea region. Today's particular pericope is about divine judgment[3] and Abraham's persistent intercession on behalf of the city. His pleading mirrors the stance Jesus says we are to have toward prayer in today's gospel. We are to be persistent. From last week's Genesis passage we are aware of the intimacy Abraham shared with Yahweh, his guest. It is because of such intimacy that Abraham (or anyone) possesses the necessary confidence to be obnoxiously persistent.

Abraham was promised that the cities would be spared if righteous people could be found. The saddest aspect to this story is that depravity was so pervasive that there were no righteous people to be found. This story ultimately became a symbol

---

[3]However, Don C. Benjamin asserts that the story of Sodom and Gomorrah is about hospitality: "strangers appear, Lot's household protects them, and they bless it with life." There was a definitive protocol regarding hospitality in antiquity. It helped to test whether a person was a friend or an enemy. The strangers pass the first test with flying colors when they decline the first invitation. They become official guests with the gesture of foot washing. Another test was to observe the strangers' table manners. If they responded appropriately it was apparent that they understood the mores of their host. However, before the test is completed (the next verses of chapter 18 and 19), the young warriors and men in leadership gather and decide on their own that the visitors are enemies. Their punishment would be rape (similar to what was experienced by David's messenger before he was released by the Ammorites). The sexual implications in that culture were not understood as they are today. Sexual activity was considered to be part of the realm of contractual agreement. Monarchs had hundred of wives because they were in contractual agreement with other nations. Homosexual or heterosexual rape was a sign of a broken treaty.

We are understandably shocked when Abraham offers his daughters in return for the strangers' lives. While not certain, scholars believe that it was an act of offering Abraham's own self to save the guests. It was believed that dead parents live on in their children. Since it is the children who must care for aged parents, by offering his daughters, he was in essence saying, "Here, take my only hope of survival. I will be destined to live a life of poverty and destitution because of the death of my daughters."

throughout biblical history of Yahweh's anger and divine retribution.

Responsorial Psalm
Psalm 138:1-2, 2-3, 6-7, 7-8

This is a psalm of praise and thanks for deliverance. It was chosen for its connection to the mercy and justice displayed by Yahweh over the Sodom and Gomorrah incident.

Second Reading
Colossians 2:12-14

This pericope is believed to be some form of liturgical prayer or hymn. One major theme of this letter is our incorporation into the death and resurrection of Jesus through baptism. This is the constant theme of Paul in his letter to the Romans that we hear proclaimed at every Easter Vigil. However, there is a difference. In Romans, Paul asserted our future resurrection with Christ. In the letter to the Colossians, the assumption is made that the resurrection has already taken place. Baptized Christians are living a resurrected existence.

In the verse, "He canceled the bond that stood against us with all its claims" (v. 14), the author is perhaps referring to the biblical notion of debtor and creditor. Some interpret it to mean the Jewish debt to obey the law. We owe God a debt we can never repay because of our sins. Jesus took our sins, which on our own we could never atone for, and literally nailed them to the cross through his death. The death of Christ, not the law, provided the atonement.

This reading is set in the situation of a community that was toying with dangerous, elitist philosophies that were undermining the gospel of Christ. Adherents of this philosophy believed in superhuman beings more powerful than Christ; they believed in circumcision and they obeyed Jewish beliefs and customs. The Pauline author asserted that the only reality is Jesus Christ crucified, who died and rose for our sins and who invites us into that same death and resurrection through our baptism. Those who believed in circumcision were stating their commitment to and incorporation in the covenant made with Abraham. The author of Colossians asserted that the

Christian circumcision is now in the form of baptism into Christ's paschal mystery, the new covenant. In the verse preceding this pericope, the Pauline author states that circumcision is nothing more than a mark on the flesh. Christian circumcision, baptism, "stripped off the flesh entirely."[4] Baptism stripped away the carnal nature of the person (sin).

Gospel
Luke 11:1-13

Jesus teaches the disciples the Lord's Prayer and instructs his disciples about prayer.

STEP 1
NAMING ONE'S EXPERIENCE

What were your first impressions? What was your first response? What grabbed your attention? How did you feel?

Each person names his or her initial impression. Statement should be brief. No reasons should be given at this time. All simply listen without agreeing or disagreeing.

STEP 2
UNDERSTANDING

In a brief statement, what do you think this gospel is trying to convey?

STEP 3
INPUT FROM VISION/STORY/TRADITION

Liturgical Context

The Fifteenth Sunday (Good Samaritan) exhorted us to make all people our neighbor, to be inclusive and open to all those in need. The Sixteenth Sunday (Mary and Martha) exhorted us that listening to God's word is the Christian's greatest activity. The Seventeenth Sunday (Lord's Prayer) teaches

---

[4]Patricia Datchuck Sanchez, *The Word We Celebrate* (Kansas City: Sheed and Ward, 1989), 350.

us that prayer is what drives us and is vital to the kingdom.

Today we open up the prayer we proclaim at every liturgy. During the mass, the Lord's Prayer functions as a prayer in preparation for reception of communion.

> Since the eucharistic celebration is the paschal meal, it is right that the faithful who are properly disposed receive the Lord's body and blood as spiritual food as he commanded. This is the purpose of the breaking of the bread and the other preparatory rites that lead directly to the communion of the people:
>
> a. Lord's Prayer: this is a petition both for daily food, which for Christians means also the eucharistic bread, and for forgiveness of sin, so that what is holy may be given to those who are holy. . . . The embolism, developing the last petition of the Lord's Prayer, begs on behalf of the entire community of the faithful, deliverance from the power of evil.[5]

Evidence of the Spirit that was requested in the Lord's Prayer occurs every time Christians gather for the holy meal. It is an ongoing memorial to Jesus' life, death, and resurrection, a continuation of the Lord's Prayer that gives us identity as Catholic Christians. This is reflected in the prayer after communion,

> Lord,
> we receive the sacrament
> which celebrates the memory
> of the death and resurrection of Christ your
>   Son.
> May this gift bring us closer to our eternal
>   salvation.[6]

The prayer of the liturgy reflects the same hope expressed in the Lord's Prayer, that the promised

future kingdom, as well as the kingdom here and now, be realized.

Are there any candidates ready for the Rite of Full Communion, Acceptance or Welcome?

Gospel Exegesis

The facilitator gives input regarding what critical biblical scholarship has to say about this text. The input includes insights as to how people would have heard the gospel in Jesus' time.

There are two forms of the Lord's prayer preserved in Christian tradition: the one used by the Jewish community in Matthew and the one used by the gentile Christian community in Luke. The Jewish prayer was eschatological, the Lukan prayer was present-centered.

The original form of the prayer was future-oriented. The prayer asked that God would bring about the eschatological kingdom to come. It was a kingdom in which all people would recognize God and his authority over the human race. Since the eschatological kingdom was sought in the first verses, the daily bread requested was believed to mean the "spiritual manna at the heavenly banquet table." The "deliverance from temptation" requested was a reference to the final battle of good vs. evil. The prayer sought divine protection from the wiles of the Evil One on that fateful day.

This is a communal prayer, the prayer of the community. The orientation is "us" rather than "me." The community prayed for the speedy arrival of the future kingdom and that all would be protected as the shift to this final age occurred. The prayer asked that this final age be ushered in immediately.

Luke's Jesus is less future-oriented and places the prayer in the context of the here and now. We are to pray for the kingdom, *now* in this place. Use of "daily bread" differs from the original form of the prayer in that it asks God to provide what is necessary to meet the daily physical needs for the mission. While the prayer certainly has implications of the coming kingdom, it is con-

---

[5]"General Introduction to the Roman Missal," in *The Liturgy Documents* (Chicago: Liturgy Training Publications, 1991), #56.

[6]Seventeenth Sunday in Ordinary Time: "Prayer After Communion," *The Sacramentary*.

cerned with the present state of affairs. The deliverance from temptation in Luke refers to the daily temptations that ensnare human beings. The prayer requests that disciples not be ensnared by the seductions of life and be prepared for the coming of the Spirit, evidence of God's reign. Thus, the prayer "gives instruction to disciples about what to pray for in the midst of ongoing historical process: daily bread, forgiveness, victory over temptation, the gift of the Holy Spirit, and the ultimate victory of God."[7]

We are to pray unceasingly because it is the way Jesus derived his spiritual strength and power. The parable gives two other reasons for persistence in prayer. The parable is regarded as a "how much more parable." If a neighbor shamelessly persists in knocking at the door and is finally answered by a reluctant host, then *how much more will* God be willing to answer our persistent requests. Why pray? Because God will answer. The second reason for prayer is also formulated in terms of "how much more." If parents would not think of giving their child a harmful gift (serpent, stone, scorpion, etc.), *how much more* would God desire to give only good gifts to his children! The *good gifts* refers to the Holy Spirit. We are to pray for the gift of the Holy Spirit.

When the disciples asked Jesus to teach them to pray, in essence they were saying, "Lord, give us an identity." Groups were identified by the way they prayed. Jesus wanted them to be bold. "Give me my future hope and give it to me *now!*" God likes his disciples to have a little spunk! If you're going to ask for something, you might as well go for it with gusto! Luke's theology insists that we are to be persistent; that we are not to take "no" for an answer. Prayer is not wimpy. It gets results.

Jesus affirms the relationship he has with his disciples. He attests that the relationship he has with his Father is the same relationship that he has with his disciples.

Proclaim the gospel again.

---

[7]Charles Talbert, *Reading Luke* (New York: Crossroad, 1992), 132.

Sometimes we gain new insights when we hear the text after the interpretation has been given. Someone from the group proclaims the gospel a second time.

STEP 4
TESTING

Conversation with the Liturgy and the Scriptures

Test your original understanding in dialogue with the text.

(You might consider breaking into smaller groups.)

Were there any new insights? Was there anything you had not considered before? How does your original understanding of this story compare with what was just shared? How does this story speak to your life?

Participants share an experience from their lives that connects with the biblical interpretation just shared.

> *In our fast-paced McDonald's world, it is difficult to imagine the kind of persistence that today's gospel suggests. We are a culture that wants instant gratification. While the gospel does suggest that we are to be bold and keep at it, it does not say that our prayers will be immediately answered. In fact, it appears to suggest the opposite. It is almost saying, "If at first you don't succeed, try and try again, and again, and again." We are so used to the fast-paced world that if we do not see results in a timely manner, we assume that God did not answer our prayers.*

> *Quite a few years ago I was involved in a very difficult, painful situation. Every day brought new challenges. Those of us involved could not see the hand of God. It seemed as if Evil was the daily victor. We prayed daily for the strength to see God in the midst of the problem and to bring about a speedy resolution. But days turned into weeks and weeks turned into months. Our prayers continued at high-pitch level even when it appeared that all had failed. It seemed as if God had abandoned us. However, over time, vindication arrived. As we look back to those days we see that God was leading us through the wall of water every step of the way. While we did not*

give up on prayer (at times prayer was the only thing left for us to do), it was very easy to lose sight of God's presence in the midst of the garbage. We were being taught the heart of today's prayer on a day-by-day basis. We asked for what we needed to survive each day and each crisis and we were given what we needed. We were to forgive those who were hurting us and recognize God's love for them as well as for us. Above all we prayed that the Lord's will would be accomplished in the midst of the chaos.

Hindsight is the best teacher. The answer to our prayers was subtle and very characteristic of God. There were no lightning bolts. The answer was characterized by the restoration of peace and harmony. We were living in the answer long before we realized it. The situation taught us that we are never to give up on prayer, that we are to trust God to provide for us in our need no matter what the situation, and that we are to embrace the cross of Christ and seek his will in the midst of all of life's difficult situations.

All share their life experience.

What was Luke saying to his community? What does he have to say to our community and to me today? What might God be creating in us through this experience of Jesus in the gospel? In what way does this gospel point to God's promise to be with us? In what way have we known death/resurrection in our experience and understanding of this gospel? What are our collective and personal responses to all of these questions? Do we still feel the same way about this text as we did when we began? Has our original understanding been stretched, challenged, or affirmed?

STEP 5
DECISION

The gospel demands a response.

How does our sharing and this biblical interpretation challenge our community today? What are the implications for modern-day living? Since this was a prayer of identity and a communal prayer, how does it challenge us as a community? What are the implications of this gospel for my life?

What am I/we/community/parish called to do in response? What is one concrete action we will take this week as a response to what we have learned and shared today?

DOCTRINAL ISSUES

What church truth/teaching/doctrinal issue could be drawn from the gospel for the Seventeenth Sunday in Ordinary Time?

Participants suggest possible doctrinal themes that flow from the readings.

Possible Doctrinal Themes

Baptism, paschal mystery, prayer, trust, suffering, images of God

Present the doctrinal material at this time.

1 The facilitator gives input on a particular doctrinal issue of his/her prior choosing. OR
2. The group chooses a doctrinal issue from the list they created. They read together from the Doctrinal Appendix.

(The doctrinal issues are found in the Doctrinal Appendix in the back of this workbook. If you are choosing an issue from this resource, please refer to it now.)

Reflection questions centered around the chosen doctrinal theme can be found at the end of each topic in the Doctrinal Appendix. The questions are based on the five-step reflection process. If you choose a topic not included in the Doctrinal Appendix, craft your own questions according to the same five-step process.

Following the reflection questions you will be reminded to return to chapter 7, "Preparing the Catechetical Session," to assist you in crafting your own session.

Closing Prayer

Let us pray
[for the faith to recognize God's presence
in our world]

Pause for silent prayer.

God our Father,
open our eyes to see your hand at work
in the splendor of creation,
in the beauty of human life.
Touched by your hand our world is holy.
Help us to cherish the gifts that surround us,
to share your blessings with our brothers and sisters,
and to experience the joy of life in your presence.
We ask this through Christ our Lord.[8]

Selected Bibliography

Benjamin, Don C. "Sodom and Gomorrah." *The Collegeville Pastoral Dictionary of Biblical Theology.* Ed. Carroll Stuhlmueller, C.P. Collegeville: The Liturgical Press, 1996.

Days of the Lord. Vol 6. Collegeville: The Liturgical Press, 1991.

"General Introduction to the Roman Missal." In *The Liturgy Documents.* Chicago: Liturgy Training Publications, 1991.

Horgan, Maurya P. "The Letter to the Colossians." In *The New Jerome Biblical Commentary.* Ed. Raymond E. Brown, S.S., Joseph A. Fitzmyer, S.J., Roland E. Murphy, O.Carm. Englewood Cliffs: Prentice Hall, 1990.

Sanchez, Patricia Datchuck. *The Word We Celebrate.* Kansas City: Sheed and Ward, 1989.

Talbert, Charles. *Reading Luke.* New York: Crossroad, 1991.

---

[8]Seventeenth Sunday in Ordinary Time: "Alternative Opening Prayer," *The Sacramentary.*

EIGHTEENTH SUNDAY IN ORDINARY TIME

INTRODUCTORY RITES

Opening Song (or Entrance Antiphon)

God, come to my help. Lord, quickly give me assistance. You are the one who helps me and sets me free: Lord, do not be long in coming. (Ps 69:2, 6)[1]

Opening Prayer

The facilitator of the session may lead the prayer. Others in the group may be asked to proclaim the readings.

Let us pray
[to the Father whose kindness never fails]

Pause for silent prayer.

God our Father,
gifts without measure flow from your goodness
to bring us your peace.
Our life is your gift.
Guide our life's journey,
for only your love makes us whole.
Keep us strong in your love.
We ask this through Christ our Lord.[2]

LITURGY OF THE WORD

Let us listen to God's word.

The readings are proclaimed.

First Reading
Ecclesiastes 1:2, 2:21-23

Ecclesiastes ("from the Greek *ekklesiastes,* referred to the one who convokes the *ekklesia* or assembly"[3]) is a commentary on the futility and transitory nature of this life. The word for vanity

refers to breath or vapor and that which is empty or transient. The author of Ecclesiastes was probably someone who preached or presided over an assembly. Whoever he was, his realism was stark and depressing. He acknowledged that when all is said and done, all one does in life is meaningless. The author was bemoaning the fact that life was without value. Only God gives meaning to life.

One scholar suggests that Ecclesiastes is the most Christian book in the entire Old Testament because it demonstrates what life apart from God is truly like. It prepares us for hearing the good news of Jesus in the gospel since it is filled with the bad news one must hear in order to embrace the good. Apart from God human life means nothing.

Responsorial Psalm
Psalm 95:1-2, 6-7, 8-9

Psalm 95 is a call to worship and a warning regarding neglect of God's word. It is the psalm used as the invitatory for the church's morning prayer. The second part of the psalm is a warning to those who have slackened off and are no longer growing in their relationship with God.

Second Reading
Colossians 3:1-5, 9-11

As stated in last week's commentary on the letter to the Colossians, baptism affords the Christian a share in Christ's resurrected life. However, today's reading reminds believers that they are not to become complacent. They must be diligent as they remain true to their baptismal calling. We are not to escape from this world only to dwell in the transcendent presence of God, but we are to dwell in God's presence while offering our lives in the service of others.

In referring to God the Creator and the fact that we are created in God's image, the Pauline writer was alluding to the creation event and in the process was refuting the gnostic teachers. The author of Colossians was affirming God's creating

---

[1]Eighteenth Sunday in Ordinary Time: "Entrance Antiphon," *The Sacramentary.*

[2]Eighteenth Sunday in Ordinary Time: "Alternative Opening Prayer," *The Sacramentary.*

[3]Patricia Datchuck Sanchez, *The Word We Celebrate* (Kansas City: Sheed and Ward, 1989), 352.

and saving action. When Christians are living their baptismal commitment, people share equally in the transforming knowledge (mind and heart) of God. Such knowledge is not just for a select few. The only knowledge that matters is Christ crucified. All people are one in God's reign. Christians are to live in daily obedience to the call and commitment of their baptism.

The pericope contains a common Hellenistic device of listing virtues and vices. The first list (v. 5) enumerates the vices and passions.[4] Sins of the intellect are included in verse 8 (not in this Sunday's pericope). Because of these sins God's retribution is coming.

The Pauline author wishes the Christian to understand how the effects of Jesus' death and resurrection are evident in their lives. The Christian responds in faith because of Christ's gratuitous act. He or she does not respond in order to "get something." The "something" has already been given and the rewards have been realized. The daily response is a result of the gift.

The "putting off the old self" was probably referring to the baptismal ritual in which the initiates took off their old clothes as a sign of turning away from sin.

Gospel
Luke 12:13-21

Jesus tells a parable about a rich man.

STEP 1
NAMING ONE'S EXPERIENCE

What were your first impressions? What was your first response? What grabbed your attention? How did you feel?

Each person names his or her initial impression. Statement should be brief. No reasons should be given at this time. All simply listen without agreeing or disagreeing.

---

[4]Maurya P. Horgan, "The Letter to the Colossians," in *The New Jerome Biblical Commentary,* ed. Raymond E. Brown, S.S., Joseph A. Fitzmyer, S.J., Roland E. Murphy, O.Carm. (Englewood Cliffs: Prentice Hall, 1990), 882.

STEP 2
UNDERSTANDING

In a brief statement, what do you think this gospel is trying to convey?

STEP 3
INPUT FROM VISION/STORY/TRADITION

Liturgical Context

The alternative opening prayer reflects the primary theme of today's gospel: "Our life is your gift." We owe our lives to the benevolence of God. The introductory rites assert our utter dependence on the one who saves us and sets us free. Psalm 95 states that God is the "rock," the foundation upon which we build our lives. The prayer after communion asks for the strength of new life from the gift of Christ's Body and Blood. We are to look forward to that future day when we will live eternally with him. The liturgy itself proclaims the implications of today's readings. Preface V in Ordinary Time echoes the Pauline author who acknowledges that it is God who is sovereign and who controls our destiny. Preface V reminds us that God is the master of our lives. We are to be stewards of all that God has given us. We are merely wayfarers on this earthly journey. Unlike the foolish rich man, Christians are to be prepared for the consummation of our lives, for it will bring us into our eternal union with God.

Gospel Exegesis

The facilitator gives input regarding what critical biblical scholarship has to say about this text. The input includes insights as to how people would have heard the gospel in Jesus' time.

In the gospel today Jesus seems to be answering Qoheleth in the first reading. The rich fool in the gospel lived his life with little concern for the things of God. He saw himself as independent and not in need of God. In the end, all of his efforts meant nothing. He ended up with nothing. It was a shock to the man to discover that it was God who ordered and controlled his life.

Luke Timothy Johnson maintains that in the reference to "no one's life" in verse 15, Luke is positing the basic distinction between life and possession. "Life is a gift of God. No amount of possessions, however abundant, can make it greater or give it security."[5] In the last verse of the pericope Luke asserts that to store wealth for oneself is not a response of faith. A response of faith would be demonstrated by sharing wealth with others.

This story takes place in a section of Luke's gospel called "on the road to Jerusalem." Jesus has been engaged in serious dialogue about the implications and challenges of the journey toward Jerusalem. Someone interjects a question that seems inconsequential in light of the other serious matters they have been discussing. Someone asks Jesus to settle an inheritance dispute. Although there are specific laws governing such disputes, Jesus is asked to comment.

Luke uses this interlude to offer commentary on the seductive power of possessions. Luke suggests that attachment to possessions is our way of dealing with our fear of the transitory nature of life. "It is out of deep fear that the acquisitive instinct grows monstrous."[6] The rich fool thought his massive crops would be his future security. However, at the end of his life his possessions were scattered like seed in the wind.

People amass goods believing them to offer security; in fact, they are more tentative than life itself. "The less you have the freer you are" is an apt description of this text's implication. The moral is: we must let go of death-clutching fear, acknowledge that *life* itself is the ultimate gift from the ultimate Giver, and realize that this life is tentative at best. We look forward to a future life in which the choices made in this life will impact our future. Not only are disciples to let go of fear, but they are to literally sell all they have and give it to the poor. This is truly the mind and spirit of the Lukan message. Believers know true freedom because of their trust and reliance on God who controls their destiny. Because of that freedom they are able to offer the gift of self to others. Such

freedom prompts them to share their possessions with others. Only then are they spiritually free. True generosity exists in the midst of spiritual freedom.

Proclaim the gospel again.

Sometimes we gain new insights when we hear the text after the interpretation has been given. Someone from the group proclaims the gospel a second time.

STEP 4
TESTING

Conversation with the Liturgy and the Scriptures

Test your original understanding in dialogue with the text.

(You might consider breaking into smaller groups.)

Were there any new insights? Was there anything you had not considered before? How does your original understanding of this story compare with what we just shared? How does this story speak to your life?

Participants share an experience from their lives that connects with the biblical interpretation just shared.

> *We used to have a Benedictine friend who constantly exhorted us: "The less you have the freer you are." When families are concerned about amassing possessions it takes up all their energy and enslaves them. A catechumen in our initiation process was an immigrant from Russia. She taught me a great deal about this parable by sharing her experience of growing up in Russia before and after the fall of communism. When capitalism emerged in Russia after the fall, the people were instantly obsessed with having all the "goods" the Western world could offer. She worked herself sick to purchase the goods that promised her so much happiness. But the goods did not deliver on their promise. She was no happier. Something was seriously missing.*
>
> *Life was barren. God was missing and she knew it. She told us that one cannot imagine what it is like to live in a culture where God has been totally oblit-*

[5]Luke Timothy Johnson, *The Gospel of Luke,* Sacra Pagina Series, Vol. 3 (Collegeville: The Liturgical Press, 1991), 199.
[6]Ibid., 201.

erated from the consciousness of its citizens. In the words of Qoheleth, "It was vanity of vanities—rubbish, nothingness!" Had it not been for the grandmothers who had transmitted the remembered stories of faith, Russia would have lost all of its awareness of God.

Elena had worked to buy new clothes. When she purchased them with her hard-earned money, she was amazed at how quickly they deteriorated. She saved and struggled to get a new and bigger apartment. No sooner had she acquired what she had dreamed about for so long than her circumstances changed. She was offered the opportunity to leave the country for a new and better life. But then she was saddled with an expensive apartment that she was unable to sell. She was not free. She felt extremely burdened by the possessions she had craved. She decided that true freedom exists only through inner poverty. Her journey toward God had begun.

It led her to us. She was pure gift. She taught us what it means to detach. Her faith in God's providence was greater than that of anyone I had ever met. Elena owned one dress, one pair of shoes, and one pair of slacks and asserted that it was all she needed. She had chosen the better portion in her relationship with God. She taught us how precious the gift of faith truly is and the price one must pay to keep it.

The challenge of today's gospel is not necessarily that we are to consider our possessions intrinsically evil, but that we are to ask ourselves the question, "How much space do they occupy in our hearts?" The lure of possessions is very seductive. Are we detached enough from the things of this world to fall with reckless abandon into the arms of our living God? It is very easy to fool ourselves. Balance is difficult to achieve. The lesson is ongoing and very challenging. Thank God for Elena.

All share their life experience.

What was Luke saying to his community? How is it a word for us today? What might God be creating in us through this story of the rich fool? In what way does this gospel point to God's promise to be with us? How does this gospel invite us/me into the paschal mystery (life, death, and resurrection)? In what way is our community challenged?

What are our collective and personal responses to all of these questions? Have we been stretched in any way as a result of sharing these readings?

STEP 5
DECISION

The gospel demands a response.

How does our sharing and this biblical interpretation challenge our community's attitudes? What are the implications of this gospel for today? In what concrete way does this gospel call our parish to action in the church, parish, neighborhood, or world? Has this conversation challenged or stretched my personal attitudes? What am I/we/community/parish called to do in response? What is one one specific action we will take this week as a response to what was learned and shared today?

DOCTRINAL ISSUES

What church truth/teaching/doctrinal issue could be drawn from the gospel for the Eighteenth Sunday in Ordinary Time?

Participants suggest possible doctrinal themes that flow from the readings.

Possible Doctrinal Themes

God the Father, baptism, Trinity, paschal mystery

Present the doctrinal material at this time.

1. The facilitator gives input on a particular doctrinal issue of his/her prior choosing. OR
2. The group chooses a doctrinal issue from the list they created. They read together from the Doctrinal Appendix.

(The doctrinal issues are found in the Doctrinal Appendix in the back of this workbook. If you are choosing an issue from this resource, please refer to it now.)

Reflection questions centered around the chosen doctrinal theme can be found at the end of each topic in the Doctrinal Appendix. The questions are based on the five-step reflection process. If you choose a topic not included in the Doctrinal Appendix, craft your own questions according to the same five-step process.

Following the reflection questions you will be reminded to return to chapter 7, "Preparing the Catechetical Session," to assist you in crafting your own session.

Closing Prayer

Father, all powerful and ever-living God,
we do well always and everywhere to give you
    thanks.
All things are of your making
all times and seasons obey your laws,
but you chose to create man in your own image,
setting him over the whole world in all its wonder.
You made man steward of creation,
to praise you day by day for the marvels of your
    wisdom and power,
through Jesus Christ, our Lord.[7]

Selected Bibliography

Days of the Lord. Vol. 6. Collegeville: The Liturgical Press, 1991.

Horgan, Maurya P. "The Letter to the Colossians." In *The New Jerome Biblical Commentary.* Ed. Raymond E. Brown, S.S., Joseph A. Fitzmyer, S.J., Roland E. Murphy, O.Carm. Englewood Cliffs: Prentice Hall, 1990.

Johnson, Luke Timothy. *The Gospel of Luke.* Sacra Pagina Series. Vol. 3. Collegeville: The Liturgical Press, 1991.

Sanchez, Patricia Datchuck. *The Word We Celebrate.* Kansas City: Sheed and Ward, 1989.

---

[7]Sundays in Ordinary Time V, Preface 33, *The Sacramentary.*

Nineteenth Sunday in Ordinary Time

INTRODUCTORY RITES

Opening Song (or Entrance Antiphon)

Lord, be true to your covenant, forget not the life of your poor ones for ever. Rise up, O God, and defend your cause; do not ignore the shouts of your enemies. (Ps 73:20, 19, 22, 23)[1]

Opening Prayer

The facilitator of the session may lead the prayer. Others in the group may be asked to proclaim the readings.

Let us pray
[that through us
others may find the way to life in Christ]

   Pause for silent prayer.

Father,
we come, reborn in the Spirit,
to celebrate our sonship in the Lord Jesus Christ.
Touch our hearts,
help them grow toward the life you have promised.
Touch our lives,
make them signs of your love for all men.
Grant this through Christ, our Lord.[2]

LITURGY OF THE WORD

Let us listen to God's word.

The readings are proclaimed.

First Reading
Wisdom 18:6-9

Even though Solomon lived a millennium before this book was written, he was given the credit for its authorship. The book was actually written in the first century B.C.E. in Hellenistic Alexandria, a major trade community and a bustling cultural, intellectual, academic, and political center. Many Jews ended up in Alexandria during the diaspora. "Living in the midst of pagans, the Jewish community was in frequent contact with all the elements of the new society that was the Hellenistic world."[3] There was a growing skepticism, a cosmopolitan, individualistic mentality, and a disdain for traditional values emerging within the society. Many Jews, who were caught in the heat of the crisis, were experiencing a serious crisis of faith. Today's letter was written to strengthen the Jewish tradition, to remind the people of their heritage, lest they become fully entrapped by the temptations of Hellenistic society and culture.

Today's Wisdom passage is about salvation history. The reader is reminded of what God accomplished through the exodus event. The people were delivered out of bondage, given their ultimate freedom, and set upon their own land. The annual pasch (Passover) was a living memorial to the God who saves and delivers. The people were heirs to the promises made to Abraham. Thus, it is God who saves, provides for, delivers, and protects his people.

Responsorial Psalm
Psalm 33:1, 12, 18-19, 20-22

This is a psalm in praise of God's action in salvation. It asserts God's election of a people, not individuals. God elected Israel. Christians inherited this election through Christ's fulfillment of the covenant. The Christian community includes the entire world.

Second Reading
Hebrews 11:1-2, 8-19 or 11:1-2, 8-12

It is generally held that the letter to the Hebrews was not written by Paul but by a Hellenistic Christian. The letter to the Hebrews asserts that worship in the old covenant has been superseded by the

---

[1] Nineteenth Sunday in Ordinary Time: "Entrance Antiphon," *The Sacramentary.*

[2] Nineteenth Sunday in Ordinary Time: "Alternative Opening Prayer," *The Sacramentary.*

[3] Addison G. Wright, S.S. "Wisdom," in *The New Jerome Biblical Commentary,* ed. Raymond E. Brown, S.S., Joseph A. Fitzmyer, S.J., Roland E. Murphy, O.Carm. (Englewood Cliffs: Prentice Hall, 1990), 511.

sacrifice of Christ on the cross.[4] A major theme of the letter is the priesthood of Christ. Primarily a theological document, the letter to the Hebrews was written as a response to the dangerous apostasy that was prevalent at the time of its writing. Most scholars believe that the intended audience of the letter was Jewish Christians and that it was written about 80-90 C.E. While some maintain that the audience was gentile, the references to Old Testament worship being superseded by the sacrifice of the cross seem more relevant to a Jewish audience. Gentiles had little experience with the old law.

Reginald Fuller states that Hebrews is often called "the roll call of the heroes of faith." But since heroes extoll their own achievements, this is not quite accurate. Hebrews attests to the role of faith in salvation history. Faith requires that believers take seriously what God promises for the future. Faith requires that we step out and follow God's will no matter where that may take us. Like Abraham we are to go forward, not knowing where we are going, assured that God will lead and provide.

The author of Hebrews intended to describe faith. A person who has faith is characterized by a certain assurance and conviction. Faith is evidence that the believer holds the deed to the promised land of future glory in heaven.

Gospel
Luke 12:32-48

Jesus exhorts the disciples about being prepared.

STEP 1
NAMING ONE'S EXPERIENCE

What were your first impressions? What was your first response? What grabbed your attention? How did you feel?

Each person names his or her initial impression. Statement should be brief. No reasons should be given at this time. All simply listen without agreeing or disagreeing.

---
[4]Myles M. Bourke, "The Epistle to the Hebrews," in *The New Jerome Biblical Commentary*, ed. Raymond E. Brown, S.S., Joseph A. Fitzmyer, S.J., Roland E. Murphy, O.Carm. (Englewood Cliffs: Prentice Hall, 1990), 921.

STEP 2
UNDERSTANDING

In a brief statement, what do you think this gospel is trying to convey?

STEP 3
INPUT FROM VISION/STORY/TRADITION

Liturgical Context

The introductory rites assert our incorporation into God's covenant and our place within salvation history. Today we remember what God has done throughout all time. We celebrate all his wonders and marvels. We are reminded of Christ's passover and our incorporation into his life, death, and resurrection. Our entire liturgy is a remembrance and a living of that reality. We remember, celebrate, and make present the sacrifice of Calvary.

The alternative opening prayer reminds us that we are children of God and that we are to grow in the life of Christ. Jesus gives us the blueprint today for that growth. We are to become detached from all that keeps us from centering on God. We are to be prepared for the "Day of the Lord" whether that be at our death or at the second coming. Each liturgy exhorts us to be prepared. "Christ has died, Christ is Risen, Christ will Come again!" "Lord, by your cross and resurrection you have set us free; you are the Savior of the world." "When we eat this bread and drink this cup we proclaim your death, Lord, until you come in glory." Each of those acclamations reminds us that it is the paschal banquet we celebrate. By waiting in hope for Christ's return, we express our willingness to to be prepared. We pray for the day when the Lord will come again.

Gospel Exegesis

The facilitator gives input regarding what critical biblical scholarship has to say about this text. The input includes insights as to how people would have heard the gospel in Jesus' time.

Chapter 12 through chapter 13:9 is a single teaching that takes place in one locale. It addresses two audiences: the disciples and the crowd. There are three or four topics addressed. Sometimes the topic is provoked by a question or is a response to a particular request. During this lengthy teaching Jesus cautions his disciples about hypocrisy. He warns them about the persecution they will encounter because of him. He challenges them to trust God for their basic needs. He asks them to give their property away and he calls them to faithfulness as they await the coming of Jesus a second time.

Detachment from possessions is seen as a preparation for the coming of the Son of Man. Luke's primary concern is what the coming of the Son of Man means for the disciples. Since it will be an unexpected event, he wants to make sure that disciples are constantly on guard and ready at all times to meet the Lord when he comes.

At this second coming the Lord still serves his guests (disciples) who recline at table. Thus, even the glorified Christ still serves at the eschatological banquet. Imagine being served at table by none other than the Lord himself.

Verses 39-48 contain a warning for the religious leaders of the house churches. Jesus insists that religious community leaders must behave lovingly toward those they serve. It is a common concern of Jesus' throughout Luke's gospel. Robert Tannehill summarizes the primary agenda of the twelfth chapter of Luke as "faithful fulfillment of leadership responsibility, willingness to suffer and right attitude toward wealth."[5]

This pericope begins with an exhortation that we are to sell what we have and give to the poor. This is a consistent theme through Luke's gospel. It is at the heart of the radical call of Christ in the gospel. He spoke his message to the rich and the not so rich. In the "Sermon on the Plain" in chapter 6 of Luke's gospel, Jesus instructed his disciples to give to everyone who asks and to lend while expecting nothing in return (6:35). In today's reading from Luke's chapter 12, Jesus told his disciples to sell their possessions and give alms.[6] Jesus was detached from his possessions and lived a life of simplicity. This simplicity provides freedom for others.

Another theme in today's reading from chapter 12 emerges in verse 35 and cuts to the heart of Christianity: Christ's passing from death to life. Christ is the New Passover and we are participants in his life, death, and resurrection—the paschal mystery. "Let your belts be fastened around your waists and your lamps be burning ready" (v. 35) is a reference to passover. This ritual action was prescribed by law for all who observed the annual Jewish Passover. The first reading recalls the exodus event and is a reminder that the people were heirs to the benefits of the exodus and its inherent blessings. Luke's connection to the exodus ritual reminds the listener that Christ is the New Covenant, the new Passover. Through his passing from this world into his new, resurrected life, he accomplished for the world the completion of God's plan for our salvation. During the time when Luke was writing there existed a hope that Jesus would return during this annual Passover commemoration.

The allusion to reclining at table was seen already fulfilled in the eucharistic banquet. Luke's community had to reconcile the fact that Jesus had not returned as quickly as expected. They were aware (as we are today) that his resurrected presence lived on in their gathering for eucharist. The ancients understood, as we do today, that the ritual gathering is an *anamnesis,* that is, a remembering that makes the reality present. For example, the Passover story has always been told in Jewish households with the understanding that, in the telling, the same saving grace that was offered to their ancestors is present for them as well. This, too, is our belief in the eucharist. Every time we gather for eucharist, when we tell the story, break the bread, and share the meal, we make real the remembered presence of Christ in our midst.

The bottom line of today's parable is preparedness. We are to be ready for the Master's return. We are given a bird's-eye view of what will happen

[5]Robert C. Tannehill, *The Narrative Unity of Luke-Acts: A Literary Interpretation,* Vol. I (Minneapolis: Augsburg Fortress, 1986), 240-251.

[6]Richard J. Cassidy, *Jesus, Politics, and Society* (Maryknoll: Orbis Books, 1978), 26-27.

to those who are aware of the implications of his return yet ignore them. While those ignorant of his promised return will receive the least punishment, all are nevertheless held responsible. It is a sobering challenge today. Are we really ready to meet Christ when he comes again?

Proclaim the gospel again.

Sometimes we gain new insights when we hear the text after the interpretation has been given. Someone from the group proclaims the gospel a second time.

STEP 4
TESTING

Conversation with the Liturgy and the Scriptures

Test your original understanding in dialogue with the text.

(You might consider breaking into smaller groups.)

How does the interpretation of the readings impact your life? Were there any new insights? Was there anything you had not considered before? How does your original understanding of these texts compare with what we just shared? How does this story speak to your life?

Participants share an experience from their lives that connects with the biblical interpretation just shared.

> *A friend of mine met an elderly couple in the grocery store. They excitedly shared the good news with her. "Guess what! Jesus is coming back again very soon!" My friend politely acknowledged the sweet enthusiasm of the couple as she mused to herself. She thought the idea fanciful. It was certainly possible that Jesus would come again soon, but even more probable was the reality that, for them, Jesus would indeed be coming soon. They were very old and infirm and probably did not have many years left before they would meet Jesus face-to-face in the hereafter.*

> *Today's gospel is about preparedness. We are to be prepared whether it be for Jesus' return or for our union with him at our death (for neither of which we know the day or hour).*

There are three themes floating through today's readings. All three themes form the heart of our Christian life: detachment, preparedness, and willingness to embrace the cross and the paschal mystery. If one is detached and living the paschal mystery it would appear to follow that one is also prepared for the coming of Christ or the end of one's life.

Across the state where I live there is a bank building that has what appears to be an image of Mary on its front. It is strikingly clear and easy to see. Scientists attest that it is there because of oxidation with the air and the salt spray from the bay. Whether it is a miracle from our heavenly mother or a scientific phenomenon makes no difference. What strikes me is that the building is barraged by hordes of pilgrims coming to see the image. Why must we chase such phenomena? We encounter a miracle every time we gather as a diverse people to share the Body and Blood of Christ. The message of the apparitions is the same as the message of the gospel: Jesus died and rose for our sins. We are to embrace the cross of Christ, share the good news, and follow Jesus. We prepare ourselves for Christ's coming or our death (whichever is first) every time we live the gospel, every time we share what we have with the poor, every time we work for justice, and every time we acknowledge our dependence on God by following the gospel.

All share their life experience.

What was Luke's message to his community? What are the implications today? In what way am I/we living or not living the message of Jesus regarding wealth, possessions, preparedness, and the paschal mystery? What might God be creating in us through this experience of Jesus in the gospel? In what way does this gospel point to God's promise to be with us? In what way have we known death/resurrection in our understanding of this gospel? How is God speaking to us as a community? Do we still feel the same way about this text as we did when we began? Has our original understanding been stretched, challenged, or affirmed?

STEP 5
DECISION

The gospel demands a response.

In what way does this gospel call us to action? Has this conversation with the exegesis changed or stretched my personal attitudes? What are the implications for my life? What am I/we/community/parish called to do in response? What is one concrete action we will take this week as a response to was learned and shared today?

DOCTRINAL ISSUES

What church truth/teaching/doctrinal issue could be drawn from the gospel for the Nineteenth Sunday in Ordinary Time?

Participants suggest possible doctrinal themes that flow from the readings.

Possible Doctrinal Themes

Paschal mystery, faith, Reign of God (present and future), cross, eschatology

Present the doctrinal material at this time.

1. The facilitator gives input on a particular doctrinal issue of his/her prior choosing. OR
2. The group chooses a doctrinal issue from the list they created. They read together from the Doctrinal Appendix.

(The doctrinal issues are found in the Doctrinal Appendix in the back of this workbook. If you are choosing an issue from this resource, please refer to it now.)

Reflection questions centered around the chosen doctrinal theme can be found at the end of each topic in the Doctrinal Appendix. The questions are based on the five-step reflection process. If you choose a topic not included in the Doctrinal Appendix, craft your own questions according to the same five-step process.

Following the reflection questions you will be reminded to return to chapter 7, "Preparing the Catechetical Session," to assist you in crafting your own session.

Closing Prayer

Let us pray.
Lord,

may the Eucharist you give us
bring us to salvation
and keep us faithful to the light of your truth.
We ask this in the name of Jesus the Lord.[7]

Selected Bibliography

Bourke, Myles M. "The Epistle to the Hebrews." In *The New Jerome Biblical Commentary.* Ed. Raymond E. Brown, S.S., Joseph A. Fitzmyer, S.J., Roland E. Murphy, O.Carm. Englewood Cliffs: Prentice Hall, 1990.

Cassidy, Richard J. *Jesus, Politics, and Society.* Maryknoll: Orbis Books, 1978.

Fuller, Reginald H. *Preaching the New Lectionary.* Collegeville: The Liturgical Press, 1974.

Sanchez, Patricia Datchuck. *The Word We Celebrate.* Kansas City: Sheed and Ward, 1989.

Tannehill, Robert C. *The Narrative Unity of Luke-Acts: A Literary Interpretation.* Vol. I. Minneapolis: Augsburg Fortress, 1986.

Wright, Addison G., S.S. "Wisdom." In *The New Jerome Biblical Commentary.* Ed. Raymond E. Brown, S.S., Joseph A. Fitzmyer, S.J., Roland E. Murphy, O.Carm. Englewood Cliffs: Prentice Hall, 1990.

---

[7]Nineteenth Sunday in Ordinary Time: "Prayer After Communion," *The Sacramentary.*

TWENTIETH SUNDAY IN ORDINARY TIME

INTRODUCTORY RITES

Opening Song (or Entrance Antiphon)

God, our protector, keep us in mind; always give strength to your people. For if we can be with you even one day, it is better than a thousand without you. (Ps 83:10-11)[1]

Opening Prayer

The facilitator of the session may lead the prayer. Others in the group may be asked to proclaim the readings.

Let us pray
[with humility and persistence]

Pause for silent prayer.

Almighty God, ever loving Father,
your care extends beyond the boundaries of race
    and nation
to the hearts of all who live.
May the walls, which prejudice raises between us,
crumble beneath the shadow of your outstretched
    arm.
We ask this through Christ, our Lord.[2]

LITURGY OF THE WORD

Let us listen to God's word.

The readings are proclaimed.

First Reading
Jeremiah 38:4-6, 8-10

For further background on the prophet Jeremiah, refer to the first reading for the Fourth Sunday in Ordinary Time. The event leading up to this pericope has to do with the encounter between Jeremiah and Zedekiah during the siege of Jerusalem in 588-587 B.C.E. Zedekiah was one of the last kings of Judah. He was a weak, spineless, puppet leader under the control of Babylon, the conquering nation. He foolishly believed that he could revolt against his powerful overlords and live to tell about it. When Jerusalem was under siege, Zedekiah asked Jeremiah what the outcome would be. Jeremiah did not give him the assurance he was hoping for. Jeremiah remained steadfast in his directive: to revolt meant suicide. Submission was the only way to survive. Jeremiah called the people to prayer and repentance. In the middle of the siege, Jeremiah was asked to summon Yahweh for help. Instead, Jeremiah insisted that Nebuchadnezzar would win, even with his crippled army. Needless to say, this did not make Zedekiah happy. Jeremiah was arrested for the treasonous act of leaving his post. Zedekiah consulted Jeremiah again, hoping for a reprieve, but his word remained steadfast. Jerusalem would fall.[3] This is where today's reading begins.

The nobles charged Jeremiah with demoralizing the troops, which would ultimately cause them to go down in defeat. So as not to cause a riot by publicly executing Jeremiah, the nobles lowered him into a pit and left him to die.

Because of the unique construction of the cistern, it would normally have been impossible for Jeremiah to escape on his own. However, King Zedekiah's Ethiopian servant pleaded for Jeremiah's life and subsequently rescued him. Thus, it was not an Israelite, but a foreigner that Yahweh used as the means to continue his plan of salvation.[4]

Reginald Fuller suggests that this text should be read in light of Jeremiah's prayer in chapter 15 in which he bemoans the suffering he has had to endure for the sake of Yahweh's word. Fuller main-

---

[1]Twentieth Sunday in Ordinary Time: "Entrance Antiphon," *The Sacramentary*.

[2]Twentieth Sunday in Ordinary Time: "Alternative Opening Prayer," *The Sacramentary*.

[3]Guy P. Couturier, C.S.C., "Jeremiah," in *The New Jerome Biblical Commentary*, ed. Raymond E. Brown, S.S., Joseph A. Fitzmyer, S.J., Roland E. Murphy, O.Carm. (Englewood Cliffs: Prentice Hall, 1990), 292-293.

[4]Patricia Datchuck Sanchez, *The Word We Celebrate* (Kansas City: Sheed and Ward, 1989), 356-357.

tains that it is not the deliverance of Jeremiah that is the connection to today's gospel but, rather, the suffering and rejection Jeremiah encountered for the sake of the word. "The passion of Jeremiah foreshadows the passion of Jesus adumbrated in the gospel reading."[5]

Responsorial Psalm
Psalm 40:2, 3, 4, 18

The main thrust of this psalm is the deliverance of the psalmist. This psalm was chosen because of its reference to the miry bog (cistern well) in the second stanza. However, deliverance is not the key message of the first reading and the gospel. Rejection is.

Second Reading
Hebrews 12:1-4

Once again the author of Hebrews gives accolades to the ancient heroes of faith of the Old Testament. Heroes like Abraham are models of faith and worthy of emulation. The letter to the Hebrews reminds the community that they must persevere in the painful, difficult situations they face. Like the athlete who commits his or her total self to the completion of the goal, so too must the Christian display similar courage, perseverance, and commitment.

The "cloud of witnesses" refers to those who stand behind the athletes to cheer them on. The witnesses were the ancient heroes of faith who had gone before to show the way. They stood in the stands to support the athletes as they moved toward their goal.

Even though the ancient heroes were to be venerated and imitated, their influence paled in comparison to the influence of Jesus' pasch. This pasch—the passion, cross, death, and resurrection of Christ—was to be the ultimate object of imitation.

The author of Hebrews reminded his readers that Jesus faced persecution and rejection (see today's gospel and Jeremiah in the first reading). The author was consoling his readers who had also been persecuted and had been rejected by both their Jewish neighbors and the Roman authorities. They were not to give up. Their persecution had not resulted in bloodshed as yet, but the Hebrews were to pray for the strength to persevere daily and endure martyrdom for the sake of the gospel, if that is where their faith should lead.

Gospel
Luke 12:49-53

Jesus warns of his coming baptism by fire. He alerts his audience that they face a time of decision. The decisions will ultimately cause chaos and disruption and pit family members against one another.

STEP 1
NAMING ONE'S EXPERIENCE

What were your first impressions? What was your first response? What grabbed your attention? How did you feel?

Each person names his or her initial impression. Statement should be brief. No reasons should be given at this time. All simply listen without agreeing or disagreeing.

STEP 2
UNDERSTANDING

In a brief statement, what do you think this gospel is trying to convey?

STEP 3
INPUT FROM VISION/STORY/TRADITION

Liturgical Context

The beautiful alternative opening prayer reflects the longing of each heart as we stand concerned over the implications of today's difficult gospel. Will our families be pitted against us? Who will choose for Christ and who will not? How many parents in our Sunday assemblies stand fearful and saddened by the proclamation of this gospel because of children who no longer profess faith in Christ? It is their deepest sorrow. Jesus does not gloss over the reali-

---

[5]Reginald H. Fuller, *Preaching the New Lectionary* (Collegeville: The Liturgical Press, 1974), 527.

ties of discipleship, but cautions us to keep our focus on him. Nothing is to deter us from our purpose. Nothing is to keep us from our intended mission: incorporation into the life and mission of Christ. The alternative opening prayer puts it all in wonderful perspective. God is bigger than our narrow, limited perceptions. We pray in confidence that God can and will change hearts. The prayer expresses our desire that God will transcend our prejudices and crumble the barriers that exist between us. The communion antiphon expresses our hope and our assurance, "With the Lord there is mercy and fullness of redemption" (Ps 129:7).

The symbol of fire alluded to in today's gospel is very close to the heart of the liturgy. Even today fire is considered a sign of God's presence. A lamp remains lit in every sanctuary as a sign of God's illuminating presence in the eucharist. Candles serve as a reminder that Christ is present in the midst of the gathered assembly. Fire is used at the Easter Vigil as a sign of God's ultimate theophany and is blessed as a symbol of the resurrected presence of Christ, the Light of the World.[6]

Gospel Exegesis

The facilitator gives input regarding what critical biblical scholarship has to say about this text. The input includes insights as to how people would have heard the gospel in Jesus' time.

This gospel is set in the context of the continuing instruction of the disciples discussed last week. The disciples were beginning to discover that following Jesus was, rather than smooth sailing, a turbulent affair. Conflicts were erupting, sometimes even in the same family.[7] It was important that

---

[6]Irene Nowell, O.S.B., "Fire," in *The Collegeville Pastoral Dictionary of Biblical Theology*, ed. Carroll Stuhlmueller, C.P. (Collegeville: The Liturgical Press, 1996), 337.

[7]Even Jesus' own family thought that he had gone insane. In Mark 3:21 we read, "He went home again, and once more such a crowd collected that they could not even have a meal. When his relatives heard of this, they set out to take charge of him, convinced that he was out of his mind." Mark clearly identifies these relatives as Jesus' mother and brothers. Jesus was obviously an embarrassment to the family. (Jerome Murphy O'Connor, "Do the Gospels Paint a Clear Picture of Jesus?" *America,* Dec. 1996), 9.

Christians keep their perspective and assert their priorities. Jesus addressed the entire gathered crowd. His message was an urgent call to conversion before it was too late.[8]

Jesus compares his mission to a baptism by fire. Scholars assert that *fire* is open to interpretation. It could mean the coming judgment when the Son of Man returns or possibly the eschatological gift of the Spirit at Pentecost.[9] Regardless, his imagery helps drive home the point: there is passionate urgency—LISTEN AND TAKE HEED!

Jesus came to bring peace, but not the peace understood in human terms. Sometimes we want to focus on the positive side of Jesus' mission rather than on the hard message. It is unthinkable that following Christ may cause divisiveness and discord in our own families. However, God will not tamper with our freedom. People are free to choose to follow Christ or not to follow him. They will either be open to the light or they will not. All must decide; people are either with Jesus or they are not.

Throughout scripture fire had multiple layers of meaning. It was used as a metaphor for God and God's protection. It was a natural symbol of both anger and judgment and connoted testing and purification.[10] Fire was the medium of the theophany with Moses (burning bush) and Israel in the desert (pillar of fire). Fire was used as a metaphor for God and God's intervention in human affairs. The use of fire in today's gospel is to assert that Jesus' mission is to purify the earth with fire.

The baptism Jesus spoke of was not the kind that incorporates Christians into the paschal mystery. Rather, Jesus' baptism in this instance is the horrifying ordeal he is about to endure for the sake of all people. It is a baptism of purification, suffering, and death. Only through such baptism will the Spirit be released as tongues of fire to emblazon the earth. Such a radical occurrence naturally will prompt controversy and discord. In the midst of the purifying fire, families stand before God and must choose.

---

[8]Luke Timothy Johnson, *The Gospel of Luke*, Sacra Pagina Series, Vol. 3 (Collegeville: The Liturgical Press, 1991), 209.

[9]Ibid.

[10]Nowell, "Fire," 334.

There was an apocalyptic tradition that believed that in the last age the family unit would disintegrate. Family members would be pitted against one another because of the moral depravity of the people. Since Jesus' death and resurrection were the fulfillment and transition into the messianic age, the disruption had begun with Christ. Christians were living in the messianic age and thus could expect familial conflict. It was a decisive moment. It is still a decisive moment.

Proclaim the gospel again.

Sometimes we gain new insights when we hear the text after the interpretation has been given. Someone from the group proclaims the gospel a second time.

STEP 4
TESTING

Conversation with the Liturgy and the Scriptures

Test your original understanding in dialogue with the text.

(You might consider breaking into smaller groups.)

Is there anything about these readings that makes you uncomfortable? How do you feel about the interpretation? Does it resonate with your original understanding of this gospel? Were there any new insights? Was there anything you had not considered before? How does this story speak to your life?

Participants share an experience from their lives that connects with the biblical interpretation just shared.

> *Someone told me the story of a couple who were divorced. One of the reasons given for the breakup was that the husband could not accept his wife's faith tradition. He found the practice of her faith to be annoying and was unwilling to discuss it with her. There was no more to be said—it was over. Their marriage was over and the reason given made no sense! The wife was devastated.*

> *This woman can speak from first-hand experience about today's gospel. Many of us experience the implications in small ways. My children sometimes ac-*

cuse me of having old-fashioned values that no longer apply (WRONG!). I have been accused of not being "spiritual enough" by people who know me only from afar. But I have never personally experienced a father turning against a mother, or a brother against a sister, or a husband against a wife.

The closest I have ever come was in the early years of marriage. I prayerfully discerned that I was to support a decision my parents felt was not in my best interest. They believed I had lost all balance in my spirituality (looking back it is possible that they were right). However hurtful that was, it in no way compares to the experience of my friend. An entire family was destroyed.

This very difficult gospel is a reminder that Christianity is not a "pie in the sky" religion. It has implications and consequences and often the price is high. Sometimes the cost is more than we can endure to pay. No wonder Jesus was speaking with such urgency. It is very easy to lose sight of the ultimate priority when one's life is crumbling before one.

All share their life experience.

What was Luke saying to his community? How is it relevant to our community today? Where are images of death, liberation, and resurrection evident in these readings? In what way are the biblical themes of exodus, creation, covenant, and community evident? Do we still feel the same way about this text as we did when we began? Has our original understanding been stretched, challenged, or affirmed?

STEP 5
DECISION

The gospel demands a response.

How is your community challenged by this conversation? Be concrete. Have you experienced conversion as a result of this sharing? What are you/your community/your parish called to do in response? Name one concrete action you will take this week as a response to what was learned and shared today.

DOCTRINAL ISSUES

What church truth/teaching/doctrinal issue could be drawn from the gospel for the Twentieth Sunday in Ordinary Time?

Participants suggest possible doctrinal themes that flow from the readings.

Possible Doctrinal Themes

Paschal mystery, cross, fire, cost of discipleship, soteriology (salvation)

Present the doctrinal material at this time.

1. The facilitator gives input on a particular doctrinal issue of his/her prior choosing. OR
2. The group chooses a doctrinal issue from the list they created. They read together from the Doctrinal Appendix.

(The doctrinal issues are found in the Doctrinal Appendix in the back of this workbook. If you are choosing an issue from this resource, please refer to it now.)

Reflection questions centered around the chosen doctrinal theme can be found at the end of each topic in the Doctrinal Appendix. The questions are based on the five-step reflection process. If you choose a topic not included in the Doctrinal Appendix, craft your own questions according to the same five-step process.

Following the reflection questions you will be reminded to return to chapter 7, "Preparing the Catechetical Session," to assist you in crafting your own session.

Closing Prayer

God our Father,
source of unity and love,
make your faithful people one in heart and mind
that your Church may live in harmony;
be steadfast in its profession of faith,
and secure in unity.
We ask this through our Lord, Jesus Christ, your
   Son,

who lives and reigns with you and the Holy Spirit,
one God for ever and ever.[11]

Lord,
as we receive the sacrament of unity,
help us live together in your household
united in mind and heart.
May we experience the peace we preach to others
and cling to the peace we receive in the eucharist.[12]

Selected Bibliography

Couturier, Guy P., C.S.C. "Jeremiah." In *The New Jerome Biblical Commentary*. Ed. Raymond E. Brown, S.S., Joseph A. Fitzmyer, S.J., Roland E. Murphy, O.Carm. Englewood Cliffs: Prentice Hall, 1990.

Johnson, Luke Timothy. *The Gospel of Luke*. Sacra Pagina Series. Vol. 3. Collegeville: The Liturgical Press, 1991.

Nowell, Irene, O.S.B. "Fire." In *The Collegeville Pastoral Dictionary of Biblical Theology*. Ed. Carroll Stuhlmueller, C.P. Collegeville: The Liturgical Press, 1996.

Sanchez, Patricia Datchuck. *The Word We Celebrate*. Kansas City: Sheed and Ward, 1989.

---

[11]Mass for Promoting Harmony: "Opening Prayer," *The Sacramentary*.

[12]Mass for Promoting Harmony: "Prayer After Communion," *The Sacramentary*.

Twenty-First Sunday in Ordinary Time

INTRODUCTORY RITES

Opening Song (or Entrance Antiphon)

Listen, Lord and answer me. Save your servant who trusts in you. I call to you all day long, have mercy on me. (Ps 85:1-3)[1]

Opening Prayer

The facilitator of the session may lead the prayer. Others in the group may be asked to proclaim the readings.
Let us pray

[with minds fixed on eternal truth]

Pause for silent prayer.

Lord our God,
all truth is from you,
and you alone bring oneness of heart.
Give your people the joy
of hearing your word in every sound
and of longing for your presence more than for
 life itself.
May all the attractions of a changing world
serve only to bring us
the peace of your kingdom which this world does
 not give.
Grant this through Christ our Lord.[2]

LITURGY OF THE WORD

Let us listen to God's word.

The readings are proclaimed.

First Reading
Isaiah 66:18-21

Isaiah 66 is considered part of Third Isaiah (ca. 5th century B.C.E.). It is believed to have been written by someone other than the authors of the

first two books. Second Isaiah (ch. 40–55) was written to support Israel during her Babylonian captivity (6th century B.C.E.) Third Isaiah was written as a prophetic book following the Babylonian exile. The tone of the book is apocalyptic. It looks forward to the creation of a new heaven and a new earth. Jerusalem will be restored and will be home to an incredible and unimaginable peace in which the lion and lamb dine at the same table. In the apocalyptic age, clear distinctions between the righteous and the unrighteous will be drawn.

Isaiah's image of the messianic age was one in which people would be gathered in Zion from all corners of the earth. In verse 19 we are told that a sign will go forth. Some scholars believe that the sign is missionary in magnitude and refers to the faithful remnant who will go forth to spread the word and gather the nations.

Responsorial Psalm
Psalm 117:1, 2

This psalm is a summons to the nations to praise Yahweh and is used by Christians to extol the universal mission Christ. Its missionary tone connects it appropriately to the first reading.

Second Reading
Hebrews 12:5-7, 11-13

The readers of the letter to the Hebrews had been Christian for a long time. They were growing frustrated and complacent. Jesus' return was not as imminent as once thought and discouragement had set in. The *discipline* spoken of in the text probably referred to prejudices and persecution experienced at the hands of their friends and non-Christian neighbors.

The theme of today's first reading and gospel is strongly universal. Hebrews, on the other hand, seems to reflect an "in-house" agenda. However, it is easily connected to the theme of universality when one realizes the implication of the Hebrew exhortation. Wherever and whenever the church suffers in any way, whether that be through serious persecution, dwindling numbers, or apathy, we are to view it as discipline. We are disciplined as a

---

[1]Twenty-First Sunday in Ordinary Time: "Entrance Antiphon," *The Sacramentary.*

[2]Twenty-First Sunday in Ordinary Time: "Alternative Opening Prayer," *The Sacramentary.*

church. This discipline is a sign of God's love of the church. (One cannot help but recall St. Theresa's complaint: "Lord, if this is how you treat your friends, it is no wonder you have so few.")

The theology of Hebrews asserts that suffering is to be seen as necessary for growth, not punishment for wrongdoing. In some cultures young males undergo rigorous, often painful rites of passage that form and strengthen them for entrance into adult life. This is the type of discipline referred to in today's pericope. It is the kind of suffering that forms the soul in the crucible of fire.

Last week the author used the imagery of the athlete competing in a race. This week the imagery shifts to the "road pilgrims traveled on their way to God."[3] Once the destination is realized, the Christian is able to place the suffering in proper perspective. A mother forgets the pain of childbirth in the joy of her new infant.

Gospel
Luke 13:22-30

Jesus speaks of the universal mission of salvation and warns people not to be complacent and presumptuous.

STEP 1
NAMING ONE'S EXPERIENCE

What were your first impressions? What was your first response? What grabbed your attention? How did you feel?

Each person names his or her initial impression. Statement should be brief. No reasons should be given at this time. All simply listen without agreeing or disagreeing.

STEP 2
UNDERSTANDING

In a brief statement, what do you think this gospel is trying to convey?

---

[3]Patricia Datchuck Sanchez, *The Word We Celebrate* (Kansas City: Sheed and Ward, 1989), 360.

STEP 3
INPUT FROM VISION/STORY/TRADITION

Liturgical Context

Today's readings are the last in a series of instructions that began on the Eighteenth Sunday. Today's gospel serves as a conclusion to Jesus' teachings on salvation, how one should live, and the choices one must make.

Today's alternative opening prayer articulates the posture we should have in response to Jesus' exhortations in today's gospel. If we truly have the joy of hearing God's word in all we do, if we long for God's presence more than for life itself, then our hearts will naturally be repentant as we recognize our total dependence on our God who saves.

The liturgy upholds the relationship we must have with God in order to make the appropriate choices necessary to live in the fullness of salvation that Christ won for us. If we take seriously Jesus' urgent challenge in today's gospel, then we will make the prayers of the introductory rites our own. We will beckon the Lord to answer our pleas. We will trust God and call on him all day long, for God gives us his mercy. Without repentant hearts we cannot pray that prayer with sincerity.

Through our sharing in the suffering of Christ we are opened to the "universal mystery of salvation: what is impossible for us is actually done by God."[4] The eucharist frees us from sin. It is the ongoing sacrament of salvation as we await the final consummation of the world. The eucharist heals us and strengthens us. The communion antiphon asserts the power of eucharist: "The Lord says: The man who eats my flesh and drinks my blood will live for ever; I shall raise him to life on the last day" (Jn 6:55). Eucharistic Prayer IV best sums up the implications of today's readings.

This would be an appropriate day to celebrate a Rite of Acceptance or the blessing of catechumens with oil.

---

[4]*Days of the Lord*, Vol. 6 (Collegeville: The Liturgical Press, 1991), 181.

Gospel Exegesis

The facilitator gives input regarding what critical biblical scholarship has to say about this text. The input includes insights as to how people would have heard the gospel in Jesus' time.

This entire section begins with a sober reminder that Jesus was on his way to Jerusalem. All warnings, reminders, and teachings are framed with the realization of where Jesus is heading. There is reason for the urgency of his message. Jesus will soon be reaching the end of his earthly sojourn. The stakes are high. Jerusalem is the place where God will effect the salvation of the people through Jesus' passion, death, and resurrection. Jerusalem is pivotal for Luke. His is the only gospel that begins and ends there.

Luke frames his entire gospel in the journey motif. It not only serves to place Jesus' story in the context of his ultimate destination, but it functions as a metaphor for the life of a Christian. Christians are formed by the journey. They learn what it means to live in the reign of God by actually living in it. There is nothing in the world that compares to it. It does not fit our worldly constraints and standards. The reign of God surprises us and turns our world view on end. God plays no favorites. Entry is not guaranteed. It is not "who you know," but how you live that determines entry. In other words, those who self-righteously think they belong at the head of the line may be surprised to find themselves ejected from the line altogether.

Someone in the crowd asked Jesus if few would be saved (v. 23). Jewish understanding of the messianic age assumed that all of Israel would be saved. "Israel's impending salvation is anticipated as unfolding at the expense of other nations, whose wealth will be seized and given to Yahweh's elect."[5] They were the "few" of biblical history and understanding. The "many" *unsaved* included sinners, tax collectors, the unclean, and gentiles. Jesus turned this bias upside down and implied that their narrow restrictions were not the way of the kingdom. Self-righteous individuals who were certain that they belonged to the *few saved* would

rather find themselves among *many unsaved*. Their status as "chosen" had created complacency and a presumption that salvation was a given.

Jesus' audience included people who had eaten with Jesus, listened to him in their towns, and perhaps offered him hospitality. Yet from the tone of the dialogue it appears that many of them were included in the list of the unsaved. The implication is: it will do them no good to have known Jesus in the past if their hearts are still unrepentant. There is no room at the table for unrepentant hearts. Religious status or past association does not guarantee a seat. Sinners, gentiles, and tax collectors would take their place. Foreigners would take their place. What an affront!

Some in the crowd were accused of being against Jesus and not responding to his message. Jesus provided an urgent warning. Tension was mounting in the story. Last week the crowd was told that even family members might turn against them. This week they are warned that if they are not careful, even they could lose the salvation Jesus is offering.[6] A decision had to be made quickly and decisively.

Proclaim the gospel again.

Sometimes we gain new insights when we hear the text after the interpretation has been given. Someone from the group proclaims the gospel a second time.

STEP 4
TESTING

Conversation with the Liturgy and the Scriptures

Test your original understanding in dialogue with the text.

(You might consider breaking into smaller groups.)

Were there any new insights? Was there anything you had not considered before? How does your original understanding of this story compare with

---

[5]J. Kenneth Kuntz, *The People of Ancient Israel* (New York: Harper and Row, 1974), 421.

[6]Robert C. Tannehill, *The Narrative Unity of Luke-Acts: A Literary Interpretation*, Vol. 1 (Minneapolis: Augsburg Fortress, 1986), 152-153.

what was just shared? How does this story speak to your life?

Participants share an experience from their lives that connects with the biblical interpretation just shared.

> *Jesus is challenging our assemblies. It is very sobering. It reminds us that we cannot sit on our laurels and assume that salvation is ours without care or concern for living the rigorous demands of discipleship. Salvation is for all people. We can choose to accept it or reject it. I often wonder what would happen if one of us were to bring a dirty, homeless person to our assembly and seat that person in the front row. Would our attitude be one of welcome or one of self-righteous indignation?*

> *Jesus' salvation is for everyone. I wonder how many of us really believe that this includes people like our homeless drug addicts and alcoholics. Jesus warns us today that we cannot be so smug that we assume that we are "in" and others are "out." To complacently make such assumptions is dangerous to our future (as proclaimed in the gospel today). Our primary concern is to live our lives according to the pattern of Jesus. Salvation is serious business. It should receive our/my serious attention.*

All share their life experience.

What was Luke's message to his community? What does he have to say to our community and to me today? There are strong images of the biblical themes of covenant, exodus, creation, and community inherent in these readings. How are these images evident? Do we still feel the same way about this text as we did when we began? Has our original understanding been stretched, challenged, or affirmed?

STEP 5
DECISION

The gospel demands a response.

How does our sharing and this biblical interpretation challenge our communal attitudes? Have we in any way experienced change as a result of this sharing? What am I/we/community/parish called to do in response to these readings? What is one concrete action we will take this week as a response to what was learned and shared today?

DOCTRINAL ISSUES

What church truth/teaching/doctrinal issue could be drawn from the gospel for the Twenty-First Sunday in Ordinary Time?

Participants suggest possible doctrinal themes that flow from the readings.

Possible Doctrinal Themes

Salvation, evangelization, reign of God, paschal mystery, discipleship

Present the doctrinal material at this time.

1. The facilitator gives input on a particular doctrinal issue of his/her prior choosing. OR
2. The group chooses a doctrinal issue from the list they created. They read together from the Doctrinal Appendix.

(The doctrinal issues are found in the Doctrinal Appendix in the back of this workbook. If you are choosing an issue from this resource, please refer to it now.)

Reflection questions centered around the chosen doctrinal theme can be found at the end of each topic in the Doctrinal Appendix. The questions are based on the five-step reflection process. If you choose a topic not included in the Doctrinal Appendix, craft your own questions according to the same five-step process.

Following the reflection questions you will be reminded to return to chapter 7, "Preparing the Catechetical Session," to assist you in crafting your own session.

Closing Prayer

Father in heaven,
it is right that we should give you thanks and
    glory...

Source of life and goodness, you have created all
  things,
to fill your creatures with every blessing
and lead all men to the joyful vision of your light...
Even when man disobeyed you and lost your
  friendship
you did not abandon him to the power of death,
but helped all men to seek and find you.
Again and again you offered a covenant to man,
and through the prophets taught him to hope for
  salvation.
Father, you so loved the world
that in the fullness of time you sent your
only Son to be our Savior.[7]

Selected Bibliography

Days of the Lord. Vol. 6. Collegeville: The Liturgical
  Press, 1991.
Fuller, Reginald H. *Preaching the New Lectionary.*
  Collegeville: The Liturgical Press, 1974.
Kuntz, J. Kenneth. *The People of Ancient Israel.* New
  York: Harper and Row, 1974.
Sanchez, Patricia Datchuck. *The Word We Celebrate.*
  Kansas City: Sheed and Ward, 1989.
Tannehill, Robert C. *The Narrative Unity of Luke-
  Acts: A Literary Interpretation.* Vol. 1. Minneapo-
  lis: Augsburg Fortress, 1986.

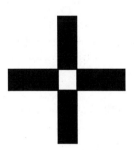

---

[7]"Eucharistic Prayer IV," *The Sacramentary.*

Twenty-Second Sunday in Ordinary Time

INTRODUCTORY RITES

Opening Song (or Entrance Antiphon)

I call to you all day long, have mercy on me, O Lord. You are good and forgiving, full of love for all who call to you. (Ps 85:3, 5)[1]

Environment

It is late summer, early fall. It is a season waiting in transition. The earth is giving up its fruits, families are gearing up to give up their leisure and return to the autumn days of school. Perhaps the standard greens of Ordinary Time can begin to turn to the deep hues of golds, purples, and yellows. Perhaps dried flowers and herbs from the gardens of parishioners may now be added to your environment. It is the time of harvest. "For the church the harvest is an intense scriptural image of the paschal mystery. Paul told us that Jesus Christ is the firstfruits of the dead. Jesus is first, but soon will come all who have died, each reaped into heaven 'in proper order' (1 Cor 15:23). The ingathering began on Calvary, as Jesus breathed forth the life-giving Spirit, and it will be completed on the final day."[2] Imaginative use of harvest images would be appropriate during these weeks.

Opening Prayer

The facilitator of the session may lead the prayer. Others in the group may be asked to proclaim the readings.

Let us pray
[to God who forgives all who call upon him].

Pause for silent prayer.

Lord God of power and might,
nothing is good which is against your will,
and all is of value which comes from your hand.
Place in our hearts a desire to please you

and fill our minds with insight into love,
so that every thought may grow in wisdom
and all our efforts may be filled with your peace.
We ask this through Christ our Lord.[3]

LITURGY OF THE WORD

Let us listen to God's word.

The readings are proclaimed.

First Reading
Sirach 3:17-18, 20, 28-29

Sirach is a book of instruction on the day-to-day living of a well-disciplined, moral life. Please refer to the first reading of the Feast of the Holy Family for further background information on the book of Sirach.

Today's pericope immediately sets the tone for how we are to hear the passage. The author identifies the reader as "my son." "Such a term is loaded with meaning. It is an invitation to adopt an attitude of attentiveness and humility—the attitude of a disciple—to the speaker."[4] This posture of humility is Sirach's most desired virtue. Contrasted with humility is pride, the deadliest sin. Humility means to pray in earnest, "more of you, Lord, and less of me." Sirach is giving a lesson in humility; thus the reason for this pericope. It is directly related to the gospel. Humility is the ultimate act of faith in which the believer abandons the self to the will and care of God. Alexander Di Lella asserts that "the high and mighty have a greater need to be humble than the lowly and weak."[5] In the history of Israel, humility is considered an openness to God's grandeur. The humble give

---

[1]Twenty-Second Sunday in Ordinary Time: "Entrance Antiphon," *The Sacramentary.*

[2]Peter Mazar, *To Crown the Year* (Chicago: Liturgy Training Publications, 1995), 176.

[3]Twenty-Second Sunday in Ordinary Time: "Alternative Opening Prayer," *The Sacramentary.*

[4]*Days of the Lord,* Vol. 6 (Collegeville: The Liturgical Press, 1991), 185.

[5]Alexander Di Lella, O.F.M., "Sirach," in *The New Jerome Biblical Commentary,* ed. Raymond E. Brown, S.S., Joseph A. Fitzmyer, S.J., Roland E. Murphy, O.Carm. (Englewood Cliffs: Prentice Hall, 1990), 499.

praise and thanks to God who provides for all their needs.

Responsorial Psalm
Psalm 68:4-5, 6-7, 10-11

This psalm is a psalm of praise and thanks for God's kindness to the poor. It is believed that rather than one single piece, this psalm is comprised of what seem to read more like chapter titles or headings. By speaking of the "poor," the psalm connects to the first reading's emphasis on humility.

Second Reading
Hebrews 12:18-19, 22-24

This is the last Sunday in Cycle C that we will read from the letter to the Hebrews. These words of exhortation suggest a moral response to living the Christian life. It is a call to safeguard one another from the danger of apostasy. It highlights the way things used to be with the ways things are now. The old way was life under the old law. The new way is life in the new covenant, which is life in heaven. The old law took place on earth; the new law resides in heaven. This reading contrasts the law and the gospel. The author speaks to those who have already won the benefits of heaven through Jesus' paschal mystery, but are still in their earthly sojourn. "He can speak of them as having already arrived."[6] The "firstborn" of verse 23 may be referring to the angels of verse 22 or to the assembly of Christian believers. The terrifying, blazing fire is a reference to the presence and word of God given at Mount Sinai. Jesus' life, death, resurrection, ascension, and sending of the Spirit in Jerusalem inaugurated the *new word*. In the process, people were offered greater access to God. Through baptism, the *firstborn* (church) are offered access to the new covenant. There is realized eschatology in this reading. Believers live in a state of the *kingdom now* and *not yet*. They have access to heaven. They live in its shadow and reality while they journey toward its glory. The faithful live in communion with the saints of old, the saints of now, and the saints to come.

---

[6]Myles M. Bourke, "The Epistle to the Hebrews," in *The New Jerome Biblical Commentary*, ed. Raymond E. Brown, S.S., Joseph A. Fitzmyer, S.J., Roland E. Murphy, O.Carm. (Englewood Cliffs: Prentice Hall, 1990), 940.

Gospel
Luke 14:1, 7-14

The parable of the guest who was invited to the wedding feast.

STEP 1
NAMING ONE'S EXPERIENCE

What were your first impressions? What was your first response? What grabbed your attention? How did you feel?

Each person names his or her initial impression. Statement should be brief. No reasons should be given at this time. All simply listen without agreeing or disagreeing.

STEP 2
UNDERSTANDING

In a brief statement, what do you think this gospel is trying to convey?

STEP 3
INPUT FROM VISION/STORY/TRADITION

Liturgical Context

For the next three Sundays we listen to most of chapter 14 and portions of chapter 15 of Luke's gospel. Contained within those verses are eight of Jesus' parables. The liturgy offers us six for our reflection. Today's parable begins with a meal and the Twenty-fourth Sunday ends with a feast. Thus they are unitive weeks that look forward to the greatest banquet of all at the end of time.

Today's gospel gives a glimpse of our moral response to God in the context of our Christianity. The eucharist is the way we live today's gospel. Do we come as the Pharisees? Do we seek places of honor in our assemblies? Is our posture one of humility or one of arrogant pride? Jesus purposely does not address the Pharisees directly, but rather in the form of parable, so as to be inclusive of anyone who displays similar behavior.

The behavior of the Pharisees is very human behavior and all people are easy prey to the temptation to exalt the self. The liturgy exalts the people of God as a sacrament of the presence of God. The people of God are inclusive of all those whom society rejects.

> They are a people called to offer God the prayers of the entire human family, a people giving thanks in Christ for the mystery of salvation by offering his sacrifice. Finally they are a people growing together in unity by sharing in Christ's Body and Blood. These people are holy by their origin, but becoming ever more holy by conscious, active participation in the mystery of the eucharist.[7]

There is no reason for any person within any ecclesial community to consider himself exalted above the general community. All are dependent on God. Humility demands that we not only be humble but that we embrace all of God's people as equals before God. It will be the humble, the poor, the blind, the crippled, and the lame who will first stand exalted at the future banquet.

Today's prayer after communion exemplifies Jesus' stance in today's gospel. "Let us pray. Lord, you renew us at your table with the bread of life. May this food strengthen us in love and help us to serve you in each other. We ask this in the name of Jesus the Lord."

Gospel Exegesis

The facilitator gives input regarding what critical biblical scholarship has to say about this text. The input includes insights as to how people would have heard the gospel in Jesus' time.

Today's gospel is a hypothetical wedding feast to which the lawyers and the Pharisees were invited. Jesus had observed their behavior at a Sabbath meal and told his parable to address such behavior. The parable presents two situations. In the first hypothetical situation the invited guest pre-

sumes to take an elevated place at the table. As a result of his presumption he is humiliated and loses face. He is sent to the lowest place at the table. The risk in choosing a place of honor lies in the possibility that a higher ranking dignitary might come along and bump the lower ranking person out of his or her exalted place to the lowest place at the table. In this highly shame-based culture, the situation presented would cause untold misery for the guest. He would want to avoid such an embarrassment at all cost.

The second situation is the guest who is honored by the host and other guests because he assumed the lowest place at the table on his own initiative. "Guests who take the lowest place are apt to be called to a higher place by their host."[8] "My friend, come up higher..." (v. 10) lets the reader in on a special intimacy between the host and this guest. "To be greeted as friend and invited higher suggests a special intimacy and, more than that, equality with the host."[9] Those who rush into the place of honor are shamed, while those who are called to the place of honor are exalted. The Christian attitude is not to be imbued with prideful self-importance.

The next piece of this pericope is not a parable, but an exhortation to Jesus' host, an important Pharisee. No longer is there any hypothetical ruse. Jesus openly tells his host not to invite the exalted, but to go out and gather in the poor, the lame, the cripples—the low-class and those who have no chance of reciprocating the kindness. There is to be no expectation of earthly reward. The reward will be given in heaven, the land of the just.

In the old law such people were excluded from priesthood (Lev 21:17-21). At Qumran, the lame, crippled, and blind are not included in the final eschatological battle or even in the final heavenly banquet. Luke extends the term "poor" to include all such marginalized.

Lest we think that Jesus was insulting his host by his accusing parable, we need to consider the cir-

---

[7]"General Instruction to the Roman Missal," #5, *The Sacramentary.*

[8]Eugene LaVerdiere, *Dining in the Kingdom of God* (Chicago: Liturgy Training Publications, 1994), 102.

[9]Luke Timothy Johnson, *The Gospel of Luke,* Sacra Pagina Series, Vol. 3 (Collegeville: The Liturgical Press, 1991), 224.

cumstances of the dinner to which Jesus had been invited. First, Jesus was eating with the same Pharisees that earlier had been trying to set a trap for him (11:31-35). Jesus was being watched. Thus, the dinner invitation was not cordial. Suspicion abounded; it was a hypocritical affair.

Jesus went on the counter-offensive with the parable about the wedding guest. The Pharisees and lawyers were the ones who had sought the places of honor. The punch line of this parable, the last line (v. 14), is the crisis moment. The earlier part of the parable was positing what was already considered proper ethical behavior. The reading from Sirach indicates that humility was a prior biblical value. Jesus' parable was not merely a moral lesson on the virtue of humility. It was a subversive, challenging word. The parabolic reversal is encountered in the last line. The Pharisees sought the places of honor so as to receive honor and respect from the other invited guests. That this was the case is clear in Jesus' words of rebuke for those who invite only people who can reciprocate the kindness. Jesus turns this on end and suggests that it is God's respect they should seek, not that of other human beings. If they do not, God will do the humbling. Their hospitality to the marginalized, with nothing expected in return, will be rewarded by God, not by other human beings.

Jesus does not directly address the offending Pharisees for their ill-advised showy behavior. Instead, he uses the parable to reach a wider audience, to give the parable general significance.[10] It is addressed to all those to whom it might apply.

Jesus' message was paradoxical. Go out and invite the blind, the poor, the lame, and the beggars to your table. Think not that you are better than they. When taking the lowest place at the table, the Christian is acting like Christ.

> Charles de Foucauld said that Jesus took last place for himself so well that no one could ever take it from him. But we know that because of this, he was exalted to the right hand of the Father in the inaccessible glory that belongs to him as Son. And yet, he allows us to share in it by traveling, with him, a similar paschal road.[11]

---

[10]*Days of the Lord*, Vol. 6, 191.

[11]Ibid., 194.

Proclaim the gospel again.

Sometimes we gain new insights when we hear the text after the interpretation has been given. Someone from the group proclaims the gospel a second time.

STEP 4
TESTING

Conversation with the Liturgy and the Scriptures

Test your original understanding in dialogue with the text.

(You might consider breaking into smaller groups.)

Were there any new insights? Was there anything you had not considered before? How does your original understanding of this story compare with what was just shared? How does this story speak to your life?

Participants share an experience from their lives that connects with the biblical interpretation just shared.

> *I am reminded of one cold night when we opened our homeless shelter. It was the night of our Advent reconciliation service. Two of the fellows asked what was going on in church. My husband told them. They asked if they would be welcomed and if they could attend. My husband took them to church. They were dirty, disheveled, and perhaps even smelled of alcohol. They sat in the back of the assembly, were somewhat observant and even mildly engaged in the liturgy. However, one of the them made a comment that prompted a quiet giggle out of the other. Two women who sat in front of them turned to them in disgust and disdain and told them that if they chose to talk again they could leave and not come back.*

> *Granted, the men should not have talked or even quietly giggled. However, I daresay a stray giggle takes place in any given assembly on any given day and ne'er a complaint is uttered. The women were incensed by the behavior of these men and appeared to be disgusted by their very presence. It was almost as if, said my husband, the presence of the men was a sacrilege to God.*

The behavior of the women seemed to betray an attitude of superiority. The paradox of the situation lay in the fact that it all took place in the midst of a reconciliation service. I am sure that any one of us might entertain feelings similar to those expressed in the actions of the women. They acted; we might only entertain the attitude. Both, however, are wrong. Humility demands that we welcome the disheveled stranger and let God do the judging. Why are we any more worthy to come before God than one of our society's rejects? Jesus says that we are not.

I am able to share the transgressions of our community because I also celebrate our gifts and our glory. There are incredible examples of service, outreach, ministry, care, and concern for all kinds of people in our parish family. If we are unable to name our sin, however, we dare not boast of our glory.

All share their life experience.

What was Luke trying to tell his community? What does he have to say to our community and to me today? What might God be creating in us through this gospel? In what way does this gospel point to God's promise to be with us? In what way have I/we known death/resurrection (transformation) in my/our experience and understanding of this gospel? How is God speaking to us as a community in this liturgy? Do we still feel the same way about this text as we did when we began? Has our original understanding been stretched, challenged, or affirmed?

STEP 5
DECISION

The gospel demands a response.

What would be the contemporary implications of what we have shared today? In what concrete way does this gospel call our parish to action in the church, parish, neighborhood, or world? Has this conversation with the exegesis changed or stretched my personal attitudes? What am I/we/community/parish called to do in response? What is one concrete action we will take this week as a response to what was learned and shared today?

DOCTRINAL ISSUES

What church truth/teaching/doctrinal issue could be drawn from the gospel for the Twenty-Second Sunday in Ordinary Time?

Participants suggest possible doctrinal themes that flow from the readings.

Possible Doctrinal Themes

Theology of eucharist, justice, discipleship, morality, sin, trust

Present the doctrinal material at this time.

1. The facilitator gives input on a particular doctrinal issue of his/her prior choosing. OR
2. The group chooses a doctrinal issue from the list they created. They read together from the Doctrinal Appendix.

(The doctrinal issues are found in the Doctrinal Appendix in the back of this workbook. If you are choosing an issue from this resource, please refer to it now.)

Reflection questions centered around the chosen doctrinal theme can be found at the end of each topic in the Doctrinal Appendix. The questions are based on the five-step reflection process. If you choose a topic not included in the Doctrinal Appendix, craft your own questions according to the same five-step process.

Following the reflection questions you will be reminded to return to chapter 7, "Preparing the Catechetical Session," to assist you in crafting your own session.

Closing Prayer

Let us pray.
Lord,
you renew us at your table with the bread of life.
May this food strengthen us in love
and help us to serve you in each other.
We ask this in the name of Jesus the Lord.[12]

---

[12]Twenty-Second Sunday in Ordinary Time: "Prayer After Communion," *The Sacramentary.*

Selected Bibliography

Bourke, Myles M. "The Epistle to the Hebrews." In *The New Jerome Biblical Commentary.* Ed. Raymond E. Brown, S.S., Joseph A. Fitzmyer, S.J., Roland E. Murphy, O.Carm. Englewood Cliffs: Prentice Hall, 1990.

Days of the Lord. Vol. 6. Collegeville: The Liturgical Press, 1991.

Di Lella, Alexander A., O.F.M. "Sirach." In *The New Jerome Biblical Commentary.* Ed. Raymond E. Brown, S.S., Joseph A. Fitzmyer, S.J., Roland E. Murphy, O.Carm. Englewood Cliffs: Prentice Hall, 1990.

Fuller, Reginald H. *Preaching the New Lectionary.* Collegeville: The Liturgical Press, 1974.

Johnson, Luke Timothy. *The Gospel of Luke.* Sacra Pagina Series. Vol. 3. Collegeville: The Liturgical Press, 1991.

LaVerdiere, Eugene. *Dining in the Kingdom of God.* Chicago: Liturgy Training Publications, 1994.

Mazar, Peter. *To Crown the Year.* Chicago: Liturgy Training Publications, 1995.

TWENTY-THIRD SUNDAY IN ORDINARY TIME

INTRODUCTORY RITES

Opening Song (or Entrance Antiphon)

Lord, you are just, and the judgments you make are right. Show mercy when you judge me, your servant. (Ps 118:137, 124)[1]

Opening Prayer

The facilitator of the session may lead the prayer. Others in the group may be asked to proclaim the readings.

Let us pray
[that we may realize the freedom God has given us in making us his sons and daughters]

Pause for silent prayer.

God our Father,
you redeem us
and make us your children in Christ.
Look upon us,
give us your freedom
and bring us to the inheritance you promised.
Grant this through our Lord Jesus Christ, your
    Son,
who lives and reigns with you and the Holy Spirit,
one God, for ever and ever.[2]

LITURGY OF THE WORD

Let us listen to God's word.

The readings are proclaimed.

First Reading
Wisdom 9:13-18

The book of Wisdom is one of the last books of the Old Testament. It is not contained in the Hebrew bible and it is believed that it was originally written in Greek. It was a popularly held belief that the book was written by Solomon, but scholars maintain that it was written long after his reign. Solomon's authorship was refuted by Origen, Eusebius, Augustine, and Jerome. Assertion of Solomon's authorship is considered a literary device. "The author of the book remains anonymous, and the most we can say is that he was a learned Greek-speaking Jew and probably a teacher, and that he was familiar with Hellenistic philosophy, rhetoric, and culture."[3]

The book was written about 60 B.C.E. in order to strengthen the faith of Jews in Alexandria. Egypt's Alexandria was the third largest city of its day. It was a cultural center with the proper climate for intellectual debate between Jewish and Greek scholars intent on testing their philosophies and methodologies. It is believed that these exchanges served as the catalyst for the creation of the Septuagint, the Greek translation of the Old Testament. Hellenistic culture was rapidly advancing. Philosophies and religions were cropping up that were attempting to define the real meaning of life. A burning issue of the day was divine retribution: how is it that the just suffer and the wicked prosper? Skepticism and individualism were rampant. There was a serious crisis of faith in which traditional values were questioned. Many Jews left the faith to embrace new modern philosophies and pagan ideologies. The book of Wisdom was the Jewish response to the Greek philosophical system that was threatening traditional Jewish life.

The style of this literature is comparable to Hellenistic literature of the time known as "didactic exhortation." Such exhortation maintains that what one learns should have an impact on the way one lives one's life. The book reflects the writing and the wisdom of an author who meditated upon the scriptures and wished to offer consolation and encouragement to his Jewish brothers and sisters.

---

[1]Twenty-Third Sunday in Ordinary Time: "Entrance Antiphon," *The Sacramentary.*

[2]Twenty-Third Sunday in Ordinary Time: "Opening Prayer," *The Sacramentary.*

[3]Addison G. Wright, S.S., "Wisdom," in *The New Jerome Biblical Commentary,* ed. Raymond E. Brown, S.S., Joseph A. Fitzmyer, S.J., Roland E. Murphy, O.Carm. (Englewood Cliffs: Prentice Hall, 1990), 510.

The book of Wisdom reflects post-exilic thought and belief in the afterlife. The afterlife was considered a place where one was cut off from God (Sheol). Thus, divine retribution was realized in the temporal world. Large families, possessions, and good fortune were signs of God's favor.

The book is divided into two parts. Sometimes the first part (1–6:21) is referred to as the *Book of Eschatology*. It deals with retribution and the benefits of seeking Wisdom above all else. The second part of the book deals with how Wisdom (Spirit of God) works in the world and how one is to find it (6:21–end).

Today's pericope hinges on an event in Solomon's life in which legend suggested that God promised the king that his prayerful request would be granted. There is an earlier and a later version of Solomon's prayer. The first is found in 1 Kings 3:6-9 where Solomon asks God for understanding. The later version is found in Chronicles 1:8-10 where Solomon asks God for the necessary wisdom to lead and govern his people. Today's Wisdom author expands on Solomon's prayer and asks for counsel. He attests that human beings are too limited to understand the mind and heart, or the counsel of God. We barely understand the things of this world, let alone the things of heaven. Only with God's Wisdom (Spirit) will we be able to even remotely understand God's instruction. Discernment is possible only through the power of the Holy Spirit.

The author is responding to Greek dualism which asserted that humanity could not understand the will of God because the evil human body drags down the good spirit-mind. It seems that the author of Wisdom is embracing the dualistic Platonic notion that body/matter is evil and the spirit is good. He is not, however. The Hebrew scriptures uphold the Genesis notion that creation is intrinsically good. He is simply stating that the body is an encumbrance when seeking to understand the will of God. "It is its finite, not its evil, character that is its drawback."[4] The Spirit of God helps humanity to transcend its finitude.

Responsorial Psalm
Psalm 90:3-4, 5-6, 12-13, 14-17

The first part of the psalm highlights the difference between God's immortality and our mortality. The last part of the psalm is a prayer that God will bless the endeavors of human beings as life is so short and transitory.

Second Reading
Philemon 9-10, 12-17

Paul's letter to Philemon was a personal note and is the shortest of Paul's letters. "In the New Testament canon, Paul's letters are arranged in order of length, from Romans to Philemon."[5] There is no question regarding Pauline authorship of this letter. Paul's letter was written to Philemon, Philemon's wife, Apphia, and Archippus (probably their son). Philemon was a Christian converted by Paul, probably in Ephesus. The slave Onesimus had run away from his master, a Christian in Colossae named Philemon. Onesimus went to be with Paul in prison, probably because he knew that his master highly regarded Paul. Paul was responsible for Onesimus's conversion to Christianity. Paul sent him back to his master with the exhortation that Onesimus was no longer a slave, but a brother. He begged Philemon to take the runaway slave back. Paul would have preferred to have Onesimus stay and help with the work of evangelization. But he recognized Philemon's right and sent the slave back to his master as a brother, not a slave. The fact that both were now Christians forged an unbreakable bond between them. They were in a new relationship. Both Philemon and Onesimus were adopted children of God, brothers, through baptism. Paul pleaded with Philemon not to punish Onesimus as the law would allow. It seems as if Paul was asking for the slave to be freed in order to work with Paul.

One reason this letter to Philemon was included in the canon of scriptures was due to Paul's command to love. Paul did not try to change the social structure of slavery. That was an impossible task.

---

[4]Reginald H. Fuller, *Preaching the New Lectionary* (Collegeville: The Liturgical Press, 1974), 66.

[5]Luke Timothy Johnson, *The Writings of the New Testament* (Minneapolis: Augsburg Fortress, 1986), 251.

But in sending the slave back to his master, with the exhortation to love and forgive and accept, Paul was seeking to transform the structure of slavery within its own context. Paul insists that Onesimus is a freed person in Christ. He is not condemning the practice of slavery, but suggests a transformation of relationships within the system of slavery. Slavery was not immoral in the consciousness of the ancient world. It was not deemed immoral until the nineteenth century.

There was to be Christian charity in all Christian relationships—since in Christ there is neither slave nor free. Thus, Christians are to live in harmony with one another. Onesimus's name means "the Profitable One." "Paul implies that this slave, now a Christian, will live up to his name."[6]

Gospel
Luke 14:25-33

Jesus tells his followers that believers must be ready to renounce all possessions in order to be disciples.

STEP 1
NAMING ONE'S EXPERIENCE

What were your first impressions? What was your first response? What grabbed your attention? How did you feel?

Each person names his or her initial impression. Statement should be brief. No reasons should be given at this time. All simply listen without agreeing or disagreeing.

STEP 2
UNDERSTANDING

In a brief statement, what do you think this gospel is trying to convey?

---

[6]Joseph A. Fitzmyer, S.J. "The Letter to Philemon," in *The New Jerome Biblical Commentary*, ed. Raymond E. Brown, S.S., Joseph A. Fitzmyer, S.J., Roland E. Murphy, O.Carm. (Englewood Cliffs: Prentice Hall, 1990), 870.

STEP 3
INPUT FROM VISION/STORY/TRADITION

Liturgical Context

Today's reading from the book of Wisdom reminds us that we can do nothing without the power of the Holy Spirit. The Spirit empowers us to know the mind and the will of God. The Spirit empowers us to speak with power and conviction. Paul converted the slave Onesimus. He asked for Christian charity in the face of what might have been a very bad situation for the slave. He stood with the slave and, although he could not change the institution of slavery, he challenged the slave's owner to transform the master/slave relationship with the love of Christ. Paul reminded Philemon that all Christians are freed people through our membership in the Body of Christ. Paul's letter reminds all Christian communities that we must speak with similar conviction when we see oppression of any kind. We may not be complacent.

The gospel takes up a similar theme. Discipleship demands that the believer bear the cross for the sake of others. While the gospel seems to be exhorting us against love (v. 25, we are to leave father, mother, wife, children, brothers, etc.), it is, on the contrary, a call to love. Preoccupation with relationships and possessions keeps us from extending love.

The alternative opening prayer draws on the justice and mercy that God bestows. "With unparalleled love" we have been saved from death. We are to show similar unparalleled love in our response to all those "slaves" in our contemporary world who cry out for us to speak for them as Paul spoke for Onesimus.

Christian Initiation

Today would be a good day to celebrate the Rite of Acceptance. The gospel calls for the disciple to take up the cross and follow Christ. It exhorts the Christian to bear the mark of Christ and to make all else in life secondary to following Christ and his gospel. The Rite of Acceptance celebrates the passage of the inquirer into the period of the catechumenate. One of the primary symbols of the rite is the signing of each candidate with the sign of the cross. The paradox of the Christian life is laid bare for reflection by all the faithful. In this initial stage of entry the candidates are welcomed, they state their intention to continue toward initiation, and they are signed with the mark of the Christian—the cross of Christ. This is not a wimpy, feel-good Christianity we celebrate. It is a Christianity that is serious about the implications of discipleship: it leads to the cross. Christianity is incorporation into the ongoing paschal mystery of Christ. Celebration of this rite for the inquirer would recognize his or her new place in the church. He or she would become a catechumen with all a catechumen's inherent rights, responsibilities, and privileges. Is there someone in your catechumenate process ready to celebrate the Rite of Acceptance?

Gospel Exegesis

The facilitator gives input regarding what critical biblical scholarship has to say about this text. The input includes insights as to how people would have heard the gospel in Jesus' time.

Discipleship is the word of the day. The gospel insists that the believer face the cost of discipleship. It demands that we willingly give our lives to Christ and the spreading of the Good News. Today's gospel reminds us that the call of the gospel is radical. Discipleship insists that believers embrace the gospel's demanding implications. The Christian must make difficult choices.

It seems that Jesus' intended audience is the crowd he has just invited to the messianic banquet, the poor, the lame, the blind. The invitation was only the first step, however. The call to follow in the Master's steps, to take up the cross, is a lifetime endeavor. Thus, the call to this radical discipleship extends to all people, not just the twelve apostles. It is the vocation of every Christian.

It appears to the reader that Jesus is asking for something beyond comprehension. The literal challenge of today's pericope is even stronger

than what appears in this translation. The literal translation says we are to *hate* our relatives. How can this be? Are we really suppose to *hate* our relatives and turn our backs on them? Luke Timothy Johnson asserts that the term *hate* (*misein* in Greek—the opposite of *agape*—love) reflects an attitude and a mode of action, not an emotion. Matthew softened the expression to "Whoever loves father or mother more than me." Luke, however, used the more original and severe wording. Luke's Christian knows exactly what the challenge of the gospel involves. Over-involvement with relationships and possessions will keep the believer from hearing, responding, and following through with God's call. Disciples cannot become so emotionally attached to their possessions and relationships that they are not free to embrace the demands of gospel living. "Part of the cost of discipleship is the willingness to forego the joys of security of family ties so as to be bound completely to Christ."[7]

In Matthew's version of this pericope we are exhorted to *accept* the cross. In Luke, we are asked to *bear* the cross. The difference highlights Luke's agenda of stressing the ongoing, continuous nature of discipleship.

The parable about building a tower is found only in Luke's gospel. In essence it asserts: Don't start the project unless you are willing to pay whatever price is necessary to complete it, even if it means giving up your very life. The bottom line of this pericope is that all the demands of life must be subordinate to the will of God. It is impossible for the disciple to follow the call of both possession and prophet. Anyone who tries will be like salt that has gone flat and loses its flavor. Attachment, for the disciple, must be only to God.

Proclaim the gospel again.

Sometimes we gain new insights when we hear the text after the interpretation has been given. Someone from the group proclaims the gospel a second time.

---

[7]Patricia Datchuck Sanchez, *The Word We Celebrate* (Kansas City: Sheed and Ward, 1989), 365.

Conversation with the Liturgy and the Scriptures

Test your original understanding in dialogue with the text.

(You might consider breaking into smaller groups.)

Did the exegesis of this week's gospel provide you with any insight you had not considered before? How does your original understanding of this story compare with what we just shared? How does this story speak to your life?

Participants share an experience from their lives that connects with the biblical interpretation just shared.

> *This is a very difficult gospel for families. At first glance it would appear that Jesus is asking us to abandon our families to follow the gospel. What we are being asked is not to allow anything to get in the way of our relationship with God. It is about priorities. It is about sticking with our call to Christian discipleship even when it is difficult. It is about upholding the gospel when everything around us tells us to give in to other pressures.*

> *Many years ago my husband and I committed to following the Christian call to discipleship no matter where that might take us. We were both from families that were very close knit. It would never have occurred to us to move away from our families. Yet, in following God's will for our lives, we did move. This move was a difficult decision. It took us away from the security of family and demanded that we trust. The move turned out to be the best thing we could have done for our lives.*

> *It is possible that another move will one day be in order. It will be difficult for our children, as this has become our family homestead. It represents security for all of us. However, if we discern that it is right for us and that it is God's call for our lives, then our challenge will be to once again trust. Even though we adore our grown children, we will need to follow the mandate of our conscience and follow what appears to be the will of God in our lives. Today's gospel simply (or maybe not so simply) asks us to put*

Christ before anything else and to take up our cross and offer our suffering for the sake of the gospel.

All share their life experience.

What was Luke trying to tell his community? What does he have to say to our community and to me today? What are the opportunities to be re-created as a result of our sharing of this gospel (creation theme)? In what way does this gospel point to God's promise to be with us (covenant)? In what way have I/we known death/resurrection in my/our experience and understanding of this gospel (exodus)? How is God speaking to us as a community? In what way is our community challenged? Do we still feel the same way about this text as we did when we began? Has our original understanding been stretched, challenged, or affirmed?

The gospel demands a response.

What are our collective and personal responses to all of the above questions? How does our sharing and this biblical interpretation challenge our community to action? In what concrete way does this gospel call our parish to action in the church, parish, neighborhood, or world? What are the implications of this liturgy for my life? What am I/we/community/parish called to do in response? What is one concrete action we will take this week as a response to what was learned and shared today?

DOCTRINAL ISSUES

What church truth/teaching/doctrinal issue could be drawn from the gospel for the Twenty-Third Sunday in Ordinary Time?

Participants suggest possible doctrinal themes that flow from the readings.

Possible Doctrinal Themes

Holy Spirit, discipleship, cross, kingdom of God, moral life

Present the doctrinal material at this time.

1. The facilitator gives input on a particular doctrinal issue of his/her prior choosing. OR
2. The group chooses a doctrinal issue from the list they created. They read together from the Doctrinal Appendix.

(The doctrinal issues are found in the Doctrinal Appendix in the back of this workbook. If you are choosing an issue from this resource, please refer to it now.)
Reflection questions centered around the chosen doctrinal theme can be found at the end of each topic in the Doctrinal Appendix. The questions are based on the five-step reflection process. If you choose a topic not included in the Doctrinal Appendix, craft your own questions according to the same five-step process.

Following the reflection questions you will be reminded to return to chapter 7, "Preparing the Catechetical Session," to assist you in crafting your own session.

Closing Prayer

Bow your heads, and pray for God's blessing.

Lord,
grant your people your protection and grace.
Give them health of mind and body,
perfect love for one another,
and make them always faithful to you.
Grant this through Christ our Lord.[8]

Selected Bibliography

Days of the Lord. Vol. 6. Collegeville: The Liturgical Press, 1991.

Fitzmyer, Joseph A., S.J. "The Letter to Philemon." In *The New Jerome Biblical Commentary.* Ed. Raymond E. Brown, S.S., Joseph A. Fitzmyer, S.J., Roland E. Murphy, O.Carm. Englewood Cliffs: Prentice Hall, 1990.

Fuller, Reginald H. *Preaching the New Lectionary.* Collegeville: The Liturgical Press, 1974.

Johnson, Luke Timothy. *The Writings of the New Testament.* Minneapolis: Augsburg Fortress, 1986.

Sanchez, Patricia Datchuck. *The Word We Celebrate.* Kansas City: Sheed and Ward, 1989.

Wright, Addison G., S.S. "Wisdom." In *The New Jerome Biblical Commentary.* Ed. Raymond E. Brown, S.S., Joseph A. Fitzmyer, S.J., Roland E. Murphy, O.Carm. Englewood Cliffs: Prentice Hall, 1990.

---

[8]"Prayer Over the People," *The Sacramentary.*

TWENTY-FOURTH SUNDAY IN ORDINARY TIME

INTRODUCTORY RITES

Opening Song (or Entrance Antiphon)

Give peace, Lord, to those who wait for you and your prophets will proclaim you as you deserve. Hear the prayers of your servant and of your people Israel. (See Sirach 36:18)[1]

Opening Prayer

The facilitator of the session may lead the prayer. Others in the group may be asked to proclaim the readings.

Let us pray
[that God will keep us faithful in his service]

Pause for silent prayer.

Almighty God,
our creator and guide,
may we serve you with all our heart
and know your forgiveness in our lives.
We ask this through our Lord
Jesus Christ, your Son,
who lives and reigns with you and the Holy Spirit,
one God, for ever and ever.[2]

LITURGY OF THE WORD

Let us listen to God's word.

The readings are proclaimed.

First Reading
Exodus 32:7-11, 13-14

In today's pericope the people are waiting for Moses at the foot of Mount Sinai. They grow impatient waiting for his return so they ask Aaron "to fashion visible tokens of deity to whom they may express their trust."[3] The calf was an ancient symbol of fertility. Yahweh views this worship as a re-

jection of the newly instituted covenant but he does not destroy them. Moses litigates on the people's behalf. Yahweh had already rescued them. To destroy them now would undermine his divine plan. Egypt would then lay claim to the position that Yahweh saved the Israelites only to kill them in the desert. If Yahweh were to kill them now, he would, in essence, be nullifying the promise made to the patriarchs. Moses, even though he spoke on their behalf, turned around and furiously dealt with his people.

Scholars believe that the incident with the golden calf was actually an anachronism. It was a later incident that was read into the earlier wilderness account. It was in fact a reference to the two calves installed by Jeroboam at shrines at Dan and Bethel. Jeroboam used the same words from this text as he led the Northern Kingdom into apostasy.[4] The calf-worship event underscores the fact that Israel, having just been marvelously delivered from bondage in Egypt, turned her back on Yahweh even as Moses was receiving the law on top of Sinai. In the midst of what was to become Israel's defining tradition, she was rebellious.

Israel understood this disobedience as representative of her nature. The rebellion in the desert was not an isolated event, but was part and parcel of Israel's intrinsic character. She sinned, Yahweh forgave. Salvation history was a chronicle of such sin and forgiveness. The relationship between God and God's people is characterized by unfaithfulness forgiven by God's unconditional faithfulness.

Scholars attest that the molten calf was not crafted for the purpose of worshiping a false idol, but was a desire to have an image that represented Yahweh. "In ancient Near Eastern iconography bulls figure prominently either as representations of

---

[1] Twenty-Fourth Sunday in Ordinary Time: "Entrance Antiphon," *The Sacramentary.*

[2] Twenty-Fourth Sunday in Ordinary Time: "Opening Prayer," *The Sacramentary.*

[3] J. Kenneth Kuntz, *The People of Ancient Israel* (New York: Harper and Row, 1974), 117.

[4] Richard J. Clifford, S.J., "Exodus," in *The New Jerome Biblical Commentary*, ed. Raymond E. Brown, S.S., Joseph A. Fitzmyer, S.J., Roland E. Murphy, O.Carm. (Englewood Cliffs: Prentice Hall, 1990), 59.

gods...or as animal thrones of deities standing upon their backs. In the people's eyes, the images represent Yahweh (hence an altar is built before them), contrary to Israel's aniconic [prohibition against icons] tradition."[5]

Patricia Sanchez reminds us of Barth's position that this event is an example of how religions can confuse the voice of the people (vox populi) with the voice of God (vox Dei). Any religion has the capacity to produce a "calf" to meet the needs of the people who are in opposition to the will of God. "Need does not create religion. Although Aaron had ordered the making of the calf in a dubious effort to salvage the faith of his people, all that resulted was a compromise that threatened the integrity of their relationship with God."[6]

Moses' intervention renewed the covenant with Abraham: the promise of land, descendants, and abundance. A major piece of this pericope deals with Moses as mediator. "He makes intercession for them by pleading the promise of God to the patriarchs....Moses foreshadows the Messianic work of Christ."[7] This defining moment in salvation history was to be the paradigm for God's relationship with humanity. God's grace is always available in the face of sin and rebellion. Later in salvation history, Jesus would be the ultimate symbol of grace conquering opposition in consummate love.

Responsorial Psalm
Psalm 51:3-4, 12-13, 17, 19

This psalm is known as an individual lament and is one of the penitential psalms. The backdrop of this psalm is David's sin with Bathsheba. As a lament, it is a prayer for pardon and the confession of sin. Verses 10-14 are a prayer for restoration and verses 15-19 are a prayer in praise of God before the community and the sacrifice of a humble heart.[8]

It (psalm 51) should be sung in Hebrew; no translation can do justice to the richness expressed by this grouping of words. *Haman*— to take "pity," to grant "mercy," —evokes the image of bending down, stooping, descending toward: a wholly free movement demanding no reciprocity. *Hesed*—"mercy," "love,"—is one of the watchwords of the covenant, practically its equivalent; not merely a sentiment of pity, but fatherly bearing, moved by active generosity. *Raham*—according to your great "mercy"— designates the very seat of compassion, the voice of blood, the love that arises from the inmost heart.[9]

Second Reading
1 Timothy 1:12-17

Robert Karris asserts that the author of the pastoral letters imagines his audience to be Christians "who want to follow Paul in the changed circumstances after his death."[10] The Christian readers of the pastoral understand themselves as Christians who seek to live the gospel in the post-apostolic era—now that their apostle, Paul, is gone. In 1 Timothy and Titus, Paul is the apostle who gives the church instructions to follow after his death so they may continue the work of the gospel and cope in the midst of suffering.

The Paul of the pastoral letters is not a herald of ecclesiastical law and order, asserts Karris. Paul did not lay down one rigid mode, style, or pattern of leadership. Paul inaugurated different models such as elders, a college of elders, and bishops. The author's agenda is to exhort the church to find a style that best suits its needs and then to get on with the business of being church. "There is emphasis on sound teaching, and the emphasis is on good conscience, on godliness, on irreproachable conduct."[11]

This is an exhortatory letter written to a church. The author gives authoritative credence to the church and household regulations contained

---

[5]Ibid.

[6]Patricia Datchuck Sanchez, *The Word We Celebrate* (Kansas City: Sheed and Ward, 1989), 366.

[7]Reginald H. Fuller, *Preaching the New Lectionary* (Collegeville: The Liturgical Press, 1974), 68.

[8]John S. Kselman, S.J. and Michael L. Barré, S.S. "Psalms," in *The New Jerome Biblical Commentary*, ed. Raymond E. Brown, S.S., Joseph A. Fitzmyer, S.J., Roland E. Murphy, O.Carm. (Englewood Cliffs: Prentice Hall, 1990), 534.

[9]*Days of the Lord*, Vol. 6 (Collegeville: The Liturgical Press, 1991), 208.

[10]Robert J. Karris, O.F.M., *The Pastoral Epistles* (Wilmington: Michael Glazier, Inc. 1979), 46.

[11]Ibid., 47.

within the epistles. The technique used to accomplish this is to make Paul the author of the letters and by using imperative verbs such as *must*.

The church is to live according to doctrine that promotes good moral living for the Christian and for society. Paul upholds himself as the example. He was a sinner and was made just, righteous through Christ. "The key message of this passage is that Paul's gospel and example promote good conduct and lead to love which stems from a heart that is single minded, a conscience that has no guilt on it, and from a faith that practices what it confesses."[12]

Gospel
Luke 15:1-32

The three parables: the lost sheep, the lost coin, and the prodigal son.

STEP 1
NAMING ONE'S EXPERIENCE

What were your first impressions? What was your first response? What grabbed your attention? How did you feel?

Each person names his or her initial impression. Statement should be brief. No reasons should be given at this time. All simply listen without agreeing or disagreeing.

STEP 2
UNDERSTANDING

In a brief statement, what do you think this gospel is trying to convey?

STEP 3
INPUT FROM VISION/STORY/TRADITION

Liturgical Context

The Twenty-Second and Twenty-Third Sundays in Ordinary Time remind us of what it means to be a

---

[12]Ibid., 53.

disciple. All of chapter 15 is proclaimed on this Sunday. Luke always has his eye fixed on our participation in the final great banquet that Christ has prepared for us. We are called to meditate upon his intended guest list and imitate Jesus' behavior toward them.

All three readings today are concerned with turning to God in repentance. Following its apostasy, Israel returned to their God in the first reading. In the second reading, Paul is jubilant over his conversion to Christ and sees himself as a model for other sinners. The gospel celebrates repentance and God's forgiveness so strongly that it emphasizes the point in triplicate. Three parables depict God seeking out the sinner.

Both the opening prayer and alternative opening prayer support the reconciliation offered by Christ in today's gospel. The opening prayer celebrates the forgiveness that is ours through Jesus. The alternative opening prayer shows us where that forgiveness must lead—to our ultimate service in God's reign. "Bring us to the dignity which distinguishes the poor in spirit and show us how great is the call to serve..." (Alternative Opening Prayer).

The liturgy for this Sunday reminds us that through the eucharist we are strengthened to carry out the mission and will of God. "Lord, may the eucharist you have given us influence our thoughts and actions. May your Spirit guide and direct us in your way" (Prayer After Communion).

Perhaps it is time for a communal reconciliation celebration.

Gospel Exegesis

The facilitator gives input regarding what critical biblical scholarship has to say about this text. The input includes insights as to how people would have heard the gospel in Jesus' time.

A major context for understanding the three parables in today's gospel is to examine the audience to whom Jesus was speaking. Tax collectors and sinners were attracted to Jesus and listened and responded to his message. Pharisees and scribes also followed Jesus, but their motives were far more sinister. They could not accept Jesus' inclusivity. How could Jesus associate with society's degenerates? Those closest to the law thought they had an edge when it came to understanding the mind and heart of God concerning sinners. Jesus turned their religious world upside down (the purpose of parables) and emphatically asserted that God not only welcomes and loves sinners but seeks after them with a vengeance. Thus, the three parables are intended to exonerate Jesus' practice of receiving sinners and eating with them. They were also a condemnation or a criticism of the Pharisees who did not seek the lost.

A digression concerning the Pharisees is in order at this time. The depiction of the Pharisees in the gospels is not an accurate depiction of Pharisees in the time of Christ. It is more reflective of the situation after the destruction of the temple in 70 C.E. when Pharisaic Judaism assumed a major leadership role and when Luke's gospel was written. "Pharisaism was a lay movement noted for its oral and accurate interpretation of the Jewish law."[13] It was not a rigid, legalistic, and hypocritical force dominant in Jesus' time. Luke uses Pharisees to thwart Jesus. Their understanding of the reign of God is opposite to Jesus' understanding. Their negative response to Jesus is intended to elicit a positive response in the readers.

Barbara Reid asserts that Jesus was not faulted for not observing strict ritual purity laws by eating with sinners. He was faulted for his attitude toward sinners.

> E. P. Sanders argues that what offended other Jews was that Jesus offered to sinners forgiveness and admission into his community without making the normal demands of restitution and commitment to the law. He shows that Jesus' offer of forgiveness was not novel: in Judaism one could always turn to God, repent, and be saved (e.g., Is 45:22).... Sanders proposes that the novelty and offense of Jesus' message was that sinners who heeded him

would be included in the reign of God even though they did not repent by making restitution, sacrifice, and turning to obedience to the law. Jesus' companionship with such people was a sign that God would save them, and, moreover, implied a claim to know whom God would include. (E. P. Sanders, *Jesus and Judaism* [Minneapolis: Augsburg Fortress, 1985])[14]

All three of the subjects in today's parables would have been considered not worthy of the effort in the mind of the scribes and Pharisees. Consider it from their perspective. Who is going to go after one lost sheep and leave the other ninety-nine unattended? Who in their right mind would turn a house upside down looking for one lost coin when there were nine others, and who would dare welcome home a son who wished the father dead, disgraced the family, and turned his back on tradition while there was still a good son at home? ABSURDITY—all of it!

In the parable of the lost sheep Jesus immediately catches the Pharisees' angry attention. He begins, "And what man among you...." He asks the Pharisees to imagine themselves as shepherds. Throughout scripture the shepherd had been used as a metaphor for God, but real shepherds did not possess good reputations. Real shepherds were believed to be dishonest pilferers. It was an insult to ask dignitaries such as the Pharisees to imagine themselves as shepherds. This further highlights the impact of the message. "Yet a disdained shepherd illustrates God's search for the lost better than the religious leaders who thought themselves upright. The parables challenge religious leaders to actively seek out the 'lost sheep,' such as tax collectors and sinners, and bring them back to the fold."[15]

The woman with the lost coin is also intended to illustrate the point that God goes to great lengths to seek out the lost. However, there is much more to this parable than meets the contemporary eye. Many often have believed this pericope to be a contrast with the rich shepherd who has a sizeable herd, and the poor woman who loses one

---

[13]Barbara E. Reid, *Women in the Gospel of Luke* (Collegeville: The Liturgical Press, 1996), 180.

[14]Ibid., 184.
[15]Ibid.

drachma, a day's wage. However, Reid asserts that people in first-century Palestine would not have seen that implication. The woman would have been considered rather well off, since she already had in her possession one third of a month's salary (ten drachmas). The poor of that time could only dream of such a luxury. "A rich-poor contrast weakens the impact of the parable. The point is that both a male character and a female one equally represent the manner in which God acts."[16]

The woman goes to great lengths and uses expensive oil in her lamp in order to find the coin; she expends great energy in looking in all the cracks and crevices of the house. The most challenging point of the parable is that God is portrayed as a woman. It has as strong an impact as that which the Pharisees experienced when Jesus asked them to put themselves in the place of the ill-reputed shepherd—it is shocking! It is far easier and more comfortable to imagine God as the loving father in the story of the prodigal son than it is to imagine God as the woman in search of the lost coin. The parable of the lost coin offers believers the opportunity to expand their image of God and more fully enter the dimension of divine mystery. "Choosing the better part is to see the woman seeking the coin as a metaphor that is equally apt for speaking of God as is 'father.' Just as the Pharisees and scribes are asked to imagine themselves as this woman, current believers, male and female, are challenged to do the same: to imitate her godly action of diligently seeking out and restoring the lost."[17]

For a thorough exegesis concerning the parable of the prodigal son and the merciful father, please refer to the Fourth Sunday of Lent. All three parables are an exhortation to all believers to seek the lost and restore them to relationship with God.

Proclaim the gospel again.

Sometimes we gain new insights when we hear the text after the interpretation has been given. Someone from the group proclaims the gospel a second time.

---

16 Ibid., 185.
17 Ibid., 189.

Conversation with the Liturgy and the Scriptures

Test your original understanding in dialogue with the text.

(You might consider breaking into smaller groups.)

Now that you've heard the exegesis, how do you feel about it? Were there any new insights? Was there anything you had not considered before? How does your original understanding of this story compare with what we just shared? How does this story speak to your life?

Participants share an experience from their lives that connects with the biblical interpretation just shared.

> *I am writing this chapter while receiving multiple collect phone calls from one of our homeless friends in the correctional institution. Since he has no money for bail, he will have to await pre-trial arraignment in jail for over three weeks. It will have cost the county a minimum of twenty thousand dollars to hold him, adjudicate him, feed him, and provide the physical plant that will house him. He will go before a judge and receive a suspended sentence and a slap on the wrist for possessing a marijuana cigarette. (This is merely my editorial comment about the absurd way our judicial system treats people who have no money.)*

> *I groaned when our homeless friend, Billy, called. I nearly did not accept the charges on the four occasions he called collect. We had been around the block with Billy before. He could be such a pain in the neck. He was calling to simply ask that we pass on a message to the people who were taking care of his dog. Knowing Billy as we do, I wanted to scream at him and tell him to "get a life." I had to chuckle when he promised me he would take us out to dinner when he got out of jail since we had been nice enough to accept his collect phone charges.*

> *Billy is a bright, young, seriously alcoholic man who gave up on life and has become accustomed to the streets. Last year, in a near-death experience, with our church community at his side, he gave up drinking. Death was his only other alternative. However,*

his life has not changed. He continues to run from his life and to live off the world. Yet, in his more serious moments, there is a spark of life left in Billy. I can still see a spark of hope in this man who would try the patience of Job.

Most people tell us to hang up on him when he calls. And we want to. However, there is always something that says, "maybe this helping hand could help him turn the corner." It did for his girlfriend. With the help of our homeless ministry she left Billy and is off the streets and working two jobs. We nearly gave up on her many times. She came to us one last time and asked for help. It was the help she was ready to accept. When will Billy be ready? Will he ever? I am sure the Pharisees looked on the sinners of Jesus' day with the same disdain. Yet, Jesus exhorts us not to give up.

Some suggest that any form of help given to people like Billy is nothing more than enabling his behavior. But people like Billy are at such a point in their lives that no one is enabling anything. All the enabling occurred long ago. They hit bottom years ago. They are so steeped in hopeless living that they not only cannot see a way out, they are sure that a way out does not even exist. "Perhaps this one last act of kindness," we say, "this one last time, and no more times; no, not ever—never again—but just this last time—is THE RIGHT TIME."

While not intending to thwart the very valid AA principle of not enabling the alcoholic, the homeless that come to us are so far gone in their disease that they have completely lost the desire for restoration. They can be beaten, cold, hungry, exposed to the dangers of the elements—no matter what befalls them, they are on a suicide track. They have absolutely no expectations. When they encounter respect they are completely thrown off guard. Our job is to seek the lost. Look at the lengths taken in today's parables. Seeking the lost in the case of our alcoholic, homeless friends means offering them respect, hope, and a lifeline if it is requested. It is Jesus' job to save them. Perhaps seeking the lost can simply be an act of human kindness, respect, and dignity offered to people who believe they long ago abdicated their own dignity.

All share their life experience.

What was Luke trying to tell his community? What does he have to say to our community and to me today? Where are the biblical images of creation, covenant, community, and exodus apparent in today's readings? Do we still feel the same way about these texts as we did when we began? Has our original understanding been stretched, challenged, or affirmed?

STEP 5
DECISION

The gospel demands a response.

How is God speaking to us as a community? In what way is our community challenged? What are our collective and personal responses to all of these questions? How does our sharing and this biblical interpretation challenge our community's attitudes? What would be a contemporary comparison to the parables in today's gospel? What would be today's response? In what concrete way does this gospel call our parish to action in the church, parish, neighborhood, or world? Has this conversation with the exegesis of this text changed or stretched me in any way? What is one concrete action we will take this week as a response to what was learned and shared today?

DOCTRINAL ISSUES

What church truth/teaching/doctrinal issue could be drawn from the gospel for the Twenty-Fourth Sunday in Ordinary Time?

Participants suggest possible doctrinal themes that flow from the readings.

Possible Doctrinal Themes

Morality, reconciliation, mercy, forgiveness, images of God

Present the doctrinal material at this time.

1. The facilitator gives input on a particular doctrinal issue of his/her prior choosing. OR
2. The group chooses a doctrinal issue from the

list they created. They read together from the Doctrinal Appendix.

(The doctrinal issues are found in the Doctrinal Appendix in the back of this workbook. If you are choosing an issue from this resource, please refer to it now.)

Reflection questions centered around the chosen doctrinal theme can be found at the end of each topic in the Doctrinal Appendix. The questions are based on the five-step reflection process. If you choose a topic not included in the Doctrinal Appendix, craft your own questions according to the same five-step process.

Following the reflection questions you will be reminded to return to chapter 7, "Preparing the Catechetical Session," to assist you in crafting your own session.

Closing Prayer

Let us pray
[for the peace which is born of faith and hope]

Pause for silent prayer.

Father in heaven, creator of all,
look down upon your people in their moments of
    need,
for you alone are the source of our peace.
Bring us to the dignity which distinguishes the
    poor in spirit
and show us how great is the call to serve,
that we may share in the peace of Christ
who offered his life in the service of all.
We ask this through Christ our Lord.[18]

Selected Bibliography

Bailey, Kenneth E. *Poet and Peasant and Through Peasant Eyes: A Literary-cultural Approach to the Parables in Luke.* Grand Rapids: William B. Eerdmans Pub. Inc., 1980.
Clifford, Richard J., S.J. "Exodus." In *The New Jerome Biblical Commentary.* Ed. Raymond E. Brown, S.S., Joseph A. Fitzmyer, S.J., Roland E. Murphy, O.Carm. Englewood Cliffs: Prentice Hall, 1990.
Days of the Lord. Vol. 6. Collegeville: The Liturgical Press, 1991.
Fuller, Reginald H. *Preaching the New Lectionary.* Collegeville: The Liturgical Press, 1974.
Karris, Robert J., O.F.M. *The Pastoral Epistles.* Wilmington: Michael Glazier, Inc. 1979.
Kselman, John S., S.J. and Michael L. Barré, S.S. "Psalms." In *The New Jerome Biblical Commentary.* Ed. Raymond E. Brown, S.S., Joseph A. Fitzmyer, S.J., Roland E. Murphy, O.Carm. Englewood Cliffs: Prentice Hall, 1990.
Kuntz, J. Kenneth. *The People of Ancient Israel.* New York: Harper and Row, 1974.
Reid, Barbara E. *Women in the Gospel of Luke.* Collegeville: The Liturgical Press, 1996.
Sanchez, Patricia Datchuck. *The Word We Celebrate.* Kansas City: Sheed and Ward, 1989.

---

[18]Twenty-Fourth Sunday in Ordinary Time: "Alternative Opening Prayer," *The Sacramentary.*

TWENTY-FIFTH SUNDAY IN ORDINARY TIME

INTRODUCTORY RITES

Opening Song (or Entrance Antiphon)

I am the Savior of all people, says the Lord. Whatever their troubles, I will answer their cry, and I will always be their Lord.[1]

Environment

We are now well into autumn. Deep fall colors and images may be incorporated into the catechetical environment.

Opening Prayer

The facilitator of the session may lead the prayer. Others in the group may be asked to proclaim the readings.

Let us pray to the Lord who is a God of love to all peoples.

Pause for silent prayer.

Father in heaven,
the perfection of justice is found in your love and
all humanity is in need of your law.
Help us to find this love in each other
that justice may be attained
through obedience to your law.
We ask this through Christ, our Lord.[2]

LITURGY OF THE WORD

Let us listen to God's word.

The readings are proclaimed.

First Reading
Amos 8:4-7

The book of Amos was probably written by his disciples after his death so that his prophetic utterances would be remembered. There were portions of the book that he probably helped compile. Amos's spoken word came first. He was terse and to the point. His words carried great weight and meaning. It is often suggested that the book of Amos was written around 722 B.C.E. It was probably written in the Southern Kingdom after the fall of the North.

Amos came from an eastern Judean village named Tekoa. He spent most of his time with shepherds in the region. Amos was by profession a dresser of sycamore trees. By puncturing their fig-like fruit he improved the quality of their taste. Amos lived outdoors and used images and metaphors from nature for the spiritual life. Amos left the South and headed to the Northern Kingdom in order to prophecy to them about their immediate need for divine correction.

There are three major sections to the book of Amos. Chapters 1–2 contain prophecies against neighboring nations as well as a word against Israel. The second portion of the book (chapters 3–6) refers to the spiritual, social, and religious degeneration of Israel. The third section (chapters 7–9) depicts Amos's five visions, the story of his argument with Amaziah, and other utterances.

In the first section, Amos rails against the sins of the farthest-away areas of the kingdom. He then cleverly levels his attack against the sins of Judah, his own Southern Kingdom; then he centers his attack on Israel herself. "Israel is judged for exploitation of the poor (2:6), immorality (2:7), senseless forms of worship (2:8), and silencing Yahweh's prophets (2:12)."[3] Amos demanded that God come down upon Israel in judgment. The strength Israel enjoyed under Jeroboam II was swiftly coming to an end.

The second section of the book is concerned with justifying why Israel was to be judged and punished. God's vengeance was to be hurled against a

---

[1] Twenty-Fifth Sunday in Ordinary Time: "Entrance Antiphon," *The Sacramentary.*

[2] Twenty-Fifth Sunday in Ordinary Time: "Opening Prayer," *The Sacramentary.*

[3] J. Kenneth Kuntz, *The People of Ancient Israel* (New York: Harper and Row, 1974), 267.

people who had failed in their social and religious obligations.

The third section deals with Amos's prophetic oracles and visions. The prophet railed against the meaningless sacrifices and public rituals while the poor remained downtrodden. The people, in their own self-righteousness, believed that they were in good standing with Yahweh. They believed the "Day of the Lord" would find them ready to receive the light of Yahweh. Amos assured them that they would find only darkness. The "Day of the Lord" was believed to be a time when Yahweh would once again crash into Israel's history and intervene on her behalf. Amos was incredulous. How could they expect the "Day of the Lord" to take place for a people whose lives did not reflect their covenant responsibilities?

Amos denounces the rich who exploit and take advantage of the poor. The merchants considered the Sabbath an intrusion into their questionable business transactions. The rich of Amos's day lived lavishly while the poor languished. Amos challenged the people of Northern Kingdom to change their ways as God's judgment was imminent.

The first reading is thematically connected to the gospel. During Amos's prophetic ministry, the Hebrew mindset was that covenant relationship with God presupposed care for the poor and oppressed. Such care was considered a sign of good discipleship. Today's gospel suggests that disciples are to seek God's kingdom with the cleverness and diligence of the unjust steward. Evidence of that discipleship could be seen in the way resources were used to build God's kingdom.

Responsorial Psalm
Psalm 113:1-2, 4-8

This psalm is connected to the first reading because of its concern for the poor. It is a hallel psalm (it begins with Alleluia) that praises God for God's mighty works and cites Yahweh's favor for the poor.

Second Reading
1 Timothy 2:1-8

We know very little about the context of Paul's letter to Timothy. This letter is considered one of the pastoral epistles. There is great debate regarding Pauline authorship. Most scholars would agree that the pastorals were probably written by a disciple of Paul's who was following the customary practice of spreading his master's message "by publishing the sort of letter he thought the master might have written had he still been alive."[4] Johnson hypothesizes about the possible circumstances of the letter: "Paul left Timothy in Ephesus on his way to Macedonia. He hopes to return soon but writes to his delegate, 'so that you may know how one ought to behave in the household of God, which is the church of the living God, the pillar and bulwark of the truth' (3:15)."[5] It appears to be a rather mature community with sound structures of leadership already in place.

Some in the community are succumbing to godless "gnosticism"; they believe that special knowledge gives them particular prominence and importance in the community. The godliness we are to assume is involvement in those things in society that promote religious and human welfare. "The 'godly' person is the one who goes to church, who has served country in military service, who is dedicated to spouse and family, who is active in civic organizations which foster the fine arts, etc. In the author's frame of reference 'ungodly' persons are the gnostics who deny the goodness of creation and human institutions."[6] This passage describes life in the kingdom of God and administration and stewardship of that life. Ministries essential to building the church are articulated and people are exhorted to pray for those in authority. No doubt the latter was in response to tension between Christians who were considered to be in non-compliance of civil law and the Roman authorities. Like the gospel, the reading from 1 Timothy stresses God's salvation for all people. God is the only source of truth. Trust and prayer will sustain God's people in oppressive circumstances.

Gospel
Luke 16:1-13

---

[4]Hubert Richards, *The Gospel According to St. Paul* (Collegeville: The Liturgical Press, 1990), 128.

[5]Luke Timothy Johnson, *The Writings of the New Testament: An Interpretation* (Minneapolis: Augsburg Fortress, 1986), 396.

[6]Robert J. Karris, *The Pastoral Epistles* (Wilmington: Michael Glazier, 1979), 100-101.

This Sunday's gospel contains the parable of the unjust steward accompanied by statements regarding the use of wealth.

STEP 1
NAMING ONE'S EXPERIENCE

What were your first impressions? What was your first response? What grabbed your attention? How did you feel?

Each person names his or her initial impression. Statement should be brief. No reasons should be given at this time. All simply listen without agreeing or disagreeing.

STEP 2
UNDERSTANDING

In a brief statement, what do you think this gospel is trying to convey?

STEP 3
INPUT FROM VISION/STORY/TRADITION

Liturgical Context

All three readings today refer in some way to stewardship. The readings from the Twenty-Fifth and the Twenty-Sixth Sundays in Ordinary time come from Luke's sixteenth chapter. These two Sundays form their own unity. Both Sundays thematically refer to the proper attitude toward money that a member of God's kingdom should have. Luke strongly maintains a "preferential option" for the poor throughout his gospel. He cautions disciples regarding the entrapments of wealth and the consequences of being unwilling to share it.

This week and next week's first readings are taken from Amos. This week's reading is taken from the third section: Amos's prophetic oracles and visions. Next week's first reading is taken from the second section of the book of Amos. The second readings for both weeks are taken from 1 Timothy and deal with the duties and responsibilities of members of God's household.

The ritual prayers for today's liturgy speak of the demands of justice. Both opening prayers ask that we be guided to love one another with God's perfect love. The alternative opening prayer suggests that we will attain justice through our obedience to God's law. The command to care for the world's less fortunate, for the oppressed, and for the downtrodden is a most ancient command. It begins with our understanding of creation and biblical justice. At the Orlando Catechetical Conference (held in the fall of 1996), the noted patristics scholar Walter Burghardt asserted that biblical justice is fidelity to the demands of relationships, to responsibilities that stem from our covenant with God.

> The Old Testament asked: what did it mean for an Israelite to live? They were united by bonds of family or covenant. In that framework or context, how is God just? God acts as God should: always faithful to his promise. God provides and God punishes violations. *God is always faithful.* When are we just? When we are in right relationship to our God, to our brothers and sisters, and to the earth. In the Genesis creation story everything was in right relationship to everything else. All were in covenant relationship with God. Because of this covenant the people of God were to welcome the stranger, feed the hungry, give a home to the alien, not because they deserved it, but because this is how God acted toward Israel. Deuteronomy said to love the stranger because God did. Justice of God, then, is fidelity to relationships, expressions of love. Not to execute justice was not to worship God.

The communion rite for the Twenty-Fifth Sunday is from Psalm 118: "You have laid down your precepts to be faithfully kept. May my footsteps be firm in keeping your command" (Ps 118:4-5). To faithfully follow God and God's precepts, we must be stewards of all God's resources: relationships, the earth, and money. Creation theology asserts that all creation is good. We are to use the gifts we have been given to further the reign of God. We are not to be mastered by the gifts, but are to share them and use them for God's glory. This sentiment is reflected in today's prayer over the gifts. "Lord, may these gifts which we now offer to show our belief and our love be pleasing to you...."

Gospel Exegesis

The facilitator gives input regarding what critical biblical scholarship has to say about this text. The input includes insights as to how people would have heard the gospel in Jesus' time.

Parables capture the attention of the listener. Original assumptions are turned upside down and conversion is invited. One is enticed into a new or renewed understanding of God and God's reign. For the early Palestinian community, the scenario in this parable was a common occurrence. Listeners were very familiar with the machinations of dishonest stewards from personal experience. In this story there is an unjust steward who was caught and then fired. That ancient community would have expected as much. However, they would also have expected the steward to be jailed immediately. When Jesus told the audience that the steward was not jailed, he captured their imagination. Customarily, the man would have gone immediately to jail. His life would have been over. No one would ever trust him enough to employ him in the future. His situation was hopeless!

The ancient peasants were tickled by stories in which the underdog gets the better of the person in power. In spite of the steward's dishonesty, the crowd would have been cheering him on. Jesus brilliantly takes the expected and turns it into the unexpected. He reverses the situation and uses it to teach the listeners a truth about God, God's kingdom, and what it means to live in that kingdom.

This parable is considered one of the most difficult to understand. It seems as if Jesus praises the steward for his unjust behavior. Kenneth Bailey suggests that this is a story about an honorable master and his not-so-honorable steward/manager. The manager is the master's agent. The renters deal directly with the manager, not the master. The steward/manager performs some unknown dishonest deed and the master finds out. The steward's silence suggests guilt. He realizes that he is in trouble. He is incapable of ditch digging and he refuses to beg. Therefore, he has to act quickly to fix his seemingly hopeless situation.

When the master does not immediately jail him, the steward realizes that the master is a man of mercy. The unjust steward cleverly devises a plan. He gathers the renters together and reduces the payments owed to the master. Renters believe this action is with the master's full approval and authority. Now the master becomes the hero of the day. The entire community sings his praise.

The steward/manager is very a clever fellow. He realizes that the only way out of his dire situation is to rely completely on the mercy of the master. In early eastern cultures, mercy and generosity were highly valued. When the master did not jail the steward, he acted mercifully. The dishonest steward saw an opportunity and seized it. He would capitalize on the master's generosity.

If the master were to tell his renters what had really happened, nullifying the manager's actions, the master would be seen as stingy, not generous or merciful. The people would have been angry that their joy had been short-lived. The steward counted heavily on the fact that a merciful, generous man would never disrupt the celebration of his renters.

The steward hoped that even if the master did not reinstate him, he would be welcomed and employed by others in the community. The people would have assumed that the manager had encouraged the master to act so benevolently.

The master called the steward/manager a wise man. The Hebrew scriptures (Old Testament) define wisdom as an *instinct for self preservation*. The steward is praised for very cleverly devising a plan that would save him and secure his future in this hopeless situation.

The parable is a wonderful commentary on the mercy and salvation offered by God. Human beings are dependent on God for life itself. The God of mercy is hope for the hopeless. We cannot be saved through our own merit. Only God can save.

The bungling steward/manager had the wisdom to count on the mercy he had experienced earlier.

Disciples are to possess similar wisdom. Disciples of Christ are to believe and trust in God's grace. The master does not praise the steward for his dishonest behavior. Rather, the master praises him for the clever way he assured and secured his future. Patricia Sanchez suggests that the steward's solution was not dishonest. He had merely surrendered his own commission, namely, the interest he as manager had added to the principal owed his master. Disciples are to be as clever and enterprising when it comes to preserving their place in God's kingdom.

This parable is called a "so much more" parable. If an unjust steward shrewdly secures his worldly future by the manipulation of wealth, so much more will God's children secure their place in the kingdom of God by using wealth to build God's kingdom.

The final section of the pericope deals with the use of money. If disciples are not good stewards of the riches loaned to them by God, how can they be good stewards of the truths entrusted to them by God? Riches are for building the kingdom of God, to serve God and God's people. Members of the early church shared their wealth. Charles Talbert states: "There was first a spontaneous and then an organized sharing of wealth within the community to meet needs."[7]

Ultimately, the message is: What matters most to God is what lies within a person's heart, i.e., radical trust in God's mercy. In the early Palestinian community, radical dependence on God was proven by the proper use of one's resources. People in relationship with God care for the poor and defenseless. In the first reading Amos resonates with this theme. Trust God, seek God's kingdom and know that only God saves. Love of God demands a response.

Proclaim the gospel again.

Sometimes we gain new insights when we hear the text after the interpretation has been given. Someone from the group proclaims the gospel a second time.

---

[7]Charles H. Talbert, *Reading Luke* (New York: Crossroad, 1992), 155.

Conversation with the Liturgy and the Scriptures

Test your original understanding in dialogue with the text.

(You might consider breaking into smaller groups.)

Now that you've heard the biblical scholarship concerning this text, how does your original interpretation fit with the opinions of scholars? Were there any new insights? Was there anything you had not considered before? What was the message to the community, then and now? How would you articulate a connection between the parable of the unjust steward and the proper use of wealth? How does this story speak to your life?

Participants share an experience from their lives that connects with the biblical interpretation just shared.

> *Today's liturgy suggests that the wise stewardship of resources is indicative of the quality of one's spiritual life. Our two-thousand family parish is an example of such stewardship. We are very blessed to have excellent fiscal health: we are debt free. In the eleven years I have been in the parish, we have built a new office complex and made significant changes to the worship space. All construction costs were paid for before construction began. We maintain a school and an expensive plant. We have a large staff, including two secretaries, a bookkeeper, a parish administrator, a DRE, a director of adult formation, a director of elderly concerns, and multiple support and maintenance staff (not to mention the school staff).*

> *Our community is committed to the sound stewardship of time, talent, and treasure. Lest this appear self-serving, we also tithe ten percent of our income to the poor. We recently built an entire school in Haiti, supported a water treatment project in third-world countries, financed the building of homes in Appalachia, built three homes for Habitat, and support many, many missionary endeavors. Our next project will be to finance a self-help project in our sister diocese in the Dominican Republic.*

We have been richly blessed with resources. But we have also been wise stewards of the resources provided. The parish is solvent, supports local, national, and global charitable concerns, and is presently in the process of building a new school.

Wealth is not evil. The love of wealth is. Wealth is very useful in promoting the reign of God. Wealth is the servant, not the master. We have been able to impact many lives through the wise use of our resources and the generosity of our parishioners.

I believe this all begins with a commitment to prayer, worship, and spirituality. The parish community places high priority on Sunday worship, the source and summit of all we do. The spiritual lives of our people are our first concern. A great investment is made and great effort is put into feeding the souls of our parishioners. All else flows from the lives of committed Christians who understand the call and the challenge of the gospel. When a community is committed to the demands of the gospel experienced in its worship, it cannot ignore the call to serve the world's less advantaged.

All share their life experience.

What was Luke trying to tell his community? What does he have to say to our community and to me today? In what way, if any, are the biblical themes of creation, community, covenant and exodus evident? What are our collective and personal responses to all of the above questions? Do we still feel the same way about this text as we did when we began? Has our original understanding been stretched, challenged, or affirmed?

STEP 5
DECISION

The gospel demands a response.

How does our sharing and this biblical interpretation challenge our community? What would be a contemporary implication or situation that speaks to today's gospel interpretation? In what specific way does this gospel call our parish to action in the church, parish, neighborhood, or world? Has this conversation with the exegesis changed or stretched my personal attitudes? What is one concrete action we will take this week as a response to what we have learned and shared today?

DOCTRINAL ISSUES

What church truth/teaching/doctrinal issue could be drawn from the gospel for the Twenty-Fifth Sunday in Ordinary Time?

Participants suggest possible doctrinal themes that flow from the readings.

Possible Doctrinal Themes

Stewardship, kingdom of God, apostolic action, images of God, justice, discipleship

Present the doctrinal material at this time.

1. The facilitator gives input on a particular doctrinal issue of his/her prior choosing. OR
2. The group chooses a doctrinal issue from the list they created. They read together from the Doctrinal Appendix.

(The doctrinal issues are found in the Doctrinal Appendix in the back of this workbook. If you are choosing an issue from this resource, please refer to it now.)

Reflection questions centered around the chosen doctrinal theme can be found at the end of each topic in the Doctrinal Appendix. The questions are based on the five-step reflection process. If you choose a topic not included in the Doctrinal Appendix, craft your own questions according to the same five-step process.

Following the reflection questions you will be reminded to return to chapter 7, "Preparing the Catechetical Session," to assist you in crafting your own session.

Closing Prayer

Lord, help us with your kindness.
Make us strong through the eucharist.

May we put into action the saving mystery we
  celebrate.
We ask this in the name of Jesus.[8]

Selected Bibliography

Bailey, Kenneth E. *Poet and Peasant and Through
  Peasant Eye.* Grand Rapids: Eerdmans Publish-
  ing Company, 1976.
Fuller, Reginald H. *Preaching the New Lectionary.*
  Collegeville: The Liturgical Press, 1974.
Sanchez, Patricia Datchuck. *The Word We Celebrate.*
  Kansas City: Sheed and Ward, 1989.
Scott, Bernard Brandon. *Hear Then the Parable.*
  Minneapolis: Augsburg Fortress, 1989.
Talbert, Charles H. *Reading Luke.* New York: Cross-
  road, 1992.

---

[8]Twenty-Fifth Sunday in Ordinary Time: "Prayer After
Communion," *The Sacramentary.*

TWENTY-SIXTH SUNDAY IN ORDINARY TIME

INTRODUCTORY RITES

Opening Song (or Entrance Antiphon)

O Lord, you had just cause to judge men as you did: because we sinned against you and disobeyed your will. But now show us your greatness of heart, and treat us with your unbounded kindness. (Dan 3:31, 29, 30, 43, 42)[1]

Opening Prayer

The facilitator of the session may lead the prayer. Others in the group may be asked to proclaim the readings.

Let us pray
[for God's forgiveness
and for the happiness it brings]

Pause for silent prayer.

Father,
you show your almighty power
in your mercy and forgiveness.
Continue to fill us with your gifts of love.
Help us to hurry toward the eternal life you
    promise
and come to share in the joys of your kingdom.
Grant this through our Lord Jesus Christ, your
    Son,
who lives and reigns with you and the Holy Spirit,
one God, for ever and ever.[2]

LITURGY OF THE WORD

Let us listen to God's word.

The readings are proclaimed.

First Reading
Amos 6:1, 4-7

Today's first reading and last week's first reading are both taken from the book of Amos. Refer to

the Twenty-Fifth Sunday for further historical background.

There are three major sections to the book of Amos. Chapters 1-2 contain prophecies against neighboring nations as well as a word against Israel. The second portion of the book (from which today's pericope is taken) refers to the spiritual, social, and religious degeneration of Israel. The third section depicts Amos's five visions, the story of his argument with Amaziah, and other utterances.

In the first section, Amos rails first against the sins of those in the farthest-away areas of the kingdom. He then cleverly levels his attack against the sins of Judah and then centers his attack on Israel herself. "Israel is judged for exploitation of the poor (2:6), immorality (2:7), senseless forms of worship (2:8), and silencing Yahweh's prophets (2:12)."[3] Amos demands that God come down upon Israel in judgment. Israel's power, might, and strength, enjoyed under Jeroboam II, were swiftly coming to an end.

The entire second section of the book is concerned with Yahweh's just judgement against Israel. God's vengeance was to be hurled against a people who had failed in their social and religious obligations. The "Day of the Lord" would result in a resounding defeat for Israel. Such would be the judgment of Yahweh against Israel for her defiant smugness.

It appeared that Amos was foretelling a justly deserved, inevitable catastrophe for Israel. Was there no hope? In spite of the consequences to come, all was not lost—Yahweh still loved Israel. Amos believed that a small remnant would be saved. He trusted that grace would ultimately remain with a very few faithful followers.

Just what was their horrible sin? The rich who had profited on the backs of the poor would find themselves cut off, the first to go into bondage in the exile. "Since they think only of enjoying the

---

[1] Twenty-Sixth Sunday in Ordinary Time: "Entrance Antiphon," *The Sacramentary.*
[2] Twenty-Sixth Sunday in Ordinary Time: "Opening Prayer," *The Sacramentary.*

[3] J. Kenneth Kuntz, *The People of Ancient Israel* (New York: Harper and Row, 1974), 267.

present life as if their precarious security rested on themselves and their riches, they take no care of the future, their own future and that of the people."[4] The bottom line of this pericope cannot be missed: Yahweh cares deeply for the plight of the poor and disadvantaged.

Responsorial Psalm
Psalm 146:7, 8-9, 9-10

This psalm is part of the last group of Alleluia psalms in the psalter. These are psalms in praise of the mighty deeds of Yahweh. Verses 9-10 denounce the excesses of the rich and depict God's eternal care for the poor and the oppressed. The psalm appropriately points us to today's gospel.[5]

Second Reading
1 Timothy 6:11-16

Today's reading, continued from last week (refer to the Twenty-Fifth Sunday), is particularly interested "in the *now* of the Christian life and its conscious orientation toward the manifestation of the Lord."[6] It deals with how we are to live in the reign of God.

Possessions of themselves are not bad; they come from God and are a gift of God. However, they are not to consume us, or fill us with self-importance. They are to be used for the benefit of others.

The noble profession of faith we all made took place in the presence of many witnesses in the ecclesial community at baptism. Our baptism is rooted in the virtues enumerated at the beginning of this pericope. Our baptism empowers us to live the Christian life in the manner described in today's reading. Our own profession of faith and the profession of Christ before Pilate remind us that we are to endure to the end of our earthly mission.

The final section of this pericope ends with what might have been a beautiful liturgical hymn in praise of the blessed and immortal King of Kings and Lord of Lords. This exclamation of faith re-

---

[4]*Days of the Lord,* Vol. 6 (Collegeville: The Liturgical Press, 1991), 230.

[5]Reginald H. Fuller, *Preaching the New Lectionary* (Collegeville: The Liturgical Press, 1974), 70.

[6]*Days of the Lord,* Vol. 6, 231.

minds us of our goal and our hope—life eternal with the Holy One of Israel.

Gospel
Luke 16:19-31

Jesus tells the Pharisees the parable about the beggar Lazarus and the rich man.

STEP 1
NAMING ONE'S EXPERIENCE

What were your first impressions? What was your first response? What grabbed your attention? How did you feel?

Each person names his or her initial impression. Statement should be brief. No reasons should be given at this time. All simply listen without agreeing or disagreeing.

STEP 2
UNDERSTANDING

In a brief statement, what do you think this gospel is trying to convey?

STEP 3
INPUT FROM VISION/STORY/TRADITION

Liturgical Context

Chapter 16 of Luke's gospel is read on the Twenty-Fourth and Twenty-Fifth Sundays. The concern of these verses is with the use of money. Thus, these two Sundays form their own internal unity. Even though Jesus addresses the Pharisees, his exhortation is not only for them but for all disciples. Last week we were challenged regarding the proper use of money. This week the challenge continues. Today we are in the second part of chapter 16. The readings from Amos and Timothy continue.

Last week's and this week's gospels issue a call and a warning, attests Charles Talbert. Luke calls disciples to be wise in their stewardship of money in order to guarantee their future. He also warns against placing too much emphasis on the acquisition of wealth and its importance. The believer is not to assume that wealth is a sign of God's favor, nor is he or she to ignore the needs of the poor. In ignoring the needs of the poor, the law and the prophets are ignored and one is cut off from God.

The alternative opening prayer asks that through God's mercy we may experience God's power as we are continually forgiven our sins. We ask that the power of God's love empower us to love and forgive others. We promote the reign of God when we love as Jesus loved and when we enter into solidarity with all people.

Gospel Exegesis

The facilitator gives input regarding what critical biblical scholarship has to say about this text. The input includes insights as to how people would have heard the gospel in Jesus' time.

Only in this parable does the principal character have a proper name. This is also the only parable in which a scene from the afterlife is depicted.[7] Both facts have a great deal to do with the interpretation of the parable.

There is evidence that the ending of the parable highlights the lack of Jewish belief in Jesus as messiah. Although the primary theme of the parable is wealth and poverty, Luke had an apologetic motive in his telling of the parable. It was intended to further belief in Jesus' resurrection. The following exegesis is based on the interpretation provided by Bernard Brandon Scott in *Hear Then the Parable.*

There is a reversal of order that takes place within the structure of the parable. The rich man begins the parable and is the first mentioned. Lazarus is last on the scene. By the end, Lazarus is first and the rich man is last. Just as the plot reverses the hierarchical order of the rich man and Lazarus, so does the actual structure of the parable.

We know the man is wealthy because he wears purple clothing, and purple is a color worn by royalty. His purple clothing places him among society's

elite. The "merry-making" of this royal personage implies a feast of the most grandiose order. It is sumptuous, an out-of-the-ordinary feast, reserved only for the most momentous occasions. Nevertheless, it is a feast that occurs *every day!*

Contrast such urban opulence with the situation of Lazarus, who has nothing but his name. His name means, "he whom God helps." The contrast is stark. The rich man has many possessions. The poor man has only his name, but it is a name that holds within it a promise of help. The story tells us that Lazarus is a beggar. During Jesus' time, beggars were considered sinners and deserving of their lot. Poverty was viewed as divine retribution.

The rich man is on the inside; the beggar, Lazarus, is on the outside, at the gate. He has no access to the goods of the world. The gate serves as entryway—it can either let in or keep out. The rich man, in a position of patron, can use the gate to either let in his client or to shut him out and cut him off. What will he do? Will he help Lazarus? Lazarus's desire to eat the rich man's table droppings contrasts with the daily feast of the rich man.

The rich man and the beggar are thus divided by society's gate that distinguishes outsiders from insiders. Since this was a limited-goods society, what there was, was all there was. There was no excess to go around. Rich and poor were in fixed positions. We are cautioned not to judge the situation in terms of contemporary biases. But what we can expect is some sort of assistance for Lazarus by the rich man. To compound Lazarus's plight, even the cursed dogs licked his sores. Dogs were considered a plague in the ancient world.

Lazarus remains passive in the story. He does not even beg, which in this society makes him even less sympathetic. At least as a beggar he would perform a meaningful function: he would provide the opportunity for others to give alms.

Those listening to the parable are hooked early on. They believe that the story is setting up a situation in which the beggar will become the client of the rich patron. However, the listener is caught off guard. Lazarus dies before the rich man can extend patron/client patronage. Even in death, Lazarus remains passive as he is carried away by

---

[7]Bernard Brandon Scott, *Hear Then the Parable* (Minneapolis: Augsburg Fortress, 1989), 141.

the angels. No mention is made of a burial for the beggar, a further scandal in antiquity.

To thicken the plot, the rich man also dies—and again the fates of the two are intertwined. Things change drastically. Roles are reversed. Lazarus's fate is lavishly described (just as was the earthly condition of the rich man). He is carried off by angels to the bosom of Abraham. The stark language of the parable merely states that the rich man was buried.

"The poor man was lifted up into the bosom of Abraham and the rich man was buried in the ground (in this world)."[8] The separation between the rich man and poor man continued after death. Lazarus was in the *bosom* and the rich man was in *Hades* (a place of torment). Now the conversation continued the stark reality of the reversal. Lazarus was named as the one who had been in misery while in the world. His name reflected what he needed—God's help. God fulfilled his need. Lest we take this parable as an indictment against the rich, it is not: Abraham was also a rich man.

The reversal of roles is further evidenced as the rich man asks Abraham if Lazarus might momentarily relieve his torture with a cool refreshing dip of water. Lazarus remains passive even in death. Abraham is the one asked for help, as he is the premier symbol of hospitality. Abraham had fed the three strangers at the Oaks of Mamre (Gen 18:1-15). Abraham's act of offering help to strangers stood in contrast to what the rich man did not do for the beggar Lazarus who had waited at the rich man's earthly gate.

The radical difference between the rich man's opulent life on earth and his indigent afterlife is depicted in his request for a drop of water. The rich man was in a place of fire, whereas Lazarus was in a place where there was cool running water. We are not to take this as a literal description of heaven and hell. It is merely intended to show the stark contrast between the life of the rich man on earth and his afterlife. Restoration was no longer a possibility. There was no chance of bridging the gap, of uniting the division between Lazarus and the rich man. The chasm was fixed forever.

The Jewish audience would have been outraged at a few of the elements of the story. The rich man was condemned with no real evidence of guilt. There was only implied guilt. Furthermore, he was offered no opportunity to atone for his sin. The Jewish audience would have been outraged that no warning was given to the rich man about the consequences of not walking through the gate to help Lazarus. Some scholars believe the piece about sending Lazarus to the rich man's five brothers was a later addition to address that concern. The piece makes the point that whether there had been a warning or not, the rich man would not have listened.

"For the parable, places in the kingdom are determined not by differences but by solidarity. In the first part of the story the rich man fails to come through the gate; in the second he asks Lazarus to come through. He never makes the motion himself even in desire. So the chasm he created remains fixed."[9]

Charles Talbert suggests that this parable challenges the belief that wealth is a sign of God's favor. Only the interior heart determines a person's status before God. The rich man neglected his responsibility to the poor. "Deuteronomy 15:4 says there should be no poor person in Israel's midst. So generosity toward the poor was counted as righteousness."[10] The parable establishes that God is righteous in the face of injustice. "The falsely exalted of this world will be humbled in the next life."[11]

Two themes emerge in the second part of the parable. The first theme is the universality of the reign of God. Everyone is invited in. The second theme is a reminder that the law regarding the poor is still in full force. If the law and the prophets do not exhort the sinner to repent, then one who returns from the dead does not stand much of a chance either.

The rich man did not pass through the gate to help his neighbor: that was his sin. In the parable, the reign of God exists in the gate. If God ends up

---

[8]Ibid., 152.

[9]Ibid., 155.

[10]Charles H. Talbert, *Reading Luke* (New York: Crossroad, 1992), 156.

[11]Scott, *Hear Then the Parable,* 158.

taking care of everything, then there is no need for a gate (metaphor for the reign of God). The parable is not about random acts of kindness; it is about the ability to be in solidarity with those on the other side of the gate. The gate is a connecting link between those on both sides. The purpose of the gate is to bring both sides into solidarity with one another. To miss the gate means we may have missed the opportunity to further the reign of God and to be in solidarity with the entire human race. The danger in missing it is that, like the rich man, we may find that it is too late for us. The *Catechism of the Catholic Church*, states that "Our Lord warns us that we shall be separated from him if we fail to meet the serious needs of the poor and the little ones who are his brethren" (#1033).

Proclaim the gospel again.

Sometimes we gain new insights when we hear the text after the interpretation has been given. Someone from the group proclaims the gospel a second time.

STEP 4
TESTING

Conversation with the Liturgy and the Scriptures

Test your original understanding in dialogue with the text.

(You might consider breaking into smaller groups.)

Now that you've heard the exegesis, how do you feel about it? Were there any new insights? Was there anything you had not considered before? How does your original understanding of this story compare with what was just shared? How does this story speak to your life?

Participants share an experience from their lives that connects with the biblical interpretation just shared.

> *Very often we are deluded into believing that our responsibility to the poor is taken care of by throwing a few shekels at the problem. It appears that today's gospel is asking for more. It is asking that we get involved. It is asking that we be in solidarity with those on the outside.*

My son has a strong heart, love, care and concern—an option for the poor. He hopes that his studies will lead to work with the poor in a third-world country. He often finds himself "fighting" with his peers over issues that have to do with the poor. He is outraged at the attitudes he encounters. In his recent sociology class, he entered into a heated debate with another young man who argued that the rich are rich because of their own great talents, and the poor are poor because of their own laziness. This young man asserted that the rich have absolutely no responsibility to the poor. The poor simply need to get better jobs if they want to improve their situation. They have the same opportunities to achieve that rich people enjoy.

My son was astounded. He was ridiculed for what was labeled as his liberal political stance. In this Catholic college setting, little credence was given to the church's theology regarding an option for the poor. He felt as if he were beating his head against a wall. His disillusionment could not be masked.

A negative attitude toward the poor is nothing new, yet it very seldom gets articulated to the degree that my son experienced it. The attitude resonates with the posture of the rich man in today's gospel. We are not only called to be in solidarity with the less fortunate, but we are to engage in efforts to change their condition. It is very easy to fall prey to rich-man thinking. Our exaggerated sense of self-importance over our accomplishments tempts us to ignore our Source. When we are in solidarity with those on the other side of the gate, we realize how close we are to the same fate. We realize that, "there but for the grace of God go I." And we realize that without God we can do nothing. Our blessings are to be shared so that others can achieve the heights of their human potential.

If there are many young people with the same attitude as the young man in my son's sociology class, our society is in for very difficult times. How do we issue a wake-up call?

All share their life experience.

What was Luke trying to tell his community? What does he have to say to your community and to you today? Where do you see images of God's covenant, the exodus (passage from bondage to freedom), creation and the people of God (community) in this reading? Do you still feel the same way about this text as you did at the beginning? Has your original understanding been stretched, challenged, or affirmed?

STEP 5
DECISION

The gospel demands a response.

How is God speaking to us as a community? In what way is our community challenged? What are our collective and personal responses to all of these questions? How does our sharing and this biblical interpretation challenge our community's attitudes? Are there any situations in our communal life that need to be challenged by today's readings? In what concrete way does this gospel call our parish to action in the church, parish, neighborhood, or world? Has this conversation with the exegesis changed or stretched my personal attitudes? What is one concrete action I will take this week as a response to what was learned and shared today?

DOCTRINAL ISSUES

What church truth/teaching/doctrinal issue could be drawn from the gospel for the Twenty-Sixth Sunday in Ordinary Time?

Participants suggest possible doctrinal themes that flow from the readings.

Possible Doctrinal Themes

Social justice, morality, kingdom of God

Present the doctrinal material at this time.

1. The facilitator gives input on a particular doctrinal issue of his/her prior choosing. OR
2. The group chooses a doctrinal issue from the list they created. They read together from the Doctrinal Appendix.

(The doctrinal issues are found in the Doctrinal Appendix in the back of this workbook. If you are choosing an issue from this resource, please refer to it now.)

Reflection questions centered around the chosen doctrinal theme can be found at the end of each topic in the Doctrinal Appendix. The questions are based on the five-step reflection process. If you choose a topic not included in the Doctrinal Appendix, craft your own questions according to the same five-step process.

Following the reflection questions you will be reminded to return to chapter 7, "Preparing the Catechetical Session," to assist you in crafting your own session.

Closing Prayer

All powerful Father,
God of goodness,
you provide for all your creation.
Give us an effective love for our brothers and
      sisters
who suffer from a lack of food.
Help us to do all we can to relieve their hunger,
that they may serve you with carefree hearts.
We ask this through our Lord Jesus Christ, your
      Son,
who lives and reigns with you and the Holy Spirit,
one God, for ever and ever.[12]

Selected Bibliography

Days of the Lord. Vol. 6. Collegeville: The Liturgical Press, 1991.
Fuller, Reginald H. *Preaching the New Lectionary.* Collegeville: The Liturgical Press, 1974.
Johnson, Luke Timothy. *The Writings of the New Testament: An Interpretation.* Minneapolis: Augsburg Fortress, 1986.
Karris, Robert J. *The Pastoral Epistles.* Wilmington: Michael Glazier, 1979.
Kuntz, J. Kenneth. *The People of Ancient Israel.* New York: Harper and Row, 1974.
Scott, Bernard Brandon. *Hear Then the Parable.* Minneapolis: Augsburg Fortress, 1989.
Talbert, Charles H. *Reading Luke.* New York: Crossroad, 1992.

---

[12]Ritual Mass #28: In Time of Famine or for Those Who Suffer from Famine: "Opening Prayer," *The Sacramentary.*

TWENTY-SEVENTH SUNDAY IN ORDINARY TIME

INTRODUCTORY RITES

Opening Song (or Entrance Antiphon)

O Lord, you have given everything its place in the world, and no one can make it otherwise. For it is your creation, the heavens and the earth and the stars: you are the Lord of all. (Est 13:9, 10-11)[1]

Environment

The feast of Michael, Gabriel, and Raphael the Archangels is on September 29. These autumn liturgical weeks are in proximity to this feast. The imagery of this span of the liturgical cycle prompts our meditation on last things, end times, and the great eschaton. Non-saccharin images of angels might be creatively incorporated into the catechetical environment. Michael is a wonderful "patron" of autumn, suggests Peter Mazar. As dragon slayer, Michael's role is to lead the dead into the new and eternal city. Gabriel, with his ram horn, will sound the trumpet and awaken the dead. Even though Gabriel is also associated with Advent, Christmas, and the Annunciation, his folklore has strong eschatological overtones that are most appropriate in the waning days of autumn. Mazar also contends that Raphael, as healer and guide in the book of Tobit, has been a beloved companion during late autumn days.

These are also harvest days. Pumpkins, squash, gourds, cucumbers, apples, etc. remind us of God's plentiful yield. We are limited only by our imaginations when it comes to using such bounty in our catechetical environment.

Opening Prayer

The facilitator of the session may lead the prayer. Others in the group may be asked to proclaim the readings.

Let us pray
[that God will forgive our failings
and bring us peace]

Pause for silent prayer.

Father,
your love for us
surpasses all our hopes and desires.
Forgive our failings,
keep us in your peace
and lead us in the way of salvation.
We ask this through our Lord Jesus Christ, your
     Son,
who lives and reigns with you and the Holy Spirit,
one God, for ever and ever.[2]

LITURGY OF THE WORD

Let us listen to God's word.

The readings are proclaimed.

First Reading
Habakkuk 1:2-3, 2:2-4

Nothing is known for sure about Habakkuk's life. The inheritance he left was his beautifully crafted oracles that demonstrate his attitude toward God. He brilliantly addressed the issue of why the evil seem to prosper and the just do not. The backdrop for Habakkuk's dialogue was the situation occurring in the late seventh and early sixth centuries. The Assyrians were oppressing God's people. They had conquered the north and were greatly impacting Judea in the south. The Judean king was controlled by the Assyrians until their defeat by Babylon in 612 B.C.E.

Scholars agree that Habakkuk considered the Babylonians to be God's instrument. Through them, God would put an end to the cycle of violence, ruin and misery. God would use the Babylonians to chastise the wickedness of his people.

The first part of today's pericope is Habakkuk's first oracle. He boldly denounced the lawlessness

---

[1]Twenty-Seventh Sunday in Ordinary Time: "Entrance Antiphon," *The Sacramentary.*

[2]Twenty-Seventh Sunday in Ordinary Time: "Alternative Opening Prayer," *The Sacramentary.*

rampant in his time. Today's reading includes Habakkuk's complaint and God's subsequent response. Was God really willing to allow the innocent to suffer in order to punish the wicked? Habakkuk was instructed to write down God's message for posterity. God's response was a word for all people—a timeless word. It was so important that Habakkuk was to write it boldly enough that a runner could read it while passing by (the first billboard!). God promised that fulfillment of his vision would be realized in due time. Faith was to be the human response to God's initiative. The faithful person need only wait for Yahweh to act. The future was in God's hands. Trust was and is the believer's expected response. "Nevertheless, the message of Habakkuk contained the declaration that divine justice is inexorable and the assurance that even if satisfying answers to perplexing questions are not always within reach, God is still worthy of man's concern and confidence."[3]

Responsorial Psalm
Psalm 95:1-2, 6-7, 8-9

Psalm 95 is referred to as an enthronement psalm. Like the other enthronement psalms, Psalm 95 exalts in the presence of Yahweh. It also proclaims Yahweh's supremacy over other gods. Verse 7 shifts in tone as it recalls the wandering in the desert and Israel's infidelity. Meribah (the name means strife) and Massah (meaning testing) are places where God tested the people.

Second Reading
2 Timothy 1:6-8, 13-14

Second Timothy is considered a personal parenetic (exhortation) letter. Paul writes his letter to encourage and admonish Timothy in his difficulties and struggles. The letter does not contain any new information. Paul merely restates what Timothy already knows and exhorts him to hold fast to what he knows to be true. It is believed that 2 Timothy, as one of the pastoral epistles, is deutero-Pauline; that is, it is derived from the Pauline school, written by a disciple or disciples of Paul. Second Timothy is much shorter than First Timothy. It is addressed to the same disciple and is a

testament to the old and imprisoned apostle Paul. "The structure for 2 Timothy therefore is (a) the presentation of Paul as model (1:3–2:13); (b) maxims for Timothy as a teacher, presented in contrast to false teachers (2:14–4:5); (c) the representation of Paul as model (4:6-18)."[4]

Poor Timothy is discouraged and is thinking about giving up preaching. Paul, his mentor and "father," is in prison and has little hope of release. Paul writes to Timothy and encourages him by remembering Timothy's tears and the faith he learned from his mother and grandmother. His concern, however, shows itself when he reminds Timothy of the qualities and dispositions to which he was called. He was not given a spirit of cowardice; he was given a spirit of "power and self-control." Paul wants to strengthen and empower his protégé so he will persevere.

Paul presents himself as a model for Timothy. Paul is an exemplary teacher, and an example of how to suffer for the sake of the gospel. Timothy should be encouraged, as God will strengthen him for his mission. The gift of faith dwells within Timothy and will uphold him on the difficult journey. The mission of the post-apostolic church is to witness, suffer, and endure for the sake of the gospel and the reign of God.

Gospel
Luke 17:5-10

Jesus teaches the apostles about faith.

STEP 1
NAMING ONE'S EXPERIENCE

What were your first impressions? What was your first response? What grabbed your attention? How did you feel?

Each person names his or her initial impression. Statement should be brief. No reasons should be given at this time. All simply listen without agreeing or disagreeing.

---

[3]J. Kenneth Kuntz, *The People of Ancient Israel* (New York: Harper and Row, 1974), 331.

[4]Luke Timothy Johnson, *The Writings of the New Testament* (Philadelphia: Fortress, 1986), 392.

In a brief statement, what do you think this gospel is trying to convey?

STEP 3
INPUT FROM VISION/STORY/TRADITION

Liturgical Context

The Lectionary has chosen the central portion of the seventeenth chapter on the teaching of the dutiful servant and the healing of the lepers (recounted only in Luke) for our celebration and reflection this week and next. The foundational message is that God's gift of salvation is a totally free, gratuitous gift for *all people* inclusively. This forms the unity and sequence between the Twenty-Seventh and Twenty-Eighth Sundays.

This is the only time we hear from Habakkuk in the Sunday Lectionary. The last line in Habakkuk was used in catechesis early in Christendom. St. Cyril of Jerusalem preached the following: "Even if you think you are faithful, you have not yet attained the perfection of faith. You must also say: 'Lord, increase our faith.' For you have hardly anything of your own, but must receive much from him.... May you already have the faith that depends on you, so that you may be drawn by the one from whom you receive this other, who does what is beyond human power."[5]

Psalm 95 reminds us that "there is no proclamation of hope or profession of faith without a firm intention of conversion."[6] The second reading has ordination overtones. It is reminiscent of a liturgical text and formula. The imposition of hands is a sign of investiture, transmission of power, and the bestowal of mission. The imposition of hands is always associated with an epiclesis (invocation of the Holy Spirit) in the Christian liturgy. It is an awakening of the gift of faith that lies within. The letter

to Timothy is a reminder to our communities that the goal of liturgy is mission. Mission demands that we lay down our lives for the sake of others and the gospel. We are all charged with the mission. The ordained, the non-ordained—all are commissioned priest, prophet, and ruler at baptism. Every baptized person is to go to any length to spread the gospel of Christ. All we need is faith the size of a mustard seed and we will have what we need to see us through to the end.

Today's liturgy is faith's clarion call. The Christian journey demands simply that we have enough faith. We will be given what we need, but we are also to pray for an increase. The alternative opening prayer echoes our cry for faith. "Let us pray before the face of God in trusting faith...." It further reminds us that God will give us what we need to courageously stand before God's truth. "Father of the world to come, your goodness is beyond what our spirit can touch and your strength is more than the mind can bear. Lead us to seek beyond our reach and give us the courage to stand before your truth...."

Christian Initiation

Today's obvious faith overtones in the liturgy provide great leaven for the celebration of the Rite of Acceptance, a Rite of Full Communion into the Catholic Church or perhaps, if desirable or beneficial, the anointing of catechumens with oil.

> Anointing of Catechumens: Care is to be taken that the catechumens understand the significance of the anointing with oil. The anointing with oil symbolizes their need for God's help and strength so that, undeterred by the bonds of the past and overcoming the opposition of the devil, they will forthrightly take the step of professing their faith and will hold fast to it unfalteringly throughout their lives. [RCIA, #99]

Gospel Exegesis

The facilitator gives input regarding what critical biblical scholarship has to say about this text. The input includes insights as to how people would have heard the gospel in Jesus' time.

---

[5]Cyril of Jerusalem (ca. 315-386), *Catéchèse*, 5:9-11; P.G.33, 315-320; in *Days of the Lord*, Vol. 6 (Collegeville: The Liturgical Press, 1991), 356.

[6]*Days of the Lord*, Vol. 6, 243.

Luke 17:1-10 is a collection of sayings that focus on two questions: a) What are the disciples called to do? b) Are they able to do it? Today's pericope responds to and answers the second question. They are able to do it if they have faith. The assumption is that the apostles, even with their little faith, have enough to do the impossible! Luke uses the expression as an example of the faith that is needed to live the moral life proposed in verses 1-4. Matthew and Mark use the saying to demonstrate Jesus' miraculous power and to promise similar power to his disciples. Luke uses it to describe the amount of faith needed to support and strengthen the life of discipleship.

Faith is a person's response to God's initiative. It is a personal response to a God with whom we are in personal relationship. God continually forgives us. We, in turn, are to respond in faith and forgive others as God forgives us. Since God continually and perpetually forgives us, we will have the faith to do what seems to be impossible.

Faith emphatically is not the magic coercion of God to do what we want God to do. It is our "co-operation with God in the action, which, by his initiative, he has indicated that he wills to perform."[7] Luke believes that the disciple is able to do what is required. He or she is not to cause another to stumble and is always to forgive others. Thus, if disciples are able to do what is required, asserts Charles Talbert, they are not able to do more than is required. The point of the parable in the pericope is that even if the disciple does all that is commanded, there is nothing out of the ordinary in that. He or she is simply doing what is expected. The slave in the story, after working a hard day in the fields, came home and served as cook and housekeeper. He did not expect thanks, because he did what he was commanded to do. When the disciple does not cause another to stumble and when he or she forgives others, he or she is doing what has been commanded and there is nothing extraordinary in that. It is possible to do even with minimal faith.

The Pharisees were full of their own self-important accomplishments. Yet, while fulfilling all the requirements of the law they still could do nothing to gain their own salvation, nor did they fulfill their duty as disciples. The parable reminds us that we are justified by faith and that our works alone cannot gain salvation. We work in the kingdom because it is expected; it is our response in faith. Work in the kingdom is ongoing. It never ceases. "In the commitment that costs no less than everything, one's quota is never reached."[8]

Proclaim the gospel again.

Sometimes we gain new insights when we hear the text after the interpretation has been given. Someone from the group proclaims the gospel a second time.

STEP 4
TESTING

Conversation with the Liturgy and the Scriptures

Test your original understanding in dialogue with the text.

(You might consider breaking into smaller groups.)

Now that you've heard the exegesis, how do you feel about it? Were there any new insights? Was there anything you had not considered before? How does your original understanding of this story compare with what was just shared? How does this story speak to your life?

Participants share an experience from their lives that connects with the biblical interpretation just shared.

> *The heart of today's liturgy is conversion. What does faith mean without a complete turning of our lives and hearts to Christ and his gospel? Lest we become overwhelmed by the responsibilities that are inherent in such radical conversion, we can take comfort in today's liturgy. God will provide what is needed. The gospel is not suggesting that the disciples go out and acquire faith under the assumption that they have none. Rather, the gospel exhorts them to understand that the "little" faith they have is enough to uproot a sycamore.*

---

[7]Charles H. Talbert, *Reading Luke* (New York: Crossroad, 1992), 163.

[8]Patricia Datchuck Sanchez, *The Word We Celebrate* (Kansas City: Sheed and Ward, 1989), 375.

The little faith we have will be sufficient for the work we are called to do. We are simply to do what is expected of us as Christians, and the rest will be provided. We need not feel righteously self-inflated over fulfilling our Christian duties and responsibilities, either. The handing over of our lives is the length we are expected to go to further the reign of God.

I am reminded of the time five years ago when our parish was trying to make the shift from a nine-month school calendar model of Christian initiation to a year-round process. The task seemed monumental. We worked and worked; we argued and debated. It seemed as if our imaginary obstacles were insurmountable. We were trying to proceed on our own steam.

In the final analysis, it was the minimal faith and vision of the team that was multiplied. When the decision to implement the ongoing process was finally made, the sycamore tree was uprooted and the transition was not only smooth, but it was less stressful than we had anticipated. We all worked very hard to implement the vision. There was a lot of skepticism. We lost some team members in the process. It was not easy.

Today's gospel is a reminder to us that the Christian life is not always smooth-going or easy. We need not feel self-exalted over our labors—they are expected. Our job is to continue, to persevere, and to provide whatever faith we can muster. God will give us the strength to stay in the journey. That, indeed, has been our experience in working with the very messy process of initiation.

All share their life experience.

What was Luke's message to his community? What does he have to say to our community and to me today? What might God be creating (creation) in us through Jesus' teaching in the gospel? In what way does this gospel point to God's promise to be with us (covenant)? In what way have I/we known death/resurrection/liberation in my/our experience and understanding of this gospel (exodus)? How is God speaking to us as a community? Do we still feel the same way about this text as we did when we began? Has our original understanding been stretched, challenged, or affirmed?

The gospel demands a response.

In what way is your community challenged? How does your sharing and this biblical interpretation challenge your community's attitudes? Are you aware of any contemporary situation that could benefit from insights from today's liturgy? In what way does this gospel call your parish to action in the church, parish, neighborhood, or world? Be concrete. Has this conversation with the exegesis changed or stretched your personal attitudes? Name one specific action you will take this week as a response to what was learned and shared today.

DOCTRINAL ISSUES

What church truth/teaching/doctrinal issue could be drawn from the gospel for the Twenty-Seventh Sunday in Ordinary Time?

Participants suggest possible doctrinal themes that flow from the readings.

Possible Doctrinal Themes

Faith, kingdom of God, discipleship, Christian witness

Present the doctrinal material at this time.

1. The facilitator gives input on a particular doctrinal issue of his/her prior choosing. OR
2. The group chooses a doctrinal issue from the list they created. They read together from the Doctrinal Appendix.

(The doctrinal issues are found in the Doctrinal Appendix in the back of this workbook. If you are choosing an issue from this resource, please refer to it now.)

Reflection questions centered around the chosen doctrinal theme can be found at the end of each topic in the Doctrinal Appendix. The questions are based on the five-step reflection process. If you choose a topic not included in the Doctrinal Appendix, craft your own questions according to the same five-step process.

Following the reflection questions you will be reminded to return to chapter 7, "Preparing the Catechetical Session," to assist you in crafting your own session.

Closing Prayer

Let us pray
[before the face of God
in trusting faith]

Almighty and eternal God,
Father of the world to come,
your goodness is beyond what our spirit can touch
and your strength is more than the mind can bear.
Lead us to seek beyond our reach
and give us the courage to stand before your
      truth.
We ask this through Christ our Lord.[9]

Selected Bibliography

Days of the Lord. Vol. 6. Collegeville: The Liturgical Press, 1991.

Fuller, Reginald H. *Preaching the New Lectionary.* Collegeville: The Liturgical Press, 1974.

Johnson, Luke Timothy. *The Writings of the New Testament.* Minneapolis: Augsburg Fortress, 1986.

Kselman, John S., S.J., and Michael L. Barré, S.S. "Psalms." In *The New Jerome Biblical Commentary.* Ed. Raymond E. Brown, S.S., Joseph A. Fitzmyer, S.J., Roland E. Murphy, O.Carm. Englewood Cliffs: Prentice Hall, 1990.

Kuntz, J. Kenneth. *The People of Ancient Israel.* New York: Harper and Row, 1974.

Mazar, Peter. *To Crown the Year.* Chicago: Liturgy Training Publications, 1995.

Sanchez, Patricia Datchuck. *The Word We Celebrate.* Kansas City: Sheed and Ward, 1989.

Talbert, Charles H. *Reading Luke.* New York: Crossroad, 1992.

---

[9]Twenty-Seventh Sunday in Ordinary Time: "Alternative Opening Prayer," *The Sacramentary.*

Twenty-Eighth Sunday in Ordinary Time

INTRODUCTORY RITES

Opening Song (or Entrance Antiphon)

If you, O Lord, laid bare our guilt, who could endure it? But you are forgiving, God of Israel. (Ps 129:3-4)[1]

Environment

Ordinary time environment continues.

Opening Prayer

The facilitator of the session may lead the prayer. Others in the group may be asked to proclaim the readings.

Let us pray
[in quiet for the grace of sincerity]

Pause for silent prayer.

Father in heaven,
the hand of your loving kindness
powerfully yet gently guides all the moments of
    our day.
Go before us in our pilgrimage of life,
anticipate our needs and prevent our falling.
Send your Spirit to unite us in faith,
that sharing in your service,
we may rejoice in your presence.
We ask this through Christ our Lord.[2]

LITURGY OF THE WORD

Let us listen to God's word.

The readings are proclaimed.

First Reading
2 Kings 5:14-17

The first and second book of Kings contain a strong theological bias: Yahweh chose Israel from among all other nations as a partner in covenant relationship. The books further maintain that Yahweh is a jealous God; there are to be no foreign gods. Yahweh alone is one. The center of worship is also one. Thus, Jerusalem is to be the central, communal worship place in Israel.

Solomon, known for his splendor, his supremacy over other rulers, and his shrewd wisdom and ability to amass a vast empire, was remembered with disdain for ignoring the centralization of worship in Jerusalem. "He was unimpressed with the mandate that Israel must worship one God within the precincts of the Jerusalem Temple."[3]

Today's pericope stars the folk-hero and prophet, Elisha, whose name means "El has saved—God is salvation" in Hebrew. Elisha was commissioned by Elijah to continue the prophetic ministry. Elisha served in the Northern Kingdom of Israel under the rule of Jehoram, Jehu, and Jehoash (ca. 850-800 B.C.E.). He was remembered for his care and concern for the poor and for those faithful few who maintained their religious roots in spite of the decadent environment and culture. The writer of 2 Kings wrote his chronicle to encourage the religious remnant who had just endured the demise of the Northern and Southern kingdoms. The stories of Elisha helped them derive meaning from their situation and to sustain their covenant faithfulness to Yahweh. Such stories were a reminder of Yahweh's promise of future messianic glory. The stories in Kings were like "anecdotes that try to show the importance of the events in which the prophets participated. A most important motif in these stories is the absolute claim that Yahweh has on Israel."[4]

In today's story we meet Namaan, an Aramean/Syrian general afflicted with leprosy, an incurable

---

[1]Twenty-Eighth Sunday in Ordinary Time: "Entrance Antiphon," *The Sacramentary.*

[2]Twenty-Eighth Sunday in Ordinary Time: "Alternative Opening Prayer," *The Sacramentary.*

[3]J. Kenneth Kuntz, *The People of Ancient Israel* (New York: Harper and Row, 1974), 201.

[4]Leslie J. Hoppe, O.F.M., "Elijah/Elisha," in *The Collegeville Pastoral Dictionary of Biblical Theology,* ed. Carroll Stuhlmueller, C.P. (Collegeville: The Liturgical Press, 1996), 254.

disease. An Israelite slave girl informed Namaan of the healing Elisha had performed. Namaan's contemporaries encouraged him to ask Elisha to cure his leprosy. Namaan was Syrian and Elisha was an Israelite. Israel and Syria enjoyed an unstable peace. The king of Israel was suspicious of Namaan, but wanted to assist the commander in his plight. Elisha rescued the situation and invited Namaan to come to his house. Elisha told Namaan, a pagan, to go down and wash seven times in the Jordan. Namaan was annoyed, but he did as he was told and was subsequently healed of his leprosy.

The healing and works of Elisha were associated with the messianic reign of salvation. Reginald Fuller calls it a "parable of man's plight from which he would only be delivered by the Messiah, i.e. by a miracle at the end of time."[5]

Namaan was converted to belief in the transcendent power of Yahweh. He vowed to worship Yahweh upon his return home. He therefore took earth from Israel with him to his home in Syria so he could build an altar. This action was in response to an ancient belief that the power of the gods was limited to their geographical area. The author of Kings makes it clear that Yahweh's power is universal: it is for all people inclusively—everywhere.

As a Syrian, Namaan was excluded from the Israelite community. His healing foreshadows the healing and salvation Christ would accomplish in the messianic reign.

Responsorial Psalm
Psalm 98:1, 2-3, 3-4

Psalm 98 is part of the collection of enthronement psalms, exultant songs of joy in praise of the incredible power of Yahweh. This power was expressed in the yearly ritual enthronement of the king. The antiphon extols the fact that the nations recognize Yahweh's power.

Second Reading
2 Timothy 2:8-13

Even if, as some scholars suggest, Paul did not write this letter, it is possible that the first part of this reading is Paul's farewell letter to Timothy. The backdrop for this letter to Timothy was a Roman prison. Paul was awaiting martyrdom. He contrasted the unchained word of God with his own fettered and bound condition. Paul believed that his own suffering would further the reign of salvation in the messianic age. "Here would be the basis for the developing scriptural understanding of the doctrine of the 'merits' of the saints: suffering offered obediently to God is like prayer in that it contributes to the furthering of God's saving purpose."[6]

Paul preached salvation through suffering not just by his word, but by his very life. Paul's suffering brought life because he endured. Paul is the perfect example of enduring for the sake of the gospel. Paul's example is not enough, however. It is the "power of the grace given him by Christ Jesus."[7] Jesus will empower and strengthen his disciples to stand firm in the midst of suffering.

While it may appear that this is a word for only Timothy or church leaders, it is actually a word for all Christians. All will suffer for the sake of the gospel. We profess this creed in our liturgy, especially in the celebration of the eucharist. Eucharist incorporates us into the suffering, death, and resurrection of Jesus. Like bread, we are taken, blessed, broken, and shared for the sake of the gospel.

Verses 11-13 are probably liturgical in origin. These hymn-like verses are introduced by the introduction, "the saying is sure." This opening formula emphasizes that the following material is worthy of the disciple's trust and will guide diligent disciples on their path and practice of the faith.

Gospel
Luke 17:11-19

Jesus heals the ten lepers, but only one returns to thank him.

---

[5]Reginald H. Fuller, *Preaching the New Lectionary* (Collegeville: The Liturgical Press, 1974), 74.

[6]Ibid., 76.

[7]Robert J. Karris, O.F.M., *The Pastoral Epistles* (Wilmington: Michael Glazier, 1979), 20.

STEP 1
NAMING ONE'S EXPERIENCE

What were your first impressions? What was your first response? What grabbed your attention? How did you feel?

Each person names his or her initial impression. Statement should be brief. No reasons should be given at this time. All simply listen without agreeing or disagreeing.

STEP 2
UNDERSTANDING

In a brief statement, what do you think this gospel is trying to convey?

STEP 3
INPUT FROM VISION/STORY/TRADITION

Liturgical Context

Today's first reading is connected to the gospel through the theme of universality evidenced in the story of Namaan, a pagan who was healed and included in God's plan of salvation. In today's gospel story nine lepers (Israelites and thus the chosen people) were healed by Jesus and did not return to give thanks. There was one who did return to give thanks—a Samaritan and an outsider. The Samaritan accepted the universal, inclusive salvation of God. So did Namaan.

We have followed Jesus on the journey to Jerusalem since the Thirteenth Sunday in Ordinary Time. It has been a theological journey. It has been a journey fraught with meaning—a journey that leads us to Jerusalem and embracing the paschal mystery of Christ. The Christian journey always looks toward Jerusalem. Jerusalem is realized as we join our dying and rising to Christ. Jerusalem is experienced and realized as the community of God's people gather to remember and make present the sacrifice made on Calvary in Jerusalem. This happens every time the church gathers to take, bless, break, and share the Body of Christ.

The prayer after communion reflects this understanding and reminds us that we share in Jesus' life through his Body and Blood. It is through the eucharist that Jesus' road to Jerusalem becomes our road to Jerusalem.

Today's liturgy serves as a constant reminder that we are healed and made whole through the awesome power of God. We can be healed without experiencing conversion, however. Conversion demands that we turn to God with a humble spirit, confess our powerlessness before God, and offer God our thanks and praise. We do this every time we gather for eucharist. In today's alternative opening prayer we ask God to guide the journey of our lives, to anticipate our weakness, and to prevent us from stumbling along the way. In order to rejoice in God's presence we must first acknowledge God as Lord of our lives. Today's gospel reminds us that we are not to be complacent about the gifts God bestows upon us. We are to respond in faith.

This might be a good day to celebrate the Rite of Anointing catechumens. God strengthens and heals us on our life's journey, but we still must respond in faith.

Gospel Exegesis

The facilitator gives input regarding what critical biblical scholarship has to say about this text. The input includes insights as to how people would have heard the gospel in Jesus' time.

The ten lepers called out to Jesus by his name (a rather unusual occurrence in the gospels). Their supplication was an incredible expression of faith. Jesus was implored by name and with a request for help only three times: by the blind man at Jericho, by the thief on Calvary (in Luke's passion narrative) who asked Jesus to remember him in the heavenly reign, and in this story of the ten lepers. Further, Luke is the only evangelist to use the title "Master" in reference to Jesus. It is a confession of his omnipotence. It was used when Peter hauled in the big catch of fish, at the transfiguration, and when the fear-struck apostles begged for deliverance in the midst of the storm. Today's gospel expresses meaning by the mere invocation of Jesus' name. There is power in Jesus' name.

Eugene LaVerdiere asserts that this story is part of a section which stresses that selfish, exclusive, and blind attitudes and expectations fail to appreciate the presence of God's reign. On the "Day of the Lord," all will be saved, just like the foreigner/outsider who returned giving thanks and praise.

Today's story takes place on the road between Samaria and Galilee. It is part of the "road to Jerusalem" section of Luke's gospel. From now on, we will hear more of the journey motif as Luke's gospel forges ahead on this Jerusalem road, the inevitable road all disciples must take.

Leprosy was considered a sign of deserved punishment for sin. Those who suffered from the disease were believed to be morally and ritually unclean. Regardless of the severity of their disease, they were cut off from society. In order to be restored to the community they had to be healed, ritually cleansed, and officially pronounced clean. Today's healing had communal implications. Jesus' healing action restored the lepers to their rightful place in the community.

Samaria is significant in today's story. Only the Samaritan returned to give God thanks for the healing received. Earlier in the gospel's travelogue, Samaria had rejected the disciples' message because Jesus was headed for Jerusalem. However, Jesus kept the disciples from praying down fire and rain upon the city. Samaritans did not believe in Jerusalem as the proper seat of religious authority. Conflict between Jews and Samaritans had endured a long history, but the schism became hostile and open after the Samaritans had built a temple on Mount Gerazim centuries before. When Jesus went to Jerusalem, he superseded Jerusalem's previous significance as the seat of religious power.

Samaritans figured significantly in the story of the Samaritan who demonstrated what it meant to be a good neighbor according to the prescription of the law. And in this story a Samaritan returned giving thanks and praise to God. In contrast to the other nine, the Samaritan is an example of what "embodies the conditions of salvation."[8] He returned in faith to praise God for blessings received.

The nine lepers, representative of Israel, had not returned giving thanks. They, like the Pharisees, failed to understand that the messianic reign had arrived and was in their midst. The messianic reign was observable through Jesus' healing. While gratitude is indeed a message of this gospel, faith is another. It is freely offered and the salvation it provides is universal—freely given to all people. Those who are willing to suffer and die will preserve their lives and be saved.

There are two miracles in this story. Ten lepers were healed and a Samaritan came to faith in Jesus. The cure of the ten was not instantaneous, but required the obedient submission to a higher authority. Namaan followed Elisha's command to wash in the Jordan and the lepers had to go and show themselves to the religious authorities. They were healed en route. The Samaritan was the only one who returned to offer thanks. Thus, Jesus could confidently state, "Your faith has saved you." The story asserts that there is a difference between healing and salvation. One can be healed without coming to faith and thus being saved.

Charles Talbert asserts that the function of this story is to highlight what conversion entails. The human response to healing and conversion is to praise God. "The meeting of a physical need led to a spiritual conversion and produced an outpouring of praise."[9] He further reminds us that the experience of healing did not necessarily save. Healing was the catalyst. The Samaritan came to faith and responded in thanks to the healing he received. Salvation was bigger than the physical cure. Healing is salvific when the healing causes a person to respond to God in relational faith.

Jesus healed non-Jews. Luke makes it clear that Jesus' mission is to the entire world, not just to a select chosen few. It is open to all. Luke uses the strangest characters to demonstrate how often the least likely person is the recipient and appropriate respondent to God's saving works.

Some scholars maintain that this gospel is a foreshadowing of the Jewish rejection of Jesus and his commandments. It hints at the eventual mission to the gentiles. Luke's purpose is missionary. It re-

[8]Eugene LaVerdiere, S.S.S., *Luke* (Wilmington: Michael Glazier Books, 1980), 215.

[9]Charles H. Talbert, *Reading Luke* (New York: Crossroad 1992), 176.

minds the disciples that the gospel is for all people inclusively. As they go forth to baptize all nations, they are to be reminded that "*ALL*" means that no one is excluded from the reign of God.

Proclaim the gospel again.

Sometimes we gain new insights when we hear the text after the interpretation has been given. Someone from the group proclaims the gospel a second time.

STEP 4
TESTING

Conversation with the Liturgy and the Scriptures

Test your original understanding in dialogue with the text.

(You might consider breaking into smaller groups.)

Now that you've heard the exegesis, how do you feel about it? Were there any new insights? Was there anything you had not considered before? How does your original understanding of this story compare with what was just shared? How does this story speak to your life?

Participants share an experience from their lives that connects with the biblical interpretation just shared.

A friend recently told me of a couple from our neighboring parish who share an incredible story of healing, salvation, and conversion. Both had enjoyed the good life. They were not particularly religious. They decided that they would leave the rat race of the world. They were outsiders of their own choosing. They sold all their possession, bought a large sailboat, and set sail to live a life of leisure and solitude far away from the madding crowd, going from exotic port to port.

One night a storm appeared out of nowhere. The waves came crashing over the sides of the boat. The small vessel nearly capsized. The winds and rain were so strong that the couple were certain they would be washed overboard. They secured ropes and tied themselves to the deck of their sailboat. They were sure to die and they knew it. They kissed each other and waited with each agonizing convulsion of

their fractured vessel to go down with their ailing craft. Death was a surety.

Yet, in those pre-death moments something marvelously strange happened to both of them. As their lives flashed before them, they were flooded with God's incredible presence. It was a moment of encounter. Fear gave way to incredulous peace. It was as if the strong hand of Yahweh stabilized the boat and held it through its crashing course throughout the interminable hours between dark and dawn.

As dawn crept over the horizon, the couple woke from their exhausted slumber, slumped over, yet still bound to the ship's deck. Death stood watch on the bow of their deck, waiting to snatch its next victim, yet it stood powerless before the firm grip of God's protective embrace.

The couple was saved on that night. They could have walked away from that boat rescued and saved, but still untouched. They chose to allow their experience to define their lives. It gave new meaning to their existence. They met Grace head on and were forever changed by the encounter. They came back praising God and giving thanks. They who had given up on the world went right back to it in order to be its servant.

Their conversion led them to give back to God what has been freely given to them—their very lives. They disembarked at the nearest port and made that parish their home. They now devote their lives to serving God's people.

How many people are saved in dramatic and not-so-dramatic ways and yet do not change their lives or return giving thanks and praise? This couple had given up on society. They had left it to pursue their own ends. Yet, a brush with eternity sent them hurling right back into it with meaning and purpose for their lives.

All share their life experience.

What was Luke trying to tell his community? What was his intention? What does he have to say to our community and to me today? What might God be creating in us through this experience of Jesus in the gospel? In what way does this gospel point to God's promise to be with us? Where do we see images of the exodus (passage from bondage to freedom or new life)? How is God speaking to us as a community? Do we still feel the same way about this text as we did when we began? Has our original understanding been stretched, challenged or affirmed?

STEP 5
DECISION

The gospel demands a response.

In what way is our community challenged? How does our sharing and this biblical interpretation challenge our community (attitudes and behaviors)? In what concrete way does this gospel call our parish to action in the church, parish, neighborhood, or world? Has this conversation with the exegesis prompted any conversion within me? What am I /we/community/parish called to do in response? What is one concrete action we will take this week as a response to what we have learned and shared today?

DOCTRINAL ISSUES

What church truth/teaching/doctrinal issue could be drawn from the gospel for the Twenty-Eighth Sunday in Ordinary Time?

Participants suggest possible doctrinal themes that flow from the readings.

Possible Doctrinal Themes

Conversion, salvation, sacrament of healing, faith, grace

Present the doctrinal material at this time.

1. The facilitator gives input on a particular doctrinal issue of his/her prior choosing. OR
2. The group chooses a doctrinal issue from the list they created. They read together from the Doctrinal Appendix.

(The doctrinal issues are found in the Doctrinal Appendix in the back of this workbook. If you are choosing an issue from this resource, please refer to it now.)

Reflection questions centered around the chosen doctrinal theme can be found at the end of each topic in the Doctrinal Appendix. The questions are based on the five-step reflection process. If you choose a topic not included in the Doctrinal Appendix, craft your own questions according to the same five-step process.

Following the reflection questions you will be reminded to return to chapter 7, "Preparing the Catechetical Session," to assist you in crafting your own session.

Closing Prayer

All powerful and ever-living God,
the lasting health of all who believe in you,
hear us as we ask your loving help for the sick;
restore their health,
that they may again offer joyful thanks in your
    Church.
Grant this through our Lord Jesus Christ, your
    Son,
who lives and reigns with you and the Holy Spirit,
one God for ever and ever.[10]

Selected Bibliography

Fuller, Reginald H. *Preaching the New Lectionary.* Collegeville: The Liturgical Press, 1974.

Hoppe, Leslie J., O.F.M. "Elijah/Elisha." In *The Collegeville Pastoral Dictionary of Biblical Theology.* Ed. Carroll Stuhlmueller, C.P. Collegeville: The Liturgical Press, 1996.

Karris, Robert J., O.F.M. *The Pastoral Epistles.* Wilmington: Michael Glazier, 1979.

Kuntz, J. Kenneth. *The People of Ancient Israel.* New York: Harper and Row, 1974.

LaVerdiere, Eugene, S.S.S. *Luke.* Wilmington: Michael Glazier Books, 1980.

Talbert, Charles H. *Reading Luke.* New York: Crossroad, 1992.

---

[10]Masses for the Sick: "Alternative Opening Prayer," *The Sacramentary.*

Twenty-Ninth Sunday in Ordinary Time

INTRODUCTORY RITES

Opening Song (or Entrance Antiphon)

I call upon you, God, for you will answer me; bend your ear and hear my prayer. Guard me as the pupil of your eye; hide me in the shade of your wings. (Ps 16:6, 8)[1]

Opening Prayer

The facilitator of the session may lead the prayer. Others in the group may be asked to proclaim the readings.

Let us pray
[to the Lord who bends close to hear
our prayer]

Pause for silent prayer

Lord our God, Father of all,
you guard us under the shadow of your wings
and search into the depths of our hearts.
Remove the blindness that cannot know you
and relieve the fear that would hide us from your
    sight.
We ask this through Christ our Lord.[2]

LITURGY OF THE WORD

Let us listen to God's word.

The readings are proclaimed.

First Reading
Exodus 17:8-13

Moses and his tribe gear up for battle in today's pericope. His opponents are the Amalekites, a fierce tribe in the vicinity of Kadesh. Descendants of Esau, they were a nomadic tribe that resided in the desert regions of the Sinai, the Negeb and the Arabah, and parts of Arabia. While actual histori-cal records of the Amalekites are not to be found outside of scriptural reference, they are Israel's constant scriptural adversary. These tribes controlled passageways used by caravans traveling between Arabia and Egypt. Until defeated by David, they served as a constant threat to Israel's attempt to settle in Canaan.

In today's story, Moses is victorious in battle against the Amalekites as long as he extends over them the rod he used to defeat Pharaoh. Yahweh is in alliance with Israel as long as Moses extends the rod. Moses' arms become extremely fatigued, however, and the advantage turns whenever he lowers his arms. The word for fatigued is the same word used to describe "his inability to function without sharing his authority."[3] Thus, Joshua and Hur enter the scene. Hur does not maintain a dominant role in the events of Exodus, but Joshua becomes Moses' most trusted servant and later his successor. The Amalekites are doomed to defeat because they seek to keep Israel from her God-given heritage. They are formally cursed in a document promulgated by Joshua, Israel's military leader. Moses built an altar and praised Yahweh for their victory.

The biblical authors were not concerned with recording historical war records for the sake of historical accuracy. The stories were told in order to make a religious statement of truth. Yahweh protects Israel and her interests. Israel's valiant efforts were supported by a loving God who intervened on their behalf. "In the incident at Rephidim, Moses was established as the mediator of his people, one upon whose endurance and faith the welfare of the entire nation depended."[4]

While the event stretches the imagination to its limit, the theological point in this situation cannot

---

[1]Twenty-Ninth Sunday in Ordinary Time: "Entrance Antiphon," *The Sacramentary.*
[2]Twenty-Ninth Sunday in Ordinary Time: "Alternative Opening Prayer," *The Sacramentary.*

[3]Richard J. Clifford, S.J., "Exodus," in *The New Jerome Biblical Commentary,* ed. Raymond E. Brown, S.S., Joseph A. Fitzmyer, S.J., Roland E. Murphy, O.Carm. (Englewood Cliffs: Prentice Hall, 1990), 51.
[4]Patricia Datchuck Sanchez, *The Word We Celebrate* (Kansas City: Sheed and Ward), 378.

be missed. Prayer works! God is powerful—we are not! God saves—we do not! This story is so fixed in our conscious imagination that we usually miss the central figure of this story. We are so locked into our gaze upon Moses' outstretched hands that we fail to see the staff in his hands. Moses is holding the "staff of God." It is God's instrument. It is through God's intervention, symbolized in the staff, that Israel is saved.

Reginald Fuller suggests that some believe Moses' connection with New Testament thought is typological. Moses is understood as a pre-figure of Christ who intercedes for the people. Another more probable interpretation is that Moses' action is understood as a symbolic action similar to the actions of prophets who influenced certain situations.

Without the staff of God raised over us in protection, our enemies will be victorious over us. While not placing God in the position of God-Warrior over our sin-caused human wars, we metaphorically use the image as a means to understand God's role in our lives. We are expected to do our part, to fight the battles against our enemies with valor, but then to expect God to uphold us with his staff when our limited efforts fail.

Responsorial Psalm
Psalm 121:1-2, 3-4, 5-6, 7-8

This is a psalm of trust. The psalmist relies on Yahweh's divine protection. The psalm asserts that God will never forsake the church. God will always guide her and be manifest to her. God may judge the church, but will never leave her.

Second Reading
2 Timothy 3:14–4:2

The primary aim of the pastoral letters was to instruct church leaders. However, the letters were also a veiled exhortation to the church at large—the faithful believers. Please refer to the Twenty-Seventh and Twenty-Eighth Sundays—second reading.

A primary motif in today's letter to Timothy is the primacy of the proclamation of God's word in the apostolic mission. This demands faithfulness to the gospel by all believers. "The apostle is not a

schoolmaster, but a servant: he receives what he must in turn pass on faithfully."[5]

The word of God is always transmitted in a community of believers. It is passed on from believer to believer. Abraham Heschel once said that there are no proofs for the existence of God, there are only witnesses. Thus, it is the community's experience and revelation of God that is passed down through the inspired word of God and thus to all believers through the transmission of that word from community to community and from person to person. Paul attests to the significance of the word handed down first from its Hebrew origins in the Old Testament, then carried on in the New Testament and furthered in the living tradition of the church.

Paul affirmed the word that Timothy's ancestors had faithfully transmitted to him. Since as a child Timothy had not been a Christian, Paul was giving credence to the authenticity of the Hebrew scriptures (OT) and their continuity with the New Testament.

Paul reminded Timothy that he had received the word as a child. The word was passed on to him by his grandmother Lois and his mother Eunice (2 Tim 1:5). We are prompted to remember and revere the evangelization efforts of all mothers and grandmothers who have gone before us. How many of us have embraced a living faith while rocking in the laps of our maternal ancestors?[6] Paul is the model preacher of the good news. He transmitted the word with his life. We are called to the same vocation.

---

[5]*Days of the Lord,* Vol. 6 (Collegeville: The Liturgical Press, 1991), 263.

[6]I am reminded of a young woman who entered our initiation process. She was a recent immigrant from Russia. Her father was a "card-carrying" Communist and forbade the word *God* to be spoken in their home. Elena shared how, as she grew into adulthood, she became aware of a hollowness and an emptiness in her life and she started to seek. She thanked God for the missionaries who helped her find what she was seeking. Elena asked us to teach her everything we could about Jesus, as she knew very little. However, as her story unfolded we discovered that Elena "knew" more than she thought. She knew of a God who loved her and protected her. She told how, even though it was unlawful to speak about God, most people were aware of God and stories about God,

Gospel

Luke 18:1-8

The parable of the unjust judge and the widow.

STEP 1
NAMING ONE'S EXPERIENCE

What were your first impressions? What was your first response? What grabbed your attention? How did you feel?

Each person names his or her initial impression. Statement should be brief. No reasons should be given at this time. All simply listen without agreeing or disagreeing.

STEP 2
UNDERSTANDING

In a brief statement, what do you think this gospel is trying to convey?

STEP 3
INPUT FROM VISION/STORY/TRADITION

Liturgical Context

There are only five Sundays left for us to encounter Luke's "sequence of events." There is a unity between the Twenty-Ninth through the Thirty-First Sundays. Included are excerpts from chapters 18 and 19. On these three Sundays we experience stories that occur only in Luke: the parable of the unjust judge and the persistent widow, the parable of the Pharisee and the tax collector, and the story of Zacchaeus. There are threads of Luke's overall doctrine woven through these three stories. They form a whole—a composite—and thus provide an internal unity between the Twenty-Ninth through the Thirty-First Sundays.

A theme emerges for Luke. "Justification comes from faith granted to the one who does not rely on his merits but opens himself to the gratuitous mercy of GOD."[7] At the National Conference of Catechetical Leaders held in Orlando, Florida in 1997, Rev. Michael Himes echoed that sentiment when he stated, "Salvation is not a movement from *not being* loved by God to a state of *being* loved by God. Rather, salvation is a movement from *not accepting* God's love to *acceptance*." In other words, God's love was always present—there was never a time when God's love was absent. There is nothing we can do to earn it; it is freely given. All we can do is graciously accept it.

An image of God as one who does justice for defenseless widows, justifies the humble, and saves sinners emerges in these three passages. Jesus is revelatory of that image. Jesus embodies such justification and salvation when he befriends the lowly, cares for those on the fringes, and seeks out the lost. These three gospel events sum up the entire Lukan message. Diligence in prayer and persistence in the face of injustice are hallmarks of the reign of God. Prayer and action are the basis of the Christian dispensation as we await Jesus' final coming in glory.

As we approach the waning days of the liturgical year, leaves begin to turn color and drop to the ground. The earth begins to prepare its winter's bed. We are reminded that life is tenuous at best, that seeds must fall to the ground and die before they can sprout again to new life. Our attention begins to turn toward the last things and our eschatological hope. Prayer and action strengthen us as we await that final glorious day. Today's readings and liturgy remind us that we are not to remain passive in our waiting, but rather are to pray with diligence, turn to God for the strength we need, spread the word of God by the example of our lives, and fight to right injustice when it bears down on us like a roaring lion.

The alternative opening prayer reminds us that it is only through our blindness and fear that God is

---

of Jesus and the events of scripture. We found this to be most amazing! "How did you learn about these things when you lived in a Communist home that forbade 'God-talk' of any kind?" "It was the grandmothers," said Elena. The grandmothers remembered the stories from their youth and passed them on to their grandchildren. "Our Russian grandmothers told us the stories and insisted that we never forget."

---

[7]*Days of the Lord,* Vol. 6, 258.

absent from our lives. Only through prayer will we prevail through such fear and blindness. "Let us pray to the Lord who bends close to hear our prayer. Lord our God, Father of all, you guard us under the shadow of your wings and search into the depths of our hearts. Remove the blindness that cannot know you and relieve the fear that would hide us from your sight." Through the celebration of the eucharist we are given the nourishment to sustain us on the journey to life's culmination. We are told that God loves us so much that he bends close to us to hear our prayer. God will do whatever it takes for us to accept the love that he freely gives.

The prayer after communion reminds us that eucharist makes a difference in our lives: "Lord, bring to perfection within us the communion we share in this sacrament. May our celebration have an effect in our lives." The effect we seek is a life of discipleship: prayer, evangelization, and action.

Gospel Exegesis

The facilitator gives input regarding what critical biblical scholarship has to say about this text. The input includes insights as to how people would have heard the gospel in Jesus' time.

The judge in today's story is concerned neither about God nor about the customary codes of human honor and shame. The judge in this story does not follow the biblical norms concerning right conduct for judges. Judges, according to 2 Chronicles 19:6-7, are to be impartial; they are to judge on behalf of God and they are not to take bribes. The woman in this story is not your typical helpless biblical widow, either. She demonstrates much *chutzpah* in her relations with the judge. She will not be put off! Care for widows was tied to covenant relationship. *Hesed* (biblical justice) demanded that widows be cared for because God desired it. Thus, widows were to be given the leftovers of the harvest and their clothing was not to be taken in payment.

Interest would have been aroused immediately by Jesus' parable. First, a woman pleading her own case (unheard of, or at least extremely rare!) would have immediately startled the audience. An-

other point of interest was the story's locale. By placing the judge in the city, the parable was immediately making a political statement. It was placing him among the "urban elite," entitled to a place of honor in that shame-based culture. Societal roles were established by that one declaration and listeners would have been acutely aware of their own lowly status. The judge was on the top of society's pile; the listeners were on the bottom. There was nothing novel about this. Yet, the parable was giving the listeners an inside scoop: this judge was shameless. By not fearing God and by not having respect for people, he was shameless. "He is an outlaw judge."[8] He was not deserving of his elevated societal status.

The parable lets the listener in on a political perspective simply by describing the next character as a widow. There was a strong biblical mandate concerning the proper treatment of widows. A widow was a person in need of special protection. In biblical times a widow was often left destitute after the death of her husband. She was not allowed to inherit the estate of her husband. However, the law demanded that she be provided for by proceeds from the estate and by remaining relatives. The law did not always play itself out in practice, however, and many widows were very poor and in need of protection. Yahweh demanded that Israel protect its widows. Those who did not protect widows were considered lawless and wicked.[9]

The judge eventually answered the woman's prodding, not out of his God-given duty, but because he was afraid she would give him a black eye (or so it appears from the text)! The phrase about violence can also be interpreted as "to slander another." The judge's good name would be battered or blackened if he did not respond to the persistent woman. The judge was expected to answer the woman because she deserved protection, yet he acted only out of personal convenience and self-preservation. According to Bernard Brandon Scott, the great irony is that the judge acted not out of fear of God or respect of people, but out of fear of a defenseless widow, the weakest member of society. In the parable, the judge was supposed

---

[8]Bernard Brandon Scott, *Hear Then the Parable* (Minneapolis: Augsburg Fortress, 1989), 180.

[9]See first reading for Thirtieth Sunday—next Sunday.

to stand for God (the traditional role of judges). This judge, however, acted out of self-preservation, not justice.

Barbara Reid suggests that if the widow is an example of persistent prayer, then the judge is a metaphor for God. However, if the woman is an image of God (like the parable of the woman searching for the lost coin), then there is a different perspective to consider.

The main thrust of the parable is the action of the widow. She keeps coming and coming. It is *in the coming* that she gets results, not because of the justice of her cause. She wears the judge down. Barbara Reid entertains the notion that the widow, *as an image of God,* is relentless in pursuing justice. It would have been quite startling to Jesus' listeners to place God in the position of a defenseless widow: God is powerful, not powerless. Reid suggests, "She embodies godly power in the midst of apparent powerlessness."[10] This is the paradox of the paschal mystery—strength in weakness, life through death. It is embodied in the life, death, and resurrection of Jesus Christ. Jesus' helplessness in the face of death conquered the demon death.

Jesus turns the expected into the unexpected, catches the listener, and in the process "shatters stereotypes and highlights the seeming powerless."[11] The widow, metaphor for God, fights for justice amidst her weakness.

Interestingly, the widow's persistence in the face of injustice is not unique to this widow. Ruth and Tamar both took action on behalf of their people, thus transcending the traditional image of the helpless widow. The widow who was no longer bound to care for home and family was given greater freedom to serve in ministerial roles, asserts Reid. "Like the widowed Anna, who spent her days in the Temple prophesying to all who were awaiting redemption (2:36-38), so this widow appears before the judge day after day, relentlessly speaking out for justice."[12]

---

[10]Barbara E. Reid, *Women in the Gospel of Luke* (Collegeville: The Liturgical Press, 1996), 192.

[11]Ibid., 194.

[12]Ibid., 193.

While persistent prayer is no doubt a worthy interpretation of this parable, courage in the face of death-dealing powers and persistence in demanding justice are also credible as well as laudable considerations.

Proclaim the gospel again.

Sometimes we gain new insights when we hear the text after the interpretation has been given. Someone from the group proclaims the gospel a second time.

Step 4
Testing

Conversation with the Liturgy and the Scriptures

Test your original understanding in dialogue with the text.

(You might consider breaking into smaller groups).

Now that you've heard what the scholars have to say about this parable, how do you feel about it? Were there any new insights? Was there anything you had not considered before? How does your original understanding of this parable compare with what we just shared? How does this story speak to your life?

Participants share an experience from their lives that connects with the biblical interpretation just shared.

> *I am reminded of a situation someone shared recently. Two people in Christian community experienced a severe fracture in their relationship. One person was in a position of power, the other was at the mercy of the person in power. The person in power used power abusively and consequently drove the other person out of the community. The action not only was an injustice toward the person, but also to the people who benefited from this person's ministry. In the spirit of today's liturgy, members of that Christian community rallied behind their oppressed friend. No one had much faith that their persistent efforts to change the situation would have an impact. However, some asserted that it was worthwhile to simply stay in the struggle (to keep coming) for as long as it might take.*

Both persistence and prayer are needed in situations where death and evil in the form of human weakness and insecurity have the upper hand. By human standards the victim in this scenario did not "win out." However, God "raises his staff" over communities that choose to stand with the oppressed. Perhaps the only "winner" was the community that persisted in its efforts to demand biblical justice. Today's parable reminds us that it is in the coming *that the reign of God is made manifest. The word of God is revealed in such communities by the action of community members' lives.*

All share their life experience.

What was Luke trying to tell his community? What does he have to say to our community and to me today? In what way are the biblical themes of creation, community, covenant, and exodus evident and what do they mean to the life of our community? In what way have I experienced transformation or a new perspective in my experience and understanding of this gospel? Do we still feel the same way about this text as we did when we began? Has our original understanding been stretched, challenged, or affirmed?

STEP 5
DECISION

The gospel demands a response.

How does this liturgy, our sharing, and this biblical interpretation challenge our community? In what concrete way does this gospel call our parish to action in the church, parish, neighborhood, or world? Has this conversation with the exegesis of the parable of the unjust judge changed or stretched my personal attitudes? What is one concrete action I will take this week as a response to what was learned and shared today?

DOCTRINAL ISSUES

What church truth/teaching/doctrinal issue could be drawn from the gospel for the Twenty-Ninth Sunday in Ordinary time?

Participants suggest possible doctrinal themes that flow from the readings.

Possible Doctrinal Themes

Prayer, justice, grace, faith, images of God, kingdom of God

Present the doctrinal material at this time.

1. The facilitator gives input on a particular doctrinal issue of his/her prior choosing. OR
2. The group chooses a doctrinal issue from the list they created. They read together from the Doctrinal Appendix.

(The doctrinal issues are found in the Doctrinal Appendix in the back of this workbook. If you are choosing an issue from this resource, please refer to it now.)

Reflection questions centered around the chosen doctrinal theme can be found at the end of each topic in the Doctrinal Appendix. The questions are based on the five-step reflection process. If you choose a topic not included in the Doctrinal Appendix, craft your own questions according to the same five-step process.

Following the reflection questions you will be reminded to return to chapter 7, "Preparing the Catechetical Session," to assist you in crafting your own session.

Closing Prayer

Let us pray
[for the gift of simplicity and joy
in our service of God and man]

Almighty and ever-living God,
our source of power and inspiration,
give us strength and joy
in serving you as followers of Christ,
who lives and reigns with you and the Holy Spirit,
one God, for ever and ever.[13]

---

[13]Twenty-Ninth Sunday in Ordinary Time: "Opening Prayer," *The Sacramentary.*

Selected Bibliography

Clifford, Richard J., S.J. "Exodus." In *The New Jerome Biblical Commentary.* Ed. Raymond E. Brown, S.S., Joseph A. Fitzmyer, S.J., Roland E. Murphy, O.Carm. Englewood Cliffs: Prentice Hall, 1990.

Days of the Lord. Vol. 6. Collegeville: The Liturgical Press, 1991.

Fuller, Reginald H. *Preaching the New Lectionary.* Collegeville: The Liturgical Press, 1974.

McKenzie, John L., S.J. *Dictionary of the Bible.* New York: Collier, 1965.

Reid, Barbara E. *Women in the Gospel of Luke.* Collegeville: The Liturgical Press, 1996.

Sanchez, Patricia Datchuck. *The Word We Celebrate.* Kansas City: Sheed and Ward, 1989.

Scott, Bernard Brandon. *Hear Then the Parable.* Minneapolis: Augsburg Fortress, 1989.

THIRTIETH SUNDAY IN ORDINARY TIME

INTRODUCTORY RITES

Opening Song (or Entrance Antiphon)

Let hearts rejoice who search for the Lord. Seek the Lord and his strength, seek always the face of the Lord. (Ps 104:3-4)[1]

Opening Prayer

The facilitator of the session may lead the prayer. Others in the group may be asked to proclaim the readings.

Let us pray
[in humble hope for salvation].

    Pause for silent prayer.

Praised be you, God and Father of our
Lord Jesus Christ.
There is no power for good
which does not come from your covenant,
and no promise to hope in,
that your love has not offered.
Strengthen our faith to accept your covenant
and give us the love to carry out your command.
We ask this through Christ our Lord.[2]

LITURGY OF THE WORD

Let us listen to God's word.

The readings are proclaimed.

First Reading
Sirach 35:12-14, 16-18

Jesus Ben Sirach lived and wrote around 180 B.C.E. He was an educated man whose main writing concerns were reflection on the Torah and practical suggestions for upright living. Sirach wrote his book in Hebrew with the intention of providing a book of instruction on the day-to-day living of a well-disciplined, moral life. His grandson translated the work into Greek around 132 B.C.E. The book

of Sirach helped preserve Jewish thought and wisdom in the midst of Hellenistic culture. It gives us a glimpse into Jewish religious and societal norms of the period prior to the Maccabean revolt (169–164 B.C.E.). He was so serious about the law's exhortations that he considered breaking the law as tantamount to breaking the covenant relationship with God. Israel's covenant relationship with Yahweh demanded biblical justice—*hesed*. *Hesed* assumed a reciprocity and required that love of one another flow out of the love of God.

Today's pericope comes from a section devoted to prayer and sacrifice. Sacrifice is understood as pleasing to God only when the one offering the sacrifice is in covenant relationship with Yahweh and is faithful to the law. "As a merely external exercise, the sacrificial cult is hypocritical and an abomination in God's eyes."[3] Sirach insists that the poor person's gift is equal in value to the rich person's gift. God has no favorites.

The New Testament parts company with Sirach's theology of a rigid merit system based on the Torah. Sirach insisted that God is impartial in his treatment of people. The rich fare no better in God's eyes than the poor. But Sirach would also disagree with the New Testament belief in gratuitous, unearned grace. For Sirach, people are justified through their observance of the law.

The book of Sirach was not accepted in the Hebrew and Protestant canons. Yet, Sirach was a Jewish favorite up until the eleventh century. Sirach has been used in Christian worship more than any other text with the exception of the psalms.

The Pharisee of today's parable had well embraced Sirach's understanding of justification. However, he did not temper it with God's mercy that found its perfect fulfillment in Christ and his paschal mystery.

Responsorial Psalm
Psalm 34:2-3, 17-18, 19, 23

---

[1]Thirtieth Sunday in Ordinary Time: "Entrance Antiphon," *The Sacramentary.*

[2]Thirtieth Sunday in Ordinary Time: "Alternative Opening Prayer," *The Sacramentary.*

[3]Patricia Datchuck Sanchez, *The Word We Celebrate* (Kansas City: Sheed and Ward, 1989), 380.

Psalm 34 is an individual song of thanks. The psalm addresses the just and invites them to join with the psalmist in praising God for God's protection and deliverance of those who trust. The psalm reflects the wisdom tradition's basic view that the righteous will be taken care of by the providential care of God.

Second Reading
2 Timothy 4:6-8, 16-18

Paul's second letter to Timothy is written in a genre similar to the farewell discourse and exhortation. It is generally believed that Paul was not the author of this letter and that it was written somewhere near the second century. It is further believed that the letter contains fragments of Paul's original words. Those authentic fragments are believed to be the words of today's second reading. Paul is awaiting death from his prison cell as he writes to Timothy. (Please refer to Twenty Seventh Sunday in Ordinary Time for further background information on 2 Timothy.) "Although he feels close to death (4:6-8), he writes to encourage and admonish his favorite delegate in *his* struggles."[4] *Life poured out like a libation* is language indicative of Greek thought. Wine and oil were often associated with the Jewish liturgy of offering sacrifice. Libations of wine and oil were also used by the Greeks and the Romans. Wine was poured on the ground in homage to gods at banquets and festive occasions. Paul adapted the pagan notion as an image of his own life being poured out in sacrifice for the sake of others.

When Paul mentioned that he had kept the faith (v. 7), he meant that through the witness of his life and adherence to the doctrine of Christ crucified he had endured in spite of persecution.

There is no new word for Timothy in this letter, simply a reiteration of what Timothy already knows and holds to be true. Paul challenges Timothy to remain steadfast and true to what he already knows.

In this fourth chapter of second Timothy, Paul presents himself as the model of suffering in hope. In spite of being opposed, Paul had remained strong in his ministry. Timothy is thus exhorted to remain steadfast through suffering and adherence to the gospel, just like Paul. Hope resonates through Paul's encouragement to Timothy. Paul is assured of God's love, God's reign, and God's protection until such time as he is taken safely to the heavenly reign. Paul would win the crown (an olive, laurel, or pine branch wreath was awarded to athletes at the end of a great feat of endurance) through his participation in Jesus' suffering, death, resurrection, and subsequent victory over evil.

In the second part of today's pericope, Paul speaks of a *first hearing* (probably a type of arraignment) to determine if charges would be leveled. It appears that no one came to Paul's defense at this first hearing. Some scholars suggest that the absence of support by Paul's Christian brothers and sisters might have been due in part to the Roman church's concerns about his orthodoxy. Paul assures Timothy that with or without their support, Jesus is with him to strengthen and uphold, *to stand by his side and give him strength* (v. 17).

Gospel
Luke 18:9-14

The Pharisee and the tax collector go to the temple to pray.

STEP 1
NAMING ONE'S EXPERIENCE

What were your first impressions? What was your first response? What grabbed your attention? How did you feel?

Each person names his or her initial impression. Statement should be brief. No reasons should be given at this time. All simply listen without agreeing or disagreeing.

STEP 2
UNDERSTANDING

In a brief statement, what do you think this gospel is trying to convey?

---

[4]Luke Timothy Johnson, *The Writings of the New Testament* (Minneapolis: Augsburg Fortress, 1986), 391.

Liturgical Context

The three readings today are about God's judgment. They remind us of the appropriate stance and posture we are to assume before God: an unabashed attitude of humility. God is a judge who cares for the poor, hears their prayer, and offers them justice. Justice comes only from God. The tax collector prayed the prayer of the poor and was offered biblical justice—*hesed*. The Pharisee did not need *hesed*—he was already just in his own eyes.

We gather around the Lord's table aware of our sinfulness. The challenge is to offer our prayer in solidarity with the tax collector, not the Pharisee.

The weeks of Ordinary Time are beginning their movement toward closure. Fall is well under way and is moving toward winter. The liturgies begin their concentration on last things. The judgment of God is an important aspect of our concentration on last things. To reflect on the end of our humanity means to reflect on our ultimate dependence on the mercy of God. The tax collector in today's parable is certain of his sinfulness. He is certain of his need for God's mercy. There are no illusions. Salvation is possible for him only through the benevolence of God.

The Pharisee, on the other hand, is certain that he has nothing to worry about—he has it under control. He has taken all the necessary steps. He has observed all the laws—he's in! It is precisely his own self-reliance that puts him at odds with his God. There is no need for God, as the Pharisee has taken care of everything himself; this is ultimate pride and arrogance.

The opening prayer reflects our utter dependence on God's love and strength: "There is no power for good which does not come from your covenant, and no promise to hope in that your love has not offered. Strengthen our faith to accept your covenant and give us the love to carry out your command." This prayer does not reflect the posture of one who believes that he or she is doing *all the right things*. It reflects the posture of one who *hopes* that God will guide him or her to do the right thing. It places the onus on God where it belongs.

Gospel Exegesis

The facilitator gives input regarding what critical biblical scholarship has to say about this text. The input includes insights as to how people would have heard the gospel in Jesus' time.

Today's parable is found only in Luke's gospel. We are immediately introduced to the Pharisees and the negative attitude they always bring to any situation. In our day, the word *phariseeism* usually means hypocrisy. However, even though the centuries have judged them harshly, particularly because of parables just like this one, there is more to the Pharisee story than first meets the eye. The Pharisees have been given a bad rap throughout history. Yes, there were bad Pharisees, but there were also good Pharisees.

Luke portrayed various images of Pharisees. Pharisees came to Jesus and warned him that Herod wanted to kill him (Lk 13:31). Gamaliel, a Pharisee and a respected teacher of the law, was a moderator between the apostles and the Sanhedrin in the Acts of the Apostles. Only one Pharisee persecuted Christians—Paul. Sadducees, as the priestly party, were the ones responsible for the death of Jesus. They were the persecutors. The Pharisees were mostly good, observant, religious people and were loved by the populace. Today's parable reflected reality. The Pharisee probably did avoid sin, fast, and pay his tithe.

Pharisees were very popular with the people and contributed greatly to Jewish life. The Pharisees attempted to make the family setting a sacred space by insisting that religious dietary and cleanliness rules be observed in the home. It is very easy for the casual observer to see only the laws and fail to see the reason the laws were established in the first place. "These regulations are not originally intended so much to supplant the Temple altogether as to sanctify family and home life by making it a Temple as well. One of the reasons that Judaism is immediately able to continue even after its central symbol, the Temple in Jerusalem, is destroyed is that the sanctuary of family and home is already established as sacred space."[5]

This parable is not necessarily highlighting the Pharisee as a hypocrite. It would be normal for the Pharisee as well as for any one of us today to thank God that we are not like the thieves and criminals that adorn the front pages of our newspapers. The average person in the ancient world would not automatically assume that the word Pharisee was synonymous with hypocrisy. John Dominic Crossan suggests a modern-day corollary. If we were to say, "A pope and a pimp went to St. Peter's to pray," no one would remotely assume self-righteousness on the part of the pope.[6] Nor should we make a similar assumption about the Pharisee. Without Luke setting up a bias in verse 9, there would be no basis for the judgment of the Pharisee.

Bernard Brandon Scott doubts whether Lukan hearers would have judged the Pharisee as unjust without Luke's introduction. Scott asserts that this parable is a commentary on the temple and the kingdom of God. The socio-political temple structure places the Pharisee on the inside and the tax collector on the outside. There is nothing to suggest that the Pharisee is not exactly what the temple standards would uphold as a pious man. The Pharisee stands in the temple, confident of his place and his rights. He is the insider who has a right to the holy space.

The tax collector, on the other hand, knows that he has no rights or place in the temple. He stands at a distance and his prayer reflects awareness of his sinfulness. So far, there is nothing that would have startled first-century listeners. All is occurring as expected. The Pharisee is pious and the tax collector remains a sinner. "So what's the big deal?"

Not until they leave the sacred space for their respective homes does the hook come crashing in on the listeners. The tax collector is named right-

eous. How could that be? Where is the tax collector's repentance?

Scott suggests that even though Luke uses the parable as an example story, in reality there is nothing to imitate. "The hearer cannot imitate the behavior of one or the other. The parable's message is simpler."[7] The parable establishes that temple standards are no longer valid when it comes to distinguishing insiders from outsiders. The parable subverts the notion that the kingdom of God resides in the temple. It overturns the prevalent principle that ". . . things associated with the temple are holy and in the kingdom, things not associated with the temple are unholy and outside the kingdom. In the parable the holy is outside the kingdom and the unholy is inside the kingdom."[8]

Another scholar suggests that the problem of the Pharisee lies in the contrast with the tax collector. One is convinced of his own righteousness while the other is convinced of his sinfulness. One man is understood to be in good relationship with God. The other knows he is not and simply awaits God's mercy. We cannot become "just" on our own power. The tax collector knows he is not just; the Pharisee is sure that he is just.

The parable is written for the listener. The listener is set up to judge the Pharisee before the parable begins. "This introduction (v. 9) sets up the character to be rejected as false, untrue to his religiosity."[9] We are easily deluded. It is easy to acknowledge and recognize feelings of righteousness and superiority when comparing ourselves with the worst of sinners. However, we can be blinded to our self-righteousness when we follow all the rules, behave as saints, and forget that we too are sinners in need of redemption. We need God. We are nothing without God's mercy. The only posture before God is humility.

The tax collector acknowledged his need before God. The Pharisee believed in his own righteousness. He received no grace, because he needed no

---

[5]Bernard J. Lee, *The Galilean Jewishness of Jesus* (New York/Mahwah: Paulist Press, 1988), 102.

[6]John Dominic Crossan, *Raid on the Articulate* (New York: Harper & Row, 1976), 108.

[7]Bernard Brandon Scott, *Hear Then the Parable* (Minneapolis: Augsburg Fortress, 1989), 97.

[8]Ibid.

[9]Ibid., 92.

grace. Reginald Fuller suggests that Jesus would never have condemned the man for his piety or applauded the tax collector for his thievery and dishonesty. "What was wrong with the Pharisee was his approach to God."[10] He lauded his own efforts; his focus was not on God's action, but on his own righteousness. The tax collector, however, waited in abject need for God's mercy.

Proclaim the gospel again.

Sometimes we gain new insights when we hear the text after the interpretation has been given. Someone from the group proclaims the gospel a second time.

STEP 4
TESTING

Conversation with the Liturgy and the Scriptures

Test your original understanding in dialogue with the text.

(You might consider breaking into smaller groups.)

Now that you've heard what the scholars have to say about this parable, how do you feel about it? Were there any new insights? Was there anything you had not considered before? How does your original understanding of this story compare with what was just shared? How does this story speak to your life?

Participants share an experience from their lives that connects with the biblical interpretation just shared.

> *We very often are fooled into thinking that the reign of God only exists in our churches or parishes. It is difficult to imagine God working in the lives of those outside the official church. We think the holiest persons are those who go to church, volunteer their time, pray, and are the pious members of our community. We often fail to see holiness in the most unexpected places—sometimes in what we would judge to be unholy.*

---

[10]Reginald H. Fuller, *Preaching the New Lectionary* (Collegeville: The Liturgical Press, 1974), 82.

When my son's friend was killed in a car accident, our family experienced holiness in the lives of teenagers who had not graced the inside of a church for a long time. Yet, holiness was evident in their care for one another, in the ways they prayed and grieved for their friend, and in the way they touched the transcendent in the midst of their pain.

I remember one young man who stood in the back of the church, with his flaming orange hair, crying like a baby, too timid to come forward, yet so much in need of consolation. In the pain of this young man was the pain and frustration of lost young people everywhere. Christ was present in this young person's loneliness and pain. This young man wept as he chastised us for not giving him an opportunity at the funeral to openly say his goodbye and tell the world what a good person his friend had been. He told us that he wasn't a church-going person; he said he probably shouldn't even be in church because it had been so long, but he had to say goodbye to his friend. He knew Adam was with God.

This young man was not an insider. With his orange hair and unkempt look, most communities would dismiss him and consider him an outsider. Yet, he was the broken, wounded presence of Christ in our midst. His family history was filled with rejection and deep wounds. In his own simple way, he was aware that he was an outsider—he didn't fit in. It was tempting to judge his fringe, far-out appearance as unworthy of our worship space.

Danny shared a very simple belief in the God he knew was with his friend. He also brought his grief, broken dreams, and young lifetime of brokenness. I reached out to him in his brokenness. In his simplicity and his child-like grief he was the face of God and embodied the sacred as I held him like a small child in my arms.

Danny acknowledged that he didn't belong in church, that he was not very religious, and that he did not like organized religion. However, he demonstrated a child-like faith in God who seemed to him like the only thing that made sense amid the chaos and senselessness. If this weird looking young man didn't belong in church, then none of us belong.

I must avoid smug self-righteousness when it comes to my relationship with God. The Dannys of the world are often closer to the heart of God because of the failure and rejection they have experienced. They instinctively know that only God cares for them since the people in their world long ago gave up that role.

It is easy to forget the Source of my life when I am so busied about all those activities that will guarantee a permanent place in eternity. The conversation goes something like this: "God, I'll get back to you later; I'm supposed to do all these things if I want to spend eternity with you. So, I just don't have the time right now. Hold that thought, though; I'll get back to you later. I have to take care of YOUR business right now—prayer, tithing, almsgiving, etc."

While God's business is indeed worthy, the engine that drives it in this case is not God—it is human self-sufficiency. How absurd! Too much self-reliance—not hypocrisy—was the blind sin of the Pharisee.

All share their life experience.

What was Luke trying to tell his community? What does he have to say to our community and to me today? What might God be creating in us through this gospel reading? In what way does this gospel point to God's promise to be with us? In what way have I known death/resurrection in my experience and understanding of this gospel? How is God speaking to us as a community? Do we still feel the same way about this text as we did when we began? Has our original understanding been stretched, challenged, or affirmed?

STEP 5
DECISION

The gospel demands a response.

How does your sharing and this biblical interpretation challenge your community's attitudes? In what way does this gospel call your parish to action in the church, parish, neighborhood, or world? Be concrete. Has this conversation with the exegesis of this parable changed or stretched your personal attitudes? Name one concrete action you will take this week as a response to what was learned and shared today.

DOCTRINAL ISSUES

What church truth/teaching/doctrinal issue could be drawn from the gospel for the Thirtieth Sunday in Ordinary Time?

Participants suggest possible doctrinal themes that flow from the readings.

Possible Doctrinal Themes

Morality, conversion, kingdom of God, discipleship, image of God, judgment of God

Present the doctrinal material at this time.

1. The facilitator gives input on a particular doctrinal issue of his/her prior choosing. OR
2. The group chooses a doctrinal issue from the list they created. They read together from the Doctrinal Appendix.

(The doctrinal issues are found in the Doctrinal Appendix in the back of this workbook. If you are choosing an issue from this resource, please refer to it now.)

Reflection questions centered around the chosen doctrinal theme can be found at the end of each topic in the Doctrinal Appendix. The questions are based on the five-step reflection process. If you choose a topic not included in the Doctrinal Appendix, craft your own questions according to the same five-step process.

Following the reflection questions you will be reminded to return to chapter 7, "Preparing the Catechetical Session," to assist you in crafting your own session.

Closing Prayer

It is truly right to give you thanks,
it is fitting that we offer you praise,
Father of mercy, faithful God.
You sent Jesus Christ your Son among us
as redeemer and Lord.
He was moved with compassion
for the poor and the powerless,
for the sick and the sinner;
he made himself neighbor to the oppressed.

By his words and actions
he proclaimed to the world
that you care for us
as a father cares for his children.
And so, with all the angels and saints
we sing the joyful hymn of praise.[11]

Selected Bibliography

Crossan, John Dominic. *Raid on the Articulate.* New York: Harper & Row, 1976.

Days of the Lord. Vol. 6. Collegeville: The Liturgical Press, 1991.

Fuller, Reginald H. *Preaching the New Lectionary.* Collegeville: The Liturgical Press, 1974.

Johnson, Luke Timothy. *The Writings of the New Testament.* Minneapolis: Augsburg Fortress, 1986.

Kselman, John S., S.J., and Michael L. Barré, S.S. "Psalms." In *The New Jerome Biblical Commentary.* Ed. Raymond E. Brown, S.S., Joseph A. Fitzmyer, S.J., Roland E. Murphy, O.Carm. Englewood Cliffs: Prentice Hall, 1990.

Lee, Bernard J. *The Galilean Jewishness of Jesus.* New York/Mahwah: Paulist Press, 1988.

Sanchez, Patricia Datchuck. *The Word We Celebrate.* Kansas City: Sheed and Ward, 1989.

Scott, Bernard Brandon. *Hear Then the Parable.* Minneapolis: Augsburg Fortress, 1989.

---

[11]Eucharistic Prayer for Masses for Various Needs and Occasions: "Preface—Jesus the Compassion of God," *The Sacramentary.*

THIRTY-FIRST SUNDAY IN ORDINARY TIME

INTRODUCTORY RITES

Opening Song (or Entrance Antiphon)

Do not abandon me, Lord. My God, do not go away from me! Hurry to help me, Lord, my savior. (Ps 37:22-23)[1]

Opening Prayer

The facilitator of the session may lead the prayer. Others in the group may be asked to proclaim the readings.

Let us pray
[that our lives will reflect our faith]

Pause for silent prayer

God of power and mercy,
only with your help can we offer you fitting service
    and praise.
May we live the faith we profess
and trust your promise of eternal life.
Grant this through our Lord Jesus Christ, your
    Son,
who lives and reigns with you and the Holy
    Spirit,
one God, for ever and ever.[2]

LITURGY OF THE WORD

Let us listen to God's word.

The readings are proclaimed.

First Reading
Wisdom 11:22–12:1

The book of Wisdom is one of the last books of the Old Testament. It is not contained in the Hebrew bible and it is believed to have been originally written in Greek. It was a popularly held be-

lief that the book was written by Solomon, but scholars maintain that it was written long after his reign. Solomon's authorship was refuted by Origen, Eusebius, Augustine, and Jerome. The assumption of Solomon's authorship in the text is a literary device. "The author of the book remains anonymous, and the most we can say is that he was a learned Greek-speaking Jew and probably a teacher, and that he was familiar with Hellenistic philosophy, rhetoric, and culture."[3]

The book was written about 60 B.C.E. in order to strengthen Jews in Alexandria. Alexandria in Egypt was the third largest city of its day. It was a cultural center and a place of intellectual debate between Jewish and Greek scholars intent on testing their philosophies and methodologies. It is believed that these exchanges served as the catalyst for the production of the Septuagint, the Old Testament translation into Greek.

Hellenistic culture was rapidly advancing. Philosophies and religions were cropping up that were attempting to define the real meaning of life. A burning issue of the day was divine retribution: how is it that the just suffer and the wicked prosper? Skepticism and individualism were rampant. There was a serious crisis of faith in which traditional values were questioned. (Sound familiar?) Many Jews left the faith to embrace new modern philosophies and pagan ideologies. The book of Wisdom was the Jewish response to the Greek philosophical system that was threatening traditional Jewish life.

The style of this literature is comparable to the Hellenistic literature of the time known as *didactic exhortation.* Such exhortation maintains that what a person learns should have an impact on the way one lives his or her life. The book reflects the writing and the wisdom of an author who meditated upon the scriptures and wished to offer consola-

---

[1]Thirty-First Sunday in Ordinary Time: "Entrance Antiphon," *The Sacramentary.*
[2]Thirty-First Sunday in Ordinary Time: "Opening Prayer," *The Sacramentary.*

[3]Addison G. Wright, S.S., "Wisdom," in *The New Jerome Biblical Commentary,* ed. Raymond E. Brown, S.S., Joseph A. Fitzmyer, S.J., Roland E. Murphy, O.Carm. (Englewood Cliffs: Prentice Hall, 1990), 510.

tion and encouragement to his Jewish brothers and sisters. "When he retells the history of his people, it is not to discover their future or explain their destiny in it. His meditation is rather concerned with God himself and his conduct with respect to humanity."[4]

The book is divided into two parts. Sometimes the first part (chapters 1–6:21) is referred to as the *Book of Eschatology*. It deals with retribution and the benefits of seeking Wisdom above all else. The second part of the book deals with how Wisdom (Spirit of God) works in the world and how one is to find it (Chapter 6:21–end).

Today's pericope is a reflection on the utter insignificance of human beings in the face of the transcendent God. God's awesome power merely highlights the incredible nature of his mercy and love. In this passage, the word *love* is used as a verb, not a noun. It is an action word: God continually creates us anew, preserves us, and forgives our sins. The point of the passage, asserts Reginald Fuller, is that even though humanity perverted the creation bestowed upon them, it is nevertheless God's creation. God's Spirit is in all things. Thus, human beings can summon their Creator and ask that God's masterful work of creation be spared from destruction. After all, what God would want to ruin his own finely crafted work of art? We can draw the conclusion that we are indeed God's work of art and, though sinful, are worth saving.

The author is responding to Greek dualism which asserted that humanity could not understand the will of God because the evil human body drags down the good spirit-mind. It seems that the author of Wisdom is embracing the dualistic Platonic notion that body/matter is evil and the spirit is good. He is not, however. The Hebrew scriptures uphold the Genesis notion that creation is intrinsically good. The Wisdom author believes the body is merely an encumbrance when seeking to understand the will of God. "It is its finite, not its evil, character that is its drawback."[5] The Spirit of God helps humanity to transcend its finitude.

---

[4]*Days of the Lord*, Vol. 6 (Collegeville: The Liturgical Press, 1991), 280.

[5]Reginald H. Fuller, *Preaching the New Lectionary* (Collegeville: The Liturgical Press, 1974), 66.

Responsorial Psalm
Psalm 145:1-2, 8-9, 10-11, 13, 14

This psalm praises Yahweh's kingship. Verses 1-10 extol God's might and God's greatness. Verse 11 praises God's eternal reign over all; and verses 14-21 focus on Yahweh's mighty deeds. The psalm is a fitting response to the first reading.

Second Reading
2 Thessalonians 1:11–2:2

The letters to the Thessalonians probably inaugurated the beginning of Christian literature (ca. 49 C.E.), asserts Luke Timothy Johnson. Paul's main issue is the "identity and integrity of the community."[6]

The purpose of Paul's letters was to encourage and support, to clarify misunderstandings, and to communicate with the communities since he was unable to be with them. A closer inspection of Thessalonians shows us a common problem Paul encountered within the churches he established. Even though the communities accepted his message, they did not always understand it.

Paul had gone to the capital city of Macedonia and preached in the Thessalonian synagogue. A few Jews were converted, and a great many gentiles and prominent Jewish women were brought into the fold of Christianity. The Jews were furious. When they were unable to find Paul, they dragged Paul's colleague, Jason, before the court. They charged Paul with treason for claiming that Jesus was a king. Paul then moved on to preach in a new area. The Thessalonians followed him there and further harassed him. Paul left Timothy and Silas, moved to Athens, was rejected there, and finally landed in Corinth, where he set up his base headquarters.

In his first letter to the Thessalonians, Paul exhorted them not to abandon the faith. The letter was a parenetic (moral exhortation) correspondence. Paul's first letter was not a response to a crisis situation, but rather sought to encourage stability and strength in the face of pending oppression.

---

[6]Luke Timothy Johnson, *The Writings of the New Testament* (Minneapolis: Augsburg Fortress, 1986), 260.

Some scholars believe that the second letter is unauthentic. Johnson refutes that notion. He insists that it is too close to the heart of the first letter to be unauthentic. Some believe that the second letter was written because the city demanded that Paul revise his first letter in order to respond to the growing, struggling community.

The second letter does seem to be responding to a crisis situation and to misunderstandings that plagued the fledgling community. In this second letter persecution is referred to in less general, more descriptive and specific terms. The description of judgment is more climactic.

The church seemed to be experiencing demoralizing fear. Church members believed the end was upon them. Some quit working in order to await Jesus' arrival. This fear was due to the community's immaturity, popular belief regarding the end times, misunderstandings of Paul's warnings and admonitions in the first letter, and an increase of persecution of the church. While Paul described the end of time in his first letter, he refused to give a timetable for its arrival. He assured the Christians in Thessalonica that they would be saved and cautioned them to be watchful and alert. This only fed their preoccupation. While Paul was simply encouraging diligence in living the Christian life, well meaning Christians interpreted *diligence, watchfulness,* and *alertness,* as postures of preparation for the immanent, final eschaton. They could not be bothered with the mundane things of life—they were compelled to devote all their energy to this one obsession! The second letter was written, therefore, to correct mistaken interpretations of Paul's first letter and to refute a false letter that was circulating at the time that asserted that the "Day of the Lord" had already arrived!

At the time there was a gnostic tendency to divide people into two subgroups: the pneumatics (those who experienced a refined, superior knowledge and enlightenment) and the psychics or *hylics* (those who belonged to this world). The hylics had no chance of being anything better than what they were—chained to the body and a life of degradation. False teachers were teaching that the gospel revealed the true nature to only an elite few (the pneumatics). One was either privileged or not. The gospel's purpose was to reveal to the pneumatic his or her true, elevated, and enlightened nature. Once people realized who they really were (the extent of their true nature), the "Day of the Lord" had arrived for them! "The elite already enjoyed immortality."[7] Gnostics believed they were already living in the reality of their resurrection.

Paul loudly responded: "No way!" The "Day of the Lord" had not yet arrived. There was still much to do and much that needed to happen. Diligence demanded day-to-day attentiveness to living the moral life. To persevere and win the prize of salvation was not due to the effort of human achievement, but rather to the gratuitous mercy of God!

Gospel
Luke 19:1-10

Zacchaeus climbed the tree to see Jesus and received mercy, love, and salvation.

STEP 1
NAMING ONE'S EXPERIENCE

What were your first impressions? What was your first response? What grabbed your attention? How did you feel?

Each person names his or her initial impression. Statement should be brief. No reasons should be given at this time. All simply listen without agreeing or disagreeing.

STEP 2
UNDERSTANDING

In a brief statement, what do you think this gospel is trying to convey?

STEP 3
INPUT FROM VISION/STORY/TRADITION

Liturgical Context
The Wisdom reading is taken out of its context for the sake of the liturgy. In this case it is intended to

---

[7]Fuller, *Preaching the New Lectionary,* 84.

be a preparation for listening and responding to today's gospel. God's mercy is unfathomable and it is freely given. God draws us to conversion. God spares creation because God loves all he has created and all creation belongs to God. God lives and moves within his creation. God chastises and teaches sinners and then God exhorts them to a new way of life. What better reflection to prepare us for the proclamation of God's love and mercy in the personal encounter between Zacchaeus and Jesus?

The "road to Jerusalem" segment is coming close to an end in Luke's gospel. The journey is in its last stages. In today's gospel Jesus is in Jericho, an oasis in the desert. This city has the lowest elevation of any city in the world. It is three hundred meters below sea level; the ascent to Jerusalem is at least 1,000 meters. It is in this desert oasis city that Jesus meets Zacchaeus and invites him to become a "son of Abraham." Jesus seeks him out and saves him.

Today's gospel reminds the reader that Jesus came to seek the lost, the outcast, the sinner, and society's rejects. Jesus ate with them and offered his life with and for them.

We share in this life through the eucharist. The earthly life of Jesus is the incarnate presence of God crashing through our human history to seek and save the lost. Reginald Fuller suggests that it is "a seeking and a saving which is a present reality in the eucharist, when the Son of Man (Jn 6:53) comes under the forms of bread and wine to seek and save the lost."[8] The communion antiphon for today's liturgy attests to this reality: "As the living Father sent me, and I live because of the Father, so he who eats my flesh and drinks my blood will live because of me" (Jn 6:58). The prayer after communion puts it in the context of our everyday lives: "Lord, you give us new hope in this eucharist. May the power of your love continue its saving work among us and bring us the joy you promise." The eucharist is the tangible reality of that love as it strengthens, nourishes, and transforms us each week.

Zacchaeus, in spite of his great sinfulness, demonstrated great faith in his response to Jesus. He went to great lengths to receive the hospitality

---

[8]Ibid., 86.

Jesus was offering. In the process of his encounter with *Love* personified, Zacchaeus was moved to a deep interior transformation: repentance of his sins. We participate in that repentance by the conversion of our interior disposition, and by the celebration of the eucharist. "God of mercy, may we offer a pure sacrifice for the forgiveness of our sins" (Prayer Over the Gifts).

Today we also begin the last letter of Paul that we will read in Cycle C. It is short, but it packs great meaning within its few pages. The two letters to the Thessalonians are the oldest letters to have been passed down to the church. The first was written about twenty years after Jesus' death, ca. 51 C.E. It reminds us of what every liturgy celebrates: watchful diligence until the Master returns. Paul's letter is most appropriate in the waning weeks of the liturgical year. It is interesting how the seasons segue one into another. The last weeks of the liturgical cycle speak of last things, just as the first weeks of the new cycle speak of last things as well as new things.

Today's liturgy is a sober reminder that the church swiftly approaches her focus on the end times, the last things, and the day of the great eschaton.

Gospel Exegesis

The facilitator gives input regarding what critical biblical scholarship has to say about this text. The input includes insights as to how people would have heard the gospel in Jesus' time.

Today's story of Zacchaeus is intended to contrast with that of the wealthy man in chapter 18 who, after having asked what he must do to enter the kingdom of God, could not make the ultimate commitment by giving his possessions away to the poor and then following Christ. Both men were powerful in their own right. The first wealthy man was a righteous person in every way except the one that mattered. He could not let go completely. He could not turn his life over to the Master's care by selling his possessions and giving the money to the poor.

Zacchaeus, on the other hand, was not considered a righteous man. He was a sinner. The tax collector was regarded as unclean and deplorable in the eyes of the community. As chief tax collector for Jericho, Zacchaeus had ingratiated himself to no one. He was held in universal contempt.

Rome auctioned off the right to collect taxes to the highest bidder. The tax collector was required to pay off all the taxes owed to Rome before he collected them. He hired agents to collect the taxes that would recoup his initial investment. The tax collector then added a hefty interest payment to the tax owed, used questionable collection methods, and in the process made a tidy (read-HUGE!) profit on his original investment. The tax collector was considered unclean, a sinner, and a lawless rogue for gouging the citizenry.

This rogue and sinner in today's story accepts the prophet with joy and is willing to give restitution to the full extent of the Torah. He is willing to give back more than the law demands of him. "When one who had cheated another confessed his guilt and volunteered to make restitution, the amount required was equal to the amount stolen plus one fifth more (Leviticus 6:5, Numbers 5, 7). However, if a person were caught in the act and then *forced* to make restitution, the amount exacted would be four or fivefold the amount stolen (Exodus 22:1-4, 2 Samuel 12:6)."[9] Of his own volition, Zacchaeus chose to pay the greater penalty, demonstrating his own responsibility for his dishonest behavior as well as his willingness to make the ultimate restitution.

The story demonstrates that appearances can be deceiving. As far as the casual observer was concerned, it appeared as if the first wealthy man (ch. 18) was the pious one, yet he was closed to the invitation of the Master. The tax collector, on the other hand, was regarded as the scum of the earth, yet in the end he was called the "child of Abraham."

Today's story is a message about the kingdom. The good news reached out, even to the branches of a treetop, to seek out and save the lost. Prior to the story of Zacchaeus there were stories of the blind man whose sight was restored and stories of the poor, the outcast, and children who were welcomed into the kingdom. Jesus reached out to receive them and they accepted his invitation. Theologian Michael Himes suggests that there is never a time when *Love* is not present; never is there a time when salvation is not already a reality. Prior to salvation the only missing ingredient is the acceptance and reception of that *Love* and salvation that are always there in the first place.

There was never a time when Jesus did not love Zacchaeus. Zacchaeus did not have to change in order for Jesus to love him. It was in response to the *Love* offered that Zacchaeus was transformed and in that transformation he was radically called to live a new way. Zacchaeus demonstrated great faith in his determination to see Jesus. Faith of that sort is capable of breaking through any humanly imposed barrier to God such as the law.

Luke warns the listener that attitudes toward possessions reveal what is in one's heart. The wealthy man was bound up with his possessions. His unwillingness to respond to the Master's invitation was indicative of his unwillingness to forego his possessions. Zacchaeus's willingness to share with the poor was indicative of a transformed heart eager to listen and respond to the voice of his Master.

Jesus' response to Zacchaeus prefigured the future Christian paradigm. "Outcasts would repent, give to the poor and be saved, over the objections of those who deemed themselves righteous."[10] Jesus told Zacchaeus that he must stay at his house (v. 5) and later he affirmed that salvation had come to that house (v. 19). Eugene LaVerdiere suggests that "to have Jesus as one's guest is to be the host of salvation."[11]

In chapter 18 the question is raised as to whether or not a rich person can be saved. The story of Zacchaeus answers the question. Of course the rich can be saved. However, the demands of salvation require that a person receive Jesus' hospitality

---

[9]Patricia Datchuck Sanchez, *The Word We Celebrate* (Kansas City: Sheed and Ward, 1989), 384.

[10]Eugene LaVerdiere, S.S.S., *Luke* (Wilmington: Michael Glazier Books, 1981), 225.
[11]Ibid.

and table fellowship, repent for acts of injustice, provide for the poor, and welcome Jesus into his or her home.

Reginald Fuller suggests that this story echoes a common theme of the synoptic gospels: Jesus ate with the outcasts of society. Scholars affirm that one certainty in the gospel portrayal of Jesus is that he ate with sinners and outcasts. In spite of the objections of the righteous, Jesus saved and will save whom he pleases. Salvation is offered for everyone—it need only be accepted.

Charles Talbert reminds us that the stories of the historical Jesus were shaped by the church's experience of the risen Christ. It is this context that enables us to understand Zacchaeus's story in terms of the conversion it invites. Jesus beckoned a person. There was something in the unknown Jesus that captured the spiritual imagination of Zacchaeus. Verses 5-7 attest that Jesus *came into* Zacchaeus. As Zacchaeus welcomed Jesus into his house, the indwelling of Jesus brought forgiveness. Talbert also states that Jesus "confirmed" Zacchaeus (vv. 8-9). That is, he gave "assurance of the reality of what transpired in the secret of the human soul. This assurance rests on two things: a transformed life (v. 8) and the witness of Jesus (v. 9)."[12]

The eschatological nature of this story rests in the salvation offered and Jesus' use of the term, *Son of Man*. Some scholars argue that Jesus probably did not use that term in relation to himself. The *Son of Man* was a heavenly being who was to appear at the end of time before the final eschaton. Jesus was an earthly being and, as such, did not identify himself as that personage. The Christian church, however, later appropriated the Jewish understanding of *Son of Man* as a reference for Christ. The reference to the *Son of Man* in this pericope is the church's mystagogical reflection on Jesus' entire life and ministry. The *Son of Man*, this eschatological, transcendent being lived, suffered, died, and rose again. This *Son of Man* came to seek out and save the lost.

Proclaim the gospel again.

_____
[12]Charles H. Talbert, *Reading Luke* (New York: Crossroad, 1992), 177.

Sometimes we gain new insights when we hear the text after the interpretation has been given. Someone from the group proclaims the gospel a second time.

STEP 4
TESTING

Conversation with the Liturgy and Scriptures

Test your original understanding in dialogue with the text.

(You might consider breaking into smaller groups.)

Was there anything in the exegesis of the Zacchaeus story that captured your imagination? Were there any new insights? Was there anything you had not considered before? How does your original understanding of this story compare with what was just shared? How does this story speak to your life?

Participants share an experience from their lives that connects with the biblical interpretation just shared.

> *Today's liturgy screams to us from the rooftops—"Do you get it yet? You may not put the Lord, your God in a box!" My imagination sent me looking for a modern-day corollary. The amazement of first-century listeners on hearing of the conversion of Zacchaeus was no less than ours would be today if someone such as the publisher of Hustler Magazine were to similarly go to great lengths to respond to the prophet Christ. In the very naming of such a scenario I betray my preexistent bias and judgment of someone I deem to be the antithesis of righteousness. But the reality of today's gospel is that the aforementioned publisher could be Zacchaeus (might already be Zacchaeus) in the flash of an eye, whereas I could be and perhaps am in league with those who refused the Savior's invitation. By my very act of judgment I set myself up as righteous—VERY DANGEROUS!*

> *In a recent news documentary on the spread of infectious diseases, I was aghast when I saw a placard that was raised in protest by well meaning Christian men and women in response to the AIDS epidemic. It read: "Don't you dare spend one dime to find a cure for AIDS—it is God's just retribution for the*

sin of homosexuality." What a dangerous place for Christians to tread: the judgment court of heaven. We cannot perceive the human heart. We do not know who is a willing recipient of God's mercy and who is not. We can safely bet that those who are self-righteous and who condemn others cut themselves off from the power of that mercy.

I am challenged every day of the week in my own home to respond to the Zacchaeus principle—and I often fail miserably. On any given day of the week I am surrounded not simply by my own teenagers, but by teenagers of various sizes, assortments, shapes, personal lifestyles, and religious leanings (or lack thereof). On any given day my space is invaded by the "long haired," the "no-haired," the "tummy tattooed," and "the eye, ear, nose and navel pierced" characters that pass through my humble abode. The dialogue that goes on in my head is often not fit for human consumption. Murmurs such as "terrorist," "pagan," "lazy," and "just plain weird" betray the welcoming, hypocritical smile on my face.

I know from first-hand experience that many of these young people have a great deal to teach me about the unconditional love and acceptance of God. I am convinced they are put in my path to teach me until such time as "I finally get it." Most of them are unchurched, but the majority of them have the kindest, most loving hearts imaginable. Most of them demonstrate great love for one another and for others. I often hear them challenge one another when they succumb to gossip about their friends. I never cease to be amazed at the pearls of wisdom that often seem to flow right from the mouth of God into their mouths and out to me. Most of them believe in a power greater than themselves whom they call God, but at the same time, turn their noses up at organized religion.

I am often annoyed to distraction because they don't look the way I think they should look and they often act impetuously and irresponsibly. They do not conform to what I believe are society's standards for upright living (in my humble, though judgmental opinion—what do I know?), and ultimately they are the first to challenge authority gone amuck—often quite prophetically.

While I do not see them giving back the fullest demands of the law in restitution for their sinful lives

(like Zacchaeus), I do believe that any one of them would give the shirt off his back to anyone in need. Most of them have "hung-out" with my husband and his friend in the homeless ministry and know the guys by name.

Today's liturgy challenges me to remember that God is in charge of the salvation business—not me! I have enough to concern myself with in tending to my own interior and outward conversion and faith response. When I look to the sin in others you can be sure that I am in desperate need of jumping into the old sycamore with Zacchaeus. Only when I can acknowledge my own sinful nature and complete dependence on God's gratuitous love will I rise above the judgments that block me from the Grace that is there for the asking and receiving.

All share their life experience.

What was Luke trying to tell his community? What does he have to say to your community and to you today? What might God be creating in you through this experience of Jesus in the gospel? In what way does this gospel point to God's promise to be with us? How does the Zacchaeus story call you to leave the bondage of sin and enter the promised land of gospel living? What is your collective and personal response to all of these questions? Do you still feel the same way about this text as you did at the beginning? Has your original understanding been stretched, challenged, or affirmed?

STEP 5
DECISION

The gospel demands a response.

In what way is our community challenged by this sharing and experience of the liturgy? In what concrete way does this gospel call our parish to action in the church, parish, neighborhood, or world? Has this conversation with the exegesis of this gospel changed or stretched my personal attitudes and/or behavior? What am I /we/community/parish called to do in response? What is one concrete action I will take this week as a response to what was learned and shared today?

DOCTRINAL ISSUES

What church truth/teaching/doctrinal issue could be drawn from the gospel for the Thirty-First Sunday in Ordinary Time?

Participants suggest possible doctrinal themes that flow from the readings.

Possible Doctrinal Themes

Salvation/soteriology, eschatology, justice, kingdom of God, Jesus Christ, the Savior of the World, repentance

Present the doctrinal material at this time.

1. The facilitator gives input on a particular doctrinal issue of his/her prior choosing. OR
2. The group chooses a doctrinal issue from the list they created. They read together from the Doctrinal Appendix.

(The doctrinal issues are found in the Doctrinal Appendix in the back of this workbook. If you are choosing an issue from this resource, please refer to it now.)

Reflection questions centered around the chosen doctrinal theme can be found at the end of each topic in the Doctrinal Appendix. The questions are based on the five-step reflection process. If you choose a topic not included in the Doctrinal Appendix, craft your own questions according to the same five-step process.

Following the reflection questions you will be reminded to return to chapter 7, "Preparing the Catechetical Session," to assist you in crafting your own session.

Closing Prayer

Let us pray
[in the presence of God, the source of every good]

> *Pause for silent prayer.*

Father in heaven, God of power and Lord of mercy,

from whose fullness we have received,
direct our steps in our everyday efforts.
May the changing moods of the human heart
and the limits which our failings impose on hope
never blind us to you, source of every good.
Faith gives us the promise of peace
and makes known the demands of love.
Remove the selfishness that blurs the vision of faith.[13]

Selected Bibliography

Days of the Lord. Vol. 6. Collegeville: The Liturgical Press, 1991.

Fuller, Reginald H. *Preaching the New Lectionary.* Collegeville: The Liturgical Press, 1974.

Johnson, Luke Timothy. *The Writings of the New Testament.* Minneapolis: Augsburg Fortress, 1986.

Kselman, John S., S.J. and Michael L. Barré, S.S. "Psalms." In *The New Jerome Biblical Commentary.* Ed. Raymond E. Brown, S.S., Joseph A. Fitzmyer, S.J., Roland E. Murphy, O.Carm. Englewood Cliffs: Prentice Hall, 1990.

LaVerdiere, Eugene, S.S.S. *Luke.* Wilmington: Michael Glazier Books, 1981.

Sanchez, Patricia Datchuck. *The Word We Celebrate.* Kansas City: Sheed and Ward, 1989.

Talbert, Charles H. *Reading Luke.* New York: Crossroad, 1992.

---

[13]Thirty-First Sunday in Ordinary Time: "Alternative Opening Prayer," *The Sacramentary.*

THIRTY-SECOND SUNDAY IN ORDINARY TIME

INTRODUCTORY RITES

Opening Song (or Entrance Antiphon)

Let my prayer come before you, Lord; listen and answer me. (Ps 87:3).[1]

Environment

This Sunday falls in or around the month of November. During November we remember the dead. Some parishes display a special book of the dead in which the names of the deceased are written and displayed near the baptismal font. The church remembers her deceased members in prayer especially during this month. While not wishing to duplicate the book of the dead used in the worship space, it still might be worthwhile to find a way to imaginatively and creatively remember the deceased relatives of those in the catechetical group. Perhaps the names could be written in calligraphy on parchment paper, or pictures of the deceased might be gathered into an album of sorts and then placed in the late autumn catechetical environment. Small votive candles in dark red, green, or amber holders might be placed throughout the environment. Perhaps the catechetical environment might include late fall flowers (fresh or dried), a cornucopia filled with the late fall harvest of corn, squash, dried grasses, and gourds.

Icons that reflect an eschatological theme might also be used during these last days. Another possibility is to place a grape vine wreath adorned with produce, wheat stalks, or dried grasses in the environment. It may then be used later to craft an Advent wreath. There are multiple sizes available. "A wreath is more than a decoration. It is an emblem of royalty, of victory, of God's reign, of the wedding band we wear to remember our fidelity to Christ."[2]

Opening Prayer

The facilitator of the session may lead the prayer. Others in the group may be asked to proclaim the readings.

Let us pray
[for health of mind and body]

Pause for silent prayer.

God of power and mercy,
protect us from all harm.
Give us freedom of spirit
and health in mind and body
to do your work on earth.
We ask this through our Lord Jesus Christ, your
    Son,
who lives and reigns with you and the Holy Spirit,
one God for ever and ever.[3]

LITURGY OF THE WORD

Let us listen to God's word.

The readings are proclaimed.

First Reading
2 Maccabees 7:1-2, 9-14

This book is named after Judas Maccabeus, the third son of the priest Mattathias, who inaugurated the Jewish revolt against the Seleucids in 167 B. C. E. The name *Maccabees* means "designated by God," an apt title for one who would so courageously lead the people in their fight for independence.

Even though Protestants regard 1 and 2 Maccabees with special esteem, the books are not included in the Protestant canon. Catholics, however, officially included the Maccabean books in the official canon because of their frequent citing in early Christian tradition by such giants as

---

[1]Thirty-Second Sunday in Ordinary Time: "Entrance Antiphon," *The Sacramentary.*

[2]Peter Mazur, *To Crown the Year* (Chicago: Liturgy Training Publications, 1995), 191.

[3]Thirty-Second Sunday in Ordinary Time: "Opening Prayer," *The Sacramentary.*

Clement of Alexandria, Hippolytus, Jerome, Augustine, and Theodoret. They were recognized by three different early councils as "sacred."

Neil McEleney asserts that 2 Maccabees was an abbreviated paraphrase of the volumes written by Jason of Cyrene. The purpose was to provide a commentary on the Judas tradition, a history of the Seleucids, and to create an archive for temple documents. Factual data was not necessarily the only aim of the book; the author also wished to entertain the reader as evidenced by his clever use of dialogue and miracles.

The purpose of 1 Maccabees was to detail Jewish history in the Seleucid Empire and in the process show how God was present and active in that history. Through trust in Yahweh, and through the leadership of Judas, Judaism was delivered from pagan oppression and Israel won her independence. The lesson for all people was to trust in Yahweh's intervention in human affairs.

The second book had a similar aim. There is more importance placed on the temple and on religious ideas, however. The author wished to strengthen Jewish faith by sharing stories of Jewish heroism under persecution. Another important purpose of 2 Maccabees was to stress the doctrine of the resurrection of the just. Since historicity was only a secondary aim of the book, the reader is not to place too much stock in its historical accuracy. Theological aims were the primary consideration. History was subservient to the lesson or theology being professed.

Today's pericope is the story of the martyrdom of the seven brothers and their mother during the persecution under Antiochus Epiphanes. The revolt, later led by Judas Maccabeus, drove the Syrian power out of Israel. Today's passage introduces us to the doctrine of the resurrection of the dead. "You accursed fiend, you are depriving us of this present life, but the King of the world will raise us up to live again forever." It is the brothers' emphatic faith in the resurrection that gives us hope. Christian faith is also rooted in hope in the resurrection.

The obvious connection with the gospel rests with the argument between Jesus and the Sadducees

regarding the resurrection. The Sadducees did not believe in resurrection of the just and attempted to dash the hopes of those who did. The seven brothers' last living testament is to their hope in their own resurrection.

Responsorial Psalm
Psalm 17:1, 5-6, 8, 15

This psalm is the personal lament of someone in great trouble. The psalmist implores God for help in the midst of his dreadful situation, yet he ends on a hopeful note. The psalmist probably did not use the term "awaking" as an expression of his belief in the afterlife. It was probably an acclamation of hope that he would be rescued from his present crisis. However, meaning is broadened when put in the context of the first reading. One can easily hear the prayer of the martyrs for vindication in the first part of the psalm, and their subsequent hope in the resurrection in the latter part.

Second Reading
2 Thessalonians 2:16–3:5

Two themes emerge in Paul's letter chosen for today's liturgy: eschatological hope and intercessory prayer. Last week Paul responded to the false letter regarding the imminent coming of the end of time. The false letter had sent terror into the hearts of the people. Paul encouraged them to remain steadfast to the gospel they had been given. They were not to become obsessed with fearful waiting for the end, but were to go about their Christian business with diligence. Today's letter reminds the people that it is Jesus himself who encourages us in our journey and our waiting. Jesus alone is the source of our eternal hope.

In the last days of the liturgical year, our focus is on the last things. The apostle expressed the hope we are to have as we reflect on our own demise, on the limitations of this earthly dwelling, and on the hopeful waiting for the Master's return. ("May God, our Father who loved us and in his mercy gave us eternal consolation and hope....")

Disciples are encouraged to join with Paul in praying that the word of God go forward. We are to intercede for the world that all will cooperate with the will of God. The word of God must go speedily that all may come to know God's will for our lives and for the salvation of the world.

Gospel
Luke 20:27-38

Jesus enters into dialogue with the Sadducees about life after death.

STEP 1
NAMING ONE'S EXPERIENCE

What were your first impressions? What was your first response? What grabbed your attention? How did you feel?

Each person names his or her initial impression. Statement should be brief. No reasons should be given at this time. All simply listen without agreeing or disagreeing.

STEP 2
UNDERSTANDING

In a brief statement, what do you think this gospel is trying to convey?

STEP 3
INPUT FROM VISION/STORY/TRADITION

Liturgical Context

Today's liturgy reminds us of our foundational truths. We are resurrection people who will share eternal life. Our eternal resting place is not merely an extension of this earthly life, but is a new existence. We will be changed, not dead. We cannot assume to know what life after death will be like, as it is a mystery. We can, however, be assured that our God is a God of the living, not the dead. God wishes that we share eternal life with him.

The eucharist is our constant participation in God's eternal life as we await the day of the Lord's coming. The word is our living guide. As a living word, it is always revealing God's will to us. The word is constantly being opened for us to encounter the risen Christ. The alternative opening prayer asks that we be shielded from the distortions of pride so that we may be led closer to the truth. An open heart and a willingness to share God's word in the midst of a discerning community will help us in our struggle to live God's word in the kingdom. The prayer after communion reminds us that we will be given the strength we need to persevere until the end. This strength comes from our sharing of Christ's Body and Blood in the eucharist. "Pour out your Spirit upon us and in the strength of this food from heaven keep us single-minded in your service."

Perhaps a Rite of Acceptance, Welcome, or a Full Communion may be celebrated on any of these last Sundays before Advent begins. A non-sacramental (or sacramental) communal reconciliation service might be celebrated in the final days of the liturgical cycle as a reminder of our need for God's mercy. When we slip into attitudes of Sadducee-ism and Pharisee-ism we are reminded that God alone saves and that God's mercy heals and restores.

The opening prayer for today's liturgy reminds us that our health and well-being depend on God's providence. The Prayer Over the People #2 in the *Sacramentary* continues the theme of health and wellness and might also be used as a prayer at some point in the catechetical session: "Lord, grant your people your protection and grace. Give them health of mind and body, perfect love for one another, and make them always faithful to you. Grant this through Christ, our Lord."

This month, when our mortality is placed prominently before us, might be an appropriate time to celebrate a communal healing service. Prayers for most situations in everyday life such as "Blessing for Times of Sickness" can be found in the *Catholic Household Blessings and Prayers*. In the *Book of Blessings* there are blessings that address human health and wellness; these include: Orders for the Blessing of Elderly People Confined to Their Homes; Order for the Blessing of the Sick; Order for the Blessing of a Person Suffering from Addiction or from Substance Abuse; Order for the Victim of Crime or Oppression. Perhaps it would be helpful to offer catechetical groups periodic reminders about appropriate liturgical celebrations for use in the home for various situations, occasions, and holidays throughout the year.

For example, there are prayers provided that are eschatologically oriented and would be appropriate during the last days of the liturgical cycle. They are found in a section entitled, "November Prayers." "During November, the church celebrates the communion of saints, intercedes for those who have died, and prepares to welcome the one Saint Francis called 'Sister Death.'"[4]

Christian Initiation

This also might be an appropriate time to celebrate a rite of anointing catechumens with the oil of catechumens. The opening prayer asks God for strength in mind and body to carry out the will of God. Since the anointing rite is intended for just such a purpose, perhaps this would be an appropriate time to celebrate it.

Gospel Exegesis

The facilitator gives input regarding what critical biblical scholarship has to say about this text. The input includes insights as to how people would have heard the gospel in Jesus' time.

Today's encounter takes place in Jerusalem. Jesus has finally arrived at the place where his earthly sojourn will culminate. Jesus speaks of the resurrection in the very place where he will give up his life. His words have power and authority. Once again Jesus is in confrontational dialogue, this time with the Sadducees. The Sadducees were the wealthy aristocracy of Jesus' day. It is believed that the Sadducees were descended from Zadok, the high priest of Solomon. Sadducees were the privileged presiders of temple rituals and sacrifices. Luke believed the Sadducees were responsible for Jesus' death. The Sadducees later persecuted the church (they hauled John and Peter before the Sanhedrin and had them imprisoned).

The Sadducees believed only in the written scriptures while Pharisees also held to the oral tradi-

---

[4]*Catholic Household Blessings and Prayers* (Washington: USCC, 1988), 181.

tion. Sadducees were the conservative fundamentalists of Jesus' day. The law and nothing but the law was their code. The oral tradition was not on the same plane as the written law. They were doctrinally and liturgically narrow in their views and practices.

They did not believe in the resurrection of the dead, the existence of angels, or the immortality of the soul because their fundamentalist leaning would not allow them to embrace anything that was not written in the Torah. "Resurrection of the dead" was not a concept found in the Pentateuch. It was a later biblical concept. Thus, the Sadducees adhered to the more traditional belief. As the elite class they enjoyed a cooperative relationship with the Romans.

The other religious party was the Pharisees. The Pharisees were descendants of the Hassidim. The Hassidim supported the Maccabean revolt discussed in the exegesis of today's first reading. Pharisees were more pastoral than the Sadducees. Their primary concern was the religious and spiritual life of the people. Sometimes legalists in their own right, the Pharisees, however, believed that doctrine was not written in stone and was subject to God's divine ongoing revelation. The works of the prophets and biblical literature written after the Pentateuch were also accepted as the inspired word of God transmitted to and through human beings.

The Pharisees were the first group to interpret the law and expand it to include all facets of human life. Jesus was primarily a Pharisee. He did, however, argue with them at times about applications of the law that imposed unnecessary burdens on people in the name of strict observance. Jesus promoted the law of love rather than rigid legalism.

Today's story has the Sadducees refuting belief in the resurrection by applying it to an old Mosaic law regarding "levirate marriages" (concerning a brother-in-law). Levirate law assured the continuance of the family line by allowing a widow to marry the brother of her dead husband. Sadducees tried to point out irreconcilable problems that would occur in the afterlife and they used the levirate law as an example. If there was an afterlife, how would the human race continue and who would be married to whom? The Sadducees used this line of reasoning to prove that there could not be an afterlife as proposed by Jesus and the Pharisees.

Jesus tells them that their thinking is very limited. The levirate marriage is something that belongs to this world—not to the next. The Sadducees are thinking in human, earthly terms.

> He begins by pointing out that levirate marriage, and marriage in general, is a condition that belongs to "this age": perpetuating the name of the dead brother (levirate), having children so the race will never die out (marriage). This does not apply to the "age to come," because those who are resurrected "are no longer liable to death!" Thus, the comparison fails.[5]

One scholar uses the comparison of a baby in a mother's womb. The baby cannot imagine a life outside the womb. It is incomprehensible. Similarly, we cannot imagine life after death—it is beyond our experience or imagination.

Jesus expresses faith in the living God, the author of all life. He further demonstrates his authority by interpreting the Mosaic law. When Moses encountered Yahweh in the burning bush he referred to God as the God *of* Abraham and the God *of* Isaac. In his argument, Jesus insists that if God is the God *of* Abraham and *of* Isaac (who were dead long before Moses), it follows then, that there must be life after death. Moses was talking about Abraham and Isaac as if they were still alive. Moses did not say, "God *was* the God of Abraham." Rather, Moses said: "God *is* the God of Abraham." It is a present-tense declaration. If God *is* the God of Abraham and Isaac, then they must be enjoying life somewhere, because God can only be the God of someone who is alive—not dead. God is a God of the living, not the dead! Jesus also refutes the notion that life after death is simply a continuation of this life as we know it. The Pharisees are obviously pleased with Jesus' interpretation as it is in harmony with their own belief in the resurrection.

Luke portrays his primary agenda in this vignette. A main concern for Luke is to view the life and ministry of Jesus in relationship to the kingdom of God. This story highlights the discrepancy between the beliefs regarding the kingdom of God and messianic expectations of the Jewish leaders and those same beliefs as understood by Luke and the post-resurrection church.

For the Jews, the kingdom of God was a political reality; allegiance was either paid to a Jewish king or the people participated in overt or covert rebellion against the emperor. "Life before God" for the Jews meant life in the earthly existence. There was no intended implication of resurrection in that phrase. A blessed life was understood to mean an abundance of earthly prosperity, longevity, and children. The only expectation of the coming messiah was that he would protect them within their borders and offer them the opportunity to prosper in the temporal world. The leaders of this political messianic kingdom (the religious leaders in power) find their reward in "earthly recognition and in public acclaim and prestige, but who cannot be content with that, and oppress others even as they parade a public piety."[6]

Luke contrasts this political, earthly kingdom with the *reign* of God ushered in by Christ. God owns all things. Everything belongs to God and must be given back to God. God is the author and fountain of all life. God did not stop revealing himself to humanity with the Moses event, but rather continues to manifest himself to all human beings. God is the author of life and gives it freely, both at birth and after death. One action is as simple for God as the next. Resurrected life is life in God as God's children. Only those preoccupied with the trappings of this world would think of reducing *life in God* to a laundry list of possessions, power, and prestige. The reign of God is the alive, active, transforming, resurrected presence of Christ's Spirit in this world. God's new kingdom is not the narrowly conceived world of self-serving, religious sovereignty imagined by the religious leaders of Jesus' time, but rather is a world turned upside down by the radical, paradoxical God who goes about the world searching

---

[5]*Days of the Lord,* Vol. 6 (Collegeville: The Liturgical Press, 1991), 298.

[6]Luke Timothy Johnson, *The Gospel of Luke,* Sacra Pagina Series, Vol. 3 (Collegeville: The Liturgical Press, 1991), 318.

after sinners on whom he can shower his abundant eternal life.

Proclaim the gospel again.

Sometimes we gain new insights when we hear the text after the interpretation has been given. Someone from the group proclaims the gospel a second time.

STEP 4
TESTING

Conversation with the Liturgy and Scriptures

Test your original understanding in dialogue with the text.

(You might consider breaking into smaller groups.)

Now that you've heard what the scholars have to say about Jesus' dialogue with the Sadducees and Luke's intention in this gospel, how do you feel about it? How does your original understanding of this gospel compare with what was just shared? Were there any new insights? Was there anything you had not considered before? How does this story speak to your life?

Participants share an experience from their lives that connects with the biblical interpretation just shared.

> *When my mother was dying there were many laborious days of suffering with her for every breath. She was dying of emphysema. There was a tremendous struggle. She was a faith-filled person. Dying, however, was very difficult. She clung to life with every forced gulp of air. Things were improving; she was getting better. They moved her out of intensive care into a regular room. For the first time in weeks we left her bedside and went home to rest. When we returned that evening she was back in intensive care. She had crashed while we were gone. She was back on the respirator we had worked so diligently to wean her off of. However, something had changed. In the place of a frenzied, frightened woman was my serene, peaceful, resolute mother. She smiled at us, and even though she could not talk, she was able to write. I still treasure her scribbled note. "God wants me here a while longer." We asked her what had happened. "I saw Jesus. He took me by the*

hand. I saw my father and then he led me back here. It is so beautiful."

We knew it was just a matter of time. We could not go with her to this new place, but she was truly ready to go on her own. Never before had my mother looked so peaceful or happy. We waited for my sister to arrive from the airport to say her last goodbyes for the second time that day. She had no sooner gotten off the plane in her hometown that morning than she had to get right back on and return to our dying mother's bedside.

In the dark hours of the night as we kept vigil at her bedside, the words "but with the dawn rejoicing," kept ringing through my ears. As the first bird chirped its early dawn "good morning," we held our mother's hand as she breathed her last and for the second time that day walked—no ran, into her Master's waiting arms.

I do not have a clue about what life after death looks like. I do know someone who's been there, however. She shared the experience with her family, if only through an incredible peace that surpasses all understanding.

In today's gospel Jesus assured us of our share in eternal life. I have the experience of my mother's last moments, the hope of God's word and my sharing in the eucharist of bread, wine, and community to sustain me as I await the day when I will be reunited with my loved ones who went before me.

My first question will be: "God, how could we have been so stupid as to worry about such trivial things as which law was right, what interpretation were we willing to defend? It was all rubbish—compared to this bliss—it was all rubbish! What fools we were!"

The bottom line is: There is a God—and we're not it! Jesus took the method used by the Sadducees to entrap him (citation of the law), turned it upside down, and used it on them to show how ludicrous their fundamentalist notions truly were. The apostle in today's second reading asks that the word of God go speedily forth. In this eschatological age, in these last days of the liturgical cycle when we reflect on last things, in this time of hopeful waiting for the Master's return, I am reminded that the kingdom of God is now. We are a resurrection people. Our job is to participate in God's reign by professing and living his word, by trusting in the life he offers, and by becoming agents of change and unity, rather than of stagnation and division. When it is all said and done, we too can hopefully claim with joy and assurance, "I have seen Jesus. He took me by the hand—it is so beautiful!"

All share their life experience.

What was Luke trying to tell his community? What does he have to say to our community and to me today? What is the implication of today's gospel for us? Does God's promise to be with us (covenant) have anything to do with today's scriptures? In what way does this gospel invite us out of bondage into freedom (exodus)? In what way is this a word for our community (people of God)? Do we still feel the same way about this text as we did when we began? Has our original understanding been stretched, challenged, or affirmed?

STEP 5
DECISION

The gospel demands a response.

In what concrete way does this gospel call our parish to action in the church, parish, neighborhood, or world? Has this conversation with the exegesis changed or stretched my personal attitudes? What are the implications for my life? What is one concrete action I will take this week as a response to what was learned and shared today?

DOCTRINAL ISSUES

What church truth/teaching/doctrinal issue could be drawn from the gospel for the Thirty-Second Sunday in Ordinary Time?

Participants suggest possible doctrinal themes that flow from the readings.

Possible Doctrinal Themes

Resurrection of the just, eschatology, soteriology, scripture interpretation, life after death

Present the doctrinal material at this time.

1. The facilitator gives input on a particular doctrinal issue of his/her prior choosing. OR
2. The group chooses a doctrinal issue from the list they created. They read together from the Doctrinal Appendix.

(The doctrinal issues are found in the Doctrinal Appendix in the back of this workbook. If you are choosing an issue from this resource, please refer to it now.)

Reflection questions centered around the chosen doctrinal theme can be found at the end of each topic in the Doctrinal Appendix. The questions are based on the five-step reflection process. If you choose a topic not included in the Doctrinal Appendix, craft your own questions according to the same five-step process.

Following the reflection questions you will be reminded to return to chapter 7, "Preparing the Catechetical Session," to assist you in crafting your own session.

Closing Prayer

Let us pray
[that our prayer rise like incense
in the presence of God]

Pause for silent prayer.

Almighty Father,
strong is your justice and great is your mercy.
Protect us in the burdens and challenges of life.
Shield our minds from the distortion of pride
and enfold our desire with the beauty of truth.
Help us to become more aware of your loving
    design
so that we may more willingly give our lives in service to all.
We ask this through Christ our Lord.[7]

Selected Bibliography

Days of the Lord. Vol. 6. Collegeville: The Liturgical Press, 1991.

---

[7]Thirty-Second Sunday in Ordinary Time: "Alternative Opening Prayer," *The Sacramentary.*

Fuller, Reginald H. *Preaching the New Lectionary.*
    Collegeville: The Liturgical Press, 1974.
Johnson, Luke Timothy. *The Gospel of Luke.* Sacra
    Pagina Series. Vol. 3. Collegeville: The Liturgi-
    cal Press, 1991.
McEleney, Neil C.S.P. "1 and 2 Maccabees." In *The
    New Jerome Biblical Commentary.* Ed. Raymond
    E. Brown, S.S., Joseph A. Fitzmyer, S.J.,
    Roland E. Murphy, O.Carm. Englewood
    Cliffs: Prentice Hall, 1990.
Sanchez, Patricia Datchuck. *The Word We Celebrate.*
    Kansas City: Sheed and Ward, 1989.

Oper

The ... not
disas ...
and ... h I
exile

Envi

Refe

Ope

The j
the g

Let
[tha

Father of
keep us f‑
for to ser‑
We ask t
    Son
who liv‑   ‑rit,
one Gc‑

Let

The

First
Mala

Virtu‑   ‑nymous
auth‑   y written
arou‑   is be‑

tiphor‑   trance An‑

'Thirty‑‑‑‑   pening
Prayer," *The Sacramentary*.

Team prayer

Creator God,
you have given each of us
the gift of life.
You have formed each of us
as unique individuals.
You have blessed each of us
with the gift of faith
and the desire to share and pass
on our faith to others.
We ask that you be with us
as we strive to use our gifts and
talents,
our energy and love
to foster the spark of faith
within those people who come to
us.
We have each answered a voice
within us
in committing to this initiation
team.
We ask that you help us to be‑
come
what we say we are: a team.
May we truly see ourselves
as one in purpose and one in
heart.
Give us the confidence to do our
part,
knowing always that you have
placed others
here to help and support us.
Amen.

lieved that the name of the book comes from a reference from 3:1—*mal' akki*, my messenger. Although the exile was over and the people had been allowed to return home, they were disheartened. With the assistance of the Syrian government the people had been given the necessary aid to rebuild the temple. Even though the temple was built, it did not guarantee communal, liturgical, or spiritual cohesiveness. The people were in disarray. The clergy were negligent, the ritual sloppy, and there was an indifference to the needs of the poor. The rich became richer and the poor became poorer.

It seemed to Malachi as if those who turned their backs on God prospered, while the God-fearing, faithful poor were barely surviving. Malachi was incensed and through his prophetic word promised that the situation would one day be overturned.

Three centuries earlier, the prophet Amos had prophesied that the "Day of the Lord" would come upon the people. The people had fantasized that it would be a day marked by great joy. God's people would reign victorious over their enemies. Amos, however, shattered their illusions. The "Day of the Lord" was to be a day of judgment for Israel. Rather than joy, there would be terror.

After the exile, fervor for the "Day of the Lord" came again to the fore. It was heralded as a day of fire and brimstone. The righteous would be saved, but the evil would be destroyed by the sun's fiery blaze. However, the same fiery sun that was to destroy the evil would be the healing agent of the righteous. Sun of justice (v. 20) literally means "sun which is justice." In ancient Persia and Egypt, the sun was depicted as a winged solar disk. This sun god was believed to be the source of light and warmth, and thus the source of all life. Biblical authors embraced the symbol of the sun god and applied it to Yahweh. Yahweh is light and life, source of all that is good, and the one who will send the wicked to be consumed in the blazing fire.

When the Christians applied the term "Sun of Justice" to Jesus, they were signifying Christ, the light and judge, who came into the world as the incarnate presence of God, and who will come again as judge of the world.

The tone of this reading is powerfully eschatological. The judgment, vindication, and the Lord's coming are thrown into full view as we say goodbye to Luke's final panoramic view of the full implications of the Christ event. Malachi sets the stage for our reflection on these very sober realities.

Responsorial Psalm
Psalm 98:5-6, 7-8, 9

This is an enthronement psalm with eschatological overtones. Yahweh will judge the earth with righteousness. This psalm expresses the joy and confidence in our King who will judge those who have loved the Lord and have remained faithful to his word.

Second Reading
2 Thessalonians 3:7-12

Today's pericope is a continuation of the exhortation from last week. It is obviously written in response to a situation. The situation concerned a gnostic belief that the "Day of the Lord" had already arrived and that certain people were living within it—in heaven. Thus, those who believed they were already living in this realized eschatology refused to work, eat, or enjoy life. This posed an incredible burden on the Christian community. Since so many folks were opting out of work, it placed an even greater burden on others to carry the load.

Many use this Thessalonian text to support their belief regarding the poor in a modern society. Reginald Fuller eloquently poses the challenge for the contemporary reader:

> Idleness today is hardly likely to be due to an over realized eschatology. It is no longer true that those who do not work are not allowed to eat, as it was in the case of subsistence level economy of New Testament times. For this very reason this passage points up an interesting problem of what is called hermeneutics. This is the problem of getting the text to say the same thing in a completely altered situation. You can no longer get the same meaning if you just report what it says *verbatim*. Its expressions have to be changed in order to put across the same idea. In a society whose economic injustices condemn a large segment of the population to unemployment, it is no good just lifting the Thessalonian text about those who refuse to work not being allowed to eat, and to use it as an argument against welfare payments. This is what fundamentalists in middle America may be sometimes tempted to do. Of course there are shirkers in all societies, and they need the warning of this text. But they are just as likely to be found among the affluent as the poor.[3]

Fuller further asserts that the hermeneutical task demands sensitivity. Christianity demands that we uphold the law of love. Thus we must remember to interpret this text and find meaning for our contemporary lives only in the context of an entirely changed situation.

Paul's letter to the Thessalonians stressed that he was the proper example to emulate. Paul worked to further the reign of God and the word of God in the world. He worked to the point of exhaustion. Paul exhorted the Thessalonians that their waiting posture was to be rooted in love and patient endurance and that they must have diligent concern for day-to-day Christian living.

Gospel
Luke 21:5-19

Jesus foretells and describes the end of the age.

STEP 1
NAMING ONE'S EXPERIENCE

What were your first impressions? What was your first response? What grabbed your attention? How did you feel?

---

[3]Reginald H. Fuller, *Preaching the New Lectionary* (Collegeville: The Liturgical Press, 1974), 95.

Each person names his or her initial impression. Statement should be brief. No reasons should be given at this time. All simply listen without agreeing or disagreeing.

STEP 2
UNDERSTANDING

In a brief statement, what do you think this gospel is trying to convey?

STEP 3
INPUT FROM VISION/STORY/TRADITION

Liturgical Context

After this Sunday and next Sunday the liturgical cycle comes to a close. There is a consistent theme of last judgment and preparation for the coming of the Lord's Nativity. The end of one liturgical cycle dovetails with the beginning of a new liturgical cycle. The Christian perspective of last judgment and coming of the Son of Man is laced with abundant joy as evidenced by the alternative opening prayer: ". . . through the future coming of your Son, our Lord Jesus Christ. Help us to drink of his truth and expand our hearts with the joy of his promises."

While today's liturgy is an extended mediation on the end of time, eschatology, and the second coming of Christ, we are not to sit back on our laurels and do nothing. We are to be diligent and to participate in the Christian life as we await Jesus' return. We are to serve the mission of Christ as expressed in the opening prayer for today's liturgy. Eucharist is our strength as we await that final glorious day of Christ's return. "Lord God, may the gifts we offer increase our love for you and bring us to eternal life. We ask this in the name of Jesus the Lord" (Prayer Over the Gifts). "Father, may we grow in love by this eucharist we have celebrated in memory of the Lord Jesus, who is Lord for ever and ever" (Prayer After Communion).

Thanksgiving often occurs on or around this Sunday. *Catholic Household Blessings and Prayers* provide prayers and blessings for use at all major holidays and observances. There is a special prayer of thanks and a suggested blessing provided for Thanksgiving Day. The *Book of Blessings* provides two orders of blessing that could be used at Thanksgiving: Order for a Blessing on the Occasion of Thanksgiving for the Harvest and Order for the Blessing of Food for Thanksgiving Day (fourth Thursday in November).

Ember Days

Throughout the church's history the church observed three days (Wednesday, Friday and Saturday) before the beginning of the spring, summer, fall, and winter seasons or at times of special need, penance, or intercession. These days were called ember days. Prayers are provided in *Catholic Household Blessings and Prayers* for special observance of the ember days. There are also prayers provided for the weekdays prior to Thanksgiving.

Eucharistic Prayer IV stresses the history of salvation and the consummation of all things in Christ Jesus. The fullness of our eschatological hope is realized in this prayer.

> Remember those who have died in the peace
>   of Christ
> and all the dead whose faith is known to you
>   alone.
> Father, in your mercy grant also to us, your
>   children,
> to enter into our heavenly inheritance
> in the company of the Virgin Mary, the
>   Mother of God,
> and your apostles and saints.
> Then, in your kingdom, freed from the cor-
>   ruption of sin and death,
> we shall sing your glory with every creature
>   through Christ our Lord . . .

Gospel Exegesis

The facilitator gives input regarding what critical biblical scholarship has to say about this text. The input includes insights as to how people would have heard the gospel in Jesus' time.

Charles Talbert suggests that Luke 19:45–21:38 forms a single unit with a specific agenda. This section begins and ends with the statement that *Jesus was teaching in the temple.* The purpose was to place God's favored messenger in confrontation with Israel. The result was the rejection of Jesus and condemnation of those who rejected him. Today's pericope functioned in Luke's gospel as the second part of Jesus' public teaching in the Jerusalem temple.

Jesus taught in response to a question posed in verse 5 regarding the adornment of the temple. Jesus responded to the question by uttering a prophecy about the coming of the end. Jesus' word echoes Micah's prophecy regarding the destruction of the temple (Mic 3:12).
Luke places the events of the end in the following order: 1) it will be a time of testimony, 2) there will be false messiahs, 3) there will be political rebellions, 4) there will be cosmic disturbances, 5) the Son of Man will come.

In response to the question posed in verse 7 (regarding the timetable of events), Luke asserts that the temple will be destroyed as part of the political upheaval, right before the end. People will know the end is near when armies surround Jerusalem. While it was a question about the temple's destruction that prompted Jesus' prophecy, Talbert suggests that Luke had a larger intention. Luke's primary agenda (in addition to discussing the destruction of the temple) was to address persecution in the time of testimony and perseverance and preparedness for the coming of the Son of Man.

Talbert states that a closer look at chapter 12 will help us fully appreciate Jesus' prophecy in today's pericope. Luke treats the issue of persecution in 12:1-12. The disciple is to avoid hypocrisy. What is in a person's heart must correspond to the person's actions. Persecution demands personal integrity. Disciples should never "give-in" in the face of impending death. God controls human destiny after death. God alone has power and control over our lives. God's enemies will be damned to Gehenna.[4]

A person's final destiny depends on that person's relationship to Christ. A disciple could be forgiven denial of the earthly Christ (after all, Peter denied the earthly Christ), but denial of the Spirit would not be forgiven. Thus, the time between the earthly ministry of Jesus and the mission of the church is clearly defined. Those who deny the risen Christ will be denying the Holy Spirit and the Spirit's power to mediate God's forgiveness. This is unforgivable in the Lukan perspective. "The disciples, who are the evangelist's primary concern here, would be rejecting the Spirit's inspiration when, required to testify before persecutors, they would, in direct opposition to the Spirit's influence, deny Christ (vv. 11-12; cf. 21:14-15; Acts 4:8, 19-20; 5:30). By denying Christ the disciples deny the Holy Spirit within and blaspheme the only one who can mediate God's forgiveness."[5]

Luke's warning of persecution in chapter 12 is to be read into Jesus' prophetic word in today's gospel. Before the end, disciples will experience persecution of the sort described in chapter 12. Disciples will be dragged before Jewish synagogue courts as well as before kings and governors. The Acts of the Apostles is the testament to such persecution. Disciples must stand firm. Martyrdom awaits them, but if they endure to the end, eternal life is the reward.

Endurance in the face of persecution was a major theme in the early Christian tradition. Luke also addressed the perseverance of the disciples as they awaited the coming of the Son of Man.

Luke's community reflected the sayings of Jesus in light of the crisis they were enduring. Jerusalem had been destroyed, the temple was gone. Jesus' life and work were placed in the context of those events. Luke believed that signs of the end were present. The temple was gone; cosmic signs were plenteous; political upheaval was a reality. The only thing left was the return of Christ.

It is in the context of Jesus' expected imminent return that we are to read today's gospel. It is how Luke wrote it. We are to be prepared at all times. Reginald Fuller confirms that, using apocalyptic literature, Luke was interpreting the "present crisis in which they were involved as the last crisis of human history, to be followed soon by its consummation."[6]

---

[4]Gehenna was a place near Jerusalem where children had been sacrificed to the god Molech. Josiah's reforms turned the place into a garbage dump. Symbolically, it was understood as a place of punishment for God's enemies.

[5]Charles H. Talbert, *Reading Luke* (New York: Crossroad, 1992), 201.

[6]Fuller, *Preaching the New Lectionary,* 96.

Apocalyptic literature functioned in a specific way. It was not written as prophecy about future events. It was written as imminent reality. True to fashion, apocalyptic literature expands in transmission. Commentary is added to what presently exists and then it is adapted to meet current situations. Sometimes the crisis at hand subsides, sometimes it gets worse. Sometimes details are added or omitted. In Mark's gospel there is minimal reference to the destruction of the temple. It is suggested that Mark did not experience the destruction firsthand but was told about it and thus included it in his gospel. Luke, on the other hand, describes it as if he had been an eyewitness. All three evangelists subscribe to an "apocalyptic theology and world view to express the horror of destruction of Jerusalem as sign and preparation for the end time."[7] Carolyn Osiek maintains that apocalyptic theology was the way the early church expressed its faith in the power of God for deliverance and salvation. Periodically throughout the history of the church apocalyptic fervor is renewed because it appeals to an intrinsic desire for peace, healing restoration, and a better world. "Because it is so vulnerable to psychic and emotional imbalance, the consequences are, unfortunately, often disastrous."[8]

We can see one example of apocalyptic fervor gone amuck in today's reading from Thessalonians. They believed the "Day of the Lord" had already arrived. The community suffered as a result. In every generation there are groups who, in their search for the utopian life, give up on this life, embrace an unbalanced vision of future realities, and come to a disastrous end. The mass suicides of cults such as Heaven's Gate and Jim Jones are examples of such extremes.

Various uses of apocalyptic literature can be observed in Christian history.

1) It is used as *criticism* against structures in society or in the church. It is sometimes used to support political power.

2) Apocalyptic is sometimes used as an expression of *hope*. It seeks to make "belonging" part of a larger historical pattern of reality, thereby offering personal meaning. The hope that human beings can improve is a great contribution of apocalyptic literature.

3) Apocalyptic is most often a message of hope in the final victory of good over evil. Apocalyptic often challenges people to a *moral decision* regarding the choice between good and evil. Endurance in the midst of suffering for the sake of good is rewarded, and persistent evil behavior is punished.

4) Apocalyptic literature seeks to foster *values* which assert that death is not the ultimate disaster.[9]

It is certain that Jesus did prophesy about the destruction of the temple. It was one of the charges brought against him. No doubt there were natural disasters experienced by the early community. The community also experienced the persecution of Peter, Paul, and James the Just. The events of the post-resurrection Christian community, when added to Jesus' known sayings, were the substantive basis of the apocalyptic material of the gospels. It is difficult to know where the authentic sayings of Jesus left off and the expanded apocalyptic material picked up.

In the rest of chapter 21, Luke exhorts disciples to pray—the opposite of losing heart. Prayer was a sign of persistence. To be constantly vigilant and prepared at all times meant that disciples were to be single-hearted, single-minded, and of single purpose. Nothing was to get in the way of their focus on Christ's return. The promise of help in the time of trial reflected Jesus' promise of the gift of the Holy Spirit.

Proclaim the gospel again.

Sometimes we gain new insights when we hear the text after the interpretation has been given. Someone from the group proclaims the gospel a second time.

---

[7]Carolyn Osiek, R.S.C.J., "Apocalyptic," in *The Collegeville Pastoral Dictionary of Biblical Theology*, ed. Carroll Stuhlmueller, C.P. (Collegeville: The Liturgical Press, 1996), 39.

[8]Ibid., 40.

[9]Zachary Hayes, O.F.M., "Apocalyptic-Pastoral Liturgical Tradition," in *The Collegeville Pastoral Dictionary of Biblical Theology*, ed. Carroll Stulmueller, C.P. (Collegeville: The Liturgical Press, 1996), 40.

Conversation with the Liturgy and Scriptures

Test your original understanding in dialogue with the text.
(You might consider breaking into smaller groups.)

Now that you've heard the exegesis of the readings in today's liturgy, how do you feel about them? Were there any new insights? Was there anything you had not considered before? How does your original understanding compare with what we just shared? How does this story speak to your life?

Participants share an experience from their lives that connects with the biblical interpretation just shared.

> *Very often when times are tough and when society experiences a spiritual void, there is a renewed vigor for apocalyptic zeal. Suffering often brings an intense desire for the consummation of the world and for Christ to come again. The last few years have given rise to just such fervor. There have been many reports that such-and-such a future day would be the end of the world. A friend of mine was recently stopped at the mall and a mutual acquaintance told her that the end of the world was going to happen on a given day. Since the day is already passed, the prophecy obviously did not come true. The ultimate absurdity of that encounter is that the person sharing the prophetic pronouncement was a very solid, active, "NORMAL" person. People will travel miles to follow after popular spiritual phenomena.*

> *I recently heard theologian Michael Himes comment that caution is in order whenever a philosophical or religious doctrine suggests that there is value in leaving the human body for another plane of existence. It is the ultimate denial of humanity and its limited condition. Human beings are in the process of dying from the moment they are born. We are all dying.*

> *All of the above examples are indicative of the spiritual void that cries out for meaning in people's lives. The teenagers in my life insist that young people are plagued by a serious lack of hope. They believe the future looks dismal. According to their perspective, the opportunities to forge successful lives (such as those enjoyed by their parents) are not available to them. There is rampant apathy and fear. Such things give rise to the apocalyptic fervor expressed in today's readings. Perhaps this is one reason young people seek out counter-cultural groups, cults, and gangs. We cannot dismiss the Thessalonian community as the equivalent of ancient weirdos. Every generation experiences groups who behave similarly.*

> *The reality of today's liturgy is that we are to approach the "Day of the Lord" with joy. Our faith gives us hope. When we chase after spiritual phenomena we miss what is under our noses. Christ is truly present in our midst—in the community, the eucharist, the word of God, and in all creation. There is no need to worry. Be prepared? Yes. Live each day as if it were our last? Of course. The rest is God's problem.*

All share their life experience.

What was Luke trying to tell his community? What does he have to say to our community and to me today? Where is there evidence of the biblical themes of creation, exodus, covenant, and people of God? What are our collective and personal responses to all of the above questions? Do we still feel the same way about this text as we did when we began? Has our original understanding been stretched, challenged, or affirmed?

The gospel demands a response.

In what way does this reflection on the last things call your parish to action in the church, parish, neighborhood, or world? Be concrete. Has this conversation with the exegesis changed or stretched your personal attitudes? What are the implications for your life? What are you/your community/your parish called to do in response? Name one concrete action you will take this week as a response to what was learned and shared today.

DOCTRINAL ISSUES

What church truth/teaching/doctrinal issue could be drawn from the gospel for the Thirty-Third Sunday in Ordinary Time?

Participants suggest possible doctrinal themes that flow from the readings.

Possible Doctrinal Themes

Eschatology, last judgment, hell, heaven, soteriology, kingdom of God

Present the doctrinal material at this time.

1. The facilitator gives input on a particular doctrinal issue of his/her prior choosing. OR
2. The group chooses a doctrinal issue from the list they created. They read together from the Doctrinal Appendix.

(The doctrinal issues are found in the Doctrinal Appendix in the back of this workbook. If you are choosing an issue from this resource, please refer to it now.)

Reflection questions centered around the chosen doctrinal theme can be found at the end of each topic in the Doctrinal Appendix. The questions are based on the five-step reflection process. If you choose a topic not included in the Doctrinal Appendix, craft your own questions according to the same five-step process.

Following the reflection questions you will be reminded to return to chapter 7, "Preparing the Catechetical Session," to assist you in crafting your own session.

Closing Prayer

Let us pray
[with hearts that long for peace]

Father in heaven,
ever-living source of all that is good,
from the beginning of time you promised man salvation
through the future coming of your Son, our Lord Jesus Christ.

Help us to drink of his truth
and expand our hearts with the joy of his promises,
so that we may serve you in faith and in love
and know for ever the joy of your presence.
We ask this through Christ our Lord.[10]

Selected Bibliography

Fuller, Reginald H. *Preaching the New Lectionary.* Collegeville: The Liturgical Press, 1974.

Hayes, Zachary, O.F.M. "Apocalyptic-Pastoral Liturgical Tradition." In *The Collegeville Pastoral Dictionary of Biblical Theology.* Ed. Carroll Stuhlmueller, C.P. Collegeville: The Liturgical Press, 1996.

Osiek, Carolyn, R.S.C.J. "Apocalyptic." In *The Collegeville Pastoral Dictionary of Biblical Theology.* Ed. Carroll Stuhlmueller, C.P. Collegeville: The Liturgical Press, 1996.

Sanchez, Patricia Datchuck. *The Word We Celebrate.* Kansas City: Sheed and Ward, 1989.

Talbert, Charles H. *Reading Luke.* New York: Crossroad, 1992.

---

[10]Thirty-Third Sunday in Ordinary Time: "Alternative Opening Prayer," *The Sacramentary.*

CHRIST THE KING—LAST SUNDAY IN ORDINARY TIME

INTRODUCTORY RITES

Opening Song (or Entrance Antiphon)

The Lamb who was slain is worthy to receive strength and divinity, wisdom and power and honor: to him be glory and power for ever. (Rev 5:12; 1:6)[1]

Environment
There need not be a special environment just for this feast. The space should reflect the overall eschatological tone of the past weeks. The liturgical color for this feast is white.

Opening Prayer

The facilitator of the session may lead the prayer. Others in the group may be asked to proclaim the readings.

Let us pray.

[that all men will acclaim
Jesus as Lord]

Pause for silent prayer.

Almighty and merciful God,
you break the power of evil
and make all things new
in your Son Jesus Christ, the King of the universe.
May all in heaven and earth acclaim your glory
and never cease to praise you.
We ask this through our Lord Jesus Christ, your
 Son,
who lives and reigns with you and the Holy
 Spirit,
one God, for ever and ever.[2]

OR:

Let us pray
[that the kingdom of Christ
may live in our hearts and come
to our world]

Pause for silent prayer.

Father all-powerful, God of love,
you have raised our Lord Jesus Christ
from death to life,
resplendent in glory as King of creation.
Open our hearts,
free all the world to rejoice in his peace,
to glory in his justice, to live in his love.
Bring all mankind together in
Jesus Christ your Son,
whose kingdom is with you and the Holy Spirit,
one God, for ever and ever.[3]

LITURGY OF THE WORD

Let us listen to God's word.

The readings are proclaimed.

First Reading
2 Samuel 5:1-3

David, a shepherd boy with hidden charismatic talents known only to God, would one day become the paradigmatic king of all time in the mind and collective consciousness of a people. David was not perfect. David was a sinner, yet he would be the one Israel would remember as leader of their splendid past. Their hopes for a glorious future were sparked by their memories of this legendary, charismatic earthly king. David was heralded as the ideal king throughout Israel's history.

As a sense of messianic hope developed in Israel, it was logical that the messiah-to-be would be referred to as the Son of David. Hebrew scriptures subscribed to two notions of kingship. Royal ideology of the Davidic court posited the king as the sacramental presence of Yahweh's reign over the people. Today's pericope is an expression of this notion. The king is a ruler who is in solidarity with his people. Thus, king as benevolent ruler and as

---

[1]Christ the King: "Entrance Antiphon," *The Sacramentary*.
[2]Christ the King: "Opening Prayer," *The Sacramentary*.

[3]Christ the King: "Alternative Opening Prayer," *The Sacramentary*.

shepherd are primary motifs in the first Old Testament theology of kingship.

The second notion distrusts human kingship. The inherent risk in having an earthly king is that sight of the sovereignty of Yahweh might be lost. Those who adhered to an anti-monarchy stance believed that the establishment of a kingship in the style of other national kingships was tantamount to rejection of Yahweh's theocratic rule of Israel. There was fear that an absolute monarchy would ultimately lead to tyranny. Israel had her share of such tyrannical kings.

David is a figure of Christ as king and as messiah. David was chosen by God. It was an unexpected, surprising choice. No one expected David to be chosen from among Jesse's sons. While it was God's choice, it was still important that Israel accept David as her ruler. The "elders" chose David for two reasons: he was shown to be a great leader and God had chosen David to be shepherd and commander of Israel. David's monarchy brought about the uniting of a people under the authority of the king. His monarchy would remain a symbol of never-failing hope even after the schism occurred. This Davidic hope gave rise to messianism. One day all the nations would be gathered under the messiah, the Son of David. Jesus, descendant of David, would be the realization of Isaiah's messianic prophecy. David was king of Israel; Jesus was king of the universe.

Responsorial Psalm
Psalm 122:1-2, 3-4, 4-5

This is known as a psalm of ascent. It was sung by pilgrims as they ascended to Jerusalem for festivals. The first part reflects the pilgrims' excitement as they arrive within Jerusalem's sacred confines. The psalmist sings of the symbolic unity of the tribes as all gather for festivals in Yahweh's temple. The gathering of the nations in Jerusalem was a symbol of post-exilic Israel's eschatological hope. The New Testament understands this to be fulfilled in the admission of the gentiles to the church.

Second Reading
Colossians 1:12-20

Today's pericope is one of the greatest christological and cosmic hymns in the New Testament.

Jesus accomplished two great works: creation and preservation. The Son of God, in his preexistent state, presided at the creation of the world and continues to preserve all creation through the power of the Spirit. The second part of the hymn exalts Christ's work of redemption. It speaks of Jesus' incarnation, the saving effects of the cross, his resurrection, and his ascension into glory and then the establishment of his Body, the church.

Jesus was heralded as the embodiment of Jewish wisdom. Jesus regarded himself in those terms (Lk 11:49). It was therefore natural that later Greek Christians identified Jesus as the incarnation of the personified wisdom of later Judaism. The wisdom of God is God going forth in the action of creation and redemption. This made it possible for Greek Christians to refute the gnostic belief that humanity needed to be saved *from* creation. They were adamant that "Jesus Christ was the redemption *of* all creation."[4] It is one and the same God who creates and redeems. Thus, Christ was truly present at creation as well as at the redemption at Calvary.

This reading is connected to the kingship of Christ in that it upholds the belief that the preexistent Christ, the eternal Son of God, who became incarnated through the person of Jesus Christ, is the "'cosmocrator'—the ruler of the universe."[5] Jesus' reign (though hidden) is proclaimed and acknowledged by the church. The world is the arena over which Christ reigns from his throne. The kingship of Christ is not just an abstract idea, asserts Reginald Fuller. "It involves the doctrines of the creation, redemption and reconciliation of the universe and of the church as the sphere where the universal reign is already acknowledged and proclaimed."[6]

Gospel
Luke 23:35-43

The penitent thief wins salvation and Christ is acknowledged King of the Jews.

---

[4]Reginald H. Fuller, *Preaching the New Lectionary* (Collegeville: The Liturgical Press, 1974), 100.
[5]Ibid.
[6]Ibid.

What were your first impressions? What was your first response? What grabbed your attention? How did you feel?

Each person names his or her initial impression. Statement should be brief. No reasons should be given at this time. All simply listen without agreeing or disagreeing.

STEP 2
UNDERSTANDING

In a brief statement, what do you think this gospel is trying to convey?

STEP 3
INPUT FROM VISION/STORY/TRADITION

Liturgical Context

This is the final Sunday of the liturgical cycle. It is the last time we encounter Jesus Christ through the lens of Luke for another two years. One of the so-called idea feasts, the feast of Christ the King serves as a finely tuned blending and climactic celebration of the major themes of Luke's gospel. There are three texts chosen just for this feast. "As opposed to the other Sundays in Ordinary Time, the Liturgy of the Word here takes the form of a triptych. The center, chief panel is the Gospel; the other panels, of the Old Testament and the epistle, are not quite on the same level as the first, but turned slightly toward it."[7]

Today's solemnity is reminiscent of the feasts of Ascension, Epiphany, and Palm Sunday. All celebrate the reign of Christ. Pope Pius XI instituted this feast in his Encyclical Letter *Quas primas*, Dec. 11, 1925, in response to the destructive forces of the age. He insisted that the only weapon against such forces and chaos is the acknowledgment of the sovereignty of Christ.

---

[7]*Days of the Lord*, Vol. 6 (Collegeville: The Liturgical Press, 1991), 314.

...It is necessary that the royal dignity of Our Lord be recognized and accepted as widely as possible. To this end it seems to Us that nothing else would help so effectively as the institution of a special feast dedicated to Christ our King. The annual celebration of the sacred mysteries is more effective in informing people about the Faith and in bringing them the joys of the spiritual life than the solemn pronouncements of the teaching Church. Documents are often read only by a few learned men; feasts move and teach all the faithful. The former speaks but once; the latter every year and forever. The former bring a saving touch to the intellect; the latter influence not only the mind but the heart and man's whole nature.[8]

At the time when the encyclical was written, the world had experienced the Bolshevik revolution in 1917, the spread of fascism, the loss of the church's political power, and the decadence of the 1920s. However, as cultural condition changed, so did the focus of this feast. The moving of the feast to the last Sunday of the liturgical cycle placed it center stage in our unfolding eschatological agenda. Thus, today this feast serves as an appropriate way to remember the Second Coming of Christ. "It is now clearer that the exalted Lord and King is the goal not only of the liturgical year but of our entire earthly pilgrimage....At the end of the liturgical year, then, stands the Lord of Glory."[9]

Adolph Adam suggests that Epiphany is the feast par excellence that remembers the kingship of Christ in the liturgy as expressed in Epiphany's entrance antiphon: "The Lord and ruler is coming; kingship is his, and government and power." He quotes W. Durig on the matter:

Only an obscuring of the content of the liturgical feast of Epiphany and an intellectualization of liturgical theology could have led Pius XI in 1925 to introduce a second Feast of Christ the King on the

---

[8]AAS 17 (1925), 593-610. In Adolf Adam, *The Liturgical Year*, trans. Matthew J. O'Connell (Collegeville: The Liturgical Press, 1990), 177.

[9]Adam, *The Liturgical Year*, 178.

last Sunday of October. This move is typical of the development that modern piety has undergone; this development becomes clear from a comparison of the two feasts. The feast of Christ the King *celebrates the general idea of Christ's kingship; it celebrates a title of honor, a name, a concept* [italics mine]. On the other hand, it is essential to the liturgical feast of Epiphany that it brings before us, in a concrete way, a royal action of Christ, an event that is an essential part of the process of salvation. On the one hand, then, an idea; on the other, the reality of the mystery of Epiphany which contains in itself the entire mystery of redemption.[10]

Reginald Fuller asserts that the feast duplicates the themes of Ascension Day and contains a distinctive emphasis on social action. According to Fuller this feast provides the liturgical support for the social teaching of the great papal encyclicals since Leo XIII.

When it was first established as a feast assigned to the last Sunday in October, there was a danger of removing the kingship of Christ from its eschatological context. Jesus' enthronement at the Ascension is the inauguration of his eschatological reign, his rule over all until he comes again in glory, and his ongoing defeat of the power of evil. By moving the feast to the last Sunday of the year, this eschatological emphasis was retained.

The events that prompted establishment of the feast had to do with the sixteen-century anniversary of the Council of Nicea's pronouncement that Christ and the Father are one and the same (consubstantiality), thus providing the basis for his kingly rule. "He [Pius XI] chose this day chiefly in view of the coming feast of All Saints; the feast of Christ the King would exalt 'before all men the glory of Him Who triumphs in His saints and His elect.'"[11] On this feast there was to be a consecration to the heart of Christ, the Redeemer.

In a decree promulgating the *editio typica* of the General Roman Calendar on March 21, 1969, *Anni liturgici ordinatione, #3760,* the feast of Christ the King was moved to a new day: "The feast of the Baptism of the Lord and Christ the King are to be celebrated on the days newly assigned to them."[12] The revised liturgical calendar moved the feast of Christ the King from the last Sunday in October to the last Sunday of the year. According to the "General Norms for the Liturgical Year and the Calendar,"

> Because of its special importance, the Sunday celebration gives way only to solemnities or feasts of the Lord. The Sundays of the seasons of Advent, Lent and Easter, however, take precedence over all solemnities and feasts of the Lord. Solemnities occurring on these Sundays are observed on the Saturday preceding.[#5]

> By its nature, Sunday excludes any other celebration's being permanently assigned to that day, with these exceptions: a. Sunday within the octave of Christmas is the feast of the Holy Family; b. Sunday following 6 January is the feast of the Baptism of the Lord; c. Sunday after Pentecost is the solemnity of the Holy Trinity; d. The last Sunday in Ordinary Time is the solemnity of Christ the King. [#6][13]

The liturgy exalts the universal reign of Christ, not just today, but in every celebration of liturgy. Today's entrance antiphon asserts Christ's divinely instituted power. Christ, the slain Lamb, is worthy to receive strength and divinity and to him be "glory and power for ever." The opening prayer expresses our confidence in Christ's exaltation and his power to reign over all creation: "You break the power of evil and make all things new. . . ." The prayer over the gifts acknowledges the sacrifice of Christ's life on the cross, a sacrifice that reconciled the world to the Father and inaugurated Christ's kingship. The preface for today's

---

[10]W. Durig, "Epiphanie," in *Ercheinung des Herrn* (Am Tisch des Wortes, Neue 118; Stuttgart, 1971), p. 12, in Adolf Adam, *The Liturgical Year,* 147.

[11]Adam, *The Liturgical Year,* 177.

[12]*Documents on the Liturgy, 1963-1979: Conciliar, Papal and Curial Texts* (Collegeville: The Liturgical Press, 1982), 1156.

[13]"General Norms for the Liturgical Year and the Calendar," in *The Liturgy Documents, 1963-1979* (Collegeville: The Liturgical Press, 1982), 1156.

liturgy echoes repeated references to the kingdom established by Christ:

> Father, all-powerful and ever-living God,
> we do well always and everywhere to give you
> thanks.
> You anointed Jesus Christ, your only Son, with
> the oil of gladness,
> as the eternal priest and universal king.
> As priest he offered his life on the altar of the
> cross
> and redeemed the human race
> by this one perfect sacrifice of peace.
> As king he claims dominion over all creation,
> that he may present you, his almighty Father,
> an eternal and universal kingdom:
> a kingdom of truth and life,
> a kingdom of holiness and grace,
> a kingdom of justice, love, and peace.[14]

The third form of the penitential rite picks up the same theme: "Lord Jesus, you rule over the kingdom of truth and life."

As Ordinary Time comes to a close and Advent begins, both dovetail in focus and we are reminded that both exalt Christ, who reigns triumphant over the world and who will come again in glory. Thus, Advent's "Solemn Blessing Over the People" is included in this session's closing prayer. It echoes today's contemplation on the reign of Christ.

Christian Initiation

The Feast of Christ the King strongly echoes the fullness of the Easter Vigil. Christ's sovereignty over all creation through his life, death, resurrection, ascension into heaven and the coming of his Spirit finds concrete expression in the passage of the elect through the waters of new birth from death to new life in baptism. The newly baptized died to the old self to rise again with Christ, Lord and Ruler of their lives. Thus, the feast of Christ the King might be an appropriate time to baptize infants and those unable to be baptized at the Easter Vigil.[15] It might also be an occasion to celebrate a Rite of Acceptance/Welcome or a Rite of Full Communion, if needed.

Today's psalm exalts the pilgrim's journey and ascent to Jerusalem. The liturgy is our pilgrimage to Jerusalem. The liturgy anticipates the heavenly banquet in the new Jerusalem. It is in this heavenly reign that Christ's kingship will be finally realized.

Gospel Exegesis

The facilitator gives input regarding what critical biblical scholarship has to say about this text. The input includes insights as to how people would have heard the gospel in Jesus' time.

Having just experienced the cosmic hymn of Christ, the "cosmocrator" in the second reading, we are jolted back to earth with the story of the thief who was the eleventh-hour recipient of Christ's benevolent reign. There is much to absorb in this gospel: the kingship of Christ, the great irony in the situation, and the salvation of the thief.

There is the inscription on the cross: "King of the Jews." It was a false charge against Jesus, perhaps placed there in mockery of him, but to those who believe in him, it is the ultimate truth of the cosmos. The thief proclaimed the kingship of Christ by requesting that Christ remember him when he enter into his reign. Jesus assured the thief a place in paradise.

Jesus' reign is named and uniquely highlighted in this gospel. The inscription on the cross and the jeers of the leaders named Christ as the King of the Jews. Luke Timothy Johnson poses an interesting question. Why would Pilate place such a charge on the cross if he had already declared Jesus innocent of the charge? Johnson names three possibilities: 1. to defend himself against a later possible charge of giving in to the demands of the crowd; 2. to mock Jesus in order to placate and please the Jewish leadership; 3. to provide a warning to other aspiring zealot revolutionaries against the empire: "This is what happens to those who call themselves 'King of the Jews.'"[16]

---

[14]Christ the King: "Preface," *The Sacramentary*.

[15]For example, fully catechized unbaptized persons (such as spouses who have attended weekly liturgy for years) might fall under this category. Since there would be no need to

delay their initiation longer than necessary, perhaps they could be initiated on this feast. The Easter Vigil remains the church's premier time for adults to celebrate baptism, confirmation and eucharist, however. (See *RCIA*, Part II, Chapter II: "Christian Initiation of Adults in Exceptional Circumstances.")

[16]Luke Timothy Johnson, *The Gospel of Luke*, Sacra Pagina Series, Vol. 3 (Collegeville: The Liturgical Press, 1991), 378.

The inscription and declaration nevertheless expressed profound truth. Jesus is sovereign over all: the religious, the penitent believer, and the universe.

Jesus was called king only once in his earthly life: at the triumphant entry into Jerusalem on the last leg of his journey to Calvary. However, Luke used the term *kingdom, Lord,* and *reign* throughout the gospel. The entire passion account points to the coming reign of God. Jesus, when questioned by the council, attested, "But from this time on the Son of Man will be seated at the right hand of the power of God" (Lk 22:69).

Luke insists that Jesus' kingdom is radically different from the world kingdoms built on power, wealth, and prestige. Crucifixion is the throne of Christ's kingdom. It is built on seeming defeat. Luke cleverly tells us that there are people present at this event who "stood there watching [*theorin*]." Luke used the verb *theorin* that meant contemplation. Why would Luke include the "*stood there watching*" folks if not to invite the reader to place himself or herself among their company? They stood there contemplating. What were they contemplating and what was the result of their contemplation? Perhaps we are to fill in the blanks. Johnson maintains that the posture of the crowd is far different from the response of the leaders. The leaders stand in abject mockery.

It was the crucifixion of the Chosen One that inaugurated his universal reign. On this feast of Christ the King, we too are invited to *stand there contemplating.* What will be our response to this contemplation?

Next to Jesus on the cross was the thief who acknowledged his own guilt yet at the same time asserted Jesus' innocence. The accusers, however, hurled accusations at Jesus. Their very accusations were ironic acclamations of Christian faith—messiah, savior, the chosen one. "He saved others; let him save himself if he is the *Messiah of God, the chosen one.*" God testified to Christ's identity and power by the very words that came out of the mouths of the accusers. What brilliant irony! The soldiers, at least, were ignorant of the implications of their actions. They were simply doing what they had been told to do. Why should they think this was different from any other execution?

The leaders, the soldiers, and one criminal jeered. One thief repented, and the people contemplated. In his last moment, the penitent thief asked for salvation from the man *Jesus,* whose name means, "God saves."[17] Such familiarity was unusual. Was he reaching out to the implication of Jesus' name, reaching for the hope it contained?

The thief asked to be remembered. In the Hebrew scriptures God was usually the object of requests to be remembered. The thief was asking that the living God, the One who had the power to save, remember him. While aware of his own sinfulness, the thief was confident that God could and would save. Jesus' assurance was stronger than the thief's request. The day of death is the day of salvation for those who believe.

"Today" is an important concept for Luke. "Today in the city of David a savior has been born...." "Today this Scripture is fulfilled in your hearing. ..." "Today salvation has come to this house...." *Today* is an ongoing reality. It is not tied to a particular static moment in Jesus' life. It embodies the reign of God *now* and *not yet.* It is the present as well as the future reality. The thief was offered paradise in the quick breath of the spoken word. Theologian Michael Himes asserts that God's love and salvation are preexistent realities. There is never a time when we are not loved or saved. We merely have to accept the love and salvation freely offered through Christ. We accept the reality that was always present.[18] The thief stepped into reality that was his for the taking. In this context, *today* is the moment of decision.

As members of the contemplating crowd, we stand before Christ of the Universe, Christ of Calvary's Throne with the same question and at the same moment of decision.

Proclaim the gospel again.

Sometimes we gain new insights when we hear the text after the interpretation has been given. Someone from the group proclaims the gospel a second time.

---

[17]In antiquity people's names reflected the entity of their being, their role, and their designation in life.

[18]Michael Himes, "Jesus Yesterday, Today and Forever: Christology Update for Catechetical Leaders," Workshop, National Conference of Catechetical Leadership, April 13–17, 1997.

Conversation with the Liturgy and Scriptures

Test your original understanding in dialogue with the text.

(You might consider breaking into smaller groups.)

Now that you've heard what the scholars have to say about the feast of Christ the King, how do you feel about it? Were there any new insights? Was there anything you had not considered before? How does your original understanding of this feast and these scriptures compare with what was just shared? How does this story speak to your life?

Participants share an experience from their lives that connects with the biblical interpretation just shared.

One of the highlights of my trip to Israel was our journey into Jerusalem. As our bus chugged up the mountainside, we sang the psalm of pilgrims, the psalm of ascent, "Let us go rejoicing to the house of the Lord. . . ." We sang amidst our surprising tears in anticipation of our arrival into Jerusalem, the ancient symbol of God's salvation history with the human race. Emotion choked us into awesome contemplation between the verses of our sung praise.

Yet in the midst of this sacred moment, we were confronted with the sober reality of this city's lure and fame—or, perhaps, infamy. Scattered on both sides of the road were rusted armored vehicles, memorials of Israel's war of independence. Men and women had given their lives fighting for this holy city. Through the ages many gave their lives for the same reason—most with varied theological reasons to support their uncommon valor.

Today the fight continues. Blood is still shed over the right to reign over this ancient city. The disputing sides of the fight all assert their God-given right to sovereignty. Yet, only God is sovereign. God's power is realized not in actions of dominance displayed by world powers intent on destruction, but through the absurdity of the cross. God's reign is manifest in the lives of faithful people of all denominations and religious leanings who follow their God and sacrifice themselves for others.

No place I have ever been reflects the cosmic reign of Christ more than the eternal city of Jerusalem. This is a holy city from whose parapets early morning voices cry out in Moslem praise of God. This is a broken city whose poor dot each entrance gate with desperate pleas for alms. This is a sacred city whose pilgrims come from the earth's far corners to contemplate the mysteries of their incarnate and transcendent God and the place where the Christ Victor redeemed the world on Golgotha hill. This is a divided city, whose violent factions continue to herald the world's need for a great and mighty King who brings peace and is Lord of all people unconditionally and inclusively. This is a cosmic city that reminds us that it is the new Jerusalem we await—one in which there will be no more weeping or tears, no more division or bloodshed, no more powers or principalities, and one in which all people will worship in unity at the throne of the Lamb.

So, what does this have to do with my life as it is lived within the confines of my own community and my family? Jerusalem reminds me of the implications of today's feast. Jesus Christ is Lord and Ruler of my life, of all life. Jerusalem simply serves as a composite symbol of every Christian's life. We are all on the road to Jerusalem in one way or another. The question is: Are we going to Jerusalem to participate in her worst and finest hour—the redemption of the cross? Or are we going to Jerusalem to be indifferent bystanders or worse yet, condemning accusers? Are we going to Jerusalem as people who stand in solidarity with the world's broken, poor, and oppressed? Or are we going to Jerusalem as self-serving power mongers? It is a question that demands a decisive answer. The answer is observed by the way we live our lives.

Christ is Lord of the Universe. We live that reality when we abandon ourselves to the authority, love, and salvation of our Cosmic, Sovereign Christ and when we accept the love and salvation that are already ours as we await the consummation of his final and conclusive act of love. How do we know if we are doing all that? We must be brutally honest as we ask ourselves the question: How are we loving those who are the most difficult to love in our midst?

All share their life experience.

What was Luke trying to tell his community? How can that be applied today? How does this liturgy call me to transformation? How are the biblical themes of creation, community, covenant and exodus evident in this celebration? Do I still feel the same way about this text as I did at the beginning? Has my original understanding been stretched, challenged, or affirmed?

STEP 5
DECISION

The gospel demands a response.

How does your sharing and this biblical liturgical interpretation challenge your community to action? Be concrete. Has this conversation with the exegesis of these scriptures changed or stretched you to growth? In what way? Name one concrete action you will take this week as a response to what was learned and shared today.

DOCTRINAL ISSUES

What church truth/teaching/doctrinal issue could be drawn from the gospel for the Feast of Christ the King?

Participants suggest possible doctrinal themes that flow from the readings.

Possible Doctrinal Themes

Jesus Christ, King of the Universe, kingdom of God, eschatology, soteriology

Present the doctrinal material at this time.

1. The facilitator gives input on a particular doctrinal issue of his/her prior choosing. OR
2. The group chooses a doctrinal issue from the list they created. They read together from the Doctrinal Appendix.

(The doctrinal issues are found in the Doctrinal Appendix in the back of this workbook. If you are choosing an issue from this resource, please refer to it now.)

Reflection questions centered around the chosen doctrinal theme can be found at the end of each

topic in the Doctrinal Appendix. The questions are based on the five-step reflection process. If you choose a topic not included in the Doctrinal Appendix, craft your own questions according to the same five-step process.

Following the reflection questions you will be reminded to return to chapter 7, "Preparing the Catechetical Session," to assist you in crafting your own session.

Closing Prayer

You believe that the Son of God once came to us;
you look for him to come again.
May his coming bring you the light of his holiness
and free you with his blessing.
(Amen.)

May God make you steadfast in faith,
joyful in hope, and untiring in love
all the days of your life.
(Amen.)

You rejoice that our Redeemer came to live with
us as man.
When he comes again in glory,
may he reward you with endless life.
(Amen.)[19]

Selected Bibliography

Adam, Adolf. *The Liturgical Year.* Trans. Matthew J. O'Connell. Collegeville: The Liturgical Press, 1990.

Days of the Lord. Vol. 6. Collegeville: The Liturgical Press, 1991.

Documents on the Liturgy 1963-1979. Collegeville: The Liturgical Press, 1982.

Fuller, Reginald H. *Preaching the New Lectionary.* Collegeville: The Liturgical Press, 1974.

Johnson, Luke Timothy. *The Gospel of Luke.* Sacra Pagina Series. Vol. 3. Collegeville: The Liturgical Press, 1991.

Sanchez, Patricia Datchuck. *The Word We Celebrate.* Kansas City: Sheed and Ward, 1989.

---

[19]"Advent Solemn Blessing," *The Sacramentary.*

SOLEMNITIES AND FEASTS

TRINITY SUNDAY

INTRODUCTORY RITES

Opening Song (or Entrance Antiphon)

Blessed be God the Father and his only begotten Son and the Holy Spirit: for he has shown that he loves us.[1]

Environment

We have just left the pinnacle season of the church year. One almost needs time to catch one's breath. It almost seems anticlimactic to go from the festive whites and golds of Easter, the red of Pentecost, to the simplicity of green with instant abruptness. But move we must. Trinity Sunday and Corpus Christi give us two opportunities to slowly ease into the ripened green of summer Ordinary Time. We are not, however, to assume that the Easter season is extended for two more weeks. Ordinary Time has definitely begun. The liturgical color of these two solemnities is white, even though Ordinary Time has returned. The profound nature of the two feasts, God's sacramental expression of love, calls for highlighted attention.

Perhaps one way to return to the longest season of the year is to replace any remaining festal flowers of the Easter season with simple green plants. What better plant to use for this feast than the shamrock, nature's own hint of the Triune God? Without verbiage, its placement in the catechetical environment is a simple reminder that all creation praises the Creator. Perhaps the stark simplicity of a white cloth adorned with nothing but the shamrock and the nearby enthronement of the scriptures would be all that is needed to capture a sense of the feast and movement into a new season.

Opening Prayer

The facilitator of the session may lead the prayer. Others in the group may be asked to proclaim the readings.

Let us pray
[to the one God, Father, Son and Spirit,
that our lives may bear witness to our faith]

Pause for silent prayer.

Father,
you sent your Word to bring us truth
and your Spirit to make us holy.
Through them we come to know the mystery of
    your life.
Help us to worship you, One God in three Per-
    sons,
by proclaiming and living our faith in you.
We ask this through our Lord Jesus Christ, your
    Son,
who lives and reigns with you and the Holy Spirit,
one God, for ever and ever.[2]

LITURGY OF THE WORD

Let us listen to God's word.

The readings are proclaimed.

First Reading
Proverbs 8:22-31

In ancient Israel there were three types of groups that inspired religious and social life: priests, prophets, and sages. Sages were talented in the art of contemplation and discernment. Their advice was treasured. "Schooled in the ways of the world, they were equipped to instruct their contemporaries in how the good life should be lived. And because they were convinced that 'the fear of the Lord is the beginning of wisdom' (Prov 9:10; cf. also Prov 1:7, Ps. 111:10, and Job 28:28), the sages had something to say about the nature and requirements of authentic religion."[3]

The sage (wise man) advised the average Israelite in how to live a well ordered, balanced life. He was not as passionate as the prophet. He perhaps agreed with the need for structures to change, but was not one to challenge the status quo. The wise man was an active member of Hebrew society. He

---

[1]Trinity Sunday: "Entrance Antiphon," *The Sacramentary.*

[2]Trinity Sunday: "Opening Prayer," *The Sacramentary.*

[3]J. Kenneth Kuntz, *The People of Ancient Israel* (New York: Harper and Row, 1974), 448.

was the privileged leader in a movement that was sweeping the Near Eastern world. The sage had his finger on the pulse of the world. He understood human needs, dreams, problems, and hopes. The wisdom movement had great impact on Hebrew thought, prayer, and history. Traces of its influence can be found in multiple genres of biblical literature. However, the books of Job, Proverbs, and Ecclesiastes are the books most often identified as the wisdom books.

Scriptural wisdom literature was of two types. The first type dealt with practical advice in living a well ordered life and offered exhortations about hard work, containment of one's emotional life, and how to get along with colleagues and companions. Wisdom literature held that a well-disciplined life was a successful life.

The second type of wisdom literature was critical and reflective. It recognized that life "happens" and that good does not always come to those who work hard and follow all the rules. The sage did not ascribe to an easy, soft orthodoxy. This literature perhaps could be the ancient version of "Why bad things happen to good people."

Both types worked in tandem to seek the meaning of life. The sage was not concerned with the historical relationship between God and God's people as were the priests and prophets. The sage was concerned with the individual as he or she existed in the community of the human race. The wise man believed that human experience had much to teach the intelligent, disciplined person.

The wisdom movement's finest hour was under the tutelage of Solomon. While it is generally held that Solomon did not write the wisdom books (as ancient tradition suggests), it is safe to assume that he influenced these writings.

The book of Proverbs could be the handbook for the "power of positive thinking." Its tone and tenor are incredibly optimistic. Proverbs 1–9 is considered the first collection. Since it is the most cohesive, well defined collection in the book, scholars believe it was written last.

The most theologically striking section of the book is the passage in today's liturgy. Wisdom is personified as Lady Wisdom, who invites people to come to her in order to acquire prudence. Lady Wisdom speaks of herself as a participant in creation's birth. She was an active agent. The Lady also claims to be active in creation's ongoing conservation. This promise of preservation is primarily directed to her relationship with the human race. The prefigured theology of Spirit prevalent in Old Testament biblical literature gives God a feminine face: Lady Wisdom.

While the doctrine of Trinity is not specifically revealed in scripture, it is foreshadowed and hinted at. In the Old Testament God is referred to as Father of Israel. God is personified throughout as Word (*dabar*), Spirit (*ruah*), Wisdom (*hokmah*), and presence (*shekinah*).

Responsorial Psalm
Psalm 8:4-5, 6-7, 8-9

Today's psalm text is from psalm 8, a hymn in praise of Yahweh the Creator. It puts in verse form the theological truth of the creation event recorded in Genesis 1. "God is creator of the whole universe and man is the crown of creation, destined for glory and honor and invested with dominion over the created order."[4] The antiphon "O Lord, our Lord, how wonderful your name in all the earth!" depicts an ancient sacramental understanding of God's name. "The 'name of God' is the sacramental bearer of divine reality."[5]

In verse five the psalmist seeks to contrast the insignificance of humanity with the transcendent majesty of God. God's splendor and glory are acclaimed and a human being appears to be "crowned" with the same glory and splendor. John Kselman suggests that perhaps this was a reference to the king; "blessed with divine attributes, he is almost a god." Paul's letter to the Hebrews lifts this passage and applies it to the person of Jesus Christ (Heb 2: 5-9).

---

[4]Reginald H. Fuller, *Preaching the New Lectionary* (Collegeville: The Liturgical Press, 1974), 41.

[5]John S. Kselman, S.J. and Michael L. Barré, S.S., "Psalms," in *The New Jerome Biblical Commentary,* ed. Raymond E. Brown, S.S., Joseph A. Fitzmyer, S.J., Roland E. Murphy, O.Carm. (Englewood Cliffs: Prentice Hall, 1990), 528.

Second Reading
Romans 5:1-5

Before Paul wrote his letter to the Romans, he had already grappled with the subject matter inherent in this letter. In his letter to the Galatians, Paul furiously defended his developing theology of the Christian kerygma. One can almost hear the echoes of his interior debate regarding the meaning of Jesus' sacrifice as it relates to the law and the prophets. Paul was reformulating his theology in light of his experience of the risen Christ in the lived experience of the gentile community. The letter to the Galatians is a rather impulsive, defensive letter. It was written from a jail cell and reflected the frenzy of his predicament. The letter to the Romans is a more refined, less exaggerated articulation of the Galatian message: in order to become transformed, all one needed to do was embrace the message of Jesus Christ. The Holy Spirit, then, would slowly begin the process of transformation.

After no doubt alienating more than a few law-abiding Jewish Christians, Paul displayed more tact, finesse, and certainly more brilliance in expressing and defining his theology to the Roman community. He was careful not to diminish or minimize the Jewish roots of his readers. However, while the letter to the Romans is certainly more conciliatory toward his Jewish audience, Paul is nevertheless determined to challenge rigid legalism and the notion of merited salvation. The letter validated Yahweh's intervention in Israel's (Old Testament) history.[6] Paul asserted that the Christian kerygma is the fulfillment of what God already accomplished in the Old Testament. Thus, according to Hubert Richards, Paul did not repudiate Judaism and the gospel was stated as its fulfillment.[7]

Paul insisted that Jesus died once and for all people. It was a complete act of gratuitous, unmerited, unconditional love. The response to such love can be nothing less than the complete offering of one's entire life to the God who loves so greatly. Human beings are justified by faith, not by observance of the law, not by their own merits. It was a difficult message to accept. Justification through the law was ingrained in people's consciousness and history. Paul was afraid that people would simply not believe they were forgiven. He felt compelled to proclaim the Good News to the entire world with determined urgency.

The letter to the Romans was written toward the end of Paul's third missionary journey. He was already planning his fourth trip and Rome was to be his home base. Paul's intention in writing to the Romans was to prepare them for his arrival and to encourage them in the midst of their struggle. The letter to the Romans is a masterful articulation of the Christian belief in the paschal mystery. It is a brilliant, systematic expression of Christian theology. Some call it "Paul's gospel."

Joseph Fitzmyer asserts that rather than a summation of Paul's doctrine, it is a presentation of the possibility of salvation offered to all people through the good news of Christ. "We *are* at peace," says Paul in the first verse of today's pericope. It is a firm proclamation of the fact that we are truly, already justified by faith in Jesus Christ. No longer are we cut off from God, because we have been reconciled to God through Christ. Through Jesus, grace is open to all and is humanity's most precious gift.

Some suggest that the term "access" means safe harbor. Paul was intent on encouraging the persecuted church in the midst of its trials to stand firm and rejoice in them. Paul wrote his letter to the Roman Church from Corinth (ca. 57-58 C.E.). He was extremely aware of the difficulties they were experiencing. Eight years earlier Claudius had expelled the Jews from Rome. Christian Jews were not exempt from the expulsion. In 54 C.E. Nero annulled Claudius's mandate and the Jews were invited to return. However, there were disputed issues between the Hellenist Christians who had been exempt from expulsion and had remained in the city and the returning Jewish Christians. Paul, aware of these tensions, was able to address them from the perspectives and insights gleaned from his own missionary efforts. He knew well the struggle, as he had experienced similar difficulties in his relationship with the Judaizers. It was from this school that Paul learned and grew in his con-

---

[6]The Galatians letter seemed to repudiate the Old Testament. His tone in the letter to the Romans is far more conciliatory to the Jews.

[7]For more information refer to: Hubert Richards, *The Gospel According to St. Paul* (Collegeville: The Liturgical Press, 1990), 87.

viction that all are offered God's free gift of salvation: human beings are justified through faith.

Thus, in today's reading, Paul insists that standing firm in the midst of such trials yields to endurance and a firm hope. For Paul, the assurance that salvation was a free gift for all inclusively was based on his belief in God's love shown to us through the power of the Holy Spirit. It was Paul's firm belief in the triune nature of God that would later be the foundation upon which theologians based the doctrine of Trinity. For Paul it was the Christian anchor: hope and endurance come through faith in the Triune God's transcendent power!

Gospel
John 16:12-15

Jesus expresses the role of the Paraclete in his farewell address.

STEP 1
NAMING ONE'S EXPERIENCE

What were your first impressions? What was your first response? What grabbed your attention? How did you feel?

Each person names his or her initial impression. Statement should be brief. No reasons should be given at this time. All simply listen without agreeing or disagreeing.

STEP 2
UNDERSTANDING

In a brief statement, what do you think this gospel is trying to convey?

STEP 3
INPUT FROM VISION/STORY/TRADITION

Liturgical Context

Trinity Sunday is one of the four solemnities of the Lord during Ordinary Time. Since these feasts are dependent upon the celebration of Easter, they are called movable solemnities of Ordinary Time. The solemnities are Trinity Sunday, Corpus Christi, Sacred Heart, and Christ the King.

Adolf Adam calls them feasts of devotion and feasts of ideas. As feasts of devotion they are expressions of a piety born in response to an internal or external trial. As idea feasts, each one extols a particular truth or specific aspect of the mystery of Christ. By stressing these truths or mysteries, the church hoped to renew and strengthen the faith of God's people.

The Arian controversies of the fourth and fifth centuries gave rise to a strong emphasis on and devotion to the Trinity in Spain and Gaul. Arius, a priest in Alexandria who died in 336, denied the divinity of Christ. As a result, faith in God the Father, Son, and Holy Spirit, and the equality of the three divine persons was threatened. The Councils of Nicea and Constantinople (381) condemned the heresy and formulated the Nicene Creed, the profession of faith recited at every Sunday Mass.

The heresy had an impact on Catholic faith and life. Preaching sought to strengthen faith in the church's doctrine regarding the Trinity. The first preface of the Trinity found its way into the liturgy in the 400s as this feast was born out of controversy. The modern preface of the Trinity appeared during the eighth century. By 800 the Mass of the Trinity was celebrated as a votive Mass for Sundays. All Sunday liturgies became more trinitarian in focus. By the year 1000 the feast of the Trinity was celebrated on the Sunday after Pentecost in Frankish and Gallic monasteries. The feast reminds the faithful of what it means when we refer to the Father, Son and Spirit: We believe in three divine persons in one God.

In the year 1077 Pope Alexander questioned the need for a special feast devoted to just the Trinity. The Pope's contention was that the Trinity is remembered and celebrated every Sunday, even every day. One hundred years later Alexander III said the same thing. However, the feast continued to exist. John XXII made it an official feast during the exile in Avignon in 1334. Adam suggests that the placement of this feast on the Sunday after Pentecost served as a mirror to reflect back on the mystery of salvation just culminated with the celebration of Pentecost.

The feast celebrates a lofty, abstract dogma that seems unrelated to our everyday lives. The overall context for approaching this feast, then, is best found in the following exhortation: "The feast is only a feast if we follow the lead of the assigned scriptures and acclaim a God of love, not dissect an arcane theological treatise."[8]

The liturgy has assigned to it three different readings and responsorial psalms for the three-year cycle. The gospel for Cycle C is taken from Jesus' farewell discourse in John's gospel. This gospel amazingly reveals the mystery of the Trinity: "All that the Father has belongs to me. That is why I said that what he [the Spirit of truth] will announce to you he will have from me." The Hebrew scriptures herald the personified Wisdom of God that was "beside God" before creation, delighting in all creation. The second reading from Romans emphasizes the effects of salvation: human beings are heirs to God's peace through Christ; they are rooted in hope and God becomes approachable. Paul claims that God's love is poured out upon us through the Spirit.

The alleluia verse is one grand summation and doxology in praise of the One, Triune God: "Glory to the Father, the Son and the Holy Spirit: to God who has been given to us." The opening prayer asks that the Father help us pray to the One God in three persons by living and proclaiming our faith. "One hears criticism about this feast because it commemorates not an event but a Christian doctrine. However, the opening prayer blends both event and doctrine: Belief in the Trinity leads us to life of the Father by experiencing the truth revealed by Jesus and the holiness of the Spirit."[9]

All liturgy professes belief in the Triune God. Never is there a liturgical celebration in which the power of the Trinity is not invoked. The Sunday assembly professes faith in the Triune God when it begins every gathering by invoking "The grace of our Lord Jesus Christ and the love of God and the fellowship of the Holy Spirit be with you all."[10] "Celebrated on the Sunday after Pentecost, it [the feast of the Trinity] is a great doxology to the Father who raised his Son and brought him into the glory where he reigns with the Holy Spirit he has sent to us. When the sequence of the Sundays in Ordinary Time is about to begin again, this feast sheds light on the face and true nature of Jesus, the Son of God, who, by his teaching and his acts, reveals the Father and leads humankind to himself in the Spirit."[11]

Symbol: Finger of God

Today's psalm refers to the finger of God. "When I behold your heavens, the work of your fingers...." The finger of God throughout the Hebrew scriptures is a term reflecting God's power. It is similar in usage to the "hand" of God, also a symbol of divine power. The term is used in the New Testament in Luke 11:20 when Jesus drives out a demon "by the finger of God." It is used in this reference as a means to show the ease with which Jesus performed such a powerful action. Matthew recounts the same event by stating that Jesus drove out demons by the Spirit of God (Mt 12:28).

Church tradition picked up both images in later patristic writings. In the fourth century St. Ambrose made the comparison of the Son and Spirit as the hand and finger of God. There was no intention to minimize their role, or to imply that they were only a small portion of God. "It expresses the unity of power among the three in all their actions."[12]

This understanding is articulated in later centuries in the hymn "Veni Creator Spiritus" (766-856). The Spirit is cited as the "finger of God's right hand." The term "finger of God" is used in Vatican II's *Dogmatic Constitution on the Church* in reference to the power of Christ's miracles as a sign that the reign of God was firmly established on this earth.

[8]Bishops' Committee on the Liturgy Secretariat, National Conference of Catholic Bishops, *Study Text 9: The Liturgical Year Celebrating the Mystery of Christ and His Saints* (Washington: USCC, 1984), 60.

[9]Stephen T. Jarrell, *Guide to the Sacramentary* (Chicago: Liturgy Training Publications, 1983), 74.

[10]Order of Mass: "Greeting," *The Sacramentary*.

[11]*Days of the Lord*, Vol. 7 (Collegeville: The Liturgical Press, 1994), 7.

[12]Dennis M. Sweetland, "Finger of God," in *The Collegeville Pastoral Dictionary of Biblical Theology*, ed. Carroll Stuhlmueller, C.P. (Collegeville: The Liturgical Press, 1996), 334.

If we were to say that there is a bottom line in this liturgy, it can be summed up in words of the entrance antiphon: Blessed be God the Father and his only begotten Son and the Holy Spirit: *for he has shown that he loves us.*

Gospel Exegesis

The facilitator gives input regarding what critical biblical scholarship has to say about this text. The input includes insights as to how people would have heard the gospel in Jesus' time.

Jesus' farewell address was for the purpose of preparing the disciples for their mission. Today's pericope centers on the role of the Holy Spirit. Jesus warned his disciples that he would undergo suffering and death before he would return to his Father. They were terrified. Their unity was dependent upon his presence. Jesus was their driving force and they knew it. He was their anchor, the one who kept them from feeling alienated, lost, and without hope.

Jesus sought to lift their fearful, mournful prospects for a future without him by promising to send the Paraclete. This Spirit would be always with them, to guide, protect, and strengthen them. They would eventually realize that the Spirit was none other than the risen presence of Jesus in their midst. According to Richard Cassidy it is significant that the term *Paraclete* is used. It is a term used only five times in the New Testament: four times in Jesus' farewell discourses between chapters 14 through 16 and once in 1 John 2:1. Cassidy maintains that it is significant that this word in Greek understanding had juridical connotations. The Paraclete was to bear witness to Christ and to help the disciples as they too bore witness to him. Jesus made his promise to the disciples right after he warned them of future persecution. "Thus, the Paraclete's role in this context can be likened to that performed by a 'defense attorney.' Subsequently, in a particularly rich passage in which Jesus consoles the disciples regarding his departure, he also alludes to the Paraclete's role in 'convincing or convicting' the world and the ruler of the world (16:8-10)."[13] What better attorney to argue on our behalf than the Spirit of God!

---

[13]Richard J. Cassidy, *John's Gospel in New Perspective* (New York: Orbis Books, 1992), 61.

Jesus' disciples were a little thick at times. Jesus was often frustrated by their lack of understanding. They did not fully grasp the implications of Jesus' mission while he was still on earth. They only minimally grasped the meaning of his often unorthodox teaching, parables, and parabolic actions. There would be another day and Jesus knew it. "I have much more to tell you, but you cannot bear it now." Raymond Brown insists that this text refers to the future day, after Jesus' resurrection, when the Spirit would come upon them and only then would they understand the full implication of Jesus' life, mission, death, and resurrection. The Spirit would not be revealing anything new, but would merely shower upon them a deeper awareness and understanding of all that Jesus had already taught them, all that they had been unable to fully grasp.

There are scholars who believe the Johannine text was referring to additional, continual revelation that would end with the death of the last apostle. Brown disagrees, reminding us that earlier, in chapter 15:15 the Johannine Jesus says that he has already revealed *everything* that the Father has told him. There is no hint of future revelation in today's verse (16:12).

In verses 13-15 the verb announce (*anangellein*) is used three times. Apocalyptic writings use that word to mean the interpretation of visions or dreams (revelation) already received. Brown suggests that a better translation of verses 13 through 15 would read: "he will reannounce to you." Again, the Spirit is not revealing a new word, but is rather breathing new life into a word already given but not fully understood. The Spirit would reveal the fullness of the Christ event in the midst of the growing, attentive Christian community.

The Spirit was the risen presence of Christ in the midst of the community. With the Spirit of truth, the community would not be led astray; they would stand firm in the face of falsehood, heresies, and other movements that claimed divine revelation.

The Spirit Jesus would send would lead the community in the path of Christ. The Spirit would be the presence of Christ. The community's response to the action of the Spirit would be evidence that they were indeed living the way of Christ: the Father would be proclaimed and Jesus' mission to the world would go forth into the world.

The Spirit was promised to be with the church for all time. That promise continues today. Jesus never abandoned us, not even at the moment of his death. The Spirit was given to the church on Calvary when water and blood poured out of Jesus' side. Water was the outpouring of his Spirit upon a sorrowful world, and blood was the sign of his continued presence through the eucharist.

Proclaim the gospel again.

Sometimes we gain new insights when we hear the text after the interpretation has been given. Someone from the group proclaims the gospel a second time.

STEP 4
TESTING

Conversation with the Liturgy and the Scriptures

Test your original understanding in dialogue with the text.

(You might consider breaking into smaller groups.)

Now that you've heard the exegesis of the readings in today's liturgy, were there any new insights? Was there anything you had not considered before? How do these readings affect your understanding of the Trinity? Has your original understanding of this feast or your understanding of the Trinity been in any way expanded as a result of this sharing? How does this liturgy speak to your life?

Participants share an experience from their lives that connects with the biblical interpretation just shared.

> *Rather than an abstract theological doctrine or concept, the Trinity is all in all, everything, the sum total, the absolute driving force in my life. All my life breath has its roots in the living, ongoing, daily, minute-to-minute presence of the Triune, transcendent, consoling presence of my God. Scriptures tell us that the Spirit groans within us: the inexpressible, what words cannot begin to formulate. The Spirit sings praise to the Father in a constant chorus within my longing heart.*

This God in community extends the love of that community to me and out to others. Love is the key force. The extent to which I love is the extent to which I reveal the Trinity to others. The Spirit gently teaches me to love, sometimes challenges me to love, and at other times drags me kicking and screaming to love.

I am struck by Paul's theology of justification through faith. I am loved. I have been loved before I knew I was loved. In my mother's womb I was cradled in the loving arms of my God. In that embryonic pool life was breathed into me, and the dabar *(word) of the Hebrew scriptures loved me into existence.*

My problem, our problem is that I/we don't believe it. My being, our being of beings has not caught up with Truth. Perhaps that is what the life quest is all about. I continually think I have to do it all. If I do enough works, if I am a good enough person, if I don't make any mistakes, then I will be worthy of God's love. Hogwash! says Paul. God will not take away God's love. We need only accept it. I continue to grow in the revelation of the might, power, and transcendence of God as I listen to the Spirit in my life.

I have come to understand that it is only on a rare occasion that I am able to fully enter into an awareness of Father God. Father God is almost too big to comprehend. But Jesus God through Spirit God gives me the sacramental means to encounter Father God's awesomeness. Jesus and Spirit bring the Father into my temporal world and make it possible for me to communicate. Trinity God helps me plug into the mystery of God according to the leanings of my soul at various times, situations, and life circumstances.

Father God peeks into my consciousness when I take time to reflect on God's grandeur and self-communication to us through creation. How can one not look out of an airplane, view a mountain range or a raging ocean, and not be captivated by the awesome power of God's finger? How can one grieve at the deathbed of a loving relative and not be touched by Jesus God who wept over his friend Lazarus and who healed the broken and consoled those who mourned? How can one not look at the conversion of a friend, the reconciliation of families, the turning away of loved ones from the ravaging oppression of addiction and not be swept off one's feet by the ruah *(breath, wind) of Spirit God's action in our lives?*

Trinity is mystery. It cannot be explained. I can only experience it in the love poured out upon me by God's incredible movement in my life. To wrap it in definition is to rob it of its power, or reduce it to human classification. The Trinity is God in all of God's mysterious, spectacular, multidimensional actions in my life, the life of my family, the life of my parish community, the life of the church, and the life of the world. All creation is a majestic amphitheater in which the Master Conductor raises his finger to conduct the ultimate Symphony of Love: God in relationship with human beings. Our only response? To jump to our feet singing and shouting, "Bravo!" " Maestro!"

Words simply cannot reflect the truth of this liturgy. All attempts fail. In the end, all any of us can say is that our words can only minimally express such transcendence. When left with nothing but human commentary, all we have is rubbish! Humanity cannot begin to capture the essence of God into a neatly defined package. All attempts have failed in the past; all will fail in the future. We can try. We have tried. If our trying helps us enter more deeply into relationship, then, try we must.

In the end, however, all I can really do is experience, rest with the experience and then allow it to transform my life. There is nothing else for me to do but go out and share it.

All share their life experience.

What was John's intention in today's gospel? How does that connect with our community and with me today? Where are the biblical images of creation, covenant, community, and exodus apparent in these readings? Do I still feel the same way about this liturgy as I did when we began? Has my original understanding been stretched, challenged, or affirmed?

STEP 5
DECISION

The gospel demands a response.

How does our sharing and this biblical interpretation challenge our community? In what concrete way does this liturgy call our parish to action in the church, parish, neighborhood, or world? Has this conversation invited transformation in my life? If so, how? What am I/we/community/parish called to do in response? What is one specific action I will take this week as a response to what was learned and shared today?

DOCTRINAL ISSUES

What church truth/teaching/doctrinal issue could be drawn from the gospel for Trinity Sunday?

Participants suggest possible doctrinal themes that flow from the readings.

Possible Doctrinal Themes

Trinity, Father, Son, Spirit, image of God, faith

Present the doctrinal material at this time.

1. The facilitator gives input on a particular doctrinal issue of his/her prior choosing. OR
2. The group chooses a doctrinal issue from the list they created. They read together from the Doctrinal Appendix.

(The doctrinal issues are found in the Doctrinal Appendix in the back of this workbook. If you are choosing an issue from this resource, please refer to it now.)

Reflection questions centered around the chosen doctrinal theme can be found at the end of each topic in the Doctrinal Appendix. The questions are based on the five-step reflection process. If you choose a topic not included in the Doctrinal Appendix, craft your own questions according to the same five-step process.

Following the reflection questions you will be reminded to return to chapter 7, "Preparing the Catechetical Session," to assist you in crafting your own session.

Closing Prayer

The Lord be with you.
(And also with you.)

Lift up your hearts.
(We lift them up to the Lord.)
Let us give thanks to the Lord our God.
(It is right to give him thanks and praise.)
Father, all-powerful and ever-living God,
we do well always and everywhere to give you
    thanks.
We joyfully proclaim our faith
in the mystery of your Godhead.
You have revealed your glory
as the glory also of your Son
and of the Holy Spirit:
three Persons equal in majesty,
undivided in splendor,
yet one Lord, one God,
ever to be adored in your everlasting glory.
And so, with all the choirs of angels in heaven
we proclaim your glory
and join in their unending hymn of praise:
Holy, holy, holy Lord, God of power and might,
heaven and earth are full of your glory.
Hosanna in the highest.
Blessed is he who comes in the name of the Lord.
Hosanna in the highest.[14]

Selected Bibliography

Adam, Adolf. *The Liturgical Year.* Trans. Matthew J.
    O'Connell. Collegeville: The Liturgical Press,
    1990.
Cassidy, Richard J. *John's Gospel in New Perspective.*
    New York: Orbis Books, 1992.
Days of the Lord. Vol. 7. Collegeville: The Liturgical
    Press, 1994.
Fuller, Reginald H. *Preaching the New Lectionary.*
    Collegeville: The Liturgical Press, 1974.
Jarrell, Stephen T. *Guide to the Sacramentary.*
    Chicago: Liturgy Training Publications, 1983.
Kselman, John S., S.J. and Michael L. Barré, S.S.
    "Psalms." In *The New Jerome Biblical Commentary.*
    Ed. Raymond E. Brown, S.S., Joseph A.
    Fitzmyer, S.J., Roland E. Murphy, O.Carm. En-
    glewood Cliffs: Prentice Hall, 1990.
Sanchez, Patricia Datchuck. *The Word We Celebrate.*
    Kansas City: Sheed and Ward, 1989.
Sweetland, Dennis M. "Finger of God." In *The Col-
    legeville Pastoral Dictionary of Biblical Theology.*
    Ed. Carroll Stuhlmueller, C.P. Collegeville:
    The Liturgical Press, 1996.

---

[14]Trinity Sunday: "Preface," *The Sacramentary.*

SOLEMNITY OF THE BODY AND BLOOD OF CHRIST (CORPUS CHRISTI)

INTRODUCTORY RITES

Opening Song (or Entrance Antiphon)

The Lord fed his people with the finest wheat and honey; their hunger was satisfied. (Ps 80:17)[1]

Opening Prayer

The facilitator of the session may lead the prayer. Others in the group may be asked to proclaim the readings.

Let us pray
[to the Lord who gives himself in the Eucharist that this sacrament may bring us salvation and peace]

Lord Jesus Christ,
you gave us the Eucharist
as the memorial of your suffering and death.
May our worship of this sacrament of your body
    and blood
help us to experience the salvation you won for us
and the peace of the kingdom
where you live with the Father and the Holy
    Spirit,
one God, for ever and ever.[2]

Alternative Opening Prayer

Let us pray
[for the willingness to make present in our world the love of Christ shown to us in the Eucharist]

Lord Jesus Christ,
we worship you living among us
in the sacrament of your body and blood.
May we offer to our Father in heaven
a solemn pledge of undivided love.
May we offer to our brothers and sisters
a life poured out in loving service of that kingdom
where you live with the Father and the Holy
    Spirit,
one God, for ever and ever.[3]

---

[1]Corpus Christi: "Entrance Antiphon," *The Sacramentary.*
[2]Corpus Christi: "Opening Prayer," *The Sacramentary.*
[3]Corpus Christi: "Alternative Opening Prayer," *The Sacramentary.*

LITURGY OF THE WORD

Let us listen to God's word.

The readings are proclaimed.

First Reading
Genesis 14:18-20

We know very little about Melchizedek other than that he was a "high priest of God" and king of Salem. Today's passage recounts an episode between Abraham and Melchizedek. Abraham had set out on an expedition to save his nephew Lot. Lot had been taken captive and all his possessions had been seized and taken as booty. With an army of only 318, Abraham had defeated his foes (four kings), rescued Lot, retrieved their possessions, and returned home.

Enter Melchizedek on the scene. It was often the custom that a king would seek approval from a victorious leader by welcoming the leader and tending to his troops. It was a means of hopefully keeping the pillage down to a bare minimum. However, Melchizedek did not seem to possess ulterior motives in his encounter with Abraham. Melchizedek, the priest-king, offered bread and wine accompanied by ritual prayers. The prayer of Melchizedek irrevocably effected what it proclaimed, because it was God who blessed. The prayer sought continued favor from God.

Abraham realized that his victory against the four kings was due to Yahweh's protection. Abraham believed that this protection was a sign that God would be with him for the rest of his life. In response to God's providential care, Abraham promised to give Melchizedek, priest of the Most High God, a tenth of everything he owned.

Abraham was a unique victor. He did not go to war to seek wealth or revenge. All Abraham asked was that his troops receive the share due them for their efforts and that Lot be recompensed for his seized possessions. Abraham did not seek or take the booty normally awarded the victor.

Abraham gave homage to Melchizedek because he spoke for the God of all creation, the author of all blessing. Melchizedek blessed Abraham with a blessing actualized and made effective by God. Later Christian writers would evoke this episode in history and consider it a prefigurement of Christ. Patristic writers would assert that the priesthood of Christ transcended human priesthood, or any human institution. Jesus' priesthood originates in God.

Melchizedek's name is etched not only in the history tablets of biblical tradition, but also in church tradition, and even in the Roman Canon (Eucharistic Prayer IV). Melchizedek, an elusive, little known character, prefigured the Christ who would establish a new covenant and intercede for the human race. Jesus would offer the blessing of his life—the effect would be irrevocable and would be the gift of God's self to the entire world—redemption. Jesus is the only true priest because of both his humanity and his divinity.

Responsorial Psalm
Psalm 110:1, 2, 3, 4

This is a royal psalm of disputed origin. Some believe it to be a psalm of the early Davidic kings. Others believe it to be a justification by the later family of Hasmoneans for their claim to kingship and priesthood. Melchizedek is used as a symbol of priest-king. The author of the letter to the Hebrews refers to this psalm as the foundation for developing a theology of Christ's priesthood. The early church had a firmly established belief in the kingship of Christ. Later writers developed an expanded christology. The church interpreted Jesus' death as the sacrificial act of a priest. Reginald Fuller reminds us that Christ is the presider at the eucharistic liturgy "as he offers himself as the sacrificial victim to the faithful."[4] St. Thomas Aquinas affirmed, "He gives himself with his own hand."

Second Reading
1 Corinthians 11:23-26

Today's second reading is the same reading used on Holy Thursday. The reading proclaims the institution of the eucharist. However, on Holy Thursday it is celebrated and understood within the context of the Sacred Triduum. On the feast of Corpus Christi the eucharist is set aside for special contemplation as an ongoing rite of the church.

This is the earliest fragment of Christian tradition preserved in the New Testament. Paul stated that he had received the tradition given in today's letter prior to his dealings with the Corinthians. He used language denoting the *passing on of tradition,* such as that which is passed on through the oral teaching of the rabbis. Paul received his revelation from the oral tradition in which human witnesses, under the inspiration of the risen Christ, shared and passed on their experience.

It is believed that today's pericope is an exegesis of a eucharistic liturgy already being celebrated. It does not completely describe the Last Supper, but rather seeks to define it in light of eucharistic theology. In the earliest celebration of the *breaking of bread,* there was a supper between the bread and the cup, as alluded to in this pericope, thus testifying to the primitive character of this text.[5]

Just as the unleavened bread was a living memorial of the events of Passover, so too is the unleavened bread of eucharist a living memorial of the events of Jesus' *passage of death to life.*

There are strong eschatological overtones in this reading. Paul reminds us of the Lord's second coming. Eucharist, for Paul and for us, was and is a ritual remembering of the cross with its effects made real and present. It is an anticipation of Jesus' second coming: "Christ has died, Christ is risen, Christ will come again."

Eucharist connects us with the salvation we presently share and the full actualization and realization of it when Jesus returns. In this we place all our hope. The mystery of Christ present in the eucharist is a both *now* and *not yet* reality—at the same time. The eucharist trumpets our hope in Christ's return. It also gives us the promise of that hope's realization.

---

[4]Reginald H. Fuller, *Preaching the New Lectionary* (Collegeville: The Liturgical Press, 1974), 43.

[5]Ibid., 17.

"If we enter this world after having participated in that sacrament, we shall enter with complete confidence into the heavenly sanctuary as if a golden armor made us invulnerable. And why speak of the life to come? *The very earth, here below, becomes heaven through this mystery.* Open therefore, open the doors of heaven, look: it is not enough to say of heaven but of the highest place of heaven, and you will see what I announced to you. I am going to show you what the treasures of highest heaven have that is most precious, treasures lying on the earth. For, if it is true that in a royal palace what is most august is neither the walls nor the gold paneling but the king on his throne, likewise in heaven itself, it is the king. Now you can see him, today, on the earth. I am not showing you angels or archangels or heaven or the heaven of heavens: I am showing you the master and Lord of all this. Do you understand that what is most precious you see on earth"? And not only do you see it but you touch it; but you do even more, you feed on it, you receive it, you take it away into your home! (St. John Chrysostom 350-407)[6]

Gospel
Luke 9:11-17

Jesus feeds loaves and fishes to the multitudes.

STEP 1
NAMING ONE'S EXPERIENCE

What were your first impressions? What was your first response? What grabbed your attention? How did you feel?

Each person names his or her initial impression. Statement should be brief. No reasons should be given at this time. All simply listen without agreeing or disagreeing.

---

[6]St. John Chrysostom (ca. 350-407), "Homelie 24 sur la Premiere lettre aux Corinthiens, 5," in A. Hamman, *La messe: Liturgies anciennes et textes liturgiques,* Lettres chretiennes 9 (Paris: Grasset, 1964), 179-180; in *Days of the Lord,* Vol. 7 (Collegeville: The Liturgical Press, 1991), 60.

STEP 2
UNDERSTANDING

In a brief statement, what do you think this gospel is trying to convey?

STEP 3
INPUT FROM VISION/STORY/TRADITION

Liturgical Context

Prior to the ninth century there was no true worship of the eucharist outside of mass. Such worship began in about the eleventh century. It grew in accord with controversies regarding the "real presence" of Jesus in the sacrament. The controversies helped define eucharistic theology: "the Eucharist is really the Body and Blood of Christ, but under the sign—the sacrament—of bread and wine."[7] Controversies over the eucharist gave birth to eucharistic devotion.

The origin of this feast dates back to the twelfth century. During that time there was an "intense cult of the Blessed Sacrament that placed particular emphasis on the real presence of 'Christ whole and entire' in the consecrated bread."[8] This strong emphasis led to the desire *to see.* Thus, in 1220 in Paris, the practice of elevating the host began.

The feast originated largely due to the vision received by an Augustinian nun who saw a shining disk with a dark spot on it. She was told that the spot was there because there was no feast to commemorate the eucharist. Consequently the Bishop of Liege introduced the feast into his diocese in 1246. In 1264 Pope Urban IV established the feast for the entire church. In his presentation intended to explain the reasons for establishing the feast (*Bull Transiturus*—the document establishing the feast), the pope put forth a balanced theology of eucharist as sacrifice and meal. Some believe that Thomas Aquinas wrote the text for the mass

---

[7]*Days of the Lord,* Vol. 7 (Collegeville: The Liturgical Press, 1994), 38.

[8]Adolf Adam, *The Liturgical Year,* trans. Matthew J. O'Connell (Collegeville: The Liturgical Press, 1990), 169.

and office. The feast did not spread very rapidly. However, Pope Clement V reintroduced it at the Council of Vienne in 1311-12.

Traditionally the feast was called "Feast of the Most Holy Body of Christ." The new Roman missal expanded the title to express the fullest understanding of the sacrament and to include the mystery of the "precious blood": "Solemnity of the Most Holy Body and Blood of Christ." However, popular usage has retained the Latin title, "Corpus Christi."

Corpus Christi is a duplication of the feast that already commemorates the sacrament of the eucharist: the day of its institution—Holy Thursday. Both feasts emphasize the redemptive effects of Jesus Christ. However, Adolf Adam insists that it is a defensible duplication, as Holy Thursday cannot quite enter into the fullness of festal joy as it is explicitly connected to Good Friday. Thus, a feast dedicated to the expression of joy in the eucharist as the "precious fruit and operative presence of the paschal mystery"[9] is certainly a laudable practice. Every Sunday celebrates the paschal mystery in its entirety in the celebration of eucharist. Notwithstanding, Adam asserts that "the objection of duplication has no place."[10]

St. Thomas Aquinas's influence is evident in the eucharistic theology woven through the presidential prayers of the proper of the mass. In his *Summa*, Thomas examines the importance of the eucharist in terms of past, present, and future. As a past reality it commemorates Jesus' sacrifice of passion, death, and resurrection. As a present reality it unites us with Christ and one another. As a future reality it anticipates "enjoyment of the divinity."

The liturgy reflects this past, present, and future understanding. The opening prayer touches the past remembrance: "You gave us the eucharist as the memorial of your suffering and death." The prayer over the gifts touches on the present reality: "Lord, may the bread and wine we offer bring your Church the unity and peace they signify." The concluding prayer connects us to the future

hope: "May we come to possess it fully in the kingdom."

The Sequence, *Lauda, Sion, Salvatorem (Zion, praise your Savior),* expresses classical eucharistic theology.

Zion, praise your Savior. Praise your leader and shepherd in hymns and canticles. Praise him as much as you can, for he is beyond all praising and you will never be able to praise him as he merits.

But today a theme worthy of particular praise is put before us—the living and life-giving bread that, without any doubt, was given to the Twelve at table during the holy supper.

Therefore let our praise be full and resounding and our soul's rejoicing full of delight and beauty, for this is the festival day to commemorate the first institution of this table.

At this table of the new King, the new law's new Pasch puts an end to the old Pasch. The new displaces the old, reality the shadow and light the darkness. Christ wanted what he did at the supper to be repeated in his memory.

And so we, in accordance with his holy directions, consecrate bread and wine to be salvation's Victim. Christ's followers know by faith that bread is changed into his flesh and wine into his blood.

Man cannot understand this, cannot perceive it; but a lively faith affirms that the change, which is outside the natural course of things, takes place. Under the different species, which are now signs only and not their own reality, there lie hid wonderful realities. His body is our food, his blood our drink.

And yet Christ remains entire under each species. The communicant receives the complete Christ—uncut, unbroken and undivided. Whether we receive one or a thousand, the one receives as much as the thousand. Nor is Christ diminished by being received.

---

[9]Ibid., 171.
[10]Ibid.

The good and the wicked alike receive him, but with the unlike destiny of life or death. To the wicked it is death, but life to the good. See how different is the result, though each receives the same.

Last of all, if the sacrament is broken, have no doubt. Remember there is as much in a fragment as in an unbroken host. There is no division of the reality, but only a breaking of the sign; nor does the breaking diminish the condition or size of the One hidden under the sign.

Behold, the bread of angels is become the pilgrim's food; truly it is bread for the sons, and is not to be cast to dogs. It was prefigured in type when Isaac was brought as an offering, when a lamb was appointed for the Pasch and when manna was given to the Jews of old.

Jesus, good shepherd and true bread, have mercy on us; feed us and guard us. Grant that we find happiness in the land of the living. You know all things, can do all things, and feed us here on earth. Make us your guests in heaven, co-heirs with you and companions of heaven's citizens. Amen. Alleluia.[11]

In the ritual prayers two images of eucharist emerge. The first is eucharist as Jesus at table with his disciples, feeding the people with the gift of himself (Preface II of the Holy Eucharist). The second image is eucharist as a gift of adoration and worship ("...we worship you living among us in the sacrament of your body and blood"—Alternative Opening Prayer). The first is more communal in nature; the second reflects a posture of private devotion. Both are valid and helpful reflections on the eucharist, but coming from the context of Sunday worship, the communal image best reflects our Sunday experience and theology of the eucharist. The opening prayer, prayer after communion and first preface reflect a theme of personal worship, strengthening and cleansing. The alternative opening prayer begins with our worship of Christ in the sacrament of his Body and Blood, and ends with the prayer that we offer our lives poured out in service of our brothers

and sisters. The second preface refers to the feeding of God's people with the gift of Christ in the eucharist. The prayer over the gifts asks that the bread and cup, signs of peace and unity, bring unity and peace to the church. The second invocation of form C of the penitential rite expresses the fullness of eucharist. "Lord Jesus, you came to gather the nations into the peace of God's kingdom: Lord have mercy. You came in word and sacrament to strengthen us in holiness: Christ have mercy. You will come in glory with salvation for your people: Lord have mercy." Eucharist gathers us as a people in unity and peace. Eucharist strengthens us and makes us holy as we await the day we will feast at the heavenly banquet.

This feast has moved from a feast of devotion to the blessed sacrament reserved in the tabernacle and presented to the people for adoration, to a celebration of eucharist. Observe the preface for Holy Thursday which reflects that focus:

Father, all-powerful and ever-living God,
we do well always and everywhere to give you
   thanks
through Jesus Christ our Lord.
He is the true and eternal priest
who established this unending sacrifice.
He offered himself as a victim for our deliverance
and taught us to make this offering in his
   memory.
As we eat his body which he gave for us,
we grow in strength.
As we drink his blood which he poured out for
   us,
we are washed clean.
Now, with angels and archangels,
and the whole company of heaven,
we sing the unending hymn of your praise.[12]

One distinguishing feature of this feast is the eucharistic procession. During the Middle Ages the procession included tableaus of the passion and Old Testament figures. During the baroque era, the procession became far more elaborate. It evolved into a public, triumphant procession of thanksgiving. Floats and scenes that had little or

_____

[11]Corpus Christi: "Sequence" (prose text), *The Lectionary.*

[12]Holy Thursday—Mass of the Lord's Supper: "Preface of Holy Eucharist I" (P47), *The Sacramentary.*

nothing to do with the eucharist became part of the procession. During the Enlightenment, this all but disappeared.

The procession is considered an exercise of devotion (*pia exercitia*) under the direction of the local ordinary. There is a recent call for a return to the practice of eucharistic processions, perhaps sparked by a renewed vision of the Vatican Council. The Council affirmed the image of God's people as a pilgrim people who could withstand the dangers of the journey only with the help and assistance of Christ.

> Our contemporaries so often suffer from the randomness of existence. If the Corpus Christi procession were properly conducted in the spirit of the liturgy, it could, more than any other procession, be or become a way of making them aware, by means of a real symbol, that they are not alone as they make their way along the difficult mountain path of life on earth, but rather that in the communion of the Church, which has the eucharistic Lord with her, going before, beside and behind her, they are on the way to eternal union with the Christ of the parousia, when "he comes on that day to be glorified in his saints, and to be marveled at in all who have believed." (2 Thes 1:10)[13]

Gospel Exegesis

The facilitator gives input regarding what critical biblical scholarship has to say about this text. The input includes insights as to how people would have heard the gospel in Jesus' time.

Today's story of the feeding of the multitudes with loaves and fishes is the only miracle story found in all four gospels. Luke establishes the context for his rendition by the question posed by Herod in a preceding verse (9): "Who is this man about whom I hear all these reports?" Luke answers the question in prophetic fashion and names Jesus the

fulfillment of all messianic hopes and dreams. His answer is prophetic, messianic, eucharistic, and eschatological. Jesus was understood as the fulfillment of Old Testament messianic prophecy. This story would remind the ancient audience of a similar feeding story in which Elisha fed 100 men with 20 loaves of bread and thereby, as God's agent, testified to God's mighty power. Today's story is also reminiscent of the feeding of Israel in the desert with manna from heaven, thus giving credence to the type of Christ Luke was attempting to portray—a "prophet like Moses."

The original intent of the story was a proclamation of the imminent reign of God. Luke has Jesus teaching about the kingdom and healing those in need—both signs of the messianic reign. This messiah-king was to usher in his reign not built on riches, power, and royal domination, but on identification with the poor, oppressed, and marginalized and on suffering and death for himself and all who would follow in his steps.

In previous chapters Jesus was someone else's formally invited dinner guest. Today Jesus hosts the banquet. This pericope is situated in a section devoted to the mission of Christ. The section's mission context informs our understanding of this gospel. The gospel gives no indication of house, home, or location of the meal. Eugene LaVerdiere suggests that "perhaps this is the way it should be for a symbolic meal of the church's missionary journey."[14] Jesus had no specific place to call home.

The other meals of earlier chapters required an invitation. This banquet required no invitation: everyone was invited. The crowds came to be fed by Jesus' teaching and nourished by his healing touch. They stayed well into the evening. It was time to find food and a place to stay. In a grand gesture of hospitality Jesus offered a banquet and instructed the Twelve to serve it.

The offer of hospitality is biblically and often universally understood to accompany the offer of food and drink. Today's story is one of five hospitality meals. Obsession with those who were the

---

[13]W. Durig, "Zur Liturgie des Fronleichnamsfeier," in *Am Tisch des Wortes*, Neue Reihe 113 (Stuttgart, 1971), p. 17; in Adolf Adam, *The Liturgical Year*, trans. Matthew J. O'Connell (Collegeville: The Liturgical Press, 1990), 169, 170.

[14]Eugene LaVerdiere, *Dining in the Kingdom of God* (Chicago: Liturgy Training Publications, 1994), 58.

privileged and non-privileged guests occupied the focus of the previous meals. The focus of this meal was the obvious immediate problem: "How are we going to feed this many people?"

This meal of Jesus' is a "great hospitality event welcoming hungry thousands for the breaking of the bread."[15] The words and expressions in the ritual action performed by Jesus were obviously taken out of an early eucharistic liturgy. *Taking . . . blessing . . . . breaking . . . . giving . . .* these are the actions of eucharist. They would be repeated at the Last Supper when Jesus, as host, would once again take, bless, break, and share himself with his disciples. Those same actions would be repeated at Emmaus.

In the other meal stories, eucharist is understood as a call to evangelize and invite people to conversion and repentance (banquet at Levi's house). Eucharist also reconciles people to God and to one another (dinner at Simon's house). Today's meal is a missionary feast. The repentant and reconciled are nourished by the Bread of Life and then sent forth to nourish others with that same Bread. Thus, today's meal stands as a prophetic sign intended to summon the church to repent, to be reconciled as a united people, and then to be sent forth for mission.

This section of Luke's gospel is intended to make a strong theological statement about the implication of the Jesus event. "The prophet Jesus has by his deeds and words created a divided response within historical Israel: the outcasts from the people have accepted him and his message, and have become disciples. A restored Israel based on repentance is starting to gather around this prophet. At the same time, however, the prophet is being rejected by the religious elite, the leadership of Israel."[16] The stage is set for establishment of future leadership in the fledgling church. Who will lead the people after Jesus is gone? Much of the agenda of this section of Luke's gospel is concerned with preparing new leadership to continue the mission of Christ to the restored people of God.

---

[15]Ibid., 58.

[16]Luke Timothy Johnson, *The Gospel of Luke,* Sacra Pagina Series, Vol. 3 (Collegeville: The Liturgical Press, 1991), 147.

The overabundance of food serves as a much needed lesson to Jesus' would-be leaders: God will provide the abundance needed for mission by God's own power, not by human design. Also, those who give out of their need receive back a far greater amount.

This story not only looks ahead to the Last Supper, but shows Christ as the one who feeds his own. Jesus' authority to preach and teach are empowered by table service—by feeding. Luke makes sure that the Twelve are given explicit instructions. The Twelve are to set the table before the people. Luke's is the only gospel to call the disciples who served the meal "the Twelve." He further highlights the symbolism by having the disciples collect twelve baskets of leftovers. The number twelve represents the twelve tribes of Israel and the twelve apostles who were being prepared for leadership in the new church.

The meals of Luke's gospel provide a firm theology of eucharist. Eucharist evangelizes, reconciles, calls to conversion and repentance, and sends us forth for mission. Church teaching insists that eucharist also commits us to the poor. When Jesus hosted a meal, all were invited, all were fed, and all were healed. The operative word is *all.* The righteous and unrighteous were offered seats at the table.

There is a strong moral imperative implicit in the eucharist. If all were fed, all were entitled to eat. There is no room for hunger in God's reign. The implication for our modern world lies in the responsibility of developed nations to be the bread basket for all hungry people of the world. It is not simply a nice suggestion. There is a moral demand—a matter of conscience—that eucharistic assemblies assume the responsibility and respond to the cries of the poor and hungry. To turn a deaf ear brings justified condemnation. One cannot eat the Bread of Life and deny basic sustenance to any of God's people.

Eucharist never fully satiates; we are always left with a hunger for more, for complete immersion and unity in the Body of Christ. We are never finished growing in and through the sacrament of eucharist. Eucharist built on a purely private personal experience of Christ is the sacrament turned inward. All sacraments are our participation in the paschal mystery of Christ. If, through our participation in the eucharist, we are unwilling to live, suffer, die, and rise for others and participate in the Spirit life of the church, eucharist then becomes a self-serving moment of personal piety rather than participation in Jesus' life.

Proclaim the gospel again.

Sometimes we gain new insights when we hear the text after the interpretation has been given. Someone from the group proclaims the gospel a second time.

STEP 4
TESTING

Conversation with the Liturgy and the Scriptures

Test your original understanding in dialogue with the text.

(You might consider breaking into smaller groups.)

Now that you've heard what the scholars have to say about the readings in this liturgy, how do you feel about it? Were there any new insights? Was there anything you had not considered before? How does your original understanding of this story compare with what we just shared? How does this story speak to your life?

Participants share an experience from their lives that connects with the biblical interpretation just shared.

> *Living and participating fully in the life of the community is one way we live Jesus' message in today's gospel. Liturgical theology asserts that a primary sign of the presence of Christ in our Sunday liturgy is the assembly. "He is present when the Church prays and sings, for he promised: 'Where two or three are gathered in my name, there I am in the midst of them'" (Constitution on the Sacred Liturgy, General Principles, #7).*

> *Thus, communities that evangelize, that call one another to repentance and conversion and reconcile themselves and one another to God and to the world are the living sign of eucharist. Communities that*

are less intent on navel gazing and in-house maintenance and more intent on offering the bread of hospitality to strangers, newcomers, outsiders, insiders, and the world's poor, hungry, and disenfranchised are a living sign of eucharist.

To lesser or greater degrees every Christian community bears the sign of eucharist within it. We never fully realize the power and effect of eucharist in our communities. But we move forward in hope. We either grow in the sign of eucharist, or we stagnate. One sign of growth is observable in the way communities reach beyond themselves, their parish borders, their city borders, perhaps their national borders to respond to the needs of the suffering global church.

Our parish is blessed with one powerful sign—Christ, the Bread of Hospitality. Hospitality is the one charism that would be universally regarded as our parish's greatest gift. Over and over again people who come say they are drawn to this parish because of the community. It is not the liturgy (though good), it is not the preaching (though good), it is not the music (though good)—certainly those things help—but it is the undefinable love and bread of hospitality extended by the community at large. It is the reason cited most often when people are attracted to our parish.

None of us is so arrogant as to assume that this is the "perfect parish." No doubt hospitality is not every person's experience. No place is perfect. However, hospitality is such a strong charism in our parish that most people comment on it, celebrate it, and experience the love of God through its power.

Every few months we invite all our newcomers to come forward after the greeting for a special blessing of welcome (Order of Blessing for New Parishioners). After celebrating eucharist, we send them from the church with a sign of our hope for them, our hospitality and our prayer support as they forge their new life in our community. After mass, we send the newcomers home with a freshly baked loaf of bread. While simply a token of our hospitality, the gesture runs the risk of becoming a self-serving expression of our grand care and concern for others. Careful discernment demands that our actions as church reflect the symbolic expression of this noble gesture of hospitality. No doubt some of those newcomers fall through the cracks. Hopefully most of them do not. Hopefully they are embraced by the love of the community. The most important thing for us to remember is that we must remain attentive. If we stop asking ourselves the question: "How are we living eucharist in our parish, city, state, nation and world?" then we risk becoming a church powered by our own engine, rather than God's.

If we were ever to stop feeding the hungry in our midst through various parish ministries, or if we were to cease empowering the hungry in such places as Haiti and the Dominican Republic, then I would worry about our soul. Similarly, if our charitable activities serve as a means to pat our proverbial backs, then also, I will worry about our heart. We can do many and wonderful things that might have nothing to do with witnessing to the love and power of God. The challenge of today's liturgy is to be attentive to the invitation posed by our celebration of eucharist and to commit through prayer and discernment to grow as a eucharistic people as our lives inch ever closer to our eschatological hope.

A friend of mine shared her whimsical image of the eschatological banquet. All the people of God are gathered around a huge, linen-covered banquet table with a meal fit for kings, queens, sheiks, and sultans. But there is a problem. There might be this lavish, bountiful meal, but there is no way to eat it. No silverware is to be found anywhere, except for one giant fork. Heaven for my friend is a banquet table in which there is only one fork, shared by all. Everyone eats or no one eats. Who are the people in our lives whom we would never think to invite to a banquet we would host? Who are the people with whom we cannot imagine sharing the same silver or a common cup? It is a scary thought.

All share their life experience.

What was Luke's message to his community in today's gospel? What are the implications for our community today? What might God be creating in us through this experience of Jesus in the gospel? In what way does this liturgy point to God's promise to be with us? In what way have I/we known death/resurrection in my/our experience and understanding of the readings for this liturgy? How is God speaking to us as a community? What are our collective and personal responses to all of these questions? How might this liturgy be calling us to pass from death to freedom and life (exodus)? Do we still feel the same way about this text as we did when we began? Has our original understanding been stretched, challenged, or affirmed?

STEP 5
DECISION

The gospel demands a response.

In what way does this gospel call your parish to action in the church, parish, neighborhood, or world? Be concrete. Has this conversation with the exegesis invited conversion and transformation within you? How? What are you/your community/your parish called to do in response? Name one specific action you will take this week as a response to what was learned and shared today.

DOCTRINAL ISSUES

What church truth/teaching/doctrinal issue could be drawn from the gospel for the Solemnity of the Body and Blood of Jesus Christ?

Participants suggest possible doctrinal themes that flow from the readings.

Possible Doctrinal Themes

Eucharist, evangelization, eucharist as forgiveness of sins, eucharist as Body of Christ

Present the doctrinal material at this time.

1. The facilitator gives input on a particular doctrinal issue of his/her prior choosing. OR
2. The group chooses a doctrinal issue from the list they created. They read together from the Doctrinal Appendix.

(The doctrinal issues are found in the Doctrinal Appendix in the back of this workbook. If you are choosing an issue from this resource, please refer to it now.)

Reflection questions centered around the chosen doctrinal theme can be found at the end of each topic in the Doctrinal Appendix. The questions are based on the five-step reflection process. If you choose a topic not included in the Doctrinal Appendix, craft your own questions according to the same five-step process.

Following the reflection questions you will be reminded to return to chapter 7, "Preparing the Catechetical Session," to assist you in crafting your own session.

Closing Prayer

Lord,
by this sacrifice of peace and praise,
mercifully cleanse us from our sins
and guide the desires of our hearts.
We ask this through Christ our Lord.[17]

OR

Father,
you have brought to fulfillment the work of our
    redemption
through the Easter mystery of Christ your Son.
May we who faithfully proclaim his death and res-
    urrection in these sacramental signs
experience the constant growth of your salvation
    in our lives.
We ask this through our Lord Jesus Christ, your
    Son, who lives and reigns with you and the
    Holy Spirit, one God for ever and ever.[18]

OR

Lord, hear our prayer for your mercy
as we celebrate this memorial of our salvation.
May this sacrament of love be for us
the sign of unity and the bond of charity.[19]

OR

Lord,
may our sharing at this holy table make us holy.
By the body and blood of Christ
join all your people in brotherly love.
Grant this through Christ our Lord.[20]

Selected Bibliography

Adam, Adolf. *The Liturgical Year.* Trans. Matthew J. O'Connell. Collegeville: The Liturgical Press, 1990.

Days of the Lord. Vol. 7. Collegeville: The Liturgical Press, 1994.

Fuller, Reginald H. *Preaching the New Lectionary.* Collegeville: The Liturgical Press, 1974.

Johnson, Luke Timothy. *The Gospel of Luke.* Sacra Pagina Series. Vol. 3. Collegeville: The Liturgical Press, 1991.

LaVerdiere, Eugene. *Dining in the Kingdom of God.* Chicago: Liturgy Training Publications, 1994.

Sanchez, Patricia Datchuck. *The Word We Celebrate.* Kansas City: Sheed and Ward, 1989.

---

[17]Masses and Prayers for Various Needs and Occasions: "For Forgiveness of Sins," *The Sacramentary.*

[18]Votive Masses, Holy Eucharist: "Opening Prayer," *The Sacramentary.*

[19]Votive Masses, Holy Eucharist: "Prayer Over the Gifts," *The Sacramentary.*

---

[20]Votive Masses, Holy Eucharist: "Prayer After Communion," *The Sacramentary.*

SOLEMNITY OF THE SACRED HEART OF JESUS

INTRODUCTORY RITES

Opening Song (or Entrance Antiphon)

The thoughts of his heart last through every generation, that he will rescue them from death and feed them in time of trouble. (Ps 32:11, 19)[1]

Opening Prayer

The facilitator of the session may lead the prayer. Others in the group may be asked to proclaim the readings.

Let us pray
[that we will respond to the love of Christ]

    Pause for silent prayer.

Father,
we rejoice in the gifts of love
we have received from the heart of Jesus your Son.
Open our hearts to share his life
and continue to bless us with his love.
We ask this through our Lord Jesus Christ, your
    Son,
who lives and reigns with you and the Holy Spirit,
one God, for ever and ever.

OR

Father,
we have wounded the heart of Jesus your Son,
but he brings us forgiveness and grace.
Help us prove our grateful love
and make amends for our sins.
We ask this through our Lord Jesus Christ, your
    Son,
who lives and reigns with you and the Holy
    Spirit,
one God forever and ever.[2]

LITURGY OF THE WORD

Let us listen to God's word.

---

[1]Sacred Heart: "Entrance Antiphon," *The Sacramentary.*
[2]Sacred Heart: "Opening Prayer," *The Sacramentary.*

The readings are proclaimed.

First Reading
Ezekiel 34:11-16

There are two threads running through this passage. The author seeks to denounce the bad rulers who have shepherded Israel and to announce that Yahweh alone will shepherd them and appoint a new ruler, David, to watch over them.

Sumerian kings from the third millennium on referred to themselves as shepherds of the people. Ezekiel allegorically refers to the lost, exiled, and defeated Israelites as lost sheep.

Yahweh was to be shepherd of the people. Biblical tradition often referred to God as Israel's shepherd. Lawrence Boadt suggests that this theme moves in three parts. First, God reverses the evil done by the evil human shepherds. Second, God is not simply a good provider, but he also defends justice and upholds the weak. Human kings may abdicate their responsibility, but God will take over to provide, defend, and uphold. However, there are both good and bad sheep in the flock and they will need to be separated.

The piece regarding David as king looks forward to the everlasting covenant made with Israel. God promises to bring forth a king from David's line who will reign in peace. The third part of the theme is that Israel will be blessed as she is obedient to the covenant.

Responsorial Psalm
Psalm 23:1-3, 3-4, 5, 6

Second Reading
Romans 5:5-11

The justified Christian is reconciled to God and experiences a peace that surpasses all understanding. This peace cannot be disturbed in the midst of difficulties. The Christian will not be disappointed in his or her hope. The justified Christian is confident in his or her salvation.

The effect of our justification in Jesus is peace. Those who have been estranged are reconciled with God. We experience such peace because Christ has reconciled us and led us into the divine presence. Christians know they are justified as evidenced by their hope. Their hope is grounded in the love of God for human beings.

The Holy Spirit pours out God's love on people. The Spirit is proof of God's love. The Spirit is the proof that the divine presence resides within the justified. On our own we can do nothing: our reconciliation is dependent upon God.

Christ died for us, once and for all. It was a gratuitous act of love. The Father's love is poured out through the Spirit and is manifested through Jesus' death. "This triadic text is a Pauline starting point for later Trinitarian dogma."[3]

Jesus' death reconciles sinners and brings them into intimacy with God. We also will share in Jesus' risen life through our justification. We are saved. Salvation is something that happens now, but it is still to come and is rooted in living the Christian life. Justification allows the reconciled to boast before God, rather than to stand in fear.

Gospel
Luke 17:3-7

Jesus goes after the lost sheep.

STEP 1
NAMING ONE'S EXPERIENCE

What were your first impressions? What was your first response? What grabbed your attention? How did you feel?

Each person names his or her initial impression. Statement should be brief. No reasons should be given at this time. All simply listen without agreeing or disagreeing.

---

[3]Joseph A. Fitzmyer, S.J., "The Letter to the Romans," in *The New Jerome Biblical Commentary,* ed. Raymond E. Brown, S.S., Joseph A. Fitzmyer, S.J., Roland E. Murphy, O.Carm. (Englewood Cliffs: Prentice Hall, 1990), 844.

STEP 2
UNDERSTANDING

In a brief statement, what do you think this gospel is trying to convey?

STEP 3
INPUT FROM VISION/STORY/TRADITION

Liturgical Context

This feast is celebrated on the third Friday after the feast of Pentecost. Since this feast takes place on a Friday, it is seldom thoroughly treated in catechetical groups. However, it is an important solemnity of the Lord and, as such, is part of the deposit of faith as it is revealed in the unfolding liturgical cycle. While most parishes will not have the luxury of meeting on this day, it would nevertheless be important that this liturgy be addressed in catechetical groups whose formation is centered on breaking open the riches of the liturgical cycle.

The feast of the Sacred Heart is a devotional feast that honors Christ for the love he showers upon humanity. That love is symbolized by his heart. The earliest origins of such a devotion can be traced back to the church Fathers who stressed certain passages in John (7:37, 19:34). Anselm and Bernard of Clairvaux also cited similar passages in the twelfth century, only to be followed by others such as Albert the Great and Bonaventure in the thirteenth century.

According to Adolf Adam, later mystics increased their devotion to the Sacred Heart and by the sixteenth century Jesuits and other groups also promoted the devotion. French Oratorians Pierre Berulle and John Eudes helped move the devotion to official levels. After receiving permission from his bishop, Eudes celebrated the first feast in honor of the Sacred Heart in his community.

Visitation nun Margaret Mary Alacoque had a series of visions encouraging her to work toward establishment of the feast on the Friday after Corpus Christi. She also promoted the observance of Fridays in honor of the Sacred Heart.

Rome did not allow the feast to be officially celebrated for another hundred years. In 1856 Pius IX established the feast as obligatory for the universal church. Pope Leo XIII raised the feast to a higher rank and consecrated the world to the Sacred Heart of Jesus. Pius XI in 1927 elevated it again and, without making it a holy day of obligation, raised it to the same status as Christmas.

In this century, Karl Rahner addressed some objections to the feast when he explained the word "heart" as a primordial concept. Rahner maintained that the word "heart" in scripture and tradition refers to the body and soul, the totality of a person. Thus, the heart of Christ refers to the complete essence of his being.

The text for this mass was compiled by Pius XI in 1928 in collaboration with Benedictine Abbot H. Quentin. An earlier focus for this feast was the passion of Christ and the mysticism of the Song of Solomon. Pius XI emphasized expiation, humanity's need for the love of Christ to redeem sin.

There are two opening prayers—one old, the other new. The new prayer, the first, acknowledges the love we have received through Christ and asks that we continue to be blessed with that love. The second acknowledges human guilt and asks that we worship Christ through the service we offer to our brothers and sisters. Love, then, is not just an internal state of being between Creator and created, but rather is demonstrated and evidenced in love extended to others.

The old concluding prayer, "we have tasted the sweetness of your loving heart," was replaced with "May this sacrament fill us with love. Draw us closer to Christ your Son and help us to recognize him in others." A new preface was assigned to the feast that centers more closely on the scriptures and the theology of the Fathers: "Lifted high on the cross, Christ gave his life for us, so much did he love us. From his wounded side flowed blood and water, and the fountain of sacramental life in the Church. To his open heart the Savior invites all men, to draw water in joy from the springs of salvation."

The three readings in Cycle C rely heavily on the biblical image of the Good Shepherd who seeks out and saves all lost sheep. This is not the only time in the liturgical cycle that we stress this image of Christ. The fourth Sunday of Easter is also devoted to the Good Shepherd.

There are other forms of devotion to the Sacred Heart: the first Fridays of each month and the eve of first Friday. There is also a votive mass for First Fridays approved at the end of the nineteenth century by Leo XIII. When properly explained within its scriptural and historical context, this feast has great pastoral value.

Gospel Exegesis

The facilitator gives input regarding what critical biblical scholarship has to say about this text. The input includes insights as to how people would have heard the gospel in Jesus' time.

Today's pericope in Luke has a twofold purpose: 1. No one is to cause a Christian to stray—to sin. 2. If one does sin or stray—go after that person. In Matthew's version, the sheep is not lost, it simply goes astray. Luke, however, has another idea; Luke's sheep is lost. Luke wants his reader to know for certain the identity of the *lost*. Verse 7 reads, "Just so I tell you, there will be more joy in heaven over one *sinner* who repents than over ninety-nine righteous persons who need no repentance." According to Charles Talbert, "The lost in Luke are sinners, the outcasts with whom Jesus eats."[4]

Proclaim the gospel again.

Sometimes we gain new insights when we hear the text after the interpretation has been given. Someone from the group proclaims the gospel a second time.

STEP 4
TESTING

Conversation with the Liturgy and the Scriptures

Test your original understanding in dialogue with the text.

---

[4]Charles H. Talbert, *Reading Luke* (New York: Crossroad, 1992), 148.

(You might consider breaking into smaller groups.)

Now that you've heard the exegesis of this liturgy, were there any new insights? Was there anything you had not considered before? How does your original understanding of this story compare with what was just shared? How does this story speak to your life?

Participants share an experience from their lives that connects with the biblical interpretation just shared.

> *Forgiveness is always there for me, for us. All I have to do is accept it. Whenever I put God on the back burner, I cut myself off from his love. Whenever I choose to remain alienated from my family, friends, and community, I am also alienated from God. The challenge of today's liturgy is that I must accept the love that God already has for me. Forgiveness is mine. I live in God's love through prayer and when I respond in love to the needs of those around me. When I move out of selfish concerns into concern for others, I am living the love I have been given. The real saints in communities are those who selflessly give of their love, concern, and compassion for hurting members of their family, parish, or wider community. There are so many people who reach out to the sick and suffering, the poor, the lonely, the bereaved. They manifest God's love. I cannot rest in my personal relationship with God and think I have "arrived." Unless I demonstrate that love with self-giving action, it is empty. I can write a beautiful piece of music that praises God. I can write eloquent words that reveal God to the world, but if I fail to love those around me, then I am not centered in the heart of Christ.*

All share their life experience.

What does this liturgy have to say to our community and to me today? In what way is our community challenged? Do we still feel the same way about this liturgy as we did when we began? Has our original understanding been stretched, challenged, or affirmed?

STEP 5
DECISION

The gospel demands a response.

How does our sharing and this biblical interpretation challenge our community and how does it challenge me? In what way does this gospel call our parish to action in the church, parish, neighborhood, or world? What is one concrete action we will take this week as a response to what was learned and shared today?

DOCTRINAL ISSUES

What church truth/teaching/doctrinal issue could be drawn from the liturgy for the feast of the Sacred Heart?

Participants suggest possible doctrinal themes that flow from the readings.

Possible Doctrinal Themes

Sacred Heart, Trinity, christology, forgiveness

Present the doctrinal material at this time.

1. The facilitator gives input on a particular doctrinal issue of his/her prior choosing. OR
2. The group chooses a doctrinal issue from the list they created. They read together from the Doctrinal Appendix.

(The doctrinal issues are found in the Doctrinal Appendix in the back of this workbook. If you are choosing an issue from this resource, please refer to it now.)

Reflection questions centered around the chosen doctrinal theme can be found at the end of each topic in the Doctrinal Appendix. The questions are based on the five-step reflection process. If you choose a topic not included in the Doctrinal Appendix, craft your own questions according to the same five-step process.

Following the reflection questions you will be reminded to return to chapter 7, "Preparing the Catechetical Session," to assist you in crafting your own session.

Closing Prayer

Father,
we honor the heart of your Son

broken by man's cruelty,
yet symbol of love's triumph,
pledge of all that man is called to be.
Teach us to see Christ in the lives we touch,
to offer him living worship
by love-filled service to our brothers and sisters.
We ask this through Christ our Lord.[5]

Selected Bibliography

Adam, Adolf. *The Liturgical Year.* Trans. Matthew J. O'Connell. Collegeville: The Liturgical Press, 1990.

Boadt, Lawrence, C.S.P. "Ezekiel." In *The New Jerome Biblical Commentary.* Ed. Raymond E. Brown, S.S., Joseph A. Fitzmyer, S.J., Roland E. Murphy, O.Carm. Englewood Cliffs: Prentice Hall, 1990.

Days of the Lord. Vol. 7. Collegeville: The Liturgical Press, 1994.

Fitzmyer, Joseph, A., S.J. "The Letter to the Romans." In *The New Jerome Biblical Commentary.* Ed. Raymond E. Brown, S.S., Joseph A. Fitzmyer, S.J., Roland E. Murphy, O.Carm. Englewood Cliffs: Prentice Hall, 1990.

Talbert, Charles H. *Reading Luke.* New York: Crossroad, 1992.

---

[5]Sacred Heart: "Alternative Opening Prayer," *The Sacramentary.*

PRESENTATION OF THE LORD (FEBRUARY 2)

INTRODUCTORY RITES

Opening Song (or Entrance Antiphon)

Within your temple, we ponder your loving kindness, O God. As your name, so also your praise reaches to the ends of the earth; your right hand is filled with justice. (Ps 47:10-11)[1]

Blessing of Candles and Procession

The Lord will come with mighty power,
and give light to the eyes of all who serve him,
    alleluia.

Forty days ago we celebrated the joyful feast of the birth of our Lord Jesus Christ. Today we recall the holy day on which he was presented in the temple, fulfilling the law of Moses and at the same time going to meet his faithful people. Led by the Spirit, Simeon and Anna came to the temple, recognized Christ as their Lord, and proclaimed him with joy.

United by the Spirit, may we now go to the house of God to welcome Christ the Lord. There we shall recognize him in the breaking of the bread until he comes again in glory.

Then the priest joins his hands and blesses the candles.

Let us pray.
God, our Father, source of all light,
today you revealed to Simeon
your Light of revelation to the nations.
Bless + these candles and make them holy.
May we who carry them to praise your glory
walk in the path of goodness
and come to the light that shines for ever.
Grant this through Christ, our Lord.[2]

Opening Prayer

The facilitator of the session may lead the prayer. Others in the group may be asked to proclaim the readings.

All powerful Father,
Christ your Son became man for us
and was presented in the temple.
May he free our hearts from sin
and bring us into your presence.
We ask this through our Lord Jesus Christ, your
    Son,
who lives and reigns with you and the Holy Spirit,
one God, for ever and ever.[3]

LITURGY OF THE WORD

Let us listen to God's word.

The readings are proclaimed.

First Reading
Malachi 3:1-4

The reading from Malachi heralds the coming of the "messenger of the covenant." This messenger comes for judgment. The coming "Day of the Lord" will accomplish the purification of the people. We are to prepare by living the covenant.

The people had returned from exile and the temple had been rebuilt, but the people's response was lackluster. Those who turned away from God would be punished in the coming "Day of the Lord." Those who suffered while the wicked prospered would enjoy vindication on the "Day of the Lord." Placing this reading within this feast makes it clear how the church understands Malachi's prophecy. The presentation of Jesus in the temple is understood as the fulfillment of Malachi's prophecy.

Responsorial Psalm
Psalm 24:7-10

Second Reading
Hebrews 2:14-18

Jesus came to be the new high priest in the new covenant. He offered his life as a perfect sacri-

---

[1]Presentation of the Lord: "Entrance Antiphon," *The Sacramentary*.

[2]Presentation of the Lord: "Blessing of Candles and Procession," *The Sacramentary*.

[3]Presentation of the Lord: "Opening Prayer," *The Sacramentary*.

fice. By doing this, Jesus reconciled humanity with God. Jesus freely surrendered to death for the salvation of the world. He did this because of his faithfulness to Yahweh. Jesus' death was a passage to his glory, not to darkness. Because of Jesus' sacrifice, we are heirs to his resurrected life. We will die, but we will live with Jesus forever. Jesus' death was real. His suffering was real. He was a human being (with both a human and divine nature) and suffered as other human beings do. Like us in every way except sin, Jesus knows our suffering and is our advocate. He strengthens us and intercedes for us as we endure the trials of this life.

Gospel
Luke 2:22-40

Mary and Joseph take Jesus and present him in the temple.

STEP 1
NAMING ONE'S EXPERIENCE

What were your first impressions? What was your first response? What grabbed your attention? How did you feel?

Each person names his or her initial impression. Statement should be brief. No reasons should be given at this time. All simply listen without agreeing or disagreeing.

STEP 2
UNDERSTANDING

In a brief statement, what do you think this gospel is trying to convey?

STEP 3
INPUT FROM VISION/STORY/TRADITION

Liturgical Context

Jesus is the center of attention in today's gospel. The feast takes place forty days after Christmas and is centered around events that took place in the Jerusalem temple.

In antiquity, a woman was considered unclean for forty days after delivering a male child (eighty days after a female). She was to go to the temple and offer the priest a lamb and a young pigeon or turtledove or, if poor, two turtledoves. This was to be her sin offering, to make her ritually clean again.

Mary was dutifully following the law when she presented her son Jesus to the temple. Firstborn male children belonged to the Lord (Ex 13:2) and were to be taken to the temple so the parents could ransom them back with money. "In keeping with these regulations Mary and Joseph brought Jesus to the temple, and Mary offered the sacrifice that 'purified' her and at the same time ransomed her firstborn."[4]

It is possible that this feast was celebrated as early as the fifth century. The feast was a continuation of the Christmas event and its focus was clearly driven by today's gospel. While it is a feast strongly connected to the Nativity, it also has a paschal orientation.

The celebration included a procession. It began as a replacement for the pagan procession of expiation that took place every five years in February. To capture the original penitential flavor of the feast, purple vestments were worn (up to the 1960).

The procession with candles reminds us that Simeon called Jesus "a revealing light to the gentiles" (Lk 2:32). This feast has also been referred to as Candlemas. In the middle of the eighth century the feast was designated the "Purification of Blessed Virgin Mary." The new calendar made clear that the feast was a feast of the Lord, not of Mary, and the change of name in 1969 captured the original intent of the feast. The blessing of candles dates back to around 1000 C.E. in Gaul.

There are two forms of procession and blessing that may be used. In the first form, people gather outside and process into church with blessed candles (perhaps singing the Canticle of Simeon, the *Nunc dimittis*: "Now Master, you may let your servant go in peace according to your word."). The simpler form has a representative group enter the church carrying candles in procession with the priest.

---

[4]Adolf Adam, *The Liturgical Year*, trans. Matthew J. O'Connell (Collegeville: The Liturgical Press, 1990), 150.

The temple events are the lens through which all the ritual prayers of the mass are viewed. The prayers of the mass reflect the biblical understanding of the feast. We are to be joyful and praise God forever, because we have seen the light of the Lord (Preface). His light has gone out to all the world. We share that light as we await the day he will return and bring us into everlasting life (Prayer After Communion).

Gospel Exegesis

The facilitator gives input regarding what critical biblical scholarship has to say about this text. The input includes insights as to how people would have heard the gospel in Jesus' time.

Today's episode with Simeon during the presentation of Jesus in the temple accomplishes far more than the actual event described. The Lord's mission and destiny are heralded and the law and the Old Testament's importance are underscored. This gospel pronounces of the mystery of Christ: "Jesus, by submitting to the prescriptions of the Law imposed on first-born sons, manifested as soon as he entered the world his obedience to God, his Father (Luke 2:49)."[5]

Simeon, representative of the just of Israel, understood salvation to be the dawning of light to all the nations. Simeon echoed the words of the prophets who attested to the universal mission of the messiah. Yet, even though this mission is inclusive of all people, it will not be easy. Those who accept Christ will be rejected, just as Christ will be rejected. Simeon prophesies about the division that will be brought about as a result of faith in Christ. Mary, as representative of all believers, is an example of a faithful servant who listens to God's word and acts upon it. We are to do the same.

The Eastern Church calls this the Feast of the Encounter. Through celebration of the liturgy and the biblical texts, we encounter the mystery of the *Living One Who Came to Bring Light to the Nations* and we are challenged to live in a radical new way because of it. God promised to send a messenger

---

[5]*Days of the Lord*, Vol. 7 (Collegeville: The Liturgical Press, 1994), 112.

to purify the temple, the priesthood, and the people. He sent his Son to be the light for the entire world.

Proclaim the gospel again.

Sometimes we gain new insights when we hear the text after the interpretation has been given. Someone from the group proclaims the gospel a second time.

STEP 4
TESTING

Conversation with the Liturgy and the Scriptures

Test your original understanding in dialogue with the text.

(You might consider breaking into smaller groups.)

How does your original understanding of this story compare with what was just shared? How does this story speak to your life?

Participants share an experience from their lives that connects with the biblical interpretation just shared.

What does this liturgy have to say to our community and to me today? Has our original understanding been stretched, challenged, or affirmed?

STEP 5
DECISION

The gospel demands a response.

In what way does this gospel call our parish to action in the church, parish, neighborhood, or world? Has this conversation with the exegesis of this liturgy changed or stretched my personal attitudes? What is one concrete action we will take this week as a response to what was learned and shared today?

DOCTRINAL ISSUES

What church truth/teaching/doctrinal issue

could be drawn from the gospel for the Presentation of the Lord?

Participants suggest possible doctrinal themes that flow from the readings.

Possible Doctrinal Themes

Mystery of Christ, incarnation, evangelization, ecumenism

Present the doctrinal material at this time.

1. The facilitator gives input on a particular doctrinal issue of his/her prior choosing. OR
2. The group chooses a doctrinal issue from the list they created. They read together from the Doctrinal Appendix.

(The doctrinal issues are found in the Doctrinal Appendix in the back of this workbook. If you are choosing an issue from this resource, please refer to it now.)

Reflection questions centered around the chosen doctrinal theme can be found at the end of each topic in the Doctrinal Appendix. The questions are based on the five-step reflection process. If you choose a topic not included in the Doctrinal Appendix, craft your own questions according to the same five-step process.

Following the reflection questions you will be reminded to return to chapter 7, "Preparing the Catechetical Session," to assist you in crafting your own session.

Closing Prayer

Lord,
you fulfilled the hope of Simeon,
who did not die
until he had been privileged to welcome the Messiah.
May this communion perfect your grace in us
and prepare us to meet Christ
when he comes to bring us into everlasting life,
for he is Lord for ever and ever.[6]

---

[6]Presentation of the Lord: "Prayer After Communion," *The Sacramentary.*

Selected Bibliography

Adam, Adolf. *The Liturgical Year.* Trans. Matthew J. O'Connell. Collegeville: The Liturgical Press, 1990.

Days of the Lord. Vol. 7. Collegeville: The Liturgical Press, 1994.

SOLEMNITY OF JOSEPH, HUSBAND OF MARY (MARCH 19)

INTRODUCTORY RITES

Opening Song (or Entrance Antiphon)

The Lord has put his faithful servant in charge of his household. (Lk 12:42).[1]

Opening Prayer

The facilitator of the session may lead the prayer. Others in the group may be asked to proclaim the readings.

Let us pray
[that the Church will continue
the saving work of Christ]

Pause for silent prayer.

Father,
you entrusted our Savior to the care of St. Joseph.
By the help of his prayers
may your Church continue to serve its Lord, Jesus Christ,
who lives and reigns with you and the Holy Spirit,
one God, for ever and ever.[2]

LITURGY OF THE WORD

Let us listen to God's word.

The readings are proclaimed.

First Reading
2 Samuel 7:4-5, 12-14, 16

Today's reading from Samuel reminds us of Yahweh's promise that David's reign would endure forever. This promise is considered typological of the promise that would be fulfilled in the messianic reign of Jesus Christ. Jesus fulfilled the promise made to David, since Joseph was a descendant of David.

---

[1]Solemnity of Joseph, Husband of Mary: "Entrance Antiphon," *The Sacramentary.*

[2]Solemnity of Joseph, Husband of Mary: "Opening Prayer," *The Sacramentary.*

Responsorial Psalm
Psalm 89:2-3, 4-5, 27, 29

This psalm is a reflection on the promise made to David: David's house would endure forever and his reign would extend for all time.

Second Reading
Romans 4:13, 16-18, 22

Joseph is called "Just in the eyes of God" *(tzaddik).* It is the greatest accolade paid to anyone in biblical tradition. Anyone who played a role in the history of salvation was considered a model to follow and was thus entitled to be called "just." Paul's letter to the Romans seeks to teach the disciple how to become "just" like the *tzaddik.* Paul used Abraham as an example.

Abraham was righteous ("just") because of his faith in God. God did not grace Abraham because of his observance of the law. Abraham was elected completely through the grace of God and trusted that God would multiply his descendants even though the aged Sarah was childless. Abraham even stood firm in his trust of Yahweh when asked to sacrifice his son, Isaac.

Paul's letter to the Romans invites the reader to share Abraham's faith. We, too, are heirs of the promise made to Abraham. Our response is complete trust.

Gospel
Matthew 1:16, 18-21, 24

Joseph obeyed the angel and took Mary as his wife.

Or Luke 2:41-51

Jesus is left behind in the temple in Jerusalem as Mary and Joseph search for him.

STEP 1
NAMING ONE'S EXPERIENCE

What were your first impressions? What was your first response? What grabbed your attention? How did you feel?

Each person names his or her initial impression. Statement should be brief. No reasons should be given at this time. All simply listen without agreeing or disagreeing.

STEP 2
UNDERSTANDING

In a brief statement, what do you think this gospel is trying to convey?

STEP 3
INPUT FROM VISION/STORY/TRADITION

Liturgical Context

The earliest evidence of observance of a devotion to Joseph, husband of Mary, can be traced back to the eighth century in Coptic calendars. A celebration taking place on March 19 occurred in the twelfth century. Bernadine of Sienna, a Franciscan, fostered the celebration of the feast in honor of St. Joseph. A church was built in honor of Joseph in Nazareth during the crusades.

By the end of the sixteenth century Pope Sixtus IV established the feast for the church universal. Pope Gregory XV made it a holy day of obligation in 1621. Pius IX named Joseph the patron and protector of the universal church in 1870.

A preface in honor of St. Joseph was introduced in 1920 and was retained in the New Missal of 1970. Pope John XXIII added St. Joseph's name to the Roman canon in 1962. Since the feast falls in Lent, permission is granted to episcopal conferences to transfer it to another time.

In 1847 Pius IX established another feast in honor of St. Joseph and placed it on the third Sunday after Easter. This feast had been celebrated by the Carmelites of Italy and France since 1860. Pius X made it a first-class feast and moved it to the third Wednesday after Easter. Since this was a duplication of the present solemnity, it was abolished by the Congregation of Rites in 1956.[3]

---

[3]Adolf Adam, *The Liturgical Year,* trans. Matthew J. O'Connell (Collegeville: The Liturgical Press, 1990), 230.

In the secular contemporary world, May 1 has been observed as a day in honor of the rights of the working person. Pius XII established a feast on May 1 in order to give the secular observance a Christian dimension. The pope also wished to highlight the rights of workers. The "Solemnity of St. Joseph the Worker, Husband of the Blessed Virgin Mary, Confessor and Patron of Working People" was retained in the new calendar as an optional memorial. The reason for reducing the rank of the feast is evidence of Rome's attempt to lessen the number of *idea feasts.*

The preface for this solemnity speaks of Joseph, the "just man" who served as protector in the infancy stages of the Incarnation event, protector of Mary, the Mother of God, and protector of Jesus, God's Son. Joseph served as earthly father in place of Jesus' natural father.

By being faithful to his mission of serving God, Joseph took his place in the annals of salvation history. Joseph is named as a wise, loyal, selfless servant. The liturgy opens by illuminating the character of Joseph: "The Lord has put his faithful servant in charge of his household" (Entrance Antiphon). We are exhorted to follow the example of Joseph in his ministry of service and care: "Father, with unselfish love St. Joseph cared for your Son, born of the Virgin Mary. May we also serve you at your altar with pure hearts" (Prayer Over the Gifts).

Flowers are allowed in church on this lenten weekday and are therefore an appropriate adornment for the St. Joseph shrine. An Italian tradition, the St. Joseph's table originated as a meal for the poor. It was offered in thanksgiving and in honor of St. Joseph for answered prayer. The meal is comprised of meatless dishes. It is a wholesome combination of the lenten disciplines of prayer, fasting, and almsgiving. *Catholic Household Blessings and Prayers* provides a litany and domestic prayer for the day. The *Book of Blessings* provides an "Order of Blessing of St. Joseph's Table." "Joseph is the patron saint of Mexico, Canada, Bohemia (in the Czech Republic) and Belgium, too. He has become known as the patron saint of the church, of fathers, of a happy death and of prayer."[4]

---

[4]Mary Ellyn Hynes, *Companion to the Calendar* (Chicago: Liturgy Training Publications, 1992), 60.

Gospel Exegesis

The facilitator gives input regarding what critical biblical scholarship has to say about this text. The input includes insights as to how people would have heard the gospel in Jesus' time.

Matthew 1:16, 18-21, 24

The genealogy of Matthew ends with Joseph, who was to play a role in God's messianic plan of salvation. Through the mediation of an angel, God revealed to Joseph the role he was to play in the lives of Mary and Jesus. It is through Joseph's genealogy that Jesus would be an heir to the promise made to David. When Jesus assumed Joseph's name, Jesus was legitimated as a descendant of David. When Joseph accepted Jesus as his son, he acknowledged Jesus' role as messiah. Joseph, as a righteous man, lived according to the law and was faithful to the will of God. All who follow Joseph's example are also righteous in the eyes of God.

Scripture does not credit Joseph with speaking a single word. Joseph's silence is the silence of one who lets God do the talking and simply and humbly follows God's commands. After the first two chapters in Matthew, Joseph is not heard from again. His role, according to Matthew, was assigned to the early life of Christ. He passed on his lineage to Jesus, he saved Jesus from Herod, and he brought his small family back to Galilee after the sojourn in Egypt. Joseph acted always at God's initiative, thus making him the personal representative of the Father at the side of the Son on earth. Joseph was a trustworthy guardian because he was faithful to God's word.

Joseph was not a wild-eyed dreamer. He was a man of action. But God revealed his intentions to Joseph through dreams, a common biblical medium of divine revelation. Joseph listened and followed God's leading. Joseph is a model for all who seek to do God's will.

Luke 2:41-51

Today's gospel from Luke serves as a transition from the infancy narratives to the adult manifestation of Christ. The event in today's story is more about Jesus than it is about his parents. It reflects and illuminates the mystery of the Incarnation and how the believer is to understand it. Jesus, Mary, and Joseph's pilgrimage to Jerusalem for the annual feast of Passover is of particular importance in the context of this passage. We are told that Jesus was twelve years old. This is Luke's way of telling the reader that Jesus was no longer a child and was now subject to the law.

The fact that Jesus remained in the temple after his parents left demonstrates Jesus' close connection to the sacred place. It was in this very same place that Jesus' future destiny would play itself out and lead to the cross on Calvary. However, in this scene, the learned teachers marvel at the wisdom of this budding would-be rabbi. We are not to sentimentalize this scene as that of a child prodigy amazing the scholars. We must look at this event through the lens of the crucifixion.

When Jesus responded to his anxious parents that he must be about his Father's business, we are told that they did not understand. They who lived with Jesus, his own parents, had to grow in understanding of his mission. As the words and experiences of Jesus' life unfolded, they would be able to reflect back on them and grow in understanding. Believers are thus encouraged in the face of their own doubts and lack of understanding.

Proclaim the gospel again.

Sometimes we gain new insights when we hear the text after the interpretation has been given. Someone from the group proclaims the gospel a second time.

STEP 4
TESTING

Conversation with the Liturgy and the Scriptures

Test your original understanding in dialogue with the text.

(You might consider breaking into smaller groups.)

How does your original understanding of this story compare with what was just shared? How does this story speak to your life?

Participants share an experience from their lives that connects with the biblical interpretation just shared.

What does this liturgy have to say to our community and to me today? Has our original understanding been stretched, challenged, or affirmed?

Step 5
Decision

The gospel demands a response.

In what way does this gospel call our parish to action in the church, parish, neighborhood, or world? Has this conversation with the exegesis of this liturgy changed or stretched our personal attitudes? What is one concrete action we will take this week as a response to what was learned and shared today?

DOCTRINAL ISSUES

What church truth/teaching/doctrinal issue could be drawn from the gospel for the Solemnity of Joseph, Husband of Mary?

Participants suggest possible doctrinal themes that flow from the readings.

Possible Doctrinal Themes

Incarnation, faith, mystery of Christ, St. Joseph, protector of the Universal Church

Present the doctrinal material at this time.

1. The facilitator gives input on a particular doctrinal issue of his/her prior choosing. OR
2. The group chooses a doctrinal issue from the list they created. They read together from the Doctrinal Appendix.

(The doctrinal issues are found in the Doctrinal Appendix in the back of this workbook. If you are choosing an issue from this resource, please refer to it now.)

Reflection questions centered around the chosen doctrinal theme can be found at the end of each topic in the Doctrinal Appendix. The questions are based on the five-step reflection process. If you choose a topic not included in the Doctrinal Appendix, craft your own questions according to the same five-step process.

Following the reflection questions you will be reminded to return to chapter 7, "Preparing the Catechetical Session," to assist you in crafting your own session.

Closing Prayer

Lord,
you nourish us at this altar
as we celebrate the feast of St. Joseph.
Protect your Church always,
and in your love watch over the gifts you have given us.
Grant this through Christ, our Lord.[5]

Selected Bibliography

Adam, Adolf. *The Liturgical Year.* Trans. Matthew J. O'Connell. Collegeville: The Liturgical Press, 1990.

Days of the Lord. Vol. 7. Collegeville: The Liturgical Press, 1994.

Hynes, Mary Ellyn. *Companion to the Calendar.* Chicago: Liturgy Training Publications, 1992.

Mick, Lawrence E. *Sourcebook.* Chicago: Liturgy Training Publications, 1994.

---

[5]Solemnity of Joseph, Husband of Mary: "Prayer After Communion," *The Sacramentary.*

SOLEMNITY OF THE ANNUNCIATION OF THE LORD (MARCH 25)

INTRODUCTORY RITES

Opening Song (or Entrance Antiphon)

As Christ came into the world, he said: Behold! I have come to do your will, O God. (Heb 10:5, 7)[1]

Opening Prayer

The facilitator of the session may lead the prayer. Others in the group may be asked to proclaim the readings.

Let us pray
[that Christ, the Word made flesh,
will make us more like him]

Pause for silent prayer.

God, our Father,
your Word became man and was born of the Virgin Mary.
May we become more like Jesus Christ,
whom we acknowledge as our redeemer, God and man.
We ask this through our Lord Jesus Christ, your Son,
who lives and reigns with you and the Holy Spirit,
one God, for ever and ever.[2]

LITURGY OF THE WORD

Let us listen to God's word.

The readings are proclaimed.

First Reading
Isaiah 7:10-14

King Ahaz was undecided on his course of action in the face of military conflict. Like other arrogant monarchs, Ahaz believed in his own self-sufficiency. He did not need the intervention of Yahweh in the affairs of state. The prophet was urging one course of action and Ahaz's advisers another. Isaiah offered a sign. Ahaz was encouraged to seek confirmation of Isaiah's promise, but his mind was already closed. It seemed to him that the obvious course of action was to make an alliance with a powerful nation and rise up against a weaker one. What could go wrong? He did not listen to the Lord's warning. Without a firm faith he would not stand.

God would keep his promise to David and the sign would remain—not to convince Ahaz, but rather to prove the truth of the prophet's word. The word referring to the *woman* with child was not the technical term for virgin. Scholars suggest that the woman, though a hazy character, is probably one of Ahaz's wives. The promised child was a sign himself. This woman would give birth to a child who would be a sign. The child would possess a unique destiny in salvation history. Isaiah's prophecy served as the foundation for Israel's messianic hope.

Christ is the obvious fulfillment of this messianic hope. Christ, Immanuel, is with us as his salvation plan unfolds before the world.

Responsorial Psalm
Psalm 40:7-8, 8-9, 10, 11

Second Reading
Hebrews 10:4-10

The letter to the Hebrews is primarily concerned with reflection upon the Jewish scriptures. The Lectionary omits a very important piece of Hebrews in which the humanity of Jesus is addressed at great length. It is perhaps the "New Testament's most profound and systematic discussion of what it means for Jesus to have been human."[3] This reading is particularly appropriate on this feast that celebrates the announcement of Jesus' birth. The reason for Christ's Incarnation is reparation for the sins of the world. With the coming of Jesus,

---

[1]Annunciation of the Lord: "Entrance Antiphon," *The Sacramentary.*

[2]Annunciation of the Lord: "Opening Prayer," *The Sacramentary.*

[3]Raymond F. Collins, *Preaching the Epistles* (New York/Mahwah: Paulist Press, 1996), 120-121.

the sacrifices of old are rendered meaningless. Jesus replaced the burnt offerings and sacrifices of the old covenant.

The Pauline community asserts that Jesus definitively assumed unto himself such oblations once and for all. One cannot meditate on the Incarnation without reflection upon the reason for it in the first place: the cross and resurrection.

Gospel
Luke 1:26-38

The angel Gabriel announces the birth of Jesus to Mary.

STEP 1
NAMING ONE'S EXPERIENCE

What were your first impressions? What was your first response? What grabbed your attention? How did you feel?

Each person names his or her initial impression. Statement should be brief. No reasons should be given at this time. All simply listen without agreeing or disagreeing.

STEP 2
UNDERSTANDING

In a brief statement, what do you think this gospel is trying to convey?

STEP 3
INPUT FROM VISION/STORY/TRADITION

Liturgical Context

The first hint of a celebration honoring the Annunciation of the Lord can be traced to the Council of Toledo in 656. Thirty years later the feast was celebrated in Rome. The March 25 date has had a dubious background. There is evidence that the feast was celebrated on December 18, a week prior to Christmas, in Spain around the year 1000. The feast is understood in the context of the Nativity

event. The reform of the Vatican Council appropriately named it a feast of the Lord.

The feast strongly resonates with a sound Mariology. Mary is the Mother of God's Son who came to save the world through the paschal mystery—death, resurrection, and glorification. She is a venerated person in the history of salvation because God chose her and graced her to be the mother of Christ. The scriptural texts, the announcement of Jesus' birth, the promised Immanuel of Isaiah, and Paul's letter to the Hebrews regarding the self-gift of Christ to the world, give us the absolute lens through which we are to view and celebrate this event. It is a Christ event—it calls us to fix our gaze on Jesus Christ, Son of God, born of the Virgin Mary.

The introductory rites open the liturgy with a proclamation of Jesus' mission: He came to do his Father's will. This liturgy celebrates the God who sent his Son to become bone and flesh, to be born of a human, virgin mother, to experience life as all human beings experience it (except for the experience of sin) and to one day allow his human body to suffer, die, and rise again for the salvation of all. The Virgin Mary gave completely of herself. She gave her very womb to bear the will of the Father in the flesh.

The liturgy knows well the longing of the human heart and that only Jesus' presence will satisfy it. Mary intercedes for the waiting world (Alternative Opening Prayer) and asks that Jesus fill the void of incompleteness. The opening prayer asks that we become more like Jesus, our redeemer, who is both human and divine. The prayer over the gifts reminds us that the Incarnation of Christ was the beginning of the church. This feast is about Christ. It is a feast of the Lord. It is the cornerstone of our faith and celebrates the primary truths of the Christian faith: Jesus, the Father's only Son, our Lord, became a man and dwelt among us. "...By the power of the Holy Spirit he was born of the Virgin Mary, and became man. For our sake he was crucified under Pontius Pilate; he suffered, died and was buried. On the third day he rose again in fulfillment of the Scriptures; he ascended into heaven and is seated at the right hand of the Father. He will come again in glory to judge the living and the dead, and his kingdom will have no end. We believe in the Holy Spirit, the Lord, the giver of life, who proceeds from the Father and the Son. With the Father and the Son he is worshiped and glorified...."[4]

Gospel Exegesis

The facilitator gives input regarding what critical biblical scholarship has to say about this text. The input includes insights as to how people would have heard the gospel in Jesus' time.

Luke's announcement story is patterned after other biblical birth announcements of extraordinary persons. The similarities are so strong that they place the contrasts in stark focus. Only twice in biblical tradition does an angel appear to a woman: Hagar (Gen 16:7-16) and Samson's mother (Judg 13: 1-25). The appearance of the angel is to announce to the reader that the events being foretold are part of God's plan of salvation for the world.

The angel's words are similar in the birth announcements of John and Jesus; there are differences, however, in the description of each child's role and identity. John is to be "great before the Lord," but Jesus will be "great and Son of the Most High." John will prepare the people, but Jesus will rule over them. John's role is temporary, Jesus' is endless. John is a prophet, Jesus is more than a prophet: he is the Son of God. Luke's readers are alerted to the graphic differences between John and Jesus and that Jesus is something far greater than a Davidic king.[5]

It is quite remarkable that Luke gave Mary such an important focus. The patriarchal biblical and secular world would have given little credence to the exalted role of a woman. Even more remarkable is the fact that it was Joseph who gave Jesus his legitimacy as heir to the Davidic dynasty. Luke Timothy Johnson maintains that Luke's intention remains unclear. It is possible that his treatment of Mary is a "historical reminiscence, special tradition, or Luke's predilection for presenting positive women figures (evident throughout his narrative)."[6]

In Matthew's account the emphasis is placed on the role of Joseph. Luke gives Mary center stage. Mary's name, a Semitic name (*Mariam* in Greek; *Miryam* in Hebrew), is derived from the Hebrew word for *height* or *summit*. In a feminine context it probably meant "excellence." It is not without significance that Mary's name is the same as that of the mother of Moses. Both are significant characters in God's salvation plan and both have similar stories. Luke tells us very little about Mary in the infancy narratives. The other characters are well introduced. Elizabeth, Joseph, Zechariah, Simeon, and Anna are all identified by their genealogy or their piety. Mary is not heralded as possessing any special characteristics. She is not called righteous, or an astute observer of the law. She is one of society's powerless: she is young in a culture that values age, a female in a man's world, and poor in an unequal economy. A woman's identity is validated through her husband and child—yet she has neither. The great paradox of this passage is that Luke understands God to be a God of surprise, "always reversing human expectations."[7]

We have to wait until the angel's proclamation before we are given a glimpse of how God considers Mary. "Hail, rejoice, Mary!" gives us a clue to her exalted status with God. We are told of her virginity and of her high standing with God. There is no question: Mary is a decent person, in spite of outward appearances. There is no hint of impropriety in Luke's gospel.

Mary is fearful at the angel's announcement. In biblical tradition, fear is a common reaction to angelic messengers. Mary is troubled that the angel said she "had found favor." She was a "favored one." That was an uncommon salutation in the New Testament. The Hebrew scriptures attest to people who were "favored": Noah, Moses, Gideon, Samuel. Perhaps Mary is troubled because a woman was being called "favored by God." A woman was named a key player in God's salvation plan. Perhaps Mary is troubled at the thought of the heavy burden usually placed on "those favored by God." The "favored of God" usually end up paying the ultimate price in their service of God.

[4]Nicene Creed, *The Sacramentary.*

[5]Luke Timothy Johnson, *The Gospel of Luke,* Sacra Pagina Series, Vol. 3 (Collegeville: The Liturgical Press, 1991), 38-39.

[6]Ibid., 39.

[7]Ibid., 39.

Gabriel's declaration to Mary that the Lord is with her is a reminder that she will participate in "God's action to save."[8] The angel announces to Mary that she is to bear a Son and tells her what she is to name him and what his role will be. Mary is incredulous. So was Zechariah. However, there is a difference. Mary's question asks how it could be possible in light of her virginity. Hers is a practical question. Zechariah's question is one of basic disbelief.

Mary's question keeps the story line in a suspenseful forward motion. Gabriel proceeds to tell her how all this will happen. The Holy Spirit will accomplish it. The Holy Spirit will overshadow and come upon her. These are not sexual metaphors for divine-human intercourse. Rather, they are simply statements that God will intervene and do what God intends.

Mary's assent, "be it done unto me according to your will," places her in the role of disciple. Disciples hear the word of God and act on it. All Mary needed to hear was the angel's assurance that it was by divine intervention, not by human design that she should be so blessed. "She prefigures her son's acceptance of God's will, despite the high price that it demands."[9]

The Incarnation is shrouded in obedience. The Son was obedient to the Father, Mary and Joseph were obedient to the word of God through the mediation of an angel. Faithful obedience to God's will is demanded of all faithful disciples. The ancient martyrologies referred to this feast as "The announcement of the divine incarnation to the Blessed Virgin Mary." Today it is less explicitly named "Annunciation of the Lord." "Today is the announcement of the first day of the new era of creation."[10]

Proclaim the gospel again.

Sometimes we gain new insights when we hear the text after the interpretation has been given. Someone from the group proclaims the gospel a second time.

---

[8]Barbara E. Reid, *Choosing the Better Part? Women in the Gospel of Luke* (Collegeville: The Liturgical Press, 1996), 67.
[9]Ibid., 69.
[10]*Days of the Lord*, Vol. 7 (Collegeville: The Liturgical Press, 1994),142.

STEP 4
TESTING

Conversation with the Liturgy and the Scriptures

Test your original understanding in dialogue with the text.

(You might consider breaking into smaller groups.)

How does your original understanding of this story compare with what was just shared? How does this story speak to your life?

Participants share an experience from their lives that connects with the biblical interpretation just shared.

What does this liturgy have to say to our community and to me today? Has our original understanding been stretched, challenged, or affirmed?

STEP 5
DECISION

The gospel demands a response.

In what concrete way does this gospel call our parish to action in the church, parish, neighborhood, or world? Has this conversation with the exegesis of this liturgy changed or stretched our personal attitudes? What is one specific action we will take this week as a response to what was learned and shared today?

DOCTRINAL ISSUES

What church truth/teaching/doctrinal issue could be drawn from the gospel for the Solemnity of the Annunciation of the Lord?

Participants suggest possible doctrinal themes that flow from the readings.

Possible Doctrinal Themes

Incarnation, Holy Spirit, role of Mary: mother of God, disciple, christology

Present the doctrinal material at this time.

1. The facilitator gives input on a particular doctrinal issue of his/her prior choosing. OR
2. The group chooses a doctrinal issue from the list they created. They read together from the Doctrinal Appendix.

(The doctrinal issues are found in the Doctrinal Appendix in the back of this workbook. If you are choosing an issue from this resource, please refer to it now.)

Reflection questions centered around the chosen doctrinal theme can be found at the end of each topic in the Doctrinal Appendix. The questions are based on the five-step reflection process. If you choose a topic not included in the Doctrinal Appendix, craft your own questions according to the same five-step process.

Following the reflection questions you will be reminded to return to chapter 7, "Preparing the Catechetical Session," to assist you in crafting your own session.

Closing Prayer

Father, all powerful and ever-living God,
we do well always and everywhere
to give you thanks through Jesus Christ our Lord.
He came to save mankind by becoming a man
    himself.
The Virgin Mary, receiving the angel's message in
    faith,
conceived by the power of the Holy Spirit
and bore your son in purest love.
In Christ, the eternal truth,
your promise to Israel was realized beyond all ex-
    pectations.
Through Christ the angels of heaven
offer their prayer of adoration
as they rejoice in your presence for ever.
May our voices be one with theirs
in their triumphant hymn of praise:
Holy, Holy, Holy Lord, God of power and might,
heaven and earth are full of your glory.
Hosanna in the highest.
Blessed is he who comes in the name of the Lord.
Hosanna in the highest.[11]

---

[11]"Annunciation: "Preface," *The Sacramentary.*

Selected Bibliography

Adam, Adolf. *The Liturgical Year.* Trans. Matthew J. O'Connell. Collegeville: The Liturgical Press, 1990.

Collins, Raymond F. *Preaching the Epistles.* New York/Mahwah: Paulist Press, 1996.

Days of the Lord. Vol. 7. Collegeville: The Liturgical Press, 1994.

Jensen, Joseph, O.S.B. "Isaiah 1-39." In *The New Jerome Biblical Commentary.* Ed. Raymond E. Brown, S.S., Joseph A. Fitzmyer, S.J., Roland E. Murphy, O.Carm. Englewood Cliffs: Prentice Hall, 1990.

Johnson, Luke Timothy. *The Gospel of Luke.* Sacra Pagina Series. Vol. 3. Collegeville: The Liturgical Press, 1991.

Reid, Barbara E. *Choosing the Better Part? Women in the Gospel of Luke.* Collegeville: The Liturgical Press, 1996.

INTRODUCTORY RITES

Opening Song (or Entrance Antiphon)

There was a man sent from God whose name was John. He came to bear witness to the light, to prepare an upright people for the Lord. (Lk 1:6-7; 17)[1]

Opening Prayer

The facilitator of the session may lead the prayer. Others in the group may be asked to proclaim the readings.

Let us pray
[that God will give us joy and peace]

Pause for silent prayer.

God, our Father,
you raised up John the Baptist,
to prepare a perfect people for Christ the Lord.
Give your Church joy in spirit
and guide those who believe in you
into the way of salvation and peace.
We ask this through our Lord Jesus Christ, your Son,
who lives and reigns with you and the Holy Spirit,
one God, for ever and ever.[2]

LITURGY OF THE WORD

Let us listen to God's word.

The readings are proclaimed.

First Reading
Isaiah 49:1-6

Isaiah foretold a *Suffering Servant,* especially chosen by God, who would suffer and in the end would lead people to salvation. In biblical history this figure eventually became associated with the messiah. Christianity easily saw the Suffering Servant to be a prefigure of Christ who suffered, died, was buried, and rose again for the salvation of the world.

The Suffering Servant figure was also reminiscent of other prophets who suffered so that others might come to recognize the Holy One upon his arrival. John the Baptist was understood as such a prophet.

His mission was difficult and discouraging. It was easy to lose heart. Prophets were acutely aware that they were driven and propelled by the power of Yahweh. The Servant in today's pericope was assured of God's confidence in the mission God had appointed him to accomplish. The prophetic message is to have everlasting consequences, reaching to the ends of the earth by the power of God. John's mission was to prepare the way for the *Anointed One of God.* His message was one of conversion and repentance. John would be misunderstood and in the end give his life for the *Word* he was sent to herald. But his message not only would reach to the ends of the earth, it would do so for all time. Today's prophetic message would extend to the end of the ages.

Responsorial Psalm
Psalm 139:1-3, 13-14, 14-15

Second Reading
Acts 13:22-26

On Paul's first missionary journey he preached in the synagogue at Pisidia. Paul addressed the people with a foundational truth that both the speaker and the audience shared: Israel was elected by God and David, also elected, was regarded as the king who found favor with God and to whom God made a promise. Unlike the political leaders of today, there were no "spin-doctors" to whitewash David's character. All of his faults were laid bare for biblical history to examine. However, David was memorialized as a larger-than-life character who repented, loved and was loyal to his God. "Idealized by the biblical tradition in chronicles that are apologies David became the figure of the Messiah himself."[3] Thus, the messiah

---

[1]Birth of John the Baptist: "Entrance Antiphon," *The Sacramentary.*

[2]Birth of John the Baptist: "Opening Prayer," *The Sacramentary.*

[3]*Days of the Lord,* Vol. 7 (Collegeville: The Liturgical Press, 1994), 156.

would come from David's dynasty and emerge from David's throne. All in Paul's audience could agree on that premise. There was nothing new until Paul spoke of the messiah in past tense terms. By implying that the messiah had already come, Paul threw them a curve. "Paul speaks in the past tense of the Messiah who has already come to Israel and identifies the Messiah with Jesus."[4]

Here is where Paul sparks controversy. This Jewish audience would not be coming with any such presupposition. Paul built on the foundation they knew and understood in order to help them see that within their cherished history lay the seeds of what God had already accomplished through Jesus. Paul's speech is an announcement that the promised messiah has indeed arrived and today sits on the Davidic throne by the power of his death and resurrection.

John heralded the advent of the Savior by preaching a baptism of repentance. He specifically gave testimony to Christ by attesting that a greater one than he was still to come. John was not the expected messiah: of this he was emphatic! He reminds us that we are to prepare our hearts for the reign of Christ in our lives. We are to turn from sin, change our lives and live the good news.

Gospel
Luke 1:57-66, 80

The birth of the Baptist is announced and he is named John.

STEP 1
NAMING ONE'S EXPERIENCE

What were your first impressions? What was your first response? What grabbed your attention? How did you feel?

Each person names his or her initial impression. Statement should be brief. No reasons should be given at this time. All simply listen without agreeing or disagreeing.

---

[4]Robert C. Tannehill, *The Narrative Unity of Luke-Acts: A Literary Interpretation*, Vol. 2 (Minneapolis: Augsburg Fortress, 1990),166.

STEP 2
UNDERSTANDING

In a brief statement, what do you think this gospel is trying to convey?

STEP 3
INPUT FROM VISION/STORY/TRADITION

Liturgical Context

Jesus himself proclaimed to the world that John was more than a prophet: "the greatest of human beings." The fact that Jesus attested to his greatness and the fact that he was a martyr won him a venerated place among the saints of the early church. He was on a par with the apostles and Stephen.

Celebration of a feast in honor of John the Baptist dates back to the fourth century. The Greeks celebrated it on January 7, the day after Epiphany, the day that commemorated the baptism of the Lord. Since John baptized Jesus in the Jordan, the celebration of his feast was placed on the day following Epiphany. The West celebrated his feast on June 24, thus placing it six months prior to the Nativity of the Lord according to the scripture attesting to this time frame (Lk 1:36a).

Six churches were built in Rome in honor of John. By the sixth century a vigil was attached to the celebration and there were three assigned masses for the day. One of the masses was to be celebrated at the baptistry *(ad fontem)*.

The East established two other feasts in his honor, but the West maintained only one of them: the Beheading of John the Baptist on August 29. His birth is still commemorated in the Byzantine Church on September 24.

The solemnity has a vigil attached to it that includes most of the prayers from the old vigil mass in addition to the inclusion of a second reading, an alleluia verse, and the special preface.[5] This

---

[5]Adolf Adam, *The Liturgical Year*, trans. Matthew J. O'Connell (Collegeville: The Liturgical Press, 1990), 234.

chapter will deal only with the mass of the day, however.

The preface for this feast depicts God's favor bestowed on John. It describes his mission, his martyrdom, and his role in salvation through Christ. The opening prayer asks that we be guided to walk the path of salvation and peace. John, we are told, prepares us to become a perfect people (notice the present tense). The teaching of John will lead us to Christ. We ask for help to live, by the action of our lives, the mystery we celebrate (Vigil Prayer Over the Gifts). This is done in the shadow of John's message of repentance and gospel living.

"In the liturgy of the Church, a 'nativity' is not a birthday. Birthdays are anniversaries of a birth. Instead, a nativity is the birth itself. Today is not John the Baptist's birthday. Today John is born. That is what we sing in the liturgy today!"[6] We remember and make present the effects, implications, and mission of John the Baptist as we celebrate this feast. He is born anew to herald the same message of repentance and conversion.

Places around the world honor the feast day in various ways. People in Europe mark the feast by staying up all night and burning "St. John's fires." In Poland candles are placed on wreaths and floated downriver. In Morocco the Muslims also light fires in his honor. In Sweden people decorate cars, buses, doors, and a Maypole with green birch twigs. The pole is hoisted in the afternoon amid shouts of joy. In Lithuania people sweeten a cheese with honey, which is reminiscent of the food eaten by John. The cheese is prepared to look like the sun.

Gospel Exegesis

The facilitator gives input regarding what critical biblical scholarship has to say about this text. The input includes insights as to how people would have heard the gospel in Jesus' time.

Today's story is less about the announcement of John's birth and more about the naming of John.

When John was named, his special identity and role in salvation history were announced. John was given his name on the day of his circumcision. It was a day of celebration and all expected John to be named after his father, Zechariah. Elizabeth, however, proclaimed that his name would be John (in obedience to the command given earlier by Gabriel). The gathered crowd was taken aback and approached Zechariah expecting him to rectify this breach of tradition. Zechariah, unable to speak, confirmed in writing that indeed the child's name was "John." The crowd was astonished!

In antiquity, people's names expressed their role, their character, and very often their mission in life. "Transcending all classifications, it is a person's proper word, speaking his unique identity and singular contribution to history."[7] However, it is not the meaning of John's name ("The Lord has been gracious") that sparks attention in this case; it is the fact that he was named by divine intervention. The fact that God intervened in John's conception and now intervened in his naming called attention to John's significant destiny. A child was born who enjoyed great favor with God. This was great news not only for his parents, but for all in their region.

Because Zechariah did not believe the angel's word that God would send them a child, he was subsequently struck dumb. His speech was restored when he responded to God's earlier directive and named his son *John*, blessing God as he did so. Everyone who heard or witnessed the event was afraid. Zechariah's ability to speak was understood by all as a sign from God that focused attention not on Zechariah's miracle, but on the person of John. All were alerted to the fact that this child was indeed favored by God and great things could be expected as a result. John's mission, however, remained cloaked in mystery.

The story ends with a fast-forward into John's adult life. We are taken to the edge of the desert to await his adult mission. The desert image alerts the reader that John is about to enter a time of preparation for his mission. In the scriptures, the

---

[6]Mary Ellyn Hynes, *Companion to the Calendar* (Chicago: Liturgy Training Publications, 1992), 94.

[7]Eugene LaVerdiere, S.S.S., *Luke* (Wilmington: Michael Glazier, 1980), 26, 27.

desert signifies a barren area with low rainfall. Sometimes it is called the wilderness. In the biblical perspective barren places are places where humans encounter God. In the Christian perspective, the desert is a symbol of inner pilgrimage leading to the experience of God.

Many of the salvific acts of the Old Testament occurred in the desert. *It was a place of death.* If people lost their way in the desert, they would surely die. *It was a place of protection and a place of testing.* In the story of Exodus, God led Israel through the desert for forty years. He fed them, provided water for their thirst, and showed them the way through the desert. God entered into a covenant with Israel and she became a people. God tested Israel through her forty-year sojourn. Many of God's dealings with Israel occurred in the desert. "Clearly the desert and God's plan for Israel were intimately bound together."[8] The desert is a place where God tests, forms, and prepares his chosen for their mission, just as God tested, formed, and prepared Israel for her mission in the promised land.

We are told that the child John grew up and matured in spirit. Such an announcement was a biblical formula used to depict the "harmonious development of a child marked before birth by divine grace and one whom 'the hand of the Lord' reposed."[9] John was destined to preach the good news of salvation from his very conception. God's favor rested on him; he could do no less.

John's mission is intimately bound to the mission of Christ. John preached conversion and repentance, thus preparing people to hear and accept Jesus' message. Today the church continues John's preaching mission. John preached a word that cost him his life. It was not a soft word, but a word that demanded *metanoia*, a complete turning of one's heart and life to God. Such preachers usually pay the ultimate price for their work. John paid with his head.

---

[8]John F. Craghan, "Desert," in *The Collegeville Pastoral Biblical Dictionary of Theology*, ed. Carroll Stuhlmueller, C.P. (Collegeville: The Liturgical Press, 1996), 216.

[9]*Days of the Lord,* Vol. 7 (Collegeville: The Liturgical Press, 1994), 159.

John reminds us that we must prepare the way for Christ to come into our hearts and to the hearts of all people everywhere. He invites us to become evangelists. John reminds us that we are to preach the good news and repent. He invites us to share the gospel and to change our lives. John reminds us that we are to give of our life-blood in pursuit of the gospel way of life. He invites us to become martyrs. John is our model who reaches out his hand and invites us to follow him, if we dare!

Proclaim the gospel again.

Sometimes we gain new insights when we hear the text after the interpretation has been given. Someone from the group proclaims the gospel a second time.

STEP 4
TESTING

Conversation with the Liturgy and the Scriptures

Test your original understanding in dialogue with the text.

(You might consider breaking into smaller groups.)

How does your original understanding of this story compare with what was just shared? How does this story speak to your life?

Participants share an experience from their lives that connects with the biblical interpretation just shared.

How does this liturgy challenge our community? How does it challenge me? Has our original understanding been stretched, challenged, or affirmed?

STEP 5
DECISION

The gospel demands a response.

In what way does this gospel call your parish to action in the church, parish, neighborhood, or world? Be concrete. Has this conversation with the exegesis of this liturgy changed or stretched your personal attitudes? Name one concrete action you will take this week as a response to what was learned and shared today.

DOCTRINAL ISSUES

What church truth/teaching/doctrinal issue could be drawn from the gospel for the Solemnity of the Birth of John the Baptist?

Participants suggest possible doctrinal themes that flow from the readings.

Possible Doctrinal Themes

Conversion, christology, repentance

Present the doctrinal material at this time.

1. The facilitator gives input on a particular doctrinal issue of his/her prior choosing. OR
2. The group chooses a doctrinal issue from the list they created. They read together from the Doctrinal Appendix.

(The doctrinal issues are found in the Doctrinal Appendix in the back of this workbook. If you are choosing an issue from this resource, please refer to it now.)

Reflection questions centered around the chosen doctrinal theme can be found at the end of each topic in the Doctrinal Appendix. The questions are based on the five-step reflection process. If you choose a topic not included in the Doctrinal Appendix, craft your own questions according to the same five-step process.

Following the reflection questions you will be reminded to return to chapter 7, "Preparing the Catechetical Session," to assist you in crafting your own session.

Closing Prayer

God our Father,
the voice of John the Baptist challenges us to repentance
and points the way to Christ the Lord.
Open our ears to hear his message,

and free our hearts
to turn from our sins and receive the life of the gospel.
We ask this through Christ our Lord.[10]

Selected Bibliography

Adam, Adolf. *The Liturgical Year.* Trans. Matthew J. O'Connell. Collegeville: The Liturgical Press, 1990.

Days of the Lord. Vol. 7. Collegeville: The Liturgical Press, 1994.

LaVerdiere, Eugene, S.S.S. *Luke.* Wilmington: Michael Glazier, 1980.

Reid, Barbara E. *Choosing the Better Part? Women in the Gospel of Luke.* Collegeville: The Liturgical Press, 1996.

Tannehill, Robert C. *The Narrative Unity of Luke-Acts: A Literary Interpretation.* Vol. 2. Minneapolis: Augsburg Fortress, 1990.

---

[10]Birth of John the Baptist: "Alternative Opening Prayer," *The Sacramentary.*

SOLEMNITY OF PETER AND PAUL, APOSTLES (JUNE 29)

INTRODUCTORY RITES

Opening Song (or Entrance Antiphon)

These men, conquering all human frailty, shed their blood and helped the Church to grow. By sharing the cup of the Lord's suffering, they became the friends of God.[1]

Opening Prayer

The facilitator of the session may lead the prayer. Others in the group may be asked to proclaim the readings.

Let us pray
[that we may remain true to the faith of the apostles]

   Pause for silent prayer.

God our Father,
today you give us the joy
of celebrating the feast of the apostles Peter and
    Paul.
Through them your Church first received the
    faith.
Keep us true to their teaching.
Grant this through our Lord Jesus Christ, your
    Son,
who lives and reigns with you and the Holy Spirit,
one God for ever and ever.[2]

LITURGY OF THE WORD

Let us listen to God's word.

The readings are proclaimed.

First Reading
Acts 12:1-11

Today's story of Peter's rescue from prison has a deeper significance than that which appears at first glance. It is a story that is reminiscent of other biblical stories of divine rescue. As such, it has a higher purpose than just relating the events of this particular story. "It [the story] recalls the power of God to rescue those chosen for God's mission, a power repeatedly demonstrated in the past."[3]

We are reminded of past events in which there is rescue from evil rulers. Peter's arrest is similar to Jesus' arrest in Luke 22:54. The reference to Passover is intentional. The reader is to make a parallel connection between Jesus' passion story and the story at hand. Jesus' disciples are experiencing the fate he assured them they would endure.

The Passover allusion also serves as a reminder of another past event, the exodus out of bondage in Egypt. The reader is asked to look below the surface for another type of exodus rescue, suggests Robert Tannehill. Peter's language in the later telling of his rescue is laced with exodus language: the Lord "rescued me from the hand of Herod." The command of the angel for Peter to rise and gird himself is reminiscent of the command to the Israelites to eat the Passover with their loins girded and sandals on their feet (Ex 12:11). The rescue of Peter serves as an exodus parable. "For the Church, it is still the time of the Exodus. During the night of this world, it prays with confidence, remembering the pasch of Christ and giving thanks for the marvels God has accomplished, including thanksgiving ahead of time for the crowning marvel: when Christ himself, and no longer an angel, will come back to 'snatch her finally and forever from the hands of all her enemies.'"[4]

Responsorial Psalm
Psalm 34:2-3, 4-5, 6-7, 8-9

---

[1] Peter and Paul, Apostles: "Entrance Antiphon," *The Sacramentary.*

[2] Peter and Paul, Apostles: "Opening Prayer," *The Sacramentary.*

[3] Robert C. Tannehill, *The Narrative Unity of Luke-Acts: A Literary Interpretation,* Vol. 2 (Minneapolis: Augsburg Fortress, 1986), 151.

[4] *Days of the Lord,* Vol. 7 (Collegeville: The Liturgical Press, 1994), 176.

Second Reading
2 Timothy 4:6-8, 17-18

Paul's second letter to Timothy is in the genre of a farewell discourse and exhortation. It is generally believed that Paul was not the author of this letter and that it was written somewhere near the second century. It is further believed that the letter contains fragments of Paul's original words. Those authentic fragments are believed to be the words of today's second reading. Paul is awaiting death from his prison cell as he writes to Timothy. (Please refer to Twenty-Seventh Sunday in Ordinary Time for further background information on 2 Timothy.) "Although he feels close to death (4:6-8), he writes to encourage and admonish his favorite delegate in *his* struggles."[5] *Life poured out like a libation* is language indicative of Greek thought. Libations of wine and oil were often associated with the Jewish liturgy of offering sacrifice. They were also used by the Greeks and the Romans. Wine was poured on the ground in homage to gods at banquets and festive occasions. Paul adapted the pagan notion as an image of his own life, being poured out in sacrifice for the sake of others.

When Paul mentioned that he had kept the faith (v. 7), he meant that through the witness of his life and adherence to the doctrine of Christ crucified, he endured in spite of persecution.

There is no new word for Timothy in this letter; it is simply a reiteration of what Timothy already knows and holds to be true. Paul challenges Timothy to remain steadfast to what he already knows.

In this fourth chapter of second Timothy, Paul presents himself as the model of suffering in hope. In spite of being opposed, Paul had remained strong in his ministry. Timothy is thus exhorted to remain steadfast through suffering and adherence to the gospel, just like Paul. Hope resonates through Paul's encouragement to Timothy. Paul is assured of God's love, God's reign, and God's protection until such time as he is taken safely to the heavenly reign. Paul would win the crown (an olive, laurel, or pine branch wreath was awarded to athletes at the end of a great feat of

endurance) through his participation in Jesus' suffering, death, resurrection, and subsequent victory over evil.

In the second part of today's pericope, Paul speaks of a *first hearing* that no doubt functioned like an arraignment to determine if charges would be leveled. It appears that no one came to Paul's defense at this first hearing. Some scholars suggest that the absence of support by Paul's Christian brothers and sisters might have been due in part to the Roman church's concerns about his orthodoxy. Paul assures Timothy that, with or without their support, Jesus was with him to strengthen and uphold, *to stand by his side and give him strength* (v. 17)

Gospel
Matthew 16:13-19

Peter confesses faith at Caesarea Philippi.

STEP 1
NAMING ONE'S EXPERIENCE

What were your first impressions? What was your first response? What grabbed your attention? How did you feel?

Each person names his or her initial impression. Statement should be brief. No reasons should be given at this time. All simply listen without agreeing or disagreeing.

STEP 2
UNDERSTANDING

In a brief statement, what do you think this gospel is trying to convey?

STEP 3
INPUT FROM VISION/STORY/TRADITION

Liturgical Context

The apostles, those first eyewitnesses to the Jesus event, were paid great homage by the early Christ-

---

[5] Luke Timothy Johnson, *The Writings of the New Testament* (Minneapolis: Augsburg Fortress, 1986), 391.

ian church. Christ hand-picked them to carry out his mission of salvation to the world. He empowered the first apostles, particularly Peter, to form, strengthen, and build the church. They were the foundation upon which the future church would be built. The early community venerated these noble saints as evidenced by the devotion of Constantine who built a church in their honor.

Origins of a feast commemorating the apostles can be traced to the East where all twelve apostles were remembered in a single feast. Individual feasts were primarily celebrated in places where the tomb of each apostle was located or in places connected with memories of certain apostles.

The two great apostles, Peter and Paul, were martyred in Rome by Nero (54–68). Paul was beheaded and Peter was crucified. Even though there is nothing to suggest that these two martyrdoms occurred simultaneously, both apostles have been remembered on the same day since the mid-third century.

Three liturgies were celebrated in Rome on this feast. Peter was commemorated at a special liturgy celebrated on Vatican Hill in the church that was named after him. Paul was honored in a liturgy on the road to Ostia at St. Paul Outside the Walls. A liturgy commemorating both apostles was celebrated at the "catacombs" (near the present-day St. Sebastian's. It is believed that this is where their bodies or their heads were kept during the persecution of Valerian). Observance of three liturgies posed a hardship for the church of the eighth century, so St. Paul's feast was moved to the next day, even though he was still remembered on June 29. However, the revised Roman calendar removed Paul's feast from the calendar (June 30) except in the place that honors his name: The Roman Basilica of St. Paul.

By the third century, a feast commemorating both apostles extended to the church in Italy and North Africa. By the fifth century most Eastern and Western countries held similar observances. St. Ambrose attested to a vigil observance as early as 397.

The revised Roman calendar maintained the vigil as a mass for the evening preceding the solemnity.

Some ritual texts such as the entrance antiphon, the second reading, the presidential prayers, and the preface are new. The opening prayer reminds us that it was through the apostles that the church received her initial faith. We ask for the strength to remain faithful to their teaching. The preface reminds us that each apostle was chosen to gather the church in unity, Peter as its fearless leader and Paul as its gifted preacher. We are reminded of the price each paid for his call to ministry. We too are called to lead and to preach the word of God by the action of our lives. Paul and Peter serve as models of faithful service.

> Father, all-powerful and ever-living God,
> we do well always and everywhere to give you thanks.
> You fill our hearts with joy
> as we honor your great apostles:
> Peter, our leader in faith,
> and Paul, its fearless preacher.
> Peter raised up the Church
> from the faithful flock of Israel.
> Paul brought your call to the nations,
> and became the teacher of the world.
> Each in his chosen way gathered into unity
> the one family of Christ.
> Both shared a martyr's death
> and are praised throughout the world.
> Now, with the apostles and all the angels and saints,
> we praise you for ever:
> Holy, holy, holy Lord, God of power might,
> heaven and earth are full of your glory.
> Hosanna in the highest.
> Blessed is he who comes in the name of the Lord.
> Hosanna in the highest.[6]

We continue to ask for their prayers in the ongoing ministry of word and sacrament in today's church reflected in the prayer over the gifts: "Lord, may your apostles join their prayers to our offering and help us to celebrate this sacrifice in love and unity."[7] We further ask that we be united in love through the breaking of bread in the sacrament of eucharist and through the teaching of the

---

[6]Peter and Paul, Apostles: "Preface," *The Sacramentary.*

[7]Peter and Paul, Apostles: "Prayer Over the Gifts," *The Sacramentary.*

apostles. We are confident that the church will be renewed through our participation in the eucharist and through listening and responding to the teaching of the apostles:

Lord,
renew the life of your Church
with the power of this sacrament.
May the breaking of bread
and the teaching of the apostles
keep us united in your love.
We ask this through Christ our Lord.[8]

The celebration of this solemnity reminds us of the church's two-fold dimension: one and universal. Peter and Paul represent the diversity of ministries to further the mission of Christ on earth. "Peter and Paul are the two pillars of the Church, the one the shepherd of Christ's flock who governs from his 'chair' at Rome, the other the missionary, the 'Apostle of Nations' who went all over the world to found ecclesial communities everywhere and to strengthen, in the course of his apostolic journeys, those he had already established."[9]

Gospel Exegesis

The facilitator gives input regarding what critical biblical scholarship has to say about this text. The input includes insights as to how people would have heard the gospel in Jesus' time.

Peter's confession of faith, Jesus' pronouncement of the rigors of discipleship, and the envisioning of the transfiguration are turning points in Jesus' ministry in all three synoptic gospels. Matthew, however, adds the investiture of Peter by Jesus as leader and rock of the church.

Jesus asked the ultimate question of his disciples: "Who do you say that I am?" In answering they would profess faith in him. Peter's insight was astounding as he answered for the whole church. Jesus was overwhelmed at Peter's insight and praised his Father for revealing this truth to one with such childlike faith. Peter professed the faith of the church and was given the keys of the kingdom of God. Until the master's return, the keys

will safeguard and protect the Master's property. When Jesus gave Peter the keys, it was a symbol of confidence. He was handing over his property for Peter. As new master of the house, Peter was to lead as a servant and steward. The apostles were fully aware that they would be held accountable for their management of the property in the master's absence. "They were given their authority only for the service of their brethren (John 13:13-17)."[10]

Jesus, as head of the kingdom, or household, exercises authority in God's name. Jesus passes authority on to the church to "mediate salvation in the time between the earthly ministry of Jesus and the future coming of the kingdom."[11]

Enormous authority is given to Peter. Citing R. H. Hiers and J. Jeremias, Benedict Viviano maintains that according to rabbinic legislation, binding and loosing may refer to exorcism of the devil, "to the juridical acts of excommunication and of definitive decision-making (a form of teaching through legislation, policy setting)."[12] The disciples are given the authority to bind and loose in verse 18, but only Peter is the foundation and only Peter is given the keys.

In the gospel of Thomas, James, the leader of the Jewish Christians, was afforded a special role of leadership. The Gentile Christians would have preferred to have had Paul named as their foundational leader. Thus, the ecumenically sensitive Matthew named Peter as the rock, thus holding both communities together in peaceful, delicate balance. It was, after all, Peter who served as spokesman for Jesus in his earthly ministry. Peter may be the keeper of the keys, but in Matthew's ecclesiology, Christ is always present in the whole church and through the power of the Holy Spirit continues to guide the church as she waits for Jesus' return.

The apostles were stewards of Christ's salvation and servants of God's servants. Even though their ministries and their personalities were different,

---

[8]Peter and Paul, Apostles: "Prayer After Communion," *The Sacramentary*.

[9]*Days of the Lord*, Vol. 7, 162.

[10]Ibid., 181.

[11]Benedict T. Viviano, O.P., "The Gospel of Matthew," in *The New Jerome Biblical Commentary*, ed. Raymond E. Brown, S.S., Joseph A. Fitzmyer, S.J., Roland E. Murphy, O.Carm. (Englewood Cliffs: Prentice Hall, 1990), 659.

[12]Ibid.

Peter and Paul had similarities. Peter denied Jesus; Paul persecuted him through his disciples. Peter was generous, presumptuous, often hesitant but steadfastly loyal. Paul was a proud Roman citizen who demanded his rightful title of apostle and owned his own fragility. Peter was loyal to the institution, but was not afraid to be challenged by the Spirit. Paul evangelized to the nations, but was resisted by his own people. Both were martyrs and gave their lives for the Christ they adored and served with ardent passion. We are to do no less.

Proclaim the gospel again.

Sometimes we gain new insights when we hear the text after the interpretation has been given. Someone from the group proclaims the gospel a second time.

STEP 4
TESTING

Conversation with the Liturgy and the Scriptures

Test your original understanding in dialogue with the text.

(You might consider breaking into smaller groups.)

How does your original understanding of this story compare with what was just shared? How does this story speak to your life?

Participants share an experience from their lives that connects with the biblical interpretation just shared.

How does this liturgy challenge your community? How does it challenge you? Has your original understanding been stretched, challenged, or affirmed?

STEP 5
DECISION

The gospel demands a response.

In what way does this gospel call your parish to action in the church, parish, neighborhood, or world? Be concrete. Has this conversation with the exegesis of this liturgy changed or stretched your personal attitudes? Name one concrete action you will take this week as a response to what was learned and shared today.

DOCTRINAL ISSUES

What church truth/teaching/doctrinal issue could be drawn from the gospel for the Solemnity of Peter and Paul, Apostles?

Participants suggest possible doctrinal themes that flow from the readings.

Possible Doctrinal Themes

Discipleship, apostleship, reign of God, martyrdom, the mystery of the church

Present the doctrinal material at this time.

1. The facilitator gives input on a particular doctrinal issue of his/her prior choosing. OR
2. The group chooses a doctrinal issue from the list they created. They read together from the Doctrinal Appendix.

(The doctrinal issues are found in the Doctrinal Appendix in the back of this workbook. If you are choosing an issue from this resource, please refer to it now.)

Reflection questions centered around the chosen doctrinal theme can be found at the end of each topic in the Doctrinal Appendix. The questions are based on the five-step reflection process. If you choose a topic not included in the Doctrinal Appendix, craft your own questions according to the same five-step process.

Following the reflection questions you will be reminded to return to chapter 7, "Preparing the Catechetical Session," to assist you in crafting your own session.

Closing Prayer

Let us pray
[one with Peter and Paul in our faith in Christ the Son of the living God]

Pause for silent prayer.

Praise to you, the God and Father of our Lord
    Jesus Christ,
who in your great mercy
have given us new birth and hope
through the power of Christ's resurrection.
Through the prayers of the apostles Peter and Paul
may we who received this faith through their
    preaching
share their joy in following the Lord
to the unfading inheritance
reserved for us in heaven.
We ask this in the name of Jesus the Lord.[13]

OR

The Lord has set you firm within his Church,
which he built upon the rock of Peter's faith.
May he bless you with a faith that never falters.
    (Amen.)

The Lord has given you knowledge of the faith
through the labors and preaching of St. Paul.
May his example inspire you to lead others to
    Christ
by the manner of your life. (Amen.)

May the keys of Peter, and the words of Paul,
their undying witness and their prayers,
lead you to the joy of that eternal home
which Peter gained by his cross, and Paul by the
    sword. (Amen.)[14]

Selected Bibliography

Adam, Adolf. *The Liturgical Year.* Trans. Matthew J.
    O'Connell. Collegeville: The Liturgical Press,
    1990.
Crosby, Michael H. *House of Disciples.* Maryknoll:
    Orbis Books, 1988.
Days of the Lord. Vol. 7. Collegeville: The Liturgical
    Press, 1994.
Johnson, Luke Timothy. *The Writings of the New Tes-
tament.* Minneapolis: Augsburg Fortress, 1986.
Tannehill, Robert C. *The Narrative Unity of Luke-
Acts: A Literary Interpretation.* Vol. 2. Minneapo-
lis: Augsburg Fortress, 1986.
Viviano, Benedict T., O.P. "The Gospel of
    Matthew." In *The New Jerome Biblical Commen-
tary.* Ed. Raymond E. Brown, S.S., Joseph A.
Fitzmyer, S.J., Roland E. Murphy, O.Carm. En-
glewood Cliffs: Prentice Hall, 1990.

---

[13]Peter and Paul, Apostles: "Alternative Opening Prayer,"
The Sacramentary.

[14]Peter and Paul, Apostles: "Solemn Blessing," *The Sacramentary.*

FEAST OF THE TRANSFIGURATION (AUGUST 6)

INTRODUCTORY RITES

Opening Song (or Entrance Antiphon)

In the shining cloud the Spirit is seen; from it the voice of the Father is heard: This is my Son, my beloved, in whom is all my delight. Listen to him. (See Mt 17:5)[1] (Or sung psalm or song)

Opening Prayer

The facilitator of the session may lead the prayer. Others in the group may be asked to proclaim the readings.

Let us pray
[that we may hear the Lord Jesus
and share his everlasting life]

Pause for silent prayer.

God our Father,
in the transfigured glory of Christ your Son,
you strengthen our faith
by confirming the witness of your prophets,
and show us the splendor of your beloved sons
    and daughters.
As we listen to the voice of your Son,
help us to become heirs to eternal life with him
who lives and reigns with you and the Holy
    Spirit,
one God, for ever and ever.[2]

LITURGY OF THE WORD

Let us listen to God's word.

The readings are proclaimed.

First Reading
Daniel 7:9-10, 13-14

The prophet is not a fortune teller. He proclaims what he hears, but even he does not fully under-

stand all there is to know about the word he has been given. With time and the passage of events, the meaning becomes clearer. The prophet and his contemporaries do not necessarily see the prophetic word as foretelling specific future events.

Often it is only hindsight that gives meaning to the biblical prophecy. The New Testament uses much of Hebrew prophecy in that way. A past prophecy helps explain the meaning of present events. Daniel's vision helps explain the full implications of what the disciples witnessed on Mount Tabor.

The church often chooses scripture in her liturgy to shed light on specific mysteries. She does not give new meaning to the texts, but she uses them to further reveal the meaning of an event, feast, or specific celebration. Jesus, the Son of Man, is the *One* Daniel heralds in his vision.

In Daniel's vision the people of God are living in the midst of persecution and oppression. To all appearances, God appears to be powerless. An ageless, ancient personage takes his place on the throne. His white hair and garment give him a radiant brilliance. All attend to this magnificent person as he passes judgment on the good and the evil. Then another person appears, one like a son of man, who has been given authority over all the earth. The Ancient One gives this person everlasting authority. The term "son of man" originally referred to every member of the human race. It eventually came to refer to a perfect man, who was an image of God and was representative of the entire human race. This new man, unlike Adam, originates from heaven. Jesus is understood in the New Testament as this Son of Man. Jesus, the Son of Man, will establish the reign Daniel proclaims in this first reading. Jesus, Son of Man, does have dominion over all the earth. Jesus' reign is everlasting and the entire world bows before him.

Responsorial Psalm
Psalm 97:1-2, 5-6, 9

The Lord is king, the most high over all the earth.

---

[1] Feast of the Transfiguration: "Entrance Antiphon," *The Sacramentary.*

[2] Feast of the Transfiguration: "Opening Prayer," *The Sacramentary.*

Second Reading
2 Peter 1:16-19

Peter is exhorting his believers to embrace the message they have been given about Christ as an authentic and true word. It is a not a myth. Peter and the other disciples witnessed Jesus' glory themselves on top of Mount Tabor. The apostles experienced the presence of the risen Christ after his death. Their testimony is true and trustworthy. The church can count on their eyewitness account. The church's faith rests on the testimony of the apostles. The Christian professes belief in the resurrection and ascension into glory of Christ and understands it as an act of prophetic fulfillment. The gospel opens to us the meaning of past prophecy, but always points us to the future. Through his life, passion, death, and resurrection, Jesus fulfilled scripture and revealed to us its deepest meaning. Even though Christ was revealed in his glory on Tabor, we still await the final glory when all will stand with him in the light of heaven. We continue to wait for his final return but are sustained and nourished by the sacrament of Christ's word in the scripture and eucharist.

Gospel
Luke 9:28-36

Jesus is transfigured before their eyes.

STEP 1
NAMING ONE'S EXPERIENCE

What were your first impressions? What was your first response? What grabbed your attention? How did you feel?

Each person names his or her initial impression. Statement should be brief. No reasons should be given at this time. All simply listen without agreeing or disagreeing.

STEP 2
UNDERSTANDING

In a brief statement, what do you think this gospel is trying to convey?

STEP 3
INPUT FROM VISION/STORY/TRADITION

Liturgical Context

The foundation for this feast rests with the fact that all three versions of the event in the synoptic gospels agree on what happened. Early in Lent our eyes are turned toward Mount Tabor in order to prepare us to encounter the glory of Christ crucified during the Triduum. Now, forty days before the feast of the Triumph of the Cross, we are once again asked to reflect in similar fashion. We are reminded that through Christ's passion and death he entered into glory. Once again, on August 6, we are invited into the glory and brilliance of Easter that reminds us of our ultimate destiny and eschatological hope—a share in the glory of Christ.

This feast dates back to the fourth century in the East. The monks of the desert were the first to pay particular attention to the transfiguration event. They reflected upon the transfigured glory of Christ as part of their mystic spirituality.

An official feast was observed in Spain around the tenth century and rapidly spread due (it is believed) to a heightened interest in the sacred sites of the Holy Land. Abbot Peter the Venerable established the feast and wrote an office for it at Cluny. Calistus III instituted it in Rome before he became pope (1455-1458). It was placed in the calendar in 1457 in thanksgiving for the victory over the Turks the previous year by John of Capistrano and John Hunyadi.

We are reminded in the opening prayer that the transfigured glory of Christ was foretold by the prophets of old. We ask that as we listen to and grow in Christ we may become heirs to his promise. The prayer over the gifts reminds us that through the power of the resurrected, glorified Christ, the gifts of bread and wine are made holy, transformed and become his body and blood.

> Lord, by the transfiguration of your Son,
> make our gifts holy,
> and by his radiant glory free us from our sins.[3]

---

[3]Feast of the Transfiguration: "Prayer Over the Gifts," *The Sacramentary.*

The celebration of this liturgy serves as a further reminder that every eucharistic liturgy is participation in the passion, death, resurrection, and ascension into the glory of Christ. Thus, through the power of Christ in the eucharist we are changed to become more like him.

> Lord,
> you revealed the true radiance of Christ
> in the glory of his transfiguration.
> May the food we receive from heaven
> change us into his image.[4]

Gospel Exegesis

The facilitator gives input regarding what critical biblical scholarship has to say about this text. The input includes insights as to how people would have heard the gospel in Jesus' time.

Reginald Fuller maintains that there are three traditional ways to interpret the pericopes of the gospel: what actually happened, how the story was orally transmitted (understood) by the Christian community, and how the evangelist used the story. Fuller suggests a fourth way to understand the texts: *how they are interpreted and what they might mean to a gathered liturgical assembly.*

Fuller names the *givens* of this story: Jesus went up to the mountain after he broke off his ministry in Galilee. There was a change in plans. We are told of a trip to Jerusalem and the meaning of the trip. "The original meaning of the incident was that it inaugurated the final stage of the ministry."[5]

In light of Fuller's fourth level of understanding, one scholar suggests an interesting interpretation of the story. The following exegesis is based on Barbara Reid's proposed scenario and interpretation of the transfiguration.[6]

In Luke's version, Jesus went up the mountain *to pray.* Mark does not say why he went up the mountain. Jesus took Peter, James and John apart by

themselves (just as he did on the day of his agony in the garden). Prior to this event, Jesus had been healing, teaching, and experiencing success in his initial mission. Tension had been building during the journey section of Luke's gospel known as "on the road to Jerusalem."

Jesus' destination now becomes more evident. He is apprehensive about having to go to Jerusalem, but he faithfully forges onward. Jesus' instructions to the disciples intensify; his mission picks up in pace and urgency. Jesus passionately challenges his followers to understand the implications of his teaching.

Jerusalem was the headquarters of religious power and authority. If things were going to change, if his mission was going to bring about the change that needed to happen, then he would have to go to the seat of religious power and authority. There was no other way; he had to go to Jerusalem. Yet, there was still so much to do in Galilee; there were still so many people searching for God and for meaning in their lives. "Should I go, should I stay?" Perhaps these concerns weighed heavily on Jesus' heart. Perhaps he was wrestling with God over the direction of his mission. Jesus knew where to find his answer and his strength: in intimate prayer with his Father. He gathered three of his disciples and together they went up the mountain to pray. Traditionally, mountains are places of profound theophanies.

Perhaps Jesus' discernment sounded something like this:

Jesus: "My loving, compassionate Father, hear me. Help me discover your will. If I stay here, I can continue my ministry to your people: praying, healing, teaching, and exorcizing. Your people are broken. They are poor, hungry and dejected. They are oppressed by systems that keep them on the bottom with no hope to rise to the top. Your precious, broken children, those most in need of your love and consolation, are even oppressed by the very religious structures that should offer them your love, hope and consolation. I must do something. There is so much more to do, I must continue; I am not finished. Loving God, if I go to Jerusalem, it is over; they will kill me."

---

[4]Feast of the Transfiguration: "Prayer After Communion," *The Sacramentary.*

[5]Reginald H. Fuller, *Preaching the New Lectionary* (Collegeville: The Liturgical Press, 1974), 4.

[6]Barbara Reid, "The Gospel of Mark in the Liturgical Year," Workshop: Church of Our Saviour, October, 1996.

God: "But, Son, you have done all you can do here; you must go to the seat of power. You must go to Jerusalem. You will understand soon enough."

Enter Moses and Elijah on the scene. Scholars have two opinions about the appearance of these two characters in the transfiguration scene. One opinion refers to the ancient tradition that believed that Moses and Elijah did not die in the natural sense, but were *taken up* into the next life and would reappear before the inauguration of the messianic age. Thus, Moses and Elijah appeared on the mountain of transfiguration because they were the *heralds* of the messianic age that Jesus was about to initiate through his death and resurrection.

A second opinion regarding the appearance of Moses and Elijah centers around Israel's foundation: the law and the prophets. Jesus was the fulfilment of all the expectations of the law and the prophetic utterances of the prophets. Those who ascribe to this second theory suggest that the departure of Moses and Elijah from Mount Tabor signaled the arrival of the messianic age. Jesus would henceforth take up where the law and the prophets left off. Faith was now to be centered in Jesus Christ—not in the law and not in the prophets.[7]

Luke is the only evangelist that allows us to eavesdrop on the mountaintop conversation. Moses and Elijah speak of the *exodus* Jesus was about to experience in Jerusalem. "They appeared in glory and spoke of his *passage* which he was about to fulfil in Jerusalem." There are two different meanings to the word *passage* (Greek: *exodus*). One meaning is liberation and the other is death.

Luke does not use the word *transfiguration.* "His face *changed* in appearance." Jesus had an "a-ha" moment, the kind that knocks us off balance, makes us shake our head in incredulity and say, "Wow!" Jesus experienced an incredible insight, and it was *reflected on his face.* All of a sudden it all made sense—Jesus understood the big picture. Now he knew what needed to happen and why. His death was not the end of his mission, but the

fulfillment of it. His death meant liberation. He had to go to Jerusalem; it was the only way. His mission on earth was accomplished. There was nothing left for him to do. He had created a living legacy, a living memorial. Jesus had to die. He had to "give his life as a ransom for the many." Through his death, the gates of heaven would be opened and his ministry of healing and liberation would last forever. It made perfect sense.

Jesus' face had to change. The revelation was so profound, the *shekina* glory so great, that it was "written all over his face"! Profound revelation often accompanied a change in facial expression, such as when Hannah learned she would have a child (1 Sam 1). Some of the stories of early martyrs reflect a changed countenance on their faces. "The members of the Sanhedrin who sat there stared at him intently. Throughout, Stephen's face seemed like that of an angel" (Acts 6:15). In other instances we are told of martyrs who went to their day of victory cheerful and *bright of countenance.* Thus, from Luke's version of the transfiguration, it is possible to conclude that the theophany on Mount Tabor was for Jesus an encounter, a turning point, and the impetus to go forward to Jerusalem, to his ultimate death.

The secondary focus in the story of the transfiguration is the disciples. They are part of the story. They are witnesses to this epiphany. They see it on Jesus' face. Peter wants to pitch a tent, to stay there, to bask in the glory (how human!). Peter wants to stay on the mountain of glory. *The whole point of the story, however, is that we need to proceed to Jerusalem; we may not stay in Galilee.* The transfiguration was for the benefit of the disciples! Someday, when they needed it most, they would reflect back on the experience and remember. In moments when the decision to stay or to go would be hanging in the balance, they would remember this night. When staying would seem more comfortable than going, they would remember this night. *This transition moment, this turning point in Jesus' life and mission would be remembered and it would urge them onward.* Unfortunately, suggests Barbara Reid, the story was told, retold, and recast as a story of transfiguration rather than as a turning point.

The final scene in today's unfolding drama opens with the familiar voice from heaven telling the dis-

---

[7]Patricia Datchuck Sanchez, *The Word We Celebrate* (Kansas City: Sheed and Ward, 1989), 286.

ciples: "This is my beloved Son, my Chosen One, listen to him." The last time we heard that *Voice* was at Jesus' baptism by John in the Jordan. It was the Spirit, not John, who baptized Jesus in the Jordan, thereby establishing and empowering his mission. Following Jesus' baptism, the Spirit led him into the desert to be tested by the devil. Jesus' desert scene was for the purpose of discerning the scope of his mission. He discovered what his mission was intended to be—a reign of service, love and self-offering.

Today's gospel brings us full circle. We are brought back to memories of Jesus' baptism. With Moses, Elijah, and the disciples, we too encounter the *Voice*. We hear the same words that inaugurated Jesus' initial mission: "This is my beloved Son, listen to him." The *Voice* first spoke to Jesus at his baptism. Now the *Voice* speaks to Jesus' companions, the disciples. "This is what it means to be 'beloved Son.'" It means head for Jerusalem.

Luke allows us to be intimate viewers of Jesus' private moments of decision. We are present at Jesus' baptism when the Spirit inaugurates his mission and empowers his ministry. We are present in the desert as the Spirit leads Jesus through the temptations that will help him discern his mission. We are present at Tabor as Jesus encounters yet another moment of decision and commitment. We are invited into the privileged intimacy as Jesus is helped to understand his final fulfillment and the ultimate consequences of his faithful mission.

Jesus went to the mountain to pray and, in the process, discovered who he was. As he tasted his future glorification, the heavens opened and the Father's *Voice* cried out: "This is my beloved Son." It was an awakening for Jesus. For the first time in salvation history, the law (Moses) and the prophets (Elijah) came together to testify to the day of fulfillment and to profess to the world, "Jesus Christ is Lord!"

Luke very cleverly invites his readers into the intimacy. There are no detached bystanders. Being privy to such profound intimacy, we are invited to embrace the journey. Every Lent is a renewed invitation to embrace the journey.

Jesus would experience one more turning point—Gethsemane. Today's gospel is cast in the light of Gethsemane. There is little question that Gethsemane is a moment of decision. Perhaps Gethsemane shows us how we should read the transfiguration event. Similarities between the two stories suggest that Luke considered them to be related. At Gethsemane and at the transfiguration, Peter, James and John go with Jesus to pray. At both events the apostles are overcome with sleep, while Jesus prays.

At Gethsemane the question of God's will erupts.

Jesus: "Father, let this pass. Surely there must be some other way! However, let your will be done, not mine."

God: "My Son, what I *will* is the liberation of all my people. I will life, not death. I do not *will* your murder, I do not *will* your death, but I *do will* the liberation of my people. Go, do what you must do, be faithful to my *Word* as you have always been faithful. Your liberating death is necessary to the resurrection. The only way is through the cross."

Some scholars assert that God never willed Jesus' death. He could not will it. Jesus' death was an immoral, evil act. God would never will an evil act. Jesus was murdered; God does not will murder. However, God did will Jesus' faithfulness. His faithfulness ultimately led to the free offering of his life in death. Jesus' death is the result of the life and ministry that preceded it.

When we seek God, the joy of our encounter is reflected on our faces. What happened to Jesus also happens to us. What do our faces say to the world? Do our faces express the paradox? We, too, have those moments in which we have to face our decisions. They may not always be life and death situations; they may simply lead to a fork in the road. What road will we take: the road less traveled or the freeway at rush hour? Will our decisions be life giving for those most in need of liberation, or will they be self-serving?

Proclaim the gospel again.

Sometimes we gain new insights when we hear the text after the interpretation has been given. Someone from the group proclaims the gospel a second time.

STEP 4
TESTING

Conversation with the Liturgy and the Scriptures

Test your original understanding in dialogue with the text.
(You might consider breaking into smaller groups.)

How does your original understanding of this story compare with what was just shared? How does this story speak to your life?

Participants share an experience from their lives that connects with the biblical interpretation just shared.

How does this liturgy challenge your community? How does it challenge you? Has your original understanding been stretched, challenged, or affirmed?

STEP 5
DECISION

The gospel demands a response.

In what way does this gospel call your parish to action in the church, parish, neighborhood, or world? Be concrete. Has this conversation with the exegesis of this liturgy changed or stretched your personal attitudes? Name one concrete action you will take this week as a response to what was learned and shared today.

DOCTRINAL ISSUES

What church truth/teaching/doctrinal issue could be drawn from the gospel for feast of the Transfiguration?

Participants suggest possible doctrinal themes that flow from the readings.

Possible Doctrinal Themes

Christology, ascension, resurrection, paschal mystery

Present the doctrinal material at this time.

1. The facilitator gives input on a particular doctrinal issue of his/her prior choosing. OR
2. The group chooses a doctrinal issue from the list they created. They read together from the Doctrinal Appendix.

(The doctrinal issues are found in the Doctrinal Appendix in the back of this workbook. If you are choosing an issue from this resource, please refer to it now.)

Reflection questions centered around the chosen doctrinal theme can be found at the end of each topic in the Doctrinal Appendix. The questions are based on the five-step reflection process. If you choose a topic not included in the Doctrinal Appendix, craft your own questions according to the same five-step process.

Following the reflection questions you will be reminded to return to chapter 7, "Preparing the Catechetical Session," to assist you in crafting your own session.

Closing Prayer

Lord,
you revealed the true radiance of Christ
in the glory of his transfiguration.
May the food we receive from heaven
change us into his image.
We ask this in the name of Jesus.[8]

Selected Bibliography

Adam, Adolf. *The Liturgical Year.* Trans. Matthew J. O'Connell. Collegeville: The Liturgical Press, 1990.

Days of the Lord. Vol. 7. Collegeville: The Liturgical Press, 1994.

Fuller, Reginald H. *Preaching the New Lectionary.* Collegeville: The Liturgical Press, 1974.

Sanchez, Patricia Datchuck. *The Word We Celebrate.* Kansas City: Sheed and Ward, 1989.

---

[8]Feast of the Transfiguration: "Prayer After Communion," *The Sacramentary.*

SOLEMNITY OF THE ASSUMPTION (AUGUST 15)

INTRODUCTORY RITES

Opening Song (or Entrance Antiphon)

All honor to you, Mary! Today you were raised above the choirs of angels to lasting glory with Christ.[1]

Opening Prayer

The facilitator of the session may lead the prayer. Others in the group may be asked to proclaim the readings.

Let us pray
[that the Virgin Mary will help us with her prayers]

Pause for silent prayer.

Almighty God,
you gave a humble virgin
the privilege of being the mother of your Son,
and crowned her with the glory of heaven.
May the prayers of the Virgin Mary
bring us to the salvation of Christ
and raise us up to eternal life.
We ask this through our Lord Jesus Christ, your
    Son,
who lives and reigns with you and the Holy
    Spirit,
one God for ever and ever. [2]

LITURGY OF THE WORD

Let us listen to God's word.

The readings are proclaimed.

First Reading
Revelation 11:19; 12:1-6, 10

This eschatological reading reminds us of previ-ous prophets who spoke of Jerusalem's and the people's promised glory in the last days. The image of a woman in the pangs of childbirth emerges as a symbol of new life that can come to pass only in the fullness of time and only after enduring unavoidable pain.

It is tempting to think that Mary is the mother about to give birth to Christ, the child about to be born. However, the author was not thinking of Mary. Christ is about to come to birth in the lives of people. It is painful because it is accompanied by sorrow, persecution, and the daily struggle to persevere. The woman is a symbol of the church who exists in the midst of God's glory, yet nevertheless is bound to the struggles of this earthly sojourn. Christ protects and strengthens her as she passes from death to life.

Even though the author of Revelation was not referring to Mary in his vision, Christian tradition has always understood the woman as an image of Mary. The meaning is not changed, however. Mary is a symbol of the church who still gives birth to Christ in the lives of the faithful. "God willed this unique and marvelous divine motherhood to be the figure and exemplar of the fecundity of the virgin Church that also becomes a mother...the Church in the sacrament of baptism somehow continues Mary's virginal motherhood. We may offer one example of this teaching from our predecessor St. Leo the Great; in one of his Christmas sermons he says: '[Christ] placed in the baptismal font the source of his own origin in the womb of the Virgin: the power of the most high and the overshadowing of the water to give rebirth to the believer.'[3] And if we want to find the same idea in liturgical

---

[1] Vigil of the Assumption: "Entrance Antiphon," *The Sacramentary.*

[2] Vigil of the Assumption: "Opening Prayer," *The Sacramentary.*

[3] Leo the Great, *Tractatus* (In Nativitate Domini) 5: CCL 138, 123: SC 22 bis, 132; see also *Tractatus* (In Nativitate Domini) 1: CCL 138, 147; SC 22 bis, 178; *Tractatus* 63 (De Passione Domini) 6: CCL 138, 386; SC 74, 82. In *Documents on the Liturgy, 1963-1979: Conciliar, Papal and Curial Texts*, Section 4: Sanctoral Cycle: A. Mary (Collegeville: The Liturgical Press, 1982), 1213.

sources, we can cite the very beautiful *Illatio* [preface] of the Mozarabic liturgy: '[Mary] carried life in her womb; the Church, in the baptismal font. In the body of Mary Christ put on flesh; in the waters of the Church the baptized put on Christ.'[4]"[5]

Responsorial Psalm
Psalm 45:10, 11, 12, 16

The queen stands at your right hand, arrayed in gold.

Second Reading
1 Corinthians 15:20-26

There is no denying that Jesus rose from the dead. This is the core of our faith: Christ conquered death once and for all. Our salvation depends on it. All will live because of Christ, the "first fruit." When the first fruits of the harvest were offered, it was considered a sample of the entire harvest. Symbolically it was a rendering of the entire harvest to God. Thus, Christ offered himself completely for the human race. In that offering the entire human race was offered with him. Christ freed Adam's heirs from the stain of his sin. Christ's act of self surrender was definitive. His death and resurrection accomplished salvation for the entire world—once and for all. We still await the final day when he will return and establish his heavenly rule forever. We continue to remain vigilant until that last and final victory over death. When Jesus comes again, death will be no longer. In one last grand act, the human race will be resurrected into everlasting glory. Mary is a sign of the hope we all share as we await that great and glorious day.

Gospel
Luke 1:39-56

Mary sets out to see Elizabeth, the baby leaps in Mary's womb, and Mary proclaims the glory of God.

---

[4]M. Ferotin, *Le Liber Mozarabicus Sacramentorum* col. 56. In *Documents on the Liturgy 1963-1979: Conciliar, Papal and Curial Texts*, Section 4: Sanctoral Cycle: A. Mary (Collegeville: The Liturgical Press, 1982), 1213.

[5]*Documents on the Liturgy 1963-1979: Conciliar, Papal and Curial Texts*, Section 4: Sanctoral Cycle: A. Mary (Collegeville: The Liturgical Press, 1982), #19, #3917, p. 1213.

STEP 1
NAMING ONE'S EXPERIENCE

What were your first impressions? What was your first response? What grabbed your attention? How did you feel?

Each person names his or her initial impression. Statement should be brief. No reasons should be given at this time. All simply listen without agreeing or disagreeing.

STEP 2
UNDERSTANDING

In a brief statement, what do you think this gospel is trying to convey?

STEP 3
INPUT FROM VISION/STORY/TRADITION

Liturgical Context

Even after they had converted to Christianity, people who had formerly been pagans continued the practice of honoring their dead. They purged the paganism from their commemoration of dead ancestors by placing their memorial celebrations within the context of their faith in Christ and his resurrection. They sang hymns to Christ and eventually began the practice of gathering near the tombs of their ancestors on anniversaries of their death. If a person had been martyred, all gathered around his or her tomb to commemorate the anniversary of that person's death. These celebrations were eventually moved into the church. Commemoration of the most famous martyrs spread to the church at large.

Veneration of martyrs continued. Added to the list were those "confessors of faith," who had not spilt their blood, but had suffered prison, exile, or forced labor for the cause of Christianity. Virgins and mystics who had given their lives to the Lord's service of prayer and solitude were also included as persons to be venerated and remembered. A life of dedication and consecration was understood as a type of martyrdom. This is how the church's practice of venerating the saints evolved.

Mary's role in scripture seemed to end with the Pentecost event. We do not hear of her again. However, in 431 the third ecumenical council at Ephesus took action that resulted in the beginning of the cult of the Virgin Mary. The council declared that Christ was both God and man, refuting the teaching of Nestorius. Mary became the "Mother of God—Theotokos." Afterward, Pope Sixtus III (432-440) built a basilica in honor of the Mother of God—"St. Mary Major." The first liturgical observance centered around the feast of the Nativity both in the East and in the West.

There is evidence of apocryphal writings dating from the fourth century telling of Jesus' appearance to Mary two years after his ascension to tell her that she would soon be assumed into heaven. There were other apocryphal writings that spoke of Mary's death and of her being carried up to heaven.

The origin of this feast occurred in Jerusalem with a celebration that took place near the location where it is believed that Mary *rested* (*koimesis,* which in Greek means either rest of sleep or sleep of death) before entering Bethlehem. By the end of the fifth century the feast (Dormition of Mary) was celebrated at Gethsemane where Mary's tomb was venerated. The feast commemorated her death and entrance into heaven.

By the end of the sixth century this was made an obligatory feast in the East. The West celebrated a similar obligatory feast remembering her motherhood on January 1 in Rome. The August 15 date was established around the year 650 and the celebration centered around the glorification of the Virgin Mary. The term *dormition* was used until 770 when the word *assumption* appeared.

Since there were no authentic witnesses to the Marian events, the reticent church of the ninth century did not insist upon adherence to the doctrine of Mary's glorification. "For a long time the magisterium remains silent: It silently observes the dialogue between the intuitions of the 'lovers' of Mary and the reticence of the theologians, who re-

spect above all the witness of the word of God, including its silences."[6] There were, however, nearly twenty feasts devoted to Mary in the Roman Calendar.

The church took a stronger position with regard to Mary in 1854 when Pius IX defined the Dogma of the Immaculate Conception and in 1950 when Pius XII defined the Assumption. The new calendar promulgated by Paul VI arranged the Marian feasts according to their importance; the feasts were "integrated in a clear way into the mystery of salvation through Christ, the true object of Christian faith and worship."[7]

> On August 15 we celebrate the glorious Assumption of Mary into heaven. It is the festival honoring the fullness of blessedness that was her destiny, the glorification of her immaculate soul and virginal body that completely conformed her to the risen Christ. This is a celebration that offers to the Church and to all humanity an exemplar and a consoling message, teaching us the fulfillment of our highest hopes: their own future glorification is happily in store for all those whom Christ has made his own brothers and sisters by taking on their "flesh and blood" (Heb. 2:14, see Gal. 4:4). The solemnity of the Assumption is continued on into the celebration of the Queenship of Mary on the octave day. She who is enthroned next to the King of Ages is contemplated as the radiant Queen and interceding Mother. These then are the four solemnities [Immaculate Conception, Mary Mother of God, the Annunciation, and the Assumption of Mary] that in their high rank as liturgical celebrations bring out the main truths related to the simple handmaid of the Lord.[8]

[6]M. Bobichon, *Marie dans la nouvelle Liturgie de la Parole,* tome 1, Pâque nouvelle (Lyon: Chalet, 1971), 110. In *Days of the Lord,* Vol. 7 (Collegeville: The Liturgical Press, 1994), 202.

[7]*Days of the Lord,* Vol 7, 202.

[8]Paul VI, Apostolic Exhortation *Marialis cultus,* on rightly grounding and increasing Marian devotion, 2 February 1974: AAS 66 (1974) 113-168; Not 10 (1974) 153-197. In *Documents on the Liturgy, 1963-1979: Conciliar, Papal and Curial Texts,* Sec-

There are two masses for this solemnity: the vigil and the day of the feast. The vigil celebration focuses on "Mary's glory and her significance in the history of salvation. The Mother of our Savior, the Son of God, is already elevated to the glory of the elect, where she bears witness to the victory over death that will shine for all those who follow Christ, who hear the word of God and observe it."[9] The mass during the day reminds us of the self-offering of Mary and the foreshadowing of that same pasche in the church. Mary's joy at the birth of her Son is intimately connected to her sorrow at his death. The mass of the day celebrates Mary as the symbol of the church and a sign for all believers who journey toward their heavenly glory with Christ. Mary is a sign of hope for us all.

Gospel Exegesis

The facilitator gives input regarding what critical biblical scholarship has to say about this text. The input includes insights as to how people would have heard the gospel in Jesus' time.

Luke is not concerned with telling us a story about two pregnant relatives who meet one last time before their babies' birth. Nor is it a story that denotes Mary's concern and care for Elizabeth in her time of need. If that were the case, Luke would not have Mary departing when Elizabeth's need is obviously the greatest. Rather, through the literary devices inherent in storytelling, Luke provides a theology of God's plan of salvation through Jesus. The two mothers-to-be are gathered in praise of God for the work God is doing in and through them. In their gathering, the theological reality that John is the precursor of Jesus and that Jesus is the Savior who is superior to John is proclaimed. This is the point of the story.

There are four literary devices commonly used in Luke/Acts to illustrate God's plan. They are: previews and reviews, repeated or highlighted scriptural references, commission statements, and interpretive statements by reliable characters. Robert Tannehill suggests that there may be de-

tails in the story that review what God has already done in the past and preview what God is about to do, "in a way that interprets these events."[10] Through the birth stories of both John and Jesus, Luke previews what God intends for humanity's redemption. Through various images and words, the reader knows that reference is being made to God's plan revealed throughout the scriptures.

Through allusions to scriptural passages and traditions, the reader is shown that "the law and the prophets are fulfilled in Jesus."[11] These same passages also express a particular understanding of God's purpose and are programs for action.[12] For example, when Elizabeth tells us that the baby leapt in her womb, the reader is reminded of the leaping of Rebekah's twin children, Jacob and Esau. According to biblical tradition, leaping in-utero foreshadowed a future relationship and "symbolized destinies that would be lived out by the children."[13] In John's leaping we are previewing a future relationship between Jesus and John.[14] Through the power of the Holy Spirit, Elizabeth is able to interpret John's leaping. John leapt in Elizabeth's womb because the destiny of the world was being fulfilled in the baby within Mary's womb.

The third literary device is the agent, the chosen instrument, "reliable persons commissioned by God to carry out God's purpose."[15] In this story both Elizabeth and Mary are those instruments. Both have been obedient to the will of God and, as a result, both bring God's intended plan of redemption to birth in the world. In biblical tradition, Mary leaving in haste refers to an "interior disposition that makes one act with fervor and zeal."[16] Mary is understood as great because of the child she will bear and is praised because of her

tion 4: Sanctoral Cycle: A. Mary (Collegeville: The Liturgical Press, 1982), #3904, p. 1208.

[9]*Days of the Lord*, Vol. 7, 203-204.

[10]Robert C. Tannehill, *The Narrative Unity of Luke-Acts: A Literary Interpretation* (Minneapolis: Augsburg Fortress, 1986), 20-38.

[11]Ibid., 21.

[12]Ibid., 22.

[13]Patricia Datchuck Sanchez, *The Word We Celebrate* (Kansas City: Sheed and Ward, 1989), 272.

[14]Karris, Robert J., O.F.M., "The Gospel According to Luke," in *The New Jerome Biblical Commentary*, ed. Raymond E. Brown, S.S., Joseph A. Fitzmyer, S.J., Roland E. Murphy, O.Carm. (Englewood Cliffs: Prentice Hall, 1990), 681.

[15]Tannehill, *The Narrative Unity of Luke-Acts*, 21.

[16]*Days of the Lord*, Vol. 1 (Collegeville: The Liturgical Press, 1991), 158.

relationship to Christ. Mary's role is christological. She has a role in God's liberating plan for the human race.

The fourth literary technique is the commission, the call and mission of the individual in question. When Elizabeth says, "...blessed is the fruit of your womb. Who am I that the mother of my Lord should come to me?" she prophesies about the mission of the child in Mary's womb. This child will bring salvation. He will be the fulfillment of God's plan. Luke wants to make it clear that both John and Jesus have a unique role to play. John will prepare the way and will be the bridge between the old covenant and the new covenant. John will help prepare hearts for giving birth to the advent of the Messiah. Jesus, however, is that messiah. Jesus is the One who will fulfill Israel's hopes. Luke insists that his community have no illusions about "who's who" in the eschatological events about to take place.

Mary and Elizabeth, two great women of scripture, listen to God and become the ultimate paradigm of disciple. In this scriptural text Mary becomes the great gift and model for the church. She listens, she responds, she obeys with fervor and zeal the voice of God and she acts on that Word. We, too, are exhorted to "go in haste," to go with zeal and fervor to live the call of the gospel and to share the mighty news it contains. Mary models for us the perfect liturgy. She listens, she gives thanks and praise, she responds in faith to the Word of God, and then she goes in haste.

Proclaim the gospel again.

Sometimes we gain new insights when we hear the text after the interpretation has been given. Someone from the group proclaims the gospel a second time.

STEP 4
TESTING

Conversation with the Liturgy and the Scriptures

Test your original understanding in dialogue with the text.

(You might consider breaking into smaller groups.)

How does your original understanding of this story compare with what was just shared? How does this story speak to your life?

Participants share an experience from their lives that connects with the biblical interpretation just shared.

How does this liturgy challenge our community? How does it challenge me? Has our original understanding been stretched, challenged, or affirmed?

STEP 5
DECISION

The gospel demands a response.

In what way does this gospel call your parish to action in the church, parish, neighborhood, or world? Be concrete. Has this conversation with the exegesis of this liturgy changed or stretched your personal attitudes? Name one concrete action you will take this week as a response to what was learned and shared today.

DOCTRINAL ISSUES

What church truth/teaching/doctrinal issue could be drawn from the gospel for the Solemnity of the Assumption of Mary?

Participants suggest possible doctrinal themes that flow from the readings.

Possible Doctrinal Themes

Mary, Mother of God, the Assumption of Mary, Mary, symbol of the church

Present the doctrinal material at this time.

1. The facilitator gives input on a particular doctrinal issue of his/her prior choosing. OR
2. The group chooses a doctrinal issue from the list they created. They read together from the Doctrinal Appendix.

(The doctrinal issues are found in the Doctrinal Appendix in the back of this workbook. If you are choosing an issue from this resource, please refer to it now.)

Reflection questions centered around the chosen doctrinal theme can be found at the end of each topic in the Doctrinal Appendix. The questions are based on the five-step reflection process. If you choose a topic not included in the Doctrinal Appendix, craft your own questions according to the same five-step process.

Following the reflection questions you will be reminded to return to chapter 7, "Preparing the Catechetical Session," to assist you in crafting your own session.

Closing Prayer

Lord,
may we who receive this sacrament of salvation
be led to the glory of heaven
by the prayers of the Virgin Mary.
We ask this in the name of Jesus the Lord.[17]

Selected Bibliography

Adam, Adolf. *The Liturgical Year.* Trans. Matthew J. O'Connell. Collegeville: The Liturgical Press, 1990.

Days of the Lord. Vol. 7. Collegeville: The Liturgical Press, 1994.

Documents on the Liturgy, 1963-1979: Conciliar, Papal and Curial Texts. Collegeville: The Liturgical Press, 1982.

Karris, Robert J., O.F.M. "The Gospel According to Luke." In *The New Jerome Biblical Commentary.* Ed. Raymond E. Brown, S.S., Joseph A. Fitzmyer, S.J., Roland E. Murphy, O.Carm. Englewood Cliffs: Prentice Hall, 1990.

Sanchez, Patricia Datchuck. *The Word We Celebrate.* Kansas City: Sheed and Ward, 1989.

Tannehill, Robert C. *The Narrative Unity of Luke-Acts: A Literary Interpretation.* Minneapolis: Augsburg Fortress, 1986.

---

[17]Solemnity of the Assumption: "Prayer after Communion," *The Sacramentary.*

FEAST OF THE TRIUMPH OF THE CROSS (SEPTEMBER 14)

INTRODUCTORY RITES

Opening Song (or Entrance Antiphon)

We should glory in the cross of our Lord Jesus Christ, for he is our salvation, our life and our resurrection; through him we are saved and made free. (See Gal 6:14)[1]

Opening Prayer

The facilitator of the session may lead the prayer. Others in the group may be asked to proclaim the readings.

Let us pray
[that the death of Christ on the cross
will bring us to the glory of the
resurrection]

> *Pause for silent prayer.*

God our Father,
in obedience to you
your only Son accepted death on the cross
for the salvation of mankind.
We acknowledge the mystery of the cross on earth.
May we receive the gift of redemption in heaven.
We ask this through our Lord Jesus Christ, your
　　Son,
who lives and reigns with you and the Holy Spirit,
one God, for ever and ever.[2]

LITURGY OF THE WORD

Let us listen to God's word.

The readings are proclaimed.

First Reading
Numbers 21:4-9

The snake was a sign of danger, confusion and even wisdom. In mythology the snake was a sign of fertility and rebirth. If a person was bitten by a snake and remained unharmed, it was a sign of some sort of divine protection. All these images creep into the telling of today's story.

The scene is the desert following Israel's escape from Egypt. The cast includes Moses and the people of Israel. The situation centers around the amnesia of Israel. The people had forgotten all that God had done for them. They obnoxiously believed that God took them to the desert to let them die. God was angered by their lack of faith and sent serpents among them. Many people died from the sting of these serpents. The people understood this tragedy to be a result of and punishment for their sin.[3] They prayed to be delivered. God told them to take a pole and fashion a serpent on the top of it. All who looked at the pole would be healed.

The serpent episode is typical of God's relationship with Israel. Israel sinned. God punished. The people repented and were converted wholeheartedly to the Lord who was ready to forgive their sins. The Christian tradition connected this reading and the image of the bronze serpent with the cross of Christ. Christ, elevated on the cross, was a sign of healing, salvation, and forgiveness.

Responsorial Psalm
Psalm 78:1-2, 34-35, 36-37, 38

Do not forget the works of the Lord!

Second Reading
Philippians 2:6-11

It is believed that Paul inserted this beautiful, previously crafted hymn into his letter to the Philippians. Some consider it a perfect expression of Pauline theology regarding the passion and death of Jesus. This hymn was probably used in ancient Christian liturgies and profoundly captures the essence and the paradox of Christian redemption. Jesus, through abject humiliation (see Fourth Sun-

---

[1]Feast of the Triumph of the Cross: "Entrance Antiphon," *The Sacramentary.*

[2]Feast of the Triumph of the Cross: "Opening Prayer," *The Sacramentary.*

[3]Israel understood all life to be ordered by God. They understood all blessings to be a result of God's benevolence and all tragedy to be a result of God's anger.

day of Lent, Cycle C, parable of prodigal son), offered the free gift of himself. Through such humiliation, salvation was won. Jesus left his rightful throne with Yahweh, descended into the midst of humanity and took the form of a slave, subject to the suffering and limitations of the human person. He allowed himself to be rejected, misunderstood, and treated like a slave and a criminal. Because of this free gift of self, this abasement, Jesus ascended back to the throne victorious. Because of the resurrection, humanity was and is offered freedom from the ravages of sin and death, and the promise of eternal life. Jesus, the perfect servant, model of all perfect servants, earned the rightful title, Lord, *Kyrios* (Greek), *Adonai* (Hebrew).

Paul was addressing the dissensions and factions in the Philippian community. He pleaded that all assume the posture of Jesus. If they would only assume the model of Christ's self-abasement, then harmony and peace would be restored to the community. Jesus could have claimed all the rights and privileges of royalty. But he did not. "He became sin"; he entered the human condition with all its defects and in the process emptied himself. The Philippian community was exhorted to embrace *kenosis,* a voluntary emptying of oneself in the manner of Jesus. Paul challenged his community to assume the humble stance of self-giver rather than give in to the lure of power and control. Jesus, emptied and poured-out, went willingly to his passion and death. We are to follow in his footsteps.

Gospel
John 3:13-17

Jesus tells Nicodemus that the Son of Man must be lifted up.

STEP 1
NAMING ONE'S EXPERIENCE

What were your first impressions? What was your first response? What grabbed your attention? How did you feel?

Each person names his or her initial impression. Statement should be brief. No reasons should be given at this time. All simply listen without agreeing or disagreeing.

STEP 2
UNDERSTANDING

In a brief statement, what do you think this gospel is trying to convey?

STEP 3
INPUT FROM VISION/STORY/TRADITION

Liturgical Context

In the early days of the church the cross was simply considered Jesus' instrument of execution. As Christianity evolved it became a multivalent symbol. It came to symbolize Christ's sacrificial death as well as Christ himself. It was also understood as a sign of Christianity.

Veneration of the cross is evidenced by the fourth century. The cross of Christ was found by Empress Helena on September 14, 320. Five years later, on September 13, two churches were consecrated in honor of the cross—Martyrium (the Church of the Cross), and the Resurrection (the Church of the Anastasis). Helena's discovered cross was displayed and venerated by the faithful on the next day, September 14, 325. The solemn observance became an annual event. Constantinople observed a similar feast by the fifth century and Rome by the seventh century. Those churches that had major relics of the cross showed the relics to the faithful in a solemn celebration called the *Exaltatio* (lifting-up).

During the eighth century, the people of Gaul celebrated a feast honoring the cross on May 3. A relic of the cross was captured by the Persians. It was subsequently recovered and carried in triumphant procession into Jerusalem. Rome placed this observance in the calendar and erroneously called it "Discovery of the Holy Cross." The September 14 feast was called "The Exaltation of the Holy Cross." The September feast was incorrectly designated as the feast to honor the restoration of the cross. Pope John XXIII rectified the situation and removed the May 3 observance from the calendar. The original meaning was restored to the September 14 feast.

The entrance antiphon gives us the theme for today's liturgy: we are to glory in the cross, for it is our salvation. The liturgy celebrates the salvation won for humanity by the sacrifice of Christ on the cross. The preface makes the comparison between the cross of Christ and the tree of paradise that was ultimately the sign of sin and death.

The cross is a sign of our identity as Christians. We sign ourselves with the cross. Catechumens are traced with the cross as a sign of God's strength and incorporation into the life of Christ. We sign ourselves with the cross when we enter and leave church; when we begin every liturgical celebration; when we eat a meal; and when we go to bed and wake up in the morning. The cross is the sign of Christ and the sign of the Christian life.

There are forty days from the feast of the Transfiguration on August 6 to the feast of the Holy Cross on September 14. This was once a period of pilgrimage to welcome the autumn season.

Gospel Exegesis

The facilitator gives input regarding what critical biblical scholarship has to say about this text. The input includes insights as to how people would have heard the gospel in Jesus' time.

Jesus was to be lifted up, like the serpent of Moses, as a sign of healing and salvation. Through the sign of the cross all who believe in Jesus will inherit eternal life. The cross, then, becomes the throne of glory, not the tool of an executioner. John insists that Jesus was "lifted up" on the cross. He uses coronation language rather than execution language. John's gospel reads like a royal liturgy. The language of crucifixion sounds like the installation of royalty upon a throne. The king is lifted up and crowned triumphant upon the throne of the cross.

Jesus willingly and knowingly went to his death. He was in control. It was a horrible death, but the torturous details are not the point of the story. Jesus, Son of Man, God-Man, saved the world from his throne of the cross. Those who looked upon Moses' serpent were saved. Those who look to the cross of Christ, believe in its power to save, and conform their lives to its power are also saved.

We are not to forget the gravity of sin, its lure and its death-dealing consequences. But today's liturgy is a joyful reminder that the cross is our hope in the midst of our sinfulness. This feast, situated halfway between the Triduum's celebration of the passion, death, and resurrection of Christ and the end of the liturgical year, serves as a midyear reality check. Every day is an opportunity to join in the sacrifice of Christ on the cross. Every liturgy remembers and makes present its saving power. Today's liturgy is an invitation to model Christ's saving action in our everyday lives. Do we love to the point of self-sacrifice, to the point of dying on the cross of our own selfishness?

Proclaim the gospel again.

Sometimes we gain new insights when we hear the text after the interpretation has been given. Someone from the group proclaims the gospel a second time.

STEP 4
TESTING

Conversation with the Liturgy and the Scriptures

Test your original understanding in dialogue with the text.

(You might consider breaking into smaller groups.)

How does your original understanding of this story compare with what was just shared? How does this story speak to your life?

Participants share an experience from their lives that connects with the biblical interpretation just shared.

How does this liturgy challenge our community? How does it challenge me? Has our original understanding been stretched, challenged, or affirmed?

STEP 5
DECISION

The gospel demands a response.

In what way does this gospel call your parish to action in the church, parish, neighborhood, or world? Be concrete. Has this conversation with the exegesis of this liturgy changed or stretched your personal attitudes? Name one concrete action you will take this week as a response to what was learned and shared today.

DOCTRINAL ISSUES

What church truth/teaching/doctrinal issue could be drawn from the gospel for Triumph of the Cross?

Participants suggest possible doctrinal themes that flow from the readings.

Possible Doctrinal Themes

Cross, redemptive suffering, paschal mystery

Present the doctrinal material at this time.

1. The facilitator gives input on a particular doctrinal issue of his/her prior choosing. OR
2. The group chooses a doctrinal issue from the list they created. They read together from the Doctrinal Appendix.

(The doctrinal issues are found in the Doctrinal Appendix in the back of this workbook. If you are choosing an issue from this resource, please refer to it now.)

Reflection questions centered around the chosen doctrinal theme can be found at the end of each topic in the Doctrinal Appendix. The questions are based on the five-step reflection process. If you choose a topic not included in the Doctrinal Appendix, craft your own questions according to the same five-step process.

Following the reflection questions you will be reminded to return to chapter 7, "Preparing the Catechetical Session," to assist you in crafting your own session.

Closing Prayer

Lord,
may this sacrifice once offered on the cross

to take away the sins of the world
now free us from our sins.
We ask this through Christ our Lord.[4]

Selected Bibliography

Adam, Adolf. *The Liturgical Year.* Trans. Matthew J. O'Connell. Collegeville: The Liturgical Press, 1990.

Days of the Lord. Vol. 7. Collegeville: The Liturgical Press, 1994.

---

[4]Feast of the Triumph of the Cross: "Prayer Over the Gifts," *The Sacramentary.*

SOLEMNITY OF ALL SAINTS (NOVEMBER 1)

INTRODUCTORY RITES

Opening Song (or Entrance Antiphon)

Let us all rejoice in the Lord and keep a festival in honor of all the saints. Let us join with the angels in joyful praise to the Son of God.[1]

Opening Prayer

The facilitator of the session may lead the prayer. Others in the group may be asked to proclaim the readings.

Let us pray
[that the prayers of all the saints
will bring us forgiveness for our sins]

Pause for silent prayer.

Father, all powerful and ever-living God,
today we rejoice in the holy men and women
of every time and place.
May their prayers bring us your forgiveness and
    love.
We ask this through our Lord Jesus Christ, your Son,
who lives and reigns with you and the Holy Spirit,
one God for ever and ever. [2]

LITURGY OF THE WORD

Let us listen to God's word.

The readings are proclaimed.

First Reading
Revelation 7:2-4, 9-14

Christ, who is risen, exalted, and appears in glory, is the primary theme of the book of Revelation. After giving a word of encouragement to the seven churches, Christ reveals the turmoil that will take place in the great battle between good and evil at the end of time.

Today's liturgy celebrates the joy of martyrs who share Christ's glorification. They shared in Christ's passion through their martyrdom. This is John's second vision in which there is a large gathering of people. In this vision, the number of people is beyond counting. The first vision was in reference to Israel. This vision refers to everyone—all nations. The palm fronds that are held by the assembled are a sign of victory.

The great trial referred to in this pericope is the tribulation that will come at the end of the age. During these latter days of tribulation, God's faithful will experience persecution. The robes represent the interior, spiritual disposition of the individual. The soiled robes represent sin and the clean robes represent holiness. This cleanliness is associated with the sacrificial death of Jesus. Through Jesus' death and resurrection, the robes (interior lives) are washed clean.

Baptism is the means through which the person is transformed, washed clean by the blood of the Lamb, and made holy. "The fundamental allusion here seems to be repentance, conversion, and baptism taken together as a transformation of the person."[3]

The image of the last tribulation or the trial is an exhortation to persevere in conversion and *metanoia*. Perseverance will give people the necessary means to endure and share in the salvation offered through Jesus' paschal mystery. Some of those who persevere will be called to martyrdom.

Responsorial Psalm
Psalm 24:1-6

Lord, this is the people that longs to see your face.

Second Reading
1 John 3:1-3

---

[1]Solemnity of All Saints: "Entrance Antiphon," *The Sacramentary.*

[2]Solemnity of All Saints: "Opening Prayer," *The Sacramentary.*

[3]Adela Yarbro Collins, "The Apocalypse (Revelation)," in *The New Jerome Biblical Commentary*, ed. Raymond E. Brown, S.S., Joseph A. Fitzmyer, S.J., Roland E. Murphy, O.Carm. (Englewood Cliffs: Prentice Hall, 1990), 1006.

John's favorite message is the love of God for his people. If we would only keep God's love in our consciousness, then we would convert our entire lives to God. The world will not understand. We are not to provoke persecution, but persecution will be ours. Without the eyes of faith, Jesus' identity is incomprehensible to the world. Through God's love we are made his children. As God's children we share his divine nature. Because we are God's children we will share his glory at the end of time.

Gospel
Matthew 5:1-12

Jesus gives us the blueprint for living in his reign: the beatitudes.

STEP 1
NAMING ONE'S EXPERIENCE

What were your first impressions? What was your first response? What grabbed your attention? How did you feel?

Each person names his or her initial impression. Statement should be brief. No reasons should be given at this time. All simply listen without agreeing or disagreeing.

STEP 2
UNDERSTANDING

In a brief statement, what do you think this gospel is trying to convey?

STEP 3
INPUT FROM VISION/STORY/TRADITION

Liturgical Context

During the fourth century, martyrs were remembered at a celebration. The day of the celebration was different in each of the churches. In Syria it was celebrated on May 13. In Antioch it was celebrated on the day after Pentecost. The Greek Orthodox still observe this day and call it "All Saints

Sunday." The Eastern Syrian liturgy observes the feast on the Friday after Easter.[4]

There is evidence that in Rome all three dates were observed. Pope Boniface IV accepted the Pantheon, a pagan temple, as a gift from Emperor Phocas. It was consecrated in honor of the Virgin Mary and martyrs on May 13, 609. Twenty-eight wagon loads of martyrs' bones were brought to the church from the catacombs. The pope named the feast assigned to May 13 the feast of All Saints.

In the eighth century in England and Ireland a feast in honor of All the Saints was celebrated on November 1. Pope Gregory IV gave permission to Louis the Pius, emperor of the West, to promulgate November 1 as the feast of "All Saints" for his entire kingdom. That date spread to the entire church and May 13 eventually disappeared. From the beginning the feast was assigned a vigil and by the fifteenth century an octave was also included. However, both vigil and octave were eliminated in the liturgical reform of 1955.

The feast remembers deceased friends, relatives, and ancestors who upon their death entered into heavenly glory. It also remembers the canonized saints. The liturgy seeks the intercessions of the saints who went before us. We ask that their prayers bring us forgiveness and love.

The feast also celebrates the Triune God who gathers the elect together in the courts of the heavenly Jerusalem to worship him. Every liturgy foreshadows our future participation in the heavenly banquet. This, however, is an extended meditation on the hope we celebrate. The praise and worship of God are at the center of this celebration.

Gospel Exegesis

The facilitator gives input regarding what critical biblical scholarship has to say about this text. The input includes insights as to how people would have heard the gospel in Jesus' time.

---

[4]Adolf Adam, *The Liturgical Year,* trans. Matthew J. O'Connell (Collegeville: The Liturgical Press, 1990), 228.

When Jesus returned from his ordeal in the desert, he went to Capernaum to announce the arrival of the messianic reign. He exhorted the people to repent. Jesus went up to a mountain and began to teach them. For Matthew, the mountain location was significant. It was a high place where human beings encounter divine authority. Moses went up the mountain to encounter God. Jesus, too, went up the mountain, the place of divine authority, and he sat down to teach the people. Matthew paints this picture with an exclamation point: he wants his audience to know that Jesus was speaking with the highest authority. He sat down to teach them as one who would rule from a royal throne.

Jesus began to exhort and encourage the people. In Jesus' reign, this is how it is to be. Jesus gives a blueprint for holiness. In a workshop given in 1995, Donald Senior noted that "The key to Matthew's gospel is that it is a call to doing things, not saying things." The sermon on the mount was a response to a crowd in need of healing. Matthew portrays Jesus as Teacher and Healer. Matthew's Jesus teaches for the transformation of people through the reign of God. Jesus' reign was not a future event, but a present reality.

There are four characteristics to the kingdom of God motif, says Senior.
1. soteriological: the kingdom is intended to rescue people from an intolerable situation.
2. theological: the kingdom reveals Israel's image of God. God cares enough to come and save Israel. God cares about the lives of the people.
3. eschatological: the final history is at hand.
4. community: the kingdom is a community effort. Individuals cannot experience the reign of God in isolation. Israel was a community. The transformation of our world was not an individual experience.[5]

Those who were listening to Jesus' message were experiencing the reign. The kingdom of God is

now! Jesus gives the Christian the blueprint for sainthood. As we await the future heavenly glory of the heavenly Jerusalem, we live in this earthly reality. Thus, we are to be meek and clean of heart. We are to thirst after justice and hunger for righteousness. All these things lead the saints of God on their way to their final resting place where they will join all those saints who went before them. Joachim Jeremias asserts that good gospel living is sign and symptom of what happens when grace seizes a child of God. Donald Senior takes it another step. "The Beatitudes are what happens when grace seizes a child of God."

Proclaim the gospel again.

Sometimes we gain new insights when we hear the text after the interpretation has been given. Someone from the group proclaims the gospel a second time.

STEP 4
TESTING

Conversation with the Liturgy and the Scriptures

Test your original understanding in dialogue with the text.

(You might consider breaking into smaller groups.)

How does your original understanding of this story compare with what was just shared? How does this story speak to your life?

Participants share an experience from their lives that connects with the biblical interpretation just shared.

How does this liturgy challenge our community? How does it challenge me? Has our original understanding been stretched, challenged, or affirmed?

STEP 5
DECISION

The gospel demands a response.

---

[5]Donald Senior, "Gospel of Matthew," Workshop, Church of Our Savior, Oct. 1995.

In what way does this gospel call your parish to action in the church, parish, neighborhood, or world? Be concrete. Has this conversation with the exegesis of this liturgy changed or stretched your personal attitudes? Name one concrete action you will take this week as a response to what was learned and shared today.

DOCTRINAL ISSUES

What church truth/teaching/doctrinal issue could be drawn from the gospel for the feast of All Saints?

Participants suggest possible doctrinal themes that flow from the readings.

Possible Doctrinal Themes

Saints, eschatology, kingdom of God, soteriology

Present the doctrinal material at this time.

1. The facilitator gives input on a particular doctrinal issue of his/her prior choosing. OR
2. The group chooses a doctrinal issue from the list they created. They read together from the Doctrinal Appendix.

(The doctrinal issues are found in the Doctrinal Appendix in the back of this workbook. If you are choosing an issue from this resource, please refer to it now.)

Reflection questions centered around the chosen doctrinal theme can be found at the end of each topic in the Doctrinal Appendix. The questions are based on the five-step reflection process. If you choose a topic not included in the Doctrinal Appendix, craft your own questions according to the same five-step process.

Following the reflection questions you will be reminded to return to chapter 7, "Preparing the Catechetical Session," to assist you in crafting your own session.

Closing Prayer

Father, holy one,
we praise your glory reflected in the saints.

May we who share at this table
be filled with your love
and prepared for the joy of your kingdom,
where Jesus is Lord for ever and ever.[6]

Selected Bibliography

Adam, Adolf. *The Liturgical Year.* Trans. Matthew J. O'Connell. Collegeville: The Liturgical Press, 1990.

Collins, Adela Yarbro. "The Apocalypse (Revelation)." In *The New Jerome Biblical Commentary.* Ed. Raymond E. Brown, S.S., Joseph A. Fitzmyer, S.J., Roland E. Murphy, O.Carm. Englewood Cliffs: Prentice Hall, 1990.

Days of the Lord. Vol. 7. Collegeville: The Liturgical Press, 1994.

------

[6]Solemnity of All Saints: "Prayer After Communion," *The Sacramentary.*

Feast of All Souls (November 2)

INTRODUCTORY RITES

Opening Song (or Entrance Antiphon)

Just as Jesus died and rose again, so will the Father bring with him those who have died in Jesus. Just as in Adam all men die, so in Christ all will be made alive. (1 Thess 4:14; 1 Cor 15:22)[1]

Opening Prayer

The facilitator of the session may lead the prayer. Others in the group may be asked to proclaim the readings.

Let us pray
[for all our departed brothers and sisters]

> *Pause for silent prayer.*

Merciful Father,
hear our prayers and console us.
As we renew our faith in your Son,
whom you raised from the dead,
strengthen our hope that all our departed brothers and sisters
will share in his resurrection,
who lives and reigns with you and the Holy Spirit,
one God, for ever and ever.[2]

LITURGY OF THE WORD

The Readings

There are no set readings for today's liturgy. The Lectionary refers us to the readings for the masses for the dead. Any of the readings from the vast repertoire may be chosen. The large number of readings shed light on and reflect the inexhaustible meaning of death. The scriptures tell the story of past communities who struggled with the pain of death and thereby appropriated meaning for their lives. The word of God is a living word that has relevance today as similar communities struggle with similar issues. Scriptures "demonstrate how revelation can and must be constantly read in light of everyday life and the thought of people of all races and cultures. In this way, Scripture appears as a powerful and sure contribution to progress of thought, offering always new perspectives and lighting up its way."[3]

With nearly fifty different scripture passages included in masses for the dead, there is not sufficient space to provide an exegesis for all of them. It is important, however, to be aware of their purpose.

The Old Testament readings reveal the mystery of death as understood by believers five centuries before the birth of Jesus. These readings reflect the yearnings, questions, and queries of believers of those ancient times, the answers they received, and the meaning they were able to appropriate from their searching inquiries. The same questions are still asked today. Reflection on the Old Testament readings helps us understand how our ancestors grappled with the same questions about death that we ask today.

The psalms provide us with a timeless prayer book. Centuries of previous generations have been strengthened, consoled, encouraged, and exhorted by their use. Jewish and Christian faith have been nourished by the psalms. The psalms are always relevant. They reflect the longing, aching, and supplication of the human heart. They speak in honest, direct, and frank terms. They are so filled with faith and trust that they hold us up when we are tempted to despair in the midst of sorrow and pain. The healing words of the psalms console us and give us the courage to speak to God in words that we might be afraid to utter. The psalms connect us with others who have cried the same tears and suffered the same anguish. They also give us the means of direct dialogue with a God who is with us in the struggles of our everyday life.

---

[1]All Souls Day: "Entrance Antiphon," *The Sacramentary.*
[2]All Souls Day: "Opening Prayer," *The Sacramentary.*

[3]*Days of the Lord*, Vol. 7 (Collegeville: The Liturgical Press, 1994), 260.

The New Testament writings include the Acts of the Apostles, the apostolic letters, and the book of Revelation. The Acts of the Apostles reflects the good news, the Christian kerygma, as proclaimed by the first Christian community. The apostolic letters are letters of encouragement written to early Christian communities who struggled with living the gospel in light of the Christ event. The letters were written to guide the faith of those first communities. The book of Revelation is a prophetic book that gives us a look at the last days and the fulfillment of the reign of Jesus Christ, the messiah. The New Testament readings in the masses for the dead are from these three literary genres. "Each one of these twenty-four texts takes up the central message of the preaching of the apostles while emphasizing one or more particular points, sometimes giving more concrete consequences of the basics of faith as proclaimed by the apostles."[4]

The gospels, beginning with Mark (ca. 64-69 C.E.) and ending with John (end of the first century), are witnesses to the life and mystery of Jesus Christ. They tell the story of his life, his teaching, and his saving actions. The evangelists were not seeking to produce historically accurate biographies, but rather to express the living faith of communities who experienced Christ and were brought to faith as a result of their experience. The gospel proclaims the good news of his life and mission. The one central message of the gospel is the paschal mystery: the life, passion, death, resurrection, ascension into glory and coming of the Spirit of Jesus Christ.

Jesus is the source of happiness. In the midst of despair, he is reason for hope. Jesus offers the human soul joy in the midst of suffering. Jesus came to save us all. He is the good shepherd who knows his sheep by name and gathers them all together to be with him. Jesus died and went to prepare a place for all of us who will one day join him and his Father in eternity.

Jesus broke the chains of death once and for all when he died on the cross. He understood death. Jesus knew that he had to die and that his death would bring about his glorification; yet he still suffered untold anguish. The human Christ gives the human race the hope to endure. Jesus suffered

---

[4]*Days of the Lord*, Vol. 7, 273.

and cried out. In our anguish we are consoled by the suffering Christ who conquered death in order for us to live eternally with him. The gospels for the masses for the dead express essential truths revealed either through Jesus' teaching or his actions. The mystery of death is laid before us and hope is placed in its path through reflection on the gospels for this day.

Liturgical Context

The pagans of antiquity kept memorials of dead relatives. Christians retained the practice of remembering their dead as long as it was consonant with their Christian faith. There is evidence of a celebration commemorating deceased relatives as early as the second century. The dead were prayed for and a mass was celebrated. The custom of the early church was to celebrate a remembrance of the deceased person three days after burial and on the one-year anniversary of the person's death. A later practice included an observance seven days following burial and then thirty and forty days after that.

In the seventh century, Bishop Isodore of Seville began a yearly commemoration of the souls of the dead. He ordered his monks to celebrate mass for this purpose on the day after Pentecost. By the ninth century the practice had spread and an office of the dead was added to the liturgy of the hours on the feast of All Saints.

In 998 "All Souls Day" was established when Abbot Odo of Cluny ordered that all monasteries celebrate a festal memorial of all the faithful departed. The practice spread but was not accepted in Rome until the thirteenth century.

Previously, if All Souls Day occurred on Sunday, the readings for the Sunday were given precedence. However, in the revised Roman Missal of 1970, the All Souls Day readings are given precedence. The missal provides three sets of prayers for this day. Each set contains an entrance antiphon, an opening prayer, a prayer over the gifts and a post-communion prayer. There are also five prefaces from which to choose.

This liturgy is intended to highlight the paschal nature of Christian death. The paschal mystery (the life, death, resurrection and ascension) of

Christ is the ultimate source of our hope. Previously used texts that hinted at the fear of God's judgment were replaced with texts that express Christian faith in the resurrection. The Easter pasch is at the heart of this celebration. All Souls Day celebrates the Christian's participation in the death and resurrection of Jesus. The entrance antiphon expresses this well: "Just as Jesus died and rose again, so will the Father bring with him all those who have died in Jesus. Just as in Adam all men die, so in Christ all will be made alive." We ask in the opening prayer that our hope be strengthened that our departed brothers and sisters will share in Christ's resurrection.

The ritual prayers reveal for us the church's perspective in relation to death, dying, and life after death. Any reflection on All Souls Day would necessarily require that the ritual texts from the liturgy of this day be prayed and reflected upon.

DOCTRINAL ISSUES

What church truth/teaching/doctrinal issue could be drawn from the celebration of All Souls Day?

Possible Doctrinal Themes

Death, eschatology, resurrection of the dead, heaven

Closing Prayer

Lord God,
may the death and resurrection of Christ
which we celebrate in this eucharist
bring the departed faithful to the peace of your
    eternal home.
We ask this in the name of Jesus.[5]

Selected Bibliography

Adam, Adolf. *The Liturgical Year.* Trans. Matthew J. O'Connell. Collegeville: The Liturgical Press, 1990.

Days of the Lord. Vol. 7. Collegeville: The Liturgical Press, 1994.

Sanchez, Patricia Datchuck. *The Word We Celebrate.* Kansas City: Sheed and Ward, 1989.

---

[5]All Souls Day: "Prayer After Communion," *The Sacramentary.*

FEAST OF THE DEDICATION OF THE BASILICA OF ST. JOHN LATERAN (NOVEMBER 9)

INTRODUCTORY RITES

Opening Song (or Entrance Antiphon)

Greatly to be feared is God in his sanctuary; he, the God of Israel, gives power and strength to his people. Blessed be God! (Ps 67:36)[1]

Opening Prayer

The facilitator of the session may lead the prayer. Others in the group may be asked to proclaim the readings.

God our Father,
from living stones, your chosen people,
you built an eternal temple to your glory.
Increase the spiritual gifts you have given to your
    Church,
so that your faithful people may continue to grow
into the new and eternal Jerusalem.
We ask this through our Lord Jesus Christ, your
    Son,
who lives and reigns with you and the Holy Spirit,
one God, for ever and ever.[2]

The Readings

The readings for today's liturgy are taken from the Commons of the Dedication of a Church.

Liturgical Context

The Basilica of St. John Lateran is the cathedral of the diocese of Rome. The pope is the bishop of this church. The name Lateran is derived from the reign of the Laterani family. The edict of Milan brought an end to persecution and Christianity became the official state religion. Older churches were refurbished and new ones were built. Emperor Constantine gave the Lateran palace and the surrounding property to the Church of Rome. He had a church built on the grounds in 324. On November 9 Pope Sylvester I dedicated the new basilica built on the site that had once housed the imperial guard. He dedicated the basilica to the Holy Redeemer. It was damaged by earthquakes in the fourth and especially the tenth centuries and was rebuilt by Sergius III (904-911).

Since the twelfth century the second titular patron of the basilica has been St. John the Baptist. Later, St. John the Evangelist was also associated with the basilica. This is why it is referred to as St. John Lateran.

The palace was the home of the bishop up until 1304 when Pope Benedict XI was forced to leave Rome because of political uprisings. His successors made Avignon their residence until 1377. During this time the Lateran palace was unused. During Nicholas V's term as pope, the church offices were moved to the Vatican. However, the Basilica of the Lateran has always been the cathedral church of the bishop of Rome, the pope. The basilica of the Lateran was damaged by fire in 1308 and again in 1361. Pope Benedict XIII consecrated it in 1726. It has since been under constant reconstruction and renovation. Clement XII (1730-1740) had an inscription placed on the basilica: this church is "Mother and Head of all the churches of the City and the world." The annual commemoration of the dedication spread throughout the church as a result of the efforts of the Augustinian hermits.

This feast holds great importance because the Basilica of St. John Lateran is the cathedral of the universal church. The cathedral is a symbol of the unity of the church gathered around its bishop. The bishop of Rome is responsible for the unity of his own diocese and the entire church. Thus, the cathedral of Rome has great significance for the entire church. "Celebrating the anniversary of the

---

[1]Common of the Dedication of a Church (A. In the Dedicated Church): "Entrance Antiphon," *The Sacramentary*.

[2]Common of the Dedication of a Church (B. Outside the Dedicated Church): "Opening Prayer A," *The Sacramentary*.

cathedral that is the mother of all others founded down through the ages is to celebrate the Lord, who founded his Church in order to gather together in unity, under the crozier of Peter and his successors, all the children of God, wherever they may live."[3]

The celebration of the anniversary of the dedication of the Lateran Basilica expresses the unity of all local parish churches with the universal Church of Rome, founded by Peter and Paul. The pope, as head of the college of bishops "presides over the charity of all the Churches throughout the world."[4]

Churches elegant and churches humble are living testament to the presence of God and the faith of those who built them. We are to remember that the people are the living stones upon which the church is built. It is the only church that will live on at the end of time—the church as people of God.

DOCTRINAL ISSUES

What church truth/teaching/doctrinal issue could be drawn from the gospel for feast of the Dedication of St. John Lateran?

Possible Doctrinal Themes

Mystery of the Church

Closing Prayer

Father,
you called your people to be your Church.
As we gather together in your name,
may we love, honor, and follow you
to eternal life in the kingdom you promise.
Grant this through our Lord Jesus Christ, your
    Son
who lives and reigns with you and the Holy Spirit,
one God, for ever and ever.[5]

Selected Bibliography

Adam, Adolf. *The Liturgical Year.* Trans. Matthew J. O'Connell. Collegeville: The Liturgical Press, 1990.

Days of the Lord. Vol. 7. Collegeville: The Liturgical Press, 1994.

---

[3]*Days of the Lord,* Vol. 7 (Collegeville: The Liturgical Press, 1994), 280.

[4]Ibid., 290.

[5]Common of the Dedication of a Church (B. Outside the Dedicated Church): "Opening Prayer B," *The Sacramentary.*

SOLEMNITY OF THE IMMACULATE CONCEPTION (DECEMBER 8)

INTRODUCTORY RITES

Opening Song (or Entrance Antiphon)

I exult for joy in the Lord, my soul rejoices in my God; for he has clothed me in the garment of salvation and robed me in the cloak of justice, like a bride adorned with her jewels. (Is 61:10)[1]

Opening Prayer

The facilitator of the session may lead the prayer. Others in the group may be asked to proclaim the readings.

Let us pray
[that through the prayers of the sinless
Virgin Mary, God will free us from our sins]

> *Pause for silent prayer.*

Father,
you prepared the Virgin Mary
to be worthy mother of your Son.
You let her share beforehand
in the salvation Christ would bring
by his death,
and kept her sinless from the first
moment of her conception.
Help us by her prayers
to live in your presence without sin.
We ask this through our Lord Jesus Christ, your
   Son,
who lives and reigns with you and the Holy
   Spirit,
one God, for ever and ever.[2]

LITURGY OF THE WORD

Let us listen to God's word.

The readings are proclaimed.

First Reading
Genesis 3:9-15, 20

The sages of Israel meditated on the relationship between God and the sinner and the nature of sin. Their reflection was based on their historical experience of God and God's people. Israel understood misfortune to be punishment for sin. When they lived outside the law, tragedy befell them. However, even when God punished them, he loved them, offered forgiveness, and promised them future blessing. The very first telling of this story of grace and sin takes place in today's story of Adam and Eve in the garden. This is the first fall from grace into sin.

Sin is an act of rebellion on the part of the created person who believes he or she can survive without God. Sin cuts the person off from God. Today's story depicts two human beings who enjoyed trusted freedom with their Creator. They chose to rebel and thus became afraid of their Creator. Awareness of nudity was a sign of their poverty and lack of protection against destruction. Sin caused a lack of communion with God. This lack of communion caused dissension between Adam and Eve.

We are given no information about the serpent who tempted Eve. The serpent was sentenced to a life of crawling on his belly because of his evil action. The serpent will continue to do battle with the human race, but he will not be victorious. He will be destroyed by the offspring of the woman. "St. Jerome's (ca. 342-420) Latin translates the Hebrew neuter with a feminine pronoun.... It is a daughter of the woman, a new Eve, who will crush the head of the serpent."[3] This interpretation probably was not the original intent of the author of Genesis, but Christian tradition has interpreted the story in light of the Christ event.

Christian tradition understands Jesus as the new Adam who conquered sin and brought salvation.

---

[1] Solemnity of the Immaculate Conception: "Entrance Antiphon," *The Sacramentary*.

[2] Solemnity of the Immaculate Conception: "Opening Prayer," *The Sacramentary*.

[3] *Days of the Lord*, Vol. 7 (Collegeville: The Liturgical Press, 1994), 300.

Mary is the new Eve, the mother of the Savior, whose victory was foretold after the fall. The Genesis reading sheds light on the mystery celebrated in this solemnity.

Responsorial Psalm
Psalm 98:1, 2-3, 3-4

Sing to the Lord a new song, for he has done marvelous deeds.

Second Reading
Ephesians 1:3-6, 11-12

The letter to the Ephesians begins with a liturgical prayer of thanksgiving. Its subject is God's plan of salvation, hidden throughout time, fulfilled in the person of Christ and revealed to all believers. Today's pericope refers especially to the Virgin Mary who was chosen beforetime to bear the Christ and to be holy in the sight of God. The apostle celebrates the work of salvation already accomplished by God through Jesus and in the Spirit. Ephesians asserts that we are chosen by God to be holy and without blemish. We are his adopted children and salvation is initiated solely through the love of God. Jesus was also part of the decision. With the Father, Jesus chose the human race for salvation just as he chose Israel as his own.

If we are so chosen, how much more, then, is Mary, the mother of Christ, chosen and blameless in the eyes of God. She is the perfect model of holiness for us.

Gospel
Luke 1:26-38

The angel appeared to Mary to tell her that she would conceive and bear a son.

STEP 1
NAMING ONE'S EXPERIENCE

What were your first impressions? What was your first response? What grabbed your attention? How did you feel?

Each person names his or her initial impression. Statement should be brief. No reasons should be given at this time. All simply listen without agreeing or disagreeing.

STEP 2
UNDERSTANDING

In a brief statement, what do you think this gospel is trying to convey?

STEP 3
INPUT FROM VISION/STORY/TRADITION

Liturgical Context

This feast celebrates the dogma that Mary was free from original sin from the first moment of her existence. Pope Pius XII promulgated the papal bull *Ineffabilis Deus* on December 8, 1854. The feast is still celebrated on this date. The doctrine of the Immaculate Conception holds that through the grace of God and the saving action of Christ, Mary was free from sin from the moment of her conception. Mary was born free of original sin.

While the Immaculate Conception is not found explicitly in scripture, there are texts that support it, such as today's Lectionary readings: victory over the serpent (Gen 3:15) and the angel's salutation to Mary as full of grace (Lk 1:28).

Special devotion to Mary that included a recognition of the uniqueness of her conception began around the seventh century in the East. In the twelfth century a feast in honor of the Immaculate Conception was celebrated in England.

However, controversy over the doctrine grew. Theologians such as Anselm, Bernard, Aquinas, and Bonaventure attested to Mary's sanctification in the womb, but they argued that she had to be affected by original sin even if for only a moment in order to be a recipient of Christ's redeeming grace. These objections were resolved by Duns Scotus (d. 1308) who asserted that Christ saves in two ways. "In one, he rescues from sin those already fallen. In the other, he preserves someone from being touched by sin even for an instant."[4] The

---

[4]Richard P. McBrien, "The Immaculate Conception," in *The Encyclopedia of Catholicism* (San Francisco: HarperCollins, 1995), 655.

Council of Trent (1545-1563) purposely eliminated Mary from the doctrine on original sin. It asserted that she was sin-free her entire life. In 1846 the United States bishops named Mary in her Immaculate Conception as patroness of the country.

This feast is christological in that it centers on the salvation offered for sinful humanity. Jesus suffered, died, and was buried for the sins of the world. The doctrine of the Immaculate Conception celebrates Christ's victory over the evil powers of the world at Mary's conception. "In her very being, through the mercy of God, the grip of evil is broken. To the Catholic imagination it is fitting that grace be freely given to her from the first moment of her existence because of her role in being the faith-filled mother of Jesus. Her yes to God brought Christ into the world, through whom the ancient sin of Adam and Eve is overturned."[5] This feast reminds us that grace is freely given and is more powerful than sin.

We are not to lose sight of the season in which this celebration is situated. "During Advent the liturgy frequently brings Mary to mind. On 8 December the solemnity of the Immaculate Conception recalls the preparation for the Savior's coming at its origins (See Is 11:1 and 10) and also the happy beginning of the Church in its beauty without spot or wrinkle."[6]

Gospel Exegesis

The facilitator gives input regarding what critical biblical scholarship has to say about this text. The input includes insights as to how people would have heard the gospel in Jesus' time.

Luke's concern in this pericope is the unusual circumstance surrounding Jesus' conception. Verse 35 asserts that Jesus would be the promised Davidic Messiah, thus the meaning of Jesus' name: "Yahweh saves." Jesus was conceived through the power of the Holy Spirit in the womb of Mary and thus is the Son of God. Jesus' birth of the virgin Mary is evidence of his humanity.

St. Augustine developed this theology when he asserted that all people are sinful because of original sin. All people need Christ's salvation. We are all heirs of original sin because of sexual generation. Christ as Savior was sinless and did not inherit original sin. Thus, Jesus could not have become human through sexual procreation. When Christ was conceived by the Holy Spirit he avoided the stain of original sin and was sinless Savior of the world.

In Greco-Roman literature the hero's greatness was often explained by a story of the hero's miraculous conception. "Jesus was what he was because he was divinely begotten."[7]

One emphasis in Luke/Acts is that Jesus descended from the Davidic monarchy and is the fulfillment of messianic Jewish prophecy. Through the paschal mystery Jesus is the glorified, exalted Son of God who sits at the right hand of his Father. Christ rules from his Father's right hand and intercedes for the people. Through the power of divine intervention (miraculous conception) Jesus was Savior of the world: he lived, suffered, died, rose again, and ascended to sit at the right hand of his Father's throne.

Proclaim the gospel again.

Sometimes we gain new insights when we hear the text after the interpretation has been given. Someone from the group proclaims the gospel a second time.

STEP 4
TESTING

Conversation with the Liturgy and the Scriptures

Test your original understanding in dialogue with the text.

(You might consider breaking into smaller groups.)

Were there any new insights? Was there anything you had not considered before? How does your

---

[5]Ibid., 656.
[6]DOL, #467, Section 4. Sanctoral Cycle: A. Mary, #3901, #3 in *Documents on the Liturgy* (Collegeville: The Liturgical Press, 1982), 1207.

---

[7]Charles H. Talbert, *Reading Luke* (New York: Crossroad, 1992), 20.

original understanding of this story compare with what was just shared? How does this story speak to your life?

Participants share an experience from their lives that connects with the biblical interpretation just shared.

What was Luke trying to tell his community? What does he have to say to our community and to me today? Do we still feel the same way about this text as we did when we began? Has our original understanding been stretched, challenged, or affirmed?

STEP 5
DECISION

The gospel demands a response.

In what way does this gospel call your parish to action in the church, parish, neighborhood, or world? Be concrete. What are you called to do in response? Name one concrete action you will take this week as a response to what was learned and shared today.

DOCTRINAL ISSUES

What church truth/teaching/doctrinal issue could be drawn from the gospel for the feast of the Immaculate Conception?

Participants suggest possible doctrinal themes that flow from the readings.

Possible Doctrinal Themes

Immaculate Conception of Mary

Present the doctrinal material at this time.

1. The facilitator gives input on a particular doctrinal issue of his/her prior choosing. OR
2. The group chooses a doctrinal issue from the list they created. They read together from the Doctrinal Appendix.

(The doctrinal issues are found in the Doctrinal Appendix in the back of this workbook. If you are choosing an issue from this resource, please refer to it now.)

Reflection questions centered around the chosen doctrinal theme can be found at the end of each topic in the Doctrinal Appendix. The questions are based on the five-step reflection process. If you choose a topic not included in the Doctrinal Appendix, craft your own questions according to the same five-step process.

Following the reflection questions you will be reminded to return to chapter 7, "Preparing the Catechetical Session," to assist you in crafting your own session.

Closing Prayer

Born of the Blessed Virgin Mary,
the Son of God redeemed mankind.
May he enrich you with his blessings.
 Response: Amen.

You received the author of life through Mary.
May you always rejoice in her loving care.
R. Amen.

You have come to rejoice at Mary's feast.
May you be filled with the joys of the Spirit
and the gifts of your eternal home.
 Response: Amen.

May almighty God bless you,
the Father, and the Son + and the Holy Spirit.
 Response: Amen.[8]

Selected Bibliography

Days of the Lord. Vol. 7. Collegeville: The Liturgical Press, 1994.
McBrien, Richard P. "The Immaculate Conception." In *The Encyclopedia of Catholicism.* San Francisco: HarperCollins, 1995.
Talbert, Charles H. *Reading Luke.* New York: Crossroad, 1992.

---

[8]Solemnity of the Immaculate Conception: "Solemn Blessing Over the People," *The Sacramentary.*

DOCTRINAL APPENDIX

DOCTRINE AND THE LITURGICAL YEAR

This appendix contains doctrinal material that flows from and surfaces out of the experience of word and worship on Sunday. The church has always revered the scriptures in much the same way as she reveres the Body of Christ. The people of God are offered the bread of life at both the table of God's word and the table of the eucharist.[1]

The Second Vatican Council's document, *The Dogmatic Constitution on Divine Revelation,* asserts that sacred scripture and tradition are intimately connected. They flow from and through one another. They have the same purpose. Scripture is God communicating with human beings through human writers by the power of the Holy Spirit. Tradition provides us with the full message of God's word given to the apostles by Jesus and the Holy Spirit. Thus, all future generations are enlightened by what was handed on to us by the apostles. Through that inheritance the Spirit strengthens us to live a gospel life and spread the good news of salvation. "Therefore both sacred Tradition and sacred Scripture are to be accepted and venerated with the same sense of devotion and reverence."[2]

The church has always considered scripture and tradition to be the primary rule of faith. Theology's foundational roots hinge on the written word of God and sacred tradition. Through both, the mystery of Christ is encountered, bringing light and life to the believer. "Therefore, the 'study of the sacred page' should be very soul of sacred theology."[3]

As an introduction to this Doctrinal Appendix, basic principles regarding the core issues of tradition will be articulated once again for review. This appendix will address the central core of the church's teaching, the hierarchy of truths that comes to us from scripture and tradition that

began with the apostles and has continued through the ages. All other teachings of our faith are rooted and find meaning in those essential, primary truths. The church has many teachings that are not included in the "hierarchy of truths." This section will focus only on those that form the basis of our faith. This in no way diminishes the fact that we are to believe all that the church holds to be true. However, some truths hold more importance than others as they are foundational to all we believe.

The General Catechetical Directory asserts that "the message of salvation has a certain hierarchy of truths which the Church has always recognized when it composed creeds or summaries of the truths of the faith. Some truths of the faith are based on others as of a higher priority and are illumined by them."[4]

The hierarchy of truths is listed in both the General and National Catechetical Directory. These truths are grouped under four headings. Once again they are:

1. The mystery of God the Father, the Son, and the Holy Spirit, Creator of all things.

2. The mystery of Christ, the incarnate Word, who was born of the Virgin Mary and who suffered, died, and rose for our salvation.

3. The mystery of the Holy Spirit, who is present in the church, sanctifying it and guiding it until the glorious coming of Christ, our Savior and Judge.

4. The mystery of the church, which is Christ's Mystical Body, in which the Virgin Mary holds a preeminent place.

All other truths are informed by and in direct relation to the hierarchy of truths. These truths

---

[1] *The Dogmatic Constitution on Divine Revelation (Dei Verbum),* in *The Documents of Vatican II,* ed. Walter M. Abbott, S.J. (New York: America Press, 1966), 125, #21.

[2] Ibid., #9.

[3] Ibid., #21, 24.

[4] General Catechetical Directory (GCD), in *The Catechetical Documents* (Chicago: Liturgy Training Publications, 1996), 33, #34.

are encountered and remembered ritually throughout the liturgical year through the Lectionary scriptures and in the feasts and seasons we celebrate.

The doctrinal issues in this appendix are thematic overviews. This chapter is not an attempt to provide a comprehensive rendering of all the articles of Catholic belief and practices. The primary sources used in this appendix are the documents of the church. All other resources provide supplemental background. We encourage you to study church documents, the rites of the church, the *Catechism of the Catholic Church,* historical context, and the related works of theologians in order to broaden your understanding.

This is not "everything you ever wanted to know about a topic." Rather, it provides a brief overview of post-biblical teaching or practice as it relates to the lived experience of past communities, flows from the gospel exegesis, and connects to the lived experience of people today. What is provided in this appendix is but a taste and is intended to provide a model that may be used to assist others in crafting doctrinal sessions not included in this workbook.

The facilitator may prepare material on a doctrinal issue or the group may choose and read together a doctrine from this appendix. The suggested themes may or may not be appropriate for each parish. It is not our intention to suggest that every parish should teach the same doctrine on a particular Sunday. Each community should decide for itself what issues of tradition are pertinent and best flow from the Sunday's readings and from the needs of the community.

This appendix will not include every doctrinal issue listed under the following list of core issues. Some of the topics are addressed within the body of the workbook, however. For example, the dominant symbols of the church are examined in the Easter Vigil section. One need only use that material in conjunction with the learning model used in these structured sessions.

The following list is a compilation of doctrinal themes that are inherent in and flow from the liturgical year.

CORE ISSUES OF FAITH IN THE LITURGICAL YEAR

Advent
Eschatology, Christ's Coming: Future, Present, Past, Son of Man, Parousia, Kingdom of God

Christmas
Incarnation, Epiphany/Manifestation, Holy Family, Christology

Lent
Renewal, Preparation, Penitence, Fasting, Conversion, Almsgiving, Practices of Prayer, Sin, Transfiguration, Grace, Providence, Soteriology

Easter Triduum
Paschal Mystery, Redemption, Vigil, Eucharist, Priesthood, Service, Justice; Dominant Symbols of the Church: Assembly, Light, Cross, Water, Oil, Laying on of Hands, Garment, Bread/Wine

Easter Season
Fifty Days, Ascension, Pentecost, Resurrection, Holy Spirit, Charisms, Ecclesiology, Discipleship, Hope

Ordinary Time
Trinity, Body and Blood of Jesus, Christian Witness, Sacraments, Death/Dying, Suffering, Beatitudes, Vocation, Moral Decision Making, Non-violence, Christian Stewardship All Saints, All Souls, Sacred Heart, Solemnity Mary Mother of God, Assumption, Immaculate Conception, Saints, Kingdom of God

DOCTRINAL TOPICS

ADVENT

See Advent Overview.

ALL SAINTS

See Feast of All Saints.

ALL SOULS

See Feast of All Souls.

ALMSGIVING

See Lenten Overview.

ASCENSION

See Easter Overview and Feast of the Ascension.

ASSUMPTION

See Feast of the Assumption.

BAPTISM

See CHRISTIAN INITIATION: Part I—Baptism (Appendix). See Easter Vigil, Symbols of Water, Light, and Garment.

BREAD

See Easter Vigil.

CONFIRMATION

See CHRISTIAN INITIATION: Part II—Confirmation (Appendix). See Easter Vigil, Symbol of Oil.

CONVERSION

See Lenten Overview and the Sundays of Lent.

CROSS

See Easter Vigil.

BODY AND BLOOD

See CHRISTIAN INITIATION: Eucharist (Appendix). See Easter Vigil, Symbol of Bread. See Feast of Corpus Christi.

CHRISTIAN INITIATION

Through the sacrament of initiation people are freed from the power of sin and evil. They die and are buried with Christ and are raised again to new life. They receive the Spirit of adoption, making them children of God. With the entire church they celebrate the memorial of Christ's death and resurrection.

Through baptism people are incorporated in the life of Christ. They are formed as God's people and are forgiven their sins. They are elevated to the dignity of adopted children. They are a new creation in Christ through water and the Spirit, and thus are called children of God.

Christians more perfectly become the image of Christ when they are signed with the gift of the Holy Spirit in confirmation. They bear witness to Christ and strive to bring others to him.

They come to the Lord's table to eat and drink his Body and Blood so they may have eternal life and show the unity of God's people. They offer themselves with Christ, thereby sharing in his paschal mystery. They pray for an outpouring of the Holy Spirit so the human race may be brought together in unity as God's people. The three sacraments bring the faithful to full stature in Christ and empower them to carry out the mission of Christ in the church and the world.[1]

I. Baptism

Natural Sign
What is your experience of water in everyday life? How might water express something about the

---

[1]Christian Initiation, *The Rites of the Catholic Church*, English translation prepared by the International Commission on English in the Liturgy (New York: Pueblo Publishing Co., 1976), p. 3, #s 1, 2.

mystery of God? What is your present understanding of baptism? How would you articulate a definition? Complete this sentence: "Baptism is...."

Tradition: Biblical, Ecclesial, and Liturgical Signs
The sacraments of initiation (baptism, confirmation, and eucharist) free us from the power of darkness and evil. We are united to Christ and his paschal mystery, his death, burial and resurrection. We are adopted children of God by the power of the Holy Spirit and are incorporated into the Body of Christ in the celebration of the memorial of the paschal mystery—the eucharist.

"Baptism incorporates us into Christ and forms us into God's people. This first sacrament pardons all our sins, rescues us from the power of darkness, and brings us to the dignity of adopted children, a new creation through water and the Holy Spirit. Hence we are called and indeed are the children of God."[2] (See Colossians 1:13; Romans 8:15; Galatians 4:5.) The three sacraments of initiation allow us to carry out the mission of Christ in the world.

Baptism initiates us into God's reign and is the gateway to eternal life. It is the first sacrament offered by Christ who later entrusted it and his gospel to the church when he exhorted his disciples to "Go and make disciples of all the nations, and baptize them in the name of the Father, and of the Son, and of the Holy Spirit" (Mt 28:19). Through baptism, we are enlightened by the Spirit of God to live the gospel.

Baptism incorporates us into the church and into the house of God (Eph 2:22). We are made a royal priesthood. We are all united through the sacramental bond of baptism. We have been signed into this unchangeable effect through the anointing with chrism in the presence of God's people. Baptism, validly celebrated even by Christians with whom we are not in full communion, may never be repeated.[3]

Through the sign of water, baptism cleanses away every stain of sin, original and personal, and offers us a share in the life of Christ. We become his adopted children. Through the water of baptism

we are reborn into Christ. The Blessed Trinity is invoked over the person who is baptized. The baptized enter into communion with the Father, the Son, and the Holy Spirit. The baptized are prepared for and led to this communion through biblical readings, the prayer of the community, and their own profession of faith in the Father, Son and Spirit.[4]

This is all accomplished through the death and resurrection of Jesus Christ. We who are baptized are united to him in his death. We are buried with Christ and then are born again to new life in Christ. Baptism remembers and makes present the death and resurrection of Jesus, his paschal mystery. Through baptism we die to sin and are born to new life.[5] (See Ephesians 5:26, 2:5-6, 2:22; 1 Peter 2:9; 2 Peter 1:4; Romans 6:4-5, 8:15; Galatians 4-5; Titus 3:5; John 3:1, 5, 6:55; Matthew 28:19.)

Through the ritual of baptism we are anointed priest, prophet, and king. As priest we are called to serve, as prophet we are called to proclaim the good news, and as royalty we are called to lead.

Water used in baptism is to be true water, pure and clean. Immersion, a more suitable symbol denoting the death and resurrection of Christ (we go down into the waters and are buried in Christ and rise out of the waters to new life), or pouring can be used to lawfully administer the sacrament. The words for the conferral of baptism are: "I baptize you in the name of the Father, and of the Son and of the Holy Spirit."[6]

Refer to the symbol of water in the Easter Vigil chapter. A similar, separate reflection process centered around the symbol of water would be recommended and would include: natural sign of water in everyday life; biblical uses of water throughout the scriptures; ecclesial understanding of water throughout the history of the church; liturgical use of water.

Testing
Were there any new insights or clarifications? What might this doctrine have to do with my

___

[2] RCIA, #2.
[3] Ibid., #4.

[4] Ibid., #5.
[5] Ibid., #6.
[6] Ibid., #23.

everyday life or the life of the community? What are the implications for living the Christian life?

Decision

What concrete action will I take as a result of this teaching?

Refer to chapter 7, "Preparing the Catechetical Session," if you intend to plan your catechetical session at this time.

II. Confirmation

Natural Sign

What is your experience of oil in everyday life? How does it speak to you about God? How would you explain the sacrament of confirmation?

Tradition: Biblical, Ecclesial, and Liturgical Signs

Confirmation is an initiation sacrament. The Rite of Confirmation #1 states that the baptized continue on the path of Christian initiation through the sacrament of confirmation. The joining of both baptism and confirmation signifies the unity of the paschal mystery, and the close connection between the work of the Son and the outpouring of the Holy Spirit. The Father, Son, and Spirit come to those who are baptized. Adults and children of catechetical age are to receive the sacraments of baptism, confirmation, and eucharist in a simple celebration.[7] The priest receives authority to confer confirmation at these celebrations from canon law itself.

The conferral of the Spirit at confirmation is the second stage of initiation, not a rite of passage into adulthood. Confirmation leads us more fully into our baptismal identity. Confirmation is not about ratifying an adult faith. It is the gift of the Spirit.

The initiatory character of confirmation and its connection with baptism and eucharist are based on the life, death, and resurrection of Christ. Confirmation is a sign of the paschal mystery. "This makes clear the specific importance of confirmation for sacramental initiation, by which the faithful members of the living Christ are incorporated into him and *configured* to him through baptism and through confirmation and the eucharist."[8]

One significant aspect of confirmation reform as set forth in the Apostolic Constitution or the Rite of Confirmation places the coming of the Spirit at Pentecost in center stage. The anointing with chrism is understood as having its basis in Jesus' baptism and the outpouring of the Spirit on the disciples at Pentecost. "The descent of the Spirit at Jesus' baptism reflects a new and extraordinary vision of the pneumatic quality of baptism itself, and the intrinsic unity of the baptismal event: baptism and the outpouring of the Spirit are one mystery and sacrament."[9]

Those who are born anew in baptism receive the inexpressible Gift, the Holy Spirit himself who imparts a special strength. Confirmation, then, is closely related to eucharist. After being signed by baptism and confirmation, the faithful are then fully incorporated into the Body of Christ through participation in the eucharist. This is signified more fully in the new sacramental formula: "Be sealed with the Gift of the Holy Spirit." The Gift *is* the Spirit, not the gifts *of* the Spirit. Thus, confirmation makes us:

1. more completely the image of Christ and fills us with his Spirit so we may bear witness to him;
2. configured to Christ and strengthened by the Holy Spirit;
3. witnesses to Christ in order to build the Body of Christ in faith and love.

Confirmation so marks the recipient with the character of Christ that, like baptism, it also cannot be repeated. The seal of the Spirit marks our total being for Christ. We are forever in the service of Christ's mission and we are promised divine protection until the final day.

Confirmation completes baptism; eucharist completes initiation. It is eucharist that fully incorporates a person into the Body of Christ. Eucharist is the repeatable sacrament of initiation [Augustine]. We grow into our identity as fully initiated members of the Body of Christ through our sharing in

---

[7]National Statutes of the RCIA, #14.

[8]"Rite of Confirmation—Apostolic Constitution," *The Rites of the Catholic Church,* English translation prepared by the International Commission on English in the Liturgy (New York: Pueblo Publishing Co., 1976), 290–297.

[9]Linda Gaupin, CDP, Ph.D., Specialized Certification for Sacramental Catechesis (Diocese of Orlando, Fla., 1996–1997), unpublished course text, 7.

the eucharist. Confirmation takes place within mass in order to stress the fundamental connection between confirmation and Christian initiation that culminates in the communion of Christ's Body and Blood. "Thus, even when confirmation is celebrated after first communion, the initiatory identity of Eucharist as the sacrament which completes initiation should be maintained."[10]

Confirmation, therefore, is not an occasion of personal commitment to an adult faith. It is not a rite of adult passage, nor is it a sacrament of maturity. "Although Confirmation is sometimes called the 'sacrament of Christian maturity,' we must not confuse adult faith with the adult age of natural growth, nor forget that the baptismal grace is a grace of free, unmerited election and does not need 'ratification' to become effective."[11]

"Some are teaching that the main reason for the Rite of Baptism for Children is that infants be allowed at some point to accept for themselves the faith. That is where confirmation comes in. Response: This is pure fantasy. The rite says no such thing. Some are teaching that confirmation 'assists the transition into adult faith... it develops experiences of faith based upon both the individual and the community.' Response: This is the purpose of the eucharist."[12]

The sacrament of confirmation is conferred by anointing the candidates with chrism on the forehead and saying the words: "Receive the Gift of the Holy Spirit." *The anointing with chrism represents the apostolic laying on of hands and the anointing with the Holy Spirit.* The laying on of hands and accompanying prayer prior to the anointing with chrism does not belong to the substance of the rite yet it is to be held in high regard.

Refer to the Rite of Confirmation (chapter 5, III) for the scriptural passages that taken together shed light on the celebration of this sacrament.

Refer to the symbol of oil in the Easter Vigil chapter. A similar, separate reflection process centered around the symbol of oil would be recommended and would include: natural sign of oil in everyday life; biblical uses of oil throughout the scriptures; ecclesial understanding of oil throughout the history of the church; liturgical use of oil.

Testing
Were there any new insights? How would you articulate a definition of confirmation now? Have your original assumptions been stretched in any way? How does this doctrine of confirmation have anything to do with living everyday life?

Decision
What action will I take as a result of today's sharing?

Refer to chapter 7, "Preparing the Catechetical Session," if you intend to plan your catechetical session at this time.

III. Eucharist

Natural Sign
What is your experience of bread and wine in everyday life? How do they speak to you about the nature of God? What is your present understanding of the sacrament of eucharist?

Tradition: Biblical, Ecclesial, and Liturgical Signs
Eucharist completes initiation. Those who have been elevated to the status of royal priesthood through baptism and configured to Christ through confirmation share with the entire community in the Lord's sacrifice of Calvary through the eucharist. The eucharist ["liturgy," *Constitution on the Sacred Liturgy*, #10] is the source and summit of all we do. All catechesis, all our efforts as Christian people lead us to full and active participation in the eucharistic banquet. Eucharist is a sacrament of unity and it strengthens the Body of Christ. The eucharistic celebration is carried out in response to the mandate of Christ to "Do this in memory of me."

In the liturgy the priest prays the words of eucharistic consecration and the bread and wine are changed into the Body and Blood of Christ. Under the appearance of bread and wine, Jesus, true God and true Man, "is substantially present, in a mysterious way, under the appearance of bread and wine."[13]

---

[10]Ibid., 9.

[11]*Catechism of the Catholic Church* (CCC), English translation by USCC-Libreria Editrice Vaticana (Liguori: Liguori Publications, 1994), 1308.

[12]Gaupin, 9.

---

[13]"Basic Teachings for Catholic Religious Education," in *The Catechetical Documents* (Chicago: Liturgy Training Publications, 1996), #12.

It is called *eucharist* (Greek: *eucharistein, eulogein*— recollection of the Jewish blessing in praise of God's work or redemption and sanctification) as it is a ritual action of praise and thanks to God.

The paschal mystery (passion, death, and resurrection of Christ) is celebrated anew in an unbloody manner through the ministry of the priests. This holy meal recalls and makes present the Last Supper and it celebrates the unity we share in Christ. It also looks toward our participation in the heavenly banquet.

Bread and wine, the two symbols of eucharist, are changed into Christ's Body and Blood through the invocation of the Holy Spirit. We are nourished by the Body and Blood of Christ so that we may become a people more acceptable to God and that we may be capable of greater love for God and one another.

In the celebration of the eucharist the church gathers to celebrate the presence of Christ in the Body of Christ, the eucharistic assembly, in the proclamation of the word, in the presiding celebrant, and in the eucharistic elements. "To accomplish so great a work, Christ is always present in his Church.... He is present in the sacrifice of the Mass, not only in the person of his minister... but especially under the eucharistic elements.... He is present in his word since it is Christ himself who speaks when the holy scriptures are read in the Church. He is present lastly, when the Church prays and sings, for he promised: 'Where two or more are gathered together in my name, there am I in the midst of them' (Mt. 18:20)."[14]

The eucharist is foreshadowed in the Hebrew scriptures in the gesture of the king-priest Melchizedek who offered bread and wine (Gen 14:18). Bread and wine were offered under the old covenant as a sign of grateful thanks for the harvest and the Creator's benevolence. Bread and wine were significant symbols in the Passover meal that remembered the liberation out of Egypt's bondage into the promised land (Deut 8:3). The miracle of the loaves and fishes foreshadowed the eucharist in the multiplication, breaking, and dis-

tribution of the loaves to the crowd, prefiguring "the superabundance of this unique bread of his Eucharist."[15]

Jesus left a pledge of his love by leaving a memorial of his death and resurrection and commanding his followers to repeat the ritual action of this memorial until his return. "The three synoptic Gospels and St. Paul have handed on to us the account of the institution of the Eucharist; St. John, for his part, reports the words of Jesus in the synagogue of Capernaum that prepare for the institution of the Eucharist: Christ calls himself the bread of life, come down from heaven."[16] Jesus instituted this memorial on the night before he would die and in the process gave new and definitive meaning to the Passover event: Jesus passed from this life to his Father through his death and resurrection. This new Passover is anticipated in the eucharist that fulfilled the Passover of the old covenant and anticipates the last Passover of the entire church at the end of the age.[17]

The eucharist, center of the church's life, proclaims the paschal mystery of Christ and makes it present. The eucharist strengthens the community of believers as they embrace the cross and move forward to their final destination in heaven, where all the "elect will be seated at the table of the kingdom."[18]

Eucharist initiates conversion again and again. It invites and causes transformation. The bread is taken, blessed, broken, and shared; we too are taken, blessed, broken, and shared and in that way participate in the paschal mystery of Jesus. Eucharist strengthens our union in Christ, forgives our sins, makes us church, and empowers us to do good, promote the gospel, and serve the needs of the world. "Eucharist commits us to the poor."[19]

Refer to the symbols of bread and wine in the Easter Vigil chapter. A similar, separate reflection process centered around the symbols of bread and wine would be recommended and would include:

---

[14] *Constitution on the Sacred Liturgy* (CSL), in *The Liturgy Documents* (Chicago: Liturgy Training Publications, 1991), #7.

[15] CCC, #1335.
[16] Ibid., #1338.
[17] Ibid., #1339-1340.
[18] Ibid., #1344.
[19] Ibid., #1397.

natural signs of bread and wine in everyday life; biblical uses of bread and wine throughout the scriptures; ecclesial understanding of symbols of bread and wine throughout the history of the church; liturgical use of bread and wine.

Testing

Were there any new insights? How would you now finish this sentence: "Eucharist is..."?
What are the implications for living Christian life? What is the challenge of eucharist?

Decision

What am I/we going to do about it? What response am I going to make?

Refer to chapter 7, "Preparing the Catechetical Session," if you intend to plan your catechetical session at this time.

CHRISTMAS

See Overview of Christmas and the Sundays of the Christmas Season.

CHRISTOLOGY

See JESUS (Appendix).

CHURCH, MYSTERY OF

Natural Sign

Have you ever had an experience of being part of a community other than your church community? What were the things that attracted you to this community? Did you ever have the sense that a community you were part of possessed corporate power?

One of the first symbols of God's presence in the world is the church. There are many interchangeable terms for church—community, church, people of God, assembly—but they are all the same reality. God is present to the world through the visible, tangible sign of God's love, the church. "As a divine reality inserted into human history, the Church is a kind of sacrament. Its unique relationship with Christ makes it both sign and instrument of God's unfathomable union with humanity and of the unity of human beings among themselves.

Part of the Church's mission is to lead people to a deeper understanding of human nature and destiny and to provide them with more profound experiences of God's presence in human affairs."[20]

Tradition: Biblical, Ecclesial, and Liturgical Signs

Please refer to Easter Vigil: Symbol of Church (p. 227), for information regarding the biblical understanding of church/community and for further historical elaboration.

The Second Vatican Council redefined our understanding of church. The following principles are a summary of our theology as articulated in *Sharing the Light of Faith: The National Catechetical Directory.* "The Church is a mystery. It is a reality imbued with the hidden presence of God (From Pope Paul VI's opening allocution at the second session [September 19, 1963]." The Church is a gift coming from the love of God, Christ's redeeming action and the power of the Holy Spirit (National Catechetical Directory [NCD], #63). "As a divine reality inserted into human history, the Church is a kind of sacrament. Its unique relationship with Christ makes it both a sign and instrument of God's unfathomable union with humanity and of the unity of human beings among themselves" (NCD, #63). "...As a mystery, the Church cannot be totally understood or fully defined. Its nature and mission are best captured in scriptural parables and images, taken from ordinary life, which not only express truth about its nature but challenge the Church: for example, to become more a People of God, a better servant, more faithful and holy, more united around the teaching authority of the hierarchy" (NCD, #63).

The church is a community of believers, the people of God. We are called to become a new people, a royal priesthood, a people claimed by God to proclaim the greatness of God (1 Pet 2:9). Jesus freed us from sin and because of the saving waters of baptism we are called to believe, worship, and witness to his saving works.

We are one body in Christ (Rom 12:5). Through Jesus' death, resurrection, and glorification, he remains a living presence and head of his church, of which we are all members. *We celebrate this identity*

---

[20]NCD, #63.

most especially in the eucharist. Through the eucharist, we become the Body and Blood of Christ.

The church is servant and has a mission to heal and reconcile as Jesus did. The church is to live the gospel through the works of mercy, assisting the needy or anyone who is in need of our help. The church as servant acts out of love and concern, not for personal glory. One way the church is servant is through her teaching ministry in which she witnesses to the gospel and the power of God in the world.

The church is a sign of the reign of God. The church is evidence that God is alive in our midst. In order to be that sign, the church "must be committed to justice, love and peace, to grace and holiness, truth and life, for these are the hallmarks of the kingdom of God" (NCD, #67).

The church is a pilgrim church. Aware of her sins, the church journeys to her final destination as she repents and overcomes patiently the trials and tribulations that come her way. In this way she demonstrates her steadfast faithfulness to the world.

"As mystery, people, one body in Christ, servant, sign of the kingdom, and pilgrim, the Church is conceived as God's family, whose members are united to Christ and led by the Spirit in their journey to the Father. The Church merits our prayerful reflection and wholehearted response" (NCD, # 68).

The church is one, holy catholic and apostolic. Unity is the substance of the church and is based on the unity of the Trinity. While unified, the church is diverse; this is expressed by the various liturgical rites within the church such as Catholic Coptic Rite, Ethiopian Rite, etc.

We express our unity through a profession of faith, apostolic succession, and the communal celebration of worship, especially the sacraments. Heresy, apostasy, and schism wound the unity of the church. The Catholic Church shares baptism, scripture, belief in the Trinity, and some sacraments with some ecclesial communities; it shares devotion to Mary, Mother of God, and some common liturgical texts with other ecclesial communities.

The symbol of church as people of God is a primary symbol in the liturgy. The gathered community is a sign of God's presence in our midst. Before the book is opened or the bread shared, God is experienced in the community. "For these people are the people of God, purchased by Christ's blood, gathered together by the Lord, nourished by the word. They are a people called to offer God the prayers of the entire human family, a people giving thanks in Christ for the mystery of salvation by offering his sacrifice. Finally, they are a people growing together into unity by sharing Christ's Body and Blood. These people are holy by their origin, but becoming ever more holy by conscious, active and fruitful participation in the mystery of the eucharist."[21] In every liturgical celebration the community is a primary experience of God's presence. We profess the mystery of the church in our ritual prayers and the creed, and through the eucharist we live its reality. Through all the ministries of the church, Christ is present. Thus, when the people participate and celebrate, the lector proclaims, the priest presides, the eucharistic minister serves, the cantor sings, the hospitality people welcome, etc., Christ is made manifest in our midst.

The church is a priestly, prophetic, and royal people. Through baptism and faith in God the church shares Christ's priestly role as leader. The church is consecrated a holy priesthood and a spiritual house. The church shares the prophetic ministry as it witnesses to God's reign in the world. The church is royal in its ministry of service to the poor and the needs of the world.

Testing
Are there any new insights? Have any of your original assumptions about church been stretched or affirmed? Does this teaching about church resonate with your experience of church in your own community? What are the areas of death/resurrection? What are some specific areas that are in need of growth?

Decision
What is the challenge and what action will I take as a result of this teaching on the mystery of the church?

---

[21]"General Instruction of the Roman Missal" (GIRM), in *The Liturgy Documents* (Chicago: Liturgy Training Publications, 1991), #5.

Refer to chapter 7, "Preparing the Catechetical Session," if you intend to plan your catechetical session at this time.

EASTER SEASON

See Overview of Easter Season, Easter Vigil, and the Sundays of Easter.

EASTER VIGIL

See Easter Vigil.

EPIPHANY

See Overview of Christmas and Feast of Epiphany.

ESCHATOLOGY

The Collegeville Pastoral Dictionary of Biblical Theology defines eschatology, from the Greek *eschatos*, last, as that which has to do with beliefs and ideas about the end time, and with the valuation of time and history in this perspective. "Most religious traditions have some set of beliefs about an ultimate future of the individual and of the earth, whether that future is envisioned as eternal, cyclic, or limited."[22]

Natural Sign

When we speak about the end of the world, what does it evoke in you? How do you feel when we speak about the end of your own world through death? If you were to articulate an understanding of what happens to us after we die, what would you say? How would you articulate an understanding of your faith tradition's belief in the afterlife and the end of time?

Tradition: Biblical, Ecclesial, and Biblical Signs

Eschatology is the area of theology that studies the last things. The last things refer to the final manifestation of God's loving relationship to humanity. Issues that fall under the umbrella of eschatology's concerns are "death, particular judgement,

heaven, hell, purgatory, Second Coming of Christ, resurrection of the body, general judgment, consummation of all things in the perfection of the Kingdom of God."[23] Richard McBrien asserts that even though future oriented, these realities have already been accomplished in the present through people who live the life awarded to them by the death and resurrection of Jesus. "Our *judgment* will be the visible manifestation of the judgment of acquittal already rendered in Jesus Christ."[24]

All of time is sanctified by God. In the Christian perspective, eschatology refers to the sanctification of future time and hinges upon the life, death, and resurrection of Jesus. Eschatology's springboard is the reality of Jesus' first entrance into human history through his Incarnation, the resulting effects, and the future promise of eternal life at the end of time.

One type of eschatology found in the New Testament is apocalyptical. That is, it alludes to the end of the world with preceding signs and wonders. The end time is seen as a time in which evil is conquered and Jesus will come again on a cloud, summoning all the faithful to their final destination: life with all the saints in the heavenly kingdom. Apocalyptic literature is often rich in symbolic language and speaks powerfully of a present reality, not just some future expectation. Berard Marthaler states: "Apocalyptic literature is purported to be a revelation of the future, whereas in actuality it was most often a commentary on the times in which it was composed."[25] The book of Revelation is an example of apocalyptic literature. Often the purpose of such literature was to offer consolation to persecuted people in present crisis situations.

Another type of eschatology in the scriptures can be found in the synoptic gospels of Matthew, Mark and Luke. This type of eschatology heralds the reign of God both now and in the future. God is celebrated as the ONE who reigns in our midst. God's presence demands nothing but the total giving of self in response: complete conversion and

---

[22]Carolyn Osiek, R.S.C.J., "Eschatology," in *The Collegeville Pastoral Dictionary of Biblical Theology,* ed. Carroll Stuhlmueller, C.P. (Collegeville: The Liturgical Press, 1996), 264.

[23]Richard P. McBrien, *Catholicism* (San Francisco: Harper Collins, 1981), 1101-1105.

[24]Ibid., 1103.

[25]Berard Marthaler, *Creed* (Mystic: Twenty Third Publications, 1987), 206.

metanoia. The kingdom of God is present when people are gathered in the name of Jesus.

Another scriptural image for eschatology is that of banquet. In the Old Testament the image of feasting was used in reference to "heavenly happiness."[26] The Last Supper was also seen as eschatological. It signaled the beginning of the last days. That which Christ was sent to do was coming to completion, beginning with the Lord's Supper. Thus, every eucharistic celebration has remembrances and reminders of our eschatological center.

Another biblical principle of eschatology appears in the gospel of John and is referred to as *realized eschatology.* The term refers to the fulfillment of that which is awaited and hoped for. Thus, those who believe in Jesus are already living in the promise and imbued with the Spirit of his very presence.

The history of eschatology in the church developed over time. It moved through stages in which there were notions that after a thousand year reign the end would come. This understanding came from a literalist view of Revelation 20. It was an understanding easily reputed in the year 1001. The end, of course, did not arrive.

Later there was great debate concerning where people would go upon their death. Questions of location came to the fore. Where would the individual soul go? Were there interim places before the final beatific vision? It is out of such debate that our understandings of purgatory and the resurrected body come.

These understandings remained intact until the advent of biblical scholarship in recent times. There was a shift away from the concept of the individual and the locale of his or her final resting place toward a broader, more inclusive understanding of eschatology. Contemporary theology thinks more in terms of humanity's final collective relationship to the Creator as a people.

More recently, Marxism criticized the *future only oriented* Christian stance as an excuse to avoid engaging in the concerns of the world. From such critique emerged the perception that indeed God and humanity were to be coworkers in the work of transforming the world. Disciples are called to be actors in the ongoing theater of life. They are to be history makers.

Lest we negate the creed of the kingdom of God *yet to come* in favor of a narrower interpretation as only meaning the kingdom of God *here and now,* the Second Vatican Council redefined the church's theology in regard to eschatology. The church defined the reign of God as a transcendent future, yet acknowledged humanity's role to be active participants in changing the present world while awaiting the coming of the next *(Dogmatic Constitution on the Church).*

Thus, we are to face death with courage and joy. We should be counseled about our belief in death, judgment, and eternity, but always with "consoling hope, as well as salutory fear."[27] The Lord's death has conquered death. In our funeral liturgy we proclaim that through the resurrection of Jesus we share in his life; we live, we die, and we shall live again. We are to look forward with hope as we realize our responsibility toward our own eternal destiny and the destiny of the world. Evangelization, spreading the reconciling good news of Jesus, is no light matter when one considers the stakes.

The following citations are a few that reflect the eschatology of Israel, the gospels, and the early church:

Hebrew Scriptures
National Eschatology: Prophet Amos—professed the fall of the Northern Kingdom (9:8); Prophet Isaiah—insisted Southern Kingdom would stand (6:13); he also foretold the messianic reign (11:1-9).
Cosmic Eschatology: Prophet Isaiah—envisioned the new heaven and new earth (65:1); Prophet Jeremiah—spoke of the void earth (4:23); Prophet Ezra spoke about the end of the world (4 Ez 7:30).
Personal Eschatology: resurrection of the dead (Dn 12:2; 2 Mac 7).

---

[26]John J. Collins, "Eschatology" in *The Collegeville Pastoral Dictionary of Biblical Theology,* ed. Carroll Stuhlmueller, C.P. (Collegeville: The Liturgical Press, 1996), 261-264.

[27]"Basic Teaching for Catholic Religious Education," #25, p. 142.

New Testament

Christ's future return (Jn 21:22-23; Acts 1:11); parousia (Mt 24:29-31; Mk 13:24-27); eschatological reign of God (Mt 13:31-32, Mk 4:30-32); eschatological banquet (Mt 26:29; Mk 14:25; Lk 22:15-16); realized eschatology (Jn 14:6; 17:3); final judgment (Rev 13:1-8; Mt 19:28; Lk 22:30; 1 Cor 6:2-3).

Testing

In what way, if any, has your original understanding regarding the end times been stretched, challenged or affirmed? Was there any new information for you? If so, what was it? In light of the material just presented, is there any implication for living the Christian life? Are there any implications for the wider church? In what way can we as church participate in helping people live in *realized eschatology*? How are the biblical themes of covenant, exodus, creation, and community evident in the post-biblical teachings about the end times, final judgment, eternal life, and resurrection of the body? In what way are these post-biblical teachings related to the scriptures of this Sunday's liturgy? In light of this sharing, how would you articulate a theology or an understanding of eschatology? Is it the same as your first understanding, or has it changed?

Decision

How does this understanding of eschatology challenge me personally? How am I living the message? In what way do I need to grow? What is one concrete action I can take this week as a response to our sharing? Prepare to share the experience next week.

Refer to chapter 7, "Preparing the Catechetical Session," if you intend to plan your catechetical session at this time.

EUCHARIST

See Christian Initiation, Part III: Eucharist (Appendix).

FASTING

See Lenten Overview.

GARMENT

See Easter Vigil, Symbol of Garment.

HOLY FAMILY

See Feast of the Holy Family.

HOLY SPIRIT

See Trinity: God as Spirit (Appendix). See Feast of Pentecost. See Easter Season Overview. See Feast of the Baptism of the Lord.

INCARNATION

The Incarnation (from the Latin, *caro*, "flesh," "enfleshing") refers to God assuming human nature. It specifically refers to God becoming a human being when Jesus was conceived by the Holy Spirit in his mother, Mary. It also refers to the mystery of Christ, as one divine person, possessing a fully human and a fully divine nature.

Natural Sign

When we speak about the Incarnation, what does it evoke in you? How do you feel about the idea of God coming to earth in the person of Jesus? If you were to articulate an understanding of Incarnation, first, do you have such an understanding, and second, what is it? How would you [or could you] articulate an understanding of your faith tradition's belief in the Incarnation?

Tradition: Biblical, Ecclesial, and Liturgical Signs

Belief in the incarnation is a foundational truth. It is among the *hierarchy of truths*. The essence of being Christian is to accept the reality and the mystery of the Incarnation. Jesus, who was one with God, entered human history and took on a human nature. We are taught that Jesus became a human being to save us from our sins, to reconcile us with God (1 Jn 4:10; 4:14). We proclaim that truth every time we pray the Nicene Creed together in liturgy.

Another reason God took human form through Jesus is so that we all could experience God's unfathomable love. We humans are very stubborn sometimes. God understands us all too well. God knew that if he did not come to us in the flesh, we would never really believe the love God has for us. Unless someone could walk with us in our struggles, suffer with us in our pain, laugh with us in our joys, we would never really own the love that God has for us. Thus, Yahweh sent his Son to endure what all human beings have to endure, the struggles of life.

Jesus, the Son of God, also came to us to show us the way to God, to show us what it means to be a holy people. Jesus is the perfect model. As our brother, he showed us how to live by the example of his own life. Through his teaching we are shown what it means to be a holy people, a royal priesthood, a people set apart. Jesus came to offer us the law of love. He gave us the great commandment of love: we are to love God and one another. We are to lay down our lives for one another, just as Jesus laid down his life for us.

God became human in order for us to share in his divine nature. "For this is why the Word became man, and the Son of God became the Son of man: so that man, by entering into communion with the Word and thus receiving divine sonship, might become a son of God."[28] Sometimes this is the most difficult reality for people. We are so sure of our wretchedness that we find it difficult to accept that we share the divine nature of God through our incorporation into Jesus' Mystical Body. We *are* holy people. To echo the words of Genesis: God created male and female and God saw that it was good. By taking human form God elevated human nature and restored human dignity.

Jesus is not a divided self, part God and part human. The mystery we celebrate is that Jesus was fully human and fully divine at the same time. The first heresies denied that Jesus was fully human (Gnostic Docetism). According to the Arian heresy, Jesus was not from the same substance as the Father. In response, the Nicean Council stated that Jesus was begotten, not made. There never was a time when Jesus was not.

Jesus, as true God and true human being, possessed a human will and intellect. This will and intellect were subject to his divine will and intellect, the same will and intellect of Father and Son. The mystery of the Incarnation "sheds light both on the mystery of God and the mystery of human life."[29] Through the mystery of the Incarnation God is so dedicated to humanity and to creation (God's handiwork) that he exploded into human history to be one with us in all things. God desired to experience our humanity in its completeness: the joys and the struggles.

The Incarnation shows us what it means to be human and gives meaning and purpose to the human life. To live is to hunger for intimate relationship with God. For this we were created. Consequently, the Incarnation is good news for the human race. It expresses the potential goodness of every human life. How could human life be anything but potentially worthy if God was willing to take its form? While there is propensity for sin in human nature, the Incarnation gives us the hope and the means to enter deeply into relationship with God. It is the kind of relationship that God envisioned and desired at the creation of the world.

The messiah came to restore the perfect harmony created by God in the genesis event. Creation's perfect harmony consisted in right ordered relationships: God's perfect justice. Perfect justice is an ordering of relationships that places human beings in reciprocal covenant relationship with God, with one another, and with creation. God and humanity were to share an unbreakable bond and as a result were to enter into a similar union with one another. They were to offer God's justice and love to the powerless and to those difficult to love by the world's standards. This love was to be extended not necessarily because such persons deserved to be loved, but because God would do as much and wished that we do no less. Humanity's response was a sign of their love for God (or lack thereof).

However, people interrupted God's plan through sin. They turned from God and lost God's just and perfect kingdom. The *Word Made Flesh* was to restore creation's justly ordered design. The peace

---

[28] St. Irenaeus, Adv. Haeres. 3, 19, 1:PG7/1, 939, in *Catechism of the Catholic Church*, p. 116, #460.

[29] Richard P. McBrien, *Encyclopedia of Catholicism* (San Francisco: HarperCollins, 1995), 659.

that accompanied Jesus' birth was nothing less than the restoration of God's first grand design. Through Jesus the relationships envisioned by God are possible.

The Advent/Christmas season highlights the Incarnation in the liturgical texts and scriptures celebrated throughout the season. Every eucharistic liturgy celebrates the Incarnation and professes it in ritual and prayer, Gloria, Creed, eucharistic prayers, etc.

Testing

In what way, if any, has your original understanding regarding the Incarnation been informed, stretched, challenged, or affirmed? Was there any new information for you? If so, what was it? In light of the material just presented, is there any implication for living the Christian life? What does this teaching have to say about the community's and your role in God's plan for the redemption of the human race? In what way is this post-biblical teaching related to the scriptures of this Sunday's liturgy? In light of this sharing, how would you articulate an understanding of the Incarnation? Is it the same as your first understanding, or has it changed?

Decision

How does this teaching about the Incarnation challenge our community? In what way is our community living the message we just shared? In what specific way is our community in need of transformation? Is there any concrete action I can take to be an agent of change in my community? How does this reflection concerning the Incarnation of Jesus challenge me personally? How am I living the message? In what way do I need to grow? What one concrete action can I take this week as a response to what we have shared?

Refer to chapter 7, "Preparing the Catechetical Session," if you intend to plan your catechetical session at this time.

JESUS

Natural Sign

Have you ever had a personal experience of Jesus in your life? Define what you believe about Jesus. What do you think the church teaches about Jesus Christ?

Tradition: Biblical, Ecclesial, and Liturgical Signs

Non-Christian sources do give testimony to the existence of Jesus. However, they give little or no historical information.

The New Testament answers the question of "Who is Jesus?" through the use of a multitude of titles that reflect his multi-faceted personhood and mission such as: Jesus the Prophet, Jesus the Suffering Servant of God, Jesus the High Priest, Jesus the Messiah, Jesus the Son of Man, Jesus the Lord, Jesus the Savior, Jesus the Word, Jesus the Son of God.

The gospels are the final, edited, redacted version of the oral and written remembrance of Christ proclaimed in the early church. The resurrection of Christ is the central pivot upon which the Christian kerygma hinges. It is the event that prompts the early church's faith in Christ as the promised messiah and Savior of the world. No one saw the resurrection, but many experienced Christ after the resurrection. Jesus' central message was the arrival of the reign of God that he proclaimed through parables, proverbial sayings, and the Lord's Prayer.

The church's understanding of Jesus grew gradually in the apostolic age especially between 100 and 700 with the primary focus centered on his nature. Doctrine in relation to Christ developed as a result of curiosity, controversies, and heresies.

The main question or problem centered around the divinity and the humanity of Christ. Belief in Jesus, the God-Man, was the cause of controversy. Jesus was both human and divine. To stress the divinity over the humanity undermines belief in Jesus' humanity. When Jesus' humanity is too greatly stressed his divinity is diminished. Balance is critical.

Heresies centered around belief in Christ's humanity and divinity prompted an articulation of the church's creed in relationship to Christ. The Council of Nicea definitively asserted the divinity of Christ and rejected the Arian heresy that stated that Jesus was made at a certain point in time. The Council attested to Jesus' oneness with the Father. The Council of Constantinople was concerned with upholding the humanity of Christ so that the effect of Christ's redemption not be minimized.

The Council of Ephesus maintained that Jesus is both God and human at the same time and that Mary, his mother, is the mother of Jesus and the Mother of God (Theotokos). The Council attested to the two natures of Jesus: human and divine at the same time. The Council of Chaldeon affirmed Jesus' two distinct natures. He is fully human and fully divine and like us in all things except sin.

Doctrine in relation to Christ was firmly established in the historical period of 100-700 and forms the basis of our christology today. The church teaches that Jesus is the Word made flesh. God took on human form in order to accomplish his plan of salvation. He became human for us that we might be reconciled with God and saved for all eternity. He became human so that we would know God's love for us and so we would have an example of holiness. Jesus taught us what it means to be fully human and fully alive.

Jesus is truly God and truly human. He became man while remaining fully divine. Belief in the passion, death, and resurrection is at the heart of the Christian kerygma. Christ loved us to death. He died and rose again for the sins of the world. The blood ritual of the old covenant was replaced by the Christ's blood, the blood of the new covenant. Christ's sacrifice surpasses all other sacrifices. None is greater. Through Christ's death we are freed from sin; through his resurrection we are raised to new and eternal life. Jesus is the second person of the Blessed Trinity.

Jesus is the centerpiece of all liturgical celebrations, blessings, sacraments, private prayer and devotions. He is the object and purpose of our gathering and the source of our prayer.

Testing

Were there any new insights? Have any of your original assumptions been stretched? How would you articulate an understanding about the church's belief in Christ in light of this presentation? What does belief in Christ have to do with everyday life?

Decision

How does this teaching about Christ challenge me personally? How am I living the message? In what way do I need to grow? What one concrete action can I take this week as a response to what was shared?

Refer to chapter 7, "Preparing the Catechetical Session," if you intend to plan your catechetical session at this time.

KINGDOM OF GOD

Natural Sign

What does the term "kingdom of God" evoke in you? What does it call to mind? Have you ever had a personal experience of God's kingdom in your life? If you were to give a definition of "the kingdom of God," what would it be? What do you think is meant by the term?

Tradition: Biblical, Ecclesial, and Liturgical Signs

The kingdom of God is now. There is evidence in scripture to make such an assertion. Jesus said that "the kingdom of God is at hand" (Mk 1:14-15). In obedience to his Father's will, Jesus initiates the kingdom of heaven in our midst, here and now, on earth.

As members of this kingdom we share in God's divine life. We call this gathering of God's people the church, the family of God. Jesus is the head of that family through his word, through signs that reveal God's reign, and through the sending of disciples to spread the good news. "The Word of the Lord is compared to a seed which is sown in a field; those who hear the Word with faith and become part of the little flock of Christ, have received the Kingdom itself" (*Lumen Gentium*, #5).

Jesus established his kingdom on earth. We are invited to be part of that kingdom by living Christ's paschal mystery. When we accept the daily dyings and risings of life, we share in Jesus' suffering, death, and resurrection.

Everyone is called to God's kingdom. It belongs to the poor and the lowly. Jesus identifies with the poor and those humble enough to hear his word. The condition for membership in God's kingdom is that we respond in love to the poor and less fortunate.

Sinners are welcome and are part of God's kingdom. They are invited to deep conversion and transformation.

We learn a great deal about God's kingdom through Jesus' parables. They challenge us to give all that we are to build God's kingdom—in word and action. "The parables highlight the social character of the kingdom. Jesus never presents the kingdom as a private affair between God and an individual. Rather, it is an active force in the world, a reconciling presence creating a sense of solidarity among people."[30]

We know the kingdom is at hand through the signs Jesus performed. Miracles strengthen faith. "The miracles of Jesus also confirm that the Kingdom has already arrived on earth" (*Lumen Gentium*, #5). We are not, however, to view them in a magical, manipulative way.

Jesus empowers the apostles to carry on his work in establishing the kingdom. That authority continues through the pope, bishops, priests, deacons, religious, and all God's people.

We live in God's kingdom now with hope in the kingdom yet to come. Through the story of the Transfiguration we are given a glimpse of God's heavenly kingdom. We will one day share in Jesus' transfigured glory when we join him in the eternal city.

We must not lose sight of that hope. Yet we live in the present. Our reality is that the kingdom of God is *now*. Jesus envisions a kingdom of peace where the lame walk, where the blind see, where people lay down their lives for one another and the poor and oppressed are cared for. When one looks at present day society it is often difficult to imagine such a kingdom. However, the kingdom of God *is at hand* when Christians gather in truth, hope and love; when they live a gospel life, repent, change their lives and spread the good news.[31]

The following gospel citations address the reign of God. The kingdom of God in Mark's gospel: "is at hand..." (1:15); purpose of the parables (4:11, 26, 30). The kingdom of God in Matthew's gospel: on earth, in heaven (6:10); parables—"kingdom is like..." (13:24, 31, 33-34, 44-45, 47; 18:23; 20:1; 22:2; 25:1). Kingdom of God in Luke's gospel: now and not yet (4:43; 8:1; 9:2, 11, 60, 62; 16:16). Kingdom of God in John's gospel: who is admitted? (3:1-5).

The kingdom of God is proclaimed at every liturgy when the gospel is proclaimed and the eucharist and the sacraments are celebrated. Every liturgy is a proclamation of the reign of God. The kingdom of God is definitely announced in the Lord's Prayer.

Testing

In what way, if any, has your original understanding regarding the kingdom of God been stretched, challenged, or affirmed? Was there any new information for you? If so, what was it? In light of the material just presented, is there any implication for living the Christian life? What does this teaching have to say about the community's and your role in God's kingdom? Who is invited? What are the signs of God's kingdom? The biblical themes of the presence of God through his covenant, the exodus, creation, and community are evident in this teaching. How are those themes connected to this understanding of the kingdom of God?

In what way is this church teaching related to the scriptures of this Sunday's liturgy? In light of this sharing, how would you articulate an understanding of the kingdom of God now? Is it the same as your first understanding, or has it changed?

Decision

How does this teaching about the kingdom of God challenge our community? In what way is our community living the message we just shared? In what specific way is our community in need of transformation? Is there any concrete action you can take to be an agent of change in your community? How does this understanding of the kingdom of God challenge you personally? How are you living the message? In what way do you need to grow? What one concrete action can you take this week as a response to this sharing?

Refer to chapter 7, "Preparing the Catechetical Session," if you intend to plan your catechetical session at this time.

LAYING ON OF HANDS

See Trinity: God as Spirit (Appendix). See Easter Vigil: Symbol of Laying on of Hands.

---

[30]Marthaler, *The Creed*, 223-227.
[31]Ibid.

LENT

See Lenten Overview and the Sundays of Lent.

LIGHT

See Easter Vigil: Symbol of Light.

MARY, MODEL FOR THE CHURCH

Natural Sign
What role, if any, does Mary play in your life? What does the image of mother evoke in you? What is your understanding of the church's teaching on Mary?

Tradition: Biblical, Ecclesial, and Liturgical Signs
The basis of the church's teaching regarding Mary is belief in Jesus Christ. As the first Christian, Mary is a model for how to reveal Christ to the world and how to live the Christian kerygma.

The *Catechism of the Catholic Church* calls Mary the "Eschatological Icon of the Church" (972). Through her we reflect upon what the church already is as it makes its journey of faith toward the final resting place in heaven.

Christ is the focus of Marian devotion. Church teaching about Mary is best summed up in the liturgical feasts of the year. Mary, Mother of God (Jan. 1) stresses the true nature of Christ—his humanity and divinity, and honors Mary as the Mother of God. The Annunciation honors the virginal conception of Christ by the power of the Spirit. The Immaculate Conception (Dec. 8) celebrates the utter graciousness of God toward humanity in that Mary was conceived without original sin due to grace, not merit. The Visitation (May 31) celebrates the working of the Spirit as Mary was inspired to visit her cousin Elizabeth. The Assumption of Mary (Aug. 15) into heaven was intended to strengthen our belief in the resurrection of the body. The feast also honors Mary who shares a unique union with God in Christ from the very beginning through the end of her life. The Queenship of Mary (August 22) honors Mary as queen and mother of the human race. Our Lady of Sorrows (September 15) remembers the suffering of Mary and reminds us that the church is united with Christ through suffering and death so that we may live eternally with him.[32]

Commentary in this workbook on the liturgical feasts honoring Mary offers a more elaborate and detailed analysis of various facets of Marian devotion. Please refer to those feasts for further insights.

Testing
Were there any new insights? Is your understanding of the role of Mary expanded or affirmed? How might the role of Mary have anything to do with your everyday life? What are the implications for living the Christian kerygma?

Decision
In what way does this teaching call me to action in my life, in the church, or in the world? What action will I take as a result?

Refer to chapter 7, "Preparing the Catechetical Session," if you intend to plan your catechetical session at this time.

MORALITY: FOUNDATIONS

Natural Sign
If you were asked what it means to live a moral life, how would you respond? Complete this sentence: "Morality is. . . ."

Tradition: Biblical, Ecclesial, and Liturgical Signs
Morality refers to behaviors that flow from an individual's principled assumptions. Both the Hebrew scriptures (Old Testament) and the Christian scriptures (New Testament) view the totality of life, secular and the spiritual, as one. The Hellenistic world (Greek) and its philosophical constructions introduced to us a sense that we are divided between matters spiritual and temporal. This is called dualism. The scriptures paint an entirely different picture, however. All life is sacred and consecrated to God's saving presence. God wishes us to be happy and whole, not divided. The Hebrew understanding of wholeness is the right ordering of relationships (*hesed*), that is, right rela-

---

[32]Linda Gaupin, CDP, Ph.D., *Catholic Faith and Life: Catechist Training* (Diocese of Orlando, Fla., 1996). Unpublished course text, 81.

tionship to God, to one another, to the earth, and to oneself.

The Christian scriptures uphold a standard that speaks of moral behavior in terms of *just actions,* such as feeding the hungry and giving drink to the thirsty. In contrast with a fundamentalist approach to morality in which morality is founded on direct biblical revelation and directives,[33] Catholic morality is based primarily on the biblical themes of creation, exodus, covenant, and cross. From a biblical and early church perspective, when one's morality was weighed, it was judged in light of discipleship. For example, before one was admitted for baptism, that person's readiness was discerned. The criteria for this discernment were based on the person's moral behavior. Was *metanoia* visible in the person's life? Was there a change, a turning from one thing toward another, a turn from one way of living to a new way of living in Christ? Early documents, such as the Didache, directed that catechumens be given clear instruction regarding the type of life they were to live after baptism. Baptism empowered them for incorporation into the life and mission of Christ.

Christian morality is based on the understanding posited by Thomas Aquinas that nature and supernature are graced by God. As human beings we possess dignity. God is infinitely present to all of life, thus all of life is graced by God. We have been told in the story of our human genesis that we are made in God's image. We are sacred because *we are,* not because of anything we have done. Jesus lives within us and teaches us what it means to be fully human. "All people seek happiness: life, peace, joy, wholeness and wholesomeness of being. The happiness human beings seek and for which they are fashioned is given in Jesus, God's supreme gift of love. He comes in the Father's name to bring the fulfillment promised to the He-

brew people and, through them, to all people everywhere. He is Himself our happiness and peace, our joy and beatitude."[34]

Through our union with God, who is communal by nature (Father, Son and Spirit), we are *social beings.* We are intended to live in relationship. As human beings we live in the community of family, church, and world. We are destined for happiness insofar as we live in right ordered relationships (*hesed*). When we respond in love to uphold the dignity of the human person we become fully human and fully alive. There is no room for an individualistic faith. We are ecclesial by nature and by design.

Our moral life is communal by nature and by design. Even our personal sins impact others in some way. Thus, our pursuit of happiness must be grounded in care and concern for others. Living a moral life demands that we uphold the ethical teaching of Christ in the gospel.

God created us with a free will. We have the power to choose the path for our lives. We are free to pattern our lives in conformity to God's will, to say yes or no to God. Human beings are free to choose between good and evil; thus we are called to responsibility. As a mature person of faith I am called to behave in a moral way because God desires it.

The church teaches that the moral law is expressed in different ways, all of which are connected. The moral law is expressed through eternal law, given by God who is the source of all law, through natural law, through revealed law (Old Covenant and New Covenant) and civil and ecclesiastical law. Moral law, then, hinges on more than the Ten Commandments. All forms of moral law find meaning in the life of Jesus.

For example, as a Christian, my choice to obey the civil law regarding the speed limit brings my Christian perspective into the choice. On a very practical level I do not disobey the civil law against speeding because I do not want to get a ticket. On a moral level, however, my choice to obey the law

---

[33]It is interesting to note that fundamentalists often ignore the biblical directive to sell all you have and give to the poor. "We don't take the bible that literally," is often the reply. In essence, they become their own redactors of biblical ethics. The result is a canon within the canon: a biblically interpreted moral code, delicatessen style. Biblical interpretation insists that the historical, cultural, and literary milieu of the text be considered when appropriating meaning for our contemporary culture.

[34]*Sharing the Light of Faith, National Catechetical Directory for Catholics of the United States* (NCD), USCC, 1979, #100.

is illumined by my relationship with Christ. I am in covenant relationship with Jesus. Jesus loves me unconditionally. I, in turn, love Jesus and wish to act according to his design. We are all God's children and are graced by God. As a child of God, I have a responsibility to care for those around me. If I choose to place anyone in danger because of my actions, my relationships are not in right order. My relationship with Christ is strained because I have violated the law of love—care and concern for others. My relationship with my neighbor has been strained because I have placed others in harm's way. My relationship to myself is strained because in order to live in *shalom*-peace[35] my life has to be ordered to the will of God. As I reflect upon the life of Jesus in the gospel, I am invited into relationship. That relationship demands a response. The response made in love helps give meaning to my life.

Testing

Were there any new insights? How would I answer the question, "Morality is…" in light of the tradition presented? What is the challenge of this doctrine?

Decision

What action will I take as a response to this presentation? How am I called to transformation? Be specific.

Refer to chapter 7, "Preparing the Catechetical Session," if you intend to plan your catechetical session at this time.

ORDINARY TIME

See Overview of Ordinary Time. See chapter 8, "Time and the Liturgical Cycle."

PAROUSIA

The term *parousia* (pronounced pahr-*oo*-see'-uh) is a Greek word meaning "presence" or "arrival." In the ancient Greek world, cities awaiting the arrival of dignitaries to their region would be awaiting their *parousia*. Paul uses the term in reference to himself when visiting the various communities. The term later was transferred to the belief in Jesus' second coming.

Natural Sign

What are your feelings in regard to the second coming of Jesus? Is it completely foreign to your experience or understanding or are you comfortable with the concept? Have you ever considered it before? What possible connection might there be to your own personal life? What might you say if asked to explain what the parousia or second coming of Jesus is about? What do you think is meant by the term?

Tradition: Biblical, Ecclesial, and Liturgical Signs

Parousia is referred to as the glorious coming of Christ a second time, but is also related to the completion of God's plan of salvation for the human race, the final arrival of God's reign, the resurrection of the body on the last day, and final judgment. The coming of Jesus is the fulfillment of all God has been doing throughout salvation history. From the very beginning, at the creation of the world, God's master plan of salvation was intended to be accomplished through the life, death, and resurrection of Jesus Christ, the Son of God. Jesus is God's spoken Word that entered the lives of human beings. "The entire economy of salvation receives its meaning from the Incarnate Word. It prepared his coming; it manifests and extends his kingdom on earth from the time of his death and resurrection up to his second glorious coming, which *will complete the work of God.*"[36] Thus, when Jesus comes again, God's plan of salvation for the human race will be completed.

Our understanding of the parousia is expressed in our core truth, "the mystery of God the Father, the Son, and the Holy Spirit, Creator of all things; the mystery of Christ, the Incarnate Word, who was born of the Virgin Mary, and who suffered, died, and rose for our salvation, the mystery of the Holy Spirit, who is present in the Church, sanctifying it and guiding it until *the glorious coming of Christ,* our Savior and Judge; and the mystery of

---

[35]When the heavenly hosts came announcing good news and peace to people of good will, *shalom*/peace was understood to mean wholeness. *Shalom* is a wholeness achieved only through the right ordering of relationships with God, one another, self, and the natural world.

[36]GCD, #41.

the Church, which is Christ's Mystical Body, in which the Virgin Mary holds a preeminent place."[37] We proclaim this truth every time we gather for liturgy when we pray the Nicene Creed, "…he will come again in glory to judge the living and the dead…." The parousia underscores the presence of Christ throughout all of salvation history, and the completion of the ultimate plan or process of salvation that began with the Incarnation, death, and resurrection of Jesus.[38]

The early church struggled with the reality that Jesus' second coming was not as imminent as they first had thought. In response, the evangelists formulated an understanding of God that put him beyond human time limitations. Believers were exhorted to view God's delay as a sign of "merciful opportunity for repentance."[39]

It is important not to consider the parousia as the return of Christ who has been absent all these long generations. "It is a breaking through of a presence that has been continuous throughout history."[40]

Jesus promised us that we would be judged at the end of time. Our hearts will be laid bare and all will be given a personal accounting of how they have or have not lived the law of love in their lives. Each person will be held accountable for the actions of his or her life and judged accordingly

Jesus reigns today in the church through the Holy Spirit. However, the entire world has yet to recognize his reign. At the end of time Jesus will prevail victorious over the evil that permeates the world. Evil will be definitively squashed.

The church embraces the basic biblical understanding that human history has a purpose and that Jesus will win out over evil. Our doctrine is essentially a message of hope and consolation in the face of what often seems to be the ultimate victory of evil over good. We will one day experience a re-versal and thus live in the eternal Presence where evil reigns no more.

The implication of the parousia is to be constantly on guard, to have our houses in order, to live in right relationship, and to assist in God's work of establishing justice in our temporal world.

Biblical passages that address the parousia (Jesus' second coming in glory and the final coming of God's reign, resurrection from the dead and final judgement) are the following:

Foreshadowed in the Old Testament:
Genesis 49:8. Numbers 23:21. Isaiah 2:2-5; 9:2; 11:6-16. Jeremiah 23:6. Daniel 7:13-14. Hosea 2:21-25. Zechariah 11:10.

New Testament:
Acts 1:11. 1 Corinthians 15:23. 1 Thessalonians 2:19; 3:13; 4:15; 5:23. 2 Thessalonians 1:7. 2 Timothy 4:1. Titus 2:13. Peter 1:7. 1 John 2:28; 3:2, 5, 8.

Gospels:
Matthew 10:23; 14:62; 16:27-28; 24:3, 27, 30, 36-37, 39. Mark 13:24. Luke 9:26; 12:40, 46; 17:20-37; 18:8; 21:27.

The parousia is addressed at every liturgical celebration that exhorts us to hope for the day when Christ will come again. ("Christ has died, Christ is risen; Christ will come again.") The season of Advent particularly looks toward that future day.

Testing
In what way, if any, has your original understanding regarding the second coming of Jesus been informed, stretched, challenged, or affirmed? Was there any new information for you? If so, what was it? In light of the material just presented, is there any implication for living the Christian life? What does this teaching have to say about the community's and your role in preparing for the parousia? In what way is this teaching related to the scriptures of this Sunday's liturgy? In light of this sharing, how would you articulate an understanding of the parousia? Is it the same as your first understanding, or has it changed?

Decision
How does this teaching about Jesus' second coming challenge our community? In what way is our

---

[37]Ibid., #43.

[38]Zachary Hayes, O.F.M., "Parousia," in *The New Dictionary of Theology*, ed. Mary Collins, Joseph A. Komonchak, Dermot A. Lane (Collegeville: The Liturgical Press, 1987), 743.

[39]Sean P. Kealy, "Parousia," in *The Collegeville Pastoral Dictionary of Biblical Theology*, ed. Carroll Stuhlmueller, C.P. (Collegeville: The Liturgical Press, 1996). 692-694.

[40]Hayes, "Parousia," 743-744.

community living the message we just shared? In what specific way is our community in need of transformation? Is there any concrete action I can take to be an agent of change in my community? How does this understanding of the parousia challenge me personally? How am I living the message? In what way do I need to grow? What one concrete action can I take this week as a response to what we have shared?

Refer to chapter 7, "Preparing the Catechetical Session," if you intend to plan your catechetical session at this time.

PASCHAL MYSTERY

Natural Sign

What images from everyday life might evoke the sense of dying and rising? If you were asked what it meant to die and rise again, how would you respond? Finish this sentence: "The paschal mystery is...."

Tradition: Biblical, Ecclesial, and Liturgical Signs

The paschal mystery refers to the essential elements of Christian redemption. It encompasses the passion, death, resurrection, and ascension of Jesus Christ that we celebrate every time we gather and especially at the church's premier celebration during Holy Week and Easter. God's plan for the salvation of the world was accomplished once and for all by the death and resurrection of Christ.

Jesus did not come to abolish the covenant, but rather to fulfill it (Mt 5:17-19). He revealed the deepest meaning of the law and reformed the sins against it (Heb 9:15). Jesus honored the temple and the Jewish feasts. Jesus used the temple to prefigure his own death as he announced the destruction of the temple and the entrance into the messianic age in which his body would become the new temple.

Jesus suffered at the hands of the chief priests and the scribes who handed him over to the authorities to be tortured and crucified (Mk 8:31; Mt 20:19). They sought his death because of his acts of forgiving sins, expelling demons, and healing people on the sabbath as well as his unusual stance regarding the ritual laws of purity. It did not sit well with the religious authorities that he ate with sinners and tax collectors. Some people even believed that Jesus was possessed and others accused him of blasphemy, false prophecy, and religious crimes punishable by the death penalty—stoning (Mk 2:7, 14-17; 3:1-6, 22; 7:14-23; 14:1. Mt 12:24. Jn 8:48; 10:20; 7:12, 52; 8:59; 10:31, 33).

God sent his only Son to demonstrate his love for us and Jesus freely died for our sins. He gave us a lasting memorial of his death and resurrection when he gave us his Body and Blood at the Last Supper. Jesus atoned for the sins of the world through his death and resurrection, thereby fulfilling the atoning mission of the Suffering Servant (CCC, #623). Jesus went down to the domain of the dead to release those who had died before him and were held captive by the power of death. He opened the doors to the heavenly kingdom.

The resurrection was attested to by the disciples who encountered Christ in his risen state. Through the resurrection Christ entered into his glory. The empty tomb and cloths are reminders that Christ escaped the power of death. Christ entered into heavenly glory in his full humanity at his ascension into heaven. Jesus went ahead of us to prepare a place for us to dwell with him for all eternity. The paschal mystery also includes the sending of the Spirit to be with the church until such time as Christ will return to judge the living and the dead according to their righteousness before God.

The paschal mystery includes salvation as foretold in the Hebrew scriptures, incorporation into Jesus' life, and the origins of the church and its sacramental life. We especially are united into the paschal mystery through the sacraments of initiation—baptism, confirmation, and eucharist.

Through the sacraments of initiation and especially through what Augustine referred to as the repeatable sacrament of initiation, eucharist, Christians are united with Christ's suffering, death and resurrection; his passover from death to life. That is, Christians reenact and make present the paschal mystery when they take up their cross and unite their joys and sorrows with those of Jesus in the daily experience of their lives.

The paschal mystery is celebrated at every liturgy. This is why the Sunday celebration of eucharist is often referred to as an Easter event and why

Easter is considered the Great Feast of Sunday. All the sacraments express incorporation into the paschal mystery of Christ.

In the sacrament of baptism an individual plunges into the life-giving waters and in so doing dies to sin and passes over into new life in Christ. Through the sacramental anointing of confirmation the Spirit is given and the person is configured to Christ, which seals him or her permanently with the life, death, and resurrection of Jesus. Through eucharist the faithful participate in the death and resurrection of Christ in the taking, blessing, breaking, and sharing of the eucharist at each eucharistic liturgy. The suffering, death, resurrection, and ascension of Christ and the sending of the Spirit are remembered and actualized at every celebration of eucharist.

Testing
Has your original understanding of the paschal mystery been affirmed, stretched or challenged? Were there any new insights? Was there anything just shared that had not occurred to you before? What are the implications for everyday life? In what way have you experienced death and resurrection in your life? What are the implications for the church? In what way does the post-biblical teaching on paschal mystery have to do with this Sunday's readings? In light of this sharing, how would you articulate an understanding of the paschal mystery? Is it the same as your first understanding, or has it changed?

Decision
In what way do we as community live the message we just shared? Are there ways we need to grow in our understanding of what was shared? Where are the specific places where transformation is needed? How does the paschal mystery challenge me personally? How am I living it? In what way do I need to grow? What one concrete action can I take this week as a response to our sharing?

Refer to chapter 7, "Preparing the Catechetical Session," if you intend to plan your catechetical session at this time.

RECONCILIATION

Natural Sign
Have you ever experienced the forgiveness of someone close to you? Please explain. What did it teach you about reconciliation? How would you complete this sentence: "Reconciliation is..."?

Tradition: Biblical, Ecclesial, and Liturgical Signs
Please refer to the Rite of Penance (#386-394) for the scripture citations that are suggested in the Rite of Penance. These scriptural texts shed light on God's mercy experienced through his healing love and reconciliation.

The church exhorts men and women to repentance so that they may turn away from sin and be converted completely to the Lord (Rite of Penance [RP], #1). We are called to reconciliation with God and the church. Every sin is an offense against God that disrupts our friendship with him. "The ultimate purpose of penance is that we should love God deeply and commit ourselves deeply to him"[41] Sinners who embrace the way of penance come back to the Father who loved us first, to Christ who gave himself up for us, and to the Spirit who has been abundantly poured upon us.

By the mystery of God's love we are joined in the bond of solidarity. The sin of one harms others and the holiness of one benefits others.[42] Penance always involves reconciliation with brothers and sisters who are harmed by our sins (RP, #5). Through the grace of Christ we are all to work for justice and peace in the world (RP, #6). Hence, we are to be cognizant of the social dimension of sin. "Men frequently join together to commit injustice (RP, #6)."

> Sin and its effects are visible everywhere: in exploitative relationships, loveless families, unjust social structures and policies, crimes by and against individuals and against creation, the oppression of the weak and the manipulation of the vulnerable, explosive tensions among nations and among ideological, racial and religious groups, and social classes, the scandalous gulf between those who waste goods and

---

[41]Paul VI, Apostolic Constitution *Paenitenini*, February 17, 1966. AAS 57 (1965), 15-16. In Rite of Penance: *The Rites of the Catholic Church*, #5.

[42]Paul VI, Apostolic Constitution *Indulgentiarum doctrina*, Jan. 1, 1967, no. 4: AAS 59 (1967), 9; see Pius XII, encyclical *Mystici Corporis*, June 29, 1943. AAS 35 (1943), 213.

resources, and those who live and die amid deprivation and underdevelopment, wars and preparations for war. Sin is a reality in the world.[43]

Thus, we are to help each other do penance by working with others to realize justice and peace for all.

There are observable effects of reconciliation. We are converted to God with our whole heart. This conversion leads to sorrow for sin and the intention to live a new life. The intent to lead a new life is expressed through confession made to the church, through due satisfaction for sin and the promise to amend one's life. Pardon is granted through the church, which works by the ministry of priests (RP, #6).

Reconciliation occurs through the four components of the sacrament of penance. 1. Contrition: we are sorry for our sins and intend to sin no more. We are completely converted to Christ and turn our lives to the holiness and love of God in order to render ourselves more like Christ. 2. Confession: we examine our sin in light of God's mercy before God; we are sorry for our sins, and our heart is to be opened to God's minister, the priest.

3. Act of penance: True conversion is completed and evidenced by satisfaction for sins committed, amendment of conduct, and reparation of injury (suited to personal condition of each penitent). 4. Absolution is given through the sign of laying on of hands. God grants pardon to the sinner in sacramental confession and penance is completed.

> In the sacrament of penance the Father receives the repentant Son who comes back to him, Christ places the lost sheep on his shoulders and brings it back to the sheepfold, and the Holy Spirit sanctifies this temple of God again or lives more fully within it. This is finally expressed in a renewed and more fervent sharing of the Lord's table, and there is great joy at the banquet of God's church over the Son who has returned from afar.[44]

The church celebrates reconciliation through liturgical signs in the following manner: Rite of Reconciliation of individual penitents, Rite of Reconciliation of Several Penitents with Individual Confession and Absolution, Rite of Reconciliation of Several Penitents with General Confession and Absolution and Various Texts Used in the Celebration of Reconciliation, including sample nonsacramental penitential celebration. "Penitential celebrations, mentioned in the Rite of Penance (#36-37), are beneficial in fostering a spirit and virtue of penance among individuals and communities; they also help in preparing for a more fruitful celebration of the sacrament of penance. However, the faithful must be reminded of the difference between these celebrations and sacramental confession and absolution."[45]

Testing
Were there any new insights? How would you answer the following question now? "Reconciliation is. . . ."? What is the challenge? How are you called to live in a new way as a result of this doctrine?

Decision
What concrete action will I take as a result of this sharing?

Refer to chapter 7, "Preparing the Catechetical Session," if you intend to plan your catechetical session at this time.

SACRAMENTALITY

Sacramentality refers to the presence and encounter of God in all spheres of relationships and human endeavors.

Natural Sign
Do you remember a time when you experienced a sense of God's presence? How do you remember it? Describe it. What happened? How do you understand the meaning of the encounter you just described?

Tradition: Biblical, Ecclesial, and Liturgical Signs
In order to better understand sacraments it would be helpful to understand the concept of sacramentality on a purely human or anthropological

---

[43]NCD, #98.
[44]Rite of Penance, #6d.

[45]Rite of Penance, Appendix II, #1.

level. Sacramentality is an activity that all human beings engage in by virtue of being in relationship. It is a process of discovery. People perform the rituals of life and in the process seek to appropriate meaning for their lives. Through sacramentality we give deeper meaning to the observable events around us. Moments of significant encounter, relational moments, form us and cause us to reflect on the meaning for our lives.

In the scriptures the word sacrament is translated "mystery." It has a broad meaning and refers to God's plan and activity, revealed in Christ, for our salvation. The word sacramentality encompasses all the ways that God reaches out to us in the world. Any object, person, or thing that somehow brings God and people into contact, that reveals God's saving love, is understood as sacrament.

Sacramentality occurs whenever there is a precious encounter, a presence of God in any situation. Sacramentality embodies everyday moments of grace that have meaning for our lives. Wherever human beings are fully alive, God is present.

By our very nature, we Catholics are a sacramental people. We regard all creation as holy. We see God's life and energy in all created things, and we particularly set aside specific symbols from our natural world to speak and celebrate that reality.

The National Catechetical Directory states that there are four signs of God's presence: natural signs, biblical signs, ecclesial signs, and liturgical signs. Sacramentality is the essence of these signs. God is present throughout all human experience, through the natural signs in everyday life. God is sacramentally present in human experiences and relationships, in art, in music, in technology. God is sacramentally present in biblical signs, in the word of God spoken through the generations. God is revealed to us sacramentally (real presence) in the scriptures. God is truly (sacramentally) present to us in the church, through the living of our faith, through our beliefs and practices and through the service we perform in his name. God is sacramentally present to us in the rites of identity, passage, and celebration that we perform in the gathering and worship of God's people, the liturgy.

Even before Christ became human, there were rituals, blessings, signs, prayers, and gestures that spoke to the people about their identity and about a sacramental presence of God. The Spirit-guided church determined seven signs to be the most important and the most authentic because within them there appeared to be the very essence and life energy of Christ. Thus, there are seven unique signs that are especially determined to be sources of God's life and grace for the uplifting of the church. They are called the seven sacraments.

Testing
Had you ever considered the concept of sacramentality before? Were there any new insights? Was there anything just shared that had not occurred to you before? What are the implications for everyday life? In what way does sacramentality have anything to do with this Sunday's readings? How would you articulate an understanding of sacramentality?

Decision
How does sacramentality impact my life? How should I respond? How does this understanding of sacramentality challenge me personally? In what way do I need to grow? What one concrete action can I take this week as a response?

Refer to chapter 7, "Preparing the Catechetical Session," if you intend to plan your catechetical session at this time.

SACRAMENTS

Sacraments are the seven designated "liturgical rites of the church through which participants experience the love and power of God (grace) that flows from Christ's Passion, death and Resurrection."[46]

Natural Sign
Call to mind a particularly meaningful sacramental rite you have experienced. (Remember that people in the initiation process may or may not have had any church rituals. Thus, they instead might be asked: "Do you have a conscious mem-

---

[46]Richard McBrien, "Sacrament," in *Encyclopedia of Catholicism* (San Francisco: HarperCollins. 1995), 1146.

ory of celebrating any church ritual or any other type of family or organization's ritual?") Please describe the experience. What happened? Based on your experience, how would you define *sacrament*? (Or, for a person in initiation, one might ask: "How would you explain the meaning of the word *ritual* in light of the experience you just shared?")

Tradition: Biblical, Ecclesial, and Liturgical Signs

The seven sacraments were not presented to us by Christ in specific formula and intent. One cannot go to the scriptures and find the as-is liturgical rituals of sacraments. Their origins are reminiscent of the so-called Jewish sacraments. However, the spirit and meaning of the sacraments can be found in scripture through the life, ministry, and paschal mystery of Christ. We celebrate the mystery of salvation through the sacraments. They point us toward our eventual participation in the great banquet of heaven.

The term sacrament (from the Latin *sacramentum*, "oath," "pledge") refers to the seven liturgical rites of the church. Through the celebration of these rites people experience the love and grace of God and share in the paschal mystery of Christ, his life, passion, death, and resurrection. The seven sacraments are baptism, confirmation, eucharist, penance, anointing of the sick, holy orders, and matrimony.

The original word, *mysterion* (Greek "mystery"), was translated into the Latin word *sacramentum*. "A sacrament was an oath of allegiance made by a soldier in the military. Sometimes the soldier was branded on the arm with a sign of the general he was to serve."[47] An early church Father, Tertullian, used this image to refer to baptism. We are permanently consigned to the mission of God "through word 'oath' and visible 'sign' (brand) made possible through sharing in the Paschal Mystery of Christ."[48]

During the Middle Ages the church designated a list of seven sacraments. Prior to that time there had been a broader understanding of sacrament. It was understood to mean the power, love, and manifestation of God in any and all circumstances. Sacraments were also referred to as mysteries. The hidden nature of sacrament reflected God's hidden plan of salvation for all the world. God's plan was realized through the paschal mystery of Christ.

The theology of sacrament was developed during the scholastic period of the church (1100-1300). God offers salvation and strengthens the church through the sacraments which are instruments of God's grace. Sacraments unify the church and make holy her people. God's action is inherent in the sacramental signs. The familiar definition was "Sacraments are an outward sign, instituted by Christ, to give grace."

To expand the scholastic understanding of sacramental theology, modern sacramental catechesis "has emphasized that *Jesus Christ is the first sacrament.*"[49] Since the power of the sacraments flows from the life, passion, death and resurrection of Jesus, he is our first sacrament. *The Church has also been referred to as sacrament since she is the living presence of Christ on earth until he comes again in glory.* The church as the Body of Christ is the instrument that "proclaims God's powerful love for humanity in and through the Paschal mystery."[50]

Christ himself, through the Holy Spirit, offers the grace and power that each sacrament expresses. Through the Holy Spirit the sacraments have the power of healing and transformation. Through the sacraments we are made more into the image of Christ. Thomas Aquinas stated: "Therefore a sacrament is a sign that commemorates what precedes it—Christ's Passion; demonstrates what is accomplished in us through Christ's Passion— grace; and prefigures what that Passion pledges to us—future glory."[51] In other words, through the sacraments, the passion of Jesus is remembered and made present. We are graced, given a share in his life, and are promised eternal life. Sacraments strengthen and empower us to cooperate with the life we have been given.

Sacraments have their genesis out of the signs and symbols of everyday life. Humanity experiences the spiri-

---

[47]Ibid.
[48]Ibid., 1147.

[49]Ibid.
[50]Ibid.
[51]St. Thomas Aquinas, *Summa theologiae*, III, 60, 3.

tual world through symbols. Language, gestures, and actions express and communicate meaning on a very basic level. The elements of creation speak to us of the power and nature of God. Fire, water, light speak to us of God's presence and God's power. Actions of everyday life, washing, anointing, breaking bread, sharing a cup, can express for us the way God graces us and the way we offer praise and thanks for all of God's saving work. God takes the gifts made from human hands and through the power of the Holy Spirit makes them holy. The elements (bread, wine, water, oil, light, laying on of hands, cross, fire) are transformed into a new reality and in the process we are changed and transformed as well. It is not magic, but it is mystery. It is mystery when the church is able by the grace of the Holy Spirit to remember past events and actions, bring those events and actions into the present through story telling and symbolic ritual, and know that the same effect of the original event is a present, experienced reality.

Sacraments are celebrations of conversion and are related to life and human experience. They possess meaning on two levels, theoretical and practical. We understand conceptually what a sacrament means and we *experience* the meaning given to it through its celebration in the community.

The sacraments are not private. They are communal by nature and by intent. The Constitution on the Sacred Liturgy states: "Liturgical services are not private functions but are celebrations of the entire Church which is 'the sacrament of unity,' namely, the holy people united and organized under the authority of the bishops. Therefore, liturgical services pertain to the whole Body of the Church. They manifest it, and have effects upon it."[52] Thus, sacraments are celebrated through active participation of all the faithful. By virtue of our baptism we are consecrated a holy people. We are anointed priest, prophet, and king and therefore "may offer spiritual sacrifices."[53] "Rites that are meant to be celebrated in common, with the faithful present and actively participating, should as far as possible be celebrated in that way rather than by an individual and quasi-privately."[54] Sacramental celebration, therefore, is a communal response

[52]CSL, #26.
[53]*Lumen Gentium* 10; cf. 1 Pet 2:45.
[54]CSL, #27.

of word, song, prayer and gesture to the God who calls us to life through Christ Jesus.

Sacraments assume celebration in faith. It is said that sacraments effect what they signify. When the celebration of a sacrament expresses a specific grace, for example, membership, cleansing, and empowerment for mission, it is not only bestowed on the person, but it is also operative in the life of the one who celebrates. However, since faith is assumed, the effects are dependent on the disposition (faith, conversion) of the individual. One either cooperates with the grace or one does not. I used to be an excellent guitar player. Over the years I have had to use my keyboard talents more than my guitar playing skills. I no longer can play as I used to play. However, if I were to invest the time and energy into the practice of the guitar, my playing would rapidly improve. Sacraments operate in somewhat similar fashion. Grace (the presence of Christ) is there for the asking, but without faith it is not necessarily evident and operative in the life of the individual.

Sacraments call us to action. They are not simply gifts for our own spiritual benefit. They are intended to build up the entire church. That can happen only when its members live and act as children of God, when they live the paschal mystery and take what they have received into the world in order to transform it.

Testing
Was there anything just shared that had not occurred to you before? Were there any new insights? What are the implications of sacraments for living your everyday life? What difference do sacraments make to the wider church? In what way have sacraments made a difference in your life? What do sacraments have to do with this Sunday's readings? How would you explain sacraments to a stranger? Has your original understanding been changed, affirmed, or challenged in any way?

Decision
How do sacraments call for a response by the community? What are the implications of sacraments for the church? How do sacraments as described in this session challenge me personally? What one concrete action can I take this week as a response to our sharing?

Refer to chapter 7, "Preparing the Catechetical Session," if you intend to plan your catechetical session at this time.

SIN

Natural Sign

When we speak about sin, what does it mean to you? Have you ever given any thought to your own sinfulness? In what way? How would you articulate an understanding of your faith tradition's belief about sin?

Tradition: Biblical, Ecclesial, and Liturgical Signs

The etymology of the word sin means to "miss the mark" or, in a religious sense, "to fall short of God's will for us."[55] Human beings were created in the image and likeness of God. As such, we are holy in God's sight. However, since the beginning of time human beings have abused the freedom given to them by God. Men and women have turned away from God and attempted to be fulfilled apart from God.[56]

Sin wreaks havoc in the lives of people. It causes great sorrow and upheaval. People sin when their actions "knowingly and deliberately violate the moral law and in a serious matter also seriously offend God."[57] Most of us have experienced a time in our lives when our actions affected another person in a negative, hurtful, or destructive way. This is sin.

Throughout the history of salvation God has intervened in the lives of men and women in order to help them in their struggle against the forces of sin and evil. Sin was, is, and always will be a part of our lives. In the Old Testament sin was usually personified in terms of a character (e.g., the serpent in the garden). For the ancients, sin resulted in humanity's foolish belief that they could get along without God, or that they could be like God. The primary motif of the Old Testament scriptures is God in relationship to a people. God entered into covenant with Israel. Israel sinned; God invited her to repent; she repented, and God rescued and liberated her.

In both the Old and the New Testaments there is very little understanding of sin in personal terms. It is most commonly understood to be communal. Serious sins such as rebellion, infidelity, and sexual misconduct were seen as disturbances to community and family order and would be reprimanded accordingly. When people revolted by turning away from God completely, the punishment was either banishment from the community or death. It was believed that sinners brought such judgment down upon themselves.[58]

Jesus' primary role through his passion, death, and resurrection, was to free the human race of the effects of sin. God is alive for us in the person of his Son. The grace given to us by Jesus is far more abundant than the sins we commit. Through repentance for our sins we can share in the love and salvation offered by Jesus.[59]

Sin is the greatest obstacle men and women face in their efforts to love God and one another. There are different types of sin. Humanity is born into original sin, the first obstacle to a life of love. We are born into the human condition, a fallen state: "human nature...fallen, stripped of the grace that clothed it, injured in its own natural powers and subjected to the dominion of death, that is transmitted to all."[60]

Human beings as individuals commit personal sins. "It is willful rejection, either partial or total, of one's role as a child of God and a member of His people. By it sinners knowingly and deliberately disobey God's command to love Him, other people, and themselves in a morally right way."[61] By sins of omission (failing to do what one should do) or commission (willfully doing what one

[55]Robert J. Schreiter, C.P.P.S., "Sin," in *The Collegeville Pastoral Dictionary of Biblical Theology,* ed. Carroll Stuhlmueller, C.P. (Collegeville: The Liturgical Press, 1996), 921-922.

[56]*Dogmatic Constitution on the Church,* in *The Documents of Vatican II,* ed. Walter M. Abbot, S.J. (New York: Guild Press, America Press, Association Press, 1966), #13.

[57]GCD, #62.

[58]James A. Fischer, "Sin-Old Testament," in *The Collegeville Pastoral Dictionary of Biblical Theology,* ed. Carroll Stuhlmueller, C.P. (Collegeville: The Liturgical Press, 1996), 916-919.

[59]GCD, #62.

[60]Pope Paul VI, *Credo of the People of God* (June 30, 1968).

[61]NCD, #98.

should not do) men and women turn from God's will. Personal sin begins within the heart of an individual and extends to behavior that defies God's greatest commandment to love God, neighbor, and self.

Grave sin, called mortal, seriously disrupts one's relationship with God. Mortal sin is committed with malice of intent, by deliberately choosing evil over good. Mortal sin assumes full consent and knowledge of the offense. Lesser sins, called venial, also impair that same relationship and can accumulate to the point of leading to more serious sin.[62]

Because God loves us, the entire human race is formed in an eternal bond of "supernatural solidarity, so much so that the sin of one harms the others just as the holiness of one benefits the others."[63] Penance calls us to reconcile with our brothers and sisters who are always harmed by our sins.[64] God calls us away from sin. This conversion constitutes a "profound change of the whole person by which one begins to consider, judge, and arrange his life according to the holiness and love of God."[65]

We are forgiven our sins and reconciled with God and one another through the sacraments of penance and eucharist. Through baptism our fallen nature is crucified with Christ so that the body of sin may be destroyed and we may no longer be slaves to sin, but rise with Christ and live for God (Rom 6:4-10). The sacrament of penance is like a second baptism. Rather than the water of baptism, there are tears of penance.[66]

The eucharist is also for the forgiveness of sins. In the liturgy we recall and make present Jesus' words, "Take and eat. This is my Body given up for you for the forgiveness of sins." We are forgiven by the death and resurrection of Jesus. We, in turn, take up our cross and offer our lives for the sins of others, just as Christ offered his life for us.

Sometimes we unconsciously trivialize the actual atrocity of sin. We reduce it to a laundry list of do's and don't's and fail to get inside the permeating and devastating aspects of another dimension of sin called *social sin*. It is very easy to relegate social sin to be out of our control, unrelated to us or our lives and, in essence, not our problem. We often fail to see that we are part of a global human village.

Sin occurs in both personal and social forms. Social sin is a concept that most of us have not had the occasion to consider. What is it? "Social sin represents, as it were, the accumulation of sinful acts that create environments of oppression, racism, and sexism, environments of sinfulness so powerful and so pervasive that no one can escape them."[67]

How do we commit social sin? Social sin has seriously impacted the lives of innocent people around the world. This sinister reality was confronted in 1983 by a group of bishops gathered at the Synod of Reconciliation. As a result of this meeting, Pope John Paul II addressed the topic of social sin in an apostolic letter resulting from this Synod, "Reconciliation and Penance," Dec. 2, 1984.

The highlight of the letter's main points are as follows:

I: The presence of social sin exists in laws, policies, and social practices that result in the failure to respect or enhance the human dignity of certain groups within society.

II: Social sin is the accumulation of personal sins. Human beings contribute to social sin in a number of ways.
   a. Actions or omissions that cause or support the evil condition, that fail to enhance human dignity. (*The School of the Americas is training guerrillas in the art of torture and warfare to use in Third World countries. That's the government's business, not mine.*)
   b. Actions or omissions that exploit the evil condition, that take advantage of people

---

[62]Ibid.

[63]Paul VI, Apostolic Constitution *Indulgentiarum doctrina*, January 1, 1967, no. 4: AAS 59 (1967), 9; see Pius XII, encyclical *Mystici Corporis*, June 29, 1943. AAS 35 (1943), 213.

[64]Rite of Penance, #5.

[65]Pope Paul VI, Apostolic Constitution *Paenitemini*, February 17, 1966.

[66]St. Ambrose, Letter 41:12: PL 16, 1116.

---

[67]Schreiter, "Sin," 921-922.

or situations for self-interest or gain. (*I think I might hire an illegal immigrant. I can get a lady to clean my house for $2.00 an hour because she is desperate.*)

c. Failure to avoid, eliminate, or at least limit the evil condition due to laziness, fear, indifference, the conspiracy of silence, or through secret complicity. ("*I know that my boss is knowingly discriminating against the minorities in my company and is falsifying records in order to get away with it. But I'll never tell anyone; it's none of my business.*")

d. Another way personal sin contributes to social sin is when I take refuge in the impossibility of changing the evil condition with the attitude that there is nothing I can do. (*Henry Thoreau was imprisoned during the Mexican War. He thought the war was an attempt to gain control of other regions for the purpose of building their slave labor pool. He would not support the war and refused to pay taxes. When his friend, Ralph Waldo Emerson visited him in prison, he asked Thoreau why he was in jail. Thoreau very indignantly asked Emerson why he was not right there with him, as he too had been opposed to the war for the same reason. How many of us are that ready to put our money where our mouth is!*)

e. When we sidestep the effort and sacrifice required to address the evil condition with the attitude, "I don't want to be bothered; it will put me out too much." (*I would like to work at the soup kitchen on Tuesdays but it is the day I get my hair and nails done. Or...I am against abortion, but it is just too much fuss to do or say anything about it. Leave that to others!*)

f. When we rationalize with regard to why we cannot engage in actions to address the evil condition by thinking, "If I do that they will have my head on the platter." (*I am very much against the practices of the World Bank because they deliberately charge interest that causes excessive suffering for the poor in Third World countries. If I take any action to speak up in any way, I will be fired from my position at the bank.*)

While social sin is communal, the responsibility belongs to individuals. Social sin is the amassment of our own personal sins. The effects of my sins are limited to those in somewhat close proximity. I sin due to an action or a failure to act and the consequences generally affect a small group of people. Personal sins are healed through the healing sacrament of reconciliation. Social sin, on the other hand, is intricate and ambiguous and affects a much larger group of people. It invades our laws, customs, and practices and thus the repercussions are immense. It is not easily healed as it usually involves a collective blindness. Sometimes social sin is even disguised as socially acceptable. We need to make it our business to see. (*A young man who grew up in New Orleans during the days of segregation was riding his daily bus. He witnessed a scene he had observed many other times: a black woman getting on the bus, only this time she attempted to enter it from the front rather than the rear. The bus driver hit the woman. For the first time this young man's eyes were opened. He saw the evil of prejudice and its effects.*)

The pope maintains that personal sin such as fear, greed, and selfishness are at the core of all social sin and that we must take responsibility for it. We respond to social sin with a communal mindset, an awareness that we are part of the human village. This begins with an inner disposition of solidarity with those who suffer any injustice, asserts the pope. One reason Jesus was killed was because of his unpopular, dangerous support for the poor and marginalized. He shook the status quo. He offered hope to the oppressed and unnerved those who were in positions of power.

The first place to begin to address our participation in social sin is to raise our consciousness to all evil, especially evil that robs human beings of their God-given right to dignity.[68]

Testing

In what way, if any, has your original understanding of sin been stretched, challenged, or affirmed? Was there any new information for you? If so, what was it? Was there anything you found to be uncomfortable about in this teaching? In light of the material just presented, is there any implication for living the Christian life? In what way is this

---

[68]Section on social sin adapted from "Grace and Sin," a presentation by Robert Duggan, North American Forum on the Catechumenate.

post-biblical teaching related to the scriptures of this Sunday's liturgy? In light of this sharing, how would you articulate a theology or understanding of sin? Is it the same as your first understanding, or has it changed?

Decision

How does this teaching about sin challenge our community? In what way do we as community live the message we just shared? Are there ways we need to grow in our understanding of what was shared? Where are the specific places where transformation is needed? Is there any concrete action I can take to be an agent of change in my community? How does this understanding of sin challenge me personally? How am I living the message? In what way do I need to grow? What is one specific action I can take this week as a response to our sharing?

Refer to chapter 7, "Preparing the Catechetical Session," if you intend to plan your catechetical session at this time.

TRINITY

Natural Sign

In what way have you experienced God in creation? How would you finish the following sentence: "The Trinity is...."?

Tradition: Biblical, Ecclesial, and Liturgical Signs

The mystery of the Trinity is essential to our faith. It is unique to the Christian faith: One God in three persons. The Hebrew scriptures do not provide a Trinitarian understanding of God. Israel contributed the concept of a mono-theistic God. In the Hebrew scriptures God is Creator, Author of all Life. Israel depicted God as Word (*dabar*), Spirit (*ruah*), Wisdom (*hokmah*), and Presence (*shekina*).

The New Testament does not clearly define the dogma of Trinity. Rarely is Jesus referred to as God, as it would identify him too closely with the Father. But his divinity is recognized. The word Trinity is not used, but there is a proclaimed experience of Triune God—Father, Son, and Spirit. This is referred to as the economic trinity—the experience of God's action in the world. Matthew's gospel has Jesus exhorting his disciples to go out and baptize all nations in the name of the Father, Son, and Spirit (28:19). The Trinity is experienced in Jesus' baptism in the Jordan when the Spirit descends upon him and the Father's voice is heard.

The apostolic age held fast to the doctrine of one God and defended this against pagan polytheism. There are references to the Trinity in early liturgies prior to a formalized doctrine on Trinity. There is a basic principle that states that from the church's prayer flows its creed (*lex orandi, lex credendi*). The church professed its belief through its prayer. The prayer of the church reflects the lived experience of the Triune God. From the experience of ritual prayer, the church formulated its official creed.

The Trinitarian creed was formulated as a result of heresies that crept into the church early in its history. Language is very limited when it comes to explaining an inexplicable mystery. Notions from philosophical origins helped formulate the theology.

There were two schools of thought emanating from the Greek and Latin Fathers. The two schools were based on the distinctions between immanent trinity and economic trinity. The economic trinity (Greek Fathers) was based on the experience of God in the world, in the history of salvation. Humanity experienced God as creator, Son as redeemer and Spirit as sanctifier. The term relates to the three "faces" or actions of God's manifestation. Economic trinity refers to the *mission* of God who sent the Son and the Spirit to accomplish the work of salvation.

Immanent trinity (Latin Fathers) refers to the relationship the Father, Son, and Spirit have with one another apart from the actions they have performed in the world. Immanent trinity centers on the "Oneness" of God, one divine nature. The inner life of God is Trinitarian. Outside the inner life, the actions of God are common to all three persons as there is only one nature. No person of the Trinity is less than the others.

The Arian heresy asserted that there was a time when Jesus *was not*. He was created by the Father. The divinity of the Holy Spirit was questioned by other heresies. The Council of Nicea (325 C.E.)

resolved the heresies by establishing a creedal statement of faith, the Nicene Creed (proclaimed in every eucharistic liturgy).

The Council asserted that there is one God of three: co-equal and co-eternal. Jesus was begotten, not made. He always was with the Father. There was never a time he was not. He was with the Father, as was the Spirit, at the creation of the world. That is, all three always existed. The three persons are distinct, but not separate. The Son is of the same substance as the Father (*homoousios*). Father, Son, and Spirit work for our redemption. The Council of Constantinople in 553 attested to the one God in three persons (consubstantial Trinity). The Council of Toledo maintained that the "three persons do not share one divinity unto themselves, but each one is whole and entire."[69] They are distinct from one another, yet one. The term used to designate this three persons and their distinctions is *hypostasis*. The Father is not the Son, the Son is not the Spirit, etc. God is one, but not solitary. The divine persons are distinct. They are distinct in the way they are related to each other. The Father generates, the Son is begotten, and the Holy Spirit proceeds.

The official church teaches that the Trinity is an absolute mystery. We do not understand it even after it has been revealed. Mystery transcends the capacity of our ordinary rational and conceptual powers. It goes beyond the scope of human imagination and everyday knowledge.

God as Father

The Father, unbegotten, acts only with the Son and the Spirit. The Father generates the Son and sends the Spirit. Jesus reveals the Father who is Father because of his relationship to Jesus, the Son. Jesus is Son only in relation to the Father.

God as Son

Jesus was eternally begotten of the Father. He was not made. Jesus is of the same essence as the Father—divine and coeternal (he always was). In John's gospel Jesus is referred to as the Word. One possible metaphor for trying to grasp the ineffable mystery is to see it in terms of the WORD image.

If Jesus is the WORD of the Father, the WORD was always a part of the Father. God but spoke the Word and a part of Godself came forth from his very being.

It is through Jesus that the Father is expressed to us in our salvation history. The Son is the same unity, substance as the Father—thus it is not Sonship as we understand it in human terms.

God as Spirit

If Jesus is the Word, the truth of God's self that comes from his very being, then who is the Spirit? The Spirit is also God. The Word was spoken and Jesus was begotten. The life force, the breath that came forth from the mouth of God was the Spirit. From the truth of God's existence came the Son, begotten of the Father. From the truth of God as revealed to us by the Son comes love, the Spirit of God. If Jesus is the Word, or Truth of who God is, the Spirit is the action of the Truth: Love.

God the Holy Spirit is another divine person who is with Jesus and the Father. The Spirit is given as gift from the Father, given to us through the Son. The Spirit communicates the Father to us and we are able to communicate in a personal relationship with the Father. The Holy Spirit is God communicating with us. Thus, the Holy Spirit is given in love and with that love comes reconciling and renewing power. The Spirit is of the same essence as the Father, but distinct. "The Spirit has the same essence of the Father, and yet is distinct from the Father and the Son. The Spirit proceeds from the Father through the Son. The procession is not a begetting, since this would lead to the supposition that there are two Sons, nor is the Spirit merely a mode [through] which the Son communicates himself to us. The Spirit originates from the Father and the Son, and has a distinct relationship to the Father and the Son."[70] Thus, they are three persons in one God, and the Spirit has a role in the saving mission throughout history.

The symbols of the Holy Spirit show us the nature and the activity of the Spirit in the church. Water signifies the Holy Spirit in baptism and is a sign of new birth. The gestation of first birth took place

---

[69]Linda Gaupin, *Catholic Faith and Life,* 46.

[70]Ibid, 49.

in water, so too, our birth in the divine life comes through water. Anointing is a sign of the presence of the Spirit. Christ in Hebrew means the *one anointed by God's Spirit*. The Holy Spirit anointed Jesus as "Christ."

By the power of the Spirit Mary conceived and Simeon could proclaim her son messiah. Through the Spirit power went out from Jesus through acts of healing and saving. The Spirit raised Jesus from the dead.

Fire as symbol signifies the transforming energy of the Spirit's actions. Jesus said of the Spirit, "I came to cast fire on the face of the earth, and would that it were already kindled." The tongues of *fire, cloud, and light* are manifestations of the Holy Spirit. They reveal God's transcendence, omnipotence and glory, (e.g., Moses on Sinai, at the tent of meeting, and the wandering in the desert).

The *seal* as symbol of the Spirit is similar to anointing. It indicates the effects of the anointing of the Spirit. The *hand* as sign of the Spirit demonstrates healing power. Jesus invokes the Spirit and heals the sick by the laying on of hands. The apostles would do the same. The *finger* is also a sign of the Holy Spirit. By the finger of God Jesus cast out demons (Lk 11:20). The dove (flood, baptism) is a traditional sign of the Spirit. Noah released a dove and the earth was again hospitable. The Spirit comes "like a dove" and remains in the purified hearts of the baptized (Mk 1:10).

What is the bottom line here? When all is said and done, it is God who created us, who sustains us, who will judge us, and who will give us eternal life. This is a God who is not removed from us. Our God is a God of absolute proximity, who is truly communicated to us in the flesh in history and within the human family. God is with us in the spiritual depths of our existence as well as in our unfolding history. God is in our everyday lives. God is the source of enlightenment and community.

We proclaim the Trinity in the liturgy in the greeting, the sign of the cross, the Gloria, the creed, the eucharistic prayers, the doxology, and the final blessings as well as in all the sacraments. Refer to the *Catechism of the Catholic Church*, #249-267.

Testing

Were there any new insights? How would you articulate an understanding of Trinity? How does this dogma have anything to do with everyday life? Have any of your original assumptions been stretched?

Decision

How does this teaching call us to action? What one action will you take as a response?

Refer to chapter 7, "Preparing the Catechetical Session," if you intend to plan your catechetical session at this time.

TRANSFIGURATION

See Feast of the Transfiguration and Second Sunday of Lent.

Bibliography

Basic Teachings for Catholic Religious Education. In *The Catechetical Documents*. Chicago: Liturgy Training Publications, 1996.

Catechism of the Catholic Church. USCC-Liberia Editrice Vaticana. Liguori: Liguori Publications, 1994.

The Collegeville Pastoral Dictionary of Biblical Theology. Ed. Carroll Stuhlmueller, C.P. Collegeville: The Liturgical Press, 1996.

Collins, John J. "Eschatology." *The Collegeville Pastoral Dictionary of Biblical Theology*. Ed. Carroll Stuhlmueller, C.P. Collegeville: The Liturgical Press, 1996.

Documents on the Liturgy, 1963–1979: Conciliar, Papal and Curial Texts. Collegeville: The Liturgical Press, 1982.

The Documents of Vatican II. Ed. Walter M. Abbot, S.J. New York: Guild Press, America Press, Association Press, 1966.

Fischer, James A. "Sin-Old Testament." In *The Collegeville Pastoral Biblical Dictionary*. Ed. Carol Stuhlmueller, C.P. Collegeville: The Liturgical Press, 1996.

Gaupin, Linda, CDP, Ph.D. *Catholic Faith and Life: Catechist Training*. Diocese of Orlando, 1996.

———. *Specialized Certification for Sacramental Catechesis: Course Text*. Diocese of Orlando,

1996–l997.

General Catechetical Directory. In *The Catechetical Documents.* Chicago: Liturgy Training Publications, 1996.

Hayes, Zachary, O.F.M. "Parousia." In *The New Dictionary of Theology.* Ed. Mary Collins, Joseph A. Komonchak and Dermot A. Lane. Collegeville: The Liturgical Press, 1987.

Kealy, Sean P. "Parousia." In *The Collegeville Pastoral Dictionary of Biblical Theology.* Ed.Carroll Stuhlmueller, C.P. Collegeville: The Liturgical Press, 1996.

The Liturgy Documents. Chicago: Liturgy Training Publications, 1990.

Marthaler, Berard L., O.F.M. *The Creed.* Mystic: Twenty-Third Publications, 1987.

McBrien, Richard, P. *Catholicism.* San Francisco: HarperCollins, 1981.

_____ . *The Encyclopedia of Catholicism.* San Francisco: HarperCollins, 1995.

National Catechetical Directory. In *The Catechetical Documents.* Chicago: Liturgy Training Publications, 1996.

The New Dictionary of Theology. Ed. Mary Collins, Joseph A. Komonchak and Dermot A. Lane. Collegeville: The Liturgical Press, 1987.

Neyrey, Jerome H., S.J. "Community." In *The Collegeville Pastoral Dictionary of Biblical Theology.* Ed. Carroll Stuhlmueller, C.P. Collegeville: The Liturgical Press, 1996.

Rite of Christian Initiation of Adults. ICEL. Chicago: Liturgy Training Publications, 1988.

Rite of Confirmation. In *Rites of the Catholic Church.* English translation prepared by ICEL. New York: Pueblo Publishing Co., 1976.

Rite of Penance. In *Rites of the Catholic Church.* English translation prepared by ICEL. New York: Pueblo Publishing Co., 1976.

Schreiter, Robert J., C.P.P.S. "Sin." In *The Collegeville Pastoral Dictionary of Biblical Theology.* Ed. Carroll Stuhlmueller, C.P. Collegeville: The Liturgical Press, 1996.

DOCTRINAL INDEX

This index of doctrinal topics lists relevant church documents and official sources. Document titles are abbreviated; for more information on these sources, see the listing of documents that follows the index.

DOCTRINAL TOPICS

ADVENT DOL 442 nos 39-42, 467 nos 3-4; CB 235; GNLY 39-42; LM 11; CCC 522-524

ALL SOULS CB 395; DOL 478

ALMSGIVING CCC 575,1032, 1434, 1438, 2101, 2447, 2462

ANOINTING AND PASTORAL CARE OF THE SICK RA Apostolic Constitution, RA 1-40; DOL 408-409, 412; NCD 127-128; SC 73-75; CCC 1520-1525

ASCENSION CCC 659-664, 668-673

ASSUMPTION DOL 467 no 6; CCC 966, 974

BAPTISM (see Christian Initiation)

BEATITUDES CCC 1716-1724; BT 19; NCD 105

BREAD GIRM 281-285; CCC 1329, 1333-1340, 1355

BODY OF CHRIST DOL 176 no 35-39, 44, 64-72; 179 no 6-8; CCC 775-776, 779, 789, 791, 792, 805, 807

CHRISTMAS GNLY 32-38; LM 95; AD 3; LM 12; CCC 525-534

CHRISTIAN INITIATION

BAPTISM RCIA INTRO 1-35; GS 11; LG 10-17; GCD 11, 57; NCD 116-117; SC 7; UR 22; DOL 301 no 33; CCC 1213-1274 (Role of baptized: priest, prophet and king CCC 901-913)

CONFIRMATION RC Apostolic Constitution, RA 1, 9, 13; RCIA INTRO 2; LG 11, GCD 11; CCC 698, 1183, 1272-1274, 1285-1314; NCD 118-119; DOL 304, 305 nos 1-19

EUCHARIST RCIA INTRO 2; LG 7, 11; DOL 169 no 58, 176 no 70, 177; GIRM INTRO 2-5; GIRM 1-2, 7-8, 62; AA 8; GCD 12, 58; NCD 120-122; CCC 1322-1405; SC 47; Influence of Eucharistic celebration on daily life: DOL 179 no 13; Adoration of eucharist: DOL 179 no 49, 50; Mystery of the eucharist: DOL 184, 185, 189, 191

CHURCH, MYSTERY LG 1-16; GCD 20-23, 65-67; DOL 4 no 3, 176 no 37-38; NCD 30, 56-59; 63-73; 93-96; TJD 12; CCC 774-776, 811-829, 1396

COMMUNION DOL 177, 179 nos 3b, 31-32, 34; 183; 188

CONFIRMATION (see Christian Initiation)

CONVERSION SC 9; DH 10; DV 5; RP 6; DOL 191, 193, 378 NCD 99, RCIA 36, 37; CCC 1989

CREATION LG 1; GCD 51; NCD 51, 85; CCC 280-314

CROSS LG 3, 38; CB 1011; DOL 176 no 34; CCC 517, 618, 662, 1235

DEATH/DYING GS 18, 22; AG 18; OCF 1-7, 18-19, 22; NCD 108; RA 26-34; SC 81; BT 25

DIGNITY OF HUMAN PERSON GS 3,12, 27; AG 18; AA 6; DH 1, 9; GCD 60

DISCIPLESHIP AA 6, 8; NCD 72, 152-154; CCC 425, 654, 618, 1816

EASTER SEASON GNLY 22-26; LM 11-102; CB 371; CCC 1169; NCD 144

EASTER TRIDUUM GNLY 18-21; LM 99; CB 295-332; 68-639; SC 102

ECUMENISM UR 1-24; DOL 6 nos 2-8, 178 no 10

ESCHATOLOGY LG 39; GCD 25; NCD 109-110; BT 25; OCF 1-8; CCC 958, 1020-1050, 1088-1090, 1402, 1662,1681; SC 8

EUCHARIST (see Christian Initiation)

EVANGELIZATION AA 6, 8; EN 6-82; AD 1-22; 35-36; RCIA 36-40; DOL 66 no 2, 189; CCC 858-859

FAITH GCD 15, 22-24 57-59; DV 5; NCD 15, 22; RCIA 211; DH 10; CCC 142-175

FASTING CCC 1434, 2043

FIRE CCC 696

GARMENT RCIA 214, 320; CCC 1243-1244

GRACE GS 57; NCD 98; CCC 1996-2005

HIERARCHY OF TRUTHS GCD 43; BR INTRO; NCD 43,47; CCC 90, 234

HOLY ORDERS PO 1-9; GCD 57; NCD 132-133

HOLY SPIRIT (see Trinity)

INCARNATION AD 3; BT 4; GCD 52-54; NCD 87; CCC 456-478, 653

JESUS (see Trinity)

JUSTICE LG 27-32, 69-72; EJFA 48-78; NCD 162, 165; CCC 1397; TJD 10-11

KINGDOM OF GOD LG 36; GS 45; CCC 541-560,675, 677

LAYING ON OF HANDS DOL 306; RC 9; RA 5-6; CCC 1288, 1668; 1556

LENT SC 109-110; GNLY 27-31; LM 13; RCIA 138

LIGHT RCIA 230, LG 1; NCD 117, CCC 699, 700, 697, 1243

LITURGICAL YEAR SC 102; GNLY 1,17; CB 228; LM 7

LITURGY SC 10; DOL 21, 22 no 19, 176 no 35; CCC 1069-1075, 1077-1124

LORD'S PRAYER GIRM 56; CCC 2601, 2777-2856

MARY, MODEL FOR THE CHURCH LG 60-69; SC 103; GCD 24; BT 24; NCD 106

MASS GIRM 1-58; DOL 176 nos 1-55; 179 3b-g, 12, 193; CCC 1332, 1382

MATRIMONY RMa 1-7; GCD 59; AA 11; NCD 131; AA 11; GS 47-52; LG 11; SC 77-78; DOL 169 no 59

MERCY OF GOD RP 1-11; CCC 1991-1992, 1994

MORALITY: FOUNDATIONS GCD 19, 63-64; NCD 101-105; BT 15,17-19

MORAL CONSCIENCE GS 15-16; NCD 103, 190; DH 3, 14

OIL RC 9; RBO 1-5; RA 5-15, 20-29; RCIA INTRO 2, 214; NCD 117; CCC 695, 1241, 1291, 1289, 1294-1296

NEW TESTAMENT DV 17-20; CCC 124-128

OLD TESTAMENT DV 14-16; CCC 121-123

ORDINARY TIME GNLY 43-44; LM 15, 103-110; CB 377-380

PASCHAL MYSTERY GS 38; RCIA INTRO 1, 5, 6; AG 38; SC 106; GIRM 2; OCF 2, 3; CCC 444-445; 654, 1067-1068, 1164, 1363-1364, 2175

PENANCE (see Reconciliation)

PENTECOST LG 4, 19-20, 24; AG 4; CCC 731-741

PRAYER SC 9-13; BT-INTRO; DOL 53, 55; NCD 140-145; CCC 2558-2565, 2566-2745; 2598-2622

PRAYER FORMS CCC 2626-2643

RECONCILIATION/PENANCE RP-INTRO, 1-11; LG 11; DOL 191; GCD 11; NCD 124-126

RESURRECTION LG 36; BT 4, 8; NCD 87 CCC 638-655

REVELATION DV 2-6, 21-24; GCD 10-14; NCD 48-55; CCC 51-67

SAINTS LG 49-51; SC 104, 111; LM 5; NCD 107; CCC 957, 2030

SACRAMENTS SC 59; DOL 169 nos 55-57; LG 11; GIRM 346; GCD 10-11, 55; NCD 97, 114; BT 10-13; CCC 1113-1130, 1145-1158

SALVATION DV 2; GCD 37-44, 62; BT 1, 5-6, 8, 22-23; NCD 85, 96; AA 5-6; GIRM 2

SCRIPTURE DV 11-26; CCC 101-133; LM 1

SERVICE/MISSION LG 27; AA 2-3, 8, 10; RCIA 75-76; TJD 27-32; DOL 179 no 13

SIN GS 13; NCD 98-99; GCD 62; BT 15-16, 19; RCIA 211; RP 5; AA 7; CCC 385-412

SOCIAL JUSTICE NCD 149-171; CCC 1928-1942

TRANSFIGURATION CCC 554-56, 568

TRANSUBSTANTIATION DOL 176 no 46-55

TRINITY GCD 1, 41, 47; DV 2; NCD 83, RCIA 200; CCC 233-260, 290-292

    FATHER LG 2-4; GCD 41; NCD 51; CCC 238-242, 248, 254, 268-274, 279, 286-288

    JESUS LG 3-4; GS 22; AD 3; DV 17; GCD, 4, 6, 8, 50, 53-55; NCD 53, 87-91; CCC 249-267; BT 4-9; GS 45

    HOLY SPIRIT LG 4, 12; AD 3; RC Apostolic Constitution, RC 2; GCD 9, 41; NCD 54, 92; BT 9; CCC 687-741, 1091-1109; 1286; 1289

SUFFERING GS 22; RA INTRO 1-3; CCC 164, 1508, 1521

WATER RCIA INTRO 5, 18-22, 213; CCC 694, 1217-1222; OCF 8

WORD OF GOD LM 1, 3, 10; DV 10-21; CCC 109-120

Note: This is by no means an exhaustive listing of topics or documentation for the topics listed. This index merely scratches the surface and serves as a point of departure for those interested in further exploration of such topics.

DOCUMENTS

AA   *Apostolicam actuositatem:* The Decree on the Apostolate of the Laity, Vatican Council II, November 18, 1965. (Can be found in *The Documents of Vatican II,* edited by Walter M. Abbot, S.J., New York: Guild Press, America Press, Association Press, 1966.)

AG   *Ad gentes:* Decree on the Church's Missionary Activity, Vatican Council II, December 7, 1965. (Can be found in *The Documents of Vatican II,* edited by Walter M. Abbot, S.J., New York: Guild Press, America Press, Association Press, 1966.)

BT   *Basic Teachings for Catholic Religious Education,* NCCB, 1973. (Can be found in *The Catechetical Documents: A Parish Resource,* Chicago: Liturgy Training Publications, 1996.)

CB   *Ceremonial of Bishops,* ICEL, 1989. (Can be found in *The Liturgy Documents: A Pastoral Resource,* Chicago: Liturgy Training Publications, 1990.)

CCC   *Catechism of the Catholic Church,* USCC-Libreria Editrice Vaticana, 1994.

DH   *Dignitatis humanae:* Declaration on Human Freedom, Vatican Council II, December 7, 1965. (Can be found in *The Documents of Vatican II,* edited by Walter M. Abbot, S.J., New York: Guild Press, America Press, Association Press, 1966.)

DOL   *Documents on the Liturgy 1963-1979, Conciliar, Papal and Curial and Liturgical Texts,* Collegeville: The Liturgical Press, 1982.

DV   *Dei verbum:* Dogmatic Constitution on Divine Revelation, Vatican Council II, Nov. 18, 1965. (Can be found in *The Documents of Vatican II,* edited by Walter M. Abbot, S.J., New York: Guild Press, America Press, Association Press, 1966.)

EJFA   *Economic Justice for All,* NCCB, 1986.

EN   *Evangelii Nuntiandi:* On Evangelization in the Modern World, Paul VI, December 8, 1975. (Can be found in *The Catechetical Documents: A Parish Resource,* Chicago: Liturgy Training Publications, 1996.)

GIRM   *General Instruction to the Roman Missal,* ICEL, 1975. (Can be found in *The Liturgy Documents: A Parish Resource,* Chicago: Liturgy Training Publications, 1990.)

GCD   *General Catechetical Directory,* Sacred Congregation for the Clergy, 1971. (Can be found in *The Catechetical Documents: A Parish Resource,* Chicago: Liturgy Training Publications, 1996.)

GS   *Gaudium et spes:* The Pastoral Constitution on the Church in the Modern World, Vatican Council II, December 7, 1965. (Can be found in *The Documents of Vatican II,* edited by Walter M. Abbot, S.J., New York: Guild Press, America Press, Association Press, 1966.)

HLS   *This Holy and Living Sacrifice for the Celebration and Reception of Communion under Both Kinds,* USCC, 1985. (Can be found in *The Liturgy Documents: A Parish Resource.* Chicago: Liturgy Training Publications, 1990.)

LG   *Lumen gentium:* Dogmatic Constitution on the Church, Vatican Council II, 1965. (Can be found in *The Documents of Vatican II,* edited by Walter M. Abbot, S.J., New York: Guild Press, America Press, Association Press, 1966.)

LM   *Lectionary For Mass: Introduction,* second editio typica, ICEL, 1985. (Can be found in *The Liturgy Documents: A Parish Resource,* Chicago: Liturgy Training Publications, 1990.)

NCD   *Sharing the Light of Faith: National Catechetical Directory,* NCCB, 1978 (Can be found in *The Catechetical Documents: A Parish Resource,* Chicago: Liturgy Training Publications, 1996.)

OCF   *Order of Christian Funerals,* ICEL, 1990.

PO   *Presbyterorum ordinis:* Decree on the Ministry and Life of Priests, Vatican Council II, 1966. (Can be found in *The Documents of Vatican II,* edited by Walter M. Abbot, S.J., New York: Guild Press, America Press, Association Press, 1966.)

RA   Rite of Anointing and Pastoral Care of the Sick, *Rites of the Catholic Church,* ICEL, 1976.

RBO   Rite of Blessing of Oils and Rite of Consecration of Chrism: Introduction, *Rites of the Catholic Church,* ICEL, 1976.

RCIA   *Rite of Christian Initiation of Adults,* ICEL, 1988.

RC   Rite of Confirmation, *Rites of the Catholic Church,* ICEL, 1976.

RMa	Rite of Marriage, *Rites of the Catholic Church,* ICEL, 1976.
RP	Rite of Penance, *Rites of the Catholic Church,* ICEL, 1976.
RO	Rite of Ordination of Deacons, Presbyters, and Bishops, *Rites of the Catholic Church,* ICEL, 1976.
SC	*Sacrosanctum concilium:* Constitution on the Sacred Liturgy, Vatican Council II, December 4, 1964. (Can be found in *The Documents of Vatican II,* edited by Walter M. Abbot, S.J., New York: Guild Press, America Press, Association Press, 1966, OR *The Liturgy Documents: A Parish Resource,* Chicago: Liturgy Training Publications, 1990.)
UR	*Unitatis redintegratio:* The Decree on Ecumenism, Vatican Council II, November 21, 1964. (Can be found in *The Documents of Vatican II,* edited by Walter M. Abbot, S.J., New York: Guild Press, America Press, Association Press, 1966.)
TJD	*To Teach as Jesus Did,* NCCB, 1972. (Can be found in *The Catechetical Documents: A Parish Resource,* Chicago: Liturgy Training Publications, 1996.)